THE OXFORD HANDBOOK OF

JURISPRUDENCE
AND PHILOSOPHY OF LAW

THE OXFORD HANDBOOK OF

JURISPRUDENCE
AND PHILOSOPHY OF LAW

Edited by

JULES COLEMAN
AND
SCOTT SHAPIRO

Associate Editor

KENNETH EINAR HIMMA

OXFORD

UNIVERSITY PRESS

Great Clarendon Street, Oxford OX2 6DP

Oxford University Press is a department of the University of Oxford.
It furthers the University's objective of excellence in research, scholarship,
and education by publishing worldwide in

Oxford New York

Auckland Cape Town Dar es Salaam Hong Kong Karachi
Kuala Lumpur Madrid Melbourne Mexico City Nairobi
New Delhi Shanghai Taipei Toronto
With offices in
Argentina Austria Brazil Chile Czech Republic France Greece
Guatemala Hungary Italy Japan South Korea Poland Portugal
Singapore Switzerland Thailand Turkey Ukraine Vietnam

ISBN 978-0-19-927097-2

Printed and bound by CPI Group (UK) Ltd, Croydon, CR0 4YY

PREFACE

....

Dictionaries, encyclopedias, and companions are all the rage in philosophical publishing these days, and the philosophy of law certainly has its share. It was not our intention to add to the growing list of titles. Rather, we wanted to put together a volume of work on the main topics in the philosophy of law that not only reported on the state of the art, but contributed to it as well.

We provided the authors with very simple instructions: give us your 'take' on the chosen topic. Ideally we wanted the chapters to canvass some of the major issues in the field and some of the prominent approaches to such issues. But we also wanted these surveys to serve as points of departure for the authors' own views. We realized that to complete such assignments, the authors would need significantly more freedom and space than encyclopedia entries or journal articles typically allow. Accordingly, we permitted the authors to write entries of any size up to 15,000 words. While most made it within that limit, several authors went significantly over, and we let these bursts of exuberance stand.

The chapters, therefore, do not aim to be comprehensive and are intentionally distinctive, as is the *Handbook* itself. Just as the authors made no effort to cover every significant issue and position, we did not attempt to include an entry on every worthwhile topic or major school of thought in the philosophy of law—and for several reasons. First, though we have produced a large book of many pages, there were space limitations none the less. The size of each chapter significantly limited the number of entries we could include. Secondly, certain important jurisprudential topics have been extensively explored in the literature in recent years and we did not believe that additional coverage would be profitable (jurisprudence does not need another essay on the normative foundations of law and economics, for example). Thirdly, a few individuals who had committed to write entries had to withdraw at late stages of the project and time constraints prevented us from securing an adequate substitute.

All in all, though, the project has emerged substantially as we imagined it: a collection of original essays on the major topics in the philosophy of law written by many of the most interesting and thoughtful researchers working today. The volume not only captures much of the jurisprudential past; it represents the current state of the philosophy of law and points us in several of the directions where it will likely be in the future.

Finally, we would be remiss if we did not acknowledge Kenneth Himma's contribution to the success of this project. Ken began as the 'anonymous' referee for the project, and soon became Associate Editor. Virtually every submission we received was eventually sent to Ken for review. Ken responded with breathtaking speed and provided the authors with copious and penetrating comments on substance, as well as helpful suggestions on style and presentation. It is a credit to Ken that most every author, including those who were initially piqued by his criticisms, told us that the referee's comments substantially improved their piece. We entirely concur.

Jules L. Coleman
Scott Shapiro

New Haven
New York

Contents

Notes on the Contributors

Larry Alexander, Warren Distinguished Professor at the University of San Diego School of Law.

Peter Benson, Professor of Law at the University of Toronto.

Brian H. Bix, Professor of Law at the University of Minnesota Law School.

Allen Buchanan, Professor of Philosophy at the University of Arizona.

Jules L. Coleman, Wesley Newcomb Hohfeld Professor of Jurisprudence at Yale Law School and Professor of Philosophy at Yale University.

Timothy A. O. Endicott, Fellow in Law at Balliol College, Oxford.

John Finnis, Professor of Law and Legal Philosophy in the University of Oxford and Robert and Frances Biolchini Professor at Notre Dame Law School.

John Gardner, Professor of Jurisprudence at the University of Oxford.

David Golove, Professor of Law at New York University School of Law.

Leslie Green, Professor of Law and Philosophy at the Osgoode Hall Law School and in the Department of Philosophy at York University, Toronto.

Kent Greenawalt, University Professor at Columbia Law School.

Kenneth Einar Himma, Lecturer in Philosophy at the University of Washington.

F. M. Kamm, Professor of Philosophy, Medicine (Bioethics), and Law School Affiliated Faculty, New York University.

Jody S. Kraus, Professor of Law at the University of Virginia Law School.

Christopher Kutz, Assistant Professor of Law in the Jurisprudence and Social Policy Program, Boalt Hall School of Law, University of California at Berkeley.

Brian Leiter, Charles I. Francis Professor of Law, Professor of Philosophy, and Director of the Law & Philosophy Program at the University of Texas at Austin.

William Lucy, Professor of Law at Keele University.

Timothy Macklem, Lecturer in Law at King's College London.

Andrei Marmor, Associate Professor at the Interdisciplinary Centre, Hertzlia, Israel, and Long-term Visiting Professor at the University of Chicago Law School.

Gerald J. Postema, Cary C. Boshamer Professor of Philosophy and Professor of Law at the University of North Carolina at Chapel Hill.

Arthur Ripstein, Professor of Law and Philosophy at the University of Toronto.

Scott J. Shapiro, Professor of Law at the Benjamin N. Cardozo School of Law, Yeshiva University.

Edward Stein, Associate Professor of Law at the Benjamin N. Cardozo School of Law, Yeshiva University.

Martin Stone, Professor of Law and Associate Professor of Philosophy at Duke University.

Jeremy Waldron, Maurice and Hilda Friedman Professor of Law, and Director of the Center for Law and Philosophy, at Columbia University.

Benjamin C. Zipursky, Associate Dean of Academic Affairs and Professor at Fordham University School of Law.

CHAPTER 1

NATURAL LAW: THE CLASSICAL TRADITION

JOHN FINNIS

INTRODUCTION

WE can speak of law wherever we can speak of obligation. Indeed, we can use the word more broadly still, and speak of law(s) wherever we can speak of normativity, that is of general directions considered as counting, or entitled to count, in one's deliberations about what to do. So, though it certainly has other meanings, 'law' can be used to refer to any criteria of right judgment in matters of practice (conduct, action), any standards for assessing options for human conduct as good or bad, right or wrong, desirable or undesirable, decent or unworthy. That is how the word is used in the term 'natural law'.

Though it too has a range of meanings, 'natural' can be used to signify that some of those criteria or standards[1] are somehow normative prior to any human choices. On this conception, these prior standards are not the product of either individual or collective choosing or positing, and cannot be repealed, however much they may be

---

[1] For economy, this chapter uses 'standards' to refer to any principles, rules, or norms which give or purport to give direction (to motivate and to sort and rank motivations) in the deliberations of someone considering what to do. So the word covers not only the 'general directions' mentioned in the preceding paragraph, and the 'criteria' mentioned in the present text sentence, but also principles and rules of positive law, and so forth.

violated, defied, or ignored. The idea is that acknowledging these standards in one's deliberations is part of what it is to be *reasonable*—as much part of reasonableness as acknowledging basic natural realities (the world's longevity, or time's one-way flow, etc.), or the requirements of logic, or the aptness or inaptness of means to clear-cut ends (recipes for cakes, remedies for deflation, strategies for battle, circuitry for chips, etc.). Persons or cultures which fail to acknowledge these standards are in that respect unreasonable, even if in many respects rational (see Sects. 10 and 18 below).

Unreasonableness of this kind is, as the saying goes, 'human, all too human'. But to speak more precisely, it is a way of being less than fully what a human person can be. And this is not the only reason for calling it 'unnatural'. Poor thinking and choosing not only fails to actualize to the full one's capacities to be intelligent and reasonable, but also results in actions and omissions which fail to respect and promote the humanity, the nature, of everyone they affect. A community in which the standards by which we identify such failure are violated is not flourishing as it might. Its members, whether they are those acting (and forbearing) or those who should have been benefited not harmed, do not fulfil their capacities. However typical of human affairs, such a condition is unnatural so far as it is disrespectful of human persons. It is unnatural *because* unreasonable, and unreasonable *because* neglectful of the good of persons, the good which is the subject-matter of practical reason's standards.

'Classic(al)' can be taken normatively or merely descriptively. Descriptively it can signify mere chronology; so 'classical natural law theory' might mean no more than the theory that emerged in 'classical times'; for us, ancient Greece. Or the description may be of conventional assessment; so 'classical natural law theory' might mean no more than the theory that is commonly taken to be the version or subclass of such theories which is typical or most commonly under discussion. Or one can use the phrase normatively, to signal one's judgment that this theory or set of ideas, however popular or unpopular, neglected or well-known, is actually sound and entitled to acceptance as guide to personal and communal life. In this chapter, I normally use the term in all three senses at once; the weight of my interest is, of course, in the normative sense and claim.

Natural law theory claims to be the *adequate* or *sound* jurisprudence (or legal philosophy), and the sound ethics and political theory. So I shall explore the theory not only in the brief section which follows but also under a further twenty-seven headings. What sorts of things does the theory say—or would it say if consistently developed—about each of the other twenty-seven topics taken up in this *Handbook*? Sketching a response to that question, I shall follow the book's order, at the expense of some repetition, and some departure from a more natural (more coherent, illuminating, fruitful) sequence of ideas and issues.

1 CLASSICAL NATURAL LAW THEORY

The thesis that, despite the variety of opinions and practices, there are indeed some true and valid standards of right conduct was philosophically (reflectively and critically) articulated by Plato. In his dialectic with sceptics Plato also found it appropriate to recapture from them the words 'nature' and 'natural'. For sceptics contended that by nature, naturally, the strong and selfish prevail over those who are weak or who weaken themselves by care for other persons, or for promises, or for their other 'responsibilities'. With resourceful brilliance Plato responded that trying to live 'naturally' or 'in line with the law of nature' by ruthless pursuit of one's desires for power or other satisfaction is self-stultifying, incoherent, and unreasonable. By nature one's desires, whether intelligent (say for knowledge and friendship), or primarily emotional (say for tasty food, sex, power, reputation, and so forth) are in need of being governed and moderated by the standards of reason. These standards extend beyond setting one's own psyche in order, and include the establishing and maintenance of a good order with, and among, one's fellows. Justice in the soul, indeed in the whole make-up of the particular individual, is the source of, and mirrors and is reflected by, justice in society. The nature of the political community is the nature of a human individual 'writ large'—and vice versa. The standards by which we judge the lustful tyrant a bad human being, a failure (as well as, and because, wicked), are *natural right, natural law*. The sceptics' 'law of nature', despite appearances (the glamour of evil), is unnatural because unreasonable. Such is the theme of Plato's *Gorgias*, his *Republic*, his *Laws*, and others of his works.[2]

The dialectic undertaken by Plato with scepticism, and with the prototypes of modern utilitarianism and pragmatism, is a dialectic carried forward more or less continuously to this day. His conceptual apparatus and argumentative strategies are employed by Aristotle, Cicero, Augustine, and Aquinas, not to mention the works of Shakespeare and many others. Indeed, some main elements of the tradition are present in Locke, Kant, and Hegel, though with such heavy concessions to scepticism about practical reason that their theories can be called no longer classical but 'modern'. This modernity was in some respects an advance on the classic understanding and on the political and legal orders sustained by theories more or less classical in kind. But in important and fundamental ways, the 'modern' conceptions are a regression from Plato's insights, back toward the pre-Socratic philosophers and sophists. Moreover, it is a modernity already passing away.

Three introductory points about the tradition of natural law theory.

1. Its guiding purpose is to answer the parallel questions of a conscientious individual or a group or a group's responsible officer (e.g. a judge): 'What should I do?'

---

[2] See John Finnis, 'Natural Law and the Ethics of Discourse', *Ratio Juris*, 12 (1999), 354–73; *American Journal of Jurisprudence*, 43 (1999), 53–73.

'What should we decide, enact, require, promote?' True, these normative questions cannot be answered well without a sound and unblinkered knowledge of the facts about the way the world works. So good descriptions, general and specific, are needed. But descriptions remain of secondary, derivative interest. The dominant concern is with *judging for oneself* what reasons are good reasons for adopting or rejecting specific kinds of option. Societies and their laws and institutions are therefore to be understood as they would be understood by a participant in deliberations about whether or not to make the choices (of actions, dispositions, institutions, practices, etc.) which shape and largely constitute that society's reality and determine its worth or worthlessness. This 'internal' point of view is dominant, and standards and norms of conduct are never constituted by the facts of convention, custom, or consensus. (Nor by the *fact* that the deliberating person accepts them.) 'Ought' is never derivable from 'is', save by virtue of some higher, more ultimate ought-premise. Positivism, as we shall see, fails to meet this demand of logic coherently. But everything that positivism reasonably wishes to insist upon is clearly, and coherently, accommodated in classical natural law theory.

2. The reason why classical natural law theory does not reduce ought to is (whether by 'deduction' or otherwise) is that in its debates with prescientific superstition and with sophistic reductions of right to might, it got clear about the irreducibility to each other of four kinds of order, to which correspond four kinds of theory: (i) orders which are what they are, independently of our thinking, that is, nature, laws of nature, and correspondingly the natural sciences and metaphysics; (ii) the order which we can bring into our thinking, and correspondingly the standards and discipline of logic; (iii) the order which we can bring into our deliberating, choosing, and acting in the open horizon of our whole life, and correspondingly the standards of morality and the reflective discipline of ethics; (iv) the order which we can bring into matter (including our own bodies) subject to our power, as means to relatively specific purposes, and correspondingly the countless techniques, crafts, and technologies.[3] Morality, and natural law (in the relevant sense of that term), cannot be reduced to, or deduced from, the principles of natural science or metaphysics, logic, or any craft.

3. None the less, the tradition has a clear understanding that one cannot reasonably affirm the equality of human beings, or the universality and binding force of human rights, unless one acknowledges that there is something about persons which distinguishes them radically from sub-rational creatures, and which, prior to any acknowledgement of 'status', is intrinsic to the factual reality of every human being, adult or immature, healthy or disabled.

---

[3] On the four kinds of knowledge/science/discipline considered in this paragraph, and their irreducibility, see e.g. Finnis, *Aquinas: Moral, Political and Legal Theory* (Oxford University Press, 1998) (hereafter *Aquinas*), ch. 2; Finnis, 'Legal Reasoning and Legal Theory', in Robert P. George (ed.), *Natural Law Theory* (Oxford: Oxford University Press, 1992), 134–57 at 139–40.

2 THE MODERN NATURAL LAW TRADITION

'Modern' might here mean 'contemporary'. But virtually all who today are willing to call their own work 'natural law theory' regard themselves as re-presenting and developing the classical tradition. Moreover, they reject the characteristic tenets of that 'modern' tradition which emerges in the 1600s and which self-consciously set aside some of the very elements of the classical tradition that today's 'new classical' theorists esteem most highly.

So I shall follow a conventional scholarly view: the modern tradition of natural law theory emerges clearly by 1660, when Samuel Pufendorf published in The Hague his *Elements of Universal Jurisprudence*.[4] Characteristic features of this kind of natural law theory can be studied there, or in Pufendorf's fuller treatise *On the Law of Nature and of Nations* (1672),[5] or in John Locke's long-unpublished *Questions concerning the Law of Nature*[6] dating apparently from around 1660 to 1664. Both writers are clearly derivative in some ways from Hugo Grotius and in other ways from Thomas Hobbes. Very tellingly, Pufendorf prominently describes Hobbes's *De Cive* (1642) (on being a citizen), which anticipates the moral and jurisprudential substance of Hobbes's more famous *Leviathan* (1651), as 'for the most part extremely acute and sound'.[7]

From Grotius's massively influential *On the Law of War and Peace* (1625), Locke and Pufendorf take the well-sounding but quite opaque idea that morality and the law's basic principles are a matter of 'conformity to rational nature'. How this nature is known, and why it is normative for anyone, these writers never carefully consider. Such fundamental questions were confronted and answered by Hobbes. But his answers treat our practical reasoning as all in the service of sub-rational passions such as fear of death, and desire to surpass others—motivations of the very kind identified by the classical tradition as in need of direction by our reason's grasp of more ultimate and better ends, of true and intrinsic goods, of really intelligent reasons for action. Hobbes proclaims his contempt for the classical search for ultimate ends or intrinsic reasons for action. Accordingly there can be for him no question of finding the source of obligation and law in the kind of necessity which we identify when we notice that some specific means is *required* by and for the sake of some end which it would be unreasonable not to judge desirable and

---

[4] *Elementorum Jurisprudentiae Universalis Libri Duo* by Samuel Pufendorf, vol. ii, *The Translation*, by William Abbott Oldfather (Oxford: Oxford University Press, 1931) (hereafter *Elements*).

[5] *De Jure Naturae et Gentium Libri Octo* by Samuel Pufendorf, vol. ii, *The Translation*, by C. H. Oldfather and W. A. Oldfather (Oxford: Oxford University Press, 1934).

[6] Ed. Robert Horwitz, Jenny Strauss Clay, and Diskin Clay (Ithaca, NY: Cornell University Press, 1990); also published as W. von Leyden (ed.), *Essays on the Law of Nature* (Oxford: Oxford University Press, 1954).

[7] Pufendorf, *Elements*, preface, p. xxx.

pursuit-worthy.[8] Rather, obligation and law are defined, by Hobbes and then by Locke and Pufendorf, as matters of superior *will*.

'No law without a legislator.'[9] No obligation without subjection to the 'will of a superior power'.[10] 'Law's formal definition' is: the declaration of a superior will.'[11] 'The rule of our actions is the will of a superior power.'[12] These definitions and axioms are meant by these founders of modern natural law theory to be as applicable to natural law, the very principles of morality, as to the positive law of states.[13] So obligation is being openly 'deduced' from fact, the fact that such and such has been willed by a superior. To be sure, when natural law (morality) is in issue, the superior, God, is assumed to be wise. But the idea of divine wisdom is given no positive role in explaining why God's commands create obligations for a rational conscience. God's *right* to legislate is explained instead by the analogy of sheer power: 'For who will deny that clay is subject to the potter's will and that the pot can be destroyed by the same hand that shaped it?'[14]

Locke, like Hobbes, is uneasily though dimly aware that 'ought' cannot be inferred from 'is' without some further 'ought'. That is to say, he is uneasily aware that the fact that conduct *was* willed by a superior, or indeed by a party to a contract, does not explain why that conduct is *now* obligatory, or indeed can ever be *obligatory* at all. So he sometimes thinks of supplementing his naked voluntarism (oughts are explained by acts of will) by the rationality of logical coherence: fundamental moral principles are tautologies, norms which it would be *self-contradictory* to deny.[15] Hobbes had ventured a similar account of the obligatoriness of his fundamental social contract, of subjection to the sovereign. His official and prominent explanation was of the form, 'clubs are trumps' (superior will and power/force). But, for anyone unimpressed by the naked assimilation of right with might and ought with is, he offers another explanation: it is *self-contradictory* not to keep a promise one has made.[16]

---

[8] What this obligation-explaining end is, in the last analysis, is considered in Sect. 7 below.

[9] Locke, *Questions*, 192–3.   [10] ibid. 158–9, 166–7.   [11] See ibid. 102–3

[12] See ibid. 204–5

[13] See e.g. Pufendorf, *Elements*, i, def. 12, sect. 17: 'For, if you have removed God from the function of administering justice, all the efficacy of . . . pacts, to the observance of which one of the contracting parties is not able to compel the other by force, will immediately expire, and everyone will measure justice by his own particular advantage. And assuredly, if we are willing to confess the truth, once the fear of divine vengeance has been removed, there appears no sufficient reason why I should be at all obligated, after the conditions governing my advantage have once changed, to furnish that thing, for the furnishing to the second party I had bound myself while my interests led in that direction; that is, of course, if I have to fear no real evil, at least from any man, in consequence of that act.'

[14] Locke, *Questions*, 165–6: 'patet . . . posse homines a rebus sensibilibus colligere *superiorem esse aliquem potentem sapientemque* qui in homines ipsos *jus habet et imperium*. Quis *enim* negabit lutum figuli *voluntati esse subjectum*, testamque eadem manu qua formata est' (emphasis added, here as elsewhere).

[15] See Locke, *Questions*, 178–9 (passage deleted by Locke in 1664).

[16] See Hobbes, *De Corpore Politico* (1650), part I, ch. 3; *Leviathan*, ch. 14; Finnis, *Natural Law and Natural Rights* (Oxford: Oxford University Press, 1980) (hereafter *NLNR*), 348–9 (quoting and analysing the relevant passages, and pointing to the fallacies of temporal equivocation and unexplained chronological preference inherent in the strategy).

The strategy of assimilating the norms of natural law (morality) with those of logic finds its principal exponent in Kant, whose *Metaphysics of Morals* (1797) is in some ways the most sophisticated exposition of modern natural law theory. Officially rejecting any reduction of *ought* to the *is* of will, Kant holds that reason alone holds sway in conscientious deliberation and action. The rational necessity decisive for this sway is the logical necessity of non-contradiction, and all Kant's efforts to explain particular kinds of obligation (promissory, proprietary, political, marital etc.) are claims that to proceed on any other 'maxim of action' would entail (self-)contradiction.[17]

Kant's reductions of moral rationality to logic all fail. They were bound to, because his basic theory lacks the concept of a substantive reason for action—a reason which is not a true judgment about natural facts, nor a logical requirement, nor a technical necessity of efficient means to a definite and realizable end. His theoretical and practical purpose is to save the content of civilization from the ravages of utilitarianism and scepticism. He articulates with novel power the radically anti-utilitarian principle that one must always treat humanity, in oneself as in others, as an end and never as a mere means. But his own official definition of 'humanity' would rob this categorical imperative of its significance. For if our humanity is, as he says, our rationality, and that rationality has no directive content save that one be consistent, we are left with neither rational motivation nor intelligent direction that could count in deliberation.

In the end, like Locke and Hume, Kant remains firmly in the grip of the assumption that what motivates us towards one purpose rather than another is our sub-rational passions. He lacks almost all the building blocks of classical natural law theory, the substantive first principles—basic reasons for action—that direct us towards bodily life and health, marriage, friendship, knowledge, and so forth,[18] as the intrinsic human goods which give us reasons (intelligent, not merely passionate motives) for action, and which, as aspects of our humanity as flesh-and-blood persons, are to be treated always as ends and never as mere means. He cannot account for the obligations and institutions which he does try to justify, let alone others which he overlooks, such as the obligation in justice to employ much of one's wealth for the relief of the needs of others. Kant's official rejection of reductions of *ought* to the *is* of will is subverted by the ambiguities of his claim that the moral law is a matter of one's legislation for oneself, ambiguities made inevitable by the absence of any substantive *ends* (*reasons for* action) in his conception of what practical reason understands.[19]

In the mid-twentieth century it became popular to distinguish classical from modern natural law theory by saying that the former works with the idea of natural *right*

[17] See *NLNR*, 349.
[18] For a list of basic goods, see e.g. Finnis, 'Is Natural Law Theory Compatible with Limited Government?', in Robert P. George (ed.), *Liberalism and Morality* (Oxford: Oxford University Press, 1996), 1–26 at 4; more fully, *Aquinas*, 79–86; earlier, Finnis, *NLNR*, 59–99.
[19] See Finnis, 'Legal Enforcement of Duties to Oneself: Kant versus Neo-Kantians', *Columbia Law Review*, 87 (1987), 433–56 at 443–5, 454–6.

but, unlike the latter, has no concept of natural or human *rights*. Some scholars added
that the concept of natural rights is inextricably bound up with the individualist voluntarism of theories which try—of course in vain, like Hobbes—to ground political
obligation in a contract of self-imposed political allegiance, and which often fail to
integrate rights to freedom with obligations both of self-restraint and of service to
others. And so the shift from classical to modern was judged by some a mere corruption of thought. But further reflection and investigation has shown that the concept,
if not the idiom, of natural or human rights is certainly present in the classical theory,
and deserves a central place in any sound moral and political theory (see further Sect.
8 below).

So the break between 'modern' and 'classical' natural law theories should be
located, fundamentally, in the loss of the classical theorists' insight that one comes to
understand human nature only by understanding human capacities, and these
capacities in turn only by understanding the acts which actualize them, and those
acts only by understanding their 'objects', that is, the goods they intend to attain.[20]
Those goods are the *reasons* we have for action, and nothing in moral, political, or
legal theory is well understood save by attending to those goods with full attention to
their intrinsic worth, the ways they fulfil and perfect human persons, and their directiveness or normativity for all thinking about what is to be done.

3 EXCLUSIVE LEGAL POSITIVISM

The notion that there are no standards of action save those created—put in place,
posited—by conventions, commands, or other such social facts was well known to
Plato and Aristotle.[21] Developing a sustained critique of any such notion was a primary objective of these philosophers and of successors of theirs such as Cicero. Today
the promoters of this radical kind of 'exclusive positivism' are the followers, conscious or unconscious, of Nietzsche or of others who like him reduce ethics and normative political or legal theory to a search for the 'genealogy', the immediate and
deeper historical (perhaps partly or wholly physiological) sources, of ethical, political, or legal standards. These standards have their immediate sources in exercises of
the will of charismatic individuals or power-seeking groups, and their deeper sources
in the supposedly will-like sub-rational drives and compulsions of domination, submission, resentment, and so forth. Such ideas about the 'genealogy of morals' are also
found among those who today promote 'pragmatism' in legal theory.

---

[20] See *Aquinas*, 29–34, 90–91.   [21] See e.g. *Nicomachean Ethics*, I: 1094b15–16.

Legal positivism is in principle a more modest proposal: that state law is, or should systematically be studied as if it were, a set of standards originated exclusively by conventions, commands, or other such social facts. As developed by Bentham, Austin, and Kelsen, legal positivism was officially neutral on the question whether, outside the law, there are moral standards whose directiveness (normativity, authority, obligatoriness) is not to be explained entirely by any social fact. Bentham and Austin certainly did not think that their utilitarian morality depended for its obligatoriness upon the say-so of any person or group, even though Austin held that the whole content of utilitarian moral requirements is also commanded by God. Until near the end of his life, Kelsen's official theory—at least when he was doing legal philosophy—was that there may be moral truths, but if so they are completely outside the field of vision of legal science or philosophy. His final position, however, was one of either complete moral scepticism or undiluted moral voluntarism: moral norms could not be other than commands of God, if God there were. Such a position was the consummation, not only of the voluntarism that ran through all Kelsen's theorizing about positive law, but also of every earlier theory which took for granted (see Sect. 2 above) that law and its obligatoriness are and must be a resultant of the will and coercive power of a superior. As Kelsen argues, this position ultimately leaves no room for a requirement of logical consistency in the law, or for any attempt to reason that a general rule ('murder is to be punished'), taken with a relevant factual proposition ('Smith murdered Jones last week'), can require a normative conclusion ('Smith is to be punished'). The only source of normativity, and therefore of the normativity of a particular norm, is positivity, that is, the actual willing of that norm by a superior; reason, even the rationality of logic and uncontroversial legal reasoning by subsumption of facts under rules, can never substitute for will.[22]

Kelsen's final positions cannot be written off as eccentricities, of merely biographical interest. Still, the exclusive legal positivism defended today by legal philosophers such as Joseph Raz, is very different.[23] While affirming that all *law* is based upon and validated by social-fact sources—the affirmation which makes it exclusive legal positivism—it accepts also that judges can and not rarely do have a legal and moral obligation to include in their judicial reasoning principles and norms which are applicable because, although not legally valid (because not hitherto posited by any social-fact source), they are, or are taken by the judge in question to be, *morally true*. Perhaps some enacted rule is directing the judge to decide certain cases according to what is fair and equitable. Or perhaps the judge considers that where substantive justice is sufficiently urgently at stake, judges are entitled to import the moral rule of justice where it is not explicitly excluded by any legally posited rule.

---

[22] Hans Kelsen, *The General Theory of Norms*, 1st pub. 1979, trans. Michael Hartney (Oxford: Oxford University Press, 1991), chs. 57–8.

[23] See, e.g., 'A postscript', in Marshall Cohen (ed.), *Ronald Dworkin and Contemporary Jurisprudence* (London: Duckworth, 1984), 81–7.

Classical natural law theory does not reject the theses that what has been posited is positive, and what has not been posited is not positive. (Indeed, the very term 'positive law' is one imported into philosophy by Aquinas, who was also the first to propose that the whole law of a political community may be considered philosophically as *positive* law.)[24] But the theses need much clarification. What does it mean to say that a rule, principle, or other standard 'has been posited by a social-fact source'? Does it mean what Kelsen finally took it to mean, that nothing short of express articulation of the very norm in all its specificity—and no kind of mere derivation (inference) or derivability—will suffice? Virtually no other positivist can be found to follow Kelsen here. But if not, which kinds of consistency-with-what-has-been-specifically-articulated by a social-fact source are necessary and sufficient to entitle a standard to be counted as 'posited'? By what criteria is one to answer that last theoretical question? Clearly, legal theorists have little reason to be content with any notion that legal theory should merely report the social facts about what has and has not been expressly posited, by actual acts of deliberate articulation, in this or that community. Raz himself goes well beyond so confined a project when he affirms that courts characteristically have the legal and/or moral duty to apply non-legal standards.

Now consider the judicial or juristic process of identifying a moral standard as one which anyone adjudicating a given case has the duty to apply even though it has not (yet) been posited by the social facts of custom, enactment, or prior adjudication. This specific moral standard will usually be a specification of some very general principle such as fairness, of rejecting favourable or unfavourable treatment which is arbitrary when measured by the principle (the Golden Rule) that like cases are to be treated alike, unlike cases differently, and one should do for others what one would have them do for oneself or for those one already favours . . . (see Sect. 10 below). But such a specification—a making more specific—of a general moral principle cannot reasonably proceed without close attention to the way classes of persons, things, and activities are already treated by the indubitably posited law. Without such attention one cannot settle what cases are alike and what different, and cannot know what classes of persons, acts, or things are already favoured, or disfavoured, by the existing positive law. The selection of the morally right standard, the morally right resolution of the case in hand, can therefore be done properly only by those who know the posited (positive) law well enough to know what new dispute-resolving standard really fits it better than any alternative standard. This selection, when thus made judicially, is in a sense 'making' new law. But this judicial responsibility, as judges regularly remind themselves (and counsel, and their readers), is significantly different from the authority of legislatures to enact wide measures of repeal, make novel classifications of persons, things, and acts, and draw bright lines of distinction which

---

[24] See Finnis, 'The Truth in Legal Positivism', in Robert P. George (ed.), *The Autonomy of Law* (Oxford: Oxford University Press, 1996), 195–214.

could reasonably have been drawn in other ways. This significant difference can reasonably be signalled by saying that the 'new' judicially adopted standard, being so narrowly controlled by the contingencies of the existing posited law, was in an important sense *already part* of the law.[25] (See further Sect. 14 below.) Exclusive legal positivism's refusal to countenance such a way of speaking is inadequately grounded.

The law has a double life, for a judge or a lawyer trying to track judicial reasoning. It exists as the sheer fact that certain people have done such and such in the past, and that certain people here and now have such and such dispositions to decide and act. These facts provide exclusive legal positivism with its account of a community's law.[26] But the law also exists as standards directive for the conscientious deliberations of those whose responsibility is to decide (do justice) according to law. From this 'internal' viewpoint, the social facts of positing yield both too little and too much. Too little, because in cases of legal *development* of the kind just sketched, those facts, while never irrelevant, must be supplemented by moral standards to be applied because true. And too much, because sometimes the social-fact sources yield standards so morally flawed that even judges sworn to follow the law should set them aside in favour of alternative norms more consistent both with moral principle (full practical reasonableness) and with all those other parts of the posited law which are consistent with moral principle.

On positivism's incoherence and redundancy, see Section 7 below.

4 INCLUSIVE LEGAL POSITIVISM

Inclusive legal positivists are unwilling to sever the question 'What is the law governing this case?' from the question 'What, according to our law, is my duty as judge in this case?' If a state's law, taken as a whole, explicitly or implicitly authorizes or requires the judges, in certain kinds of case, to ask themselves what morality requires in circumstances of this kind, then the moral standard(s) answering that question—or at least the moral conclusions applicable in such circumstances—have legal as well as moral authority. The moral standard(s) are to that extent, and for that reason, to be counted as part of our law. They are, as some say, 'included' within or 'incorporated' into the community's law. The exclusive legal positivist (to recall) insists that

[25] See Finnis, 'The Fairy Tale's Moral', *Law Quarterly Review*, 115 (1999), 170–5 at 174–5.

[26] Raz rightly begins to leave behind the view that legal theory should attend only to what is posited in social-fact sources, when he affirms that law is systemic, so that the content of what counts as 'expressly posited' is settled by the content of *other* norms and principles of the system. For this entails that, even if these other standards are each posited by social facts, no law-makers, judicial or otherwise, do or can settle by themselves the legal content and effect of their act (social fact) of positing.

such standards, even if controlling the judges' duty in such a case, remain outside the law, excluded from it by their lack (at least hitherto) of social-fact pedigree.

Those who work in the classical natural law tradition suspect that the disputes between exclusive and inclusive legal positivists are a fruitless demarcation dispute, little more than a squabble about the word 'law' or 'legal system'. As was stated at the end of Section 3, law in general, and the law of a particular community past or present, can be profitably considered in one or other of two basic ways. It can be considered as a complex fact about the opinions and practices of a set or persons at some time, prioritizing (usually) the beliefs and practices of those members of the community who are professionally concerned with law as judges, legal advisers, bailiffs, police, and so forth. In describing this complex fact, one will observe that these people treat the law as a reason for action, and one will perhaps describe the law as they do, as a set of reasons (some authorizing, some obligating, some both) which are systematized by interrelationships of derivation, interpretative constraint, or other kinds of interdependence, and which purport to give coherent guidance. But since one is ultimately concerned with the facts about this set of people's belief and practice, one will not need to make judgments about whether the system's standards are indeed coherent, or whether its most basic rules of validation, authorization, origination, or recognition satisfyingly account for the system's other standards or give anyone a truly reasonable, rationally sufficient reason for acting in a specific way, whether as judge, citizen, or otherwise.

Alternatively, law and the law of a particular community can be considered precisely as good reasons for action. But, when deliberation runs its course, the really good and only truly sufficient *reasons* we have for action (and forbearance from action) are moral reasons: that is what it is for a reason to be moral, in the eyes of anyone who intends to think and act with the autonomy, the self-determination and conscientiousness, that the classical tradition makes central.[27] And it is obvious that, *for the purposes of this kind of consideration*, nothing will count as law unless it is in line with morality's requirements, both positive and negative. Morality, for reasons to be indicated (see Sect. 7 below), requires that we concern ourselves with making, executing, complying with, and maintaining positive, social-fact source-based and pedigreed laws, and that we keep them coherent with each other. These positive laws add something, indeed much, to morality's inherent directives. What is added is specific to the community, time, and place in question, even if it is, as it doubtless often should be, the same in content as other specific communities' positive-law standards on the relevant matters.

Classical natural law theory is primarily concerned with this second kind of enquiry. But it has respect for descriptive, historical, 'sociological' considerations of the first kind, and seeks to benefit from them. Classical natural law theory also, as we shall see (Sect. 5 below), offers reason for considering *general* descriptions of law

---

[27] See Plato, *Gorgias*; Aquinas, *Summa Theologiae*, I–II, prol.; *Aquinas*, 20, 124–5.

fruitful only if their basic conceptual structure is, self-consciously and critically, derived from that understanding of *good reasons* which enquiries of the second kind make it their business to reach by open debate and critical assessment.

Anyone who makes and adheres steadily to this basic distinction between enquiries about what *is* (or *was*, or *is likely*) and enquiries about what *ought* to be will notice that much of the debate among legal positivists arises from, or at least involves, an inattention to the distinction. Indeed, much of the contemporary jurisprudential literature swings back and forth between the rigorously descriptive ('external' to conscience) and the rigorously normative ('internal' to conscience), offering various but always incoherent mixes of the two. A rigorously descriptive understanding of Ruritania's law can do no more than report that it is widely or in some other way *accepted* in Ruritania that in certain circumstances the judges should settle cases by applying standards which they judge morally true even though unpedigreed—that is, not hitherto certified by any social-fact source of law.

Suppose that the rule of recognition so reported includes in its own terms the statement that any unpedigreed standard which the judges are required or authorized by this rule of recognition to apply (because considered by them to be morally true) shall be taken and declared by the judges to be *an integral part of the community's law*. What reason have exclusive positivists to say that such a rule of recognition is somehow false to the nature of law? Suppose, on the other hand, that Ruritania's rule of recognition stipulates (*a*) that under certain conditions its judges are *required* to apply an unpedigreed standard because they consider it *morally true*, but also (*b*) that in doing so they shall treat that standard *not* as an *integral part* of Ruritanian law, but rather as analogous to those rules of foreign states which are applicable in Ruritanian courts by virtue of the choice-of-law rules in Ruritania's law of Conflicts of Laws. (Stipulation (*b*) could well have legal consequences, e.g. in cases concerning the retrospective applicability of the standard, or its use in assessing whether there has been a 'mistake of law' for the purposes of rules of limitation of action, or restitution.) What reason have inclusive legal positivists to say that part (*b*) of such a rule of recognition is somehow false to the nature of law?

Can a dispute between rival 'isms' in legal philosophy have serious theoretical content if it could be affected by what a particular community declares to be its law? No truth about law seems to be systematically at stake in contemporary disputes between exclusive and inclusive legal positivists. The central dispute seems not worth pursuing. Provided one makes oneself clear and unambiguous to one's readers, it matters not at all whether one defines positive law as (*a*) all and only the pedigreed standards or as (*b*) all and only the standards applicable by judges acting as such. Either definition has its advantages and inconveniences. Counting as law only (*a*) what has been pedigreed has the inconveniences already mentioned: the relationship between legal duty and the duty of courts seems to fall outside the 'science' or 'philosophy' *of law*, and there seems no way of specifying precisely what counts as 'pedigreed' ('derived', 'derivable', etc.) short of the late-Kelsenian amputation of most of juristic thought and method (i.e. all reasoning from one standard to another, or from systematic consistency) by virtue of the demand that there be a specific act of will to pedigree each and every proposition of law. Counting as law (*b*) whatever standards the courts have a judicial duty to enforce has the inconvenience that it cannot be done well—critically and sufficiently—without undertaking precisely the task, and following substantially the route, of classical natural law theory.

Law's 'positivity' was first articulated, embraced, and explained by the classical natural law theorists.[28] Legal positiv*ism* identifies itself as a challenge to natural law theories. It has had, say, 225 years[29] to make its challenge intelligible. The best its contemporary exponents can offer as a statement of its challenge seems to be: 'there is no necessary connection between law and morality'.[30] But classical natural law theory has always enthusiastically affirmed that statement. Some *laws* are utterly unjust, utterly immoral; the fact that something is declared or enacted as law by the social sources authorized or recognized as sources of valid law in no way entails that it is (or is even regarded by anyone as) morally acceptable or is even relevant to a consideration of someone's moral responsibilities (whether in truth, or according to some conventional or idiosyncratic understanding). There is no necessary connection between law and morality or moral responsibility. The claim that natural law theories overlook some of the social facts relevant to law is simply, and demonstrably, false.

So the statement meant to define legal positivism is badly in need of clarification. (See further Sect. 7 below.) More fundamentally still, no genuine clarification is possible without considering *both* terms of the alleged disjunction: law *and* morality. That there is *no* necessary connection, in any relevant sense of 'connection' and 'necessity', could not be rationally affirmed without steady, critical attention to *what morality has to say* about law, either in general or as the law of particular communities. What basis is there for asserting, or implying, or allowing it to be thought, that lawyers, judges, and other citizens or subjects of the law should not, or need not, be concerned—precisely when considering how the law bears on their responsibilities

---

[28] See Sect. 3 at n. 24 above.

[29] That is, since Jeremy Bentham, *A Comment on the Commentaries* (London, 1776).

[30] Thus Jules L. Coleman and Brian Leiter, 'Legal Positivism', in Dennis Patterson, *A Companion to Philosophy of Law and Legal Theory* (Oxford and Cambridge, Mass., Blackwell, 1996), 241. They add one other 'central belief' and one further 'commitment'. (i) The central belief is that 'what counts as law in any particular society is fundamentally a matter of social fact or convention ("the social thesis")'. On this the classical natural law theorist will comment that it is equivocal between (*a*) the tautologous proposition that what is counted as law in a particular society is counted as law in that society, and (*b*) the false proposition that what counts as law for fully reasonable persons (e.g. fully reasonable judges) deliberating about their responsibilities is all and only what is counted as law by others in that society—false because *ought* (e.g. the ought of reasonable responsibility) is not entailed by *is* (and see Sect. 7 below). (ii) The further commitment is 'a commitment to the idea that the phenomena comprising the domain at issue (for example, law . . .) must be accessible to the human mind'. This commitment is fully shared by classical natural law theory, which defines natural law as principles accessible to the human mind, and positive law as rules devised by human minds (either reasserting those principles and/or supplementing them by 'specification').

as lawyers and so forth—with the question what *morality* has to say about law, and about what is *entitled* to count as law? And where is a student of law going to find such a steady, critical attention to morality as it bears on law, and on the very idea of law, and on particular laws, other than in an enquiry which, whatever its label, extends as ambitiously far as classical natural law theory does?

If you want to be 'positivist', 'rigorously descriptive' about law as a kind of social fact, you had better be positivist, rigorously descriptive, about morality, too. It is careless of 'inclusive legal positivists' to assume that any legal system whose pedigreed sources refer its judges to 'morality' ('justice' etc.) is a legal system that includes *morality*. What that legal system, descriptively regarded, includes is: what that community or those judges think moral, a set of beliefs which, morally regarded, may well be radically immoral. There is no halfway house, as inclusive legal positivists seem to suppose, between considering law and morality as social facts (as *beliefs about* reasons for action, and practices corresponding to such beliefs) and considering them as reasons for action (genuine reasons).[31] Considered precisely as genuine *reasons* for action, positive laws are social facts which count as reasons—as positive law—just in so far as morality makes their social sources and their social-fact content count.

5 METHODOLOGY

There is much uncertainty in contemporary jurisprudence about whether its subject-matter is (*a*) the *concept* of law, or rather (*b*) law as a social reality and/or as a kind of reason for action, of which people including theorists have more and less adequate concepts.[32] Late twentieth-century legal theory's paradigm text is called *The Concept of Law*.[33] But despite the definite article ('the'), Hart's book takes it as obvious that there exist many concepts of law, and even of the law of sophisticated nation states. The book does not for a moment try to establish that there exists in some communities, large or

[31] There is a third or 'halfway house' way of *articulating* law or morality, the 'detached' or 'professional' statement in which one speaks *as if* one were articulating standards as genuine reasons for action, while in fact reserving one's opinion. And indeed there are many other ways of speaking, including lying, play-acting, and so forth. None of this affects the position stated in the text.

[32] See e.g. Joseph Raz, 'Two Views of the Nature of the Theory of Law: A Partial Comparison', *Legal Theory*, 4 (1998), 249–82 at 280: 'legal philosophy . . . merely explains the concept that exists independently of it'; 256: 'having a concept can fall well short of a thorough knowledge of *the nature of the thing* it is a concept of . . . a philosophical explanation . . . aims at improving [people's] understanding *of the concept* in one respect or another' (emphases added; Raz's italicizing of the first three words removed). But see also n. 35 below.

[33] H. L. A. Hart, *The Concept of Law* (Oxford: Oxford University Press, 1961, 2nd edn. 1994).

small, a concept of law which is entitled to be called 'the' concept of law. Instead it attends to the reality of law, both as a 'social phenomenon' and as a characteristic kind of 'reason for action', and—with notable if incomplete success—seeks by doing so to arrive at an 'improved understanding', a *better concept*, of law. Hart might more accurately, if less elegantly, have called his book *A New and Improved Concept of Law*.

Such an uncertainty about subject-matter is an uncertainty about method. One cause of the uncertainty is that, as was said in Section 3 above, law has a double life. More precisely, there is the law that exists as reportable facts about the ideas and practices of a community. And there is the law that is a set of reasons for action which count in the deliberations of someone who, in the circumstances of a particular community, is deliberating with full reasonableness about what to do. For such a person, a purported reason is a *reason* only if it is a reason which is *good* precisely as a reason. Somewhat similarly, for logicians an invalid argument towards a conclusion is *no* argument, no reason for affirming the conclusion. To be sure, the reasons which we call our law are profoundly and in almost every detail shaped by our community's present and past ideas and practices. But what makes a reason a good reason for action can, in the last analysis, never be a fact, such as facts about what a certain community does or thinks. No *ought* from a mere *is*. So, once again (see Sects. 3 and 4) there are two distinct kinds of worthwhile enquiry about law, not one. There is inquiry about law *as* a matter of fact, that is, about what is in fact, reasonably or unreasonably, counted as law in particular communities and sub-communities. And there is inquiry about the laws *as* giving reasons (= good reasons) for acting as, say, a judge.

It is of course possible to understand and describe a person's or a people's reasons for action without oneself regarding them as sound reasons. One can 'adopt' another's viewpoint without 'endorsing' it, describe evaluations without evaluating, and so on. But if one aspires to say something *general* about human affairs, and to get beyond an endless newsreel, a listing and reproduction of other people's ideas in their conceptual idiom, one must judge which concepts better illuminate the human situation, and which purported reasons for action are more important for understanding human conduct and opportunities. Does *any* idea of law earn its place in general accounts of human affairs, or should it be replaced, in such accounts, with a concept such as domination, or socialization, or relationships of production and consumption? And if it earns its place, why so, and in what form? Command of superiors? Rules for efficient survival? Or for dispute resolution? Or for common good? And so on.

Classical natural law theory, as Aristotle's work makes plain, considers that the proper method in social sciences, including the political theory of which legal theory is a part (see Sect. 6), requires that the selection of concepts for use in general descriptions and explanations be guided by the very same criteria that the theorist employs when judging what is *good* for a society (and therefore also what is *bad* for it), that is, when judging what are good reasons for actions in the kinds of situation encountered by and in the theorist's own society. There is thus an inherent, if often unrecognized, dependence of descriptive general social theory (such as Hart's *The Concept of Law*) upon the conscientious evaluations of the person who is now not deliberating but rather theorizing (describing, explaining, analysing).

Notwithstanding Hart's claims to descriptive neutrality or value-freedom, his actual method abundantly verifies what classical theory asserts. *General* description and explanation are necessarily dependent on evaluations presumed to be shared between writer and reader. Rightly Hart proceeds at every point by identifying social functions, benefits, amenities, defects and their remedies, and so forth. Without these appeals to value, to good reasons for action, his arguments against rival descriptive and explanatory theories of law could hardly begin let alone succeed. There are no grounds for thinking that it could be otherwise. The history of legal theories which, like Bentham's or Kelsen's, attempted to base themselves on bare fact is a history of definitions which manage to combine arbitrariness with lack of explanatory power.[34] And we need not accept Raz's claim[35] that we can come to know the 'essential nature' or 'essential properties' of law without considering what kind of other rule(s), institution(s) or, in general, social arrangement(s) and corresponding reason(s) for action, it would be valuable to have to overcome or alleviate the evils of anarchy, tyranny, and the 'rule of men'. Nor his equivalent claim that 'law has' its essential nature or properties otherwise than in virtue of requirements of practical reason, that is, of the reasons there are for action: human goods.

The classical concepts of analogy and focal meaning, used extensively by Plato and articulated by Aristotle and Aquinas, enable theory to proceed on this basis without suppressing or even obscuring any of the evils, deviations, perversions, and vicious practices or institutions which disfigure human affairs. The immature, the decayed, the parasitic, and the morally corrupted instances of constitutions, or friendship, or legal system, are not allowed to force a thinning down of the account of the good kinds of constitution, friendship, law, etc., but appear in the account, none the less, as what they are: as not *fully* constitutions, law, and so on—not central cases of

---

[34] There is a moment in Bentham's thought when he half sees the intrinsic connection between understanding law and evaluating it: see his *An Introduction to the Principles of Morals and Legislation* (first printed 1780, ed. Wilfrid Harrison, Oxford: Basil Blackwell, 1967), 401 (ch. 16, para. 57); likewise paras 48–57 of his *A Fragment on Government* (first published 1776, ed. Harrison 1967), 23–5. But his official and stable view of general descriptive jurisprudence is the raw, barren, and reality-obscuring empiricism of his *Of Laws in General*, ed. Hart (University of London, Athlone Press, 1970).

[35] Joseph Raz, 'Postema on Law's Autonomy and Public Practical Reasons: A Critical Comment', *Legal Theory*, 4 (1998), 1–20 at 16. But cf. Raz, 'Two Views of the Nature of the Theory of Law', n. 31, at 267: 'Hart . . . denied that the explanation of the nature of law is evaluative. For him it was a 'descriptive' enterprise. For reasons explained by John Finnis [*NLNR*, ch. 1], I believe that Hart is mistaken here, and Dworkin is right that the explanation of the nature of law involves evaluative considerations.' Still Raz, like other contemporary positivists who acknowledge the necessity of such 'evaluation', insists that it need not and should not or does not extend to *moral* evaluation. Like Hart's insistence that the evaluation which is intrinsic to the concept of law can and should be limited to 'survival', all such attempts to truncate practical reason (evaluation) seem arbitrary.

those kinds of human reality and human purposefulness, and not within the focal meaning of those terms.[36]

This method is used throughout my *Natural Law and Natural Rights*: see especially the definition of law, and my explanation of the ways in which reaching such a definition differs from 'describing a concept'. The classical method is vindicated in general terms in chapter 1 of that book, and its bearing on the remarkable mistakes of interpretation made by positivists when they glance at classical texts is explained in the penultimate chapter (on unjust laws).

6 ON THE RELATIONSHIP BETWEEN LEGAL AND POLITICAL PHILOSOPHY

Aristotle's treatment of law appears in both parts of his 'philosophy of human affairs': in book V of his *Ethics*, in book III and other parts of his *Politics*, and as the subject-matter of his careful bridging passage between the two treatises (the final pages of *Ethics*, book X). Aquinas's main treatment appears in two prominent parts of his vast treatise on human self-determination (part II of his *Summa Theologiae*): a treatment dedicated to over forty issues about law as a kind of guide to co-ordination (qq. 90–7 of part I–II), and a treatment of rights, adjudication, and many related aspects of justice (in the midst of part II–II, esp. qq. 57–71).

As these analyses and syntheses suggest, both legal philosophy and political philosophy are parts of aspects of a wider enterprise, no part of which can safely be pursued without some attention to the others and to the character of the whole. That wider enterprise could be characterized as Aristotle does: 'philosophy of human affairs'. Or, more pointedly, as Aquinas does: the study of human action as self-determined and self-determining. Neither characterization in any way excludes the analysis of those aspects of human make-up, motivation, and behaviour that are biological, physiological, and in many respects similar to the life of other animals and organisms. But in focusing specifically upon the implications of human *freedom of choice*, Aquinas is putting squarely on the table, for critical analysis and appropria-

---

[36] There is no suggestion here that to understand *any* term, one must identify one instance (or type of instance) as central or paradigmatic, and one meaning as focal. On the contrary, the identification of meanings as 'focal' and instances or types as 'central' is always *relative* to some viewpoint or specific line of inquiry or focus of interest, and so has a particular importance in the social sciences, in so far as their subject-matter is constituted by what people have chosen to do: Finnis, 'Reason, Authority and Friendship in Law and Morals', in B. Y. Khanbai, R. S. Katz, and R. A. Pineau, *Jowett Papers 1968–1969* (Oxford: Blackwell, 1970), 101–24 at 101; *NLNR*, 11; *Aquinas*, 45–6: '*Judged by the standards appropriate for evaluating human actions as reasonable or unreasonable*, some constitutions are central . . .'.

tion, that feature of human reality which makes sense of practical philosophy's distinctive concern with understanding action from 'the internal point of view', that is, precisely as action is understood by the acting person who deliberates, identifies intelligent options, chooses, and successfully or unsuccessfully carries out the intention(s) so adopted.

Those who thus deliberate with intelligence, honesty, and care about what to do find good reasons to respect and promote the well-being not only of themselves but of the members of their family, of their neighbourhood, and of their economic associates and associations. The critical reflective analysis of those reasons is what Aristotle called ethics. In the first instance this is the ethics which focuses on the core of an individual's self-determination, virtue, or viciousness, and so forth. This focus tends to abstract somewhat from the full range of *inter-personal* associations whose flourishing is intrinsic, not merely instrumental, to any individual's well-being. So the study of the ethical ideas of, for example, justice, or marriage, broadens out into the practical philosophy of households, their 'economy', and its relationship to the wider network of economic relations which we follow Aristotle in calling economics. But the reasoning about what to do—about what anyone should regard as a responsibility—cannot rest there. Problems of justice between contracting parties (including spouses), between injurer and injured (including parent and child), between property-holder and trespasser, and so forth, and similarly problems of co-ordinating action—be it for defence of the whole network of neighbourhoods and associations, or to facilitate exchange, productive enterprise, and fair distribution of wealth—all call for the institution and maintenance of an all-embracing association of the kind we call political community or state. Ethical philosophy, without any essential shift in its normative, good-reason-seeking purpose and method, extends into political philosophy. And since the problems of administering justice, and of co-ordination for defence and economic welfare, cannot reasonably be resolved without new norms of conduct, new procedures for enforcing morality's perennial requirements, and new procedures for introducing and maintaining those new norms and procedures appropriately, political philosophy must include a theory of law.

In so far as it is a matter of acknowledging genuinely good reasons for action, the philosophy of politics and law cannot but be as normative as ethics itself, of which it is a specialized extension. In so far, however, as ethics is a matter of reasonable ways of thinking, both ethics in general and political and legal philosophy in particular draw upon logic, a distinct because wider discipline. Similarly, in so far as ethics and the rest of practical philosophy guide the conduct of flesh-and-blood people, they draw also upon the understanding of nature which we call science and Aristotelians used to call natural philosophy. And finally, in so far as law's ethically warranted response to the problems of social life mentioned in the previous paragraph involves the *creation* of new norms and institutions by the manipulation of language and of other conventional devices such as voting systems, jurisdictional boundaries, and so forth, legal philosophy has the character of other non-ethical 'arts'—techniques and technologies for attaining goals far more limited than ethics' unbounded horizon of human good. So, just as technologies cannot be reduced to ethics (nor technologies and ethics to logic or natural science), so legal theory cannot be reduced without remainder to ethics or to political philosophy in general.

'Legal realism' tends to reduce its subject-matter and method to natural science. Kantian legal theory tends to reduce its subject-matter, and its method, to logic. Positivisms of various kinds, to the extent that they are not simply incoherent (see Sects. 4 above and 7 below), reduce legal theory to a kind of technology. Natural law theory seeks to avoid all these kinds of reductionism. And its centrepiece is its explanation of why, and how law, though dependent on its ethical reasonableness for its worth and its normativity or authority, *cannot be reduced to ethics*, or any deduction from ethics, but is in large part genuinely created, fully positive. That strategy of explanation is sketched in the following section.

7 AUTHORITY

> Now we can see the problem with the natural lawyer's account of authority. For in order to be law, a norm must be required by morality. Morality has authority, in the sense that the fact that a norm is a requirement of morality gives agents a (perhaps overriding) reason to comply with it. If morality has authority, and legal norms are necessarily moral, then law has authority too.
>
> This argument for the authority of law, however, is actually fatal to it, because it makes law's authority redundant on morality's. . . . if all legal requirements are also moral requirements (as the natural lawyer would have it) then the fact that a norm is a norm of law does not provide citizens with an additional reason for acting. Natural law theory, then, fails to account for the authority of law.[37]

The criticism entirely fails. No natural law theory of law has ever claimed that 'in order to be law, a norm must be required by morality', or that 'all legal requirements are also'—independently of being validly posited as law—'moral requirements'. Natural law theorists hold that the contents of a just and validly enacted rule of law such as 'Do not exceed 35 m.p.h. in city streets' are *not* required by morality until validly posited by the legal authority with jurisdiction (legal authority) to make such a rule. The centrepiece of natural law theory of law is its explanation of how the mak-

---

[37] Jules L. Coleman and Brian Leiter, 'Legal Positivism', in Dennis Patterson, *A Companion to Philosophy of Law and Legal Theory* (Oxford and Cambridge, Mass.: Blackwell, 1996), 244.

ing of 'purely positive' law can create moral obligations which did *not* exist until the moment of enactment. Unfortunately, Coleman and Leiter's error, thoroughgoing as it is, has many precedents. Kelsen, particularly, used to claim that, according to natural law theory, positive law is a mere 'copy' of natural law and 'merely reproduces the true law which is already somehow in existence'; the claim has been shown to be mere travesty.[38] Like Coleman and Leiter, Kelsen cited no text to support his claims about what natural law theory says, because (as he had every opportunity to know) none could be cited.

As the fifty-five years of Kelsen's jurisprudence abundantly illustrate, positivism's efforts to explain the law's authority are doomed to fail. For, as Coleman and Leiter rightly say, 'A practical authority is a person or institution whose directives provide individuals with *a reason for* acting (in compliance with those dictates);'[39] and they might have added, a reason that is not merely a replica, for each individual, of that individual's self-interested 'prudential reasons' for so acting. But, as they ought (but fail) to acknowledge, no facts, however complex, can by themselves provide a *reason for* acting, let alone an *ought* of the kind that could speak with authority against an individual's self-interest. (To repeat, 'authority' that does no more than track the 'I want' of self-interest is redundant for the individual addressed, and futile for the community.) No *ought* from a mere *is*. So, since positivism prides itself on dealing only in facts, it deprives itself of the only conceivable *source* of reasons for action (oughts), namely true and intrinsic values (basic human goods, and the propositional first principles of practical reason that direct us to those goods as to-be-pursued, and point to what damages them as to-be-shunned).

The incoherence of positivism—its inherent and self-imposed incapacity to succeed in the explanatory task it sets itself—is nicely illustrated by Coleman and Leiter's effort to explain 'the authority of the rule of recognition'.[40] They preface this explanation with the remark that 'we all recognize cases of binding laws that are morally reprehensible (for example, the laws that supported apartheid in South Africa)'.[41] So we can conveniently test their explanations of this bindingness, this authoritativeness, by asking how such explanations could figure in the deliberations of an official (say Nelson Mandela when practising as an advocate of the Supreme Court) in South Africa in those days. Mandela (let us imagine) asks Coleman and Leiter *why* (and whether) the South African rule of recognition, which he knows is the propositional content of the attitudes accompanying and supporting the massive fact of convergent official behaviour in South Africa, gives him a reason for action of a kind that he could reasonably judge authoritative. How does this fact of convergent official behaviour, he asks, make the law not merely *accepted as* legally authoritative but actually *authoritative as law* for him or anyone else who recognizes its injustice? Coleman and

[38] Kelsen, *General Theory of Law and State* (Harvard University Press, 1945), 416; Finnis, *NLNR*, 28.
[39] 'Legal Positivism', n. 37 above, at 243 (emphasis added). For 'dictate' read directive or prescription (e.g. enactment, judicial judgment, etc.).
[40] ibid. 248.   [41] ibid. 243.

Leiter's explanation goes like this: (1) Often your self-interest requires you to co-ordinate your behaviour with that of these officials or of other people who are in fact acting in line with those officials. (But Mandela is enquiring about authoritative directions, not guides to self-interest. Self-interest requires co-operation with local gangsters, but their directions are not authoritative.) (2) Moreover, if you think that those officials are trying to do what morality requires, you have reason to follow their lead. (Mandela will not think so, and will be right.) (3) You may 'believe that the rule of recognition provides something like the right standards for evaluating the validity of norms subordinate to it'.[42] (He rightly does not.) (4) '. . . quite apart from [your] views about the substantive merits of the rule of recognition itself . . . [t]he avoidance of confusion and mayhem, as well as the conditions of liberal stability require co-ordination among officials.' Here at last Coleman and Leiter offer a reason of the relevant kind, a reason which could be rationally debated by being confronted with reasons of the same kind. The requirement asserted in the quoted sentence goes far beyond the 'fact of convergent behaviour'; it acknowledges strong evaluations of order, peace, and justice ('liberalism'); it is indeed nothing if not a moral requirement. It is *available* to explain the law's authoritativeness only if the 'separability thesis'[43] is recognized as an equivocation between defensible and indefensible theses, and Coleman and Leiter's favoured, 'positivist' interpretation of it is abandoned as the mistake it is. In jurisprudence, there is a name for a theory of law that undertakes to identify and debate, openly and critically, the moral principles and requirements which respond to *deliberating persons'* request to be shown why a legal rule, validly enacted, is binding and authoritative *for them*, precisely as law. That name, for good and ill, is 'natural law theory'.

Coleman and Leiter might reply that I am confusing legal with moral authority. But this reply depends upon the mistaken view—one which, as we have seen, they starkly hold—that positive law as understood in natural law theory adds nothing to pre-existing moral requirements. Once we acknowledge that very many (not all!) legal requirements would not be moral requirements unless legally created in accordance with the law's own criteria of legal validity, we can readily see the sense in saying that the law's authoritativeness, in the focal sense of 'authoritative', is nothing other than its moral authoritativeness. To repeat, most of our laws would have no moral authority unless they were legally valid, positive laws. So their moral authority is also truly *legal* authority. Laws that, because of their injustice, are without moral authoritativeness, are not legally authoritative in the focal sense of 'authoritative'. Their 'authority' is in the end no more than the 'authority' of the Syndicate, of powerful people who can *oblige* you to comply with their will on pain of unpleasant consequences, but who cannot create what any self-respecting person would count as a genuine obligation. (See also Sect. 13 below.)

---

[42] 'Legal Positivism', n. 37 above, at 248.   [43] See Sect. 4 text at n. 30 above.

Natural law theory's central strategy for explaining the law's authority points to the under-determinacy (far short of sheer indeterminacy) of most if not all of practical reason's requirements in the field of open-ended (not merely technological) self-determination by individuals and societies. Indeed, the more benevolent and intelligent people are, the more they will come up with good but incompatible (non-compossible) schemes of social co-ordination (including always the 'negative' co-ordination of mutual forbearances) at the political level—property, currency, defence, legal procedure, and so forth. Unanimity on the merits of particular schemes being thus practically unavailable, but co-ordination around *some* scheme(s) being required for common good (justice, peace, welfare), these good people have sufficient reason to acknowledge authority, that is, an accepted and acceptable procedure for selecting particular schemes of co-ordination with which, once they are so selected, each reasonable member of the community is morally obligated to co-operate *precisely because they have been selected*—that is, precisely as *legally* obligatory for the morally decent conscience.

This is the source of the content-independence and peremptoriness that Hart, in his late work, rightly acknowledged as characteristic of legal reasons for action, and as the essence of their authoritativeness. And as the explanation shows, this content-independence and peremptoriness is neither unconditional nor exceptionless. A sufficient degree of injustice in content will negate the peremptoriness-for-conscience. *Pace* Coleman and Leiter, the laws of South Africa, or some of them, were not binding, albeit widely *regarded and treated and enforced as* binding. Positivism never coherently reaches beyond reporting attitudes and convergent behaviour (perhaps the sophisticated and articulate attitudes that constitute a set of rules of recognition, change, and adjudication). It has nothing to say to officials or private citizens who want to judge whether, when, and why the authority and obligatoriness *claimed* and *enforced* by those who are *acting as* officials of a legal system, and by their directives, are indeed *authoritative reasons* for their own conscientious action. Positivism, at this point, does no more than repeat (i) what any competent lawyer—including every legally competent adherent of natural law theory—would say are (or are not) intra-systemically valid laws, imposing 'legal requirements' and (ii) what any streetwise observer would warn are the likely consequences of non-compliance. It cannot explain the authoritativeness, for an official's or a private citizen's conscience (ultimate rational judgment), of these alleged and imposed requirements, nor their lack of such authority when radically unjust. Positivism is not only incoherent. It is also redundant.

For all their sophistication, contemporary legal positivisms are essentially in the position adopted by Austin in his brutal, *and irrelevant*, account of the authoritativeness of wicked laws: if I say that laws gravely contrary to morality are not binding, 'the Court of Justice will demonstrate the inconclusiveness of my reasoning by hanging me up, in pursuance of the law of which I have impugned the validity'.[44]

---

[44] Austin, *The Province of Jurisprudence Determined*, 1st pub. 1832, ed. Hart (London, 1954), 185; see Finnis, *NLNR*, 354–5.

8 RIGHTS

Jurisprudence progresses as well as regresses. The late nineteenth-century analysis of rights which Hohfeld brought to completion makes a notable advance in clarity. But rights of each of the four Hohfeldian types are spoken of by Aquinas,[45] as well as by the civilian lawyers of his age (and indeed of earlier ages). The word 'right' translates the Latin *ius* or *jus*, the root of the words 'justice', 'jurist', 'juridical', and 'jurisprudence'. Though Aquinas does not use the plural forms of the word *ius* as often as we use the plural 'rights', it is a sheer mistake to claim, as some have, that he lacked or repudiated the concept of rights in the modern sense, in which a right is 'subjective' in the sense of belonging to someone (the subject of the right). When he defines justice as the steady willingness to give to others *what is theirs*, Aquinas immediately goes on to treat that phrase as synonymous with *their right* (*ius suum*); hence he treats a right/rights (*ius/iura*) as subjective. (He also uses the word to speak of 'objective' right, that is, what interpersonal action or relationship is *right*—morally or legally, depending upon the context.)[46]

Hobbes, who inspired much in Benthamite and Austinian positivism, spurned the classical juristic tradition and defined 'right' as liberty in the sense of sheer absence of duty. So people have most rights in the state of nature where they have no duties. This move exemplifies regression in legal and, more generally, in political and moral philosophy. Fortunately, the mistake is quite obvious. If no one has any duties to or in respect of others, it will be more accurate to say that no one has any rights at all. For everyone, in such a state of affairs, is subject to being destroyed or abused by everyone and anyone else, and everyone's actions can be impeded as much as any person or group cares, and is able, to arrange. The truth is that the concept of a right makes little sense save as (the Hohfeldian claim-right) a correlative of someone else's duty, or (the Hohfeldian liberty) as protected by someone else's duty of non-interference, or (the Hohfeldian power) as promoted by the duty of officials and others to recognize and effectuate one's acts-in-the-law (or their ethical counterparts), or (the Hohfeldian immunity) as protected by a similar duty of officials and others not to recognize another's juridical acts as it purportedly bears on my position.

It does not follow, as some have supposed, that in the classical view duty is conceptually or otherwise prior to right(s). Duties to others are (by definition) duties in justice, and justice is (by definition) the willingness to give to others their *right(s)*. So duties, at least to others, and rights are interdefined; neither is prior to the other. One does not really understand the relevant concept of duty unless one has an understanding of that factual and normative equality of human beings which is the foundation of justice; the concept of right(s) gives normative recognition to that equality. To the extent that the school of 'modern natural law' defined rights rather unilater-

---

[45] See *Aquinas*, 133 n. 10, 134 n. 12.   [46] See Finnis, *NLNR*, 206, 228; *Aquinas*, 132–8.

ally in terms of liberty and/or power, conceived as properties of the subject, it ran the risk of obscuring the essential correlativity of, or interdependence with, duties and, in general, with right relationships between persons.

Though the phrase 'human rights' is rather recent, and he never happens to use the exactly equivalent phrase 'natural rights' (plural), Aquinas clearly has the concept of human rights. For he articulates a series of precepts or norms of justice which concern, he says, what is owed to *everyone alike*.[47]

More fundamental than either rights or duties, and also indispensable for rationally determining what rights people have, are the first principles of practical reason which identify the basic reasons for action, directing us towards the basic human goods. No theory of rights is grounded or, even in outline, complete unless it attends to the question of the basic aspects of human well-being. No theory of human rights can be satisfactory unless it attends to the question what real features of human reality make us each, in the relevant sense(s), the equal of other human beings, and make it the case that other creatures in this world are not our equals and lack the rights we have. Contemporary legal philosophy (and legal theory: see Sect. 27 below) is marred by its inattention to the human person,[48] an inattention exemplified (one may think) by this *Handbook*'s selection of topics, and reparable only by taking up again the systematically complex and ambitious enterprise pursued by classical natural law theory.

9 INSTITUTIONALITY

The clustered meanings of our word 'institution', as of its Latin root *institutio*, point to salient features of laws, and of many things that law concerns: they are *made*, originated, established, instituted; they establish a pattern, arrangement, *order*, system, constitution, and/or organization; they *last* while persons and/or their actions come and go. For those are the salient features of the quite various kinds of reality we call institutions: slavery, contract, property, banking, this bank (undertaking or building), the courts, jury trial, ritual suicide, Friday dressing-down, and so forth. Roman jurists such as Gaius and Tribonian did much to transmit the word to the modern world by calling their books of foundational instruction *Institut[ion]es*: books to initiate the student in the *principles* (the rational origins or foundations) and the *established* ideas and practices which give a legal system its shape both as something

---

[47] See *Aquinas*, 136 ('*indifferenter omnibus debitum*').
[48] See Finnis, 'The Priority of Persons', in Jeremy Horder (ed.), *Oxford Essays in Jurisprudence: Fourth Series* (Oxford: Oxford University Press, 2000), 1–15.

distinct from other kinds of social arrangement and as something different from other legal systems.

Thus an exploration of the many facets of law's institutionality will be an exploration of the twin roles of reasonableness and rationally under-determined choice in the positing and maintaining of even a thoroughly decent legal system. It will also be an exploration of the ways in which law is both secondary or even subordinate to, while regulating, other social institutions which it does not institute, whether they be reasonable and good (like proper forms of marriage and family, or less ambitious kinds of promising, not to mention religious communities and practices), or unreasonable, vicious, and harmful (like prostitution, slavery, or the vendetta). We should not imagine that market institutions or marriages or corporations await the emergence of 'power-conferring' rules of law. Legal rules are often ratificatory and regulative rather than truly constitutive, whatever their legal form and their role in creating the law's versions of the social practices and institutions upon which it, so to speak, supervenes. This ratificatory and regulatory role is often highly desirable as a means of preserving peace and fairness. But, for all their originality and variability, the law's institutions—to the extent that they are reasonable and give rise to claims on conscience—remain dependent upon foundational moral principles which pick out the requirements of a reasonableness attentive to the basic human goods and the human characteristics of freedom of choice within constraints of bodiliness and emotionality, maturation, mortality, the shape and dynamics of the environment, and so forth.

Time and positivity: the law's institutional character is an emblem of law's aspiration to bring into the present and the foreseeable future an order rooted in the past, the past of some originating event (such as conception or birth) or act, usually but not always a juridical act—an act intended precisely to change legal relationships—such as accepting a contractual offer, incorporating a company or acquiring shares in it, settling a trust, and so forth. As the events of revolution and *coup d'état* remind constitutional theorists, judges, and practitioners from time to time, not even the most self-referentially elaborate and complete set of constitutional provisions can make provision adequate for all contingencies in the life of that ongoing institution, the state (the political community).[49]

10 Reasons

Hart set jurisprudence firmly on the road back—or rather, forward—to the point where it will rejoin the classical tradition. For his central message is that law and all its

---

[49] See Finnis, *NLNR*, 275–6 and citations in 275 n. 7.

constitutive elements and concepts must be understood, in jurisprudence as in life, from the internal point of view (see Sect. 1). And what is the internal point of view? It is the way of thinking of someone who treats a rule as a *reason for* action (and not simply as a prediction or basis for prediction). Hart's neglected but important later works, notably some of his *Essays on Bentham*,[50] recast his entire theory of law even more firmly as a theory of a particular kind of reason for action—reasons that are peremptorily normative by virtue not of their content but of their relationship to other, authoritative rules (of change, adjudication, and above all recognition).

Hart goes further. He offers an account of the *reasons* people have to introduce these authorizing rules (of change, adjudication, and recognition) and treat them as authoritative. The reasons are, in short, that social life without them is very defective—dispute-ridden, unadaptable to change, and so forth. These 'secondary' rules are reasonable precisely as remedies for such defects. But he goes further yet, and offers reasons for the 'primary' rules whose contribution to desirable social life is so enhanced by the secondary rules. The primary rules, he says, are rationally required for the sake of 'survival'. We should note, however, that besides his official categories of primary, obligation-imposing rules against violence, theft, and fraud, and secondary rules of legislation, adjudication, and law-recognition, Hart gives prominence to another vast category of rules: those that confer more or less *private* powers of changing one's normative position by contracting, conveying, and so forth. There is *reason* to introduce these and acknowledge their authority, for the sake of their immense 'amenity'—they are a 'step forward' as important as the wheel, he says.

All this brings Hart well within the territory of classical natural law theory.[51] But he declines to settle down as a citizen there. (1) Basic goods and reasons for acting besides 'survival' he declares 'controversial', and he declines to enter the classical dialectic showing how unreasonable and unrealistic it is to treat survival as the sole basic reason for acting. (2) The good reasons there are for benefiting society by having law (secondary as well as primary rules, etc.) he treats as entitled to no priority in accounting for the internal attitude of allegiance to the society and its law; people, including judges, 'can' conform for other 'reasons' such as careerism, blind conformism, uncritical traditionalism, and so forth. He never responds to the classical objection that, though these alternative motivations can and do indeed exist, and may be widespread, they can never have the justificatory or even the descriptive-explanatory power of the good reasons there are for introducing and upholding law *against* the pull of careerism or other forms of selfish self-interest, and *against* conformism to old ways and traditions. When thinking of the variety of law-like social institutions, he firmly and most beneficially employs the distinction between central

---

[50] H. L. A. Hart, *Essays on Bentham: Studies in Jurisprudence and Political Theory* (Oxford: Oxford University Press, 1982), especially the final essay and essay VII.

[51] For these purposes it does not matter that, as indicated in Section 9, natural law theorists would rightly have reservations about the inference which some might draw from Hart, that people did not have the capacity to, say, marry until there were 'power-conferring' legal rules about marriage.

and secondary cases, and between focal and analogous meanings. But he never recognizes how the facts of varied motivation can, likewise, be best accommodated if one acknowledges central and secondary cases *of the internal attitude*.

Thus Hart sets us on the road of understanding law as a kind of good reason for action, but balks at a full-blooded, open, critical consideration of what kinds of reason for action are really reasonable, really good as reasons. The whole ambition of natural law theory is to be precisely such a consideration.

The road lies open once one notices the error in Hume's claim that reason can only be the slave of—cannot motivate save as directing means to satisfy or respond to—the passions.[52] Emotions are involved in human action but *need not* be the exclusive or even primary ultimate motivating factor. Far better fitted for that role are the basic intelligible human goods, the intelligent opportunities of real improvement and flourishing as a person with other persons. These intrinsic goods were introduced in Section 2 above.[53] Their intelligibility, as benefiting and perfective of human persons, is the source of their directiveness, their counting as *reasons for* action. It is also the source of the further question: what is one to do, and what are the requirements of practical reasonableness,[54] given the multiplicity of basic human goods and of persons who could actualize them in their lives? The nub of the answer to that question is that one must not cut back on the directiveness of the basic reasons for action. Their combined or integral directiveness, while it is not another good or additional reason to add to the list, can be articulated as this principle: in all one's deliberating and acting, one ought to choose and in other ways will those and only those possibilities the willing of which is compatible with integral human fulfilment—that is, the fulfilment of all human beings and their communities, in all the basic human goods.[55] This is the master principle of morality, and it can also be formulated as the primary principle of human rights: other persons, so far as satisfying their needs is dependent on one's choosing and other willing, have a right that one's choosing and other willing remain open to integral human fulfilment.

All other moral principles are specifications of this master moral principle. The Kantian imperative that in every act one regard oneself as legislating for 'a kingdom of ends' ('a whole of ends in systematic conjunction') is an intimation of it; so too is Christianity's first principle, love of neighbour as oneself for the sake of the Kingdom; the Aristotelian conception of *eudaimonia* as ultimate end, and the utilitarian injunction to seek 'the greatest good/happiness of the greatest number' are other, less

---

[52] See e.g. Robert P. George, *In Defence of Natural Law* (Oxford: Oxford University Press, 1999), ch. 1. For Hume's own violations of the logical truth (often called, with some naivety, Hume's law) that *ought* cannot be deduced from *is*, see Finnis, *NLNR*, 36–8, 41–2.

[53] See n. 18 above.

[54] In *NLNR*, ch. 5 the requirements of practical reasonableness are presented as if they were each self-evident, but they should rather be understood as specifications of the unifying master principle of openness to integral human fulfilment: see *Aquinas*, ch. 4.

[55] On this 'master principle of morality', see, e.g. Finnis, J. Boyle and G. Grisez, *Nuclear Deterrence, Morality, and Realism* (Oxford: Oxford University Press, 1987), 281–8.

happy attempts to articulate it. *Integral human fulfilment* can be thought of as a kind of ultimate point (end) of human life and action, but only in the sense that it is at the heart of the master principle.

How is the first principle of morality specified into less abstract moral standards? How is its rational prescription shaped into definite responsibilities? Integral human fulfilment is not a vast state of affairs which might be projected as the goal (end) of a worldwide billion-year plan. Rather, what the master principle prescribes is that one not narrow voluntarily the range of people and goods one cares about by following non-rational motives, that is, motives not grounded in intelligible requirements of the basic reasons for action. One type of non-rational motive is hostile feelings such as anger and hatred towards oneself or others. A person or group motivated by feelings of, for example, revenge does not have a will open to integral human fulfilment. So a first specification of the master principle is: do not answer injury with injury. This principle is treated as foundational in all decent legal systems and is quite compatible with standards of just compensation (even by self-help), and of retributive punishment to restore the balance of fairness between wrongdoers and the law-abiding (see Sects. 20–2 and 26 below).

A second strategic specification of morality's master principle is the principle which every form of consequentialist, proportionalist, utilitarian, or other purportedly aggregative moral theory is tailor-made to reject: do not do evil—choose to destroy, damage, or impede some instance of a basic human good—that good may come.[56] This is the foundation of truly inviolable human rights and is the backbone of decent legal systems, for these legal systems exclude unconditionally the killing or harming of innocent human persons as a means to any end, public or private; and on the basis of analogous specifications of the master moral principle exclude unconditionally the use of perjured testimony, the choice to render false judgment or other judicial or official support of fraud, rape even for the sake of national security, and chattel slavery. A necessary part of the defence of every such specification of morality's primary principle is the critique of aggregative ethical methods, which all claim to identify greater goods which outweigh the evil done, and all fail by overlooking the incommensurability of persons, of the basic goods of persons, and of the transitive with the intransitive effects of choosing.[57]

A third principle giving relative specificity to the morality's master principle is the Golden Rule, the core principle of fairness: 'Do to others as you would have them do to you; do not impose on others what you would not want to be obliged by them to accept'. For a will marked by egoism or other partiality cannot be open to integral

---

[56] For some explanation and defence of this principle, see Finnis, 'Commensuration and Public Reason', in Ruth Chang (ed.), *Incommensurability, Incomparability, and Practical Reason* (Cambridge, Mass.: Harvard University Press, 1997), 215–33 at 226; more extensively, Finnis *et al.*, *Nuclear Deterrence*, chs. 9 and 10.

[57] See e.g. Finnis, 'Commensuration and Public Reason', n. 56 above, at 218–23; *Fundamentals of Ethics* (Oxford: Georgetown University Press and Oxford University Press, 1983), 109–42.

human fulfilment. This rational principle of impartiality[58] by no means excludes all forms and corresponding feelings of preference for oneself and those who are near and dear (e.g. parental responsibility for, and consequent prioritizing of, their children); it excludes preferences motivated by desires, aversions, or hostilities that do not correspond to intelligible aspects of the real *reasons* for action, the basic human goods instantiated in the lives of other human beings as in the lives of oneself or those close to one's heart.

11 FORMALISM

Law cannot fulfil its co-ordinating and other directive functions unless it is promulgated. Even if it could, it would normally be unfair to some if not all of the law's subjects for it to remain unpublished. Moreover, it is normally unfair for officials, including courts, not to apply the rules that were published to and taken by the law's subjects as applicable to circumstances of the kind now before the court or other official. That the law have a public 'form' is, in both these ways, at the heart of the idea of a rule of rules ('. . . of law') and not of personal discretion ('. . . of men'). And that the products of law-making be treated as valid, as law, only if made in accordance with a determinate 'manner and form' is equally essential to the law's desirable positivity and the desirable limitation of political rulers and their officials by law. One should be able to know much if not all of the law by attending, and in large measure only by attending, to its form—rather than to the unpublished intentions of its makers, or to its or their purposes, or to its justice or other value. If all this were not so, positive law would be redundant; but it is not redundant (see Sects. 3, 6–7 above); so form and formalities come as part of the very idea of having law.

Very occasionally a theory of law will describe itself as 'formalist'. Thus Ernest Weinrib offers, under that label, an account of certain institutions, such as the Law of Tort, which he considers can be understood only if one sets aside all questions about their point, their value or social utility. Their intelligibility and ideal reality is independent of any value they may have, and is trans-historical in the sense that it is independent also of the purposes of particular communities. But both the metaphysics and the illuminating power of this thesis are highly questionable. Apart from the existence of laws and legal institutions in the minds and dispositions of particular persons and communities, the only reality of laws and legal institutions—but this is

---

[58] See further 'Commensuration and Public Reason', 227–9, showing, *inter alia*, how the content of this rational standard is usually supplied, in specific cases, by sub-rational factors (taste for risk, conventions, etc.).

also their *primary* reality—is *as reasons for action* which are good because intelligibly related to (albeit usually not deducible from!) the basic reasons for action, the basic goods, the intrinsic values at stake in human action, and to their integral unfolding in moral standards.

Usually 'formalist' is an epithet applied with hostile intent by those who consider someone's actual or recommended adjudicative method insufficiently attentive to the unexpressed intentions or further purposes of law-makers, or to the considerations of justice, mercy, and/or some other aspect of human welfare.[59] Since much (though not all) of the law exists by virtue of a *determinatio* which cannot rightly claim to be the uniquely reasonable (morally required) resolution of a social problem (see Sect. 7 above), the question how much is 'too much' or 'too little' judicial attention to evaluations not expressed in the form of the *determinatio* (the legislation or prior judgment(s) or practices) is itself a question largely for *determinatio*, not deduction or insight into the self-evident nor any other intellectual process capable of yielding a uniquely correct answer. It is, in short, a question about which very little can usefully be said in abstraction from particular legal systems and particular kinds of issues arising within them.

12 PRAGMATISM

The term 'pragmatism' was introduced into the discourse of philosophers by Charles Sanders Peirce in 1878, to express a complex of ideas about logic (good thinking) which he had developed since 1867. In 1903 he gave at Harvard a series of seven lectures on 'Pragmatism as a Principle and Method of Right Thinking'.[60] These lectures enable their readers to see that a pragmatism which is true to the insights and arguments of its founder is compatible with, indeed a kind of continuation of, key philosophical methods and findings of Plato, Aristotle, and other proponents of classical natural law theory.

For there Peirce explains that 'the question of Pragmatism is the Question of Abduction'. Abduction he distinguishes from induction and deduction, as one of the three modes of inference, of moving soundly in one's thinking. Peirce's explains abduction as insight into data, into 'a mass of facts before us', which we find 'a

---

[59] On Roberto Unger's accusations of formalism in our law, see Finnis, 'On "The Critical Legal Studies Movement"', in John Eekelaar and John Bell (eds.), *Oxford Essays in Jurisprudence, Third Series* (Oxford: Oxford University Press, 1987), 145–65.

[60] Charles Sanders Peirce, *Pragmatism as a Principle and Method of Right Thinking: The 1903 Harvard Lectures on Pragmatism*, ed. Patricia Ann Turrisi (Albany, NY: State University of New York Press, 1997). William James invited Peirce, and suggested the title.

confused snarl, an impenetrable jungle', until 'it occurs to us that if we were to assume something to be true that we do not know to be true, these facts would arrange themselves luminously. That is *abduction*.'[61] The core of Peirce's 'abduction' is (we can say) what Aristotle called *nous* and Aquinas *intellectus*: insight, understanding that is neither deduction nor induction in the modern senses of that term, but is into data of experience, not a mere data-less 'intuition'.

Peirce understands logic as properly normative, as directed and directing towards and by the good of truth, as the object(ive) of the human activity of thinking. 'Every man is fully satisfied that there is such a thing as truth, or he would not ask any question. *That* truth consists in a conformity to something *independent of his thinking it to be so*, or of any man's opinion on that subject.'[62] Since logic is a human activity guided by and towards a good to be attained (the logical goodness of enabling attainment of the cognitive good of truth), logic is subordinated to (though not a mere instrument of!) another, wider knowledge of normativity: ethics. And ethics, considered as norms of human action, is in turn based upon what Peirce (eccentrically) calls aesthetics—a knowledge of what is 'admirable *per se*'.[63] Truth and knowledge of it is, therefore, one of these *per se*, intrinsic goods.

True pragmatism is thus worlds removed from the 'pragmatism' of those, such as Richard Rorty or Richard Posner, on whose lips the term signifies a (self-refuting) scepticism about truth, and a wilful embrace of logical incoherence and other forms of overt arbitrariness in assertion. Such 'pragmatism', since it openly reduces assertion to an instrument of want-satisfaction or other drives, is no part of philosophy. (Of course, just as an unjust law is part of the law, and bad science is part of science, so base pragmatism *is* part of philosophy!) What needs to be said about it, for philosophical purposes, has been said in Plato's analysis of base rhetoric, in the first of his primary discussions of natural law, the *Gorgias*.[64] True pragmatism, recalled albeit incompletely by Jürgen Habermas, understands that there is a fruitful investigation of the presuppositions and preconditions of the human actions (freely chosen) of thinking reasonably (accurately, logically, responsibly) and discoursing authentically. And among the first of those preconditions is that one understand, by an unmediated *insight* into one's experience of inclination and possibility, that understanding, reasonableness, and knowledge are not merely possibilities but also an opportunity of participating in a basic human good, and thus a true *reason* for action. The occurrence of such insights and their consolidation and unfolding in practical reason is a child's reaching the age of reason.

---

[61] *Pragmatism as a Principle and Method of Right Thinking*, 282.

[62] ibid, 255 (emphasis in original).

[63] ibid. 118–19. The classical theorists are less willing to subordinate *any* of the four kinds of 'science' to the other three (e.g. logic to ethics).

[64] For a consideration of the *Gorgias* and the ethics of discourse (as distinct from base rhetoric), in dialogue with Jürgen Habermas (not a pragmatist in the base sense), see Finnis, 'Natural Law and the Ethics of Discourse', n. 2 above.

13 LAW AND OBLIGATION

Once it is understood that the positivity of law is a reality (and a concept, and an ideal) vigorously promoted, if not also invented, by adherents of 'natural law' (objective morality), it will be readily understood that the disjunction 'legal obligation' versus 'moral obligation' is far too crude. There is, rather, a unique kind of moral obligation which obtains only as a property of, or resultant from, *positive* laws. This can be called 'legal-moral obligation', or 'legal obligation in the moral sense'. It is to be distinguished from, though normally it tracks, the 'intra-systemic legal obligation' which particular rules of law declare themselves (or are declared by other legal rules) to create, and which legal institutions also declare and take as a ground for punishments and penalties.

In recent years some jurists have argued that it is logically or conceptually possible to uncouple the concepts of authority and obligation. Rulers and their officials might be acknowledged as having authority, including moral authority to make and enforce law, and the right not to be usurped, while at the same time none of their laws, not even those imposing intra-systemic legal obligations, would create any legal obligation in the moral sense (though some of them might, of course, coincide in content with moral norms obligatory even in the absence of the law). It should be conceded that this is conceptually possible. But it should be denied that the resulting conceptions of authority and legal obligation correspond to any historical community attitudes or practices available for description. More importantly, the proposed new concepts do not pick out any reasonable kind of option, any kind of social arrangement or set of dispositions that might serve the goods for the sake of which law exists and is worth instituting, maintaining, or restoring.[65]

The discussion of authority in Section 7 above underlined the impotence of positivism to provide any account of it that could rationally satisfy those whom law most concerns—those who (for example, as judges) have the realistic opportunity to evade what the law seeks authoritatively to require of them. No *ought* from mere *is*, however complex. The same must therefore be true, even more obviously, of obligation. As Hart became vividly aware,[66] his own account of the law's obligatoriness—even of its intra-systemic obligation—was deeply unsatisfying. His own critique of Austin had pivoted on the radical difference between *being obliged* (the *is* of 'I am threatened' plus the fact or sub-rational motivation of fear) and being *under an obligation* (an *ought*). But his own explanation of legal obligation in terms of insistent social pressure motivated by *other people's* beliefs about importance yielded no more plausible

---

[65] For the suggestion and response discussed in this paragraph, see Rolf Sartorius, 'Positivism and the Foundations of Legal Authority', in Ruth Gavison (ed.), *Issues in Contemporary Legal Philosophy* (Oxford: Oxford University Press, 1987), 43–61; Finnis, 'Comment', ibid. 62–75.

[66] See e.g. Hart, *Essays on Bentham*, 266–7.

bridge to the *ought* in need of explanation. Similarly, his account of the rule of recognition as a sheer fact about convergent official dispositions and practices 'worked' by abandoning the internal attitude—the reasonable concern with reasons for action—at its decisive moment. Hart's reasons for suspending all the legal system's *oughts* from the sheer *is* of official practice are weak. Undoubtedly, some or even many officials and others can abandon the search for good reasons for allegiance to law, and make do with sub-rational motivations such as conformism, traditionalism, or careerism. But such attitudes fail to make full sense of the law's demands. The central case of reasons is not what are commonly accepted as reasons but reasons good *as reasons*. The central case of the internal attitude is the rationally warranted acceptance of law as obligatory in conscience, as speaking with true authority at the moment of choice. Only a natural law theory traces the rational warrant for such an acceptance.

Nor is it true that classical natural law theory merely puts off the evil day by suspending all reasons and obligations from an ultimate *fact*, God's will. That may, as we saw, be true of some 'modern' natural law theories (Sect. 2 above). But when Aquinas, following Augustine, says that the natural moral law (and thus all just human, positive law) has its obligatoriness 'from the eternal law' he is referring not to a divine command but rather to the intelligibility, goodness, beauty, and rational attractiveness of the great scheme of things chosen, in creating, by divine *wisdom*.[67] The normativity of the obligatory is the normativity of the first principle of practical reason or natural law: good is to be pursued and done, and bad avoided—the referents of this 'good' being given by practical reason's other first principles, the basic reasons for action (Sects. 2, 10 above). The reason why a particular option for action or forbearance is obligatory is always, ultimately: if I do not choose this option I do not coherently, reasonably, respect the integral human fulfilment—the good of all human persons and communities—to which I am directed by the ensemble of the only *reasons* I or others have for choosing anything.

14 ADJUDICATION

The primary responsibility of courts is to apply the law. The ethics of this process of adjudication were of intense concern to classical natural law theorists such as Aquinas. Judges must be concerned to establish the truth about what was done by the parties. But this responsibility, while never detachable from its goal—correspondence with the reality of past acts and facts—is to be carried out in accordance with

---

[67] See Aquinas, *Summa Theologiae*, I–II, q. 96, a. 4; *Aquinas*, 307–12.

rules of evidence and proof. These rules have a number of purposes. One is to give effect to the presumption of innocence, which is itself a specific form of the general principle of reason that one should love one's neighbour as oneself. Another purpose of the rules of evidence is to preserve the fundamental equality of the parties by lessening the risk that one party will gain an advantage over the other by surprise, rhetorical superiority, or other such means. A further purpose is to lessen the risk that the trier of fact, whether judge or jury, will be distracted by emotional or other non-rational responsiveness to features of the case not truly relevant to the goal of doing justice by applying the positive law on the basis of true facts. The classical theorists were impressed by the risk that persons adjudicating in the emotionally engaging circumstances of particular facts and parties will be deflected from that goal.

Some pessimism, or realism, about the balanced impartiality of judges/jurors inclined the classical theorists to favour legislation—if you like, codification—over common law methods of making the *determinationes* by which natural law is non-deductively specified into rules and institutions of a particular community's positive law. Here we reach the secondary responsibility and function of judges: the interpretation and development of our law. As the discussion of 'exclusive legal positivism' shows (Sect. 3 above), this will involve considerations which somehow go beyond what is already fully specified and determined in the social-fact sources (prior legislation and precedent). But the aspiration that there be a rule, a governance, of *law* and not 'of men' (particular judges) demands that every reference back to, and reasoning forward from, morality's permanent standards be tempered by, and filtered through coherent maintenance of, the community's existing law 'as a whole' including its many sheer *determinationes* (Sects. 7 and 11 above).

The moral backbone of the law is a small number of strict and exceptionless rules against intentional harm, and lying (Sect. 10 above). Much of the rest of the frame and flesh of the law involves giving specificity to broad affirmative responsibilities of care and fairness. This specificity results in particular systems of transactional, procedural, and property law. The reasonableness of these particular standards and institutions is not of the form 'inevitably required by reason (morality)' but rather of the form 'adopted by our law by choice from among the range of reasonable options'. But once *these* options have been chosen, the rational requirements of coherence strongly limit the range of reasonable options for further specification and development. (See further Sect. 25 below.)

Short of a radical refashioning of a whole area of law, such as a legislature can undertake, legal development should proceed by what Coke called that 'artificial reason of the law'[68] which is peculiarly the responsibility of judges. For judges are simply persons dedicated to, and intellectually and morally equipped for, deciding as, so to speak, voices of the law and thus of the community rather than of themselves as individuals. Their responsibility to do justice between the parties—to make a

---

[68] *Prohibitions del Roy* (1608), 12 Co. Rep. 64.

morally *sound* and justified resolution of the case—is always to be harmonized with the responsibility to make that resolution also *fit*—at least, not contradict—the community's existing law, considered as a whole and to the extent that it is morally tolerable. One traditional way of pointing towards this requirement of fit was the principle that in resolving interpretative uncertainties, judges must ask what those who made the law in its existing forms and expressions *would have* enacted (within the limits of reasonableness) *if* they had attended to the circumstances in question.

While we should thus broadly accept some main elements of Ronald Dworkin's account of adjudication, we should reject his thesis that even in hard cases there is to be presumed to be a single legally right answer. That thesis exaggerates both the specificity of morality's own standards and the linguistic and purposive determinacy of most posited rules. The requirements of moral soundness and fit with the posited law and its social-fact sources are requirements which eliminate countless logically possible resolutions of the case, and yield a uniquely correct legal resolution of all easy cases. But in a hard case they will characteristically leave more than one answer which is morally and legally right, that is, *not wrong*. Dworkin is right to observe that as a judge one will usually, even in a hard case on a divided bench, consider that one of the answers presents itself as compelling. But this results from the fact that each judge adds to the fully posited set of laws a set of presumptions about matters which are or involve guesses about the future, for example, about the consequences of adhering to 'states' rights' in an era of international economic interdependence or national economic dislocation, or of joining a speculative political venture such as the European Union, or of the supreme court's defying the desires and expectations of the national executive, and so on. Presumptions of this kind should be and usually are fairly stable in the mind of an individual judge, and lend that judge's own deliberations a specificity and inevitability which in some degree outrun the law's specificity.

Each of these two broad purposes and aspects of adjudication—application to facts, and interpretative development—requires some submerging of the judge's own mind, including moral preferences and factual beliefs, in favour of the community's. In the tradition this was dramatized in the moral and legal rule, defended by Aquinas and many but not all others, that judges must adjudicate in line with the legally admissible evidence, and without regard to facts which the law does not permit to be put in evidence even if they happen to be known to be true by the judge, as an individual.[69]

Much judicial reasoning takes the form of deciding that the relevant facts in new case *B* are analogous to those in previously decided case *A* and so should be treated in the same way. Such 'reasoning by analogy' has been found puzzling by theorists who observe that as reasoning it seems to have the pattern of a well-known fallacy. The puzzle is resolved by noticing that what warrants warranted appeals to analogy is not

---

[69] *Aquinas*, 250; Aquinas, *Summa Theologiae* II–II, q. 67, a. 2, q. 64, a. 6 ad 3.

a pattern of reasoning, but an *insight*[70] into some standard—perhaps never noticed or articulated before—which justifies *both* the earlier decision in A and the corresponding decision in B, and is appropriately coherent with the rest of the law and with sound practical judgment at large.

15 LAW AND EPISTEMOLOGY

The law's positivity allows wide scope for 'deeming'. Some such deeming is morally and legally inevitable: for example, facts once determined by proper process must thereafter be taken to be true, and unchallengeably true after time for appeals or collateral challenges has passed. Some deeming is not inevitable but may be reasonable: for example, a court, to get jurisdiction and do justice otherwise unattainable, may deem that events occurred at a place where, in truth, they did not. But examples of fictions only serve to highlight the law's general epistemology. Events really occur and can be truly judged to have occurred. Some beliefs about events, and about good and evil, right and wrong, are false. Some accounts of events are lies because the persons giving them know, or can be known to believe, that they do not correspond to the realities they purport to describe. Some beliefs about what is choiceworthy are so contrary to the truth, so wrong and unreasonable, that anyone who acts upon one of them can and should be blamed and, where appropriate, penalized for doing so. Our law's epistemology is the common-sense realism about facts and values that, with reflective critical refinements, characterizes the classic tradition of natural law theory.

As we have seen (Sect. 1 above), the tradition distinguishes forcefully between truths about the order of nature, truths about logic, truths about the reasonable order of human action (principles of ethics, politics, law), and truths about the technically or artistically effective. Truths of the third (moral) order cannot be reduced to truths of any other kind, not even truths of nature. For the nature of human beings is such that fulfilment is a matter of self-determination by free choices (and accompanying judgments of worth) in the open horizon of the human goods; so the full measure and character of human fulfilment, and the full meaning and implications of practical reason's first principles, cannot be fully known in advance of those choices and judgments and their carrying out in action by individuals and communities. But the nature of a being that can be fulfilled cannot be adequately known otherwise than by knowing what is that kind of being's *fulfilment*. So philosophical anthropology,

---

[70] This kind of insight is an instance of what Peirce called abduction: Sect. 12 above.

knowledge of human nature in the first order, requires for its completion the practical, third-order knowledge we call ethics and political theory.

Hume's and Kant's writings amply display their authors' insightfulness. So it is very significant that the epistemological cause of their critiques of, and departures from, the classical theory of reality and value is their denial or neglect of *insight*, by which one adds to the data of experience and inclination an *understanding* of some fact or value. Such understanding is none the less authentic in those instances—which are of fundamental importance—when it can and must be attained without benefit of reasoning (but rather makes reasoning possible). Rejection of all *self-evidence* as arbitrary, spooky, fishy, or tautological, formal, and empty is self-refuting, as the epistemologies stemming from Hume and Kant all ultimately are.

16 LAW AND LANGUAGE

Since one can fail to express what one means, and can struggle to find words to convey what one has in mind, and since language expands closely in the wake of advancing knowledge and (real or apparent) understanding, it is clear that language is never truly fundamental. Still, our intellectual endeavours make little progress without the assistance of language and the shared and shareable insights, beliefs, and judgments it conveys. Among our intellectual endeavours are, of course, our law, and our discourses *de lege lata,* and *de lege ferenda*, and *de lege reformanda*—about what the law is, what law there should be, and on improving the laws we have.

Language, the transmission of meaning from mind to mind by material (audible, visible, tactile) symbols, manifests in its own way our remarkable nature as beings who are, at once and in a radically *unitary* way, both spiritual and material. This duality without dualism is the source not only of opportunities, such as play, the creative arts, and marriage, but also of limitations. Among those limitations is the indeterminacy, better the under-determinacy, the vagueness inherent both in our purposes and in the language by which we may try to articulate and promote them. By the language of legislation and precedent-forming judicial arguments, we make the countless *determinationes* morally required to give effect to our moral responsibility to love (respect and promote the well-being of) our neighbour as ourselves. But those acts of specification never altogether eliminate vagueness, or the need for further determinations which must seek an appropriate fit not only with the *determinatio* being interpreted, but also with the relevant remainder of our law, and the continuing or perhaps new requirements and implications of relevant moral truths. As was said in Section 14 above, the classic theory of *determinatio* acknowledges plainly that in a good many cases there is no *one* right answer, but rather a number of right (not-wrong) answers, one of which must, for purposes of legislating or judging, be selected by a process designed both to be fair in its process of choosing between alternative reasonable (not-wrong) answers, and to minimize the risk that one of the countless *wrong* answers will be adopted. Semantic vagueness is one, but only one, of the causes of this pervasive under-determinacy of law.

More basic than the meanings 'of words' are the meanings, the intentions, of speakers and other users of words. Interpretation of legal language is in the service of co-operation and justice amongst the persons who are now or will be members of the community whose law it is. The special, 'legal' instrument of that co-operation is the making and maintaining of legal rules by law's 'social sources'—persons acting with certain kinds of intention. So the intentions of the founders, 'original intent', is always relevant. But it was their responsibility to use language in a way that would be understood reliably and in line with any conventional and professional expectations about and modes of interpretation. So the language of texts has a certain independence—not absolute or unconditional—from the minds of the law-makers. And both those aspects of legal interpretation remain within the framework of law's overriding purpose to promote common good by respecting rights and legitimate interests. This theme is pursued a little further in Section 27's remarks on constitutional and statutory interpretation.

17 LAW AND OBJECTIVITY

As bodily beings we have a bias in favour of understanding objectivity on the model of bodily objects and seeing (or otherwise sensing) them. Empiricist philosophy of every kind—not to be confused with empirical natural science and empirical common sense—trades on this bias. And empiricism was a very important assumption and premise in the work of contemporary legal positivism's main founder, Jeremy Bentham. In less naïve forms it remains an important under-tow in contemporary jurisprudence.

Objectivity is not properly understood on the model of a cat's seeing or anticipating a saucer of milk. Already the objectivity of meaning, and of successful transmission and understanding of meaning, is beyond empiricism's explanatory resources (and renders empiricist philosophizing self-refuting). Objectivity, rather, is a matter of openness to the data, and willingness to entertain all relevant questions, and to subject every insight to the critique of further questions. It is a matter of our intellectual operations being free from all biases that would make the attainment of truth—

the goal of enquiry—less likely. To the extent that we as subjects (acting persons) have this openness and this freedom from truth-obscuring biases, we are being objective, our enquiries and judgments are objective, not merely subjective, and, subject to occasional error and deception, the realities we affirm and the goods we judge to be truly pursuit-worthy and beneficial are objectively what we judge them to be.

There are no sound reasons for thinking that judgments about goods, 'value-judgments', are doomed to be merely subjective. Philosophical efforts, such as John Mackie's, to treat them as 'too queer' to be objective fail because they overlook the 'queerness'—relative to the animal norm of clearly seeing a material object—of many other kinds of judgment, for example, about logical validity, or truth in natural scientific theory and in historical investigation, or about intersubjective meaning.[71]

18 LAW AND RATIONAL CHOICE

There are at least three important and distinct senses of the ambiguous term 'rational choice'. (1) Choice is rational when it is fully reasonable, that is, complies with all the requirements of practical reasonableness and so is morally upright. (2) Choice is rational in a thinner sense of 'rational' when it is rationally motivated in the sense that its object has been envisaged by practical intelligence and has rational appeal even if it is in some respect(s) motivated ultimately by feeling or emotion rather than by reason, the feelings or emotions having to some extent fettered and instrumental-ized reason. (3) Choices are 'rational' in a special sense invented by 'game' or 'deci-sion' theorists in the mid-twentieth century, to signify decision and action which is technically or technologically right, by the standards of some art or technique for assessing the most cost-effective way of attaining a relevant technical objective; such a decision typically will be one for which, within the game, the technique 'rationally chosen' is a 'dominant' reason, one which, being commensurable with the reasons for alternative options, includes all the benefit they offer and some more.[72]

This complexity of senses causes much misunderstanding. Sense (3) is the only sense in which economics and game or decision theory, as such, employ the phrase. But common sense often uses it in sense (2). And the philosophers of the great tradi-tion use it in sense (1), arguing that choices of the other two kinds are less than fully, or even adequately, rational. The classical argument is Plato's *Republic*, in which

---

[71] See Finnis, *Fundamentals of Ethics*, n. 57 above, at 57–66.

[72] On 'rationality' in game theory and social-choice theory, see Finnis, 'The Authority of Law in the Predicament of Contemporary Social Theory', *Notre Dame Journal of Law, Ethics & Public Policy*, 1 (1984), 115–37 at 129–33; 'Natural Law & Legal Reasoning', in Robert P. George (ed.), *Natural Law Theory: Contemporary Essays* (Oxford: Oxford University Press, 1992), 134–57.

Socrates' young interlocutors most forcefully challenge him to show that justice and the other virtues opposed to egoism—opposed by egoism!—make sense even when one's justice and virtue puts one at the mercy of unscrupulous egoists and their emotion-driven supporters. The whole sweep of the dialogue is concerned, not to propose 'ideal states', but to meet the young men's challenge by showing that egoism is self-defeating, and self-defeating because it overthrows the constitutional rule (sway) of reason over the other forces in the egoist's soul, leaving egoists—tyrants—at the mercy of anarchic inner drives, lusts, and terrors, their psyches at once swollen and starved. Reason, when not subordinated by less intelligent powers, aligns one with the truths overlooked or defied by egoism. The basic human goods which give one all the reasons one can have for intelligent choices are goods for everyone, not just for me. And one of the basic human goods is the friendship that consistent egoism renders impossible.

The essence of friendship is this: A is interested in B's well-being for B's sake, and B in A's for A's sake; and so A has reason to be interested in A's own well-being not only for its own sake but also for B's; and B likewise. So the interest of neither person comes to rest solely on that person's own well-being, nor solely on the other person's well-being. Thus the relationship of interest (will, choice, action, affection) is, and is directed towards, a truly *common good*. This common good gives their relationship its self-sufficient point. Egoistic self-love is transcended. Or rather, it becomes clear that egoism is a form of self-mutilation, a dead-end deviation from the way to integral human fulfilment.[73]

There is a natural friendship, affectively thin but real and intelligent, of every person with every other person. Thus friendship and justice meet, or share a common intelligibility. The 'Prisoners' Dilemma' or Hobbesian player who regards as satisfactory or 'rationally preferable' the outcome in which he himself gets off scot-free and the other player is imprisoned for life is unreasonable. Conversely, game-theoretical or economistic models of rational choice yield no determinate strategy or outcome when the players' preferences include a concern for the fairness and decency of the outcome—a concern for *common* good. So, though they have their utility as highlighting risks and unwanted side-effects, they cannot substitute for the comprehensive theory of rational choice: natural law theory.

19 LAW AND SEXUALITY

State law and government are morally limited; they have no proper jurisdiction beyond the maintenance of justice and peace. That is the position reached by natural

[73] See *Aquinas*, 111–17.

law theory when Aquinas[74] left behind the Platonic–Aristotelian thesis[75] that the role of state law is to do everything needed to improve citizens' well-being, including their good character. When the compulsory jurisdiction of the state is no longer conceived on the model of parenting young children, it becomes clear that the law should not punish sexually corrupt adults for acts they do alone or together in complete privacy and with full consent.

Since some ethical theories and ideas popular today deny that there is an ethics of sexuality as such, it is necessary to indicate why some kinds of choice to engage in sex acts alone or between consenting adults can be corrupt. Indeed, without such an explanation, it will prove impossible to explain why sex acts between adults and willing children are child abuse rather than an agreeable form of play or (as some ancient Greeks maintained) of loving and educating.

There is a form of life—call it marriage—in which a male and a female, each of the age of reason and sexual maturity, agree to live together permanently, co-ordinating the whole of their lives by reference to the needs and true interests of each other and of any offspring of their union, and actualizing, experiencing, and expressing this mutual commitment by marital intercourse. A sex act is any act intended to lead to one's own or another's sexual satisfaction, and *marital* intercourse is a sex act which in its intentions and kind is apt to actualize, express, and allow the spouses to experience their friendship, commitment, and openness to procreation of offspring. Since willingness to accept and nurture children if they are conceived by marital intercourse is an integral aspect of the rationale of marriage—is what makes sense of its commitment to exclusiveness and permanence—no sex act can be marital unless it not only expresses the spouses' commitment in friendship but also is of a generative kind. For only a consensual act of the generative kind can express the couple's openness to procreation.[76] And even an act of the generative kind will be non-marital if either of the spouses is willing, even conditionally, to engage in the same performances with someone outside of marriage.[77] For if one has such a willingness, one *cannot* make—though, as many do, one can *hope* in vain to make—one's intercourse with one's spouse an expressing and experiencing of one's communion with and commitment to one's partner in *our marriage.* One's will being thus divided, one's sex

---

[74] See the texts and analysis in *Aquinas*, 222–54.

[75] e.g. Aristotle, *Politics*, III: 1280a31–1281a; VII: 1332a28–b12; *Nicomachean Ethics*, V: 1130b23–6; X: 1179b32–1180a5.

[76] Such intercourse—a sex act which includes the man's depositing and the woman's taking his semen into her generative tract—can be of the generative kind even if the persons know or believe that they happen to be sterile: see Aquinas, *Quodlibet*, XI q. 9, a. 2 ad 1 and other texts cited and explained in Finnis, 'The Good of Marriage and the Morality of Sexual Relations: Some Philosophical and Historical Observations', *American Journal of Jurisprudence*, 42 (1998), 97–134 at 126–9; *Aquinas*, 150, 181. See also Robert P. George, *In Defense of Natural Law* (Oxford: Oxford University Press, 1999), 139–83, especially 140–7, 156.

[77] For much fuller versions and discussions of the argument sketched in this sentence, and in the next paragraph, and of the argument's roots in Aquinas, see *Aquinas*, 148–54; Finnis, 'The Good of Marriage', 118–26.

act is one of the many kinds of sex act that lack the integrity of a truly marital act, the integrity of a union in which the uniting of organs is a uniting of bodies, emotions, senses, intelligence, and willed commitment. That lack of integrity is what is meant by 'sexually corrupt'.

Marriage is a basic form of human good.[78] It is a friendship, a relationship which is not a mere means to generating and nurturing children, as some inadequate natural law theories have taken it to be. And the procreativeness which, if children come, will be the relationship's completion is not a mere means to the satisfaction of the couple, as many today take it to be. So it is a relationship which is an *intrinsic* good, with two constitutive and mutually supportive aspects, friendship and procreation. Spouses' agreement to sharing of life includes agreement to engage together in marital intercourse whenever it is mutually agreeable and not unreasonable; this is a matter of mutual right. Kant grossly confused this right with dominion—a person's property relationship to a subpersonal thing—over one's spouse's body. (Much modern thought shares Locke's and Kant's erroneous assumption that one's living body is not oneself but something that belongs to the self/person.)

Integral to the good of marriage is this committed willingness[79] to actualize together, and enable each other to experience, the good of our marriage, in the intended joy[80] of authentically marital acts. Where the couple's sex acts are not authentically marital, the intelligibility of their marriage is disintegrated: their sex acts are unhinged from their mutual commitment. This unhinging and disintegration runs contrary to both of the goods constitutive of the complex basic good of marriage: not only the good of marital friendship but also the good of the children whose whole formation as persons is so deeply benefited by the context of a good marriage, and so vulnerable to everything that harms the marriage.

Therefore, the conscience of any spouse who really understands the good(s) of marriage must reject, among other things, any kind of willingness, however conditional, to engage in non-marital sex acts. And since even *approving* (regarding as morally reasonable) the sex acts of the unmarried entails a willingness, albeit conditional, to engage in non-marital sex acts, every clear-headed spouse must disapprove all such acts. Moreover, since such disapproval is required by the good of marriage, and the good of marriage is truly a basic human good and an essential component of the common good, respect for the good of marriage requires even the unmarried, and those who for some good reason will never marry, to reject non-marital sex acts and judge them a wrong kind of choice.

[78] See *Aquinas*, 82, 146 n. 58.

[79] This *positive* willingness, together with resolve *not* to engage in sex acts outside marriage (adultery), is what the tradition meant by *fides*, which is thus much richer than the modern 'fidelity': see *Aquinas*, 144–7; Finnis, 'The Good of Marriage', 106–11.

[80] See Aquinas, *In 1 Cor.*, 7.1 ad v. 5 [325], and the discussion of pleasure as motive for and good aspect of marital intercourse in Finnis, 'The Good of Marriage', 102–11; *Aquinas*, 143–7.

It follows that a very important part of the education of children is fitting them, emotionally and intellectually, for authentic marriage or, if their vocational choices or other circumstances of their life prevent them from marrying, for respect for the good of marriage by withholding their consent or approval from non-marital sex acts. Wilfully allowing children in one's care to become sexually corrupt—to develop a disposition to approve of sex acts disintegrated from the good of marriage—is a great injustice to them, since it blocks their genuine participation in a basic human good. Parents and others responsible for the education of children are entitled to assistance in fulfilling their responsibilities in justice. It is a fundamental responsibility of the state's government and law—here Aristotle was correct[81]—to afford them its assistance, by coercively prohibiting, for example, every kind of paedophilia, any kind of publication or distribution of pornography to children, any teaching by public employees or agencies that non-marital (e.g. homosexual)[82] sex can be reasonable, and any maintenance of places of resort arranged for non-marital sex whose public and deliberate availability for that purpose would suggest to children that such activities are approvable. A government and legal system which, having the resources to undertake these responsibilities, deliberately turns aside from them in the name of choice or pluralism or freedom of expression is mistaken about what the relevant human rights truly are, and is seriously unjust.

Similar considerations of justice to children require strenuous state support for the contract of marriage, and for mothers who devote their time to maintaining a home in preference to taking employment which will in most cases be less significant and worthwhile for the common good. The state's opposition to abuses such as polygamy is warranted by the other aspect of the good of marriage, the friendship which calls for a genuine and far-reaching *equality* between the spouses. It is of high importance for the common good that the intelligibility and worth of marriage be preserved in the minds of children and adults alike by prohibiting the appropriation of the title of marriages, and of any privileges commensurate to the heavy burdens of marriage, by relationships which, like so-called 'same-sex marriage', lack an essential part of marriage's rationale and are entered upon by people who almost universally[83] reject the constant exclusivity which is essential to marital fidelity and integrity (and so to justice to children). As Aristotle rightly said, 'human beings are by nature more conjugal than political'.[84] This centrality of the good of marriage to reasonable forms of life and community, and so to human fulfilment, is the reason why so many aspects of

[81] See also *NLNR*, 216–17, 222–3, on public morality and paternalism that is legitimate because for the sake of children.

[82] On the rejection of homosexual sex acts by Plato, Aristotle, Plutarch, and other masters of the classical natural law theory, see Finnis, 'Law, Morality, and "Sexual Orientation"', *Notre Dame Law Review*, 69 (1994), 1049–76; a revised and shortened version, with replies to some objections, is in John Corvino (ed.), *Same Sex: Debating the Ethics, Science, and Culture of Homosexuality* (Lanham, Maryland, Boulder, Colo., New York, Oxford: Rowman & Littlefield, 1997), 31–43. See also ' "Shameless Acts" in Colorado: Abuse of Scholarship in Constitutional Cases', *Academic Questions*, 7/4 (1994), 10–41 at 19–41.

[83] See Finnis, 'The Good of Marriage', 130–4.   [84] *Nicomachean Ethics*, VIII: 1162a17–18.

what promotes it, like what undermines or assaults it, are within the jurisdiction of state law and government despite that jurisdiction's limitation to peace and justice.

20 Philosophy of Tort Law

Many contemporary legal theorists seem to value only one part of classical legal theory, a part that is among its weakest: Aristotle's account of corrective justice. True, Aristotle is right to say that the restoration of a wrongfully disturbed equality between one person and another is the principle requiring tortfeasors to compensate those whom they have wrongfully subjected to harm or loss, and that that principle is an essentially true principle of justice even though its concern to restore equality differs from the concern to maintain equality in distributing some shared stock of benefits or burdens among a set of persons.[85] But he has little or nothing helpful to say by way of response to the decisive and difficult questions: are persons drastically unequal in, say, wealth to be treated as having been *equals* immediately prior to the tort? How is a tortious to be distinguished from an inculpable or non-tortious caus-ing of loss? What measure of compensation restores the hypothesized pre-existing equality when both the fault and (independently) the resources of defendants differ so greatly relative to any given scale of loss?

Tort law's distinctive project of compensation is clearly dependent upon a prior set of judgments about what forms of interaction between persons are acceptable within a given community. But the priority of those judgments may be more logical than chronological: to some extent, a community should and does form its judgments of acceptability *in* the context of tort claims. Still, prior to such communal judgments are, in many contexts, judgments made in individual or other private deliberations about what is worthwhile and what threatens the worthwhile, and about what levels of risk of loss of the worthwhile are acceptable in different contexts. The backbone of tort is a set of moral—natural law—principles identifying as wrongful all choices precisely to harm or to deceive. But the flesh-and-blood of tort is a set of standards embodying both 'natural law' elements and 'positive elements'. The former reflect a more or less adequate understanding of the basic and intrinsic aspects of human well-being and the main social structures conducive to that well-being. (These aspects and structures are what tort theorists often call 'interests'.) The 'positive' ele-ments in tort reflect more or less conventional—could-reasonably-be different—choices of ways of pursuing the basic human goods, choices among alternative designs for the social structures and interactions promotive of well-being, and

---

[85] *Nicomachean Ethics,* V: 1131b25–1132b20.

choices among differing kinds and levels of risk of undesirable side-effects of those
alternative kinds of structure and ways of acting.

A sound tort law identifies as tortious every act *intended* precisely to cause harm to
another person: the American doctrine that malice makes tortious is sound, the
English rejection of it unsound (and half-hearted).[86] But an accurate understanding
of *intention* identifies as an *un*intended *side-effect* many fully foreseeable and foreseen consequences of a choice. The law-school doctrine that what is foreseen is
intended is an undesirable fiction, as is the similar doctrine that the intended
includes whatever is reasonably foreseeable as certain or highly probable.
Responsibility for one's actions' side-effects—foreseen or foreseeable—is morally
and humanly different in kind from responsibility for what one intends, and therefore ought to be regarded as a distinct kind of basis for tortious liability. In principle,
our law does treat it as distinct, first by dividing tort into the intentional and the negligent, and then by analysing the latter with the primarily normative apparatus of
duties and standards of care and remoteness of causation.

The norms appropriately at work in those phases of tort's analysis of loss-causing
incidents are, then, partly the permanently valid principles and norms of true morality, and partly the norms a community adopts by its choices of forms of life.[87] The
principles and norms of natural law neither require nor exclude choices such as our
community's choice to allow heavy vehicles to be propelled along the highways at
speeds greatly exceeding walking pace. Nor choices such as a hypothetical community's choice to set the speed limit for motor vehicles at 4 m.p.h. But such rationally
under-determined choices once made—as they inevitably are by practice and usage
if not by legislation or by courts adjudicating claims in trespass or negligence—provide a rationally determinate measure (at least presumptively or defeasibly applicable) for identifying many of tort law's duties and standards of care, and many of
tort's demarcations between actionable and remote losses. All this is a paradigm of
the interplay of morality and *determinatio*—of 'natural' and 'positive'—which is
classical natural law theory's central theme (see Sect. 14 above).

On the whole, the developed common law of tort, like the developed civil law of
delict, embodies a true understanding of persons, of their worth, of their efficacious
freedom to choose well or badly, and of the common good promoted by individual
initiative and enterprise in community with and partly for the sake of other persons.
The classic name for that true practical understanding of principles is natural law. It
does not follow, however, that all the main features of our tort law are fully in line
with the requirements of reasonableness—with natural law. How, for example, can it
be just to require defendants to compensate to a measure that takes no account whatever of either the defendant's or the plaintiff's means to compensate or bear the loss,

---

[86] See Finnis, 'Intention in Tort Law', in David Owen (ed.), *Philosophical Foundations of Tort Law*
(Oxford: Oxford University Press, 1995), 229–48.

[87] See Patrick Kelley, 'Who Decides? Community Safety Conventions at the Heart of Tort Liability',
Cleveland State Law Review, 38 (1990), 315.

and no account whatever of the innocence or viciousness of the parties' conduct in respects not causally relevant to the actionable harm or loss? Should not tort law, without abandoning its central structure, incorporate some modifying principles of the kind which elsewhere in our law, as in natural law theory, are called equity?

21 PHILOSOPHY OF CONTRACT LAW

The distinction between the duties of care and compensation specified, regulated, and enforced by tort law and the duties of performance and compensation specified, regulated, and enforced by contract is not a complete separation. Quite reasonably there are torts such as interfering in certain ways with contractual relationships. Still, the distinction is clear, sound, and should not be expected to wither away. The 'death of contract', heralded a generation ago, was rightly ignored by those whom it most concerned: businesspeople willing to sue and expecting to be sued on even purely executory (wholly unperformed) contracts. For there is good reason to treat certain kinds of agreement voluntarily entered into as creating, from the moment of agreement (or other agreed commencement), a set of obligations, and of correlative rights which pertain, from that moment, to the legally protected holdings (wealth) of the right-holder.

Historically, legal systems have been cautious about undertaking the responsibility of regulating and enforcing informal, let alone purely executory informal agreements. This is neither surprising nor sign of stupidity or superstition. Legal systems have many prior, more urgent responsibilities and, as lawyers in advanced legal systems easily forget, the existence of a clearly identifiable moral obligation does not entail that the state's legal organs have a moral responsibility to concern themselves with it. Affirmative responsibilities are always subject to circumstances. Nevertheless, the moral obligations creatable by agreement are obligations of justice, upholding justice is what the state's organs are essentially for, and the underlying moral obligations created by voluntary agreements are the rational basis for the legal obligations which are the heart of what we call contract. The moral obligations created by trustees' voluntary assumptions of responsibility are analogous to those central to contract, and are similarly the rational basis for much of the law of trusts. When the common law's old doctrines of privity and consideration are relaxed, it becomes obvious that contract and trusts are more deeply similar and interrelated than their usual doctrinal, institutional, and pedagogical separation would suggest.

So too, contract and property are deeply interconnected at the level of principle. The 'chose in action' constituted by breach of even a purely executory contract is positive law's witness to the moral truth that one's freedom, dignity, and power as a person includes one's capacity to enrich other specific persons here and now by choosing to confer on them the present rights correlative to (entailed by) one's assuming (undertaking) the responsibility of doing them some future specific service. Still, persons are radically superior to all subpersonal realities, and property law is rightly distinct in so far as its paradigmatic subject-matter is subpersonal realities, not obligations of service, obligations which should never be treated as a kind of subpersonal thing. This insight rightly informs much of the remedial part of the law of contract, most obviously its aversion to ordering specific performance of *stricto sensu* personal service.

Essential to an account of the morally binding force of voluntarily assuming responsibility by promising or agreeing is some account of the benefits reasonably foreseeable from division of labour and co-operation. It is this benefit of co-operation between people who are *not* in *stricto sensu* partnership that gives to voluntary assumptions of responsibility (within limits) the normative significance they purport to have, and makes them reasonable kinds of act, neither mumbo-jumbo nor self-enslavement. The kind of benefit at stake is essentially a kind of control over the future, a kind of security which is not so much warding off anticipated harms as positively improving the well-being of all the parties. Hobbesian, Lockian, and Kantian efforts to explain promissory obligation by appeals to extrinsic sanctions, the supposed logic of self-consistency, and/or the metaphysics of personhood, all look the wrong way. They all fail for want of the key idea of a common good in which the parties attain individual benefits by the service of a co-operation which can be asynchronous and reliably extend well beyond the present, while not being committed to a common project such as *stricto sensu* partners share in.[88] The same key idea gives us reason to say that Oliver Wendell Holmes's conception of contracts as creating no more than the disjunctive legal obligation to either-perform-or-pay-damages is, while not incoherent or incapable of being adopted by a legal system, none the less neither accurate as an account of common, civil, or international law, nor at all desirable as an alternative.

Just as tort law presupposes certain truths about human action and intentionality which are often denied by theoretical sceptics, so contract presupposes all these and also some further, related truths about the intelligibility of language and the accessibility of other people's meanings, beliefs, and intentions. Even the so-called 'objective' test employed in analysing offers or acceptances takes as decisive what a reasonable person, in the context, would have judged to be the speaker's actual ('subjective') meaning and intent.

---

[88] Such a project need not be, and typically is not, entered upon out of motives of generosity (*liberalitas*), but once agreed upon by promise or contract is a matter of the virtue of strict justice and the vice of injustice, not generosity or meanness. Contrast James Gordley, *The Philosophical Origins of Modern Contract Doctrine* (Oxford: Clarendon Press, 1991).

22 PHILOSOPHY OF THE CRIMINAL LAW

A just law of crimes cannot be adequately understood and justified without under-standing some main elements in (i) political theory, (ii) moral theory, (iii) the meta-physics of persons and their acts, and (iv) a common-sense awareness of the culture and dispositions of a given community's triers of fact (judges or juries). Classical nat-ural law theory, in its contemporary forms, addresses these issues explicitly, and jus-tifies the sharp distinction between criminal and civil law which is characteristic of modern legal systems but not of ancient or even medieval practice and theory.

That the state's law and government 'monopolize force' (as Kelsen puts it), or alone have the right to authorize and administer the irrevocably and deliberately harmful measures we call punishment (as Aquinas more accurately holds), is a decisive ele-ment in political theory, descriptive or normative. Legal theory must be regarded as incorporating and extending this element when it seeks to give an account of (*a*) the proper limits of the criminal law's prohibitive and affirmative requirements, and (*b*) the point and justice of imposing punishment when those requirements are violated. The criminal law's first function, of identifying what subjects *must* refrain from (or, in a few cases, do), is justified only by the premise that none of the other persons exer-cising legitimate, for example, parental or corporate directorial, authority, and no other legitimate kinds of measure save this, are likely to be either effective or fair in identifying, and seeking to avert or reduce, the prospect that some subjects will otherwise be treated *unjustly* by others.[89]

The criminal law's second function, of authorising and requiring the imposition of punitive measures against those judicially found to have violated its requirements, is best understood as an element in the state's wider function of upholding, and where necessary making and re-making, a just distribution of benefits and burdens. The burden of complying with the law's just requirements falls, in fairness, on all the law's subjects, indeed all persons within its territorial jurisdiction. Whenever crimes which could justly be punished are committed, the offenders are helping themselves to the advantage of, at their own arbitrary will, renouncing that burden. The advan-tage they thereby illicitly and unfairly gain is precisely the advantage of a kind of free-dom to do as they please, to follow their own preferences and choices in preference to the way laid down for all by the law. Pursuant to the state's function of maintaining distributive justice, the state's authorities can therefore be justified in coercively depriving offenders of this kind of advantage, so that the balance of advantage and disadvantage, between them and the law-abiding—a balance disturbed by the volun-tary criminal act—is restored and rectified. This balance-restoring deprivation is of precisely the kind of advantage the offenders took: of excessive freedom. Just punish-ment is not essentially a matter of inflicting pain, but rather of repressing the will, the

---

[89] *Aquinas*, 239–52.

freedom, of offenders. (Nothing other than this line of thought can make sense of the opaque notion that crimes or criminals *deserve* punishment.)

Retribution, therefore, is the general justifying aim of punishment.[90] The opportunity to use retributively justified punishments to deter and reform is only a bonus side-effect, and measures intended to deter and/or reform cannot rightly be more deleterious to the convicted offenders' interests than can be justified by retributive considerations. And retribution's intrinsic relation to the state's unique function and authority to uphold a fair pattern of relevant advantages and disadvantages explains why criminal law is so distinct from civil. In civil or private law, the victim of wrongdoing seeks redress from the wrongdoer, as a rectification of a pre-existing relationship between them presupposed to be fair. But in criminal proceedings, the wrongdoer's victim has no proper standing save as a witness, for here it is the interests of the law-abiding (normally including the victim) that are to be vindicated as a matter of restoring justice *to them*.

The criminal law's main general doctrines, about voluntariness, acts, and *mens rea*, are tightly connected with the retributive theory's understanding of what it is in offences that warrants punishment. Of course, the theory in turn, like the doctrines, rests on an understanding of what is involved in persons *acting* (rather than just behaving, as in sleep walking). It rests particularly on an understanding that the paradigm of action is the *carrying out* of a *choice*, a specific *intention* adopted as an envisaged means to some envisaged end, some wider intention. That carrying out is typically—and in all cases that are within the proper scope of the criminal law—by bodily movements (though there are certainly acts, such as prayer or mental calculation, where there is no movement of the acting person). Many of the conundrums of criminal law theory concern the question of demarcating items of behaviour from *the act*,[91] and demarcating the act from what it causes, its *consequences*. Many offences, though by no means all, are legally defined in terms not only of kinds of intention and of bodily movement, but also of kinds of effect. The criminal law thereby creates for itself—and for good reason—problems that do not arise in purely moral reflection, in which what is intended, generally (as end) and specifically (as means), is decisive for judgment more or less independently of what in fact happens or fails to happen as a result.

In criminal law doctrine and practice much confusion arises from the reluctance of those who administer it to differentiate clearly between *behaviour* and *action* (behaviour precisely *as* the execution of a choice), and between action and *consequences*, particularly when readily foreseeable but unintended consequences are impressively harmful and the intentions and other motivations of the accused are opaque to observers.

---

[90] See *Aquinas*, 210–15; *NLNR*, 262–4.

[91] See Finnis, 'Intention and Side-Effects', in R. G. Frey and Christopher W. Morris (eds.), *Liability and Responsibility: Essays in Law and Morals* (Cambridge: Cambridge University Press, 1991), 32–64.

23 PHILOSOPHY OF PROPERTY LAW

Property in all the forms known to legal doctrine is a defined set of normative relationships between people considered precisely in so far as one or more of them is or might be concerned with some part of the world—some resource—which can be put to human use. The relevant kinds of concern with a resource (a *res* or thing) may, of course, be quite indirect and contingent, as in the case of money, shares, futures, patents, and the like. But always the ultimate source of the value of such intangibles is their potentiality to confer control over resources and the use of these resources to promote some (real or supposed) intrinsic good of a human person.

Although legal doctrine, for good technical reasons, contrasts *rights between persons* with *rights over things*, rights of the latter kind are always reducible to combinations of rights between persons, and always have as their primary point the regulating of relationships between persons (e.g. the exclusion of non-owners from the thing and its use). The entire law of property, every property right and relationship, and every item of property, is wholly in the service of human persons and just relationships between persons. No kind of physical relationship between particular persons and particular things—original and/or long-standing 'occupation', creation by personal labour working on other things, invention—constitutes by itself a normatively sufficient reason to acknowledge or rule that those persons have property in those things, still less that they rightly have 'absolute' ownership such as Roman *dominium* or common law fee simple in possession. The world's resources pre-exist all of us, and since we are all fundamentally each other's equals as persons the only reasonable normative baseline is that all those resources are to be treated at all times as for the benefit of everyone.

So property rights in all their forms (i) give particular persons rights to the use and/or fruits of resources in priority to all other persons (who are so far forth excluded from such enjoyment of the thing), but (ii) at the same time are morally subject to a kind of inchoate trust, mortgage, lien, or usufruct in favour of *all other persons*. This moral burden on property holdings is given legal *specificatio* by the various norms of private and public law—varying, like the forms of property right themselves, from system to system—which qualify owners' priority of enjoyment and control: nuisance, prescriptive easements, taxation, eminent domain, 'antitrust' (anti-monopoly law), and so forth.

Hence the classical natural law tradition accepts the position articulated in Aristotle's apparently paradoxical slogan: property is to be private in possession but common (shared) in use.[92] This sounds paradoxical, since the point of possession is use, and the point of making possession private—the point of *appropriating* resources and rights to resources to particular people to the exclusion of others—is

[92] *Politics*, II: 1263a25, a 38.

(as Aristotle's and Aquinas's famous discussions[93] make clear and the sad experience of two generations of Bolshevism super-abundantly confirms) to provide incentives to careful, prudent, but dynamic and forward-looking management and exploitation of those resources. Such incentives lie in the owners' priority of use and enjoyment. How then can use rightly be called common? How can it be said that non-owners, who have contributed nothing to the creation or cultivation and management of the thing, have some right to participate in its enjoyment? The answer lies in the idea already mentioned, that the owners' rights of enjoyment, though conferring sufficient priority and benefit to incentivize owners to care and cultivation, are qualified by a residuary quasi-trust for the benefit of all whose needs might reasonably be served by some share in the resource's use or fruits. The institutions of redistributive taxation are the devices perhaps most characteristic of modern legal systems' recognition of this moral burden on private property. Provided that the point of the institution of property—the well-being of persons—is kept always in view, the Aristotelian dictum escapes paradox and prescribes an appropriate balance between naïve communism and raw capitalism. The fact that no such balance can be expected to be simply optimal, or permanently even appropriate, does not entail that the search for appropriate balance is pointless.

Just as various technical contours of a legal system's institutions of property are delineated not in the treatise on property but under the heading of tort (conversion, trespass . . .) and contract (passing of title in sale . . .), so the rules enforcing the orderly subjection of all owners' rights to the interests and moral rights of the needy are found in many corners of the law. Many legal systems contain no explicit qualification of the laws of theft to accommodate the starving—a qualification prominent in the writings of moralists in the tradition ('in necessity, all things are common'[94]). Such a lack can be justified, if at all, only by robust countervailing practices of prosecutorial and sentencing discretion. Forgetfulness of the tradition seems to contribute to the heavy weather recent jurists have made of *Vincent v. Lake Erie Transportation*.[95]

24 PHILOSOPHY OF INTERNATIONAL LAW

Whether or not coined for English by Bentham, the term 'International law' translates the term *Jus inter gentes* which emerges in the sixteenth-century renovation of

[93] *Politics*, II: 1262b36–1263b26; Aquinas, *Summa Theologiae*, II–II q. 66, a. 2; *Aquinas*, 188–90.

[94] *Aquinas*, 190–6; Grotius, *De Jure Belli ac Pacis*, II. ii. 6; Pufendorf, *De Jure Naturae*, II. vi. 5–8 (n. 5 above, pp. 301–9).

[95] 124 N.W. 221 (Minn. 1910): saving one's life in a storm by attaching one's ship to another's wharf is no trespass, even if it creates an obligation to compensate for damage thereby done to the wharf.

natural law theory after the breakdown of a unitary secular-ecclesiastical Christendom. Articulated in succeeding centuries as a law between *states* rather than nations or peoples as such, international law manifests in its contemporary development both the underlying complexity of human community—a complexity far exceeding the multiplicity of states—and the inaccuracy of the thought that a state is, without qualification, a *perfecta communitas*, a complete community entitled to constitute the ultimate and unconditional horizon of a just person's allegiance. Has an individual person, or a group which is not a state, standing to move international organs as a subject of international law with substantive and procedural rights derived from international law? Has an international organization such as the United Nations an international personality comparable to that of a state, and are its rights in international law limited to those conceded to it by the states party to its establishment? Can the same be said of a non-governmental organization such as the International Red Cross? If 'persons' other than states can be subjects of international law rights, can they also be creators of international law rules, as states can?

These issues have driven many of the developments in international law during the past fifty years. They all emerge from a developing understanding that new interdependencies, economic, environmental, and cultural, are bringing into being a worldwide human community that might in principle become a *perfecta communitas* equipped to supervise the doing of justice everywhere. On occasion, as at Nuremberg in 1945–6, such issues have laid bare the natural law foundations which alone could justify holding that some conduct can be, and concretely was, a 'crime against humanity', triable internationally.

Why is state law and government, with jurisdiction over the families, neighbourhoods, and other associations within a distinct and economically viable territory, needed and justified? Most fundamentally by the need for an authority that can be expected to administer coercive and irreparable punishments with the justice of impartiality and care for truth.[96] Historically, it seems that states and their governments have very often been constituted by a sheer taking of authority unauthorized by any pre-existing legal title or any other moral claim other than the prospect of being, *de facto*, likely to succeed in securing a degree of co-ordination and co-operation sufficient to allow justice to be not merely desired and ordered but actually done.[97] There is today no central-case type of international legislative, executive, or judicial authority because no person or group is capable of taking power, in the above sense, and because states tacitly concur in judging that no existing or envisageable authority could be relied upon to act with an effective justice sufficient to merit a general transfer or subordination of state jurisdiction to it.

Hence agreements (treaties) and to a lesser extent customary practice (especially of states) remain the primary sources of international law, which remains both descriptively and morally a relatively undeveloped, non-central case of law. Still, it

---

[96] *Aquinas*, 247–52.   [97] Finnis, *NLNR*, 245–52.

should not be called simply a primitive legal system; so far as they go, international legal processes are sophisticated applications of 'the general principles of law recognized by civilized nations'[98] and of those techniques for stabilizing practical thought, and for rendering it an instrument of commonality and co-operation, which we call legal doctrine, as evidenced in the 'judicial decisions and the teachings of the most highly qualified publicists of the various nations'.[99] In these formulae, the terms 'recognized' and 'civilized', if not also 'qualified', point towards the assumption— fully justified—that there are true principles—traditionally called natural law— underlying this and every other legal order, principle, and doctrine.

25 PHILOSOPHY OF THE COMMON LAW

The term 'common law' is found in Euripedes and Plato, and is well known (as *ius commune*) in legal and political thought in medieval civil (Roman law) and ecclesiastical law, in a meaning substantially the same as one aspect of its meaning in English legal and political thought: the general law of the realm, as distinct from local and personal customs pertaining to a family, or calling, or district. But another aspect of the common law is perhaps more significant: its distinction from statutes or other enactments—from law made by a body whose authority and primary function is precisely to change the law of the realm.

Lawyers in the tradition called common law in distinction from Roman or civil law have reflected for nearly a thousand years on the common law's nature. The history of their reflections shows that there has never been a stable, articulate, coherent, and generally accepted account of the place or roles in its make-up of sources such as reason (moral principle), antiquity (permanence), popular custom, judicial precedent, or professional experience, opinion, and practice.[100] Nevertheless, two dimensions of the common law are identified, in one way or another, by everyone. The common law which it is the responsibility of the superior courts of justice to administer is a law which is inherently related to, indeed in some sense drawn from, *reason*, and it is somehow a matter of *usage*.

Each of these dimensions is complex. *Reason* signifies the principles of reasonable choice and action which have been called natural law or (with the same meaning and reference) law of reason or morality or human rights and human decency, or equity,

[98] Statute of the International Court of Justice, art. 38(1)(*d*).
[99] ibid., art. 38(1)(*e*).
[100] This is amply demonstrated for the period 1150–1630 by J. W. Tubbs, *The Common Law Mind: Medieval and Early Modern Conceptions* (Baltimore and London: Johns Hopkins University Press, 2000).

fairness, and justice. But the 'reason' of the common law has often been taken to include the 'artificial reason' of a learned profession, leaving unclarified the question how far this is a matter of moral wisdom based on more than ordinary experience, and how far it is a matter of technical doctrines, institutions, and practices *posited* by choices of professional lawyers who could reasonably have chosen differently. In the latter sense, the common law's 'reason' merges with the second main dimension, usage, but retains the special sense that the doctrines and so forth posited by the legal profession's practices are subject to a requirement of internal consistency and coherence with each other. (See also Sects. 3 and 14 above.)

Most of the old common lawyers' confused and shifting discussions of common law's nature could have been clarified by a firm grasp of the Thomistic idea that practical reason's principles need to be extended and applied by *determinatio*.[101] As was noted towards the end of Section 3 and in Section 14 above, one of the unchanging principles that underlie any justifiable *determinatio* is the principle that like cases are to be decided alike. That grounds the common law's acceptance of norms of *stare decisis* (judicial precedent), an acceptance which crystallized almost as soon as the preconditions (especially printed law reports) were in place. For judges confronted by an issue not settled by the plain meaning of a constitution or statute ought to try to settle it in the way that it would be settled by any other judges hearing the case on the same day in the same realm. (That is part of what is involved in administering *common* law, and common law judges often think of their realm as, for some purposes, as wide as 'the common law world'.) But such synchronic (counterfactual) consistency of decisions requires that there be some standard of decision besides the statutes and any given judge's moral response to the issue. The standard needs to be *salient*—identifiable by all and more easily identifiable than the answer to the question in issue. The fact that the issue has in the past been resolved in a particular way by judge(s) in the same general legal context is salient and so provides a standard presumptively and defeasibly appropriate for resolving the issue here and now.

26 PRIVATE WRONGS AND RECOURSE

The law of private wrongs and remedies, of which tort law is one of the central types, certainly cannot be justified or well described by theories which overlook its

---

[101] Chief Justice Sir John Fortescue's discussion of maxims, in his *De Laudibus Legum Angliae* (*c*.1469), appeals to Aristotle's conception of self-evident principles, and Fortescue's discussion of political community in *The Governance of England* (1475) appeals to Aquinas's conception of limited government (see Finnis, 'Is Natural Law Theory Compatible with Limited Government?', n. 18 above), but he fails to advert to Aquinas's development of Aristotle on law's derivation from principle by *determinatio*.

fundamental structure as a set of primary and correlative rights and duties (e.g. not to be defamed and not to defame) whose violation ('breach') is taken to *warrant* the recognition that P, whose primary right was violated, thereby acquires a remedial right of action at law for compensation, and that D, having been in breach of a primary duty, correlatively becomes liable, at P's suit, to make such compensation to P. Breach of duty is violation of right and '*cause* of action'.

Any account which explains remedial rights, not as consequences of violation of primary rights but as means to maximizing social wealth or some other value (e.g. by reducing wasteful precautions and/or transaction costs incurred in attempted exchanges of rights), will fail to make sense of the pervasive rules and doctrines of our law of tort which deny P a remedial right where D's breach of duty to T foreseeably caused harm to P but involved no breach of any primary duty to P. So economistic analyses of tort, though helpfully drawing attention to certain side-effects of legal rules and proceedings, will not do. But equally, theories which put on the mantle of Aristotelian 'corrective justice' have failed to fill the gaps in Aristotle's account: its insufficient attention to the *primary* rights and duties which make wrongs identifiable as wrongs, and its neglect to explain just how breach of primary right *warrants* tort's normal judicial order of fully compensatory damages.

The recent account[102] of tort as founded on a 'principle of civil recourse' was offered as descriptive and 'conceptual', and disclaimed any 'normative' or justificatory purpose. Its critique of rival accounts powerfully demonstrated that economistic, utilitarian, and (in different ways) Aristotelian corrective justice theories do not make sense of tort's structure and many of its rules. And the account's middle-level analysis of that structure rightly pointed to the way in which social conventions and other norms of fairness give some determinacy to tort's primary rights and duties.[103] But at its deepest level, this theory of civil recourse fails by overlooking the radical dependence of descriptive or conceptual analysis on unrestricted critical engagement with issues of evaluation—with the normative truths which are the sole rational source of justifications (or condemnations). For a theory or account aspiring to any interesting level of generality cannot sufficiently 'make sense of' any rules or institutional structures without showing them to be warranted—if they are—by principles which the theorist not only can 'suggest' have 'certain appealing normative justifications'[104] but can reasonably judge to *be justified* in the rich sense of justification sought by a conscientious judge deliberating about changing the whole life of D, or P, or both by making or refusing an award of damages. In the absence of such full-blooded normative justification the defeated rivals can reclaim the field of battle by

---

[102] Benjamin C. Zipursky, 'Rights, Wrongs and Recourse in the Law of Torts', *Vanderbilt Law Review*, 51 (1998), 1–100.

[103] Benjamin C. Zipursky, 'Legal Malpractice and the Structure of Negligence Law', *Fordham Law Review*, 67 (1998), 649–90 at 679–80. See more generally at n. 102 above.

[104] Zipursky, 'Rights, Wrongs and Recourse', 97.

denouncing as anachronisms those features of the law unaccounted for—not shown to be justified, or shown to be unjustifiable—by their rival accounts.

As a justification for tort's structure, the theory of recourse would be rejected by the classical theory of natural law. At its root the theory of recourse treats as worthy the emotional impulse of a victim of wrongdoing to 'get even',[105] by 'act[ing] against'—having recourse against—the rights-violator.[106] This impulse is in most if not all respects contrary to the true principle, do not answer injury with injury (Sect. 10 above). The recourse theory fails to explain why P's impulse should be allowed for when it is a desire to seize the wrongdoer's goods but not when it is a desire to impose on D a hurt or harm like what P has suffered. It leaves unexplained why the remedial right of action granted by the law in recognition of and substitution for P's emotional impulse should extend, as it does in tort, to full compensation for all foreseeable losses. But at the same time, though treating P's remedial rights as independent of any supposed moral duty of D to *volunteer* full compensation, the theory provides no support for the thought (see Sect. 20 above) that our law is simplistic, unbalanced, and to some extent unjust and unjustifiable in maintaining a quasi-universal rule of *full* compensation for foreseeable losses caused by D's breach of duty to P, however minor that breach and whatever the relative resources of P and D. Moreover, the recourse theory questionably offers to justify the institution of punitive damages, a part of the law of tort which, in its American forms, seems unjustifiably to commingle private with public (especially but not only criminal) law; even the more restrained forms of the institution of punitive damages, elsewhere in the common-law world, can be justified only to the extent that the institution amounts (if it does) to awarding damages for a distinct though hitherto implicit wrong of contempt for P's personality, much like the Roman law delict (tort) of *Injuria*.

The recourse theory rightly identifies central features of our law of tort which have long been misunderstood or undervalued, and central issues of explanation or justification of those features. But it leaves those issues scarcely resolved. The needed resolution will have to recognize that not every feature of tort can be justified; some of the features in need of reform are of very long standing, but others are recent importations under the influence of economistic and other 'policy-oriented' approaches. Resolution will come from recognition that, like other parts of the law but in its own distinctive way, tort law's foundations are judgments about what kinds of relationship between people are fair and reasonable, both generically and in particular kinds of context. These judgments are the main basis for recognizing primary rights and duties. The remedial right to compensation in the event of D's violation of P's right invokes a further judgment about fairness and reasonableness in re-establishing the fair relationship between them that D's conduct ruptured. Very often—but by no

---

[105] What Zipursky calls a desire for retribution has nothing to do with the retribution argued for in the account of crime and punishment proposed in Sect. 22 above, a theory in which the desires of the victim, and even the *desires* of the law-abiding, have no normative significance.

[106] Zipursky, 'Rights, Wrongs and Recourse', 85.

means always—remedial fairness calls for that restoration of equality which is the rationale for what tort law (and in many cases only tort law) provides: *D* so far as possible restoring *P* to the position *P* would have enjoyed had *D*'s breach of duty to *P* not occurred.

27 CONSTITUTIONAL AND STATUTORY INTERPRETATION

Interpretation of texts and other statements is sometimes simply historical: what did a given author or set of authors intend to communicate in their text or other statement? That question, even when it concerns a text with multiple authorship, often has a determinate answer in whose accuracy one can reasonably have high confidence. (If you think this claim is over-optimistic, you have understood it and done your bit to verify it.) Often, however, the question cannot be given so determinate and reliable an answer, other than: we do not know and have no means of knowing what the author(s) intended to communicate on such-and-such a matter, to which their text seems more or less closely relevant. Often this uncertainty has its source in the limitations which make human beings unable to foresee all relevant issues or to address exhaustively even those issues they do foresee.

In adjudication and the practice of law, interpretation of constitutional and statutory texts and statements can never reasonably be exclusively historical. Constitutions and statutes arise for consideration—indeed, exist as *law*—only in a context of the interpreter's intention to serve persons and their well-being, the common good, for example, by doing justice according to law as a judge. Constitutions and statutes call for historically accurate understanding, so far as it is possible. To say otherwise is to deny their authority to *settle* any of the questions of social life which need to be settled by law. But constitutions and statutes—and what those who enacted them wrote, said, and intended to communicate and to bring about— also need to be interpreted as parts of a whole of immense complexity and scope: the community's constituent settlements and compromises amongst its constituent peoples, its past investments of every kind, its present needs including the overcoming of present sources of conflict, the wisdom and craftsmanship, and narrow-mindedness and selfishness, of its legal organs and other elites, and many other aspects of its common good. It is only as parts of this whole, conceived of as oriented to the present and future common good, that constitutions and enactments have any legal authority whatsoever, or any claim, legal or moral, to guide anyone's present deliberations.

Since law and legal thought are entitled to little respect or consideration unless they serve, or can be brought to serve, every person whom they could benefit, all the basic human rights should be regarded as controlling every otherwise open question of interpretation. The basic error of the Supreme Court in *Dred Scott v Sandford*[107] was to approach the interpretation of the Constitution's provision, for example, in relation to the congressional power of naturalization, without a strong presumption that, whatever the assumptions and expectations of its makers, every constitutional provision must, if possible, be understood as consistent with such basic human rights as to recognition as a legal person. An essentially identical error is made by those judges, such as Justice Scalia, who interpret the Fourteenth Amendment's unelaborated references to 'persons' as permitting states to treat as non-persons and to authorize the killing, or the enslavement (in embryo banks), of the unborn, whom these same judges know to be in reality human persons.[108]

When unequivocal violations of fundamental human rights are not in issue, very little of wide generality can be said to resolve determinately the many issues of interpretation which call for a proper balance to be made between fidelity to the text, fidelity to the intentions of its makers, fidelity to the historic law, consistency with other parts of the law, respect for the division of constitutional responsibilities between legislatures, courts, and administrative agencies, the needs of present and foreseeable future persons, and the judge's own hunches about the likely consequences of alternative decisions and alternative developments of the law.

28 RESPONSIBILITY

The abstract noun 'responsibility' emerges only towards the end of the eighteenth century; its first user recorded in the *Oxford English Dictionary* is Hamilton, followed by Burke. But this word from the Enlightenment richly conveys a cluster of insights each of which the enlightened philosophies of Hume, Kant, Bentham sought to banish, or rendered needlessly obscure. They are insights familiar to common sense, today as much as with Plato and his interlocutors. They are essential to making sense of the idea of obligation, with which this chapter began.

A first insight is that one can really bring about, *cause*, effects in the world, including benefits and harms to one's fellows, one's neighbour, and any or all other human persons. None of this is well explained in terms of observed constant conjunctions.

---

[107] (1857) 60 U.S. 693; Finnis, 'The Priority of Persons', n. 48 above, at 7–8.
[108] See Finnis, 'Public Reason, Abortion, and Cloning', *Valparaiso University Law Review*, 32 (1998), 361–82 at 373–4.

One's causal power, not least one's mind's power over matter, is a reality one both experiences and understands (albeit not in a fully explanatory way) in every act by which one carries out what one intended, for example, to say to one's class the audible words 'Hume and Mill refuted classical natural law theories'.

A second insight is that when A's conduct has harmed B, it is sometimes true (albeit sometimes not) that A is answerable, *liable*, to B, that is to say, ought to do something to rectify the present relationship between them and to restore a former, more appropriate relationship. Sometimes this ought is entailed by some rule of a legal system under which A can be required to answer—*respond* . . . in Latin and then modern languages—to B's complaint, both by denying or acknowledging his causal responsibility for B's harm, and by repudiating or accepting his duty to compensate B in some measure.

Liability-responsibility thus has at its core an instance of a wider insight: one may, and often or in some respects always does, stand in such a relationship to other human persons that one has the *role*, function, obligation to render them some service, perhaps only of taking care not to harm them, perhaps of positively caring for them in some way, as the person responsible for the advancement of their well-being in some or all respects. This is associated with the important practical truth that government, properly understood and carried on, is not a matter of lording it over others but of doing them some service, so that—speaking always of the central case, from conscience's internal point of view—*authority over* is a consequence of *responsibility for*. Authority ('power'), like law itself, is a means to an end which those in authority are responsible for promoting, the common good of (all who pertain to) the community in and over which they have whatever authority they do have.

A fourth insight is that what one does, and thereby what one causes, is peculiarly one's own if and only if one had the *capacity* to choose to do otherwise. One is, then, a responsible agent if one has this capacity of free choice between open alternatives— that is, if there are occasions when one envisages alternative options and nothing (whether inside or outside oneself), save one's choice of one option in preference to others, settles what one does. This status of capacity responsibility is, not etymologically but really (ontologically, metaphysically), at the core of the cluster of realities understood in the insights articulated in the fourfold analogy of responsibility.

All this leaves, of course, much to be said to explain the cluster's interrelationships and implications. But here this chapter reaches the limit of its transgression of limits. The classical theory of natural law is open to development and new insights in every dimension. So one can expect succeeding chapters in this *Handbook* to add much of value to this chapter, and to correct it in various respects without overturning any of the main classical theses it has rearticulated.

CHAPTER 2

NATURAL LAW: THE MODERN TRADITION

BRIAN H. BIX

Natural law theory is a mode of thinking systematically about the connections between the cosmic order, morality, and law, which, in one form or another, has been around for thousands of years. Different natural law theories can have quite disparate objectives: for example, offering claims generally about correct action and choice (morality, moral theory); offering claims about how one comes to correct moral knowledge (epistemology, moral meta-theory); and offering claims about the proper understanding of law and legal institutions (legal theory). As will be discussed, natural law has also played a central role in the development of modern political theory (regarding the role and limits of government and regarding natural rights)[1] and international law.

I am grateful to Matthew D. Adler, Jules L. Coleman, David Orgon Coolidge, Neil Duxbury, John M. Finnis, Robert P. George, Steven P. Goldberg, Philip A. Hamburger, Matthew H. Kramer, Nancy Levit, David J. Luban, Linda R. Meyer, Thomas H. Morawetz, Scott Shapiro, Malcolm B. E. Smith, Adam Tomkins, Robert W. Tuttle, Kenneth I. Winston, and an anonymous reader, for their comments and suggestions.

[1] It is not coincidental that the American Declaration of Independence (1776) claims authority from 'the Laws of Nature' and refers to the 'unalienable rights' of 'Life, Liberty, and the pursuit of Happiness'. Similarly, the French Declaration of the Rights of Man (1789) declares 'the natural, inalienable, and sacred rights of man'. (The idiosyncratic equation of natural law with pursuing happiness in the American document may derive from the work of Jean Jacques Burlamaqui (1694–1748). See Jean

The focus of this chapter is on the more recent works on natural law theory, particularly those that concentrate on discussing (the implications of natural law for) positive law.[2] However, it is difficult to understand the origin and direction of the modern works without having a strong sense of the tradition from which they arose, so the chapter will begin with a brief history and overview of natural law theories.

One can find important aspects of the natural law approach in Plato (c.429–347 BC),[3] Aristotle (384–322 BC),[4] and Cicero (106–43 BC);[5] it is given systematic form by Thomas Aquinas (c.1225–74).[6] In the medieval period and through the Renaissance, with the work of writers such as Francisco Suárez (1548–1617), Hugo Grotius (1583–1645), Samuel Pufendorf (1632–94), John Locke (1632–1704), and Jean-Jacques Rousseau (1712–78), natural law and natural rights theories were integral parts of theological, moral, legal, and political thought. The role natural law has played in broader religious, moral, and political debates has, perhaps unsurprisingly, varied considerably.[7] Sometimes it has been identified with a particular established religion, or more generally with the status quo, while at other times it has been used as a support by those advocating radical change. Similarly, at times, those writing in the natural law tradition have seemed most concerned with the individual-based question, how is one to live a good ('moral,' 'virtuous') life?;[8] at other times, the concern has been broader—social or international: what norms can we find under which we can all get along, given our different values and ideas about the good?[9]

Jacques Burlamaqui, *The Principles of Natural and Political Law*, trans. Thomas Nugent, 5th edn. (Cambridge: Cambridge University Press, 1807), in particular part I, chapter V).

[2] Law created or 'posited' by human beings for their (self-)governance is often referred to as '*positive* law', to be contrasted with '*natural* law', which consists of moral principles derived from a 'higher' or 'more basic' source.

[3] Plato, *Laws*, book IV, 715b, in Plato, *The Collected Dialogues*, ed. E. Hamilton and H. Cairns (Princeton: Princeton University Press, 1961), 1306.

[4] Aristotle, *Nicomachean Ethics*, book V, 7: 1134b18–1135a5, in *The Complete Works of Aristotle*, ii, 1790–1, ed. J. Barnes (Princeton: Princeton University Press, 1984). One can also find references to natural law-like views in ancient Greek drama. See e.g. Sophocles, *Antigone*, in *The Oedipus Plays of Sophocles*, trans. P. Roche (New York: New American Library, 1958), 210.

[5] Cicero, *Republic*, III. xxii. 33 and *Laws*, II. v. 11–12, in *De Re Publica; De Legibus*, trans. C. W. Keyes (Cambridge, Mass.: Harvard University Press, 1928), 211, 383, 385.

[6] Thomas Aquinas, *Summa Theologiae*, I.II (first part of the second part), Questions 90–7, in *Thomas Aquinas, The Treatise on Law*, ed. R. J. Henle (Notre Dame: University of Notre Dame Press, 1993).

[7] One commentator has written regarding one grouping of natural law theories: 'the different natural law theories were potent weapons in a variety of moral, theological and political battles and they were, in large measure, shaped for such purposes'. Knud Haakonssen, 'The Significance of Protestant Natural-Law Theory', unpublished MS, presented at the Hester Seminar, 'Natural Law Theory: Historical and Contemporary Issues', Wake Forest University, Nov. 1997, at p. 1.

[8] In the terms of one commentator, many natural law theorists can be seen as 'see[ing] morals within a metaphysical framework'. Haakonssen, 'The Significance of Protestant Natural-Law Theory', 4.

[9] Jerome Schneewind calls this last theme 'The Grotian Problematic', J. B. Schneewind, *The Invention of Autonomy* (Cambridge: Cambridge University Press, 1998), 70–3, and he finds it not only in Grotius, but also in nearly every significant natural law theorist since Grotius. It also clearly foreshadows some ideas of the contemporary theorist, John Rawls. See e.g. John Rawls, 'The Idea of an Overlapping Consensus', in *Collected Papers* (Cambridge, Mass.: Harvard University Press, 1999), 421–48.

Some of the modern legal theorists who identify themselves with the natural law tradition seem to have objectives and approaches distinctly different from those classically associated with natural law. Most of the classical theorists were basically moral or political theorists, asking: how does one act morally? Or, more specifically, what are one's moral obligations *as* a citizen within a state, or as a state official? And, what are the limits of legitimate (that is, moral) governmental action?[10] By contrast, some (but far from all) of the modern theorists working within the tradition[11] are social theorists or legal theorists, narrowly understood. Their primary dispute is with other approaches to explaining or understanding society and law. In fact, much of modern natural law theory has developed in reaction to legal positivism, an alternative approach to theorizing about law. As will be discussed, one can see the two different types of natural law—natural law as moral/political theory and natural law as legal/social theory—as connected at a basic level: as both exemplifying a view of (civil) law not merely as governing, but also as being governed.[12]

1 TRADITIONAL NATURAL LAW THEORY

1.1 Definition

What makes a theory a 'natural law' theory?[13] There are almost as many answers to the question as there are theorists writing about natural law theory, or calling them-

[10] Natural law theorists are often concerned with moral matters one step removed, that is, matters of 'meta-theory': e.g. how does one go about *determining* what morality requires?; and, what is it in the world that makes a statement about morality true or false? For example, both Aquinas' *Summa Theologiae* and John Finnis's *Natural Law and Natural Rights* (Oxford: Clarendon Press, 1980) are largely devoted to such questions.

[11] In an earlier article on natural law theory, I distinguished the moral/political theorists in the tradition from the legal/social theorists under the titles of 'traditional' versus 'modern' natural law theory (labels I now find more distracting than helpful). See Brian Bix, 'Natural Law Theory', in *A Companion to Philosophy of Law and Legal Theory*, ed. Dennis Patterson (Oxford: Blackwell, 1996), 223–40. A similar distinction can be found in Philip Soper, 'Some Natural Confusions About Natural Law', *Michigan Law Review*, 90 (1992), 2393, 2394–403.

[12] By connected, I do not mean a matter of logical entailment, or any other bind so strong that it would be incoherent to adhere to one view while dissenting from the other. As will be made clear, one can consistently agree with a natural law view of morality while refusing to take a natural law position on social and legal theory, and vice versa. I mean to assert only that there is a general similarity of attitude or approach among the various theories that go under the name 'natural law'.

[13] One might wonder why it matters whether something is called 'natural law' or not, or what criteria are used for including or excluding theories from the category. The short answer is, that it does not (or should not) matter at all. A label is just a label, and a theory rises and falls on its own merits, not on the approach, school or tradition with which it is associated. That said, (1) it is a natural and

selves 'natural law theorists'. Some of the proffered definitions are quite broad. According to some commentators who identify themselves as 'natural law theorists', all that seems to be required for a theory to fit into that category is that it views values as objective and accessible to human reason.[14] Such a view might exclude very little: almost every moral theory could qualify as a natural law theory, give or take the most hardened moral relativism, scepticism, or non-cognitivism.[15] Of course, in the case of John Finnis (1940–), and many other self-described natural law theorists, their claim for inclusion in the category is supported by their consciously working within a particular tradition,[16] citing, discussing, and elaborating the views of prominent predecessors.[17]

Many commentators define the category more narrowly, by offering more content to the word 'natural'.[18] Even here, though, the explanations of 'natural' can diverge radically: for example, (1) that moral principles can be read off of 'Nature' or a nor-

understandable reaction to the vast complexity of life (and almost comparably complex theoretical literature) to deal with things in categories rather than individually; (2) there are times when one can usefully describe attributes, and strengths and weaknesses, of a particular category of theories; and (3) some theorists take pride in working out of a particular tradition, and seeing themselves as continuing a project initiated by some great thinker of the past (whether that thinker be Thomas Aquinas, Thomas Hobbes, Hans Kelsen, or H. L. A. Hart).

[14] See Finnis, *Natural Law and Natural Rights*, 23–5; Philip Soper, 'Legal Theory and the Problem of Definition' (book review), *University of Chicago Law Review*, 50 (1983), 1170, 1173–5 (discussing Finnis's position).

[15] See e.g. Soper, 'Legal Theory and the Problem of Definition', 1174–5 and n. 21; see also Russell Hittinger, 'Varieties of Minimalist Natural Law Theory', *American Journal of Jurisprudence*, 34 (1989), 133–5. Under the broader definition, deontological theories, for example, would not seem to be excluded, and even Utilitarians and other consequentialists could argue that they believe that moral truths are objective and accessible to reason. Some discussions of natural law expressly exclude deontological theories and 'aggregative conception[s] of the right and the just' from the tradition on other grounds. See e.g. John Finnis, 'Natural Law', in *Routledge Encyclopedia of Philosophy*, vi (London: Routledge, 1998), 685–90, at 687; see also Robert P. George, 'Natural Law Ethics', in *A Companion to Philosophy of Religion* , ed. Philip L. Quinn and Charles Taliaferro (Oxford: Blackwell, 1997), 460–5, at 462–3.

[16] On this matter, one should also note: 'Historically there is not really *a* tradition of natural law, but several tradition*s*.' Russell Hittinger, 'Introduction', in Yves R. Simon, *The Tradition of Natural Law*, ed. Vukan Kuic (New York: Fordham University Press, 1965), xiii–xxxii, at p. xix.

[17] Cf. Robert P. George, *In Defense of Natural Law* (1999), 1. Finnis is adamant that he is offering a theory of natural law, and not a history of other theories that have come under that name. Finnis, *Natural Law and Natural Rights*, 24–5. At the same time, his text (and many of his other works) includes pervasive references to and discussions of Augustine, Aquinas, Gabriel Vazquez, Francisco Suárez, Francisco de Vitoria, Germain Grisez, and many others who have worked within the tradition.

[18] On such a basis, one eminent natural law theorist, Russell Hittinger, can hint that John Finnis and Germain Grisez do not fit within the fold. See Russell Hittinger, *A Critique of the New Natural Law Theory* (Notre Dame: University of Notre Dame Press, 1987), 8 (arguing that the Grisez–Finnis approach does not qualify because natural law 'requires a commitment to law as in some way "natural", and nature as in some way normative').

matively charged universe;[19] (2) that moral principles are tied to human nature—and 'nature' here is used to indicate either the search for basic or common human characteristics or (to the extent that this is different) some discussion of human teleology, our purpose or objective within a larger, usually divine, plan;[20] and (3) that there is a kind of knowledge of moral truth that we all have by our nature as human beings.[21]

A further sharp division exists within the classical natural law tradition, among those who purport to be interpreting and applying Aquinas's ideas. As characterized by one participant in the debate, the question is whether the 'knowledge of the reasonable, the good, and the right is derived from prior knowledge of human nature or what is "natural" for human beings' or whether 'something in the moral domain is "natural" for human beings and in accord with human nature precisely in so far as it can be judged to be *reasonable*; and something in this realm of discourse is "unnatural" and morally wrong just in so far as it is *unreasonable*'.[22] It is not that one side claims a linkage between human nature and the good and the right, and the other side does not; it is more a matter of epistemology—the path to knowledge. One side claims that we come to know what is right and good by investigating human nature, while the other side argues that knowledge of the good and the right comes by

---

[19] See, e.g., Lloyd L. Weinreb, *Natural Law and Justice* (Cambridge, Mass.: Harvard University Press, 1987), 15–42; Ronald R. Garet, 'Natural Law and Creation Stories', in *Religion, Morality and the Law, Nomos XXX*, ed. J. Roland Pennock and John W. Chapman (New York: New York University Press, 1988), 218–62, at 219–20 ('The underlying notion is that careful observation of nature permits us to understand which regime or basic social structure is best suited to beings such as ourselves'). This is a position found not only in some forms of Western natural law theory, but also in some theorists within the Chinese neo-Confucian tradition. See e.g. Tu Wei-Ming, *Neo-Confucian Thought in Action* (Berkeley, Calif.: University of California Press, 1976), 167–8 (discussing Chu Hsi's interpretation of the concept of *ko-wu*, 'the investigation of things').

[20] The contrast in perspectives is exemplified by the way Suárez seemed to view the moral theologian as the likely expert for determining the laws of nature, while Pufendorf considered the inquiry an entirely secular one in which a moral theologian would have no place. See Schneewind, *The Invention of Autonomy*, 131.

One could see as a basic divide, not merely among natural law theorists, but among moral/virtue theorists generally, between the classical teleological writers, like Aristotle and Aquinas, and most of the later writers, roughly from Grotius on. The classical writers had a strong sense of human teleology and for that reason could and did equate what people should do and what was in their interest. Later writers saw the world in a way which is now conventional: with the claims of morality generally at odds with the claims of self-interest (even enlightened and considered self-interest). See Stephen Darwall, 'Law and Autonomy: From Imposition to Self-Legislation', unpublished MS.

[21] One can find this view, for example, in the work of the modern French natural law theorist, Jacques Maritain (1882–1973). According to Maritain's view: 'The first principles of this [natural] law are known *connaturally*, not rationally or through concepts—by an activity that Maritain, following Aquinas, called "synderesis". Thus, "natural law" is "natural" because it not only reflects human nature, but is known naturally. Maritain acknowledges, however, that knowledge of the natural law varies throughout humanity and according to individuals' capacities and abilities, and he speaks of growth in an individual's or a collectivity's moral awareness.' William Sweet, 'Jacques Maritain', in *Stanford Encyclopedia of Philosophy*, fall 2001 edn., at http://plato.stanford.edu.

[22] George, 'Natural Law Ethics', 462.

another path (usually a combination of rationality and empirical observation),[23] even if the 'basic human goods and moral norms *are* what they are because human nature *is* what it is'.[24] One obvious advantage of *not* trying to derive moral truths from descriptive claims about human nature is that one need not confront the objection (summarized in Sect. 1.5 below) that this involves an inappropriate derivation of 'ought' from 'is'.[25]

One might sense a broad, perhaps metaphoric notion that unites the various forms of traditional natural law, and may even tie natural law moral/political theories to natural law legal/social theories.[26] The focus within natural law is away from conventional law, from civil law, to something higher or (to change the image) more basic that rules or guides, perhaps teleologically. In the voluntarist forms of traditional natural law,[27] it is divine commands creating moral standards; in some forms of Thomistic natural law, it is an ideal towards which humans, by their nature, strive; in recent natural law legal theories, it is the sense to which conventional legal rules are approximations of what law really is (Ronald Dworkin) or what law must try to be (Lon Fuller). Also, in most traditional natural law theories, natural law is not understood by analogy to (or as an imperfect version of) positive law, but rather the other way around: that it is natural law which is the primary focus, and positive law which should be understood by analogy to, or as an imperfect version of, natural law.[28]

1.2 Natural Law and God

Natural law theory has become associated for many people with religious belief, in part because of the long period during which those associated with the Catholic Church were the main elaborators and defenders of that tradition.[29]

[23] The more complicated point is explaining how such knowledge *is* obtained. Robert George writes of 'non-inferential acts of understanding wherein we grasp self-evident truths'. Robert P. George, *In Defense of Natural Law* (Oxford: Clarendon Press, 1999), 87; see also Finnis, *Natural Law and Natural Rights*, 59–80.

[24] George, *In Defense of Natural Law*, 85; see also Russell Hittinger, *A Critique of the New Natural Law Theory* (1987), 10–20 (summarizing the Grisez–Finnis critique of more traditional Thomistic approaches).

[25] See Finnis, *Natural Law and Natural Rights*, 33–6.

[26] I am grateful to Robert Tuttle for the basic idea of this paragraph. For other approximations of the same point, see e.g. Hittinger, 'Introduction', in Simon, *The Tradition of Natural Law*; Alexander Passerin d'Entrèves, *Natural Law*, 1st pub. 1951 (New Brunswick: Transaction Publishers, 1994).

[27] 'Voluntarism' has been defined as '[t]he theological position that all values are so through being chosen by God . . .'. Simon Blackburn, *The Oxford Dictionary of Philosophy* (1994), 396. (Blackburn also notes that a number of quite different philosophical and theological positions also carry the label 'voluntarism'.)

[28] See Russell Hittinger, 'Natural Law as "Law": Reflections on the Occasion of "Veritatis Splendor"', *American Journal of Jurisprudence*, 39 (1994), 1.

[29] An association between the Catholic Church and natural law theory continues, of course, as recently exemplified by Pope John Paul II's encyclicals, 'Veritatis Splendor' (6 Aug. 1993) and 'Fides et Ratio' (14 Sept. 1998).

However, most of the important writers within this tradition have gone to some lengths to dissociate the principles of natural law from belief in a particular religious tradition or from belief in a (certain kind of) deity. Grotius may have been the first to make the statement plainly: 'What we have been saying would have a degree of validity even if we should concede that which cannot be conceded without the utmost wickedness, that there is no God, or that the affairs of men are of no concern to Him'.[30]

The context of seventeenth- and eighteenth-century writing on natural law may help to explain the diminished role of God in their theories. Some of the writers were reacting against and trying to escape the theological disputes and wars (particularly, though not exclusively, Protestant versus Catholic) of the time, and were searching for a way to ground a moral or political philosophy that could avoid such disputes. Similarly, some theorists were searching for principles from which an international law could be constructed, principles which could be accepted by nations and peoples of very different faiths.[31] Finally, political theorists were looking for a basis to justify and limit government, but in a way more favourable to individual liberty, and these theorists feared that a religious grounding would tend towards theocratic, authoritarian rule. All three developments within natural law theory required a reduced role of God—reduced, but usually not eliminated altogether, for God was often a handy basis for grounding ultimate duties and rights.[32]

Contemporary writers within this tradition are often equally insistent about being able to offer 'a theory of natural law without needing to advert to the question of God's existence or nature or will'.[33] Yet one can still find theorists within the tradition who take the opposite position: that one cannot understand the notion of natural *law* without positing a supernatural being who is ordering compliance.[34]

[30] Hugo Grotius, *De Jure Belli Ac Pacis Libri Tres*, trans. Francis W. Kelsey (Oxford: Clarendon Press, 1925) (1625) ('Prolegomena', para. 11), 13. The position can probably be traced back to earlier writers, including Gregor of Rimini (*c.*1300–58), Francisco de Vitoria (1492/94–1546), and Francisco Suárez. See Finnis, *Natural Law and Natural Rights*, 54. Suárez's summary of Gregory of Rimini's position is quoted in Schneewind, *The Invention of Autonomy*, 60. For an argument that Grotius's role in this debate has been overstated, see ibid. at 67–8, 73–5.

[31] The ideas of laws that bound all nations had roots that long predate the seventeenth century, see e.g. J. M. Kelly, *A Short History of Western Legal Theory* (1992), 77–8, 110–11, 156–8, 199–202, but modern international law as we know it began with Grotius. Ibid., at 241–3.

[32] John Locke may be an example: in his *Second Treatise of Government* (1690) § 6, people's ultimate duties ('to preserve [one]self [and] . . . the rest of Mankind') derive from God's wishes. A theorist could try to build a moral theory without God, based merely on 'reason' or prudence or the like, as theorists have tried from Hobbes to the present day, but the difficulties of the task are well known.

[33] Finnis, *Natural Law and Natural Rights*, 49; see also Michael S. Moore, 'Good without God', in *Natural Law, Liberalism, and Morality*, ed. Robert P. George (Oxford: Clarendon Press, 1996), 221–70.

[34] See e.g. Garet, 'Natural Law and Creation Stories', 236–7. See also John T. Noonan, Jr., 'The Natural Law Banner', in *Natural Law and Contemporary Public Policy*, ed. David F. Forte (Washington: Georgetown University Press, 1998), 380–3, at 382: 'The *ressentiment* nourished against natural law [by unbelievers] arises because one who says "nature" says "creatureliness", and creatures require a Creator. Law requires a lawgiver, and one who speaks of a law governing human purposes speaks of a Lawgiver transcending the state and individual desires.'

The role of God within various natural law theories also allows one to differentiate such theories along the lines of the relative prevalence of 'will' or 'reason'.[35] At one extreme is 'voluntarism',[36] a sub-category of natural law theories in which God—and, in particular, God's will—plays an important role. One can go back to Plato's Socrates, who asks Euthyphro, 'Is what is holy holy because the gods approve it, or do they approve it because it is holy?'[37] Voluntarism is the position that something is good or morally required because—and only because—God has ordered that we do it (or bad/morally prohibited because of His prohibition). Voluntarism of one type or another appears regularly in the history of natural law theory. For example, the important seventeenth-century natural law theorist, Samuel Pufendorf, offered a voluntarist view, which one commentator has summarized as follows: '[G]iven that we have the nature God gave us, certain laws must be valid for us, but only God's will determined our nature. As a result, our nature indicates God's will for us. Hence observable facts about ourselves show us what laws God commands us to obey.'[38] The opposite extreme, a reason-based approach, would equate virtue with reasonableness rather than tying it to the 'will' or orders of any entity.[39] There is also a form of natural law theory that seems to take a compromise between a 'will' approach and a 'reason' approach: this form asserts that actions are intrinsically good or bad, but we are only obligated to pursue the good because God so commands us; this was Francisco Suárez's view.[40]

[35] 'Will' (or 'fiat') refers to choices of individuals or institutions, and the argument that the normative world is different because of such choices (e.g., the orders of a sovereign or an individual's signing a contract), generally without taking into account the content or the moral worth of those choices. 'Reason', by contrast, is an argument based on the merit of an action or interaction or institution, generally without regard to whether it was chosen or under what circumstances it was chosen. While the contrast between will and reason can be helpful in analysing a number of topics within moral, legal and political theory, see e.g. Vernon J. Bourke, *Will in Western Thought: An Historico-Critical Survey* (New York: Sheed and Ward, 1964); Francis Oakley, 'Medieval Theories of Natural Law: William of Ockham and the Significance of the Voluntarist Tradition', *Natural Law Forum*, 6 (1961), 65; Brian Bix, *Jurisprudence: Theory and Context*, 2nd edn. (London: Sweet & Maxwell, 1999), 121–6; Lon L. Fuller, 'Reason and Fiat in Case Law', *Harvard Law Review*, 59 (1946), 376, the contrast is rarely as sharp or as obvious as it is within alternative approaches to traditional natural law theory.

[36] See above n. 27.

[37] Plato, *Euthyphro* 10a, in *The Collected Dialogues*, ed. Edith Hamilton and Huntington Cairns, trans. Lane Cooper (1961), 178. The words are echoed in the summary John Duns Scotus (1266–1308) gives of a position of Aquinas: 'for Thomas, Duns Scotus says, "what is commanded [in the Decalog] is not good merely because it is commanded, but commanded because it is good in itself".' Schneewind, *The Invention of Autonomy*, 23, quoting John Duns Scotus, *Duns Scotus on the Will and Morality*, ed. and trans. Allan B. Wolter (1986), 273.

[38] J. B. Schneewind, 'Samuel Pufendorf', in *The Cambridge Dictionary of Philosophy*, ed. Robert Audi (Cambridge; Cambridge University Press, 1995), 664.

[39] See e.g. the view of Robert George, summarized in the text accompanying n. 24, above.

[40] See Francisco Suárez, *On Law and God the Lawgiver*, book II, ch. VI, excerpted in J. B. Schneewind (ed.), *Moral Philosophy from Montaigne to Kant*, i (Cambridge: Cambridge University Press, 1990), 76–9; see also Schneewind, *The Invention of Autonomy*, 60–2; T. H. Irwin, 'Obligation, Rightness, and Natural Law: Suarez and Some Critics', unpublished MS, presented at the Hester Seminar, 'Natural Law Theory:

1.3 Natural Law and Natural Rights

Many people coming to the discussion assume that the two lines of thought, natural law and natural rights, are interchangeable, or at least closely connected. This view may reflect a modern perspective, which sees rights as primary, or views rights and duties as simple correlates.[41] There are other, and older, perspectives, however, in which talk of duties was not so strongly connected with talk of rights, or in which the duties were primary and the correlative rights were not analytically important because they were held by society, the state, or God.

A common view within the literature is that the natural law and natural rights traditions developed as competing views of the world, not logically inconsistent, but reflecting different attitudes towards man's place within society. According to this view, the natural law tradition posits a normatively ordered universe and the normative order described often involves all individuals in society having a set place and corresponding duties. By contrast, natural rights theories often deny or downplay a view of society as a whole *except as* a function of individuals and their rights.

The matter remains highly controversial.[42] One should also be careful not to overstate whatever differences there might be between the two different perspectives on society. A traditional natural law theorist like Aquinas, with his tendencies towards an organic view of society, still refers to individual rights—for example, to choose a vocation, to choose whether and whom to marry, and whether to subscribe to a particular religious faith.[43] Further, one can arguably find sufficient resources as much in Aquinas as in Locke to justify disobedience and rebellion against tyranny.[44]

Still, it seems hard to deny that the natural rights approach, as it developed, encouraged and reinforced an individualistic way of perceiving political and social

Historical and Contemporary Issues', Wake Forest University, Nov. 1997 (discussing Suárez's position, and showing how it depends on a narrow understanding of 'obligation').

[41] On rights generally, see e.g. Matthew H. Kramer, N. E. Simmonds, and Hillel Steiner, *A Debate Over Rights: Philosophical Enquiries* (Oxford: Clarendon Press, 1998); the most important modern discussion of rights in the legal literature is by Wesley Hohfeld, who suggested that the concept of 'right' has been used in a number of different ways, only one of which would be understood as correlating to another person's duty. See Wesley Hohfeld, 'Some Fundamental Legal Conceptions as Applied in Judicial Reasoning', *Yale Law Journal*, 23 (1913), 16; 'Fundamental Legal Conceptions as Applied in Judicial Reasoning', *Yale Law Journal*, 26 (1917), 710.

[42] In an important work that challenges many accepted views about natural law and natural rights, Brian Tierney offers a historical analysis of rights and natural rights discourse, tracing the idea of rights (what European commentators often call 'subjective rights') back to the twelfth century, with fuller development in the thirteenth and fourteenth century. Brian Tierney, *The Idea of Natural Rights: Studies on Natural Rights, Natural Law, and Church Law 1150–1625* (Atlanta, Georgia: Scholars Press, 1997). Tierney rejects the view, summarized above, of natural law and natural rights as historically having been competing theories; he sees them instead as having been complementary theories.

[43] John Finnis, Aquinas: *Moral, Political and Legal Theory* (Oxford: Oxford University Press, 1998), 172 and nn. 179–81 (summarizing Aquinas's views and giving citations to his texts); see generally ibid. at 132–80 ('Towards Human Rights').

[44] ibid. at 272–4, 287–91.

realities in a way that traditional natural law approaches did not.[45] One can also sometimes find natural rights and natural law analyses in tension, if not in complete conflict. Michael Zuckert has described the way that traditional natural law theory tends towards discussions of duties, while the natural rights analyses of John Locke (and Thomas Hobbes before him) tends towards discussions of liberties.[46] A great deal will necessarily depend on the particular social and political context, and natural rights will not always be the hero of the drama; for example, one can find historical examples of 'natural rights' undermining civil liberties.[47]

The development of the idea of natural rights is a vast topic on its own, and cannot be discussed at any length here.[48] However, one should note at a minimum the obvious connection or parallel between talk of 'natural rights' (a label some avoid in part because of the apparent connection with natural law theories) and the more common or more fashionable references to 'human rights'.[49]

1.4 Connection with Law

Contrary to a lay person's expectations, natural law theory often has little if anything to do with 'law' as that term is conventionally used.[50] The 'law' in natural law theory

[45] See e.g. d'Entrèves, *Natural Law*, 51–62. One could, in a sense, consider this discussion as being relevant to the later Sect. 1.5, 'Opponents Actual and Potential', in that the political strand of natural law theory, which increasingly emphasized natural rights, began to work against the tradition from which it arose. The primary focus became liberty and rights against government, rather than duties or the organic nature of society. By the time one gets to Burlamaqui's inalienable right to pursue happiness, see above n. 1, the original moral strand of natural law had been left far behind.

[46] See Michael P. Zuckert, 'Do Natural Rights Derive From Natural Law?', *Harvard Journal of Law and Public Policy*, 20 (1997), 695.

[47] See Richard Tuck, 'The Dangers of Natural Rights', *Harvard Journal of Law and Public Policy*, 20 (1997), 683. Tuck cites Britain's recent use of citizens' right to security as a justification for taking away the procedural rights of suspected terrorists, ibid. at 691, and the fact that the early natural rights theorists, Grotius, Pufendorf, and Hobbes, 'explicitly defended slavery and absolutism'. Ibid. at 684 (fn. omitted).

[48] One suggestive approach comes from Knud Haakonssen: 'the contemporary . . . idea of rights derives from early modern Protestant natural law combined with English Common-Law notions and must count as a major part of the former's "significance" '. Knud Haakonssen, 'The Significance of Protestant Natural-Law Theory', unpublished MS, presented at the Hester Seminar, 'Natural Law Theory: Historical and Contemporary Issues', Wake Forest University, Nov. 1997, at 17.

[49] See e.g. Finnis, *Natural Law and Natural Rights*, 198–9; Soper, 'Legal Theory and the Problem of Definition', 1174.

[50] However, as a moral and political theory, natural law theory has regularly been brought out in discussions of the moral and political controversies of the day. See e.g. David F. Forte (ed.), *Natural Law and Contemporary Public Policy* (Washington, DC: Georgetown University Press, 1998); George, *In Defense of Natural Law*, 123–245 ('Moral and Political Questions').

In the United States, natural law theory is often raised in regards to questions of interpretation of the United States Constitution, with theorists in sharp disagreement on what relevance, if any, natural law theory might have on this question. See e.g. Randy E. Barnett, 'Getting Normative: The Role of Natural Rights in Constitutional Adjudication', in *Natural Law, Liberalism, and Morality*, ed. Robert P. George

usually refers to the orders or principles laid down by higher powers that we should follow. However, traditional natural law theorists have had some important influences on thinking about 'human' or 'positive' law,[51] in particular through their ideas regarding moral problems relating to (human) law. Best known is probably Aquinas's discussions of the obligations of officials and citizens,[52] a set of arguments that has been further elaborated by other writers, including, recently, John Finnis.[53] Aquinas defines (positive) law as 'a certain dictate of reason for the Common Good, made by him who has the care of the community and promulgated'.[54] Aquinas holds that officials are directed to pass legislation consistent with natural law. Sometimes the positive law can be derived directly from natural law principles, while at other times the officials will have some choice or discretion in the determination of specific rules from more general principles.[55] Positive laws consistent with natural law 'have the power of binding in conscience'.[56] Unjust laws do not create moral obligations, though one might have an obligation to comply publicly with such laws if this is necessary to prevent a greater evil.[57]

(1996), 151–79; Walter Berns, 'The Illegitimacy of Appeals to Natural Law in Constitutional Interpretation', in ibid. 181–93; Christopher Wolfe, 'Judicial Review', in *Natural Law and Contemporary Public Policy*, 157–89; George, *In Defense of Natural Law*, 110–11; 'Symposium on Natural Law', *Southern California Interdisciplinary Law Journal*, 4 (1995), 455–738; cf. G. Edward White, *Earl Warren* (Oxford: Oxford University Press, 1982), 222–30, 354–67 (describing the 'natural law' aspects of Chief Justice Warren's approach to constitutional interpretation).

[51] One of the most important such influences, already noted, was natural law's foundational importance in the development of international law, as theorists began to wonder what principles could apply to disputes between nations (or between parties who were citizens of different nations), especially when the parties had different political or religious beliefs. See e.g. Schneewind, *The Invention of Autonomy*, 70–3.

[52] Aquinas, *Summa Theologiae*, q. 96, art. 4; see also Finnis, *Aquinas*, 266–74.

[53] Finnis, *Natural Law and Natural Rights*, 354–66.

[54] Aquinas, *Summa Theologiae*, q. 90, art. 4, corpus.

[55] Aquinas, *Summa Theologiae*, q. 95, art. 2, corpus. On Aquinas's notion of *determinatio*, the concretization by rational but rationally under-determined choice, see Finnis, *Aquinas*, 267–71.

John Locke may be presenting an idea similar to Aquinas's '*determinatio*' when he writes: 'The Obligations of the Law of Nature, cease not in Society, but only in many Cases are drawn closer, and have by Human Laws known Penalties annexed to them, to inforce their observation'. John Locke, *Two Treatises of Government*, ii: ch. 11, § 135 (1690); cf. Jeremy Waldron, *The Dignity of Legislation* (Cambridge: Cambridge University Press, 1999), 63–91 (arguing that Locke's text refers to a level of choice and responsibility more substantial than Aquinas's '*determinatio*').

[56] Aquinas, *Summa Theologiae*, q. 96, art. 4, corpus. To be more precise, Aquinas said that 'just laws' have the power of binding in conscience, and he lists three ways in which a law can fail to be just: it does not pertain to the common good, the lawmaker was acting *ultra vires*, or the burdens of the law are unequally distributed in the community. Aquinas, *Summa Theologiae*, q. 96, art. 4, corpus.

[57] See ibid. q. 93, art. 3, reply 2. For a modern treatment on similar lines, see Finnis, *Natural Law and Natural Rights*, 354–62.

The above discussion is connected with the expression '*lex iniusta non est lex*' ('an unjust law is no law at all'), which is—often imprecisely, if not quite erroneously—ascribed to natural law theorists. The expression is true, and indeed somewhat banal, when understood as saying that unjust laws are not laws 'in the fullest sense,' in that they do not create moral obligations to obey them in the way that just laws do. See Norman Kretzmann, 'Lex Iniusta Non Est Lex: Laws on Trial in Aquinas' Court of Conscience',

Many opponents of natural law theory portray it as arguing that immoral laws necessarily lack *legal* validity. That is, it is not merely the case that one has no *moral* obligation to obey, but one also has no *legal* obligation. Occasionally one even finds an assertion along those lines (or at least one open to such interpretations) among the less sophisticated advocates of natural law theory. William Blackstone (1723–80) offers the following comment in passing in his *Commentaries*: 'no human laws are of any validity, if contrary to [the law of nature]'.[58] This comment was taken by John Austin (1790–1859), perhaps unfairly, as being about *legal* validity. There are (at least) two major problems with a claim that injustice necessarily or always negates the *legal* validity of a rule. First, if one is using a normal understanding of 'legal validity', the assertion is simply empirically false. Consider Austin's response to Blackstone:

Suppose an act innocuous, or positively beneficial, be prohibited by the sovereign under the penalty of death; if I commit this act, I shall be tried and condemned, and if I object to the sentence, that it is contrary to the law of God . . . the Court of Justice will demonstrate the inconclusiveness of my reasoning by hanging me up, in pursuance of the law of which I have impugned the validity.[59]

While this is slightly overstated,[60] the basic point is that the concept of 'legal validity' is closely tied to what is recognized as binding in a given society and what the state enforces, and it seems fairly clear that there are plenty of societies where immoral laws are recognized as binding and are enforced. Someone might answer that these immoral laws are not *really* legally valid, and the officials are making a mistake when they treat the rules as if they were legally valid.[61] However, this is just to play games

American Journal of Jurisprudence, 33 (1988), 99; Finnis, *Natural Law and Natural Rights*, 363–6; Bix, *Jurisprudence: Theory and Context*, 64–6.

One can find commentators (often writers who do not consider themselves part of the natural law tradition) who argue that laws that are not just *can* sometimes carry normative weight. See e.g. Philip Soper, 'Legal Systems, Normative Systems and the Paradoxes of Positivism', *Canadian Journal of Law and Jurisprudence*, 8 (1995) 363, 375–6 ('the State does no wrong . . . in acting on (enforcing) the norms which, in good faith, it believes are necessary to govern society', though the claim is lost for truly wicked laws); Jeremy Waldron, 'Lex Satis Iusta', *Notre Dame Law Review*, 75 (2000), 1829 (some unjust laws can create an obligation to obey them). For a critique of Soper's view, see Joseph Raz, 'The Morality of Obedience' (book review), *Michigan Law Review*, 83 (1985), 732.

[58] William Blackstone, *Commentaries on the Laws of England*, I.41 (1765–9). For a sympathetic portrayal of Blackstone's approach to natural law theory, see John Finnis, 'Blackstone's Theoretical Intentions', *Natural Law Forum*, 12 (1967), 163; see also Daniel J. Boorstin, *The Mysterious Science of the Law* (Chicago: University of Chicago Press, 1941), 48–59.

[59] John Austin, *The Province of Jurisprudence Determined*, ed. W. E. Rumble (Cambridge: Cambridge University Press, 1995) (1832), lecture V at p. 158.

[60] It too quickly rushes an equivalence between enforcement and legal validity, leaving no room for the concept of legal mistake (whether through error, corruption, or abuse of power). See Brian Bix, *Law, Language, and Legal Determinacy* (Oxford: Clarendon Press, 1993), 85–6; Brian Bix, 'On Description and Legal Reasoning', in *Rules and Reasoning*, ed. Linda Meyer (Oxford: Hart Publishing, 1999), 7, 17–19.

[61] A different kind of claim would be that *in a particular legal system*, certain legal principles, perhaps of a constitutional nature, ensure that no immoral enactment is (legally) valid under that system. However, note that this is a contingent claim about a particular legal system, not a general or conceptual claim about the nature of law.

with words, and confusing games at that. 'Legal validity' is the term we use to refer to *whatever* is conventionally recognized as binding; to say that all the officials could be wrong about what is legally valid is close to nonsense. The interlocutor seems to be saying that immoral rules *ought not* to be recognized as binding—but this merely translates into either a proposal for reform of the society's legal practices, or a restatement of the traditional natural law point that immoral laws create no *moral* obligations,[62] whatever legal obligations they might create.[63]

The second problem, clearly pointed out by Philip Soper,[64] is that judgments under a natural law standard, if incorporated into a legal system, would have to be made by fallible individuals working within fallible institutions. No matter how able or virtuous the decision-makers, the decisions would have whatever significance they did by *choice*—this is what the authorized panel decided—rather than by reason. However well-intended the institution or the overall system, the result is a legal positivist product (law because a certain authorized actor so declared) rather than a natural law product.

Finally, one should note, on a quite different theme, that natural law and natural rights thinking have influenced the development of legal doctrines—in particular, core notions of constitutional rights and civil liberties—and that influence continues to be felt today.[65]

1.5 Opponents Actual and Potential

A variety of challenges has been brought to the general project of natural law theory, or to some of its more prominent variations. While the full consideration and

---

[62] Of course, many people who do *not* subscribe to natural law theory would agree that immoral laws do not create moral obligations. At least at a general level, it is not a controversial view, and natural law theorists have never claimed (or assumed) otherwise. It is only some opponents of natural law who have portrayed the natural law position on immoral laws as unusual or controversial.

[63] This last is arguably what Blackstone was attempting to convey, as might be made clearer by seeing Blackstone's quote in context: 'The law of nature, being coeval with mankind and dictated by God himself, is of course superior in obligation to any other. It is binding over all the globe in all countries, and at all times: no human laws are of any validity, if contrary to this; and such of them as are valid derive all their force, and all their authority, mediately or immediately, from this original.' William Blackstone, *Commentaries on the Laws of England*, i: 41.

[64] Philip Soper, 'Some Natural Confusions About Natural Law', *Michigan Law Review*, 90 (1992), 2393, 2412–13.

[65] See e.g. *State v Joyner*, 625 A.2d 791, 800–3 (Ct. 1993) (referring to historical understandings of natural law and natural rights doctrine in the course of interpreting a state constitutional requirement); *State v Ganim*, 660 A.2d 742, 762–5 (Ct. 1995) (discussing the historical influence of natural law thinking on the development of Connecticut law); ibid. at 801–2 (Berdon, J., dissenting) (same); see generally Philip A. Hamburger, 'Natural Rights, Natural Law, and American Constitutions', *Yale Law Journal*, 102 (1993), 907.

evaluation of these challenges is the work of many volumes, it may be of value at least to mention some of the writers and themes.[66]

Thomas Hobbes (1588–1679) affirmed the existence of natural law,[67] but stated that individuals entering civil society will voluntarily surrender their rights to act on (their own interpretations of) it,[68] for the exercise of such rights would lead to chaos, a return to the war of all against all that entering civil society was meant to avoid.[69] Further, many commentators have noted that even Hobbes's affirmation of natural law seemed hedged, or perhaps ironic.[70]

In his *Treatise of Human Nature*, David Hume (1711–76) famously commented on the relation between 'is' and 'ought', that it seemed 'altogether inconceivable that this

[66] Such a list should include philosophical teachings that, though not directed specifically at natural law doctrines, could be thought to push thinkers in a different direction: for example, (1) 'Ockham's razor', or the principle of parsimony, associated with William Ockham (sometimes spelled 'Occam') (*c*.1285–1347), which holds that 'entities should not be multiplied beyond necessity' in the construction of theories, Robert Audi (ed.), *The Cambridge Dictionary of Philosophy* (Cambridge: Cambridge University Press, 1995), 545; and (2) the methodology of radical doubt used by René Descartes (1596–1650) in his *Meditations on First Philosophy* (1641). Some have viewed Ockham's nominalism as the force which 'reduc[ed] Thomas's conception of ordered justice to the competing interests and claims of individuals', thus leading to the (natural) rights analysis of later centuries. Charles J. Reid, Jr., 'The Medieval Origins of the Western Natural Rights Tradition: The Achievement of Brian Tierney' (book review), *Cornell Law Review*, 83 (1998), 437, 438–9. However, this view of the role of Ockham is strongly contested, in particular by Tierney. See Tierney, *The Idea of Natural Rights*, 195–203.

A list of opponents, or those who (unintentionally) supplied arguments to opponents, might also include Charles-Louis de Secondat, Baron de Montesquieu (1689–1755), whose work, *On the Spirit of the Laws* (1748), emphasized the *differences* in the laws of different countries, and ascribed these differences to the particular geography, trade, history, etc., of each land; and Auguste Comte (1798–1857), who made similar claims in the context of developing a more scientific, empirically based approach to studying societies.

[67] Some would go further: emphasizing Hobbes's role in the development of natural law thinking, arguing that 'modern natural law theory begins with Hobbes rather than Grotius'. Norberto Bobbio, *Thomas Hobbes and the Natural Law Tradition* (Chicago: University of Chicago Press, 1993), 149.

[68] Excepting the right to defend oneself against a clear threat of death, a right Hobbes generally treats as inalienable. For a discussion of Hobbes's view on the topic, see Richard Tuck, *Natural Rights Theories: Their Origin and Development* (Cambridge: Cambridge University Press, 1979), 119–25.

[69] See Thomas Hobbes, *Leviathan*, ed. Richard Tuck (Cambridge: Cambridge University Press, 1996) (1651), chs. 18, 26, 29; Thomas Hobbes, *Behemoth or the Long Parliament*, ed. Ferdinand Tönnies (Chicago: University of Chicago Press, 1990; 1st pub. 1679), 50 ('It if be lawfull then for subjects to resist the king, when he commands anything that is against the Scripture, that is, contrary to the command of God, and to be judge of the meaning of Scripture, it is *impossible* that the life of any King, or the peace of any Christian kingdom, can long be secure'); see also Richard Tuck, 'Introduction', in *Leviathan*, pp. ix, xxviii. On a slightly different theme, the necessity of sovereign command to make natural law into actual law, see Hobbes, *Leviathan*, ch. 26, at 191 ('The Authority of writers, without the Authority of the Common-wealth, maketh not their opinions Law, be they never so true. . . . For though it be naturally reasonable; yet it is by the Soveraigne Power that it is Law').

[70] In one well-known deflationary passage, Hobbes refers to natural law as mere theories of prudence, before offering a partial retraction. Hobbes, *Leviathan*, ch. 15, at 111 ('These dictates of Reason, men use to call by the name of Lawes, but improperly: for they are but Conclusions, or Theoremes concerning what conduceth to the conservation and defence of themselves. . . . But yet if we consider the same Theoremes, as delivered in the word of God, that by right commandeth all things; then are they properly called Lawes').

new relation ["ought"] can be derived from others, which are entirely different from it'.[71] That is, one cannot derive an evaluative or prescriptive conclusion from purely descriptive or empirical premises.[72] To the extent that this is correct (and it has always been a matter of great controversy within philosophy), it undermines a major strand of the natural law theory tradition: that which seeks to derive moral prescriptions from statements about the nature of human beings or the nature of the world. In fact, by many accounts, Hume's argument, and similar challenges, did much to push natural law theory to the sidelines of moral philosophy.

2 MODERN NATURAL LAW THEORY

2.1 Introduction

Many of the important recent writers in natural law theory, like Jacques Maritain[73] and John Finnis, have continued to work within the tradition that goes back to Aquinas (and beyond), focusing primarily on ethics and meta-ethics. What may be most distinctive in the recent work done under the name 'natural law theory' are those writers who have offered not a general ethical theory (with implications for law and policy), but instead a narrowly focused theory of the nature of (positive) law. This section will offer overviews of both types of modern natural law theories.

A key moment in modern natural law theory is the exchange between H. L. A. Hart (1907–92) and Lon Fuller (1902–78) in the *Harvard Law Review* in 1958.[74] Hart located the boundary between legal positivism and natural law theory at the conceptual separation of law and morality—that is, that the question of whether something (either a rule or a whole system) was 'law' was conceptually separate from its moral merit.[75]

[71] David Hume, *Treatise of Human Nature*, iii: 1.1 (1739).

[72] There is some controversy over whether Hume's statement should be read this strongly. A second interpretation (taking the quotation in its larger context), supported by a number of commentators, is that Hume was concerned not about the move from the factual to the normative, but rather the move from any true statement (whether factual or moral) to statements about motivation. See, e.g., Stephen Buckle, *Natural Law and the Theory of Property* (Oxford; Clarendon Press, 1991), 282–3; see also Finnis, *Natural Law and Natural Rights*, 37–48.

[73] See e.g. Jacques Maritain, *The Rights of Man and Natural Law* (New York: Charles Scribner's Sons, 1943).

[74] H. L. A. Hart, 'Positivism and the Separation of Law and Morals', *Harvard Law Review*, 71 (1958), 593; Lon Fuller, 'Positivism and Fidelity to Law—A Response to Professor Hart', *Harvard Law Review*, 71 (1958), 630.

[75] To put the same matter a different way, the claim denies that legal systems *must* condition the validity of legal norms on their passing some moral test (legal positivists disagree among themselves regarding whether legal systems *can* condition validity on morality—this is the debate between 'inclusive' and 'exclusive' legal positivism, discussed elsewhere in this volume).

A number of writers—most prominently, Lon Fuller and Ronald Dworkin—have been willing to take on legal positivism on its own terms: arguing that one *cannot* conceptually separate law and morality.

Modern natural law theorists have offered the following responses to legal positivism:

1. Law is best understood, at least in part, as a teleological concept:[76] a concept or institution that can be properly understood only when the ultimate objective is kept in mind—here, the ultimate objective being a *just* society.[77] This is in sharp contrast to the generally descriptive, largely empirical, morally neutral approach one finds among the legal positivists.

2. Though the legal positivists might be able to offer what appears to be a simpler model of law (a model that bears a better-than-passing resemblance to law in practice), a view of law that included more about the moral claims[78] and moral aspirations of law[79] would be a more complete, and therefore better, theory of law.[80]

In both cases, the basic claim is that a (natural law) theory of law that incorporates moral evaluation or other aspects of morality will be superior to a legal positivist theory, because the fuller, richer natural law theory includes or reflects aspects of our practice and experience of law that a (legal positivist) theory, avoiding such elements, cannot.[81]

---

[76] On the use and value of teleological explanations, see Larry Wright, *Teleological Explanations* (Berkeley, Calif.: University of California Press, 1976).

[77] See e.g. Kenneth Winston, 'The Ideal Element in a Definition of Law', *Law and Philosophy*, 5 (1986), 89.

[78] See e.g. Soper, 'Searching for Positivism', 1756 ('That we would be puzzled about what to call standards that have no moral consequence at all is some evidence that the moral qualification is not contingent but part of the essence of law.').

[79] Arguably a legal positivist can incorporate assertions about the moral claims of law, for that can be stated in a neutral way, without evaluation of the claims. In fact, the legal positivist Joseph Raz includes just such an element in his theory of law. See Joseph Raz, *Ethics in the Public Domain* (Oxford: Clarendon Press, 1994), 199 ('every legal system claims that it possesses legitimate authority'). The moral aspirations of law, however, when incorporated into a *critical* (evaluative, not merely descriptive) theory of law, crosses the line of moral neutrality.

[80] One can find similar arguments offered by John Finnis, *Natural Law and Natural Rights*, 11–18, and Philip Soper, 'Searching for Positivism', 1753–7.

[81] One response to this argument might be that in considering the relative merit of alternative theories, detail and level of accuracy are not the only values; simplicity of a model is a countervailing value. See e.g. W. J. Waluchow, *Inclusive Legal Positivism* (Oxford: Clarendon Press, 1994), 19–21.

Linguistic usage may add an additional (if perhaps weak) argument for natural law theory: the reason we may resist calling what the Nazis had as 'law' is that the term is not merely descriptive—it is not like saying, this is a table, but it is not well-constructed. The term 'law' has deep connections with morality, or at least with justice, and to give some social institution that label inevitably carries with it some amount of moral praise.

2.2 Lon Fuller

2.2.1 *Critique of Legal Positivism*

Fuller's criticism of legal positivism can be summarized as follows: (*a*) legal positivism treats law as an object—an object of study, like any other such subject of scientific or quasi-scientific investigation—when it is better understood as a process or function; (*b*) legal positivism seems to believe or assume, falsely, that the existence or non-existence of the law is a matter of moral indifference; and (*c*) legal positivism presents law as a 'one-way projection of authority', when it is better understood as involving reciprocity between officials and citizens.

Law as Object versus Law as Process

For Fuller, law is not merely an object or entity, to be studied dispassionately under a microscope; law is a human project, with an implied goal—and an implied *moral* goal—the ability of people to coexist and cooperate within society.[82] It is not merely that law has an ideal, but that one cannot truly understand law unless one understands the (*moral*) ideal towards which it is striving (there are many human activities, from painting to jogging to boxing, that are hard to understand unless one knows the objective or ideal towards which the participants are striving). Law is the 'enterprise of subjecting human conduct to the governance of rules'.[83] Law thus is a *process*, to be contrasted with the slightly different process of *managerial direction* (the latter can be specific rather than general, and is more attuned to attaining the objectives of the 'rulemaker'—as contrasted with law, whose purpose is primarily helping citizens to coexist, cooperate, and thrive—though, even with managerial direction, it is unwise to make rules that oppress or confuse).[84]

The standard way to define or categorize objects is by assigning essential characteristics: for example, a substance is 'gold' if it has a certain chemical composition, and an animal is a mammal if it is warm-blooded and suckles its young. A completely different approach to defining or categorizing objects would be by their *function*: '[a]nything that mows hay is a mower, whatever its structural features';[85] everything

---

[82] Fuller, *The Morality of Law*, 123. Similarly, Fuller would insist, legal theory is not mere description: 'definitions of "what law really is" are not mere images of some datum of experience, but direction posts for the application of human energies'. Fuller, 'Positivism and Fidelity to Law', 632.

[83] Fuller, *The Morality of Law*, 96. 'Unlike most modern theories of law, this view treats law as an activity and regards a legal system as the product of a sustained purposive effort.' Ibid. at 106.

Though the quotation in the text certainly has the appearance of a definition or conceptual analysis of law (and Fuller even refers to it later, ibid., as '[t]he only formula that might be called a definition of law offered in these writings'), it should be noted that Fuller seemed to have little regard for the project of 'defining law'. See Winston, 'The Ideal Element in a Definition of Law', 91.

[84] Fuller, *The Morality of Law*, 207–10.

[85] See Michael S. Moore, 'Law as a Functional Kind', in *Natural Law Theory: Contemporary Essays*, ed. Robert P. George (Oxford: Clarendon Press, 1992), 188–242, at 207.

that cuts food is a knife, and so on. Fuller's approach to law can be seen as rejecting the notion that 'law' is best understood in the first sense, as an object that can be analysed down to its component parts. Instead, he would argue, law is better understood as being the official response to certain kinds of problems—in particular, the guidance and coordination of citizens' actions in society.[86]

Once one takes a 'functional' approach to law, then the mantra often ascribed to natural law theory, 'an unjust law is no law at all',[87] *begins* to make sense. We would certainly understand someone who says that a long thin metal object that cannot cut (cannot even slice butter) is 'hardly a knife'. Similarly, if one starts with the view that law is about guiding behaviour, one could well say of a purported legal system that is so badly constructed and badly run—for example, containing many obscure, retroactive, or contradictory legal rules, with judicial applications of legal rules that do not match the content of those rules—that citizens could not alter their behaviour to comply with the law, that such a system was not really 'law'.[88] The final step between this functional view and 'an unjust law is no law at all' is to understand the sense in which Fuller's procedural approach touches on *aspects* of justice, though not all of it.[89]

Existence and Non-existence of Law: A Moral Good

Fuller portrays legal positivism as assuming that the existence or non-existence of 'law' within a society is a matter of moral indifference.[90] Fuller argues that such assumptions are false: that, at a minimum, living a good life requires a societal structure that only a sound legal system can provide.[91] The manner in which the existence of law, or the existence of 'law in its fullest sense', can effectuate certain moral goods will be discussed further below, in the evaluation of Fuller's affirmative programme.

---

[86] Fuller does not expressly reject an institutional element to understanding law, cf. e.g. Neil MacCormick and Ota Weinberger, *An Institutional Theory of Law: New Approaches to Legal Positivism* (Dordrecht: Kluwer Academic Publishers, 1986), and much of his work in fact involves exploring the institutional structure and resulting strengths and weaknesses of many legal processes. See Lon L. Fuller, *The Principles of Social Order*, ed. Kenneth I. Winston (Durham, N.C.: Duke University Press, 1981) (a selection of Fuller's essays). However, at one point he comments: 'there are theories that concentrate on the hierarchic structure that is commonly thought to organize and direct the activity I have called law, though again without recognizing that this structure is itself a product of the activity it is thought to put in order'. Fuller, *The Morality of Law*, 118.

[87] See above n. 57.

[88] Fuller's point is grounded on a procedural understanding of the nature of law; a substantive variation of the same 'functional argument' can be given: that legal rules are intended to give reasons for action; immoral legal rules fail to give reasons for action, and thus fail to be law (in its fullest sense), as one might say that logically invalid arguments, which fail to give reasons for belief, are not really arguments. John M. Finnis, 'Problems in the Philosophy of Law', in *The Oxford Companion to Philosophy*, ed. Ted Honderich (Oxford: Oxford University Press, 1995), 468–72, at 469.

[89] Fuller describes his discussion of the internal morality of law as 'a procedural, as distinguished from a substantive natural law'. Fuller, *The Morality of Law*, 96. The question of whether one can describe the internal morality of law as being connected with justice or morality will be taken up below, in Sect. 2.2.3.

[90] Fuller, *The Morality of Law*, 204.   [91] ibid. at 204–7.

One-Way Projection of Authority

Fuller argues that legal positivism sees laws mostly as a 'one-way projection of authority'—one party giving orders, and other parties complying. This is most obvious in John Austin's work, with its reduction of law to the commands of a sovereign,[92] but later legal positivists are arguably not that different. This view of law, Fuller states, is a basic misunderstanding: for so much of law, so much of a fully functioning legal system, depends on there being a *reciprocity of duties between citizens and lawgivers*: 'the existence of a relatively stable reciprocity of expectations between lawgiver and subject is part of the very idea of a functioning legal order'.[93] Only when citizens and officials cooperate, each fulfilling his or her own functions, can law work. For example, officials promise, expressly or implicitly, to enforce the rules as promulgated and to make the demands on citizens reasonable and consistent; to the extent that officials violate these duties, the smooth running of society will begin to break down.

Fuller discusses the choice between the flexibility and power of broad discretion (directly granted, or hidden in the use of vague or inconsistently applied rules) as against the clear guidance of always following a lucidly written rule—how managers in large companies and tyrants in wicked legal systems find a use for lack of guidance and arbitrary will. We find this to be wrong in a legal system, but our criticism is not that arbitrary discretion is not 'efficacious'—it is quite useful for some purposes, but it is contrary to the morality intrinsic to lawmaking.[94]

2.2.2 *Fuller's Alternative: The Internal Morality of Law*

Fuller's affirmative analysis develops from his evaluation of the shortcomings of legal positivism. In the place of legal positivism, he offers an analysis that focuses on law as a process, a process that emphasizes the importance of the interaction between officials and citizens, and that makes more transparent the way in which a legal order can be instrumental to the attainment of other goods.

Fuller offers a list of eight 'principles of legality', which would both serve as criteria for testing the minimal duties of a government, and also set the objective of excellence towards which a good government would strive.[95] Fuller's eight criteria are as follows:

- the rules must be general;
- the rules must be promulgated;

---

[92] See Austin, *The Province of Jurisprudence Determined*.

[93] Fuller, *The Morality of Law*, 209; see also ibid. at 39–40 ('[T]here is a kind of reciprocity between government and the citizen with respect to the observance of rules. Government says to the citizen in effect, "These are the rules we expect you to follow. If you follow them, you have our assurance that they are the rules that will be applied to your conduct." When this bond of reciprocity is broken, nothing is left on which to ground the citizen's duty to observe the rules.' (fn. omitted)).

[94] ibid. at 212–14.

[95] See ibid. at 41–2.

- retroactive rulemaking and application must be minimized;[96]
- the rules must be understandable;
- they should not be contradictory;
- they should not be impossible to obey;
- the rules should remain relatively constant through time;
- there should be a congruence between the rules as announced and as applied.[97]

Following the principles makes it easier for a lawmaker to guide the behaviour of its citizens (and for citizens to be able to plan their activities knowing what they need to do to stay on the right side of the law).[98]

Some of Fuller's eight principles[99] are best seen as minimal requirements, for which there is no excuse for less than full compliance—for example, laws that require the impossible or contradict one another. Others, such as the minimizing of retroactive legislation, the full promulgation of laws, and the understandability of the laws, are best seen as ideals to which legal systems should always strive, but which we should not expect the systems to meet perfectly.[100]

To the extent that one sees law as a process, as a means of guiding and coordinating human behaviour within society, this process will be more successful to the extent that Fuller's eight principles are met. In this sense, one could also speak of systems that are 'more legal' or 'less legal'. At one point, Fuller talks of rule systems as 'being legal' to a greater or lesser extent; at other times, he seems to imagine some threshold beneath which a rule system no longer qualifies as 'legal'.[101] In any event, the basic point is the same—that rule systems that substantially comply with the eight requirements are '*legal* systems', *in the sense that* they are likely to succeed in guiding the behaviour of their citizens; rule systems that do not substantially comply with the eight requirements are not 'legal systems', in the sense that they are unlikely to be able to guide citizen behaviour. (It is worth noting one difference between Fuller's analysis and that of at least some legal positivists and traditional natural law theorists: while some theorists inquire about possible moral tests for

---

[96] Obviously, it is impossible to conform one's behaviour to norms promulgated after the fact; but Fuller understood that judicial decision-making will often have some retroactive elements. Fuller's point was that, at a minimum, governments needed to be aware of the injustice of such retroactive actions, and to work to keep them as infrequent as possible. See ibid. at 56–62.

[97] See ibid. at 46–91. The wording used in the text sometimes varies slightly from that used by Fuller.

[98] As Robert Summers argued in Fuller's name: 'Sufficient compliance with the principles of legality necessarily guarantees, to the extent of that compliance, the realization of a moral value . . . that the citizens will have a *fair* opportunity to obey the law [whether the law is moral or immoral].' Robert S. Summers, *Lon L. Fuller* (Stanford: Stanford University Press, 1984), 37.

[99] Cf. Joseph Raz's similar list of 'principles which can be derived from the basic idea of the rule of law'. Joseph Raz, *The Authority of Law* (Oxford: Clarendon Press, 1979), 214–19.

[100] On promulgation and understandability, the ideal is for all citizens to know all of their legal obligations fully and precisely, without the need of consulting a lawyer. It seems that even (or especially) in modern, developed countries, we are very far from that ideal.

[101] See e.g. Fuller, *The Morality of Law*, 39.

both legal systems and individual legal norms, Fuller is focused only on the system as a whole.)[102]

2.2.3 *Criticisms*

H. L. A. Hart, in a review of Fuller's *The Morality of Law*,[103] argues that Fuller has shown that law, to some extent, operates as a process, with an objective—the objective being to guide behaviour. Hart has no argument with this as far as it goes, nor does he doubt that following Fuller's eight guidelines would make a legal system better able to guide citizen behaviour.[104] What Hart objects to is calling this 'morality'— it is merely efficacy or efficiency, a morally neutral value as important to wicked people and governments as to virtuous ones (one could easily, Hart famously notes, have an '[internal] morality of poisoning').[105] If a legal system has evil ends, like Nazi Germany or Apartheid South Africa, then following Fuller's guidelines will allow the government to be more efficient in achieving those evil ends.[106]

A number of replies could be offered (many of which Fuller in fact gives on his own behalf):

1. As others have noted, 'playing by the rules of the game'—or playing the game fairly, is itself an integral part of justice, even if far from all of it[107] (by analogy: it is still of some moral value to keep one's promise, even if it was a promise to do something bad). Fuller gives the example from the former Soviet Union, where the lawmakers were once so concerned about the increase in certain kinds of economic crime that they substantially raised the penalty, and to show how seriously

---

[102] See e.g. ibid. ('A total failure in any one of these eight directions does not simply result in a bad system of law; it results in something that is not properly called a legal system at all . . .').

[103] H. L. A. Hart, 'Lon L. Fuller: The Morality of Law', in *Essays in Jurisprudence and Philosophy* (Oxford: Clarendon Press, 1983), 343–64.

[104] ibid. at 347–9.   [105] ibid. at 350.   [106] ibid. at 349–53.

Matthew Kramer raises a different line of criticism: following Fuller's principles of legality might only lead consistently to the best results in the (unlikely) circumstance of a legal system that is always and only serving virtuous objectives. Where a law or set of laws is less than morally optimal, procedural deviations from what the laws (and Fuller's principles) would seem to require might actually have a morally good effect. Matthew Kramer, 'Scrupulousness without Scruples: A Critique of Lon Fuller and His Defenders', *Oxford Journal of Legal Studies*, 18 (1998), 235, 239–43. An analogous point might be made through the example of promise-keeping. Most people assume that keeping promises is a morally good thing. However, when considering someone who has made promises whose content is wicked, or at least less than morally optimal, it is possible that breaking the promises will create morally better consequences than keeping them.

One possible response to this line of argument is to question its implied premise: that the value of Fuller's approach depends (or depends exclusively) on its usefulness as a proxy for consequentialist evaluations. As discussed earlier, Fuller's approach—a functionalist or teleological view of law—might be both better understood and entirely defensible simply as a better or more complete view of the nature of law.

[107] See Weinreb, *Natural Law and Justice*, 185–94. Weinreb argues that justice is best thought of as an often-uneasy combination of 'entitlement' (his term for the following of the rules laid down) and desert. Ibid. at 184–223.

they took this kind of crime, they made the increase in sentence retroactive for those already in prison for those offences. The lawyers in the Soviet Union, not a country normally known for its adherence to procedural justice, protested that this was unjust.[108]

This is not just a question of 'efficacy'—if it were, one might applaud the extra deterrent power that might come if a potential criminal knew that her actions might lead to even worse consequences than are now advertised.[109] If retroactive lawmaking is to be criticized, it is not at the level of efficacy, but at the level of justice and morality.

2. Certain kinds of evil are arguably less likely when proper procedures are followed: for example, courts may be more likely to come up with just decisions when judges know that they must give public reasons for their decisions (certain forms of corruption may be hard to rationalize). Also, as one commentator has observed, 'a wicked government's decision to act within the procedural constraints of the rule of law affords the general population at least some measure of security'.[110]

3. Fuller once wrote that he could not believe that a legal system that was procedurally just would not also be substantively just.[111] Certainly, a correlation exists (at least in the negative sense that countries that care little for one are likely to care little for the other), but there have also been countries that have promulgated evil in an efficient and meticulous way. On most accounts, Fuller's faith in a strong connection between procedural and substantive justice is an optimistic, but peripheral part of his theory.[112] However, some commentators have treated it as central, arguing that Fuller's theory stands or falls based on its (dubious) merit.[113]

2.3 Ronald Dworkin

Ronald Dworkin (1931–) has been an immensely influential figure in English-language legal philosophy, and also in political and moral philosophy. In legal philosophy, his early work offered wide-ranging criticisms of H. L. A. Hart's version of

---

[108] Fuller, *The Morality of Law*, 202–3.

[109] See ibid. at 203 ('Now it is reasonable to suppose, I think, that the [objecting] Soviet lawyer was not asserting that the action of the authorities was an ineffective measure for combating economic crime.').

[110] George, *In Defense of Natural Law*, 114.

[111] Fuller, 'Positivism and Fidelity to Law', 636.

[112] See e.g. Bix, *Jurisprudence: Theory and Context*, 76–7. One can find mixed evidence from Fuller's own writings regarding his views on this connection. At one point, he downplays the connection: 'I have never asserted that there is any logical contradiction in the notion of achieving evil, at least some kinds of evil, through means that fully respect all the demands of legality'. Lon Fuller, *A Reply to Professors Cohen and Dworkin*, Vill. L. Rev., 10 (1965), 660, 664. Elsewhere in his writings, however, he denies that there were many, or perhaps any, actual historical examples of such combinations. Fuller, *The Morality of Law*, 154.

[113] See Anthony J. Sebok, *Legal Positivism in American Jurisprudence* (Cambridge: Cambridge University Press, 1998), 163–7.

legal positivism,[114] a critique from which Dworkin built his own theory of law.[115] In later works, that theory was re-characterized as an interpretive theory of law.[116]

According to Dworkin's approach, to determine what the law requires—what the law 'is'—one finds the best interpretation available of the relevant legal data: legislative acts, judicial decisions, constitutional texts, and so on.[117] As an interpretation, the theory must adequately fit the relevant data (e.g. it cannot dismiss too many old judicial decisions as 'mistakes'); additionally, to be a *good* interpretation, it must also do well on the scale of moral value.[118] Dworkin also argues that this approach (which he calls 'constructive interpretation')[119] is as appropriate for legal theorists discussing the nature of law as it is for lawyers and judges discussing what the law requires on a particular matter.[120]

The literature on Dworkin's work is vast.[121] This is not the place to revisit extensively that already well-travelled territory. Instead, this section will focus on Dworkin's work only in a tangential way: discussing the way in which his work could be said to be a natural law theory, and what Dworkin's own work might indicate about the need or the viability of such a project.

Dworkin does not normally use the label 'natural law' for his own work. In fact, with the prominent exception of one lecture, later published as an article,[122] he has avoided referring to 'natural law' entirely, either as a description of his own work, or as an approach to contrast with his own. In that one reference, however, Dworkin concedes that his work might warrant the label 'natural law': 'If the crude description of natural law I just gave is correct, that any theory that makes the content of law sometimes depend on the correct answer to some moral question is a natural law theory, then I am guilty of natural law'.[123]

---

[114] See H. L. A. Hart, *The Concept of Law*, 2nd edn. (Oxford: Oxford University Press, 1994).

[115] Ronald Dworkin, *Taking Rights Seriously* (Cambridge, Mass.: Harvard University Press, 1977).

[116] See Ronald Dworkin, *Law's Empire* (Cambridge, Mass.: Harvard University Press, 1986).

[117] See ibid. at 225–8, 245–58.

[118] There are additional complications: (1) the values of 'fit' and 'moral value' must both be considered in comparing alternative tenable theories, with the relative weights of those two factors varying in different areas of the law, ibid. at 228–58; and (2) Dworkin also speaks of a value of 'Integrity'—that judges should prefer an interpretation that makes the legal system speak with a unified 'voice'. Ibid. at 225.

[119] See ibid. at 52 ('constructive interpretation is a matter of imposing purpose on an object or practice in order to make of it the best possible example of the form or genre to which it is taken to belong').

[120] See e.g. Ronald Dworkin, 'Legal Theory and the Problem of Sense', in *Issues in Contemporary Legal Philosophy*, ed. Ruth Gavison (Oxford: Clarendon Press, 1987), 9, 13–15.

[121] See e.g. Marshall Cohen (ed.), *Ronald Dworkin and Contemporary Jurisprudence* (Totowa, N.J.: Rowman & Allanheld, 1983); Andrei Marmor, *Interpretation and Legal Theory* (Oxford: Clarendon Press, 1992); Bix, *Law, Language and Legal Determinacy*, 77–132; Stephen Guest, *Ronald Dworkin*, 2nd edn. (Edinburgh: Edinburgh University Press, 1997).

[122] Ronald Dworkin, '"Natural" Law Revisited', *University of Florida Law Review*, 34 (1982), 165.

[123] ibid. at 165. Dworkin offers no opinion on whether this view of natural law theory is historically accurate or succeeds in distinguishing legal positivism.

Dworkin is a natural law theorist in the sense that his approach to law and to legal theory rejects a strict ('conceptual' or 'necessary') separation between law and morality. To deny a strict separation, of course, is not to affirm an equivalence; Dworkin does not assert that once one knows what morality requires then one also knows the content of the legal system (*no* natural law theorist, traditional or otherwise, makes *that* claim). The argument of conceptual connection is that moral evaluations are a necessary part of determining the content of a legal system. Under Dworkin's approach, the choice between tenable interpretations of past official actions may easily come down to a determination of which interpretation presents the legal system as better morally. Thus, within Dworkin's approach, one cannot determine 'what law is' without considering moral or evaluative matters.[124]

Dworkin's approach also has connections with other natural law approaches in that 'what law *really* is' is something different from the official decisions that most people conventionally associate with the term. Recall that for Dworkin all past official acts—including promulgated statutes and judicial decisions—are merely 'preinterpretive data'[125] to be used in constructing the best theory of what the law requires regarding some issue. Judicial decisions are thus, under this view, only fallible guesses at what the law 'really is', what it actually requires. There is some ideal towards which (the better) judicial decisions are striving.[126]

The similarities and differences between Dworkin and Fuller are instructive.[127] The convergence of their views is mostly at the broadest level: both believe that law cannot be properly understood without morality, especially the moral values towards which all law necessarily aspires. By way of difference, Fuller is more concerned with the 'form' and 'process' of law, while Dworkin's work focuses on the

---

[124] Here it is important to note Dworkin's equation of 'law' with 'what judges are obligated to apply'. See e.g. Ronald Dworkin, 'A Reply by Ronald Dworkin', in *Ronald Dworkin & Contemporary Jurisprudence*, ed. Marshall Cohen (Totowa, N.J.: Rowman & Allanheld, 1983), 247, 262. This is a controversial and significant point, significant because of the contrary perspective of the legal positivist, Joseph Raz. Raz would have 'law' defined in a legal positivist way, without reference to moral or evaluative terms, but has no objection to the idea that judges are often authorized or obligated to include moral terms as part of their decisions. See Joseph Raz, 'Legal Principles and the Nature of Law', in *Ronald Dworkin & Contemporary Jurisprudence*, 73, 84–5; Joseph Raz, 'Postema on Law's Autonomy and Public Practical Reasons: A Critical Comment', *Legal Theory*, 4 (1998), 1.

[125] See e.g. Ronald Dworkin, *Law's Empire*, 65–6.

[126] Dworkin is thus sympathetic to the idea that law 'works itself pure'. *Omychund v Barker* (1744) 26 E.R. 15 at 23.

[127] Dworkin for a long time has been strangely silent about Fuller. Long before Dworkin developed his interpretive approach to law, he wrote some articles critical of Fuller's approach. See Ronald Dworkin, 'The Elusive Morality of Law', *Villanova Law Review*, 10 (1965), 631; Ronald Dworkin, 'Philosophy, Morality, and Law—Observations Prompted by Professor Fuller's Novel Claim', *University of Pennsylvania Law Review*, 113 (1965), 668. (Fuller responded to some of the points raised by Dworkin in the 'Reply to Critics', which appears in the revised edition of *The Morality of Law*. Fuller, *The Morality of Law*, 198–202, 221–3, 238–40.) As noted in the text, Dworkin's later, interpretive work converges in some ways with Fuller's approach to law; however, Fuller is rarely if ever mentioned (e.g. his name does not appear in the detailed index of *Law's Empire*).

interpretive process he believes to be central both to determining what the law (substantively) requires *and* to understanding law generally.

2.4 John Finnis

John Finnis may be the theorist within the classical natural law tradition best known to modern English-language legal theorists.[128] His work, in particular, *Natural Law and Natural Rights*,[129] consciously works within the tradition of Thomas Aquinas,[130] emphasizing moral philosophy and meta-theory, while also contributing to contemporary debates about the nature of law.

2.4.1 *Moral Theory*

Overview[131]

Finnis builds his moral theory from a foundation of 'basic goods', goods we value for their own sake, 'aspects of authentic human flourishing, . . . real (intelligent) reason[s] for action'.[132] In *Natural Law and Natural Rights*, Finnis lists seven: life,[133] knowledge, play, aesthetic experience, sociability (friendship), practical reasonableness, and 'religion'.[134] These are ends and purposes we can and do choose for their

---

[128] If one were speaking more about natural law in a broader sense (as this chapter does), a sense that would include Dworkin, then he would likely get the title as 'the best-known natural law theorist' in contemporary English-language legal theory.

[129] John Finnis, *Natural Law and Natural Rights* (Oxford: Clarendon Press, 1980).

[130] Finnis has also written a detailed commentary on Aquinas. John Finnis, *Aquinas: Moral, Political, and Legal Theory* (1998).

Finnis's own work is grounded directly on Aquinas, and also indirectly, through Germain Grisez's 'representation and development of classical arguments'. See ibid. at p. viii; see also Germain Grisez, 'The First Principle of Practical Reason: A Commentary on the *Summa Theologiae*, 1–2, Question 94, Article 2', *Natural Law Forum*, 10 (1965), 168. The extent to which Finnis's account is consistent with or deviates from Aquinas's teaching is a matter of contention. See e.g. Russell Hittinger, *A Critique of the New Natural Law Theory* (1987) (criticizing Grisez and Finnis).

[131] The focus will be on Finnis's general discussions of natural law theory, which centre on moral philosophy in the broadest sense. Finnis has also written two texts on morality and ethics in a more narrow sense of those terms. John Finnis, *Fundamentals of Ethics* (Washington, DC: Georgetown University Press, 1983); John Finnis, *Moral Absolutes: Tradition, Revision, and Truth* (Washington, DC: Catholic University of America Press, 1991).

[132] Finnis, *Natural Law and Natural Rights*, 64; cf. Aquinas, *Summa Theologiae*, q. 94, art. 2 (discussing the apprehension of human goods through Practical Reason).

[133] 'Life' includes 'every aspect of vitality' including physical health and procreation. Finnis, *Natural Law and Natural Rights*, 86–7.

[134] ibid. at 86–90. The quotation marks around 'religion' are in the original, and signify that it is meant to include all forms of inquiry about human nature and its place within the universe, even if the result of such inquiries may, for some, be a kind of atheism or existentialism. Ibid. at 89–90.

Finnis notes that there may be other ways of listing or characterizing the basic goods, but he does not think that there are other basic goods that could not be fitted within his list of seven. Ibid. at 90–2. Finnis in fact offers a slightly different list in John M. Finnis, 'Is Natural Law Compatible with Limited

own sake, not merely (or always) as a means to other ends and purposes. It is not that no one ever seeks a basic good, say, friendship, as a means to another end, but that the basic goods are those (few) ends and purposes that one can intelligibly choose for their own sake.[135]

According to Finnis, the basic goods are grounded in human nature, not directly, in the sense of being read off a metaphysical theory, but indirectly, in the sense that '[t]he basic forms of good grasped by practical understanding are what is good for human beings with the nature they have'.[136] Importantly, for Finnis there is 'no objective hierarchy' among the basic goods,[137] though an individual in his or her own life can choose to give more importance to one or some than to others.[138]

There are then nine intermediate principles (principles which Finnis labels 'the basic requirements of practical reasonableness'), 'to guide the transition from judgments about human goods to judgments about the right thing to do here and now':[139]

- adopting a coherent plan of life;
- having no arbitrary preferences among values;
- having no arbitrary preferences among persons;
- maintaining a certain detachment from the specific and limited projects one undertakes;
- not abandoning one's commitments lightly;
- not wasting one's opportunities by using inefficient methods;
- not choosing to do something that of itself does nothing but damage or impede the realization of or participation in one or more of the basic goods;
- fostering the common good of one's community;
- acting in accordance with one's conscience.[140]

Finnis's approach is thus teleological, but not in the way in which some natural theories are—there is no single human (or superhuman) ideal towards which everyone must aspire.[141] The prescription is rather more general: 'In voluntarily acting for

Government?', in *Natural Law, Liberalism, and Morality*, ed. Robert P. George (Oxford: Clarendon Press, 1996), 1–26, at 4.

[135] Consider some goods whose value is clearly only instrumental: if a person reported that she was collecting money or medicine not for the good that might be done with such objects, either in the short term or the long term, but just in order to have more of those items, one might rightly question her rationality or sanity.

[136] Finnis, *Natural Law and Natural Rights*, 34; see Finnis, *Aquinas*, 90–4; see also George, *A Defense of Natural Law Theory*, 83–91 ('Natural Law and Human Nature').

[137] Finnis, *Natural Law and Natural Rights*, 92. Finnis adds: 'each [basic good], when we focus on it, can reasonably be regarded as the most important'. Ibid.

[138] See ibid. at 93–4.   [139] Finnis, *Fundamentals of Ethics*, 70.

[140] Finnis, *Natural Law and Natural Rights*, 100–26.

[141] See, e.g., Finnis, *Aquinas*, 314–19; John M. Finnis, 'Natural Law and the "Is"—"Ought" Question: An Invitation to Professor Veatch', *Catholic Lawyer*, 26 (1981), 266; George, *In Defense of Natural Law*, 50–2. For a contrary position, emphasizing a hierarchy among values and a stronger role for a sense of man's final end, see Hittinger, *A Critique of the New Natural Law Theory*, 65–198.

human goods and avoiding what is opposed to them, one ought to choose and other-wise will those and only those possibilities whose willing is compatible with integral human fulfillment'.[142]

Finnis holds the list of basic goods and the principles of practical reasonableness to be 'self-evident', but by that he does not mean that they are obvious or intuitive or that all reasonable people will immediately assent.[143] 'Self-evidence' means primar-ily that the truths in question are not derived from any more fundamental truth; they are 'grasped by intelligent reflection on data presented by experience', supported indirectly by speculative and dialectical arguments.[144]

Criticism

Finnis's moral theory has been subject to a number of criticisms, representing a variety of alternative views (and the number of controversial areas in which Finnis has been an active disputant). Only two among the many lines of criticism will be sampled here.

One line of criticism, or at least questioning, is whether Finnis's combination of 'basic human goods' and 'basic requirements of practical reasonableness' are suf-ficient to come up with answers (and to come up with the *right* answers) to the important moral questions we face.[145] That is, the argument is that Finnis's approach does not have sufficient resources to reach (determinate) answers on difficult moral questions.

From critics who offer alternative readings of the natural law tradition generally, or of Aquinas's views in particular, the challenge regarding the *adequacy* of Finnis's approach is often connected with claims about its *exegetical accuracy*.[146] In terms dis-cussed earlier, the exegetical question is whether Aquinas is best understood as con-structing a teleological view based directly on a view of human nature, or is best understood as offering a kind of 'virtue ethics'—that there are certain goods basic to human flourishing, that we know or discover by using reason, and whose connection to human nature is (more) indirect.[147] The sufficiency criticism is that we can find

---

[142] Finnis, *Moral Absolutes*, 45 (fn. omitted); see George, *In Defense of Natural Law*, 51 ('The concept of integral human fulfillment . . . is not meant to indicate a supreme good above or apart from the basic goods.').

[143] Finnis, *Natural Law and Natural Rights*, 64–9; see also George, *In Defense of Natural Law*, 43–5, 61–6, 85–90, 262–6.

[144] George, *In Defense of Natural Law*, 61–3.

[145] At least those questions that *have* answers. It is common ground among Finnis and many of his critics that there are important questions that may have no single, unique right answer (as a moral mat-ter), due either to the plurality of goods or (to the extent this is a different point) the incommensurabil-ity of goods.

[146] See e.g. Ralph McInerny, 'The Principles of Natural Law', *American Journal of Jurisprudence*, 25 (1980), 1; Henry B. Veatch, 'Book Review', *American Journal of Jurisprudence*, 26 (1981), 247, 255–9.

[147] On this debate, see e.g. Hittinger, *A Critique of the New Natural Law Theory*; George, *In Defense of Natural Law*, 59–75 (responding to Hittinger); McInerny, 'The Principles of Natural Law'; John Finnis and Germain Grisez, 'The Basic Principles of Natural Law: A Reply to Ralph McInerny', *American Journal of Jurisprudence*, 26 (1981), 21.

the answers to the difficult moral questions only once we have a full-fledged teleology with an ordered hierarchy of goods, rather than Finnis's list of equally basic goods.[148]

A quite different line of criticism is offered by Steven Smith, who suggests that Finnis's approach to 'the basic goods' (and Finnis's use of such concepts in his writings on sexual issues) reflects a too-great divide between the idea of 'the good' and actual persons' desires and experiences.[149] Smith notes not only the absence of 'pleasure' as a 'basic good', a good sought for its own sake,[150] but also the strangely *non-empirical* status of claims like the following: '[H]omosexual conduct (and indeed all extra-marital sexual gratification) is radically incapable of participating in, actualizing, the common good of friendship'.[151] By non-empirical status, Smith means that, in the context of Finnis's writings, it seems clear that Finnis would not consider the claim about homosexual conduct to be rebutted by testimony from homosexual couples claiming that their intimate conduct *is* a way of maintaining, expressing, and strengthening friendship.[152] However, Smith argues, as the gap grows between 'being a good' and 'being experienced as a good', the potential for disconnection grows between academic morality and our actual moral concerns.[153]

2.4.2 *Legal Theory*[154]

Law plays a role within Finnis's moral theory, in that there are certain common goods that are best obtained through the specific kind of social coordination that law offers,[155] and there is a sense in which participation in the community and in the common good of building a (political) community is an integral part of living a good life.[156] Finnis also discusses legal theory in the narrower sense of the term. In analyzing the concept of law, he agrees with the general approach of H. L. A. Hart: that one should look at 'law' (or 'legal system') in its fullest or highest form, rather than in some lowest common denominator of all systems we might consider 'legal';[157] and that such an approach must incorporate the perspective of participants. However,

---

[148] See e.g. Russell Hittinger, 'Varieties of Minimalist Natural Law Theory', *American Journal of Jurisprudence*, 34 (1989), 133; Hittinger, *A Critique of the New Natural Law Theory*, 74–89.

[149] Steven D. Smith, 'Natural Law and Contemporary Moral Thought: A Guide from the Perplexed' (book review), *American Journal of Jurisprudence*, 42 (1997), 299, 316–21. One could concede the point and still note that Finnis's approach does a better job than Kantian deontological theories in trying to connect morality with a view of human well-being. See George, *In Defense of Natural Law*, 60–1.

[150] Cf. Finnis, *Natural Law and Natural Rights*, 95–7 ('Is Pleasure the Point of It All?').

[151] John Finnis, 'Is Natural Law Compatible with Limited Government?', ed. Robert P. George (1996), 12–13 (emphasis omitted).

[152] Smith, 'Natural Law and Contemporary Moral Thought', 316–19.   [153] ibid. at 319–21.

[154] Along with moral theory and legal theory, Finnis has also written on political theory. See e.g, Finnis, 'Is Natural Law Compatible with Limited Government?'.

[155] Finnis, *Natural Law and Natural Rights*, 260–4; John M. Finnis, 'Law as Co-ordination', *Ratio Juris*, 2 (1989), 97.

[156] See Finnis, *Natural Law and Natural Rights*, 164–5, 260–4; Veatch, 'Book Review', 252–3.

[157] Finnis, *Natural Law and Natural Rights*, 3–11; cf. Hart, *The Concept of Law*, 3–4, 15–17.

Finnis narrows and strengthens Hart's 'internal perspective':[158] it is 'the viewpoint of those who not only appeal to practical reasonableness but also *are* practically reasonable'.[159] According to Finnis, one must select the 'internal viewpoint' according to the idea of 'central case' (the concept in its fullest sense), and that this will direct one away from a morally neutral perspective: 'If there is a point of view in which legal obligation is treated as at least presumptively a moral obligation . . . , a viewpoint in which the establishment and maintenance of legal as distinct from discretionary or statically customary order is regarded as a moral ideal if not a compelling demand of justice, then such viewpoint will constitute the central case of the legal viewpoint'.[160] This may seem a minor modification, to Hart's approach, but it is one sufficient to move a theorist across the border, from legal positivism (law conceptually separated from morality) to natural law theory (moral evaluation central to understanding law).

Finnis's criticism of legal positivism, implicit in his views on 'internal perspectives' and express in other writings,[161] is that a proper theory of law will require moral evaluation. The basic claim is the same sort of teleological argument discussed earlier in relation to Fuller's work: one cannot fully understand a reason-giving activity like law without the (moral) evaluation of what it would mean for the official statements and enactments to give citizens a *good* reason for action.[162]

2.5 Michael Moore

Michael Moore (1943–) offers a theory of law and legal practice built around metaphysical realism.[163] Metaphysical realism is generally understood as a claim about

[158] See Hart, *The Concept of Law*, 87–91.   [159] Finnis, *Natural Law and Natural Rights*, 15.

[160] ibid. at 14–15; see also Finnis, *Aquinas*, 257–8.

[161] See John Finnis, 'On the Incoherence of Legal Positivism', *Notre Dame Law Review*, 75 (2000), 1597; see also John M. Finnis, 'Problems of the Philosophy of Law', in *Oxford Companion to Philosophy*, ed. Ted Honderich (Oxford: Oxford University Press, 1995), 468, 469.

[162] For a more detailed discussion of Finnis's view of the debate between legal positivism and natural law theory, see Brian Bix, 'On the Dividing Line Between Natural Law Theory and Legal Positivism', *Notre Dame Law Review*, 75 (2000), 1613.

[163] See Michael S. Moore, 'Good without God', in *Natural Law, Liberalism, and Morality*, ed. Robert P. George (Oxford: Clarendon Press, 1996), 221–70; 'Law as a Functional Kind', in *Natural Law Theories: New Essays*, ed. Robert P. George (Oxford: Clarendon Press, 1992), 188–242; 'Moral Reality Revisited', *Michigan Law Review*, 90 (1992), 2424; 'The Interpretive Turn in Modern Theory: A Turn for the Worse?', *Stanford Law Review*, 41 (1989), 871 (hereinafter Moore, 'Interpretive Turn'); 'Precedent, Induction, and Ethical Generalization', in *Precedent in Law*, ed. Laurence Goldstein (Oxford: Clarendon Press, 1987), 183–213 (hereinafter, Moore, 'Precedent'); 'Metaphysics, Epistemology and Legal Theory', *Southern California Law Review*, 60 (1987), 453 (book review); 'A Natural Law Theory of Interpretation', *Southern California Law Review*, 58 (1985), 277 (hereinafter, Moore, 'Interpretation'); 'Moral Reality', *Wisconsin Law Review*, (1982), 1061; and 'The Semantics of Judging', *Southern California Law Review*, 54 (1982), 151. Moore's articles 'Metaphysics, Epistemology and Legal Theory'; 'Law as a Functional Kind'; and 'Interpretive Turn' are reproduced in Michael Moore, *Educating Oneself in Public: Critical Essays in Jurisprudence* (Oxford: Oxford University Press, 2000), 247–423. For an extended critical overview of Moore's approach, see Bix, *Law, Language, and Legal Determinacy*, 133–77.

ontology—that our words refer to objects whose existence and properties are independent of conventional beliefs or observers' beliefs about the objects.[164] Moore's own views on metaphysical realism emphasize ontological commitments, but also includes views regarding truth, reference, morality, and meaning.[165] Moore does not assert *merely* that there are right answers to moral questions (though he certainly asserts that);[166] on ontological matters, he posits the existence of 'moral entities such as rights and duties, virtues and vices, and moral qualities such as goodness and badness' as well as 'moral kinds' (a moral analogue to natural kinds).[167] On meaning, he equates terms, including evaluative terms like 'justice', with 'natural kinds' or 'natural kinds of events'; in such cases, the meaning is held to be supplied by 'the best scientific theory we can muster' about the kind in question.[168] Moore, however, is not a Platonist on all matters: he favours a coherence theory in epistemology,[169] and he views law not as a natural kind, but as a 'functional kind'.[170]

Moore's challenge to those who are not metaphysical realists is to claim that metaphysical realism is the correct approach,[171] and that this approach requires us to modify our views about the nature of law and how legal institutions should operate.[172] The question might be characterized: how should/would we—as lawyers, judges, legislators, citizens—act differently if we believed, and took seriously, the notion of unique right answers to moral questions, and determinate referents to most concepts (whether moral, legal, or natural-kind terms)?

[164] Michael Dummett has argued that realism would be better understood as a claim about meaning and truth, in particular the application of bivalence to all statements within an area of discourse. See e.g. Michael Dummett, *The Seas of Language* (1993), 230–76. Most people who are realists about an area of discourse under a semantics-based definition will also be realists under an ontology-based definition. There are yet other (different, but overlapping) understandings of metaphysical realism. For a good, brief overview, see Simon Blackburn, *The Oxford Dictionary of Philosophy* (1994), 319–20 ('realism/anti-realism').

[165] Moore, 'Moral Reality Revisited', 2432–40.

[166] See e.g. Moore, 'Interpretation', 286.

[167] Moore, 'Precedent', 208. On 'natural kinds', see Hilary Putnam, 'The Meaning of "Meaning"', in *Mind, Language and Reality* (Cambridge: Cambridge University Press, 1975), 215–71.

[168] Moore, 'Interpretation', 291–301; Moore, 'Moral Reality Revisited', 2436–40. Even with terms like the legal concept of 'malice' (not to be confused with the everyday-speech use of that term), Moore argues that this term 'picks out some thing in the world' and might be thought of as an example of a 'moral kind'. Moore, 'Interpretation', 333.

[169] See e.g. Moore, 'Interpretation', 312; Moore, 'Precedent', 197–8, 208–9.

[170] See Moore, 'Law as a Functional Kind'. 'Unlike nominal kinds, items making up a functional kind have a nature that they share that is richer than the "nature" of merely sharing a common name in some language. Unlike natural kinds the nature that such items share is a function and not a structure'. Ibid. at 208.

[171] Sometimes he argues or implies that most of us are already metaphysical realists, however much we might deny it. See Moore, 'Interpretation', 322–6, 397–8. If one defines metaphysical realism broadly enough, this is likely to be true (as indicated earlier, a similar claim could also be made for 'natural law theory', defined broadly enough).

[172] Moore, 'Interpretive Turn', 873, 881–90; Moore, 'Moral Reality Revisited', 2468–91.

A robust belief in the existence and accessibility of moral truth, in a metaphysically realist sense, helps and hinders legal analysis in a number of ways:

1. Some of the notorious paradoxes and indeterminacies of precedential (common law) reasoning may fall away if we believe (or assume) that there are 'moral kinds'.[173] Then the proper way to (re)characterize the holding of a past case is as describing the application of a relevant moral kind;[174] additionally, the indeterminacy of characterization, that any judicial decision can be restated at different levels of generality, falls away, at least in principle, for the *correct* level of generality is that of the moral kind.[175] Under Moore's approach, common law legal reasoning is understood as all-things-considered moral reasoning—while emphasizing that one of those factors to be considered is the 'institutional' or 'rule of law' argument, an argument that may result in the entrenchment of some past wrong decisions, because morality does take seriously people's reliance interests.[176]

2. The equally troublesome problems with determining the legislative intentions of the groups who enacted legislation (or created constitutional language)[177] might be circumvented if the lawmakers 'should be held to have the same linguistic intentions as other language users, namely [metaphysically] realist ones'.[178] The lawmakers' intentions regarding the meaning or application of the terms they use (beyond their realist intentions that words be understood according to their 'real' meaning) are not relevant.[179] To put the same point a different way, judges should guide their interpretation of legal terms (whether of statutory, constitutional, or common law origin) according to a metaphysically realist theory of meaning— according to 'the real nature of the things to which the words refer and not by the conventions governing the ordinary usage of those words'.[180] Moore goes farther, arguing that even the stipulated definitions within legislation are not to be given special deference; to the contrary, those definitions should be treated as mere 'conventional glosses' on the 'real' meaning of terms (and it should be assumed that this is how legislators wanted those definitions to be treated).[181]

[173] Moore, 'Precedent'.

[174] See ibid.; see also Moore, 'Interpretation', 358–76. More precisely, most of the use for the concept of 'holdings' falls away. Moore, 'Precedent', 210–13. What we are doing at each step—both in deciding cases, and in describing past decisions—is trying to state 'truths of the common law'. Ibid. at 210.

[175] Of course, believing that there are moral kinds, even if that belief becomes widespread, offers no guarantee that people will agree on what the moral kind *is* for a particular line of legal or precedential reasoning.

[176] Moore, 'Precedent', 210.

[177] See e.g. Dworkin, *Law's Empire*, 313–99; Moore, 'Interpretation', 338–58; Antonin Scalia, *A Matter of Interpretation* (1997).

[178] Moore, 'Interpretation', 323.   [179] ibid. at 338–58.

[180] ibid. at 287. Again, as with the analysis of precedent, while metaphysical realism regarding legislative interpretation may change the type of questions being asked, and remove some insoluble problems, it by no means guarantees consensus.

[181] ibid. at 331–8, 383.

3. More generally, legal reasoning and interpretation should be derived from 'the moral reality' (and never merely from people's conventional beliefs regarding moral matters).[182]

4. Moral realism, like any other form of right-answer theory (e.g. Ronald Dworkin's),[183] would direct judges to keep looking for the unique right answer to the difficult questions they face, rather than giving up the matter on the basis of policy or personal preference.[184]

An interesting aspect of Moore's approach, already noted, is that he prefers a coherence-theory approach to knowledge. This sometimes leaves him vulnerable to the charge that his moral realism, at least its ontological aspect, is doing no work.[185] When he contrasts his moral realist view with 'conventionalist' forms of coherence reasoning, he argues for the superiority of the former because it has room for 'mistake' and justifies the final conclusions not by mere 'conventional acceptance' but 'by correspondence with what there is'.[186] However, if our only way of determining 'what there is' is coherence with conventional beliefs, then the differences may seem to be more in packaging than in substance.

Moore offers a variety of responses to this line of argument. First, he concedes that his theory is one focused on ontology (what there is), not epistemology (what we know and how we justify our claims of knowledge), but he considers this concession far from fatal.[187] Secondly, he argues that metaphysical realism *explains* our beliefs and practices better than alternative approaches; that is, the theory is important because it is *true*, even if it would not or did not affect our practices.[188] Thirdly, he argues that moral realism may be of value in that it can *justify* existing practices that might seem problematic under a different moral or metaphysical view of the world.[189] A related point: if judges see themselves as acting on the basis of 'the true nature of things' rather than merely acting on the basis of personal idiosyncratic beliefs or conventional beliefs, this will (rightfully) affect the attitude the judges carry towards the legitimacy of their actions.[190] Fourthly, he reaffirms his assertion that

---

[182] Moore, 'Interpretation', 286–8.

[183] See e.g. Dworkin, *Taking Rights Seriously*, 123–30. Moore offers a strong argument that Dworkin cannot maintain both his opposition to metaphysical realism and his 'right answer thesis'. Moore, 'Metaphysics, Epistemology and Legal Theory', 475–94.

[184] Moore, 'Interpretation', 308; Moore, 'Moral Reality Revisited', 2480, 2484–7.

[185] See Bix, *Law, Language, and Legal Determinacy*, 148–50. For Moore's response to this line of argument, see Moore, 'Moral Reality Revisited', 2470–91.

[186] Moore, 'Precedent', 209.   [187] See Moore, 'Moral Reality Revisited', 2470–2.

[188] See e.g. ibid. at 2452–68, 2471–2, 2511–18.

[189] See Moore, 'Moral Reality Revisited', 2472 ('moral realism can make sense of some of our adjudicatory practices such as judicial review—and thereby give us a reason to continue them, or modify them, as the case may be—that moral conventionalism and moral skepticism cannot').

[190] ibid. at 2469–91. This argument is tied in with the claim that moral realism can justify unconventional, indeed revolutionary, responses to moral, legal, and political questions, in a way that non-realist approaches cannot. See ibid.

metaphysical and moral realism *do make a difference* to how judges (should) act[191] (a view summarized elsewhere in this section).

One category of questions that is prominently raised by Moore's work, but that is relevant to many other modern writers within the natural law tradition, is the extent to which questions of moral philosophy or meaning can or should pre-empt other apparently political or institutional issues. Sometimes theorists seem to be arguing that once one understands the truth regarding metaphysical realism or the like, certain traditional questions about institutional roles and legal processes will be seen to be easily resolved or, perhaps, irrelevant. These are matters on which Moore himself is usually sensitive: for example, to what extent should a judge decline to reach the morally correct common law decision because prior judicial decisions came out the other way?[192] In other words, should judges affirm wrong or partly wrong decisions in deference to 'rule of law' values or similar concerns about consistency, reliance, predictability, equality, and the like? A comparable question arises elsewhere in judicial reasoning, in particular in constitutional interpretation: to what extent should judges (who ascribe to natural law thinking) act on the view that the natural law is a part of the country's foundational law, or otherwise incorporate natural law learning into (all) legal interpretations, even (or especially) if prior judicial decisions have taken a different view?[193] While it is hard to find real-world advocates for the extreme view that natural law truths should always trump institutional, 'rule of law' reasons for adhering to mistaken precedent, one *can* find prominent natural law theorists arguing for a position on the other extreme, that the natural law tradition offers *no* views on judicial decision-making other than to instruct judges to defer to whatever the institutional and interpretative rules are within the legal system in question.[194]

2.6 Other Natural Law Legal Theories

There are a variety of other recent theories of law that might fit into the category of natural law. Late in his book, *The Concept of Law*, in the course of describing where law and morality overlap, H. L. A. Hart introduces the notion of 'the minimum content of natural law'.[195] The discussion occurred in the context of offering an overview of the various ways in which morality and law *do* overlap (overlaps consistent with the legal positivist dogma that there is no 'necessary' or 'conceptual' connection between the two). Hart speculates that any system of law or conventional morality that does not offer at least minimal protections (e.g. against violent assault) to at least

191 See e.g. ibid. at 2480–91.
192 See e.g. Moore, 'Precedent', 201–4, 209–10; Moore, 'Interpretation', 372.
193 Cf. Sebok, *Legal Positivism in American Jurisprudence*, 222–30 (describing 'strong epistemic natural law' approaches to constitutional interpretation).
194 For this view, see e.g. George, *In Defense of Natural Law*, 102–12; see also Wolfe, 'Judicial Review'.
195 Hart, *The Concept of Law*, 193–200.

some significant minority of the population (as might be done in societies where an elite minority rules, while the majority population is enslaved or otherwise treated as second-class citizens) could not long survive. While there is a slight resemblance, more in title than in substance, between Hart's discussion and traditional natural law theory, the similarities do not run very deep.[196] Hart is making an empirical claim— though one that purports to cover human society for as long as human beings and human societies have the (contingent) scarcities, needs, and vulnerabilities that we have now.[197] He is not offering a moral theory or a conceptual argument; he does not claim that anything follows for criteria of legal validity or for how people should act within legal systems.[198]

Randy Barnett has offered a provocative twist to the traditional natural law approach.[199] Whereas many writers in this tradition advance theories along the line of 'given human nature and/or the nature of the cosmos, certain things follow (pre-scriptively)', Barnett's analysis follows the argument structure, 'given human nature, if one wants to obtain certain generally accepted social goals (security, prosperity, liberty, etc.), certain institutions and rules should be established'. What results in Barnett's work is a liberal-libertarian programme that will not be to every person's liking, but one might none the less appreciate the novel adaptation of a natural-law-like method of analysis and investigation.

A number of other approaches merit mention, though they can only be summarized briefly. Lloyd Weinreb has tried to reconstruct the original (that is, ancient Greek) understanding of natural law theory, natural law theory as viewing a normative order within nature.[200] Ernest Weinrib has analysed private law in terms borrowed from Aristotle and Kant—that private law has a set form from which we can determine, generally if not exhaustively, the moral obligations parties owe one another and the proper doctrinal rules and institutional structures that should be established.[201] Deryck Beyleveld and Roger Brownsword have put forward a legal

---

[196] For an interesting presentation of a different view, developing Hart's discussion in the direction of a more substantial (and more traditional) natural law approach, see Kenneth I. Winston, 'Introduction', in Lon L. Fuller, *The Principles of Social Order*, ed. Kenneth I. Winston (Durham, N.C.: Duke University Press, 1981), 11–44, at 24–6; see also Randy E. Barnett, *The Structure of Liberty* (Oxford: Clarendon Press, 1998), 10–12.

[197] See Hart, *The Concept of Law*, 199–200 ('for the adequate description not only of law but of many other social institutions, a place must be reserved, besides definitions and ordinary statements of fact, for a third category of statements: those the truth of which is contingent on human beings and the world they live in retaining the salient characteristics they have').

[198] See ibid. at 193–200; Bix, *Jurisprudence: Theory and Context*, 43–4.

[199] Randy E. Barnett, *The Structure of Liberty: Justice and the Rule of Law* (1998). For a detailed critique, see Lawrence B. Solum, 'The Foundations of Liberty' (book review), *Michigan Law Review*, 97 (1999), 1780.

[200] Weinreb, *Natural Law and Justice*. For a critical analysis of Weinreb's approach, see Robert P. George, 'Recent Criticism of Natural Law Theory' (book review), *University of Chicago Law Review*, 55 (1988), 1371, 1372–1407.

[201] Ernest J. Weinrib, *The Idea of Private Law* (Cambridge, Mass.: Harvard University Press, 1995).

theory based on Alan Gewirth's writings in moral philosophy.[202] And Richard Dien Winfield[203] and Alan Brudner[204] have offered theories of law grounded in a Hegelian view of society and law's role within it.

3 NATURAL LAW'S PLACE IN JURISPRUDENCE

It is time to take stock. How does natural law fit within the broader context of modern legal philosophy? The next section considers the boundary-drawing question of how, if at all, one can distinguish natural law theories of law from the (other) mainstream theory of law, legal positivism. The boundary confusions arise primarily from two sources: (*a*) the debate *within* legal positivism regarding the role of moral norms in law; and (*b*) efforts of some legal positivist theories to consider or explain the reason-giving aspects of law, while retaining whatever it is that makes theories 'legal positivist' rather than 'natural law'. In the final section, the chapter will consider more generally what role natural law theory does or should play within modern analytical jurisprudence.

3.1 Relationship with Legal Positivism

3.1.1 *Traditional Natural Law Theory and Legal Positivism*

The founder of modern legal positivism, H. L. A. Hart, offered the opinion that there was little if anything within a traditional natural law theory like that of John Finnis with which a legal positivist must disagree.[205] A similar assertion of general agreement has been offered by another prominent legal positivist, Neil MacCormick.[206] Finnis has returned the favour, in a sense, asserting that traditional natural law theory

---

[202] Deryck Beyleveld and Roger Brownsword, *Law as a Moral Judgment* (London: Sweet & Maxwell, 1986).

[203] Richard Dien Winfield, *Law in Civil Society* (Kansas: University Press of Kansas, 1995).

[204] Alan Brudner, *The Unity of the Common Law: Studies in Hegelian Jurisprudence* (Berkeley, Calif.: University of California Press, 1995).

[205] See H. L. A. Hart, *Essays in Jurisprudence and Philosophy* (Oxford: Clarendon Press, 1983), 10–11 (Finnis's natural law theory as being 'in many respects complementary to rather than a rival to positivist legal theory').

[206] Neil MacCormick, 'Natural Law and the Separation of Law and Morals', in *Natural Law Theory: Contemporary Essays*, ed. Robert P. George (Oxford: Clarendon Press, 1992), 105–33.

would be able to accept and affirm most of the statements that have been offered as tenets of legal positivism.[207]

Even if one accepts that traditional natural law theory might be compatible with legal positivism, one should consider the argument that traditional natural law theory—and, indeed, any comprehensive moral or ethical theory—undermines the project of legal positivism. The argument, generally, is that law might be best seen as part of a larger normative enterprise: with the larger normative theory determining what rules should be enacted, how the legal system should be run, and how citizens and officials should act within the system. When describing a reason-giving institution like law, it would seem natural to distinguish (morally) good reasons from bad reasons, and if one believes that one has a moral theory at hand (of a natural law kind or otherwise) for making such distinctions, the choice to avoid such distinctions and evaluations seems strange.[208] All of the modern natural law theorists discussed in this essay—Fuller, Dworkin, Finnis, and Moore—have confronted, in one way or another, the extent to which moral issues should, or must, be considered when constructing a proper descriptive theory of law.

Finally, one should note Roger Shiner's argument, that as legal positivist theories become more sophisticated (to meet weaknesses in and criticisms of simpler forms of the theory), the resulting theories verge on natural law theories, in the sense that they come close to incorporating moral elements and moral evaluation within descriptive theories of law.[209] Shiner's point may be most obvious in some recent efforts by legal positivists to discuss the normative aspects of law in a detached and descriptive manner. The most prominent example may be H. L. A. Hart's use of the internal aspect of rules and law in his legal theory, which allowed theory *to take into account* the fact that participants in the practice 'accept' the legal norms as reasons for action, without in turn *endorsing* that judgment.[210] Consider also Joseph Raz, who, within his legal theory, builds much of his analysis from the assertion that 'every legal system claims that it possesses legitimate authority'.[211] (It is important in this context to emphasize the '*claim*' in the phrase 'claim . . . [to] possess legitimate authority', for Raz certainly does not believe that all legal systems *in fact* 'possess legitimate authority'.)[212] According to Raz, much follows from this truth about legal systems, because even to

[207] See John Finnis, 'The Truth in Legal Positivism', in *The Autonomy of Law: Essays in Legal Positivism*, ed. Robert P. George (Oxford: Clarendon Press, 1996), 195–214, at 203–5.

[208] See e.g. Winfield, *Law in Civil Society*, 2 ('Only by adopting a normatively indifferent stance can one entertain law as a discrete object of investigation warranting separate study'); a similar point is made in John M. Finnis, 'Problems in the Philosophy of Law'; see also the earlier discussion of Finnis's views, in Sect. 2.4.2.

[209] Roger A. Shiner, *Norm and Nature: The Movements of Legal Thought* (Oxford: Clarendon Press, 1992).

[210] Hart, *The Concept of Law*, 55–8, 91–9; see Brian Bix, 'H. L. A. Hart and the Hermeneutic Turn in Legal Theory', *SMU L. Rev.*, 52 (1999), 167.

[211] Raz, *Ethics in the Public Domain*, 199.

[212] Raz has elsewhere argued eloquently *against* the proposition that even just legal systems create a general obligation of obedience. See e.g. ibid. at 325–38; Raz, *The Authority of Law*, 233–49.

have the capacity to be authoritative law must offer guidance that can be followed without reference to the general (moral and prudential) reasons that the guidance was meant to supplant.[213] The point is not to evaluate the value or truth of Raz's argument,[214] but only to point out how Raz uses an aspiration that could easily be characterized as moral, the claim to possess legitimate authority, in a way that does not seem to 'taint' the moral neutrality of his analysis.

Relevant to the above discussion, one should note a problem frequently overlooked, or at least under-emphasized, in legal theory: the extent to which the claims being made about law are *special* to law, or are rather only a particular instance of a more general truth—for example, about all social institutions or all normative systems.[215] For example, consider the argument of critics of legal positivism, that it is inadvisable or impossible to separate the description of legal systems from their evaluation. If this argument is valid, it would seem likely (though by no means certain) that it would apply equally well to attempts to separate the description and evaluation of conventional morality.[216] One should be suspicious of theories that offer claims that purport to apply solely to law. One should test these claims in the context of other social institutions and other normative systems; to the extent that the claims do not seem valid in those other or broader contexts, there would be reason to doubt their validity in the legal context.[217]

3.1.2 *Modern Natural Law Theory and Inclusive Legal Positivism*

A number of countries have judicial review of the validity of legislation, that review grounded on a written constitution or some other source of higher principle. Some critics of legal positivism, in particular Ronald Dworkin, have argued that legal positivism cannot account adequately for such practices, and what is needed instead is a theory that does not claim a sharp separation of law and morality.[218]

Evaluating the merits of the criticism depends in part on interpreting the legal positivist claim that no necessary or conceptual connection exists between law and morality. Does this mean merely that moral evaluation *need not* be part of the test of

---

[213] See Raz, *Ethics in the Public Domain*, 199–204.

[214] For a variety of perspectives of Raz's argument, see e.g. Brian Leiter, 'Realism, Hard Positivism, and Conceptual Analysis', *Legal Theory*, 4 (1998), 533, 540–4; Waluchow, *Inclusive Legal Positivism*, 123–40; Jules L. Coleman, 'Incorporationism, Conventionality, and the Practical Difference Thesis', *Legal Theory*, 4 (1998), 381, 413–20.

[215] See e.g. Bix, *Jurisprudence: Theory and Context*, 7–8; Philip Soper, 'Legal Systems, Normative Systems, and the Paradoxes of Positivism', *Canadian Journal of Law and Jurisprudence*, 8 (1995), 363, 373; William Lucy, *Understanding and Explaining Adjudication* (Oxford: Oxford University Press, 1999), 17–38.

[216] Soper, 'Legal Systems, Normative Systems and the Paradoxes of Positivism', 373.

[217] Cf. Raz, *Ethics in the Public Domain*, 238–43 (analysing the general nature of rights: emphasizing some of the problems of building a theory based on what happens with *legal* rights, and discussing the question of whether legal rights are best understood as a sub-category of institution-based rights or, alternatively, as a sub-category of moral rights).

[218] See Dworkin, *Taking Rights Seriously*, 1–130.

legal validity (but *may* be part of such a test in particular legal systems),[219] or does it mean that moral evaluation *can never* be part of the test for legal validity?[220] The first perspective is that of 'inclusive' legal positivism;[221] the second is 'exclusive' legal positivism. Both views are discussed at length elsewhere in this book, but for the moment it is worth noting that both views see themselves as forms of legal positivism, to be distinguished from natural law theory. At the level of criteria of legal validity, the difference between inclusive legal positivism and some forms of natural law theory is one of modality: inclusive legal positivists argue that moral criteria *can* but *need not be* part of the test for whether a norm is legally valid, while some natural law theorists would argue that moral criteria are *always* and *necessarily* part of the test for legal validity. At the level of theory, inclusive legal positivists advocate a morally neutral description or conceptual analysis of law, while natural law theorists argue that law is best understood teleologically, within the context of a larger moral analysis. While the differences between inclusive legal positivism and some modern, law-focused versions of natural law theory might seem slight, they are differences of theoretical significance.

3.2 The Role of Natural Law Theory

As reviewed in Part I, natural law was historically an approach to morality, one centrally grounded on a certain view of metaphysics and/or epistemology, but none the less a theory of morality.[222] It might seem fair to wonder why *this* form of moral theory should receive special attention within jurisprudence, treating it as a major school of jurisprudence to which all other schools of thought must reply, while other approaches to morality do not get similar treatment. One rarely if ever sees reference to 'utilitarian legal theory' or 'deontological legal theory', and references to 'Kantian legal theory'[223] and 'Hegelian legal theory'[224] are only slightly more common.

However, as discussed earlier (Sect. 2.1), 'natural law' has, within the jurisprudential community, come to mean any theory in which moral evaluation is considered

---

[219] A somewhat different perspective on the same inclusive legal positivist view is that moral principles can be part of the test for legal validity if and only if this is authorized by some social convention (e.g. a written constitution or an earlier authoritative judicial ruling).

[220] Of course, by the claimed separation of law and morality, legal positivists do not mean to deny that morality does and should play a role in the creation and evaluation of legal rules and legal decisions. See e.g. Hart, *The Concept of Law*, 203–6.

[221] This is also known as 'incorporationism', 'soft legal positivism', and 'soft conventionalism'.

[222] As discussed in Part 1, what was distinctive or important about many traditional natural law theories was their *meta*-theoretical elements—their views on how one goes about finding moral truth—*not* for the moral conclusions they offered.

[223] See 'Symposium on Kantian Legal Theory', *Columbia Law Review*, 87 (1987), 419.

[224] See Brudner, *The Unity of the Common Law: Studies in Hegelian Jurisprudence*; Drucilla Cornell, Michel Rosenfeld, and David Gray Carlson (eds.), *Hegel and Legal Theory* (New York: Routledge, 1991).

central or necessary to *either* determining the content of legal rules, evaluating the legal status of particular rules or rule systems, or the analysis of the nature of law. One should note how divergent a group of claims this includes: (1) the old naive natural law theorists who had no particular views about adjudication or about theory-formation, but who believed that a rule or rule system should not gain the appellation 'law' unless and until it had met certain moral criteria; (2) institutional competence theorists like Lon Fuller and the legal process school,[225] who equate the label 'law' less with moral criteria than with criteria of institutional design and procedures followed; and (3) Ronald Dworkin and like-minded theorists who prescribe morality-laden processes for adjudication, prescriptions which could, in principle, be separated from any principles of theory-construction or any claims regarding when to call something law.[226] All of these have been clumped together in many discussions because, and only because, legal positivism has set the agenda for modern English-language jurisprudential debate, and legal positivism has set a morality-free approach to a variety of jurisprudential questions.

Two basic questions should be asked when evaluating the writers and debates summarized in this essay: (1) What criteria could be offered to judge the debates? and (2) What is at stake in the debates? In the arguments for and against the older and more traditional natural law theories, the nature of the claims are relatively easy to discern. Those natural law theorists are offering (*a*) a moral claim—this is how one should act; (*b*) a meta-ethical claim—this is how one goes about deciding moral questions; and/or (*c*) a meta-theoretical claim regarding legal philosophy—that one should approach the study of law through a perspective of practical reasoning or some form of teleological analysis. The nature of the claims in the debates surrounding many of the modern theories that carry the label 'natural law' are sometimes less well articulated and less obvious.

Much of the awkwardness of natural law theory's place within modern jurisprudence may be attributed to the mutual confusions between academics who specialize in legal theory and those natural law theorists (narrowly understood) who may be most comfortable with moral theory or metaphysics.[227] Some legal philosophers do not take the time to understand the rich moral-philosophy context from which natural law legal theories derive; similarly, some natural law theorists enter debates

---

[225] See e.g, Henry M. Hart, Jr. and Albert M. Sacks, *The Legal Process: Basic Problems in the Making and Application of the Law*, ed. William N. Eskridge, Jr. and Philip P. Frickey (Westbury, N.Y.: Foundation Press, 1994).

[226] Putting aside for the moment the fact that Dworkin himself does not view his theory as simple prescription, but rather as an interpretation which views current practices in their best possible light. Many theorists with views on adjudication similar to Dworkin's do not characterize their prescriptions as interpretations of current practices.

[227] Cf. Finnis, 'On the Incoherence of Legal Positivism', 1607–8 (criticizing the characterization of natural law theory by two prominent legal theorists) with ibid. at 1605 (discussing 'inclusive legal positivism' in a way that misunderstands its basic point).

about the nature of law without a full appreciation of the traditions within analytical jurisprudence.

Conclusion

Much of the natural law tradition is grounded in moral philosophy, a point too easily forgotten when natural law theory is brought into debates in other areas, and this forgetting has caused much of the misunderstanding of natural law doctrines within the jurisprudential literature. Natural law theory, in all of its permutations, *does* have things to say to and about legal theory. Perhaps the most important idea modern natural law theorists have brought to jurisprudence is that views of law that take into account law's moral aspirations offer a fuller, and thus better, understanding of that social institution, compared to views that ignore or marginalize such considerations.

FURTHER READING

Barnett, Randy E., 'A Law Professor's Guide to Natural Law and Natural Rights', *Harvard Journal of Law and Public Policy*, 20 (1997), 655.

—— *The Structure of Liberty: Justice and the Rule of Law* (New York: Oxford University Press, 1998).

Beyleveld, Deryck, and Brownsword, Roger, *Law as a Moral Judgment* (London: Sweet & Maxwell, 1986).

Bix, Brian, 'Natural Law Theory', in *A Companion to Philosophy of Law and Legal Theory*, ed. Dennis Patterson, 223–40 (Oxford: Blackwell, 1996).

—— 'On the Dividing Line Between Natural Law Theory and Legal Positivism', *Notre Dame Law Review*, 75 (2000), 1613.

Bobbio, Norberto, *Thomas Hobbes and the Natural Law Tradition*, trans. Daniela Gobetti (Chicago: University of Chicago Press, 1993).

Brudner, Alan, T*he Unity of the Common Law: Studies in Hegelian Jurisprudence* (Berkeley: University of California Press, 1995).

Buckle, Stephen, *Natural Law and the Theory of Property: Grotius to Hume* (Oxford: Clarendon Press, 1991).

Covell, Charles, *The Defence of Natural Law* (New York: St Martin's Press, 1994).

Curley, Edwin M., 'The State of Nature and Its Law in Hobbes and Spinoza', *Philosophical Topics*, 19 (1991), 97.

Del Vecchio, Giorgio, *The Formal Bases of Law*, 1st pub. 1914 (South Hackensack, NJ: Rothman Reprints, 1969).

d'Entrèves, Alexander Passerin, *Natural Law: An Introduction to Legal Philosophy*, 1st pub. 1951 (New Brunswick: Transaction Publishers, 1994).

Dworkin, Ronald, *Taking Rights Seriously* (London: Duckworth, 1977).

—— ' "Natural" Law Revisited', *University of Florida Law Review*, 34 (1982), 165.

—— *A Matter of Principle* (Cambridge, Mass.: Harvard University Press, 1985).

—— *Law's Empire* (Cambridge, Mass.: Harvard University Press, 1986).

Feinberg, Joel, 'The Central Tenets of Natural Law Theory', unpublished manuscript.

Finnis, John M., 'Blackstone's Theoretical Intentions', *Natural Law Forum*, 12 (1967), 163.

—— *Natural Law and Natural Rights* (Oxford: Clarendon Press, 1980).

—— (ed.), *Natural Law*, 2 vols. (New York: New York University Press, 1991).

—— 'The Truth in Legal Positivism', in *The Autonomy of Law: Essays on Legal Positivism*, ed. R. George (Oxford: Clarendon Press, 1996), 195–214.

—— *Aquinas: Moral, Political, and Legal Theory* (Oxford: Oxford University Press, 1998).

—— 'Natural Law', in *Routledge Encyclopedia of Philosophy*, vi (London: Routledge, 1998), 685–90.

—— 'On the Incoherence of Legal Positivism', *Notre Dame Law Review*, 75 (2000), 1597.

—— and Grisez, Germain, 'The Basic Principles of Natural Law: A Reply to Ralph McInerny', *American Journal of Jurisprudence*, 26 (1981), 21.

Forte, David F. (ed.), *Natural Law and Contemporary Public Policy* (Washington, DC: Georgetown University Press, 1998).

Fuller, Lon L., *The Morality of Law*, rev. edn. (New Haven: Yale University Press, 1969).

—— *The Principles of Social Order*, ed. Kenneth I. Winston (Durham, NC: Duke University Press, 1981).

Garet, Ronald R., 'Natural Law and Creation Stories', in *Religion, Morality and the Law, Nomos XXX*, ed. J. Roland Pennock and John W. Chapman (New York: New York University Press, 1988), 218–62.

George, Robert P., *Natural Law Theory: Contemporary Essays* (Oxford: Clarendon Press, 1992).

—— (ed.), *The Autonomy of Law: Essays on Legal Positivism* (Oxford: Clarendon Press, 1996).

—— *Natural Law, Liberalism, and Morality: Contemporary Essays* (Oxford: Clarendon Press, 1996).

—— 'Natural Law Ethics', in *A Companion to Philosophy of Religion*, ed. Philip L. Quinn and Charles Taliaferro (Oxford: Blackwell, 1997).

—— *In Defense of Natural Law* (Oxford: Clarendon Press, 1999).

Grisez, Germain G., 'The First Principle of Practical Reason: A Commentary on the *Summa theologiae*, 1–2, Question 94, Article 2', *Natural Law Forum*, 10 (1965), 168.

—— Boyle, Joseph, and Finnis, John, 'Practical Principles, Moral Truth, and Ultimate Ends', *American Journal of Jurisprudence*, 32 (1987), 99.

Grotius, Hugo, *De Jure Belli Ac Pacis Libri Tres*, trans. Francis W. Kelsey (Oxford: Clarendon Press, 1925).

Haakonssen, Knud, *Natural Law and Moral Philosophy: From Grotius to the Scottish Enlightenment* (Cambridge: Cambridge University Press, 1996).

—— 'The Significance of Protestant Natural-Law Theory', unpublished manuscript, presented at the Hester Seminar, 'Natural Law Theory: Historical and Contemporary Issues', Wake Forest University, Nov. 1997.

Hamburger, Philip A., 'Natural Rights, Natural Law, and American Constitutions', *Yale Law Journal*, 102 (1993), 907.

Hittinger, Russell, *A Critique of the New Natural Law Theory* (Notre Dame: University of Notre Dame Press, 1987).

—— 'Natural Law as "Law": Reflections on the Occasion of "Veritatis Splendor"', *American Journal of Jurisprudence*, 39 (1994), 1.

Hittinger, Russell, 'Varieties of Minimalist Natural Law Theory', *American Journal of Jurisprudence*, 34 (1989), 133.

Kelsen, Hans, 'The Natural-Law Doctrine before the Tribunal of Science', in *What is Justice?* (Berkeley: University of California Press, 1971), 137–73.

Kmiec, Douglas W., 'Natural-Law Originalism—Or Why Justice Scalia (Almost) Gets It Right', *Harvard Journal of Law and Public Policy*, 20 (1997), 627.

Lisska, Anthony J., *Aquinas's Theory of Natural Law: An Analytic Reconstruction* (Oxford: Oxford University Press, 1998).

Lyons, David, 'Moral Aspects of Legal Theory', *Midwest Studies in Philosophy*, 7 (1982), 223, repr. in *Moral Aspects of Legal Theory: Essays on Law, Justice, and Political Responsibility* (Cambridge: Cambridge University Press, 1993), 64–101.

McInerny, Ralph M., *St. Thomas Aquinas* (Notre Dame: University of Notre Dame Press, 1982).

—— 'Saint Thomas Aquinas', in *Stanford Encyclopedia of Philosophy*, http://plato.stanford.edu

Maritain, Jacques, THE RIGHTS OF MAN AND NATURAL LAW (New York: Charles Scribner's Sons, 1943).

Moore, Michael S., 'A Natural Law Theory of Interpretation', *Southern California Law Review*, 58 (1985), 277.

—— 'Precedent, Induction, and Ethical Generalization', in *Precedent in Law*, ed. Laurence Goldstein (Oxford: Clarendon Press, 1987), 183–213.

—— 'Law as a Functional Kind', in *Natural Law Theories: New Essays*, ed. Robert P. George (Oxford: Clarendon Press, 1992), 188–242.

—— 'Moral Reality Revisited', *Michigan Law Review*, 90 (1992), 2424.

—— 'Good Without God', in *Natural Law, Liberalism, and Morality*, ed. Robert P. George (Oxford: Clarendon Press, 1996), 221–70.

—— *Educating Oneself in Public: Critical Essays in Jurisprudence* (Oxford: Oxford University Press, 2000).

Novak, David, *Natural Law in Judaism* (Cambridge: Cambridge University Press, 1998).

'Propter Honoris Respectum: John Finnis', *Notre Dame Law Review*, 75 (2000), 1597–892.

Pufendorf, Samuel, *On the Duty of Man and Citizen According to Natural Law*, 1st pub. 1673, ed. James Tully, trans. Michael Silverthorne (Cambridge: Cambridge University Press, 1991).

Rommen, Heinrich A., *The Natural Law: A Study in Legal and Social History and Philosophy*, 1st pub. 1936; introd. by Russell Hittinger (Indianapolis: Liberty Fund, 1998).

Ross, Alf, 'Validity and the Conflict between Legal Positivism and Natural Law', in *Normativity and Norms: Critical Perspectives on Kelsenian Themes*, ed. Stanley L. Paulson and Bonnie Litschewski-Paulson (Oxford: Clarendon Press, 1999), 147–63.

Schneewind, Jerome (ed.), *Moral Philosophy from Montaigne to Kant: An Anthology*, i and ii (Cambridge: Cambridge University Press, 1990).

—— 'Kant and Natural Law Ethics', *Ethics*, 104 (1993), 53.

—— *The Invention of Autonomy: A History of Modern Moral Philosophy* (Cambridge: Cambridge University Press, 1998).

Shiner, Roger, *Norm and Nature: The Movements of Legal Thought* (Oxford: Clarendon Press, 1992).

Simon, Yves René Marie, *The Tradition of Natural Law: A Philosopher's Reflections*, ed. Vukan Kuic, introd. by Russell Hittinger (New York: Fordham University Press, 1992).

Soper, Philip, 'Legal Theory and the Problem of Definition' (book review), *University of Chicago Law Review*, 50 (1983), 1170.

—— 'Making Sense of Modern Jurisprudence: The Paradox of Positivism and the Challenge for Natural Law', *Creighton Law Review*, 22 (1988), 67.

—— 'Some Natural Confusions About Natural Law', *Michigan Law Review*, 90 (1992), 2393.

'Special Issue on Lon Fuller', *Law and Philosophy*, 13 (1994), 253–418.

Strauss, Leo, *Natural Right and History* (Chicago: University of Chicago Press, 1953).

Suárez, Francisco, *Selections from Three Works of Francisco Suárez*, 2 vols. (Oxford: Clarendon Press, 1944).

Summers, Robert S., *Lon L. Fuller* (Stanford, Calif.: Stanford University Press, 1984).

Sweet, William, 'Jacques Maritain', in *Stanford Encyclopedia of Philosophy*, http://plato.stanford.edu

Tierney, Brian, *The Idea of Natural Rights: Studies on Natural Rights, Natural Law and Church Law* (Atlanta: Scholars Press, 1997), 1150–625.

Tuck, Richard, *Natural Rights Theories: Their Origin and Development* (Cambridge: Cambridge University Press, 1979).

—— 'The Dangers of Natural Rights', *Harvard Journal of Law and Public Policy*, 20 (1997), 683.

Veatch, Henry B., 'Book Review', *American Journal of Jurisprudence*, 26 (1981), 247.

Weinreb, Lloyd L., *Natural Law and Justice* (Cambridge, Mass.: Harvard University Press 1987).

Weinrib, Ernest J., *The Idea of Private Law* (Cambridge, Mass.: Harvard University Press, 1995).

Wieacker, Franz, *A History of Private Law in Europe: with particular reference to Germany*, trans. Tony Weir (Oxford: Clarendon Press, 1995), 199–256.

Winfield, Richard Dien, *Law in Civil Society* (Lawrence, Kan.: University Press of Kansas, 1995).

Winston, Kenneth I., 'The Ideal Element in a Definition of Law', *Law and Philosophy*, 5 (1986), 89.

Wolfe, Christopher, 'Judicial Review', in *Natural Law and Contemporary Public Policy*, ed. David F. Forte (Washington, DC: Georgetown University Press, 1998).

Wright, R. George, 'Natural Law in the Post-Modern Era' (book review), *American Journal of Jurisprudence*, 36 (1991), 203.

Wueste, Daniel E., 'Fuller's Processual Philosophy of Law' (book review), *Cornell Law Review*, 71 (1986), 1205.

Zuckert, Michael P., 'Do Natural Rights Derive From Natural Law?', *Harvard Journal of Law and Public Policy*, 20 (1997), 695.

CHAPTER 3

EXCLUSIVE LEGAL POSITIVISM

ANDREI MARMOR

Most contemporary legal positivists share the view that there are conventional rules of recognition, namely, conventions which determine certain facts or events that are taken to yield established ways for the creation, modification, and annulment of legal standards. These facts are the *sources of law* conventionally identified as such in each and every modern legal system. The purpose of this chapter is to consider some of the conceptual relations between the conventionally identified sources of law and the idea of legal validity. In particular, I will strive to defend here a 'strong' or 'exclusive' version of legal positivism, mainly against its 'inclusive' or 'incorporatist' rivals.

The kind of exclusive positivism I have in mind would basically hold that legal validity is exhausted by reference to the conventional sources of law: all law is source based, and anything which is not source based is not law. This formulation is, of course, much too crude and we shall have to refine it as we go along. For the time being, however, it suffices for the purpose of defining the main controversies about legal validity, and these are basically about the relations between law and morality. Exclusive positivism denies, whereas inclusive positivism accepts, that there can be instances where determining what the law is, follow from moral considerations about that which it is there to settle. Contemporary anti-positivists, like Dworkin, claim that determining what the law is *always* requires such moral considerations about what the law should be, and thus they reject the sources thesis as incoherent.

I am indebted to Jules Coleman, Joseph Raz, and Scott Shapiro for discussing with me many of the issues presented in this chapter.

Though both Dworkin and inclusive legal positivists share the view that there are close relations between morality and legal validity, they differ on the grounds of these relations. Dworkin maintains that the dependence of legal validity on moral considerations is an essential feature of law which basically derives from law's profound interpretative nature. Inclusive positivism, on the other hand, maintains that such a dependence of legal validity on moral considerations is a contingent matter; it does not derive from the nature of law or of legal reasoning as such. Inclusive positivists claim that moral considerations affect legal validity only in certain cases, namely, in those which follow from the rules of recognition which happen to prevail in a given legal system. In other words the relevance of morality is determined in any legal system by the contingent content of that society's rules of recognition. As opposed to both these views, exclusive legal positivism maintains that a norm is never rendered legally valid solely in virtue of its moral content. Legal validity, according to this view which I will strive to defend here, is entirely dependent on the conventionally recognized sources of law.

A First Look at The Sources Thesis

Why should we think that legal validity is exhausted by reference to the conventionally identified sources of law? Why is it the case that a norm is not legally valid unless it derives its validity from one of the conventionally identified sources? There are two basic arguments supporting the sources thesis which I would like to defend here. The first argument derives directly from the conventional foundation of law, which I have articulated elsewhere in greater detail.[1] The second argument was presented by Joseph Raz, and it concerns the authoritative nature of law.

Before we proceed, however, a few clarifications about the concept of legal validity are called for. To begin with, it should not be assumed that legal validity is co-extensive with the membership of norms in a legal system. The latter is more restricted; norms can be legally valid even if they do not belong to the legal system in which they are applied. Norms of public international law can be valid in a certain legal system, even if they do not belong to it. Similarly, according to familiar provisions of private international law, it is often the case that the legal norms of a foreign country are legally valid with regards to a given dispute, and bear on its legal consequences. These foreign norms, however, do not gain membership in the legal system which applies them.

Could it be said, then, that the legally valid norms are those norms which judges (and other officials) are legally bound to apply? This would seem to be a mistake. Judges may be legally bound to apply norms and other considerations which are not,

---

[1] See my 'Legal Conventionalism', *Legal Theory*, 4 (1998), 509.

by themselves, legally valid, and vice versa; there may be legally valid norms judges are not bound to apply (e.g. because the issue is not justiciable, etc.).

It seems that the best way to define legal validity is by its affinity with truth. This is partly suggested by the fact that validity is a phase-sortal concept: norms can either be legally valid, or not. Legal validity, like truth, does not admit of degrees. (I am neither denying, nor suggesting, that legal validity is logically bivalent, or that it excludes the possibility of indeterminacy. I am only suggesting here that legal validity does not admit of degrees.) Thus, we can say, uncontroversially, I hope, that a norm, say N, is legally valid in a system S, at time T, if and only if, the proposition— 'According to the law of system S, at time T, N'—is true. Part of what is entailed by the conventional foundations of the law is, that the truth conditions of propositions of this kind are reducible to truths about social conventions combined with truths about particular facts or events.

This brings us to the first argument for the sources thesis. The argument is based on the conventional foundations of law and the essentially constitutive nature of the conventions of recognition. I have argued elsewhere at some length that it is an essential element of such a social practice like law, that it is founded on constitutive conventions, namely, on a set of conventions which determine what the practice is, and how one goes about engaging in it. The rules of recognition of modern legal systems define the ways in which law is to be created, and they define them in ways which tie the creation of law to certain conventionally established sources.[2] Why couldn't it be the case, then, that such conventions also constitute ways of recognizing law simply by moral or political argument? Basically, this cannot be the case because there is nothing the conventions could constitute there. There is no role constitutive conventions can play in determining that people should act according to moral reasons. Politics, morality, ethics, and similar considerations bear on our practical reasoning regardless of conventions. Constitutive conventions can make a difference only by determining specific ways in which such moral, political, and other types of concerns become part of law, that is, part of a conventionally established social practice. And this is precisely what the conventions of recognition do: they constitute practices of making law, changing it, applying it to novel cases, and the like.

Actually, this is not so simple. Conventions do play significant roles in shaping some of our moral conceptions, particularly with respect to the so-called 'thick' moral concepts. The content of such thick concepts as 'shame', 'chastity', 'politeness', and so on, is partly determined by social conventions. I do not wish to deny this. The point here is different, namely, that constitutive conventions have no role to play in determining that we should act according to moral reasons. Moral and other practical reasons are there to be acted upon, regardless of conventions. Conventions can constitute part (but only a part!) of what it means to act morally in this or that situation. But they cannot constitute reasons for acting according to reasons.

---

[2] 'Legal Conventionalism', n. 1 above.

It is easy to misunderstand the constitutive function of the conventions of recognition by assuming that it is essentially motivated by an epistemic concern with certainty about the law. A widespread view attributed to positivism is that unless law is conventionally identified, it would be uncertain, and hence it would either defeat its own rationale in rendering certain all that which morality and prudence leave fuzzy or controversial, or else the law would face difficulties in fulfilling its putative social or moral-political functions.[3] Both these concerns about the certainty of law are beside the point. The function or point of constitutive conventions does not consist in rendering certain, or unequivocal, aspects of our lives which would otherwise remain uncertain and fuzzy; their point is to constitute a social domain which is valuable and worth engaging in. The constitutive conventions of theatre, for example, are not there to render more certain and concrete some pre-existing but vague conception of theatre, which had been there before the conventions were in place, as it were. Without the constitutive conventions, there is no theatre (nor concept of theatre). And without the constitutive conventions of recognition, there is no practice of law. Thus, by claiming that the rationale of the constitutive conventions of law is to determine ways in which moral and political reasoning become part of law, we need not think that the function of such conventions is to turn something vague and fuzzy into something more certain and concrete. It is not the preoccupation with certainty that matters here, but the idea of a social practice which is constituted by conventions. The conventions determine what the practice is; their function is constitutive and not epistemic.

I venture to guess that some critics have made this mistake because they tend to confuse the function of the rules of recognition, which is constitutive of what counts as law, with the various social and political functions of the law itself, which is a different issue altogether. It is certainly true that amongst the numerous functions and purposes of law in our society, it serves many which have an epistemic character. Certainty and predictability are among the values law is able to enhance in numerous areas, and part of its legitimacy can be derived from such epistemic functions it serves (that is, of course, to the extent that the law is legitimate). But none of this bears on the particular role of the rules of recognition, which is, again, constitutive and not epistemic.

So now we can return to the main argument. Conventions, I have argued, cannot determine ways of making law simply by moral and political arguments, because

---

[3] It should be admitted that Hart's own characterization of the rules of recognition in the fifth chapter of *The Concept of Law* (Oxford: Oxford University Press, 1961; 2nd edn. 1994), emphasizing their role in solving the problem of uncertainty in the recognition of law, could certainly give rise to this interpretation. Hart's account, however, is ambiguous. According to one possible, and to my mind, plausible, interpretation, we can read Hart's idea about the epistemic aspect of the rules of recognition as an historical speculation, suggesting that the emergence of those rules was driven, in large part, by the need of certainty in the identification of law. According to another interpretation, which is less plausible, enhancing certainty is the function or rationale or such rules. See also Hart's postscript published in the second edition, p. 251.

there is no constitutive function they can possibly have there. Conventions cannot constitute reasons for acting according to moral reasons; they can only shape the particular ways in which actions (or opinions, etc.) form a well-structured social practice.[4] Perhaps I should add that there is no co-ordinative function conventions can fulfil here either. A co-ordination convention in the realm of moral-political reasoning can only determine *who* it is that we should listen to when we must reach an agreement on how to act, and we cannot reach it on our own, as it were. But then the convention does not make law depend on moral considerations. On the contrary, it makes it depend on the decision of the agent (or some other decision procedure) who has been assigned by the convention to determine the outcome in such cases.

The essential point, however, is this: conventions cannot constitute a practice which consists in the expectation that people who engage in the practice do that which they would have reason to do regardless of the practice. Now, it is true that the constitutive conventions themselves are prone to be affected by the values inherent in the practice which is constituted by them. But this is an historical process which involves a gradual change of the conventions themselves. From an historical perspective, constitutive conventions tend to be under constant interpretative pressure, which is partly due to external needs and values of a changing world, and partly due to novel interpretations of those same values which are inherent in the practice. But this is always a slow, gradual, almost invisible process that takes place over time, and it results in changes of the conventions themselves.[5] Evaluative arguments, good and ingenious as they may be, do not, by themselves, constitute conventions, even if they are generally accepted as good arguments. Even if people realize that 'It ought to be that it is a convention that *P*', it simply does not follow that 'It is a convention that *P*' (though in due course, a *P* convention may emerge). In other words, the dynamic aspect of conventionally constituted practices, like law and artistic genres, does not undermine their conventional foundation. And once we admit the conventional foundation of law, it no longer makes sense to say that the law can be identified as such on the basis of moral or political considerations alone.

Let us turn now to the second argument for the sources thesis, suggested by Raz and based on his conception of authority.[6] The basic insight of Raz's argument is, that the law is an authoritative social institution. The law, Raz claims, is a *de facto* authority. However, it is also essential to law that it must be held to *claim legitimate* authority. Any particular legal system may fail, of course, in its fulfilment of this claim. But the law is the kind of institution which necessarily claims to be a legitimate authority.[7] Now, it is a necessary condition of an authority's legitimacy that it be able to

---

[4] I don't want to deny, of course, that there are particular moral and political concerns which are created by the existence of certain legal institutions.

[5] With one major exception: a revolution. Accounting for revolutionary changes of legal systems is a serious challenge for conventionalism, but I cannot hope to face it here.

[6] See J. Raz, *Ethics in the Public Domain* (Oxford: Oxford University Press, 1994), ch. 9.

[7] In chapter 2 of my book *Positive Law and Objective Values* (Oxford: Oxford University Press, 2001), I argue that law's claim to legitimacy necessarily follows from its authoritative nature.

prescribe for its subjects reasons for action that the subjects would be better off complying with, as compared to their attempts to act on those reasons directly, without the mediation of the authority's directive. This is what Raz calls the authority's essential mediating role. Hence it follows that for something to be able to claim legitimate authority, it must be of *the kind of thing* capable of claiming it, namely, capable of fulfilling such a mediating role.

What kinds of things can claim legitimate authority? There are at least two such features necessary for authority-capacity, and each one of them is sufficient to support the sources thesis: first, for something to be able to claim legitimate authority, it must be the case that its directives are *identifiable* as such, namely, as authoritative directives, without the necessity to rely on those same reasons which the authoritative directive is there to replace. If this condition is not met, namely, if it is impossible to identify the authoritative directive as such without relying on those same reasons the authority was meant to rely on, then the authority could not fulfil its essential, mediating role; it could not make the practical difference it is there to make. Note that this argument does not concern the efficacy of authorities. The point is not that unless authoritative directives can be recognized as such, authorities could not function effectively. The argument is based on the rationale of authorities within our practical reasoning. Authorities are there to make a practical difference, and they could not make such a difference unless the authority's directive can be recognized as such without recourse to the reasons it is there to decide upon.

Secondly, but this is an argument I will not attempt to substantiate here, for something to be able to claim legitimate authority, it must be the case that the authority is capable of forming an opinion on how its subjects ought to behave, distinct from the subjects' own reasoning about their reasons for action.[8] In other words, a practical authority, like law, must be basically personal authority, in the sense that there cannot be an authority without an author.

Now, it is not difficult to see that this conception of legal authority entails the sources thesis, since it requires that the law, *qua* an authoritative resolution, be identifiable on its own terms, that is, without having to rely on those same considerations which the law is there to settle. Therefore a norm is legally valid (i.e. authoritative) only if its validity does not derive from moral or other evaluative considerations about that which it is there to settle.

There is, of course, much more to be said about these two arguments for the sources thesis. For now, however, it suffices to see how both Raz's argument from the authoritative nature of law and the conventional foundation of law at least initially support the sources thesis. It is now time to consider the alternative view, namely, the idea of inclusive positivism.

---

[8] See my 'Authorities and Persons', *Legal Theory*, 1 (1995), 337.

INCLUSIVE LEGAL POSITIVISM

Inclusive, legal positivism is not one doctrine, but several, closely related ones, and I will distinguish them shortly. There are two main points, however, which are characteristic of inclusive positivism: first, unlike Dworkin's theory, inclusive positivism adheres to the basic idea that law is recognized as such on the basis of social conventions. In other words, inclusive positivism subscribes to the thesis about the conventional foundation of law.[9] Secondly, and this is what distinguishes the soft from the strong version of positivism, it seems to share a conviction that at least some of Dworkin's arguments against the sources thesis are sound. Inclusive positivists agree with Dworkin that there must be more to law than that which derives from the conventionally identified sources of law. Some moral or political principles are valid law, just in virtue of being sound moral principles. Before I turn to distinguish between the various doctrines that have emerged from this general conviction, however, I would like to provide a brief sketch of the main motivations which underlie it, and the reasons for the uneasiness many positivists feel with respect to the strong interpretation of the sources thesis.

Why are legal philosophers drawn to think that moral principles can be legal norms, just by virtue of being the correct moral principles that apply to the circumstances? Roughly speaking, I think that there are two main motivations for holding such a view: first, because judges say so. Secondly, because it seems that the law itself prescribes it. Let me try to explain both of these points.

Much of the plausibility of the criticism of the sources thesis derives from judicial rhetoric. In the Anglo-American legal systems (and many others) one often finds judicial rhetoric which seems to support the view that there is more to law than that which derives from its conventionally established sources. There are numerous moral and political principles judges feel bound to rely on, and apply to their decisions, whose validity cannot be traced back to the conventional sources of law. True, some of those principles have become part of law by incorporation through precedent, which is a conventional source of law. But at least judicial rhetoric seems to suggest that often it is not in virtue of their source that judges regard certain principles as legally binding, but in virtue of their content.

The argument does not end, however, with pointing to judicial rhetoric. It is more sophisticated than this. It claims that it is on positivism's own terms that such rhetoric ought to be taken seriously. After all, it is the conventionalists—as opposed to the natural lawyers—who claim that the law simply is what judges and lawyers

---

[9] See e.g. J. Coleman, 'Second Thoughts and Other First Impressions', in B. Bix (ed.), *Analyzing Law: New Essays in Legal Theory* (Oxford: Oxford University Press, 1998), 257; H. L. A. Hart, *The Concept of Law*, postscript, 2nd edn., ed. J. Raz and P. Bulloch (Oxford: Oxford University Press, 1994), 234.

think that it is.[10] Since it is a fact that the judges themselves think that there is more to law than that which derives from conventionally established sources, the sources thesis is undermined on conventionalism's own grounds.

A similar line of reasoning is suggested by the second argument. Instead of relying on judicial rhetoric, it relies on the content of the law itself. Many critics of the sources thesis think that we simply cannot do away with the vast number of occasions where the law itself makes the legal validity of norms depend on moral and political considerations, particularly, though not exclusively, in the realm of constitutional law. After all, it is a remarkable feature of modern constitutional documents that they prescribe moral and political reasoning for the purposes of determining the legal validity of norms. And it is a common practice of constitutional adjudication to turn this into reality, namely, by validating or invalidating norms on the grounds of moral and political principles.[11] Isn't all this is too familiar and too central to the functioning of modern legal systems to be swept away by a dogmatic adherence to the sources thesis? It is in a way, then, the desire to bring theory in line with the practice, which motivates inclusive positivism. Legal practice strikes many conventionalists to be much more affected by moral reasoning than the sources thesis would seem to allow. The essential question is, however, whether we can make sense of this inclusive positivist theory. As I have already indicated, it is not one doctrine, but several, and it is now time to distinguish between them.

There are, basically, three versions of inclusive positivism that I will take up in turn. The first maintains that the rules of recognition need not exclusively consist of source constraints on legal validity; they may also incorporate, in addition to the sources of law, moral principles as criteria of legality. The second and third versions do concede that such source constraints are inevitable, but they attempt to incorporate morality either by claiming that entailed law is also law or, as the more popular version has it, that the law itself can explicitly incorporate morality as a validity condition, on the grounds of its own sources.

The first and strongest version of inclusive positivism maintains that the rules of recognition need not turn the validity of legal norms to depend exclusively on conventionally identified sources (though they would typically do that as well).[12] A rule of recognition, on this view, can take the following form: the law is whatever follows from sources $S_{i...n}$, and whatever follows from the correct moral reasons—or some specific subset of such reasons—that apply to the circumstances.[13]

---

[10] This is not quite accurate: conventionalism is committed to the view that the content of law is what judges and lawyers think that it is. It is not committed to the view that judges' views on the nature of their activity is conclusive of anything. As I have argued elsewhere, people can follow conventions even if they are not aware of the conventional nature of the rules they follow. See n. 1 above.

[11] See, e.g. W. J. Waluchow, *Inclusive Legal Positivism* (Oxford: Oxford University Press, 1994), 113–17.

[12] Hart, postscript, p. 250; recently advanced by Jules Coleman, see e.g. 'Second Thoughts and Other First Impressions', *Concept of Law*, n. 9 above.

[13] Coleman has made it very clear, though, that he does not think that inclusive positivism is a necessary feature of law: it is possible, he claims, for a legal system to exist, whose rules of recognition prescribe

We have already seen what the initial motivation for holding such a view would be, namely, that it would seem to be more in accord with contemporary judicial rhetoric, and perhaps even more so, with (the rhetoric of) contemporary constitutional law, particularly in the major Western democracies. But the question is, whether there are any arguments which could support such a view, and still remain faithful to the conventional foundation of law, that inclusive positivism adheres to. As a matter of fact, we have already noted one main reason why the answer must be negative. The source constraint which is embodied in the rules of recognition is not a peculiarity of particular legal systems, or even of law, as such. It stems from the constitutive nature of the conventions of recognition: it simply makes no sense to suggest that conventions can constitute a practice which partly consists in the expectation that people do that which they have reasons to do regardless of the practice.

As a possible rejoinder to this line of reasoning consider the following argument. The rules of recognition are conventional rules. Like other rules, their application to particular cases can be controversial, morally, politically, or otherwise. Therefore, the argument concludes, it may well be a matter of moral or political argument determining what a rule of recognition actually prescribes in particular cases, and therefore it is at least sometimes the case that determining what the law is, depends on moral considerations about what it ought to be.[14]

This argument is almost persuasive. After all, rules and conventions can always be controversial, and some of those controversies are bound to rely on moral considerations. But the main flaw in the argument under consideration is that it assumes that there is a potential gap between the convention, which is a rule, and its application, a gap that can be bridged by moral or political arguments. The main reply to this is, that there is no such a gap. The convention is constituted by the practice of its application to particular cases. It is not the case that we first have a rule-formulation, say that convention 'R' prescribes so and so, and then we try to make up our minds how to apply R to particular cases (and then, as this story goes, sometimes we know the answer, and sometimes we argue about it). Conventions are what they are, because there is a practice of applying the rule to certain cases; it is the application of the rule which constitutes its very existence. Once it is not clear to the norm subjects whether the convention applies to a certain case or not, then there is no conventional solution to that matter, and at least as far as the convention is concerned, this is the end of it. People can have different views about the convention they would want to have in those circumstances (or how, otherwise, they would like to solve the problem they face), but they cannot have an intelligent argument about what the convention *really*

source-based law as the exclusive conditions of legality. The thesis which acknowledges this possibility he dubbed 'Negative Positivism'. He is less clear, however, about the question whether source constraints are necessary or not. Namely, whether he thinks that it could be the case that the rules of recognition do not embody any source constraints whatsoever. Could the rule of recognition only prescribe that law is whatever is morally the right thing to do, or something like this?

[14] If I understand it correctly, this is, at least, part of Coleman's argument.

requires in those controversial cases. The only reality there is to a convention is the actual practice of its application; a social practice. In the case of conventional rules, there is no gap between the rule and its application, a gap which could be bridged by an interpretative reasoning preferring one application to another. Once the application of a convention is not clear there is no convention on that matter.

To illustrate this by a simple example, consider the conventions of a natural language. It is a convention of the English language that the time of day at 9 a.m. is appropriately called 'morning' and it is not clear, from that convention's perspective, whether one can apply the notion of 'morning' to 11.30 a.m. or not. Does it make any sense to ask what is it that the notational convention of 'morning' really requires in the latter case? Hardly. The only thing we could say is that people would not be making a mistake either way, and that if it is important for some reason or other whether 11.30 is 'morning' or not (and one can easily imagine situations where it would be, e.g. in some legal context), then one must decide either way according to the appropriate considerations which would apply to the circumstances, given the fact that as far as the notational convention goes, it could go either way.[15]

Similar examples are abundant in law. Take, for instance, the rules of recognition concerning the doctrine of precedent. In all the jurisdictions which have such conventions, they would normally include some notion about the life expectancy of precedents; how far back in history one could go in search of a binding precedent. Different jurisdictions have different conventions about these matters. But of course, no such convention can be very accurate. Once we face a borderline case, the only thing to say about it is that it is a borderline case, namely, that there is no convention about that matter and that the question must be answered on its merits.

Perhaps there is a better argument to make here. Suppose the conventions of recognition somehow presuppose some general constraints on legal validity which consist in adherence to some shared communal values, or certain conceptions of fairness, or the like. Could it not then be controversial what those, for example, conceptions of fairness really require? And if so, would it not be a case where the appropriate *application* of the rule of recognition turns on moral arguments?

Conventions can, of course, determine their application conditional upon other, non-conventional considerations. It is a widely shared convention, for instance, that one should greet (in a conventionally recognized manner) one's friends and acquaintances when meeting with them. The application of this greeting convention depends, of course, on our ability to determine who is, and who is not, one's acquaintance. This is partly a matter of convention too, but not entirely. People may

---

[15] Morning may be a vague concept. The so-called epistemic theories of vagueness maintain that there is a truth of the matter about borderline cases, only that it is not knowable. (See e.g. T. Williamson, *Vagueness* (London: Routledge, 1994).) I don't find epistemic theories of vagueness persuasive, but it is not part of my argument here. The borderline cases of conventional rules need not stem from vagueness, and the argument here need not take sides of any of the philosophical debates about the nature of vague concepts. The argument relies on the nature of conventions.

have different views on what is considered sufficient acquaintance for the purposes of the greeting convention, and they may form such views on the basis of, *inter alia*, evaluative considerations. So now suppose that two people disagree about the application of the greeting convention, and that such a disagreement stems from different views they have about what 'sufficient acquaintance' consists in. One party claims that a one-time casual previous acquaintance is sufficient, and the other denies it. Of course in one sense it is not a mistake to say that they disagree about the application of the greeting convention. As a matter of fact, they would apply it differently under certain circumstances. But essentially the situation here is not different from the notational convention we have encountered earlier. As far as the greeting convention goes, neither party would make a mistake. None of them could claim that his or her view is *the conventional* one. The content of a convention is exhausted by the social practice which consists in the application of the convention. We can never say that 'it is a convention that *P*' *because* it ought to be that *P*. Hence it is not really the greeting convention's application which is controversial here, although it may well be the case that people would apply the convention differently under certain circumstances. To the extent that there is a genuine disagreement about such differences in application it is a disagreement about what the convention ought to be, and not about what it is; it is a disagreement about how to apply the convention to novel cases, which is, basically, a disagreement about how to change, or extend, the convention.

But can it not be the case that people understand a convention differently, and that one understanding is better than the other? Of course this can happen. People can have a genuine and significant disagreement, for example, over the question of what is the point of the convention, and there may well be better and worse answers to such questions. A better grasp of the point of something is also a better grasp of the nature of that thing. Similar considerations apply to the formulation of a convention, its history, its functions, rationale, and a great many other aspects. In other words, I am not denying that the nature of a convention can be controversial. Anything which is meaningful can be controversial. It is not the possibility of controversy that I object to. The only wrong assumption of the argument under consideration is that there is a potential gap between the convention, and its application, a gap which can be bridged by the correct, or true, moral considerations. A convention consists in what people do, as a matter of following a rule. This leaves open the possibility that we would have different interpretations of what people do, and what this doing really amounts to. Hence the room for controversy. But it makes no sense to say that there *is* a convention about doing *A*, even if people substantially disagree on the question whether doing *A* is prescribed by the convention or not.[16]

So the idea that judges and lawyers can have genuine arguments about what the rules of recognition *really require* in controversial cases, and that such a phenomenon

---

[16] There is an obvious distinction between disagreement and misunderstanding. People can, of course, misunderstand a convention. Note, however, that it cannot be the case that most everybody misunderstands a convention. Conventions are, essentially, what people take them to be.

shows how morality can determine what the law is, involves a misunderstanding of the concept of a convention. It is incompatible with the conventional foundation of law that inclusive positivism adheres to.[17]

The search for a middle ground between Dworkin's legal theory and strong-positivism has engendered two further versions of inclusive positivism. Let me concentrate first on the more popular version of it. This version concedes that legal validity is basically source based, but it also insists that the conventional sources themselves often include a specific reference to moral considerations which bear on the legal validity of norms. Source-based law often incorporates morality on its own terms, as it were.[18] Here is a simple model of this line of thought: suppose the conventions of recognition in a legal system S_i, prescribe that law is whatever Rex tells you to do. Suppose further, that Rex had decreed, as a matter of fact, that in cases of type X people should do the right thing, or that they should behave in a fair and just manner. Or else, suppose that Rex had prescribed that none of his own laws shall be valid unless they meet certain moral constraints, like fairness or equality. In both cases, such incorporatists would maintain, the conditions of legal validity are clearly affected by moral considerations. It is at least sometimes true in S_i, that the validity of a legal norm depends on its moral merit, and hence strong-positivism must be false.

This version of inclusive positivism embodies two advantages. First, if true, it would seem to constitute a very good answer to some of Dworkin's objections to legal positivism, that is, without giving in to his rejection of legal positivism as such. All we would have to show is, that in those legal systems we are familiar with and that Dworkin focuses on, explicit source-based reference to morality is not a rare phenomenon. If this is true, as it certainly seems to be in the case of American law, Dworkin's counter-examples to legal positivism, based on judicial rhetoric and the law itself, are easily explicable on positivist grounds. True, we would say, morality does bear on legal validity pretty much in the way Dworkin depicts, but this follows from the sources thesis itself, it does not necessarily go against it. Secondly, this version of inclusive positivism, unlike its stronger relative, does seem to be consistent with the conventional foundation of law. It does not make the incoherent claim that conventions can establish practices which are there regardless of conventions. The conventions are there to establish the sources of law, and in this they have fulfilled

[17] What actually happened here is, that inclusive positivists have made the mistake of trying to turn one of Dworkin's most important arguments against the conventional foundation of law on its head. It was Dworkin who insisted that there is law in such controversial cases, and hence it makes no sense to assume that legal norms derive their validity from conventional rules of recognition. When the convention's application is controversial, there is no convention on the matter. Since judges and lawyers assume that there is, nevertheless, law in such cases, it follows that the law cannot derive its validity from conventions. My argument shows that the inclusive positivist argument under consideration is not a coherent reply to Dworkin. Either Dworkin is right, namely, that there is law in such controversial cases, in which case, conventionalism is false, or else, strong-positivism is right, in which case, the appropriate conclusion is that there is no law in controversial cases, judges' rhetoric notwithstanding. There is no middle ground here, at least as far as this argument is concerned.

[18] See e.g. Waluchow, *Inclusive Legal Positivism*, n. 11 above.

their constitutive rationale. This does not seem to preclude the possibility that the sources of law make it, as a matter of fact, either mandatory or permissible that the validity of other legal norms depend on morality.

THE ARGUMENT FROM AUTHORITY

There are two main ways in which inclusive positivists can claim that morality bears on what the law is. One type of phenomenon that they typically have in mind, is what can be called 'conditional validity': this is the type of cases where the law imposes certain moral or political constraints, like equality, or fairness, and so on, on the legal validity of norms in general, that is, either with respect to all the norms of the system, or some specific sub-type of norms (e.g. like state, as opposed to federal legislation, or administrative norms as opposed to federal legislation, etc.). In this type of cases the law seems to make the validity of otherwise source-based law *conditional* upon meeting certain moral constraints. This is, allegedly, the typical case of the familiar constitutional provisions conditioning the validity of all legislation on meeting certain prescribed moral and political constraints. The second type of situation, which by want of a better idea I will call 'content validity', consists of those cases where the law is supposed to be simply what morality, or justice, or some other relevant values, dictate. The legislature may decree, for instance, that in cases of type *x*, the law is whatever morality requires. Suppose, for instance, that the law only prescribes that in cases of type *x*, one party should pay 'just compensation' to another party, 'just' meaning whatever *is just* according to the relevant moral considerations. Allegedly, then, in such a case the answer to the question what kind of compensation a party should pay to another is simply determined by the appropriate moral reasons.

Both phenomena of conditional and content validity are familiar aspects of modern legal systems. There is, after all, nothing there to stop legislatures or judges from using the language of moral and political values in their prescriptions of what the law requires. And they often do that. The question is how to interpret these phenomena. Inclusive positivism asks us to take them at face value: what the law says is what it does, namely, it requires us to decide what the law is on the basis of moral or political considerations. Hence the law is what those moral and political considerations really require. But this cannot be quite right, even at face value. At the same time that the law incorporates morality into itself, as it were, it also assigns somebody the role of determining, officially and authoritatively, what the moral considerations require, namely judges. After all, it is never simply up to us, as the subjects of law, to decide for ourselves what just compensation really is, or whether to abide by a given law if it seems to infringe a constitutional requirement of fairness, or whatever. It is always the judges who decide these matters, and it is only their decision which could carry any authoritative weight.

This last point was not meant to be a conclusive argument against inclusive positivism. It was only meant to show that the issues are rather complicated, and that there is very little that we can draw from face-value interpretations of the situation, not to speak of conclusions. Eventually, and I think most legal philosophers admit as much, the argument turns on the sense we can make of the authoritative nature of law: can it be the case that a norm is authoritative, if it requires the norm subjects to decide what the norm is, on the basis of those considerations which the norm is there to settle? At least on the basis of Raz's theory of authority, the answer is clearly 'no'.

Brian Leiter correctly identifies three main arguments which have been offered as rejoinders to Raz's argument from authority.[19] First, it has been claimed that Raz conflates two possible ways in which an authority's subjects may be required to rely on moral reasoning in order to determine what the authority has prescribed, and only one of them undermines the rationale of authority itself. Coleman writes, for example, that 'not every morality condition of legality directs us to the law's underlying or justifying conditions. Thus, on the assumption that authority precludes identification by appealing to its justifying or dependent reasons, not every Incorporationist rule of recognition will be incompatible with the possibility of legal authority.'[20] A rule prescribing, for example, a general condition of fairness for the validity of all other rules, requires the authority's subjects to rely on moral considerations in determining what the law is, but it 'does not direct us to the dependent reasons that would justify any particular legal rule'.[21]

The truth is that it is not quite clear what the relevant distinction is. Undoubtedly, legal authorities can be limited. Judges, officials, and even the legislature, are typically limited authorities. They may exercise their authority only within specified areas, or on specified grounds, or according to some specified procedures. The argument under consideration seems to add that such limits on the exercise of a legal authority may also consist of moral constraints, established and recognized as such by the conventional sources of law of the pertinent legal system, and it contends that such moral limits do not undermine the authoritative nature of law. But how does any of this show that a norm can be a legal norm just in virtue of its moral content? Raz's argument from authority does not aim to exclude any type of evaluative or moral consideration from legal discourse. It only aims to prove that morality cannot determine what the law is.

According to exclusive legal positivism, legal norms are products of authoritative resolutions; every legal norm consists of an authoritative directive. This does not

---

[19] 'Realism, Hard Positivism, and Conceptual Analysis', *Legal Theory*, 4 (1998), 533.

[20] See Coleman, 'Incorporationism, Conventionality, and The Practical Difference Thesis', *Legal Theory*, 4 (1998), 381, at 414. A similar argument was presented by Waluchow, *Inclusive Legal Positivism*, n. 11 above, at 129–40.

[21] Coleman, 'Incorporationism'.

entail that everything a legal authority decrees is law; authorities may transgress their legal powers. Now, the argument under consideration claims that such powers can sometimes be specified in evaluative, moral terms. The legal power of authorities can be constrained by moral considerations, if (but only if) such considerations derive from the rules of recognition. This is true: legal powers can be constrained by moral criteria. But for law to emerge, the power must be exercised. This is what the sources thesis amounts to: law can only derive from authoritative sources. Constraints, of the moral or any other kind, by themselves do not determine the law; they only prescribe ways in which the law can be changed. Thus, even if it is true that some of the constraints which determine the legal powers of authorities are evaluative or moral in kind, it does not undermine the sources thesis, since it does not entail that a norm can be a legal norm just in virtue of its moral content.

Perhaps Coleman can restrict his conclusion to the negation of legal validity, arguing that although moral considerations cannot, by themselves, establish the legal validity of a norm, they can, nevertheless, establish that a norm is legally not valid as it transgresses a moral constraint. The main problem with this view is, however, that it would require the introduction of a notion of prima-facie validity. The negation of legal validity on moral grounds would only make sense if we thought that the pertinent norm is at least prima-facie valid. Furthermore, since most, if not all, legal norms can be defeated, allegedly, by such moral constraints, it would mean that most norms in a legal system are only prima-facie valid. Such a view, however, would beg many more questions than it can hope to answer. To begin with, it would render the idea of legal validity far less certain than it actually is, since it would always make the conclusion about the legal validity of a norm depend on truths about morality.[22] More importantly, however, such a view is inconsistent with the authoritative nature of law, and for those same reasons we have observed above: legal authority is there to make a practical difference, and it could not purport to make such a difference if authoritative directives are only prima-facie valid, often awaiting, as it were, the confirmation of their validity on grounds which the putative subjects of the authority should figure out for themselves. It is as if the authority said: 'do what I say, unless what I say goes against moral reasons'. Legal validity is not a prima-facie construct. Legal authority is needed precisely because it is there to render conclusive, that is, at least from a legal point of view, prima-facie reasons which apply to the putative subjects.

To illustrate the problem, consider a standard case where the legal validity of a norm is questioned on moral grounds along the lines suggested by the argument under consideration. Suppose that an authoritative resolution has been rendered, say, by the Supreme Court, deciding that the norm is legally valid. Now suppose that the moral reasoning of the Supreme Court was at fault, and that the relevant moral reasons would actually call for the invalidation of the norm. Let us assume, for the

---

[22] This problem is all too familiar and I will not try to develop it further here.

sake of the illustration, that this is what has happened with the constitutional challenge to capital punishment in the USA; that is, let us assume that from a moral point
of view, capital punishment is really cruel, and therefore it should not be valid.
Nevertheless, unfortunately the Supreme Court decided otherwise. Would we have
to maintain that laws prescribing capital punishment in the USA today are actually
not legally valid? (And if so, what is the practical significance of the authority of the
Supreme Court, which has decided otherwise?) Natural law mythology is too high a
price to pay for such an argument. It is much more natural to say that in such cases,
the Supreme Court has been given the legal power to change the law according to
moral considerations, and that the change it introduced into the law was not a
morally desirable one. On this idea of morally directed power I will expound later.

Coleman offers another argument against Raz's argument from authority, based
on a distinction he draws between two possible roles that we can assign to the rules of
recognition. One is basically epistemic and the other is concerned with the notion of
legal validity. The epistemic role consists in enabling the citizens and the judiciary to
identify the relevant legal norms that apply to them. This, Coleman claims, is at best
of secondary importance. Few people know the rules of recognition of their country
anyway, and even if they do, it is hardly of great importance. The philosophical significance of the rules of recognition, the role that they are there to fulfil, is not a matter of epistemology, but of validity. The rules of recognition determine which norms
are legally valid and not, how people would come to realize this.[23] The argument
from authority, Coleman claims, 'imposes essentially epistemic constraints. It has to
do with the ways in which people figure out what the law is and what it demands of
them. The argument from authority isn't about what can count as law'.[24] But these
epistemic constraints, Coleman claims, are beside the point. The rules of recognition
need not be concerned with the question of how ordinary citizens identify what the
law requires of them; it is not a tool that serves this purpose. Since Raz's argument
concerns only this last, epistemic issue, it does not impose an analytic-conceptual
constraint on the legal validity of norms, and hence it fails as an argument against
inclusive positivism.

What actually fails here, however, is this argument, since it fails to notice that epistemic arguments can have non-epistemic, conceptual, conclusions. Raz's argument
from authority is such a case. What matters for our purposes is that the law be able
to make a practical difference, and this is a conceptual point. More precisely, it is

---

[23] Scott Shapiro has argued that in the case of judges, the two potential functions of the rules of recognition actually coincide, and hence the argument fails on its own terms. See S. Shapiro, 'The Difference
that Rules Make', in B. Bix (ed.), *Analysing Case Law: New Essays in Legal Theory* (Oxford: Oxford
University Press, 1998), 33 at 60. I am not entirely convinced by this argument, however. As I have argued
above, the function of the constitutive rules of recognition is not epistemic, and I don't think that this
changes where judges are concerned. The constitutive rules of chess, for example, serve the same functions for the players, as for the umpire in the game: they constitute what the game is. The constitutive
conventions, whether in chess or in the law, simply define the rules of the game.

[24] See 'Second Thoughts and Other First Impressions', n. 9 above.

something that follows from the essentially authoritative nature of the law. The fact that nothing can make such a difference unless certain epistemic constraints are assumed, namely, that the authoritative directive must be such that people *can* identify it without having to rely on those same reasons which the authoritative directive is there to settle, does not entail that the conclusion of this argument is epistemic. The conclusion is a conceptual one. It imposes a conceptual constraint on the kinds of things that can count as authoritative prescriptions.

There is nothing philosophically puzzling, or unique, about such arguments. In fact, a very similar line of reasoning applies to constitutive conventions as well. It is true about constitutive conventions too, that they must be recognizable as such. Consider, for example, the conventions constituting a structured game, like chess, or soccer. Part of what it means to play such structured games is, that the players *follow* certain rules. This requires that the rules and conventions be recognizable as such. People can only follow conventional rules which they can recognize as such, namely, as rules to be followed. This is not only a point about how people go about learning to play the game, or in identifying its rules. It is also a point about what games essentially are.[25]

Finally, the third type of argument which is suggested as a rejoinder to Raz's argument from authority is based on the rejection of Raz's thesis that authoritative directives engender exclusionary reasons for action. If authoritative directives are not exclusionary reasons, so this argument continues, then the fact that law is essentially authoritative does not entail that we must be able to identify the law without having to rely on those same considerations which the law is there to settle.[26]

Elsewhere I have already argued that this argument misses its target.[27] Raz's conclusion that it does not make sense to identify the law on the basis of those same considerations which the law is there to settle, follows from the fact that the rationale of practical authorities must take into account the ways in which authorities create partly content-independent reasons for action. For the putative subjects of an authority, it must be practically significant that the directive has been actually issued by an authority, and their reasons for action must take this fact into account. This entails that the putative subjects of an authority must be able to recognize the authoritative directive as such, namely, as an authoritative directive, regardless of the particular merits of the directive itself. True, Raz believes that the best explanation of this feature of authorities is given by his account of exclusionary reasons. But even if he is wrong about this particular aspect of the explanation, the conclusion remains, namely, that authoritative directives must be recognizable as such without having to

---

[25] Coleman is cautious not to confuse the question: what can count as a practical authority, with the different, and irrelevant question: what is required for an authority to be an efficient authority. As Coleman rightly concedes, Raz's argument does not depend on such considerations of efficiency.

[26] See e.g. R. M. Dworkin, *Law's Empire* (Cambridge, Mass.: Harvard University Press, 1986), at 429; Waluchow, *Inclusive Legal Positivism*, n. 11 above, at e.g. 136.

[27] *Interpretation and Legal Theory* (Oxford: Oxford University Press), 118.

rely on the dependent reasons, since this conclusion derives from the fact that authoritative directives must be taken to entail partly content-independent reasons for action. Whether this content-independence of reasons is best explained as a species of exclusionary reasons, or not, bears on a different question—what kind of obligations authoritative directives engender?—but this is beside the point.

Even if we reject, as we should, the criticisms of Raz's argument from authority, it still remains an open question how best to interpret those phenomena inclusive positivists point at, namely, the pervasive reference to morality in the law. It is, after all, quite unlikely that all this talk of moral and political constraints on legal validity, prevalent in legal practice, is sheer nonsense. I want to suggest that it is meaningful indeed, but not in the way inclusive positivists have envisaged. I will mainly concentrate on what I have called 'conditional validity', but I take it that with the appropriate modifications, this account will apply to content validity as well.

Joseph Raz has long suggested the following solution: legal rules which prescribe that the validity of other legal rules depend on certain moral or political considerations, actually function as power-conferring rules, granting to the judiciary *limited* and *guided* legislative power. In effect, such power-conferring provisions prescribe to judges that they should legislate new legal standards, sometimes in addition to the existing ones, but often to the effect of modifying or nullifying existing norms. Now, the main function of the moral precepts embodied in such power-conferring rules is to limit either the *kind of purposes* judges should take into consideration in their legislative function, or *the kind of reasons* they should rely upon when justifying it or, typically, both. Consider, for example, the Eighth Amendment of the US Constitution forbidding 'cruel and unusual punishment'. Presumably, the question what kinds of punishment are cruel, is a moral one. The purpose of this constitutional provision is to require judges to invalidate legal institutions which amount to cruel forms of punishment. But the judges' power to modify, change, or invalidate existing legal norms is guided by certain aims and by certain types of permissible justifications. They are not given the power to modify existing practices of punishment on grounds of economic efficiency, for example, even if those considerations are sound. The judges' power is thus limited and guided by prescribing a certain type of considerations they may rely upon.

Such guided and limited power-conferring rules Raz called 'directed power'.[28] Power is directed here in two respects: first, it is circumscribed by its legally prescribed aims and reasons. Secondly, it is a kind of power which the norm subjects (i.e. judges or other officials) have a legal duty to exercise. Unlike the typical case of a power-conferring rule, which leaves it entirely to the norm subjects' will whether to exercise the power or not, such a directed power makes it obligatory to exercise it. As Raz pointed out in detail, such directed power-conferring rules are ubiquitous in the law, and they often apply to legislators, as well as to numerous officials, and not only

---

[28] Raz, *Ethics in the Public Domain*, n. 6 above, ch. 10.

to judges. The essential point, however, is this: even when power-conferring rules are directed in both ways we mentioned, their exercise *changes* the law. Whenever one makes use of a legal power one introduces a change in the law in the form of creating new rights and duties which have not been hitherto part of the law. This simply follows from the logic of the concept of a legal power, and it is true of the exercise of power both in the private and the public law. The whole idea of a power-conferring norm is to provide the norm subjects and legal officials with a tool to introduce a change in the law. And this, of course, is true of judicial power as well. When judges are granted a directed power to interpret the law according to certain moral considerations, they are given the power to change the law in a limited and guided manner.

An obvious difficulty seems to present itself here: if this is so simple, why it is not generally recognized as such. Why the smoke-screen? The answer is not difficult to surmise: for reasons which have to do with institutional convenience, and perhaps with historical contingencies, it is typically the case that judges' legislative powers must be exercised retrospectively: not only with respect to the particular parties in front of them, but often with respect to many other parties who may have relied on the nullified or modified norm long before any litigation commenced. It is typically the case, as a matter of legal doctrine, that when judges declare a certain legislative act unconstitutional, for example, their decision renders the act *void ab intitio*. As a kind of legislative power, such retroactive legislation is problematic indeed. First, because it creates the impression that we must have been wrong about the way in which we had previously understood the law. Mainly, however, it is a political issue: it is, politically, extremely inconvenient to admit that judicial authorities have such a tremendous legislative power which is retroactive in its effect. Hence the smoke-screen.

The power-conferring function of moral concepts embodied in the law is not their only function, although it is the most important one, particularly in the context of conditional validity. Another, typical use of moral terminology in the law concerns the reference it aims to make to certain conventions of a community's morality. In other words, legal reference to moral terms often embodies no more than a reference to positive morality. Thus, when a law refers to such notions as 'indecency', or 'obscenity', and the like, it may well do no more than prescribe a reference to certain values which happen to prevail in the community, assumed to be widely shared and recognized as such. In such cases the legal reference to positive morality is not different in essence from other numerous references the law makes to social conventions, assuming (sometimes wrongly) that its subjects know perfectly well what those conventions are.[29] Interestingly, however, such a technique of legislative reference to moral conventions is rather precarious. It always faces the 'danger' that judges will actually interpret the reference to moral concepts in the former way I have suggested, namely, as a power-conferring rule, enabling them to change the law in accordance

---

[29] The references to matters of sexual morality, which, until quite recently, have been pervasively used in criminal codes, is a good example of such a reliance on conventions of communal morality.

with what they deem as the correct moral values which apply to the case. And this often happens.

ENTAILED LAW?

There is, finally, another version of inclusive positivism we should briefly consider. This version maintains that law is basically source based, but it also incorporates those norms which are *entailed* by source-based law. I am not quite sure whether this version of inclusive positivism is actually maintained by inclusive positivists, or was it only invented (and repudiated) by Joseph Raz.[30] In any case, since it does seem to carry some plausibility, we should dwell on it for a moment. The basic idea is rather simple, and it may seem to be in accord with the conventional foundation of law: suppose a legal system, say, S_i, contains the norms $N_{i\ldots n}$. Suppose further, that norms $N_{i\ldots n}$ entail the truth of a further norm, say, N_x. May we not conclude, then, that N_x is also legally valid in S_i? But what would it mean to say that N_x is entailed by $N_{i\ldots n}$? There are several possibilities here. On the most restricted notion of entailment, one would think of it only in terms of logical entailment. (Coupled, I presume, with certain truths about facts.) On the least restricted notion, one could also think of it as moral-evaluative entailment. If it is the case, for instance, that the norms $N_{i\ldots n}$ embody, or manifest, a moral principle M, and M morally requires N_x, then N_x is also part of S_i. This latter view brings us much closer, of course, both to Dworkin's views and to the kind of inclusive positivism we have earlier considered.

Despite the considerable differences between these two views of entailment, and perhaps other possible views in between these two extremes, they share a crucial assumption: namely, that the law is necessarily coherent. It is imperative to note that it is not the value of coherence that is the issue here; for establishing the conclusion that entailed law is also law, it is not enough to assume that coherence is an important (even over-riding) value, that legal interpretation must be guided by. The assumption under consideration here is much stronger than that. It is the assumption that the law is, as a matter of necessity, coherent; it cannot be anything else. Otherwise, if it only maintains that coherence is a value, then the fact that a norm is entailed by other legal norms could not lead to the conclusion that it *is* a legal norm in virtue of such an entailment; only that it should be.

Therefore, the only question we should ask now is whether it makes any sense to assume that the law is necessarily coherent, logically, or otherwise. A negative answer to this question is hardly deniable. Coherence might be a necessary requirement that

---

[30] See his *Ethics in the Public Domain*, n. 6 above, at 210–14.

we ascribe to theories, as such. The incoherence of a theory normally indicates that part of it is false. But the law is not a theoretical domain. It is a practical one, where the numerous complexities of our lives are regulated by norms, decisions, and force. It may well be desirable (to some extent!) that these regulations be shaped in a coherent fashion, but it certainly cannot be assumed to be so, by necessity. A priori, the law need not be coherent at all.

Well, this is not quite accurate. Some measure of coherence is a practical necessity. If the law commonly and pervasively prescribed conflicting norms and decisions, it would have created so much confusion that it would make it practically impossible to abide by its rules. This, of course, is a matter of degree. Neither perfect harmony, nor total confusion, are feasible options. There is always *some level* of compliance without which law would not be possible, and there is *some level* of coherence without which such compliance would not be possible. But the question where the line is, is not one for philosophers to answer. Determining law's actual level of tolerance of incompliance and confusion is a matter for sociologists to indulge in. For our purposes it suffices to realize that there is some such level of tolerance, and that there is no necessity in law's being logically, or otherwise, coherent. If this is accepted, it immediately follows that there is no reason to assume that entailed law is law, just in virtue of such an entailment relation, whatever its precise nature was meant to be.

As a closing remark for this chapter, let me say what it is that can be concluded from our discussion so far, and what would be premature to conclude. I have tried to present here at least the initial plausibility of a certain version of legal positivism, which is best captured by the idea of the sources thesis. This version of positivism, I have tried to show, derives from two main considerations: first and foremost, it derives from the conventional foundation of the law and the nature of social conventions. Secondly, it is reinforced by the Razian insight that the law is essentially an authoritative social practice, and it must be held to be able to make a practical difference in that respect. These two considerations, I have argued, suffice to show that the inclusive version of legal positivism, which was meant to form a middle-ground between exclusive legal positivism and Dworkin's anti-positivist doctrine, is untenable. There is no such a middle ground. Dworkin's anti-positivist doctrine, however, has not been answered. I have shown that at least some objections to the sources thesis, deriving from Dworkin's insights, are ill founded. But there are, of course, many other arguments which still await to be discussed in detail.

CHAPTER 4

INCLUSIVE LEGAL POSITIVISM

KENNETH EINAR HIMMA

THE conceptual foundation of legal positivism consists in three commitments: the Social Fact Thesis, the Conventionality Thesis, and the Separability Thesis. The Social Fact Thesis asserts that the existence of law is made possible by certain kinds of social fact. The Conventionality Thesis claims that the criteria of validity are conventional in character. The Separability Thesis, at the most general level, denies that there is necessary overlap between law and morality.

While the Separability Thesis thus implies that there are no *necessary* moral criteria of legal validity, it leaves open the question of whether there are *possible* moral criteria of validity. Inclusive legal positivists (also known as soft positivists and incorporationists) believe there can be such criteria; that is, they believe there are conceptually possible legal systems in which the criteria for legal validity include (or incorporate) moral principles. Prominent inclusive positivists include H. L. A. Hart, Jules Coleman, W. J. Waluchow, and Matthew Kramer. Exclusive legal positivists (also known as hard positivists) deny there can be moral criteria of validity. Exclusive positivists, like Joseph Raz, Scott Shapiro, and Andrei Marmor, claim the existence and content of law can always be determined by reference to social sources.

1 Conceptual Foundations
of Positivism

1.1 The Social Fact Thesis

The most fundamental of positivism's core commitments is the Social Fact Thesis, which asserts that law is, in essence, a social creation or artefact. What distinguishes legal norms from non-legal norms, according to this thesis, is that the former instantiate a property that makes reference to some social fact. The occurrence of the relevant social fact, then, is what ultimately explains the existence of a legal system and constitutes it as an artefact.

While all positivists are committed to the Social Fact Thesis, they differ with respect to which social fact is essential to the explanation of legal validity. Following Jeremy Bentham, John Austin argues that the distinguishing feature of a legal system is the presence of a sovereign who is habitually obeyed by most people in the society but who is not in the habit of obeying anyone else. On Austin's view, a rule R is legally valid (i.e. is a law) in a society S if and only if (1) R is the command of the sovereign in S; and (2) R is backed up by the threat of a sanction. Thus, the social fact that explains the existence of any legal system, on Austin's view, is the presence of a sovereign willing and able to impose a sanction for non-compliance with its commands.

Hart rejects Austin's version of the Social Fact Thesis for a number of reasons[1] but chief among them is that it overlooks the existence of meta-rules that have as their subject matter the first-order rules themselves:

[Meta-rules] may all be said to be on a different level from the [first-order] rules, for they are all *about* such rules; in the sense that while [first-order] rules are concerned with the actions that individuals must or must not do, these [meta-]rules are all concerned with the [first-order] rules themselves. They specify the way in which the [first-order] rules may be conclusively ascertained, introduced, eliminated, varied, and the fact of their violation conclusively determined.[2]

---

[1] Hart also believes that Austin's theory explains only the existence of first-order rules that require or prohibit certain kinds of behaviour. On Hart's view, Austin overlooks another kind of first-order rule that confers the power to create, modify, and extinguish rights and obligations, like those governing the creation of contracts.

[2] H. L. A. Hart, *The Concept of Law*, 2nd edn. (Oxford: Clarendon Press, 1994), 92. Hereinafter referred to as *CL*. Hart makes the distinction in terms of primary and secondary rules but he seems to use the term 'secondary rules' in two different ways. First, he uses 'secondary rules' to denote 'power-conferring rules' that enable individuals to alter existing legal relations; in contrast, 'primary rules' are rules that require or prohibit certain behaviours on the part of citizens. On this usage, the rules of contract are secondary rules. Elsewhere he uses 'secondary rules' to denote rules about rules. On this usage, the rules of contract are not secondary rules. I find the latter usage more apt and will use the terms 'first-order' and 'meta-' to capture it.

Hart distinguishes three types of meta-rules that mark the transition from primitive forms of law to full-blown legal systems: (1) the rule of recognition, which 'specif[ies] some feature or features possession of which by a suggested rule is taken as a conclusive affirmative indication that it is a rule of the group' (*CL*, 92); (2) the rule of change, which enables a society to create, remove, and modify valid norms; and (3) the rule of adjudication, which provides a mechanism for determining whether a valid norm has been violated. On Hart's view, then, every society with a full-blown legal system has a meta-rule of recognition that provides criteria for making, changing, and adjudicating legally valid norms.

What ultimately goes wrong with Austin's version of the Pedigree Thesis, then, is this. Because Austin takes first-order criminal law as paradigmatic of all legal content, he believes that the presence of a coercive sovereign is essential to explaining the existence of law. Since Austin thus explains all law as originating from the sovereign, he fails to notice that the claim that first-order legal content originates with the sovereign defines a legal meta-norm and hence overlooks the possibility of other meta-rules of recognition than the one that validates only coercive sovereign commands. While this may be one possible rule of recognition, Hart believes there are many other possibilities; it is up to each society to decide on the content of its validity criteria.

On Hart's view, then, it is the presence of a binding rule of recognition, and not the presence of a sovereign able to coerce compliance, that brings a legal system into existence. And, for Hart, there is a binding rule of recognition *RoR* in a society *S* when two conditions are satisfied: (1) the criteria of validity contained in *RoR* are accepted by officials in *S* as standards of official conduct; and (2) citizens in *S* generally comply with first-order rules validated by *RoR*. Thus, according to Hart's version of the Social Fact Thesis, the existence of a rule of recognition satisfying (1) and (2) is the social fact that gives rise to law.

Thus construed, the Social Fact Thesis explains the authority of the validity criteria in terms of some set of social facts and thereby conceptualizes law as an artefact.[3] On Hart's version of the thesis, the relevant social fact is the acceptance of the officials; on Austin's version, the relevant social fact is the sovereign's ability to coerce compliance. But, in any event, since the validity criteria are authoritative in virtue of instantiating some social property, the legal system to which they give rise is a human creation. According to the Social Fact Thesis, then, it is a conceptual truth that law is a social artefact.

Although the Social Fact Thesis is most usefully construed as explaining the authority of the validity criteria, it can also be construed as explaining the authority of *first-order legal norms*. On this construction of Austin's version of the thesis, a first-order legal norm is valid because it is the command of a sovereign who backs it up

---

[3] Raz construes the term 'authority' as having moral content. An authority is, on this usage, morally legitimate. See Section 6, below, for a discussion of Raz's views. As I use the term here, 'authority' should not be construed as connoting moral legitimacy.

with a sanction. It is the validity of first-order norms, rather than the authority of the meta-norm, that is being explained in terms of the relevant social fact; such norms are valid because they instantiate a complex social property involving the sovereign, her intentions, and her subjects.[4]

This second version of the Social Fact Thesis operates at the same level as the so-called Pedigree Thesis. According to the Pedigree Thesis, the rule of recognition provides criteria that validate only norms enacted in accordance with certain procedural requirements; on this view, a norm is legally valid in virtue of having the right kind of source or pedigree. Austin subscribes to the Pedigree Thesis; on his view, the appropriate source that gives rise to legal validity is the sovereign. Raz's Source Thesis also seems to be a version of the Pedigree Thesis. Since the Pedigree Thesis explains the validity of first-order norms in terms of social facts, it implies this version of the Social Fact Thesis.

Nevertheless, this version of the Social Fact Thesis does not imply the Pedigree Thesis. There could be a rule of recognition, for example, that validates those norms that have an appropriate pedigree together with norms ('derived norms') that stand in some logical (or moral) relationship to norms having an appropriate pedigree. At bottom, the validity of every legal norm can be explained in terms of some social fact; for the validity of the derived norms depends on their standing in the appropriate relation to norms that are valid in virtue of some social fact. On this account, if the legal status of the underlying pedigreed norm changes, so does the legal status of the derived norm. The validity of the derived norm thus depends, we might say, *immediately* on the relation of its content to the content of the pedigreed norm but *ultimately* on the instantiation by the pedigreed norm of the relevant social facts. Thus, while this version of the Social Fact Thesis operates on the same level as the Pedigree Thesis, the two theses are not identical.

All positivists accept the Social Fact Thesis as it pertains to the authority of the meta-rule; this is part of the shared foundation that distinguishes legal positivism from other conceptual theories of law. While many positivists accept the Social Fact Thesis as it pertains to the validity of first-order rules, not all do. In fact, the distinction between exclusive and inclusive positivism can be expressed in terms of this version of the Social Fact Thesis. Exclusive positivists accept, while inclusive positivists reject, the second version of the Social Fact Thesis. As we will see, some inclusive positivists believe there can be norms that are legally valid in virtue of their moral content—regardless of whether such norms bear a logical relationship to norms having an appropriate pedigree.

---

[4] Hart rejects this version of the thesis since he allows for the possibility of moral criteria of validity. Thus, as Coleman points out, 'the two aspects of the Social Fact Thesis—that law must be identifiable by social facts and that the rule that sets out the criteria of legality is a social rule—are independent of one another'. Jules L. Coleman, 'Second Thoughts and Other First Impressions', in Brian Bix (ed.), *Analyzing Law: New Essays in Legal Theory* (Oxford: Clarendon Press, 1998), 257–322, 264. Hereinafter referred to as *ST*.

Even so, it is important to bear in mind that Hartian inclusive positivists must none the less accept that in every conceptually possible legal system there will be institutions that allow for the existence of first-order norms that are valid, at least partly, because of some social fact. There simply could not be a legal system in which the meta-rule of recognition is exhausted by content-based criteria of validity. On Hart's view, for example, the simple rule 'all and only moral rules are legally valid' could not be a rule of recognition because it does not provide any mechanism for changing and adjudicating law. Such a system of rules, on Hart's view, would be at best a rudimentary or primitive form of law; but it would not be a legal system because it lacks the appropriate institutional machinery for making, changing, and adjudicating law.[5]

Accordingly, Hart's theory of law correctly requires the presence of certain institutions by which law can be manufactured, modified, and adjudicated. This, as we shall see, should not be construed to preclude in Hart's theory a rule of recognition that can validate some norms solely in virtue of content. But this does imply that the rule of recognition must define certain institutional structures, like legislatures and courts, that make possible the existence of first-order norms that are valid, at least partly, in virtue of social pedigree. For this reason, there could not exist a legal system defined *entirely* by the meta-rule 'all and only moral rules are legally valid'.

Hart, then, accepts a modified version of the Social Fact Thesis as it operates to explain the validity of first-order norms: in every conceptually possible legal system, there are institutions making possible the existence of legal norms that are valid, at least partly, because some social conditions are satisfied. And given the plausibility of this thesis, it must also be attributed to inclusive positivism generally.

1.2 The Conventionality Theses

1.2.1 *The Weak Conventionality Thesis*

The Weak Conventionality Thesis supplements Hart's version of the Social Fact Thesis with a deeper and more detailed account of the social fact that explains the authority of the validity criteria. What explains the authority of the validity criteria in any conceptually possible legal system, according to this thesis, is that such criteria constitute the terms of a social convention among the persons who function as officials. As Coleman describes the thesis, 'law is made possible by an interdependent

---

[5] Hart concedes 'it is . . . possible to imagine a society without a legislature, courts, or officials of any kind' (*CL*, 91). The problem, however, is that such a system contains exactly the defects that the institution of law is intended to correct. As Hart would put it, such a simple system of rules is too 'static' as there is no formal mechanism for changing rules (*CL*, 92). Likewise, this simple system is 'inefficient' because there is no formal mechanism by which social pressure is brought to bear on non-compliance (*CL*, 93). Thus, Hart would characterize such a system as a primitive or rudimentary system of law.

convergence of behavior and attitude . . . among individuals expressed in a social or conventional rule'.[6]

The existence of a social convention depends on a convergence of *both* behaviour and attitude.[7] Many people, for example, converge on putting both socks on before putting on shoes, but it would be incorrect to characterize such behaviour as constituting a convention; for no one would be inclined to criticize someone who puts a sock and shoe on one foot before dressing the other foot. But if people were suddenly to view deviating behaviour with respect to the order of putting on shoes and socks as a ground for censure, that would be enough to constitute a certain way of putting on socks and shoes as a convention. A social convention, then, is constituted by a convergence of both behaviour and attitude: in addition to conforming behaviour, there must be a shared belief that non-compliance is a legitimate ground for criticism.

The existence of law, then, is made possible by a convergence of behaviour and attitude. As Hart puts the point, 'those rules of behaviour which are valid according to the system's ultimate criteria of validity must be generally obeyed, and . . . its rules of recognition specifying the criteria of legal validity and its rules of change and adjudication must be effectively accepted as common public standards of official behaviour by its officials' (*CL*, 113). Thus, the Weak Conventionality Thesis explains the existence of law in terms of there being a *conventional* rule of recognition which validates norms that are minimally efficacious in regulating citizen behaviour.

While nearly all positivists, exclusive and inclusive alike, agree that the criteria of validity are authoritative in virtue of a social convention of some kind,[8] they disagree on the character of the convention that confers authority on the criteria of validity. At one point, Coleman entertained the view that the criteria of validity are best characterized as a coordination convention:

The rule of recognition solves the coordination problem of settling on a particular set of criteria of validity. If it is a good idea to have law at all, then it is clearly better that some set of criteria be agreed upon than that there be no agreement, even if individuals differ from one another as to their ranking of the options. (*ICP*, 398)

Thus, once it is established that a system of law is desirable for some reason (which may or may not relate to the solution of a coordination problem), it will be necessary to agree on a set of criteria for determining what properties a norm must have to be law. Different individuals might, of course, prefer different criteria but each presumably has a stronger preference for the state of affairs in which the same criteria are recognized by all officials than for the state of affairs in which each official recognizes her own favoured criteria.

    [6] Jules Coleman, 'Incorporationism, Conventionality, and the Practical Difference Thesis', *Legal Theory*, 4/4 (Dec. 1998), 381–426, 383. Hereinafter referred to as *ICP*.
    [7] Austin, then, does not accept the Weak Conventionality Thesis; for a mere convergence of behaviour (i.e. a habit of obedience) is enough, on his view, to support a legal system.
    [8] Leslie Green is a notable exception. See e.g. Leslie Green, 'Positivism and Conventionalism', *Canadian Journal of Law and Jurisprudence*, 12/1 (Jan. 1999), 35–52.

In response, Marmor rejects the idea that the conventional rule of recognition can be modelled as a solution to a coordination problem:

It seems rather awkward to claim that the rules constituting the game of chess are solutions to a recurrent coordination problem. Antecedent to the game of chess, there was simply no problem to solve. . . . 'Let's have a competitive intellectual game' or something like this is not a coordination problem. . . . If it were, then 'Let's have a just Constitution' would also be a coordination problem, and, of course, it is not.[9]

The problem, on Marmor's view, is that the existence of a coordination convention assumes that parties have a stronger preference for agreement on a solution than for any particular substantive solution. But, as he points out, people are not indifferent with respect to the content of the validity criteria: 'It matters a great deal to all of us, who makes the law, and how it is to be enacted' (*LC*, 517).

Instead, Marmor characterizes the rule of recognition as a constitutive convention. Constitutive conventions are distinguished from coordination conventions in that the former 'constitute the point or value of the activity itself, and it is in this sense that we can talk about autonomous practices' (*LC*, 521). Just as, according to Marmor, the conventional rules of chess create or constitute the autonomous game of chess, the conventional criteria of validity create or constitute the autonomous social practice of law.

For different reasons, Coleman rejects his earlier view that the rule of recognition is necessarily a coordination convention. According to Coleman, 'It would place an arbitrary and baseless constraint on our concept of law to stipulate that the social practice among officials necessary for the existence of a Rule of Recognition must always be representable as a game of partial conflict'.[10] The idea here is that while a rule of recognition is partly constituted by a convergence of attitude, the relevant attitude need not be supported by a preference set that makes possible a solution to a coordination problem.[11] As Coleman points out, 'the large majority [of our social or conventional practices] cannot be modeled as solutions to partial conflict games' (*POP*, 94).

Coleman believes that an explanation of law's conventional character must be sought at a higher level of abstraction. Following Scott Shapiro, Coleman argues that the conventional meta-rule of recognition is most plausibly thought of as being a shared cooperative activity (SCA).[12] Coleman identifies three characteristic features

[9] Andrei Marmor, 'Legal Conventionalism', *Legal Theory*, 4/4 (Dec. 1998), 509–32, 521. Hereinafter referred to as *LC*.

[10] Jules L. Coleman, *The Practice of Principle: In Defence of A Pragmatist Approach to Legal Theory*, The Clarendon Lectures in Law (Oxford: Oxford University Press, 2000), 94. Hereinafter referred to as *POP*.

[11] Coleman describes the structure of such a preference set as follows: 'Although each person's first preference is that all apply his favored set [of validity criteria], each prefers (second) that all apply the *same* set—regardless of which one it is—over the (third-ranked) alternative of applying her own first-choice set while others apply their own (which is to say, the alternative of having no legal system at all)' (*POP*, 92).

[12] See Scott J. Shapiro, 'Law, Plans and Practical Reason', *Legal Theory*, 8/4 (Dec. 2000), 387. The concept of an SCA owes to Michael E. Bratman. See Bratman, 'Shared Cooperative Activity', *Philosophical Review*, 101/2 (Apr. 1992).

of an SCA: (1) each participant in an SCA attempts to conform her behaviour to the behaviour of the other participants; (2) each participant is committed to the joint activity; and (3) each participant is committed to supporting the efforts of the other participants to play their appropriate roles within the joint activity. An SCA, then, enables participants to coordinate their behaviour and also provides ' "a background framework that structures relevant bargaining" between [participants] about how the joint activity is to proceed' (*POP*, 97).

What is conceptually essential to the social practice constituting a conventional rule of recognition, then, is that it has the normative structure of an SCA. It is a conceptual truth about law that officials must coordinate their behaviour with one another in various ways that are responsive to the intentions and actions of the others; what a judge, for example, does in a particular case depends on what other judges have done in similar cases. Similarly, it is a conceptual truth that officials be committed to the joint activity and to supporting one another; officials responsible for promulgating laws require an assurance of continuing support from officials responsible for enforcing and executing those laws. In the absence of the normative features constitutive of an SCA, according to Coleman, legal practice is not conceptually possible.[13]

1.2.2 *The Strong Conventionality Thesis*

Following Hart, Coleman holds that it is a conceptual truth about law that the rule of recognition imposes a legal duty on officials to conform to its criteria of validity. Thus, Coleman and Hart subscribe to:

> The Strong Conventionality Thesis: the conventional rule of recognition is a duty-imposing rule.

The Strong Conventionality Thesis asserts that officials are *obligated* to apply the requirements of the rule of recognition in discharging their official functions and that it is the rule of recognition that autonomously gives rise to this obligation. Of course, officials might also be *morally* obligated to apply the rule of recognition; but whether or not there is such an obligation is a contingent matter that depends on its content. In contrast, it is part of the very nature of law, according to the Strong Conventionality Thesis, that the rule of recognition autonomously obligates officials to conform to its criteria of validity.

Though Raz and Marmor accept that the criteria of validity are conventional and hence accept the Weak Conventionality Thesis, each rejects the Strong

---

[13] Coleman concedes there are conceptually possible legal systems in which the rule of recognition is a constitutive convention but finds this theoretically unhelpful. On his view, the notion of a constitutive convention leaves unexplained why officials would jointly commit to such a rule. In contrast, the notion of a coordinating convention can help to explain such a commitment: in so far as commitment to a shared set of validity criteria is necessary to solve an important coordination problem, officials have a reason to make such a commitment.

Conventionality Thesis. Raz, for example, rejects the Hartian view that the criteria of validity constitute part of the law:

It seems to me that to answer the question whether a certain suggested law exists as a law in a certain legal system one must ultimately refer not to a law but to a jurisprudential criterion. Ultimately one must refer to a general statement that does not describe a law but a general truth about law.[14]

Hart and Coleman, of course, deny the rule of recognition is valid (the idea that the criteria of validity could themselves be valid is incoherent) but hold it is part of the law. In contrast, Raz believes that the criteria of validity are neither valid nor part of the law. While the criteria of validity can be expressed in a propositional rule of recognition, they do not operate to regulate the behaviour of officials. Hence, on Raz's view, the rule of recognition is really no rule at all: it neither imposes duties nor guides (in the relevant sense) official behaviour.

Marmor is more adamant in rejecting the Strong Conventionality Thesis, believing that a social convention, by itself, can never give rise to an obligation:

From a moral or political point of view, the rules of recognition, by themselves, cannot be regarded as sources of obligation. Whether judges, or anybody else, should or should not respect the rules of recognition of a legal system is purely a moral issue that can only be resolved by moral arguments. . . . And this is more generally so: the existence of a social practice, in itself, does not provide anyone with an obligation to engage in the practice. (*LC*, 530)[15]

On Marmor's view, a constitutive convention can give rise to an institution that has its own values and objectives but can never give rise to a self-supporting reason to participate in that institution: '[just as] the constitutive rules of soccer cannot settle for me the question whether I should play soccer or not[,] the rules of recognition cannot settle for the judge, or anyone else for that matter, whether one should play by the rules of law or not' (*LC*, 530).

Ironically, Marmor's scepticism about the ability of a convention to autonomously give rise to an obligation may ultimately derive from Hart's own reasons for rejecting Austin's account of legal obligation. Hart famously rejected Austin's view on the ground that the institutional application of coercive force can no more give rise to an obligation than can the application of coercive force by a gunman. To paraphrase

[14] Joseph Raz, *The Concept of a Legal System*, 2nd edn. (Oxford: Clarendon Press, 1980), 200.

[15] Notably, Raz does not share Marmor's scepticism about the possibility of a social convention that gives rise to an obligation. Consider, for example, Raz's views about what he calls the attitude of respect for law: '[T]he practical respect which some people have for the law is itself a reason to obey the law. The fact that this respect has no ordinary external foundation is acknowledged by the submission that there is no obligation to respect the law even of a good legal system. Respecting the law in such societies is merely permissible. Yet those who respect the law have a reason to obey, indeed are under an obligation to obey. Their attitude of respect is their reason—the source of their obligation. The claim is not merely that they recognize such an obligation, not merely that they think they are bound by an obligation. It is that they really are under an obligation.' Joseph Raz, *The Authority of Law* (Oxford: Clarendon Press, 1979), 253. In so far as a social convention is supported by the appropriate attitude of respect, that convention could, on Raz's view, give rise to an obligation.

Hart, the command of a gunman can *oblige* compliance, but it can never *obligate* compliance.

Unfortunately, Hart failed to provide theoretical resources to insulate his view from his own criticism of Austin. As is readily evident, the situation is no different if the gunman takes the internal point of view towards his authority to make such a threat. Despite the gunman's belief that he is entitled to make the threat, the victim is obliged, but not obligated, to comply with the gunman's orders. The gunman's behaviour is no less coercive simply because he believes he is entitled to make the threat. Likewise, a system of law is no less coercive simply because the officials take the internal point of view towards the rule of recognition.

While the point of Coleman's analysis of the rule of recognition as an SCA is to make explicit the normative structure of the supporting social practice, it also goes a long way in the direction of rescuing Hart from his own criticism of Austin. Part of the problem for Hart is that his analysis of the internal point of view seems unable to explain how a rule of recognition could give rise to autonomous obligations.[16] To take the internal point of view towards the rule can involve no more than regarding it as a standard for criticizing deviating behaviour; indeed, Hart believes that an official can accept the rule of recognition for any reason at all, including purely prudential reasons. But, by itself, one person's unilateral acceptance of a rule as a standard cannot obligate her to abide by the rule; for example, an official whose attitude towards the rule of recognition changes cannot thereby extinguish her obligations under the rule. For this reason, a mere convergence of independent acceptances among officials cannot obligate any of them to abide by the rule.[17]

It is here that the notion of an SCA might contribute to an explanation of how a social practice can give rise to obligations. The notion of an SCA involves more than just a convergence of unilateral acceptances of the rule of recognition. It involves a joint *commitment* on the part of the participants to the activity governed by the rule of recognition. As Coleman puts the point with respect to judges, '[t]he best explanation of judges' responsiveness to one another is their commitment to the goal of making possible the existence of a durable legal practice' (*POP*, 97). And there is no mystery (at least not one that a legal theorist is obliged to solve) about how joint commitments can give rise to obligations; in so far as such commitments induce reliance and a justified set of expectations (whether explicitly or not), they can give rise to

---

[16] It can, however, provide a more limited explanation of the normativity of the rule of recognition. For it is clear that the behaviour of one person A can give another person B a reason to act. To the extent that B has a preference that her behaviour conforms to the behaviour of A, A's doing φ can clearly give rise to a reason in B to also do φ. Further, to the extent that A is committed to regarding B's behaviour as a standard against which to criticize deviations, B's doing φ can provide a weightier reason for A to do φ than it would if A's commitment to doing what B does was merely a preference that A's and B's behaviour converge. Thus, taking the internal point of view towards the behaviour of others can provide a reason to do as the others do.

[17] But note that Coleman has argued Hart never intended his analysis of the internal point of view to explain how social rules give rise to obligations. See *ICP*, 400.

obligations. Thus, if it is a conceptual truth that every rule of recognition has the structure of an SCA, it is also a conceptual truth that every rule of recognition imposes an institutional obligation on the part of officials.

Nevertheless, while Coleman's analysis shows how a Hartian rule of recognition could give rise to obligations on the part of officials, it provides only a partial defence of Hart against his own criticism of Austin. The mere fact that the *officials* commit themselves to legal activity cannot give rise to an obligation on the part of *citizens* to comply with the laws made by officials as part of this commitment. An SCA, for example, may obligate members of a religious community to evaluate even the behaviour of non-members on the basis of religious laws but it cannot obligate non-members to abide by those laws. Thus, if Hart's gunman example is a valid criticism of Austin, a minimal legal system in which there is no commitment on the part of citizens to pursuing a legal system cannot give rise to an obligation on the part of citizens to abide by its laws. To the extent that such laws are enforced by the state's police power, Hart's minimal legal system, even supplemented with the notion of an SCA, is no less coercive than the Austinian legal system.[18]

1.3 The Separability Thesis

The final thesis comprising the foundation of positivism is the Separability Thesis. In its most general form, the Separability Thesis asserts that law and morality are conceptually distinct. This abstract formulation can be interpreted in a number of ways. For example, Klaus Füßer interprets it as making a meta-level claim that the definition of law must be entirely free of moral notions.[19] This interpretation implies that any reference to moral considerations in defining the related notions of law, legal validity, and legal system is inconsistent with the Separability Thesis.

More commonly, the Separability Thesis is interpreted as making an object-level claim about the existence conditions for legal validity. According to the object-level interpretation of the Separability Thesis, it is not a conceptual truth that the validity criteria include moral principles.[20] Thus, the object-level interpretation asserts that there exists a conceptually possible legal system in which the legal validity of a norm

[18] Solving this problem might ultimately require rejecting Hart's view that a legal system cannot be purely coercive—a move that strikes me as the correct one. It is one thing to claim that legal obligation is not *essentially* coercive; it is another to say that legal obligation *cannot be* purely coercive. Hart seems to have overstated the shortcomings in Austin's theory of law. For a discussion of this point, see Kenneth Einar Himma, 'Law's Claim of Legitimate Authority', in Jules Coleman (ed.), *The Postscript: Essays on the Postscript to the Concept of Law* (Oxford: Oxford University Press, forthcoming); and Matthew H. Kramer, 'Requirements, Reasons, and Raz: Legal Positivism and Legal Duties', *Ethics*, 109/1 (Jan. 1999).

[19] Klaus Füßer, 'Farewell to "Legal Positivism": The Separation Thesis Unravelling', in Robert P. George, *The Autonomy of Law: Essays on Legal Positivism* (Oxford: Clarendon Press, 1996), 119–62.

[20] Notice that, thus construed, the Separability Thesis is a straightforward logical consequence of the Weak Conventionality Thesis.

does not depend on its moral merits. In other words, the Separability Thesis asserts that there exists at least one conceptually possible legal system in which the criteria of validity are exclusively source- or pedigree-based.

2 HISTORICAL OVERVIEW OF THE INCORPORATION THESIS

Positivism's Separability Thesis denies that the legality of a norm necessarily depends on its substantive moral merits; as H. L. A. Hart puts it, 'it is in no sense a necessary truth that laws reproduce or satisfy certain demands of morality, though in fact they have often done so' (*CL*, 185–6). Accordingly, the Separability Thesis implies it is logically possible for something that constitutes a legal system to exclude moral norms from the criteria that determine whether a standard is legally valid. In such a legal system, it is neither a necessary nor a sufficient condition for a norm to be legally valid that it conform to (or cohere with) a set of moral norms.

Knowing there can be legal systems without moral criteria of validity, however, does not tell us anything about whether there can be legal systems *with* moral criteria of validity. Inclusive positivists subscribe to the Incorporation Thesis, according to which there are conceptually possible legal systems in which the validity criteria include substantive moral norms. In such legal systems, whether a norm is legally valid depends, at least in part, on the logical relation of its content to the content of the relevant moral norms.

There are two components to the Incorporation Thesis corresponding to two ways in which the validity of a norm could depend on the moral merits of its content. According to the Sufficiency Component, there are conceptually possible legal systems in which it is a sufficient condition for a norm to be legally valid that it reproduces the content of some moral principle. The Sufficiency Component allows, then, that an unpromulgated norm might be legally valid in virtue of its moral content. According to the Necessity Component, there are conceptually possible legal systems in which it is a necessary condition for a norm to be legally valid that its content be consistent with some set of moral norms.[21] Thus, the Necessity Component allows

---

[21] Note that the relevant logical relation differs in each of the components. While the relevant relation in the Necessity Component is the consistency relation, the relevant notion in the Sufficiency Component is the conformity relation. The Sufficiency Component could not use the consistency relation because it would validate inconsistent norms; there are many propositions P such that P and $\sim P$ are each consistent with morality. A law that requires drivers to drive on the right side of the road is no less consistent with moral principles than a law that requires drivers to drive on the left side. Likewise, the

morality to serve as a constraint on promulgated law; it is not enough for a norm to be valid that its content stands in the appropriate logical relation to the content of some moral norms.

The Necessity Component of the Incorporation Thesis was first articulated in Hart's debate with Lon L. Fuller. In *The Morality of Law*, Fuller argued that the conceptual function of law is to guide behaviour.[22] To be capable of performing law's conceptual function, on Fuller's view, a system of rules must satisfy the following principles: (P1) the rules must be expressed in general terms; (P2) the rules must be publicly promulgated; (P3) the rules must be (for the most part) prospective in effect; (P4) the rules must be expressed in understandable terms; (P5) the rules must be consistent with one another; (P6) the rules must not require conduct beyond the powers of the affected parties; (P7) the rules must not be changed so frequently that the subject cannot rely on them; and (P8) the rules must be administered in a manner consistent with their wording (*ML*, 39). No system of rules that fails minimally to satisfy these 'principles of legality', according to Fuller, can achieve law's purpose of achieving social order through the use of rules that guide behaviour.

Fuller believed his functionalist theory of law had an important advantage over Hart's theory: the principles of legality operate as moral constraints on the behaviour of lawmakers and hence show that, contra Austin, lawmakers do not necessarily have unlimited discretion to make law. On Fuller's view, Hart's notion of a rule of recognition is inconsistent with any kind of constraint on enacted legislation: 'Hart seems to read into this characterization [of the rule of recognition] the . . . notion that the rule cannot contain any express or tacit provision to the effect that the authority it confers can be withdrawn' (*ML*, 137). In so far as there is no way to restrict lawmaking authority in Hart's theory, he is committed to unlimited lawmaking discretion—a proposition that is difficult to reconcile with what appear to be constraints on enacted law in many legal systems.

In response, Hart denied Fuller's assumption that a rule of recognition cannot contain substantive constraints on lawmaking behaviour: '[A] constitution could include in its restrictions on the legislative power even of its supreme legislature not only conformity with due process but a completely general provision that its legal power should lapse if its enactments ever conflicted with principles of morality and justice'.[23] Hart here is making two distinct claims: (1) the content of legislation can be constrained by moral principles, such as due process; and (2) the power of the legislature can be revoked if it fails to make legislation in conformity with morality.

Necessity Component could not use the conformity relation because it would result in too few norms—at least in modern legal systems. Many laws are intended as solutions to coordination problems and hence do not reproduce the content of some moral norm.

[22] Lon L. Fuller, *The Morality of Law* (New Haven: Yale University Press, 1963). Hereinafter referred to as *ML*.

[23] H. L. A. Hart, 'Book Review of *The Morality of Law*', *Harvard Law Review*, 78 (1965), 1281, reprinted in H. L. A. Hart, *Essays in Jurisprudence and Philosophy* (Oxford: Clarendon Press, 1983), 361.

Whether these two claims are ultimately equivalent is not clear; but the first is just the Necessity Component of the Incorporation Thesis.

The Sufficiency Component of the Incorporation Thesis was, in contrast, developed later in response to Dworkin's analysis of *Riggs v Palmer* (the 'Original Problem').[24] In *Riggs*, the court considered the question of whether a murderer should be allowed to take under his victim's will. At the time the case was decided, neither the statutes nor the case law governing wills expressly prohibited such takings. Despite this, the court declined to award the defendant his gift under the will on the ground that doing so would be inconsistent with the principle that no person should profit from her own wrong (the *Riggs* principle). Since the judges would 'rightfully' have been criticized for failure to consider this principle, the *Riggs* principle must, according to Dworkin, be characterized as part of the community's law.

Dworkin argues that the status of the *Riggs* principle as law is inconsistent with positivism because the validity of a principle cannot derive from pedigree- or source-based criteria: '[e]ven though principles draw support from the official acts of legal institutions, they do not have a simple or direct enough connection with these acts to frame that connection in terms of criteria specified by some ultimate master rule of recognition' (*TRS*, 41). What explains the validity of the *Riggs* principle, on Dworkin's view, is not its pedigree or source, but rather its content: the principle that no person should profit from her own wrong is legally valid because it is a moral requirement of fairness.

The positivist has a number of moves available in response.[25] For example, the positivist can argue that the judges in *Riggs* reached outside the law in deciding the case on the basis of the moral principle that no person shall profit from her own wrong. The *Riggs* principle, on this line of reasoning, is neither legally valid nor legally binding (in the way a law of another country might be legally binding on a judge in a case involving that country's law). The judges in *Riggs* were free to apply or ignore this principle as they saw fit in the exercise of strong judicial discretion. But this, of course, is not a plausible response. The sheer prevalence of such principles in judicial decision-making and the expectations of the public in regard to such practices suggest that judges are *bound* to consider such principles in deciding hard cases—even if Dworkin turns out to be wrong in thinking they are part of the law.

David Lyons adopts a different strategy; on his view, Dworkin's criticism rests on a caricature of Hart's positivism:

Dworkin's critique . . . turns upon a fundamental misconception of legal positivism, namely, that the positivists' use of 'pedigree' as a test for legal standards excludes tests of 'content.' . . . Hart claims that we can think of every legal system as having a 'rule of recognition,' which, if it were formulated, would state the ultimate criteria that officials actually use in validating legal standards. . . . Hart seems to place no limits on the sort of test that might be employed by

---

[24] Ronald Dworkin, *Taking Rights Seriously* (Cambridge, Mass.: Harvard University Press, 1977). Hereinafter referred to as *TRS*.

[25] The following discussion owes an obvious debt to Coleman's discussion of the issue in *ICP*.

officials, and the reason is simple: unlike other legal rules, the rule of recognition may be said to exist only by virtue of the actual practice of officials. Nothing else determines the content of this rule. The tests for law in a system are whatever officials make them—and Hart suggests no limits on the possibilities.[26]

Inasmuch as there are no constraints on the content of a rule of recognition, a rule of recognition can incorporate validity criteria that make moral merit a sufficient condition for legal validity. Thus, as Philip Soper points out, there is nothing in Hart that would logically preclude a rule of recognition that provides that all disputes are to be settled as justice required.[27]

Hart is generally taken as accepting the Sufficiency Component, but he has never clearly and unambiguously endorsed it. The closest Hart has come to embracing the Sufficiency Component is in his remarks in the postscript where he rejects 'plain-fact' positivism in favour of the Incorporation Thesis:

Dworkin in attributing to me a doctrine of 'plain-fact positivism' has mistakenly treated my theory . . . as requiring . . . that the criteria of validity which the rule provides should consist exclusively of the specific kind of plain fact which he calls 'pedigree' matters. . . . [This] ignores my explicit acknowledgement that the rule of recognition may incorporate as criteria of legal validity conformity with moral principles or substantive values. (*CL*, 250).

Thus, according to Hart, Dworkin's view that positivism is committed to exclusively source-based criteria of validity misunderstands Hart's theory: 'there is nothing in my [theory that suggests the] . . . criteria provided by the rule of recognition must be solely matters of pedigree; they may instead be substantive constraints on the content of legislation such as the Sixteenth or Nineteenth Amendments to the United States Constitution' (*CL*, 250).

While it is clear from this passage that Hart supports the Necessity Component, it is not quite as clear that he endorses the Sufficiency Component.[28] Nevertheless, Hart is most plausibly construed as being committed to both components. First, as Lyons points out, Hart rejects the idea that there are any constraints on the content of the social practice giving rise to the rule of recognition; indeed, Hart himself asserts that '[t]here is . . . no logical restriction on the content of the rule of recognition'.[29] Secondly, as Coleman argues, Hart's point in reaffirming the Incorporation Thesis in response to Dworkin was to show that positivism could accommodate his view that

[26] David Lyons, 'Principles, Positivism, and Legal Theory', *Yale Law Journal*, 87 (1977), 415, 423–4. See also Jules Coleman, 'Negative and Positive Positivism', *Journal of Legal Studies*, 11 (1982), 139, reprinted in Marshall Cohen, *Ronald Dworkin and Contemporary Jurisprudence* (Totowa, NJ: Rowman & Allanheld, 1983). Hereinafter referred to as *NAPP*. Coleman was not the first to articulate the Sufficiency Component as a solution to the Original Problem but is, more than anyone else, responsible for its subsequent development and importance in legal philosophy.

[27] Philip Soper, 'Legal Theory and the Obligation of a Judge: The Hart/Dworkin Dispute', *Michigan Law Review*, 75 (Jan. 1977), 473.

[28] Some inclusive positivists, such as Waluchow and Kramer, endorse only the Necessity Component of the Incorporation Thesis.

[29] Hart, 'Book Review of *The Morality of Law*', 361.

the *Riggs* principle is legally valid because it is a moral requirement of fairness.[30] Since only the Sufficiency Component can accommodate Dworkin's analysis of *Riggs*, Hart is most plausibly construed as adopting both components of the Incorporation Thesis.

Exclusive positivists adopt a different strategy for responding to the Original Problem. They reject Dworkin's analysis of *Riggs*, arguing instead that the authority of the *Riggs* principle must be explained in terms of its having an authoritative source. Thus, exclusive positivists deny the Incorporation Thesis and subscribe instead to the Source Thesis, according to which the existence and content of law can always be determined by reference to its sources without recourse to moral argument.

Nevertheless, denying the Incorporation Thesis does not commit exclusive positivists to denying the obvious fact that legal systems often include validity criteria that are described using moral language. Exclusive positivists concede, as they must, both that criteria of validity often contain moral language and that judges often engage in moral argumentation in making decisions about the validity of judicial and legislative acts.

What exclusive positivists deny is that the presence of moral language in a rule of recognition succeeds in making moral requirements part of the law; otherwise put, they deny that ostensibly moral provisions in a rule of recognition succeed in incorporating moral content into the validity criteria.[31] Instead, they argue that such provisions, if part of the law, must be construed as directions that courts consider moral norms under certain circumstances. Exclusive positivists, for example, construe the Eighth Amendment as requiring that judges consider moral standards prohibiting cruelty in determining whether to allow certain punishments to be administered; these moral standards are binding but not law. Complying with this directive, of course, will require judges to engage in precisely the sort of moral argument that seems to be common in constitutional cases. But exclusive positivists insist that judicial rulings on such matters necessarily involve creating new law in the exercise of

[30] See, generally, *PoP*, Chapter 8.

[31] But it is important to note that the Source Thesis does not commit the exclusive positivist to claiming it is never possible for law to incorporate morality. The Source Thesis and the Incorporation Thesis are claims about what can be included in a *rule of recognition*. The Source Thesis, by its own terms, claims only that the criteria of validity consists entirely of source-based standards relating to the procedural conditions under which law can be promulgated. Thus, while the Source Thesis precludes incorporation of moral content into the rule of recognition, there is nothing in the Source Thesis, by itself, that commits the exclusive positivist to denying that the law can incorporate moral principles as first-order rules.

And some exclusive positivists explicitly allow for the possibility that moral principles can be incorporated into the law as long as they have an authoritative source—and do not function as criteria of validity. As Scott Shapiro, describes the view, '[t]he promise-keeping rule, for example, may only become law when some authoritative body duly enacts or practices it; if the promise-keeping rule lacks a direct social pedigree, it may never count as a legal norm'. Scott J. Shapiro, 'The Difference that Rules Make', in Brian Bix (ed.), *Analyzing Law: New Essays in Legal Theory* (Oxford: Clarendon Press, 1998), 57.

judicial discretion. Thus, on this view, provisions of the rule of recognition that include moral language succeed, at most, in incorporating into the law judicial holdings about morality.[32]

Inclusive positivists may appear to have the stronger view; for their interpretation of the relevant legal practices seems easier to reconcile with both the language of directives that include moral terms and the associated practices of lawyers and judges.[33] After all, the Eighth Amendment asserts that 'cruel and unusual punishment [shall not be] inflicted' and not that 'judges should consult the moral notion of cruelty in deciding whether to uphold a punishment'. But critics of inclusive positivism have developed a number of arguments purporting to show that inclusive legal positivism is conceptually incoherent. According to these critics, who range from anti-positivists like Dworkin to exclusive positivists like Raz and Shapiro, inclusive positivism is untenable because the Incorporation Thesis is inconsistent with other basic commitments of positivism.

3 THE INCORPORATION THESIS AND THE SOCIAL FACT THESIS

In 'The Model of Rules I', Dworkin anticipates the Hartian solution to the Original Problem and rejects it. On his view, the validity of legal principles cannot be explained by a rule of recognition that defines purely social criteria of validity:

[W]e could not devise any formula for testing how much and what kind of institutional support is necessary to make a principle a legal principle, still less to fix its weight at a particular order of magnitude. We argue for a particular principle by grappling with a whole set of shifting, developing and interacting standards . . . about institutional responsibility, statutory interpretation, the persuasive force of various sorts of precedent, the relation of all these to contemporary moral practices, and hosts of other such standards. We could not bolt all of

---

[32] For this reason, exclusive positivism cannot be falsified by the obvious fact that written constitutions often contain clauses that are expressed using moral language.

[33] Many theorists, like Waluchow, accept the Necessity Component because of its descriptive accuracy; the Necessity Component more tightly coheres than other positivist theories with the empirical fact that constitutional provisions frequently include moral language that constrains legislative lawmaking. For these theorists, the Incorporation Thesis enjoys a special epistemic status: in so far as a claim C about legal practice conflicts with the Incorporation Thesis, that constitutes a prima facie reason for rejecting C. Coleman rejects this view: '[T]he dispute between exclusive and inclusive legal positivists cannot be resolved on descriptive grounds, for the simple reason that the dispute is not a descriptive one' (POP, 109). The issue for Coleman is whether there exists a coherent *conceptual* framework that includes the Incorporation Thesis.

these together into a single 'rule,' even a complex one, and if we could the result would bear little relation to Hart's picture of a rule of recognition. (*TRS*, 40–1)[34]

The problem with Hart's solution, then, is that a rule of recognition cannot specify how much weight a principle should receive because its weight can be determined only by complex strategies of moral reasoning that cannot be expressed in a rule of recognition.

This line of criticism presupposes that the conceptual function of a rule of recognition is to provide a test that decides all questions of law. Indeed, as Dworkin frequently describes Hart's view, it is a conceptual truth that 'in every legal system some commonly-accepted test does exist for law, in the shape of a social rule, and this is enough to distinguish legal from moral rules and principles' (*TRS*, 60). But, according to Dworkin, there cannot be a test for resolving questions of law involving standards with the dimension of weight: the role that such standards play in legal reasoning is too complex to be captured by something as simple as a test.

Dworkin's argument here fails because there is nothing in the concept of a rule of recognition that commits the positivist to claiming it provides a test that eliminates uncertainty about what legally valid norms and principles require. Thus, Hart writes:

> [Many of Dworkin's criticisms] rest on a misunderstanding of the function of the rule. It assumes that the rule is meant to determine completely the legal result in particular cases, so that any legal issue arising in any case could simply be solved by mere appeal to the criteria or tests provided by the rule. But this is a misconception. (*CL*, 258)

Indeed, Hart believes that uncertainty with respect to what the law requires is inevitable: '[w]hichever device . . . is chosen for the communication of standards of behaviour, these, however smoothly they work over the great mass of ordinary cases, will, at some point where their application is in question, prove indeterminate; they will have what has been termed an *open texture*' (*CL*, 127–8). Where a legal dispute involves a question of law implicating a rule's open texture, 'uncertainties as to the form of behaviour required by them may break out in particular concrete cases' (*CL*, 126).

Moreover, as Coleman points out, a rule of recognition need not serve any identification function at all: 'The rule of recognition sets out validity or membership conditions. It may, but it need not, serve an epistemic role. It may, but it need not, provide the vehicle through which individuals identify the law and its content' (*ICP*, 416). As a matter of empirical fact, most ordinary citizens and lawyers do not directly use the rule of recognition as an identification rule. Instead they rely on official and

---

[34] Strictly speaking, Dworkin's criticism here applies to *any* attempt to explain the legal validity of moral principles in terms of a rule of recognition, including exclusivist attempts to explain the binding authority of such principles in terms of formal promulgation. See Joseph Raz, 'Legal Principles and the Limits of Law', *Yale Law Journal*, 81 (1972), 823. Nevertheless, I include a short discussion of this criticism here because of its historical importance and because the claim that moral principles can be legally valid in virtue of source (as opposed to content) is mildly incorporationist.

unofficial reporters identifying sentences that were purportedly enacted in accordance with the rule of recognition. While such individuals rely indirectly on the rule of recognition by trusting that these reporters accurately reproduce sentences satisfying the validation conditions of the rule, they are not using the rule of recognition directly to identify sentences that give rise to valid law. Of course, this does not preclude using the rule of recognition as an identification rule, but it does show that the rule of recognition need not serve as such.

What is essential to the concept of a rule of recognition is that it provides the conditions that must be satisfied by a norm for it to count as legally valid. Thus, the rule of recognition sets out *validation* conditions: a legal norm has the property of validity because and only because it satisfies the criteria contained in the rule of recognition. For example, the rule prohibiting intentional killing in Washington is valid because and only because it was enacted by the legislature according to the procedures described in the rule of recognition. Dworkin's criticism, then, fails not only to the extent that it assumes that the rule of recognition must provide a test for identifying questions of law, but also to the extent that it assumes the rule of recognition must set out *identification* conditions.

4 The Incorporation Thesis and the Weak Conventionality Thesis

Exclusive and inclusive positivists flesh out the Weak Conventionality Thesis in different ways, but the basic idea is this: the criteria of legal validity are established by a social convention in the form of a rule of recognition. If legal standards are distinguished from non-legal standards in that the former satisfy, while the latter do not, the criteria established by a conventional rule of recognition, it follows that the validity criteria are exhausted by the conventional rule of recognition in the following sense: for every proposition P, P is legally valid if and only if it satisfies the criteria articulated in the conventional rule of recognition.

Dworkin believes that certain kinds of disagreement about law are inconsistent with Hart's characterization of the rule of recognition as a 'social rule'. As a social (or conventional) rule, the rule of recognition has an external and internal aspect. The external aspect consists in general obedience to the norms satisfying its validity criteria; the internal aspect consists in its acceptance by officials as a standard of official behaviour. On Dworkin's view, this element of Hart's theory entails that there cannot be any disagreement about the content of the rule of recognition:

Hart's qualification . . . that the rule of recognition may be uncertain at particular points . . . undermines [his theory]. . . . If judges are in fact divided about what they must do if a subsequent Parliament tries to repeal an entrenched rule, then it is not uncertain whether any social rule [of recognition] governs that decision; on the contrary, it is certain that none does. (*TRS*, 61–2)

As Dworkin reads Hart, the requirements of a social rule simply cannot be controversial: 'two people whose rules differ . . . cannot be appealing to the same social rule, and at least one of them cannot be appealing to any social rule at all' (*TRS*, 55).

The problem here arises because of the rule of recognition's internal aspect. Disagreement among citizens about the content of the rule of recognition presents no problem because Hart's theory does not assume that they accept or understand the rule, but disagreement among officials is another story. In so far as the rule's internal aspect is defined by a critical reflective attitude towards the rule, it seems to entail understanding of the rule's contents. Since Hart requires that officials adopt a critical reflective attitude towards the *same* rule, it seems to follow that they share an understanding of the contents of the rule of recognition. But if the rule of recognition exhausts the criteria for legal validity and is constituted by a shared understanding among officials, it is not clear how there could be disagreement among officials about the rule's content.

The exclusive positivist has a straightforward response: the disagreements to which Dworkin refers are not disagreements about what the rule of recognition *is*; rather they are disagreements about what it *should be*. This response implicitly concedes Dworkin's claim that if there is disagreement about what a conventional rule requires, there is no convention and hence no rule on the issue; on this view, the presence of controversy about the content of a convention signals a gap in the content of the convention. For this reason, controversy about what the rule of recognition requires in some circumstance signals a gap in the content of the rule of recognition; the rule has simply run out. Such disagreements among officials, then, are about what the content of the rule of recognition *should be*.

But the inclusive positivist cannot rest on such a response. Moral norms are not usually thought of as being conventional. On traditional understandings of critical morality, the requirements of a moral norm can be determinate even when people disagree about what the norm requires. Thus, in so far as the inclusive positivist holds that the rule of recognition incorporates the content of a moral norm in the sense that it makes *that* norm part of the meta-rule, it will not do merely to claim that controversy about the meta-rule indicates a gap in its content. For if the relevant provision is just some moral norm, there can be controversy about what that provision requires in a given case without it implying that the provision is indeterminate. Thus, the inclusive positivist needs to explain how there could be controversy about a rule of recognition that incorporates moral content.

Coleman provides such an explanation. As Coleman points out, if the rule of recognition is a social rule, then Hart's view implies there must be general agreement among the officials of a legal system about what standards constitute the rule of recognition. But it does not imply there cannot be disagreement as to what those standards require in any given instance:

> The controversy among judges does not arise over the content of the rule of recognition itself. It arises over which norms satisfy the standards set forth in it. The divergence in behavior among officials as exemplified in their identifying different standards as legal ones does not establish their failure to accept the same rule of recognition. On the contrary, judges accept the same truth conditions for propositions of law. . . . They disagree about which propositions satisfy those conditions. (*NAPP*, 156)

Coleman, then, distinguishes two kinds of disagreement practitioners can have about the rule of recognition: (1) disagreement about what standards constitute the rule of recognition; and (2) disagreement about what propositions satisfy those standards. On Coleman's view, Hart's analysis of social rules implies only that (1) is impossible.

5 THE INCORPORATION THESIS AND THE SEPARABILITY THESIS

Hart's response to the criticisms raised by Fuller and Dworkin is, as we have seen, to adopt the Incorporation Thesis, but Hart is not entirely comfortable with this strategy. A few pages later, Hart qualifies his endorsement of the Incorporation Thesis: 'if it is an open question whether moral principles and values have objective standing, it must also be an open question whether "soft positivist" provisions purporting to include conformity with them among the tests for existing law can have that effect or instead, can only constitute directions to courts to make law in accordance with morality' (*CL*, 254).

Hart's concern here is that the Incorporation Thesis presupposes the objectivity of moral norms (i.e., that moral principles have objective standing or are objectively true). Hart believes that legal norms can constrain judicial decision-making only if such norms have objective content (i.e. only if there is an objectively correct answer to what the norm requires). If a legal norm lacks such content, then there is no possibility of the judge making a mistake about its content; thus, it is up to the judge to determine content on the basis of extralegal considerations. Determining the content of such a norm, then, necessarily involves legislating, rather than just judging. Thus, if moral norms lack objective standing, then the only way, on Hart's view, to give effect to a legal norm containing moral language is to treat it as directing the judge to exercise his 'law-making discretion in accordance with his best understanding of morality' (*CL*, 253). Since it is an open question whether moral objectivism is true, it is an open question whether a rule of recognition can incorporate moral criteria of validity.

Dworkin, however, argues that a commitment to moral objectivism is problematic for positivism because it is inconsistent with the Separability Thesis's claim that 'the objective standing of propositions of law [is] independent of any controversial moral theory either of meta-ethics or of moral ontology' (*TRS*, 349). As Dworkin sees it, the Separability Thesis 'promis[es an] ontological separation of law from morals' (*TRS*, 348–9). On this view of the Separability Thesis, there can be no overlap between questions about the existence of *any* law-related standard or institution and questions about morality. Any intersection of legal and moral validity at even the level of *contingent* description would violate the Separability Thesis, thus construed, because questions about whether a standard is legally valid are ontological questions about whether that standard, so to speak, exists as a law.

This line of criticism misconstrues Hart's version of the Separability Thesis. As Hart expresses this thesis, 'it is in no sense a necessary truth that laws reproduce or satisfy certain demands of morality, though in fact they have often done so' (*CL*, 185–6). Hart's articulation of the Separability Thesis is weaker than Dworkin's version in an important respect: whereas Dworkin interprets the Separability Thesis as implying there *cannot* be any moral constraints on legal validity, Hart interprets it as implying only that there *need not* be any moral constraints on legal validity.

Dworkin's criticism, then, presupposes an implausibly broad construction of the Separability Thesis; there is simply no reason to think that the Separability Thesis, by itself, promises a complete ontological separation of law and morality. Indeed, most positivists follow Hart in claiming that the criteria for legal validity must, as a conceptual matter, include rules for making, changing, and adjudicating laws. But apart from that conceptual restriction, it is up to each society to decide what standards will make up its criteria of validity. The point of the Separability Thesis is to emphasize that there are no necessary substantive moral constraints on what standards a society can include in its criteria of validity. For this reason, the Separability Thesis implies there is a conceptually possible legal system without moral standards in its validity criteria, but leaves open the issue of whether there is a conceptually possible legal system *with* moral standards in its validity criteria.[35]

---

[35] Exclusive positivists, of course, deny this possibility, but for reasons that have nothing to do with the intuitions that (1) 'the existence of a law is one thing, its merit another' and (2) the notions of law and morality are conceptually distinct, which motivate the Separability Thesis. As we will see in the next section, Raz subscribes to the Source Thesis because he believes the Incorporation Thesis is inconsistent with the nature of authority. Dworkin and Raz each reject inclusive positivism but for different reasons.

6 THE INCORPORATION THESIS AND THE NATURE OF AUTHORITY

6.1 The Nature of Authority

At the foundation of the Razian critique of inclusive positivism is the view that law necessarily claims legitimate authority (the Authority Thesis).[36] Raz concedes that law's claim of authority is often false, but he insists this claim is 'part of the nature of law': 'though a legal system may not have legitimate authority, or though its legitimate authority may not be as extensive as it claims, every legal system claims that it possesses legitimate authority' (*ALM*, 215). The Authority Thesis, then, purports to state a conceptual truth about law: it is part of the very concept of law that law claims legitimate authority.

On Raz's view, the Authority Thesis implies that, as a conceptual matter, law must be *capable* of possessing legitimate authority: 'If the claim to authority is part of the nature of law, then whatever else the law is it must be capable of possessing authority' (*ALM*, 215). A normative system that is not the kind of thing capable of possessing authority is conceptually disqualified from being a legal system.

To be capable of possessing authority, the law must be able to 'mediate between people and the right reasons that apply to them' (*ALM*, 214). According to Raz's 'service conception of authority', the conceptual point or function of authority is to stand between subjects and the reasons that apply to them by providing directives that reflect those reasons. A normative system that cannot perform this mediating function is incapable of possessing authority and is hence conceptually disqualified from being a legal system.

Crucial to Raz's service conception of authority is the special status that authority purports to have in practical deliberations. Unlike the advice of a third person, which provides one reason to be weighed in the balance with other reasons, an authoritative directive replaces—or preempts—those other reasons:

The [authority's] decision is for the [subjects] a reason for action. They ought to do as he says because he says so. . . . [But] it is not just another reason to be added to the others, a reason to stand alongside the others when one reckons which way is better supported by reason. . . . The [authority's] decision is also meant to replace the reasons on which it depends. In agreeing to obey his decision, the [subjects] agreed to follow his judgment of the balance of reasons rather than their own. Henceforth his decision will settle for them what to do. (*ALM*, 212–13)

On Raz's view, then, the conceptual function of authority implies that authoritative directives play (or should play) this special role in practical deliberation. Thus,

---

[36] Joseph Raz, 'Authority, Law, and Morality', *The Monist*, 68/3 (1985), in Raz, *Ethics in the Public Domain* (Oxford: Clarendon Press, 1994). References are to the reprint. Hereinafter identified as *ALM*.

according to the Preemption Thesis, 'the fact that an authority requires performance of an action is a reason for its performance which is not to be added to all other relevant reasons when assessing what to do, but should replace some of them' (*ALM*, 214).

Raz believes that these conceptual features of authority determine the conditions under which an authority is morally legitimate. Given that authority is supposed to 'serve' its subjects, there is no reason to accept an authority unless two conditions are satisfied. First, according to the Normal Justification Thesis (NJT), it must be the case that the disputant 'is likely to better comply with reasons which apply to him (other than the alleged authoritative directives) if he accepts the directives of the alleged authority as authoritatively binding, and tries to follow them, than if he tries to follow the reasons which apply to him directly' (*ALM*, 214). Secondly, according to the Dependence Thesis, authoritative directives should be based on reasons that already apply to the subjects.

Of course, NJT and the Dependence Thesis also apply to advice in so far as the point of advice, as seems plausible, is to serve the advisees; for this reason, any implications of just these two theses also apply to advice. For example, NJT and the Dependence Thesis imply that a service directive must be presented as someone's view about how people should behave—which is true, of course, of both authority and advice. But when NJT and the Dependence Thesis are combined with the Preemption Thesis, which distinguishes advice from authority, they imply that authoritative directives have a property that distinguishes them from merely advisory directives:

> The Identification Thesis: It must always be possible to identify the existence and content of an authoritative directive without recourse to the dependent reasons that justify that directive.

Inability to identify the existence or content of advisory statements without recourse to the reasons that justify that advice might diminish the utility of those statements *qua* advice, but it does not conceptually disqualify those statements from being advice. But inability to identify the existence or content of a directive without recourse to its dependent justification conceptually disqualifies that directive from being authority.

The reason for this somewhat surprising result is that the conceptual point of authority is to benefit subjects by providing directives that reflect the balance of applicable reasons and *preempt* the subjects' judgments about that balance. A directive that *cannot* be identified by the subject without recourse to the balance of reasons is *incapable* of preempting that balance in the deliberations of the subject. Thus, as Raz points out, subjects of authority 'can benefit by its decisions only if they can establish their existence and content in ways which do not depend on raising the very same issues which the authority is there to settle' (*ALM*, 219).

Raz argues that the Identification and Authority Theses are inconsistent with the Incorporation Thesis. Since law necessarily claims authority, the law must be capable of possessing legitimate authority and hence, according to the Identification Thesis, be identifiable without recourse to the dependent reasons justifying the law. But the content of a moral norm cannot be identified without recourse to the reasons justifying that norm. To determine what the law *is*, for example, under a recognition rule that validates only enacted norms consistent with the requirements of justice, we must identify the moral requirements of justice that ultimately justify *that law*. We cannot determine the validity of, say, an enacted norm prohibiting the killing of innocent persons without recourse to the requirements of justice as they pertain to such killings. This implies that the content of a moral rule cannot be incorporated into the rule of recognition because the law *qua* authority is supposed to settle disputes about what the law requires. If the Identification and Authority Theses are true, then the Incorporation Thesis must be false.

Schematically, Raz's argument can be summarized as follows:

1. The conceptual point of an authoritative directive is to preempt the balance of reasons it reflects.
2. It is a necessary condition for authority to be legitimate that (1) the Dependence Thesis be satisfied and (2) NJT be satisfied.
3. If premises 1 and 2 are true, then it is a necessary condition for authority to be legitimate that the existence and content of an authoritative directive can always be identified without recourse to the dependent reasons justifying the directive.
4. Therefore, it is a necessary condition for authority to be legitimate that the existence and content of an authoritative directive can always be identified without recourse to the dependent reasons justifying the directive. (From 1, 2, 3)
5. It is a conceptual truth that law claims legitimate authority.
6. If it is a conceptual truth that law claims legitimate authority, then law is the sort of thing that is always capable of being legitimate authority.
7. If law is the sort of thing that is always capable of being legitimate authority, then law must be capable of satisfying the necessary condition for authority to be legitimate.
8. Therefore, if law is the sort of thing that is always capable of being legitimate authority, then the existence and content of a legally authoritative directive can always be identified without recourse to the dependent reasons justifying the directive. (From 4, 7)
9. Therefore, if it is a conceptual truth that law claims legitimate authority, then the existence and content of a legally authoritative directive can always be identified without recourse to the dependent reasons justifying the directive. (From 6, 8)
10. Therefore, the existence and content of a legally authoritative directive can always be identified without recourse to the dependent reasons justifying the directive. (From 5, 9)
11. The existence and content of a legal norm validated by moral criteria of validity *cannot* be identified without recourse to the dependent reasons justifying that norm.

12. If premises 10 and 11 are true, then the Incorporation Thesis is false.

13. Therefore, the Incorporation Thesis is false. (From 10, 11, 12)

6.2 Coleman's Compatibility Argument

Coleman rejects Raz's view that the Incorporation Thesis is inconsistent with the set of theses making up the service conception of authority. On Coleman's view, it is not necessarily true that a legal norm authoritative in virtue of its moral merits can be identified only by recourse to the dependent reasons justifying that norm. Consider, for example, a legal system with the rule of recognition that 'only enacted norms that treat individuals fairly are legally valid' and a valid legal prohibition on intentional killing. According to Coleman:

Certain reasons of fairness and equality (for example, does the law offer fair opportunities for appeal?, is it fairly administered?, etc.) are not part of the justification for laws prohibiting murder. A prohibition against murder would be justified or defensible just because it violates Mill's Harm Principle, or because murder violates the Categorical Imperative, or because it is inefficient . . . or whatever. On the other hand, it is perfectly sensible that no particular prohibition could count as law unless it met certain requirements of fairness and equal treatment in its administration. This is just another way of saying that the evaluative considerations that go to the legality of a rule need not coincide with those that go to the underlying merits of the rule. (*ST*, 271)

While recourse to considerations of fairness may be necessary to identify the murder prohibition as a legal norm, one can none the less identify the murder norm without recourse to its dependent justification because considerations of fairness are irrelevant with respect to that norm's justification. Thus, even if *all* of Raz's central claims about authority are true, '[e]valuative criteria of legality as such do not vitiate law's claim to authority' (*ST*, 271).

In response, Brian Leiter argues that merely pointing to one example of an inclusively validated norm that can be identified without recourse to the dependent reasons justifying adoption of the rule cannot defeat the Razian objection. On Leiter's view, 'it suffices to defeat Soft Positivism as a theory compatible with the law's authority if there exists *any* case in which the dependent reasons are the same as the moral reasons that are required to identify what the law is; that there remain some cases where these reasons "may" be different is irrelevant'.[37] Accordingly, Leiter concludes Coleman has it backwards: one contrary case shows 'that Soft Positivism is incompatible with the (in-principle) authority of law'.[38]

---

[37] Brian Leiter, 'Realism, Positivism, and Conceptual Analysis', *Legal Theory*, 4/4 (Dec. 1998), 541.

[38] Leiter, 'Realism, Positivism, and Conceptual Analysis', 542.

6.3 The Preemption Thesis

Waluchow attempts to reconcile the Incorporation Thesis with the Authority Thesis by challenging the claim that authoritative directives necessarily provide preemptive reasons. Waluchow believes that the Canadian Charter is an inclusive rule of recognition that can exert authority without providing preemptive (i.e. exclusionary) reasons. Thus, for example, he points out that the Canadian Supreme Court held in *Regina v Oakes* that a Charter right can be limited provided that the objectives of doing so are 'sufficiently important' and that there is no other way to achieve those objectives. On the basis of such examples, Waluchow concludes that 'Charter rights . . . are not fully exclusionary, but they do enjoy a very heavy presumption in their favor'.[39]

But Waluchow's observation that the scope of a constitutional right can be limited by other kinds of value cannot, by itself, defeat the Razian critique. For Raz concedes that exclusionary directives may sometimes operate in precisely this way:

An exclusionary reason may exclude all or only a certain class of first-order reasons. The scope of an exclusionary reason is the class of reasons it excludes. Just as any reason has an intrinsic strength which can be affected by strength-affecting reasons so every second-order reason has, as well as a strength, an intrinsic scope which can be affected by scope-affecting reasons.[40]

Accordingly, Raz can respond that the reasons provided by the Canadian Charter are exclusionary but none the less have a limited scope that excludes the more important values that can justify limiting a Charter right. Just as a sergeant's command must yield to commands by higher-ranking servicemen, the protections of the Canadian Charter must yield to protections of more important values.

Heidi Hurd adopts a more aggressive strategy against the Preemption Thesis; whereas Waluchow wishes to show there are forms of authority that do not provide preemptive reasons, Hurd argues that the very notion of a pre-emptive reason as it functions in Raz's theory is conceptually incoherent. Hurd believes that if Raz is correct, then obedience to authority is irrational because it contradicts the principle that an agent should act in accordance with the balance of reasons.[41] In so far as the Razian account of authority requires an agent to comply with an authoritative directive regardless of whether the directive conforms to the balance of reasons, it violates this central principle of rationality by requiring the agent to ignore reasons that would otherwise apply to her.

Such implications need not cause theoretical anxiety, on Hurd's view, because Raz's concept of a content-independent preemptive reason is incoherent. Hurd

---

[39] Wilfrid Waluchow, 'Authority and the Practical Difference Thesis: A Defense of Inclusive Legal Positivism', *Legal Theory*, 6/1 (Mar. 2000), 45–82, at 58.

[40] Joseph Raz, *Practical Reasons and Norms* (Princeton: Princeton University Press, 1990), 46.

[41] Heidi M. Hurd, 'Challenging Authority', *Yale Law Journal*, 100 (1991), 1611. Hereinafter referred to as *CA*.

believes that Raz's theory of authority implies that if an action is rational solely because it is commanded by a legitimate practical authority acting within the scope of such authority, then any action commanded by a legitimate practical authority acting within the scope of such authority is rational. But this implies that 'in order to judge whether indeed an authority is acting legitimately one must balance the reasons for action in each case in which a law applies so as to police the ability of the claimed authority to order action in conformity with that balance' (*CA*, 1633). For to determine whether the authority is legitimate and acting within the scope of her authority, the agent must determine whether the conditions of NJT are satisfied— and this requires the agent to balance the reasons that apply.

Such a result is problematic for Raz, according to Hurd, because it is inconsistent with the Preemption Thesis:

If (1) the rationality of abiding by a practical authority depends upon the legitimacy of that authority, and (2) the legitimacy of a practical authority can be established only by balancing the first-order content-dependent reasons for action, and (3) practical authority bars one from balancing those first-order content-dependent reasons, then practical authority cannot be rational. (*CA*, 1633)

The idea is as follows: the agent must balance the first-order reasons in each case of an authoritative directive to determine whether the conditions of NJT apply, but the Pre-emption Thesis bars the agent from balancing those first-order reasons.

Hurd's reasoning, however, equates Raz's notion of a preemptive reason with Hart's notion of a peremptory reason for action. As Hart describes this notion:

The commander's expression of will . . . is not intended to function within the hearer's deliberations as a reason for doing the act, not even as the strongest or dominant reason, for that would presuppose that independent deliberation was to go on, whereas the commander intends to cut off or exclude it. This I think is precisely what is meant by speaking of a command as 'requiring' action and calling a command a 'peremptory' form of address. Indeed, the word 'peremptory' in fact just means cutting off deliberation, debate, or argument.[42]

Thus, a peremptory reason *P*, as Hart defines the term, operates to preclude, forbid, or cut off deliberation on the balance of reasons that *P* is intended to replace.

But the Hartian notion of a peremptory reason is much stronger than the Razian notion of a preemptive reason. For there is nothing in Raz's notion of a preemptive reason that precludes the agent from thinking about the balance of reasons. What a preemptive reason precludes the agent from doing is *acting* on her perception of the balance of reasons; an agent may deliberate if she wishes on the balance of reasons, but may not act on the outcome of such a deliberation.[43] To put it in Razian terms, a preemptive reason *replaces* the agent's own judgment of the balance of reasons in the

---

[42] H. L. A. Hart, 'Commands and Authoritative Legal Reasons', in Hart, *Essays in Bentham* (Oxford: Clarendon Press, 1982), 253.

[43] More specifically, it precludes the agent from *deciding* what to do (and hence from *acting*) on her judgment of the balance of reasons.

agent's deliberation of what to do. But this ultimately precludes the agent only from *acting* on her perception of the balance of reasons; unlike Hart's account, it does not bar her from deliberating on the balance of reasons. If Raz's service conception of authority is ultimately untenable, it is not because he commits himself to the contradictory premises that Hurd identifies.

6.4 The Normal Justification Thesis

Hurd's critique of Raz is ultimately grounded in the assumption that NJT is a principle of practical rationality. Indeed, she views Raz as attempting to answer the question of when it is rational for a person to accept authority: 'The question that must be answered [by Raz's theory], then, is this: Why would it ever be rational to act solely because one has been told to do so' (*CA*, 1627)? On her view, it cannot be rational to act solely for such a reason because 'if an action is rational solely *because* it has been commanded, then any action that is commanded is rational' (*CA*, 1628)—and she believes, plausibly enough, that the consequent of this conditional is clearly false.

But Raz does not intend NJT as a practical thesis; rather he intends NJT as 'a *moral* thesis about the type of argument which could be used to establish the *legitimacy* of authority'.[44] As Raz correctly understands it, the notion of legitimacy is a moral notion: 'No system is a system of law unless it includes a claim of legitimacy, or *moral* authority. That means that it claims that legal requirements are morally binding, that is that legal obligations are real (moral) obligations arising out of the law.'[45] Likewise, he argues: 'If [a legal system] lacks the moral attributes required to endow it with legitimate authority then it has none. . . . To claim authority it must be . . . a system of a kind which is capable in principle of possessing the requisite moral properties of authority' (*ALM*, 215).

The notion of moral legitimacy is related to the notion of a preemptive reason, on Raz's view, in the following way. It is generally thought that what it means to say that an authority is legitimate is that there exists a general moral obligation to obey a directive of the authority *because* it originates with the authority.[46] Accordingly, the moral obligation to obey the directives of legitimate authority has to do with the *source* of the directive—and not with its content. Of course, the content of a law can *also* give rise to a moral obligation to obey, as is the case with a law prohibiting

[44] Joseph Raz, 'Authority and Justification', *Philosophy & Public Affairs*, 14/1 (winter 1985), 18; emphasis added.
[45] Joseph Raz, 'Hart on Moral Rights and Legal Duties', *Oxford Journal of Legal Studies*, 4/1 (spring 1984), 131 (emphasis added).
[46] For a contrary view, see William A. Edmundson, 'Legitimate Authority without Political Obligation', *Law and Philosophy*, 17/1 (Jan. 1998), 43–60. On Edmundson's view, to say that an authority *A* is legitimate over a person *P* is to say that *P* has a moral obligation to refrain from interfering with *A*'s efforts to 'administer' her directives.

murder, but this has nothing to do with the moral authority of a legal system to issue directives. Construed as a moral thesis, then, NJT states the conditions under which authoritative directives give rise to content-independent moral obligations to obey.

Raz believes that moral obligations function (or should function) in the mind of a moral agent as preemptive reasons for action. In so far as the agent has a moral obligation to do *A*, it is morally impermissible for her to refrain from doing *A*. It follows, *a fortiori*, that in so far as the agent has a moral obligation to do *A*, it is morally impermissible for her to refrain from doing *A* regardless of how she sees the balance of reasons. Thus, a moral obligation to do *A* operates to bar the agent from acting on her perception of the balance of reasons. For this reason, if successful in stating the conditions under which *de facto* authority is legitimate, NJT would also succeed in stating the conditions under which authoritative directives function (or should function) as preemptive reasons for action.

Moreover, if it is rational for an agent to comply with a moral obligation even when it conflicts with her perception of the balance of reasons minus the reason provided by the obligation, then NJT also shows how it can be rational for an agent to follow the directives of a legitimate authority. In so far as the directives of a morally legitimate authority give rise to moral obligations, it is rational for the agent to comply with those directives—even when they conflict with the agent's perception of the balance of reasons. Thus, NJT provides the conditions under which it is rational to treat the directives of authority as providing a preemptive reason for action.

One can, however, argue that NJT fails as an account of morally legitimate authority because satisfaction of NJT is neither sufficient nor necessary to give rise to a content-independent moral obligation to obey. The mere fact that complying with an authority's directives is more likely to conduce to the demands of right reason than not complying can perhaps *oblige* a person to obey the authority, but it cannot morally *obligate* her to do so. Nor can it provide a moral justification for using coercive means to enforce those directives against that person.

Suppose, for the sake of simplicity, that right reason demands that we always comply with moral standards. Suppose also that *X* is infallible in determining what is required by morality. While it is true that I am morally obligated to comply with moral standards, this does not imply that I am morally obligated to obey *X*. Of course, if *X* is morally infallible, I am morally obligated to comply with the directives of *X* because of the *content* of *X*'s directives—but not because *X* is the source of the directives. Here it is important to remember that Raz's account of legitimate authority involves a content-independent obligation to follow authoritative directives. While I am obligated to conform my behaviour to the content of what *X* directs because the content conforms to morality, *X*'s moral infallibility alone cannot give rise to a content-independent moral obligation on my part to obey *X*. Thus, satisfaction of NJT is not sufficient for morally legitimate authority.

Nor is it necessary. If you and I consent to abide by the directive of an authority and forgo options that would otherwise be available to us, our mutual consent morally obligates us to comply with the authority's decision. There are different ways to explain how this gives rise to a moral obligation on the part of each of us to obey the directives. One might take, for example, a strict contractarian view and conceptualize our mutual consent as a contract that gives rise to the obligation. Or one might argue it would be unfair to allow someone to reap a benefit from disobedience when others forgo that benefit. But however this is done, a key element in the legitimacy of authority is typically thought to rest on the express or implied consent of all persons over whom the authority is thought to be legitimate.

Of course, there are limits on the extent to which consent gives rise to moral obligations—even if that consent is bargained for or relied upon by other people. As Raz points out, consent to regard a directive as authoritative presupposes certain restrictions on the considerations by which an authority determines which directives to issue. In ordinary circumstances, for example, consent to an authority presupposes that she may not decide issues on the basis of a coin-flip. Likewise, mutual consent and reliance is not enough to rescue a bargain if it is extremely unfair to one of the parties. But these are exceptional circumstances and not the general rule with respect to the relation between consent and authority. If the parties are capable of giving effective consent to authority and the consent is secured fairly, then the conditions articulated by NJT are not necessary for consent to authority to give rise to a moral obligation to obey the directives of that authority.

6.5 The Authority Thesis

Many inclusive positivists attempt to defend the Incorporation Thesis against the Razian critique by challenging the Authority Thesis.[47] For example, Philip Soper argues that 'nothing in the practice of law as we now know it would change if the state, convinced by arguments that there is no duty to obey law *qua* law, openly announced that it was abandoning any such claim'.[48] Soper gives four reasons in support of this claim: (1) the duty to obey the law is not usually expressed in a legal norm; (2) abandoning the view that the state claims citizens have a moral duty to obey law does not mean the state must abandon its view about the moral merits of the law; (3) a state could openly adopt the bad man's point of view with respect to its rules; and (4) a legal system can survive on the strength of coercion alone and hence need not claim moral authority.

Soper's defence of inclusive positivism, however, misunderstands the character of the Authority Thesis. Soper's argument that abandoning the claim to moral

---

[47] See Kenneth Einar Himma, 'Law's Claim of Legitimate Authority', in Jules Coleman (ed.), *Hart's Postscript: Essays on the Postscript to the Concept of Law* (Oxford: Oxford University Press, 2001) for a discussion of the Authority Thesis.

[48] Philip Soper, 'Law's Normative Claims', in Robert P. George, *The Autonomy of Law* (Oxford: Clarendon Press, 1996), 215–47. Hereinafter referred to as *LNC*.

authority would not result in any practical changes construes the Authority Thesis as a view about what a legal system must claim in order to be efficacious. For Soper's point is that if the state openly repudiated a claim to authority, we would not notice any change in the day-to-day workings of the legal system. But the Authority Thesis neither asserts nor implies that legal systems claiming authority are more likely to be efficacious than legal systems not claiming authority because the Authority Thesis is a *conceptual* claim—and not an empirical claim; it is, on Raz's view, 'part of the nature of law' that law claims legitimate authority. Thus, Raz can concede we would not notice any differences in the day-to-day functioning of a legal system *S* if it abandoned any claim to authority, but argue that the abandonment of that claim implies the abandonment of *S*'s status as a *legal* system.

What is needed to rebut the Authority Thesis is an example of a system of rules that makes no claim to moral authority yet is plausibly characterized as a legal system; in other words, what is needed is a counterexample to the Authority Thesis. Matthew Kramer attempts such a rebuttal:

> Of course, an organized-crime syndicate such as the Mafia might well exert control over most aspects of life in a certain region, with dictates that are just as broadly applicable and lasting as the mandates of a veritable legal system. . . . If the Mafia's system of exercising far-reaching control does indeed very substantially partake of the key qualities [of durability and generality], and if it also meets some relevant test for efficacy (whatever that test might be), then it ought to be classified as a legal system. Or, at any rate, the appropriateness of such a classification should not be denied merely because the Mafia's officials make no pretensions to moral admissibility.[49]

Nevertheless, this is unsuccessful as a response to the Authority Thesis because it is not *clearly* a counterexample. In other words, it is just not obvious that the Mafia system should be characterized as a legal system. As a result, Raz could respond, quite plausibly, that the last sentence in the quoted passage simply begs the question.

A more promising example is as follows. Suppose there is a society *S* that is as much like ours as is consistent with the following properties: the lawmakers and law-subjects in *S*, being philosophically sophisticated, have seen all the arguments and counter-arguments for the claim that law can be legitimate. As a result, the residents of *S* and officials are all sceptical that law can ever give rise to a content-independent moral obligation to obey law. Thus, citizens and officials of *S* refrain from using the potentially misleading terms 'authority', 'duty', 'obligation', and 'right', relying instead on terms like 'official', 'required', 'mandatory', 'non-optional', and 'permitted' (as opposed to 'permissible').

Both of Hart's minimum conditions for the existence of a legal system are satisfied in *S*. The officials of *S* adopt the internal point of view towards the rule of recognition out of a sense that, as a practical matter, something must be done to regulate behaviour. Indeed, *all* the law-subjects of *S* believe it is in everyone's interest to structure a

---

[49] Kramer, 'Requirements, Reasons, and Raz', 394.

system of rules around the conventions adopted by the officials—and, thus, also take the internal point of view towards the criteria of validity. And, recognizing the advantages associated with having a system of rules for regulating behaviour, the law-subjects generally obey the directives validated by the rule of recognition.

What plausible, non-question-begging reason could there be to deny that this system of rules is a legal system? The only notable difference between the two systems of rules is that the officials in one system believe their system is legitimate, while the officials in *S* lack such a belief—a difference that seems irrelevant to the classification of the latter. All of the major institutions are there: a rule of recognition that creates the institutions which make possible the creation, modification, and adjudication of law. All of the citizens of *S* accept the determinations of the officials as strong reasons for action. The rules of *S* are obeyed to precisely the same extent as they are in this society. Given these observations, it makes sense to characterize *S* as having a legal system because it has all of the pieces necessary to create efficacious regulations for governing behaviour—even though there is nothing that could be construed as an institutional claim to legitimate authority. If this is correct, the Authority Thesis is false.

7 THE INCORPORATION THESIS AND THE PRACTICAL DIFFERENCE THESIS

7.1 The Case against Hartian Functionalism

Shapiro argues that the Incorporation Thesis conflicts with one of Hart's fundamental commitments, namely his view that the conceptual function of law is to guide behaviour. As Hart puts the matter, 'it [is] quite vain to seek any more specific purpose which law *as such* serves beyond providing guides to human conduct and standards of criticism of such conduct' (*CL*, 249; emphasis added). According to Hart's functionalism, then, any system of rules incapable of guiding behaviour is conceptually disqualified from being a legal system.

Shapiro identifies two ways in which a norm can guide behaviour. First, a norm *R* motivationally guides a person *P* if and only if *P*'s conformity to *R* is motivated by the fact that *R* requires the behaviour in question. *P* is motivationally guided by *R*, then, just in case *P* conforms to *R* because he accepts *P* as a standard of conduct—and not because, say, he is afraid of sanctions. Secondly, *R* epistemically guides *P* if and only if *P* 'learns of his legal obligations from [*R*] . . . and conforms to [*R*]'.[50] For *R* to

---

[50] Scott J. Shapiro, 'On Hart's Way Out', *Legal Theory*, 4/4 (Dec. 1998), 469–508, at 490. Hereinafter referred to as *HWO*.

epistemically guide P, then, R need not motivate compliance: as long as P learns of his obligations from R, it does not matter that P complies with R out of fear of sanctions.

Shapiro argues that Hart's minimum conditions for the existence of a legal system commit him to a particular account of how officials are guided by rules. As we have seen, Hart believes a legal system comes into existence when (1) officials take the internal point of view towards a conventional rule of recognition; and (2) citizens generally obey the laws valid under the rule of recognition. But this seems to imply that law performs its conceptual function of guiding behaviour differently according to whether one is an official or an ordinary citizen. Since Hart's minimum conditions require that citizens generally obey the law without requiring any specific motivation, first-order legal norms must be capable of epistemically guiding citizens. In contrast, since Hart's minimum conditions require that officials accept the rule of recognition as a standard of official behaviour, the rule of recognition must be capable of motivationally guiding officials.

It follows, on Shapiro's view, that Hart is committed to the Practical Difference Thesis (PDT), according to which every legal norm must be capable of making a practical difference in the deliberation of an agent by providing either motivational or epistemic guidance. Since Hart's minimum conditions for the existence of a legal system imply that every legal norm must be capable of making a practical difference in judicial deliberations by providing motivational guidance, it follows that any norm incapable of motivationally guiding a judge is conceptually disqualified from being law.

Shapiro argues that this implication is inconsistent with a commitment to the Incorporation Thesis because it is impossible for a judge to be motivationally guided by both an inclusive rule of recognition and the rules validated by it. As we will see, Shapiro offers separate arguments for necessity and sufficiency rules, but the basic strategy is as follows. Suppose that RoR is a rule of recognition that contains moral criteria of validity and that R is valid in virtue of its moral merit. If the judge is motivationally guided by RoR, then she will be motivated to decide the case in a way that is morally meritorious. But once she is motivated to decide the case in a way that is morally meritorious, R cannot provide any further motivation. For, by hypothesis, the judge will do what is morally meritorious regardless of whether she appeals to R (which, again, is valid because of its moral merit). Appeal to R *cannot* make a practical difference because the reasons provided by R are already contained in RoR. Thus, the Incorporation Thesis is inconsistent with the Practical Difference Thesis.

Schematically, Shapiro's argument can be summarized as follows:

1. The conceptual function of law is to guide behaviour (the Functionalist Thesis).
2. If the Functionalist Thesis is true, then a norm incapable of making a practical difference in the structure of deliberations is conceptually disqualified from being a law.
3. Therefore, a norm incapable of making a practical difference in the structure of deliberations is conceptually disqualified from being a law (PDT). (From 1, 2)

4. Hart's minimum conditions for the existence of a legal system imply that the rule of recognition makes a practical difference by motivationally guiding officials and that valid first-order norms make a practical difference by epistemically guiding citizens.

5. Therefore, a rule that is incapable of motivationally guiding officials is conceptually disqualified from being a rule of recognition. (From 3, 4)

6. A judge cannot simultaneously be motivationally guided by a rule of recognition incorporating moral criteria of validity and by a norm valid under that rule of recognition (the Impossibility Thesis).

7. Therefore, a rule that incorporates moral criteria of validity is conceptually disqualified from being a rule of recognition. (From 5, 6)

8. The Incorporation Thesis allows that there can exist rules of recognition that incorporate moral criteria of validity.

9. Therefore, if the Practical Difference Thesis is true, then the Incorporation Thesis is false. (From 3, 7, 8)

10. Therefore, if the Functionalist Thesis is true, then the Incorporation Thesis is false. (From 2, 9)

Shapiro concludes that '[e]xclusive legal positivism . . . is forced on the legal positivist who is committed to a functionalist conception of law' (*HWO*, 507).

7.2 Coleman's Response to Shapiro

Coleman offers a conservative response to Shapiro's argument. Coleman accepts that Shapiro's argument establishes the inconsistency of PDT with the Incorporation Thesis but denies that an inclusive positivist should abandon the Incorporation Thesis in favour of PDT:

> There seems to be a difference between the status of the claim that persistence and continuity are necessary features of law and the claim that capacity to make a practical difference is. It is not possible to imagine law lacking persistence, continuity, and their implications: institutionality, secondary rules, an internal aspect. It is less clear that rules are incapable of being legally valid or binding simply because they are incapable of guiding behaviour. We might say, then, that the claim that law is a normative social practice implies that most law most of the time makes a practical difference. (*ICP*, 424–5)

The claim that law makes a practical difference, according to Coleman, is at most an empirical claim about what law typically does: 'it is just not part of our concept of law that capacity for practical difference is a condition of legality, though a general capacity to make a practical difference is a feature of law generally' (*ICP*, 425).

Of course, if Shapiro's premise 2 is correct and the Practical Difference Thesis is a logical consequence of the view that the conceptual function of law is to guide behaviour, then Coleman must also give up functionalism.[51] Though it seems that law, being an artefact of sorts, must have a distinguishing function and that guiding behaviour is the most intuitive candidate for that function, Coleman rejects the idea that law has a conceptual function on the ground that it amounts to an unacceptable metaphysical essentialism (*POP*, 145). Thus, Coleman concedes the soundness of Shapiro's argument but argues that the inclusive positivist should reject functionalism and the PDT.

7.3 The Necessity Component

Of the two components to the Incorporation Thesis, the Necessity Component is the weaker one relative to exclusive positivism because it, unlike the Sufficiency Component, operates only on norms that have an appropriate social source. But despite its theoretical proximity to exclusive positivism, Shapiro believes the Necessity Component is inconsistent with PDT.

The argument is as follows. Suppose that *NRoR* validates all and only rules that (1) are enacted by the legislature according to certain procedures and (2) are not grossly unfair. And suppose that the legislature enacts R_{mw}, which requires employers to pay wages of at least \$6 per hour. Assume R_{mw} is not grossly unfair and is hence valid under *NRoR*. According to Shapiro, if the judge is motivationally guided by *NRoR*, she cannot simultaneously be motivationally guided by R_{mw}:

> Can the minimum-wage rule at least motivationally guide a judge? The answer to this question is . . . 'no.' Recall that a rule motivationally guides conduct when it is taken as a peremptory reason for action; it follows that a rule cannot motivationally guide if the agent is required to deliberate about the merits of applying the rule. As the application of the minimum-wage rule depends, pursuant to the inclusive rule of recognition, on the [judge] first assessing whether the rule is grossly unfair, he cannot treat the rule as a peremptory reason for action and hence cannot be motivationally guided by it. (*HWO*, 501)

In so far as R_{mw} is intended to motivationally guide judicial behaviour by providing a peremptory reason that *precludes* deliberation on the moral merits of R_{mw}, it follows that R_{mw} cannot motivationally guide behaviour because *NRoR* requires that the judge deliberate on the merits of R_{mw} as a precondition for applying it.

The problem here arises because, as we have seen, Hart's account of peremptory reasons *bars* the judge from deliberating on the moral merits of R_{mw}.[52] Insofar as a rule of recognition requires deliberation on the merits of a law as a precondition to

---

[51] But notice that the sentence 'the conceptual function of law is to guide behavior' is ambiguous between the function of law as an institution (or the function of a legal system) and the function of law considered as an individual norm. The former does not imply a commitment to PDT. See Kenneth Einar Himma, 'H. L. A. Hart and the Practical Difference Thesis', *Legal Theory*, 6/1 (Mar. 2000), 1–43.

[52] See nn. 48–50, above.

applying it, that law cannot even purport to provide peremptory reasons because peremptory reasons *preclude* such deliberation. Since, for Hart, law motivationally guides behaviour by providing peremptory reasons, any law that must be morally assessed as a precondition of applying it is incapable of motivationally guiding behaviour in the Hartian sense.

But notice that there is nothing in the Conventionality, Social Fact, and Separability Theses that commits Hart to the view that the only way in which law can provide motivational guidance is by foreclosing deliberations on the merits of a rule. Nor is there anything in Hart's general views about the rule of recognition's having an internal aspect that commits him to defining this important idea in terms of official acceptance of *peremptory* authority. While there may be other features of Hart's theory that saddle him with such an account of motivational guidance,[53] these features are extraneous to the central commitments of inclusive positivism. If this is correct, then an inclusive positivist can respond to Shapiro by rejecting Hart's theory of peremptory reasons as an account of how law motivationally guides behaviour.

Indeed, once we reject Hart's account of peremptory reasons as an account of motivational guidance, we can see how a judge can simultaneously be guided by $NRoR$ and R_{mw}. Suppose it would be grossly unfair to employees to allow employers to pay less than \$4 per hour and grossly unfair to employers to require them to pay more than \$9 per hour. Suppose an employee sues an employer under R_{mw}, alleging that the employer is paying only \$5.50 per hour in violation of the minimum-wage requirement. Suppose further the judge requires the employer to pay employees the difference between what they would have received had they been paid \$6 per hour and what they actually received—and does so because R_{mw} constrains her to do so.

Under these suppositions, there seems to be room for R_{mw} to make a practical difference in the deliberation of the judge. On Shapiro's view, to determine whether a rule makes a practical difference, we must consider what the agent would do if she did not appeal to the rule; if she would do exactly the same thing without appealing to the rule, the rule does not make a practical difference. But notice that there is no reason to think that the judge's decision would have been the same without appeal to R_{mw}. R_{mw} requires employers to pay \$6 per hour but, by hypothesis, it would not be grossly unfair for them to pay \$5.50 per hour. Thus, there is no guarantee that a judge who is motivated by $NRoR$ would do the same thing if she did not appeal to R_{mw}. Indeed, the judge's decision would have been different had R_{mw} required \$7 per hour (which, by hypothesis, is not grossly unfair). Thus, it is possible for the judge to be motivationally guided by $NRoR$ and R_{mw}.

Here it is worth noting that norms valid under exclusive rules of recognition can make a practical difference because exclusive validity criteria leave judges with what Shapiro calls 'elbow room'. A judge can be motivationally guided by both the

[53] Shapiro believes that Hart cannot rethink his theory of peremptory reasons without having to rethink other aspects of his theory. See Scott Shapiro, 'Law, Morality and the Guidance of Conduct', *Legal Theory*, 6/2 (June 2000), 62–3. Hereinafter referred to as *LMG*. References are to the manuscript.

exclusive rule of recognition and a rule valid under it because 'it is always up to [the judge] to imagine that the norm no longer exists' (*HWO*, 498). If the norm no longer exists or is replaced by some other norm, then the judge has a reason for doing something different. According to Shapiro, '[i]t is this "elbow room" carved out by dynamic rules of recognition that allows the primary legal rules to make practical differences' (*HWO*, 498).

But, as the example above shows, necessity rules leave exactly the same kind of elbow room. In so far as necessity rules require that legislative enactments be consistent with some set of moral principles, they are dynamic because, in most instances, there will be more than just one rule governing a behaviour that is consistent with the relevant moral principles. There are, for example, many ways that a state could regulate the flow of traffic on an interstate highway consistent with the Eighth Amendment to the Constitution. Thus, a judge who is motivated by a necessity rule can simultaneously be motivated by a rule valid under it because the judge can always imagine that the rule no longer exists or is replaced by some other rule. As long as the positivist rejects the view that law provides peremptory reasons, she may accept the Necessity Component as a means of explaining the operation of constitutional provisions like the Eighth Amendment.

7.4 The Sufficiency Component

While Shapiro's argument against the Necessity Component is directed at Hart's account of peremptory reasons, Shapiro's argument against the Sufficiency Component targets other possible accounts of motivational guidance and is hence considerably more powerful. Let *SRoR* be a sufficiency rule that asserts that 'judges are bound to apply moral norms in hard cases' and let R_{com} be the moral norm that one person A should compensate another person B when A's behaviour wrongfully results in injuries to B. R_{com} is valid in virtue of its moral content under *SRoR*. Now suppose that the judge must decide whether John should compensate Tom for injuries he sustained when he slipped on ice that formed on John's sidewalk and that R_{com} is the only relevant rule. Suppose further that the judge is motivationally guided by *SRoR*.

On Shapiro's view, the judge cannot simultaneously be motivationally guided by R_{com} 'because the judge will act in exactly the same way whether he or she personally consults the moral principle or not' (*HWO*, 496). For a judge who is motivationally guided by *SRoR* would be motivated to decide the case in accordance with morality—and morality requires that John compensate Tom. Thus, if the judge is motivationally guided by *SRoR*, R_{com} cannot make a practical difference: 'Guidance by the inclusive rule of recognition *by itself* is always sufficient to give the judge the right answer' (*HWO*, 496).

One might object that the judge would have behaved differently if morality did not require John to compensate Tom; otherwise put, one might object that the judge would have decided the case differently had R_{com} not been a rule. But Shapiro responds that it is simply not possible for R_{com} not to be a rule under a sufficiency rule that validates all and only moral principles. Exclusive rules of recognition leave elbow room with respect to R_{com} because whether R_{com} is valid depends *entirely* on whether it has the appropriate social source—and this is a contingent matter; though R_{com} is a moral requirement of corrective justice, a legislature could none the less decline to enact R_{com}. Under an exclusive rule of recognition that validates R_{com}, then, a judge has the requisite elbow room with respect to R_{com} because 'it is always up to us to imagine that the norm $[R_{com}]$ no longer exists'. Thus, exclusive rules of recognition are 'dynamic' in the sense that what rules are validated by an exclusive rule is a purely contingent matter.

And this, on Shapiro's view, distinguishes exclusive rules of recognition from inclusive rules of recognition:

In contrast to the exclusive rule of recognition, the inclusive one is static. The set of possible motivated actions is fixed at its inception and never varies. The reason for this is simple: morality is a static system—it has no 'rule of change.' Morality differs dramatically from law in this respect. While legal rules routinely change over time, moral rules do not. It is incoherent, for example, to say that promises no longer need be kept. If promises must be honored today, they must be honored tomorrow. (*HWO*, 498)

What distinguishes sufficiency rules from exclusive rules of recognition, then, is as follows: while it is a contingent matter as to what rules are valid under an exclusive rule of recognition, it is not a contingent matter as to what rules are valid under a sufficiency rule of recognition.

Nevertheless, Shapiro's argument here problematically assumes the falsity of normative ethical relativism. According to normative ethical relativism, cultures manufacture morality in the following sense: what is right or wrong in any given culture is determined entirely by what most people in the culture believe. Thus, for example, abortion is morally wrong in a culture at time *t* if and only if most people believe at *t* that abortion is wrong. But if normative ethical relativism is true, it follows, contra Shapiro, that morality is a dynamic system in which moral rules can change and hence leave sufficient elbow room for a judge 'to imagine that the norm $[R_{com}]$ no longer exists'.

In response, Shapiro argues that normative ethical relativism will not rescue the inclusive positivist; for if it were true, 'inclusive legal positivism would collapse into exclusive legal positivism, as both would demand that legal norms have social sources and are valid in virtue of those sources' (*LMG*, 25). This, however, overstates the consequences of normative ethical relativism on legal positivism. Exclusive positivists claim it is a conceptual truth about law that it has an *institutional* source that serves as a pedigree for law. What is needed to validate a norm, according to exclusive positivism, is (1) some kind of intentional act (2) expressed in an institutional context that conforms to the conventional criteria of validity. Norms that are valid in virtue of what people in the culture generally believe satisfy neither of these conditions. While the truth of normative ethical relativism would require rethinking the distinction between inclusive and exclusive positivism, it is not because the distinction between the two would collapse.[54]

In any event, Shapiro has a much stronger response to the objection: even if it is possible for R_{com} not to be a moral rule, R_{com} cannot motivationally guide a judge who is motivationally guided by $SRoR$. On Shapiro's view, R_{com} motivationally guides a judge to do a if and only if the judge might not have done a had she not appealed to R_{com}. But if the judge is motivationally guided by $SRoR$, she will do what morality requires, whether this is determined objectively or intersubjectively, even if she does not appeal to R_{com}. Thus, regardless of whether normative ethical relativism is true, the judge cannot be motivationally guided by both $SRoR$ and R_{com}.

7.5 Motivational Guidance and Judicial Decision

Shapiro's arguments critically rely on the claim that PDT implies that judges must be motivationally guided by first-order legal norms. As we have seen, Shapiro rejects the possibility of there being an inclusive rule of recognition because a judge who is motivationally guided by such a rule cannot simultaneously be motivationally guided by any first-order norm it validates. Once the judge is motivated by an inclusive rule of recognition, on Shapiro's view, there is no room for a first-order norm to motivationally guide the judge because the rule of recognition determines what the judge will do.

But one can reasonably wonder why any plausible version of PDT would require judges to be motivationally guided by first-order norms. Here it is important to note that, according to Hart, the rule of recognition is addressed only to officials and hence defines the legal duties of officials *qua* officials. In contrast, first-order legal norms do not generally define legal duties that apply to officials *qua* officials. Thus, when a judge evaluates a citizen's conduct under a first-order norm, her behaviour satisfies a duty defined by the rule of recognition. It does not satisfy a duty defined by the relevant first-order legal norm; the first-order legal norm, by its own terms, defines the defendant's duty—and that is why that norm is relevant.

Hart's commitments to the internal point of view and the Strong Conventionality Thesis seem to imply, as Shapiro points out, that judges must be motivationally guided by the rule of recognition. A judge who takes the internal point of view

---

[54] To see this, note that one could argue that the Razian conception of authority is still inconsistent with the Incorporation Thesis. For under an inclusive rule of recognition, identifying the law would require a person to deliberate on its 'merits'—though its merits would be defined in terms of an empirical property, namely what people in the culture believe. And this remains inconsistent with the conceptual point of authority, which is to settle issues about what right reason requires.

towards a rule of recognition that defines her duties necessarily takes the rule as a reason for doing what it demands *of her*.

However, it is not clear how judges could be motivationally guided by rules that are not addressed to them and hence do not *define* their legal duties. To be motivationally guided by a rule, on Shapiro's view, is to 'conform' to the rule because of its status as a rule. But a judge who evaluates a defendant's conduct under a first-order rule is not *conforming* to the first-order rule; rather she is conforming to the rule of recognition that requires her to determine whether the defendant's conduct *conforms* to that first-order rule. In so far as the judge cannot, strictly speaking, conform *qua* judge to that first-order rule, it is not clear why PDT should be construed as requiring that the judge be motivationally guided by such rules.[55]

Of course, as Shapiro points out, some first-order norms are addressed to judges (*LMG*, 30). Consider, again, the principle, made famous in *Riggs v. Palmer*, that no person should be allowed to profit from her own wrong. By its own terms, the *Riggs* principle seems to direct judges to take action to prevent a person from profiting from her own wrong and is hence addressed clearly to judges and not to citizens.

But this observation, though correct, cannot vindicate Shapiro's argument against inclusive positivism. What is needed to falsify the Incorporation Thesis is an argument that shows that judges must *always* be motivationally guided by first-order norms. That some first-order norms are addressed to judges and hence must be capable of motivationally guiding their behaviour does not imply that *all* first-order norms must be capable of motivationally guiding judicial behaviour. If this is correct, then Shapiro's argument shows, at most, that first-order norms addressed to judges cannot be legally valid in virtue of moral content; such norms are either invalid, valid in virtue of source, or must be construed as being addressed to subjects.[56] This implies a conceptual restriction on the content of inclusive rules of recognition, but it does not logically preclude the possibility of moral criteria of validity.

---

[55] See Himma, 'H. L. A. Hart and the Practical Difference Thesis', 34–9, for a detailed discussion of this line of criticism. Shapiro believes that Hart holds the view that first-order norms motivationally guide behaviour. Thus, for example, Shapiro points out that Hart claims that 'it is surely evident that for the most part decisions, like the chess-player's moves, are reached either by genuine effort to conform to rules consciously taken as guiding standards of decisions or, if intuitively reached, are justified by rules which the judge was antecedently disposed to observe and whose relevance to the case in hand would generally be acknowledged' (*CL*, 141; cited at *LMG*, 27).

I doubt that Hart's views on the various forms of guidance were sufficiently developed to make these isolated remarks reliable evidence one way or another. Indeed, part of what makes Shapiro's work on the topic so important is that he has formulated distinctions not previously made in the literature. I suspect there is much in Shapiro's work that would have impressed even Hart as pure innovation. In any event, I do not want to make any claims here about what Hart did or did not believe. Rather, I am arguing only that the core of Hart's theory permits him to deny that judges must be, in Shapiro's sense, guided by first-order norms and that he should deny this strong claim.

[56] Thus construed, the *Riggs* principle would state that it is wrong for a person to profit from her own culpable conduct.

CHAPTER 5

FORMALISM

MARTIN STONE

General propositions do not decide concrete cases.

Holmes

1 INTRODUCTORY

EVER since Holmes penned his critical aphorisms and Pound ridiculed 'mechanical jurisprudence', few terms have been used more often to criticize legal thought and practice than the terms 'formalism' and 'formalistic'. It is said that Holmes initiated a 'large scale revolt against formalism'.[1] Whether or not this is accurate, it must be allowed that the *notion* of such a revolt has been an obsession in American jurisprudence, something expressed in the fact that while 'formalism' is widely considered to have been dismantled by the Realists, it continues to be attacked by each generation of theorists. Like the treatment of neurosis or the death of God, the critique of formalism seems somehow interminable.[2]

I am grateful to Jules Coleman, Arthur Jacobsen, Steven Perry, Robert Post, Scott Shapiro, and Ben Zipursky for helpful comments on an earlier draft.

[1] Morton White, *Social Thought in America: The Revolt Against Formalism* (Oxford: Oxford University Press, 1947), 11; see also, Grant Gilmore, *The Ages of American Law* (New Haven: Yale University Press, 1977), 12.

[2] The idea that 'formalism has already been thoroughly discredited' is often cited at the beginning of a fresh attack on it. See Michael S. Moore, 'The Semantics of Judging', *Southern California Law Review*, 54 (1981), 151, 153.

Yet for all its notoriety, a precise statement of the formalist's mistake is not easy to find. Holmes's maxim is often presented as capturing—and, by negation, correcting—the core of that mistake; yet it hardly seems clear whom Holmes's words are supposed to be informing, or of what. The voluminous literature opposing 'formalism' is not apt to make things more perspicuous. First, one encounters various 'formalist' theses which appear to be little more than scarecrows. How could such theses have seemed worth the ongoing efforts to deny them? Secondly, the various theses one encounters do not exhibit the unity which reports of a 'large-scale revolt' seem to suggest.

This study concerns 'formalism' as it appears as a term of criticism in the tradition of thought originating with Holmes and the Realists.[3] The remainder of this introduction presents two examples of the first difficulty in grasping the aim of this tradition (scarecrows), and it then briefly elaborates the second difficulty (the varieties of formalism). These difficulties set the agenda. Part I critically surveys what various writers since Holmes have meant by 'formalism', placing the various types of formalism in relation to one another. Part II (which appears separately) is more interventionist: it offers directions for addressing two broad questions which are threaded throughout the previous tapestry of formalisms, those of (1) the desirability and (2) the very possibility of judicial adherence to rules. Surfacing in both parts is a proposal concerning the target notion of formalism—that is, concerning what we might call 'formalism' if we wish to give the name to a distinctive doctrine that is worth disputing. Provisionally stated, formalism's target notion is that private law is morally intelligible in non-reductive terms. The point here is not to make the use of the term 'formalism' more tidy than it is.[4] The proposal serves its purpose if it helps to motivate certain features of post-Holmesian thought which would otherwise seem puzzling. Just how the proposal helps in this regard is something to be seen. But, to set the stage, it is with a statement of the puzzles that our study commences.

1.1 Scarecrows: Deduction and Mechanism

(*a*) References to 'deduction' and 'logic' are legion in the literature on formalism. The formalist is supposed to require these to play a role in judicial decision which (it turns out) they cannot play. Hence, according to a renowned historian, 'the demonstration [by John Dewey] that deductive logic could not provide a self-executing way to move

---

[3] As various commentators have pointed out, 'formalism' is almost always a term of opprobrium, so its positive doctrine, if there is one, must largely be gleaned from its critics. Two notable exceptions to this are Frederick Schauer, 'Formalism', *Yale Law Journal*, 97 (1988), 509, and Ernest J. Weinrib, 'Legal Formalism: On the Immanent Rationality of Law', *Yale Law Journal*, 97 (1988), 949.

[4] Nor of course does this proposal concerning the target of 'formalism' purport to capture everything that every jurisprudential writer has called 'formalism'. This is a point against it, however, only on the doubtful assumption that there is such a unity to be captured.

from the general to the particular' was among 'the most important contributions' to the post-Holmesian revolt.[5]

It is not clear what 'self-executing' means here, but does it matter? The formalist's thought—namely, that particular judgments ('Jones piled the hay negligently') can be deduced from general rules ('Negligence is the failure to take reasonable care')— seems sufficiently absurd even without this qualification. Dewey does assert—but does not 'demonstrate'—the negation of this thought.[6] Understandably, no argument struck him as required. Nor is any legal knowledge required. For the point is also that the judgment '*this* is red' is not logically derivable from general statements which make no reference to the red item in question. 'Logic' as H. L. A. Hart put it, 'is silent about how to classify particulars';[7] it takes us from rules only to further rules, not to applicative judgments about particulars. Kant (who, for Holmes, was *the* archetypal formalist) made the same point:

General logic contains and can contain no rules for judgment. . . . If it sought to give general instructions how we are to subsume under these rules, that is, to distinguish whether something does or does not come under them, that could only be by means of another rule. This, in turn, for the very reason that it is a rule, again demands guidance from judgment. And thus it appears that, though understanding is capable of being instructed, and of being equipped with rules, judgment is a peculiar talent which can be practised only, and cannot be taught.[8]

In so far as a 'demonstration' of Dewey's point is to be found, it lies here, in the thought that the idea of 'logical' rules for making judgments about particulars involves us—since judgment would be needed to apply such rules—in a hopeless regress. This regress need not afflict more narrowly applicable rules of judgment: any explanation or interpretation of a concept or rule (e.g. 'Negligence is the failure to take reasonable care') is just such a rule of judgment. But such explanations or interpretations must come to an end somewhere; we cannot intelligibly explain the correctness of particular judgments, or teach someone to make them, by making a

---

[5] Morton J. Horowitz, *The Transformation of American Law 1870–1960* (Oxford: Oxford University Press, 1992), 200. Horowitz also credits this demonstration to Felix Cohen. On formalism as a false deductivism, see also ibid. 16; Roberto Unger, *Knowledge and Politics* (New York: The Free Press, 1975), 92; Margaret Jane Radin, 'Reconsidering the Rule of Law', *Boston University Law Review*, 69 (1989), 781, 793.

[6] See John Dewey, 'Logical Method and Law', *Cornell Law Quarterly*, 10 (1924), 17, 22. Dewey's main point is that judges should treat legal rules as instruments of social policy; the illusion of their deductive applicability, he seems to think, impedes this.

[7] H. L. A. Hart, 'Positivism and the Separation of Law and Morals', *Harvard Law Review*, 71 (1958), 583, 630.

[8] Immanuel Kant, *Critique of Pure Reason*, trans. Norman Kemp Smith (New York: St Martin's Press, 1929), A133/B172 ; cf. Kant, 'On the Common Saying: "This May be True in Theory, but it does not Apply in Practice" ' in Kant, *Political Writings*, ed. Hans Reiss (Cambridge: Cambridge University Press, 1970), 61. One might call the regress to which Kant draws attention a 'demonstration' (of the impossibility of moving by logic from general norms to particular judgments); but it seems more accurate to say that what Kant demonstrates is that there is no intelligible claim about logic asserted or denied here at all.

perfectly *general* use of the idea of rules for applying concepts or rules.[9] Hence 'general logic', as Kant puts it, '*can* contain no rules for judgment'. The thought is not just that 'logic is silent about how to classify particulars' (which might, without more, be cause for alarm), but that we do not so much as have an idea of what it would be for rules possessing the generality of 'logic' to speak to this—or *fail* to speak to it, for that matter, either.

(*b*) If, despite these considerations, the thought that judges do not 'deduce' their decisions from legal rules still struck someone as a substantial *claim*, we might not be surprised if they were to try to clarify it like this: 'The law is not a machine and the judges are not machine-tenders';[10] 'provisions have [not been] made in advance for legal principles, so that it is merely necessary to put the facts into the machine and draw therefrom an appropriate decision'.[11] The formalist, as these quotations indicate, is often accused of thinking that judges apply legal rules 'mechanically'.[12] Perhaps this is what 'self-executing' was getting at.

But it seems implausible, if not comical, to imagine someone, the so-called 'formalist', recognizing this as an account of what she was thinking. ('Yes, a machine, just what I had in mind'!) If any rule-application can be called 'mechanical', it is perhaps the sort which requires little thought or effort. In this sense, '$y = x + 2$' is 'mechanically applicable', but not '$y = x^2 + 3x - 7$' (at least for some values of 'x' or 'y'). This has notably nothing to do with whether a rule determines a single answer or is laid down 'in advance'.[13] Moreover, if someone wanted to say that the law always provides an answer, or that legal rules sometimes compel judges to reach certain decisions, then appeal to a mechanism would be quite unsuited to her purposes. For mechanisms sometimes break down or malfunction; the necessity they exhibit is much *softer* than that which might have seemed to be in play whenever the law speaks of rules or other normative items not subject to natural vicissitudes. Talk of decisional 'mechanisms' might be just an evocative way of re-describing such *normative* constraints. But if talk of 'mechanisms' goes beyond this, the implication would be that, for a formalist, a judicial decision is never justified but, at best, excusable as a causally determined effect. Clearly this is not what the formalist (or the critic attempting to capture the formalist's view) has in mind. If legal rules sometimes justify a decision,

[9] This is also one of the points of Wittgenstein's discussion of 'accord with a rule' in L. Wittgenstein, *Philosophical Investigations*, trans. G. E. M. Anscombe (Oxford: Blackwell, 1958), §§ 138–202.

[10] Jerome Frank, *Law and the Modern Mind* (Glouster, Mass.: Peter Smith, 1970), 129.

[11] Haines, 'General Observations on the Effects of Personal, Political, and Economic Influences in the Decisions of Judges', *Illinois Law Review*, 17 (1922), 96.

[12] Cf. Duncan Kennedy, 'Legal Formality', *Journal of Legal Studies*, 2 (1973), 351, 359; Roscoe Pound, 'Mechanical Jurisprudence', *Columbia Law Review*, 8 (1908), 605. For an especially vivid version of this accusation, see Burt Neuborne, 'Of Sausage Factories and Syllogism Machines: Formalism, Realism, and Exclusionary Selection Techniques', *New York University Law Review*, 67 (1992), 419, 421.

[13] Both of these rules are determinate for every case of x; '$y^2 = x$' is not, though it is sometimes mechanically decidable.

they present a form of rational, not causal necessitation—though their application is not, on that account, a matter of logical inference either.

It might be suggested that the point of these assaults on formalism is really just to correct the impression that the law can always be applied thoughtlessly or effortlessly. But again, whose impression needed correcting? That a rule justifies a decision does not imply that everyone endeavouring to follow the rule will agree; and the need for thought and effort is often obvious, as anyone who has filed a tax return must know, even in cases where people always do agree.[14] Further, as we shall see, 'formalism' is often associated with the view that legal reasoning is a distinctive art, requiring special training and experience, and not merely an exercise of a general capacity to recognize facts and draw valid inferences.[15] This seems especially inhospitable ground for the view that there is something mechanical or self-executing about it.

1.2 The Varieties of Formalism

Part of the campaign against formalism thus looks like an effortless assault on undefended positions.[16] But even when this is not so, formalists seem to fall into a troubling variety of criss-crossing camps. According to the literature, a legal formalist is on hand whenever someone:[17]

(1) defends the equal right of all persons to own property and to exchange their property and labour with others through contract; or, rather, defends these or other private law principles relating property owners (e.g., *the duty of reasonable care, sic utere tuo . . .*) in a non-reductive way;[18]

(2) seeks to gain theoretical information and/or practical guidance concerning law through attention to its 'form' as opposed to its (historically and geographically variable) content, and hence without regard for the detailed findings of history, sociology, anthropology, and so on;[19]

[14] See Joseph Raz, *The Authority of Law* (Oxford: Clarendon Press, 1979), 182.

[15] For a classical expression of this view, see Edward Coke, *Coke's Rep.*, 12; 4th edn. 1738, 63, 64–5.

[16] Cf. Ronald Dworkin on the critics of 'mechanical jurisprudence': 'Their difficulty lies in finding practitioners to ridicule. So far they have had little luck in caging and exhibiting mechanical jurisprudists (all specimens captured—even Blackstone and Joseph Beale—had to be released after careful reading of their texts.') 'The Model of Rules I', in *Taking Rights Seriously* (Cambridge, Mass.: Harvard University Press, 1978), 15–16. I know of only two instances in which the general deducibility of legal conclusions appears to be asserted: John M. Zane, 'German Legal Philosophy', *Michigan Law Review*, 16 (1916), 288, 338; and Friedrich A. Hayek, *The Constitution of Liberty* (Chicago: University of Chicago Press, 1960), 213–14. But both authors are best understood, I think, as saying merely that judicial deliberation can always be cast in the form of a *syllogism*. On this distinction, see Sect. 4.3 below.

[17] This is not meant to be a complete list, nor of course are the items on it perfectly clear just as they stand.

[18] See Ernest J. Weinrib, *The Idea of Private Law* (Cambridge, Mass.: Harvard University Press, 1995).

[19] See Judith N. Shklar, *Legalism: Law, Morals, and Political Trials* (Cambridge, Mass.: Harvard University Press, 1964), 33–4: 'the idea of treating law as . . . identifiable without any reference to the

(3) fails to decide legal cases in light of social policy; or adheres to a legal rule without regard to its background reasons; or denies that courts should have the power to make exceptions to rules in light of the purposes they serve;[20]

(4) maintains that there are cases in which the application of a legal rule is clear without *interpretation*, or asserts that the law affords a basis for resolving some cases without appeal to 'policy' or 'morality';[21]

(5) believes that all cases are legally regulated (that the law is complete and univocal), or that a judge need never go outside the law and exercise a law-creating power in order to make a decision;[22]

(6) asserts that legal validity is content-independent, or that the law can be identified on the basis of distinct sources, without recourse to moral or political argument;[23]

(7) denies that the law, or some region of it, is to be understood as an instrument of social policy. ('Formalism' is supposed to be opposed to 'instrumentalism'.)[24]

Post-Holmesian criticism has sometimes featured an unhappy figure called 'the formalist' who goes in for this entire list—say, for deductivism, formal equality, the ahistorical study of law, socially unresponsive decision-making, the autonomy of law and legal reasoning, and so on. Formalism, it is said, encompasses all the major issues 'in

content, aim, and development of the rules that compose it, is the very essence of formalism, for formalism does not just involve treating law mechanically as a matter of logical deductions from given premises …').

[20] See H. L. A. Hart, *The Concept of Law* (Oxford: Clarendon Press, 1961), 129; Larry Alexander, ' "With Me, It's all er Nuthin": Formalism in Law and Morality', *University of Chicago Law Review*, 66 (1999), 530, 531; Frederick Schauer, 'Formalism'; Roberto Unger, *Law in Modern Society: Toward a Criticism of Social Theory* (New York: Free Press, 1976), 204; Robert Summers, *Instrumentalism and American Legal Theory* (Ithaca, NY: Cornell University Press, 1982), 136–74.

[21] See Stanley E. Fish, *Doing What Comes Naturally: Change, Rhetoric and the Practice of Theory in Literary and Legal Studies* (Durham: Duke University Press, 1989), 153, 2–32; Roberto Unger, *Knowledge and Politics*, 93; Hart, *Concept of Law*, 124–30; Mark Tushnet, 'Anti-Formalism in Recent Constitutional Theory', *Michigan Law Review*, 83 (1985), 1502, 1506–7; Duncan Kennedy, *A Critique of Adjudication, Fin de Siecle* (Cambridge, Mass.: Harvard University Press, 1997), 105, 109; Roberto Unger, *The Critical Legal Studies Movement* (Cambridge, Mass.: Harvard University Press, 1986), 1; Roberto Unger, *What Should Legal Analysis Become* (London: Verso, 1996), 41–2; Gary Peller, 'The Metaphysics of American Law', *California Law Review*, 73 (1985), 1152; Thomas C. Grey, 'Langdell's Orthodoxy', *University of Pittsburgh Law Review*, 45 (1983), 1.

[22] See Hart, *Concept of Law*, ch. 7; Grey, 'Langdell's Orthodoxy'; Morton J. Horowitz, *The Transformation of American Law 1870–1960* (Oxford: Oxford University Press, 1992), 199; Brian Leiter, 'Review Essay: Positivism, Formalism, Realism', *Columbia Law Review*, 99 (1999), 1145–6; David Lyons, 'Legal Formalism and Instrumentalism—A Pathological Study', in *Moral Aspects of Legal Theory* (Cambridge: Cambridge University Press, 1993), 41; Summers, *Instrumentalism and American Legal Theory*, 137–74.

[23] See Anthony J. Sebok, *Legal Positivism in American Jurisprudence* (Cambridge: Cambridge University Press, 1998); Shklar, *Legalism*, 33–4; Horowitz, *The Transformation of American Law*, 9, 16.

[24] See Ernest J. Weinrib, 'Legal Formalism: On the Immanent Rationality of Law', *Yale Law Journal*, 97 (1988), 949; Weinrib, *The Idea of Private Law*; Horowitz, *The Transformation of American Law*, 254; Oliver Wendell Holmes, 'Law in Science and Science in Law', *Harvard Law Review*, 12 (1889), 443, 460; Summers, *Instrumentalism in American Legal Thought*, 137–75.

the history of the modern Western rule of law'; its 'destruction . . . brings in its wake the ruin of all other liberal doctrines of adjudication'.[25] Given this promiscuous use of 'formalism', a strong counter-measure was perhaps only to be expected. 'Formalism', it has become tempting to say, is 'little more than a loosely employed term of abuse',[26] one 'used to describe any judicial decision, style of legal thinking, or legal theory with which the user of the term disagrees'.[27] In fact, these inflationary and deflationary assertions are made in one another's image. Common to both is the implausible assumption that we must look for the meaning of formalism in some common factor of its various employments. Could we not allow that the term 'formalism' may be well-applied in each instance (and that each instance may bear connections to the others), but still insist that '*the* formalist' is a character to be found only in legal mythology? We are bound to locate him there once we realize that major legal theorists who subscribed to some of our standard formalisms explicitly rejected others, and that Legal Positivists, Thomists, Kantians, and Marxists are all formalists in at least one of the standard ways.[28]

These cautions to legal theory against a tendency arising among some of its historians are reinforced by a further consideration which suggests that there is no 'legal formalist', even as an ideal type, who would go in for the entire list, nor any 'anti-formalist' who should reject it entirely. The fact is that even this limited list does not present a consistent set of attitudes. The formalisms surveyed below are not unfamiliar, but the inconsistencies involved in criticizing them *en masse* often go unnoticed. Our survey is organized around three such inconsistencies.

2 THEORY OR PRACTICE?

2.1 The Desirability and Possibility of 'Blind' Adherence to Rules

Sometimes a judge's way of making decisions is criticized as 'formalistic'. Judges, it is said, should not be overly rule-bound, but should decide in ways that are sensitive to

---

[25] Unger, *Law in Modern Society*, 203; Unger, *Knowledge and Politics*, 92.

[26] A. W. Brian Simpson, 'Legal Iconoclasts and Legal Ideals', *University of Cincinnati Law Review*, 58 (1990), 819, 834.

[27] Schauer, 'Formalism', 510. Schauer considers but does not himself draw this conclusion.

[28] Thus, one could point out that Kant and Hegel embrace (1) and (2) but reject (6); that Pashukanis embraces (2) but rejects (6) and (1); that Austin, Kelsen, Hart, and Raz embrace (2) and (6) but express no definite opinion on (1); that Dworkin affirms (5) but rejects (6) and perhaps (2) as well; that Aquinas also rejects (6) but—following Aristotle—accepts (2) and rejects (5); that Kelsen and Hart reject (5) and criticize the practice described in (3), etc. One could go on with such map-making, but there is little to be learned from it beyond the negative lesson of the need to observe differences.

the aims and needs the law is meant to serve. (Of course, we are not unambivalent about this: judges are also criticized for acting *ultra vires*, for stepping beyond the rules.)[29] Here 'formalism' refers to a purportedly undesirable form of legal practice, and the point of the criticism is, naturally, reform. This may mean that a particular court should change its approach to making decisions, or that the decisional norms operating throughout a whole legal system should be changed.[30] In either case, we will call this variety of formalism 'overly rule-bound decision making' (ORBD).

Elsewhere in the literature, formalism refers not to a form of legal practice, but to a purportedly mistaken piece of *theory*: to a doctrine concerning what one aspect of legal practice—the application of rules—consists in. According to this doctrine, a judge can sometimes apply the rules without (as the critic of this sort of formalism is apt to say) 'interpreting' them. Provisionally, we shall take this to mean that a judge need not always consider the rules in light of some purposes or policies they might serve.[31] As is well known, H. L. A. Hart defended this doctrine. He claimed that legal rules have a central 'core' of meaning, and that when the facts of a case fall within this core (an 'easy case'), the rule determines what is to be done, and hence can be applied by the judge without his having recourse to any desired social aim.[32] Hart himself would not have described this doctrine as 'formalist'. But that is how it is often described by those who object to it.[33] We shall call it 'easy case formalism' (ECF).

Holmes's maxim ('General propositions do not decide concrete cases') has seemed serviceable to critics of both 'formalist' doctrines. Directed against ORBD, the maxim says that general rules do not (always) *correctly* decide particular cases; rather, the rules need sometimes to be modified in light of the reasons directly engaged by those cases. Aimed at ECF, the maxim says that legal rules do not determine what is to be done *anyway*, except by way of some further interpretive choice. (Holmes himself tended to describe the grounds of such choice as 'policy'.) But can the maxim really play this dual role? Can one intelligibly oppose both ORBD and ECF?

That the former refers to a purportedly undesirable practice of applying legal rules, and the latter to a purportedly mistaken conception of what applying rules consists in, does not, just in itself, bespeak any conflict between them. People sometimes go wrong in practice because they misconceive what they are doing. Yet in the

---

[29] The ambivalence bears on the question of the merits of 'formalistic' decision-making. I plan to take this up in a sequel to the present chapter.

[30] The details of such systemic and inter-systemic formalism are explored by Schauer, 'Formalism'.

[31] In fact, it is not easy to see what 'interpreting a rule', conceived as a universal requirement, is supposed to be, or how it differs, except in name, from 'applying a rule'. The provisional formulation will allow us not to get stuck on this at the outset. I discuss the problems with 'interpretation' as a universal requirement in Stone, 'Focusing the Law; What Legal Interpretation is Not", in A. Marmor, *Law and Interpretation: Essays in Legal Philosophy* (Oxford: Clarendon Press, 1992), and 'Wittgenstein on Deconstruction', in A. Gary and R. Read, *The New Wittgenstein* (London: Routledge, 2000).

[32] Hart, 'Positivism and the Separation of Law and Morals', esp. 614–15; Hart, *The Concept of Law*, ch. 7.

[33] See e.g. Lon Fuller, 'Positivism and Fidelity to Law—A Reply to Professor Hart', *Harvard Law Review*, 71 (1958), 630, 638 ; Michael Moore, 'The Semantics of Judging', esp 273–81.

present instance there is a conflict. For the heart of the criticism of ORBD is that a judge adheres ('blindly') to a legal rule, even when it would be better, from the point of view of the aims which recommend the rule, to create an exception or to 'interpret' the rule so as to render it inapplicable to the particular case. Obviously, such a criticism would make no sense unless what a rule required was sometimes capable of conflicting with what it would appear best to do on the basis of the aims underlying the rule, and hence also unless the meaning of the rule was sometimes independently ascertainable. Criticism of ORBD, in short, presupposes that adherence to legal rules is sometimes frustrating. But critics of ECF assail this presupposition. 'It is an illusion', they say, 'to think that legal rules have this sort of autonomous power to frustrate our purposes; they only *seem* to compel us to reach determinate judgments when there exists a general agreement about the desirability of interpreting them one way or another'. Since opposition to ORBD presupposes ECF, one cannot intelligibly oppose them both.[34]

2.2 The Equivocal Criticism of ECF

But there is a tendency to get mixed up here. Specifically, there is a tendency for opponents of ECF to cast their criticism in a way which fails to discriminate between these two 'formalist' targets. The case against ECF then seems to gain cogency from the engagement of worries about ORBD—at least as long as one fails to notice the equivocation. Recall, for example, the famous question which Fuller, one of the prominent critics of ECF, put to Hart:

What would Professor Hart say if some local patriots wanted to mount on a pedestal in the park a truck used in World War II, while other citizens, regarding the proposed memorial as an eye-sore, support their stand by the 'no vehicle' rule? Does this truck, in perfect working order, fall within the core or the penumbra?[35]

The implications of this question are not as clear as Fuller seems to have thought. One might answer: 'If the truck falls within the core of the "no vehicle" rule, it presents a case in which fidelity to the rule arguably produces an undesirable result. So conceived, the case might turn us against ORBD, but the argument does not adversely touch—it rather presupposes—ECF. Perhaps, however, the truck falls within the penumbra. In that case, making an intelligent decision might require interpreting the rule in light of what it is good for. But does this mean that *every rule always* must be so interpreted? Clearly not. So however the question—core or penumbra?—is answered, ECF goes unharmed.'

---

[34] Of course, both doctrines may be sound. In that case legal rules would have the power to frustrate judges who apply them, and it would be a good thing, too, that the practice of applying them was often one of enduring such frustration rather than circumventing it through 'interpretation' or other means.

[35] Fuller, 'Positivism and Fidelity to Law', 663.

Naturally, this will be felt to have missed the (rhetorical) point of Fuller's question, namely that it is uncertain *how* the case is to be classified. The trouble for ECF, it will be said, resides in this classificatory uncertainty, not in one or another resolution of it. But if Fuller's question was meant to elicit such uncertainty, doesn't this make the question (logically) strange? The possibility of such uncertainty is, after all, Hart's doctrine of the penumbra. If it is doubtful whether the 'no vehicle' rule applies in this case, then surely the case does *not* fall within the core of the rule (if it falls under the rule at all).

This is supported by the following consideration. A different conclusion (i.e. uncertainty) would require that we have some grip on what constitutes the semantic 'core' of a rule which is something other than for its application to be clear or unclear, case by case. Given such an independent grip, we would have *two* criteria for the meaning of a rule, and we might then be in the sort of doubt Fuller imagines whenever the criteria conflict. But what could this second criterion be which would lead us to say that although it was unclear whether a rule applied in a particular case, the facts of the case none the less fall within the core of its meaning? It might be thought that standard explanations of the terms of the rule—for example, 'a vehicle is any motorized car or truck suitable for transporting cargo or passengers, etc.'—are what set up the potential conflict. Thinking of such explanations, we are apt to feel that the memorial truck falls within the rule's core of meaning. But such explanations are either irrelevant (it is not, after all, the use of the word 'vehicle' in other contexts which concerns the judge), or they comprise, in effect, an interpretive rider to the rule and thus recreate the problem: our grasp of what constitutes 'the core' of this rule-cum-rider must come, it seems, by way of *its* application being clear, case by case.[36] So if it is unclear, as Fuller suggests, whether the 'no vehicle' rule, however formulated, enjoins the proposed memorial, shouldn't we say that the case falls within the rule's penumbra?[37]

[36] This does not mean that questions about the meaning of a legal rule are unrelated to how the terms of the rule are used in other contexts. As Hart emphasized, the terms of a legal rule could not mean what they do if they were not used in certain standard ways elsewhere. See *Concept of Law*, ch. 7.

[37] Someone may want to say that 'a vehicle is a vehicle', and that if we manage to entertain doubts about the application of the 'no-vehicle' rule in this case, that is only because we are already reading the rule in light of a question about what its aim might be. This seems right, but it suggests that such terms as 'aim' or 'purpose' are too crude for the distinctions we need here. Why should Hart not be able to allow that a legal rule would not be intelligible except against a background of aims it can be understood to advance? The distinction between easy and hard cases would be drawn against this background; it need not be understood as a distinction between rules which require this background and rules which somehow do not. It is possible, as Andrei Marmor suggests, that Fuller himself might be read as intending nothing more than this. See Marmor, *Interpretation and Legal Theory* (Oxford: Clarendon Press, 1992), 130 n. 13. But there are passages which suggest that he intends something much stronger (see e.g. Fuller, 'Positivism and Fidelity to Law', 665–6). It should be remembered that one of the familiar purposes people have in laying down a rule is to decide certain cases in advance so that they need not reason about what advancing their aims requires case by case. It would seem peculiar and paradoxical if the purposive background of language use—which Fuller feels Hart ignores—were such as to prevent people from using language in ways which realize such purposes.

It seems that Fuller needed to have it both ways. His example belongs to a class of jurisprudential chestnuts which seem distinctive in their power to evoke conflicting temptations.[38] On the one hand, one wants to say that it is unclear what the rule requires; on the other hand, there is a temptation to think that this is, after all, perfectly clear, only the result of adhering to the rule would be unwelcome or absurd. In short, while seeming to present an indeterminate rule, such examples also engage our dissatisfaction with ORBD.

Why such an example seemed serviceable to Fuller is perhaps not hard to see. Remember what the example is meant to prove: a rule has no core of meaning except by way of inquiry into what it is good for. (Is the 'no vehicle' rule good for preserving quiet, or for preventing large obstructions, or for pedestrian safety . . . ?)[39] The trouble is that this is a universal proposition. How can the need to interpret, in light of social aims, *this* rule in *this* case so much as appear to suggest anything about the possibility-conditions of following a rule in general?[40] The answer is: by having it both ways. By eliciting recognition of a different universal thesis—namely, that the literal or strict application of any legal rule may sometimes lead to unwelcome results—the example could *seem* to suggest a quite general need for purposive interpretation (i.e. to avoid potentially unwelcome results), while at once remaining an example of the need to interpret an indeterminate rule.

To make this clearer, suppose that someone, not fully aware of the potential inconsistency, was disposed to see the situation Fuller describes as (*a*) a core instance of a rule which requires an unwelcome result, *and* as (*b*) a case in which there is no knowing what the rule requires, anyway, without interpreting it in light of what it is good for. The rejection of ECF might now understandably seem to follow. First, seeing the situation as (*a*), one concludes that a judge must read every legal rule in light of its purpose if he is not to risk producing an unwelcome result. Next, seeing the situation as (*b*), one draws apparently the same conclusion in a case in which the legal rule is genuinely indeterminate: in such a case, the judge must again interpret the rule (otherwise, his decision will avoid absurdity, if it does, only by luck). Finally, one takes the latter conclusion to be an instance of the first conclusion. Does the argument not show that no legal rule determines what is to be done apart from an absurdity-avoiding consideration of what the rule is good for? The answer is that (1) this conclusion is equivocal between a *normative* claim about how judges ought to decide cases (whether they should apply the rules, revise them, create an exception, etc.) and a *conceptual* claim about what it is to understand and apply a legal rule; and (2) it is only because the conclusion, as stated, equivocally straddles these claims that one can

---

[38] *Riggs v Palmer*, 22 N.E. 188 (N.Y. 1889) (the murdering heir) and Pufendorf's surgeon (discussed in *Riggs*) would be other members of this class.

[39] 'What can this rule be for? What evil does it seek to avert? What good is it intended to promote? . . . It is in light of this "ought" that we must decide what the rule "is".' Fuller, 'Positivism and Fidelity to Law', 665–6.

[40] Of course, far from denying any *less-than universal* version of the interpretivist claim, that is just what Hart's distinction between core and penumbra was meant to assert. See *Concept of Law*, ch. 7.

fail to notice the *non sequitur* involved in moving from (*a*) the thought that the purposes behind any rule might be frustrated by applying it *simpliciter* to (*b*) the conclusion that there is no such thing as applying it *simpliciter*.

To be sure, Fuller himself never urged that it is undesirable for judges to adhere strictly to legal rules. Rather, he sought to oppose ORBD by arguing against the conceptual possibility of such a thing. The present point is that his example would never have been felt to generalize in the appropriate way if it had not lent itself to raising doubts about two different theses: first, that judges should always strictly follow the legal rules; secondly, that it is *always* possible for them to do so, even without considering what the purpose of the rules might be.[41] In post-Fullerian criticisms of ECF, the supposed undesirability of strict adherence to rules is sometimes adduced more explicitly in support of the claim that there is a ubiquitous need for purposive interpretation. The following argument is not uncommon:

1. Any legal rule, no matter how carefully drafted, can, if strictly applied, produce undesirable results.
2. In applying legal rules, judges should always try to avoid undesirable results.
3. Hence in applying a legal rule, a judge must always consider the rule's purpose and consider whether that purpose would be furthered or frustrated by a strict application of the rule.
4. So the application of any legal rule requires that it be interpreted in light of its purpose.
5. So the meaning of a legal rule is therefore unavailable except by way of purposive interpretation.
6. So ECF is mistaken.

By dispensing with unclarities about what cases like that of the memorial truck are supposed to show, this schema makes the difficulty (of taking such cases to refute ECF) plain by exhibiting the central equivocation involved. In brief: (4) is entailed by the preceding premises only if it is construed as a claim about how judges ought to decide cases. But (5) follows from (4), only when the latter is construed as a claim about what applying a legal rule consists in. That it is undesirable for judges to adhere strictly to rules does not mean that it is impossible for them to do so. But (4) (like our previous formula, 'no legal rule determines what is to be done') can be used to express either sort of claim, so it disguises the fact that the argument really does nothing more than assert this implausible equivalence.[42]

---

[41] Each of these theses is indeed quite doubtful, but neither, of course, was put forward by Hart.

[42] Cf. Summers, *Instrumentalism in American Legal Theory*, 169: '[W]hen judges . . . lay down a rule, one can, within limits, understand its content. But this sort of understanding is significantly incomplete. Without an appreciation of the reasons for the rule, one will usually be unable to determine its justified scope.' Summers perhaps only means that understanding the applicable legal rules is, just by itself, insufficient to reach an appropriate legal decision, for there remains the question of whether even clearly applicable legal rules should be applied when they give undesired results. But if so, his reference to 'a sort of understanding' which is 'incomplete' precisely confuses this normative claim (directed towards legal practice) with a conceptual claim (concerning what it is to understand a rule). Although Michael Moore

2.3 Two Motives for the Confusion

Why this confusion? It seems insufficient to say that ORBD and ECF are confused because they are both called 'formalism'. Without some other motive for confusion, the intellectual demands of keeping things distinct in thought which are not distinct in speech are not that great.[43] Moreover, this explanation might plausibly be said to get matters backward: the doctrine of easy cases would not have been associated with 'formalism' had it not been confused with ORBD—so both are called formalism *because* they are confused.[44] This returns the question of the motive for confusing them.

(*a*) *Intellectual fashion.* Perhaps a familiar sort of fashion is at work here, whereby the practices to which one objects *must* turn out to be rooted in theoretical mistakes about more 'foundational' matters, for example, about what grasping the meaning of a rule consists in. One could not, it was suggested, intelligibly oppose ECF and continue to criticize judicial adherence to rules as 'formalistic'. But, in keeping with the fashion, someone might wish to say that a judicial tendency to ORBD flows from an acceptance of ECF; and if that is true, it might understandably look as if one way to criticize ORBD would be to show that the notions of an 'easy case' or 'plain meaning' do not have the substance judges are inclined to credit them with, that the judicial conception of these things is a naïve one, in that it fails to take account of their (interpretive) conditions of possibility.

The response to such a 'foundationalist' criticism of ORBD should now be clear. Certainly people sometimes think that a rule compels them to reach certain conclusions when in fact they are making an interpretive choice. But if we wanted to point out the truth to them, we should hardly describe the situation as one in which they were rigidly adhering to the rule. That is how *they* see it, but they see it incorrectly. If the illusion is pervasive, as the critic of ECF maintains, then there is *never* any such thing as 'rigidly adhering to a rule', only one's thinking there is. (Indeed, if this still meant anything at all, it would perhaps simply be that a judge has carried out the mandatory exercise of his interpretive powers in an undesirable way.) Moreover, even a judge who mistakenly thinks he can follow a rule *simpliciter* is not thereby compelled to decide in the way he thinks of as 'following the rule'. Believing that the rule requires such and such, whether he *should* follow the rule will present itself to him as a question about the particular circumstances, the decisional norms of the legal

reads Fuller's claim as a normative one—'urging judges to disregard [the meaning of a rule] when it does not fit their notion of the rule's purpose' ('The Semantics of Judging', 277)—I think his argument against 'formalism' does not fully avoid the confusion described, for he takes this normative claim to contradict Hart (who in fact had little to say, it seems, about how judges should decide cases).

[43] No one supposes, for example, that an idealist, in the Berkeleyian sense, is someone who has an overly rosy expectation of what the future will bring.

[44] Hart after all presented the notion of an 'easy case' as part of a *criticism* of 'formalism'—as an attempt to limit the domain of its rightful claims. See *Concept of Law*, ch. 7.

system, and the morality of judging. If it is true that legal rules settle nothing except by way of an interpretive choice, then someone's naïvety about this explains why he regards one or another choice as simply required by the rule. But this neither makes it correct to describe him (from our knowing point of view) as rigidly following the rule, nor does it entail that he must go in for what he would describe as that (from his deluded one).

(*b*) *The theory of adjudication.* A more substantial cause of the present confusion might be found in different legal-theoretical needs for the notion of an 'easy case'. Hart introduced this notion not to advance a claim about how judges should decide cases, but to defend a thesis about the concept of law—namely, that law consists in a combination of different types of rules—against a form of 'rule-scepticism' which threatened to undermine it. For this limited purpose, it sufficed to define an 'easy case' as one that fell within the semantic core of a legal rule, and a hard case, by contrast, as one that did not. The theory of adjudication, however, must concern itself with at least two different ways in which a case might be hard. First, there may be reasonable doubts about what the rules require. Secondly, there may be doubts about what should be done, even when it is clear what the rules require. The first type of case is presented when a court must apply a rule which is vague or ambiguous; the second, when, under a legal system's norms of decision, a court has the option of revising or creating an exception to a rule upon a rule when the rule requires an undesirable result. Distinguishing these two types of hard case amounts to distinguishing ECF and ORBD. But a potential source of confusion lies in the fact that it may be useful, for purposes of a theory of adjudication, to define an 'easy' case as one which is not 'hard' in *either* of these two ways. And this—combined with the fact that some hard cases evoke, as we have seen, a temptation to say both that there are reasons to set aside the legally required result *and* that the legal rules are indeterminate—can lead to the impression that whenever a jurisprudential writer speaks of a case as 'easy', he must mean to exclude the doubts associated with both forms of hardness; or worse, that these forms of hardness are one and the same, the simple negation of the properties found in an adjudicationally easy case.

Of course, this is a fallacy. Not every uncertainty about whether to adhere to a legal rule can be an uncertainty, calling for 'interpretive' resolution, about the 'meaning' of the rule. If it were—if such practical uncertainty generally eroded our grip on what a rule requires—it would be obscure why we should be interested in having rules (i.e. why we should have the *concept* of 'a rule' that we do) when the same results might as well be achieved by asking in each case what it is best to do. To avoid eliding the difference that rules can make, it needs to be stressed that, for the theory of adjudication, an 'easy case' is a derivative idea, formed by alternating and then negating everything that can make a case hard. There is no such thing, in contrast, as a hard case comprised of the negation of everything that makes a case adjudicationally easy—for example, a case in which a rule is at once indeterminate and determines an unwanted result—though it is just this conceptual mongrel which issues from the union of the two complaints about 'formalism' that we have considered.

2.4 Logic Again

This first part of our survey has established that the object of the complaint about 'formalism' cannot be both the doctrine of easy cases and the practice of strict adherence to rules.

Curiously, both doctrine and practice have been stigmatized as involving an 'excessive use' or 'overestimation' of logic. This adds to the puzzle (concerning the identification of 'formalism' with a false reliance on 'logic') with which we began. For logic obviously no more tells one *whether* to adhere to a rule than it does how to subsume particulars under it. And even if it is true that, when a legal rule is indeterminate, judges should always exploit this fact to further social policies, a judge who fails to do so is not, in any familiar sense, being more or less 'logical' in his decision.[45] As for the more general contrast, which appears in the assault on formalism, between 'interpretation' (or 'policy') and the deductive applicability of rules, this requires a longer discussion, which we reserve for later (Sect. 4).

3 LEGAL POSITIVISM OR LEGAL DETERMINACY?

The forms of formalism considered so far concern theoretical and practical aspects of rule-based adjudication. Sometimes, however, the views which attract the label 'formalism' belong to a more general part of legal theory, that which seeks to explain the concept of law. This section examines the source of a long-standing association between 'formalism' and the legal positivist's explanation of the concept of law.

---

[45] See H. L. A Hart, 'Problems of the Philosophy of Law', in *Essays in Jurisprudence and Philosophy* (Oxford: Clarendon Press, 1983), 104. Someone who complains about the judicial abuse of 'logic' may simply mean that legal decision-making should be flexible and not bound by rules. 'Logic' figures in this complaint as a paradigm of inflexibility. But of course the sense in which the 'laws of logic' might be said to be 'inflexible'—namely, that there is no thought which is alien to them—is inimical to the purposes of someone who wishes to say that judges should be prepared to modify the law.

3.1 Preliminary: Formal Study/Formal Sources

One basis for the association was already touched on. Hart (who defended a form of positivism) is sometimes considered a 'formalist' on account of his doctrine of easy cases. Without more, this label seems prejudicial and distracting, for, in at least two other standard senses, Hart must be considered one of formalism's opponents. First, he disapproves of ORBD. Secondly, he advises that there are bound to be, in any legal system, cases which, due to indeterminacy in the rules, call for a legally unregulated decision. In fact, there are two other aspects of Hart's theory which have attracted the label 'formalist' to it, and before turning to what is most distinctive in the positivist's explanation of law, it will be helpful to distinguish them. They involve a commitment to (1) the formal (culture-independent) study of law and (2) the formal (content-independent) validity of laws. The *study* of law is formal if it focuses on the law's essential or structural characteristics, as opposed to those characteristics which may vary across culture or time.[46] An account of *legal validity* is formal if it entails that there can be a test for identifying valid law which is indifferent to the law's material content, for example, to whether the law is politically desirable, moral, or just.[47]

It is easy to fall into thinking that these are the same, but that is a mistake. Anyone committed, like Hart and Kelsen, to distinguishing the formal validity of a legal order from the political and moral content of particular laws, also believes that there is at least one thing (namely, the conditions of legal validity) to be learned from the formal study of law, even if they think there is little to be learned in this way about the law's content. The converse, however, is not as clear. For there are celebrated theorists who profess to be studying the law's essential characteristics but who do not embrace a purely formal account of legality. According to Kant, for example, a *Rechtslehre* must describe 'the foundations of any possible positive legislation' and thereby go beyond the empirical-historical study of 'what the laws say or have said at a certain time and at a certain place'.[48] This description of the task of legal theory would suit Kelsen or Hart as well. But Kant also finds the concept of law to be internally related to the freedom or self-determination of rational agents, and this implies, for him, a content, namely, the right to own property and other rights associated with private law. Similarly, Pashukanis, while enjoining Marxists to study 'the [universality and] fundamental essence of the legal form' (and not simply 'the material content of legal regulation in different historical epochs'), also criticized (as 'formalistic') Kelsen's view that the legal order is capable of having almost any content. Contractual

---

[46] Cf. Weinrib, 'Legal Formalism', 957–66; Hart, *Concept of Law*, 'Postscript', 239–40.

[47] Cf. Hans Kelsen, *Introduction to the Problems of Legal Theory*, trans. Bonnie Paulson and Stanley Paulson (Oxford: Oxford University Press, 1992), 25; Hegel, *Prefatory Lectures on the Philosophy of Law*, *Clio*, 8: 49, 62 (trans. A. Brudner, 1978) (quoted in Weinrib, 'Legal Formalism', 954).

[48] Immanuel Kant, *The Metaphysical Elements of Justice (Part I of The Metaphysics of Morals)*, trans. John Ladd (Indianapolis: Bobbs-Merrill, 1965), 34.

relations between commodity owners, he argued (broadly following Kant), are the 'cell-form' of all legal relations.[49]

The distinction between these kinds of formality might need no remarking were it not for a tendency, originating with the Realists, to level at 'the formalist' the vague charge of neglecting history and society in his understanding of law. 'Formalism', according to one contemporary, is 'the dogma that legal forms can be understood apart from their social context'.[50] This sounds like an objection to the formal study of law, but can it really be so? No doubt, the law exhibits many variations, which it may be profitable to study, in different cultures and times. But this does not contradict the thought that these variations share a general form, any more than the fact that there are different genres of music or different social moralities entails that there is nothing to say about music or morality in general. Indeed, it may plausibly be said that the law's variability *requires* there to be something of a more formal and general sort to say, for it shows that we are prepared to treat the concept of law as an abstract unity applicable to just *such-and-such* instances. Where variation is intelligible, so, it would seem, is the idea of form.[51] Those who object to the general study of 'legal forms' are probably supposing that this incurs a commitment to the systemic isolation of legality from questions of moral and political content.[52] Yet it has also been suggested that positivism, in being committed to such isolation, is itself the product of a failure to focus the study of law on the essential properties that constitute its form.[53] Since these cannot both be true, it seems best to recognize that neither positivists nor their opponents have any monopoly on the formal study of law, and that what is at issue between them is rather what conclusions, if any, concerning the law's content can be derived from such formal study. In any case, positivism should not be branded as 'formalism' simply because it involves a formal and general study of law. If anything, it might be preferable to reserve the term 'formal-*ism*' for the more ambitious type of formal study which claims also to discover necessary features of the law's content.

3.2 The Sources Thesis as the Basic Formalist Commitment

We shall consider the thesis that every valid proposition of law has a social source (or that what is law is a social fact, the identification of which involves no moral or political argument), to be what is most distinctive in the positivist's explanation of law.[54] It

[49] See E. Pashukanis, *Law and Marxism: A General Theory*, trans. Barbara Einhorn (London: Pluto Press, 1978), 49–54. For Kelsen's rejection of the Kantian thesis, see e.g. Kelsen, *Introduction to the Problems of Legal Theory*, 39–53.

[50] Robert Gordon, 'Critical Legal Histories', *Stanford Law Review*, 36 (1984), 57, 68.

[51] Cf. Giorgio Del Vecchio, *The Formal Bases of Law*, trans. John Lisle (Boston: The Boston Book Company, 1914).

[52] See e.g. Shklar, *Legalism*, 33–4.   [53] See e.g. Weinrib, 'Legal Formalism', 955–6.

[54] See Raz, *The Authority of Law*, 38.

has been argued (with considerable historical subtlety) that this thesis deserves to be considered also the core of what American jurisprudence has called 'formalism'.[55] The argument has two steps. First, a formalist is said to accept the easy case thesis. Secondly, this thesis is said to derive its interest from the attempt to isolate authoritative legal norms from the larger universe of moral, political, and other normative considerations. Apart from such an attempt at isolation, the thought goes, it would not matter whether recourse to policies and purposes was always needed to decide a case. But given the attempt, one is bound to deny that such recourse is always needed—otherwise no legal result would be traceable back to a legally authoritative source. On this account, then, the 'sources thesis' underlies and motivates the formalist commitment to 'easy cases'; and the essence of formalism is considered to lie in the isolation of the legal system, in the 'autonomy of law', as is sometimes said, from morality and politics.

(*a*) *Fuller's argument.* It was Fuller who first suggested a connection between formalism (as a theory of legal reasoning) and positivism (as an explanation of the concept of law). Hart's defence of the distinction between the law as it is and the law as it (morally) ought to be (the 'separability thesis'), Fuller said, 'necessarily leads in the direction of formalism'.[56] We have already encountered one of Fuller's premises, his rejection of ECF. Placing this premise in argumentative context, Fuller's thought is that (1) Hart's 'separability thesis' entails ECF (i.e., it entails that judges can identify and apply legal rules without considering what they 'ought to be'), but (2) ECF is untenable, so (3) the separability thesis is untenable. In short, positivism entails formalism, so the untenability of formalism requires the rejection of positivism.

Various writers have attacked this argument's second premise.[57] That premise can gain no support from the purported undesirability of ORBD, with which it is sometimes confused (Sect. 2). But the argument is shaky, for reasons Hart pointed out, even if this premise is accepted. First, the purported error of ECF seems to undermine the separability thesis only on the assumption that the purposes and policies to which judges would have to appeal (if ECF is mistaken) are themselves to be considered part of the law. Secondly, even if it were true that the meaning of a legal rule is available only by way of purposive interpretation, that would only show that judges must apply the law in light of *some* purposes, not that these purposes must necessarily be moral ones.[58] In 1934, Carl Schmitt wrote that 'every interpretation [of the law] must be an interpretation according to National Socialism'. That seems sufficient to suggest that the fact (if such it be) that legal norms are inextricably interwoven, at the point of application, with purposes and policies, is as serviceable to the friends of good as it is to those of evil.[59]

[55] See Sebok, *Legal Positivism in American Jurisprudence.*
[56] Fuller, 'Positivism and Fidelity to Law', 638.
[57] See e.g. Andrei Marmor, *Interpretation and Legal Theory,* 124–54.
[58] See Hart, 'Positivism and the Separation of Law and Morals'.
[59] Schmitt's remark is quoted in I. Muller, *Hitler's Justice: The Courts of the Third Reich* (Cambridge, Mass.: Harvard University Press, 1991), 70. Not surprisingly, formalism in the sense of 'rigid adherence

(*b*) *Redirecting Fuller's argument.* Still, someone might wonder whether there isn't a good point to be salvaged from Fuller's association of positivism with formalism. Fuller focused on the positivist's 'separability thesis'. Suppose Hart is right in suggesting that this thesis is clouded by the ('anti-formalist') requirement of purposive interpretation only if the purposes and policies on which judges must rely are themselves to be considered law. For a positivist who accepts the sources thesis, they are not necessarily to be considered law. But might not the anti-formalist requirement be aimed against this (arguably)[60] much more fundamental positivist thesis? According to the sources thesis, the considerations of morality and policy which show up in legal reasoning are to be considered law only under special conditions. The bounds of the law are given by a certain type of social fact, the presence of which can be independently determined, so that when a judge is required to apply 'moral' considerations in order to resolve a case, he is in fact often changing or developing the law. With respect to this thesis, an anti-formalist challenger, inspired by Fuller, might ask: 'Would there be any *point* in regimenting the concept of law in this way if it were really true that in every case a judge can decide what the law requires only in light of (her sense of) what the law 'ought' to be?' If the answer to this question were 'no', then it might at least be said that positivism does depend, as Fuller maintained, on ECF, such that if ECF is untenable, positivism is as well.

But the answer to this redirected Fullerian challenge is not so clear. It depends, first of all, on what the motivation of the sources thesis is, on why we might wish to make the need for moral assessment the crucial factor in a test for the limits of law. Perhaps *some* arguments for the sources thesis cannot tolerate the Fullerian criticism of 'easy cases' (assuming that criticism were otherwise sound). It has been said, for example, that the sources thesis clarifies what is involved in our sense that a central function of law is to provide authoritative public standards by which persons are bound even in the face of disputes about the justification of those standards.[61] Perhaps the sources thesis, so motivated, would be undercut if there really were a ubiquitous need for recourse to (justifying) purposes and policies in order to decide whether the law requires *this* or *that*. But a discussion would be needed at this point of the considerations which make the sources thesis compelling.

There is, however, something odd about any argument which purports to call the sources thesis into question on the basis of the need for morality and policy to resolve indeterminacy in the application of the law. Such arguments seem in fact to presuppose that thesis. For doesn't talk of legal indeterminacy presuppose a concept of law which draws the limits of law more narrowly than all the considerations which judges ought to use in deciding cases? Absent a statement of what those limits are, it seems natural to think that all those who, since the Realists, have stressed the law-making

to legal rules' appears, in some contexts, as a judicial weapon in the fight against fascism. See Guido Calabresi, 'Two Functions of Formalism', *University of Chicago Law Review*, 67 (2000), 479.

[60] See Raz, *Authority of Law*, 38.   [61] Ibid. 52.

function of the judge, or the need for the judge to go beyond the law and make decisions on the basis of morality or policy, have all (whatever they may have said) been positivists in the sense clarified by the sources thesis.

3.3 Positivism and Indeterminacy

Someone might feel that this way of construing Fuller's argument (as invoking the law's indeterminacy) does not do it justice. Fuller's point, it might be said, is not that in applying purposes and policies, legal reasoning must go beyond the law, but that it must go beyond the law as the *positivist* mistakenly conceives it. Hence his argument might be construed as one towards the boundlessness of legal reasons. Since 'it is in light of [an] "ought" that we must decide what the [legal] rule is',[62] the law consists of all those normative considerations which judges should use in making their decisions. This makes the law *determinate*—or at least no less so than practical reason in general.

There is much in Fuller that seems to be at odds with this reading, but it is instructive to consider it here as a possible position, for it involves a variety of adjudicational formalism which is arguably *stronger* than the one Fuller attributed to Hart. Hart's claim, to review, was that in *some cases* a judicial decision can be regarded as faithful to the law even without the interpretive aid of purposes or policies. Fuller's rejection of this claim affects the separability thesis, we allowed, only on the assumption that the purposes or policies to which judges must purportedly have recourse are themselves to be considered part of the law. This led to the suggestion that the argument should be redirected towards the sources thesis, which allows purposes on policies to count as law only on special conditions. But now if one rejects the sources theses in favour of a concept of law which embraces all the considerations which must come into play in reaching determinate judgments—if the appropriateness of a consideration to the resolution of a case is enough to make it into law—one will have gone well beyond Hart's modest 'easy case' thesis to the claim that the law determines, at least as well as reason itself does, what is to be done in all cases. Of course, this striking claim is itself standardly referred to as 'formalism'.

At this point, the association of positivism and formalism looks like a matter of definitional fiat. Someone might say that whereas Hart's doctrine of easy cases is 'formalistic', the view that there are no legally unregulated cases is not, since the latter view does not isolate the law from the larger universe of moral and political norms. But the label doesn't matter—it merely shows what someone is determined to call 'formalism'. Here the interests of clarity seem best served by dropping the label and discussing positivism in its own terms. A label is only a label, of course; but when it comes laden with associations, its needlessness is a reason to avoid it.

---

[62] Fuller, 'Positivism and Fidelity to Law', 665–6.

We can summarize our findings here as follows. It is difficult to see how 'formalism' could betoken at once (*a*) the positivist's thesis of the limits of law *and* (*b*) the view that judges can reach a decision in every case without having to go beyond the law. These views do not directly occlude one another. But the assertion that the law is indeterminate, which anti-formalism in one guise is supposed to champion, presupposes some test, of the sort positivism supplies, for the limits of law. Conversely, if one's concept of law is such as to limit the law to authoritative sources, it will seem implausible, on account of the renowned indeterminacies affecting legal norms, to think that legal reasoning need never go beyond the law. Legal indeterminacy, in short, presupposes, if not positivism, at least some alternative way of drawing the limits of law well short of all the relevant judicial-decisional considerations; and positivism, the most developed account there is of these limits, makes legal indeterminacy practically inevitable.

3.4   Formalism: The Autonomy of Law or of Legal Reasoning?

To conclude this second part of our survey, a brief comment on positivism's favourability to claims of legal indeterminacy seems in order. Objecting to the identification of positivism and formalism, one recent writer has insisted that 'if positivism is one's theory of law, nothing substantial follows about one's theory of adjudication', for the sources thesis, central to positivism, 'is silent on legal reasoning'.[63] This is understandable as a response to the mistaken identification of positivism and formalism, and it is perhaps even unobjectionable taken strictly *à la lettre*, but it is itself misleading. For the falsity of one ('formalist') view of adjudication—namely, that judicial reasoning never goes beyond the law—*does* follow from the sources thesis, given two weak assumptions, even if it does not follow by an immediate inference.[64]

The first assumption is that the law's determinacy does not set the limits of a court's obligation to render a decision. If this were not true—if courts were free to refuse to decide whenever the law was indeterminate or gappy—they might indeed confine themselves merely to saying what the law requires, even when the only answer is 'the law is silent'. In that case, the positivist limitation of law and the formalist view that judges only unfold its meaning would sit happily together. But this is not any legal system we know. It goes against our basic commitment to the idea that a court should find for one of the parties in some non-arbitrary way.[65] The second

---

[63]   Leiter, 'Review Essay: Positivism, Formalism, Realism', 1150, 1152.

[64]   See Joseph Raz, 'On the Autonomy of Legal Reasoning', in *Ethics in the Public Domain: Essays in the Morality of Law and Politics* (Oxford: Clarendon Press, 1994), to which I am indebted in the paragraph which follows.

[65]   See Raz, 'On the Autonomy of Legal Reasoning', 334. Hence, indeterminacy is never an appropriate ground for a court's refusal to decide. This should be distinguished from the situation where a higher-order legal norm requires a court to resolve indeterminacies in favour of one of the parties; in such a case, the law is not indeterminate.

assumption, now widely accepted, is that any regime of source-based law will be sub-ject to indeterminacies and gaps.[66] It follows from these assumptions that legal rea-soning cannot confine itself to source-based material, and hence, given the sources thesis, that it must go beyond law to morality or policy. Someone might try to avoid this conclusion by stipulating that 'legal reasoning' is always reasoning about what the law requires and nothing more. That would make the formalist view (that legal reasoning never goes beyond the law) true by definition. But then one will either say that in cases where the law is indeterminate, judges must go beyond legal sources and *thereby beyond 'legal' reasoning* (which sounds odd), or, keeping to the common-sense view (that legal reasoning is what judges do in deciding cases), one will have to close off all gaps and indeterminacies by massively expanding the class of considera-tions which count as law. In either case, there is a disjunction between the positivist's source-based limitation of law and the formalist's view that judges merely unfold the law's meaning; between the so-called 'autonomy of law' (its normative isolation, its regulation of its own limits) and the so-called 'autonomy of legal reasoning'.

4 DEDUCTIVISM OR ANTI-INSTRUMENTALISM?

4.1 Background: The Realist's Focus on Judicially Elaborated Private Law

The last part of our survey presents a curious tension within post-Holmesian thought rather than a straightforward inconsistency. Resolving the tension sheds light on the problem mentioned in the beginning: nothing seems either less hidden or more insistently exposed since Holmes than that judges do not deduce their deci-sions from legal rules. The problem is to motivate the felt need to expose this, given the obviousness of the fact that logic is silent about the chief task of legal reasoning, the classification of particulars.

Consider the following:

It is a commonplace that law is 'political.' Ever since the realists debunked 'formalism' in legal reasoning, the received learning has been that legal analysis cannot be neutral and determi-nate, that general propositions of law cannot decide particular cases. Some policy judgment or value choice necessarily intervenes. It is 'transcendental nonsense' to believe that it could be any other way.[67]

---

[66] See Hart, *Concept of Law*, ch. 7.   [67] Peller, 'The Metaphysics of American Law', 1152.

A central strand in the critique of formalism finds the law to be pervasively inde-terminate in a way that must be managed by reference to the 'political'. Typically, this strand (*a*) presents the deducibility of judgments in particular cases as a privileged paradigm—a sort of gold standard—of what it would mean for legal norms to be 'determinate', (*b*) finds that in most or all cases this standard cannot be satisfied, and (*c*) concludes that some 'policy judgment'—some reference to desired social goals—must mediate between legal norms and their application in particular cases.[68] Two general points may help to locate this line of thought more precisely.

(1) First, its chief focus was originally private law—tort, contract, and property[69]—or rather a 'classical' picture of private law, conceived by the Realists as entailing: (i) private law's independence from the type of prudential reasoning (con-cerning means to socially common ends) which was supposed to be the task of pub-lic rule, and (ii) the belief that moral limits on state power were *therefore* available not merely as a matter of political prudence and the general good, but as a matter of a law given prior to political ends. The Realist assertion of a ubiquitous need to understand and apply the law as an instrument of social policy comprised a *reductionist* response to this picture. The point was to exhibit private law as a form of public, administra-tive law (a use of common means in pursuit of common ends), and thereby to liber-ate the state from purportedly imaginary 'juridical' constraints while reshaping private law into a functionally rational instrument of social welfare.[70] (Legal realism

[68] Cf. Allan C. Hutchinson, 'Democracy and Determinacy: An Essay on Legal Interpretation', *University of Miami Law Review*, 43 (1988), 541, 558: '[T]here simply does not exist a necessary and ade-quate connection between legal outcomes and doctrinal material. . . . [T]here can be no law without interpretation, no interpretation without judges, and no judges without politics.'

[69] A second focus was on constitutional doctrines which regulate the boundary between public and private. See William Fisher, Morton Horowitz and Thomas Reed (eds.), *American Legal Realism* (New York: Oxford University Press, 1993), 76–129. It seems notable that 'the proposition that legal rules can be understood only with reference to the purposes they serve', was first announced by Fuller in an argu-ment to the effect that the rule of awarding damages for breach of contract is, in itself, indeterminate, and so must be understood and applied as an instrument of 'social policy'. L. Fuller and W. R. Perdue, 'The Reliance Interest in Contract Damages', *Yale Law Journal*, 46 (1936), 52

[70] These points make it understandable why *Lochner v New York*, 198 US 45 (1905), which found the private law principle of freedom of contract to be entrenched in the Fourteenth Amendment, should have come to be regarded by the Realists as a paradigm of 'formalism'. Certainly Justice Peckham's opin-ion does not purport to 'deduce' that principle from the textual reference to 'liberty'; nor is there any-thing 'mechanical' about his finding it there. But if contractual rights and obligations are correctly understood as functional instruments of social purposes (or if they are mere 'predictions' of the inci-dence of public power), then it must be doubtful that the Fourteenth Amendment entrenches them when the state, as society's agent, declares that they no longer serve its purpose. So it is perhaps just the classical picture of private law in which Lochner's reputed 'formalism' really consists. Cf. Cass Sunstein, 'Lochner's Legacy', *Columbia Law Review*, 87 (1987), 873. Four years after Lochner was decided, Pound described it as reflecting a form of legal thought 'which exaggerates private right at the expense of public right' and which involves 'mechanical jurisprudence, a condition of juristic thought and judicial action in which deduction from conceptions has produced a cloud of rules that obscures the principles from which they were drawn, in which conceptions are developed logically at the expense of practical results . . .'. Pound, 'Liberty of Contract', *Yale Law Journal*, 18 (1909), 454. Pound's alignment of the complaint about the priority of private law with references to mechanism, logic and deduction seems

appears to have been blind to the possibility of *non-reductive* responses to classical assertions of private law's priority—for example, questioning whether (i) really incurs a commitment to (ii). Along with some of the 'classical' jurists, the Realists seem to have taken this for granted.)

(2) Secondly, since private law was mainly judicially elaborated common law, the claim that 'policy judgments' were required for its specification was aimed not just at the law's academic defenders but at the self-understanding of its judges as well. According to Holmes, for example, the choice between the negligence principle (which requires proof of the defendant's failure to take 'reasonable care') and strict liability (which does not) 'is a concealed, half conscious battle on the question of legislative *policy*, and if any one thinks that it can be settled *deductively* . . . I only can say that I think he is theoretically wrong, and that I am certain that his conclusion will not be accepted in practice. . . .'[71] These terms of judicial criticism persist to the present day. The bad ('formalist') judge engages in the pretence that the general, structural concepts of private law (e.g. '*alienum non laedas*') determine the result (or the rule) to be applied in particular (types of) cases. At best, he is deceived, otherwise only 'half-conscious', 'concealing' what he knows, acting in bad faith.[72] The good ('Realist') judge reveals the policy-driven interpretation which must willy-nilly be made if there is to be an intelligent decision or an intelligent selection of rules. Here are two examples of self-conscious realism in judging:

What we do mean by the word 'proximate' is, that because of convenience, of public policy, of a rough sense of justice, the law arbitrarily declines to trace a series of events beyond a certain point. This is not logic. It is practical politics. (Andrews in *Palsgraf*)[73]

Whenever the courts draw a line to mark out the bounds of duty, they do it as a matter of policy. . . .Whenever the courts set bounds to the damages recoverable—saying that they are, or are not, too remote—they do it as a matter of policy . . . (Denning in *Spartan Steel*)[74]

Using such concepts as 'proximate cause' and 'duty', the law distinguishes, on a case-by-case basis, between the proper consequences of negligent action and its merely fortuitous upshots. According to these judges, the indeterminacy of these concepts requires that the exercise of applying them be conceived as one of prudential reasoning towards political goals. Thus Denning resolves the question of a negligent

---

puzzling. What could be less mechanical than Lochner's application of the due process clause to minimum hour laws?

[71] Oliver Wendell Holmes, 'The Path of the Law', in *Collected Legal Papers* (New York: Harcourt, Brace and Company, 1920), 182–3.

[72] For modern redeployment of these terms, see e.g. E. H. Levi, *An Introduction to Legal Reasoning* (Chicago: University of Chicago Press, 1949), 1–4; Kennedy, *A Critique of Adjudication*. Of course, some theorists applaud rather than criticize the covert pursuit of policy objectives through legal 'rhetoric'. Cf. Guido Calebresi, 'Concerning Cause and the Law of Torts: An Essay for Harry Kalven, Jr.', *University of Chicago Law Review*, 69 (1975), 69, 107.

[73] *Palsgraf v Long Island Railroad Co.*, 248 NY 339, 162 NE 99 (1928).

[74] *Spartan Steel & Alloys Ltd. v Martin & Co.*, 1 QB at 27, 37 (1973).

contractor's duty to protect the plaintiff from economic loss on the grounds that it would be socially desirable if such losses were widely distributed. There are similar decisions following Andrews.[75] In each case, an interpretive recourse to 'policy' is supposed to be required if some general legal concept is to be non-arbitrarily applied.

The line of anti-formalist thought to be considered here is thus something more than an assault on a naïve 'deductivism'. It associates the idea that particular judgments can be reached deductively with a classical understanding of private law, and it contrasts this classical understanding with the application of the law as an instrument of social policy. These associations and contrasts are familiar. But they are also, on reflection, puzzling. We shall consider two puzzles in turn. First, the inference from 'indeterminacy' to the specification of legal norms in light of policy seems dubious. Secondly, the contrast between 'deductive' and 'policy-based' decision seems neither exhaustive (are there no other alternatives?) nor even exclusive: the demand for 'policy' to resolve problems of applicative judgment seems best understood, we shall suggest, as itself a demand for a deductive procedure.

4.2 The Dubious Inference from Indeterminacy to Policy

In everyday settings, the idea that problems of situational judgement are problems of 'policy', to be resolved in light of some independent goals, does not—to say the least—come naturally to common sense. Suppose Richard must decide whether to help his friend where this means missing some opportunity for professional advancement. The question concerns, among other things, the obligations of friendship. Here we are accustomed to thinking that there may be no decision procedure available to Richard other than this: he must try to read the salience of the facts of the situation in light of the general concerns (friendship, another's need, his own work, etc.) it brings into play. Analogies may help, but it is not to be supposed that they will establish a rule (e.g. 'in circumstances ABC, do so-and-so') which makes it unnecessary for Richard to try to understand the relevant concerns in light of *this* situation's concrete demands. All this, perplexing to the practical agent as it sometimes is, is commonplace.

Do such familiar problems of judgment arise because the relevant concerns are 'indeterminate'? If this means they are nowhere taught or explained in a way which affords deductive access to judgment, it may be allowed that they are 'indeterminate'. But it would be strange to conclude from this that some supplemental recourse to 'policy' is needed. That makes it sound as if all the existing explanations of 'friendship' had somehow left something out. Suppose Richard, putting on his policy hat, hits upon the supplemental idea that the purpose of friendship is to 'enhance an

---

[75] See e.g. *Petitions of the Kinsman Transit Co.*, 383 F 2d 708 (1964), esp. 725–6.

individual's ability to maximize his satisfactions'.[76] People are well advised to cultivate friendships because, by doing so, they will be happy, as measured in some more
basic currency. Richard might think this idea an advance since (whatever else is to be
said for or against it) it at least converts his problem from one of casuistry to calculation: given sufficient information (e.g. the opportunity costs of helping his friend,
etc.), he could *demonstrate* what friendship really requires. Perhaps Richard has been
reading Sidgwick, who cites the prospect of moving from casuistry to calculation as
an argument for utilitarianism over 'common sense morality':

[W]here the current formula [of Common Sense Morality] is not sufficiently precise for the
guidance of conduct, while at the same time difficulties and perplexities arise in the attempt
to give it additional precision, the Utilitarian method solves these difficulties and perplexities. . . .

The Utilitarian . . . endeavour[s] to show the Intuitionist that the principles of Truth, Justice,
etc. have only a dependent and subordinate validity: arguing either that the principle is really
only affirmed by Common Sense as a general rule admitting of exceptions and qualifications
. . . and that we require some further principle for systematizing these exceptions and qualifications; or that the fundamental notion is vague and needs further determination, as in the
case of Justice; and further, that the different rules are liable to conflict with each other, and
that we require some higher principle to decide the issue thus raised. . . . Here, as elsewhere,
Utilitarianism at once supports the different reasons commonly put forward as absolute, and
also brings them theoretically to a common measure, so that *in any particular case we have a
principle of decision between conflicting political arguments* [emphasis added].[77]

According to Sidgwick, 'common sense' stands in need of 'some further principle'
(which Utilitarianism can supply) which would yield a decision-procedure for particular cases.[78] But doesn't this beg the question of the sort of precision we should
expect the common-sense principles to have in the first place? Recourse to 'some further principle' might be said to be required *if* one is already a utilitarian, in secure
possession of the knowledge that the terms of common sense were only blunt markers of utility anyway, bits of sound (but incomplete) advice given to those embarking
on life's maximizing journey. It is hard to see how such a requirement could stand on
its own to recommend the utilitarian reduction. Were Richard really to decide what
to do on the basis of his 'satisfaction-maximization' theory of friendship, surely common sense would be entitled to say that he hasn't brought the relevant concern—
friendship—into view.[79] If such recourse to 'policy' is excluded in so far as Richard

[76] Richard Posner, *Economic Analysis of Law*, 2nd edn. (Boston: Little, Brown and Co., 1977), 185–6.

[77] Henry Sidgwick, *Methods of Ethics* (Chicago: University of Chicago Press, 1962), 421, 444, 425.

[78] The looked-for procedure is implicitly a deductive one. For it is hard to see how a 'further principle' which did not afford deductive access to judgment would be an improvement over the terms of
common-sense, or why (on the assumption that 'common sense' requires a 'further principle') such a
'further principle' would not itself require a 'further principle' to make *it* determinate, and so on.

[79] Someone sensitive to reasons of friendship is not routinely willing to trade it off against other
generic satisfactions. See Joseph Raz, *The Morality of Freedom* (Oxford: Oxford University Press, 1986),
352–3.

keeps *this* concern in view, the fact that the inherited explanations of it do not afford deductive access to judgment does not suggest that anything is *missing* from them. If that is what it means for them to be 'indeterminate', they are not indeterminate. They are as precise as they can be without ceasing to be what they are—namely, explanations of friendship, not rules-of-thumb for maximizing more basic satisfactions.[80]

These considerations do not, by themselves, imply that private law doctrines are not instrumental ones. Nor do they suggest that, in elaborating the law, judges do not 'legislate'. What is in question is a view with which the issue of 'judicial legislation' seems to have been (starting with Holmes) fatally confused, namely, whether judges inevitably confront 'policy' questions whenever it is uncertain what a legal norm requires. The question of 'judicial legislation' is a question about the conceptual limits of law (Sects. 3.2–3.3). Even if it is resolved in a way favourable to the view that many judicial decisions are 'not law' until enacted by a court, nothing follows from this about the appropriate *grounds* of decision.[81] As Holmes and the Realists knew all too well, traditional judges confronting an 'indeterminate' norm do not simply put on their policy-making hats, even if their view is that they must make new law. They attempt to understand the meaning of the relevant norm in light of what the situation demands; they argue, by analogy, for the salience of certain facts, and they try to find principles which have some toe-hold in the existing law. All this is commonplace; so too is the fact that there may be competing analogies and principles, and other practical perplexities.[82] But the question of whether such traditional procedures are mistakenly 'formalistic' is just the question of whether the notional 'indeterminacy' of a legal norm means that intelligent judgment must supply itself with some independent ground of decision (Sidgwick: 'some further principle'). Reflection on everyday practical thinking suggests that this is not generally the case. It suggests that the inference from the indeterminacy of a norm to the need for premises of 'policy' is not generally valid. Must it be different with law?

[80] A version of Sidgwick's question-begging argument is a crucial point of support in Shavell and Kaplow's claim that there is no good for the law to do except that of advancing social welfare defined in Paratonian terms. See Louis Kaplow and Steven Shavell, *Principles of Fairness versus Human Welfare: On the Evaluation of Legal Policy*, Harvard Law School, Law-Econ Discussion Paper No. 277, SSRN Electronic Paper Collection (2000). The only consideration they advance in support of this claim is the observation that any other candidate goods are 'indeterminate' with respect to the selection of legal rules and therefore leave everything to 'intuition'. I think it is merely scientism (a prejudicial demand for practical matters to have the sort of intelligibility found in the natural sciences) which makes this look like a good argument, but the point would require a longer discussion than is possible here. Cf. Sidgwick, *Methods of Ethics*, 425: 'Utilitarians are . . . called upon to show a natural transition from the Morality of Common Sense to Utilitarianism, somewhat like the transition in special branches of practice from trained instinct . . . to the technical method that embodies and applies the conclusions of science: so that Utilitarianism may be presented as the scientifically complete and systematically reflective form of [the] regulation of conduct'.

[81] Otherwise put: if judges must have recourse to policy, then they must legislate; but from the fact that judges legislate, it doesn't follow that they must have recourse to policy.

[82] See Roberto Unger, *The Critical Legal Studies Movement* (Cambridge, Mass.: Harvard University Press, 1983), 8–9.

4.3 The Doubtful Contrast between Deductive and Policy-Based Decision Procedures

Realist judges are apt to suggest that decisions on grounds of policy are inevitable in applying general legal norms, because the only other possibility would be to pretend that judgment is accessible by means of deduction. (Andrews: 'This is not logic. It is practical politics.') But this seems implausible. If Richard does not put into play any 'policy' to resolve the question of his obligations as a friend, are we to think that he purports to 'deduce' the answer from the concept of friendship instead?

The issue has been muddied by a confusion, again of Holmesian origins, between the idea of a deductive decision procedure and that of a 'legal syllogism'. In the classical practical syllogism, the major premise refers to some good to be achieved and the minor premise to some feature of the situation indicating something doable to advance that good. (It is fitting to help a friend in need/By doing x I can help a friend in need/So I shall do x). It is true that judges sometimes cast their deliberations into something resembling this form, and that they thereby (sometimes) exhibit their decision as deducible from a legal rule along with another fact-stating premise. But this is an irrelevancy which should have fooled no one into thinking that judges purport to access their judgments deductively. For obviously the selection of just certain facts as what matters about the situation, and the classification of those facts in terms of the relevant rule often require a kind of discernment which is more than a capacity to draw logical inferences or recognize that certain facts obtain. This is bound to be the case when the conditions set out in the rule have the featureless generality of such private law principles as 'reasonable care' or 'reasonable forseeability'. Since the formation of a minor premise which will co-operate with such principles to produce a deductive argument for the legal conclusion exhibits a selective take on what matters about the situation (and not just a recognition of what the facts are), one might say that classical legal reasoning is distinctively 'practical' as opposed to 'theoretical': it requires thought about what matters and not just about what is true. This distinction will be useful momentarily in clarifying the idea of a 'deductive decision procedure'. Deductive reasoning is sometimes practical (it may concern what to do), but it is not *proprietary* to the practical. So to say that judges (pretend to) deduce their decisions is to say, among other things, that (they pretend) there is nothing distinctively practical about legal reasoning.

That a judge casts his deliberations into the form of a syllogism and refers to no 'policy' does not (*pace* Holmes) touch the question of whether he purports to be able to reach his decision by deductive means, for the syllogistic structure is, in itself, neutral between deductive reasoning and reasoning which—involving thought about what matters and not just what is true—is distinctively practical. Moreover, the syllogistic structure is equally available for characterizing classical legal casuistry *and* the policy-based reasoning of judges like Andrews and Denning. These considerations suggest that deductive and policy-based procedures do not exhaust the legal possibilities. But they also suggest that we should not assume that these describe *exclusive* possibilities. We should not assume, that is, but *ask*, whether the Realist demand that private law doctrines be applied as instruments of social policy is well understood as a demand for judges to drop a deductive pretence and acknowledge an irreducibly practical task. Might not the meaning of this demand be just the reverse: an attack on the proposition—which was never disguised in the classical procedures—that legal reasoning must confront practical tasks, in favour of a demand to certify its results by the operations of a purely theoretical-deductive rationality?

Consider one bit of contemporary 'Realism' about private law, the interpretation of 'reasonable care' as socially cost-justified spending on accident prevention. Such an understanding of the law has not, of course, eliminated the need for juries (or, in appellate cases, judges) to make judgments of 'reasonableness'. But the classical casuistry of reasonableness persists, according to instrumentalists, only for contingent reasons. As Judge Posner explains:

[T]he parties do not give the jury the information required to quantify the variables that the Hand formula picks out as relevant. That is why the formula has greater analytic than operational significance. Conceptual as well as practical difficulties in monetizing personal injuries may continue to frustrate efforts to measure expected accidents costs with the precision that is possible, in principle at least, in measuring the other side of the equation—the cost or burden of precaution. For many years to come juries may be forced to make rough judgments of reasonableness, intuiting rather than measuring . . . [these] factors.[83]

This presents judgments of reasonableness as a kind of 'second-best' way of hitting a target which could, in principle, be more exactly located by purely theoretical means; it says that such judgments are correct just when they are the ones that would be reached on the basis of informed calculations, starting with the premise that law's purpose is to bring about 'cost-effective spending on accident prevention'. If the relevant information were available, then a judge might put this premise into operation. The result would be not merely a bit of legal reasoning which could be cast in syllogistic form; it would also be an instance of something we might intelligibly call a 'deductive decision procedure'. For given this premise, the correctness of particular legal rulings could be demonstrated given only the addition of factual information about what would lead to what. In fact, the interest of such an understanding of the law does not really depend on whether the information needed to operationalize it will be available in some realistic future. (If it did, law and economics would be much less interesting to people than it is.) It seems clear that another motivation for developing such an understanding of the law (its 'analytic significance' as Posner says) is to vindicate the very notion of correct legal judgment by showing that the law's 'intuitively' based rulings could, in principle, be validated by means of an argument which did not involve any thinking of a distinctively practical kind. Such a motivation seems

---

[83]   *McCarty v Pheasant Run, Inc.*, 826 F 2d 1554 (7 Cir. 1987).

intelligible against the background of scepticism, itself prominent in the Realists, about our entitlement to the notion of correctness in the kind of practical thought which involves the situational specification of norms.

4.4 The Main Tension: Instrumentalism, on the one hand, and the Attack on Judicial 'Deduction' on the other

All of this points to a tension between two familiarly conjoined elements in the revolt against formalism. Formalism is supposed to consist in a deductive procedure for applying legal norms, and it is supposed to contrast with the understanding and application of law as an instrument of social policy. The received learning even presents these as the same: 'Formalism . . . is the theory that all questions of law can be resolved by deduction, that is, without resort to policy . . .'.[84] But doesn't this get things backwards? *On the one hand,* in the classical picture, private law was organized around a few relatively abstract principles (e.g. 'reasonableness', *'sic utere tuo,* etc.') which, even taken along with their common law glosses, could not plausibly be supposed to furnish deductive access to all legal decisions. The practical problem when such principles came into play was essentially specificatory (it was to say what it would be in this, or in a like, situation to realize them), and for this, jurisprudence, in an older sense of the word, a form of thought dependent on analogy and judgment, and directed towards the elaboration of the content of principles in light of concrete situational demands, was required.[85] *On the other hand,* the requirement that the specific content of such common law principles be determined by recourse to 'policy' did present the prospect of a legal decision procedure which might genuinely be called 'deductive'. For a defining feature of a 'policy' (like loss-spreading or efficient deterrence) as opposed to a principle (like proximate cause or reasonableness) is that there is no special problem about what it would be to realize it in a particular case.[86]

---

[84] Kennedy, *Critique of Adjudication,* 105. Kennedy later says that he is using ' "policy" to denote all non-deductive factors' (109). I suppose this means that he is using 'policy' as a catch-all term for all *sources* of decision that are not law (in legal theory 'morality' is sometimes used this way as well). But this leaves unexplained why his name for legal sources should be 'deductive factors'. Deduction is a type of reasoning, not a special source of decision, and some non-legal sources are much more likely to furnish deductive access to judgment than is the law. Cf. Roberto Unger: 'Legal reasoning is formalistic when the mere invocation of rules and the deduction of conclusions from them is believed sufficient for every authoritative legal choice. It is purposive when the decision about how to apply a rule depends on a judgment of how most effectively to achieve the purposes ascribed to the rule.' *Law in Modern Society,* 194. Again, this seems odd because 'the mere invocation of [legal] rules' is often patently unserviceable for 'the deduction of conclusions'; whereas a redirection of legal reasoning onto questions about the efficacy of one or another decision for bringing about a purpose ascribed to a rule can, as my examples in the text suggest, sometimes be expected to yield deductive procedures.

[85] *Prudentia* was Aquinas's term for Aristotle's *phronesis,* often translated as 'practical wisdom'.

[86] This is certainly not the only way the term 'public policy' is used, but it is constitutive of the interest of 'policy' in the Realist argument from indeterminacy to policy.

The practical problem when such policy goals come into play is mainly one of the expected efficacy of the various means which might be adopted to bring them about; and this means that once such goals are postulated, the correctness of any legal ruling can, in principle, be established by procedures of reasoning which require only the application of empirical knowledge about cause and effect.

It looks like a mistake, then, to think that, sometime in the twentieth century, a discovered need to resort to 'policy' interrupts a previous ('classical' or 'formalist') fantasy of being able to resolve all legal questions by deduction.[87] For it seems more accurate to say that it is the resort to policy which first makes such a fantasy possible. Only when the law is understood as an instrument of policy does the possibility of deductively accessible judgments begin to come into view.

This tension in post-Holmesian thought was already latent in Holmes who, while proclaiming the platitude that the problems of legal reasoning are not those of logical transitions from statements of principle and fact to conclusions, also maintained that common law principles were more or less covert renderings of social policies which good judges should bear in mind.[88] Those who, following Holmes, have denounced deductivism and championed instrumentalism (both in the name of opposition to 'formalism') might be surprised to realize, on reflection, that the interpretation of 'society's good' as Kaldor–Hicks efficiency, and the identification of the 'inner nature' or 'true grounds'[89] of the common law with the pursuit of this good, is just about the only thing in the history of legal thought that answers to the view standardly attributed to the formalist: that of legal reasoning as the deductive application of a gapless system of rules. Only the contemporary economic perfection of the functionalist strand of Legal Realism comes close to something that could be said to make logic 'the life of the law'.[90]

4.5 The Tension Resolved

What is going on here? Why did those who criticized the 'formalist' view that legal reasoning could be deductive also typically urge judges to understand and apply legal rules as instruments of policy? How could such critics stress the need for recourse to interpretive premises of policy on account of the impossibility of a deductive

[87] Cf. Unger, *What Should Legal Analysis Become*, 42–3.

[88] See Holmes, 'The Path of Law', 180, 181, 184; and Holmes, 'Law in Science and Science in Law', *Harvard Law Review*, 12 (1899), 443, 460.

[89] Richard Posner, *The Problems of Jurisprudence* (Cambridge, Mass.: Harvard University Press), 361.

[90] Posner has recognized this: 'If the positive economic theory of the common law is right, the common law is a logical system, and deductive logic—formal reasoning—can be used (by the judge) to reach demonstrably correct results in particular cases or (by the scholar) to demonstrate the correctness of results in particular cases'. Hence, economic analysis of law is 'the modern exemplar of formalism'. Legal Formalism, Legal Realism and the Interpretation of Statutes and the Constitution', *Case Western Reserve Law Review*, 37 (1986), 179, 181, 185.

decision procedure, when such premises seem to be themselves a way of making legal judgment deductively available? This may sound like a paradox, as if the critic of formalism were denying in one breath the possibility he is affirming in the next. In fact, it is possible to understand such a critic. To do so requires an answer to two questions:

1. Why would someone think that those engaged in classical legal casuistry must have been purporting to be able to deduce their decisions in particular cases from general legal rules?
2. Why would someone think that any intelligent application of a quite general norm must refer to some desired goals which can be grasped independently of the norm in question?

The answer to the first question would explain the recurrently felt need to deny that deduction is the core of legal reasoning when scarcely anyone can be found who asserts this. The answer to the second question would explain the recurrent view that the 'indeterminacy' of legal norms must be managed by recourse to policy. Both thoughts, being unintuitive, must be theoretically motivated. And both can be motivated by an assumption which may be called 'deductivism':

> (D) In a disagreement about the application of a norm, we are not entitled to regard one or another judgment as objectively correct (i.e. as genuinely required by the norm and the practical situation) unless we can exhibit that judgment as the conclusion of a deductive argument, the premises of which would be (*a*) some agreed-upon elaboration of the norm in question and (*b*) some characterization of the facts which does not presuppose the correctness of one or the other disputed judgment.

Intuitively, (D) says that the notion of a correct resolution of a disagreement in judgment is available only if we are able to prove one or another judgment, that is, to make it argumentatively compelling from a position outside the disagreement in question.[91]

Given (D), the propositions embedded in (1) and (2) above naturally follow. The first proposition follows from (D) in so far as traditional judges claimed, at least implicitly, to be making correct judgments about what the law requires. Suppose a traditional judge rules that the plaintiff's injury is 'unforeseeable' or 'insufficiently direct', and therefore beyond the scope of the defendant's duty of care. Although the judge might cast his reasoning in syllogistic form and support it by analogy to other cases, there is no question of a deductive procedure here—*unless* one views his decision in light of (D). If one does, one becomes obliged to think either that the judge (*a*) is really (contrary to what he claims) making a creative choice concerning what constitutes a 'direct' or 'foreseeable' injury; or (*b*) purporting to have an understanding of the content of these notions which, if fully spelled out, would be accepted by the

---

[91] For a similar finding concerning the assumption which seems to be operating in discussions of 'formalism', see Lyons, 'Legal Formalism and Instrumentalism', 51.

disputing parties and would rationally compel them, in view of the facts, to reach the same judgment.[92] Assuming that the judge presents himself as saying what the law requires (and not making a choice), (D) thus makes it inevitable to regard him as purporting to have an understanding of the law from which his ruling could, in principle, be deduced.

The second proposition—which requires judicial recourse to premises of policy whenever a legal rule is not deductively applicable—follows from (D) in the same way. Such premises are simply what are needed to elevate any legal rule to the level of deductive applicability, or to turn the syllogism in which it figures into a proof; and this is imperative, given (D), if we are to regard an application of the rule as something more than an unexplained choice. Thus, given (D), it becomes natural to think of the problem of legal judgment, not as one of reading the demands of the particular situation in light of general norms (like 'reasonable foreseeability'), but as one of getting (at least covertly, under rhetorical cover of such norms) the right policy into play; and hence to think of disputes about what such norms require as disputes about what policies the law should follow (as being rationally resolvable, and therefore understandable as genuine disputes, only in such terms).

4.6 Illustration: Economic Functionalism and CLS as Two Ways of Inheriting the Critique of Formalism

Someone might balk at what these considerations seem to imply, namely, that there is a direct line of inheritance from Holmesian/Realist anti-formalism to functionalist accounts of private law, like Posner's, where there is no obstacle, other than an empirical one, to spelling out the law's content as a set of deductively applicable rules which determine a correct answer in every case. They might protest: 'Isn't this the very essence of formalism? Aren't the true inheritors of post-Holmesian thought those Critics who reject such a picture of legal determinacy in favour of the view that every application of the notion of a "legally correct answer" is really a political and ideological assertion of will?'

But there is no need to choose here between these rivals; both may be regarded as inheriting the same Holmesian framework.[93] Common to both is the premise that *if* the problems of specifying abstract legal norms are capable of rational resolution, they must be regarded as problems about what policies the law should pursue and be resolved in such terms. The difference is that Posner affirms, while the Critics deny,

---

[92] If, in its fully spelled-out version, the judge's concept of proximate cause was not accepted by the parties, that would show that there was no genuine dispute about a matter of application—the parties were operating with different concepts.

[93] Edmund Kitch is right that 'law and economics evolved out of the agenda of legal realism'. Kitch, 'The Intellectual Foundations of Law and Economics', *Journal of Legal Education*, 33 (1983), 184.

that the problems of legal specification are resolvable in such terms. Posner is sanguine about this (and hence sanguine about private law as a functionally rational instrument of policy) because he thinks there is just one goal which the law should pursue, 'wealth-maximization'.[94] For the Critics, in contrast, once the specification of legal norms is understood to require recourse to policy, too many conflicting visions of what good the law might do compete for recognition for doctrinal reasoning ever to be (or become) anything more than what the Realists said it was—a disguised form of political contest.[95] Of course, Posner hopes to validate specific legal doctrines on the basis of an argument which refers to a *basic* good, something every society may be presumed to want. But for such an argument to succeed, the single-minded pursuit of this goal would have to be at least less normatively controversial than the legal doctrines that are to be validated as means of bringing it about; and this the Critics, citing the plurality of worthwhile goals the law might pursue, have rightly doubted.

This dispute is perhaps easily resolvable in favour of the Critics by anyone who does not share Posner's monism about legal value (or, as it seems, about value). Our present task, however, is only to make visible the framework of thought which these parties share. For both, the problem of how abstract doctrines of private law are to be applied in particular cases is to be conceived, not (as it appeared to classical legal thought) as one of expressing the content of such doctrines by saying what they require in contingent situations, but rather as one of deciding which already fully understood goals the law should be trying to advance (and, of course, of estimating the efficacy of particular legal rulings in advancing them). It is (D) which makes it seem that the problems of legal reasoning *must* be conceived in this way.

4.7 Summary: The Idea of a Deductively Applicable Rule

To take stock, it may be useful to comment on and to illustrate the notion of 'deductive applicability', for this notion has played a central role in this part of our survey. Recall the long-standing complaint: the formalist thinks that logic alone enables a judge to determine what a legal rule requires in a particular case. This seemed puzzling (Sect. 1.1). How could anyone realistically be supposed to think this when logic is obviously silent about how to classify particulars? Doubtless, there may be rules for

---

[94] Similarly, many Realists affirmed that legal reasoning might become an applied 'science of policy'. Naturally, this prospect comes nearer into reach if one is willing to suppose that the State has 'ultimately' only one aim. See Richard Posner, 'The Concept of Corrective Justice in Recent Theories of Tort Law', *Journal of Legal Studies*, 10 (1981), 187, 206.

[95] On the break between CLS and the Realist attraction to 'policy science', see Peller, 'Metaphysics of American Law'; Guyora Binder, 'Critical Legal Studies', in Dennis Patterson (ed.), *A Companion to Philosophy of Law and Legal Theory* (Cambridge, Mass.: Blackwell Publishers, 1996). The break should not be exaggerated. It takes place within the common assumption that the elaboration of legal doctrine must consist in the selection and implementation of social policies.

applying rules, but such rules (interpretations or explanations) must come to an end somewhere; at some point, an applicative judgment, not a logical inference, is required. To clarify the grounds of the complaint against the formalist, our discussion made use of a somewhat different notion—that of a 'deductively applicable' rule. Although there is no such thing as a rule which is connected to particular judgments through mere logical inference, it can nonetheless make sense to distinguish between rules which afford deductive access to judgment and those which do not. Our aim was to mark a distinction between rules like

(1a) The defendant is negligent just when he fails to spend the last dollar on safety precautions that would have brought a greater expected return in accident prevention;

(2a) The defendant is the proximate cause of injury to the plaintiff just when he is a better conduit of loss-spreading than the plaintiff;

(3a) Do not exceed 60 m.p.h. while driving;

(4a) Stop at red lights;

and rules like

(1b) The defendant is negligent just when he fails to take the care of a reasonable person under the circumstances;

(2b) The defendant is the proximate cause of injury to the plaintiff just when that injury is a reasonably foreseeable consequence of his action;

(3b) Do not drive at an unreasonable speed;

(4b) Exercise reasonable care for the safety of others while driving;

the former, but not the latter, being 'deductively applicable'. In this use of the term, it makes no sense to ask whether legal rules, as such, are deductively applicable—some are and some aren't. But what exactly is the difference between the rules in group (*a*) and group (*b*)?

All of these rules are 'general propositions'—all present a standard of correctness for innumerable particular cases—and thus cannot intelligibly be regarded as connected to their instances apart from applicative judgments. Hence the mark of a rule which is 'deductively applicable' is *not* that it determines what is required in particular cases as a matter of 'logic' or in a way that is 'self-executing', if this means that the rule somehow takes care of itself. Is the 'deductive applicability' of a rule a matter of sociological agreement in judgments? People do tend to agree about the operations of deductive reasoning, but it is not their agreement which makes a rule deductively applicable.[96] In the course of our discussion we rejected another suggestion, namely that a judicial decision is 'deductive' in so far as it can be represented as the conclusion of a syllogism in which the major premise states a rule of law and the minor premise characterizes the facts. This makes deducibility too cheap. For the application of *any* legal rule can be cast into this form, thereby exhibiting the route to a legal

[96] In fact, there is apt to be a great deal of disagreement about which actions are 'negligent' or a 'proximate cause' under rules (1a) or (2a).

conclusion as a deduction from the rule ('A person is liable if he φ's; X φ-ed; so X is liable').

What, then, is the difference between (*a*) and (*b*) type rules, such that we want to say that one is deductively applicable and the other not? It must be remembered that we want to say this with a view to illuminating a central aspect of anti-formalist thought; other purposes may call for the expression 'deductive applicability' to be put to a different or more restricted use. Our suggestion was that the difference lies in the kind of thinking needed to select a suitable minor premise. Type (*b*) rules require a distinctively practical form of thinking which tries to see what is salient in the facts of a case in light of a correct, but (as it appears) not fully codifiable understanding of the relevant rule.

To illustrate this, consider what is involved in applying rule (2*b*), the rule limiting civil liability to 'foreseeable' injury. As is often pointed out, judgments about 'foreseeability' are sensitive to how generally or specifically certain features of the situation (namely, the class of person endangered, the type of danger, and its manner of occurrence) are described. These are features of any practical situation—any action can be described in such terms. Described generally enough—for example, as the creation of a risk of *some* injury, *somehow*, to *someone*—the situation will engage a concern for the defendant's freedom to act. For the prospect of injury, so described, we may want to say, is always 'foreseeable'. If it is wrongful for the defendant to have created such a general risk, it must be wrongful for him to have acted just *as such* (for all action carries such a general risk). Described more specifically—for example, as the creation of a risk of just such a micro-fracture occurring to Mr *X* in just such-and-such a manner—the situation will engage a concern for the plaintiff's security. For the prospect of injury, so described, we may want to say, is never 'foreseeable'.[97] If an action were wrongful only when such a prospect is foreseeable, then the defendant's entitlement to act would be without bounds. The observation that 'foreseeability' is sensitive in this way to action-descriptions is often accompanied by the further suggestion that the idea of 'foreseeability' is (therefore) impotent or empty as a 'test' of liability.[98] Yet it is hard to see how any rule could be an expression of justice or fairness if it were *not* sensitive to the features of situations which bring these two concerns—one person's freedom and another's security—into play. One might say that the 'foreseeability' rule calls for a judge to form a minor premise by selecting those features of the situation which are salient as a matter of these concerns. The judge must read what matters in the situation in light of a conception (of which 'foreseeability' is itself already a partial specification) of what justice or fairness requires.[99]

[97] Unless perhaps the actor is performing surgery.

[98] An exception to this is Clarence Morris. See 'Duty, Negligence, and Causation', *University of Pennsylvania Law Review*, 101 (1952), 189.

[99] I describe the structure of such judgments in 'The Significance of Doing and Suffering', in Gerald Postema (ed.), *Philosophy and Tort Law* (Cambridge: Cambridge University Press, 2001).

No such distinctively practical problems arise in applying type (a) rules. The terms of the rules themselves either directly describe the appropriate minor premise once the facts are known ($3a$, $4a$), or else call only for the application of empirical information about what legal interventions will lead to what ($1a$, $2a$). There is no special problem, for example, about what it would be in particular cases to 'spread losses', only a technical problem about how to bring this about. So here disputes about legal decision are apt to be either technical disputes about the efficacy of means, or else disputes (not about the law's application at all) about whether 'loss-spreading' was the right goal to put into play.

The difference between these two types of rules comes into especially sharp focus whenever a judge approaches a hard case—say, about the scope of the defendant's duty of care—in a self-consciously 'realistic' way. Employing a rule like ($2b$), the notionally 'formalist' judge goes over the facts from various angles, trying out different descriptions of them and testing these descriptions in light of analogies to clear or settled cases. At length, she says that ('in her view') the situation requires a judgment for one or the other party. (This qualifying phrase expresses an appropriate modesty; it does not mean that her judgment is about her own beliefs as opposed to what the rule requires.) The realist, as we have seen, finds the rule to be hopelessly indeterminate and so 'interprets' it in a way that turns the problem into one of applying a rule like ($2a$) instead. This seems bewildering to the formalist. The law offers no standing invitation to sue parties who happen to be good conduits for spreading losses. So how can one of the parties' superiority as a loss-spreader render it a fit target for liability? This contingency has apparently nothing to do, the formalist reasons, with the features of the situation which brought the concept of 'proximate cause' (as a specification of the concern for fairness) into play. But to the Realist, the assertion that fairness requires one or another judgment in the case looks, as we know, disingenuous or naïve. Why cross the gap from the generality of 'foreseeability' to the particularity of judgment in just *this* way? If no compelling argument *proves* that a different judgment is incorrect or undesirable, haven't reasons for judgment run out? Hence the familiar dilemma, a signature of Realism: either the 'formalist' judge must have some unstated reason for her decision, or she must be merely leaping across a gap (between the generality of a rule and the particularity of a judgment) in the mistaken belief that the legal rule carries her across of its own accord.

Given (D), these are indeed the only options. In effect, (D) says that a judge's applicative judgment is a *mere judgment* (and not an exercise of reasoning) unless the reasons for it can be spelled out as an (a)-type rule. Excluded is the possibility that the judgment 'this is what the situation requires' can sometimes be a way of expressing one's reasons for decision. Innocent of (D), the formalist will ask: isn't this the sort of expression of reasons we should sometimes expect if the reasons in question are to be ones of justice or fairness and not something else? On this view, the need for situational judgment is not a lack or defect in the legal rule, as if the rule somehow still left the appropriate grounds of decision out of account. Rather, it is constitutive of the rule's legal appropriateness, for it bespeaks the rule's intelligible sensitivity to aspects of the situation which engage a concern for transactional fairness. Might not the 'foreseeability' rule have just the degree of exactness appropriate to *this* concern? The common law is, after all, replete with the discovery that it is sometimes mistaken to expect some more exact rule to be laid down prior to the contingent situations in which judgment is required. The law teaches that to demand such exactness is sometimes to fail to grasp what matters about those situations—the aim of judgment— not to grasp it more determinately.[100]

Both sides to this dispute, it should be stressed, accept that notions such as 'foreseeability' do not afford a deductive test of liability.[101] They agree, that is, that even with all the concretizing glosses that other cases may provide, there is no cause to think that the content of such notions (or of the idea of justice they express) can, absent recourse to 'policy', be codified or spelled out in the form of a rule which will make judgment deductively available. But on the 'formalist' view, this means only that notions like 'foreseeability' afford material for good legal syllogisms, not deductive proofs. Whether this also means, as the realist claims, that the problem of specifying such notions in light of contingent facts must really, 'at bottom',[102] be one of deciding which more or less already completely specified goals society ought to pursue, is a question that turns on the acceptability of (D) and the privilege it bestows on (*a*)-type rules.

As indicated, our purpose here has been to make intelligible a central strand in the post-Holmesian assault on 'formalism'. Consider again Holmes's remark, 'General propositions do not decide concrete cases', the rallying cry of anti-formalism if there is one. Why does this strike people as a deep thing to say?[103] One possibility is that the remark merely restates the commonplace—shared by Dewey, Hart, and Kant—that an applicative judgment (a Kantian 'synthesis of intuitions') is required in every case. So construed, Holmes would be making a 'grammatical' remark (in Wittgenstein's sense) about what a 'case' is and what a 'general proposition' is, and his point would range indifferently over both our (*a*) and (*b*)-type rules. This is a natural reading, and its possibility may be part of what gives Holmes's remark its air of undeniable truth. But of course this is not the way the remark has been understood whenever it has been found serviceable to the anti-formalist cause. The standard reading says that concrete decisions cannot be *deduced* from general legal propositions; there is a standing gap between them which must be closed by interpretation or by premises of

---

[100] This teaching notably runs counter to one of Holmes's view. See Oliver Wendell Holmes, *The Common Law*, ed. Mark DeWolfe Howe (Cambridge, Mass.: Harvard University Press, 1963), 98–9. But the lesson is present in (for example), the progressive elimination of special duty rules (e.g. regarding emotional harm or entrants onto land) in favour of the more abstract 'reasonable care' formula.

[101] There are, of course, other canonical glosses on proximate cause—e.g. directness—but, like 'foreseeability', they are intelligibly sensitive to descriptions of action and thus fail to provide a deductive decision procedure.

[102] Holmes, *The Common Law*, 32.

[103] Jerome Frank framed it as an epigraph in his *Law and the Modern Mind*.

'policy'.[104] So construed, the remark draws a distinction between two kinds of 'legal propositions'—those which *do* decide concrete cases and those more *general* ones which, absent further premises, do not. This is the distinction we have been spelling out. Perhaps someone's attraction to Holmes's remark would evaporate once its sense was made perspicuous in this way. So perhaps the perceived serviceability of the remark in fact depends on one's not being very clear about what it means: say, on its seeming *at once* to have the obviousness of the commonplace about applicative judgment, *and* to draw a substantial distinction between more and less specific grounds of legal decision—between rules which make judgment deductively accessible and those which do not. Be that as it may, once the framework of thought which informs the standard reading is made explicit, two matters are explained which would otherwise remain puzzling: first, why traditional judges were thought to be under the illusion that they were making 'deductions', and secondly, why, according to the same line of criticism, judges must have recourse to 'policy' if they are intelligently to reach determinate conclusions. Simply put, the explanation is that those who put forward these criticisms of 'legal formalism' were Deductivists.

From our survey, it seems that one would often do well, when 'formalism' appears as a term of criticism, to ask one or more of the following questions. Is the object of criticism a mistaken theory of rule-application or an undesirable practice of applying rules? Is the objection aimed at the formal study of law or merely at the formal isolation of the legal system? Does the criticism refer to the autonomy of legal reasons (a doctrine the positivist, in limiting law to social sources, embraces) or to the autonomy of legal reasoning (a doctrine the positivist, for the same reason, is bound to deny)? And does the critic really mean to unmask a mistake about the deductive nature of legal reasoning? Or is his aim rather to bolster a functionalist understanding of the law on the grounds that only such an understanding could attain to (what he sees as) the gold standard of deductive applicability?

Clearly, 'formalism' is prone to ambiguity. Yet putting aside, as we advised, the association of formalism with positivism, and allowing that there need be nothing 'formalistic' about the formal study of law, a loose centre of gravity will be discernible. The difficulties which attract the label 'formalism', it can be said, are ones we get into over the fact that where there is law, there are also authoritative (i.e. judicial) decisions concerning what it is to follow the law in contingent situations. Both the *desirability* and *possibility* of judicial adherence to rules come into doubt, with the latter doubt taking two characteristic forms. According to some theorists, all legal rules are indeterminate (a purposive interpretation is needed in every case), whereas according to others, this is true only of a particular subset of legal rules, those which are not sufficiently relativized to specific situations so as to be 'deductively applicable'. These issues (concerning the desirability and possibility of judicial rule-

---

[104]   See e.g. Horowitz, *The Transformation of American Law*, 202.

following) were reflected in three possible renderings of Holmes's maxim. (1) Legal rules do not determine a 'correct' result (from the point of view of background reasons) in all cases. (2) There is a quite general gap between a rule and its application, a gap which an 'interpretation' of the rule is needed to fill. (3) There is no such general gap, but there is a gap between *general* rules—that is, rules not sufficiently relativized to specific situations—and the results in particular cases.

If these claims represent, as opponents of formalism say, the received post-Realist learning,[105] that learning stands in need of criticism, for all of these claims are problematic, even apart from—what our survey stressed—their collective inconsistency. A critical discussion remains, however, for another occasion.

[105] See Peller, *The Metaphysics of American Law*, 1152.

CHAPTER 6

ADJUDICATION

WILLIAM LUCY

The Supreme Court in *Bakke*, as on occasion in other cases, played
the role of a peacemaking or truce-keeping body by negotiating its
way through an impasse of conflict, not by invoking our shared
moral first principles. For our society as a whole has none.

(A. MacIntyre, *After Virtue*, 1981: 236)

Law is something more than mere will exerted as an act of power.

(*Hurtado v California* (1884) 110 U. S. 516, pp. 535–6)[1]

Law is the dictate of reason determining every rational being to that
which is congruous and convenient for the nature thereof.

(Viscount Stair, *Institutions of the Law of Scotland*, 1893, I. i.1)

1 GREAT EXPECTATIONS

WHAT *do* we and what *should* we expect from adjudication, from judges deciding
cases? A pack of answers jostle for attention: impartiality, consistency, predictability,
fairness, justice, rationality and legitimacy. If we expect adjudication to embody all

Thanks to Steven Brown and Kenneth Himma for comments and thoughts. A much earlier version benefited from the thoughts of John Gardner and Matthew Kramer. The arguments herein are much
extended and revised versions of some that appear in chapter 4 of my *Understanding and Explaining
Adjudication* (Oxford: Clarendon Press, 1999).

[1] Cited in T. R. S. Allan, 'The Rule of Law as the Rule of Reason: Consent and Constitutionalism', *Law
Quarterly Review*, 115 (1999), 221–44.

these supposed virtues—and the list is surely not an eccentric one—then judges deciding cases face a demanding task. So, too, do those who reflect upon and theorize about adjudication (this class can of course include those who 'do' adjudication) and for at least two reasons. First, the *inter se* connections between the various answers to our initial question are startlingly complex; secondly, each answer itself is pregnant with difficulty and even superficial analysis brings into play many of the central questions of ancient and contemporary legal and political philosophy.

Only two of these answers are considered in what follows; indeed, they structure the whole of the chapter. This parsimony is not entirely a result of pressures of space, for there is a sense in which two of the answers proffered—that adjudication is and should be both rational and legitimate—inform the rest. Consider first the claim that we take adjudication to be a rational process. Exactly what this might mean will be examined at some length below, but for now note that many of the other expectations held of adjudication are only virtues when infused with the light of rationality. Consistency might signify either blind and stubborn adherence to some principle, belief, or course of conduct, or admirable integrity in thought, sentiment, and action. What often makes the difference between virtue and vice is the rationality of the belief or conduct in question. Much the same can be said of predictability. That residents of Königsberg could be sure their local philosopher would appear in town each day at exactly the same time, might evidence either a victim of heteronomous appetites or a man whose life was as much a product of the thorough application of reason as his work. That impartiality is valued when connected in some way with reason seems obvious, since it surely explains much of our resistance—in contexts rather more serious than that of games and play—to resolving issues by flipping coins.[2] If impartiality alone is what we value here, what possible objection can there be to the flip of a coin or throw of a die?

Legitimacy takes us to the core of the notion of authority and its cognate concepts. Whatever the exact nature of the claim that adjudication must be legitimate is, it is clear that judicial and other decisions can be fair, just, impartial, and yet still not create a legitimate obligation to obey. This indeed is as it should be when some decisions and actions are borne in mind. My neighbour's recommendation for disciplining my rowdy children might be impartial in its treatment of them and fair and just in its prescribed penalties. But it is surely not the case that I have a duty to obey her. By contrast, whatever else might be expected of adjudication, it is a near unshakeable assumption that the exercise of political force (imprisonment, fines, injunctions, orders to pay damages) which almost always succeeds a judicial decision, derives legitimacy from the decision. The decision is therefore the most likely source of the obligation to obey.

[2] In a recent murder trial in Kentucky jurors had no such reservations: the *Guardian*, 26 Apr. 2000: 16.

If rationality is the lodestar illuminating many of our expectations of adjudication, legitimacy is often assumed to be its brightest satellite. A close connection between the two is taken for granted: consider how easy is the move from a claim like 'adjudication is a pre-eminently rational method of resolving disputes' to 'adjudication is therefore a prima-facie legitimate process'. The strength of the 'therefore' derives from some situations in which rationality, in the form of expertise, seemingly produces authority: could there be an expert, an 'authority', whose judgments were always wrong? It would be hazardous to assume that in other contexts there must be such a close connection between rationality and authority and part of our task here is to consider how far these two expectations of adjudication are separable.[3] Rather than star and satellite, there might instead be two different planets.

2 THE CURRENT DEBATE

2.1 Easy Cases, Hard Cases, and Discretion

These two expectations (hereinafter the rationality and legitimacy conditions) have informed much contemporary Anglo-American legal and political philosophy. While the rationality condition is a pervasive but often implicit theme within legal philosophy, the legitimacy condition is a central concern of political philosophy. The rationality of adjudication has been a primary concern of two of the best-known and most influential contemporary jurists (Ronald Dworkin and Neil MacCormick) and has featured in the writing of another major figure (Joseph Raz), who has also devoted considerable attention to the question of legitimacy. As we will see, although these jurists differ on some issues, they believe that the rationality and legitimacy conditions can be satisfied by adjudication; they therefore agree that adjudication is a relatively determinate, predictable, and in some degree fair means of resolving disputes. This shared belief is sufficient reason to characterize the various and occasionally incompatible claims about adjudication made by Ronald Dworkin, Neil MacCormick and Joseph Raz as 'non-sceptical' and to dub them 'non-sceptics'. They are not the only non-sceptics in the legal academy but they are among the most

---

[3] J. Habermas notably runs together the two expectations. He says that 'the claim to legitimacy [Habermas's equivalent to the legitimacy expectation] requires decisions that are . . . rationally grounded [his equivalent to the rationality expectation] . . . so that all participants can accept them as rational decisions': *Between Facts and Norms* (Cambridge: Polity Press, 1996), 198. So, too, does K. Kress, who assumes that the indeterminacy of doctrine (which undermines the rationality expectation) entails a lack of legitimacy: 'Legal Indeterminacy', *California Law Review*, 77 (1989), 283–337, at 285–95.

notable. Nor is their non-sceptical position on adjudication the only one available—the sceptical position will be examined in due course.

There are at least three standard topics through which non-sceptics have addressed the rationality and legitimacy conditions: easy cases, hard cases, and judicial discretion.[4] While preoccupation with the topic of hard cases is perhaps the hallmark of contemporary legal philosophy, some attention must initially be given to what they supposedly contrast with, namely, easy cases. The third topic will be tackled during the discussion of the second, since it is often assumed that judicial discretion is in play in hard cases.

Non-sceptics agree that easy cases exist, but few give sustained attention either to their identification or to the ways in which they are and should be decided. Dworkin's treatment is characteristic: easy cases figure just a couple of times in *Law's Empire* and the examples are quite uninformative. For Dworkin such cases raise very simple legal questions—such as the respective speed limits in Connecticut and California—the answers to which are completely obvious.[5] Were questions of this nature necessary and sufficient to qualify a case as easy, then such cases are, on the basis of the law reports and perhaps legal practice, very rare indeed. Admittedly, Dworkin's concern in commenting on easy cases is with more general matters, in particular defending his account of law as integrity, so criticism of his treatment is not entirely appropriate. His lack of concern with easy cases is, however, characteristic of much non-sceptical legal philosophy in which difficult, controversial, and, preferably, constitutional cases dominate the discussion of adjudication.

In this context, MacCormick's analysis of easy cases is refreshingly different, being one of the most detailed and illuminating accounts available.[6] Unlike Dworkin, he gives sustained attention to the identification of easy cases and, by contrast with both Raz and Dworkin, he offers a scrupulous analysis of the way in which decisions in such cases can be justified. MacCormick makes and defends two claims. First, that easy cases exist when there is no dispute about the relevant facts or the applicable law (it is clear, unambiguous and undoubtedly relevant to the case in question). Secondly, that decisions in easy cases are in principle capable of deductive justification. At least part of MacCormick's first claim is clearly consistent with, and most likely implied by, Dworkin's examples of easy cases. Difficult it is to imagine any more important precondition for an easy case than that the law and facts be beyond doubt. But whereas Dworkin is content to say merely that decisions in easy cases are reached almost unreflectively and justified when in accord with the requirements of law as

---

[4] There are, of course, other topics that could be explored if time and space permitted. The three considered in the text have, however, been subject to a great deal of attention and do not seep too far into the territory of other chapters in this volume.

[5] R. Dworkin, *Law's Empire* (London: Fontana 1986), 266, 353–4, and 449 n. 14. Referred to hereinafter, in both text and notes, as *LE*.

[6] See N. MacCormick, *Legal Reasoning and Legal Theory* (Oxford: Clarendon Press, 1978; rev. edn., 1993), chs. II and III. Hereinafter referred to in both text and notes as *LRLT* with accompanying page numbers.

integrity (*LE*, 266 and 353–4), MacCormick strives to show that easy case decisions are in principle deductively justifiable.

This effort requires the conversion of propositions of law into the form of open hypotheticals (if *p* then *q*, where *p* is a statement of facts or description of some situation and *q* is a legal consequence), the affirmation of a fact situation or description ('*p*'), and the derivation of a conclusion ('therefore *q*'). This structure provides a deductively valid syllogism and, says MacCormick, a judicial decision in an easy case can be translated into a web of such syllogisms so that the court's order (for example, damages for the plaintiff in the amount of £*X*) follows as a deductively valid conclusion. If easy cases only raised questions as simple as that of the speed limit in some jurisdiction, MacCormick's effort to translate them into webs of deductive syllogisms would be pointless; one would do. However, as MacCormick's analysis of the *Daniels* case shows (*LRLT*, ch. II), easy cases are neither as uncomplicated nor as uninteresting as Dworkin assumes. (Raz, like MacCormick, accepts that easy cases— 'regulated cases' in his terminology—can be complex.)[7]

MacCormick argues that decisions in easy cases are justified thus: the decisions arrived at are deductively valid. If, when judges decide easy cases (i) the applicable law and the relevant facts are unambiguous; and (ii) those propositions of law and relevant facts can properly take the form of the premises of a deductive syllogism; and (iii) those premises are true and the moves within the syllogism valid, then the decision has a powerful justification. For, the reasons that lead to the decision are not only explicitly stated, but also constitute steps which, within the structure of the judgment, necessitate or compel the conclusion reached. The rational power of the judgment is that the premises cannot be accepted and the conclusion rejected without contradiction. Thus, in a sense, the judge has 'no choice' or just 'has to' reach that conclusion and this sometimes gives cause for regret (see *LRLT*, 37).

It is important to appreciate that the possibility of deductive justification in easy cases presupposes three things. First, that propositions of law can be translated into the logical form deductive justification requires. The account has been criticized on this issue but the burden of the criticism has not been such as to deny the possibility of deductive justification. Rather, the suitability of the translation MacCormick carried out has been questioned and he now accepts that predicate rather than propositional logic is a better means of achieving his ends (*LRLT*, p. xv; MacCormick's critics on this point are listed at *LRLT*, p. xvii). Note that MacCormick only aims to show that deductive justification is in principle possible; he is committed to no view as to its incidence, except that it does indeed sometimes occur. Nor can his account be refuted by reference to the fact that easy case decisions rarely if ever explicitly take logical (propositional or predicate) form. That they are capable of taking such form, without misrepresentation or addition, but with some slight restructuring or rearrangement, is sufficient for his case to stand.

[7] J. Raz, *The Authority of Law* (Oxford: Clarendon Press, 1979), 182; referred to hereinafter, in both text and notes, as *AL*.

The second presupposition is that judges have a duty to apply relevant, clear and unambiguous propositions of law when deciding cases. Hence, although Lewis J. felt his decision in *Daniels* was harsh on one defendant, since she was in no sense at fault, that was the effect of the law and he was duty bound to apply it. In the absence of such a duty, Lewis J. might well have reached a different conclusion. And, indeed, acting extra-judicially, he would no doubt be as receptive to the argument from unfairness as anyone else. Although our non-legal decision-making is not entirely free from something like a duty of fidelity to our pre-established precepts, the duty is undoubt-edly less demanding there and free from the political significance of the judicial duty to apply relevant, clear, and unambiguous propositions of law. From a non-sceptical perspective neither the existence nor desirability of the judicial duty to apply the law is in dispute; controversy arises, though, as to the precise contours and range of the duty when the topic of judicial discretion is broached.

This brings into play the third presupposition, namely, that propositions of law can indeed be relevant, clear and unambiguous. In so far as some sceptics have denied, usually under the rubric of indeterminacy, that there are easy cases, they are committed also to denying that propositions of law can be relevant (to the case in hand), clear, and unambiguous.[8] This position is untenable when understood as a denial of the possibility of easy cases: MacCormick's treatment of *Daniels* is an exam-ple sufficient to refute it. However, taken in a more modest sense, the claim is not one with which our group of non-sceptics would disagree. The modest sense holds that the following claim is false: once an easy case, always an easy case. That is, it accepts the possibility that easy cases can become hard and that hard cases can become easy.

How is this possible? A moment's reflection on the nature of propositions of law shows that it is not solely the language in which they are formulated that allows them to be regarded as clear and unambiguous. They are in most legal systems taken as having a purpose or range of purposes and form part of a network or system of propositions of law also taken to fulfil some purpose or set of purposes. This provides the context within which particular propositions of law are understood and from which they derive much of their meaning. What is true of propositions of law is also true of simpler, non-legal rules. It seems obvious to us that the injunction 'Dogs must be carried on the escalator' is wrongly applied when used to prevent those without dogs from using the escalator. This is not solely a result of the words used. In fact, the words used do not on their face discriminate between this interpretation of the rule and one which insists that, if anyone using the escalator has a dog with them, then it (the dog) must be carried. Rather, the first interpretation of the rule seems obviously incorrect, and hence an easy case (the rule is relevant to instances in which people ride the escalator with dogs, it is clear and unambiguous because, *inter alia*, we all know the meaning of 'dogs', 'carried', 'escalator', etc.) largely because of an

---

[8]   At least one sceptic maintains that all cases are hard: see M. Kelman, *A Guide to Critical Legal Studies* (Cambridge, Mass.: Harvard University Press, 1987), 4. Compare D. Kennedy, *A Critique of Adjudication* (Cambridge, Mass.: Harvard University Press, 1997), 60.

assumption about its purpose. It seems that at this particular historical juncture, with our range of values and traditions about human dignity and animal welfare, the obvious purpose of this rule is to protect dogs and passengers from harm. The rule is not regarded as the least bit contestable or controversial in our current socio-cultural and political context.

That context can change. So, too, can the context in which propositions of law are interpreted. To be regarded as relevant, clear, and unambiguous, a proposition of law must be accepted as either beyond question or at least not worth challenging by (at a minimum) the members of the legal community. To be beyond question or unworthy of challenge, the proposition of law must be either regarded as in some sense normatively acceptable or unreflectively or habitually adhered to by, at a minimum, the legal community and, perhaps, segments of the wider community. When the proposition is challenged, either as a result of increased awareness of its effects or a greater appreciation of its normative shortcomings both within the legal community and beyond, it will no longer be regarded as obviously relevant, clear, and unambiguous. What was once accepted as an easy case and hence unworthy of argument—for example, that husbands cannot rape their wives in English criminal law—becomes harder, more controversial, and, perhaps, eventually overturned. Hence, the distinction between easy cases and hard cases is not absolute; it is a matter of degree. This is what our non-sceptics believe (*LRLT*, 198, 228; *LE*, 354; *AL*, 182) and they are surely right. So, too, are sceptics, in so far as their reservations about the easy case/hard case dichotomy are taken in this modest way.

For Raz an easy case is most likely to be a 'regulated case' (*AL*, 181). 'Most likely' because he eschews the language of easy and hard cases in favour of that of regulated and unregulated cases, there being some doubt as to whether his terminology can be translated into, for example, MacCormick's without distortion. However, some of his remarks about regulated cases justify the claim that they are similar to easy cases in some important respects. Holding that '[a] dispute is regulated if questions of the form: "In this case should the court decide that p?" have a correct legal answer' (ibid.), surely commits Raz to accepting that regulated cases are easy in exactly the way as Dworkin's examples. But in so far as Dworkin maintains that there is a single correct answer in most hard cases, and in so far as the latter fall into Raz's category of unregulated disputes, the two cannot agree.

Another possible divergence between Raz's account of regulated cases and Dworkin and MacCormick's analyses of easy cases concerns the extent of the judicial powers of distinguishing and overruling precedents. For Raz these powers exist in both regulated and unregulated cases (*AL*, 183). However, Dworkin's and MacCormick's discussions of easy cases suggest that such powers are either very limited or non-existent. Recall that, for Dworkin, easy cases raise questions the answer to which every competent lawyer knows and accepts and that, for MacCormick, the applicable law in such cases is relevant, clear and unambiguous. In these circumstances, arguments distinguishing or overruling precedents are unlikely to gain any purchase. At stake in this dispute are two different accounts of where judicial powers of reformulating and changing the law reside. For MacCormick and Dworkin such powers are confined to the realm of hard case adjudication; for Raz, too, these powers reside there but are also in play in regulated (which are to some extent easy) cases. Superficially Raz's seems the more radical view in so far as it implies that, in judges' hands, the law is almost always malleable. This may be deceptive, though, since if the category of hard cases is extensive, as it seems to be in the analyses provided by MacCormick and Dworkin, the overall degree of malleability might be the same.

MacCormick's analysis of easy cases—they exist when there is a relevant, clear, and unambiguous proposition of law applicable to the case (let us ignore, hereinafter, controversy over questions of fact)—is the best non-sceptical account available. This is encouraging, since it can be doubly effective. It serves not only to provide a plausible account of what easy cases look like but also supplies an economical characterization of hard cases. The characterization holds that hard cases are not easy: one or other of the conditions for an easy case is lacking. For MacCormick this is certainly true. Hard cases arise on his account when courts face one or other of three problems which ensure that there is doubt as to the applicable law. The first is the problem of relevancy: is there an applicable proposition of law in this case? The second, that of interpretation: which from a range of apparently applicable propositions of law, or which from a range of competing interpretations of an apparently applicable proposition of law, applies in this case? The third, which is simply a variation of the second, is the problem of classification: does the apparently applicable proposition of law actually apply to the facts of this case? (*LRLT*, 68–9, 95, and 203).

There is little in this characterization of hard cases with which other non-sceptics would disagree, although it is again the case that, by contrast with Dworkin's treatment, MacCormick's is much more precise. There is also considerable similarity and overlap between MacCormick's characterization of hard cases and Raz's account of unregulated disputes, although there are some differences that are not entirely the result of their differing terminologies.

That Dworkin's characterization of hard cases is much the same as MacCormick's becomes clear not solely as a result of any sustained analysis of the notion by Dworkin, but principally as a consequence of reflection upon the examples he adduces. This is because there is very little explicit analysis of the conditions for hard cases in Dworkin's work. In his early work he was content to assert simply that hard cases are those 'in which reasonable lawyers . . . disagree' and 'where no settled rule dictates a decision either way'.[9] He said much the same thing in subsequent work (*LE*, 353), but added that hard cases arise when judges cannot discriminate between competing legal arguments by reference to a threshold test of 'fit'. This test requires that any legal argument must be consistent with 'the brute facts of legal history' (*LE*, 255), but when more than one argument satisfies it, the case is hard. From these remarks,

[9] R. Dworkin, *Taking Rights Seriously* (London: Duckworth, 1978), pp. xiv, 83.

it seems that Dworkin thinks hard cases arise on at least three grounds: lawyerly dis-agreement; absence of a clearly applicable proposition of law; and lack of determinate guidance from the legal record.

The first is not a good guide, in itself, as to whether or not a case is hard until such time as the grounds for disagreement are unearthed. When this is done, and once it is assumed that the lawyers in question are both acting in good faith and masters of the relevant law, it is likely that their disagreement is a function of one or both of the other grounds of a hard case. Why, after all, would reasonable lawyers disagree in a case when there was some obviously applicable, unambiguous proposition of law or when (what seems to be almost the same thing) the legal record was univocal on the issue? These two grounds are not exactly the same, since the absence of *a* settled and clearly applicable proposition of law in a case need not always result from the legal record's compatibility with a range of competing propositions of law. The lack of a settled and obviously applicable proposition of law could be a consequence of the fact that such a proposition has not heretofore been developed; it is quite new and has not as yet been regarded as part of the legal record. This is an extreme instance of what MacCormick calls the problem of relevancy and which Dworkin comes close to ignoring, save for the fact that some of the cases he adduces as examples of hard cases undoubtedly embody it (*LE*, 23–9). Dworkin's third ground for a hard case—the legal record does not discriminate between two or more interpretations of a proposition of law, or two conflicting propositions of law—raises almost exactly the same issues as MacCormick's problems of interpretation and classification. This again becomes obvious once the actual cases Dworkin refers to are examined (*LE*, 15–20).

Raz, too, accepts that unregulated cases arise on the same grounds as hard cases; for purposes of identification the two can therefore be regarded as the same. Hence unregulated cases, just like hard cases, come into being either when 'the law applying to . . . [them] has gaps' (*AL*, 181) or when the relevant law is riddled with 'intended or unintended indeterminacy of language and intention' (*AL*, 193). The first situation is obviously coextensive with MacCormick's problem of relevancy while the second overlaps with both the problems of classification and interpretation. A third instance in which unregulated cases arise is, says Raz, 'slightly different' from the others: it 'is the indeterminacy of . . . cases falling under two conflicting rules' (*AL*, 193). And, while it is indeed different from the gap situation, and only very slightly different from indeterminacy of language and intention, it is exactly the same as MacCormick's problem of interpretation. That the difference between Raz's second and third grounds for hard cases is very slight is clear from the fact that the problem presented by the second is structurally the same as that raised by the third. In both instances the question facing the court is 'how is the law to be interpreted?' Admittedly, in one instance the need for interpretation arises as a result of vagueness in the law while in the other it springs from an apparent conflict between proposi-tions of law, but this is unlikely to affect the substance of the issue. The only instance in which it might would be where a legal system has specific rules tackling vagueness (for example, among its rules of statutory interpretation) and none for coping with conflicts. Even then the substantive question need not change; an additional layer of rules (those dealing with vagueness) might simply be added into the interpretative mix while the question faced by the court remains 'how is the law to be interpreted?'

The topic of judicial discretion often arises within discussions of the nature of hard cases, since some, including Raz, appear to regard discretion as a defining condition of such cases. This is not to say that judicial discretion only exists in hard cases, since it clearly can be conferred upon judges by, for example, statutes and be exercised without difficulty. There could, that is, be easy cases in which the court has discretion: for example, there is no doubt as to what the applicable proposition of law requires or allows, since it unambiguously confers discretion on the court in some matter. But this raises an obvious question: what is meant by discretion in the legal context? Dworkin provided a seminal analysis that identified three relevant senses. Discretion can refer to a situation in which one has a non-reviewable power to make a decision; to the use of judgment when making a decision; or to those instances of decision-making in which there are no applicable rules or standards.[10] These three senses, the first two of which Dworkin dubs different types of 'weak' discretion and the third of which he calls 'strong' discretion, can coexist. The dog show judge will not only need to use judgment in deciding the best of breed, where what is meant is that the decision is in no sense automatic or unreflective but requires the consideration and weighing of various and often competing criteria (weak sense 1). She may also, in making that decision, be the final arbiter (weak sense 2). In addition, some decisions she may have to make, such as whether to judge Airedales or Boxers first, may be completely ungoverned by any standard or rule: in such a situation she has discretion in the strong sense.

Since Raz defines regulated cases in part by reference to the absence of discretion—they 'fall under a common law or statutory rule which does not require judicial discretion for the determination of the dispute (rules referring to what is reasonable or just, etc., do require such discretion)' (*AL*, 181)—it is tempting to hold that he regards unregulated (hard) cases as ones in which discretion exists. While this may be correct, it is difficult to be sure what Raz means by discretion. He accepts that judgment (weak sense 1 of discretion) is in play in both regulated and unregulated cases (*AL*, 182). Its presence cannot, therefore, distinguish these two types of case. Presumably, he would not accept the view that discretion in the second weak sense (an instance of non-reviewable decision-making) distinguishes unregulated from regulated cases since judges may have a non-reviewable decision-making power both when propositions of law determine and when they do not determine a decision. If the absence of discretion is a condition for a regulated case and its presence a condition for an unregulated case, then Raz must have strong discretion in mind. While this is consonant with some of Raz's characterizations of regulated and unregulated cases—in the

---

[10] R. Dworkin, *Taking Rights Seriously* (London: Duckworth, 1978), 31–4, 68–71 and 327–30.

former the law provides a solution, in the latter it does not—it is inconsistent with others: for example, '[u]nregulated disputes . . . are subject to laws applying to them and guiding the courts as to their solution' (*AL*, 181).

The most that can be said is, insofar as Raz thinks the existence of strong discretion is a condition for a hard or unregulated case to exist (and we cannot be sure he does), then his view conflicts with that of Dworkin and MacCormick. While they accept that judgment is undoubtedly a feature of hard cases, they deny that judges have strong discretion when deciding any kind of case unless explicitly granted it by some legal provision.[11] This denial is most likely animated by three related worries. One relates to the judicial duty to apply the law, one raises questions as to the legitimacy of judicial decision-making in absence of this duty and a third, weighing on Dworkin in particular, asks whether a party to a hard case has a right to win. If adjudication takes place within the realm of strong discretion, then the courts appear to be acting beyond the law instead of applying it, and their authority for so acting seems doubtful unless explicitly granted discretion by some legal provision. However, if these worries hold sway here, they are surely just as compelling in the face of the problem of relevancy. The only difference that Dworkin and MacCormick would presumably point to is this: the problem of relevancy is resolved by reference to constraining propositions (and arguments) of law, although no such proposition obviously and conclusively disposes of the case. Presumably, where strong discretion exists, no such propositions pertain. And, for Dworkin, where no such propositions pertain, a baleful consequence is that a party to the case cannot be said to have a right to win. They have simply a chance to triumph dependent upon how the judges exercise their (strong) discretion. On this view, adjudication becomes similar to a lottery.

Dworkin and MacCormick are not completely unanimous on the topic of discretion. This is because MacCormick suggests that another sense of discretion, beyond the three already distinguished, holds sway in hard case adjudication (*LRLT*, 249). The difficulty is that he provides little helpful guidance as to what this fourth sense might embody, other than hinting that it resides between strong discretion and weak sense 1 (*LRLT*, 251). This is regrettable since the existence of such a fourth sense and the elucidation of its contours constitutes the key to resolving the dispute between Dworkin and his opponents about discretion. Such elucidation would serve to rid discussions of adjudication of a topic that has in the main been obfuscatory: discretion is undoubtedly part of most major legal systems and the issues it raises are not unique to the domain of adjudication. Such issues would be best tackled in their own right.[12]

It is obvious from the discussion so far that, despite their slightly different argots, non-sceptics agree on what makes a hard case, although disagreement might exist on the role of discretion in such cases. Non-sceptics also agree about what easy cases

[11] R. Dworkin, *Taking Rights Seriously* (London: Duckworth, 1978); *LRLT*, 249.
[12] The task has been started: see K. Hawkins (ed.), *The Uses of Discretion* (Oxford: Clarendon Press, 1992) and D. Galligan, *Discretionary Powers* (Oxford: Clarendon Press, 1986).

look like, save that Raz thinks there may be more room for judicial creativity therein than either Dworkin or MacCormick. Since there is so much overlap between these non-sceptical accounts, are there any grounds for accepting one and rejecting one or both of the others? All seem well rooted in the practice they purport to describe; all have an appreciation and detailed grasp of the legal systems they analyse. No one account seems particularly reductive nor contrary to experience. They all, in Dworkin's language, satisfy a version of the 'fit' requirement: all are to some degree true to the practice they purport to characterize. Where they might be distinguished, however, is on the basis of their claims about how hard cases are and should be decided. That issue beckons. Furthermore, it is one about which two of our non-sceptics certainly disagree.

The main burden of Dworkin's and MacCormick's work is the same. They develop schemata of reasons and arguments that judges do and should employ in deciding hard cases, criticizing and sometimes reconstructing particular decisions in light of those schemata. And, while all non-sceptics agree that judges deciding hard cases do so *relatively* constrained by propositions of law *relatively* determinative of the case before them, Dworkin and MacCormick disagree as to how the reasons which move judges from a relatively to a completely determinate position on some matter are best understood. MacCormick categorizes the reasons judges do and should use to close this gap as coherence, consistency, and consequentialist considerations. Judges deploy such considerations in order to solve the problems of relevancy, interpretation, and classification that define hard cases. Consequentialist, coherence, and consistency considerations constitute the realm of 'second-order justification' (*LRLT*, 100), the realm in which judges have to choose a relevant proposition of law to apply in the instant hard case. It is a realm which 'must therefore involve justifying choices; choices between rival possible rulings' (ibid.).

Arguments from consistency and coherence are similar in that both embody intra-systemic considerations. That is, they involve assessing rival legal arguments in a hard case by reference to their effects within the legal system. They differ in that the scope of arguments of coherence is broader than that of arguments of consistency. Arguments of the latter kind embody 'a fundamental judicial commandment: Thou shalt not controvert established and binding rules of law' (*LRLT*, 195). The effect of this commandment is that any argument in a hard case that does so controvert an established and binding rule of the legal system is likely to face acute difficulties. That is not to say that such arguments are never accepted by the courts. Rather, they are only likely to be accepted, says MacCormick, when also supported by consequentialist and coherence arguments. The latter are broader than consistency arguments because they test, reject or commend an argument in a hard case by reference to its resonance (or lack of it) with the principles and values of the wider legal system, not just those in play in the particular area of law in which the hard case has arisen. MacCormick says such arguments rest on the assumption 'that the multitudinous rules of a developed legal system should "make sense" when taken together' (*LRLT*, 152).

By contrast, consequentialist arguments are extra-systemic, looking to the effects of a hard case ruling one way or another on society as a whole. They are not overly concerned with what makes sense within the legal system but 'with what makes sense in the world' (*LRLT*, 103). Such considerations are crucial according to MacCormick because in many hard cases considerations of consistency and coherence do not completely determine the decision (*LRLT*, 110). But how are judges to decide whether or not a decision one way or the other in a hard case 'makes sense in the world'? The criterion of sense is yielded by evaluating the consequences in the world of the competing possible decisions: 'choosing between rival possible rulings in a case involves choosing between what are to be conceived of as rival models for, rival patterns of, human conduct in . . . society' (*LRLT*, 104). At least part of this process of evaluation involves a rule-utilitarian calculation of the effects of a decision one way or another upon the welfare or preference satisfaction of the whole community, or a substantial segment thereof. Not only is this move dangerous because it threatens to import utilitarianism's well-documented problems; it also assumes that 'consequences' are easily identifiable.[13]

MacCormick's assessment of the significance of consequentialist arguments in hard cases illustrates a point of disagreement with Dworkin. According to Dworkin in hard cases '[j]udges must make their . . . decisions on grounds of principle, not policy' (*LE*, 244). Arguments of principle have the following structure: they 'justify a political decision by showing that the decision respects or secures some individual or group right'.[14] These arguments are derived from an interpretation of the law that fits 'the brute facts of legal history' and 'which shows the community's structure of institutions and decisions—its public standards as a whole—in a better light from the standpoint of political morality' than any other (*LE*, 255–6). Opposed to arguments of principle are arguments of policy, which Dworkin thinks are not and should not be the basis of judicial decision-making. Policy arguments 'justify a political decision by showing that the decision advances or protects some collective goal of the community as a whole'.[15] Understood thus, they are structurally very similar to the consequentialist arguments MacCormick thinks are at the core of hard case decision-making. Hence while MacCormick and Dworkin disagree on which type of reason is the most important in hard case decision-making, they nevertheless offer partially

---

[13]   MacCormick is not entirely comfortable with utilitarianism, of whatever kind, but he nevertheless invokes it: *LRLT*, 115–16 and 105 n. 1 (see also p. xv). For excellent introductions to the difficulties utilitarianism (and its close relative, consequentialism) raises see J. J. C. Smart and B. Williams, *Utilitarianism: For and Against* (Cambridge: Cambridge University Press, 1973); S. Scheffler (ed.), *Consequentialism and its Critics* (Oxford: Clarendon Press, 1988). On the slipperiness of consequences in the legal context see B. Rudden, 'Consequences', *Juridical Review*, 24 (1979), 193–205.

[14]   R. Dworkin, *Taking Rights Seriously*, n. 9 above, p. 82 (see also p. 90). Note that Dworkin is unclear about the relevance of rights-based arguments to hard cases in the criminal law: see his *A Matter of Principle* (Oxford: Clarendon Press, 1985), ch. 3.

[15]   *Taking Rights Seriously*, n. 9 above, p. 82.

overlapping typologies since, for example, considerations of consistency and coherence bear more than a passing resemblance to the requirement of 'fit'.

Dworkin also makes two important additional claims about hard case adjudication: first, it is a process that allows a plurality of answers and yet, secondly, that there are right answers in such cases. The first point appears inevitable when the nature of the decision required in a hard case is understood. Recall that in such cases the threshold test of fit with the legal record does not determine an answer; judges then have to choose the answer they think shows the legal record in its best possible moral and political light. At this point, judges'

own moral and political convictions are . . . directly engaged. But the political judgment . . . [they] must make is . . . complex and will sometimes set one department of [their] . . . political morality against another: [their] . . . decision[s] will reflect not only [their] . . . opinions about justice and fairness but . . . [their] higher-order convictions about how these ideals should be compromised when they compete. Questions of fit arise at this stage . . . as well, because even when an interpretation survives the threshold requirement, any infelicities of fit will count against it. . . . Different judges will disagree about each of these issues and will accordingly take different views of what the law of their community, properly understood, really is. (*LE*, 256)

The right answer claim sits uneasily with the last remark since an immediate reaction to the affirmation of both is: how can there be a single right answer when different judges take different views of what the law really is? Of course, it would be an error to assume that disagreement is conclusive evidence of the fact that there is no right answer. The fact of disagreement can indeed be evidence that a right answer exists, if it is accepted that there is an issue or claim about which disputants are in genuine disagreement. Presumably, that disagreement turns on whether or not the issue or claim in question is true or false, right or wrong. But while Dworkin may be keen to show that it is false that there is no right answer in hard cases, he has yet to tackle adequately the possibility that there can be a range of right answers in such cases.[16] On the basis of the remarks like those just quoted, that does seem to be his position, although he has yet to recognize it. It may well be that his right answer claim amounts to little more than this: that for each judge there will be a single right answer in a hard case, although one judge's right answer need not be the same as another judge's right answer.

Unlike Dworkin and MacCormick, Raz does not offer a schema of reasons and argument-types that judges do and should use when deciding unregulated cases. He is concerned mainly with two other issues. The first is the weight of the reasons judges

[16] Dworkin's right answers claim has been by far the most controversial aspect of his account of how hard cases are and should be decided. For his position see *A Matter of Principle*, n. 14 above, ch. 5; pp. 275–8 of 'A Reply by Ronald Dworkin', in M. Cohen (ed.), *Ronald Dworkin and Contemporary Jurisprudence* (London: Duckworth, 1984); and *LE*, 412–13. For a flavour of the criticisms see *LRLT*, 246–55; A. D. Woozley, 'No Right Answer', ch. 8 of Cohen, *Ronald Dworkin*; J. Finnis, 'On Reason and Authority in *Law's Empire*', *Law and Philosophy*, 6 (1987), 357–80, at 370–80; and B. Bix, *Law, Language and Legal Determinacy* (Oxford: Clarendon Press, 1993), ch. 4.

might use and how, if at all, they relate to moral reasons. This focus is, of course, a consequence of Raz's defence of the strong sources thesis against those versions of legal positivism committed to 'incorporationism'.[17] Such a defence requires some account of the ways in which moral values permeate the law.

The second issue is the nature of the power judges have in unregulated cases. Raz holds that it is undoubtedly a law-making power which, although in some respects similar to the law-making power of legislators, is more limited. Hence, in hard cases 'courts act and should act just as legislators do, namely, they should adopt those rules they think best' (*AL*, 197). But in so doing, the courts do not have a completely free hand, since '[u]nregulated disputes are . . . partly regulated, hence the court has to apply existing law as well as to make new law' (*AL*, 182). Again, 'in every case in which the court makes new law it also applies laws restricting and guiding its law-creating activities'; powers of distinguishing and overruling are similarly 'circumscribed and hedged by legal limitations' (*AL*, 195). However, it seems that these limitations and hedges do not often reside in legal doctrine, for Raz, but are principally found in the institutional framework in which the courts exist. What constrains courts' law-making in unregulated cases is the fact that they are not well placed to carry out wide-ranging reform: they cannot, in one decision, hope to achieve what the legislature can in a programme of law reform. Hence the courts face a choice in utilizing their law-making powers 'between partial reform and conservatism' (*AL*, 201), whereas legislatures always have the option of radical reform open to them.

Raz apparently holds that it is not legal doctrine but this feature of institutional structure, in conjunction with the convention of argument by analogy, which constitutes the primary restriction upon the range of decisions open to courts in unregulated cases. For, once his account of the courts' powers of distinguishing and overruling in both regulated and unregulated cases is accepted, legal doctrine is left with very little constraining power. Doctrine can limit the decisions of the courts only where it provides a clear proposition of law that fits exactly the case that has arisen and where the courts either cannot or do not desire to distinguish or overrule. This is another illustration of how malleable Raz takes the law to be, even in regulated cases, and it undoubtedly sets him apart from both MacCormick and Dworkin. While they accept that the law develops in the course of hard case decision-making, they are far more circumspect than Raz about characterizing such development as law-making, probably as a result of their denial of strong discretion. In so far as Dworkin and MacCormick accept that there is a form of law-making in hard cases (Dworkin has always been especially uncomfortable with the thought), they are anxious to emphasize how restricted it is (*LRLT*, 79–80, 101–8; *LE*, 401–3). This is probably explicable on the ground that Dworkin in particular is rather more troubled

---

[17] J. Raz, *Ethics in the Public Domain* (Oxford: Clarendon Press, 1994), ch. 13. Incorporationism has been expounded most often and elegantly by J. Coleman. See his 'Authority and Reason', ch. 10 of R. George (ed.), *The Autonomy of Law* (Oxford, Clarendon Press, 1996).

than Raz by the arguments from retroactivity and democracy often directed at judicial law-making (*AL*, 198; *LE*, 258–60, 398–9).[18]

It is issues such as these, in addition to different views as to the priority of individual rights and overall welfare in dispute resolution, which throw into relief the competing moral and political ambitions that might be entertained for law and adjudication. Such ambitions come to the fore in any attempt to choose between different accounts of the ways in which judges do and should decide hard cases. Hence, while non-sceptics agree on many matters relating to the identification of such cases, the role of discretion within them, and their incidence, their ambitions for adjudication sometimes set them apart. Such different ambitions can only be assessed from the perspective of wider moral-cum-political accounts of the role of the state and its law.

It is time to change focus. The debate among non-sceptics about easy cases, hard cases, and judicial discretion is fascinating but too deep an immersion in its details runs the risk of losing sight of what is at stake. Why devote so much time and ink to these issues? Answering this question brings us back to the rationality and legitimacy conditions.

2.2 Justification, Rationality, and Legitimacy

Easy and hard case adjudication almost always brings about the exercise of force: the imposition of fines, sentences, orders to make compensation or repayment, and many other interventions. It is therefore a practice and institution ripe for justification and that must entail, at the very least, some account of the reasons for the act or acts of force. Inter-subjective justification of action without reasons is all but unintelligible, being akin to inter-subjective communication without some kind of language. Inter-subjective justification of *coercive* action without reasons is every bit as unintelligible. The requirement that the justification for an action at least involves some account of the reasons for it does not, of course, extend to the intelligibility of the action. Actions can be explained without a statement of the reasons that justify them, since a statement of the causes of an action need not include the reasons that justify it, for there might be none. For example, an action such as my physically attacking an officious neighbour can be a product of (caused by) factors Z, Y and X, and thus perfectly explicable, yet be beyond the justificatory pale because undoubtedly wrong. It is, however, both common and confusing to speak of reasons for an action without discriminating between reasons as causes and reasons as justifications.[19] While reasons as causes and reasons as justifications can overlap, there is no

[18] See also *Taking Rights Seriously*, n. 9 above, pp. 82–90 and 123–30; *A Matter of Principle*, n. 14 above, ch. 1; and R. Dworkin, *Freedom's Law* (Oxford: Clarendon Press, 1996), intro.

[19] This should not be read as denying that reasons can be causes (on which see D. Davidson, *Essays on Actions and Events* (Oxford: Clarendon Press, 1980), essays 1, 3, and 6).

necessary connection between them. Since it is an exercise of coercive force, or at least initiates such force, the reasons that adjudication requires are, in the first instance, justificatory.

From this perspective easy case and hard case decisions are exactly alike: both stand in need of justification since both can unleash the coercive power of the state. The account MacCormick provides of the way in which easy case decisions can be justified constitutes the beginning of a response to this worry. If easy case decisions are shown to be rationally justified by the reasons provided for them, and justified in the form of a web of deductively valid syllogisms, then progress has been made along the path of justification. That goal is certainly closer than if such decisions were entirely lacking rational support. Hard case decisions and decisions within the realm of strong discretion stand in need of additional justification. This is not because the force unleashed by such decisions is any more severe or morally troubling than in easy cases. Rather, it is because in addition to unleashing force, courts in these instances take a stand on what they take the law to be. In hard cases in particular, where there is doubt as to whether or not there is an applicable proposition of law, or where it is unclear which proposition out of a range of competing propositions of law applies, or which out of a range of different interpretations of an agreed proposition of law applies, the decision taken constitutes a choice and, as such, is ripe for justification. Furthermore, since there is controversy about which choices should be made in hard cases, the judges that decide them undoubtedly take a stand on a contested matter. It is not unreasonable to expect some account of the grounds (the reasons) for this stand.

As a matter of fact, Anglo-American adjudicative practice is organized so as to attempt to satisfy this expectation, since appellate court judges state the reasons for their decisions in a fairly discursive written text. Indeed, that text is most often arrived at as a result of hearing and then considering the weight of the reasons presented by opposing counsel for and against a decision one way or the other. The text is rarely uniform, since each judge usually presents his own reasons for his decision. The judges might well disagree on the decision and thus over the reasons supporting it, or agree on the decision but reach it via different reasons or, fairly rarely, agree on both the decision and the reasons for it. In other jurisdictions, by contrast, adjudicative practice is far more declaratory and much less discursive, appellate court judges being expected to offer a unanimous and brief declaration of the applicable law and its consequences in the particular case.[20]

Given the close connection between justification and reasons, it is surely correct to regard justification as the fulcrum of questions about the rationality of adjudication. It is therefore unsurprising that non-sceptical accounts of easy and hard case adjudi-

---

[20] Judgments of the French Cour de cassation are striking examples. Although the decisions of the court must be justified under Article 455 of the Code of Civil Practice, this is often done very briefly. The court does not cite or discuss precedents: see ch. 4 of N. MacCormick and R. S. Summers, *Interpreting Precedents: A Comparative Study* (Ashgate: Dartmouth, 1997).

cation spend much time attending to the structure of the arguments offered in such cases, assessing the types and weight of the reasons judges use when deciding them. Their principal concern is to show how such decisions are and can be justified, both in general terms and within the context of particular cases, and that, of course, requires consideration of the reasons adduced for them. Hence the attempt to show that adjudication satisfies what was earlier called the rationality condition animates almost all non-sceptical work in this area. However, we will see that the rationality condition is often under-analysed by non-sceptics.

If providing the reasons for an action or decision constitutes, in most instances, a sizeable step towards justifying the decision or action, is it not the case that what was earlier called the legitimacy condition is redundant? This is most likely to be so when we think solely in terms of *rational* justification. Think of run-of-the-mill actions or decisions: identifying and stating my reasons for going to the cinema rather than the opera makes the question of the legitimacy of the decision redundant. The issue of legitimacy brings into play questions about my right to do what I do or to decide how I have decided. In this instance, knowledge of my reasons (I particularly like the movies of director *X* and one is now showing; I despise the operas of composer *Y*, one of which is being performed) and some knowledge of my situation (I am not, for example, a doctor on call nor a parent with child-care responsibilities), make questions about the legitimacy of my action and decision otiose. However, it is not the case that having and articulating the reasons for my actions and decisions always make questions of legitimacy redundant. Far from it, as is obvious if my reason for going to the cinema rather than the opera was to kill the projectionist. Here the notion of justification comes into play in the guise of entitlement rather than solely in the guise of reasons for action. And it is justification in terms of entitlement—do I have a right or the authority to kill the projectionist?—that the legitimacy condition incorporates.

So, while in many instances there is an overlap between providing reasons for my action or decision and showing that the action and decision is one I am entitled to take, the overlap is not necessary. Hence, the non-sceptical effort to elucidate and evaluate the reasons courts offer for their decisions—the effort to show that adjudication satisfies some or other version of the rationality condition—will not of itself show that either adjudication in general, or particular judicial decisions, are legitimate. Furthermore, the issue of legitimacy is especially pressing within the context of the exercise of state power. Since the power so exercised is regarded as particularly worrisome (the power to, *inter alia*, remove one's liberty if not actually one's life), the question of its legitimacy is especially significant. It may well be that showing judges have good reasons for their decisions in both hard and easy cases falls far short of justifying that which flows from those decisions such as, for example, the exercise of force compelling the defendant to pay damages or imprisoning her. Such actions might never be politically or morally justifiable, might always be illegitimate, even though the decisions on which they rest are rationally justifiable. More difficult, though, is the case of a legitimate action or decision entirely unsupported by reasons. It seems almost inconceivable that, for example, some political action could be legitimate, by which we at least mean someone was entitled to do it, and yet be incapable of rational justification.

The topic of hard cases and that of judicial discretion are usually thought most likely to bring the legitimacy condition into play. These topics raise the spectre of legitimacy in an obvious way: when judges decide hard cases, and when they have (strong) discretion, they seem to the hasty to operate free from the constraints of law. And if judges are so operating, there is an obvious question about their entitlement to do so within a democratic system bolstered by a traditional understanding of the separation of powers. The haste involved in this move is that of regarding constraint by law as being an all or nothing matter. Judges are either completely bound by the law to decide a case in one way or they are completely free to decide it whatever way they wish. While non-sceptics accept that hard cases are ones in which there are a range of doubts about the applicable law, they are keen to show—indeed it is the primary burden of the schemata they develop about how judges do and should decide hard cases—that the law undoubtedly constrains (albeit it not completely) the decisions judges can make. This is as true for Dworkin and MacCormick as it is for Raz. It may seem especially surprising that Raz sees the process of deciding unregulated cases as being to some degree constrained by law, since he is clear that this is a law-making process which also might involve strong discretion. Dworkin and MacCormick, remember, see no role for strong discretion in adjudication. That the process of deciding hard or unregulated cases is constrained to some extent by law, and that judges lack strong discretion, do not make questions about the legitimacy of adjudication irrelevant; rather they make such questions a little more tractable. As already noted, such questions can arise regardless of the rationality of adjudication.

The rationality and legitimacy conditions are two distinct requirements that adjudication might be expected to satisfy, although in some situations they clearly overlap. The disjunction between them is important since it explains the structure of the rest of the chapter, which divides into two principal parts. The first (Sect. 3) offers a more sustained analysis than heretofore of what the rationality condition might entail. It identifies three versions of the condition and considers whether non-sceptical accounts can show that adjudication satisfies them. It concludes that two of the three accounts cannot, by virtue of their strong value pluralism, accommodate a stringent version of the condition.

The topic of value pluralism is introduced as a test for non-sceptical accounts of adjudication for two reasons. First, the idea of value pluralism is one that non-sceptics accept and which is now almost a shibboleth of contemporary legal, moral and political philosophy. Yet its acceptance has especially important implications for these theorists' accounts of adjudication which they do not seem to appreciate. Secondly, the standard topics addressed by non-sceptical accounts of adjudication— hard cases, easy cases, discretion, and so on—have over the course of the last thirty years been fairly thoroughly analysed. The areas of dispute and agreement are, as the previous part of this section aspired to demonstrate, clear. There is little that could usefully be said about them here.

The second part of the chapter (Sect. 4) examines the nature of the legitimacy condition. In particular, it seeks to determine whether that condition can be satisfied when the stringent version of the rationality condition is not (the latter condition cannot be satisfied when value pluralism holds). This necessitates consideration of a number of accounts of the nature of political legitimacy (or authority) and an analysis of their impact, if any, upon the problem of rationally deficient judicial decisions. However, before turning to these issues our statement of the current Anglo-American debate about adjudication must be completed. The sceptical challenge and some of its constituents must be introduced.

2.3 Determinacy, Indeterminacy, and the Sceptical Challenge

That group of contemporary jurists whose work embodies 'the sceptical challenge' deny that law in general and adjudication in particular can satisfy the rationality and legitimacy conditions. In general terms, sceptics are united in the belief that law is an undesirable or, more modestly, not pre-eminently desirable, means of 'subjecting human conduct to the governance of rules'[21] and that adjudication is an undesirable, or not pre-eminently desirable, means of resolving disputes about those rules. This challenge must not be misunderstood—it is not a paean to arbitrary power. Rather, most proponents of the challenge would accept Lon Fuller's strictures on the desirability of law over systems of arbitrary power.[22] The question the challenge places on the jurisprudential agenda is this: are law and adjudication pre-eminently desirable means of subjecting human conduct to the governance of rules, and of resolving disputes about those rules, from among the class of non-arbitrary ways of so subjecting human conduct and resolving disputes? Legal fetishism's grip is often felt when considering this question, since some find it impossible to think of non-legal ways of subjecting human conduct to the governance of rules.[23] But, although much depends upon the contours of the 'legal' here, there are clearly ways of organizing social life and resolving disputes—for example, mediation, citizens' forums or juries, mass voting, community participation—quite different to law and adjudication and not necessarily the same as systems of arbitrary power.

[21] The phrase belongs to L. Fuller: see *The Morality of Law* (New Haven: Yale University Press, rev. edn., 1969), 96.

[22] ibid., ch. II.

[23] See I. Balbus, 'Commodity Form and Legal Form: An Essay on the "Relative Autonomy" of the Law', ch. 3 of C. Reasons and R. Rich (eds.), *The Sociology of Law: A Conflict Perspective* (Toronto: Butterworths, 1978), esp. 83–5.

It is in their regard for other means of organizing social life and resolving disputes that proponents of the sceptical challenge signal their doubt that the legitimacy condition can be satisfied. In pointing out the supposedly anti-democratic nature of constitutional adjudication, the desirability of removing law from the lexicon of political power and of replacing judges with mediators, they imply that current systems of law and adjudication suffer from a legitimacy deficit.[24] The sceptical challenge imperils the rationality condition by means of a family of arguments about the indeterminacy of legal doctrine and, hence, of adjudication. Overall, this family of arguments denies that there is 'a method of legal justification that contrasts with open-ended disputes about the basic terms of social life, disputes that people call ideological, philosophical, or visionary'.[25] Talk of determinacy and indeterminacy in this context is potentially quite confusing and it is worthwhile to offer some analysis of how the notions are best understood.

The first point to note highlights the relation between the justifiability and rationality of judicial decision-making and its determinacy and indeterminacy. The relation is simply that often 'determinacy' is used as a synonym for the rationality or justifiability of a judicial decision. This was done in Subsection 2.1, above, when it was said that MacCormick offered a typology of reasons which move judges from a relatively to a completely *determinate* position in a hard case. In this formulation the notion of determinacy is a product of the power of the reasons which purportedly justify the decision whereas the idea of indeterminacy signifies the alleged weakness of those reasons. Determinacy and indeterminacy therefore highlight this property of a judicial decision: the relative weight of the reasons adduced to justify the decision. This property of judicial decisions is, of course, a property of legal doctrine also, since decisions are made within the medium of doctrine. It is almost inconceivable that legal doctrine could provide conclusive reasons for a decision (e.g. *Y* is in breach of contract) and yet the judicial decision in the same case not be based on such conclusive reasons. Almost, but not completely, since the court could be mistaken as to what doctrine requires. When speaking of particular instances of adjudication as determinate or indeterminate, sceptics most often have in mind the situation where

[24] 'The state, and with it the judge, are destined to disappear as people come to feel their brotherhood . . . Arbitrators are an improvement; mediators even better': D. Kennedy, 'Form and Substance in Private Law Adjudication', *Harvard Law Review*, 89 (1976), 1685–778, at 1771. 'An idiom of popular power could be developed, along with an accessible thesaurus of public empowerment to replace the elite lexicon of the law . . . [T]o achieve this state of affairs we must enhance and extend [but] also quieten certain voices. For instance, lawyers will have to adopt a more humble tone and speak *sotto voce*, if at all': A. Hutchinson, *Dwelling on the Threshold: Critical Essays on Modern Legal Thought* (Toronto: Carswell, 1988). See also M. Tushnet, *Taking the Constitution Away from the Courts* (Princeton, Princeton University Press, 1999).

[25] R. M. Unger, *The Critical Legal Studies Movement* (Cambridge, Mass.: Harvard University Press, 1986), 1. For a taster of the variety of this kind of argument see: J. Singer, 'The Player and the Cards: Nihilism and Legal Theory', *Yale Law Journal*, 94 (1984), 1–70; G. Peller, 'The Metaphysics of American Law', *California Law Review*, 73 (1985), 1152–290; and D. Kennedy, *A Critique of Adjudication*, n. 8 above, chs. 2–8.

doctrinal indeterminacy (doctrine does not provide good reasons for a decision one way or another) produces indeterminacy in the decision (judges are not successful in producing good reasons for the decision they reach). Predicated of a system of adjudication and doctrine, determinacy and indeterminacy refer to the number of decisions in the system that are or could be well supported by reasons; such systems can therefore be more or less determinate or indeterminate.

This is not the only sense determinacy and indeterminacy could have in this context. The notions could quite plausibly refer to the *predictability* of either adjudicative *outcomes* or *processes*. If it is supposed, for example, that a particular judge always decides hard cases in favour of attractive women, his decisions are determinate, where what is meant is 'predictable'. Equally, if a judge sometimes tackles criminal justice cases from a 'crime control perspective' and sometimes from an 'individual justice perspective', her future decisions in this area could be properly regarded as indeterminate, that is, unpredictable.[26] Predictability can also, of course, be a product of meaning. Since we are all currently more or less certain what the injunction 'Dogs must be carried on the escalator' means, our decisions in applying the rule will undoubtedly be fairly predictable. However, those who use the language of indeterminacy most often—proponents of the sceptical challenge—do not and cannot use it in the lack of predictability sense. This is because they simultaneously affirm both that adjudication is predictable and that it is indeterminate. It is both uncharitable and displays undue haste in the analysis of sceptics' arguments to assume that there must be a contradiction here.[27] The basis of the mistake is to equate indeterminacy with a lack of predictability. Yet, when indeterminacy is defined narrowly, as referring to a justification or rationality deficit, we can see that there is no contradiction between sceptics' claims about widespread indeterminacy in law and adjudication, on the one hand, and their affirmations of the predictability of adjudicative outcomes, on the other. Hence, it is idle pointing to easy—that is, completely predictable—hypothetical case outcomes (e.g. that the first paragraph of this chapter does not defame Gore Vidal) in an attempt to refute sceptical indeterminacy arguments.[28]

Both sceptics and non-sceptics affirm that adjudication is a relatively predictable process. Both camps agree that, given adequate knowledge and understanding of the law, academics, practitioners, and observers can form fairly stable expectations about the outcomes of the vast majority of cases. Yet, while accepting that the outcomes of cases are quite predictable, the reasons sceptics and non-sceptics offer in explanation are radically different. For non-sceptics, one reason why adjudication is reasonably predictable and certain is because the choices judges make are in

[26] I am stealing A. Norrie's terminology: see his *Crime, Reason and Punishment* (London: Weidenfeld and Nicolson, 1993), chs. 1 and 2. My use of his terminology is trite; his arguments are not.

[27] For examples of such haste, see Kress, n. 3 above, pp. 296–7 and L. Solum, 'On the Indeterminacy Crisis: Critiquing Legal Dogma', *University of Chicago Law Review*, 54 (1987), 462–503, at 471–2.

[28] The example belongs to Solum, 'On the Indeterminary Crisis', 471.

principle justifiable, drawing upon a limited range of reason-types and arguments. Contrary to this view, sceptics hold that although judges may believe their choices are justifiable, this belief—inculcated through socialization perhaps prior to, but certainly during, professional and academic legal training—is a mistake. The choices open to judges cannot be justified—cannot be supported by reasons—because of the truth of language or value (or some other kind of) indeterminacy. The choices judges make are nevertheless predictable because as a class they share a range of values and assumptions upon which those choices are based.[29]

The various components of the sceptical challenge are not closely analysed in what follows. The challenge hangs like a brooding omnipresence over the chapter since part of the task undertaken is that of considering whether or not those prima-facie unsympathetic to it have the resources, in their accounts of adjudication and authority, to stop it in its tracks. That task requires an analysis of non-sceptical work but not a fine-grained explication of the grounds of the sceptical challenge. Demonstrating that adjudication is indeed a pre-eminently rational and legitimate means of resolving disputes would, in so far as these properties are regarded as virtues, constitute a compelling rejoinder to that challenge.

3   THE RATIONALITY CONDITION

3.1   An Outline

Undiscriminating talk of rationality in the context of adjudication can obscure a number of issues and possibilities. Two steps must therefore be taken at the outset. First, some of the ways in which talk of rationality can function in this context must be elucidated. It can function in at least three ways. The first is conceptual: here talk of the rationality of adjudication is concerned with the ways in which it can, if at all, be a rational process. This, of course, requires some account of what rationality might mean in this context and that is provided in what follows, the main burden of which is an assessment of the ways, if any, hard case decision-making can be rational in the face of value pluralism. Talk about the rationality of adjudication clearly functions in another way, which can be called empirical. The principal issue here

---

[29] For many sceptics these values and assumptions are ideologies and hence socially determined; they are not rationally articulated and assented to, nor could they be so, given the truth of value indeterminacy: see D. Kairys (ed.), *The Politics of Law: A Progressive Critique* (New York: Pantheon, 1982), 15; Singer, 'The Player and the Cards', n. 25 above, pp. 19–25; Kelman, *A Guide to Critical Legal Studies*, n. 8 above, p. 4 and pp. 46–7; M. Tushnet, 'Defending the Indeterminacy Thesis', ch. 11 of B. Bix (ed.), *Analyzing Law* (Oxford: Clarendon Press, 1998).

concerns which, if any, actual instances of adjudication are rational. This involves an evaluation of particular judicial decisions in light of some account of the nature of rationality. Empirical talk about the rationality of adjudication therefore presupposes a conceptual account of the nature of rationality (how else can the rationality of particular decisions be assessed?). It is not directly in play in what follows. The third way in which rationality talk can function is normatively: here the existence or degree of rationality in adjudication is regarded as commendable in so far as rationality is itself regarded as a desirable feature of human life, institutions and practices. From this perspective the absence of rationality in aspects of our life, institutions, and practices is baleful. When the topic is adjudication, normative rationality talk usually serves as comparison and critique. Adjudication is either compared with other means of resolving disputes and found wanting in its degree of rationality, or the actual practice of adjudication is compared to allegedly common perceptions of its rationality and a disjunction affirmed. These two instances of normative rationality talk animate the second limb of the sceptical challenge. They are in play in what follows, but only in the same way as the challenge itself: a brooding omnipresence rather than a fully articulated argument.

Secondly, some attention must be given to what it might mean to say that adjudication is a rational process of decision-making. It might mean at least three different things, which we can identify and label as ascending steps on a rationality ladder. The lowest rung on the ladder is that of having reason(s) for action and decision. In this situation, an action X is rational if and only if an agent (A) believes there is a reason or reasons for it, such reason or reasons being compatible with the existence of countervailing reason or reasons. In response to the question 'why X?' there is a reply available to A such that it states her reason(s) for X-ing. Since our concern is with justification, and justification can only take place within the realm of reasons, this is as it should be. There may, of course, be reasons for X which operate at a non-justificatory level—X may be the product of a number of specifiable causes—and of which A is unaware. Furthermore, undoubtedly there can be other justificatory reasons for X of which A is unaware. All that is required by having reason(s) is that A had some reason(s) for X-ing, of which she was aware, and which she could articulate as a response to the question 'why X?'

As an indicator of rationality, the requirement of having reasons might be dismissed as being too lax, as ruling out almost nothing. But it does rule out some things. For, in order to have reason(s) for X-ing, A cannot do X purely unreflectively, at least in the first instance. A must know of the reason(s) for X before or at the time of X-ing; subsequently, A may do X unreflectively by assuming that, since she had reason(s) to X in the past, she has reason(s) to X in the future in relevantly similar situations. To be rational in this sense, X-ing cannot be a product of pure intuition, prejudice, bias, or completely unreflective habit. If it is, then A has no reason(s) for X-ing that she is aware of, except when her reason is: 'everyone else does X in this situation'. This, of course, is A's reason and is the product of some degree of reflection; it is not purely a product of prejudice, bias, or unthinking deference to custom. It therefore counts as having reason(s) to X.

Applied to judicial decision-making, this requirement would seem to be far too lenient. Although it would rule out much that we expect to be excluded from adjudication—judges openly tracking their prejudices, arriving at decisions solely by fiat rather than reason—it does not seem sufficient to allow adjudication to come close to living up to its publicity, both in the academy and the wider world. If courts are forums of principle, and if law schools do indeed preach 'faith in the power of reason', then a more demanding account of rationality must be sought.[30] The second rung on the rationality ladder is that of sorting reasons. It incorporates the two conditions constitutive of the first rung, namely, (i) A must believe that there is a reason or that there are reasons to X; and (ii) A must be capable of articulating the reason or reasons in response to the question 'why X?'. In addition, sorting reasons requires (iii) that A either takes steps to determine that R (the reason) or $Ra–Rz$ (the reasons) to X are genuine or is told of those steps; and (iv) that A therefore knows, or is informed of, many, most, or all of the reasons, putative and genuine, to X. The third requirement of sorting genuine from putative reasons for X implies the fourth, knowledge of the range of reasons that might support X-ing. But there need not be a plurality of reasons for X-ing in order for A to sort reason(s). A variant of the process of sorting can be carried out when there is only one reason ($R1$) to X, provided A takes steps to establish that $R1$ is indeed the only genuine reason to X. Talk of sorting reason(s) is a little strained for, since there is only one reason for X-ing, there is no process of winnowing wheat from chaff within the class of reasons. Yet there is an analogous process, namely, that of winnowing a genuine reason from the class of factors that might lead to X (prejudice, bias, etc.), not all of which are reasons.

While apparently more demanding than simply having reasons, sorting reasons is not the most stringent account of the rationality of adjudication. Although it insists that the decisions judges reach be based upon genuine reasons and thus requires sorting and evaluation of the reasons that might support the decision, it is possible to go further. The third rung on the rationality ladder is that of weighing reasons. It incorporates the four requirements of sorting reasons and adds a fifth, namely, that of weighing the genuine reasons for X-ing. On this account, A is rational when she X's only on the basis of either the strongest, most weighty reason in the class of genuine reasons for X-ing, or on the basis of the collection of reasons that together are weightiest. Weighing reasons to X only makes sense when there is a plurality of genuine reasons to X. Such plurality also makes sense of those situations, in adjudication and beyond, in which it seems that a choice either way is plausible, supported by reasons, and thus in no sense obviously wrong. In such situations it seems appropriate to speak of agents having adequate reasons to X, where what is meant is that there are

---

[30] The Dworkinian trope can be found almost anywhere in his work on adjudication; the quotation, a statement of the then Dean of Yale Law School, Anthony Kronman, is from P. Schlag, *The Enchantment of Reason* (Durham, NC: Duke University Press, 1998), 19.

reasons for X-ing which do not make refraining from X-ing irrational. If sorting reasons places agents within the domain of adequate reasons, then weighing reasons brings agents within the domain of compelling reasons, reasons that require X on pain of irrationality.[31] Compelling reasons for X not only rationally require X, they also provide the best—the weightiest, most powerful—reasons for X. When X is supported by compelling reasons there is no better justification for X-ing, although there may be other explanations of X-ing. Were adjudication rational in this sense, then judicial decisions would be supported by compelling reasons. It would be commonplace to find judges sorting and evaluating the reasons for and against a decision one way or another in a hard case, this effort being informed by the desire to find the best possible reason or reasons for the decision. Decisions based upon compelling reasons would be well placed to quell the legal controversy hard cases raise.

These three steps capture different senses of what may be meant when adjudication is claimed to be rational and, hence, constitute three different versions of the rationality condition. It is not our job, as yet, to choose between them, but it should at least be shown that they are plausible and independent. As to the first issue, it might be maintained that these three accounts of the rationality of adjudication are implausible because they take no account of either the rules of standard logic or the axioms of rational choice theory. That is true. But this is not because these rules and axioms are irrelevant here; rather, it is because they are presupposed by the different versions of the rationality condition. The rules of standard logic are the skeleton upon which the flesh of rational judicial (and all other) decisions hang; this is true also of many of the axioms of rational choice theory. The qualification in the latter instance is a result of the fact that some of those axioms are contested since they appear to distort significant features of actual, perhaps fairly common, judicial and other choice situations. There are two responses to this, neither of which is particularly helpful. In light of the apparent disjunction between the axioms of rational choice and some actual choice situations, the first proclaims 'so much the worse for actual choices', whereas the second claims 'so much the worse for rational choice theory'.[32] For present purposes, we will assume that rational choice axioms and assumptions about reflexivity and completeness, and about consistency and stability of preferences and reasons, inform the three versions of the rationality condition.

But, it may be asked, are there actually three distinct versions of the rationality condition here? It might be argued that they collapse into one another. For example, the distinction between having reason(s) and sorting reason(s) is illusory if having

[31] The terminology of adequate and compelling reasons and the account of the difference between them derives from J. Raz, *Engaging Reason* (Oxford: Clarendon Press, 1999), 9, 47–9, 63–6, 94–105 and 116–17.

[32] For some helpful discussions of rational choice axioms and some of their difficulties see: S. Hargreaves Heap, M. Hollis, B. Lyons, R. Sugden, and A. Weale, *The Theory of Choice* (Oxford: Blackwell, 1992); B. Chapman, 'The Rational and the Reasonable: Social Choice Theory and Adjudication', *University of Chicago Law Review*, 61 (1994), 41–122; and R. Nozick, *The Nature of Rationality* (Princeton: Princeton University Press, 1993).

reasons means having genuine reasons. In a sense this is quite intelligible, since having reasons is often assumed to mean having good (i.e. *genuine*) reasons. Although we sometimes make this connection, it is also true that we also often recognize a disjunction here, since the process of thinking reasons *N*, *O* and *P* support *X* but, on further reflection, concluding that only *P* supports *X*, is familiar. We make a distinction between putative and genuine reasons which usually marks a process of rational and reflective ascent. The distinction between sorting reasons and weighing reasons might be questioned in the following way: if *A* has genuine reasons to *X*, then those reasons all have weight and it makes no sense to maintain, further, that genuine reasons may have different weights.

The problem here is making sense of the claim supporting the objection, namely, that reasons have non-specifiable weight. It is envisaged that genuine reasons constitute a class which has weight *qua* class and which presumably can be compared to the weight of other classes of consideration. Some explanation of how inter-class weighing is possible is therefore required. Furthermore, while it is said that each member of the class of genuine reasons has weight, it is supposed that the weight of these reasons cannot be compared and ranked. The idea of weighing reasons certainly implies some scale by which weight can be compared and assessed and it is this that proponents of the objection might deny. As a general claim, about all reasons in all contexts, this denial is surely too sweeping; the structure of our practical reasoning and language endorses the possibility of weighing reasons. While this is hardly a proof that weighing reasons is sensible, it surely requires that we take the possibility seriously until thoroughly discredited. This point does not rest upon a bald affirmation that weighing is always and ever possible, whatever the context.

The next steps in the argument can now be taken. There are four, formulated as responses to four questions. The first briefly demonstrates the plausibility of the claim—another shibboleth of the non-sceptical jurist—that values are in play in both law and adjudication. The second unpacks the notion of strong value pluralism, while the third demonstrates who, among contemporary theorists of adjudication, are strong value pluralists. And the fourth, premised upon the suppositions that values do have a role in adjudication and that strong value pluralism is true, illustrates one *adverse* consequence strong value pluralism has for non-sceptical accounts of adjudication. The argument is that the affirmation of strong value pluralism in adjudication makes it impossible to affirm the stringent version of the rationality condition. Hence, embracing strong value pluralism ensures that the second part of the sceptical challenge is very difficult to meet.

3.2 Value Pluralism and the Rationality Condition

3.2.1 *Is Adjudication Value-Laden?*

That values are implicated within the practice of adjudication can be demonstrated by reference to some examples and by invoking an old and almost uncontested jurisprudential lesson about the nature of rule application and interpretation.

Two kinds of example illustrate the point. The first consists of those propositions of law that invoke and require interpretation of moral concepts and their constitutive values. Propositions of law that include notions such as, *inter alia*, good faith, dishonesty, reasonableness, and fairness are obvious instances. Secondly, even when dealing with propositions of law that do not explicitly incorporate any moral concepts or other kind of normative values, judges often interpret and apply those propositions in the light of generic rule of law values. These values take the form of, for example, rather abstract notions such as consistency (with other propositions of law and decisions, so that like cases be treated alike) or more specific principles such as that criminal law statutes are to be interpreted restrictively.

Now it might be the case that legal systems exist that do not incorporate values in either of the two ways—so familiar in Anglo-American legal systems—just noted. A compelling jurisprudential lesson suggests that, whether incorporated into propositions of law in the ways suggested by our examples or not, values are apparently unavoidably implicated within the process of rule application and interpretation. The lesson begins with some over-simplified instances of rule application and interpretation. The examples used are rules like: 'dogs must be carried on the escalator', 'no vehicles in the park', and 'no blood to be spilled in the streets'.[33] Setting aside issues about core and penumbral meanings, the interpretation and application of these rules in particular cases will, it is said, unavoidably implicate values of some kind. This is because being able to apply these rules in particular situations assumes some understanding of their point, purpose, or value. It is only by reference to such understandings that we can decide whether or not the park warden's pick-up truck, a war veteran's memorial jeep, children's roller skates, and the postman's bicycle are excluded from the park. The lesson, that even elementary instances of rule interpretation and application such as these depend upon an account of the point, purpose, or value of the rule, seems undeniable. Furthermore, the lesson holds when applied to the much more complex and interrelated rules and standards we find in actually existing legal systems and holds, *a fortiori*, if the rules and standards in question raise any of the issues constitutive of hard cases. Obviously, the lesson gives no

---

[33] The last two of these well-worn examples occur in, *inter alia*, L. Fuller, 'Positivism and Fidelity to Law—A Reply to Professor Hart', *Harvard Law Review*, 71 (1958), 630–74, 661–9; H. L. A. Hart, *The Concept of Law*, 2nd edn. (Oxford: Clarendon Press, 1994), 62–72; R. M. Unger, *Knowledge and Politics* (New York: The Free Press, 1975), 92.

guidance on either the number of cases that are hard or the number in which values play a role.

3.2.2 *What is Value Pluralism?*

The strongest and most interesting answer to this question consists of the plurality, conflict, and incomparability claims. A weaker, but not the weakest, answer comprises only the plurality and conflict claims. The very weakest answer makes just the plurality claim (it must do so to be regarded as an instance of pluralism). Taken alone, the plurality claim is the least interesting of the three because, within the sphere of thought about moral, political, and other values, it is one with which just about everyone could agree. It holds, obviously, that our world contains a multiplicity of values. Those—let us call them value monists and include among their ilk utilitarians—who hold that moral and political thought embraces only one ultimate and fundamental value, could quite easily accept this claim with the following caveat. It is that the multiplicity of values evidenced in our thought and language are less fundamental, particular manifestations of some single fundamental value. Similarly, those who have reasons for rejecting single value views of the human world—we will label them value pluralists—accept the plurality claim. By contrast with value monists, however, strong value pluralists conjoin the plurality claim with the conflict and incomparability claims, which they take to constitute a competing, putative truth about the nature of values.

The conflict claim insists that some or all of our important values conflict. It usually has two dimensions. The first is an observation about the human world. Its basis is that some value conflict is a consequence of the fact that the world does not bend itself to our purposes: '[i]t is beyond argument that the world as we know it gives us grounds for regret and conflict even if we do what is to be done . . . The present world, and those worlds we should think we could bring about, are worlds of conflict'.[34] If a world could be engineered in which conflict-creating features were absent, a world, for example, without scarcity of resources, then on this view value conflict would be reduced. For it is features of the world, and not our values, that create much value conflict. However, the second dimension of the conflict claim locates a source of value conflict not solely in features of the world, such as scarcity, but in the nature of values themselves. It holds that there are good reasons for accepting values that are substantively very different and which can quite plausibly conflict, in the sense of requiring incompatible courses of action in particular situations.

The incomparability claim maintains that some value conflicts cannot be resolved because the values in play are in some sense incapable of or beyond comparison. The

---

[34] M. Stocker, *Plural and Conflicting Values* (Oxford: Clarendon Press, 1990), 125. For slightly different statements of the same point see: B. Williams, *Problems of the Self* (Cambridge: Cambridge University Press, 1973), 166, 170–1, 181 and his *Moral Luck* (Cambridge: Cambridge University Press, 1981), 74–5. Williams, however, seems to think this is the only interesting source of value conflict.

standard strategy adopted to demonstrate the truth of incomparability (the language of incommensurability is often used) is this: the claim is asserted in conjunction with both the conflict claim and some actual or hypothetical examples of the phenomenon.[35] The strategy suffers from an obvious weakness, namely, the exact nature of the alleged incomparability is rarely analysed, it being in some cases simply assumed to follow from a broader doctrine about the nature of moral values.[36] Since the thrust of the incomparability claim (when conjoined with the other two) is so significant—it implies that there is no obviously rational way of resolving some instances of value conflict—its exact content requires detailed elucidation. Raz is one of the few proponents of the claim who actually attempts to elucidate the nature of the relationship between incomparable values (he is not content just to affirm incomparability and point to some examples of it). He is concerned to do this because, quite rightly, he wants to determine whether or not there is conceptual room for talk of values being incomparable or incommensurable (like Raz, I regard these two words as synonyms).[37] In order to do some distinctive conceptual work for us, the notion of value incommensurability must refer to something other than the difficulty we sometimes have in choosing between conflicting values, since that process does not need that label in order to become salient for us. Similarly, the notion of incommensurability will be redundant if it merely refers to the possibility that conflicting values can sometimes be of exactly equal weight. For how does the notion of incommensurability, used in this sense, convey more than talk of 'conflict between values of equal weight'?

Raz holds that 'A and B are incommensurate if it is neither true that one is better than the other nor true that they are of equal value' (MF, 322).[38] Obviously, this entails the claim that there is no neutral metric with which to value them should one have to choose between them. Since there is no way in which incommensurable values can themselves be valued and a choice made between them on the basis of a

---

[35] See e.g. J. O. Urmson, 'A Defence of Intuitionism', *Aristotelian Society Proceedings*, 75 (1975), 111–19, at 111 (the incomparability claim: there is 'no explicit method, no priority rules, for weighing . . . principles against one another'); 116–17 (both dimensions of the conflict claim); and 118–19 (examples). That Urmson accepts both dimensions of the conflict claim is clear, although some of the examples of conflict he uses (see 116–17) suggest that he thinks value conflict is a product of certain contingencies occurring in the world. Yet he also speaks as if conflict were simply a result of systematic tensions and inconsistencies *within* our moral thought ('I am inclined . . . to believe that there is a certain strain and disharmony within the moral requirements I must acknowledge and that there could be a decision-procedure only *within an harmonious set of moral beliefs*': 119, emphasis added). For another account of incomparability that tackles both dimensions see C. Sunstein, 'Incommensurability and Valuation in Law', *Michigan Law Review*, 92 (1994), 779–861.

[36] Urmson, above, thinks it flows from moral intuitionism, a doctrine that many other proponents of the incomparability claim do not accept: see Stocker and Williams, n. 34 above, and T. Nagel, *Mortal Questions* (Cambridge: Cambridge University Press, 1979), ch. 9.

[37] There are risks in so doing which can be avoided by noting the strain in using incomparability as a synonym for incommensurability: see R. Chang, 'Introduction', in R. Chang (ed.), *Incommensurability, Incomparability, and Practical Reason* (Cambridge, Mass.: Harvard University Press, 1997).

[38] *MF* in the text and notes refers to J. Raz, *The Morality of Freedom* (Oxford: Clarendon Press, 1986).

higher level evaluation, it seems that the choice between them cannot be made by reference to compelling reasons. Raz is unambiguous on this point: '[w]here the considerations for and against two alternatives are incommensurate, reason is indeterminate. It provides no better case for one alternative than for the other. . . . Incommensurability speaks not of what does escape reason but of what must elude it' (*MF*, 333–4). This is not to say that the choice is completely uninformed by reason and hence arbitrary and random. Rather, it is to say that the reasons one has for a choice one way or another do not completely determine that choice: one has reasons for choosing both options.[39]

Having sketched what value pluralism is, it will be worth noting what it is not so as to avoid any confusion. It is not—at least, not necessarily—a thesis about the foundation and justification of values. That is, it need not commit one to any particular position about how we can have knowledge and beliefs about moral, political, or other values. Rather, in its strongest version it holds only that there is a plurality of values, some of which can conflict, the conflict being in some sense insoluble. Nothing has to follow from this about the foundation and possibility of knowledge of values. So, for example, within the limited sphere of moral values, affirming value pluralism carries no meta-ethical commitments about how knowledge of those values can be established. One could just as easily affirm value pluralism in conjunction with a non-cognitivist position about the nature of moral values (which would make a claim along these lines: moral values cannot be rationally established, having their basis not in reason but in either our desires or sentiments) as a moral realist position (holding that there are facts in the world that make certain statements about moral values either true or false). This is not to deny that some meta-ethical theories are more and some less sympathetic to strong value pluralism. One can say, on purely contingent grounds, that the more rationalist one's meta-ethics, the less room one has for insoluble conflicts between moral values.[40] This does not *have* to be the case: the link is merely contingent.

3.2.3 *Who Affirms Value Pluralism?*

Given that the strongest version of value pluralism makes the three claims just sketched, who affirms that doctrine? MacCormick and Raz do, while Dworkin does not (he affirms a weaker version of value pluralism).

The textual evidence to show that MacCormick is a strong value pluralist is both plentiful and, with one exception, unambiguous. He is committed to the plurality and conflict claims by virtue of statements such as these:

---

[39] This explains away the apparent inconsistency between Raz's statement (ibid.), and his remarks (at 338, 339 and 352) that a choice between incommensurable options can be 'reasoned'. It is therefore wrong but not altogether rare to think that choices between incommensurables are arbitrary.

[40] B. Williams, *Problems of the Self*, n. 34 above, notes this contingent link: pp. 204–5.

I go along with Hume in supposing that a determinant factor in our assent to some or another normative principle lies in our affective nature, in our sentiments, predispositions of will . . . That people have different affective natures, differences of sentiment, passion can then be adduced in explanation of fundamental moral disagreement. (*LRLT*, 5)

Furthermore, '[h]onest and reasonable people can and do differ even upon ultimate matters of principle, each having reasons which seem to him or her good for the view to which he or she adheres' but 'the reasons which can be given are not in their nature conclusive' (ibid.). MacCormick is equally unambiguous in stating that the plurality and conflict claims are general truths manifest *within* the process of adjudication. Hence his value pluralism cannot be regarded as applicable to the general realm of value-talk but inapplicable to some specific instances, such as judicial value-talk. So, for example, MacCormick says that the consequentialist arguments judges invoke to decide hard cases are 'in part at least *subjective*' (*LRLT*, 105; emphasis in the original). Why? Because

[j]udges evaluating consequences of rival possible rulings may give different weight to different criteria of evaluation, differ as to the degree of perceived injustice, or of predicted inconvenience which will arise from adoption or rejection of a given ruling. Not surprisingly, they differ, sometimes sharply and even passionately, in relation to their final judgement of the acceptability or unacceptability all things considered of a ruling under scrutiny. At this point we reach the bedrock of value preferences which inform our reasoning *but which are not demonstrable by it. At this level there can simply be irresolvable differences of opinion between people of good will and reason.* (*LRLT*, 105–6; emphasis added)

The only ambiguity about MacCormick's invocation of the plurality and conflict claims arises because of his subsequent renunciation of the Humean account of the foundation of moral and, presumably, other values (*LRLT*, p. xvi).[41] In so far as that account is *one* of the reasons underlying MacCormick's invocation of these claims, then its rejection partially imperils those claims. Moreover, the danger is partial in another sense. For MacCormick has as yet only stated his dissatisfaction with the Humean account; he has articulated no alternative to it. It is equally unclear how far, if at all, MacCormick's rejection of the Humean account impacts upon his commitment to the incomparability claim. He certainly appears committed to some version of that claim, as the following statements—again about judges' consequentialist arguments—make clear. Those arguments are, says MacCormick, 'intrinsically *evaluative*' (*LRLT*, 105). That is, they

ask [. . .] about the acceptability or unacceptability of . . . consequences. *There is however no reason to assume that . . . [they] involve [. . .] evaluation in terms of a single scale,* such as the

---

[41] This is contained in the new foreword to the 1993 reprinting of *LRLT*. That MacCormick travelled this road to Damascus late in his thinking about adjudication is clear from the fact that in essays published several years after the first edition of *LRLT* he was still an unreconstructed Humean. See his 'Contemporary Legal Philosophy: The Rediscovery of Practical Reason', *Journal of Law and Society*, 10 (1983), 1–18, 13–14 and (with O. Weinberger) *An Institutional Theory of Law* (Dordrecht: D. Reidel, 1986), 193–6 and 204–5.

Benthamite scale of supposedly measurable aggregates of pleasures and pains. Judges characteristically refer to criteria such as 'justice', 'common sense', 'public policy', and 'convenience' or 'expediency' in weighing the case for and against given rules. *It should not be
assumed without proof that these really all boil down to the same thing.* (*LRLT*, ibid.; emphasis
added)

MacCormick is less equivocal in his discussion of whether or not there can be a single right answer to a hard case. He says that consequentialist 'evaluation *does not* use
a single scale of measurable values . . . *It involves multiple criteria . . .*' (*LRLT*, 252–3;
emphasis added; see also 114–15). Because this is so, then in hard cases 'we find ourselves faced with a disagreement which it is in principle impossible to send to any theoretical "Hercules" for objective resolution by delivery of the right answer' (254).
Presumably, the existence of multiple scales for the evaluation of the consequences of
a decision means that there can be no single right decision, for what is right on one
scale may well be wrong on another. To regard this talk of a plurality of scales of evaluation as expressing a commitment to the incomparability claim is surely neither
unfair nor perverse. For if, as seems obvious from MacCormick's remarks, he is not
making the simple points that value judgments can sometimes be either very difficult
or be 'tied', then what else—other than some version of the incomparability claim—
could he have in mind?

Thus it seems safe to conclude both that MacCormick is a strong value pluralist
and that he believes value pluralism arises within the adjudicative context. What evidence is there to suggest that Raz shares this view? It is found in his political philosophy and establishes beyond doubt that he affirms the plurality, conflict, and (as we
already know) incomparability claims (*MF*, chs. 13 and 14).[42] The only doubt about
Raz's value pluralism is this: does he accept that it arises within the adjudicative context? The question is not otiose because it is quite possible to affirm value pluralism
and hold that some segments of value-talk are beyond its range. It might, for example, be that within a context of general value pluralism there are some realms in which
only one agreed value holds sway, those realms being created by specific groups or
institutions or simply being a product of consensus. Judicial value-talk could be one
such realm. Two points serve to show that Raz thinks it is not such a realm.

The first notes Raz's remarks that values and, in particular, moral judgments play
a role within the process of adjudication. Speaking of unregulated cases, Raz says
'judges do rely and should rely on their own moral judgement' (*AL*, 199). He holds
that 'it is our normal view that judges use moral arguments . . . when developing the
law' (*AL*, 49). Those arguments, when brought to bear on the question of whether or
not an 'authority' should be overruled, consist of *inter alia* an assessment of the benefits and disadvantages of a new ruling (*AL*, 190 and 114).[43] It is therefore no surprise

---

[42] The plurality and conflict claims also appear in J. Raz, *Practical Reason and Norms* (Princeton:
Princeton University Press, 1990), 159.

[43] Raz is a little more specific on this issue in 'Facing Up: A Reply', *Southern California Law Review*, 62
(1989), 1153–235, 1208–9.

that for Raz '[l]egal reasoning is an instance of moral reasoning' (*EPD*, 324).[44] The nature of the legal standards with which judges operate guarantees that values have a role in adjudication. This is because, as we have already noted, some legal standards embody moral and other values. Raz accepts this but with one caveat (*EPD*, 227–8). For, in order to maintain his version of legal positivism, which relies upon the 'strong social thesis' (*AL*, 45–7), he has to insist that 'while the rule [or legal standard] referring to morality is indeed law . . . the morality to which it refers is not thereby incorporated into law' (*AL*, 46). This, of course, does not contradict the claim that adjudication is a value-laden process. It simply highlights Raz's point that the identification of law is not a matter of moral judgment whereas the process of law-making, a form of which occurs when judges decide unregulated cases, is. The second point highlights the occasions when Raz says incomparability arises within the adjudicative context. He says, for example, that in some instances the reasons judges have for deciding an unregulated dispute one way rather than another 'are incommensurate as to strength . . . [;] [n]either is stronger nor are they equal in strength' (*AL*, 75). If those reasons are generated by incommensurable values then this is to be expected. And Raz does indeed suggest that judges can be faced with a choice between incommensurable values (*EPD*, 322–3).

It is therefore reasonably clear both that Raz is a strong value pluralist and that, on the basis of statements like those above, he thinks value pluralism arises within the adjudicative context. We can be equally certain that Dworkin does not. That is because, although Dworkin makes both the plurality and conflict claims, he denies—albeit sometimes with a hint of equivocation—the incomparability claim. The plurality and conflict claims appear many times in Dworkin's work. He holds that there are a plurality of moral positions about issues such as homosexuality, pornography, and abortion that can conflict.[45] He also thinks that conceptions of the good life, which are surely agglomerations of moral and other values, differ between members of the same political community, this truth being one reason why a version of liberalism grounded upon a right to equal concern and respect is preferable to any other.[46] Furthermore, Dworkin's interpretative account of law contains many indications that it is 'Protestant'.[47] This means that accounts of law offered in the course of both adjudication and theorizing depend upon the values of the adjudicator or theorist and that values differ significantly between members of the same community. Hence '[f]or every route Hercules took from . . . general conception to a particular verdict, another lawyer or judge who began in the same conception would find a different route and end in a different place' (*LE*, 412; see also 411 and 413).

---

[44] *EPD* in both text and notes refers to J. Raz, *Ethics in the Public Domain*, n. 17 above.

[45] See *Taking Rights Seriously*, n. 9 above, pp. 248–9 and *A Matter of Principle*, n. 14 above, p. 203.

[46] *A Matter of Principle*, n. 14 above, p. 191 and pp. 193–4.

[47] The phrase belongs to G. Postema, '"Protestant" Interpretation and Social Practices', *Law and Philosophy*, 6 (1987), 283–319, esp. pp. 300–19.

A Protestant account of interpretation is therefore one that appears to endorse both the plurality and conflict claims. However, there is no endorsement of the incomparability claim in Dworkin's work. There are instead some more or less qualified denials of that claim. This is not particularly surprising when it is noted that Dworkin's commitment to the right answer thesis is conjoined with the affirmation that hard case adjudication is a value-laden process. For, were Dworkin to embrace incomparability, then, obviously, it would be possible for the values in play within adjudication to be incomparable. That being so, it would be very difficult if not impossible to claim, on something like Raz's definition of incomparability, that there was a single right answer in hard cases in which incomparable values were in play. No wonder, then, that in responding to John Mackie's criticisms Dworkin says that 'my thesis [about right answers and the assumption that ties will be rare in hard cases] . . . presupposes a conception of morality other than some conception according to which different moral theories are frequently incommensurate'.[48] Dworkin has gone further than this elsewhere, expressing the view that no argument has yet established widespread incommensurability within moral and political theory.[49] He has also cast doubts, albeit *en passant*, upon the relevance of incommensurability to adjudication.[50] Thus it is impossible to maintain that Dworkin is a strong value pluralist. The problem that flows from affirming that doctrine, the elucidation of which is the burden of the following subsection, does not trouble him.

3.2.4 *Why Worry about Value Pluralism?*

What follows from the fact that MacCormick and Raz, among other non-sceptical theorists of adjudication, affirm strong value pluralism?[51] In so far as values and value choices are unavoidably part of hard case adjudication, and in so far as some or all of those values conflict and are incomparable, then some judicial choices cannot be rationally justified. What is meant by the latter is that a choice one way or the other cannot be based upon compelling reasons: in the face of incommensurability reason is indeterminate. There is, in relation to these judicial choices, a rationality or justification deficit. That is not to say that such choices are either random or arbitrary. Choices based upon incommensurable reasons or between incommensurable values are still informed by, still based upon, reason. However, in the face of incommensurability, no single choice is given salience by virtue of reason: there is no rational

---

[48] 'A Reply by Ronald Dworkin' in M. Cohen, n. 16 above, p. 272. For more of the same see *A Matter of Principle*, n. 14 above, pp. 143–5.

[49] *A Matter of Principle*, n. 14 above, pp. 144–5.

[50] In P. Amselek and N. MacCormick (eds.), *Controversies about Law's Ontology* (Edinburgh: Edinburgh University Press, 1991), 88–90. See also B. Bix, n. 16 above, p. 97, where we learn that Dworkin expressed numerous reservations about incommensurability in lectures.

[51] Two other examples are: J. Levin, *How Judges Reason* (New York: Peter Lang, 1992) and J. Finnis, 'Natural Law and Legal Reasoning', ch. 6 of R. P. George (ed.), *Natural Law Theory: Contemporary Essays* (Oxford: Clarendon Press, 1992).

compulsion to choose X rather than Y. However, choosing X rather than Y does not show that favouring Y would be a mistake.

It might be maintained that, nevertheless, the choice between X and Y is in a sense arbitrary because it cannot be made by reference to reasons. 'In a sense' because the choice is, in another and, perhaps, the usual sense, not arbitrary at all: there are reasons supporting both X and Y and the choice of one or the other is therefore rooted in reason(s). The extended sense holds that, because the choice between X and Y is not compelled by reason(s), it is arbitrary. The risks with this extended usage are that the central instance of arbitrariness will come to be ignored or regarded as similar to the extended instance. This is worrying since the central instance is an example of inattentiveness to or disregard of reason(s) and that, from the viewpoint of respect for rationality, is much worse than the extended instance. In the latter, the limits of reason(s) have been reached; this presupposes that reason(s) have been attended to and, in the end, found wanting. Decisions made without any concern for reason(s) are quite different; they are truly arbitrary. It is thus better to drop the extended sense of arbitrariness in favour of some sort of locution as 'reason has run out'.

So, of what consequence is it that reason runs out in those hard cases that involve a choice between incommensurables? What follows, in other words, from affirming that strong value pluralism holds sway in some instances of adjudication? Simply this: that neither MacCormick, nor Raz, nor other strong value pluralists can easily and directly meet the second part of the sceptical challenge. It holds, remember, that there is no method of legal justification different from that which holds sway in the open-ended, ideological-cum-visionary disputes about the basic terms of social life. And by 'different from', proponents of the challenge mean 'more rational than'. If, because of widespread incommensurability and those features apparently structurally analogous to it,[52] hard case adjudication is not compelled by reasons, then it cannot satisfy the most stringent rationality condition. That condition is a matter of weighing reasons: it holds that the indicator of rationality is that decision-making and action is rational only when compelled by reasons. Weighing reasons requires that one does X for the strongest reasons available from the class of relevant reasons; the strongest reasons to X are those that make failing to X irrational.

Since adjudication in the face of incommensurability is not arbitrary or non-rational, it qualifies as a rational process, but only in the sense of either having reasons or sorting reasons. The first and weakest version of the rationality condition, that of having reasons, could easily be satisfied by adjudication: just about all the decisions we are likely to see in hard cases are supported by reasons. Judges simply cannot, according to the institutional conventions and citizens' expectations, explicitly decide cases by whim or on the basis of their prejudices. Indeed, close examination of hard case adjudication in common law jurisdictions suggests it is rational in

---

[52] The fact that judicial decisions might function as *determinationes* rather than requirements of reason is one such feature: see Finnis, ibid. and R. George, *In Defense of Natural Law* (Oxford: Clarendon, 1999), 108–9.

the more demanding sense of sorting reasons. This version of the rationality condition requires not only that decisions and actions are based on reasons rather than prejudices or hunches, but that they are based on genuine reasons. Determining which are and which are not genuine reasons for X-ing yields a set of adequate reasons for X-ing, that is, a set of reasons which support X-ing, but of which it cannot be said that one or more requires X-ing. Since it cannot be said that one or more reason requires X, then it is not irrational to refrain from X-ing in the face of adequate reasons for X-ing. This is surely the same situation as that faced by judges (or anyone else) deciding between incommensurables.

The existence of incommensurability in adjudication entails that the process can be rational in the sense of both having reasons and sorting reasons, but not in the sense of weighing reasons. It is therefore unlikely that adjudication is any more rational than many non-legal and non-arbitrary means of formulating and resolving disputes. Positions adopted in political disputes and forums, or taken up in negotiation and mediation, and votes cast in ballots, are all likely to be rational in the sense of having reasons and sorting reasons. Indeed, the more formal and public these other means of dispute formulation and resolution are, the more they seem designed to mark the move from decision-making on the ground of having reasons to that of sorting reasons. The point of rules of order and participation is surely not just to ensure participants a voice in the decision-making process, but also to create an environment in which their reasons can be articulated and tested in discussion.

Many non-sceptical jurists think it a mistake to expect hard case adjudication to satisfy any higher standard of rationality than that of sorting reason(s). This modest response to the sceptical challenge has often depended upon rather weak arguments.[53] However, there is one philosophically ambitious account of the nature of practical reason, agency, and the will that *appears*, but ultimately is not, better able to support the modest response. It belongs to Raz. He defends a classical conception of agency and the will which holds 'that the paradigmatic human action is one taken because, of all the options the agent considers rationally eligible, he chooses to perform it' (*ER*, 47).[54] By contrast, the rationalist conception 'holds that paradigmatic human action is action taken because, of all the options open to the agent, it was, in the agent's view, supported by the strongest reason' (ibid.). The latter conception 'regards reason as requiring action, whereas the [former] regards reason as rendering options eligible' (ibid.). On the classical conception, any option from the range of eligible options identified by reason can be taken, and it is the agent's will that determines which: this conception 'regards typical choices and actions as determined by a will that is informed and constrained by reason but plays an autonomous role in action' (*ER*, 48). On the rationalist account, the will has no such—or very little—autonomy. The will can, on this view, be

[53] Two examples: Levin, n. 51 above and S. Burton, *Judging in Good Faith* (Cambridge: Cambridge University Press, 1992). I have discussed both in my *Understanding and Explaining Adjudication* (Oxford: Clarendon Press, 1999), 153–63.
[54] References to *ER* in both text and notes are to *Engaging Reason*, n. 31 above

much the same as it is on the classical view, namely, a compound of socialization, deep-seated traits, and 'deep evaluation', but it is essentially a product of reason or entirely shackled by it.[55] The classical view regards the will rather like a weather vane, pointing agents in one direction or another within the field of adequate reasons. Yet the wind of reason does not, on this view, completely determine the direction of the vane whereas, on the rationalist view, no other force can or should move it. Since the classical conception allows that reasons for eligible options can be in some sense inert, it comfortably accommodates incommensurability by allowing the will of an agent the power to confer salience on one incommensurable reason or option over another (*ER*, 48–9). On the rationalist account, incommensurability is only ever a disturbing and rare possibility in practical reasoning.

Clearly there is an obvious correlation between the classical conception of reason, agency, and the will and the rationality condition understood as a matter of sorting reasons; there is also a clear overlap between the rationalist conception and the rationality condition taken as requiring weighing reasons. Placing the two versions of the rationality condition within the wider context of different conceptions of reason, agency, and the will can add to their plausibility. They derive a degree of support from these conceptions because they are shown to have resonance with a number of other related beliefs. Furthermore, one or other version of the rationality condition could be in some degree undermined by this process. In particular, if Raz's account of the classical conception of reason, agency, and the will is powerful, and his objections to the rationalist account compelling, a defence of the stringent version of the rationality condition seems unlikely. Indeed, if it is conceded that the classical conception is powerful because it resonates better than the alternative with our experience of choice and action in most ordinary situations, undertaking such a defence begins to look like a labour of Canute. Nevertheless, a partial defence will be attempted here and it has two steps.

The first explains why the defence is partial. We have noted that the rationalist conception holds that reason requires or compels actions whereas on the classical conception reason usually simply highlights eligible actions. But it would be a mistake to take this as constituting an impermeable boundary between the two conceptions. Raz rightly notes that even on the classical conception reason can sometimes require or compel action:

[w]e exercise our will when we endorse the verdict of reason that we *must* perform an action, and we do so, whether willingly, reluctantly, or regretting the need, etc. According to the classical conception, however, *the most typical exercise* or manifestation of the will is in choosing among options that reason merely renders eligible. (*ER*, 48; emphasis added)

Since reason can sometimes work in this way on the classical conception, a defence of a stringent version of the rationality condition could be mounted from within that

[55] By deep evaluation I have in mind something like the process of formulating second-order volitions outlined by H. Frankfurt, *The Importance of What We Care About* (Cambridge: Cambridge University Press, 1988), ch. 2.

conception itself. That is what is undertaken below. However, Raz may be hinting at a deeper truth in accepting that echoes of the rationalist conception are found within or can be accommodated by the classical conception. The truth may be that both conceptions are to some degree part of the structure of our practical reasoning, although each has a context in which it is more appropriate than the other and each is often mistakenly extended beyond that context. His objections to the rationalist conception could therefore be read not as complete refutations of that conception, which they do not actually look like, but rather as complaints about its over-extension. Whether or not this line of thought is helpful or plausible need not, however, detain us further since the defence of the stringent version of the rationality condition that follows does not rest upon it.

The second step in the defence consists of highlighting some contexts in which it might be thought desirable to have decisions and actions compelled by reasons. It therefore shows situations in which either the classical conception adopts an uncharacteristically stringent account of rationality (weighing reason(s)) or in which the rationalist conception of practical reason, agency, and the will operates. Yet talk of 'situations' and 'contexts' is a little misleading here since the crucial factor determining our preference for decisions and actions compelled by, rather than based on, reasons is the seriousness of the consequences of the decision or action. Where such a decision or action has a vitally significant effect on others, in the sense that it has an immediate and adverse impact upon the life chances and quality of life of those affected by it, a higher standard of rationality is required than of 'ordinary' decisions and actions. There are at least two familiar situations in which actions and decisions with these consequences are made.

The first concerns the decision-making process leading to the adoption of one or other serious and invasive medical procedure. A doctor (A) has reason to do X, where X is saving B's life, and B's life is threatened by Z. Imagine that Z is caused by either c or d, and if caused by c the way of doing X is p, whereas if caused by d, the way of doing X is q. If it can be said that A has adequate reason to do either p or q, would it be acceptable that A's will—which is 'informed and constrained by reason but plays an autonomous role in action' (ER, 48)—determines which treatment is adopted? It seems unlikely that it would. It seems entirely appropriate that A's will determines the reasons she acts upon when deciding whether to take a skiing or a hiking holiday, whether to go to the cinema or stay home reading, or even more important choices such as whether or not to have children or which career to pursue. These decisions, although undoubtedly to some extent other-regarding, are within the personal sphere and it seems odd to require adherence to a stringent standard of rationality therein, essentially because doing so would denude the 'authenticity' of A's decisions, robbing them of the marks of her character.[56] All that is required for these decisions

[56] On this kind of authenticity see C. Taylor, *The Ethics of Authenticity* (Cambridge, Mass.: Harvard University Press, 1991), 25–80.

to be intelligible and justifiable is knowledge of the reasons A has for them and knowledge of A's character.

When A makes a medical decision of the kind envisaged, things seem quite different. First, because her role with regard to B is clearly one that confers upon her significant power and (intellectual) authority over B. Second, because the effects of A's decision and action upon B could not be more significant. For these reasons at least, A's decision-making might be held to a higher standard of rationality than in the personal sphere. We might require that the decision between p and q be made not on the basis of A's will, but on the basis of A's efforts to establish compelling reasons for either p or q. This requirement does not, of course, guarantee that there will indeed be compelling reasons for choosing either p or q: the reasons for p and for q might in the end be incommensurable. But insisting upon a search for compelling reasons rules out a somewhat hasty resort to A's will as the driving force of decision and action. The gravity or seriousness of the decision, its obviously other-regarding nature, and the fact that, in making it, A occupies a role with significant power over B, seems to demand at least this.

Claiming that in this decision situation A is simply charged with the task of turning conditional reasons into non-conditional reasons, does not reduce the power of the argument. It could be said that A has conditional reason to do p and q but that further reflection shows that she actually has non-conditional reason to do p. This does not impact at all upon the point that in situations such as these it is reasonable to expect the decision to be compelled by rather than based on reasons, if it is accepted that the difference between a conditional reason and a non-conditional reason is something like that between an adequate and a compelling reason. The latter, remember, is a reason that requires action and, if not acted upon, grounds an accusation of irrationality. The former confers eligibility on some option or other but does not require it; not taking the option does not therefore ground a charge of irrationality. If a conditional reason is inert in the same way as an adequate reason, and thus does not lead to action until the condition is satisfied or until the will is engaged, the analogy partially holds. If a non-conditional reason requires action, then the analogy is complete.

The second situation in which decision and action might be required to satisfy the most stringent standard of rationality shares all the features of the first: the decision-maker's (J's) decision is other-regarding; J usually has intellectual authority over those affected by the decision (P and D); and J's decision and action has extremely significant consequences for the lives of P and D. There is, however, the following difference: it is often thought that J, unlike A, has political authority over those affected by his decisions. It is often assumed that P and D have an obligation to accept J's decision and an obligation not to frustrate the actions that flow from it. J is, of course, a judge and the action-cum-decision is a judicial decision. Since '[l]egal interpretation [often] takes place within a field of pain and death', since 'legal interpretative acts signal and occasion the imposition of violence upon others', it is no more appropriate to allow the will or character of the decision-maker to determine the choice between options here than it is in the medical example.[57] If *J* has reasons for deciding in favour of *P* and reasons in favour of *D*, it seems reasonable to expect *J* either to determine which bundle of reasons is the weightiest (which amounts to analysing whether the case is indeed one involving a conflict between incommensurables) or to eschew decision altogether. Why?

Because the alternative to these two possibilities is that *J*'s will or character determines the choice between options. Furthermore, certain expectations and assumptions that correlate around the admittedly difficult idea of the rule of the law support this. Take, for example, the claim that it is desirable to be governed by the rule of law and not of men. Despite the obvious absurdities that a literal interpretation of this idea might generate, one thing it would quite sensibly seem to endorse would be that the interpretation and application of the law not turn upon the will or character (or, we might add, the biases or prejudices) of judges. Certainly it seems inappropriate that the will of certain individuals determines the reasons which unleash the coercive power of the state. The situation would perhaps be less morally worrisome were the decision unleashing such force compelled by reasons.

Raz appreciates the difficulties of allowing the will of judges to determine their decisions:

[t]he fact that … [judicial decisions] are taken by bureaucratic institutions, by people not acting for themselves but fulfilling a role of trust, gives rise to certain additional considerations. It may be unacceptable that people when acting as judges should simply express their will, their inclination or taste favouring one solution over another. … [I]t may be unacceptable that their private tastes should determine rules about duties of disclosure of information in contract formation, or standards of care in negligence. If so, we need an artificial system of reasoning which could help determine cases where natural reason runs out, thus assuring the public that the decisions are no mere expression of personal preference on the part of the judges. (*EPD*, 323)

These remarks raise only two cavils: first, that in light of the argument above they are unduly hesitant and, secondly, calling in aid an artificial reason of the law is confusing and unnecessary. Confusing because its components—'doctrinal reasons, reasons of system, local simplicity and coherence' (*EPD*, ibid.)—are most likely to be least helpful in hard cases and because claims about the artificial reason of the law often serve to mystify rather than clarify. Raz is driven to seek such an artificial reason of the law because he thinks 'natural reason runs out' (*EPD*, 324). This is unsurprising if he conceives natural reason along the lines of the classical model of practical reason, agency, and the will, for on this conception widespread incommensurability is possible and likely, and reason cannot compel choices between incommensurables. But rather than some odd, artificial reason of law being prayed in aid here, Raz could

---

[57] The quotations are from R. Cover, 'Violence and the Word', *Yale Law Journal*, 95 (1986), 1601–29, 1601.

instead invoke the rationalist model of practical reason, agency, and the will and accept that it holds sway in this context and that it might hold sway in others. Hence recourse to some 'artificial reason' of the law is unnecessary. The plausibility of this point, however, depends entirely on the supposition that both rationalist and classical conceptions are rooted in our practical reason, that neither is irremediably wrong, and that each might bring advantages in different contexts. Of course, the overall argument of this section need not turn upon this point, since it has already been noted that Raz seemingly endorses the possibility that even the classical conception can require that some actions and decisions be compelled by reasons. The argument simply highlights some situations in which this requirement seems justified.

It is time to recap. This section began with an analysis of the rationality condition. It moved on to show that the existence of incommensurability in hard case adjudication ensures that adjudication cannot be rational in the strong sense: it cannot satisfy the most stringent rationality condition. A consequence is that part of the sceptical challenge cannot be quickly and easily silenced. An argument was then considered which might have supported a modest response to the sceptical challenge. The response holds it is a mistake to expect adjudication to be rational in the stringent sense. It was shown that the argument thought capable of supporting that response does so only in a limited way and that, in so far as the argument accepts it is sometimes appropriate to require decisions and actions be compelled by reasons, it actually undermines the modest response. The following oddity was also discovered. Raz, the author of the argument that appeared to, but did not, support the modest response, demonstrates the need for adjudication to satisfy the most stringent rationality condition and also claims that incommensurability is a significant factor in adjudication. He thereby appears to undermine the possibility of adjudication satisfying such a stringent rationality condition. This is a difficult position to sustain, undoubtedly requiring more by way of elucidation and support.

4 THE LEGITIMACY CONDITION

4.1 The Question

Could it be maintained that, even though judicial decisions resting upon incommensurability cannot satisfy the most stringent rationality condition, they are nevertheless legitimate and create an obligation to act in accordance with their content? Doing so might minimize the discomfort caused by the rationality deficit unearthed in Section 3 and also respond to the first part of the sceptical challenge. This strategy depends for its success upon: (i) a plausible account of the conceptual and normative contours of the notion of legitimate authority; (ii) the applicability of such an account to rationally indeterminate judicial decisions. Our conclusion is that the arguments to support the strategy lack plausibility. Before turning to those arguments in the next subsection, two points must be clarified.

First, we must be clear about the contours of the legitimacy condition. It holds that propositions of law can in some circumstances generate an obligation to obey, to act in accord with their content. (Note that in this formulation and in those that follow 'authority' and 'legitimacy' are used interchangeably; we are primarily concerned with legitimate not *de facto* authority, even though it is probably true that any person or group having the former needs the latter.) By contrast, sceptics seemingly endorse the illegitimacy condition: it simply denies that propositions of law—judicial or statutory—can be authoritative. This undoubtedly underlies sceptics' support of other means of dispute formulation and resolution.

It is often thought that affirming the rationality condition commits one to affirming the legitimacy condition. Since the latter holds that judicial decisions and other sources of propositions of law can in some circumstances be authoritative, can, that is, generate an obligation to obey and hence presumably give good reasons for acting in accord with their content, it depends upon the truth of rationality condition. Now the circumstances in which propositions of law can have authority will vary according to the account of political authority espoused and there are many such accounts available to us, being more or less plausible. However, given the close relationship between intellectual and practical authority (of which political authority is but a species), it seems plausible to hold that one condition for the latter is that the rule or direction offered up as authoritative is justifiable in principle and practice. In this way we may be led to think that affirming the rationality condition entails the legitimacy condition. This would be a mistake. For the fulfilment of the rationality condition is only one possible condition for a rule or directive to have legitimate authority and then, perhaps, not even a necessary condition. At least, this is the case if we accept that mistaken directives, rules, or decisions can sometimes have authority and thus generate an obligation to obey. Pending a more thorough discussion of this possibility, it appears sensible to draw a bright line between the rationality and legitimacy conditions.

The second point is that, although the question tackled here—can rationally indeterminate judicial decisions (those resting upon a choice between incommensurable values) be legitimate?—appears disarmingly simple, no easy answer is available. This is because the question brings in its wake at least two others separable only in a heuristic sense: conceptually, what does the notion of authority entail? Normatively, how, exactly, can authority be justified?[58] Answering these conceptual and normative questions will prove even more difficult if jurists and philosophers disagree about the contours of the concept of, and the best justification for, legitimate authority.

---

[58] For Raz's treatment of the relationship between the two questions see *MF*, 62–6.

There are indeed many accounts of legitimacy compatible with non-sceptical accounts of law and adjudication which constraints of time and space dictate cannot be considered. Moreover, other considerations also reduce the list of candidates for consideration.[59] So, for example, Dworkin's account of authority is significantly incomplete. He aims to move the notion of fraternal or associative obligation up the agenda of political and legal philosophy and to show that notion can support an obligation to obey the law. This is laudable since it 'asks those who challenge the very possibility of political legitimacy to broaden their attack and either deny all associative obligations or show why political obligation cannot be associative. It asks those who defend legitimacy to test their claims on a new and expanded field of argument' (*LE*, 207). But the incompleteness of the argument is evident at this precise spot, for the link between associative obligations and the obligation to obey the law appears problematic.

Demonstrating this does not require a denial of either the existence or importance of associative obligations, such as those that arise by virtue of family or religious or geographical ties, as well as those arising from other roles agents may occupy. It is undoubtedly the case that few if any of these obligations are fully consensual and therefore unlikely that their binding power derives from agents' choices. However, it seems that these obligations are qualitatively different from those involved in the obligation to obey the law of the contemporary state: between adults, fraternal obligations rarely, if ever, come with great coercive capacity attached. Failure to comply with one's fraternal obligations does not by definition trigger the coercive apparatus of the state, though it might of course lead to some informal sanction within the group or community in which the obligation holds. One's obligation to obey the law, though, is in principle an obligation with coercion attached. This is not to say that whenever one fails to discharge that obligation coercion always follows: nothing could be further from the truth in contemporary societies. But it is to say that in principle such coercion can always follow, by definition. For what marks the law and the obligation it claims as distinctive in our practical reasoning is its pre-emptory demand—backed up by force—for obedience. The law rarely comes to us in the form of conditional requests—'if you don't mind, please drive at 30 m.p.h.'—with no sanction attached.

The point is that the obligation to obey brings in its wake a more dangerous and threatening range of coercive power than that which exists within fraternal contexts. There is no need to pretend that force and coercion do not exist in fraternal contexts: we know of monstrosities carried out in families, often in the name of filial

[59] Habermas's account of legitimacy can be ruled out as being overambitious. In itself, of course, ambition is not a fault, but the range of Habermas's account of legitimacy, drawing as it does on the whole corpus of his work in social, political and moral philosophy, is such that it cannot be adequately dealt with here. Indeed, Habermas's discussion generates some difficult snags peripheral to present concerns, such as the true degree of similarity between his and Dworkin's work, and the effort to either reconstruct or simply just find his reasons for refusing to distinguish between rationality and legitimacy conditions: see n. 3 above, chs. 5 and 6.

or related obligation. Yet taken in the round, the power available to the state appears much more pervasive and threatening, and the option of exit much more difficult to access. Although it is often said that one can pick one's friends but not one's family, it needs also be noted that it is easier to escape or even change one's family than it is to avoid the coercive power of the state. Hence, while fraternal obligation is clearly an important feature of our life, and has coercive aspects, the attempt to justify or even explain political obligation by reference to it overlooks a very significant difference between them.

Philip Soper's case for authority is incomplete because it does not generate a prima-facie plausible account of the nature of the obligation to obey the law. He holds 'the features that should be sufficient to establish political obligation . . . are (1) the fact that the enterprise of law in general—including the particular system, defective though it may be, that confronts an individual—is better than no law at all; and (2) a good faith effort by those in charge to govern in the interests of the entire community, including the dissenting individual'.[60] As to the second feature, '[i]t is the claim of justice, rather then [sic] justice in fact' that is significant.[61] Soper's problem is making the transition from either of these claims to the claim that there is indeed an obligation to obey. It seems that both claims can be accepted yet the question whether there is an obligation to obey not be answered affirmatively. Some think the most Soper establishes is that the existence of a legal directive is one factor, among others, impinging upon the process of practical reasoning. It can influence our decision whether or not to act in a particular way but does not give us a protected or exclusionary reason for action.[62] And, if legal directives do not generate a reason of the latter type, how, then, can they be said to generate an obligation?

Beyond this difficulty, further analysis of Soper's position discloses that two arguments might generate the supposed obligation to obey. One is a duty deriving from the fact that a job needs to be done—the job of authoritative co-ordination—and, since the makers of legal directives are doing that job in good faith, we should obey them. The other is a duty not to frustrate and upset people who are doing their best. If the makers of legal directives are doing their best, in good faith, then we should obey them. Yet neither argument on its own looks compelling nor is it clear that they can be consistently combined. Finally, note that each argument supporting the obligation to obey only has weight, on Soper's account, if it is indeed true that the enterprise of law is in general better than no law. Soper assumes this, but he does not seem

[60] P. Soper, *A Theory of Law* (Cambridge, Mass.: Harvard University Press, 1984), 80. Soper has developed his account and defended it against some critics in, *inter alia*, 'Legal Theory and the Claim of Authority', *Philosophy and Public Affairs*, 18 (1989), 209–37 and 'The Moral Value of Law', *Michigan Law Review*, 84 (1986), 63–86.

[61] Soper, *A Theory*, p. 55.

[62] The argument put here is developed by J. Raz, 'The Morality of Obedience', *Michigan Law Review*, 83 (1985), 732–49 and S. Burton, 'Law, Obligation, and a Good Faith Claim of Justice', *California Law Review*, 73 (1985), 1956–83. The points made in the remainder of this paragraph are all derived from Raz's essay.

to appreciate the problematic nature of the assumption. It might look reasonable if the deck is stacked against a reasonable and pacifist anarchism by assuming, as Soper often does, that the options here are either law or the most solitary, most nasty, and most brutish state of nature. This contrast is hardly tenable. As we know from legal anthropologists, the distinction is better put in terms of 'formal' legal regulation and protection as opposed to 'informal' social customs and norms. A choice between these two possibilities is unlikely to be obviously and always made in favour of the former.

4.2 Modified Conventionalism

What of the remaining accounts of legitimacy? Our focus is restricted to the accounts of authority offered by Raz and MacCormick, the reason being that their work on adjudication made an analysis of the legitimacy condition necessary. They do not agree on every aspect of the nature of and justification for authority. In particular, MacCormick does not share Raz's account of the nature of the reasons for action that authorities generate, although the grounds of this disagreement have yet to be thoroughly unpacked.[63] However, both offer similar accounts of authority in that they regard as crucial to the justification of authority an alleged authority's capacity to solve co-ordination or co-operation problems. Note, though, that MacCormick's remarks on authority court a problem Raz avoids. It is that the argument from capacity to solve co-ordination or co-operation problems—let us, following standard practice, call such accounts of the nature and justification of authority 'conventionalist'—invites a number of objections which MacCormick does nothing to quell.[64]

By contrast, Raz's account of authority avoids the snags ensnaring standard conventionalist accounts by amending one of their crucial features. His account should therefore be labelled modified conventionalism. 'Conventionalism', because it shares two features with standard conventionalist accounts of authority, namely, an emphasis upon the role of practical authorities in solving co-ordination problems and the claim that the content of the solutions to such problems—their substantive rightness or wrongness—does not always determine their success *qua* solutions. 'Modified',

[63] MacCormick's objection is reported in his review of *MF*: 'Access to the Goods', *Times Literary Supplement*, 5 June 1987, 599.

[64] Standard conventionalist accounts of the nature of and justification for authority invoke game-theoretical conceptions of co-ordination problems, Prisoner's Dilemmas and their solutions. They are expertly discussed and criticized by L. Green, 'Authority and Convention', *Philosophical Quarterly*, 35 (1985), 329–46. Neither standard nor modified conventionalist accounts of authority should be confused with the interpretation of law Dworkin calls conventionalism: see *LE*, ch. 4. MacCormick's support for conventionalist accounts of authority is found in: *Legal Right and Social Democracy* (Oxford: Clarendon Press, 1982), 76–80; 'Contemporary Legal Philosophy', n. 41 above, p. 10; and 'Legal Reasoning and Practical Reason', *Midwest Studies in Philosophy*, 7 (1982), 271–86, 281–2.

because the notion of a co-ordination problem is here understood in a non-standard way.

Modified conventionalism is an account of practical and not theoretical authority. That is, it concentrates upon the nature of and justification for authorities that purport to generate reasons for action and not, or not exclusively, those that generate reasons for beliefs. This is to deny neither that reasons for action and for belief can be closely related nor that there are degrees of overlap between theoretical and practical authority.[65] For example, the authoritative directive 'do X' is, of course, reason to believe that an authority has issued that directive and a meteorological expert's statement that it will rain is reason to take one's umbrella. But it is quite possible that some reasons for belief have no impact whatsoever on the reasons for action agents have. Reasons to believe that there is a ninth planet in the solar system will have little or no influence on the practical reasoning of agents who are not in the least interested in astronomy. According to Raz, practical authority impacts upon agents' practical reasoning in a dramatic way: for a person or group to have practical authority over another involves having 'a right to rule, where that is understood as correlated with an obligation to obey on the part of those subject to the authority' (*MF*, 23). This right to rule creates obligations to act independently of one's calculation of the merits or demerits of the action in question. Authoritative utterances are, for agents subject to them, exclusionary reasons: that is, 'reasons for not acting on the balance of reasons as they see it, even when they are right'.[66] Of course, this does not rule out agents' determining what they think is required on the balance of reasons. Rather, it rules out agents' compliance with authoritative directives being conditional upon their weighing of the reasons pro and con.

Moreover, the reasons that an authority acts upon are, in an important sense, reasons applicable to the agents subject to authority. So, although agents subject to authority ought to do as the authority says just because the authority says so, this directive is the result of the authority's weighing of reasons that are applicable to the agents themselves. When an authority says 'do X', that 'is not . . . just another reason to be added to the others when one reckons which way [doing X or not X] is better supported by reason. The . . . [authority's] decision is meant to be based on the other reasons, to sum them up and to reflect their outcome' (*MF*, 41). Hence, authoritative directives generate reasons that are also 'dependent reasons' (ibid.), where what is meant is that those directives are based upon the authority's assessment of the reasons for and against the conduct, those reasons being applicable to agents and authority alike. In addition, authoritative decisions and directives are 'pre-emptive reasons' in the sense that they 'replace the reasons on which . . . [they] depend [. . . :] [t]he point is that reasons that could have been relied upon to justify action before

    65   For Raz's thoughts on the relationship see pp. 2–3, 4–5 and 9–10 of the introduction to J. Raz (ed.), *Authority* (Oxford: Basil Blackwell, 1990).
    66   Raz, *Practical Reason and Norms*, n. 42 above, p. 64. Raz offers further thoughts on exclusionary reasons in the postscript, pp. 178–99.

... [the] decision cannot be relied upon once the decision is given' (*MF*, 42). Within agents' practical reasoning the authority's decision takes the place of those reasons. It is therefore not merely one reason for an action to be taken in conjunction with the other reasons for that action.

The way in which authority can be justified, according to Raz, is through 'the normal justification thesis'.[67] It holds that

the normal way to establish that a person has authority over another person involves showing that the alleged subject is likely better to comply with reasons which apply to him (other than the alleged authoritative directives) if he accepts the directives of the alleged authority as authoritatively binding and tries to follow them, rather than by trying to follow the reasons that apply to him directly. (*MF*, 53)

Clearly, this way of justifying authority works only if it is true, first, that authorities invoke dependent reasons and, secondly, that authorities are indeed better placed than agents subject to them to recognize the reasons agents have for acting. It need not be the case that authorities, to be justified, must *always* be better able than agents to determine the reasons agents have. Rather

[a]n authority is justified ... if it is *more likely than its subjects* to act correctly for right reasons ... If every time a directive is mistaken, i.e. every time it fails to reflect reason correctly, it were open to challenge as mistaken, the advantage gained by accepting the authority as a more reliable and successful guide to right reason would disappear. (*MF*, 61; emphasis added)

Authorities do not have to be infallible in order to be legitimate.

In what instances are authorities better placed than agents themselves to determine the reasons agents have for acting? The most obvious instance will be that in which the authority is not just a practical but also a theoretical authority. In this situation the authority's expertise will by definition ensure that it is in a better position than agents to determine which reasons are and are not applicable. Another, more complex, situation in which an authority may be better placed to determine the reasons applicable to agents than agents themselves is that in which co-ordination between agents is necessary to ensure that certain benefits are obtained.[68] In this situation the authority must be better than agents are at determining both when problems of co-ordination exist and how they can be solved. Co-ordination here is not to be thought of in technical, game-theoretical terms but as a common-sense idea understood thus.[69] Co-ordination 'means getting people to act in ways which are sensitive to the way others are guided, or are likely, to act, so that benefits can be

[67] There are, according to Raz, other 'secondary' arguments that can in some circumstances be used in addition to, and, rarely, instead of, the normal justification thesis to justify authority: *MF*, 80–99. These arguments—invoking, *inter alia*, the idea of consent—are not examined here because they have no obvious role in relation to indeterminate judicial decisions.

[68] These examples and much of the next two paragraphs are informed by Raz's discussion in 'Facing Up', n. 43 above, pp. 1179–94.

[69] Game-theoretical conceptions of co-ordination problems and their solutions, which are the fulcrum of standard conventionalism, must be avoided by Raz and others, such as John Finnis, because the

expected which are less likely if they act without co-ordinating their efforts, i.e., with-out basing their own actions on a view as to how others should or are likely to act'.[70] Co-ordination in this sense can be desirable for at least two reasons. First, it can ensure that a good that would be lost were agents to try to bring it about without co-ordinating their efforts will be achieved. Secondly, although co-ordination may not make a difference to the achievement or not of a particular good (e.g. because a minority can bring it about), it is nevertheless desirable that all agents co-ordinate and contribute to bringing about the good for reasons of justice or morality (e.g. it is unfair for the minority to take up the burden of bringing about the good even though they can).

Note that in this second situation the claim that authorities may be better than agents at knowing when the need for co-ordination arises and how that need should be fulfilled is based upon both an authority's expertise (or theoretical authority) and agents' weakness or lack of expertise. Raz imagines agents reasoning thus:

[k]nowing the limits of my knowledge and understanding, and being aware of the danger that my judgement will be affected by bias, and my performance by the weakness of my resolve, I am aware of the possibility that another person, or organisation, might be better able to judge when there are strong or sufficient reasons for social co-ordination in which I should partici-pate.[71]

If that other person or organization is free from bias and is of stronger will than the agent, then there is good reason to follow its directives:

[i]n such a case I should adopt a rule to follow the instructions of such a person or body, to regard them as authorities within certain specified bounds. The rule will be justified by the fact that following it will lead me to participate in justified co-ordinated social behaviour more reliably than if I should try to decide for myself when the conditions of a co-ordination problem exist, and when I should follow a certain course of conduct as a way of participating in a justified co-ordinative practice.[72]

Now if it is the case that many people are in the position of this particular agent, then they have a reason to adopt a general co-ordinative practice to adopt the directives of a certain body within certain limits. For doing so allows all

to establish and preserve co-ordinative practices which would otherwise evade . . . [their] grasp. The reason is that by sharing the knowledge that . . . all [have] assigned to this body the

---

properties of such problems and their solutions are such as to make authority unnecessary. It has also been persuasively argued that justifications of authority premised upon game-theoretical accounts of co-ordination problems cannot account for some features of most legal systems: see L. Green, n. 64 above and his 'Law, Co-ordination and the Common Good', *Oxford Journal of Legal Studies*, 3 (1983), 299–324. See also J. Finnis, 'Law as Co-ordination', *Ratio Juris*, 2 (1989), 97–104, esp. 99–101. Kenneth Himma has raised some serious doubts as to whether, given the very modified nature of Raz's modified conventionalism, it is appropriately regarded as a conventionalist account of authority at all. I persist with the terminology here simply to avoid both creating another set of labels and a long reconstruction (or re-translation) of the existing terminology.

[70] 'Facing Up', n. 43 above, p. 1189.   [71] ibid. 1192.   [72] ibid.

power to decide . . when co-ordination problems . . . exist and the responsibility to make generally known its proposed solutions, . . [they] solve the problem of making sure [that co-ordination problems are recognized and resolved].[73]

Raz calls rules that set up a person or body as capable of authoritatively determining whether or not there is a co-ordination problem and, if there is, what should be done in response to it, 'second order co-ordinative practices'. Such 'rules justify the legitimacy of an authority . . . in accordance with the normal justification thesis. They enable all of us to solve co-ordination problems better than we might when we try to judge for ourselves whether there is a co-ordination problem and whether the . . . conditions for its solution are met'.[74]

Does modified conventionalism show that the state, its government, and its legal system can be, and sometimes or perhaps always are, legitimate? In particular, can it serve to confer legitimacy on judicial decisions that fail to satisfy the stringent rationality condition? An affirmative answer to the first, general question would make providing an affirmative answer to the second, specific question a reasonably easy task. It would, however, be a mistake to think that an affirmative answer to the first question entails an affirmative answer to the second. That is because it would be quite coherent to claim that the legal system of a particular state is, on the whole, legitimate, except for those parts of it constituted by judge-made law. (The plausibility of this claim would, of course, depend upon the definition and amount of 'judge-made law' within the jurisdiction in question.) Nevertheless, if a general argument can be provided showing under what circumstances legal systems can be and sometimes are legitimate, then an important part of the task of attempting to show the legitimacy of rationally indeterminate judicial decisions within particular legal systems has been accomplished.

Unfortunately, modified conventionalism does not provide an affirmative answer to the general question. Modified conventionalism 'denies the existence of a *general* obligation to obey the law even in a reasonably just society' (*MF*, 70; emphasis added). Prima facie, the law of such a society lacks legitimacy. This point should not be exaggerated. Modified conventionalism will indeed generate an obligation to obey the law in some circumstances even though it cannot generate a 'blanket' obligation. This is because the normal justification thesis is responsive to, first, the capacities of both subject and authority to uncover the reasons for action they have and, secondly, the circumstances in which these capacities are exercised. To determine whether or not the state, its legal system or any other institution or person legitimately has authority,

[t]he test is . . . : does following the authority's instructions improve conformity with reason? For every person the question has to be asked afresh, and for every one it has to be asked in a manner which admits of various qualifications. An expert pharmacologist may not be subject to the authority of the government in matters of the safety of drugs, an inhabitant of a little

---

[73] ibid.   [74] ibid. 1193.

village by a river may not be subject to its authority in matters of navigation and conservation of the river by the banks of which he has spent all his life. (*MF*, 74)

So, although it is the case that there is no general obligation to obey the law, particular agents may have an obligation to obey particular laws in particular circumstances. Furthermore, if there is a particular kind of situation that affects many agents—for example, when collective action is subject to co-ordination problems—and in which: (i) the state is better at recognizing the reasons agents have for acting than agents themselves; and (ii) is able, through a particular law or corpus of laws, both to tell agents that and to announce a solution to the problem, then in those circumstances the state and its law are legitimate.

Even if we take this as an albeit circumscribed affirmative answer to the general question, a number of other questions must be answered affirmatively before it can be maintained that indeterminate judicial decisions are legitimate. These other questions are: can indeterminate judicial decisions generate exclusionary reasons for action? Can the reasons they generate be dependent and pre-emptive? And, finally, can they satisfy the normal justification thesis? In what follows, the latter question is the focus while the other two are overlooked. This is not because they are unimportant. Rather, formulating an answer to the third question sheds a good deal of light upon the others since they overlap. If, therefore, there is—as the argument that follows seeks to show—doubt as to whether the third question can be answered in the affirmative, then answers to the other questions might become redundant.

Indeterminate judicial decisions might satisfy the normal justification thesis in three ways. The first two—the direct and indirect arguments—are fairly obvious and are related while the third is independent of them and quite ambitious. Although the third (fallibility) argument is not a success, it requires rather more elucidation than the other two. The direct argument would show that the general class or particular instances of indeterminate judicial decisions and the directives that issue from them (decision in favour of *A* for reasons *e*, *f* and *g*; therefore damages in the amount of £x to be paid by *B* to *A*) function so as to allow agents subject to them to comply with the reasons they have for acting more effectively than they would were they to try to determine those reasons for themselves. The indirect argument attempts to demonstrate that either a particular judicial decision and directive or a general class thereof serve to show that the parties and those affected by the dispute: (i) were in the grip of a co-ordination problem that they were unaware of; and (ii) that they had reason to co-operate which they were either unaware of or incapable of realizing. If, furthermore, the decision and directive solved the co-ordination problem by ensuring actual co-operation between the parties to the dispute and those affected by it, then the normal justification thesis must have been satisfied. The fallibility argument holds that the reasons modified conventionalism uses to show that mistaken directives are authoritative can be used to show that indeterminate judicial decisions and the directives that flow from them are also authoritative. In order to do justice to these arguments they will be treated separately.

4.2.1 *The Direct Argument*

This argument maintains that indeterminate judicial decisions can satisfy the legitimacy condition in an immediate way, by simply directing the parties in dispute to the reasons that are applicable to them but which they have, for one reason or another, failed to perceive. To be plausible this argument must assume that the parties either do not know they have reasons for action or are unaware that the reasons for action they have and the values that generate them are incommensurate. If this assumption is not made, then an indeterminate judicial decision cannot possibly satisfy the normal justification thesis. Remember that for present purposes an indeterminate judicial decision is one that rests upon a choice between two or more incommensurables. When faced with a choice between incommensurables 'reason is indeterminate. It provides no better case for one alternative than for the other' (*MF*, 333). Now if the parties in dispute know this, how can an indeterminate judicial decision enable them 'better to comply with the reasons which apply to ... [them]' (*MF*, 53) than if they did not accept the decision?

The answer is that it cannot. It merely repeats what the parties already know, namely, that the reasons and values applicable to them are incommensurable. By contrast, where the parties are unaware either of the existence or of the nature of the reasons and values applicable to them, an indeterminate judicial decision that highlights one or other of these facts allows the parties better to comply with the reasons and values applicable to them. It may be thought, though, that where the decision merely highlights the nature of the reasons applicable to the parties by showing that they are incommensurable, the normal justification thesis will not be satisfied. For in this situation the decision cannot be said to make the parties better able *to comply* with reason because, in highlighting the incommensurability of reasons, the decision does not facilitate compliance with them. Rather, it only highlights their nature. However, this objection is misguided in so far as a proper understanding of the nature of the reasons applicable to one is a necessary prerequisite to acting upon, and hence complying with, those reasons.

The conclusion that, in order for indeterminate judicial decisions to satisfy the normal justification thesis, the parties to the dispute must be ignorant in the two senses noted, could be objected to on another, apparently more compelling, ground. It might be maintained, for example, that the discussion so far has concentrated upon the judicial *decision* to the exclusion of the *directive* that follows from it.[75] And that, of course, is rarely ambiguous even though the decision from which it flows is

---

[75] W. Edmundson has drawn a distinction along similar lines, but with quite different consequences. He argues there is no obligation to obey the law (which would, presumably include judicial decisions) but that there is a duty to refrain from frustrating the performance of administrative prerogatives (the actions of those acting under the law, like police officers, representatives of the court, etc., implementing the law). The central snag here is maintaining the distinction between actions and omissions or refrainings, on which Edmundson's argument depends. Since it is very often the case that actions can be

not compelled by reason. It could be said, furthermore, that the directive can satisfy the normal justification thesis even though the decision does not and even though the parties know that their dispute is one based upon a conflict of incommensurable reasons or values. How? There seem to be only two possibilities here. The first holds that the directive simply brings the dispute to an end and in so doing satisfies the normal justification thesis because there are good reasons, applicable to the parties, to resolve the dispute. The directive can do this even when the parties in dispute know that the reasons and values applicable to them are incommensurable and that they are beset by a co-ordination problem they have good reasons to avoid. For in this situation the parties could nevertheless be in dispute about the best way in which to solve the problem and it is that dispute the directive curtails. However, there is a snag that besets this response. It can be briefly stated in the form of a question: if there are good reasons to bring the dispute to an end—and hence to make a choice and issue a directive one way rather than another—is the dispute really between incommensurables? Since this snag also besets versions of the indirect argument it will be examined in the following subsection.

The second possibility modifies the first by insisting that the parties are *unwittingly* in the thrall of a co-ordination problem. It then holds that the directive which flows from the indeterminate judicial decision satisfies the normal justification thesis because it *solves* a co-ordination problem the parties did not perceive or could not resolve and which they had good reasons to overcome (there being good reasons to co-operate). Since this response invokes the authority's greater ability at spotting and solving co-ordination disputes, it is in fact an indirect justificatory argument and best treated in the following subsection. As will be seen, it succumbs to the disabling problem that besets all versions of the indirect argument. Are there any other ways in which a directive that issues from an indeterminate judicial decision could satisfy the normal justification thesis? If we assume that the parties to the dispute know the nature of the reasons applicable to them and in play in the dispute, then it is difficult to imagine an affirmative answer.

4.2.2 *The Indirect Argument*

This argument holds that indeterminate judicial decisions and the directives flowing from them satisfy the normal justification thesis by identifying and solving co-ordination problems. Such decisions and directives identify the reasons the parties in dispute have to act—the reasons, that is, they have for co-operating—and direct the parties how co-operation can be facilitated. For this argument to be plausible at least

re-described as refrainings and vice versa, and it is likely that the distinction is not written into our notion of causality but rather a consequence of normative positions, his argument looks problematic. See his *Three Anarchical Fallacies: An Essay on Political Authority* (Cambridge: Cambridge University Press, 1998), chs. 1–3. Although occasionally aware of the slipperiness of action/refraining distinction, he appears unaware of the difficulty it poses for his argument: see e.g. pp. 50–6.

two hurdles must be cleared. I sketch the grounds for thinking these hurdles might be surmounted and conclude that, even if they are, this argument cannot demonstrate that indeterminate judicial decisions satisfy the normal justification thesis without denying the existence of incommensurability. In seeking to avail themselves of this indirect argument, strong value pluralists therefore face an uncomfortable dilemma. Its horns are these: either apparently indeterminate judicial decisions satisfy the normal justification thesis by recognizing and solving co-ordination problems, but in so doing serve to deny incommensurability; or they do not satisfy the normal justification thesis, in which case they lack legitimacy.

The first hurdle is that it must be appropriate to regard the parties' dispute—a dispute rooted in incommensurability of reasons and values—as a co-ordination problem. In the ordinary (not game-theoretical) sense that means the dispute, whether the parties know it or not, is about identifying the ways in which they should co-ordinate their action in order to obtain benefits that would not, in absence of co-operation, be forthcoming. It is not difficult to imagine how disputes rooted in incommensurability create co-ordination problems. Where the reasons and values applicable to the parties are incommensurable, then they do not have compelling reasons to prefer one reason or value to another. The parties therefore lack compelling reason to act one way (e.g. so as to bring about co-operation) or the other (so as to thwart co-operation). Now, it cannot be said in advance of an examination of the structure of particular disputes rooted in incommensurability that they will all satisfy this condition. But, given that the condition is not a demanding one, it is not reckless to assume that it will often be satisfied. When it is, the claim is that indeterminate judicial decisions rooted in incommensurability, or the directive flowing from them, solve the co-ordination problems to which incommensurability gives rise.

However, such decisions and directives must do a little more than that. They must surmount a second hurdle and actually fulfil the normal justification thesis. Doing that requires the decisions and directives dissipate the parties ignorance of one or more of the following facts: (i) the fact that the reasons and values in play in their dispute are incommensurable; (ii) the fact that they are beset by a co-ordination problem; (iii) the fact that they have good reason to overcome that co-ordination problem. If the parties to the dispute are ignorant of one of these facts, then it is more than likely that they will also be ignorant of one or more of the others. Similarly, if the parties are aware of one—for example, that their dispute rests upon incommensurability—then they will surely be aware of one or more of the others: in this example, that incommensurability is one important consideration preventing them from co-operating and hence bringing them into dispute. It just does not seem plausible that the parties could be aware of incommensurability but unaware of the fact that they are beset by a co-ordination problem or vice versa. Were it the case that the parties in dispute know some or all of these facts, an indeterminate judicial decision would merely reiterate that point. It tells the parties what they already know and is therefore incapable of satisfying the normal justification thesis. For how can an indeterminate judicial *decision*, one that rests upon incommensurability and the co-ordination problem it generates, both of which the parties already know about, allow the parties better to comply with reason?

An objection that does not reject the normal justification thesis could be made to the direction the discussion of this second hurdle has taken. It begins by noting that the *directive* that flows from the indeterminate judicial decision has been overlooked. It claims that this directive can satisfy the normal justification thesis even when the decision does not and even when the parties know the applicable reasons are incommensurable and that they are beset by a co-ordination problem. For the directive *solves* the problem: the directive forces the parties to co-operate because they have good reasons to do so. Since the directives that flow from judicial decisions rarely say 'do either *X* or *Y* or *Z*' but generally state unambiguously that one action must be taken or refrained from, they seem admirably suited to solving co-ordination problems. They unambiguously direct the parties how to act. If that way of acting solves the co-ordination problem and there are good reasons to want that—reasons found in the good of, or good that flows from, co-operation—then the normal justification thesis is undoubtedly satisfied.

This objection is instructive, but for what its proponents would surely regard as the wrong reasons. For it serves to show not that the indirect argument works but instead that, whether it relates to judicial decisions or directives, it must in this context fail. Why? Recall that the basis of the disputes in question is incommensurability of reasons and values. Further, that is why the parties in dispute face a co-ordination problem. Remember also that when the choice between reasons and values is incommensurable, then it is a choice not compelled by reason: 'incommensurability speaks not of what does escape reason but of what must elude it' (*MF*, 334). The indirect argument surely denies this. In order to satisfy the normal justification thesis, the indirect argument must show that the parties in dispute have good reason to co-operate, or that they have missed the fact that they are beset by a co-ordination problem and there are good reasons to co-operate. Those reasons are found in the benefit or good that flows from co-operation or which is internal to it. Are these good reasons to co-operate also good reasons to choose one value or to act upon one reason, on one side of an incommensurable choice, rather than the value and reason on the other side?

The situation we are imagining is one in which (i) the parties are in dispute because the reasons and values applicable to them are incommensurable; and (ii) the parties are beset by a co-ordination problem by virtue of that incommensurability. If there are good reasons for avoiding the co-ordination problem in (ii), reasons found in the good inherent in or flowing from co-operation and highlighted either by the judicial decision or directive, then there must be good reasons for exercising the choice in (i) one way. The choice in (i) is allegedly between incommensurable reasons and values—incommensurability is supposedly the basis of the parties' disagreement.

But if reasons exist to solve the co-ordination problem in (ii), which is based on the supposed incommensurability in (i), surely they also constitute reasons to resolve the choice in (i) one way rather than another. It therefore appears that the choice (i) is not after all between incommensurables but is a choice compelled by reasons. The choice only temporarily eluded reason and then presumably as a result of oversight. A possible response to this is that the reasons for resolving the co-ordination dispute in (ii) are quite independent of the incommensurable reasons and values in play in (i). Therefore, the reasons the parties have to co-operate are not capable of affecting the choice in (i) in any way. But if this is so, it seems that the practical impact of incommensurability will be almost non-existent in such situations, since the reasons to co-operate in (ii) will hold. The fact that incommensurability operates in (i) will matter not a jot if the parties always have reasons to co-operate. In addition, the effort to draw a bright line between the reasons to co-operate in (ii) and the allegedly incommensurable choice in (i) seems artificially rigid and untrue to experience, where reasons often have a wide sphere of influence.

The conclusion here is that versions of the indirect argument fail. This is because one crucial feature of the choice situation is that disputes and decisions are premised upon incommensurability. Indirect arguments do not work because they either end up denying that feature or invoke an artificial and compartmentalized account of the role of reasons. Moreover, indirect arguments fail for these reasons whether their proponents have in mind indeterminate judicial decisions or the directives that flow from them.

4.2.3 *The Fallibility Argument*

This argument raises the following question in the hope that the answer to it is equally applicable to indeterminate judicial decisions and directives: why are mistaken directives authoritative? We have already noted that modified conventionalism makes conceptual room for mistaken but supposedly authoritative directives. We need to examine how this is possible. If it is possible, and if the same reasons that make mistaken directives authoritative can also serve to make indeterminate judicial decisions and the directives that flow from them authoritative, then strong value pluralism and the legitimacy condition can both be affirmed without difficulty.

The first task is to get clear about the ways in which supposedly authoritative directives can be mistaken. From Raz's discussion it seems that there are three ways. One such mistake ensures that the directive can have no authority at all: '[m]istakes which ... [authorities] make about factors which determine the limits of their jurisdiction render their directives void. They are not binding as authoritative directives ...' (*MF*, 62). Such mistakes can henceforth be ignored. The other two kinds of mistake are not explicitly distinguished and labelled by Raz but his remarks are such as to show that he does implicitly draw a distinction and that he is (although he may not recognize it) committed to treating the two types of mistake in very different ways. An objection to Raz's account of authority holds that a directive based upon a mistake about the reasons justifying the directive is robbed of its authority.

Raz responds thus: '[r]easons which authoritative directives should, but fail to, reflect are none the less among the reasons which justify holding the directive binding' (*MF*, 61). The type of mistake Raz has in mind here is what can be called an *Ealing* mistake: there is a good directive, in the sense that there are good reasons for it, based upon a mistaken assessment of its justifying reasons. That is, the authority issues a directive in the belief that it is justified by reasons *Q* when in fact only reasons *U* can justify the directive. Since, let us suppose, reasons *U* obtain, we are faced with a situation that can crudely be described as one in which we have the right directive justified by the wrong reasons, there being good reasons available. Raz thinks that in this situation the directive can be authoritative and, if it is, it must satisfy the normal justification thesis. The second kind of mistake we can call a *Wednesbury* mistake. Here an authority issues a directive that is mistaken in the sense that there are no good reasons for it at all: this situation can be characterized, albeit crudely, as consisting of the wrong directive and the wrong reasons.[76] Raz seems to have such a scenario in mind when he imagines a 'legitimate authority . . . [being] limited by the condition that its directives are not binding if *clearly wrong*' (*MF*, 62; emphasis added). Somewhat strangely, Raz completes this remark with the caveat that 'I wish to express no opinion on whether it is so limited' (ibid.). He does not consider whether or not such directives could satisfy the normal justification thesis.

What reasons does Raz have to support the claim that *Ealing* directives satisfy the normal justification thesis? There are two, his argument beginning with a statement of the thesis and ending with a warning about losing its advantages:

An authority is justified . . . if it is more likely than its subjects to act correctly for the right reasons. That is how the subjects' reasons figure in the justification, both when they are correctly reflected in a particular directive and when they are not. If every time a directive is mistaken, i.e. every time it fails to reflect reason correctly, it were open to challenge as mistaken, the advantage gained by accepting the authority as a more reliable and successful guide to right reason would disappear. (*MF*, 61)

Now this restatement of the normal justification thesis seems intended to illustrate the point that an authority need not *always* be a better assessor of the right reasons applicable to agents than agents themselves are. Hence, in a number of cases the authority will be wrong. How does this establish that wrong directives are authoritative? The argument shows merely that, if we are satisfied that an authority tracks right reason in the majority of cases, then we ought to accept its authority in the majority

---

[76] The labels are drawn from two English administrative law cases: *Associated Provincial Picture House Ltd. v Wednesbury Corporation* [1948] 1 K.B. 223 (under which a 'wrong' directive based upon the 'wrong' reasons would certainly come to grief) and *R. v Ealing LBC ex p. Times Newspapers Ltd.* (1986) 85 LGR 316 (in which an otherwise justifiable decision was made for the 'wrong' reasons). It would, however, be a mistake to think that there is any straightforward overlap between the types of mistake identified in the text and those that will trigger judicial review of administrative action.

of cases. The most it could establish beyond this is a fairly weak presumption in favour of all the authority's directives. The argument would take the following form: since in the majority of cases the authority tracks right reason and the majority of its directives are therefore authoritative, *all* its directives should be presumed to be authoritative. The reason why this can only be a weak presumption in favour of the authority is obvious—the fact that the authority has tracked right reason in a majority of cases in the past cannot guarantee that it will continue to do so either in the present or the future. So some *Ealing* directives might be taken to be authoritative on the basis of this presumption, but only some and, one must assume, only for a limited time. If the authority is continuously mistaken its directives surely cannot satisfy the normal justification thesis. The fact that this argument falls far short of establishing that all *Ealing* directives are authoritative should not surprise us.[77] For this kind of limited claim fits snugly with Raz's view that there is no general obligation to obey the law. Rather, the existence of any obligation depends, *inter alia*, on the circumstances of both subject and authority (see *MF*, 70 and 74).

Raz's second reason to show that *Ealing* directives are authoritative is also a little shaky. It consists of the truism that when directives are mistaken we will lose the advantage of acting in accordance with an authority. But it is equally true that once an authority issues directives that are *ultra vires*, the advantage of authority is lost. What this amounts to is that when authorities act contrary to the normal justification thesis, their directives lack authority. In that case we will indeed lose the benefits of authority, but avoiding that loss surely cannot justify, under the normal justification thesis, unconditional compliance with mistaken or *ultra vires* directives. So, the most Raz establishes is that some *Ealing* directives might be authoritative because covered by the weak presumption. That is not a secure basis for the claim that all such directives are authoritative.

Were we to consider what a particular *Ealing* directive that fell within the weak presumption must look like in order to convincingly satisfy the normal justification thesis, we would have to return to the two alternative conditions that indeterminate judicial decisions must satisfy. Since these are conditions that any directive must satisfy, one or other of them needs be satisfied by *Ealing* directives. The conditions are: either (i) the directive must function so as to allow agents subject to them to comply with the reasons they have for acting more effectively than they would were they to try to determine those reasons for themselves; or (ii) the directive must show that agents were in the grip of a co-ordination problem they were unaware of, and that they had reasons to co-operate of which they were either unaware or incapable of realizing. Now, in so far as *Ealing* directives are based upon a mistaken account of the

---

[77] For a similar argument that all mistaken directives cannot be taken to be authoritative see: S. Perry, 'Second-Order Reasons, Uncertainty and Legal Theory', *Southern California Law Review*, 62 (1989), 913–94, 933–6. D. Regan also raises the problematic status of mistaken directives at pp. 1030–1 of his essay 'Authority and Value' in the same volume. Raz's reply (n. 43 above) hardly mentions mistaken directives at all.

reasons justifying directives, they cannot completely satisfy the first condition. How can a directive that rests upon such a mistake allow the agents subject to it to comply with the reasons that apply to them more effectively than if they attempted to determine those reasons for themselves? It could do so only in this situation: by invoking reasons not truly applicable to agents, the directive somehow hinted at, or pointed agents in the direction of, reasons truly applicable to them. This is much more likely in the case of *Ealing* as opposed to *Wednesbury* directives because the former direct agents to act in accord with right reason(s), even though the directives are based upon a misunderstanding of that or those reason(s). *Ealing* directives could partially satisfy the second condition in that, though mistaken as to why co-ordination was worthwhile, they could nevertheless solve the co-ordination problem. (If the directive solved the problem and did so because it was based upon an accurate account of the reasons why co-ordination was worthwhile, it would not, *ex hypothesi*, be mistaken.) Hence, even when they fall within the weak presumption *Ealing* directives can only partially satisfy the normal justification thesis.

By contrast, it is unlikely that *Wednesbury* directives could satisfy the normal justification thesis at all. While there are some good reasons available to justify *Ealing* directives, no such reasons support *Wednesbury* directives. So as to be sure that the latter type of mistaken directive does not satisfy the normal justification thesis, consider again the two alternative conditions any directive must satisfy in order to be legitimate. The first condition need not delay us long. Since *Ealing* directives are unlikely to, or will only partially, satisfy it, then there is no hope that *Wednesbury* directives will. If there are no good reasons for the directive, how can it help agents track right reason better than they otherwise would? And, whereas *Ealing* directives can partially satisfy the second condition—they solve the co-ordination problem and ensure co-operation even though they are based upon a misunderstanding of the reasons for co-operation—*Wednesbury* directives cannot. These directives, remember, are wrong, both about the reasons for co-operation and the nature of the directive required to bring about co-operation. The seemingly insurmountable difficulties that ensnare any attempt to show that *Wednesbury* directives satisfy the normal justification thesis make Raz's caveat about 'clearly wrong' directives extremely puzzling. For, it seems that if they are clearly wrong in the *Wednesbury* sense, then they just cannot be legitimate, unless covered by the weak presumption. And the life of the weak presumption will, of course, be much shorter with regard to *Wednesbury* than to *Ealing* directives.

The argument to show that mistaken directives are legitimate is, then, rather limited. Using this argument to show that indeterminate directives are also legitimate is not therefore a promising strategy. Particular mistaken (*Ealing*) directives can only partially satisfy the normal justification thesis and then only if they either fall within the realm of the weak presumption or unintentionally point agents to the reasons applicable to them. So far, it might seem that although weak as a means of establishing the legitimacy of indeterminate judicial decisions and directives, this argument is no weaker than the direct argument. Therefore, it might be thought that the fallibility argument shows that indeterminate judicial decisions and directives are legitimate. This would be a mistake, for the following reason. It consists of highlighting the way in which *Ealing* directives can partially satisfy the normal justification thesis. They do so by solving a co-ordination dispute albeit on the basis of a mistaken account of the reasons why the dispute should be solved (we are faced, remember, with the right directive but the wrong reasons). The crucial point here is that there are, even though the authority has got them wrong, *good reasons* to solve the dispute one way or another. And, as we have noted in our discussion of the indirect argument, if there are good reasons to solve a dispute supposedly based upon incommensurability one way rather than another, that must call into question the fact that we are indeed dealing with a conflict between incommensurables. The difficulty that scuppers the indirect argument arises here also and disables the fallibility argument.

The yield from the direct, indirect, and fallibility arguments is not great. The direct argument can only show that indeterminate judicial decisions and their directives are legitimate when the parties in dispute are misguided about either the existence or nature of the reasons and values applicable to them. It is thus a very limited success, the authority of decisions and directives completely dependent, as is the normal justification thesis in general, upon the knowledge, abilities, and context of the parties to whom they are applicable. By contrast, the indirect and fallibility arguments are not ultimately even partially successful: neither can show that indeterminate judicial decisions are legitimate without denying that those decisions are indeterminate.

The obvious question that now arises is this: why worry about this meagre yield? The content of the answer is different but the overall refrain familiar: part of the sceptical challenge cannot be met or, more accurately, can be met but only in a very limited way. The relevant part of the sceptical challenge is, of course, that which questions the legitimacy of law and adjudication. For sceptics, judicial decisions lack real legitimacy although mechanisms beyond and within the law serve to generate an appearance of legitimacy.[78] In this vein David Kairys observes that '[t]he judge makes a choice, and legal reasoning provides *a stylised rationalisation that legitimates* that choice within the legal and social order'; adjudication is one of the 'many areas of our lives . . . [in which] essentially social and political judgements gain legitimacy from notions of expertise and analysis that *falsely purport* to be objective, neutral, and quasi-scientific'.[79] Similarly, Unger holds that deceit is necessary if judicial decisions are to be regarded as authoritative: '[t]he concealment of . . . assumptions is vital to the *persuasive authority* of the dominant legal ideas; seemingly uncontroversial technical conceptions commonly depend upon highly controversial, nontechnical

[78] See Kelman, n. 8 above, 262–8 and ch. 9.
[79] These two statements—the emphasis is added—are from D. Kairys, 'Law and Politics', *George Washington Law Review*, 52 (1984), 243–62, 246 and *The Politics of Law*, n. 29 above, p. 17.

premises'. The legitimacy of these assumptions cannot stand the light of day: they are 'made controversial if not implausible in the very process of being exposed'.[80]

As we have seen, non-sceptics can show that the legitimacy condition is satisfied only in very limited circumstances. This, of course, is an answer to the sceptics but it is not as powerful as could be hoped. It could be maintained that this is not really a cause for worry, since legal systems in which indeterminate judicial decisions exist may well satisfy the normal justification thesis even though those particular decisions do not. This strategy insists, as Raz himself sometimes does, that it is not individual directives which should be tested for legitimacy but the overall legal system of which they are part. And, it might be said, the system as a whole better enables citizens to track the requirement of right reason(s) than they would if operating under their own lights. This could well be true, but it seems neutral between two possibilities. One has already been mentioned—if a legal system as a whole is legitimate, why worry about those particular instances where it is not? Another is more likely to occupy sceptics: those instances in which a system lacks legitimacy are especially worrying.[81]

5 CONCLUSION

The arguments herein are easily summarized. Sections 1 and 2 served to introduce the rationality and legitimacy conditions and situate them within contemporary sceptical and non-sceptical accounts of adjudication. The remaining two sections were on the whole concerned with non-sceptical accounts of adjudication only. Section 3 argued that non-sceptics who claim incommensurability plays a role in adjudication cannot also claim that adjudication is, in a stringent sense, rational. Section 4 argued that it is difficult to show that rationally indeterminate judicial decisions are legitimate. So what? Failure to show that hard case adjudication is a stringently rational and legitimate process means that a response to the sceptical challenge is hard to come by. This raises a host of questions about the ultimate power and plausibility of that challenge, but we must not overlook the target at which it is aimed. It is the idea that law and adjudication are pre-eminently desirable means of both subjecting human conduct to the governance of rules and of resolving disputes about those rules. The argument here has moved a few steps towards the conclusion that law and adjudication may not be as pre-eminently desirable as often assumed, since they are

---

[80] The two quotations are from Unger, n. 25 above, pp. 88 and 89 respectively. The emphasis is added.

[81] The underlying issue here is that of how Raz's normal justification thesis should be interpreted. It was acutely elucidated for me by Kenneth Himma.

not obviously more rational nor more legitimate than other non-arbitrary means of organizing our collective life and resolving disputes. To be valid, that conclusion depends upon an analysis of the rationality and legitimacy of these other means of organizing life and resolving disputes. Nothing has been said about such matters here. The conclusion that adjudication is in some respects not obviously better than other means of resolving disputes is, in itself, neither liberating nor disturbing. Whether it is viewed one way or the other depends upon the range of expectations we have of law and adjudication and, equally important, the degree of faith we invest in them.

CHAPTER 7

CONSTITUTIONAL AND STATUTORY INTERPRETATION

KENT GREENAWALT

1 INTRODUCTION

STATUTES and constitutions declare legal duties and legal rights. Judges and executive officials must interpret what they provide. Controversy exists about how official interpreters do, and should, perform this task and about how to theorize their practice. This chapter suggests what is relatively settled about statutory and constitutional interpretation, and what is subject to genuine disagreement.

Written constitutions and statutes provide authoritative directions for officials and citizens within liberal democracies (as well as other forms of government). These directions are not merely advisory; others are legally bound to comply. When courts interpret statutes and constitutions, they ordinarily construe a provision that seems directly applicable in accordance with other relevant provisions, related legal doctrines, and legal principles governing interpretation.

In common law countries, one very important principle of law is that courts should follow precedents that they or superior courts have established in earlier cases. Though it could be otherwise, courts follow precedents that concern constitutional and statutory law, as well as judicially developed common law. The doctrine of precedent—with its distinction between holdings that bind and non-binding dictum, and its conditions for overruling—is a vital aspect of statutory and constitutional interpretation. Though I say a few words about precedents in statutory and constitutional cases, I do not explain the practice of precedent, which is treated elsewhere.

Anyone who discusses legal interpretation must face a preliminary question about what constitutes 'interpretation'. I take an inclusive approach, one that fits traditional legal usage; but I should note some narrower possibilities. One approach is that 'interpretation' is not required when the text is clear and decision is simple; it takes place only when decision is difficult.

Another approach is that 'interpretation' involves discerning the original meaning of a statutory or constitutional provision. Other criteria may be relevant to how wise judges should decide cases, but they involve something other than interpretation. According to this account, the question of how a free speech ruling would fit with current practice *might* be relevant to what a court should do, but it would have nothing to do with what the First Amendment means.[1]

Yet a third approach distinguishes between discerning conventional practices and usages of language, for example, determining what lawyers understand by the privilege against self-incrimination, and 'interpreting' the broad significance of a text or practice, deciding how the privilege against self-incrimination relates to basic notions of fairness in the criminal process and to personal autonomy in a free society. Some authors argue that judges rarely interpret in this grander sense;[2] others claim that such interpretation is at the root of what judges do.[3] About this dispute, one can say that what lies on the surface of judicial action in many cases, including some difficult cases, is textual exegesis or the parameters of a settled practice, not interpretation in this deeper sense. In other cases, opinions reveal that judges are assessing the underlying rationale of texts and practices.

A final approach divides the interpretation of concepts from their application. On this view, a determination of whether a legal concept applies or does not apply to a borderline case is not itself a matter of interpretation.

In discussing the bases for judicial decisions, I do not restrict the label 'interpretation' to difficult cases, to inquiries about original meaning, or to evaluations of the deep significance of a text or practice. Also, because the practical import of a concept often depends on the situations to which it is applied, I treat questions of application as aspects of 'interpretation'. Thus, deciding whether a search of an automobile's glove compartment is 'unreasonable' involves interpretation of the constitutional ban on unreasonable searches and seizures.

I do not include as interpretation, however, the discretionary application of concepts that plainly leave a wide range of choice to courts or administrative agencies.

---

[1] See Gary Lawson, 'On Reading Recipes . . . and the Constitution', *Georgetown Law Journal*, 85 (1997), 1823–4.

[2] Dennis Patterson, *Law and Truth* (New York: Oxford University Press, 1996).

[3] Ronald Dworkin, *Law's Empire* (Cambridge, Mass.: Belknap Press, 1986).

Thus, if a statute requires that power companies be able to charge a 'fair rate', an agency or court may set one of a number of rates as 'fair' in the circumstances. The choice of the exact rate to charge is not mainly one of interpreting the statute (though some rates will be precluded by the statute's meaning).

Statutory and constitutional interpretation share commonalities. Both involve the construction of legally authoritative texts. For each, one must puzzle about the relationship between theory and practice. Judges, other officials, lawyers, and scholars interpret statutory and constitutional provisions. Although they must decide whether some materials, such as legislative history, matter for interpretation, they may proceed without any full-blown self-conscious theory that fits together everything they take into account. Numbers of scholars, and some judges, have developed theories, more or less comprehensive, about the point of statutory or constitutional interpretation. These theories explain why various criteria for decision should be given weight. How do such theories relate to desirable practice?

The most sceptical approach to theory of this sort is that it is crude and unhelpful—that judges and critics alike would do better to focus on nuances of the practices in which they are involved, forgoing the presumption of believing that comprehensive theories are insightful and can guide. The most ambitious claims for theory are that it is indispensable for sound decision, that all judges should think carefully about the theoretical justifications for their practice. Among a range of intermediate positions, perhaps the most straightforward is the following. Theory can be valuable and influential over time, but it belongs mainly to scholars and law journals. The performance of most judges, lacking much theoretical training, will not be improved if they try to work through deeper questions about their practice. In their actual decisions, judges will often implicitly side with one theory against another, but at least for many problems of theory, judges need not try to resolve them self-consciously.

People who think carefully about theory and practice will develop nuances in these positions. Judges are better equipped to think about some theoretical issues than others. Certain competing theories have sharply variant practical implications; other competing theories about how to conceptualize what judges do, or should do, have no opposing implications for practice. I avoid the question of just how self-conscious judges and lawyers should be about theoretical inquiries. I assume that efforts to build comprehensive theories can be valuable, that many theoretical disagreements have practical implications, and that over time the acceptance of theories influences practice. But I also assume that many able judges immersed in practice can decide wisely, without self-consciously working out many of the deeper theoretical implications of the choices they make.

One general point about theories of statutory and constitutional interpretation deserves mention. A theorist might distinguish a descriptive account of how judges do interpret statutes within any legal system from an appraisal of how they should interpret. He might, for example, say that in the United States, judges give weight to what actual legislators subjectively intended about the coverage of statutes, but they should not do so. However, descriptive and normative theories connect with each other in critical respects. Within legal systems, people rely to a degree on the continuation of existing practices; reasonable reliance constitutes a strong argument for maintaining prevailing interpretive practices. A second connection between descriptive and normative accounts is that when practices themselves are uncertain or various judges engage in different practices, a theorist may conceptualize present practices in light of what he thinks are sound practices, blurring normative and descriptive elements. Whether this aspect of interpreting practices is inevitable, it is common. Finally, when judges or legal scholars recommend shifts from particular legal practices, they claim support in broader features of the legal and political system. Almost always they say that if one understands the fundamental nature of the system, one will see that the practices they challenge are out of line. Thus, they rely on the system itself—a kind of 'is'—to support an 'ought'—the proposed changes in practice. Thus, threads of 'is' and 'ought' are interwoven in most theories of statutory and constitutional interpretation.

Although statutory and constitutional interpretation resemble each other in many respects, typical instances of the two forms of interpretation differ significantly. The differences concern the authority of constitutional and statutory provisions, the political legitimacy of the bodies enacting them, the generality of the textual language, the age of the provisions, and the ease with which political bodies can override what the courts decide. Any analysis of the two forms of interpretation must attend to these differences. In the United States, constitutional interpretation receives great public attention, and lies close to the heart of our political system. But statutory interpretation is also highly important. More significantly for our purposes, what statutory interpretation involves is less complex than what constitutional interpretation involves. Because the nuances of constitutional interpretation are most easily understood against a background of statutory interpretation, I begin with the latter. But most of the theoretical issues I pose for interpreting statutes have very close analogues in respect to constitutional interpretation.

2 STATUTORY INTERPRETATION

2.1 The General Parameters

Statutory interpretation involves the construction and application of provisions adopted by legislatures. The language of statutes is clear in its import for many circumstances. Citizens, perhaps with the help of simplifying directives or numerical tables, are able to learn their legal duties. Landlords, for example, can find out how many days notice they must give tenants to leave if they wish to take over apartments for their own use. With tax forms, people who have calculated their income know how much income tax they owe. When legal duties are clear, courts usually need not declare them, although judges do instruct juries about legal duties even when the only dispute in a case concerns what factually occurred.

When statutory rights and duties are unclear, courts usually are not the initial interpreters. Private individuals and companies, and their lawyers, decide what they should do and what benefits they may claim from others. Administrative agencies issue detailed regulations implementing more general statutory provisions. Often these agencies also engage in quasi-adjudicative decisions, resolving contested issues before they reach court. But in common law countries, courts are the final inter-preters of what statutes provide. (In many civil law systems, separate courts deal with issues of administrative law, but that is rare in common law systems.)

Among the most fundamental theoretical issues in statutory interpretation are these three: is meaning fixed at enactment or does it evolve? How far is meaning determined by reader understanding, how far by a legislative intent discerned partly by other elements? What is the comparative importance of specific narrow objectives and broader legislative purposes? Accompanying these theoretical questions are related questions about the sources courts should use to determine statutory mean-ing. Similar theoretical issues and questions about sources arise in constitutional interpretation.

The theoretical questions about interpreting statutes and constitutions suggest more general questions about the meaning of human communications; and scholars of philosophy of language, linguistics, literary theory, religious hermeneutics, and other fields discuss analogous issues. Many of them also ask whether the meaning of a communication can change over time, whether original meaning is determined by what a speaker intends or what a listener understands, whether specific objectives, such as allowing the death penalty, matter more than broad purposes, such as elimi-nating cruel punishments. Various answers offered for the most general philosophic questions or for particular fields outside law do not resolve the crucial issues about statutory interpretation. We need to see why.

Many ordinary communications have immediate practical purposes. The speaker wants to convey his thoughts or feelings or to request some action. Communication and response are fleeting in time. Other communications last. What some poets write is read centuries later. People in political authority also issue directives that last.

In ordinary discourse, speakers try to communicate in light of what listeners will understand; listeners apprehend what speakers say in light of what they think the speakers' purposes are. The intent of speakers and the understanding of listeners coa-lesce. But things can go wrong or a communication may be incomplete. Something goes wrong when a speaker's intent differs from how the listener understands his words. A communication is incomplete if it fails to indicate how a subject it covers (in some sense) should be resolved. A simple example of incompleteness would be parents, going out for the evening, who instruct their teenage daughter to go to bed at 11 o'clock when the 9 o'clock movie is over. The parents do not realize that on this night the 9 o'clock movie on television lasts until 12 o'clock. The daughter has to decide whether her parents were mainly concerned about an 11 o'clock bedtime or were willing to have her watch the end of that movie. Suppose the parents actually want her to go to bed at 11 o'clock but the daughter reasonably concludes that, because it is Saturday and her parents have allowed her to stay up until midnight on some other Saturdays, she may watch until 12 o'clock. What did the instructions themselves mean?

One approach to the problems of failure, incompleteness, and endurance over time is that the intention of the speaker, or writer, controls. He communicated; perhaps the communication means what he intended. An alternative approach is that the communication means what a listener would understand it to mean. For this purpose, one might ask about the meanings words typically express or focus on a reasonable listener in this context. On either approach, if the speaker says, 'Shut the door', when he wants a window shut, the speaker's intent is 'Shut the window', but his communication means 'Shut the door' (at least if a door is available to shut). Once we introduce the understanding of listeners or readers, the question arises whether the meaning of a communication can shift over time as readers of later years interpret words written earlier. And, if reader understanding is crucial, what if different readers have different understandings? Analysis becomes more complex still if the writer wants and expects various readers to understand his communication differently. What does such a communication mean?

A theorist might deal with these problems by developing a general theory about the meaning of communications. He would need an account that covers private letters—for which he might be tempted to find that meaning is fixed when the letter is written—and poetry written for a large audience—for which he would be attracted to an idea of meaning that differs with various readers and changes over time. Once our theorist arrived at a general theory about meaning, he would fit statutes into that theory.

We can quickly realize that what might constitute 'meaning' according to some general philosophic theory might not be exactly what courts should regard as controlling for the practical consequences of a legal system, a system in which the state uses its police power to coerce compliance. For instance, someone drawn to an author's intent approach to meaning might recognize that old statutory language fails to give modern citizens fair warning as to just what behaviour is prohibited. He might conclude that someone should not now be treated as a criminal for acting in a way that she would not realize is forbidden by the language, though the original understanding of the language would cover that action.

If the theorist wished to maintain a constant approach to meaning, he would need to distinguish between what a statute 'means' and everything else that judges should deem relevant in determining the statute's practical effect. He would distinguish statutory interpretation as an inquiry into meaning from assessment of everything that matters for a final decision in a statutory case.

Proceeding in this way raises two powerful objectives. The first lies in general philosophic considerations. Why should we assume that meaning is constant over a wide range of communications? Why is it not possible that meaning for letters is different from meaning for poetry? Perhaps the most persuasive general philosophic account is that the 'meaning' of communications depends on the nature of the communications involved—that many important inquiries about meaning must be field specific?

The second general objection lies in traditions of law I have already mentioned. Lawyers speak of the meaning of a statute as conforming with how a statute should be applied. They do not say, 'The meaning of the statute supports plaintiff's case, but defendant wins because of other considerations'. (Courts do use such language in the law of trusts, which contains special principles when a charitable trust cannot be implemented according to its terms.) With statutes, judges and lawyers speak of meaning and practical application as coinciding. Were legal theorists to differentiate 'meaning' from all else that matters for how a provision should be applied, they would employ a dichotomy unfamiliar to lawyers and judges. That, in itself, is not a crushing objection, but it is a serious disadvantage.

Given the tradition in law that desirable performance and application follow statutory meaning, it is convenient to treat interpretation of meaning as involving all that judges take into account when they decide how to understand a statutory provision. Thus, legal traditions, as well as doubts that any general theory can plausibly treat all communications similarly, support the view that statutory interpretation, and the 'meaning' of statutes, includes all the considerations that move judges to develop an understanding of statutory provisions as they apply in practice.

We can see then, that a theory about how judges *should* interpret statutes, a theory about how they should decide what statutes mean, cannot depend entirely on some general philosophy about the use of language. Such a philosophy may illuminate various subjects, such as how people expect authoritative rules of different types to be understood; but the main ingredients of a theory of statutory interpretation depend on analysis of legal systems, and more precisely, on analysis of how courts and legislatures should relate to each other within particular political orders. What is apt for liberal democracies with an independent judiciary may not be apt for a dictatorship in which interpretative officials are directly responsible to the ruler. Not only are interpretive approaches likely to differ in the two kinds of systems, different interpretive approaches will fit best with the normative premises of each system. More importantly, what is apt for Great Britain, with its cabinet system of government and careful legislative drafting, may not be apt for the United States, with its separate political branches and uneven drafting. Issues about statutory interpretation need to be resolved mainly in terms of political and legal theory, not some general philosophy of language.

2.2 Evolutionary versus Fixed Meaning

Should the meaning of statutes be regarded as fixed or subject to change? When judges interpret statutes soon after their enactment, circumstances will not have changed enough to raise most questions about a possible evolution in meaning; these questions arise with older enactments. To understand opposing positions, we need to be clear what is not in dispute.

If someone asks whether the meaning that judges assign to some statutory provisions has changed over time, the answer is 'yes'. The debated questions are whether judges do, and should, employ an interpretive methodology that embraces evolving meaning. Should judges implicitly say, 'We now hold this provision to mean x, but perhaps it should have been given a different meaning shortly after adoption'? An evolutionist says, 'Yes, statutes are pieces of a complex legal system, and their meaning appropriately changes, as does the meaning of common law principles'. An originalist says, 'No; statutes should be taken to mean what they originally meant, and they should be applied accordingly. Legislatures should change statutes, not courts.'

The gulf between the typical 'evolutionist' and the typical 'originalist' is less wide than these fictional remarks suggest. Legislatures adopt some provisions with open-ended phrases that definitely envision that those who apply the law will make judgments consonant with changing circumstances; the originalist agrees that the coverage of such provisions appropriately changes over time.

Even for provisions without this intrinsic flexibility, authoritative judicial precedents may establish a meaning that differs from what judges now deciding a case believe was the probable original meaning. In that event, originalists acknowledge that modern judges should (generally) follow the precedents rather than insisting on their understanding of the original meaning. Similarly, when administrative agencies have assigned a reasonable meaning to unclear statutory provisions, courts may adhere to that meaning, rather than adopt the meaning they would, on balance, find to be the most likely original meaning. Such deference to administrative interpretation may be warranted partly because the agency has a good sense of original meaning or is implementing flexible language, but the deference is also based on a view that administrative agencies are partners of the courts in interpreting statutes and developing the law. Thus, courts may follow agency interpretations not only when they think agencies have discretion to interpret one way or another but also, sometimes, when they think the agency interpretations are probably mistaken. (Exactly when courts should defer to agencies *is controversial*; originalists regard the circumstances for deference as more restricted than do evolutionists.)

Finally, originalists acknowledge that fair warning matters and that unclear statutory provisions should be fitted into the existing corpus of law. Especially in criminal cases, judges should not employ an original meaning if that now fails to give adequate warning. And significant changes in the surrounding body of law can affect how judges should understand an unclear statutory provision.

In these various respects, most originalists accede to forms of evolution in mean-ing. They acknowledge not only that such changes in meaning do occur but that they should occur. What evolutionists must concede to originalists is that judges rarely talk about changed meaning.

What then divides 'originalists' from 'evolutionists'? They may disagree over the circumstances when judges should accept meanings other than those they would dis-cern as original meanings, over what factors judges may take into account, and over the weight to be given to reasons in favour of change. They may also disagree about how to conceptualize judicial acceptance of a non-original meaning.

On the conceptual point, an originalist might claim that the legal 'meaning' of a statutory provision does not really change, that what modern judges are doing is deferring to the mistaken interpretations of meaning by others (as when they follow precedents or administrative rulings) or giving effect to considerations other than meaning (as when they decline to apply language that now fails to give fair warning).

If we realize that author's intention does not necessarily determine meaning, that reader understanding can matter for what language means, we have no reason to rule out the possibility that *modern* reader understanding can make a difference, and thus no reason to rule out the possibility that legal meaning can change over time. And, once we see that judges appropriately *treat* provisions as having a meaning that varies from the original one, we will find no reason in general philosophy to doubt that the meaning can actually change. From the standpoint of legal and political theory, what is of prime significance is how judges actually treat statutory provisions, not whether they see themselves (or theorists see them) as accepting changed meaning or decid-ing on the basis of considerations other than actual meaning.

Originalists differ with evolutionists over substance in being more likely to accede to changes in meaning only when they think the coverage of provisions is genuinely uncertain in the first place. Except perhaps when deferring to precedents, an origi-nalist judge will not decide against a meaning she thinks is evident, or plain. That is, an administrative decision or change in the surrounding body of law will not lead her to deviate from a plain meaning. An evolutionist will find more provisions to be uncertain in coverage, and thus susceptible to change in meaning, than will an origi-nalist. An evolutionist will also sometimes be willing to accept change in meaning, although the original meaning was not uncertain.

Originalists are likely to deny that changed social facts, other than changes in the law, can generate changed statutory meanings. They will deny that the shifting nor-mative appraisals of judges are a proper basis for new interpretations, unless a provi-sion explicitly leaves room for such appraisals.

Finally, even when an originalist concedes that judges may take account of argu-ments that are not based on original meaning, he will give more weight to the indica-tors of original meaning than will an evolutionist, who may regard original meaning as having slight significance as a statute ages.

All originalists and most evolutionists share one important point. They reject an account of meaning that fits a common modern version of meaning for poetry and other literary works. If meaning depends on reader understanding, why not say that meaning actually varies with the understanding of each reader? If you and I find different meanings in a poem, perhaps all one can say is that the poem has different meanings. Not only does the poem have different meanings, individual readers may have no good reason to try to find a meaning that will satisfy other readers.

A sceptic about legal reasoning may believe that the meaning of legal texts similarly comes down to the subjective reactions of individual readers. On this view, the reasons judges assign to adopt one meaning over another are a cloak that conceals subjective reaction. In its most extreme form, this position is definitely mistaken. Given the conventions of natural language and of law, many statutory provisions, cast in fairly precise terms, do require one understanding in context and exclude others. But this reality leaves open the possibility that over some range in which reasonable competing arguments can be made about meaning, interpretation and meaning are determined by individual subjective responses. Since the language of literary works, even poems, also exerts constraint on the meaning people reasonably find in them, the sceptic can conclude that law is really not so different in this respect from poetry.

Few theorists, however, urge this analogy to poetry as apt from the inside—as a guide for those who make authoritative decisions about legal meaning. Perhaps a judge should try to get the personal feel of a statute, as a reader gets the feel of a poem; but the judge cannot rest there. Her decision, with that of colleagues, determines whom the state will coerce; and it establishes meaning for future cases. The judge must consider whether her response is idiosyncratic or whether the reasons that move her would or should move other judges. The judge aims for a meaning that other judges would also appropriately find. Whether the meaning is 'original' or based partly on non-original factors, the judge seeks an interpretation that is sound for judges generally.

2.3 Readers' Understanding and Legislators' Intent

One of the most widely discussed issues in statutory interpretation is the nature and status of legislative intent. On examination, this issue turns largely on the relative importance of legislators' ideas about what they have enacted and readers' understandings of enactments. A vital aspect of the issue concerns the sources on which judges should draw.

To unpeel the elements of this broad issue, it helps to begin with the reminder that, in ordinary communication, speaker's (writer's) intent and listener (reader) understanding will substantially coalesce. What the listener understands is what the speaker has meant to communicate. If an outsider is aware of a communication and its social context, his best evidence of what the speaker intends is what a typical listener would understand by the speaker's words. An outsider could have special knowledge about a particular speaker and listener that would lead him to conclude that their understandings diverge, but this would be unusual. The outsider will be likely to reach differing judgments about speaker intent and listener understanding only if he has information about the speaker's intent that is not available to the listener. Commonly that information consists of remarks by the speaker made before or after she has communicated, about what she was trying to say. To revert to our example of parents telling their teenage daughter to go to bed at 11 o'clock when the 9 o'clock movie is over, the parents might say to friends, 'We've got really concerned about how tired she is. We're insisting that she stay up no later than 11.' The friends would be confident that the parents did not intend their daughter to watch the last hour of the movie that ends at 12 o'clock, although the daughter might be left in doubt by the instructions themselves.

How does this analysis apply to statutory interpretation? If judges rely entirely on the statutory text understood in light of social circumstances that are known to readers, they will have little basis to conclude that legislators intended something different from what readers would understand. Any theoretical debate about the comparative importance of the intent of legislators and the understanding of readers would lack practical significance. The theoretical debate has practical bite if judges may use sources to discern what legislators intended that ordinary readers would not employ.

2.3.1 *Evidences of Legislative Intent*

Individual legislators may declare their aims before or after they adopt a law. Everyone is suspicious of post-enactment statements, which are not subject to review and disagreement by other legislators before an act is passed. As a consequence, the main source for evidence of legislative intent (apart from text and context) is what is called legislative history, materials from the process of enactment that indicate how a bill is understood. The primary sources are reports of committees that screen and revise bills, statements made by sponsors on the floor of the legislature about what bills mean, and actual changes in the texts of bills as they proceed towards passage. These materials are, in a sense, available to readers; but a search of them is time-consuming and it is usually hard to extract what is relevant for a particular legal issue.

If a judge consults these materials, but assumes they do not also underlie the understanding of ordinary readers of the statutory text, she may determine that legislators were trying to do something at variance with what a typical reader of the text would conclude. The debate over the role of legislators' intent and reader understanding in statutory interpretation, thus, links substantially to the debate about the use of legislative history.

Those who assume that reader understanding is what matters for statutory meaning are likely to accord legislative history little or no role. Those who believe legislative intent has independent significance are likely to support the use of legislative history.

We must be careful, however, not to *equate* the place of legislative history with the more theoretical question about legislative intent. Some theorists who believe the actual intent of legislators about the scope of the law they have enacted is irrelevant still find value in the judicial use of legislative history. That history may reveal independent facts that contribute to sound interpretation and may indicate something about broader public attitudes. Further, pieces of legislative history may appropriately have a conventional weight in interpretation that does not depend on the states of mind of legislators.

Some of the arguments against use of legislative history do not directly challenge the possible significance of legislators' intents. The most common argument against judicial use of legislative history is that its exploration is time consuming and usually unproductive and that most bits of modern legislative history represent, not the considered views of important legislators, but the interests of lobbyists who have persuaded legislative assistants to insert constructions of provisions that are favourable to their interests.

I consider the issue of legislative intent on the assumption that some materials may be available to discern that intent that would not form a part of reader understanding. On this assumption, should legislators' intent control, should reader understanding control, or is each independently relevant?

2.3.2 *The Obvious Importance of Reader Understanding*

We can begin with reader understanding. Without doubt it has importance. Laws restrict human behaviour, and the legislature has no power to restrict behaviour without adopting statutes. If legislators must adopt statutes to restrict behaviour, they cannot successfully do so if citizens lack a basis in the law to apprehend the restrictions. More to the point for difficult cases, if statutory language leaves uncertain which acts are forbidden and which allowed, a reader's judgment about the language should matter for a judge's best interpretation of a provision. At least when modern reader understanding is not readily distinguishable from how readers at the time of adoption would have understood language, a law's original meaning should not rest exclusively on legislators' intent, it should include reader understanding. (One might believe that for very old laws what should matter is modern reader understanding along with what legislators originally intended, that original reader understanding should have little or no independent significance.)

Depending on the kind of statute adopted, the relevant 'reader' might be an ordinary person, an expert in a field such as atomic energy, or a lawyer. A criminal law directed at ordinary people differs from procedural rules for lawyers, and both differ from legislation regulating highly technical subjects. Now, considering that ordinary people rarely read statutes, someone might doubt whether their understanding, as opposed to that of lawyers, should ever matter. But people should be able to understand on their own why they have committed a crime or violated someone's rights, even if they have not read a statute in advance. In any event, for most purposes, the understanding of lawyers will not differ greatly from the understanding of ordinary well-educated speakers of English.

How should a judge conceive the reader of statutory language? For provisions that are complex but yield their meaning to careful analysis, she should assume a reader who is intelligent and makes the effort to unlock the complicated puzzle of the language. But there are no experts in the meaning of ordinary words and phrases (except those who comprehend the way others understand—such as compilers of dictionaries). The judge's basic task is to try to understand the text as would readers who confront it. (One can conceive of readers constructed normatively who give the best reading possible to statutory language, but this is to move away from a genuine reader understanding approach towards one in which a judge constructs the best normative reading.)

A judge who asks how a reader would understand a text must pay some attention to social context and legislative purpose. A reader will view a text against social context. He will have some sense of the problems a law was meant to address, and some idea of legislative purposes, and will interpret the language accordingly. Thus, a judge using a reader approach will need to determine what sources to use to discern the social context of a statute, and the purposes a reader would attribute to the statute. The judge might rely, for example, on analyses of social problems in newspapers and magazines or a President's State of the Union address.

For modern legislation, and modern reactions to older legislation, a judge may be bold enough to assume that she adequately replicates what a reader would understand. Her reading can be a reader's reading. But this will not work for the original understanding of much older legislation. A judge cannot intuitively grasp all of what the reader of a time long past would have understood; she needs to make a conscious attempt to recapture older understandings. But just how should she do this? Should she posit a single reader of the period or recognize that different readers may have understood crucial words or phrases differently? Should she conceive of a well-educated reader or one with a rudimentary education? Should her reader represent normatively desirable attitudes or average attitudes? To take an extreme example, if readers in 1830 assumed that members of the 'white race' were superior to all others, is a provision of uncertain coverage, adopted in 1830, now to be read accordingly? And exactly what states of mind of a reader, present or past, should our judge take as the attitudes that count for understanding? I return to these problems after surveying the more familiar analogous problems about legislative intent.

2.3.3 *Deviation from Textual Language*

Another important interpretive problem about textual understanding warrants mention. When, if ever, should judges construe language differently from what the words of a provision seem on the face of it to say? There is general agreement that judges should fill in omitted words, when no one doubts that a word, such as 'no', has been omitted by mistake. More controversially, judges also try to interpret language in a way that corresponds with basic policies underlying a statute and with funda-mental principles of justice. In one famous case, the Supreme Court construed a law that barred employers from making contracts with aliens 'to perform labor or service of any kind in the United States'.[4] Although the specific statutory language was broad enough to cover the church's contract with a British minister, the Court said the statute was aimed at manual labourers, not at brain toilers, and especially not at min-isters of the gospel. Justice Antonia Scala, a prominent 'textualist' (i.e. an originalist who relies on textual meaning, not legislative intent), has expressed powerful dis-agreement with the approach of that case:[5] when specific words are relatively clear, courts should follow them, leaving legislatures to correct their own mistakes.

2.3.4 The Possible Relevance of Legislators' Intents

Judges in various common law countries have adopted different postures towards legislators' intent and the resources of legislative history. For most of the twentieth century British courts declined to look at internal legislative materials; the American Supreme Court used them extensively to discern the objectives of Congress. At the beginning of a new century, a majority of Supreme Court Justices still rely on legisla-tive history, but others, led by Justice Scalia, do not. Among the reasons for opposing that use are these: (1) The materials of legislative history are an unreliable indication of attitudes within the legislature. (2) Legislators can regulate only by voting on statutes; they should not control meaning by inserting their points of view in legisla-tive history. (3) Judicial reliance on legislative history contravenes the necessity of adoption of legislation by two houses and the executive. (4) The concept of legislative intent is itself misconceived.

The first ground of opposition has great practical importance, but presents few troublesome theoretical questions. The materials of legislative history may be a good or bad reflector of what legislators believe. Judicial investigation of the materials may or may not often be illuminating about specific understandings of particular provi-sions and about broader purposes that underlie a statute. Judges and scholars have to assess the value of legislative history against the costs of judges considering it and of lawyers combing it for relevant information. Part of this evaluation involves a deci-sion as to whether committee reports need reflect the views of legislators themselves to be significant or may appropriately be given weight because they reflect the views of active staff members.

---

[4] *Church of the Holy Trinity v United States*, 143 US 457 (1892).
[5] Antonin Scalia, *A Matter of Interpretation: Federal Courts and the Law: An Essay* (Princeton, NJ: Princeton University Press, 1996), 18–23.

The other three objections are ones that, in principle, legislators' intentions should not make a difference. These objections raise general questions about instructions and rules, and narrower questions about political life and legal systems.

In respect to the general questions about instructions and rules, suppose that one person has a relationship of authority over another. If the subject's job were to try to carry out all the desires of the person with authority, the latter's verbal instructions would mainly serve as a means to indicate her desires. When the subject recognizes that the authority's instructions were unclear, or somehow knows that she did not intend results clearly called for by the instructions, the subject will be guided by the authority's intent. The argument that the implications of the instructions themselves should control has force only if the subject's job is to follow instructions, not to carry out an authority's every perceived wish.

Legislatures can act only by adopting the language of statutes; citizens need not do what legislators wish if the legislators have failed to adopt statutory language. Thus, the argument that only the statutory language should count passes this initial hurdle that instructions may be merely evidence of desires.

However, even when people are at liberty to do what they wish, or think is best, unless limited by instructions, relationships vary. A subject may have no relevant interests of his own opposed to those of the person in authority over him, and the authority may possess greater competence or may enjoy a greater legitimacy because she has been assigned responsibility by others. A patient has entrusted his medical care to a doctor. The doctor gives instructions about treatment to a nurse and to a doctor who is filling in for her. The nurse is less expert; the second doctor, though as skilled and experienced as the first doctor, has less responsibility for this patient's treatment. Both the nurse and second doctor should follow the first doctor's instructions according to her intent, if they happen to discover that intent.

In other circumstances, one person has authority to limit what a subject can do by issuing instructions, but the latter has interests of his own and the liberty to pursue these interests, except as instructed to the contrary. Employees, for instance, may be free to dress as they choose, except as their bosses restrict them. A worker might reasonably say he is not successfully restricted unless the terms of his boss's instructions do so, that he need not act in accord with her intent, if that intent is more confining than the apparent force of the instructions taken by themselves. The worker may assert that he has a range of liberty that can only be confined by instructions that by themselves tell him what to do. The lesson of these informal analogies is that the importance of the intent of someone issuing instructions depends on the reasons why the person has authority and on that person's relation to those subject to her.

Laws vary among themselves in respect to relations between legislatures and those subject to the laws. Some statutes are instructions to the executive branch from the legislature, a body with greater political authority, to carry out broad public policies. Other statutes restrict the liberty of individuals in ways the individuals disapprove or dislike. If an inquiry about relationships were to determine whether the language of statutes should itself be controlling or legislative intent should also count, the right answer would depend on the statute involved. Instead of concluding that intent is irrelevant because legislatures can regulate only by adopting language, judges would consider all those directly affected by a statute, before deciding whether they should reach beyond the guiding textual language to rely on an intent discoverable from outside the text.

The worry that reliance on legislative history in the United States bypasses a formal process of approval rests partly on the assumption that the Constitution, requiring acceptance by two legislative bodies and the President, was designed to make legislation difficult. Judges who use legislative history give weight to indications of meaning that have not been approved in the required way. It is a partial answer to this worry that judges usually employ legislative history to reach conclusions that are unclear from statutory provisions themselves. Using such material to interpret what has been adopted is not quite the same as allowing members in one house to legislate by their legislative history. Against an ideal of adoption by two houses and the executive, judicial use of legislative history to infer legislative intent may have a flaw, but the flaw is not grave enough to reject legislative history on that ground.

2.3.5 *How to Understand Legislative Intent*

The claim that legislative intent is wholly misconceived, that the concept is actually incoherent, is yet another objection to courts relying upon legislative history to reveal intent. To evaluate this objection, we must examine just how legislative intent might be understood. It might reflect the actual mental states of legislators, embody an objective notion of a reasonable legislator, or function as a construct based on conventions about what materials count. Many opinions read as if legislative intent reflects the actual mental states of legislators, but that idea has been powerfully challenged.

I suggest how we might best develop a mental states version of legislative intent, and offer some qualifications, before inquiring whether adoption of an objective or conventional approach avoids the perceived difficulties with a mental states account.

One might take the concept of legislative intent as an illustration of the broad theoretical issue of what constitutes a group intent. One would try to sketch the parameters of 'group intents' and then decide whether the attitudes of legislators towards a piece of legislation qualify. This way of proceeding, however, would be misguided.

As to whether a group can ever have an 'intent', the answer is 'yes'. It is not that the group as such has a mental state; it is that members of a group share the same mental state. If all (or nearly all) members of a group knowingly share an intent that relates to function of the group, the group (in this sense) has that intent. Our parents had a shared intent about the bedtime of their teenage daughter and all the members of a team might share an intent to play in a certain way.

Under these strict conditions, legislators would rarely have a shared intent about the coverage of specific statutory provisions. We might proceed to ask whether groups may have intents under less stringent conditions that legislators would more often satisfy. But the crucial question for interpretation is not whether a legislature has a group intent, it is whether judges should take into account the attitudes of legislators in interpreting statutes.

This exercise might be appropriate, perhaps because the intents of a minority of individual legislators should matter, even if the conditions for having a group intent are not satisfied. (And the exercise might be inappropriate even if the conditions are satisfied.) Once we focus on what courts may profitably take into account, we shall see not only that 'group intent' is a red herring, we can grasp that judges might be influenced by something more complex than a simple, single mental state held by some number of legislators.

Some clarifications are in order. (1) The relevant mental states might concern broad purposes of statutes as well as beliefs about the coverage of particular provisions. (2) If judges reach conclusions about actual mental states, these must be based on probabilities, not certainties. (3) Judges will base judgments about actual mental states mainly on expressions or manifestations of some kind. It would be a reasonable requirement, given the nature of legislation, that these manifestations must occur prior to adoption of legislation.

When one considers what mental state should count as an intent, two obvious candidates are 'hopes' and 'expectations'. But each proves inapt. A legislator might agree to language that she knows is designed to prohibit particular behaviour. She does not favour this prohibition, but has gone along with it in order to obtain support for aspects of the statute she endorses. She hopes the courts will construe the provision contrary to the way in which she understands it. Her hopes do not reflect her relevant intent. Suppose another legislator expects courts, unsympathetic to the aims of legislation, to construe a provision contrary to his hopes and to his understanding of what it accomplishes. His expectations do not reflect his relevant intent.

The state of mind that is much more relevant than hopes or expectations is the legislator's understanding about what the statute does, his opinion about how courts *should* interpret its language. It might be objected that this approach sets up a vicious circle. The legislator's understanding is based on how he thinks courts should interpret, on everything courts should take into account. Courts would interpret on the basis of legislators' understandings of how they (the courts) should interpret.

If there is a circle at all here, it is not vicious, because the judicial function certainly encompasses much more than guesses about what legislators think judges should do. Legislators' intents are only one basis for judicial interpretation. Judges are influenced but not controlled by how they think legislators believe they should interpret. Further, judges may decide to give more weight to legislators' views about the straightforward significance of statutory language than to their views about the subtle nuances of judicial interpretation.

What if a legislator believes courts should interpret in one way, but he accepts as settled a contrary practice courts have established? Judges should be guided by the legislator's view of how specific language or broad purposes should be understood, given interpretive practices he takes as settled. (In cases that are otherwise very close, legislators' hopes might also figure to some degree.)

Whose views should count and what weight should judges accord them? Contrary to what is sometimes assumed, the views of those who vote against a bill may matter. A legislature is a co-operative body, not simply a collection of majority voters. A legislator may participate in drafting legislation and endorse what a particular provision does, but vote against the final bill because it has other objectionable features. The legislator's view of what the provision does should be relevant. Even if she opposed that very provision, her understanding carries importance if she has joined in the effort to formulate the language.

The views of legislators who have actually considered a provision matter more than the views of passive participants (even if one could guess accurately what the passive participants thought). If one takes the temper of a group, one ordinarily gives special weight to the views of those who are most active and best informed. Moreover, legislators themselves do approve (or would approve if they thought about it) a system in which their own views matter most for the statutes with which they are most actively involved.

Given the conditions of modern legislation, do any views count other than those of legislators? In so far as members choose to rely on the judgments of their staff and of members of the executive branch who propose legislation, courts should also take those views into account. Indeed, if a judge thinks of legislation as a complex process involving many actors other than the legislators themselves, she may deem significant the views of staff members and executive officials who have participated in drafting, even apart from some notion of implicit delegation by legislators.

Judges who consider the actual views of legislators are under strong pressure to consider their hypothetical views as well. By hypothetical views, I mean the views actual legislators would have had if they had asked themselves questions they did not address. One reason judges might address hypothetical attitudes concerns passive and silent legislators. Often judges may have little basis to know whether these legislators actually had a view. But judges may be able to say that if the committee members and other dominant legislators had a particular opinion, it *either* was shared (an actual understanding) or would have been shared (a hypothetical understanding) by most other legislators. Probably the views of an informed minority should be relevant by themselves. But if virtually all those who express themselves agree, judges who count hypothetical understandings can (usually) assume that most legislators would have had a similar view.

Public choice theorists have objected to judges relying on hypothetical *votes*. Because of the arbitrary order in which options may be considered and because of strategic voting, one cannot be confident how any legislator would have voted on an issue, unless one knows the context of the vote. Reliance on the kind of hypothetical understanding I have suggested seems largely (though perhaps not entirely) to avoid these problems. The question posed is what a legislator would have thought about a provision, given the provision (and surrounding law) as it was when adopted. Answering this question may be hard but it is not much subject to the difficulties with hypothetical votes.

A mental states version of legislative intent, as developed here, is feasible; it is not incoherent. If judges try to discern and combine the crucial understandings in a nuanced way, they will concededly be unable to formulate exactly what they are doing, but this inability characterizes much practical reasoning. Judges may, none the less, be able to make sensitive assessments both of legislators' understandings and of how these should weigh against other interpretive factors.

Giving conventional weight to pieces of legislative history may be an alternative to a mental states approach. The idea of conventional weight is that certain sources have conventionally, over the years, come to have a significance for interpretation. On this account, courts assign explanatory importance to committee reports and other statements, not because these connect in any particular way to mental states, but because earlier judicial interpreters have treated them in this way. A serious problem with this account as a radical alternative to a mental states approach is that the pieces of legislative history that are accorded the most weight are just those that have best reflected the attitudes of key legislators. Further, a strong argument for giving these pieces of history less weight than in the past has been that they no longer well reflect legislators' attitudes. An account that draws some connection between conventional weight and mental states is more appealing than one that conceives a total divorce. Here is one such account.

The materials that courts have given the most weight are those that have best indicated the attitudes of key legislators. In typical cases, judges have a rough idea how much weight to assign to committee reports, sponsors' statements, and other indications of intent, and they do not worry much about just how accurately the materials reflect mental states in individual cases. However, were judges to possess some powerful indication in a case that standard materials poorly reflect mental states, and that other materials are more revealing, judges would consider these other materials. A rough correlation, thus, exists between conventional weight and mental states. Were judges to perceive the correlations as changing drastically, conventional weight would change.

A different alternative to a mental states account is the construction of a reasonable legislator. Legislative intent would be the intent a reasonable legislator would have. Just how far this construction escapes inquiry into mental states depends on how the reasonable legislator is conceived. If the reasonable legislator is taken as the average legislator, judges could make judgments (mainly empirical judgments) about what he would think only by considering the likely attitudes of most actual legislators, or the attitudes of most people who might occupy the position of legislator. Questions about whose and what mental states matter would not go away, though they would be somewhat transformed. If the reasonable legislator is taken as superior to most ordinary legislators—better informed, more careful, more attuned to public values—then the judge's conclusion about what the reasonable legislator would think would depend less on assumptions about ordinary legislators. The judicial inquiry would then be mainly normative. Even in that event, the reasonable legislator would presumably be responsive to social problems actually perceived by people. In constructing the purposes that a reasonable legislator would ascribe to a statute, a judge would have to evaluate which problems were perceived by citizens and legislators. That aspect of the inquiry would be empirical, and would concern itself with mental states.

2.3.6 *Reader Understanding and Relevant Mental States*

It remains to return briefly to reader understanding approaches, to examine some problems about mental states that should be clearer now that we have explored various approaches to legislative intent.

Readers understand statutory provisions in context. They need to grasp the social context of legislation in order to understand its purposes. If the purposes are disputed, readers must assess them according to their estimate of the likely attitudes of legislators, based on whatever sources the readers use, or according to some construct of how a reasonable legislator would react. Even the latter construct, as I have indicated, does not wholly escape inquiry into likely mental states.

More serious difficulties face the judge who is constructing the relevant reader. Readers of statutory texts may have hopes, expectations, and views about proper interpretation that may split in the same manner as the views of legislators. A judge who employs a reader understanding approach must stand ready in some instances to say what states of mind matter. And if one asks how readers of a statute, living at the time of its adoption, would have understood a provision, the answer may be that different readers would have understood it differently.

Here is an example. Title VII of the 1964 Civil Rights Act provides that employers and unions may not 'discriminate' on grounds of race, gender, and so on. One sense of 'discriminate' involves any unfavourable classification; but some people think that one cannot 'discriminate' against members of the dominant group, that classifications that favour those who have previously been oppressed do not discriminate against those who have benefited from oppression. The difference over the meaning of 'discriminate' has an obvious bearing on whether the crucial statutory sections allow employers and unions to undertake affirmative action that favours members of previously victimized groups. Looking to the purposes of the law will not settle this issue, because some readers will discern a primary purpose to help the previous victims of discrimination, while other readers will believe the main aim was to eliminate all categorization along the lines of race and gender.

The judge who adopts a 'reader understanding' approach must decide implicitly how to weight the views of different readers or how to combine those readers into one representative reasonable reader. In either event, problems of mental states and their combinations are present in reader approaches, as well as in inquiries about legislative intent. The difficulties of resolving such problems cannot be a decisive reason to consider reader understanding to the exclusion of legislative intent.

2.4   The Relevance of Purpose

A crucial question about any approach to the meaning of a statute is how much weight to give to purposes, as contrasted with the language of particular provisions and indications of specific intent. Most legislation is the product of compromise; it is not surprising that some provisions may be out of line with a law's broad purposes. If the language of a provision clearly indicates a result, courts will give it effect even if it lies in tension with a statute's more general aims.

The more troublesome interpretive problems are these. (1) The language of the provision could be read in one of two ways; the first conforms with indications in the legislative history about what results were intended under the provision, the second better carries out the act's broad purposes revealed by the legislative history. (2) The statutory language could bear a number of meanings; one of these seems the most natural reading of the specific provision, but another fits better with underlying purposes.

The first problem can be formulated in this way. When judges look outside the text to discern the aims of the legislature, should they pay more attention to purposes or specific intent? The argument in favour of specific intent is that what committee reports and other legislative materials say about specific resolutions is more focused than what they say about purposes. One argument for emphasis on purposes is that statements about purpose are less subject to manipulation by interested legislators than are claims about specific resolutions. Another argument is that the development of a rational law is best served by judges concentrating on legislative purposes; this is especially true as statutes age and conditions change. In their influential work on statutory interpretation, Henry Hart and Albert Sacks urged that the primary use of legislative history was to ascertain legislative purposes.[6] Critics have objected that this approach is not faithful to legislative compromise and encourages judges to follow their own policy views under the guise of finding amorphous purposes.

Issues about the place of purpose may also arise when judges do not rely on legislative history. Should judges prefer the reading of a narrow provision that is most natural even when that reading fits awkwardly with purposes that are stated in a preamble or are obviously implicit in the body of the statute as a whole? Judges and scholars who emphasize the priority of text tend to be concerned with restricting

---

[6] Henry M. Hart, Jr. and Albert M. Sacks, *The Legal Process: Basic Problems in the Making and Application of Law* (Cambridge, Mass.: tentative edition, 1958).

judicial discretion; they believe judges should generally stick to what the immediately relevant text seems to say rather than relying heavily on vague statements of purpose.

3 Constitutional Interpretation

3.1 Issues and Possibilities

Virtually every problem about statutory interpretation also comes up in constitutional interpretation, but crucial differences between most statutes and most constitutional provisions affect the dominant issues and persuasive positions. Three central features of the American Constitution are that it is much older than most statutes, it has many open-ended and vague provisions, and it is difficult to amend.

Partly as a consequence of these features, people worry about the political legitimacy of judges interpreting constitutional provisions and imposing their interpretations on the rest of the government. These features and concerns are related in the following (made up) attack on frequent judicial invalidation of statutes: 'Why should non-elected courts prevent legislatures from enacting the will of the people, relying on an ancient document whose wording is unclear and whose adoption was by unrepresentative politicians?'

In this chapter, I treat these central features of American constitutionalism as the setting within which to consider problems of constitutional interpretation. But I should emphasize that matters are different in some other constitutional regimes. The American Constitution was adopted in 1789 and the Bill of Rights followed two years later. The balance of federal and state power was significantly altered by the Fourteenth Amendment, adopted in 1868 after the Civil War. As a consequence, the bulk of the national constitution was adopted more than 200 years ago, and its most important later amendment is more than 130 years old. Only male land holders had the vote in most states when the Constitution and Bill of Rights were adopted, and the great majority of blacks were living in slavery. Representation was broader by 1868, but women lacked the vote.

The American Constitution is very difficult to amend. The most common method requires a two-thirds vote of each house of Congress and approval in three-quarters of the state legislatures. The difficulty of formal amendment is one reason why the early provisions have shown such staying power.

The language of many of the crucial provisions of the Constitution is sparse. Congress has the power 'To regulate Commerce with foreign Nations, and among the several States, and with the Indian Tribes . . .'[7] 'Congress shall make no law affecting

---

[7] US Constitution, Art. I, §8, cl. 3.

the establishment of religion or prohibiting the free exercise thereof. . . .'[8] This language does not provide a detailed code about how to treat problems.

The constitutions of many countries, and of many American states, are more modern, more detailed, and more amendable. These differences could well influence just how their provisions should be interpreted.

Before I turn to troublesome issues of constitutional interpretation, I note some kinds of systems in which 'constitutions' have a status different from that in the United States, and I touch on some of the constitutional responsibilities of non-judicial officials.

Some legal systems, such as Great Britain, lack a comprehensive written constitution. Judges may invoke settled constitutional practices when they interpret laws, but they cannot say that legislation enacted by Parliament is invalid. The legislature acting with the approval of the king or queen, is supreme. Some countries have written constitutions that are understood to constrain legislators and other officials. But courts do not enforce provisions of the written constitution against legislative acts; rather they accept those acts as valid.

In the United States, the prevailing assumption has been that an enacted part of the Constitution is valid until it is repealed by subsequent amendment. In India, by contrast, provisions of the Constitution have been declared invalid because they conflict with the principles of more important parts of the Constitution.[9]

Bruce Ackerman has proposed that the American Constitution may be amended by other than the formal means, through a combination of legislative action and public approval.[10] The Supreme Court has never acknowledged such authority, and, given the difficulties of judicial delineation of when informal amendment has taken place, it seems unlikely to do so. But a theorist may none the less contend that written judicial opinions that give a modern cast to ancient provisions are disingenuous efforts to conceal the reality of informal amendment. In what follows, I concentrate on interpretation of the written constitution, neglecting both the possibility that enacted, unrepealed constitutional provisions may be invalid, and the possibility that what, on occasion, courts really interpret is an unacknowledged informal amendment.

My discussion focuses on constitutional interpretation in systems in which courts interpret a written constitution and have the authority to declare statutes and executive actions (such as unlawful searches) unconstitutional. But this focus should not

---

[8] US Constitution, Amendment I.

[9] *Gopalan, A.K. v State of Mad.*, AIR 1950 SC 27, 93; *Moinuddin v Uttar Pradesh*, AIR 1960 All. 484; *Venkataramara v Mysore*, AIR 1958 SC 255. See M. Jain, *Indian Constitutional Cases*, 4th edn. (Bombay: N. M. Tripathi Private Ltd., 1987), 853.

[10] *We the People: Vol. I, Foundations* (Cambridge, Mass.: Belknap Press, 1991); *We the People: Volume II Transformations* (Cambridge, Mass.: Belknap Press, 1998). See Akhil Reed Amar, *The Bill of Rights: Creation and Reconstruction* (New Haven: Yale University Press, 1998). On the unsuitability of Ackerman's theory for judicial recognition, see Greenawalt, 'Dualism and its Status', *Ethics*, 104(3) (1994), 480–99.

obscure the reality that even in such systems other officials also interpret the constitution. Legislators decide whether a bill they might adopt passes constitutional muster and high police officers decide what investigative techniques are constitutionally permitted.

In the United States, whole areas of constitutional law are left to nonjudicial bodies. The Constitution provides that Presidents may be impeached, convicted, and removed from office for 'Treason, Bribery, or other high Crimes and Misdemeanors'.[11] Deciding how to classify forms of official misbehaviour involves constitutional interpretation; but, according to traditional understanding, courts will not review determinations that the House of Representatives and the Senate make about impeachable behaviour. Thus, even in systems in which courts enforce most provisions of written constitutions, they may not enforce every aspect of those constitutions.

Within the areas in which courts are active, two interesting questions arise about how other officials should regard their constitutional responsibilities. The first is how far legislators and executive officials should regard themselves as constrained by the constitutional determinations of courts. Without doubt, they should comply with what judges decide in any individual case, but should they also take a court's announced rule of law as controlling their behaviour more generally?

In all common law countries, other officials are largely guided by judicial interpretations; but suppose members of Congress think the Supreme Court has made a mistake in holding a statute invalid? May they appropriately re-enact similar legislation? When the *Dred Scott* decision held the Missouri Compromise invalid, because it purported to free slaves who had been brought by masters into free territories, Abraham Lincoln responded that he did not take the principles the Supreme Court announced as ones Congress had to follow.[12] It is one thing to say that courts should apply the Constitution in their decisions, another to say that their opinions bind other branches of government. In recent decades, the Supreme Court has spoken as if its decisions lay down authoritative principles for all branches of government.[13]

A second question about attitudes of non-judicial officials is how they should regard the Constitution as regulating their behaviour.[14] In some areas of American constitutional law, a statute's validity can depend on the reasons why legislators adopted it. For example, a law enacted in order to promote a religious objective violates the Establishment Clause. But judges are hesitant to decide that religious objectives underlay a statute that can be justified on non-religious grounds, and, in any event, the religious objectives of a few legislators would not render an entire statute

[11] US Constitution, Art. II, §4.
[12] See the Seventh Joint Debate at Alton, 15 Oct. 1858. Cited in Harold Holzer (ed.), *The Lincoln–Douglas Debates* (New York: Harper Collins, 1993), 360–2.
[13] See e.g. *Cooper v Aaron* 358.
[14] See generally Paul Brest, 'The Conscientious Legislator's Guide to Constitutional Interpretation', *Stanford Law Review*, 27 (1975), 585.

invalid. Suppose a single legislator would not vote for a law that provides aid to private religious schools, except that she believes the aid will promote religious truth. She knows that other legislators have secular reasons for supporting the bill—better education for children—and that a court will not declare the law invalid because it is based on an impermissible purpose. At least if she accepts the idea that the Constitution bars religious objectives for statutes, she probably has a constitutional obligation not to vote for the law, even if she knows that her vote in favour will not lead to judicial invalidation. I do not further pursue these questions about how non-judicial officials should conceive their fidelity to the Constitution.

3.2 Fundamental Questions of Political Legitimacy

Judicial review of the validity of legislative action under the federal Constitution generates two related problems of legitimacy. One problem, the more straightforward, concerns judicial interpretation. The Constitution is a kind of higher law, a law that all actors in the government should observe. If legislators and the executive are faithful to their roles and oaths of office, they will try to comply with the Constitution. In many respects the precise requirements of the Constitution are not clear. If Congress adopts a law and the President signs it, two branches of government have made a judgment that the law is constitutional. Why should the judiciary, a third non-elected branch, be able to say that the law is invalid, and, given the difficulty of amendment, effectively prevent such a law from being implemented? Why should judges not regard the decisions that the coordinate branches reach about the constitutionality of their own activities as conclusive? When legislators adopt statutes, is not the deliberate decision of the supreme elected body more important than the opinions of a majority of nine justices?

A closer analysis must distinguish among kinds of constitutional issues. Ours is a polity that is federal and whose national executive is independent from Congress. Some federal body needs to be able to say when states have overstepped their powers *vis-à-vis* the national government, and, within the national government, one may need an adjudicative body to settle disputes about authority between the legislature and executive. The Supreme Court and other federal courts are appropriate bodies to perform these functions.

The more doubtful instances of review occur when someone claims that the national Congress has exceeded its power *vis-à-vis* the states, that Congress has infringed individual rights, or that a state has infringed individual rights. The system of government would not break down if courts accepted these exercises of legislative power.

Someone might complain that any sketch of an argument against review based on political authority misses the point. Whatever we might recommend for a country adopting a new constitution, the United States has a constitution that gives courts the authority to review all kinds of constitutional issues. If the Constitution confers this authority, courts must exercise it.

Conceivably arguments against review were once relevant to analysis of whether the Constitution provided for judicial review of Congressional statutes, a power that is not explicit in the constitutional text. But that issue was settled long ago, in the famous case of *Marbary v Madison*,[15] and probably according to the design of the framers. Given that review is now firmly entrenched, its wisdom and political legitimacy might seem irrelevant to how modern judges should perform their duties.

Here is how the concern about political legitimacy connects to theories of interpretation. If judicial review of statutes is itself suspect, then judges who exercise this power should do so very cautiously. In the case of reasonable doubt, they should accept what the legislature has done.

In one of the best-known and most influential law review articles, James Bradley Thayer argued that Congress has the primary (though not exclusive) authority to interpret the constitutionality of its actions, and that its determinations are entitled to respect.[16] Courts can disregard a statute only 'when those who have the right to make laws have not merely made a mistake, but have made a very clear one,—so clear that it is not open to rational question'.[17] Courts should not make their own straightforward judgments about constitutionality, but should reach a 'conclusion as to what judgment is permissible to another department which the constitution has charged with the duty of making it'.[18] For long periods of the past century, various critics of the Court's decisions restricting congressional power *vis-à-vis* the states and upholding economic and individual (non-economic) rights have claimed that judges should restrain themselves and defer to the resolutions of legislatures.[19]

Related issues of political legitimacy, often raised as objections to judges imposing their wills too freely on legislators, go back to the basic idea of constitutional constraint. Why should a modern democratic government be limited in its decisions by the judgments of unrepresentative men who died long ago? We need to separate the three strands of this complaint: the inappropriateness of constitutional restraint; the unfairness of one generation restricting later generations; and the unrepresentativeness of a country's founders.

Should modern governments ever be restrained by written constitutions? In principle, there is no good reason why societies should not declare that some dispositions are off limits for transient majorities of legislative bodies; and for many societies this may be a wise policy. At a time of sober reflection, the members of a society, or the

---

[15] *Marbary v Madison*, 5 US 137, 1 Cranch 137 (1803).
[16] Thayer, 'The Origin and Scope of the American Doctrine of Constitutional Law', *Harvard Law Review*, 7 (1893), 129, 136.
[17] ibid. 144.   [18] ibid.
[19] For a recent argument against judicial review, see Mark Tushnet, *Taking the Constitution Away From the Courts* (Princeton, NJ: Princeton University Press, 1999).

great majority of their representatives, may decide to take certain political issues off the table of legislative choice, to prevent the legislature from giving way to passions or parochial interests. Such a reservation is particularly important to preserve the fairness of the political process itself and the equitable consideration of the interests of all citizens.

Should one generation be able to bind another? This troubling question yields no simple answer. A minor point is that, in truth, a society does not have separate generations but interlocking generations. At no single moment in time does the generation of constitution-makers give way to the *next* generation, and so on. But the problem that we live under a constitution whose major parts were adopted by persons no longer alive remains.

The best answer to the question of why we should feel bound is that a constitution must prove itself over time as valuable in the life of each generation. One reason why an old constitution is now valuable, and thus is binding, is that it provides a shared set of answers to fundamental political questions. A society must have some ground rules, and it is very difficult to get agreement on new ones. Moreover, as American history shows, a sense of the historical continuity of a constitution can have considerable value for a feeling of community. The legitimacy of the Constitution derives partly from its being in place and partly from its ancient origin. But it legitimately constrains the people of our time because it contributes to our social life.

The problem of unrepresentativeness has a similar answer. What counts over time is what the Constitution provides and how well that fits the notions of justice of subsequent generations. If some very important interests were not represented, that is a reason to be sceptical both that those interests were then fairly treated and that similar interests now receive appropriate constitutional protection. But the test for us now is content, not fairness of representation in origin.

We can easily see how these concerns about the legitimacy of an overarching constitution could affect interpretation. If someone doubts the wisdom of much restraint of democratically elected bodies, he will want the restraints that do exist to be understood modestly. Thus, the fact that a written constitution restrains present majorities may combine with the countermajoritarian feature of judicial review to counsel restraint by courts, to counsel broad acceptance of what legislatures have chosen. Concerns about the legitimacy of an *old* Constitution can work similarly, to promote a relaxed view of its restrictions. Perhaps judges should exercise judicial restraint, not invalidating all legislation the Constitution was designed to prevent and certainly not reaching out to invalidate other legislation an originalist would deem acceptable.

Worries about unrepresentativeness might work differently, to suggest a variable approach to interpretation. Perhaps judges should ask whether any particular provision resulted from unfair representation and whether the provision continues to impinge unfairly on interests like those that were not represented. If the answer to both questions is 'yes', judges might minimize or expand the import of the provision accordingly. Here is a crude example. The original Constitution provides that 'No state shall pass any . . . Law impairing the Obligation of Contracts'.[20] This formulation may have been a consequence of unjust representation of property and business interests. That might be a reason to interpret the restriction narrowly, not to prevent modern legislative relief for poor debtors.

Beliefs about failures of representation could lead judges, instead, to broaden vague constitutional protections to protect interests that were not adequately represented when the provisions were adopted. Thus, the modern Supreme Court has interpreted the Equal Protection Clause of the Fourteenth Amendment to protect equality for women, although any such protection was far from the minds of the men who adopted the amendment.

3.3 The Countermajoritarian Difficulty

A substantial amount of discourse about constitutional law in the twentieth century has taken up what has been referred to as the 'countermajoritarian difficulty'. The main focus has been on the undemocratic character of judicial review, but we have seen that the nature of an enduring written constitution itself presents a problem for majoritarian democracy. When, during the first third of the century, a politically conservative Supreme Court was striking down federal and state legislation designed to promote economic justice, many liberals and legal scholars supported Thayer's approach: judges should defer to the decisions of legislatures. In widely read work published in the 1950s and 1960s, Alexander Bickel urged, among other things, that the Supreme Court should be cautious about confronting the political branches, that it should employ 'passive virtues' to avoid deciding many issues for which the principled resolution would be rejection of popular legislative initiatives.[21]

During the late 1930s and 1940s, the Supreme Court began to read the Constitution to provide little restraint when Congress impinged on state power and when states regulated economic interests. At the same time, the Court provided increasing protection under the free speech and free press clauses, under the criminal process sections of the Bill of Rights, and, for blacks and other minorities, under the Equal Protection Clause of the Fourteenth Amendment. Within the Supreme Court and outside, people advanced justifications for the Court's reading some rights expansively and others narrowly. Formulations differed, but the basic idea was that courts need to protect the integrity of the political process and to assure that powerful majorities do not gang up on disadvantaged minorities. This approach was first

[20] US Constitution, Art. I, § 10.
[21] See, especially, Alexander Bickel, *The Least Dangerous Branch: The Supreme Court at the Bar of Politics*, 2nd edn. (New Haven: Yale University Press, 1986); Alexander Bickel, *The Morality of Consent* (New Haven: Yale University Press, 1975).

suggested in a Supreme Court opinion in a famous footnote, footnote 4 in *United States v Carolone Products*;[22] its fullest scholarly development was by John Hart Ely, who wrote that open-ended claims of the Constitution should be understood as 'representation reinforcing'.[23]

During the last part of the twentieth century, some scholars, most notably Ronald Dworkin, have challenged the underlying premises of the 'countermajoritarian difficulty'. Dworkin has argued that the fundamental nature of democracy is not having decisions made by majoritarian votes in legislatures, but affording equal concern and respect for citizens.[24] On his view, if courts reach resolutions that promote equal concern and respect, there is no sacrifice of democratic values.

If one assumes that legislatures are more fairly representative of the population than are courts, this position is overstated. When disagreements exist over what is just and useful in a society, there is *some benefit* to having these disagreements debated and resolved in politically responsible bodies. Jeremy Waldron has argued that, since no one is morally infallible, it is more appropriate for the moral views of democratically elected legislators to implement broad constitutional language than for a few unelected judges to do so.[25] Democracy has something to do with who makes decisions, and the most democratic forms of decision are by the people themselves or their elected representatives. If we believed that, over time, we could project constitutional outcomes from legislatures and courts that were equally good and just and that yielded equally clear constitutional principles, we should probably choose decision by legislatures. So, judicial invalidation of legislation carries some cost in terms of democratic values.

Offsetting gains, however, may make such a practice appropriate and desirable in a democracy. Most simply, on some important issues, one may reasonably trust courts more than legislatures. Many constitutional guarantees are designedly countermajoritarian. If temporary majorities, or legislators seeking political gain at the expense of hated minorities, are likely to give way to passion in suppressing unpopular speech, that is a solid basis to have courts determining the constitutional boundaries of free speech.

A more subtle point involves the interplay of legislative and judicial decision. Judicial invalidation may promote some values even if legislatures and courts are equally protective of those values. Free speech provides an apt illustration. If Congress chooses to allow speech to be free, a court will not declare *that choice* to be invalid. Those who prefer that speech be suppressed rarely have a constitutional argument that it *must* be suppressed. Thus, whenever Congress chooses in favour of

[22] 304 US 144, 152 n. 4 (1938).
[23] Ely, *Democracy and Distrust: A Theory of Judicial Review* (Cambridge, Mass.: Harvard University Press, 1980).
[24] Dworkin, *Freedom's Law: The Moral Reading of the American Constitution* (Cambridge, Mass.: Harvard University Press, 1996). A different formulation of this view might be that democracy is morally legitimate only to the extent that it embodies equal concern and respect.
[25] Jeremy Waldron, *Law and Disagreement* (Oxford: Oxford University Press, 1999).

freedom, its choice will stand. The issue of invalidation emerges when Congress chooses to suppress speech. If the courts defer to Congress, the choice to suppress will rarely be overturned. Non-deferential courts will invalidate more statutes that suppress speech. Thus, active judicial invalidation will promote greater freedom of speech than the alternative, even if Congress cares as much about free speech as the courts.

I should enter two caveats, however. This conclusion would not follow if the practice of judicial invalidation caused Congress to care less about free speech, to leave its protection to the courts. Further, my analysis does not apply when both parties to a political or legal dispute have competing claims of constitutional right, as when a free exercise claim to special treatment is met with an argument that special treatment would violate the Establishment Clause.

Any analysis of judicial review in an actual political system should be realistic about what legislatures are like in that system. No one believes that legislatures come close to perfectly representing constituents. If legislatures are too often insensitive to minorities, bend to vested interests, and are touched by corruption (and one does not think that would change much if judicial review ended), one may conclude that courts are not so much less representative than legislatures. (Of course, one must also look at courts as they are, not as they ideally should be.) An appraisal of what set of institutions and authorities best fulfils democratic values needs to take account of actualities as well as ideals.

Finally, a possible virtue of judicial resolution is its principled manner. Members of society may learn about fundamental values from the sustained, disciplined analysis that judicial opinions provide. On the other hand, the argumentative form of those opinions tends to put down those who hold opposing views, and may discourage accommodation and compromise.

In summary, although robust judicial review may involve some cost in terms of values of democracy, that cost may be substantially outweighed by the contributions review can make to democracy. It may be instructive in this regard that among liberal democracies since World War II, the movement among national governments (Germany, Canada, and the Republic of South Africa are notable examples) and in transnational organizations, such as the European Community, has been towards judicial review, not away from it.

Questions about legitimacy illuminate how issues we examined for statutory interpretation vary in their constitutional context. Should constitutional interpretation be evolutionary or originalist? We may contrast evolutionary interpretation with strict originalism and moderate originalism, terms I develop below. I suggest that strict originalism is not defensible, and that a plausible form of moderate originalism is not too different in practice from a moderate evolutionary approach.

3.4 Undisputed Features of Constitutional Interpretation

It is helpful to begin with some undisputed features of constitutional interpretation. Much more often than is true with statutes, the crucial constitutional language in a case comes down to a general formulation, such as the two religion clauses I have quoted. With respect to most of the key phrases in the Constitution, extensive prior litigation has developed more specific doctrines than the constitutional language provides. Much constitutional adjudication turns out to be more about the outcomes and doctrines of closely related cases than any fresh examination of the original clauses.[26] A student of free speech law meets concepts like viewpoint discrimination, public forum, and compelling interest that are crucial modern doctrines but that have no place in the Free Speech Clause itself, in the history that preceded it, or in the contemporaneous writings of the framers. I do not say these are inappropriate principles, only that they are not to be found in any easy way in the textual provision.

Another undisputed feature of constitutional interpretation is that protections must be read to deal with some circumstances that the founding generation did not foresee. In the most extreme examples, a new technology creates a reality no one then conceived. Thus, the First Amendment guarantees freedom of the press; people in 1789 had no idea of radio or television, much less the internet. The Fourth Amendment protects against unreasonable searches; no one then imagined electronic surveillance. Constitutional principles must apply to technical realities beyond the ken of the framers' generation.

Some provisions of the Constitution may have been designedly left open to changing values. A number of Supreme Court decisions have explicitly treated the cruel and unusual punishment clause in this way.

As many, many cases reflect, original understanding (of some kind) is relevant; the controversial issue is whether original understanding (of some kind) should control.

Existing bodies of constitutional law also matter. An originalist thinks that modern judges should aim to carry out the original understanding, that Supreme Court Justices should never have self-consciously departed from that understanding. To put the point this way, however, leaves open what modern Justices should do about solidly entrenched bodies of constitutional law that they believe have departed from the original understanding. Should they now declare that the Free Speech and Free Press Clauses cover only prior restraints, if they think that was the original understanding? Should they overrule *Brown v Board of Education* if they think people of the time assumed racially segregated schools were consistent with the Equal Protection Clause of the Fourteenth Amendment? A very few scholars have suggested that the modern Supreme Court should abandon bodies of law that are out of line with the original understanding, but most originalist scholars and all originalist Justices assume that judges work within the context of precedents and doctrines built up over

[26] See Charles Fried, 'Constitutional Doctrine', *Harvard Law Review*, 107 (1994), 140.

time. Although justices should not build upon and expand mistaken directions, they should not throw away all settled standards that fit poorly with original understanding.[27] Thus, virtually everyone agrees that some adherence to precedent and settled doctrine should qualify an originalist approach to constitutional interpretation.

Finally, at least among judges and most scholars, there is agreement that decisions in constitutional cases should be principled. In a widely read lecture that became controversial because of its challenge to the Supreme Court's reasoning in *Brown v Board of Education*,[28] Herbert Wechsler asserted that a primary requisite of judicial reasoning is that it be genuinely principled.[29] Although Wechsler's phrase 'neutral principles' led some to believe that he thought judges could decide cases without making controversial assessments of value, that was not his thesis. Rather, he indicated that a judicial opinion should honestly state the grounds of decision, that the decision should rest on a general principle that reaches other cases; that the judges should be willing to decide as the principle indicates.[30] Thus, if in a case involving a civil rights activist whose speech led some members of his audience to hit police officers, the Court said one cannot be punished for speech unless one actually urges others to commit crimes, it should announce such a principle only if it thinks it should apply the principle to members of the Ku Klux Klan and Communist Party as well.

When I say that judges and most scholars agree that constitutional decisions, like other judicial decisions, should be principled in this respect, I mean that they agree that this is the ordinary standard at which judges should aim. People disagree over how demanding the counsel of candour should be,[31] over the circumstances, if any, in which candour should give way to the interests of achieving majority opinions or concealing the degree of a court's innovation.[32]

A more radical critique of judicial principles is that they conceal just how political constitutional decisions are. As this critique is made by critical legal scholars, critical feminists, and critical race theorists, the claim is that apparently neutral principles serve the interests of the dominant class (gender) (race) at the expense of those who

[27] See Henry P. Monaghan, 'Stare Decisis and Constitutional Adjudication', *Columbia Law Review*, 88 (1988), 723. No one of whom I am aware is less willing to accept 'mistaken' precedents than Raoul Berger, 'Original Intent and Boris Bittler', *Indiana Law Journal*, 66 (1991), 723.

[28] 347 US 483 (1954).

[29] Herbert Wechsler, 'Toward Neutral Principles of Constitutional Law', *Harvard Law Review*, 73 (1959), 1.

[30] See Kent Greenawalt, 'The Enduring Significance of Neutral Principles', *Columbia Law Review*, 78 (1978), 982; Martin Golding, 'Principled Decision Making and the Supreme Court', *Columbia Law Review*, 63 (1963), 35.

[31] See David Shapiro, 'In Defense of Judicial Candor', *Harvard Law Review*, 100 (1987), 731; Henry Monaghan, 'Taking Supreme Court Decisions Seriously', *Maryland Law Review*, 39 (1979), 1, 22–6; Scott C. Idleman, 'A Prudential Theory of Judicial Candor', *Texas Law Review*, 73 (1995), 1307.

[32] See Eugene V. Rostow, *The Sovereign Prerogative: The Supreme Court and the Quest for Law* (New Haven: Yale University Press, 1962).

are oppressed.[33] Such a critique may underlie proposals to shift responsibilities away from courts,[34] it could be a basis to introduce more explicit political evaluations or 'narrative' approaches into judicial opinions.[35] But, given the long tradition of judicial opinions that claim to state principles that rise above immediate political controversies, no one expects a radical shift away from opinions that rely on principles. And most observers continue to think that the aspiration to decide according to principles is a worthy one.

With these features of constitutional adjudication in hand, we can address what divides originalists from evolutionists who believe in a 'Living Constitution'.

3.5 Original Understanding

If one talks about original understanding, just what kind of understanding matters? An originalist must address this question, but so also must anyone who thinks that original understanding counts for interpretation, even if it is not necessarily decisive. When we face this general question, a range of more discrete questions emerges: whose understanding, what subject of understanding, what kind of attitude, what level of understanding, what reason for following that understanding? Some of these questions are closely similar to ones we examined for statutory interpretation; others vary significantly in the constitutional context.

3.5.1 *Why Follow Original Intent?*

The question why judges *should* follow original intent bears on how the other questions might be answered. I shall here put aside the question of why original understanding should be given some weight, and focus on the question whether the original understanding should be afforded decisive significance.

One answer to the question of why judges should concentrate on original understanding is that this strategy of interpretation restrains judges, and unconstrained judicial discretion is an evil greatly to be feared. Another answer is that this approach allows desirable latitude for the political branches. A third answer is that officials must be faithful to the Constitution, and originalism represents fidelity. I shall take these answers in reverse order.

---

[33] See e.g. Charles R. Lawrence III, 'Race, Multiculturalism, and the Jurisprudence of Transformation', *Stanford Law Review*, 47 (1995), 819. Catherine MacKinnon, *Toward a Feminist Theory of the State* (Cambridge, Mass.: Harvard University Press, 1989); ead., 'Feminism, Marxism, Method, and the State: Toward Feminist Jurisprudence', *Signs*, 8 (1983), 635.

[34] See Tushnet, n. 19 above.

[35] On narrative generally, see e.g. Richard Delgado, 'Storytelling for Oppositionists and Others: A Plea for Narrative', *Michigan Law Review*, 87 (1989), 2411; Kim Lane Scheppele, 'Foreword: Telling Stories', *Michigan Law Review*, 87 (1989), 2073; Julius G. Getman, 'Voices', *Texas Law Review*, 66 (1988), 577; Lynne N. Henderson, 'Legality and Empathy', *Michigan Law Review*, 86 (1987), 1574.

The possibility of fidelity ties in with the problems of legitimacy we have already examined. As I indicated earlier, our obligation to comply with the Constitution comes from its value in the lives of our and future generations. *We* have no duty of compliance to people who lived long ago; our duties lie to our contemporaries and our successors. But, it might be said, our generation has accepted the Constitution as the structure of government, therefore we owe other members of our present society fidelity to it. This conclusion alone is not enough to get us to originalism.

We have to ask first how our generation has accepted the Constitution. If judges have engaged in non-originalist decisions, say protecting a right to have abortions and forbidding classifications that disfavour women, and most citizens approve of these decisions, it can hardly be said that originalism is a central aspect of the constitutionalism that is now agreed upon.[36]

Originalism must be defended as achieving desirable values, not on the ground that modern acceptance of the Constitution creates some obvious duty of fidelity to the original understanding.

By itself, originalism does not necessarily lead courts to be deferential to the political branches. Nevertheless, under either or both of two plausible premises, originalism fits well with the idea that legislatures should have broad latitude. The simplest premise is one Thayer advanced. The constitutional design was to make Congress the primary judge of its own authority. A deferential attitude towards legislation conforms with that design.

The second premise is more complex. In most important areas, the original understanding restricted Congress and state legislatures less than the modern Supreme Court has done. Thus, for example, the Free Speech Clause and the Equal Protection Clause had much less scope than the modern Court has given them. If the Supreme Court followed an originalist philosophy, legislatures would have greater freedom than they would be likely to have under a competing approach.

This conclusion is not true across the board. Under the original understanding of the Commerce Clause, Congress would be more restricted than it is now, and an originalist approach to the 'Contracts Clause' would limit state legislatures more than has modern Supreme Court interpretation.

Even in areas where originalist interpretation would restrict legislatures less than have modern judicial decisions, it would be more restrictive than some alternatives. Most obviously, it would be more restrictive of legislatures than an interpretive approach under which judges gave extreme deference to all legislative determinations.

Whether or not originalism promotes deference, it does restrict judges, or so proponents like Justice Antonin Scalia claim.[37] On their view, judges must seek an

---

[36] Matters become somewhat more complicated if one thinks that courts consistently employ an originalist rhetoric that persuades citizens, who do not quite acknowledge that a number of decisions they like fail under originalist standards.

[37] Antonin Scalia, *A Matter of Interpretation*.

objective original understanding rather than writing their own moral and political proclivities into the Constitution.

Just what kind of originalism someone adopts will depend partly on the reasons that he embraces originalism. Similarly, for someone who is not an originalist, the reasons to give original understanding some weight will help determine what original understanding matters. With these insights, we can tackle narrower, more specific questions about original understanding.

3.5.2 *Adopters and Readers*

The question about 'whose understanding' resembles the same question about statutory interpretation, but has less practical significance. We may start with the divide between readers and 'writers'. Most Supreme Court cases that refer to views at the time the Constitution was adopted have concentrated on the Framers (including, notably, in church–state cases, Thomas Jefferson, who did not participate in drafting the Bill of Rights, but who did draft the influential predecessor, the Virginia Statute for Religious Liberty). The Constitution was drafted and prepared at the Philadelphia Convention and ratified within state conventions. Since ratification was crucial to the Constitution's coming into force, there is no ground to disregard the views of ratifiers in preference to those at the Philadelphia Convention. Thus, if we seek the intent of those who adopted the Constitution, we must include all the adopters (proposers and ratifiers). Similarly, for constitutional amendments, we must include not only those in Congress who voted on the amendments but those in state legislatures that approved them.

Set against the adopters, we have the general population of 'readers'. We might ask how readers of particular constitutional language would have understood it. In contrast to most ordinary statutory language, the reader's understanding of the most widely interpreted parts of the Constitution could not be formed primarily from a parsing of what terms mean in ordinary English. (This comment is also true about *some* statutory language.) To understand what the right not to 'be compelled in any criminal case to be a witness against himself'[38] means, for example, one would require a sense of the practices to which the language refers.[39] Similarly, the relation of the Free Speech and Free Press Clauses to the law of seditious libel is a matter of understanding history more than of understanding ordinary English.

For some matters in the original Constitution, people's actual views may have been informed as much by writings such as the Federalist Papers as by the language of the document. This is not to say that common understanding of words may never play a part—a generous sense of the term 'necessary' plays a role in the construction of the

---

[38] US Constitution, Amendment V.

[39] For example, the language seems clearly to provide that a criminal defendant need not testify, but may a witness in a civil case be compelled to admit to crimes? The language itself is not revealing.

Necessary and Proper Clause in *McCulloch v Maryland*[40]—but it figures much less than in textual interpretation of statutes.

We have little evidence that the proposers viewed provisions differently from the ratifiers and the citizenry, and less evidence that the ratifiers had a view different from citizens at large. Of course, we do not know that all these groups had similar views, but judges must rely on the views they find expressed. Thus, so long as judicial conclusions do not depend on the opinions of one or two prominent founders, judges need worry less about exactly whose understanding matters than with respect to statutory interpretation.

With constitutional amendments that were preceded by detailed Congressional debates that would not have been available to state legislatures, interpreters may have more basis to gauge a special understanding of the proposers that may not have been shared by ratifiers or citizens.

If the question whose understanding counts has limited practical bite, it nevertheless possesses theoretical interest. Issues of fair notice to readers of a time long past *now* seem irrelevant. One can, of course, maintain that law is public, and that original reader understanding continues to be of some importance; but if the Constitution, and most amendments, represent a coherent design of government, perhaps what those responsible for the design understood should *now* matter more than how provisions would have been seen by typical readers of the public 200 years ago.

This observation *may* suggest a more general point: that when a document ages, the understanding of those who adopted it should increase in significance *vis-à-vis* the understanding of original readers. If this is a sound view, the crucial 'original understanding' may itself shift over time, as the views of adopters increase in importance relative to those of original readers.

One significant issue is whether the views of framers expressed *after adoption* should have any significance. A leading example is use in church–state cases of a letter of Jefferson's written after the Bill of Rights was adopted, which uses the phrase 'wall of separation'.[41] One might say that judges should consider no statements that were unavailable to the adopters at the time they acted, since such statements could not indicate meaning to the adopters and could not then be rebutted by those with a different understanding. However, some of these later statements may shed light on understandings at the time amendments were adopted.

On occasion, courts refer to legislation enacted shortly after the passage of constitutional provisions as evidence of how the provisions were understood. This usage is less subject to the idiosyncracies of individual proposers, because it takes majorities in both houses to produce legislation.

---

[40]   17 US (4 Wheat.) 316 (1819).
[41]   *Everson v Board of Education*, 330 US 1, 16 (1947). The expression was used earlier in *Reynolds v United States*, 98 US 145 (1878).

3.5.3 *What Attitude?*

By 'what kind of attitude', I refer to the distinction between hopes, expectations, and beliefs about how a provision should be understood. I assume that, as with statutory interpretation, the most important state of mind is how someone, adopter or citizen, believed that a provision should be understood.

3.5.4 *Attitudes about Coverage and Interpretation*

This brings us to the two most troublesome questions: what subject of understanding and what level of understanding? By the subject of understanding, I mean roughly to distinguish attitudes about interpretation from attitudes about coverage. Most of the adopters, *and* at least some lawyers in the general public, entertained ideas about how judges should interpret authoritative legal language, as well as ideas about what the Constitution would be taken to require. Of course, none had experience with written constitutions as the structure for federal governments, but they were familiar with statutes and colonial charters. Some scholars claim that up to the time the Constitution was adopted, judges had interpreted the language of statutes flexibly, paying little or no attention to what the legislators who adopted the statute intended and not reading the language in a strict or narrow way.[42] If so, it is reasonable to suppose that people who adopted or read the Constitution conceived that it would be interpreted accordingly, conceived, that is, that the content of its provisions would be construed in an evolutionary way.

If this hypothesis is accurate, judges who stick rigidly to the views of the founding generation about the content of constitutional provisions are not being faithful to their overall understanding. Thus, if the framers wrote provisions designed to encourage later judges to make their own moral evaluations—what Ronald Dworkin calls 'the moral reading of the Constitution'[43]—then judges who freely implement shifting moral judgments are following the original understanding. For someone whose reason for originalism is fidelity to the founders, this historical question about their interpretive ideas carries great significance.

But an originalist who thinks Justices should adhere to the original views about coverage might deflect this historical argument in the following way. Whatever members of the founding generation believed, *our* well-founded notions of desirable judicial performance and restraint lead us to conclude that judges interpreting authoritative texts should stick to what the adopters and original readers believed about the scope of the language. Thus, originalist judges should follow original views about content, not original views about the nature of judicial authority. The plausibility of this position lies in the claimed values of originalism which we have already examined.

---

[42] See H. Jefferson Powell, 'The Original Understanding of Original Intent', *Harvard Law Review*, 98 (1985), 885.

[43] Dworkin, *Freedom's Law*, n. 24 above.

3.5.5 *Levels of Understanding*

The related question about levels of understanding is perhaps even more central. This question parallels the distinction between purpose and specific intent in statutory interpretation. Members of the founding generation had views about specific practices the Constitution forbade; they also had ideas about the purposes of the provisions and the reasons for their adoption. Suppose that modern judges believe the reasons and purposes behind a prohibition cover practices the founding generation thought were acceptable *and* that they, the judges, need not stretch the actual textual language greatly to cover the practices. Should judges declare these practices to be unconstitutional? According to what we may call a narrow or strict originalism, modern judges should take as crucial the practices the founders thought were forbidden.[44] According to a moderate originalism, modern judges should be mainly guided by purposes and reasons. A moderate originalist might emphasize a very general level of judgment—protect whatever speech promotes liberal democracy and the spread of truth—or some intermediate middle level—protect speech whose prohibition raises the dangers the founders feared from the crime of seditious libel.

The more abstract the level of reference, the harder in practice it becomes to distinguish a judge who is a moderate originalist from one who accepts evolutionary interpretation of a 'living constitution'. The 'moral reading' approach is an example. If a judge finds in the Constitution certain very general values, such as the equality of citizens, and applies these to modern circumstances according to her own moral evaluation, is she a moderate originalist or an evolutionist? Does this depend on her own self-understanding, whether she thinks she is engaged in originalist interpretation or something else?

This example may suggest doubt that this categorization between moderate originalists and evolutionists is itself very useful. Perhaps for constitutional interpretation, instead of employing these general labels, we would do better to focus on exactly what it is that judges should take from the founders and what evaluations they should draw from contemporary moral and political standards or make on the basis of their own moral and political judgment.

One effort in this direction is Laurence Lessig's idea of translation, that modern judges should try to understand constitutional judgments in the context of the founder's generation and then apply those judgments to the very different contexts of modern life.[45] In Lessig's own hands, the notion of translation gives modern judges

---

[44] An illuminating categorization of various approaches is Paul Brest, 'The Misconceived Quest for the Original Understanding', *Boston University Law Review*, 60 (1980), 204. See also Daniel A. Farber, 'The Originalism Debate: A Guide for the Perplexed', *Ohio State Law Journal*, 49 (1989), 1085.

[45] Lawrence Lessig, 'Fidelity in Translation', *Texas Law Review*, 71 (1993), 1165; 'Understanding Changed Readings: Fidelity and Theory', *Stanford Law Review*, 47 (1995), 395.

considerable latitude, but one can imagine a version that instructs judges to stick closely to the founders' values, leaving judges much less room to respond to changing assumptions about values.

Judges who make a point of calling themselves originalists tend to emphasize the specific practices the founders thought the Constitution forbade. As I have said, virtually all originalists do acknowledge that constitutional principles may apply to new technologies, but a narrow or strict originalist would insist that the principles applied to the new technologies should (so far as possible) be the principles accepted by the founding generation. Such an approach, faithfully followed, puts *more* constraint on modern judges than does a moderate originalism that allows for greater development of new principles as social conditions and values change. The major problem with narrow or specific practice originalism is that it may be *too constraining* when a written Constitution is hard to amend.

I can make these abstract points best in terms of some specific examples. The adopters of the Fourteenth Amendment, and people at the time, did not think the Equal Protection Clause forbade public schools segregated by race (they also did not think the clause forbade special measures to favour former slaves). The decision in *Brown v Board of Education* is hard to defend according to narrow originalism. However, a moderate originalist may take the Equal Protection Clause as representing judgments that blacks should not be treated by the state as inferior and should have access equal to whites for important state services; recognizing the modern place of public schools, the universal motivating assumptions about racial subordination that lie behind segregation, and the damage that a stigma of inferiority can cause for children, he may find it easy to conclude that school segregation is now unconstitutional.

At the time the First Amendment was adopted, no one thought it restricted damages for ordinary defamation (libel and slander). In the 1960s huge awards for libel of officials in southern states threatened free discussion of the civil rights movement and official reactions to marches and demonstrations. The Supreme Court decided, in *New York Times v Sullivan*,[46] that the First Amendment was meant to bar the crime of seditious libel, a crime that penalized harsh criticism of the government. If public officials could successfully sue newspapers for innocent mistakes of fact regarding government activities, criticism of government could be sharply curtailed. Thus, the Court protected defamation of public officials in their public functions, except when statements were knowingly false or made in reckless disregard of the truth. Again, the result was one a narrow originalist could not easily defend, but one that fitted comfortably with moderate originalism.

The controversial decision creating a constitutional right to abortion was plainly mistaken according to narrow originalists and even difficult to justify for moderate

---

[46] *New York Times v Sullivan*, 376 US 254 (1964).

originalists.[47] In the crucial case of *Roe v Wade*,[48] the Supreme Court relied mainly on the Fourteenth Amendment's Due Process Clause. Although a few courts prior to that amendment had said that 'Due Process' includes *some* substantive limits as well as procedural requirements, the clause's main thrust was procedural, and one could not draw out of it any general protection of autonomous decision in personal matters. The decision is consistent with moderate originalism only if one casts the relevant constitutional values at a highly abstract level.

The application of the Equal Protection Clause to women presents somewhat similar issues. People in the generation of the Fourteenth Amendment, who denied women the vote, barred them from vocations, and sharply restricted their rights of property, did not assume the Equal Protection Clause would preclude classifications treating women and men differently. One needs to cast the original constitutional value at a high level of abstraction to cover equality for women (and for some other disadvantaged groups to whom protection has been extended). At least in this instance, however, the constitutional language comfortably fits the extension, since the clause itself is not explicitly restricted.

An interesting test of anyone's theory is how they regard the argument that capital punishment may be 'cruel and unusual'. People in the founding generation and at the time of the Fourteenth Amendment clearly accepted capital punishment, and the Constitution itself definitely contemplates its imposition. For example, the Fifth and Fourteenth Amendments forbid the taking of '*life*, liberty, or property without due process of law' (thus, implying that life may be taken with due process). Someone can argue that the founders themselves had a flexible view of 'cruel punishment' and might have envisioned that some day capital punishment, among other punishments, could be so regarded. But one may wonder whether a moderate originalism should allow the Constitution to be interpreted to reject practices whose permissibility the Constitution itself clearly presupposes.

3.5.6 *Structural Inferences*

I have written thus far as if judges are always focusing on single constitutional provisions (or two closely related provisions, such as the Free Exercise and Establishment Clauses), but an accepted form of constitutional argument relies on fundamental structures of the Constitution.[49] Just as one statutory provision is interpreted in light of surrounding provision and the purpose of the statute as a whole, so also one consitutional provision is properly interpreted in light of other provisions and the basic structures of the Constitution. But occasionally the Supreme Court has gone further,

[47] If the Ninth Amendment or the Privileges and Immunities Clause of the Fourteenth Amendment was designed to protect some pervasive zone of personal life, a moderate originalist might believe that abortion now fits within that zone.

[48] 410 US 113 (1973).

[49] See Charles Black, *Structure and Relationship in Constitutional Law* (Baton Rouge: Louisiana State University Press, 1969).

and declared a constitutional right that does not rest on any particular provision. Prior to adoption of the Fourteenth Amendment, the Supreme Court declared that states could not interfere with the freedom of citizens to travel to the seat of the national government.[50] In the majority opinion in *Griswold v Connecticut*,[51] Justice Douglas found a right of married couples to use contraceptives in the 'penumbras' of a number of the Bill of Rights.

Any of the various theories about legitimate constitutional interpretation can find some place for arguments from structure, but a strict originalist will give them less scope than might a moderate originalist or evolutionary theorist. A strict originalist would find an argument from structure to be persuasive only if it is persuasive about the rights and duties the Constitution was originally understood to create.[52] A moderate originalist could declare rights beyond those originally conceived, so long as the new rights flowed from the values and practices of the original Constitution. An evolutionary theorist could decide that new rights fitted well with the Constitution as a whole, as it is now understood.

Given the difficulty of amendment, the symbolic importance of the Constitution, and the desirability of continuity over time, during which sweeping changes in social relations and dominant values occur, a rigorously narrow originalist approach to constitutional interpretation is misguided. A plausible originalism must focus on broad constitutional principles, and how these may be applied to changing conditions. If a constitution is to survive over centuries with relatively few amendments, judges either must practise a moderate originalism that sometimes (at least) takes original constitutional values at a fairly high level of abstraction, or they must practise an evolutionary approach that places considerable emphasis on continuity with values underlying the Constitution. At the edges, these two forms of practice become nearly indistinguishable.

3.6 The Modern Reader

It remains to comment on two aspects of constitutional interpretation I have thus far touched upon only briefly. One aspect is the role of the modern reader; the other aspect is the common law quality of much constitutional adjudication.

When one thinks of most constitutional issues, modern reader understanding of the text matters less than it does for typical statutory interpretation. This is so for two reasons. Constitutional provisions mainly restrict government actions. Citizens do

---

[50]   *Crandall v Nevada*, 73 US 35 (1867).

[51]   381 US 479 (1985). It may be worth noting that only one other Justice joined the Douglas opinion without joining any other. For discussion of recent cases, see Brannon P. Denning and Glenn Harlan Reynolds, 'Comfortably Penumbral', *Boston University Law Review*, 77 (1997), 1089.

[52]   More precisely, one would have to consider the understanding at the time the most recent relevant provisions were adopted.

not usually rely on them in the way that they rely on what statutes forbid, allow, and give them a right to. I do not mean to say such reliance never occurs. A newspaper publisher might violate a law prohibiting publication of information on how to make bombs, in the belief that the law infringes freedom of the press. The wisdom of the publisher's constitutional judgment may depend on the accuracy of his confidence that he will not be punished. But citizens do not often rely in this way on the privilege against self-incrimination or the establishment clause. Their individual behaviour is not guided by their constitutional interpretation. Fair warning is less important for most constitutional claims than for most statutory claims.

The second reason why modern reader understanding *of the text* matters less in constitutional cases is that neither modern readers nor their lawyers come to the constitutional text standing by itself. If they did, the general words of most crucial clauses would fail to give much guidance. In any event, modern understanding is deeply influenced by interpretive decisions over the years. Justices may reasonably worry about withdrawing protections previous decisions have afforded, as with the constitutional right to have abortions, but the issue is not how modern readers would grasp the constitutional text standing alone, the issue concerns the reliance of citizens on what the modern Court has announced.

3.7 Common Law Aspects of Constitutional Interpretation

For judges, as well as citizens, constitutional adjudication is incremental. Constitutional rights in practice have more to do with what courts have decided over the years than with what the original document says and what members of the founding generation believed. As so stated, this point is perfectly consistent with originalist interpretation. If clauses of constitutions (and statutes) are highly general, courts attempting to carry out the original understanding may need to develop sets of ancillary doctrines and distinctions not found in the text. After many cases have been decided, new decisions may apply and refine these doctrines without any reference back to the original understanding.

But the common law quality of much constitutional adjudication *also* suggests a model of restraint that differs from originalism. Judges developing the common law are restrained by the holdings and principles of prior decisions. Perhaps, as David Strauss has urged,[53] the most important restraint on judges in constitutional adjudication is of the same kind. This restraint can exist *even if* decisions have developed the law in a way that is hard to justify on originalist grounds.

The self-conscious evolutionist, thus, has some answer to the charge that he abandons judicial restraint. He can point out that originalist judges are less constrained

---

[53] David A. Strauss, 'Common Law Constitutional Interpretation', *University of Chicago Law Review*, 63 (1996), 877.

than originalist theory supposes, both because it is so difficult to pin down original understandings and because the only plausible version of originalism, some version of moderate originalism, leaves so much latitude to modern judges in choosing the level of principles and in applying those principles to modern life. Originalist approaches afford even less constraint because judges must decide how much to accept of the existing body of decisional law that they do not think can be justified on originalist grounds.

The evolutionist, who thinks judges should recognize a 'Living Constitution', believes it is much better simply to admit that in many areas the law has drifted from what can be justified by any genuinely constraining originalism, and to recognize that constraint lies in judges preserving reasonable continuity with what their predecessors have done. On this vision, constitutional law develops out of an original constitution, but over time develops in some respects that are not easy to connect to the words of that constitution or the understandings of the founding generation. Such a pattern is not to be regretted as a series of errors that, for reasons of continuity, judges should not now correct, but as what amounts to healthy development of law for a constitution that endures for centuries.

CHAPTER 8

....

METHODOLOGY

....

JULES L. COLEMAN

ARGUABLY, the most familiar way in which philosophy contributes to our understanding of legal practice is by providing an analysis of the concepts that are central to it—including, of course, the concept of law itself.[1] In the 'Postscript' to *The Concept of Law*, Hart famously defends what he calls 'descriptive jurisprudence', his (as it turns out) unfortunate label for the methodological approach that he takes to conceptual analysis of law. Just as famously, Ronald Dworkin rejects the possibility of a descriptive jurisprudence, and argues instead that a philosophical theory of law is necessarily an activity of first-order moral/political philosophy. Jurisprudence is normative, not descriptive.[2] This is not—at least not on its face—a debate about the

---

[1] I have in the main sought to present and explore the methodological questions of jurisprudence in the terms in which the central participants (e.g. Dworkin, Perry, and posthumously, Hart) have formulated them. These are not the terms in which I have come to conceptualize them. I believe that we cannot appreciate fully the central concerns of jurisprudence without first disentangling issues of the meta-semantics and semantics of 'law' from those of jurisprudence. While I am convinced that such an approach is significantly more promising than anything that is reflected in the familiar formulations of the issues, presenting these issues from my own perspective in the context of this essay would have been inappropriate for two reasons. First, setting out an alternative and unfamiliar framework would have required so much by the way of analytic preliminaries that the essay would have become unmanageably long. Secondly, by and large, the issues can still be usefully explored and sorted out within the current framework. Where that is not the case, I indicate in substantive footnotes. The reader interested in the alternative approach to jurisprudence is directed to 'Law' with Ori Simchen (essay on file with authors) and Jules Coleman and Ori Simchen, *The Language of Law* (forthcoming, Harvard University Press, 2002).

[2] It is hard to identify who is responsible for introducing the phrases 'normative' and 'descriptive' as ways of characterizing the differences in approaches to the philosophical analysis of law. While it is clear that there are two apparently different takes on the project of jurisprudence, it is less clear how

substantive theory of law or of the concept of it, but rather a dispute about the methodology of theory construction in legal philosophy in particular, and perhaps in philosophy more generally. While there may be no issue more prominent in the recent literature than this dispute between the proponents of descriptive and normative jurisprudence, it is difficult to frame the debate in a way that would justify the attention it has received, or the passions that have arisen on both sides of the divide.

In characterizing his project as 'descriptive', Hart intended to make a very narrow and, to his mind, unobjectionable claim—that a jurisprudential theory need not warrant the inference from legality to moral legitimacy. By his lights, any other approach to analysing the concept of law runs the risk of begging the question as to the legitimacy of law, and so in describing his project as 'descriptive', he takes himself to be doing no more than what is necessary to avoid begging that question. Nothing Hart says rules out the possibility that some or all forms of governance that fall within the concept's extension are morally legitimate, worthy of endorsement, or capable of generating moral obligations to obey; he meant only to rule out the inference from legality to legitimacy. Accurately or not, Hart takes Dworkin to be imposing the constraint that an adequate theory of the concept of law is one in which its instances are at least prima-facie morally legitimate or worthy of endorsement; and in referring to his project as descriptive, Hart meant only to dissociate himself from that kind of project.

Like Dworkin, Stephen Perry has argued that Hart's jurisprudence is normative, not descriptive. Perry begins with Hart's provocative remark, in the Preface to *The Concept of Law*, that his project of analytic jurisprudence might also be characterized as 'descriptive sociology'. As Perry reads him, there is little evidence that Hart was actually engaged in a social scientific inquiry of any sort: he seeks to uncover no law-like regularities that would support appropriate counterfactuals, nor does he measure his project by the norms usually governing such inquiry—for example, by its predictive accuracy.[3] If Hart is not engaged in social science as such, then what else might he mean by referring to his project as 'descriptive sociology'?

One possible answer is that like J. L. Austin, Hart believed that we could secure knowledge of the world by exploring the way we talk about it. So a descriptive soci-

---

meaningfully to formulate the difference, and why it matters. Among the aims of this chapter is to match the level of passion the debate has engendered with a commensurate level of clarity.

[3] In contrast, Scott Shapiro argues that there is ample evidence that Hart did have certain social scientific ambitions. In particular, Shapiro takes Hart to be committed to a functionalist account of law that is very much social scientific in its aims and methods. Shapiro argues that Hart's functionalism provides the best account of the argument in chapter 5 of *The Concept of Law* (Oxford: Clarendon Press) that all legal systems in their mature form will consist of a union of primary and secondary rules. See S. Shapiro, 'On Hart's Way Out', *Legal Theory*, 4/4 (1998), and 'Law, Morality and The Guidance of Conduct', *Legal Theory*, 6/2 (2000). See also Jules L. Coleman, *The Practice of Principle* (Oxford University Press, 2001), ch. 10.

ology in this context turns out to be a sociological study of the use of language—in particular, of the various, intelligible uses made of the expression, 'law'. The job of the descriptive theorist—or the conceptual analyst, in this sense—is to investigate usage and to report his findings. So conceived, the aim of descriptive jurisprudence is to identify shared criteria for applying the noun 'law' to schemes of governance.

While the meaning of a term or of the concept it expresses is of course intimately bound up with its use, that subtle relationship could never be captured by a simple reporting project aimed at tabulating commonalities of shared usage. Such a project could in most cases yield only a vague and ambiguous notion. Hart's aim is not to report on usage, but to analyse the concept of law. To analyse the concept of law is, among other things, to rationalize the concept by articulating criteria for its use that enable us to be more precise than we could otherwise be in using the expression 'law'. Such a project is normative both in its construction and its ambition. It answers to norms of theory construction and aims to discipline use and structure thought. If this is the sense in which we are to understand the claim that jurisprudence must be 'normative', then any account or theory of the concept of law is normative, but that is hardly a revelation, and certainly not something Hart or anyone else would contest. In short Hart can, and surely would, accept the normativity of conceptual analysis of law while insisting—quite rightly—that his is a project of descriptive jurisprudence—by which he means only that it is not undertaken with the goal of warranting an inference from legality to legitimacy. If such an inference is warranted, it will be on substantive, and not conceptual or logical grounds.

If normative jurisprudence asserts no more than that the analysis of the concept of law is a norm-governed activity and aims to regulate use and discipline thought, then normative jurisprudence is a rather innocent claim that no one—least of all Hart—would reject. On the other hand, if we accept Hart's formulation, a jurisprudence is normative if and only if it warrants an inference from legality to legitimacy—or takes warranting such an inference as an adequacy condition. Any other methodology is descriptive. On the first formulation, it is impossible for jurisprudence not to be normative, whereas on the second formulation it is extremely unlikely that jurisprudence could be normative. One would be hard pressed to say that the issue has been adequately joined. Let's see if we can do better than this.

We can distinguish between two very different kinds of challenges to the method of descriptive conceptual analysis attributed among others to Hart. One family of critics objects to conceptual analysis, the other to its alleged descriptivism. Those who object to the conceptualistic dimension of the method see conceptual analysis as a relic of the 'linguistic turn' in philosophy. That Hart practised conceptual analysis is—given the period in which he wrote—an excusable error. As for the rest of us, conceptual projects are an unpardonable sin. These critics, Brian Leiter most notable among them, claim that conceptual analysis is very likely fruitless, and is in any event unilluminating, and that conceptual analysis best go the way of linguistic analysis. As linguistic philosophy has given way to naturalism, so too conceptual jurisprudence; it must give way to a naturalized jurisprudence.[4]

Other critics, like Ronald Dworkin and Stephen Perry, do not appear to deny the potential informativeness of philosophical analysis; they deny instead its descriptivist pretensions. For them, a philosophical analysis of law is fruitful in part because it necessarily invokes contestable premises of political morality.

Neither of these objections is persuasive. If there are good grounds for expressing doubt about Hart's methodology—and there may well be—they are not the grounds that those who propose a naturalized or a normative jurisprudence have advanced. This chapter proceeds as follows. In Section 1, I consider the case for normative jurisprudence. In doing so, I develop and assess many of the arguments advanced by its most ardent and competent advocates. Neither these nor a broad range of other promising arguments I construct are persuasive. Many, however, are extremely insightful, and exploring them in detail repays the effort. In Section 2 I assess Leiter's claims on behalf of naturalism. We begin with Dworkin's arguments for a normative jurisprudence.

1. Normative Jurisprudence

1.1 The Semantic Sting

Dworkin is the most important proponent of normative jurisprudence, and his most famous argument for the claim that jurisprudence is normative is the Semantic Sting. According to Dworkin, Positivism is not only a substantive view of the kind of thing law is, it is underwritten by a certain semantics of concepts, and related accounts of both what it is to understand a concept's meaning and to retrieve its content. He labels that web of commitments 'criterial semantics'. According to his formulation of criterial semantics, 'we follow shared rules . . . in using any word: these rules set out criteria that supply the word's meaning'.[5] Knowing the meaning of a concept is evidenced by a certain kind of understanding. Because the meaning of concepts is given by the shared criteria of their application, to understand the meaning is to know what

---

[4] Naturalists, like Leiter, tend to identify all forms of distinctively philosophical theorizing about law with a priori 'intuition pumping'. In doing so, the 'naturalist' relies on too narrow a conception of naturalism while offering a diminished conception of the philosophical project. I cannot address these concerns in detail here, but I will have occasion to say a bit more about the projects of analytic philosophy below.

[5] *Law's Empire* (Cambridge, Mass.: Belknap Press of Harvard University Press), 31.

those criteria are. So understood, the point of the jurisprudential project is to identify the shared criteria for properly applying the concept law.

Law, however, is an 'essentially contested' concept in the sense that competent language users disagree not only about whether this or that scheme of governance—for
example, Nazi Germany—is an instance of law, and about what the criteria for applying the concept of law *ought* to be; they disagree also about what the criteria for applying the concept of law are. If competent language users can intelligibly disagree about
the criteria for applying a concept that they share, then the meaning of the concept
cannot be fixed by shared criteria for applying it; and the project of jurisprudence
cannot consist in identifying what those shared criteria are.

The Semantic Sting thus undermines a criterial semantics of concepts generally, of
the concept of law, in particular, and the substantive legal positivism that it underwrites. In this way, the Semantic Sting Argument paves the way for the view that law
is an interpretive concept. In determining what law is we do not identify shared criteria for the application of the term. Instead we defend certain substantive normative
premises and orient our analysis of what law is according to them.

In a constructive interpretation, we begin with a pre-theoretic account or understanding of the practice. That understanding restricts the set of values or purposes we
might reasonably attribute to it. Once a value or function is ascribed to the practice,
it fixes the content of the practice. In this sense, the practice points us to the function
or purpose most appropriate to its interpretation, and that purpose in turn fixes the
extension of the noun that denotes the relevant practice. This is the way in which fit
and value figure in constructive interpretation. When it comes to law, Dworkin is
committed to the claim that the purpose or function that best illuminates our legal
practice is that of justifying, guiding, and constraining the coercive power of the state.
In interpreting what law is we orient our interpretation of it towards the goal of
revealing it in its best light—that is, as something that is the best of its kind that it can
be—which in this context amounts to interpreting it as something that serves its purpose well, or expresses well the value attributed to it. Since the point or purpose that
we impute to law is that of justifying and limiting the state's exercise of coercive force,
the substantive argument that we must undertake in order to retrieve the content of
the concept of law will necessarily appeal to norms of political morality. Thus,
jurisprudence is and must be normative.

There are two components to this argument for normative jurisprudence. The first
is the Semantic Sting; the second is the nature of constructive interpretation. The two
components of the argument are connected as follows. A philosophical analysis of a
practice—in this case law—can take the form of either a criterial semantics or a constructive interpretation. The failure of criterial semantics entails interpretivism. A constructive interpretation of law in turn requires a normative jurisprudence. Whereas the
Semantic Sting Argument is not sufficient to establish normative jurisprudence,
Dworkin takes it to be necessary to doing so. In evaluating his argument for normative
jurisprudence, we should begin with the Semantic Sting Argument itself.

The first problem with the Semantic Sting Argument is that it is simply not valid. It could only be valid were it true that the semantics of concepts must be either criterial or interpretive. Only then could the failure of a criterial semantics entail interpretivism. Of course, these are not the only two alternatives, and so the failure of criterial semantics does not entail interpretivism.[6]

Of greater concern is the fact that if criterial semantics is mistaken, Dworkin has provided no reason for thinking so, and even less reason for attributing such a semantics to Hart. As Dworkin characterizes it, criterial semantics holds that the meaning of a concept is fixed by the existence of shared criteria. The phrase 'shared criteria of application' is ambiguous between an individualistic and a community-wide interpretation. On the individualistic interpretation, the criteria are shared in the sense that each competent language speaker knows the rules for applying the concept or concept-word. On the community-wide interpretation, to say that the criteria are shared is just to say that the community has a rule for applying the concept or concept-word, though, no particular competent language speaker need know what the rule is. As everyone from Wittgenstein to Putnam and Raz has pointed out, the individualistic conception of criterialism is hopeless. Meaning is social in a way that individualistic criterialism characterizes inappropriately.[7] On the other hand, Dworkin must attribute the individual interpretation of criterial semantics to positivism, for without it, the fact that individuals disagree about what the criteria for applying a concept are, is inconsequential for the criterialist.[8]

Nor can the demand that those who share the same concept and understand its meaning share a kind of theoretical knowledge in the form of a capacity to formulate rules for applying the concept fairly be attributed to Hart. Such a view of meaning puts a logical positivist spin on the later Wittgenstein, and represents neither a plausible interpretation of Hart nor of Wittgenstein.[9] To be sure, Dworkin is free to define criterial semantics as he pleases and to saddle it with unmanageable burdens. In doing so, however, he makes any argument, including the Semantic Sting, correspondingly less interesting—its consequences that much weaker.

The Semantic Sting Argument is further undermined by a failure adequately to attend to the difference between the content of *the law* (of a particular community) and the content of the *concept* of law (or of law, a kind of social practice), the consequence of which is that Dworkin argues for one conclusion, while his goal is to estab-

---

[6] This is one reason why we might interpret the Semantic Sting along the lines suggested to me by Mark Greenberg. In this reading, the point of the Semantic Sting is to eliminate a kind of natural competition for interpretivism. Were criterial semantics correct that would make pursuing an interpretivist strategy pointless. The Semantic Sting does not establish intepretivism; it helps motivate it.

[7] Joseph Raz, 'Two Views of the Nature of Law: A Partial Comparison', in Jules Coleman (ed.), *Hart's Postscript* (Oxford: Oxford University Press, 2001).

[8] This argument is fully developed in Coleman and Simchen, *The Language of Law*. There we also explain why even the community-wide conception of criterialism fails to give the meaning of nouns like 'law'.

[9] See Coleman and Simchen, *Content and the Language of Law*.

lish the other. According to Dworkin's formulation of criterial semantics, 'we follow shared rules . . . in using any word: these rules set out criteria that supply the word's meaning'.[10] Thus, the 'very meaning of the word "law" makes *law* depend on certain specific criteria, and that any lawyer who rejected or challenged those criteria would be speaking self-contradictory nonsense'.[11] Of course, the meaning of the word 'law' may depend on specific shared criteria even if the law of a particular community does not depend on shared criteria of any sort. And thus a lawyer who challenged what the criteria of legality were in his community could hardly be accused (even by a criterial semanticist) of speaking 'self-contradictory nonsense'.

From the outset, Dworkin runs together two distinct notions: the application conditions of the term 'law' (or the semantic content of the concept of law or the nature of law), on the one hand; and the criteria of legality in a particular community, on the other. The following assertion is supposed to clinch the case against the criterial semanticist, but reveals instead the extent of the confusion. 'If legal argument is mainly or even partly about pivotal cases', he writes, 'then lawyers cannot all be using the same factual criteria for deciding when propositions of law are true and false. Their arguments would be mainly or partly about which criteria they should use.'[12] He concludes, 'if two lawyers are actually following different rules in using the word "law", using different factual criteria to decide when a proposition of law is true or false, then each must mean something different from the other when he says what the law is'.[13]

Dworkin takes the first two clauses—'If two lawyers are actually following different rules in using the word "law"', and 'using different factual criteria to decide when a proposition of law is true or false'—to come to the same thing, for both are thought to entail the conclusion that 'each must mean something different from the other when he says what the law is'. However, while it may be true on a criterial semantics that two individuals who follow different rules for applying the word or concept 'law' must be assigning different meanings to it, it hardly follows that two people who are using different factual criteria to decide whether a proposition of law is true or false must be assigning different meanings to the term 'law', or employing different concepts of law.

Two people can use different factual criteria for determining whether or not something is legally binding without disagreeing about the meaning of the concept; two people can agree on the factual criteria without disagreeing on the concept. This is obvious once one realizes that the factual criteria for determining whether or not a proposition of law is true or false are indexed to particular legal systems, whereas the criteria for the semantic content of the concept of law are not. So you and I can share the same concept of law, but because we practise law in different communities, we can 'disagree' (in an uninteresting sense) about the factual criteria for determining the truth or falsity of particular propositions of law.

---

[10] *Law's Empire*, 31.   [11] ibid. 31.   [12] ibid. 41.   [13] ibid. 41.

By the same token, you and I can practise law in the same community and agree on what the criteria are in our community, and yet disagree about the general concept of law. Thus, we can agree that a rule that violates the Equal Protection Clause of the Fourteenth Amendment is not valid law, but disagree about the concept of law. You believe that the best explanation of this fact is that substantive morality is a criterion of legality whether or not such a constraint is practised (you are a natural lawyer) and I believe that the best explanation of this fact is that there is a conventional practice of refusing to treat as binding rules that fail a test of substantive equality. I am conventionalist about the concept and you are not. What we disagree about is how best to explain the practice; we need not disagree, though we likely may do, about what the criteria of legality in the community are.

Can you and I disagree about the criteria of legality in our (common) community without thereby disagreeing about the meaning of law? In other words, is a criterial semantics compatible with disagreement between lawyers (and other competent language users) about the criteria of legality in their community? This I take it is the case Dworkin is most concerned about. Unfortunately for Dworkin, the answer is that of course you and I can disagree about the criteria of legality in our community without our disagreeing about the criteria for application of the term 'law'. Here is an obvious example. You and I disagree about what the criteria of legal validity in our community are, but we share the same criteria for applying the term 'law'. What we share is the view that law is a contestable concept in that wherever there is law, what the law is is always a matter of potential dispute, and requires an interpretive practice. Indeed our disagreement about what the criteria of legality in our community are makes perfectly good sense to us in part because such disagreement is part of our shared understanding of the kind of thing law is.

Thus, it looks like Dworkin misdiagnoses the situation in which we disagree about the criteria of legality in our community. Our disagreement tells us nothing about which semantic theory of the concept of law is correct. If positivism as a substantive theory of the concept of law claims that the conditions of legality are exhausted by shared criteria of legal validity, then our disagreement is some evidence for the claim that in some legal communities the criteria of legality are not exhausted by shared criteria, or that the criteria are not shared in the way in which a conventionalist or positivist picture requires them to be. Thus, properly understood, disagreement about the criteria of legality in a community may count against substantive positivism, but disagreement about what the criteria of law are in a community has no bearing on a semantic theory or methodological claims.[14]

The Semantic Sting component of the argument for normative jurisprudence cannot be sustained. The argument is invalid. Moreover, only a logical positivist reading of Hart warrants attributing criterial semantics to him. Such a reading is fair

---

[14] Kenneth Himma makes very much the same point. See Kenneth Himma, 'Ambiguously Sting', *Legal Theory*, 7/1 (2001).

neither to Hart nor to Wittgenstein or J. L. Austin, the two philosophers whose influence on Hart was greatest.[15] In addition, the argument confuses the nature of the content of *law* (the practice or the concept of it) with the content of *the law* of a particular community.[16]

Dworkin has nowhere repudiated the Semantic Sting; and it is quite clear that its soundness is the linchpin of his argument for normative jurisprudence. Still, if *we* are to treat Dworkin's argument for normative jurisprudence with the care it deserves, then we need to disassociate it from the Semantic Sting. The failure of criterial semantics, in other words, cannot be our grounds for concluding that law is an interpretive concept. It remains a fair question to ask of Dworkin what, in the face of the collapse of the Semantic Sting, grounds the argument for interpretivism. Let's set that issue aside and simply assume that law is an interpretative concept.

Even so, it does not follow from the fact that law is an interpretive concept, that any interpretation of it requires a foray into substantive moral/political philosophy. More argument is needed. The required argument begins with the innocent and uncontroversial claim that the norms appropriate to an interpretation of something depend on the kind of thing the object of interpretation is. This means that we need some pre-interpretive account of the kind of thing law is sufficient to anchor an interpretation of it. This is presumably the status of the claim that law's function is to justify and limit the coercive power of the state. This imputation of a justificatory function to law is the premise that orients our analysis of the concept of law towards substantive political argument.[17] Even this imputation of law's proper function is not enough to guarantee normative jurisprudence. To generate the claim that jurisprudence requires a commitment to a substantive moral/political theory, we need as well an application of the principle of charity.

Let's take a closer look at how these two premises—law's justificatory function and the principle of charity—must operate in the argument. In maintaining that the function of law is to justify coercion, one must be claiming that this is an essential or central property of law—not just a role that law can play, or a function that some,

---

[15] In this regard, see Coleman and Simchen, *The Language of Law*.

[16] We have two ways of interpreting Dworkin. We can read him as simply failing to understand a familiar distinction between what *law* is and what *the* law is. Such an interpretation is amply warranted by the text. Or we can interpret him as resisting the claim that there is a meaningful distinction to be drawn between the two. On this latter interpretation, Dworkin should be read as arguing that the familiar distinction between what law is and what the law around here is, is meaningful only within an Archimedean philosophical stance that ought to be abandoned. There is ample textual support in Dworkin's essays published after *Law's Empire* (as well as hints of it in LE) for this interpretation. Given the choice between interpreting Dworkin as overlooking a familiar philosophical distinction or as his resisting its significance in light of a particularly interesting philosophical stance, I opt for the latter. But not simply as a matter of charity. It is the better interpretation all around, but one that requires that we revamp our ordinary understanding of the argument in *Law's Empire*. These are among the issues taken up in detail in *The Language of Law*, and in 'Law'.

[17] For a discussion of the appropriateness of attributing to Dworkin the claim that law has an essential justificatory function, see below pp. 321–3.

many, or most communities happen to assign to law. If the justification of coercion were not a part of our concept of law as such, then why should an analysis of the concept be oriented towards explaining law in the light of that function? A hammer, for example, can serve any number of functions—it can be a murder weapon or a paperweight—but the capacity of hammers to be used in these ways, and in that sense to serve these functions, is hardly a part of our concept of a hammer, and we would not expect an account of what hammers are to be oriented towards providing an explanation of these capacities. If the function Dworkin attributes to law is necessary in order to orient our analysis of the concept, then we have to assume that this function is a property of law as such. But that is not something that can be assumed without argument; and one argument that is not available is that this essential feature of the concept is revealed in the process of a constructive interpretation of it. For the function must be presupposed before we can begin to apply that method, and cannot be a consequence of applying it.

Let's now turn to the principle of charity. The method of constructive interpretation requires that we display the object of interpretation in its best light. The interpretation of law is oriented towards the aim of the justificatory function—that is, towards the status of moral justification. To understand the law in its best light, given the imputed function, is to treat law as in the main serving its justificatory function well. Any account of what law is requires us to appeal to substantive norms of political morality in so far as it 'must explain how what it takes to be law provides a general justification for the exercise of coercive authority by the state'.[18]

When we conjoin the premise that jurisprudence is interpretative with these two additional premises—that law's essential function is to justify and limit the coercive power of the state and the principle of charity in interpreting what law is in the light of that function—we have an argument for normative jurisprudence—the claim that an analysis of the concept of law must invoke substantive or contestable premises of political morality.

But how seriously can we take this argument? At every crucial point, the inferences emerge from thin air. First, we start with a function —the justification of the state's coercive power—that orients the analysis towards moral premises. But we are given no argument that this function is an essential element of the concept—which it must be if an analysis of law is to be oriented towards moral/political theory.[19] Then we move from the fact that our analysis of the concept is an interpretation to the conclusion that in order to understand what law is, we must understand it as largely *suc-*

---

[18]   *Law's Empire*, 218.

[19]   Dworkin does not explicitly claim that the *essential* function of law is to justify coercion. Indeed, he rejects, as one should, essentialism about law. On the other hand, without such a claim, his defence of normative jurisprudence would be doomed. Therefore, I am not saying that Dworkin explicitly attributes an essential justificatory function to law: I am merely suggesting that such a *claim* must be presupposed by the best interpretation of the argument in *Law's Empire* for normative jurisprudence. For a fuller discussion, see below .

ceeding in justifying the state's police power. This move requires a specific, and rather dubious, understanding of how to apply the principle of charity in such a context. After all, for Davidson the principle of charity is motivated and defended as a precondition of understanding behaviour as linguistic—that is, as conveying or having meaning. There is no reason why Davidson's argument should warrant applying the principle of charity as grounds for attributing success to law in fulfilling its function.

Normative jurisprudence makes two distinct but related claims. The first of these is that one has to appeal to a substantive, moral/political theory in order to explain what law is—and thus to be in a position to provide the truth conditions for propositions of law. The second claim is that this methodological stance should be in principle compatible with a range of substantive theories of what law is—including most importantly, legal positivism as well as Dworkin's own interpretivism.

Central to my characterization of Dworkin's argument is attributing to him the view that law has an essential justificatory function. Some have objected to my interpretation. In fact, we can distinguish among at least three plausible interpretations of Dworkin's claim that the function of law is 'to guide and constrain the power of government'. Some, like Jeremy Waldron, have suggested to me that in referring to law's function as guiding and constraining the power of government, Dworkin is merely pointing out an important and prevalent feature of our legal practice: namely, that 'law insists that force not be used or withheld except as licensed or required by individual rights and responsibilities flowing from past political discussions about when collective force is justified'.[20] Legal practice has a justificatory *element*, not a justificatory function—a justificatory element, moreover, that is historical. Law's backward looking, justificatory structure is an important feature of it that any analysis of law must be able to explain. Understood in this way, Dworkin's claim that law's function is to guide and constrain police power expresses an *adequacy condition* for any substantive theory of law, not a methodological constraint on theorizing about what law is.

In effect, this reading of Dworkin takes him to be making the same kinds of points that Hart pressed against Austin. Hart suggested that any account of law would have to make sense of the historical dimension of legal authority, while making intelligible law's discourse of rights and obligations. Against Austin, Hart pressed these features of law's claim to authority as adequacy conditions of a substantive account of law, not as considerations that would call for a particular methodology of jurisprudence. As Hart argued, the resources available in Austin's account of law, while adequate to explain how law could compel action, were nevertheless inadequate to explain law's claim to impose obligations of compliance with its directives. Moreover, by identifying law with commands, Austin's account lacked the resources to explain the relevant historical dimension of our practices of legal authorization.

---

[20] *Law's Empire*, 93.

Hart faulted Austin's substantive theory of law, not his methodology. On Waldron's suggested interpretation, Dworkin is pressing similar adequacy conditions for an account of law. The justification of any particular judicial decision depends in part on its relation to past political actions. Any theory of law must illuminate this feature of it. Dworkin may be right to insist on this as an adequacy condition on a substantive theory of law, but in doing so, he imposes a burden on the resources of a theory, not on the manner of determining what those resources are.

If we read Dworkin's claims about law's justificatory function as Waldron suggests, then they do not figure in a defence of normative jurisprudence. They impose no constraints on methodology, and, therefore, none that would call for a normative jurisprudence. Without such constraints, moreover, this reading of Dworkin's claims about law's justificatory 'function' renders the relationship between the first and second parts of *Law's Empire* mysterious. If the methodological claim is not established, why would legal positivism and pragmatism have to be reformulated as interpretive theories? Dworkin's claim that they must be depends on his establishing normative jurisprudence. Establishing that requires more of the claim of law's function than this reading attributes to it. It requires that we treat Dworkin's claim about law's justificatory function as constraining the method of jurisprudence, not its substance.

Instead of interpreting the claim that law has a justificatory function as expressing an adequacy condition for a substantive theory of law, we might interpret it as an interpretative 'proposal'. The thought is that to understand law we need to attribute some value, function, or purpose to it. There is no essential, best or most apt function or value to ascribe to law. Different plausible attributes of functions yield different interpretations, all of which are in principle capable of bearing theoretical 'fruit'. At least on this reading, Dworkin's claims about law's function bear on the interpretative method of jurisprudence.

I take this suggestion up in more detail below.[21] For now, it is enough to note that, read in this way, interpretivism does not lead to a normative jurisprudence. Whether interpreting law *requires* that we appeal to a substantive moral/political theory depends on the value/function/purpose we attribute to law. And on this reading of Dworkin, any interpretation that bears fruit is a plausible, insightful one. Secondly, while Dworkin may have a range of interests in mind in pursuing an interpretative jurisprudence, he is typically read by his most ardent supporters, like Nicos Stavropoulos, as committed to providing the truth conditions for propositions of law. This reading of Dworkin's claims about the function of law is incompatible with both of these projects to which he is explicitly committed, and for obvious reasons.

This leaves us with the interpretation I have offered above. This reading of Dworkin's claims about the function of law is the only one of the three that supports an argument for normative jurisprudence. It is also the only one that is compatible with the semantic projects of the book, and the one that explains best the connection

---

[21] See pp. 333–5.

among the various parts of the book. It is only because jurisprudence must be normative in Dworkin's sense that all jurisprudential theories—including positivism—must be reformulated as interpretive theories.[22]

To this point, we have no reason for thinking that the function of law is to justify the coercive power of the state, nor a reason for thinking that we need to treat the claim law makes as true. We could overcome these problems if we could establish in some other way that law is the sort of thing that necessarily possesses a moral property sufficiently strong to impute to it a property of being generally justified as such. If it were not a part of our concept of law that it has some moral property that warrants that imputation, what would be the reason for interpreting the concept in that way? On the other hand, if we begin by assuming that law as such has the sort of necessary moral property that orients an analysis of the concept of it in a way that would support the central claim of normative jurisprudence, it may turn out that the normativity of jurisprudence is incompatible with many substantive theories of the concept. That means the methodology would beg questions about the truth of underlying substantive theories of the concept. This would violate the second tenet of normative jurisprudence; namely, its compatibility with a wide range of different substantive theories of law.

It looks as if we can proceed down either of two paths in looking for a defence of normative jurisprudence, both with obvious barriers to their success. The first is to identify a moral property that law necessarily has that will orient an analysis of the concept to principles of political morality. The worry here is that normative jurisprudence will turn out not to be compatible with a range of plausible substantive theories of the concept, and thus that the costs—from a theoretical point of

---

[22] It is not as if this interpretation of Dworkin would otherwise lack support from the text itself. He writes '[a] conception of law must explain how what it takes to be law provides a general justification for the exercise of coercive power by the state' (*Law's Empire*, 218).

I have to confess a dilemma in evaluating Dworkin's arguments for normative jurisprudence. The argument in *Law's Empire* has two basic problems: one methodological, the other substantive. The book begins with Dworkin asking how to understand jurisprudential theories. Once he establishes that all jurisprudential theories are interpretive, he reformulates the competitors to 'law-as-integrity' (i.e. positivism and pragmatism) as interpretive theories. The two problems are these. First, the argument he offers for jurisprudence as interpretive is unsound and appears to rely on a confusion between 'law' and law. Second, Dworkin's anti-Archimedeanism that comes to the fore in his later essays is entirely inconsistent with the way the argument for normative jurisprudence is constructed in *Law's Empire*. That argument relies on distinguishing the methodological from the substantive questions, but the central claim of anti-Archimedeanism is that we cannot ask questions about the proper method of jurisprudence apart from a substantive defence of a particular jurisprudence. So if we interpret *Law's Empire* on its own terms, we have an inadequate argument for normative jurisprudence that is in fact inconsistent with what turns out to be Dworkin's basic philosophical stance. On the other hand, if we read *Law's Empire* through the lens of his anti-Archimedeanism, we would have to substantially revise our reading of it. Here and in the *Practice of Principle*, I opt for the conventional reading of *Law's Empire* and object accordingly. Liberated from the conventional formulations, I defend the better interpretation—one that makes Dworkin consistent and philosophically subtle—even radical, but at the expense of the standard reading of *Law's Empire*. See Coleman and Simchen, 'Law', and *The Language of Law*.

view—of pursuing this strategy of argument will be too high. The alternative is to see if we can construct an argument for the normativity of jurisprudence that does not rely on law necessarily possessing any moral properties at all. The worry here is that no such argument exists, for if law is not the sort of thing that necessarily possesses moral properties, why would an analysis of what law is necessarily invoke moral premises. Do our accounts of table, chair, knowledge, or the like require moral premises? One suspects not and that is because our concept of each of these is not of something that possesses any necessary moral properties. Why invoke moral premises in our account of something we have no grounds for thinking has an essential moral property?

Unless law contains a necessary moral property that so orients our analysis of it, why must our analysis of what it is require moral argument? On the other hand, if normative jurisprudence depends on law having necessary moral properties, then normative jurisprudence as a methodological thesis may not be compatible with a broad range of plausible substantive views about the nature of law. Though these are ample grounds for scepticism about the prospects of success, let's see if we can construct plausible arguments employing both strategies. Let's begin with an argument for normative jurisprudence that attributes no necessary moral property to law.

One promising approach begins with the claim that an analysis of the kind of thing law is should be oriented towards the self-conception of participants in the legal system. It is, after all, a central claim even for legal positivism that in order for law to exist there must be practices of identification (I prefer, validation), legislation, and adjudication that are accepted from an internal point of view by the relevant officials. To accept these rules from the internal point of view is to be committed to them, to treat them as reasons for acting, as legitimate standards of conduct. Perhaps the conception of law that informs the relevant officials' actions—their understanding of the meaning of their actions, of what it is that they are doing—is the lens through which we can best see the kind of thing law is.

We can characterize the self-conception of legal participants in a variety of different ways, but it is plausible that any adequate characterization would emphasize the claim that law is understood by its practitioners as a special kind of justification-centred activity—one that seeks to justify a coercive police power. Those whose self-conception we are focusing on see the law as a sincere attempt to track the demands of political legitimacy. It would be hard for them to understand what they were doing if they did not see themselves as engaged in an activity that aimed to offer a genuine justification for the exercise of police power. This aim is only imperfectly realizable in practice, however, since legal practice is also constrained by the authoritative sources that constitute the distinctive identity, history, and culture of a particular legal system. The relevant legal actors understand law not only as justification-centred, but also as constrained by the history of an institution—their law—that is (at least to some significant extent) continuous over time.

Can we get from this self-understanding to a normative jurisprudence? Here is one suggestion.[23] Were it not for the peculiar institutional history of the law of any particular community, every participant in its legal system would believe that she exercised power in a way that actually did track the demands of political morality or of justice, broadly conceived.[24] When questions of law arose, participants would simply go straight to the applicable moral/political norms. The institutional history creates a potential gap between what is morally required (or would be morally required absent any institutional history) and what the law in fact requires, because what the law requires must 'fit' the institutional history: it must be the case that the new legal pronouncements and the old ones are seen as pronouncements of one and the same institution—the legal system—which is continuous over time. Law must, in this sense, display a certain integrity. The principle of charity now enters in the following way. In order to reconcile the necessary belief that their practice has a justificatory aim with the necessary belief that it is a practice that is continuous over time, participants *must* believe that the prior pronouncements were by and large morally justified. Otherwise they would have to give up either most of the prior pronouncements, or the justificatory aim—and both are necessary parts of their self-understanding as participants in a *legal* system. So the concept of law, seen through the lens of the participants of any legal institution, is the concept of something that is by and large morally justified.[25] Therefore, wherever we have law, it must be the case that the law of that community must be at least by and large legitimate—because its practitioners necessarily see it that way. That is the working hypothesis of all the relevant participants and if we are to understand law as the result of their actions, then we must see it as they do. And thus we must engage in moral argument to determine whether a community has law in the relevant sense. Jurisprudence must be normative.

If one of our worries about the previous argument was that it needed but could not warrant either law's justificatory function or the principle of charity, then one thing to be said on behalf of the Self-Conception Argument is that both are justified as conceptual components of the self-understanding of participants (at least of some and perhaps most key participants) in a legal system. Moreover, the Self-Conception Argument has the additional advantage of getting us to a normative jurisprudence from premises that do not attribute any necessary moral properties to law.

Still, however seductive it may appear at first blush, the Self-Conception Argument is inadequate to the task at hand. To be sure, we may demand as an adequacy condition of an analysis of the concept of law that it have resources adequate to

[23] This chapter considers only one version of what I am calling the Self-Conception Argument. I take up two more sophisticated and related versions elsewhere. See Coleman and Simchen, *The Language of Law*.

[24] Within the bounds of her cognitive capacities.

[25] 'By and large' is intentionally vague. Nothing here turns on this.

explain the self-understandings of participants;[26] but this does not mean that we must *credit* those self-understandings in the context of trying to understand what the practice is. Indeed, there are good reasons for suspicion in this context, for we might worry that participants in the practice are too close to it—that they have too much invested in seeing it in a way that legitimates their lives and actions. By crediting the internal point of view of officials in this way, we in effect preclude the possibility of false consciousness or bad faith. This disregards what would seem to be a natural psychological pressure to regard as justified one's participation in a practice that involves the use of coercive force to resolve disputes and to enforce a specific distribution of social burdens and benefits. The alternative would be for the participants to see themselves as thugs, extortionists, and racketeers. But we don't have to assume the possibility of bad faith or false consciousness to see the problem with crediting the self-understanding of participants. All we have to do is to admit their fallibility, the possibility that they might have got it terribly wrong, and have, despite their good faith efforts, adopted patterns of behaviour that cannot be morally justified.

It might be argued on Davidsonian grounds that there is something incoherent in the idea that the practitioners of a legal system could be systematically mistaken about the sorts of assertions that they would (indeed, must) make concerning their practice. Davidson has advanced powerful arguments for the view that in order to understand an individual's behaviour as language—that is, as expressing propositions with meanings—we must regard most of the claims that she makes as true.[27] The idea of a competent language user being systematically mistaken is incoherent. Perhaps something similar could be argued about the claims that practitioners in a legal system would make. We must credit most of their assertions if we want to hang onto the idea that they are practising law.

But this is surely a misapplication of the principle of charity. Let us grant that there are a priori reasons showing that the whole set of assertions that members of a culture or linguistic community would endorse must be regarded as mostly true if we are to regard them as assertions in the first place. It does not follow that the claims embedded in *specific* cultural institutions and practices must be regarded as mostly true—otherwise it looks as though we could secure a priori proof of the existence of God by applying the principle of charity to the claims that are made within the practice of religion.[28] It is simply implausible to assert that we *must* credit the self-understanding of

---

[26] Just as we might demand that it explain the historical dimension of justificatory argument in adjudication.

[27] I take up how best to understand the principle of charity, in Coleman and Simchen, *op. cit.*, *The Language of Law*.

[28] It might be argued that as an empirical matter, people do not adopt and maintain a practice in pursuit of a given aim unless the practice is generally reliable—that is, tends to succeed in its aim. But of course law, like religion, can have lots of different aims—even if law must always have the aim to justify and religion the aim to worship or otherwise to placate a supernatural being. But it is possible that succeeding at some of the *contingent* aims makes such an institution worth keeping and in that sense explains its persistence—even if it often or usually or even necessarily fails of its essential aim. For

legal practitioners in order to make sense of the claim that they are practising law.[29] If we are looking for an argument that an analysis of what law is must invoke substantive premises of political morality without first attributing any necessary moral properties of law, then the Self-Conception argument we just considered is of the right sort, but not up to the task.[30]

example, the practice of burning up animals in order to make God happy lasted (or has lasted) for quite a while, yet arguably has never made God happy (though it may have fostered group solidarity and produced the belief that God was being made happy—potential contributions to human flourishing). Even if the practice of law in some community fails systematically of its putatively essential aim to justify the use of force, it is possible that the benefits to some of being able to guide the behaviour of others—or the common benefits of coordination that law provides—might enable such a misguided legal system to reproduce itself and to persist over time.

[29] The points in the previous paragraph were all suggested by Eric Cavallero.

[30] In conversation, Seana Shiffrin has suggested to me an extremely novel and interesting variation of the Self-Conception Argument. As I have formulated it, the Self-Conception Argument begins with the relevant participants' (officials) self-understanding of law. On Shiffrin's variation, we begin not with the officials' understanding of law but with the members of a political community's conception of *themselves*. In doing so, we apply what Shiffrin refers to as a principle of moral charity, which is to say that our actors see themselves in the best light as moral agents. This means, for example, that they see themselves as regulating affairs among one another on terms supported by appropriate principles of justice. They seek to have these principles and other regulative ideals reflected in their political institutions, including the law. They then ask themselves 'given my self conception, what kinds of institutions can I participate in?' Whatever else it is, law is a coercive institution; the judgments it reaches, the conduct it prohibits and requires, are enforceable by force and violence. What would have to be true—at least as an aspirational matter—of legal institutions before an individual who conceives of herself as a moral agent in the relevant sense would participate in it? Arguably, an individual so (self-) conceived would participate in legal institutions only in so far as the exercise of coercive power tolerably approximated or tracked the conditions of political legitimacy.

Of course, no legal institution will perfectly track those conditions. Departures from the ideal might have many sources. Moral agents in our sense are merely idealizations of ourselves; we are not angels, nor are idealizations of us. Our motives can be at least in part selfish. Moreover, even angels can suffer cognitive limitations. The best-laid plans of the best of us acting with the best of intentions can nevertheless go awry. All this (and more) can lead to any actual legal system falling short of its ideals. Still, whether or not a set of coercively enforceable rules constitutes law or a legal system is, in part, a moral and not simply a factual question. The answer necessarily depends on the extent to which the practice satisfies the conditions of political legitimacy. This line of argument suggests, moreover, that legality is not an all or nothing matter.

Shiffrin's suggestion amounts to what I would call 'jurisprudence-as-ideal-theory'. In so referring to it, I mean to draw attention to the thought that if we want to understand what legal institutions and practices are we need to see them as partially aspirational expressions of forms of associations—schemes of cooperation and coordination—to which 'idealized' versions of ourselves could commit and participate in. Instead of jurisprudence commencing with the application of a principle of interpretive charity by officials to the set of authoritative pronouncements they are bound by and which they must interpret, jurisprudence begins with a principle of 'moral charity'—an aspirational self-conception of members of the political community.

Not only does jurisprudence-as-ideal-theory explain the normative dimension of jurisprudence, it also explains why in determining the content of the law judges apply the interpretative principle of charity to the set of 'past political acts'. Like others who are prepared to participate in and commit to legal institutions, judges are prepared to do so only to the extent to which the institutions reasonably approximate the conditions of political legitimacy. This suggests that in interpreting the relevant authoritative texts, 'moral judges' will seek to make of the law the best it can be. In doing so, they aim to realize the

But perhaps we have given up too quickly on arguments that begin by attributing a necessary moral property to law. I, for one, have long held that what troubles positivists is not the claim that law has some necessary moral property, but the stronger claim that the moral property law necessarily has (or is said to have) is sufficiently strong to warrant an inference from legality to legitimacy. In other words, I simply reject the claim that a positivist must assert that there is no necessary connection between law and morality. Positivism denies the very different claim that the legality of a norm must depend on its having a certain kind of moral property—one that implicates its *legitimacy*. If I am right—and I will assume for the sake of constructing an argument on behalf of normative jurisprudence that I am—then it may be possible in principle to identify a moral property that law necessarily has and that is strong enough to orient the analysis of the concept of it towards substantive principles of political morality, yet weak enough not to warrant an inference from legality to legitimacy. In that way we might nevertheless get to a normative jurisprudence from the existence of a necessary moral property law has, while hanging onto the claim that, at least in principle, a normative jurisprudence is compatible with the range of important substantive theories of the concept of law—including, most importantly, legal positivism.

One argument that might succeed in both of these aims rests on the idea that the predicate 'law' functions in our normative discourse as what I will call a 'predicate of weak commendation'. Articulating and developing this feature of 'law' may prove to be the best way of understanding what drives the normative/descriptive jurisprudence debate.

When we speak of law, we mean a form of governance that constitutes a distinctive normative relationship between the governing individuals or institutions, and those who are governed by them. The way that law structures this relationship is different from, and in some sense morally preferable to, the relationship between, for example, the ruling powers and the subject population in the case of a military occupation. More generally, governance by law is preferable to governance by force and fear. Any plausible account of law must not only make plain the differences among these forms of governance, it must do so in a way that explains—or enables us to explain—why we believe legal governance is morally attractive. We can capture this condition by saying that law is a 'predicate of commendation'.[31]

In characterizing law this way, we do not mean to imply that legal authority is always morally legitimate or justified, or even that any actual instance of it is. We certainly need not claim that the law in a particular community is justified merely in virtue of its status as law. Law is, in this sense, a predicate of *weak* commendation, and

---

aspirational dimensions of law and to narrow the gap between the law as it is and as an institution to which moral agents can commit and in which they can participate fully.

[31] 'Law' is not a predicate of course; 'is law' is. I am taking a few syntactic liberties in order to ease exposition.

we may contrast it with a predicate of strong commendation such as 'justice'. A theory of justice would be implausible on its face if its extension included morally undesirable social, political, or economic arrangements. The property of moral legitimacy is an essential, or a central feature of our concept of justice, and an argument to the effect that an analysis of justice picks out some morally illegitimate social arrangement is a strong argument for the inadequacy of that analysis. By contrast, laws—and perhaps even legal systems—can be morally illegitimate, and more often than we would care to believe, probably are. None the less, we seem inclined to acknowledge that there is something commendable about legal governance as such.

An argument for normative jurisprudence begins with this weak commendation feature of the predicate, law. If law is a predicate of weak commendation, then one could argue that the best explanation of how it is that law plays this role in our normative discourse is that law has a moral property adequate to warrant 'law's' linguistic role. That is, there must be some moral property that law has that provides the explanation of the fact that 'law' plays this commendation role in our normative discourse. Every instance of law must possess this moral property, M—something weaker, perhaps, than either moral legitimacy or prima-facie legitimacy. If law has such a property, an analysis of the concept of law should specify what this property M is—and in doing so, the analysis must appeal to moral argument in two ways: in specifying the content of M, the analysis must reveal how or why that property is morally attractive; and the overall analysis must be such that it picks out only things that have the property M. Thus, in selecting the other elements of the analysis of law, theorists are constrained to select a set of elements that are sufficient for, or at the very least consistent with, M. Succeeding in that is an adequacy condition for an analysis of law, and necessarily entails engaging in substantive moral argument.

This sounds like a case for normative jurisprudence, so let us consider the point more carefully. We have already granted the first premise, that law is a predicate of weak commendation. This is simply a fact about the role that 'law' plays in our normative discourse. In acknowledging this, we leave open the question of how 'law' plays this role. One answer is that provided in the foregoing argument, namely, that there is a moral property, M, that law necessarily has, and it is the existence of that property that explains how 'law' could serve as a predicate of commendation in our normative discourse. 'Law' plays a commendation role in our normative discourse because the concept of law is the concept of something with a certain morally attractive property.

Clearly, the property of being morally legitimate would suffice to explain 'law's' commendation function, but few normative jurisprudents would wish to endorse the inference from legality to moral legitimacy. There are other values for M that might also explain the commendation feature. Before we explore various possible values for M, we need first to consider whether the existence of an essential moral property is the only way we can make sense of the commending role 'law' plays in our normative discourse.

It could be argued, for example, that the commendation feature of law is simply an induction over experience. The historical record provides us with examples of a variety of different kinds of governance, legal and otherwise, and the legal ones seem to be preferable on balance. Or perhaps it is something even less creditable: a short-sighted induction. Maybe recent legal systems have been better than their alternatives. For one reason or another, we have formed positive associations about the concept, and that is what explains the role that 'law' plays in our normative discourse. However, this is just an accidental feature of law, and has no bearing on the content of the concept or on the proper method of jurisprudence.

The point is debatable, but I do not want to defend it here. The immediate rejoinder will be that if we have inductively based beliefs about the moral attractiveness of law, these beliefs are not to be explained by mere historical contingency—by brute facts about how various forms of governance happen to have worked out. If law is associated historically with a more humane or just form of governance than its alternatives, that fact is owing to something inherent in the nature of law. Indeed, it is not clear that we should even accept the claim that our beliefs about the attractiveness of law are inductively based in the first place. It is not obvious that the historical record—whether on a long or a short view—presents an unambiguously attractive picture of legal governance, or that the commendation feature really depends on the record's doing so. It seems likelier that the explanation of the commendation feature lies not in what laws and legal systems have actually been, but rather, in what they *can potentially be.* That is to say, inherent in the nature of law is the potential for a kind of governance that is more morally attractive than alternatives. Our concept of law is the concept of something that has the inherent potential to achieve, realize, or take the form of a certain ideal of governance.

The suggestion now is that the morally attractive property of law is *its inherent potential to realize or to manifest an ideal of governance.* As a potential, it need not be realized in every instance of law, and that explains once and for all why the argument for normative jurisprudence need not endorse the inference from legality to legitimacy. Yet at the same time, if this potential is an essential or central feature of our concept of law, an analysis of law must appeal to moral argument.

One way of distinguishing different forms of governance is in terms of the structure of the relationship between, as we might put it, 'ruler' and 'ruled'. The idea of law imposes constraints not only on the ruled, but also on the ruler. To be sure, a legal system need not be effective in constraining the exercise of the ruler's power, and may even stipulate that the law imposes no such constraints; but in so far as a ruler exercises purely arbitrary power, he or she does not govern by law. Law thus implies a kind of reciprocity between ruler and ruled. Legal rules are, as such, general in their scope and application, knowable in advance, and susceptible of compliance. These features indicate that under law, the governed are, in some perhaps very modest and limited sense, treated as autonomous agents capable of deliberating and acting on the basis of reasons. This normative relationship between ruler and ruled under law is morally preferable to alternatives, and this inherent feature of law explains why 'law' functions within our normative discourse as a predicate of commendation.

We can understand a range of important legal theories as alternative attempts to explicate the inherent potential of law to realize a morally attractive ideal of governance. Dworkin's assertion that law is a practice that aims to justify the state's exercise of coercive force could be seen as a way of explicating a morally attractive potential of law: certainly a state that recognizes an obligation to justify its coercive actions is capable of being better, morally, than a state that fails to recognize any such obligation. Raz's view of law as something that necessarily claims to mediate between persons and the reasons that apply to them contains similar resources. For it conceives of law's relationship to citizens as capable of serving their interest in meeting the demands of right reason, conceives of law as figuring in the deliberations of autonomous agents, and so on. Whatever their differences, Dworkin and Raz allow us to understand the moral attractiveness of a kind of governance that law has the inherent potential to realize. At the same time, neither view rests on the claim that law must always realize this potential, and thus neither view succumbs to the pitfall of endorsing an inference from legality to moral legitimacy.

Even Hart's analysis enables us to explain the inherent potential of law to realize an attractive form of governance. For in positing, as the function of law, the guidance of conduct by rules that are reasons, Hart posits a function that can be understood, perhaps in a variety of different ways, as morally attractive. The moral attractiveness of law's putative guidance function is perhaps at a higher level of generality than Dworkin's or Raz's accounts of what is morally attractive about legal governance, but all are suitable to reveal that law is necessarily the sort of thing with the inherent potential of realizing a morally attractive form of governance.

The argument from commendation may now be summarized as follows. Law is a predicate of weak commendation. This is because it is a part of our concept of law that it is morally attractive as such, from which it follows that every instance of law has some morally attractive property M. That property is the inherent potential of law to realize an ideal of governance. The relevant ideal can be specified in different, perhaps competing ways, and at different levels of generality; but any analysis of the concept of law must invoke substantive moral premises in order to explain the nature of M, and to orient the analysis towards only those practices that have M. Thus all jurisprudence must be normative.

Though extremely illuminating, the argument is beset by two fatal flaws. The first lies in the way we are to understand the idea of the inherent potential of law. Let us grant that law does have the inherent potential to realize a variety of moral ideals that other forms of governance cannot realize, and that this distinguishes law from other forms of governance. Is this inherent potential really a part of our concept of law? We should not be led astray by the metaphysical resonance of an expression like 'inherent potential'. There are ways of understanding that expression that do have metaphysical implications, but the initial plausibility of the foregoing argument depends on a more straightforward and metaphysically innocent sense of law's 'inherent potential'.

Law just is the kind of thing that can realize some attractive ideals. That fact about law is not necessarily part of our concept of it. After all, a hammer is the kind of thing that can be a murder weapon, a paperweight, or a commodity. Religion is the kind of thing that can stir murderous passions. Medicine is the kind of thing that can form the basis of a lucrative economic sector—doing so is, in that sense, an 'inherent potential' of medicine. However, the fact that a thing, by its nature, has certain capacities or can be used for various ends or as a part of various projects does not entail that all or any of those capacities, ends, or projects are a part of our concept of that thing. The only point we must grant about the 'inherent potential' of law to realize an attractive moral ideal of governance is the fact that law is the kind of thing with the capacity to do so. But that alone is sufficient to explain the commendation role that 'law' plays in our normative discourse. Nothing follows from this about the content of our concept of law. Thus, the commendation argument errs when it assumes that a particularly interesting capacity of law is in fact a part of our concept of it. An argument is needed to show that that is the case, and none appears to be forthcoming.

Of course, if we were to give an analysis of the concept of a hammer that did not shed light on its capacity to be used as a paperweight, that would be a prima-facie inadequacy of the analysis. If we were to analyse the concept of religion in a way that failed to account for the capacity of religion to stir murderous passions, we would have grounds to fault that analysis too. It does not follow that an analysis of either concept must rely on, invoke, or appeal to these capacities in identifying the central features of the concepts. By the same token, an analysis of law should help us to understand what we find morally attractive about it, and an analysis that failed to do so would be lacking. But this condition does not imply that we must appeal to moral argument in order to provide an adequate analysis of law. It is sufficient if, at the end of the day, the analysis we offer helps us to understand the morally attractive capacities of law.

In my own work, especially, in *The Practice of Principle*, I have offered a theory of law that involves a variety of elements, some familiar, some not, that can be conjoined in a way that explains why governance by law is preferable to alternative forms of governance. If one is moved by the moral ideals of autonomy and dignity, then one can see how the elements of my analysis constitute a thing (law) that has the capacity for accommodating those ideals in ways that other forms of governance cannot or cannot as well. If one is moved by the ways in which effective organization can enhance human welfare, then it is plain to see that law, understood in terms of the analysis I offer, can be conducive to those ends. But autonomy, dignity, and welfare do not enter at any point into the analysis that I offer, nor do any other moral properties. These ideals are external to the concept of law; law happens to be the kind of thing that can serve them well. The capacity to do so is, in a metaphysically innocent sense, an inherent potential of law. This implies nothing about how the analysis of law must proceed, and the analysis I have offered makes no appeal to any of the values that make law attractive.

These considerations illustrate the second, related flaw of the commendation argument. That law serves as a predicate of commendation is a fact about its use that any theory of law might well be required to make intelligible in much the same way that a theory of law must contain resources adequate to make intelligible the normativity of legal discourse. One can do either without attributing moral properties to law itself; nor must the values law is capable of serving and the forms of governance it is capable of instantiating direct us towards law's most prominent or central features. Whatever those elements turn out to be on a particular theory, they need to be capable of explaining a variety of facts about law, the commendation role of 'law' in our normative discourse being one of them.

Neither the Self-Conception Argument nor the Commendation Argument is adequate to establish the claims of normative jurisprudence. Neither succeeds where the Semantic Sting has failed. Though all fall short of their intended mark, they reflect different kinds of philosophical approaches one might take to exploring the nature of jurisprudence—its aims, its philosophical foundations, and the criteria suitable to assessing its theories. The Semantic Sting attempts to draw a conclusion about how the concept of law is to be theorized about from claims about the meaning conditions of concepts generally. The Self-Conception Argument suggests that if we want to understand or grasp the concept of law we need to look first to the self understandings of those who are central participants in the practice—a special category of what we might think of as (to use a familiar phrase from the philosophy of language) 'competent language users'. The Commendation Argument leads with the suggestion that if we want to understand law (the thing), we should investigate the roles 'law' (the word) plays in our language.

Before moving on to consider Perry's more 'particularistic' arguments to the effect that Hart is himself a normative jurisprudent, let me introduce one last general argument for a normative jurisprudence. As noted earlier, in discussing the claim that the function of law is to justify and limit the coercive authority of the state, Dworkin writes

Our discussions about law by and large assume, I suggest, that the most abstract and fundamental point of legal practice is to guide and constrain the power of government in the following way. Law insists that force not be used or withheld except as licensed or required by individual rights and responsibilities flowing from past political decisions about when collective force is justified.[32]

Instead of understanding Dworkin as imputing to law a function that is an essential feature of it and thus one which demands that we orient our analysis of law around it—a function that is discernible a priori or otherwise defensible transcendentally as a precondition of our capacity to discuss and evaluate law—we can ascribe to him a

---

[32] *Law's Empire*, 93.

somewhat different strategy of argument. On this reading, Dworkin is presenting a plausible case for orienting an analysis or theory of the concept of law around a particular conception of its function. The argument for imputing this function to law is that it helps us understand discussions about law—how it is that we are talking about the same thing both when we express our agreements and disagreements about it: what it is, what value it serves, when it is justified, and so on.

Arguably, there are other ways of thinking about the point, purpose, or function of law that can be recommended on similar grounds. So we might think of law as having the function of coordinating behaviour, of sustaining cooperative interaction, or as allowing for a certain realization of the self, and so on. In imputing a function or point to law in this sense, we then orient our analysis of the concept accordingly and see what picture emerges of the kind of practice law. Thus, instead of reading him as claiming that the function of justifying and limiting the coercive authority of the state is an essential feature of law, discernible a priori by reflecting on our concept of it, we can read Dworkin as making only a provisional claim about the concept of law. This claim could be part of an account that acknowledges that there are many possible functions or values that we can associate with law. Attributing one or another function to law will orient the analysis of the concept in a particular way—identifying particular features of law as salient, while relegating others to subsidiary roles. Thus, different theories of the concept will fall out of different attributions of a function, purpose or value. We then choose among the different conceptions according to appropriate criteria for assessing the theories of concept of law.

No doubt. The problem is that applying this line of argument doesn't yield a normative jurisprudence. If anything, we would choose among such theories of the concept in the light of the role the concept plays in our general theory of the world. Does thinking about law as oriented primarily towards the guidance of conduct, the relationship between agents and reasons, for example, fit better with other concepts cognate to law and with other human practices in, so to speak, the immediate social neighbourhood of law? Or does thinking about law in terms of political power and obligation provide a better fit? Here, the norms for evaluating the theories are pragmatic, theoretical, epistemic, and discursive.

It is very clear that understood in this way, there is no reason at all why all jurisprudential theories would necessarily invoke moral argument. It is clearer still, I hope, that the choice among conflicting conceptions of the concept is not made on grounds of political morality. The grounds are broadly speaking epistemic and discursive. We are choosing a theory of the concept—the best theory of the concept—as part of a construction of a general theory of the world and the concepts we employ to structure it. Different theories of the concept allow us to nest law and the concept of it differently: some emphasizing its centrality to the guidance of conduct; others to the theory of political obligation; others to an ideal of the person that can be realized only given certain social forms and institutions. If we pursue this tack, we are not in the business of carving the universe at its joints; we are not trying to gain access to or pick out metaphysically essential properties of law that are prior to our analysis of the concept, and that serve to orient it. Rather, this project appears committed roughly to an ontology of law that follows from the relevant epistemology of it. And while it is natural to read Dworkin, for one, as having a constructivist ontology of law, I doubt that pursuing this project along the lines I have just described can warrant a normative jurisprudence. For even if interpretivism is a normative epistemology in Dworkin's sense it falls short of requiring moral and political argument. Let us turn now from a set of abstract considerations for a normative jurisprudence, to arguments designed to show that H. L. A. Hart—clearly everyone's poster child for descriptive jurisprudence—was in fact a closet normative jurisprudent.

1.2 Perry and Hart

We can distinguish among three related but distinct arguments that Perry advances in support of his claim that Hart appeals to substantive moral and political argument early, often and prominently in developing his theory of the concept of law. These are: (1) the 'Subject Matter Argument'; (2) the 'Internal Point of View Argument'; and (3) the 'Function Argument'. Let us consider each in turn.[33]

The claim that jurisprudence is normative could be understood as the claim that before conceptual analysis can even begin we need to appeal to some norm or standard in order to pick out the features of law to which the concept of law must answer. We need to identify, if only in a provisional and revisable form, which features of law are central to the concept of it.[34] We need reasons for including law's claim to authority and its institutional nature while excluding the fact that judges usually wear robes. This process of selecting the salient features of law to which the concept is expected to answer is inevitably normative. It reflects not only different and distinct philosophical interests, but may reflect different and distinct conceptions of the point or purpose of law as well.

It is one thing to claim that normative considerations figure in the project of identifying the features of law that any theory of law must account for; quite another to claim that the norms to which one must appeal are those of political morality. Hart quite clearly appeals to epistemic norms in identifying those features of law the concept must answer to. This is obvious from chapter 1 of *The Concept of Law*, where Hart tells us that an adequate theory of law will enable us to see the connections and differences between law and systems of sanctioning on the one hand; and between law and morality on the other; and that such an account will reveal as well the relationship between law and rules. For if we want to understand the role of law in our deliberative

---

[33] The labels are mine, not Perry's. They are designed primarily to facilitate exposition.

[34] See Stephen R. Perry, 'Interpretation and Methodology in Legal Theory', in Andrei Marmor (ed.), *Law and Interpretation: Essays in Legal Philosophy* (Oxford: Clarendon Press, 1995), 97–135.

lives, then we need better to understand the way rules govern conduct. In effect, Hart is claiming that a range of theoretical norms, such as consilience and unification, govern theory construction in law. A theory of law must explain law's relationship to a range of cognate concepts in the normative and practical domains. This is why the concepts of coercion, rule, institutionality, deliberation, and agency are important for a philosophical theory of law, whereas the wearing of robes by judges is not. Even if other theorists might appeal to principles of political morality to identify the features of legal practice that a theory of the concept should explain, Hart does not.

It may be worthwhile in this context to revisit for a moment Hart's provocative claim that analytic jurisprudence is a kind of 'descriptive sociology'. I want to consider two possible interpretations of this claim, both of which explain the sense in which there is a social scientific aspect to Hart's project, but neither of which reduces the claim that analytic jurisprudence is descriptive sociology to the crude descriptivist project typically attributed to him. I will identify yet a third interpretation below. For Hart, the investigation of usage is not, as some have claimed, oriented towards identifying some set of shared criteria that fix the application conditions of the term 'law'. Rather, the investigation of usage serves to provide, in a provisional and revisable way, certain paradigm cases of law, as well as helping to single out what features of law need to be explained. Descriptive sociology enters not at the stage of providing the theory of the concept, but at the preliminary stage of providing the raw materials about which one is to theorize.

Investigating common usage may allow a theorist to construct a 'folk theory' of the concept of law, a more or less comprehensive (if incompletely articulated or rationalized) understanding of law's important features: rules, adjudicatory machinery, coercion, and the like. Conceptual analysis should be responsive to the folk theory—sometimes by vindicating its claims, by showing the connection among the elements and their relationships to one another, and at other times by requiring revisions in it.

Hart's reference to descriptive sociology may convey a bolder and more interesting claim as well, one that calls to mind Hilary Putnam's important discussion of the division of linguistic labour. In any culture characterized by expert discourses, what ordinary speakers mean by a given expression may just be whatever the relevant experts mean; indeed, the majority of ordinary speakers can even be wrong, if they tend to make false assumptions about what the experts mean by words like 'beech', 'lymphoma' or 'operating system'. In other words, it may turn out that ordinary use lacks the resources for constructing anything like a folk theory of the concept of law—usage may instead reveal only broad disagreement and confusion about the extension of the term 'law'. This would not mean that the philosopher has no choice but to substitute a contestable conception of law defensible only by appeal to substantive moral and political judgments. Rather, conceptual analysis can take its bearings from expert discourses such as social scientific inquiry.

Economists, historians, sociologists, political scientists, and anthropologists all study law—both from the internal and external points of view. In doing so, they work with their own paradigms of law, which they may revise in the light of the theories they construct and in ways that are responsive to the interests that motivate their inquiries. By attending to these inquiries outside of or beyond philosophy, we can obtain a rich and valuable picture of the forms of governance and organization that have been characterized as constituting law in different times and places, and under very different circumstances. A philosophical inquiry into the concept of law should be able to illuminate something about the practices that have been picked out as law in the social sciences, while explaining the importance of and the connections between the features that have figured prominently in the accounts of various social sciences.

In the end, the purposes of philosophical inquiry need not, and probably will not, fully coincide with all of the purposes of the social sciences;[35] but a satisfactory philosophical account should be continuous with these more naturalistic inquiries. Thus, Hart appears to have ample normative resources for identifying the features of law for which an adequate jurisprudential theory should account: he appeals to the epistemic norms of unification, consilience, systematicity, and the like; and he may also appeal to the social sciences as independent theoretical inquiries that a philosophical theory of law should heed. Yet none of this involves appeal to moral argument.

According to Perry, Hart's arguments against Holmes and Dworkin rely on the view that law has a proper function—specifically, the guidance of conduct through rules that are reasons for acting. As a shorthand notation, we will say that according to Perry, Hart thought that the function of law was the guidance of conduct. According to Perry, this commitment in turn shaped Hart's view about how to think about what law is, the importance of rules to law, and so on. In contrast, Dworkin appears to attribute no guidance function to law (other than to officials). Instead, he claims that the function of law is to limit and justify the coercive authority of the state. Holmes probably agreed with Hart that law serves a guidance function, but he emphasized law's use of sanctions, rather than its commitment to rules, as central to its fulfilling that function. It is clear, according to Perry, that Hart's arguments against Holmes and Dworkin must depend on sorting out these disputes in a particular way: by establishing—contra Dworkin—that the proper function of law is guidance; and—contra Holmes—that the function of law is to guide by rules that are reasons, and not by sanctions that are not. On Perry's reading, then, Hart's account of what needs to be explained about law depends on his substantive view about the proper function of law, a conception that must be defended by substantive political argument.

Perry's claims about Hart are most clear in his interpretation of Hart's objection to Holmes.[36] Any theory of law will have to account for the role it plays in the lives of

---

[35] More on this below in the context of so-called naturalistic jurisprudence.

[36] The discussion here follows the structure of the debate between Perry and Shapiro in their essays that appear in Stephen J. Burton (ed.), *The Path of the Law* (Cambridge: Cambridge University Press, 2000). Many of the objections I offer to Perry's account appeared first in Shapiro's critique of Perry, and are more fully developed there.

individuals who relate to law from both the first- and the third-person perspectives. The first-person perspective is that of the individual who is a participant in the legal practice. An account of law that seeks to employ the methods of the natural sciences will miss the role legal standards play in the deliberative and practical lives of those governed by law. It will look for regularities of behaviour, associating various incentives or sanctions with changes in behaviour. Such approaches to the study of law are typically reductive. They take a concept like 'legal rule' and give it content in terms of statistical regularities associating the probability of sanctions and the likelihood of certain behaviour. Thus, to say that there is a legal rule that people ought not do X is to say that if individuals do X, there is a probability P that they will have some legal sanction S visited upon them.

Hart's complaint about such formulations of law is not that they are unilluminating or inapt; they may be useful for a range of scientific purposes, including formulating hypotheses about how behaviour will be affected by changes in the frequency or quality of sanctions, and so on. Rather, Hart's complaint is that, whatever their virtues may be, these accounts lack the resources to explain various aspects of the first-person perspective on law. For in reducing rules to probabilities of sanctions, they leave no room for understanding compliance with law for the reason that the law requires it. To borrow his phrase, they define the internal point of view out of existence.

Hart's primary target was the Scandinavian Realists, like Alf Ross. The Scandinavians were not just reductionists; they were also moral or evaluative sceptics, and their scepticism about the content of evaluative judgments grew out of their logical, and not their legal positivism. As they understood it, the only meaningful propositions were those with empirical content and thus those testable before the tribunal of experience. Moral and normative language generally lacks cognitive content, and is instead to be analysed non-cognitively as prescriptions, or as expressions of attitudes. To scientize the law and its normative discourse, they found it necessary to reinterpret the language of the law in a way that attributed cognitive content to it. Thus, legal norms were viewed as elliptical ways of expressing the likelihood that conduct would meet with certain unhappy results. Instead of expressing anything fundamental about law, the legal language of rights, duties, privileges, and liberties is reducible to statements reporting probabilities of sanction. Hart argued that such an analysis of law lacks the resources necessary to account for the fact that at least some individuals comply with the law for the reason that the law requires it. Law has an internal dimension that these analyses simply cannot capture, and it is in that sense that they define the internal point of view out of existence. To understand law is to understand the way in which it can and often does figure in one's deliberations about what one ought to do, and not merely as shorthand for predictions that are accessible to external observers about what judges and other officials will do.

The jurisprudence of Oliver Wendell Holmes, as Hart understands it, is limited to the same meagre resources—sanction and behaviour—as those available to the

Scandinavian Realists. Unlike the Scandinavian Realists, who seek merely to uncover causal connections and law-like regularities suitable to a scientific inquiry, Holmes looks to unmask the role law plays in the deliberative process of those who see the law from the first-person perspective. To this end, he introduces the concept of the 'bad man'. The bad man's concern is not to identify the reasons that law provides, but rather to avoid the sanctions with which the law threatens him. Thus, although legal statements remain reducible to predictions of sanctions, the sanctions themselves are understood as entering into the deliberative processes of the 'bad man'.

Despite this first-person element of Holmes's account, Hart levels against him the same objection with which he criticizes the Scandinavian Realists—he takes Holmes to task for defining the internal point of view out of existence. Perry finds this to be puzzling at best. After all, the Scandinavians seek to uncover law-like regularities in behaviour that are available to the external, social-scientific observer. Holmes, in contrast, seeks to understand the law from the perspective of those governed by it. Indeed, Holmes's entire project would seem to be aimed at giving a distinctive content to the internal point of view. Perry concludes that Hart's objection isn't really that Holmes defines the internal point of view out of existence; rather, Holmes has 'the wrong kind' of internal point of view. On Hart's account, the legal rule itself—which represents a social judgment about what ought to be done—is the reason for acting; whereas Holmes locates the reason law provides in the threat of sanction. The former account captures a morally more attractive form of guidance—a form that presupposes a conception of the person as an autonomous agent capable of acting on the basis of rules that are reasons, and not merely as a calculating animal, responsive to threats.[37]

Perry's critique of Hart mistakes a conceptual argument for a moral one. Hart has two main conceptual motivations for rejecting sanction accounts. In the first place, it cannot be denied that individuals sometimes act for the reason that the law requires it, and Holmes lacks the conceptual resources to account for that. Hart is not faulting Holmes for having a morally unattractive account of the internal point of view; he is quite justifiably faulting Holmes for not being able to account for obvious facts about the way in which the law sometimes figures in human deliberation and action.[38]

---

[37] In fact, Hart does not presuppose any more than Holmes does about the nature of the person or of human motivation. Hart assumes only that persons are capable of acting on the basis of reasons. If Holmes's bad man is a deliberative agent—as he must be on Perry's account—then Holmes assumes as much about the nature of the person as Hart does. Nor, of course, does Hart deny that individuals living under the law sometimes act for the purpose of avoiding sanction.

[38] Perry's argument goes astray because of a certain ambiguity in the phrase 'the internal point of view'. We might mean by that expression, roughly, 'the insider's point of view' or 'the first person point of view'. On the other hand, we might mean 'the committed point of view', or the point of view of one who adopts the rule as a reason for action. There is nothing more clear in *The Concept of Law* than that Hart means by the internal point of view the second of these senses. There are many points of view that are internal in the first sense. The point of view of Holmes's bad man is internal in the first sense, but not

Moreover, for Hart, the theoretical role of the internal point of view goes beyond the need to make conceptual room for an obvious empirical fact about the experience of living under law; the internal point of view is also necessary in order to explain the very possibility of law—for Hart maintains that law depends on the existence of criteria of legality that are practised from the internal point of view. All sanction and predictive theories lack the resources to explain the possibility of legal authority, for they cannot explain the existence conditions of legal rules authorizing sanctions, or the existence of rules specifying the rules to which sanctions can attach. Sanction theories are not merely undesirable or incomplete; they are incoherent. They depend on the claim that laws are sanctions, but cannot explain how sanctioning is possible.[39]

In sum, whereas Perry claims that Hart must be defending a particular conception of the internal point of view against Holmes on substantive moral or political grounds, the fact is that moral and political considerations have nothing to do with either the argument Hart makes or the arguments a positivist would need or want to make against Holmes. If Hart actually relies on the claim that law has a proper function in order to derive the elements of his substantive theory of law, then we will have to look elsewhere to find evidence of it.

To this end, Perry introduces what I call the 'function of law' argument.[40] Hart explicitly claims that it is futile to search for any function of law more specific than the guidance of conduct. By contrast, Dworkin maintains that law has the function of employing and constraining the use of the coercive authority of the state in a way that at least makes sense of law's claim to legitimacy. This difference between Hart and Dworkin can shed light on their respective theories of the concept of law and their differing views about legal content. For Dworkin any interpretation of legal practice must operate within the parameters of trying to show the law in its best light; the positivist is committed to no such claim. On the other hand, the disagreement between Inclusive and Exclusive Legal positivists makes sense only within the context of the claim that legal norms must be capable of making a practical difference in terms of guidance, that is, a difference in the reasons the law provides to those subject to its demands. We cannot choose between positivism and Dworkin's interpretivism without determining who is right about law's proper function. Yet that dispute is not itself factual. If the disagreement between Hart and Dworkin is not a factual one about law's actual function, then it must be a normative one about law's proper function. Thus, the substantive considerations that support one or another conception of law's proper function are part of every theory of the concept of law and determine its content.

in the second. In accusing both the Scandinavian Realists and Holmes of defining the internal point of view out of existence, he has this second sense in mind. The argument to this point follows Scott Shapiro's critique of Perry.

[39] For a full development of this line of argument, see *The Practice of Principle*, especially chapter 7.

[40] See Stephen R. Perry, 'The Varieties of Legal Positivism', in *Canadian Journal of Law and Jurisprudence*, 9 (July 1996), 361–81.

Law is a human construction capable of satisfying a variety of human interests and needs (though it can serve evil as well as desirable or valuable ends). It is one thing, however, to claim that law can bring about certain desirable states of affairs, or that it can achieve certain ends—and something else altogether to claim that law has a function. Not every goal or end or product of a process is its function. The idea of a thing's function can be specified in a variety of ways; we can assign functions to things, as when the hammer on my desk functions as a paperweight. We can design things or kinds of things to have functions—for example, hammers have the function of driving nails. These are stories in which things get their functions from the uses we intend for them. However, things can have functions that are not related to intentions in that way—for example, the hand has the function of grasping, or of enabling us to grasp things. The story that connects hands with their function can invoke intentions (divine design); but we can also tell a causal story that explains how a certain outcome—the capacity to grasp things—is part of a causal/evolutionary explanation of the existence and shape of the hand.

In ascribing to law the function of guiding conduct, Shapiro suggests (and I concur) that we should not read Hart as advancing any sort of moral argument about law's proper function. Instead, we should understand him to be offering a certain kind of functional explanation of law.[41] This type of explanation is familiar in the social sciences, and is a sort of hybrid incorporating both intentional and non-intentional elements. Hart never elaborated the formal structure of the explanation, but the basic idea is that law's capacity to guide conduct effectively is part of the explanation of its existence and persistence, as well as of the shape law takes in its mature forms.

The elements of such an explanatory appeal to law's guidance function are present in chapter 5 of the *Concept of Law*. If law consisted only of primary rules imposing obligations—rules that guide epistemically by marking certain standards as those to which one must comply—then guidance would be 'inefficient' in at least three ways. First, there would be uncertainty about which rules had the authoritative marking; a more effective scheme of guidance would have a reliable way of identifying which standards bore the relevant mark. Secondly, legal guidance would be static and unresponsive to changing circumstances and interests; the capacity to amend, alter, and abandon certain rules and introduce new ones allows for a more effective form of guidance. Finally, it would be unclear in some circumstance what the rules required of us; it would be more effective if disputes about law's requirements could be resolved authoritatively. It is plausible to think that the effectiveness of these elements for guiding conduct is part of the explanation of why they are widespread and enduring features of mature legal systems. Individuals acting over time have developed the

---

[41] This is the third and most important sense in which there is a social science dimension to Hart's project. Much of the credit for noticing and developing the importance of this train of thought to Hart's overall theory should go to Scott Shapiro. See his two essays cited earlier.

structures of law in order to serve those various ends—morally worthy ones as well as morally worthless ones—because law can serve those ends more effectively than other forms of governance. Societies that can function effectively in various ways have tended to endure and their institutions have spread through various processes of diffusion. Thus, ascribing to law the function of guiding conduct enables us to understand why mature legal systems take the form of a union of primary and secondary rules.

It is possible to read Hart's argument in chapter 5 of *The Concept of Law* as a kind of social-scientific/functionalist explanation of law. This explanation reinforces the philosophical analysis of law as a union of primary and secondary rules, and makes the philosophical theory continuous with a standard social scientific explanation. Wherever law arises, no matter the historical and cultural differences, no matter the particular human ends it may serve, we can expect it to acquire roughly the same structure in its mature form. This generality is among the notable strengths of Hart's account. Contrary to Perry, there is nothing in Hart's argument to suggest that the moral attractiveness of guiding conduct through rules is the basis for his view that such guidance is the function of law.[42]

Whatever their general interest, none of Perry's arguments actually establishes that Hart engaged in substantive moral and political argument in identifying the salient features of his theory of the concept of law. Hart identifies in a preliminary way those features of law that an analysis of the concept must be responsive to by applying familiar norms of theory construction, not by applying those of political morality. His conception of the centrality of the internal point of view rests on conceptual claims about the possibility of legal authority and logic of reasons. Again, there is nothing in his argument that suggests a moral or political foundation for the internal point of view. Finally, his claim is not that law has a proper guidance function that must be defended by its moral or political attractiveness; rather by attributing to law a guidance function, we can more adequately understand why law arises, persists over time, and takes the shape it does in its mature forms. If Perry's arguments fail to capture the actual arguments that underwrite Hart's commitments to these salient features of law—its commitment to rules, the internal point of view, and the guidance function—they cannot support a claim for a more general normative jurisprudence.

---

[42] The claim that Hart relies on a moral argument fails to take seriously his explicitly positivist commitments. It is ironic that commentators who embrace a Dworkinian interpretivist project sometimes appear unwilling to apply the charitable principles that govern such a project to their reading of Hart. One would think that those principles would require us to read Hart in a way that strengthens and deepens his consistently positivist themes. Though positivists may be mere Agatha Christies to Dworkin's Shakespeare, it is uncharitable to interpret a positivist project as a second-rate production of Hamlet when it could be interpreted as a perfectly satisfying murder mystery.

2 Conceptual Analysis and Naturalism

2.1 Conceptual Analysis

Hart and many legal philosophers who have followed him take themselves to be engaged in a familiar philosophical project of conceptual analysis. Epistemologists analyse the concepts of knowledge and epistemic justification; philosophers of language the concepts of truth and meaning; metaphysicians the concept of the real; ethicists the concept of value; political philosophers the concepts of justice and authority, and so on. Philosophers of law are no different; they analyse the concept of law (and other concepts central to legal practice). As I suggested earlier, critics of Hart's methodology have advanced two different kinds of arguments against him. Critics like Dworkin and Perry reject Hart's claims to descriptivism. These critics deny that normative austerity is appropriate to jurisprudence. The concept of law, unlike the concepts of knowledge, truth, objectivity, meaning, and the real, calls for controversial moral and political argument. In this regard the concept of law is more like the concept of the good, or better, the concept of justice. Perry's twist on this objection is in arguing that not only is an analysis of the concept of law an exercise in political morality, Hart's own arguments belie his stated commitment to the contrary.

No one denies that law matters in people's practical lives; and our account of what law is should be able to illuminate the ways it does—its importance and value to those governed by law. But it is, as I argued above, simply a mistake to think that this entails anything about the nature of how jurisprudence must proceed. It establishes something of an adequacy condition on a theory, and not a methodological constraint on theorizing.

It is time to turn our attention to the second objection to the method of jurisprudence associated not just with Hart but with the vast majority of those who followed him—critics as well as proponents of legal positivism. Those like Dworkin and Perry who defend a normative jurisprudence have the burden of explaining how analysing law is different from analysing the concepts that are central to the core areas of philosophy, like meaning, truth, and knowledge. In contrast, those like Brian Leiter, who reject Hart's methodology, do so because, in their view, law is no different from knowledge, truth, and meaning. Leiter's objection is not, therefore, to Hart's commitment to descriptivism; his objection is to Hart's commitment to a philosophy of Conceptual Analysis. As Leiter sees it, Conceptual Analysis is as fruitless to the legal philosopher as it is to the epistemologist or the semanticist. The difference is that whereas epistemologists, philosophers of language, mind, and science, as well as metaphysicians and even ethicists, have seen that progress in philosophy can be made only by replacing conceptual projects with naturalistic ones, philosophers of law remain caught in a time warp. Hart can be excused, or at the least, forgiven for pursuing the linguistic project of Conceptual Analysis; we do not interpret him fairly if we fail to appreciate the influence of the linguistic turn on his scholarship. On the other hand, if jurisprudence today is to make progress it has to abandon the conceptual projects in favour of naturalistic ones—or so Leiter contends. Philosophy of law must get out of the grip of a failed Conceptual Analysis.

There are two components of Leiter's project. The first concerns the rejection of Conceptual Analysis and with it the major strands of analytic jurisprudence. The second concerns the prospects for a naturalized jurisprudence. I agree with Leiter that we need to abandon the specific project of Conceptual Analysis. But to reject Conceptual Analysis is to reject neither conceptual analysis nor analytic jurisprudence. In addition, I have grave doubts about the prospects of a naturalistic jurisprudence. Both of my points are tied together by the additional fact that the very possibility of a naturalized jurisprudence depends on a non-trivial component of analytic jurisprudence of just the sort the naturalist would have us abandon.

Let's consider both parts of his project, beginning with the rejection of analytic jurisprudence. Analytic jurisprudence for Leiter is identified with the projects of Conceptual Analysis. The aim of Conceptual Analysis is to uncover interesting and informative truths about the concepts we employ to make the world rationally intelligible to us. The basic idea is that concepts are reified objects of thought that structure our experience and make the world rationally intelligible to us, and because they are shared are essential to our ability to communicate with one another. It is nowadays a commonplace in philosophy that Quine has presented several compelling arguments adequate to undermine the projects of Conceptual Analysis.

It may be worth summarizing how the most powerful of these arguments goes. This is the argument from confirmation holism. Suppose one advances an empirical hypothesis, 'H', and seeks to test it by empirical evidence. Suppose 'H' would normally be thought to be confirmed by 'E', but the evidence gathered is 'not-E.' One might have thought that 'not-E' disconfirms 'H', and given 'not-E', someone who had previously believed that 'H' would now have to revise his beliefs and abandon 'H'. Quine shows that it is in fact possible for someone who holds 'H' to maintain both 'H' and 'not-E', provided he is prepared to make adjustments or revisions elsewhere in his system of beliefs. Evidence confirms or disconfirms one's theories (world-views or systems of belief) taken as a whole, not individually. This is confirmation holism. And on a natural, related view of meaning, confirmation holism entails meaning holism.

One's theories of the world will include putative analytic truths as well as synthetic claims. All are, therefore, subject to confirmation by evidence. This means that analytic as well as synthetic statements are subject to the tribunal of empirical evidence. Thus, so-called analytic statements as well as synthetic ones are subject to revision in the light of recalcitrant experience. Rather than saying that analytic truths are immune from the tribunal of experience, we should say instead that they stand at a greater distance or remove from experience than do other beliefs.

This argument has two consequences for the project of Conceptual Analysis, both of which are often viewed as devastating to it. First, because all claims are subject to the tribunal of experience, there is no special non-empirical philosophical domain of analysis: no special way in which philosophy can illuminate the nature of things. If there are no analytic truths, then there are no conceptual truths: nothing necessarily true about our concepts; nothing that is necessarily true of our concepts of table, art, music, or law. Secondly, to the extent that the truth of various assertions are embedded within theories or systems of beliefs, we have to give up the idea that there are reified concepts that are the bearers of meaning, out of which the meaning of propositions is to be determined. It is a language as a whole that has meaning, and the component parts of a language get their meaning in the context of their place in a language. Thus, not only must we abandon the search for analytic or conceptual truths; in a post-Quinean philosophy we also have to abandon the view of concepts as reified objects and atomistic bearers of meaning.

It is important to note, of course, that philosophy proceeds apace post-Quine, and does so on many fronts. Epistemologists are still offering analyses of knowledge; philosophers of language offer analyses of meaning and truth, and so on. If we accept the main thrust of Quine's objections, the question is not whether we have a right to do what we do, but how we are to conceptualize what it is we are doing. No one who pursues analytic projects in jurisprudence or elsewhere in philosophy must abandon them. We simply need to be careful in the way we express what we are doing.[43]

The ambitious form of naturalism asserts that a priori conceptual analysis of law is a fruitless activity in which progress is illusory at best. A more modest naturalism denies only that certain important aspects of legal theory can be fruitfully addressed

[43] Suppose we take criterialism to hold that there are correct rules for applying terms like 'law'. These rules provide the meaning of the terms and are, in effect, definitions that state analytic truths—truths that rely on the meaning of terms. By identifying positivism with criterialism, Dworkin associates it with a familiar conception of philosophy according to which its aim is to uncover analytic truths that reveal the essential features of the things we use the terms to refer to. The rules for applying 'law' thereby specify what must be true for something to fall within its extension. These analytic or conceptual truths reveal the essence of law. In rejecting criterialism in favour of normative jurisprudence, Dworkin is rejecting a picture of the philosophical enterprise that relies on the analytic/synthetic distinction. His doing so fits nicely with many of the Quinean features of his philosophy (save Quine's behaviourism). Notice now that Leiter's rejection of analytic jurisprudence has the same foundation—the rejection of the analytic/synthetic distinction. Whereas, Dworkin takes the rejection of the analytic/synthetic distinction to call for philosophy as normative theory—what I think he once referred to as 'philosophy-as-interpretation', Leiter takes the rejection of analyticity to imply a conception of philosophy-as-science (or in the case of law, of philosophy-as-social science). Both Dworkin's and Leiter's conceptions of the philosophic project are over-reactions to the rejection of the analytic/synthetic distinction. Both rely on overly narrow views of the possibilities of descriptive projects within philosophy in the wake of the rejection of the analytic/synthetic distinction. Once we sort out the relationship between jurisprudence and meta-semantics of 'law', a range of descriptive and normative projects for jurisprudence are made available. These points are fully developed in *The Language of Law*, and in 'Law'—the basic similarity between Leiter and Dworkin having first been brought to my attention by my co-author, Ori Simchen.

by a priori analysis. Ambitious naturalists would have us abandon philosophical jurisprudence altogether in favour of a social science of law; modest naturalism claims that analytic jurisprudence need not be abandoned, for it may play a secondary role within an overall naturalistic project.

Within the province of jurisprudence proper, Leiter's focus is on the theory of adjudication; and more specifically, on the issue of determinacy with regard to adjudicatory content. A theory of adjudication seeks to identify the norms that, if correctly followed by judges, will yield all and only those outcomes that are warranted by the set of authoritative legal standards binding on them. For every dispute, there are three possible outcomes warranted by law. These are: 'plaintiff wins', 'defendant wins', or 'indeterminate'—that is, the law does not determine who wins.[44] A theory of adjudication, then, aims to identify the function, if it exists, that takes as inputs the set of authoritative or binding standards and yields as its output the right answer to each legal dispute for which there is a right answer as a matter of law. The theory should give the answer 'plaintiff wins' to all and only those cases in which the plaintiff does have the best argument as a matter of law; the answer 'defendant wins' when the same is true of the defendant; and the answer 'indeterminate' when the available legal materials fail uniquely to warrant either result.

Leiter claims that no amount of philosophical reflection on the concepts of law and adjudication, or on the idea of a right answer, will reveal that function—if indeed such a unique function exists in our or any other legal system. If there are norms determining when particular answers are right, they are not accessible by reflection on concepts; if such norms exist, they are instead internal to the practice of adjudication itself.

Much of Leiter's argument draws on the claims of confirmation holism. According to confirmation holism, the relationship between evidence and belief (or theory) is holistic, in the sense that all evidence tests—that is, confirms or disconfirms—a set of beliefs as a whole, and not an individual belief or hypothesis. That is because by making adjustments or revisions elsewhere in one's stock or web of beliefs, any evidence can be reconciled with the belief or hypothesis it might otherwise be thought to disconfirm. How willing one is to abandon any particular belief in the face of recalcitrant evidence is a function of how central the belief is to one's web of beliefs—that is, how many other beliefs it supports and to what extent it does so—and of the relative advantages of the new theory in enabling one to make one's way through the world.

Considerations like these suggest that there is no point in looking a priori for norms regulating proper reasoning. Rather than employing armchair reflection to determine the test of justified belief, we should investigate the processes by which cognizers come to hold the beliefs they have, and the factors that contribute to their reliability. The analytic philosophical project of epistemology is replaced by a (social)

---

[44] This last possibility is denied by those who maintain that there are always right answers as a matter of law.

scientific (in this case, psychological) project. The analogy with the theory of adjudication is reasonably straightforward. The theory of adjudication is the philosophical activity of trying to determine, by reflection on the concepts of law, content, interpretation, and the like, the set of norms of proper adjudication. Applying them will yield uniquely warranted outcomes when such outcomes exist. The claim of naturalized jurisprudence is that an analytic theory of adjudication encounters the same difficulties as those that doom analytic epistemology. Any number of inconsistent outputs are compatible with the set of adjudicatory inputs, and there are a large number of interpretive principles or ways of organizing the inputs that are themselves internally consistent and that warrant different outcomes. There are no unique interpretive principles and there is no philosophically respectable way of picking one out as correct.

Leiter concludes that we need to replace or supplement legal philosophy with sociology, psychology, anthropology, or economics of law. We should turn away from philosophy to an appropriate social scientific inquiry—one that looks to uncovering law-like regularities in decision-making, or one which seeks to identify which norms, if any, are internal to the practice of adjudication. Leiter does not deny that there may be such norms—only that philosophy has a role to play in determining what they are or in justifying them.

There is nothing objectionable about a sociological, psychological, or a psychosocial jurisprudence. No philosopher of law could quarrel with a project of trying to uncover law-like regularities in judicial decision-making. Such social scientific laws of judging—if any could be discovered—might render judgment more predictable, which could have the salutary effect of facilitating coordination and planning; a social science of adjudication would also be valuable on purely theoretical grounds, as a way of making law and legal practice more rationally intelligible.

There are, however, several powerful objections to the suggestion that analytic jurisprudence must give way to a naturalized jurisprudence: that the philosophy of law should be replaced by the social science of law or rendered subservient to it. The first is that a naturalized project can proceed only after a good deal of philosophical spadework has been done. The second is that there is no reason to suppose that social scientific theories will seek to explain the phenomena of special interest to jurisprudence; less reason for believing that they will succeed if they do. Still less reason, I fear, for thinking that social science will succeed at illuminating even those puzzles to which it addresses itself. Let's consider these objections in turn

Leiter is himself aware that the project of a naturalized jurisprudence requires an analytic jurisprudential component, but he underestimates its extent. The very idea of an adjudicatory function operating on authoritative legal standards presupposes that we have criteria for determining what the authoritative legal standards are. Thus, the naturalist is committed as a conceptual matter to the existence of a test of legality. Moreover, not every view about the nature of the test of legality is consistent with the naturalist project. The naturalist cannot, for example, accept the Dworkinian theory of the criteria of legality, for that account falls out of Dworkin's theory of legal content.[45] If Dworkin is right that the content of the law is fully determinate, then the naturalist cannot possibly be right. This encumbers the naturalist with the burden of presenting a philosophical argument against Dworkin's entire jurisprudential project. The naturalist is thus in the same boat with every other analytic philosopher of law—his project requires analytic legal philosophy as much as Raz's or mine does.

These considerations suggest—though they do not demonstrate—that naturalized jurisprudence presupposes a positivist conception of how to think about the criteria of legality. But that places naturalism within positivism, and positivism, however attractive, is of course, a controversial substantive jurisprudential view. More importantly, these considerations suggest that naturalism will be plausible only if positivism is. And thus rather than escaping the work of traditional analytic jurisprudence, naturalism relies upon it. In that case, naturalism could not be entertained as serious alternative to analytic jurisprudence.

It is a further question, of course, whether the naturalist must defend a particular view about the content of the criteria of legality, and in so doing come out on one or the other side of the inclusive/exclusive positivism divide.[46] In one of his essays, Leiter suggests that the American legal realists—prescient naturalists on his reading—were implicitly exclusive, or what he called 'hard' positivists.[47] It is not obvious to me why legal realists or any other putative naturalist would have to come out in favour of exclusive legal positivism, but if Leiter is right, then his naturalism is grounded on a specific resolution to another, in this case, quite subtle and specialized, debate in analytic jurisprudence between inclusive and exclusive legal positivism: one that implicates particular views about how to understand legal normativity. This strikes me as quite a lot of analytic legal philosophy as a precondition for a jurisprudential view that is supposed to be an alternative to analytic legal philosophy—a dispute moreover that invokes the significance of the difference between legal validity and legality that social scientists of law are neither interested in nor particularly well suited to adjudicate.

However the naturalist comes out on the inclusive/exclusive legal positivism question, he is committed to the claim that the Rule of Recognition (or, more generally conceived, the test of legality) has determinate content. If the Rule of Recognition did not have determinate content, then it would be impossible to identify the set of adjudicatory inputs. But if the Rule of Recognition has determinate legal content, how is it that the rules that are valid under it do not? If the Rule of Recognition can pick out certain standards of conduct as official or legally authorized, why is it that legal rules valid under the Rule of Recognition cannot pick out

---

[45] This point is developed in *The Practice of Principle*, ch. 11.
[46] See chs. 8–10 of *The Practice of Principle*
[47] See Brian Leiter, 'Realism, Hard Posivitism and Conceptual Analysis', *Legal Theory*, 4/4 (1998).

acts as legally mandatory, prohibited, or permissible?[48] It is no help to say that while the rule of recognition and rules valid under it all have determinate legal content, the law has no determinate content. That would involve defending a claim about the nature of legal content that would be on its face controversial, if not implausible. Indeed, if particular legal rules are extremely indeterminate, then we could infer perhaps that legal guidance content is often indeterminate—that is, the rules would not offer adequate guidance to citizens and others whose behaviour is regulated by the rules. But this would tell us nothing about legal *adjudicatory* content.[49] For there may be very well entrenched practices in communities for resolving disputes in the face of guidance indeterminacy.[50] To be sure, those practices or norms are not discerned by a priori reflection on the nature of content or adjudication. But that is just what a positivist theory of adjudicatory content already tells us: that the 'function' that takes as its inputs 'official legal pronouncements' and gives as its outputs 'decisions in particular cases as a matter of law' will depend on the particular practices of different legal systems. Positivism entails the view that we cannot determine adjudicatory content a priori. In this sense, naturalism is no replacement for legal positivism; a limited form of naturalism is if anything a corollary of a positivist theory of legal content.

Whatever the function might be that, in a particular community, yields adjudicatory outputs from legal inputs—we cannot discover or present a theory of that function unless we first have a theory of law telling us what is true of law as such.[51] Thus,

---

[48] I first heard this objection pressed against Leiter both by Scott Shapiro and Roberta Romano. In response, Leiter could argue that there is nothing implausible in the suggestion that the Rule of Recognition has determinate content while rules valid under it do not—after all, they are different kinds of rules. One picks out rules, the other picks out behaviour as conforming to or failing to conform to the rules. So the former picks out propositional objects while the latter picks out actions. That might explain how the former can be determinate while the latter not. It is not obvious a priori why picking out rules should be easier than picking out acts that fall under rules—in part because in the legal context the rules that are being picked out are created by actions, and so what one is really picking out are rule-making acts; so there is no real difference.

Still, Leiter could respond that it isn't in the nature of rules in general or legal rules in particular that if any are determinate, all must be. Some rules can be determinate and others not. Indeed; but the burden is clearly shifted to Leiter to explain why the Rule of Recognition should be determinate while rules subordinate to it not. The burden is great, since Leiter's argument for the indeterminacy of rules subordinate to the Rule of Recognition is based on the range of available non unique interpretive principles. That issue applies equally to the Rule of Recognition.

[49] See ch. 11 of *Practice of Principle* for this important distinction.

[50] In other words, indeterminate particular legal inputs may mean that ordinary folk cannot reliably determine what actions the rule requires of them or what liberties and rights it confers on them. From their perspective, the rules are inadequate grounds. But this tells us nothing at all about whether the adjudicatory content of the law is indeterminate, for it tells us nothing about how disputes under the rules are to be resolved by officials. A great deal of guidance indeterminacy is compatible with adjudicatory determinacy. Leiter's thesis concerns the latter, not the former kind of indeterminacy.

[51] In other words, as I pointed out in chapter 11 of *Practice of Principle*, we cannot infer from 'adjudicatory content' to '*legal* adjudicatory content'. There is a premise missing, namely that whatever judges are required to decide in a case—or whatever they do decide in a case—states or expresses the law. We can have good reasons for reserving the category of law to a subset of official acts—even those mandated

the naturalist cannot, simply by focusing on adjudication, avoid the fundamental question of analytic jurisprudence to which every theory of law is addressed.

Having argued that we cannot abandon analytic jurisprudence by pursuing a naturalistic jurisprudence, let's now turn to the prospects of success for a naturalized jurisprudence. There is, of course, a quick and dirty way to get from confirmation holism to naturalism. All beliefs must face the tribunal of experience. All are revisable in the light of recalcitrant empirical evidence. There is no privileged place left for philosophy. If there are norms regulating inquiry, they are norms that are internal to the practice of inquiry: and so on. The truth of all claims ultimately depends on empirical evidence. Why not turn all inquiry over to the empirical sciences. This is the reading of Quine that gets us not only to naturalism, but to the end of philosophy as well.

One reason for turning inquiry over to science is that scientific theories provide more compelling and illuminating explanations of empirical phenomena. These are explanations in terms of natural, causal laws. The first problem is that not every natural or empirical fact is explainable by natural laws. Not every fact is covered by a law. Secondly, and much more importantly, there is absolutely no reason to believe that the facts that interest us as philosophers and social theorists are the facts that social and natural scientific theories are interested in addressing or are designed to address. Is there a social scientific theory that is interested in the difference between validity and legality, between rules that are binding on an official and those that are binding because they are part of the community's law. What social scientific inquiry calls for an explanation of that difference?

Next, not every explanation by a naturalistic theory is an explanation for us. Not every natural explanation increases or deepens our understanding. The explanations at the micro level of particle physics or field theory are not likely to be illuminating of much of our experience even if they are good explanations in the formal sense. Finally, when it comes to the practices of law, what reason do we have for relying on the success of social scientific theories. What social science paradigm has succeeded in delivering the goods (to use one of Leiter's pet phrases) in the way natural science has.

There are, in other words, very good reasons for not turning all inquiry about law over to the social scientists. There is nothing that Leiter has argued that suggests that we must. We can agree with Leiter that the old-fashioned projects of Conceptual Analysis are rendered fruitless if not literally impossible post-Quine. It is arguable whether anyone in modern legal philosophy could be stuck with the project of Conceptual Analysis in the undesirable sense. No contemporary jurisprudential project of which I am aware must be so construed: not Raz's, not Dworkin's, and certainly not mine. If I am right, the kind of analytic or conceptual philosophy that

by legal sources. Raz, for one, claims that only those acts or rules that can be practical authorities are law, and given his theory of practical authority, not all rules or decisions mandated by authoritative sources will be law. And this requires an account of what is conceptually true of law.

informs our work is part of what is necessary for Leiter's own very interesting and important project of naturalized jurisprudence to get off the ground. Leiter gives us no reason to abandon conceptual analysis; at the same time he gives every indication of relying on it himself. And a good thing too, since there is no reason to think that philosophical inquiry and the puzzles that motivate it are likely to be fruitfully illuminated, let alone resolved, by turning them over to the social sciences.

CHAPTER 9

LEGAL AND POLITICAL PHILOSOPHY

JEREMY WALDRON

1 LAW AND POLITICS

MIGHT legal philosophy be conceived as a branch of political philosophy? There is evidently some connection between them. The legal system is part of the political system, and it would be odd for the student of politics to profess no interest at all in its operations. Laws and their enforcement, constitutions, legislatures, courts, adjudication, legal reasoning, the rule of law, and so on—these are respectable subjects of political inquiry. Legislatures and courts are *political* institutions; the rule of law is a *political* ideal; adjudication and legal reasoning are practices and techniques which are part of the *political* culture of the societies in which they flourish. Sure, they are not the only topics of interest to students of politics: students of politics are interested also in non-legal institutions such as parties, non-legal ideals like liberty and prosperity, non-legal practices like electioneering and lobbying, as well as non-legal phenomena like power and war. Still, the topics studied by legal scholars are a formidable subset of the topics that ought to be of interest to a student of politics.

So: from the fact that legal institutions are a subset of political institutions and must be taken into account by anyone who studies political institutions, it would not be unreasonable to infer that legal theory is, or ought to amount to, a substantial chunk of the general theory of politics. The relation between the subject-matters—law an aspect of politics—seems to dictate the relation between disciplines—legal theory must be a branch or a subset of political theory.

I don't mean to be provocative when I call law and legal institutions, ideals, and practices 'political'. Sometimes when people say 'Law is political', they mean that cases are being decided on the basis of judges' partisan views on questions of public policy or on the basis of judges' party-political or ideological allegiances. Or, in a slightly more abstract version of the accusation, they mean that people are managing to evade the force of mechanisms designed to ensure that controversial decisions are taken by legislatures or at constitutional conventions and not by officials like judges. Or they may mean that, for all their pretensions to neutrality and objectivity, legal principles and doctrines conceal substantive and controversial political commitments. But none of these is what I meant in my opening paragraph (though surely all these things *may* be true).

I meant only to emphasize that an understanding—whether it is an empirical, an analytical, or a normative understanding—of institutions and practices in a given society from which no one would withhold the term 'political' is bound to be incomplete without an understanding of institutions and practices from which no one would withhold the term 'legal'. We can't understand political culture without considering the role that judges play in articulating public values. And we can't understand political power in a given society without grasping (among other things) the constraints that legal institutions and practices impose upon the choices and decisions of political leaders. That's true of empirical understanding and it's also true of normative theorizing: for example, one cannot deploy the concept of democracy in the real world without considering the balance that should be struck between issues decided by representative institutions and issues decided by courts; and a discussion of values like liberty, justice, and equality, if it is not to be impossibly abstract, will have an eye to the legalistic character of the structures in which these values are most familiarly embodied.

2 INTERDEPENDENCE

It is one thing to say that a comprehensive study of political institutions must pay attention to law. It doesn't follow that the study of law (doctrinal or philosophical) implicates the study of politics. Law may be part of politics but, for all that has been said, it may be a relatively self-contained part. The legal scholar and the legal theorist may do their work quite independently of political science and political theory. If what I said in Section 1 is correct, the political scientist and the political theorist should pay attention to the work of their counterparts in law, but not necessarily vice versa. The relation may be like that of naval history to military history: naval history is part of military history, and the practitioners of the latter need to understand what is going on in the former. But it is perfectly consistent with this that the naval historians think of their remit as relatively limited, informed only by the broadest or sketchiest understanding of non-maritime aspects of military history. The naval historian may say: 'There is a division of labour among historians. My friend the military historian has responsibility for a bigger picture than I do: he has to bring together what I do, and what the historians of land and air campaigns do. But my job—as a naval historian—is to take responsibility only for one little piece of the jigsaw.'[1]

Let me stick with this analogy for a moment. What I have imagined the naval historian saying is not implausible. But it is easy to see how it might be criticized. Someone might say: 'Though some degree of specialization is sensible, still it is not sensible for the naval historian to blind himself to aspects of general military history which have a bearing on the way naval power is constituted and naval campaigns are conducted. For one thing, navies, armies, and air forces compete for resources from the same national budgets. For another thing, naval strategy is unintelligible apart from its contribution to grand strategy, involving all elements of a country's armed forces. Even below the level of grand strategy, naval operations are often specifically oriented to support other non-naval military operations, such as sea-borne invasions or the bombardment of coastal towns and fortifications. Since matters which are not specifically naval in these ways pervade an understanding of naval matters, it is quite implausible to suppose that expertise in the field of naval history could be secured without considerable expertise in military history generally.'

Something similar may be true of the relation between law and politics, and between legal theory and political theory. Unless the legal scholar understands the relation between legal doctrines and institutions, on the one hand, and the wider political context on the other, his understanding of law and of the way in which particular legal doctrines work will be inconclusive or impoverished, in a formalistic sort of way. Let me give a couple of preliminary examples.

1. Jurisprudence pays a great deal of attention to the differences between rules and standards, the different demands that they make on judicial reasoning, and the different difficulties that they pose.[2] Rules give rise to issues about vagueness and open

---

[1] Notice that the analogy here is different from and more straightforward than the more common philosophical analogy between biology and physics. In the case of biology and physics, there are interesting issues of supervenience and reducibility which arise because of the difference in ontological level between the entities studied in the respective sciences. In the case of law and politics (and, analogously, in the case of naval and military history) the entities studied are of the same level and category—in each case, people, and their interactions, institutions, and ideas. The relation is one of part to whole, rather than micro to macro.

[2] See e.g. Henry M. Hart, Jr. and Albert M. Sachs, *The Legal Process: Basic Problems in the Making and Application of Law*, ed. William N. Eskridge, Jr. and Philip P. Frickey (Westbury, NY: Foundation Press, 1994), 138–43. See also Kathleen Sullivan, 'The Supreme Court, 1991 Term—Foreword: The Justices of

texture, and their application poses problems about under- and over-inclusiveness in relation to the purposes that might be imputed to them. Standards occasion disputes about the exercise of evaluative judgment by judges and other norm-appliers, and they pose hard questions about whose values the judge should use in applying a term like 'reasonable' to some contested situation: his own values, or the values of the person or institution that laid down the standard, or values that he sees as prevalent in society (whether or not he agrees with them)?

Sometimes it is a matter of choice or judgment whether to read a given provision as a rule or a standard.[3] I mean it is a matter of choice or judgment about which of these sets of difficulties, demands, and conundrums a judge should buy into in his understanding of a given provision. Now we know that, from the lawmaker's perspective, one way to approach the choice between rules and standards is to pose questions about where various powers of decision are best located. Rules are chosen, for example, where there is reason to think that the lawmaker will do a better job of determining which cases should be subject to a given legal consequence by an *ex ante* determination than the law-applier will do on the basis of a response to individual cases as they present themselves.[4] In other words, the decision is made by comparing institution A's competence at doing task T by means M with institution B's competence at doing task T by means N. Institutional competence is not the only consideration. We prefer that tax rates be specified numerically by Congress, rather than by the Director of the Internal Revenue Service reviewing individual files under a general standard like 'reasonable contribution', for reasons that have to do with legitimacy rather than with competence. Even if the Congress has to take advice on what the effect of different rates would be, still we think that rates set other than by the authority of representative legislature would be illegitimate. This is perhaps an easy case. In other situations, however, there may be genuine uncertainty whether the importance of legitimacy is adequately respected by the specification of a standard by the representative body (telling a subordinate agency, for example, what factors to take into account, but leaving the detailed balancing to the agency), or whether it requires the specification of a rule.

Decisions like these cannot be made without a great deal of attention to what existing institutions are like, and what the conditions of their legitimacy are and ought to

Rules and Standards', *Harvard Law Review*, 106 (1992), 24; Antonin Scalia, 'The Rule of Law as a Law of Rules', *University of Chicago Law Review*, 56 (1989), 1175; and Duncan Kennedy, 'Form and Substance in Private Law Adjudication', *Harvard Law Review*, 89 (1976), 1685. Note that the distinction between rules and standards is different from the distinction between rules and principles highlighted in Ronald Dworkin's early work: see Ronald Dworkin, *Taking Rights Seriously* (1977), 22–8 and 71–80.

[3] e.g. the constitutional prohibition on bills of attainder—US Constitution, Art. I, 9(3)—may be read as prohibiting only those acts of Congress that satisfy a certain technical definition, or it may be read as prohibiting any act which is objectionable on the sort of grounds that an act of attainder is objectionable.

[4] See Frederick Schauer, 'Rules and the Rule of Law', *Harvard Journal of Law and Public Policy*, 14 (1991), 645, at 679 ff., and also Frederick Schauer, *Playing by the Rules* (Oxford: Clarendon Press, 1991), ch.7.

be. These are matters of politics, political culture, and political philosophy. It would seem to follow that a judge or legal scholar who is making an argument that a particular provision, even one laid down long ago, should be read now (or continue to be read) as a rule rather than a standard or vice versa must avail himself of similar political resources.[5] And taking it one step further: general jurisprudence in this field, addressing the way in which judges should approach issues like the one just stated, must also be informed by knowledge and understanding about institutional competence in general, or about political legitimacy in general, that legal theory cannot supply on its own.[6]

2. My second preliminary example is more esoteric. It concerns an issue in the philosophical debate between legal positivists like Joseph Raz and anti-positivists like Ronald Dworkin. The issue is about whether there can be moral criteria of legal validity. Suppose some provision, T, of a tax statute might be read in two ways, T_1 and T_2, so far as its impact on a given set of circumstances is concerned. According to Dworkin, the way to identify the right answer to the question—'Is T_1 the law or T_2?'—is to choose between them on the ground of which represents T (or the tax scheme as a whole) in the best light: which makes T the best or the fairest requirement?[7] We decide which is best; and on the basis of that we decide what is the law. Raz responds that if we proceed in this way we cannot sensibly regard law as purporting *authoritatively* to settle the question of what would be a good or a fair (or the best or the fairest) tax scheme. One must already have settled that for oneself in order to use the Dworkin approach.[8] By insisting on this kind of moral criterion for legal validity,

---

[5] Thus e.g. debates about Ronald Dworkin's so-called 'moral reading' of certain Constitutional provisions may, in some cases, not be settled by an appeal to the text alone. (Does the First Amendment protect only things the Framers would have recognized as religions, construing 'religion' as a descriptive term, or does it protect things which may be judged importantly analogous to religions, in which case the free exercise clause instructs us to make a judgment of importance?) Questions like these must be settled by an appeal to the text *plus* a consideration of the competence and legitimacy implications of reading some text as a standard rather than a rule. (For 'the moral reading', see Ronald Dworkin, *Freedom's Law: The Moral Reading of the American Constitution* (Cambridge, Mass.: Harvard University Press, 1996), 7 ff.

[6] This may not be true of all interpretative arguments. Some theorists argue in the case in favour of 'original intent' simply by appealing to the character of law-making as an intentional act, without reference to any political considerations about institutional competence or legitimacy. See e.g. Stanley Fish, 'Play of Surfaces: Theory and Law', in *Legal Hermeneutics: History, Theory and Practice*, ed. Gregory Leyh (Berkeley: University of California Press, 1992), 298–9.

[7] Ronald Dworkin, *Law's Empire* (Cambridge, Mass.: Harvard University Press, 1986), 255–6: 'Hard cases arise, for any judge, when his threshold test [of fit] does not discriminate between two or more interpretations of some statute or line of cases. Then he must choose between eligible interpretations by asking which shows the community's structure of institutions and decisions—its public standards as a whole—in a better light from the standpoint of political morality. His own moral and political convictions are now directly engaged.'

[8] Joseph Raz, 'Authority, Law, and Morality', in his collection *Ethics in the Public Domain: Essays in the Morality of Law and Politics* (Oxford: Clarendon Press, 1994), 194, at 209: '[T]he identification of much of law depends, according to Dworkin's analysis, on considerations which are the very same considerations which the law is there to settle'.

Dworkin's approach fails to present law as a possible source of guidance in respect of the moral issues it addresses, says Raz.

Is this a compelling objection to Dworkin's theory? Raz thinks it is, because in his view law claims authority for itself to settle matters such as these. He believes authoritativeness is one of the most important aspects of law's self-presentation. Of course, says Raz, a law or a legal system may *in fact* lack legitimate authority: that may be the upshot of our application to it of the normative test for authority explicated, for example, in his own 'normal justification thesis'.[9] But it necessarily *claims* authority. If this claim is not to be nonsensical, Raz says, then law must have certain structural features: its directives must be capable of being identified in a way that is independent of the reasons that they are supposed to be based on. '[T]he subjects of any authority ... can benefit by its decisions only if they can establish their existence and content in ways which do not depend on raising the very same issues which the authority is there to settle'.[10]

Raz's objection would be undercut, however, if law did not make this sort of claim to authority, or if—even though it did—no one took that aspect of law seriously, that is, if it were not a prominent or important aspect of the concept of law in ordinary use. Now Raz says:

> The claims the law makes for itself are evident from the language it adopts and from the opinions expressed by its spokesmen, i.e. by the institutions of the law. The law's claim to authority is manifested by the fact that legal institutions are officially designated as 'authorities'....[11]

That much can be discerned by a philosopher (or any superficial observer). But whether these claims should be taken seriously, what role they play in the life of the law and in determining the place that law occupies in society—none of these issues can be settled except by paying attention to matters that are in the domain of political science (how law is in fact regarded) or political philosophy (how law ought to be regarded).[12] So—once again—we see that an issue in jurisprudence cannot be evaluated without paying attention to matters outside jurisprudence in the narrowest sense.

The examples I set out in Section 2 were designed to show that some legal issues cannot adequately be thought through or theorized except in a way that takes seriously empirical and theoretical work focused on the broader political and institutional context. Law is part of a political system, and it works as part of that system. It is not like a self-contained prefabricated component which is just plugged in, so to speak. It works in a way that is sensitive to other aspects of the political system's functioning.

---

[9] For 'the normal justification thesis', see ibid. 198, and also Joseph Raz, *The Morality of Freedom* (Oxford: Clarendon Press, 1986), 38–69.

[10] Raz, *Authority, Law, and Morality*, 203. [11] ibid. 199.

[12] An analogy: in most countries, what used to be called the Ministry of War is now called the Ministry of *Defence*. Whether this nomenclature—analogous to Raz's observations in the passage quoted about the linguistic association of 'law' and 'authority'—tells us anything (even something conceptual) about the role of the military is an open question.

This point need not be construed as a way of subordinating law to political science or legal theory to political theory. On the contrary, it implies that legal theory may sometimes help set the agenda for political theory, as legal theorists identify important non-jurisprudential questions that they (*qua* legal theorists) need answered. In this regard they may reinforce the importance of work already being done in political science—for example, on institutional competence—or prompt new work that requires students of politics and society to focus on features of the phenomena they study—features like the authority claims that law makes—which might have escaped them, had it not been for the legal theorist's discernment of their significance.

Beyond the particular examples I have mentioned (and others like them), it is arguable that there are also some more pervasive and programmatic connections between the agendas of legal and political theory. In Section 4, I want to say something about what some may consider the minimal relation between positivist jurisprudence and political theory: the aspects of political stability and effectiveness that must be considered part of the criteria for the existence of a system of law. In Section 5, I want to consider the connections (if any) between legal and political philosophy indicated by the fact that 'the rule of law' is widely regarded as an important political ideal, and I shall connect that too with the controversy among philosophers of law as to whether legal theory should have any contribution to make to our discussion of the issue of political obligation. Finally, Sections 6 and 7 will address some questions of methodology that arise out of this discussion.

3 Substantive Values

Before proceeding with any of that, I want to say something briefly about an array of connections between legal and political philosophy (and indeed also between legal and moral philosophy) that is almost too obvious to bear discussion in a 'meta'-piece like this.

The terms 'legal philosophy' and 'legal theory' are sometimes used to refer to the business of discussing what the law ought to be: I mean, the discussion of what laws should be enacted, what laws should be repealed, what decisions upheld and what decisions overruled, what constitutional amendments should be contemplated, and what general schemes for law reform should be adopted. Most of those who engage in it believe that this business is unthinkable apart from the invocation of values and principles that are also studied in political and moral philosophy, such as freedom, well-being, justice, equality, and respect (not to mention a host of mid-level evaluative concepts like need, harm, dignity, desert, community, etc.).

Now, when a law is opposed in legislative debate on the grounds that it will undermine liberty, or when a particular doctrinal interpretation is favoured in a brief or a
judicial opinion on the ground that it pays more attention to considerations of desert
than the alternative interpretations, there need not be much in the way of *philosophy*
going on. Moral philosophy does not happen every time someone mentions a principle or appeals to a value. And conversely, much of what goes on in moral philosophy—and I believe in political philosophy too[13]—goes on and ought to go on in a
form that is fairly distant from the concerns of the legislator or the judge. I don't just
mean that moral philosophers are interested mainly in personal virtue, which is
something that lawmakers should stay away from.[14] I do think it is very important,
for reasons I explain in Section 6, for there to be a mediated rather than a direct relation between moral and legal philosophy, even in the areas where moral ideas are evidently relevant. Mainly what I mean, though, is that, even with regard to moral
values, philosophers have a distinct set of tasks to address—issues in meta-ethics,
issues about truth-conditions, objectivity, and cognitivist versus non-cognitivist
analyses—whose direct practical relevance to political and legal choices may be quite
limited.

In recent years, however, a lot of philosophical energy has been devoted to the systematic exploration of exactly the values that lawmakers might appeal to, at a level of
discourse not much more abstract than the level at which real-life political and legal
discourse is conducted. The example of John Rawls's *A Theory of Justice* inspired not
only the development of other 'grand theories' of political value and political morality,[15] which offered philosophically well-worked-out grounds for thinking about
basic rights and the foundations of the welfare state. It inspired also, at a slightly less
grand level, a type of patient and rigorous philosophical examination of concepts
and issues that promised genuine pay-offs in mid-level legal decision-making.[16] Our
views about 'the best interests of the child' in family law could now be referred to
philosophical discussions of interests and well-being, and our discussions of the
alleged 'harmfulness' of pornography could now be referred to sustained philosophical discussions of harm and the harm principle.

This was not a startlingly new phenomenon. The great precedent was the influence
of utilitarianism as a comprehensive theory of law reform in England in the early

[13] See Jeremy Waldron, 'What Plato Would Allow', in *Nomos XXXVII: Theory and Practice*, ed. Ian
Shapiro and Judith Wagner DeCew (New York: New York University Press, 1995), 138–78.

[14] For the classic distinction between philosophizing about personal morality and philosophizing
about political values, see Immanuel Kant, *The Metaphysics of Morals*, trans. Mary Gregor (Cambridge:
Cambridge University Press, 1991), 45–54 and 181–4.

[15] John Rawls, *A Theory of Justice* (Cambridge, Mass.: Cambridge University Press, 1971); Robert
Nozick, *Anarchy, State and Utopia* (Oxford: Blackwell, 1974); Bruce Ackerman, *Social Justice in the
Liberal State* (New Haven: Yale University Press, 1980); Ronald Dworkin, *Sovereign Virtue: The Theory
and Practice of Equality* (Cambridge, Mass.: Harvard University Press, 2000).

[16] See e.g. the four volumes of Joel Feinberg, *The Moral Limits of the Criminal Law* (New York: Oxford
University Press, 1984–8).

decades of the nineteenth century. The distinctive thing about the late-twentieth-century revival of philosophy and public affairs, was that it represented, first in Rawls's theory, but also in many of the responses to Rawls, the development of philosophically well-worked-out alternatives to utilitarian theory (not just variations on a theme but genuine alternatives).

Moreover, not only has work of this character now come to pervade moral and political philosophy, but legal scholars are also increasingly responsive to it. Legal reform proposals that fail to refer to philosophical discussion are regarded in some legal circles as inadequately theorized, and for that reason condemned as unsatisfactory. And it is not just an external or synthetic match-up. Those who take responsibility for doctrinal analysis are now open to the idea that one can find in the law immanent doctrines and concepts that might match the ideas that were being developed in moral philosophy. This 'matching' would of course not be a coincidence. On the legal side, it might reflect the historic influence of moral ideas on the law, and on the philosophical side, it might also reflect the reverse influence, of legal practice on philosophical theory-building, mediated perhaps under the auspices of reflective equilibrium.[17]

The match might be at the level of substance or form.[18] And it might occur not only at the level of norms but also at the level of background ideas that inform our thinking about norms—ideas like causation and responsibility. Thus, for example, in the jurisprudence of tort law, scholars have been able to show that substantive doctrines, background ideals, and formal structures are all better explained in terms of normative theories of corrective justice than in terms (say) of quasi-utilitarian economic ideals such as wealth-maximization.[19] Admittedly these scholars also want to resist any simplistic reduction of the specific norms of corrective justice into some general theory of distributive social justice.[20] But their grounds for resisting this are themselves theorems in political philosophy, substantive theses about justice in their own right.

This section has concerned what we call in the trade *special jurisprudence*—that is, jurisprudence focused on specific topics in law such as tort liability or criminal attempts.[21] For the remainder of this chapter I want to return to the topic of general jurisprudence, and to the question of what relation we might expect between general

[17] See Norman Daniels, 'Wide Reflective Equilibrium and Theory Acceptance in Ethics', *Journal of Philosophy*, 76 (1979), 256.

[18] But note that some modern formalists deny that respect for the inherent form of, say, tort doctrine requires or admits of any reinforcement from the form of normative conceptions of justice developed in political philosophy: see Ernest J. Weinrib, 'Legal Formalism: On the Immanent Rationality of Law', *Yale Law Journal* 97 (1988), 949.

[19] See Jules L. Coleman, *Risks and Wrongs* (Cambridge: Cambridge University Press, 1992), 197–385.

[20] See ibid. 350 ff.

[21] This contrast between general and special jurisprudence (i.e. the philosophy of law as such versus the philosophy of particular legal topics such as tort liability) differs from the distinction between general (or universal) and particular (or local) jurisprudence (i.e. the philosophy of law as such versus the philosophy relevant to the law of particular jurisdictions such as England or the United States).

discussions of law as such—the very idea of law—and the concepts and values that are studied in political philosophy.

4 Existence Conditions

One of the most difficult questions that the legal philosopher asks is: what is it for law to exist? The question can be asked about a particular law or about a whole legal system, though usually we answer a question about the existence conditions for a particular law by referring the questioner to the existence conditions for a legal system and then on to that legal system's conditions for recognizing something as valid law within that system.

When we talk about the existence of positive law—about there being law governing some area of action, or interaction, or conflict—we have in mind existence at a particular time and place, in relation to a specific community or group of real people. That reference is crucial, in a number of ways. It is important for understanding the content, meaning and implications of the provision in question: what does the statute, on its own terms, purport to do? Whose conduct does it purport to govern? But equally if not more important, for the legal positivist, is the *reality* of the connection between the provision in question and the time, place, and people to which it is supposed to apply. Does the provision have any actual effect in the real world, or is it just 'law' on paper? Without the appropriate real connection, law has only a notional reality.

For example, if I wanted to waste your time, I could formulate a normative provision right now from which one could infer, as a strictly textual matter, the time, place, and subject class to which the 'law' is supposed to apply:

> *The Finger-in-the-Ear Act*: (1) This Act applies to all men who reside in New England. (2) At some time on his twenty-first birthday, every person to whom this Act applies shall put his finger in his ear and keep it there for two minutes. (3) Anyone who fails to do this shall pay a fine of $100 to the New Haven Home for Stray Dogs. (4) This Act shall commence on the first day of April, 2001.

Standing by itself, of course, this 'statute' is anomalous. But it might be thought of as enacted pursuant to a legislative norm of something I shall call 'the New England legal system':

> *New England Legislative Supremacy Principle*: Any provision enacted in New England, by being written in a publishable philosophical paper and spell-checked twice, shall be law in New England as soon as it is brought to the attention of any resident in New England other than the person who wrote it.

And if I wanted to waste more of your time than I have already, I could elaborate this 'legal system' at some length, nesting norms inside norms, showing how some norms entered into the validity conditions of other norms, adding subsidiary norms to interpret and enforce the primary norms, and so on. All this, though, would be an idiotic and futile exercise. It would hold no interest whatever, since the system of norms is purely notional and does not have the appropriate real relation to the people, places, and times to which its various provisions purport to apply.

What is that relation in the case of law? What makes a law *real* law? The answer to this question should help us not just with the silly task of dismissing the Finger-in-the-Ear Act, but also to address important questions about purported laws and legal systems in real-world situations that are marginal from the point of view of jurisprudential and political theory: law in the international arena; the laws of war; *ancien régime* law during a revolutionary period; law in times of civil conflict; legal obsolescence; widespread defiance and unenforceability of a particular law; and so on.

Traditional forms of legal positivism used the notion of *sovereignty* to specify the appropriate external relation between the provisions of a legal system considered notionally as norms and the independent reality of people, power, and behaviour in the world. 'Every positive law', said Austin, 'is set by a sovereign person, or a sovereign body of persons, to a member or members of the independent political society wherein the person or body is sovereign or supreme'.[22] That last-mentioned *sovereignty* or *supremacy* is understood not in terms of a postulated norm—like my New England Legislative Supremacy Principle—but in terms of a certain political reality:

> The superiority which is styled sovereignty ... is distinguished from other superiority ... by the following marks or characters.—1. the bulk of a given society are in a habit of obedience or submission to a *determinate* and *common* superior: let that common superior be a certain individual person, or a certain body or aggregate of individual persons. 2. That certain individual, or that certain body of individuals, is *not* in a habit of obedience to a determinate human superior.[23]

These are factual tests—vague, certainly, as Austin acknowledges (and I want to say more about that in a moment),[24] but vague like a factual predicate in political science such as 'powerful' or 'influential'. The term 'sovereign' is not, for Austin, a predicate whose use reflects the application of a legal norm (like 'authoritative' or 'valid'). His use of 'sovereignty' is thus different from the use of 'legal sovereignty' in A. V. Dicey's constitutional jurisprudence, in which the sovereignty of the British parliament is understood as the upshot of a legal principle, not the application of a factual test.[25]

---

[22] John Austin, *The Province of Jurisprudence Determined*, ed. Wilfrid E. Rumble (Cambridge: Cambridge University Press, 1995), 165.

[23] ibid. 166 (emphasis in original).   [24] See ibid. 173–5.

[25] See A. V. Dicey, *Introduction to the Study of the Law of the Constitution* (Indianapolis: Liberty Classics, 1982), 26–30, where Dicey distinguishes legal sovereignty from political sovereignty (which he defines, ibid. 27, as '[t]hat body ... in a state the will of which is ultimately obeyed by the citizens of the state').

Some may say that this is just an empirical matter. But the significance of the fact that traditional positivists always invoke a real-world sense of 'sovereignty' as the pivot of their jurisprudence is not only that they may need the help of the political scientist to apply that term empirically in certain cases. True—there may be an empirical problem.[26] But the important point is about the *meaning* of the vague empirical expression: what does 'sovereign' actually imply? Instead of implying that *the bulk* of a given society are in a habit of obedience to a common superior, it might be taken to imply that *all but a few* of the members of a given society are in a habit of obedience to a common superior. Both the emphasized terms are empirical and both are vague; but the choice between them is still significant and it is not itself an empirical matter. Now why would one opt for the former criterion (obedience by *the bulk*) rather than the latter criterion (obedience by *all but a few*) as one's factual test of sovereignty? The answer can only be: because our political theory or our political philosophy indicates the salience of 'bulk' rather than 'all but a few'. For example, our political theory may have this among its theorems: institutions can survive, keep the peace, secure expectations, and so on, even if some proportion less than all-but-a-few of the members of a given community habitually obey, provided the bulk of them do. And given a certain sort of Hobbesian or Humean approach to politics, we may regard fulfilment of these tasks as sufficient, for the purposes of real-world efficacy.

Someone may say that this is too obvious to count as a connection between legal and political philosophy. If they mean that we may reach the same conclusion implicitly without much thought or argument, then I guess they are right. But of course that wouldn't indicate that political theory was doing no work; it would indicate only that the work it did was being taken for granted.

It is not hard to see how the definition of 'sovereign' might become controversial. Though his test is vague, Austin is prepared to say that neither the submission of a people to an occupying army (e.g. France occupied by the Allies in 1815), nor the submission of the ruler of a small state to a regional hegemon (e.g. the deference of Saxony to the Holy Alliance after 1815), constitutes sovereignty. '[S]ince the commands and obedience were comparatively rare and transient' in these situations, they were 'not sufficient to constitute the relation of sovereignty and subjection'.[27] There may be deference and compliance but there is no *habit* of obedience. Well, we may

---

[26] Austin, *The Province of Jurisprudence*, 173.

[27] And as I said also a moment ago, Austin does acknowledge the vagueness of the term 'sovereign' (ibid. 167): '[I]n order that the bulk of its members may render obedience to a common superior, how many of its members, or what proportion of its members, must render obedience to one and the same superior? And, assuming that the bulk of its members render obedience to common superior, how often must they render it, and how long must they render it, in order that that obedience may be habitual?— Now since these questions cannot be answered precisely, the positive mark of sovereignty and independent political society is a fallible test of specific or particular cases. It would not enable us to determine of every independent society, whether it were political or natural.' This means that even after the political scientist has given us all the information he can about obedience-behaviour, it may still be impossible to say (as it often is with vague empirical predicates) whether a given political community has a sovereign and thus (on Austin's account) a legal system or not.

ask, why is *habit* so important? Once again, it is a philosophical not an empirical issue. The answer must be something along the following lines: the distinctive and important tasks of law—tasks like institution-building and economy-framing—cannot be performed without a regular and reliable mode of submission. In the absence of an answer of this sort, which is undoubtedly a contribution from political philosophy, the legal philosopher would be at a loss as to what to say about this most pivotal of terms.

The situation is no different in twentieth-century jurisprudence. The idea of the sovereign is abandoned in the positivist legal theories of Hans Kelsen, H. L. A. Hart, and Joseph Raz. But all three jurists recognize the need for an empirical test of the effectiveness or efficacy of law. In Kelsen's case, this is at considerable cost to the 'purity' of his theory (which, if left to its own devices, would afford him no basis for dismissing a suitably elaborated version of my New England legal system, with its own presupposed '*grundnorm*' and a validity test which the Finger-in-the-Ear Act would satisfy).[28] Kelsen's theory holds that although '[a] minimum of effectiveness is a condition of validity', and 'effectiveness has to join the positing of a legal norm if the norm is not to lose its validity',[29] the overall condition of efficacy is systemic:

[A] legal order does not lose its validity when a single legal norm loses its effectiveness. A legal order is regarded as valid if its norms are *by and large* effective (that is, actually applied and obeyed).... Effectiveness is a condition for the validity—but it is not validity.... [T]he problem of the relation between validity and effectiveness of the legal order coincides with the more familiar problem of the relationship between law and power or right and might. [T]he solution attempted here is merely the scientifically exact formulation of the old truism that right cannot exist without might and yet is not identical with might. Right (the law), according to the theory here developed, is a certain order (or organization) of might.[30]

Joseph Raz, I think, is right to observe that Kelsen does not adequately explain how the degree of requisite efficacy is to be determined.[31] Kelsen simply announces a standard—'*by and large* effective (that is, actually applied and obeyed)'—without explanation or elaboration. Elsewhere Raz remarks that of all the conditions for the existence and identity of legal systems, efficacy is 'the least studied and least understood', and he suggests that this might be because 'there is not much which legal philosophy can contribute in this respect'[32]—or at least contribute on its own. He

---

[28] Hans Kelsen, *The Pure Theory of Law* (Gloucester, Mass.: Peter Smith, 1989), 10–12 (ch. I, sect. 4.c) and 208–14 (ch. 5, sect. 34.f–g).

[29] ibid. at 11.

[30] ibid. 212–14 (emphasis in the original). See also Hans Kelsen, *Introduction to the Problems of Legal Theory*, trans. Bonnie Litschewski Paulson and Stanley L. Paulson (Oxford: Clarendon Press, 1992), 59–61.

[31] Joseph Raz, *The Concept of a Legal System: An Introduction to the Theory of Legal System*, 2nd edn. (Oxford: Clarendon Press, 1980), 93.

[32] Joseph Raz, *The Authority of Law: Essays on Law and Morality* (Oxford: Clarendon Press, 1979), 42. (However Raz's own discussion in *Concept of a Legal System*, 203–8 is very suggestive.)

thinks a lot of work must be done in this regard by the sociology of law.[33] But I suspect that *that* contribution in turn depends on an elaborated sense of the conditions on which and the auspices under which the partial efficacy of a system of norms in a society is of interest to us. The sociologists and the philosophers of law study and classify, in their different ways, interesting phenomena; and at least part of our theory of what is *interesting* in this field (perhaps the objective part) is constructed in political philosophy.[34]

H. L. A. Hart's book *The Concept of Law* proposes a two-part test of efficacy as a necessary condition for the existence in a society of a system of positive law:

On the one hand, those rules of behaviour which are valid according to the system's ultimate criteria of validity must be generally obeyed, and on the other hand, its rules of recognition specifying the criteria of legal validity and its rules of change and adjudication must be effectively accepted as common public standards by its officials. . . . The first condition is the only one which private citizens need satisfy: they may obey each for his part only and from any motive whatever. . . . The second condition must also be satisfied by the officials of the system. They must regard these as common standards of official behaviour and appraise critically their own and each other's deviations as lapses.[35]

This account has two noticeable features which might be occasions for controversy. First, there is the suggestion that a legal system can exist in a community even when those who are governed by it (ordinary members of the community) know nothing of the secondary rules governing validity, legal recognition, and so on. Hart acknowledges that '[t]he society in which this was so might be deplorably sheeplike; and the sheep might end in the slaughter-house'.[36] But he sees little reason for withholding the term 'legal system' from such a situation. Someone might dissent from this, however, on the ground that talk of the law of a community must mean something more than the existence of a set of alien principles with which the population, for whatever reason, happen to comply. Debate about this would undoubtedly engage issues in political as well as legal philosophy.

Secondly, there is the suggestion that a legal system exists only where the officials orient themselves internally to the same secondary rules, as a matter of common acceptance of the standards embodied in those rules. Now it is not clear what this amounts to: does it mean that the judges must treat the secondary rules as conventions, and that it is not enough for there to be a convergence of independent judgments among them about (say) the appropriateness of recognizing a representative body as a legislature?[37] Nor is it clear how we would defend any particular interpretation of this requirement,

---

[33] Raz, *Authority of Law*, 44.

[34] See also Raz's essay 'The Institutional Nature of Law', in ibid. 103 ff.

[35] H. L. A. Hart, *The Concept of Law*, 2nd edn., ed. Joseph Raz and Penelope Bulloch (Oxford: Clarendon Press, 1994), 116–17.

[36] ibid. 117. See also Jeremy Waldron, 'All We Like Sheep', *Canadian Journal of Law and Jurisprudence*, 12 (1999), 169.

[37] Hart, *Concept of Law*, 116. See also the discussion in the 'Postscript', ibid. at 255–7, responding to some criticisms in Dworkin, *Law's Empire*, 130–9.

without venturing beyond the rather narrow confines of legal theory, considered as something separate from the general theory of political and social organization.

I suspect Hart thought that all these questions could be resolved as a matter of open-ended pragmatics, for he says it would be 'pointless' to make statements about people's rights and duties based on the primary and secondary rules of a system of law if the efficacy condition did not obtain.[38] But there are questions to be asked about this implicit pragmatism. Does it follow there are as many efficacy conditions as there are distinct points or intelligible purposes of making statements about legal rights and duties? Or do we tailor our (one) efficacy condition for the lowest pragmatic level—the reason for talking about legal duties that most closely approximates point-lessness without actually losing its point? Or are we rather privileging a subset of the points or intelligible purposes that people may have for talking about legal rights and duties, and orienting our condition of efficacy to those? If so—and I think this third alternative far more plausible than the other two—then arriving at the best account of *why* that subset is privileged may require us to draw on a political philosopher's account of why law matters in society.

So far I have focused on sovereignty and efficacy, as conceptual ingredients of legal philosophy, whose analysis may require input from political philosophy. The points I have made, though, can be generalized to cover other jurisprudential concepts as well. In general, one would expect that a full political theory (one that includes a theory of law) will make the relation between legal concepts and political concepts transparent. Thomas Hobbes's account of the role of rules of recognition for positive law provides a fine example. We are familiar with the idea of a rule of recognition, as one of the secondary rules constituting a legal system, from H. L. A. Hart's jurisprudence in *The Concept of Law*.[39] But the idea also played a role in Thomas Hobbes's philosophy of law, written some 300 years before Hart's.

Like Hart, Hobbes distinguished between the judgment a person might make concerning the morality of a rule and the judgment he might make concerning its legal validity. For Hobbes the importance of this distinction lay in the social value of having a single shared framework for dispute resolution even in the midst of moral disagreement: people who disagree about right and wrong, just and unjust, can nevertheless agree on the need to organize social life on the basis of one set of determinate answers to those questions, even if many of them individually judge those determinate answers to be unwise or morally incorrect. That the measure one thinks wicked is nevertheless *a valid law* is a judgment that alerts a person disposed to disobey the measure (e.g. on moral grounds) to the dangers of unilateral and uncoordinated action in a context of disagreement.[40]

On this basis, one can see the importance of rules of recognition in Hobbes's theory. The business of legislating addresses the problem of competition between

---

[38] Hart, *Concept of Law*, 103–4.   [39] ibid. 94–6.
[40] See generally, Thomas Hobbes, *Leviathan*, ed. Richard Tuck (Cambridge: Cambridge University Press, 1988), chs. 17–26.

rival views and interests. Different people hold and are willing to fight for rival definitions of justice and the common good (whether because their particular definition
advances their material interests or simply because they are, in some other fashion,
attached to a particular definition). That is the context that makes legislation necessary, but it is also the context that makes secondary rules like rules of recognition
necessary. We need a rule of recognition on Hobbes's account primarily because
there is disagreement in the community as to what ought to be taken as a point of
coordination for action by individuals in the community. The practice of accepting
and obeying sovereign commands will not work to mitigate the Hobbesian state of
nature unless there is some reliable way of disentangling the question 'What did the
sovereign command?' from the question 'What is the best basis on which we might
coordinate?' Says Hobbes:

Nor is it enough the Law be written and published; but also that there be manifest signs, that
it proceedeth from the will of the Soveraign. For private men, when they have or think they
have force enough to secure their unjust designes, and convoy them safely to their ambitious
ends, may publish for Lawes what they please without, or against the Legislative Authority.
There is therefore requisite, not only a Declaration of the law, but also sufficient signes of the
Author, and Authority.[41]

Such signs, Hobbes says, will depend on accessible criteria of validity such as
'publique Registers, publique Counsels, publique Ministers, and publique Seals'.[42]
On this account, the apparatus of legal recognition is oriented to a compelling and
substantive political end—the end of ensuring that when someone faces what purports to be a legal demand, he can ascertain whether that demand really *is* playing the
role which Hobbesian law and Hobbesian legal validity aspire to play so far as the
diminution of social conflict is concerned. In other words, there has to be some way
of distinguishing real legislation from forged legislation, real laws from fake laws. If
someone rides into my village and announces, 'It is now the law that we all have to
worship as Presbyterians', I am going to insist on examining the authenticity of the
'statutory text' that he is waving. If I recognize it as authentic, then I will understand
that we are settling on Presbyterian forms of worship in order to put an end to our
otherwise internecine religious conflicts. But if the person who made the announce-
ment cannot produce authentication, then his 'proclamation' will have to be dismissed as just another stratagem in the religious wars, not (as a law would be) a way
of ending them.

The general point illustrated by Hobbes's discussion is that one's account of rules
of recognition is necessarily connected to one's account of what ultimately matters
about the process of lawmaking. For Hobbes what ultimately matters in lawmaking

[41] ibid. 189.
[42] Hobbes went on to describe these registers, seals, etc. as the means 'by which all laws are sufficiently
verified, verified, I say, not authorized, for the verification is but the testimony and the record, not the
authority of the law' (ibid.). (I read this as pointing to the distinction between rules of legal change and
rules of recognition. Compare the endnote on this issue in Hart, *Concept of Law*, 294.)

is univocality, determinacy, decisiveness, and the resolution of social conflict; without that, he thinks, we are no better off with law than we would be without it. What one needs to know, therefore, in the way of recognition, is that the purported law really does have the features of univocality, determinacy, and so on associated with Hobbesian sovereignty. If everyone is announcing laws on their own authority without reference to a sovereign, we might as well have no law at all so far as the Hobbesian theory is concerned. The state of nature would simply reproduce itself as a war of rival pseudo laws and we would be back where we began, before there was any authoritative lawmaking at all. This is the background from political philosophy that explains the substantive, not just the formal or system-theoretic, importance of this most prominent of modern jurisprudential ideas.[43]

To this, someone might object that Hobbes's political theory tells us only what sort of *system of command* is desirable for a society; they might say it is a *separate* question—one to be dealt with in jurisprudence, not political philosophy—whether such a system of command, paraded as desirable by Hobbes, corresponds to *the concept of law*. This objection I find quite unconvincing. It presupposes that the concept of law may be elaborated in isolation from any consideration of the functions served by law or the good of law and legal system for the societies that have it. It supposes that we might first give an account of the concept of law, and then be pleasantly surprised when it turned out—entirely contingently—that law served some useful purpose. Indeed, it supposes that one's account of the concept of law might be comprehensive and complete—with nothing lacking—even though no attempt whatever had been made to raise or answer questions about what law or legal system might contribute to the societies in which they are found. I will discuss this as a general issue of methodology in the section that follows. For the moment, however, let me say that I find it difficult to imagine what motivates such a resolutely narrow approach, unless it is some sort of terror that if political considerations are introduced at *any* stage in jurisprudence, they will overwhelm the entire enterprise and show us perhaps that the critics of law were right after all, and that everything has always been political all the way along; and that we must prevent at all costs. As I indicated at the end of Section 1, this sort of 'Maginot Line mentality'[44] seems to be based on a fearful misunderstanding of the force of the word 'political'.

---

[43] See also Jeremy Waldron, *Law and Disagreement* (Oxford: Clarendon Press, 1999), 38–42.

[44] Adapting a phrase from Charles Taylor, 'What's Wrong with Negative Liberty?' in *The Idea of Freedom: Essays in Honour of Isaiah Berlin*, ed. Alan Ryan (Oxford: Oxford University Press, 1979), 179.

5 NORMATIVE POSITIVISM

Be that as it may, the controversy about whether the philosophy of law can afford to neglect this political element has established itself as a major fault-line in modern jurisprudence. Of course there has always been the opposition between defenders of legal positivism and defenders of natural law. The latter are committed dogmatically to the view that law, in its essence, is oriented to human good, so that there is no question of any separation of the disciplines. The dispute about that natural law position is perfectly familiar. It amounts to a debate about the positivist's separability thesis— 'that it is in no sense a necessary truth that laws reproduce or satisfy certain demands of morality'.[45]

What is remarkable about the present debate, however, is that it is now also a debate *within* positivism. A number of legal positivists have become convinced that major claims within their tradition—including the separability thesis itself—can be grasped and illuminated only on the basis of certain normative commitments. They take their lead in this from Hobbes and Bentham—positivists who gave great prominence in their legal philosophy to the evils that might be expected to afflict societies whose members were unable to disentangle their judgments about what was required or permitted by the law of their society from their individual judgements about justice and morality. Theorists like Gerald J. Postema,[46] and others who take this view,[47] are no longer willing to subscribe to the order of priorities laid down by H. L. A. Hart:

My account is *descriptive* in that it is morally neutral and has no justificatory aims: it does not seek to justify or commend on moral or other grounds the forms and structures which appear in my general account of law, though a clear understanding of these is, I think, an important preliminary to any useful moral criticism of law.[48]

On the contrary they agree with some of the critics of positivism (such as Ronald Dworkin) that what one brings to the moral criticism of law is a concept of law already suffused with normative understanding.[49]

Those positivists who oppose this 'normative' view do so on several grounds. First, they deny that the fact that the extension of a concept is uncertain or controversial means that normative considerations must be imported from political philosophy to

---

[45] Hart, *Concept of Law*, 185–6.

[46] Gerald A. Postema, *Bentham and the Common Law Tradition* (Oxford: Clarendon Press, 1986), 328 ff.

[47] See e.g. Neil MacCormick, 'A Moralistic Case for A-moralistic Law', *Valparaiso Law Review*, 20 (1985), 1; Tom Campbell, *The Legal Theory of Ethical Positivism* (Brookfield, Vt.: Dartmouth, 1996); Stephen Perry, 'Interpretation and Methodology in Legal Theory', in *Law and Interpretation: Essays in Legal Philosophy*, ed. Andrei Marmor (Oxford: Clarendon Press, 1997), 129–31; and Waldron, *Law and Disagreement*, 166–8.

[48] Hart, *Concept of Law*, 240.   [49] See Dworkin, *Law's Empire*, 90.

settle the matter.[50] Secondly, they deny the equivalence of an inquiry into the essence of law with an enquiry into what is interesting and important about law. Or if there is any equivalence here, they say it obtains at such a broad level of generality—for example, what is interesting about law is that it 'provides guidance'—as to leave everything in political philosophy as it was before. An analogy may help to illuminate this line of argument. In 'Politics as a Vocation', Max Weber argued that

the state cannot be defined in terms of its ends. There is scarcely any task that some political association has not taken in hand, and there is no task that one could say has always been exclusive and peculiar to those associations which are designated as political ones: today the state, or historically, those associations which have been the predecessors of the modern state. Ultimately, one can define the modern state sociologically only in terms of the specific *means* peculiar to it. . . .[51]

And Weber went on to give his famous definition of the state as 'a human community that (successfully) claims the monopoly of the legitimate use of physical force within a given territory'.[52] Weber thinks this sort of definition is more illuminating than a teleological one, because it leaves it as an open question, with regard to any postulated function, F: 'Should the state take on F?' For even if the pursuit of F helps explain why people set up organizations with this shape and with these sorts of means available to them, still it does not follow that such organizations are bound to F or restricted to F. Similarly, one might argue, in the case of law: even if modern positive law configures itself as it does for the sort of reasons Hobbes thought important or the sort of reasons Bentham thought important, it could nevertheless depart from these aims and still be regarded as law. For this reason, it is important—these positivists believe—to maintain some logical distance between analytic jurisprudence and political philosophy or at least that part of political philosophy which asks what aims are worth pursuing by means of law.

Unsurprisingly, many of these issues play out in the form of a controversy about the nature of concepts (and conceptual analysis) in jurisprudence. Everyone agrees that the task of the philosopher of law (at least in general jurisprudence) is to advance our understanding of *law, legal system, constitution, validity, adjudication, legal obligation,* and so on as concepts. Many people infer from this that it is not the legal philosopher's task to figure what the law ought to be or what values or ideologies should be embodied in a country's constitution or legal code. If that *is* a philosopher's job, they say, it's the job of the moral or the political philosopher; the task of general jurisprudence is to see to it that we have a clear understanding of the legal concepts, which can then be brought to the (quite separate) normative or evaluative enterprise. On this account, there *is* a clear division of labour between the disciplines.

[50] See Jules Coleman, 'Incorporationism, Conventionality, and the Practical Difference Thesis', *Legal Theory*, 4 (1998), 381, at 389.
[51] Max Weber, 'Politics as a Vocation', in *From Max Weber: Essays in Sociology*, ed. H. H. Gerth and C. Wright Mills (London: Routledge & Kegan Paul, 1970), 77–8.
[52] ibid. 78.

Can this bright line be sustained? Everything depends on what the concepts in question—*law*, *legal system*, and so on—turn out to be like. Suppose *law* is a concept like *hospital*, rather than a concept like *state* (in Weber's sense). One of the meanings given for 'hospital' in the *Oxford English Dictionary* is '[a]ny institution or establishment for the care of the sick or wounded, or of those who require medical treatment'.[53] On this account of the meaning, no one understands the term 'hospital' unless he understands what hospitals are *for*. To describe one's establishment as a hospital is to hold out the promise of healing and care.[54] Similarly, some have argued that the concept *law* holds out a promise of justice or attention to the common good. This is not necessarily confined to the natural law tradition.[55] Philip Selznick, an eminent sociologist of law, has insisted that although law is not necessarily just, 'it does promise justice', and we make a serious mistake in legal theory, says Selznick, if we fail to notice or explicate that promise.[56]

The implications of this line of argument (which I shall call the 'hospital' thesis) for the relation between legal and political philosophy are quite complicated. At one extreme, it might be argued that the hospital thesis breaks down the barrier between conceptual analysis in jurisprudence and a substantial chunk of normative argument in political philosophy. If we accept the strongest version of a conceptual connection between law and justice we might conclude (with St Augustine), that 'a law that was unjust wouldn't seem to be law'.[57] And if that is accepted then a policy proposal to change a just provision into an unjust provision would be tantamount to a proposal to shift to law from non-law.[58] The theory of justice, then, would be a substantial concern of jurisprudence, and there would thus be a great overlap between the disciplines. Even if we only accepted Selznick's less ambitious version, we might still have to test a system's aspirations against an account of justice in order to establish whether the system should be regarded as law. That is, we would have to look at what the system aspires to (say, economic efficiency), and ask whether that might plausibly be regarded as an aspiration to justice.

[53] *Oxford English Dictionary*, 2nd edn. (online): meaning (3a) for 'hospital, *sb*'.

[54] It might turn out that the procedures actually used in a given institution, making this promise, are harmful to the patients. Now if their harmfulness is known and intended, that belies the sincerity of the description: we assume that Dr Mengele is being ironic when he talks about his clinic at Auschwitz as a 'hospital'. But we don't withdraw the term the instant the mere fact of harmfulness is discovered, if we are sure that the institution in question has healing and care as its aim.

[55] For the modern natural law tradition, see John Finnis, *Natural Law and Natural Rights* (Oxford: Clarendon Press, 1980).

[56] Philip Selznick, *The Moral Commonwealth: Social Theory and the Promise of Community* (Berkeley: University of California Press, 1992), 443–4.

[57] Augustine, *On the Freedom of Will*, I, v, 11, quoted in Finnis, *Natural Law and Natural Rights*, 363.

[58] For a more subtle version of this, see Finnis, *Natural Law and Natural Rights*, 9–18 and 351–66, on the distinction between central (focal) and non-central (non-focal) sense of 'law', and the relation of that distinction to values like *justice* and *the common good*, which are often studied in political philosophy.

At the other extreme, the hospital thesis might be persuasive in a form that connects law with values (like formal justice or legal coherence or due process) that are
not studied in any other discipline or that have always been primarily studied in
jurisprudence, rather than values like justice or the common good. These intra-legal
connections may have few or no implications for normative legal change or legal policy, or if they do, they may complement rather than duplicate whatever normative
work is going on in political philosophy.

In between these extremes, there is the possibility that an analysis of the concepts
of law will reveal a connection to values which are in the *first* instance internal to
jurisprudence in the way just described, but which also have a significance that goes
beyond that. Lon Fuller's thesis of 'the internal morality of law' seems to be in this
intermediate category. Fuller maintains that the analysis of *law* reveals connections
to values or principles like generality, prospectivity, transparency, and predictability.[59] These are themselves strictly legalistic values—part of law's *internal* morality.
But they also embody respect for certain values that are not confined in that way:

Every departure from the principles of the law's inner morality is an affront to man's dignity
as a responsible agent. To judge his actions by unpublished or retrospective laws, or to order
him to do an act that is impossible, is to convey to him your indifference to his powers of self-
determination.[60]

In Fuller's estimation, respect for these values is associated with reluctance to inflict
certain sorts of cruelties and inhumanities; it is no accident that the enthusiastic and
murderous tyranny of the Nazi party in Germany was accompanied by a catastrophic
decline in observance of these internal demands of legality.[61] H. L. A. Hart concedes
the connection between Fuller's principles and the concept of law, but he dismisses
the connection's moral significance on the ground that respect for these legal values
provides no guarantee of respect for non-legal values like justice and humanity:
Fuller's internal morality of law, he says, 'is unfortunately compatible with very great
iniquity'.[62]

Something like this intermediate position—connecting law to legal values, which
are then revealed to have non-legal significance as well—may also be developed from
the opposite direction, from the political philosophy side. 'The rule of law' is sometimes treated as the name of an important *political* ideal, which of course mentions
law and regards law as important, but is not usually elaborated as a matter of
jurisprudential analysis. Still, an analysis of the rule-of-law ideal must inevitably
reach across from political philosophy to jurisprudence. Analysis of this ideal

[59] Lon L. Fuller, *The Morality of Law*, rev. edn. (New Haven: Yale University Press, 1969), 33–94.
[60] ibid. 162.
[61] Lon L. Fuller, 'Positivism and Fidelity to Law—a Reply to Professor Hart', *Harvard Law Review*, 71
(1958), 630, at 648–61.
[62] Hart, *Concept of Law*, 207. (For a more helpful response to the Fuller argument, see Finnis, *Natural
Law and Natural Rights*, 273–4: 'A tyranny devoted to pernicious ends has no self-sufficient *reason* to
submit itself to the discipline of operating consistently through the demanding processes of law. . .').

involves three things: (i) it picks out a complex (and sometimes contested) cluster of connected ideas about governance, such as the subjection of the state to legal restraints, the idea of legal equality ('one law for all'), the procedural requirements of due process, and the importance of government on the basis of public and relatively stable rules laid down in advance; (ii) it accounts for the importance of those ideas, for example, in terms of the connection between publicity and predictability, on the one hand, and autonomy, on the other; and (iii) it associates them, understood in this light, with the characterization of the governance system in question as a system of law.[63] Steps (i) and (ii) can be confined to political philosophy. But if step (iii) found no resonance in jurisprudence, the distinctive character of the ideal of the rule of law would be seriously undermined.[64] This doesn't mean necessarily that the jurisprudential analysis of law must be conducted with the rule of law ideal in mind (though, as I have argued elsewhere, that is not an implausible methodology).[65] But it does indicate the importance of some back-and-forth between analytical strategy in the one discipline and analytical strategy in the other.

A more obvious connection between the two disciplines concerns the problem of political obligation. It is one of the central tasks of political philosophy to ascertain the nature, basis, and limits of a person's obligation (if any) to obey the laws that apply to him. Most jurists in the positivist tradition have been at pains to insist on a gulf of separation between the discussion of this problem in political philosophy and the analysis of law in jurisprudence. They have rejected the claim of Lon Fuller, for example, that we need 'a definition of law that will make meaningful the obligation of fidelity to law' and that jurisprudential analysis must display law 'as something deserving loyalty . . . it cannot be a simple fiat of power or a repetitive pattern discernible in the behaviour of state officials'.[66] It might be thought that this rejection follows directly from the positivist's separability thesis, 'that it is in no sense a necessary truth that laws reproduce or satisfy certain demands of morality'.[67] But in fact, the separability thesis may be understood as a thesis about the moral content of laws considered one-by-one, leaving open the possibility that law as a form must be understood in a way that explains the claim it characteristically makes on our allegiance.

Or the connection may be more subtle. Ronald Dworkin has argued that certain features endemic to law such as its concern for *stare decisis* and other forms of principled consistency (what he calls 'integrity') are unintelligible apart from a consideration of the conditions under which laws could make a plausible moral claim on our

---

[63] The classic account is F. A. Hayek, *The Constitution of Liberty* (London: Macmillan, 1960), 148 ff.

[64] Joseph Raz comes close to this in his article 'The Rule of Law and its Virtue', in *Authority of Law*. Raz seems to see no difficulty with the prospect of a system of governance being identified as a legal system and yet having few or none of the specific virtues associated with the rule of law ideal.

[65] See Waldron, 'Normative (or Ethical) Positivism', in *Hart's Postscript: Essays on the Postscript to the Concept of Law*, ed. Jules Coleman (Oxford: Oxford University Press, 2001), 411–33, at 419–22.

[66] Fuller, 'Positivism and Fidelity to Law', 632 and 635.   [67] Hart, *Concept of Law*, 185–6.

obedience. Dworkin thinks that a philosopher of law indifferent to the latter question (i.e. indifferent to the answers that the political philosopher came up with) would be at a loss to explain the care and persistence with which lawyers and judges seek continuity between the decision currently and the standards and decisions to which the community has already committed itself. His argument to this effect is quite complex: it consists in establishing a connection between an approach to political obligation which is sometimes called 'the principle of fair play'[68] and the idea of community, on the one hand, and a connection between the idea of community and a lawyerly respect for consistency, on the other.[69] Whether the two connections obtain in just the form that Dworkin asserts, and whether the two senses of community match in the appropriate way, is of course a question for debate.[70] But Dworkin's underlying methodology is uncompromising. He insists that it is not possible to do serious work in jurisprudence—not even serious analytical work—unless one is prepared to cross over in this way into the terrain of political philosophy, where we argue about why law matters. Without that evaluative dimension, Dworkin argues, our analysis becomes purely 'semantic', and risks leaving us in a situation where the philosopher of law has no option but to say that those who promote rival conceptions of law are simply talking past each other.[71]

6 ANALYTIC METHODOLOGY

The issues about the relation between legal philosophy and political philosophy, outlined in Sections 4 to 5 remain open, and the arguments I have sketched and the positions (such as they are) that I have taken in this chapter are still very controversial among philosophers of law. What about methodology? Can anything more conclusive be said about similarities and dissimilarities among the methodologies used in these two connected branches of philosophy?

The answer is complicated by the fact that neither of the disciplines we are considering is entirely self-contained. Legal philosophy presents itself as a beleaguered

---

[68] See A. John Simmons, *Moral Principles and Political Obligations* (Princeton: Princeton University Press, 1979) 101 ff.

[69] Dworkin, *Law's Empire*, 190–216.

[70] See e.g. Denise Reaume, 'Is Integrity a Virtue?', *University of Toronto Law Journal*, 39 (1989), 380; Stephen A. Gardbaum, 'Law, Politics, and the Claims of Community', *Michigan Law Review*, 90 (1992), 685; and Larry Alexander and Ken Kress, 'Against Legal Principles', *Iowa Law Review*, 82 (1997), 739.

[71] See Dworkin's account of 'the semantic sting', ibid. 31–46. (Hart's response to this critique distinguishes brusquely but unconvincingly between the semantic meaning of a concept and the criteria for its application: Hart, *Concept of Law*, 246. He leaves it quite unclear whether he accepts Dworkin's account of what it would be to develop a theory of criteria for application of a concept like *law*.)

island of methodological rigour in a chaotic ocean usually referred to as 'legal theory'. The practitioners of legal philosophy often comport themselves like the inhabitants of a small Pacific island or atoll threatened by something like global warming: the waters of sloppy thinking are rising all around them and they must huddle closer and closer together on the vanishingly small piece of high ground that they currently occupy. They know that their methods of conceptual analysis and rigorous argument are cheerfully ignored elsewhere in legal theory. Non-philosophical 'theorists' use flashy jargon, they tell stories or 'narratives', they conjure up images, and they make a public exhibition of their commitments and their loyalties; they cite one another as authorities, or to win favours, or to advance one another's careers; and they don't seem to be burdened in any of this by compunctions about truth or validity. When they are presenting some position that they hold, they don't necessarily make an argument; rather they rely on the embarrassment they can inflict on an opponent from any one of a variety of disparate sources—personal, political, sexual, only occasionally logical—rather than on the inherent strength of the reasons that have persuaded them or the cogency of the connections between them. They move carelessly back and forth between causal, doctrinal, logical, and psychological connections, seldom pausing to note the significance of the shift for the sort of case they are making. And despite all this, or because of it, they are terrifically successful. That's the image of legal theory that most legal philosophers have. It is not without its merits. But it is suffused with resentment, and I believe that this resentment (together with the apprehensions about 'the political' discussed at the end of Section 4, above) explains a lot about the legal philosopher's view of the relation between the two disciplines.

More affirmatively, legal philosophers pride themselves on using the analytic methods developed in other areas of philosophy, particularly moral philosophy and the philosophy of language. Indeed efforts are often made to import not just methodologies, but whole topics, into the philosophy of law, so that issues in jurisprudence can be recast in a way that is not just respectable, but substantively recognizable by the standards of philosophers working outside the legal academy. So, for example, questions about the norms that ought to govern judicial reasoning are recast as questions about objectivity,[72] questions about the nature of legal validity are presented as though they were analogous to (or as though they actually *were*) questions about a proposition's truth-conditions,[73] and questions about the over- and under-inclusiveness of rules are recast as questions about vagueness or maybe as questions about Wittgensteinian rule-following.[74]

---

[72] See e.g. *Objectivity in Law and Morals*, ed. Brian Leiter (Cambridge: Cambridge University Press, 2001).

[73] See e.g. Michael S. Moore, 'Metaphysics, Epistemology and Legal Theory', *Southern California Law Review*, 60 (1987), 453 and Jules L. Coleman and Brian Leiter, 'Determinacy, Objectivity, and Authority', *University of Pennsylvania Law Review*, 142 (1993), 549.

[74] Here, though, legal philosophers sometimes entertain each other by pointing out howlers and shortcomings in legal *theorists'* deployment of Wittgensteinian arguments about rule-following. Some

It is noteworthy, in all of this, that although philosophers of law model their methods on those used elsewhere in philosophy, *political* philosophy is not usually where they look for a model. This is partly because political philosophy is regarded as a sort of stepchild in the philosophical family—not really philosophy at all, more like political theory. At best political philosophy is treated as 'applied moral philosophy', and many working in jurisprudence seem inclined to try cutting out the middle man, to deal with moral philosophy direct.

Methodologically, this is perhaps a mistake. When a disputed question of value is raised in moral philosophy—a question about the nature of harm or well-being, for example—those who address it tend to proceed as though there were a right answer to the question. Of course, they do not agree on what the right answer is; otherwise there would be no philosophical dispute. But the notion of a right answer still does important work. It operates in the argument as the notion of something not necessarily identical with anyone's opinion in the matter, which affords an objective basis for determining the truth or acceptability of any given opinion in the matter. And it can work as an algebraic placeholder too, as we move from issue to issue, tracing the role that the right answer to one question might play in constraining or determining the right answer to another. I may accept the following proposition

(1) The right answer to question Q_1 is a function of the right answer, x, to question Q_2

even though I do not know what the value of x is. That is, even if I have a strong opinion on Q_2, I will not make the sophomoric error of confusing (1) with

(2) The right answer to Q_1 is a function of the answer that I give to Q_2 (i.e., what I think is the value of x)

or even, more modestly, with

(3) The right answer to Q_1 is a function of the answer that somebody gives to Q_2 (i.e. what somebody, y, thinks is the value of x).

Every moral philosopher worth his salt knows that there is a difference between the first of these propositions and the other two. To fail to grasp the difference, or to insist that (3), say, is more important than (1), is to give the impression of not taking objectivity seriously. And no philosopher wants to be caught doing that.

Yet in politics and—I believe very strongly—in law too, propositions of type (3) are almost always more important than propositions of type (1). Politics has deadlines in which questions must be answered and the answers acted on. We may all agree that O. J. Simpson should be denied custody of his children if *in fact* he murdered their mother (and not otherwise), and we may agree that this is an objective question. But in the real world of courts and lawsuits and deadlines, settling the custody of his children has to be a response to someone else's (y's) *determination* that he did (or didn't)

do both. See e.g. Brian Leiter, 'Intellectual Voyeurism in Legal Scholarship', *Yale Journal of Law and the Humanities*, 4 (1992), 79.

murder the children's mother. No doubt there is an important issue about who (or what institution) that should be. But it would be fatuous to insist—in the spirit of (1), above—that it is not anyone's determination that should count, but the objective fact of the matter. Sophomore philosophy students often annoy their professors by asking 'Well, *who decides* what the right answer to Q₂ is?' when their professor says something like (1). But in political philosophy, that is not necessarily an annoyance. Often it is more or less the heart of the matter. In the contested issues of politics, objective truth never manifests itself *in propria persona*; it presents itself always as someone's opinion, usually someone's contested opinion; and it cannot be made politically effective, nor the condition for any political action unless someone's determination is taken for practical purposes as the truth of the matter. It doesn't follow that the phrase 'objectively true' is meaningless nor even that it has no use in politics. But those who bandy it about (having gotten used to its importance in moral philosophy) need to remember that the existence of an objectively right answer to a given question is so far just a matter of ontology: *nothing in the way of social or political or legal decision is settled* when we insist that some issue be governed by the right answer to some question.[75]

For this reason, political philosophy is intensely interested in decision-procedures (procedures like majority-rule), *even on issues that may be conceived as objective*.[76] This interest is anathema from the point of view of the moral philosopher, who is (rightly) interested in the truth about value, not just in the popularity of propositions about value. But law has to align itself with politics in this regard, and jurists whose methodological orientation is entirely in moral philosophy may find themselves seduced into all sorts of problematic positions, if they do not take this into account.[77]

7 Law, Theory, and History

Political philosophy fades into moral philosophy on the one hand, and on the other hand it is associated with something slightly different called political theory.[78] Where

---

[75] See Jeremy Waldron, 'Moral Truth and Judicial Review', *American Journal of Jurisprudence*, 43 (1998), 75. See also Waldron, *Law and Disagreement*, 180 ff., and Dworkin, *Law's Empire*, 76–85.

[76] But cf. David Estlund, 'Making Truth Safe for Democracy', in *The Idea of Democracy*, ed. David Copp, Jean Hampton, and John E. Romer (Cambridge: Cambridge University Press, 1993).

[77] The most common of these problematic positions taken by legal philosophers whose training is in moral philosophy involves the belief that when an issue is voted on in a court, greater respect is being paid to the existence of an objective right answer, than when the same issue is voted on in a legislature or by the people at large. See Waldron, 'Moral Truth', 80 ff.

[78] One rule of thumb is that political theorists work in political science departments, they seldom have philosophical training, and they spend much more time immersed in a canon of great books than political philosophers do.

does legal philosophy stand in regard to political theory? Working in both disciplines, I find that the practitioners are often surprisingly ignorant of each other's work.

Let me return for a moment to the controversy we discussed in Sections 4 to 5 about the concept of law and the nature of conceptual analysis in jurisprudence. To a student of politics, debates of this sort are very familiar. Political scientists and political theorists have spent a considerable amount of energy in the last forty or fifty years arguing about the possibility of a 'neutral' or 'value-free' analysis of the main concepts used in the study of politics, concepts like *power, class, party, bureaucracy, interest-group*, and *participation*. For example, some political theorists say that the concept *power* cannot be given a neutral analysis, but must be associated with the sense of reproach that is usually conveyed when we say that the powerful are prevailing in some political situation. Our concepts reflect our interests and our values, they say, and to the extent that we favour equality and oppose coercion, 'the attribution of power to a segment of the society functions more as an accusation than as a normatively neutral description of the political process'.[79] Against this, other political theorists have insisted that the variety of normative standpoints means we cannot align a concept like power with any norms or values in particular:

those who 'share' the concept of power do not necessarily share the same 'commitments' with respect to specific power situations. Someone who attributes power to a given person or group P may 'accuse' P of wrongdoing; and someone else may hold that it is P's moral right. . . . That there can be, and often are, differences in moral outlook would alone justify our attempt to construct a language of political inquiry that could be used by all political scientists regardless of their ethical or ideological views.[80]

Notice that the author of the passage just quoted—Felix Oppenheim—is not claiming that a neutral analysis gives a good account of ordinary usage. It may well be true that the ordinary usage of terms such as 'power' *is* heavily value-laden. Rather, Oppenheim is defending the enterprise of *constructing* a neutral language of politics, which attempts (as far as possible) to precipitate out of the chaos of ordinary usage a descriptive meaning for each of these terms which might then provide a basis for the clear formulation of both empirical hypotheses and normative principles in political science.

Against this suggestion, the opponents of neutral analysis have made a number of points. They make a hermeneutic argument: since political science is a matter of understanding human agents and interactions in the context of belief, purpose, value, and intention, it cannot use terminology that is as divorced from the ordinary usage of political agents as Oppenheim's reconstructive approach aspires to be. The neutral approach seeks a scientific language in which descriptive content is precipitated out of its evaluative use. But, as Richard Bernstein puts it, in order to write social science literature antiseptically in a language of 'pure description', we would likely

---

[79] William Connolly, *The Terms of Political Discourse* (Lexington, Mass.: Heath, 1974), 6 and 126.
[80] Felix Oppenheim, *Political Concepts: A Reconstruction* (Oxford: Blackwell, 1981), 151–2.

end up with 'an artificial and emasculated vocabulary bearing little or no relation to the ways in which we . . . speak about human action'.[81] (From this point of view, Oppenheim's riposte that nobody reproaches atomic physicists for writing and speaking in terms that *their* subjects don't understand ironically clinches the point for his—i.e. Oppenheim's—opponent.)[82]

Opponents of conceptual neutrality in political science have also been at pains to insist that it is not a question of associating a concept like power with a particular moral or ideological *view*. It is a matter of there being certain very general values in the background when concepts like these are being used. Humans are interested in who has power or who hasn't because they have an affirmative interest in their own and perhaps others' agency. (Similarly, we might say in jurisprudence, our interest in law is informed by some very broad human interests in peace and predictability, rather than by any particular theory of justice or the social good.)

Secondly, the non-neutralists doubt whether the neutralist analysis can be carried through successfully without impoverishing our understanding of what goes on in the language of politics. They deny that it is necessarily an advance in clarity or understanding to prescind from the normative and ideological controversies that surround the use of political terms. Neutralists like Oppenheim believe that we should represent such controversies as a matter of different attitudes to a common content. But many normativists believe that this neglects the important phenomenon of 'essential contestability'. An essentially contestable term is one whose proper use involves endless normative debate about its proper use.[83] Such terms mediate and relate ideological, linguistic, and meta-scientific controversies to one another. By attempting to make them redundant in that capacity, the neutralist suppresses important reflexive dimensions of the language of politics.

Even for an evaluative term that is not essentially contested, it may be impossible to understand why a certain set of empirical attributes are clustered together in a concept in just the way they are, without reflecting on the human interests and values that inform the use of that concept. To the rigorously descriptive eye, the concept might seem odd and shapeless until we grasp, in a sense, its point.[84] And if we insist

[81] Richard Bernstein, *The Restructuring of Social and Political Theory* (London: Methuen, 1979), 78. See also Charles Taylor, 'Neutrality in Political Science', in his collection *Philosophy and the Human Sciences: Philosophical Papers* (Cambridge: Cambridge University Press, 1985), 58.

[82] Oppenheim, *Political Concepts*, 187.

[83] See W. G. Gallie, 'Essentially Contested Concepts', *Proceedings of the Aristotelian Society*, 56 (1955–6), 167. Connolly, *Terms of Political Discourse*, chs. 1 and 6, provides an excellent introduction to the importance of this idea in political science and political theory.

[84] There is a similar debate in moral philosophy. There, non-cognitivists sometimes assume that moral positions are subjective responses to factual features of the world; and their strategy is to analyse moral concepts into a descriptive component (referring some fact about the world) and an evaluative component (indicating some subjective response to that fact). So, for example, the term 'courage' refers descriptively to a certain steadfastness in the face of danger, and it connotes evaluatively an attitude of approval to that character-trait. But many moral cognitivists have their doubts about the general applicability of this pattern of analysis. Such doubts are expressed by John McDowell, in 'Non-Cognitivism

on using only concepts that satisfy some scientific or logical criterion of 'well-formedness' *apart* from any consideration of the values that might have shaped them, then again we will end up impoverishing our political vocabulary and our political culture, as the neutralist enterprise feeds back into the ordinary language of politics and makes it harder for people to express or to remain familiar with complex and embedded evaluations.

It is evident that all of these considerations and arguments might be applied to jurisprudential debate about the analysis of the concept of law and legal system, which we discussed in Sections 4 to 5. (They might be applied not necessarily to determine any particular outcome but at least to add illumination.) We know that the concepts at stake in the jurisprudential debate have many of the features that political theorists have had to think hard about in the political theory debate. But the former has been conducted in a way that is oddly isolated from the latter. This is perhaps less so on the non-neutralist side in jurisprudence: Ronald Dworkin, for one, has been willing to consider theoretical ideas about essential contestability in developing his position that the interpretation of legal concepts necessarily engages issues of value;[85] and Stephen Perry has invoked arguments from the philosophy of social science to bolster his contention that jurisprudence necessarily includes a functionalist component, and that this means it cannot possibly be purely descriptive.[86] Their neutralist opponents, by contrast, resolutely ignore these resources, convinced as usual that showing any interest in the political theory debate would already be giving the game away.

The final difference worth mentioning between the methods used in legal philosophy and those used in political philosophy (at least at the 'theory' end of political philosophy) concerns the attitude taken to the history of the subject. Political theory is characteristically studied by reading a 'canon' of great books, ranging from the seminal texts of ancient political science (Plato's *Republic*, Aristotle's *Politics*) through the classics of the early modern period (Machiavelli's *Prince*, Hobbes's *Leviathan*, Locke's *Second Treatise*) to the works of the European Enlightenment and beyond (Rousseau's *Social Contract*, *The Federalist Papers*, Kant's *Rechtslehre*, and Hegel's *Philosophy of Right*). One does political theory by interpreting, grappling with, and building upon the ideas developed in these works. Sure there are also conceptual and problematic ways of approaching the discipline—through the analysis of *power*, as we have seen, and other concepts like *liberty* and *democracy*, or through the

and Rule-Following', in *Wittgenstein: To Follow a Rule*, ed. Steven Holtzman and Christopher Leich (London: Routledge & Kegan Paul, 1981), 144: 'Now it seems reasonable to be skeptical about whether the disentangling manoeuvre here envisaged can always be effected: specifically, about whether, corresponding to any value concept, one can always isolate a genuine feature of the world—by the appropriate standard of genuineness: that is, a feature that is there anyway, independently of anyone's value-experience being as it is—to be that to which competent users of the concept are to be regarded as responding when they use it; that which is left in the world when one peels off the reflection of the appropriate attitude'.

[85] Dworkin, *Taking Rights Seriously*, 103.   [86] Perry, 'Interpretation and Methodology', 107.

pursuit of certain familiar problems like the basis of the obligation to obey the law. But even there, the discussion tends to be canonical in flavour, responding to familiar positions that can be attributed to thinkers like Plato, Locke, or Rousseau. In legal philosophy, by contrast, particularly as it is practised in the UK and America, there is less of a sense of a canon of great books stretching back to the dawn of time. If there is a canonical work it is H. L. A. Hart's book, *The Concept of Law*, which analytical jurists read over and over (and then squabble among themselves as to what it means and whose position now is closest to what Hart's is taken to be).[87] Since Hart developed his theory by criticizing the nineteenth-century jurisprudence of John Austin, there is also some half-hearted discussion of Austin's work. Beyond that, however, the 'canon' of legal philosophy is attenuated or non-existent. We know a little about Bentham as a precursor of Austin; and we all have a couple of passages up our sleeves to quote from Aquinas or Augustine when we want to raise the spectre of natural law. But only recently have these theorists been studied in any detail from a legal point of view.[88] For the rest, the artificial boundary between political theory and legal philosophy which I have been deploring in this chapter has meant that the jurisprudence of theorists like Plato, Cicero, Machiavelli, Hobbes, Locke, Hume, Kant, Hegel, and Savigny, is largely neglected.

I have heard it said that this is a good thing: it means we can study the problems of legal philosophy directly, undistracted by a purely antiquarian interest in the history of ideas. But these analytic discussions tend to be flat and repetitive in consequence, revolving in smaller and smaller circles among a diminishing band of acolytes. Worse still, they are in danger of becoming uninterestingly parochial from a philosophical point of view, as we distance ourselves from the intellectual resources that would enable us to grasp conceptions of law and controversies about law other than our own conceptions and our own controversies, and law itself as something with a history that transcends our particular problems and anxieties. Students of politics have long recognized that what they understand as politics here and now needs to be leavened with a healthy sense of how others have thought about the matter.[89] Perhaps it is past time—I think it is well past time—for analytical jurisprudence to do the same.

[87] For examples, see the disagreements over the interpretation of Hart's jurisprudence in the special issues of *Legal Theory*, vol. 4/3–4 (1998) devoted to discussion of the 'Postscript' to *The Concept of Law*.
[88] See Postema, *Bentham and the Common Law Tradition* (on Bentham) and Finnis, *Natural Law and Natural Rights*, on the detail of the natural law tradition.
[89] See John Dunn, *The Cunning of Unreason: Making Sense of Politics* (New York: Basic Books, 2000).

CHAPTER 10

AUTHORITY

SCOTT J. SHAPIRO

THE Babylonian Talmud tells of a dispute between Rabbi Eliezer and the other rabbis over the ritual cleanliness of a tiled oven.[1] Rabbi Eliezer argued at length that the oven was clean, but failed to persuade his colleagues. Having tried every conceivable argument, Rabbi Eliezer said to the rabbis: 'If the Law agrees with me, let this carob-tree prove it!' whereupon the carob-tree was torn from its roots and landed 100 cubits away.[2] The rabbis answered: 'No proof can be brought from a carob-tree'. Rabbi Eliezer tried again: 'If the Law agrees with me, let the stream of water prove it!' and behold, the stream obliged and reversed direction. Undaunted, the rabbis responded: 'No proof can be brought from a stream of water'. Rabbi Eliezer came back a third time: 'If the Law agrees with me, let the walls of the schoolhouse prove it'. As before, Rabbi Eliezer's request was granted and the wall started to fall. But Rabbi Joshua rebuked the wall, saying: 'When the scholars are engaged in a legal dispute, what have ye to interfere?'

At his wits' end, Rabbi Eliezer exclaimed: 'If the Law agrees with me, let it be proved from Heaven!' whereupon a voice from heaven cried out: 'Why do ye dispute with Rabbi Eliezer, seeing that in all matters the Law agrees with him!' But Rabbi Joshua replied: ' "It is not in Heaven" '.[3] Rabbi Jeremiah explained this to mean that once God gave the Torah to Moses on Mount Sinai, Heavenly voices no longer have any say in legal matters. The Torah confers on the rabbis the exclusive

I would like to thank Bruce Ackerman, Jules Coleman, David Golove, Peter Hilal, Ken Himma and Michael Moore for helpful comments on earlier drafts of this chapter.

[1] Baba Metzia, 59b.
[2] For some reason, the Talmud adds that others claim that the carob-tree landed 400 cubits away.
[3] Deuteronomy 30: 12.

authority to decide legal questions and requires that internal disputes be resolved by majority vote. After Rabbi Eliezer refused to back down, he is summarily excommunicated.

This story brings out, in a particularly striking way, the paradoxical nature of authority. Authorities claim a right of immense power, one, it would seem, that they could not possibly possess. Authorities claim the right to impose their will on others regardless of whether their judgments are correct. In doing so, they appear to place themselves above the truth—their right does not seem to depend on their being right. In the dispute between Eliezer and the rabbis, the rabbis had incontrovertible proof that they were wrong and nevertheless continued to demand that Eliezer accept their interpretation of the law. This sounded, at least to Eliezer, as though the rabbis were arrogantly asserting a power greater than that of Heaven. If the rabbis are wrong, he reasoned, they should submit to God, not require submission from others.

Eliezer may be recorded history's first philosophical anarchist. Philosophical anarchists argue that no claim to legitimate authority can be vindicated. How can someone have the right, they wonder, to force another to do something wrong? The obligation to act correctly should always trump the obligation to act otherwise. To the philosophical anarchist, 'legitimate authority' is a contradiction in terms.

Philosophical anarchists delight in pointing out that the claims of authority are problematic even in situations when those in power are right. For when someone in authority commands another to act as they should act, their directives are redundant. They would not harm, but they would not help either. Thus, even if the rabbis had relented and declared the oven ritually clean, Eliezer would have had no reason to submit to their authority. Eliezer should accept that the oven is ritually clean because it is ritually clean, not because the rabbis said it is.

The challenge posed by the philosophical anarchists turns out to be as powerful as it is simple: when authorities are wrong, they cannot have the power to obligate others—when they are right, their power to obligate is meaningless. It would seem that the institution of authority is either pernicious or otiose.

This argument is so powerful, in fact, that it should make one suspicious. For if the argument is sound, then those who believe in authority are not just wrong—they are incoherent. This conclusion seems too strong, however: those who believe that they are obligated to obey are not believing nonsense. In the end, no such obligation may actually exist; but it seems inconceivable that such an obligation could exist.

Most theorists writing today assume that common sense is correct and that the anarchist challenge can be met. They disagree, however, on how to meet it. In this chapter, we will discuss the many 'solutions' that have been offered on authority's behalf. The responses fall roughly into one of two groups: those who believe that problems arise due to certain naïve views about the nature of authority and rationality and that revision in this understanding is required, and those who maintain that the puzzle can be unravelled without any radical changes.

After a discussion of the paradox (or as we shall see paradoxes), we will examine two revisionist strategies.[4] The first approach denies that legitimate authorities have the right to impose obligations when they are wrong. Indeed, it denies that legitimate authorities have the right to impose obligations at all. The directives of legitimate authorities are treated either as justified threats backed by sanctions or pieces of expert advice. The paradoxes, on this view, simply dissolve—because authorities never possess the power to impose obligations, *a fortiori* they never possess the power to impose obligations when they are wrong.

The second approach we will explore accepts the basic premise of the paradoxes, namely, that legitimate authorities have the power to obligate even when wrong. But it argues that the paradoxes arise because that premise is conjoined with a tacit, but false, assumption about the nature of rationality. According to this assumption, agents must always act on the merits of the case at hand. Instead, this approach maintains that agents can, under certain conditions, have reasons to ignore the desirable or undesirable properties of actions. There is nothing paradoxical, therefore, about requiring obedience to mistaken directives, because the directives are reasons not to act on the reasons that make the directives mistaken.

Unsurprisingly, we will see that these responses bring additional problems in their wake. For if we deny that authorities ever possess the power to obligate, can we make sense of social institutions such as the Law that contain copious quantities of prohibitions, requirements, permissions, rights, and powers? Likewise, is it coherent to claim that we can have reason to ignore reasons for action?

In an effort to avoid these problems, others have attempted to solve the paradoxes without revisionism. While they concede that legitimate authorities have the power to obligate even when they are wrong, they argue that standard theories of rationality and morality can accommodate this right. Their strategy centres on the claim that authoritative directives of legitimate authority are efficient decision-making tools. By guiding conduct by legitimate authority, subjects are more likely to choose the right results than the wrong results. But, these theorists argue, subjects must take the bad with the good—subjects can benefit from the right results only if they choose the wrong results as well. The rationality of obeying a mistaken directive is, therefore, no more paradoxical than the rationality of paying a price for a gamble, when the price is less than or equal to the gamble's expected value.

While this approach is appealing, I will argue that it ultimately will not do. The paradoxes of authority cannot be solved within standard theories of rationality and morality—some revisions are necessary. Which revisions are necessary, I will claim, depends on one's underlying theory of legitimacy. For accounts that tie the legitimacy of authority to its ability to provide instrumentally valuable directives, I will

---

[4] These approaches are revisionist in the sense that they seek to revise the understanding of authority presupposed by the paradoxes. They do not argue that our concept of legitimate authority must be reworked, only that the paradoxes employ a concept that, although appearing to be, is not in fact our concept.

suggest that the standard account of authority's effect on practical reasoning be modified. Instead of seeing authoritative directives as instruments that willing subjects use to make decisions, they ought to be understood as causal constraints on action. Those who obey directives in order to instrumentally benefit from them do not choose to obey—having submitted to authority, disobedience is no longer an option. Authoritative directives can be justified in instrumental terms when, and only when, they forestall decision-making.

For accounts of authority that tie legitimacy to the moral obligation to respect collective decision-making procedures, I will suggest that we modify our views about the nature of moral autonomy. In certain circumstances, the fact that another has demanded that we act in a certain way can indeed give us a reason to so act. Rather than a violation of autonomy, obedience can actually show due respect for the value of autonomy.

In this chapter, I will attempt to justify these assertions and to demonstrate how their acceptance solves the paradoxes of authority within the different frameworks of legitimate authority. While these revisions may be somewhat drastic, I will argue that they constitute the best response to the philosophical anarchist's challenge.

1 THE PARADOXES OF AUTHORITY

1.1 Authority and Autonomy

In his *In Defense of Anarchism*, Robert Paul Wolff argued that legitimate authority and moral autonomy are logically incompatible.[5] His discussion is worth examining in detail, not only because it is the *locus classicus* for the philosophical anarchist attack on authority, but also because it contains a more subtle analysis of the concept of authority than many of authority's defenders provide.

Wolff begins his discussion by distinguishing between power and authority.[6] To have power is to have the ability to compel compliance. To have authority is to have the right to rule. A gunman has power, but he does not have authority. He can coerce his victim to cooperate by threat of force, but he is unable to impose the moral obligation to comply.[7]

---

[5] See Robert Paul Wolff, *In Defense of Anarchy* (1970). The relevant sections of Wolff's monograph are excerpted as 'The Conflict between Authority and Autonomy', in *Authority*, ed. Joseph Raz (New York: New York University Press, 1990). All citations in this chapter will be made with reference to this excerpt.

[6] Wolff, above n. 5: 20.

[7] Unlike authority, power cannot be honoured in the breach: one can cheat at one's taxes, but one cannot cheat a thief.

As Wolff points out, someone can have authority in one of two senses.[8] One can have authority by possessing the moral right to rule. The exercise of such a right, if it exists, gives rise to moral obligations to obey. A ruler can, therefore, claim authority and fail to have it in this sense. The Supreme Soviet Legislature claimed the authority to rule the Soviet Union, but it lacked the moral right to do so. It lacked legitimate, or *de jure*, authority.

Alternatively, one can have authority simply in virtue of the fact that one is regarded to be a legitimate authority. The Supreme Soviet, for example, did enjoy a measure of acceptance by many of the Soviet people. They believed that the Supreme Soviet possessed *de jure* authority, although they were mistaken—it merely had *de facto* authority.

Wolff is primarily interested in the phenomenon of *de jure* authority. This is so for two reasons. First, the concept of *de facto* authority logically presupposes the concept of *de jure* authority. *De facto* authorities are those who are believed to be *de jure* authorities. Secondly, no one contests that *de facto* authority exists. The philosophical anarchist is interested in *de jure* authority—she wants to show that the moral obligation to obey the law can never obtain.

To have the right to rule, according to Wolff, is to have the right to be obeyed. To obey a command is to perform the act commanded for the reason that it was commanded. Commands, therefore, differ from arguments.[9] Arguments are meant to persuade. They attempt to convince the person that they ought to act in certain ways and they do this by presenting to the interlocutor the reasons that make the recommendations worthy. Commands, on the other hand, are not designed to convince their addressees of the wisdom of their contents. Subjects who obey them do so not because they believe that the actions commanded are worthy of obedience, but rather in virtue of the fact that they were so commanded.

It is possible, therefore, for someone to choose to comply with a command without obeying it.[10] This happens when the command makes the subject aware that he has reasons for performing the act commanded and acts for these reasons, rather than because of the command. To acknowledge someone's claim to authority,

---

[8] Wolff, at 21. Wolff neglects to mention a third sense in which someone can have authority. *X* may have authority just in case rules exist that confer authority on *X*. All legal authorities have authority in this sense. This concept of authority, at least when applied to the law, generates paradoxes of its own, for any attempt to establish its existence generates a 'chicken–egg' paradox. The puzzle can be stated as follows: *X* can possess authority in the third sense only when legal rules confer such authority. But legal rules exist only when someone with legal authority creates such rules. Who, then, is this person that creates these rules that confers authority on *X*? It can't be *X*, because *X* does not have authority before the rules confer it. Yet, if it is someone other than *X*, then we can ask the same questions about that person that we asked about *X*. We are led either into a vicious circle or an infinite regress. See 'On Hart's Way Out', *Legal Theory*, 4 (1998), 454, reprinted in *Readings in the Philosophy of Law*, ed. J. Coleman (New York: Garland Publishing, 2000) and, with revisions, Hart's Postscript to The Concept of Law, ed. J. Coleman (Oxford: Oxford University Press, 2001).

[9] ibid. at 22.   [10] ibid.

according to Wolff, is to recognize that their right resides in their person.[11] They possess their normative power in virtue of who they are, rather than in virtue of what they command.

Having set out his conception of authority, Wolff proceeds to present his account of moral autonomy. For Wolff, an autonomous person is not someone who is merely responsible for her actions. Rather, such a person also *takes* responsibility for her actions.[12] A person takes responsibility whenever she attempts to determine what she morally ought to do. An autonomous agent, according to Wolff, is a deliberating agent.

Unlike many who have seen autonomy as a necessary condition for moral responsibility, or as the capacity to choose, Wolff treats it as an independent moral duty. Every person is charged with examining every aspect of his moral life: he must constantly gather new information, scrutinize his motives, critique his desires, and evaluate his options in light of this reflection. One who acts without assessing the merits of so acting fails to take responsibility for his actions, and to this extent, is violating their duty to act autonomously.[13]

It follows from Wolff's definition of moral autonomy that no one can obey authority and remain autonomous. A person obeys a command when he conforms for the reason that another has so commanded. An autonomous person, however, never acts for the reason that another has so commanded. He acts only when he is convinced that, on the merits, action is appropriate. Hence, an autonomous agent can never submit to another's authority. As Wolff puts it: 'The defining mark of the state is authority, the right to be ruled. The primary obligation of man is autonomy, the refusal to be ruled.'[14]

Although the autonomous agent cannot obey authority, Wolff is quick to add that he does not necessarily disobey authority.[15] If the autonomous agent thinks there are good moral reasons to pay taxes, then he will believe that he should pay his taxes. But that person does not accept the obligation because the law requires him to pay his taxes. He believes that he should pay his taxes because he believes this to be the right thing to do independent of the law's demands.

1.2 Preliminary Assessment

Wolff's argument appears to be valid: given his premises, his conclusion seems to follow. However, his premises are dubious. For example, it is not obvious that one should think of autonomy as a duty. To whom do we owe this duty? It is strange to think that I am morally bound to act autonomously for another's sake. Why would anyone care why I act correctly, as long as I act correctly?

---

[11] ibid. But see discussion in Sect. 2.2 below. [12] ibid. at 25. [13] ibid. at 28–9.
[14] ibid. at 29. [15] ibid.

Even if one does accept that there is a duty to act autonomously, it is doubtful that Wolff's formulation should be accepted. Why must a person deliberate about every moral action? Shouldn't he defer to another's judgment when that judgment is better than his? The idea that a person must weigh the balance of reasons every time a moral decision arises is not only dangerous in cases of informational asymmetries or cognitive disabilities but is also terribly wasteful. Surely it is possible to direct one's energies in a more productive manner.

To be sure, there is such a thing as over-reliance on authority. To cede too much decision-making to others is both foolhardy and morally irresponsible. Moreover, the more one depends on another's judgment, the greater the chance that one will lose the ability to make judgments for oneself and the more vulnerable one becomes to manipulation. Finally, the faculties of judgment and self-reflection are distinctively human capabilities, the exercise of which contribute in an essentially way to human flourishing. To sacrifice them is, in some real sense, to forfeit one's humanity. This 'dehumanizing' effect of authority especially concerned William Godwin, the first 'modern' philosophical anarchist.

Man is the ornament of the universe, only in proportion as he consults his judgment.... But, where I make the voluntary surrender of my understanding, and commit my conscience to another man's keeping, the consequence is clear. I then become the most mischievous and pernicious of animals. I annihilate my individuality as a man, and dispose my force as an animal to him among my neighbors, who shall happen to excel in imposture and artifice, and to be least under restraint from the scruples of integrity and justice.[16]

While the dangers of reliance on authority are real, it is important not to exaggerate them. The world is simply too complex for anyone to live one's life completely unaided by experts of one kind or another. Even Wolff admits that '[t]here are great, perhaps insurmountable, obstacles to the achievement of a complete and rational autonomy in the modern world'.[17] Complete autonomy, in Wolff's sense, is simply not an option. If authority is inconsistent with autonomy, then so much the worse for autonomy.

It is interesting to note that Kant himself did not see a clash between authority and autonomy. He famously argued that those subject to authority ought to question its demands, but this public use of reason should not prevent them from acting on them. Enlightenment is precluded both when authority demands blind obedience *and* when subjects do not respond with unconditional compliance.

The citizen cannot refuse to pay the taxes imposed upon him; presumptuous criticism of such taxes, where someone is called upon to pay them, may be punished as an outrage which could lead to general insubordination. Nonetheless, the same citizen does not contravene his civil obligations if, as a learned individual, he publicly voices his thoughts on the impropriety or even injustice of such fiscal measures.[18]

[16] William Godwin, *Enquiry concerning Political Justice*, ed. K. Carter (Oxford: Clarendon Press, 1971), 122.   [17] ibid.
[18] Kant, 'An Answer to the Question: What is Enlightenment?', in H. Reiss (ed.), *Kant: Political Writings* (Cambridge: Cambridge University Press, 1991).

Wolff's formulation of the anarchist's challenge is unconvincing because his understanding of autonomy is implausible. We should, however, be careful not to dismiss Wolff's argument too quickly, for on any credible conception of autonomy, the tension between it and authority is hard to ignore. After all, 'autonomy' literally means 'self-law-giving'. The autonomous person does not act simply because another has told him to do so—he acts only when convinced that action is appropriate. To be autonomous, in other words, involves taking *oneself* as the ultimate authority on moral questions. This commitment seems to leave no logical space for external authorities to occupy. As the proverb goes, one cannot serve two masters.

With this in mind, I think it is possible to give a more charitable reading to Wolff's objections. We should first distinguish, in a way that Wolff fails to do, between two different features of authoritative directives. We can say, following H. L. A. Hart, that authoritative directives are intended to be both 'peremptory' and 'content-independent' reasons for action.[19] A 'peremptory' reason is a reason that cuts off or excludes deliberation. A command is intended to be a peremptory reason, in that once the command has been issued, the subject is expected to stop assessing the merits of the action in question. One who weighs the pros and cons of obeying an order is not taking the order in the way that it was meant to be taken.

Authoritative directives differ from ordinary reasons, not only because they purport to preclude deliberation. Directives are intended to be 'content-independent' reasons for action, meaning that they are supposed to be reasons simply because they have been issued and not because they direct subjects to perform actions that are independently justifiable. One who obeys a command treats the command as a content-independent reason, because he complies for the reason that he was commanded, not because he has reasons to act on the content of that command. For example, if Jim takes out the garbage because his father commanded him to do so, then he is treating the command as a content-independent reason.

Content-independent reasons for complying with a directive should be contrasted with 'content-dependent' reasons. A content-dependent reason is a reason for conforming to a directive because the directive has a certain content. If the garbage smells, Jim will have a reason for taking out the garbage that is independent of the fact that his father commanded him to do so. By taking out the garbage, he will have removed an unpleasant odour from the house. Jim, therefore, has two reasons to listen to his father's command: the command is a content-independent reason, while the unpleasant odour is a content-dependent reason.

Although Wolff appears to object solely to the peremptory nature of authority, I think that it is the combination of peremptoriness and content-independence that offends him. Authority and autonomy clash not simply because one who obeys does not deliberate. The problem is also that such a person believes that the fact that he was

---

[19] H. L. A. Hart, 'Commands and Authoritative Legal Reasons', in *Essays on Bentham* (Oxford: Clarendon Press, 1982), 253–5.

ordered to act in a certain way gives him a reason to so act. He takes the will of another as his reason, indeed the only reason, rather than the merits of the case at hand.[20] Such a person, therefore, will think that he has a ready defence to any charge of improper behaviour. While the person will agree that he performed an otherwise morally indefensible act, he will plead that the reasonableness of his obedience must be viewed in a content-independent manner: whether he had reason to follow orders cannot be judged based on the content of those orders. It is the fact that he was commanded to act, rather than what he was commanded to do, which gave him a conclusive reason to do as he did.

An autonomous person, by contrast, never treats a command as a content-independent and peremptory (hereinafter 'CIP') reason for action. The demands of authority mean nothing to the autonomous agent, for such a person never allows his will to be determined by the will of another. She cares solely about the act commanded, not the command itself, and will acquiesce only when convinced that there are good reasons to act on the content of the command. According to this interpretation, autonomy and authority are incompatible because obedience to authority requires acting on CIP reasons, whereas the autonomous person does not acknowledge the existence of such reasons.

One benefit of seeing Wolff's argument in this way is that our previous objections are no longer sufficient to meet his challenge. Autonomy is not conceived as a separate duty that morality imposes upon us and that we owe to others. To say that everyone should act in a morally autonomous manner is to make a claim about the *space of reasons*. Autonomous agents are those who recognize that the only reasons that exist are either content-dependent or non-peremptory ones. Moral autonomy is important because it is important that people act on reasons and not act on non-reasons.

Moreover, on this account, reliance on experts does not necessarily lead to heteronomy. While expert advice is a CIP reason for believing that the expert is correct—one believes what the expert says because the expert has said it—the purpose of giving advice is to alert the advisee that the recommended course is supported by the balance of content-dependent reasons. When the advisee draws this inference and acts on it, the agent will be acting for content-dependent reasons, even if he does not know what they are.

Most importantly, this interpretation shows that the philosophical anarchist's anxiety about authority is not frivolous: their worry is that people will treat authoritative directives as CIP reasons for action and, in so doing, fail to take the appropriate responsibility for their actions. They will attempt to justify their conduct by pleading that they were 'just following orders'. This type of defence not only seems cowardly, but strictly speaking irrelevant. How can an act be made acceptable simply

[20]   See e.g. Wolff, above n. 5: 26 ('The autonomous man, insofar as he is autonomous, is not subject to the will of another. He may do what another tells him, but not *because* he had been told to do it.' (emphasis in original)).

because someone else said that it is acceptable? Authorities may have the power to change positive law, but no one (maybe not even God) has the ability to change the moral law. As Godwin put the point: 'The most crowded forum, or the most venerable senate, cannot make one proposition a rule of justice that was not substantially so, previously to their decision'.[21]

Yet, the philosophical anarchist reminds us, without admitting that Nuremberg defences are sometimes good justifications, it is hard to see how *de jure* authority is possible. The legitimacy of authority stands or falls on whether a subject can justify his actions by pleading that he was 'just following orders'. Legitimate authority is possible, in other words, only when CIP reasons are possible.

1.3 Authority and Rationality

It is sometimes thought that Wolff's challenge to authority is merely a special case of a more general paradox, one that purports to show the incompatibility of authority and rationality. The general argument is familiar: consider any directive issued by an authority and any action *A* required by that directive. Either the balance of reasons supports *A* or it does not. If the balance of reasons supports *A*, an agent should perform *A*, but not because *A* is required by the directive, rather because agents should always act according to the balance of reasons. On the other hand, if the balance of reasons does not support *A*, then an agent should not perform the action because agents should never act against the balance of reasons. It would seem, therefore, that authoritative directives can never be reasons for action—if a directive gives the right result, the directive is irrelevant; if the directive gives the wrong result, then the obedience to the directive is unreasonable.

Since authoritative directives can never be reasons for action, it follows that rational agents can never obey authority. The proof: rational agents always aim to act on undefeated reasons and act in accordance with that aim. If an agent were to obey an authority, they would either have to believe that they had an undefeated reason to obey or believe that they didn't have an undefeated reason but would have obeyed anyway. If the former were true, then the agent would have irrational beliefs, given that according to the first argument, authoritative directives can never be reasons for action. If the latter were true, then the agent would not be acting in accordance with the aim of acting on undefeated reasons. Hence, it seems that rational agents can never obey authority.

If the above arguments are sound, it would follow that moral agents can never rationally guide their conduct by authoritative directives. Since morality requires that agents act on the balance of *moral* reasons, obedience to authority can never be rationally justified for moral agents: whenever a directive required an action

---

[21] Godwin, above n. 16: 88.

supported by the balance of moral reasons, that directive would be morally irrelevant; otherwise, it would be morally pernicious. Authoritative directives can never be moral reasons for action and, hence, it would be irrational for any moral agent to obey authority.

Such 'derivative' arguments are possible because rationality is essentially a *formal* ideal. Rationality does not mandate conformity to any particular substantive standard—it simply requires that an agent live up to the agent's substantive standards. The paradox attempts to show the incompatibility of rationality and authority by demonstrating that authoritative directives will clash with any substantive standard: either the directive in question conforms to the given standard, in which case it is redundant, or it conflicts with the standard, in which case the standard requires non-conformity. To generate a contradiction between authority and any specific normative standard, one need only plug the standard into the equation and out will pop the desired *reductio*.

While Wolff's challenge appears to be such a derivative argument, it is important to see that it is not. This becomes evident when it is noted that the concept of rationality is at right angles to that of autonomy. To be rational is to aim to act on undefeated reasons and to act in accordance with that aim. To be autonomous, by contrast, is to aim to act on non-CIP reasons and to act in accordance with that aim. It does not follow, therefore, that a rational agent is an autonomous agent. If an agent believes that he has an undefeated CIP reason for action, then he will be acting rationally but not autonomously if he acts for this reason. Conversely, autonomous agents are not necessarily rational. If an agent acts on a content-dependent reason that, by his own lights, is defeated, then he will be acting autonomously but irrationally.

It should come as no surprise, therefore, that one can challenge the rationality of authority and not its effects on autonomy. The paradox of authority and rationality attempts to show the impossibility of having an undefeated reason to obey authority and, hence, the irrationality of believing that one has such a reason. It does not attack the content-independent and/or peremptory nature of authoritative directives. Likewise, one can object to authority because it engenders heteronomy, not irrationality. The problem with obedience, according to our interpretation of Wolff's challenge, is that authoritative directives are not CIP reasons, not that it would be incoherent to believe that they are undefeated reasons.

Given that these critiques differ from each other, one should not expect that the solution to one challenge will constitute an effective reply to the other. To see this, consider the following response to the paradox of authority and rationality: the social contract theory, the response begins, is a coherent theory of political obligation. A rational agent might regard it as true, even if it is in fact false. Assume, then, that an agent accepts the social contract theory as true. According to this agent, someone possesses legitimate authority over another when the latter has consented to be ruled by the former. Because the consent generates a promissory obligation to abide by the demands of the authority, any directive issued gives subjects who have consented a reason to act in accordance with it. Assume that this person consents to be governed by an authority. He will now regard any directive issued as a conclusive reason for action. Consequently, it might be rational for him to comply with a command whose content, by his own lights, is not supported by the balance of content-dependent reasons. From that agent's perspective, even though the balance of content-dependent reasons would not support conformity, the balance of all reasons—content-dependent reasons as well as the content-independent reason—might tilt in the direction of obedience. In this way, it may be rational to obey authority even when they are wrong about the content of their directives.

This response, however, will not work against Wolff's challenge. Wolff's argument, as we have seen, is predicated on the idea that there are no such things as CIP reasons for action. The above response would, therefore, beg the question. After all, consent itself purports to give rise to CIP reasons for action. Subjects who consent to be governed by an authority are obligated, under the social contract theory, simply in virtue of their consent. One cannot show how a CIP reason is possible by producing another (alleged) CIP reason. One must first establish that my will can give me a reason to act against the balance of reasons. But if authorities lack the power to change the moral law, how can I have the power to do so?

I don't mean to imply that Wolff's autonomy paradox is harder to answer than the rationality paradox. They are simply different critiques and, as such, each may require different solutions. Unfortunately, those who respond to philosophical anarchism do not always make it clear to which paradox they are responding. We will try to rectify this by treating the two basic paradoxes separately and asking, for every response by the defenders of authority, whether the solution is adequate to either or both.

2 Weakening Authority

Whenever faced with the clash of two concepts, one can always try to relieve the tension by weakening the formulation of one of the concepts involved. In the case of the anarchists' paradoxes, the most obvious candidate is the one given to authority. First, because the concept of authority appears in both of the basic paradoxes, one might be able to kill two birds with one stone. Secondly, and more importantly, the formulations of rationality and autonomy seem innocuous enough, at least as compared to that of authority. As we have mentioned, to be rational is to aim to act on the balance of reasons. Rationality simply imposes the obligation on every agent to live up to the substantive standards to which he is committed. Likewise, autonomy has been characterized as requiring that agents stick to the merits of the case at hand and not simply act because another has told one to do so. The plausibility of these ideas is readily apparent.

By contrast, the standard characterization of authority wears paradox on its sleeve. To possess legitimate authority, one might recall, is to have the right to rule. The right to rule implies the right to be obeyed. To have the right to be obeyed is to have the power to impose obligations irrespective of content. Those who possess legitimate authority, therefore, have the moral power to obligate others to obey even when their directives contain the *wrong* content. To say the very least, the power to obligate independent of content seems odd. As Godwin remarked: 'There cannot be a more absurd proposition, than that which affirms the right of doing wrong'.[22]

Weakening the standard characterization of authority, therefore, seems like a promising strategy. If it can be shown that authorities never claim the power to obligate, then the paradoxes could be completely sidestepped. Rationality would not clash with legitimate authority because authorities would never require agents to act against the balance of reasons. Indeed, authorities would never require agents to act at all. Likewise, autonomy would be consistent with legitimate authority because their pronouncements would not be, nor would anyone claim them to be, CIP reasons for conformity.

In the next sections we will explore two strategies for severing the connection between legitimate authority and the right to require conduct in a content-independent manner. The first approach seeks to decouple the right to rule from the right to be obeyed. The right to rule consists in the exclusive privilege that legitimate authorities possess to coerce others to conform to their demands. On this view, the authorization to use force does not imply the power to impose obligations. The second strategy denies that legitimate authorities even have the right to rule, let alone the right to be obeyed. Legitimate authorities issue neither directives nor threats. Their pronouncements constitute expert advice: rather than creating obligations, they simply inform us about their existence.

I will argue that neither approach is successful. To weaken the concept of authority in these ways is to eviscerate it. Without attributing to legitimate authorities the power to impose obligations, it would be impossible not only to account for many of the claims authorities do make, but also the claims that they need to make in order to save themselves from paradox.

2.1 The Right to Rule

Following Hohfeld, we can distinguish between two senses of the word 'right'.[23] To say that someone has a right to perform some act with respect to another might, in the first instance, refer to a privilege. A right-holder has a privilege against another to

---

[22] Godwin, above n. 16: 88.
[23] Wesley Newcombe Hohfeld, 'Fundamental Legal Conceptions as Applied in Judicial Reasoning', ed. W. W. Cook (New Haven: Yale University Press, 1923), 35.

perform an act when the right-holder is not under a duty to that person not to perform that act. For example, I have the privilege against you to enter my home in that I am not under a duty to you not to enter my home.

Alternatively, one might mean by the right-ascription that the right-holder has the normative power over the other person with respect to a certain set of acts. A right-holder has a power over another to perform a certain act when the right-holder has the ability to change the normative relations between the person and the right-holder. To say that I have the normative power to lease my house to you is to claim that I can change your duties to, and privileges against, me *vis-à-vis* the house. Whereas previously you did not have the privilege to enter my house, after the execution of the lease, you are no longer under a duty not to enter. My right to lease the house to you, where the right is understood as a power, leads to your right to enter the house, where the right is understood as a privilege.

When we said that to possess legitimate authority is to have the moral right to rule, should we take this right to be a privilege or a power? Until now, we have been assuming that legitimate authorities possess a moral power over their subjects. Robert Ladenson has suggested, however, that the right to rule should be understood as the exclusive moral privilege to rule.[24] Legitimate authorities are those who have the ability to force others to comply with their demands and who are morally permitted (i.e. not under a moral duty not) to exercise this ability. On this view, authorities do not purport to create moral obligations to obey. Rather, authoritative directives are threats backed by sanctions. Legitimate authorities differ from gangsters in that the former are morally permitted to issue such threats and punish non-conformity, as opposed to the latter who are under a moral duty not to act similarly.

According to Ladenson, someone has legitimate authority whenever they have (non-normative) power to coerce and that power justifies the exercise of that power. Why would the mere possession of power justify the exercise of the power? Why think that might can make right? Ladenson offers a 'Hobbesian' answer.[25] If some institution has the power to coerce, then they, and only they, have the ability to solve certain problems, like maintaining social order. Only the strongest in society can keep others from engaging in the types of conflicts that threaten to destabilize and destroy society.

Ladenson does not go so far as to claim that those with power are justified in using this power in any manner they choose. The Nazis were not morally permitted to engage in genocide, even though they were justified in their effort to enforce the existing traffic laws.[26] Authorities may claim legitimate authority in certain areas but fail to possess it. Someone has *de facto* authority just in case they have the ability to enforce their threats and those threatened are aware of this ability. This does not, all by itself, confer upon them *de jure* authority.

---

[24] Robert Ladenson, 'A Defense of a Hobbesian Conception of Law', *Philosophy and Public Affairs*, 9 (1980), reprinted in *Authority*, above n. 5.

[25] ibid. at 38.   [26] ibid. at 39.

The virtue of Ladenson's account is that it easily solves the paradoxes of authority. The paradoxes arise only when it is assumed that authorities claim the normative power to create reasons for action. As we saw, the nature of such a power seems utterly mysterious. Ladenson, however, rejects the core assumption of power: authorities claim the moral permission to threaten and punish, not the moral power to obligate and permit. Since the normativity of sanctions is anything but mysterious, Ladenson is able to explain how authoritative guidance can be a reason-giving activity. It is the threat of punishment, rather than the imposition of obligation, that provides the reason for subjects to obey authorities.

On Ladenson's model it is apparent how authoritative guidance can both be relevant and rational. Authoritative directives are relevant to practical reasoning whenever the balance of reasons is shifted in favour of conformity due to a threatened penalty. Authorities supply a reason to obey that the agent did not have before the authoritative intervention and render conformity rational. Through the coercive machinery of the state, authorities can be seen to make differences to the practical reasoning of agents.

Nor would obedience to authority compromise the autonomy of the agent. On Ladenson's conception, authoritative directives are not peremptory reasons for action. Those who issue threats offer their intended victims the choice whether to comply ('your money or your life'), although the choice is obviously not one between equally appealing options. More importantly, threats are not content-independent reasons.[27] Agents never obey simply because they are told to do so—an empty threat, for example, gives the victim no reason to acquiesce. Because the only reason that figures in deliberation is the threatened sanction, the moral autonomy of an agent is not thereby at risk. In fact, even Godwin believed that agents are permitted to obey authorities when threatened: 'Nothing can be more certain, that an action, suppose of inferior moment or utility, which for its own sake might be right to be performed, it may become my duty to neglect, if I know that by performing it I shall incur the penalty of death'.[28]

Any attempt to downgrade the claims of authority from power to privilege must, however, contend with one salient feature of the law's self-presentation, namely, that it does not merely speak the language of threats, but also of obligation. The law does not simply threaten citizens with imprisonment if they, say, use recreational drugs— it 'forbids' their use. Those who violate the law are 'guilty' of an 'offence' and are held 'responsible' for their 'wrongdoing'. Any sanction assessed is neither a tax nor a user fee, but a 'penalty'. The fact that legal authorities employ the moral concepts of

---

[27] Compare this to Hobbes's own characterization of authoritative directives: 'A command is when a man saith do this or do not do this yet without expecting any other reason that the will of him that said it'. That is, Hobbes took commands to be content-independent reasons for action. The only Hobbesian element of Ladenson's account, therefore, is the justification he offers for state coercion, not the account of authority itself.

[28] Godwin, above n. 16: 120.

obligation, permission, power and immunity strongly suggests that they do not merely claim the moral permission to carry out its threats.[29] Legal officials are generally morally comfortable following through on the law's threat because they believe that all are morally obligated to abide by the law and that it is fitting to punish those who fail to live up to their obligations.

Even from the perspective of power politics, Ladenson's proposal is implausible. As Weber pointed out, political power must always seek at least the appearance of moral power if it is to be secured and maintained. This is so because authorities routinely impose considerable costs on their citizens. Not only do they forbid countless actions, and, to a lesser degree, require citizens to provide aid to each other under certain circumstances, but they create a whole set of affirmative obligations that citizens owe to the state itself. They range from the mildly annoying, such as the duties to register one's vehicle and to sit on a jury, to the onerous, such as the requirements to pay one's taxes and to support one's family, as well as the life-threatening, such as the obligations to testify under subpoena against the defendant in a murder trial and to respond to military conscription.

Authorities use many strategies in order to influence people to pay these costs. Perhaps the most cost-effective approach is ideological. By claiming the power to obligate, rather than simply the permission to coerce, authorities attempt to persuade their subjects to comply out of a sense of moral duty. The greater the number of people who accept the law's authority to impose such duties, the fewer the resources that the state must devote to the enforcement of its laws. Once the state has won its people's hearts and minds, their bodies will follow. To be sure, legitimation strategies presuppose the existence of considerable machinery of education, indoctrination, and manipulation. The dissemination of ideology is, like anything else, not cost-free. Yet, the use of brute force also presumes a vast apparatus of prevention, detection, and retribution. Even at the current state of technology, law enforcement is still extremely labour-intensive, requiring a large network of police, investigators, prosecutors, and correction officers, in addition to an extensive system of jails and other correctional facilities. A society that invested all of its resources in intimidation and none in persuasion would quickly bankrupt itself.

But expense is not the only consideration that obliges authorities to legitimate themselves. The machinery that the state erects to reward those who comply and punish those who don't must be manned by at least some who recognize the state's legitimacy and remain loyal to its ideology. It is simply not possible to have 'threats all the way down'. At some point, someone has to carry out the will of the authority

[29] For a powerful elaboration of this criticism, see Joseph Raz, 'Authority and Justification', in *Authority*, above n. 5. Ladenson might reply that the law's cooptation of the language of obligation does not imply that legal authorities claim that their subjects are morally obligated to comply. Such deontic vocabulary might be used in a purely technical sense—*X* is legally obligated to do *A*, in this technical sense, just in case there exists a legal rule or rules that requires such conduct. For a discussion and defence of this semantic conception of legal obligation, see H. L. A. Hart, 'Legal Duty and Obligation', in *Essays on Bentham* and Hart, above n. 19, at 266.

because he feels not only obliged, but morally obligated to do so. The paradoxes of authority can then be turned on those who support this state bureaucracy: why would it be rational for any bureaucrat to heed the directives of authorities to enforce their threats against another? Either the balance of reasons supports enforcing the threat or it doesn't. If the former is the case, then enforcement is reasonable, but not because the bureaucrat was directed to enforce the threat, but because the balance of reasons supports enforcement; if the latter is the case, then enforcement is unreasonable.

It would seem, therefore, that Ladenson's approach to authority cannot be defended by appealing to the fact that, if true, it would supply a solution to the paradoxes of authority. For, as we have just seen, Ladenson's approach is itself vulnerable to similar problems. Rather than solving the paradoxes, his account suppresses them in one context and fails to prevent them from reappearing in others. The day of reckoning is not averted, just merely postponed.

There are two lessons that we should take away from this discussion. First, it is not possible to solve the paradoxes of authority by attempting to interpret obedience as being mere responses to threats. The enforcement of threats issued by those in power is itself an activity whose rationality and morality must be established. Secondly, it is important to distinguish between the concepts of having 'authority over a person' and of having the 'authority to act' or, to put the matter slightly differently, between having authority and merely being authorized. To have authority is to have a normative power to change another's normative relations. To be authorized is simply to be permitted by someone who has authority to act in a certain manner. The secretary is authorized to open her boss's mail. But she has no power in this regard. As Raz has aptly put the point, Ladenson's approach equates what the state may do with what the secretary may do.[30] However, as we have seen, non-normative power over a person and the authority to exercise that power does not add up to, nor can it substitute for, the authority over a person.

2.2 Theoretical Authorities

According to the first horn of the paradox of authority and rationality, if the balance of reasons supports the content of a directive, then the directive is redundant. In response, one might call into question the idea that a directive is irrelevant just because it gives the correct solution to a normative problem. An authoritative directive might be relevant if an agent could use it to solve the problem for herself. By applying the directive, she would be able to arrive at the right conclusion rather than having to deliberate about the merits of the case at hand.

---

[30]   Joseph Raz, 'Introduction' in *Authority*, above n. 5: 4.

This response attempts to locate the legitimacy of authority in its epistemic instrumentality. Agents have reasons to obey authorities whenever their directives are conclusive reasons to believe that the directed acts are reasonable. Authoritative directives, in turn, would achieve this epistemic status whenever their source was an expert in the regulated area. Authorities would be legitimate, on this view, just in case their pronouncements constituted expert advice.

This suggests that practical authority, that is, authority concerning what *ought* to be the case, might be grounded in theoretical authority, that is, authority concerning what *is* the case. This idea is as old as Western philosophy itself. In *The Republic*, Plato argued that a just society must be governed by philosophers. Plato's view was based both on his high esteem of philosophers and his low opinion of everyone else. The philosophers must rule the just city because only they had access to the truth and could be trusted to act for the common good.

[T]he simple and moderate desires, guided by reason and right judgement and reflection, are to be found in a minority who have the best natural gifts and best education. . . . This feature too you can see in our state, where the desires of the less respectable majority are controlled by the desires and the wisdom of the superior minority.[31]

One need not share Plato's social theory in order to see the virtues in this approach. Reducing practical to theoretical authority is attractive not only because it is conceptually economical, but also because the rationality of relying on theoretical authority seems unproblematic. When some person knows more about a subject that one does, it makes good sense to defer to that person's judgment; by doing so, one will do better than if one relied on one's own judgment. Moreover, as we mentioned earlier, reliance on theoretical authority is compatible with autonomy. Someone who acts on authoritative advice may do so because he believes that reliance is supported by the balance of content-dependent reasons.

While this strategy has its benefits, it seems vulnerable to a number of serious objections. First, it is an essential feature of expert–advisee relationships that advisees should not act on expert advice when they know them to be wrong. If I regard the weatherman as a theoretical authority on the weather, I should take an umbrella with me when I see it rain even though he might have forecasted clear skies. There is no value in deferring to theoretical authority when one knows them to be wrong—one relies on theoretical authorities because, and only because, one wants to know what is right. By contrast, practical authorities claim the right to obligate even when they are wrong. In Eliezer's case, the rabbis required Eliezer to defer even though he knew, and they knew, that they were wrong. This did not deter them, however, from asserting their authority. It would seem that practical authority cannot be reduced to theoretical authority, in so far as each aims to influence practical reasoning in very different ways.

[31] Plato, *The Republic*, trans. Desmonde Lee (London: Penguin, 1955), 202. For a contemporary expression of the epistemic account, see Heidi Hurd, 'Challenging Authority', *Yale Law Journal*, 100 (1991), 1611.

Secondly, the epistemic approach badly misinterprets the claims of political authorities. Political authorities claim that their directives are more than mere reasons to believe—they claim that they are reasons to act. One does not comply with an order simply by believing that the order was justified; one must act on this belief. Conversely, authorities generally do not punish failures of belief, only failures of action. Unless authorities punish thought crime, it is not against the law to think that the law on any subject is mistaken.

It is unlikely, however, that proponents of the epistemic approach will be moved by these arguments. As to the first objection, they will surely respond that this is not so much an argument against, as a wholesale rejection of, their position. Those who reduce practical to theoretical authority are eager to deny that legitimate authorities bind irrespective of content. A critic makes no headway by pointing to the fact that legitimate authorities have the power to bind even when wrong, given that this 'fact' is precisely what the epistemic approach wants to challenge. The Talmudic story, therefore, cannot be used as a refutation of the epistemic position when it has yet to be established that the rabbis' assertion of legitimate authority was coherent.

Proponents of the epistemic account admit that subjects can be required to act even when they think that the authorities are wrong. For if authorities are legitimate when their judgments are more reliable than their subjects, they are more likely to be right when their subjects think that they are wrong. The crucial word here is 'think'— when subjects 'know' that they are wrong, as when a voice from heaven tells them so, they should not defer.

Proponents of the epistemic approach will also argue that the second objection misses the mark because it badly misrepresents their account of authority. Those who attempt to reduce legitimate practical to theoretical authority do not claim that authoritative directives are nothing but reasons to believe. They agree that political authorities require action. Their claim, rather, is that when authorities are legitimate, their directives are *also* conclusive reasons to believe that their content is justified. Indeed, their directives are reasons to act because, and only because, they are reasons to believe.

While these responses are effective, they raise additional problems. According to the epistemic account, A has practical authority over B in domain C if and only if A is more expert than B on C topics. However, if expertise is necessary for legitimate authority, it follows that many areas of the law cannot possibly be legitimate. As is well known, one of the most vital functions authorities serve is to solve coordination problems: they establish rules of the road, standards for weights and measures, uniform currencies, and so on. In a coordination problem, the parties have an interest in working in a concerted fashion, but given that there is more than one acceptable way of doing so, they must figure out which of these strategies will enable them to coordinate behaviour. For example, a motorist wants to drive on the same side of the road as all other motorists. However, because both the left and right sides are equally good choices, he will have problems knowing on which side of the street others will drive and, hence, on which side he should drive. Authorities are able to solve coordination problems because they can designate one of the strategies as the choice for all to follow. In marking one of the combinations as binding on all, everyone's expectations are focused on that combination and the informational problems are overcome. Motorists know that they should drive on the right side of the road because the law has selected this side by imposing a rule requiring it. A motorist should drive on the right side because he knows that others will drive on the right given that they expect him to do likewise.

The ability of authorities to solve coordination problems, therefore, does not stem from any expertise.[32] By hypothesis, coordination problems arise because of the multiplicity of acceptable joint strategies. When the law designates the right side of the road as the proper way to drive, it does not do so because the right side is better than the left—the law was needed precisely because the right side was as good as the left. Legal authorities do not act as experts in this regard because there is nothing over which to exercise their expertise. The law's ability to solve coordination problems stems in large part from the fact that their subjects look to them as the solvers of coordination problems.[33]

Epistemic accounts are deficient because they are unable to account for the authority of law in situations where expertise is irrelevant. Worse still, they cannot legitimize legal authority even in cases where expertise is highly desirable. The reason is simple: the authority of the law, as opposed to the expert, is impersonal. When a legal official claims authority to issue a directive, the source of that authority resides in the office from which the directive will emanate. From the legal point of view, everyone must listen to President Bush because he is the President, not because he is Bush.

By contrast, the authority of an expert is entirely personal. If one should listen to an expert, it is because of the expert's superior knowledge or skill. Smith should listen to Doctor Jones, because he is Jones, not because he is a doctor. The personal nature of expertise is reflected in the fact that theoretical, as opposed to legal, authority cannot be granted, transferred, delegated, acquired, inherited, or usurped. Only in a metaphorical sense do experts 'appoint' their successors.

Because the legitimacy of an official's authority is impersonal, dependent as it is on the legitimacy of the office, the personal qualities of any official can contribute nothing to the legitimacy of the official's authority. The office is made no more legitimate

---

[32] Expertise might, however, be required in order to identify the existence of situations where coordination is necessary. See Joseph Raz, 'Facing Up: A Reply', *Southern California Law Review*, 62 (1989), 1153, 1192.

[33] It might be argued that in coordination problems authoritative directives are reasons to believe that others will act on the coordination solution, even though they are not expert advice. As I will argue in Section 6.3, authoritative directives could not solve coordination problems if it were commonly believed that everyone treated them as evidence of other people's behaviour and that they were rational.

because of the expertise of its current occupant. To be sure, one has a reason to defer to an official when that official is an expert. But the reason to defer to the official is due to her expert, not official, status. If the law's claim to authority is to be vindicated, the existence of the obligation to obey must not depend on the personalities of those demanding obedience.

3 Pre-empting Reasons

It would seem that the paradoxes of authority cannot be solved by weakening the concept of authority in the ways previously contemplated. If legitimate authorities exist, they have the normative power to obligate their subjects. We will now explore a less obvious, but far more interesting and sophisticated, attempt at solving the paradoxes. Joseph Raz has argued that the culprit is not the assumption that authorities can obligate, or that they can obligate irrespective of their content, but a false picture about the nature of rationality and the impact that authority has on practical reasoning. Once the distinctive contribution that authoritative directives make to the rationality of compliance is recognized, the problems of authority easily dissolve.

3.1 The Service Conception of Authority

According to Raz, it is an essential feature of the law that it claims legitimate authority to regulate the conduct of its subjects. It does not merely assert the privilege to threaten or the credentials to issue advice, but the moral right to obligate, permit, empower, and immunize.

On Raz's view, although the law necessarily claims legitimate authority, it does not necessarily possess it. The law's claim to authority can be, and quite often is, false. According to what Raz calls the 'service' conception of authority, political authorities possess legitimacy only when, and to the extent that, they serve their subjects.[34] Authorities work for us, not the other way around.

In what precisely does this service consist? On Raz's interpretation of the service conception, it is the distinctive task of political authorities to mediate between people and the reasons that apply to them. That is, their role is to consider the reasons that apply to their subjects and to formulate or ratify directives that will enable their subjects to conform to the balance of those reasons. Authorities are legitimate when their

---

[34] Joseph Raz, *The Morality of Freedom* (1986), 56.

subjects are in need of such mediating services and authorities satisfy these needs. Governments exercise their authority, therefore, not by building bridges, educating children, or repelling foreign invaders, but rather by producing and validating norms that allow their subjects to conform to Reason.

More precisely, Raz's 'service' conception is constituted by two theses about the nature and role of authority. The first concerns the type of reasons that should guide authorities when regulating conduct. According to Raz, all authoritative directives should be based, in the main, on reasons that independently apply to the subjects of the directives. Raz calls these reasons 'dependent reasons' and the above condition the 'Dependence Thesis'.[35]

Raz distinguishes the Dependence Thesis from the idea that authorities should serve the interests of their subjects.[36] A military commander ought to act on the basis of reasons that apply to the soldiers (e.g. defence of country) even though his commands might not be in the interests of the soldiers. Raz also points out that the Dependence Thesis specifies the way that authorities should legislate and adjudicate, not the way they actually do.[37] Obviously, many exercises of authority are not based on dependent reasons.

The second half of the service conception concerns the type of argument that must be offered in order to justify authority. According to the 'Normal Justification Thesis', authorities are legitimate when their subjects are more likely to conform to the balance of reasons that apply to them if they comply with their directives than if they attempted to conform to that balance directly.[38] The legitimacy of authority, therefore, is based on the instrumental rationality of the law. By following the law, agents are more likely to do what they are supposed to do than if they tried to act reasonably by themselves.

The Normal Justification Thesis specifies the condition that authorities must satisfy in order to be deemed legitimate. This is a stringent test and one that probably no authority has ever completely passed. It is unlikely that in *every* case some authority will be in a better position than *every* one of their subjects either to assess the demands of Reason or to provide guidance in satisfying such demands. Raz does, however, countenance the possibility of partial legitimacy, that is, where an authority is legitimate with respect to some areas of regulation but not others.[39] Some authority might, for example, be legitimate with respect to the regulation of worker safety, but not sexual morality. Raz also allows that an authority might be legitimate for some subjects and not for others. I might be bound by certain legal regulations designed to protect public health, while my doctor might not. Everything depends on whether the subjects will do better by complying with the law than if they tried to conform to Reason directly.

---

[35] ibid. at 42–53.   [36] ibid. at 48.   [37] ibid. at 47.   [38] ibid. at 53.
[39] ibid. at 73–5

3.2   The Pre-emptive Thesis

Perhaps Raz's best-known claim about the nature of authority is that authoritative directives are unlike ordinary reasons in that they are not only reasons to act in accordance with their content, but also reasons to pre-empt other reasons for action. They are examples of what he calls 'pre-emptive' reasons. When authorities require performance of an action, their directives are not merely added to the balance of reasons, but they also exclude these reasons and take their place. Raz calls this idea the 'Pre-emptive Thesis'.[40]

According to Raz, the Pre-emptive Thesis follows from both the Dependence and the Normal Justification Theses. The Dependence Thesis states that authoritative directives should be based on the balance of dependent reasons. Because these directives are meant to reflect dependent reasons, they cannot be counted along their side. To do so would amount to counting some of the dependent reasons twice.[41] Authoritative directives must replace dependent reasons because it is their function to represent them.

Likewise, the Normal Justification Thesis states that authoritative directives are binding just in case subjects would be more likely to conform with the balance of dependent reasons by complying with the directives than if they attempted to conform to the balance directly. If authoritative directives of a legitimate authority did not pre-empt the underlying dependent reasons, then it would be rationally acceptable for a subject to consider such reasons when deciding how to act. In so doing, however, the subject would be deliberating about the merits of the case and forming a judgment about what ought to be done. Yet, if the authority is legitimate, it is rationally unacceptable for the subject to rely on their own judgments rather than the authoritative directives themselves.[42] Hence, if the Normal Justification Thesis is true, so is the Pre-emptive Thesis.

Raz illustrates these points using the example of arbitration.[43] Since the arbitrator's decision is supposed to reflect the merits of the case at hand, one who considered it along with the merits would be making a mistake in normative arithmetic, for he would be counting some of the merits twice—once directly and once through the decision that is designed to incorporate their force. Moreover, parties use arbitrators to resolve their disputes whenever they find that they are unable to resolve their conflict by themselves, or when doing so would be too costly. They give the arbitrator the power to decide authoritatively who is right and, in so doing, they relinquish the right to challenge the decision. To consider the arbitrator's decision as an ordinary reason to be added to the balance along with the other merits would vitiate the purpose of the arbitration. The decision is supposed to eliminate the need to deliberate and debate the merits of the case that they have submitted.

---

[40] Joseph Raz, *The Morality of Freedom* (1986), at 57.   [41] ibid. at 58.   [42] ibid. at 61.
[43] ibid. at 41–2.

Because authoritative directives pre-empt only those reasons they are meant to reflect, they will lack pre-emptive force in situations where authorities are unable or unwilling to track the balance of dependent reasons. An arbitrator's rulings, for example, need not be followed if she is drunk or has been bribed or if new evidence of great importance later pops up.[44] Likewise, because authoritative directives have pre-emptive force in order to prevent agents from acting directly on the merits, directives will fail to pre-empt just in case subjects can determine that an error is made without scrutinizing the underlying merits of the case. Raz argues that authoritative directives may not be binding if they are 'clearly wrong'. A clear mistake is a mistake that may not deviate substantially from the balance of reasons but wears its error on its face.[45] This is to be distinguished from a great mistake which does indeed deviate greatly from the balance of reasons and whose detection as an error requires the agent to deliberate on the underlying dependent reasons putatively supporting the claim.

Raz illustrate the difference between the two types of mistakes using the case of adding integers. If an authority tells the agent that the sum is an integer, the only way to detect a great error in the sum may be to actually add all of the integers and then compare the results. On the other hand, if the answer presented were a fraction then it would be clear that the authority had made a mistake. In such a case, the dictates of rationality do not require that the agent believe clear mistakes, but would urge the acceptance of great mistakes.

3.3 The Justification of the State

Raz mentions five scenarios where political authorities are able to achieve legitimacy under the Normal Justification Thesis.[46] The first involves cases where expert advice is needed and authorities possess the requisite competence. Regulations that deal with the approval of pharmaceuticals, for example, are typically based on the expertise and information that the government possesses but that the ordinary citizen lacks. By deferring to such directives, subjects are likely to do better than if they tried to figure out for themselves which drugs are safe and effective.

The next two classes of cases involve situations where authorities compensate for various shortfalls of rationality. In some situations, authorities may be less easily swayed by temptation and bias than their subjects. In other cases, deliberation may be costly, either because it generates anxiety, fatigue, or redirects cognitive and emotional resources from other endeavours. By relying on authorities, subjects will be able to avoid the costs that surround the attempt to conform to the balance of the reasons that apply to them.

[44] ibid. at 42.
[45] ibid. at 62. ('Establishing that something is clearly wrong does not require going through the underlying reasoning.')
[46] ibid. at 75.

The fourth class concerns cases where authorities are in a superior position to provide solutions to coordination problems. Authorities, for example, are generally better at setting the rules of the road than are drivers. Although not always true—sometimes informal conventions are more efficient—it is often the case that top-down solutions are superior to bottom-up ones, and when they are, authoritative solutions will be legitimate and binding on participants.

The last class concerns prisoner's dilemmas. In a prisoner's dilemma, each player does better if all cooperate than if all defect; in contrast to coordination problems, however, each does best if the others cooperate, but he defects. Therefore, if everyone acted so as to achieve the best result, that is, unilateral defection, they will bring about an outcome that is individually suboptimal, that is, universal defection. In order to achieve the efficient solution, authorities can issue directives that require the players to cooperate. For example, if there were no laws requiring me to pay taxes, it would not be rational for anyone voluntarily to contribute money for the general upkeep of society. As a result, there would be no money available for the upkeep of society. However, according to Raz, once laws are passed requiring everyone to pay taxes, everyone will have a reason to pay their taxes. While everyone might not comply, they will at least have reasons to comply, something they did not have before the laws were enacted.

3.4 Razian Solutions to the Paradoxes

An enormous virtue of Raz's theory of authority is that it provides powerful solutions to the paradoxes of authority. The solutions, as one might guess, rest on the two distinctive claims that Raz makes about authority: first, that they are justified primarily on instrumental grounds, and secondly, that their directives have pre-emptive force.

Before we discuss Raz's solutions to the paradoxes, however, we must first translate his terminology into ours. I will assume that when Raz speaks of 'dependent' reasons, he is referring to what I have called 'content-dependent' reasons. Aside from linguistic affinities, both sorts of reasons share the same feature: they are reason that apply to subjects independently of the existence of authoritative directives.

With respect to pre-emptive reasons, however, Raz denies that they are the same as peremptory reasons. A peremptory reason is a reason not to *deliberate* about other reasons, whereas a pre-emptive reason is a reason not to *act* on other reasons. Raz faults Hart for thinking that submission to authority requires the actual surrender of judgment, instead of just the forfeit of the right to act on that judgment.[47] One obeys an order even when one thinks that directive is wrong.

I think that Raz is misinterpreting Hart's, indeed even the ordinary, notion of 'deliberation'. To deliberate is not simply to engage in the thought process of weigh-

---

[47] Joseph Raz, *The Morality of Freedom* (1986), at 39.

ing pros and cons. Rather, deliberation is essentially action-guiding. One who deliberates does so with the aim of forming an intention to act on the results of that deliberation. A peremptory reason is not, then, a reason not to think about other reasons, but a reason not to form an intention based on them.

In another way, though, Raz is right that a pre-emptive reason is different from a peremptory one. A pre-emptive reason is not simply a reason not to act on other reasons. It is a reason that *replaces* those reasons. A peremptory reason, by contrast, simply excludes certain reasons from serious consideration. It does not replace them in deliberation.

Nevertheless, a peremptory reason that is also content-independent, i.e., a CIP reason, has the same normative force as a pre-emptive reason. The peremptory nature of the CIP reason will exclude only content-dependent reasons for action—given that it is a content-independent reason, it will not exclude itself. A CIP reason, therefore, is a reason to exclude other conflicting reasons as well as a reason for acting in accordance with its content, just like a pre-emptive reason.

We are now in a position to discuss the paradox of authority and rationality. Assume that a legitimate authority issues a directive to some agent requiring him to do an action that is already supported by the balance of reasons. The agent should surely conform to the directive in this instance. But is its existence relevant to his practical reasoning? It is on Raz's theory. According to the Normal Justification Thesis, since the authority is legitimate, its directives make it more likely that the agent will do better in terms of the reasons that apply to him by complying with the directives than if he tried to act in accordance with these reasons directly. The directive, therefore, is a reason for action, because through its guidance, the agent increases his chances of acting in accordance with the balance of content-dependent reasons.

Assume, on the other hand, that the content of the directive is not supported by the balance of reasons. Should an agent follow the directive? The answer here is 'Yes' again, for according to the Pre-emptive Thesis, directives issued by legitimate authorities are not merely added to the balance of dependent reasons but replace certain of these reasons. As a result of this exclusion, the dependent reasons that counsel against conforming to the directive are no longer relevant. The only reasons that count are those that are left in the balance, which, in this case, happen to be the authoritative directive.

The possibility of rational obedience to legitimate authority is thereby secured. If an agent believes that he will do better in terms of the reasons that apply to him by deferring to directives issued than by deliberating, he is rationally required to defer to each directive irrespective of his judgments about the balance of dependent reasons.

Unfortunately, when we turn to the paradox of authority and autonomy, we must resort to speculation. The reason is that Raz's understanding of autonomy differs from the one we have been considering. Raz sometimes considers autonomy to be a principle of practical reason, at other times to be a capacity for, or the exercise of, self-determination. When understood as a practical principle, it is a rational, not a moral, one. '[O]ne's right and duty to act on one's judgement of what ought to be done, *all things considered . . .* I shall call the principle of autonomy.'[48] Raz adds in a footnote that '[i]t is clear that this principle of autonomy is not really a moral principle but a principle of rationality'.[49] Under this conception of autonomy, the paradox of authority and autonomy is a simple variant of the paradox of authority and rationality and can be resolved in the same way.

When authority is seen as a capacity for self-determination, it is inevitable that authority and the exercise of autonomy will clash. If one's actions are self-determined, they cannot, at the same time, be determined by authority. Raz recognizes this conflict, but is not particularly alarmed by it, seeing it as involving a trade-off. Many times, one should sacrifice one's right to act on one's judgments when they are inferior to another's. Yet, it is sometimes better to act on one's inferior judgments just because they are one's judgments. Without making mistakes, one can never develop the capacities necessary for autonomous action in other spheres of life.

Although Raz does not consider autonomy in the same way we have, that is, as a thesis about the space of reasons, I think it is clear that Raz is sympathetic to the same basic concerns. After all, it is core commitment of his service conception that legitimate authorities are *deontically conservative*: '[A]uthorities do not have the right to impose completely independent duties on people . . . their directives should reflect dependent reasons which are binding on those people in any case'.[50]

While we don't know his response to the paradox of authority and autonomy, we can construct a 'Razian' response. A Razian might deny that an agent is heteronomous just because they act on a pre-emptive reason. Heteronomy results not from acting on CIP reasons, but from knowingly failing to conform to content-dependent reasons. If a directive passes the test laid out in the Normal Justification Thesis, then its content-independent and peremptory nature is justified by its ability to engender conformity with the balance of content-dependent reasons for action. One can, therefore, act on a CIP and content-dependent reasons at the same time. One would not be obeying *simply* because another told one to do so, but because by doing as one is told, one would be more likely to be acting on undefeated content-dependent reasons.

4 Is Pre-emption Necessary?

Raz's theory provides a powerful response to the paradoxes of authority, as we have seen, because it combines an *instrumental* approach to authoritative directives with a

---

[48] Joseph Raz, *The Authority of Law* (Oxford: Clarendon Press, 1979), 27.
[49] ibid.   [50] *Authority*, above n. 5: 135.

hierarchical theory of rationality.[51] On the one hand, it is the function of authoritative directives to maximize conformity to the balance of content-dependent reasons. Yet, it is not necessary for any authoritative directive to actually fulfil such a function. As long as it is rational for someone to accept an authority as legitimate within a certain domain, it is rational to guide one's conduct by any directive issued concerning that domain, even when conformity to such a directive is not, by the agent's own lights, supported by the balance of content-dependent reasons.

The success of Raz's response depends, then, on whether an instrumental approach to authoritative directives is compatible with a hierarchical theory of rationality. The worry here is this: if authoritative directives are supposed to maximize conformity to the balance of content-dependent reasons, how can one have a reason to guide one's behaviour by a directive when it does not do what it is supposed to do? As the act-utilitarians have argued in a similar context, to follow through on a rule when it gives suboptimal results is to engage in a form of 'rule-worship'.[52] If authoritative directives are instrumental reasons for action, they cannot, at the same time, be pre-emptive reasons for action; alternatively, if the Normal Justification Thesis is true, then the Pre-emptive Thesis cannot be.

As we have seen, Raz presented two arguments to show that the instrumentality of directives entails its pre-emptive effect—one based on the Dependence Thesis and the other on the Normal Justification Thesis. Critics have responded primarily to the second of these arguments. They have attempted to show that authoritative directives can be instrumentally valuable even if they do not pre-empt the reasons they are supposed to reflect. In this next section, we will explore this possibility.

4.1 The Simple Model

As we saw in the last section, Raz argued that the Pre-emptive Thesis follows from the Normal Justification Thesis: if authoritative directives did not pre-empt dependent reasons, it would be rationally acceptable for a subject to try to conform to the balance of dependent reasons, which is precisely what the Normal Justification Thesis declares to be rationally unacceptable. Notice that this argument assumes that there are only two options: either a subject completely defers to an authoritative directive or she completely ignores it and deliberates in its absence. Yet, these two alternatives do not seem to exhaust all the possibilities.

Consider, for example, cases where practical authorities are theoretical authorities on a certain subject. Authoritative pronouncements are, then, reasons to believe that

[51] Raz's theory is notably similar to Rawls's presentation of rule-utilitarianism. See John Rawls, 'Two Concepts of Rules', in *Theories of Ethics*, ed. Philippa Foot (Oxford: Oxford University Press, 1967).

[52] See e.g. J. J. C. Smart, 'Outline of a Theory of Utilitarian Ethics', in *Utilitarianism: For and Against*, ed. J. J. C. Smart and Bernard Williams (Cambridge: Cambridge University Press, 1973).

the balance of content-dependent reasons supports conformity. To comply with an authoritative directive might involve treating it as strong evidence regarding the balance of content-dependent reasons and to act on the basis of it, as well as all of the other available evidence. Authoritative directives would not pre-empt the reasons they are meant to reflect—they would be additional reasons that lend their support to the pro-content side of the balance and would be considered alongside all of the other content-dependent reasons.

Let us call this account of authority the 'Simple Model'. The Simple Model treats an authoritative directive as it would any other reason: as a first-order normative consideration that is added to the balance of reasons and that can be considered alongside the other content-dependent reasons. In the case of legitimate authority, the weight of the authoritative reasons is great—great enough, in fact, to outweigh any other contrary reason.

At least at first glance, the Simple Model easily handles situations where practical authorities are also theoretical authorities: it treats their directives as strong first-order reasons to believe that the balance of content-dependent reasons supports conformity. A similar analysis can be given for directives that are used to cut down on deliberation costs and to compensate for cognitive incapacities. In these cases as well the directives are weighty first-order reasons to believe that the balance of reasons supports the content of the directives and are strong enough, given the costs of deliberation on the merits, to outweigh any contrary reason.

With regard to coordination problems, the Simple Model sees authoritative directives as creating salience. The equilibrium specified by the content of the directive is made more conspicuous by the issuance of the directive and this 'marking off' focuses the attention of all players on that solution. Each player not only focuses on that solution, but expects that others will similarly focus and expects that others will expect them to similarly focus. As with the other cases, legitimate authoritative directives do not pre-empt the underlying reasons supporting one solution over another—they are simply very powerful reasons to act accordingly which outweigh the reasons to act differently.

An advocate of the Simple Model would argue that, contrary to Raz's argument, one who treats authoritative directives as the Simple Model suggests would not undo the benefits of relying on legitimate authority. For read through the lens of the Simple Model, the Normal Justification Thesis states that an authority is legitimate just in case assigning significant weight to their directives enables one to do better than if one did not assign it any weight at all. An authority is justified in coordination cases, for example, just in case treating the authoritative directive as marking off the salient strategy and hence adding it to the balance of reasons allows one to do better than if one did not treat the content of the directive as salient but tried to solve the coordination problem by oneself. The Normal Justification Thesis would not, therefore, entail the Pre-emptive Thesis, given that the instrumentality of authority can be tapped even without pre-emption.

4.2 Variations: Transformation, Reweightings, and Presumptions

The Simple Model is but one of the many possible alternatives to Raz's Pre-emption Model. Some proposals represent subtle variations on the Simple Model, while others propose more radical departures that closely resemble Raz's approach. What they all have in common is that they reject the Pre-emptive Thesis, that is, that authoritative directives must completely pre-empt the reasons they are meant to reflect.

Beginning with subtle variations of the Simple Model, some theorists have argued that authoritative directives have transformative powers: it is their function to alter the set of content-dependent reasons. When, for example, authoritative directives constitute strong evidence that the balance of content-dependent reasons supports conformity, they are weighty reasons to believe that other reasons are not in fact reasons and hence are not entitled to their place in the balance. On this Transformative Model, authoritative directives that are used to compensate for irrationality do not pre-empt any content-dependent reason. They are reasons not to act on untrustworthy *beliefs* not as reasons to remove a bona fide reason from the balance of reasons. As Heidi Hurd argues, '[o]ne's condition of incompetence is but evidence of the fact that in working out these content-dependent reasons, one may not be employing true premises'.[53]

In coordination cases, the authoritative directive focuses attention away from other options to the content of the directive. Whatever reasons players had for acting on the other options, they no longer have. Consider Leslie Green's analysis of coordination norms:

Given a generally shared expectation that one alternative will be followed, there is no longer any appeal whatsoever in [acting in a different way], for in doing so one would be swimming against the tide which, by hypothesis, one has no interest in doing. But note: these non-options (i.e., those that are not salient) leave no practical trace—one does not hanker after them, and they exert no residual attraction from any point of view; they are simply outweighed. To achieve an equilibrium by appealing to or creating a conventional norm, one need only act on the balance of first order reasons.[54]

More complicated are proposals that treat authoritative directives as second-order reasons that affect the weight of the first-order reasons that they are meant to reflect.

---

[53] Hurd, 'Challenging Authority', above n. 31: 1624. See also D. S. Clarke, Jr., 'Exclusionary Reasons', *Mind*, 62 (1977), 253.

[54] Leslie Green, *The Authority of the State* (1988), 113–14. For similar analyses, see Donald Regan, 'Authority and Value: Reflections on Raz's Morality of Freedom', *Southern California Law Review*, 62 (1989), 995, 1027; Heidi Hurd, 'Sovereignty in Silence', *Yale Law Journal*, 99 (1990), 1016–19; Larry Alexander, 'Law and Exclusionary Reasons', *Philosophical Topics*, 7 (1990), 18.

Stephen Perry calls such reasons 'reweighting' reasons.[55] A reweighting reason is a reason to act 'as if' another reason had a certain weight. A subject who regarded an authoritative directive as strong evidence as to which actions were reasonable might, according to Perry, reweight the content-dependent reasons, transferring some of the weight from reasons that don't support the content of the directive to others that do.

Perry's reweighting reasons are generalizations of Raz's pre-emptive reasons. An exclusionary reason is a limit case of a reweighting reason, one that transfers all of the weight of certain reasons that do not support its content to those that do. Aside from pre-emptive reasons, therefore, reweighting reasons do not pre-empt the reasons upon which they operate.

In addition to functioning as reweighting reasons, Perry also claims that authoritative directives may take the form of presumptions, or as he calls them, 'epistemically bounded' reasons.[56] On this model, those who rely on authoritative directives presume that the content of the directives are supported by the balance of reasons. Such presumptions do not completely pre-empt the underlying reasons, in so far as they can be rebutted in certain circumstances. Perry believes that authoritative directives establish thresholds of credibility that pre-empt inquiry into the underlying reasons just in case no reason of a sufficiently weighty sort exceeds the threshold. Other advocates of the Presumption Model, such as Fred Schauer, believe that these presumptions can be rebutted by taking a 'perfunctory glimpse'[57] at the content-dependent reasons to determine whether there exists a good enough reason to doubt the reliability of the presumption.

As with the Simple Model, these alternative proposals permit subjects to benefit instrumentally from authority without the need for complete pre-emption. Suitably reinterpreted according to these models, the Normal Justification Thesis legitimates authority just in case treating authoritative directives as weighty first-order/second-order reweighting/presumptive reasons and then acting on the basis of the resulting balance of reasons the subject is more likely to conform to the balance of content-dependent reasons than if he did not treat them in this manner. In situations where such a condition is satisfied, a subject who acts on the basis of her judgments about the balance of reasons would not be undoing the work of authority, but rather would be harnessing the value of authority and using it as it ought to be used.

---

[55] Stephen Perry, 'Second Order Reasons, Uncertainty and Legal Theory', *Southern California Law Review*, 62 (1989), 913. See also, Stephen Perry, 'Judicial Obligation, Precedent and the Common Law', *Oxford Journal of Legal Studies*, 7 (1987), 215.

[56] See Perry, 'Second-Order Reason', above n. 55: 94.

[57] See Fred Schauer, *Playing by the Rules: An Examination of Rule-Based Decision-Making in Law and in Life* (1991), 91.

4.3 Is Pre-emption Rational?

Not only have Raz's critics argued that the instrumental benefits of authoritative directives can be secured without pre-emption, they claim that people do not generally treat authoritative directives as pre-emptive reasons.[58] It is a well-known fact about certain legal systems, for example, that judges have the power to depart from established rules. Common law judges may refuse to follow a precedent under certain circumstances, for example, if the rule is obsolete or sufficiently unjust. But if judges treat legal rules as pre-emptive reasons, and if pre-emptive reasons always defeat reasons which fall within their scope no matter how strong the first-order reasons, a judge would be barred for ever from acting on reasons that favour departing from the rules. It would then seem as if the pre-emptive nature of legal rules is incompatible with the revisibility of the common law.

Not only is it doubtful that judges treat precedents as pre-emptive reasons, but Raz's critics argue that they should not. Common law doctrines would become entrenched and the flexibility of the law to adapt to new circumstances would be greatly diminished. Michael Moore, for example, claims that 'Raz' account suffers from [this] defect . . . some cases that a judge ought to overrule won't be overruled. . . . The judicial obligation is to overrule whenever the balance of reasons (including the reasons inclining against overruling given by the rule-of-law values) make it the right thing to do.'[59]

By contrast, on the alternative models we have been discussing, judges should depart from legal rules just in case reasons exist that are powerful enough to override the reasons to adhere to such rules. Similarly, subjects should disobey any directives that are not supported either by the balance of first-order reasons, the balance of reweighted first-order reasons, or the presumed balance of first-order reasons, respectively. The benefit of these accounts, therefore, is that they attempt to account for the virtue of relying on authority without succumbing to the vice of rule-worship.

We might sum up these criticisms by seeing them as attacking Raz's solution to the paradox of authority and rationality. When the balance of content-dependent reasons supports conformity to an authoritative directive, Raz has not shown why authoritative directives must be understood as pre-emptive reasons rather than weighty first-order reasons, reweighting second-order reasons or presumptions. On the other hand, when the balance of content-dependent reasons supports non-conformity, Raz has not shown how authoritative directives can make normative considerations that are otherwise relevant in their absence completely irrelevant in their presence.

[58] See e.g. Stephen Perry, 'Judicial Obligation', above n. 55; Schauer, above n. 57: 91.
[59] Michael Moore, 'Authority, Law and Razian Reasons', *Southern California Law Review*, 62 (1989), 827, 867. See also, Perry, above n. 55: 963.

4.4 Double Counting and Prisoner's Dilemmas

Raz's critics have largely ignored his argument from double-counting. They have also failed to respond to his analysis of authoritative solutions to prisoner's dilemmas. In this section, I would briefly like to examine whether these arguments are effective.

According to the argument from double-counting, authoritative directives must be pre-emptive in order to avoid counting dependent reasons twice. Because authoritative directives are supposed to reflect dependent reasons, these reasons cannot have independent weight along with directives in the balance. By attempting to reflect dependent reasons, they must replace them.

This argument, however, is both too weak and too strong. It is too weak in that it establishes only that when a subject is *certain* that the directive tracks the balance of dependent reasons, he should not count the directive and the dependent reasons together. This indeed would involve double-counting. However, if a subject is not convinced that the directives issued will fully reflect the balance of dependent reasons, then an agent might consider the dependent reasons as a check against the possibility of error. A subject might reason as follows: 'Because the authority in question is highly reliable, I will give great weight to the authoritative directive in my deliberations. But since there is a chance that the authority might have made a mistake, I will also consider any reasons that might militate against obedience when judging how to act. If there is a reason sufficiently great to disobey, then I will conclude that the directive was not successful in reflecting the balance of reasons and I will disobey.' The dependent reasons are not here being counted twice—rather they are being used to ensure that they are at least counted once.

The argument is also too strong, for if valid, all forms of advice would have pre-emptive status. Those who dispense ordinary advice also purport to base their recommendations solely on dependent reasons. It would follow, according to the double-counting argument, that ordinary advice is also a pre-emptive reason, for it cannot be considered a first-order reason for belief without counting reasons twice. This would lead to absurdity—any piece of credible advice would defeat all of the advisee's reasons for belief as long as he knew that the adviser considered them in her judgment.

As for Raz's analysis of prisoner's dilemmas, recall that he argued that authoritative directives can be used to solve such problems if they pre-empted the reasons for defecting. While he believes that pre-emption by an authoritative directive is sufficient to solve a prisoner's dilemma, he clearly does not think that they are necessary. As Hobbes argued, authorities can solve prisoner's dilemmas by sanctioning defection, that is, by realigning preference so that defection is not only socially, but individually, suboptimal. What is unique about Raz's analysis is his suggestion that sanctions are not the only way to bring individual and social rationality in line—authoritative directives may also accomplish through their pre-emptive power.

While this is an intriguing proposal, much more needs to be said in order to over-come the following objection. In a prisoner's dilemma, it is in each player's interest to defect instead of cooperate. If Reason requires that agents act on their interests, then it would seem that an authoritative directive demanding cooperation would be demanding action contrary to Reason. However, if Reason instead requires agents to act for the collective good—either because acting on the collective good is a good itself or is an indirect way of maximizing conformity to one's own interests—then players ought to cooperate regardless of whether there is an authoritative directive.[60] Guidance by authoritative directives once again seems to be either irrational or irrelevant.

5 The Decision and Constraint Models

The debate between Raz and his critics is a long-standing one and it is not possible to do justice to its subtlety and complexity in this chapter. Rather than rehearse the responses and counter-responses in that dialectic, I would like to present an argument that, to my knowledge, has not been previously made and that aims to show that, at least in certain circumstances, authoritative directives cannot be pre-emptive reasons. If authoritative directives are capable of serving their functions, it is not in virtue of their alleged pre-emptive force.

This argument, however, will give no solace to Raz's critics. For I will claim that this argument demonstrates that the models advanced by Raz's critics are inadequate as well. The mistake made by all of these accounts of authority is their assumption that willing obedience to authoritative directives is the outcome of some form of decision-making.

As an alternative account, I will suggest that authoritative directives are instrumentally valuable when, and only when, they are capable of affecting the feasibility of non-conformity. When a subject commits himself to following an authority in order to benefit from its directives, that person attempts to constrain his future self to act on the demands of the authority, whatever they may be. If successful, the subject will not be choosing to obey when the directive is issued—when ordered, the subject will have no choice but to obey.

---

[60] To be sure, authoritative directives may help coordinate behaviour between players so that each can act on the same cooperative solution. Directives might even make the players aware that they are involved in a prisoner's dilemma. However, authorities would not be solving prisoner's dilemmas *per se*, but rather coordination problems or informational shortfalls.

In the following sections, I will generalize the suggestion to other cases of authoritative guidance. I will argue that authoritative directives are instrumentally valuable to rational agents in normal cases if and only if they are causal constraints on action. I will try to show, in other words, that authoritative directives could not perform the functions they are normally thought to serve if subjects had, or believed they had, the choice whether or not to obey. I will then argue that what I call the Constraint Model is the key to solving the paradoxes within a framework of authority that ties legitimacy to the instrumentality of authoritative directives.

5.1 Is Pre-emption Sufficient?

Charlie wakes up one morning, notices that his room-mate Larry is overweight and gives him some friendly advice. 'Hey, Larry, you're looking pretty plump. You really need to work out.' Larry looks over at Charlie and returns the favour. 'Charlie, you ain't looking too good yourself. It wouldn't hurt you to visit the gym once in a while either.' Unfortunately, each knows that the other speaks the truth. They both realize that they should lose weight and that the only way to do this is by going to the gym and exercising.

Turning over a new leaf, Charlie decides to stop by the gym on his way to work every day and exercise. Larry, however, is worried. He knows that he has tried to follow such a regimen in the past but has always failed. After voicing his concerns to Charlie, Charlie suggests that Larry hire a personal trainer. Larry is encouraged by the thought and so hires Sonnie, an ex-marine drill sergeant, for the necessary motivation.

The next morning, promptly at six o'clock, Sonny arrives at the apartment to pick Larry up for the gym. Larry says that he is very tired and, although he knows that he should work out, he tells Sonny to come back tomorrow. Sonny barks back: 'If you don't commit yourself to following my orders, you will never get into shape. And I won't be involved with a loser.' Larry sees the wisdom in Sonny's plan and so commits to following his every command.

Assume that Sonny orders Larry to go to the gym. According to Raz's theory, Larry will regard this directive as a reason for not acting on the reasons for staying at home. But can he have such a reason? An authoritative directive is a pre-emptive reason if and only if the subject is likely to do better by pre-empting certain reasons and acting on the resulting balance than if he tried to comply with the first-order reasons directly. However, regardless of whether Larry pre-empts certain reasons or not, the balance points in the same direction, that is, towards the option of going to the gym. After all, the reasons for staying at home are outweighed by the reasons for going to the gym and Larry is painfully aware of this. Indeed, that is why Larry hired Sonny—because he knows that he should go to the gym to lose weight instead of lazing around the house. Doesn't this show that the order isn't a reason for not acting for certain reasons, because even if Larry considered these first-order reasons in deliberation, Reason would still recommend that he work out?

This same point might be made by comparing Larry's situation with that of Charlie. Both have the same first-order reasons for action. Both have reasons to go to the gym that are stronger than those for not going and both know this. From the perspective of the first-order balance of reasons, there is no difference between the two. Yet, only Larry needs Sonny. Hence, the value of authority to Larry cannot be traced to the benefits of pre-emption given that pre-emption would give the same results for Charlie as well.

Larry's case is not simply a problem for Raz's theory—it generalizes to all other accounts that we have surveyed. According to the Simple Model, for example, Sonny's order is a first-order reason for Larry to comply if and only if Larry would be likely to do better by assigning the order significant weight and acting on the resulting balance than if he did not assign it such weight. If so, then Sonny's order is not a reason for action because the balance with or without the directive points towards going to the gym.

Why do all of the models we have discussed fail to account for the normativity of Sonny's order? I believe that the problem stems from several tacit assumptions made by all of these models. The first assumption is that people who submit themselves to authority are free not to follow them if they so wish. Nevertheless, these people *choose* to obey. Each act of compliance involves a choice to comply.

The second assumption is that authoritative directives affect practical reasoning by affecting a subject's preferences over options, or beliefs about those preferences. Therefore, when an agent accepts an authority's legitimacy and is ordered to act in a certain manner, the agent must believe that he prefers conformity to non-conformity. Moreover, if he were not so ordered, he might have come to the opposite judgment.

Putting these two assumptions together we get: when a subject obeys a directive issued by an authority deemed legitimate, he chooses to obey because he now prefers to conform than not conform. For example, when someone heeds a command issued by someone deemed to be a theoretical authority, that person uses the pronouncement as some sort of reason to believe that he prefers or ought to prefer conformity to non-conformity and decides to act on that belief. Let us call this account of authoritative guidance the 'Decision Model'.

The Decision Model has great intuitive appeal. Unfortunately, it is also false, as Larry's case demonstrates. If the function of authoritative directives were to affect preferences, or beliefs about preferences, then Sonny's order would be pointless. By hypothesis, Larry prefers and knows that he prefers to go to the gym. He does not need to rerank his options—they are in perfect alignment. Larry is not having trouble with his preferences but with his *ability* to act on those preferences. The Decision Model is unable to explain how authorities can help people like Larry.[61]

[61] As Sidney Morgenbesser pointed out to me, people like Larry who know what they ought to do, but are unable to do it, are known in Yiddish as 'schlemiels'.

5.2 Constraining Your Future Self

I would like to suggest that the Decision Model cannot account for the normativity of Sonny's order because it ignores the essential 'volitional' aspect of directives. Directives are not tools for making decisions—they are a way of preventing decisions from being made. When someone submits to authority, the aim is to constrain his future self to act in accordance with the demands of some third party. Should that act of commitment be successful, the agent becomes unable to act contrary to the will of the authority.

The suggestion is that submitting to authority involves trying to do to yourself internally what Ulysses was able to do externally when he lashed himself to the mast. It is to forgo later choice by the operation of the Will, but it is as real as using some pre-commitment mechanism.[62] According to what I shall call the 'Constraint Model', authoritative pronouncements are relevant to practical reasoning because, and only because, they affect feasibility. A directive, once issued, is not a factor to be considered in future deliberation about whether to comply. After submission, the agent no longer deliberates about whether to comply. The subject merely figures out which action counts as the implementation of the rule.

Understood game-theoretically, a rational agent who must consider his future actions is strategically interacting with another agent—his later self. When an agent submits to authority, his present self attempts to constrain the actions of his future self. In this 'game', the present self makes the first move and the future self will be barred from acting contrary to such a rule if the present self's actions are successful.

Several clarifications should be made about this proposal. The Constraint Model does not maintain that someone who submits to authority can never disobey. This, of course, would be absurd. When someone submits to an authority, they must sincerely attempt to constrain their future selves. That does not mean that they have constrained themselves, only that they attempted to do so. They might be wrong—the constraint might not have taken. Or it might take, but later lapse. The Constraint Model deals only with successful submission, where the agent actually follows through on the directives issued.

The Constraint Model also does not hold that authoritative directives cause us to conform to them. Because obedience is an intentional action, the subject has to act and act for a reason. Rather, according to the Constraint Model, authoritative directives causally constrain non-conformity—they prevent us from breaking them.

---

[62] See, e.g., Stanley Milgram, *Obedience to Authority* (New York: Harper & Row, 1974), 134. ('Since the agentic shift is largely a state of mind some will say that his shift in attitude is not a real alteration in the state of the person. I would argue, however, that these shifts in individuals are precisely equivalent to those major alterations in the logic systems of the automata considered earlier. Of course, we do not have toggle switches emerging from our bodies, and shifts are synaptically effected, but this makes them no less real.') But see Section 6.4, where I argue that there are some important differences between authoritative submission and pre-commitment.

When a subject obeys an authority deemed legitimate, she acts for reasons even though she does not make choices by so doing. Obedience is intentional, but not free, action.

Because the Constraint Model locates the functionality of authoritative directives in their ability to affect the feasibility of non-conformity, it is able to account for the instrumental value of Sonny's order. As we mentioned, Larry's problem lies not with his preferences but with his ability to act on those preferences. Sonny's order enables him to act on his preferences by cutting off his ability to act on temptation. By Sonny's ordering Larry to the gym, staying at home becomes infeasible—working out becomes the only available option. Charlie, on the other hand, has no need for Sonny because the feasibility of staying home poses him no practical difficulties. His knowledge that this option is suboptimal is sufficient to prevent him from exercising the option.

Not only can the Constraint Model account for the instrumental value of Sonny's order, but it also easily solves the paradox of authority and rationality. To see this, assume that an agent is committed to an authority in order to benefit from its directives. Assume further that the authority issues a directive that, according to the agent's own lights, is not supported by the balance of reasons. Is it rational for the agent to comply? According to the Constraint Model, it is. For, on this view, when an agent successfully submits to authority to benefit from its directives, that agent has no choice but to apply the directive when she recognizes that it is applicable. Compliance is the only feasible option and, hence, is the only optimal option.

Assume now that the directive is, by the agent's own lights, supported by the balance of content-dependent reasons. Is the directive relevant to the agent's practical reasoning? Again, on the Constraint Model, it is. According to the Constraint Model, authoritative directives affect practical reasoning by transforming the set of feasible options, not the preferences over those options, or beliefs about those preferences. Hence, even if the agent preferred to conform prior to the issuance of the directive, once the directive is issued, it will leave its practical mark—what once was feasible is no longer feasible.

The Constraint Model also constitutes an effective response to the paradox of authority and autonomy. The will of another possesses *normative* power, on this view, because of its *causal* power. The directives of the authority constitute reasons to obey given that the directives render disobedience infeasible—the directives make conformity the best options by default. Ironically, authority is reconciled with autonomy by showing how committed subjects are not autonomous, in the sense of not being in full control of their actions.

To be sure, it is morally permissible to abdicate control over one's actions only if one has a good moral reason to do so. One cannot absolve oneself of responsibility simply by claiming that one had no choice but to follow orders, when one made the choice not to have a choice. We have seen one example where agents can have good reasons to constrain their future selves to heed the demands of others. In the next sections, we will see others.

6 The Inadequacies of Decision Models

The Decision Model is incapable of explaining the normativity of Sonny's order. This demonstrates, at the very least, that it cannot provide a general framework for understanding the rationality of authoritative guidance, in so far as it is false in some contexts. However, this might not appear so damaging. One could argue that cases like Larry's are unusual and that authorities are normally unnecessary in situations where agents know what they ought to do. They are valuable, for the most part, in cases where agents require information of some sort, either because they lack expertise, cognitive resources, or advantageous positioning to coordinate behaviour.

In the next sections, I will argue that not only is the Decision Model false in some type of cases, it is false in all types of cases. In a broad range of normal situations, subjects cannot rationally defer to experts, compensate for shortfalls in rationality, or coordinate behaviour if they used authoritative pronouncements to make decisions.

In order to present these arguments, I will resort to the techniques of rational choice theory. The models of practical reasoning that we have been utilizing up to this point, unfortunately, are simply not robust enough, representationally or analytically, to handle the complexities of the practical situations at issue. The 'balance of reasons', after all, is only a metaphor—it cannot be made to do the work to which many have put it. Although no model of practical reasoning will command universal assent, my hope is that the general principles of probability and utility theory that I will employ are sufficiently acceptable so as to lend plausibility to my conclusions.

6.1 Authoritative Advice[63]

It is customary to distinguish between two different grades of ignorance: risk and uncertainty.[64] In situations involving risk, the agent does not know which of several states of affairs have or will obtain, but does assign a unique probability value to each of the possible states. One who ascribes fifty/fifty odds to a coin landing heads or tails is acting under conditions of risk.

Cases of uncertainty involve a greater degree of ignorance. In these situations, the agent does not know enough in order to assign unique probability values to every, or perhaps any, states of affairs. A person who had no idea whether a coin was fair might not even assign fifty/fifty odds to its landing heads or tails.

---

[63] The argument of this section was much improved by comments I received from Bruce Ackerman.

[64] See e.g. R. Duncan Luce and Howard Raiffa, *Games and Decisions* (New York: Dove Publishing, 1958), ch. 13.

Following Isaac Levi, we can model uncertainty using 'indeterminate' probabilities.[65] Instead of treating the uncertain agent as not assigning any probability values to the states, we imagine that he has ascribed many possible values. The agent's epistemic state is represented by a *set* of probability distributions, each one of which the agent has refused to rule out as admissible. Someone who did not know whether a coin is fair might admit as possible every coherent probability distribution, that is, would disjunctively assign to the state 'coin lands heads' the entire interval $[0, 1]$. An advantage of using Levi's interpretation is that it allows one to recognize, and represent, various degrees of uncertainty. An agent can be radically uncertain, that is, when he suspends judgment between every probability distribution and hence accepts every one as admissible, or merely mildly uncertain, that is, when he rules out some, but not every, possible distribution.

Under conditions of ignorance, it is normal to seek out experts and defer to their recommendations. By relying on their superior knowledge and judgment, we can compensate for our own lack of information and experience. The Decision Model has no problem accounting for the normativity of expert advice under conditions of risk. When an agent attributes a unique probability value to some proposition, he can choose to treat authoritative advice regarding that proposition as evidence and update using Bayesian Conditionalization.[66] If the expert asserts the truth of the proposition, then the agent, if rational, will increase the probability assigned to the proposition. The amount of the increase, and the corresponding decrease with respect to the contrary propositions, will be determined by Bayes Theorem and will be a function of the reliability attributed to the expert's judgments and the prior probability assigned to the proposition in question.

However, under conditions of uncertainty, deferring to experts will not normally be a rational strategy. To see this, I will present an argument developed by Levi. Levi has shown that it is usually not possible for a rational agent to harness the informational value of theoretical authorities if the agent were free not to follow the advice, but nevertheless treats the advice as reliable evidence.[67]

Levi's argument can be made clear by the following example. Suppose Tony is sick and must decide whether to take a certain antibiotic he finds in his medicine chest. Tony has very little medical knowledge; in fact, he is radically uncertain about the proposition, call it h, that the pill will make him feel better. That is, he does not assign

[65] See Isaac Levi, 'On Indeterminate Probabilities', in *Decisions and Revisions* (Cambridge: Cambridge University Press, 1984).

[66] Bayesian Conditionalization: let $p(\cdot)$ be X's probability function and $p_e(\cdot)$ be the probability function which results when X learns that e is true and incorporates it into his background theory. Then $p_e(h) = [p(e|h) * p(h)] / p(e)$. $p(h)$ is known as the prior probability of h, $p_e(h)$ as the posterior probability of h given e and $p(e|h)$ as the likelihood of e given h.

[67] See e.g. Isaac Levi, *The Enterprise of Knowledge* (Cambridge, Mass.: MIT Press, 1980), 296–8, 399–423. See also Isaac Levi, 'Induction as Self Correcting According to Peirce', in *Science, Belief and Behavior*, ed. Hugh Mellor (Cambridge: Cambridge University Press, 1980), 127.

unique odds to h, but rather completely suspends judgment on what the appropriate odds should be.

Suppose that Tony believes that his doctor is right 90 per cent of the time. It would seem reasonable for Tony to trust his doctor's recommendation about the pill. However, as Levi points out, if Tony treats his doctor's recommendation as evidence and updates by Bayesian Conditionalization, he will learn nothing and his probabilities will remain maximally indeterminate.

To prove Levi's assertion, assume for the purposes of contradiction that Tony's probabilities are maximally indeterminate before he learns his doctor's recommendation, call this report e, but not after. That must mean that Tony rules out some probability function $p_e(\cdot)$. Let $p_e(h) = x$. However, $p_e(\cdot)$ can be obtained via Bayesian Conditionalization from the function $p(\cdot)$, where $p(h) = x * p(e)/p(e|h)$. We know that Tony does not initially rule out this function because his initial epistemic state is maximally indeterminate. Hence, when Tony starts with maximally indeterminate probabilities, he will end up with maximally indeterminate probabilities if he updates his probability state via Bayesian Conditionalization.

All is not lost. Tony can decide ahead of time to constrain his future self to assign a probability 0.9 to h when the report e is made. As Levi describes it, Tony does not treat e as 'evidence' which he incorporates into his background theory and off which he conditionalizes. Rather, he treats it as a causal 'input', and constrains himself to follow through on a routine to which he has previously committed. Because of his doctor's reliability, this 'up front' choice not to accept e as evidence allows Tony to benefit from the medical advice.

Levi's argument, therefore, demonstrates that the Decision Model cannot account for the normativity of the doctor's advice, for it would be irrational for Tony to accept his doctor's recommendation as true absent a constraint to do so. When making epistemic decisions, agents are required to update each admissible probability distribution via Bayesian Conditionalization and, hence, those with maximally indeterminate probabilities cannot extract the information value of authoritative recommendations. Deference to authority in these situations is therefore irrational according to the Decision Model, but not the Constraint Model.

The same conclusion can be extended to cases of milder uncertainty. If Tony were to rule out the outlying probability distributions, say, those that assign prior probabilities of less than 0.1 to any possible state, it might still not be rational for Tony to defer to his doctor. For with respect to each non-excluded distribution that assigns h a low prior probability, conditionalization might not shift enough probability mass from $-h$ to h so that the posterior probability of h exceeds the threshold for belief acceptance. In such cases, Tony ought to continue suspending judgment on h[68] and not accept as true the reliable evidence of his doctor.

[68] Tony should accept h as true only if every admissible probability distribution attributes to h a probability value that exceeds whatever threshold value is appropriate for acceptance.

Levi's argument, I believe, undercuts the cogency of the Decision Model in cases involving authoritative advice. Any model of practical reasoning should permit agents to accept authoritative advice in conditions of uncertainty, radical or otherwise. As we have seen, however, the Decision Model will not validate acceptance of expert advice when the agent's epistemic state is highly indeterminate.

Yet, Levi's argument can be used to support Raz's contention that it is proper to distinguish between two types of advice, ordinary and authoritative, and that such a distinction is one of kind, not degree. In situations of risk or mild uncertainty, advice given may be treated like any other piece of evidence. Such ordinary advice can be used to compute posterior probabilities from prior probabilities and likelihoods in accordance with Bayesian Conditionalization. By contrast, when the agent faces more radical types of uncertainty, and the advice emanates from a highly reliable source, the agent must commit himself in advance to accept as true the recommendation of the expert. It is only by constraining our future selves that we may rationally yield to authoritative advice when our present epistemic states are highly indeterminate.

6.2 Compensating for Shortfalls in Rationality

In some situations, authorities are instrumentally valuable because they save us from having to engage in costly and risky deliberation. We can simply follow their pronouncements and be reasonably confident that we will be making the right selection most of the time. What happens when authorities give the wrong answer? According to the Decision Model, it may still be rational for the agent to decide to follow their recommendation. Directives that cut down on deliberation costs are likened to rational gambles: whenever the expected costs of deliberation exceed the expected benefits, an agent should rationally choose to follow directives in every applicable case. Losing a bet does not betray irrationality if it was rational for the gambler to have taken his chances.

Consider the following example. Liz hates deciding what to order when in a restaurant. She also thinks that waiters' culinary judgments tend to be as reliable as her own. She figures, therefore, that it would be better for her, all things considered, to treat their evaluations as authoritative rather than to agonize over what to eat.

According to the Decision Model, each time Liz follows through on a waiter's recommendation, she is making a rational decision. Even though Liz will pass up a terrific dish every so often by following the waiter (let's say that she believes that the waiter will mention a great special 5 per cent of the time), it is none the less an acceptable risk given that the probability of such an occurrence is low relative to the savings that she can expect to accrue by not deliberating.

The problem with this reasoning is that it's fallacious: once Liz knows the specials, then the probability that a terrific dish is being offered is no longer 0.05—it is either

1 or 0. Probabilities must always be computed relative to the total evidence available to the agent and, relative to the evidence available to Liz, either there is a terrific dish being offered or there isn't. Either deliberation is worth it or it isn't. She is no longer engaged in decision-making under risk—she is facing a decision problem under certainty. The waiter's recommendation is useless to her now, because the only way she can know whether to follow the directive, that is, whether it gives the right answer, is to deliberate. If the waiter gives the wrong advice, then it is irrational for her to decide to apply it.

Lest there be confusion on this matter, I am not claiming that the total evidence requirement demands that Liz deliberate. It merely requires that her choice be one that would be endorsed by ideal deliberation on all the available evidence. Liz is now in a pickle: the only way she can know whether to deliberate is to deliberate. At this point, the principles of rationality offer no guidance; whatever she decides to do is not irrational.

If, on the other hand, Liz were constrained to follow the waiter's recommendation, the probability that it pays to deliberate is irrelevant. Liz will be forced to conform regardless of the probabilities of success *ex post*. This constrained behaviour is optimal from an *ex ante* perspective and, hence, her decision to commit, as well as her following through on her commitment, are rational acts.

Once again, the Decision Model is unable to account for the normativity of authoritative directives. When agents have open minds, they are required to maximize expected utility. Only by committing oneself in advance to accept the direction of an authority can that direction be a reason for action.

6.3 Coordination

According to the Decision Model, authoritative directives affect practical reasoning in a coordination game by providing evidence about the activities of the other players. Authoritative directives are capable of providing evidence of others' activities because they create 'salience'. The rule requiring drivers to stop at a stop sign, for example, makes the joint strategy 'driver approaching stop sign stops, crosswise traffic proceeds' conspicuous to all. The rule thus constitutes good evidence that crosswise traffic may be crossing the intersection when I approach the stop sign, making it rational for me to decide to stop.

I would like to challenge this analysis. First, I will argue that authorities do not solve coordination problems by creating salience. Salience is one way of solving a coordination problem, authority another. Secondly, I will try to show that, assuming that players commonly believe that each other are rational, authoritative directives could not constitute evidence of others' activities and hence could not solve coordination problems. If authorities are able to solve coordination problems, the Decision Model cannot be correct.

To see why salience is the wrong concept to employ with respect to authoritative solutions to coordination problems, it would be best to consider briefly the reasons that the concept of salience was first introduced. In the *Strategy of Conflict*, Thomas Schelling was interested in correcting the dominant tendency in game theory that viewed all instances of conflict as cases of pure conflict. As he pointed out, many important strategic situations involve non-zero-sum components. It is often in the parties' interest to cooperate. The rub is that in many strategic situations, explicit bargaining is not feasible. Because the existence of conflict frequently leads to a breakdown in communication, the mutual selection of a coordination equilibrium cannot be had by a simple verbal manifestation of intention. A meeting of the minds must take place by a process of imaginative second-guessing, each trying to figure out what the other agent would expect him to select knowing that the other knows that he knows this.[69]

The main work to be done in tacit bargaining, therefore, is guesswork. Each side tries to guess what the other will guess. The option which possesses the property of 'being most easily guessed' Schelling called the 'salient' option. Salience is, therefore, a function not so much of the uniqueness of an option, but rather its conspicuousness. Each side must know that the option stands out in some respect, drawing and focusing attention, and each party must know that the other knows this.

To call tacit bargaining an exercise in guesswork is not to claim that the parties cannot be fairly confident that coordination will be achieved. Experimental studies have shown that humans are remarkably good tacit bargainers. The point is that the coordination of expectations in these cases is not achieved by a process of communication. Each side must guess what the other is thinking, given that there has been no explicit revelation of intention.

It is crucial to note that salience calculations are required as a compensation for the lack of communication. 'The concept of "coordination" that has been developed here for tacit bargaining does not seem directly applicable to explicitly bargaining. There is no apparent need for intuitive rapport when speech can be used; and the adventitious clues that coordinate thoughts and influenced the outcome in the tacit case revert to the status of incidental details.'[70] It is a mistake to say that when two parties

---

[69] One of Schelling's examples of a 'mixed-motive' game involves the case of chemical warfare. Given that the nations fighting in World War II all had an interest in limiting the number of casualties that would result, some mutual restraint on the use of nerve gas was known by all parties to be desirable to all parties. Yet, the number of possible prohibitions were considerable, e.g., 'No Gas', 'Some Gas', 'Gas only used on military personnel', 'Gas only to be used in self-defence', etc. Communication between the various warring factions was impossible at the beginning of the conflict and testing of the various options could not be had, considering that one failure of coordination could have prevented subsequent cooperation (it's hard for an army to restrain itself from gassing an army who has just gassed it). Tacit bargaining resulted. Of all the rules that could be selected, the absolute proscription of the use of nerve gas was the simplest. Each side conjectured that the other would pick the rule that the other could guess they would guess, and since one rule was the most conspicuous in its simplicity, it served as a focal point for agreement.

[70] Thomas Schelling, *The Strategy of Conflict* (Cambridge, Mass.: Harvard University Press, 1960), 67.

agree to follow a given course of action, they each act on the same option because that option is now most salient. In these situations, salience is otiose.

Just as it is a mistake to talk about salience in the context of explicit bargaining, so too is it when discussing authoritative direction. Authority is appropriate in coordination contexts because it remedies the problems of non-communication. Given the obvious transaction costs associated with explicit bargaining, many coordination problems have to be solved absent two-sided verbal interaction. To overcome this, the authority acts as a one-sided signalling mechanism,[71] allowing the parties to solve their coordination problem through the use of a shared algorithm. An authority no more makes an option salient than do two people who agree to select one course of action make that course of action salient. In both cases, the parties have a settled technique that allows them to effortlessly solve a problem that, absent such a procedure, would be rather more difficult, if not impossible, to circumvent.

The argument against the Decision Model is not simply that its supporters have used the wrong technical concept, that is, salience, but rather that saying that authority sometimes or always creates salience masks the unique way that coordination problems can be solved in such cases. First, and most importantly, when authorities are involved, the answers to coordination problems are settled in advance. Authorities take the guesswork out of coordinating behaviour. Secondly, considerations that would have been relevant to establish salience become irrelevant in authoritative contexts. Authoritative solutions, therefore, tend to be more stable than their salient counterparts given that directives are not invalidated by changes in their content's conspicuousness.

Supporters of the Decision Model might accept this objection and admit that authoritative directives do not create salience. Yet, they might nevertheless argue that, however authoritative directives focus attention on equilibria, the fact that they do focus attention gives each person a reason to believe that others will choose to act in accordance with the equilibria. Authoritative directives are capable of solving coordination problems because they can sometimes constitute strong evidence that others will conform to the directive, thus making it rational to choose to conform as well.

However, this still will not do. For if we assume that the players are rational and commonly believe in each other's rationality, the Decision Model does not yield the result that it would be rational for any player to follow such directives. Consider the following chain of reasoning: the Decision Model claims that it is rational for a player, call him X, to decide to comply with such a directive when, and only when, X can establish that it provides good evidence about other players' behaviour. But the directive provides good evidence about others' behaviour only when it would be rational

---

[71] With a 'one-sided' signalling mechanism, signalling is performed in order to coordinate the actions of members of the audience, whereas with a 'two-sided' mechanism the transmission is meant to coordinate the actions of the communicator and audience. See generally, David Lewis, *Convention* (Cambridge, Mass.: Harvard University Press, 1969), 122, *passim*.

for others to follow it. However, if these players are rational, the question of whether it is rational for them to follow the directive is the same as whether it is rational for X to follow the directive. Hence, X can establish that the directive constitutes good evidence only if X can first establish that it is rational for him to follow the directive.

X has now travelled in a circle. If X wants to establish the rationality of his following the directive, it seems that he must already know that it is rational for him to follow the directive. But since he is trying to establish the rationality of following the directive, he cannot assume the proposition for the purpose of proving it. So, if X does not already believe that it is rational for him to follow the directive, he will never come to that conclusion.

The conclusion I think that we should draw from this argument is that coordinating rules cannot solve coordination problems if the players are rational and it is commonly believed that every player is rational and treats the directives simply as evidence about the other players' behaviour. The players must believe that at least some of the other players either (1) treat the directives as constraints on action or (2) believe that at least some of the other players treat them as constraints on action. The fact that some players are committed to the authority ensures that they will follow the rules and these commitments, or at least the beliefs that some are so committed, will enable the appropriate expectations to form so that coordination may take place.

6.4 Feasibility[72]

The central, and as yet unanalysed, concept of the Constraint Model is, of course, 'feasibility'—disregarding a directive is seen as 'infeasible', as not being an 'option' available to the agent. It is, therefore, important that I say at least a few words about the concept of 'feasibility' that the Constraint Model employs.

We will say that a course of action is a feasible option for an agent if and only if that agent has the ability to perform that action *for a reason*. A course of action is infeasible, therefore, whenever the agent cannot perform the action for a reason—that is, when that action is not a possible intentional action.

Now, if we were to speculate about the mechanisms by which authoritative directives render disobedience infeasible, two possibilities come to mind. First, submitting to an authority might be the psychological counterpart of pre-commitment, where the agent is physically disabled from moving his body in certain ways. This physical disability would not be imposed by some external device, but would be generated from 'within' by purely psychological means.

I am inclined to think that this approach is unpromising, at least if we attend to the phenomenology of rule-guided behaviour in general. One normally does not think

---

[72] This section is adapted from Sect. 7 of 'The Difference That Rules Make', *Analyzing Law: New Essays in Legal Theory*, ed. B. Bix (Oxford: Clarendon Press, 1998).

that commitment to an authority or to a personal rule induces a form of physical paralysis. When someone adopts a rule never to take another drink of alcohol in a bar, he does not think that somehow he will be physically precluded from ordering the drink. It is not as if he thinks that if he opens his mouth, he will not be able to utter the words 'I'll have a beer' or if he does get a beer, his hand will be frozen in the down position. In this respect, he is unlike Ulysses: Ulysses can intend to break free of the rope and try to do so. Rule-guidance, on the other hand, seems more like a constraint on the will, on effective intention-formation. If John does intend to drink alcohol, he will probably end up doing so.

I would like to suggest instead that authoritative directives normally prevent agents from 'willing' disobedience to its demands, not by physically disabling the will's expression. How might these constraints on the will arise? First, the directive, coupled with the commitment to the authority, might prevent the agent from considering the reasons for disobeying. The reasons for disobeying would, in other words, be 'repressed' by the directive. This repression blocks the possibility of intentional action contrary to the directive—the agent, being unaware of reasons for not complying, would be unable to disobey for a reason. Secondly, the directive, coupled with the commitment to the authority, might disable the person's normal psychological inhibitions. An agent in the grip of an authority might no longer be able to withstand certain emotional pressures, such as guilt and shame, even though the agent would be aware of the important reasons for not complying.

All of this is speculation, of course, but I do think it is plausible speculation. If one thinks about the abilities of the human mind, undoubtedly one of its powers is that of repression. We normally hide 'reasons for action' from ourselves all the time. Awareness of all the reasons we had for acting one way rather than another would simply be too painful to bear. I am suggesting that when we submit to authority in order to benefit from them instrumentally, we harness this ability, at least sometimes, to repress certain facts and wishes from our practical reasoning. With respect to rules, the most common expression indicative of this process is: 'I have a rule against doing this so I am not even going to think about acting otherwise'. By refusing to think about it, one guarantees that one cannot break one's rules for reasons.

Most of the time, however, we aren't even aware of repressing reasons for violating our commitments. We simply follow rules and directives without any struggle or conflict, even in situations where if we thought about it, we would be deeply disturbed by our actions. They become almost like habits in that they can be executed virtually without thinking.

The ability to repress reasons is not one that everyone has nor do they have it to the same degree. Nor is the need to repress reasons as important in some people as in others, chiefly because all people do not monitor their actions with the same frequency. As control theorists say, some have longer 'feedback loops'. In situations where the need for guidance is most acute, for example, in the military, people need to be trained to lengthen their feedback loops. Boot camp consists in training people to ignore their instincts, to react first rather than think. This is accomplished partly through the complete regimentation of life and partly through the compelled performance of absurd tasks like cleaning floors with toothbrushes. The easiest way to get people to repress reasons is, therefore, to stop them from prompting themselves for reasons in the first place.

As for disinhibition, it is well known that people who act subject to orders can be made to act in monstrous ways. It is not that they don't realize what they are doing; rather, they seem to be unable to oppose the demands of the authority issuing the directives. In reporting on the results of his famous obedience experiments in the 1960s, Stanley Milgram vividly described this phenomenon. In these experiments, Milgram wanted to see how far ordinary people would go in hurting others when being ordered by an authority to do so. The subjects were told that they were to participate in an experiment on learning and negative reinforcement. Whenever the supposed learner would make a mistake, the subject was directed by the leader of the experiment to administer an increasing series of electric shocks to punish the learner for the mistake. To Milgram's suprise, many of the subjects followed the leader's orders and administered what the subjects thought were extremely painful shocks. What was even more surprising is that the subjects often expressed great reservations about continuing with the experiment but followed through anyway because they were ordered to do so. This is Milgram's description:

Some people interpret the experimental situation as one in which the subject, in a highly rational manner, can weigh the conflicting values in the situation, process the factors according to some mental calculus, and base his actions on the outcome of this equation. Thus, the subject's predicament is reduced to a problem of rational decision making. This analysis ignores a crucial aspect of behaviour illuminated by the experiments. Though many subjects make the intellectual decision that they should not give any more shocks to the learner, they are frequently unable to transform this conviction into actions. Viewing these subjects in the laboratory, one can sense their intense inner struggle to extricate themselves from the authority, while ill-defined but powerful bonds hold them at the shock generator. One subject tells the experimenter: 'He can't stand it. I'm not going to kill that man in there. You hear him hollering in there. He's hollering. He can't stand it.' Although at the verbal level the subject has resolved not to go on, he continues to act in accord with the experimenter's commands. Many subjects make tentative movements toward disobedience but then seem restrained, as if by a bond.[73]

Milgram hypothesized that by accepting the authority of another, one relinquishes the ability to inhibit actions in light of one's own values: 'The inhibitory mechanisms which are vital when the individual element functions by itself become secondary to the need to cede control to the coordinating component'.[74] He subscribed, in other words, to the Constraint Model.

In some sense, it is irrelevant whether the mechanisms I have described are present in normal functioning humans. Strictly speaking, authoritative directives can serve

[73] Stanley Milgram, above n. 62: 148–9.   [74] ibid. at 129.

the benefits they are meant to serve just in case we think that we have the ability to constrain our future selves. Whether we can actually do such a thing is another matter. We might be wrong in our belief that authorities can give rational agents reasons for action, but this belief is neither incoherent nor implausible.

6.5 Interim Conclusion

In the previous sections, I argued that, in a broad range of standard cases, the Decision Model cannot account for the instrumental potential that authoritative directives hold for rational agents. I also argued that the Constraint Model does provide an adequate explanation. Rational agents can benefit from the directives provided them only if they do not make choices about whether to obey individual directives. They may make choices to commit themselves to the authority—but those choices are choices not to make future choices.

Moreover, I suggested that the Constraint Model can provide an adequate resolution to the paradoxes of authority. When authoritative directives give the wrong results, it is neither irrational nor immoral for the committed subject to comply, given that compliance is the only feasible option. When authoritative directives give the right results, the directive is relevant to practical reasoning in so far as it affects the feasibility of non-conformity.

However, this argument is not sufficient to end the discussion of the paradoxes. For even if one were to accept the truth of the Constraint Model, the philosophical anarchist might still argue that the paradoxes remain. The Constraint Model solves the paradoxes only when a particular theory of legitimate authority is presupposed, namely, one that embraces the Normal Justification Thesis. If the legitimacy of an authority were not dependent on its ability to generate instrumentally valuable directives, the paradoxes would remain unsolved. For the Constraint Model has nothing to say about obedience that is not motivated by the desire to harness the instrumental potential of directives. It is consistent with the Constraint Model that individuals who obey directives despite their lack of instrumental value are making decisions to obey. If so, the paradoxes remain: how can it be reasonable/morally acceptable for agents to choose to obey directives that are mistaken?

The paradoxes remain, of course, only if it is possible for an authority to be legitimate despite its inability to generate instrumentally valuable directives. As I will argue in the next section, we must take this possibility seriously.

7 SERVING THE GOVERNED

Despite all of the critical attention focused on Raz's theory of authority, few have challenged the validity of the Normal Justification Thesis. Raz's critics have, by and large, accepted his claim that authorities are legitimate just in case subjects are likely to do better in terms of the reasons that independently apply to them by deferring to their directives than if subjects attempted to conform to these reasons directly. The main bone of contention, as we have seen, has centred on the Pre-emptive, not the Normal Justification, Thesis.

The appeal of the Normal Justification Thesis, I believe, stems from its being an expression of the Service Conception. According to the Service Conception, it is the function of authorities to serve the governed. The Normal Justification Thesis regards this service as consisting in the provision of directives to subjects so that they might better conform to the reasons that bind them.

The idea that authorities are in our service, not vice versa, is one of the most important ideas to have emerged from the Enlightenment.[75] Enlightenment thought rejected the notion that authorities derive their power from superior birth or social status. Indeed, it has been the burden of modern political theory to explain how authorities can have the power they claim to have despite the fact that no individual is 'better' than any other. The Service Conception provides the standard response to this dilemma: authorities have the power to tell us what to do because we benefit from their having such power.

As I will argue, however, the Normal Justification Thesis is but *one* expression of the Service Conception. Accordingly, I will distinguish between two different models of service, one that treats the function of authority as mediating between reasons and persons, and another that understands their role as arbitrating between rival parties. I will argue that the traditional liberal understanding of service consists not in mediation but in arbitration. Rather than capturing a dominant theme of traditional liberal thought, the Normal Justification Thesis represents a somewhat radical understanding of the function that legitimate authorities are meant to serve.

It is not, of course, an argument against the Normal Justification Thesis that it breaks with tradition. Rather, I will argue that Raz's theory of authority is flawed because of the inadequate justificatory role that it accords to democratic decision-making. According to the Normal Justification Thesis, the value of various schemes of power-sharing in a society is understood primarily in instrumental terms—one structure of government is more legitimate than another when one is more likely to track the balance of dependent reasons than another. Consequently, democratic

---

[75] Or, as I should say, 're-emerged', as the Service Conception was an important theme in classical political thought.

structures are preferable to undemocratic ones just in case the former generate 'better' directives than the latter.

However, I will suggest that the value of democratic decision-making does not lie in its instrumental value. Rather, democratic procedures are capable of possessing legitimate authority because they represent power-sharing arrangements that are fair. Rather than violating one's autonomy, heeding rules that one believes to be mistaken can be an affirmation of the value of autonomy in general. It shows respect for the rational faculties of others, recognizes the fairness of accepting burdens in cooperative ventures, and supports the equality in distribution of power through society.

7.1 Mediation and Arbitration

Authorities can serve their subjects in one of two ways. First, they might serve their subjects through the guidance that their directives provide, that is, by enabling subjects to achieve benefits that they would not have been able to achieve without the directives. In this chapter, we have seen the many benefits that authoritative guidance can secure via its directives, that is, dispense valuable information, compensate for cognitive shortcomings, economize on deliberation costs, combat weakness of the will, and coordinate behaviour.

Secondly, authorities might serve their subjects by providing them with a way to resolve their disputes on normative matters. Disagreements between parties can be settled by appealing to the authoritative determinations of a certain person or persons, such as clergy, teachers, parents, officials, courts, legislatures, or agencies. On this account, success is not measured by the content of the directives issued. Rather, authorities serve their function when the directives issued are capable of resolving actual or potential disputes.

Accordingly, we can distinguish between two service conceptions of authority. The first, which might be called the 'Mediation Model', understands the function of authority to be the mediation between reasons and persons. Authorities are legitimate for a subject to the extent that authorities serve this function effectively, that is, the subject is better off in terms of the reasons that bind her by complying with directives provided than if she attempted to conform to those reasons directly. The chief proponent of the Mediation Model is, of course, Joseph Raz.

According to what might be called the 'Arbitration Model', the function of authority is to act as an arbitrator between subjects. Authorities are legitimate for a given subject just in case the acceptance of the process as binding by some of the parties generates a moral obligation for the subject to abide by the outcome. The type of acceptance, the parties that must accept the process, and the nature of the moral obligation generated by such acceptance will vary depending on the type of Arbitration Model. A social contract theorist, for example, would understand the acceptance as an act of consent by the subject and the obligation generated to be a promissory one. A fair play theorist, on the other hand, would understand the acceptance as the willing receipt of the benefits of the process by the subject and the obligation generated would be one of fairness, that is, that parties must shoulder the burdens of a process when they also willingly accept its benefits.

The Mediation and Arbitration Models differ in three respects. Most obviously, they differ in the main function attributed to authorities. For the Mediation Model, the function is one of mediation between reasons and persons; for the Arbitration Model it is of arbitration between rival parties. Secondly, these models differ in the relationship they draw between the function of authority and its legitimation. In a Mediation Model, the relationship between function and legitimation is direct: authorities are legitimate for a subject if and only if they serve their mediating function for that subject. In an Arbitration Model, by contrast, authorities are not necessarily legitimate for a subject simply because they successfully resolve disputes involving that subject. The connection is more indirect: the arbitration function gives parties reason to accept the outcome of the process and it is this acceptance, not the successful performance of the dispute-resolution, that lends legitimacy to the process.

Thirdly, the models differ in terms of the ultimate grounds of legitimation. In the Mediation Model, authorities are ultimately legitimated by dependent reasons. When facing legitimate authority, each subject is likely to do better in terms of the reasons that bind him if he complies with the directives than if he did not comply. In the Arbitration Model, subjects might do worse in terms of the dependent reasons. What binds subjects is the acceptance of the process as binding by some of the parties.

The contrast between the two models might be summed up as follows. In the Mediation Model, obedience itself is instrumentally valuable. In the Arbitration Model, the parties do not benefit through their obedience. Obedience, rather, is the moral *price* that parties must pay in order to secure the compliance of others.[76]

7.2 Mediation and Democracy

The Arbitration Model has surely been the dominant account of authority in modern liberal theory. The classical liberal theorists such as Hobbes, Locke and Kant believed that the foundation of legitimate authority lay with their ability to arbitrate disputes. The move from the state of nature to civil society, they argued, was necessitated by the costs associated with anarchy, that is, with the absence of a person or persons to which feuding parties could appeal in order to resolve their disputes. It is the

[76] In addition to these two accounts, we might imagine a third mixed model of authority. The 'Mixed Model' is a disjunctive combination of the Mediation and Arbitration Models. It legitimates authority just in case it either successfully mediates between reasons and persons or the commitment on behalf of the subjects to abide by the determinations of authority actually generates a moral obligation to obey.

function of authorities to serve their subjects, but not primarily through their issuing instrumentally valuable directives, but rather by the fact that they issue directives at all. Ideally, of course, the directives issued should be morally appropriate and conducive to the common good. Yet, the obligation to obey these directives does not depend on their meeting, or even coming close to, this ideal.

Despite its fringe status in modern liberal theory, the Mediation Model has found a toe-hold and is gaining momentum. Unfortunately, this is not the occasion for a full investigation of the Mediation Model as compared to the Arbitration Model. I would, however, like to suggest that the Mediation Model might be less plausible than has hitherto been thought.

According to the Mediation Model, the legitimacy of authority is determined exclusively by its ability to provide instrumentally valuable directives. The origins of the authoritative regime seem to be irrelevant, at least from the standpoint of the obligation to obey. Institutions, as we have seen, are measured primarily in instrumental terms—one structure is more legitimate than another just in case the former leads to more effective mediation than the latter.

However, this instrumental conception ignores the intrinsic value of democracy. The legitimacy of rule is generally not judged exclusively, or maybe even primarily, by its *output*, but rather by its *input*, that is, by whether the regime has been determined, and is supported, by the populace. Platonic political theory has been derided for centuries precisely because of its top-down structure. Despite the philosopher-king's excellent mediation skills, his right to rule is defective because those over whom he rules have no say in whether he should have such a right.

The Arbitration Model, by contrast, has room to accommodate the importance that democratic rule plays in legitimating authority. To see this, we must return to the paradoxes of authority.

7.3 Arbitration and the Paradoxes of Authority

The Mediation Model attempts to solve the paradoxes of authority, as we have seen, by taking a thoroughly instrumental approach to authoritative directives. This strategy will not work for the Arbitration Model, however, as the normativity of directives does not depend on their instrumental value. The Arbitration Model sanctions obedience, for example, even when the directive is not supported by the balance of content-dependent reasons, subjects are aware of this and have the ability not to comply. We must see, then, whether obedience to authority can be rendered compatible with both rationality and autonomy.

Let us begin with the paradox of authority and rationality. Assume that a legitimate authority issues a directive that is supported by the balance of content-dependent reasons. Does the directive give a subject a reason for action? Yes, according to the Arbitration Model. Because the subject is morally obligated to comply with the outcome of legitimate processes, he will have an additional reason to comply. Should the subject disobey the authority, he will have committed two offences: he will have performed an action that, independent of the directive, he should not have performed and will have violated his moral obligation to obey.

Assume now that the directive is not supported by the balance of content-dependent reasons. Can obedience nevertheless be reasonable? On the Arbitration Model, it can. Since each subject is morally obligated to comply, the directive constitutes a content-independent reason for action. The balance of all reasons, content-dependent as well as independent, would then tip in the direction of obedience, even though it would have tipped in the opposite direction had the directive not been issued.

Notice that the Arbitration Model supplies a solution to the paradox of authority and rationality regardless of whether it is true. For as long as an agent thinks it is true, it will be rational for him to obey.

By contrast, the Arbitration Model must be true in order for it to provide a solution to the paradox of authority and autonomy. For it will not be enough to demonstrate the coherence of subjects believing that they can have moral obligations to comply with the results of arbitration. It must be shown that such obligations actually exist.

Consider, for example, the social contract variant of the Arbitration Model. One might be tempted to answer the paradox of authority and autonomy by arguing that the promissory obligation engendered by consent provides subjects with reasons to act contrary to the balance of content-dependent reasons. However, as we saw in Section 2, this response is question-begging. If some person's will cannot give me a reason to do what ordinarily would be wrong, how can my own will give me such licence? Since consent also purports to give rise to content-independent and peremptory reasons for action, the social contract account merely pushes the paradox one step back, namely, how can the mere fact that I have consented to abide by the results of some process give me a good enough reason to abide by the results of that process.

In what follows, I will suggest that the moral obligation to obey authority can be generated under certain conditions in a liberal democratic polity. Roughly, the idea is deference to democratically elected authority under conditions of meaningful freedom is deference to a power-sharing arrangement that is *socially necessary, empowering,* and *fair.* By disobeying, subjects are unilaterally, and hence unreasonably, setting the terms and direction of social cooperation.

A sketch of this argument begins with the truism that social cooperation is not, as a practical matter, possible without the availability of procedures for the resolution of conflict. Disagreements between parties as to the appropriate terms of social interaction and the division of social surplus would either forestall or derail individual and joint pursuits. And absent acceptable resolution, disputes would fester into outright feuds and internecine battles would likely threaten the very survival of the community.

Democratic decision procedures, of course, constitute only a small subset of possible dispute resolution mechanisms. However, they distinguish themselves by the degree to which they empower the citizenry. In liberal democracies, citizens are granted the power to exert control over their lives by allowing them, through the franchise, to affect the terms of social cooperation and the direction of collective pursuits. They may affect the shape of the social landscape either directly, by plebiscite, or, more familiarly, indirectly, by the election of representatives. The protection of free speech also enables citizens to influence the social structure and objectives by permitting them the opportunity to persuade their rivals, and the uncommitted, of their views. As opposed to oracles, trials by ordeal, or coin flips, therefore, democratic procedures allow individuals some input into the resolution of their disputes. Democracies give expression to, and create opportunities for the exercise of, the individual's autonomous capacities.

Finally, democratic processes that take place under conditions of meaningful freedom constitute fair procedures for the resolution of disputes. These processes are fair because power is shared in a roughly equal manner. Equal power-sharing consists, first, in the equal voting power that individuals, or groups to which they belong, have in the selection of policies or election of representatives. Secondly, equality of power is determined by the equal and meaningful opportunity that individuals, or groups to which they belong, possess to express their views and to persuade others as to the value of their positions.

My claim is not that all democratic processes are fair, only those that take place under conditions of meaningful freedom. The fact that a society extends the franchise to all citizens and protects their right to free speech does not entail that the distribution of political power is fair. As is well known, the right of free speech actually has the potential to diminish substantially the ability of citizens to have their voices heard in public debate. In *Buckley v Valeo*,[77] for example, the United States Supreme Court held that the First Amendment prohibits mandatory ceilings on campaign expenditures, although limits on contributions are constitutionally acceptable. As a result of this ruling, enormous sums of money have found their way into political campaigns, primarily through the use of so-called 'soft money' raised and spent by political interest groups on behalf of certain candidates. Many have argued that the influence of money on political discourse has had a morally destructive effect, allowing certain groups to dominate public debate while effectively drowning out other voices.[78] Whether the present situation in the United States falls short of the conditions of 'meaningful freedom', and if so, what are the appropriate

[77] 424 US 1 (1976).

[78] See e.g. Ronald Dworkin, 'The Curse of American Politics', *New York Review of Books* (17 Oct. 1996), at 19; David A. Strauss, 'Corruption, Equality, and Campaign Finance Reform', *Columbia Law Review*, 94 (1994), 1369; Cass R. Sunstein, *Democracy and the Problem of Free Speech* (New York: The Free Press, 1993), 94–101; John Rawls, *Political Liberalism* (New York: Columbia University Press, 1993), 356–63.

remedies,[79] are questions well beyond the scope of this chapter. I will assume, however, that such conditions are attainable in modern society, although I admit that such a proposition is far from self-evident.

7.4 Democracy and Autonomy

The last step in the argument is the claim that it is unreasonable for an individual not to abide by socially necessary, empowering, and fair procedures. To motivate this assertion, consider the objection that might offer to challenge it.[80] One might argue that it is an unreasonable infringement on personal liberty to require individuals to be bound by a procedure that they did not voluntarily accept. No one has the right to demand that others shoulder burdens when those benefits have been thrust upon them.

This objection, however, lacks merit. It ignores the fact that personal liberty has value only when schemes of social cooperation are already in place. One cannot complain that one's ability to pursue projects in the manner one sees fit would be overburdened when the meaningful ability to pursue those projects depends on everyone else's restraint.[81] The very assertion of personal liberty indicates that the objector willingly accepts the benefits of such procedures. The objector, in other words, wants to have his cake and eat it too.

One who disagrees with the outcomes of a socially necessary, empowering, and fair procedure, and thus disregards it, acts, we might say, like a dictator: he unilaterally 'dictates' the terms of social interaction to others and thereby exercises inappropriate control over the lives of his fellow citizens. It is no defence for the rebel to point out that the procedure produced an incorrect result—for whether it did or not, it is not 'up to him' to impose his own judgment on others.

The conclusion I would like to draw is that disobedience to the democratic will, at least under certain circumstances, amounts to an unreasonable arrogation of power.[82] Those who act in such unreasonable manners deprive those in the majority

[79] It is fair to say that most commentators believe that *Buckley* was wrongly decided and they urge its overruling. In addition to the sources cited in the previous footnote, see C. Edwin Baker, 'Campaign Expenditures and Free Speech', *Harv. C.R.-C.L. L. Rev.*, 33 (1998), 1; Owen M. Fiss, 'Money and Politics', *Columbia Law Review*, 97 (1977), 2470; Edward B. Foley, 'Equal-Dollars-Per-Voter: A Constitutional Principle of Campaign Finance', *Columbia Law Review*, 94 (1994), 1204; Richard L. Hasen, 'Clipping Coupons for Democracy: An Egalitarian/Public Choice Defense of Campaign Finance Vouchers', *California Law Review*, 84 (1996), 1; Burt Neuborne, 'Buckley's Analytical Flaws', *J.L. & Pol'y*, 6 (1997), 111. For a fascinating reform proposal that does not require the overruling of *Buckley*, see Bruce Ackerman and Ian Ayres, *Voting with Dollars* (forthcoming).

[80] See e.g. Robert Nozick, *Anarchy, State, and Utopia* (New York: Basic Books, 1974), 90–6.

[81] I am ignoring here the case of the so-called 'internal exile' whose interest in personal liberty does not depend on a pre-existing scheme of social cooperation for its fulfilment.

[82] For a similar view about the nature of the obligation that democratic governments impose on their citizens, see Thomas Christiano, *The Rule of the Many* (Boulder, Colo.: Westview Press, 1996).

of three important goods. First, they deny the majority the outcome that they had a right to expect. Secondly, they deny the majority the control over their lives that they had the right to exercise. Thirdly, they deny the majority the respect due to them as equal participants in a fair power-sharing arrangement.

Somewhat surprisingly, it turns out that submission to authority, rather than leading inexorably to the violation of autonomy, actually manifests respect for autonomy, understood here as the power to control one's life. Deferring to democratically elected authority or selected policies under conditions of meaningful freedom is deferring to one's fellow citizen. In doing so, one pays respect to the importance that people are allotted a certain control over their lives and the fairness of sharing that power equally.

By contrast, the Mediation Model underestimates the important contribution that democratic decision-making can make to bolstering, and preserving, of individual autonomy. Politics is not just about getting it right—it is also about participating in a communal activity where all voices have the opportunity to be heard and where each voice can make a difference. As Learned Hand famously wrote:

> For myself I would find it most irksome to be ruled by a bevy of Platonic Guardians, even if I knew how to choose them, which I assuredly do not. If they were in charge, I should miss the stimulus of living in a society where I have, at least theoretically, some part in the direction of public affairs. Of course, I know how illusory would be the belief that my vote determined anything; but nevertheless when I go to the polls I have a satisfaction in the sense that we are all engaged in a common venture.[83]

I would like to end this section by issuing a brief disclaimer. I am not arguing that citizens in a democratic republic, even under conditions of meaningful freedom, ought to defer to the will of the majority in every instance. Indeed, the fact that autonomy and fairness play such significant roles in grounding the obligation to obey democratic procedures suggests that the scope of the obligation is itself limited by those very concerns. Whenever democracies insert themselves too deeply into our personal affairs, disenfranchise segments of the citizenry, or discriminate against the politically powerless, the obligation to obey the offending rules ends.

My aim in this section was to sketch a solution to the paradoxes of authority. The paradoxes attempt to demonstrate that authorities are incapable of morally obligating their subjects. An adequate resolution of the paradoxes, therefore, need not map out the entire sphere of legitimate power—it need only show that there is such a sphere. The paradoxes will have been solved if one can show that, at least under some circumstance, authorities have the power to obligate irrespective of content.

I have tried to dispel the cloud of paradox by suggesting that the claims of democratic authority be viewed through the lens of autonomy. If the autonomy of citizens is to be assured, democratic authorities must have the moral right to obligate even when wrong. For a world in which individuals had the right to balk at collective

---

[83] Learned Hand, *The Bill of Rights* (Cambridge: Harvard University Press, 1958), 73–4.

decisions just because they believe them to be misguided is a world in which no one has the power to affect the terms and direction of social cooperation. Individuals have control over their social lives only to the extent that those with whom they disagree nevertheless decide to comply. Individuals are autonomous, in other words, only when they can get others to act just because they, or their representatives, said so.

8 CONCLUSION

Let us return to the dispute between Eliezer and the Rabbis. Was Eliezer right not to submit to the mistaken judgment of the Rabbis? I think it is fair to say that Eliezer acted badly. If he truly cared about the Will of God, he would have submitted, for God had willed that legal decisions are to be decided by majority vote.

Eliezer manifested a vice that is not uncommon among the pious, a vice which might be called 'excessive purism'. Excessive purists always insist on acting in the technically right manner. They refuse to corrupt themselves, to dirty their hands by descending to the level of the lumpenproletariat and to act as the benighted do. However, as I have tried to argue, one can have reasons to abide by the will of another, even when one knows that they are wrong. To loftily stay above the fray can manifest extreme disrespect for one's fellow citizens.

Perhaps the dangers of excessive purism in matters of authority are slight compared with the sins of the opposite extreme, namely, apathy, sloth and servility. A sceptical attitude towards authority is perhaps the healthiest stance to take. But such scepticism, I have tried to suggest, can go too far.

CHAPTER 11

REASONS

JOHN GARDNER
TIMOTHY MACKLEM

In differentiating human beings from other animals Aristotle emphasizes human excellence in the closely connected faculties of speech and reason.[1] We may think of these faculties, in their most developed form, as the distinctively human ways of relating to the world. One, the faculty of speech, provides us with a distinctive way of imposing ourselves on the world. The other, the faculty of reason, is the distinctive channel through which the world, in return, imposes itself on us.

Of all human practices the practice of the law serves most clearly to bring to a head the question of *how* the two faculties are connected. Many of the timeless problems of jurisprudence revolve around the puzzling way in which legal speech creates legal reasons and the consequent difficulty that legal reasons are often encoded in legal speech. Recent jurisprudential fashion has played up the speech side of the equation. Starting with Hart's interest in the philosophy of language in general and the theory of speech-acts in particular, through Dworkin's engagement with the theory of interpretation, through the sceptical application of literary theory to the law by Fish and others, and culminating in the current rebirth of interest in legal aesthetics and legal form, the study of legal reasoning has increasingly come to be regarded as subsidiary

This chapter was defended in whole or in part, by one or both of us, in seminars at University College London, the University of Toronto, Rutgers University, and New York University. We are grateful to all who participated. Constrained by space, we have said nothing here to allay the most far-reaching queries and objections that were raised on these occasions. We hope to have the chance to tackle some of them elsewhere. Meanwhile, we owe special thanks to Grant Lamond for his extremely testing interrogations, which forced us to come clean on many issues.

[1] Aristotle, *Politics* 1253[a]7 ff.; *Rhetoric* 1355[b]1 ff.

to the study of legal discourse. Partly this has been a reflection of a more general change in cultural mood, a growing sense that reason *per se* has somehow let us down, that rationalist optimism had held out a false promise of progress. But in part it was also an understandable reaction to the scientistic aspirations of nineteenth- and early twentieth-century jurisprudence, which rightly struck many as having suppressed the creative, world-constructing dimension of legal life in favour of an arid preoccupation with total rationalization.

This trend in the philosophy of law mirrors philosophical fashion more generally. Although there has been a good deal of important recent work on reasons and rationality, the subject has found itself swimming against the stronger current of interest in language and interpretation.[2] Like other fashions, however, this one too often feeds off the most preposterous, stilted version of the fashion that came before it. Rationality is routinely represented, therefore, as a false prison of our own construction. Sometimes it is as if the idea itself is being burdened with all the elementary errors of all those who ever sought to understand it.[3] Various forms of scepticism about rationality flourish in this climate. What the sceptics set themselves against is often a bizarre caricature unrecognizable as a human faculty, let alone as a human excellence. If rationality were as the sceptics say it is we would have every reason to doubt its importance to our self-understanding as human beings. But fortunately rationality is not as it is represented either by its most incautious enthusiasts or by the detractors who make capital out of that incaution, and properly understood its significance is still every bit as inescapable as Aristotle held it to be.

In this chapter we will highlight some aspects of the role of reasons in human life that have often been misunderstood. Some of the misunderstandings came of the exaggerated expectations of rationality's enthusiasts, while others came of sceptical overreactions to that enthusiasm. We begin by reasserting, against the sceptics, the classical idea that as rational beings we are beings in the world responding to the world (Sect. 1). Responding to reasons is responding to facts, not responding to one's own grasp or one's own construction of the facts. But as the chapter goes on certain widely touted supposed implications of this view that reasons inhabit the realm of fact are refined, doubted, or flatly denied. The much-misunderstood contrast between fact and value is nuanced (Sect. 2), allowing a clearer view of the relationship between reasons and values (Sect. 3). The sense in which, in spite of their facticity, reasons can somehow be personal to each of us is explained (Sect. 4). The rationalistic urge to suppose that in view of the importance of reasons everything should be

---

[2] The interpretivist turn can be glimpsed, for example, in the tendency to read claims that values are incommensurable as claims about the inconsistency of rival interpretations of the world, rather than as the kinds of claims about rational force set out in Sect. 7 below. For criticisms of this general interpretative turn in practical philosophy see e.g. Michael S. Moore, 'The Interpretive Turn in Modern Theory: A Turn for the Worse?', *Stanford Law Review*, 41 (1989), 871; Joseph Raz, 'Morality as Interpretation', *Ethics*, 101 (1991), 392.

[3] For a subtle negotiation of this tendency as it figures in feminist thinking see Genevieve Lloyd, *The Man of Reason*, 2nd edn. (London: Routledge, 1993).

done by reasoning with those reasons is deflated (Sect. 5). Steps are then taken to alleviate the anxiety that reasons are fundamentally constraining, with a broadside against the analysis of reasons as mandatory (Sect. 6) and an explanation of the importance of incommensurability (Sect. 7). Finally, in the light of all these manoeuvres, the contrast sometimes drawn between being reasonable and being rational is subjected to critique (Sect. 8). The net result is to reaffirm that the special kind of responsiveness to the world that lies in being a rational being is not all there is to being a human being, even though one is not a fully fledged human being without it. Rationality itself also makes space for the speaking, creating, constructing agent.

By and large our examples are not drawn from the law and the specific attention we give to legal reasons and legal reasoning is extremely limited. We are among those who believe that, in spite of its important place at the interface of speech and reason, there is no special legal mode of rationality nor any special legal linguistics. Legal thought and action is subject to the same fundamental doctrines and principles of rationality (and legal utterance to the same fundamental rules of language) as the rest of human life. This view will not be defended here, but to justify the place of this chapter in this book it must be assumed.

1 Reasons and Facts

A solitary man leaves the darkness of the Embankment and hurries onto Waterloo Bridge, looking over his shoulder repeatedly. Reaching the middle he stops suddenly, looks first behind, then in front of him, and makes a lunge for the river. Caught by a passer-by at the last moment he struggles for freedom, crying out that he is being pursued from all sides by men with machetes. In fact he is not. Does he nevertheless have the reason that he says he has to jump into the river? If men with machetes were indeed pursuing him he would have that reason to jump into the river, assuming only that his chances against the river are better than his chances against the machetes. Does the fact that no one is pursuing him mean that he doesn't have the reason to jump that he thinks he has? Is his belief still a reason even though deluded?

A year later, after successful treatment for paranoia, the man (call him A) is reunited with his rescuer. He thanks the rescuer profusely, apologizes for the trouble that he caused, and explains that at the time he was under the impression that he was being chased by men with machetes. In fact he had no reason to jump and every reason not to. He was ill at that stage and acting irrationally. Is he right so to denounce the reason he gave at the moment of his rescue? Or did his belief, that he was being pursued to the point of death, however deluded it may have been, constitute a reason to jump into the river?

Which testimony should we trust? Concerning a particular moment in his life, the moment when he was about to jump from the bridge, *A* has said different things at different times. On the bridge itself he maintained that he had a reason, but a year later he said that he had none. The contradiction between these statements cannot be escaped by drawing attention to the lapse in time between the two claims. It goes without saying that *A* had no reason to jump into the river after his cure. The question is only whether he had such a reason at the moment when he was about to jump. At that moment he said yes, later he said no. Which statement is true?

It is tempting to decide in favour of what he originally said on the bridge. It is tempting to conclude that his belief at that time, although false, was a reason for him to do as he did. After all, only that belief *explains* what he did. And isn't it the job of reasons to explain? Yet notice that neither on the bridge nor afterwards did *A* himself rely on his belief as a reason. On the bridge he pointed to the presence of his pursuers, not to the presence of his belief in their presence. Afterwards he pointed to the absence of any pursuers, not (as he might if he were 'in denial') to the absence of his belief in their presence. When he cited his earlier belief as an explanation of his conduct on the bridge it was just to deny that that belief was a reason for his conduct. In fact what he said was that he had acted irrationally, because his actions had been based on a deluded belief.

It might be thought that the problem here, the explanation of why the earlier belief was not a reason, is precisely that the belief in question was deluded. The poor fellow was out of his mind. Perhaps things would be different if he had been acting on a belief that had some basis in fact. Wouldn't *such* a belief be a reason? Perhaps. Take a different sort of story, then, one in which there is no delusion, no bridge, no attempt to leap into the river. Suppose that in the darkness of the Embankment, a man sees a small knot of burly men turn onto the path in front of him, men who look very like men with whom he has just had an altercation in a pub. They are too close now for him to turn tail and retreat. If he strikes quickly, so as to take out the largest of them, he may be able to break through to a busy, well-lit road just ahead. If he does not strike he will be overwhelmed, or so he thinks. In the event he strikes, and thereby succeeds in reaching the road ahead, only to be intercepted there by a policeman.

In fact, and as the policeman soon establishes, the burly men were German tourists, hoping to enjoy what they took to be the romance of the riverside, seeking directions to the nearest Underground station from one whom they took to be a friendly local resident. Informed of this, our man (call him *B*) is embarrassed and extremely apologetic, but maintains that this was a genuine case of mistaken identity. The burly men may have been tourists, but in the darkness of the Embankment, not far from the pub where an altercation had taken place shortly before, their size and number gave him every reason to believe that they were the men with whom he had quarrelled, and from whom he might well expect an attack. Does this mean that *B* had reason to strike them as he did?

The salient difference between A's case and B's case is that B goes on to defend his mistaken belief in terms of the reasons that he had for holding it. He was not deluded all the way down. He really did have an altercation, and the burly men who approached him really did look like the men in the pub. Although still apologetic, he does not denounce his former self-explanation as irrational in the way that A, cured of his paranoia, did. But the fact that B does not regard himself as having been irrational does not mean that he still thinks that he had a reason, in the form of his mistaken belief, to attack the German tourists.[4] It is compatible with his making a more modest claim. It is compatible with his admitting that he had no such reason, but nevertheless asserting that he had reason to believe, as he did believe, that he had such a reason. His rationality lay in the fact that he responded correctly to reasons for belief rather than to reasons for action. Having responded correctly to reasons for belief he naturally, as a rational agent, responded to the reasons for action that he was led to believe he had. But still, just like A, in truth he had no such reasons.[5]

The contrast here is between having reasons for action and having reasons to believe that one has reasons for action. It corresponds to the distinction, well known to all lawyers, between justifications and excuses. One *justifies* one's actions by reference to the reasons one had for acting. One's actions are *excused* in terms of the reasons one had for believing that one had reasons for action. To be exact, the paradigm excuse is that one had a justified belief in justification. This excusatory case is sometimes known to lawyers as a case of 'putative' or 'perspectival' justification.[6] The qualifications 'putative' and 'perspectival' show that something less than a real justification for the action is involved. This means, to our minds, that something less than a real reason for the action is involved. Instead it is a real reason for belief that there is a reason for action.

We should make clear that not all excuses are belief-based. Some are based on the argument that one acted unjustifiably on the strength of justified emotions such as anger and fear. These are adaptations of the same basic idea, however, the idea that from the inside of one's anger, or fear, as from the inside of one's erroneous belief, actions seem justified which in fact are not. Nevertheless the anger or fear or erroneous belief may itself be justified, and that is the ground of one's excuse.[7] Such excusatory cases, of which B's is an example, differ from cases like A's. A is not

[4] Compare Derek Parfit's remark that something 'not deserving the extreme charge "irrational" [may be] open to rational criticism': Parfit, *Reasons and Persons* (Oxford: Oxford University Press, 1984), 119.
[5] In one idiom A and B alike had *explanatory* (or *motivating*) reasons but not *guiding* (or *normative*) reasons. Although this idiom has its uses we have avoided it here in favour of the idiom according to which A and B lacked reasons for their actions but regarded themselves as having them, this regard being the explanation for their actions. To put it simply: as we present it, all reasons are guiding reasons. For the other way of speaking, see Michael Smith, *The Moral Problem* (Oxford: Blackwell, 1994); also many of the contributions to Garrett Cullity and Berys Gaut, *Ethics and Practical Reason* (Oxford: Clarendon Press, 1997).
[6] See e.g. Suzanne Uniacke, *Permissible Killing* (Cambridge: Cambridge University Press, 1994).
[7] John Gardner, 'The Gist of Excuses', *Buffalo Criminal Law Review*, 1 (1998), 575.

responsible for his paranoid actions, with the result that those actions do not call for justification or excuse, for the expectation of justification and excuse applies only to responsible agents.[8] This is what *A* is trying to convey when he apologetically denounces his deluded actions as having been performed in the grip of irrationality. By contrast *B* is asserting his responsibility when he apologetically pleads his mistaken but justified belief as an excuse for his admittedly unjustified action. In defending his actions he has no wish to see his rationality impugned, even though he admits his error.

These thoughts tend to corroborate the claim that reasons for action are facts rather than beliefs. Or at any rate, they lend support to the proposal that *false* beliefs are not reasons for actions, even if they are beliefs which one has every reason to hold. Neither *B* nor *A* had the reasons that at the time of their action they believed themselves to have, because their beliefs departed from the facts. Admittedly this does not quite eliminate the possibility that reasons for action are beliefs rather than facts. Perhaps reasons for action are *true* beliefs.

Consider a new example, then, one in which reasons are present but corresponding beliefs are absent. Suppose that a young woman, newly appointed to a position as a television presenter, has had the misfortune to attract the interest of a celebrity stalker, a man who is preparing to kill her. She knows nothing of this stalker, let alone of his murderous intentions. The police, however, have learned from their sources all about this man and his intentions, and they have been told that there is a letter bomb on its way to her. Having failed to intercept the bomb, do they have reason to warn the young woman, call her *C*, not to touch the post until they reach her house?

Of course they do. Who would deny it? But exactly what reason do they have? It is part of the very idea of a warning, like the idea of advice, that it draws another person's attention to the reasons that, according to the warner or adviser, the other person *already has*. For what they do to count as a warning, therefore, the police must be drawing *C*'s attention to a reason that, according to them, *C* already has not to open her post. The reason is that there is a bomb in it. Of course *C* is unaware of this reason. The police know of it and she does not. But if reasons were (true) beliefs then *C* would have no reason not to open her post until she knew (and hence truly believed) that there was a bomb in it, and so would have no reason not to open her post until she was warned not to do so. From this it follows that her reason not to open her post could not possibly be a reason for the police to equip her with that knowledge. In other words, they have nothing to warn her of. This conclusion is bizarre. It follows that the fact that *C* does not yet have the belief that she is in danger cannot be an obstacle to her having a reason to avoid that danger. The reason (for *C* not to open the post and for the police to warn *C* not to do so) is the fact that there is a bomb in the

---

[8] Notice that it does not follow from this proposition that *A* is beyond the pale of justification and excuse right across his life. He is beyond the pale only in respect of those actions performed on the strength of his paranoid delusions. On this point see Anthony Kenny, *Freewill and Responsibility* (London: Routledge, 1978), 80–4.

post, not C's true belief in that fact, a belief which, at the time when it is needed to justify the warning, C does not yet possess.

So reasons, it appears, are facts not beliefs. One of the most common objections to this view comes of the connection that we already drew attention to, between reasons and justifications. If C has the same reason whether or not she knows of it, wouldn't it follow that all else being equal she would be justified in not opening her post even if blissfully unaware of its contents? This would suggest that one is justified whenever one accidentally engages in the course of action that reason would support, irrespective of one's reasoning. This conclusion seems too much too bear. Fortunately we have no need to bear it. There are at least two independent conditions that must be satisfied to establish that one was justified in what one did. First, one must show that reasons did indeed support the course of action that one has engaged in. Secondly, one must show that one acted *for* one of those supporting reasons.[9] It follows that C is not justified in declining to open her post if she is not aware of any reasons not to, for in that case she cannot act *for* such reasons. Nevertheless the reasons exist and are capable of contributing to the meeting of the first condition, whether or not she is aware of them. So the fact that unknown justifications are not justifications is in no way incompatible with the claim that reasons are facts, not beliefs.

Those who are committed to the opposite idea, that reasons are beliefs, and yet who find that conclusion unpalatable with respect to certain beliefs, particularly with respect to the paranoid belief held by A (that he was being pursued by men with machetes), must exclude certain beliefs from the realm of reason without appealing to a relationship between those beliefs and the facts. In order to achieve this, and so save their position, they need to appeal to the quality of those beliefs *as beliefs*. They need to appeal to what we might call the 'beliefness' of those beliefs, where this quality does not lie in the relationship between those beliefs and the facts, that is in their facticity. Can they do so? The very contrast between beliefness and facticity is an odd one, since it is in the nature of a belief that it aims at the facts, so that it might be thought that whatever beliefness is, it is necessarily proportionate to facticity. The thought, we suggest, is well founded. In truth what these adversaries of ours need to appeal to in order to identify a reason (or absence of a reason) are facts (or the absence of facts), and accordingly the arguments that they actually offer are plausible just to the extent that those arguments make an admitted or tacit appeal to the relationship between beliefs and facts, that is, to the facticity of the beliefs.

In spite of elaborate attempts to show that there is something wrong with A's beliefs independent of the facts, such that A does not have the reason to jump that he takes himself to have, in the end the only way to isolate an error in A's reasoning is by reference to the facts. Is there anything else wrong with A's beliefs? Are they incoherent with his other beliefs, or does he fail to believe that his beliefs are justified, to pick

---

[9] The second requirement is defended in John Gardner, 'Justifications and Reasons', in A. P. Simester and A. T. H. Smith (eds.), *Harm and Culpability* (Oxford: Clarendon Press, 1996).

two criteria that have sometimes been suggested as tests for beliefness? Not a bit of it. His disorder is not a form of dementia or compulsion. He is not confused within himself, or reluctantly struggling against alien impulses. On the contrary, he is at ease with his consistent but deluded view of the world. His belief in the presence of men with machetes is irrational, not because it is incoherent or alien, and hence deficient in beliefness, but just to the extent that it is deluded, that is, remote from the facts. The allure of appeals to coherence, or to second-order cognitive endorsement, or to any other relations among beliefs, comes of the tacit links between these tests and authentic tests of facticity. People are lulled into thinking that coherent or endorsed beliefs are more likely to be true (and *vice versa*) and it is on the basis of that truth that they are drawn to such explanations of rationality. But they should not be so lulled. *A*'s lack of rationality relative to *B* lies in a lack of connectedness to the facts. The real reason why *B* is so anxious to distance himself from the accusation of irrationality is that he does not admit to being that detached from the facts and therefore from the world. The gist of *B*'s excuse is that he was very nearly fully connected to the facts. For reasons are facts.

2 FACTS AND VALUES

It may be said, even by those who agree that reasons are facts as opposed to beliefs, that this only tells half the story. A *complete* reason is actually made up of two components, it may be said, and only one of these is the admittedly factual component. The other component is *evaluative*. In answer to a request for reasons we sometimes state only the factual component (that there is a bomb in *C*'s post) but at other times state only the evaluative component (that *C*'s being blown up by a bomb would be terrible). Which of these we choose to state and so emphasize depends upon which of them our interlocutor can be expected to already regard as obvious, so as to go without saying. Sometimes both components are complex and call for expression. But typically one will suffice. Nevertheless, it is said, the other component always lurks in the background.[10]

We agree that many statements of reasons are incomplete because they take certain things for granted. Suppose that *D* is asked by a friend whom she meets in the wine

[10] The most common version of the view according to which every complete reason cannot but have two components is the view according to which every reason comprises a pro-attitude and a belief. This view is owed first and foremost to Donald Davidson, 'Actions, Reasons and Causes', in Davidson, *Essays on Actions and Events* (Oxford: Clarendon Press, 1980), and has been adopted by many others, including, for example, Philip Pettit and Michael Smith, 'Backgrounding Desire', *Philosophical Review*, 99 (1990), 565.

shop why she is buying a bottle of Trebbiano. Suppose that *D*'s answer is simply that she is having spaghetti vongole for dinner. Her friend is baffled. Is Trebbiano an ingredient in spaghetti vongole, he asks? No, says *D*, but it is a spectacular accompaniment to that dish. This response makes clear that her original answer was not a complete statement of her reason for buying Trebbiano, or to put it another way, did not state a complete reason for buying Trebbiano. Her complete reason has two components, one *operative* and the other *auxiliary*.[11] The operative component of her reason is that Trebbiano is a spectacular accompaniment to spaghetti vongole. The auxiliary component is that she is having spaghetti vongole for dinner. Together these components add up to a complete reason for her to buy Trebbiano. It is not the only possible (complete) reason to buy Trebbiano, nor the only possible reason to buy Trebbiano that contains the auxiliary component that *D* is having spaghetti vongole for dinner. As her bemused friend's question revealed, it might be a reason to buy Trebbiano that according to some recipes Trebbiano is an ingredient of spaghetti vongole rather than an accompaniment to it, and that *D*'s partner has decided to make spaghetti vongole according to one of those recipes. Similarly the same operative premiss may be combined with a variety of different auxiliary ones. The fact that Trebbiano is a spectacular accompaniment to spaghetti vongole might also be a reason to *make* spaghetti vongole, if *D* and her partner have not yet decided on the menu for dinner and Trebbiano is what they are drinking tonight.

But is it true that every complete reason comprises both these components? Consider the operative premiss that *D* mentions by way of further explanation for her choice of wine, namely, that Trebbiano is a spectacular accompaniment to spaghetti vongole. Isn't this a complete reason for a different action from the one that *D* is performing, namely, to try the combination of the two? It would not be a complete reason for buying Trebbiano or for having spaghetti vongole, for the reason for those actions is incomplete in the absence of an auxiliary component, that *D* and her partner are having spaghetti vongole tonight, or have already opened a bottle of Trebbiano. Yet the operative premiss is indeed a complete reason for trying the combination of the two and can be recognized as such by *D*'s friend. For example, that premiss is all that *D*'s friend needs to offer by way of explanation the following week when he is asked by his partner why he is so insistent on this particular combination of food and drink. Doesn't this show that while every auxiliary premiss needs an operative premiss to complete it as a reason, the reverse does not hold true?

A natural response to this contention might be to try to show that even this reason (that Trebbiano is a spectacular accompaniment to spaghetti vongole) breaks down into two components, that what we have paraded as an operative premiss is in fact an operative premiss and an auxiliary premiss combined. To state that Trebbiano is a spectacular accompaniment to spaghetti vongole, it might be contended, is to incor-

---

[11]   We borrow this terminology from Joseph Raz, *Practical Reason and Norms*, 2nd edn. (Princeton, NJ: Princeton University Press, 1990), 33–5.

porate by reference an unstated operative premiss, that spectacular combinations of food and drink are always worth trying, relative to which the stated and supposedly complete reason is strictly speaking only an auxiliary premiss. But this response fails. The new suggested operative premiss is vacuous. Not only does it go without saying that spectacular combinations are always worth trying, but the reason that it goes without saying is that the idea that they are always worth trying is built into the idea that they are spectacular. In other words the proposition is analytic. Having said that Trebbiano is a spectacular accompaniment to spaghetti vongole, one adds nothing at all by way of further explanation of why one is trying that combination, let alone anything *operative*, by adding that spectacular combinations are worth trying.

Perhaps it is possible to find some other ingenious way of breaking down the complete reason that Trebbiano is a spectacular accompaniment to spaghetti vongole into two components, one genuinely operative, the other genuinely auxiliary. All that we are saying is that a point will always come at which further dismantling of successive operative premisses introduces a vacuity. At that point the vacuous pseudo-operative premiss drops out, what was presented as the auxiliary premiss turns out still to be operative, and that operative premiss is a complete reason in its own right.

This is not to diminish the rational importance of auxiliary premisses. It leaves their central role intact, which is their role in practical reason*ing*. Their role is to transmit the force of one complete reason for action to another action, namely, an action that will contribute to the performance of the first. For example, buying Trebbiano contributes to trying the spectacular combination of Trebbiano and spaghetti vongole just in case one is already planning spaghetti vongole for dinner. Likewise *A*'s jumping into the river contributes to his escaping men with machetes just in case there are men with machetes in pursuit of him and the river will carry him away from them at less peril to himself. In these cases, as in all others, the auxiliary premiss is a reason for action given the operative premiss. It is a reason for performing the action which in fact will contribute to the performance of the further action for which the operative premiss is a complete reason. That is why explanations citing auxiliary premisses, such as the explanations offered by *A*, *B* and *C*, are capable, if the auxiliary premisses are true, of being rational explanations.

At this point it might be said that we have cast doubt on our own claims in the previous section. We maintained there that reasons are facts. We then started this section by raising a challenge to that view, namely, the challenge that facts tell only half the story. What they tell is the auxiliary half of the story. The operative half of the story, the challenge continues, is evaluative rather than factual. In arguing that operative premisses can be complete reasons without relying on auxiliary premisses haven't we confirmed that some reasons do not have factual components? In the case of such reasons it is surely not even a *half* truth to say, as we said, that reasons are facts?

In endorsing the distinction between operative and auxiliary premisses, however, we did not endorse the view that operative premisses are not facts. What is true is that operative premisses are evaluative, but they are evaluative precisely because the facts that go to make them up are value-laden facts. They are facts like the fact that Trebbiano is a spectacular accompaniment to spaghetti vongole, or the fact that the Lake District is beautiful, or the fact that the Thames is dangerous. The elemental error of those who try to break down every complete reason into operative and auxiliary components is the error of thinking that while there may be mixtures of facts and values there are no true compounds of the two. It is always possible, it is said, to separate the factual from the evaluative without changing the character of either and without slipping into vacuity. Yet one need not believe in the strong thesis that all evaluative properties are supervenient upon factual ones to deny that such separation is always possible.[12] Either way, holding that all reasons are value-laden is in no way incompatible with holding that all reasons are facts, through and through.

3 REASONS AND VALUES

So it seems that all reasons are value-laden. Every complete reason contains an operative component which reveals the value that would be served by the action for which it is a reason. If this is true it raises the question of the relationship between reasons and values. In particular it may bring to mind a contentious thesis that we could call *proportionalism*. Proportionalism is a thesis that holds the relationship between reasons and values to be constant. According to proportionalism, to be exact, one always has more reason to perform the more valuable of any two actions. Some proportionalists hold that this doctrine is analytically true, because statements of reasons are simply synonymous with statements of values. In other words they define reasons as values or values as reasons.[13] Other proportionalists hold that this doctrine is a synthetic truth, in that reasons track values or values track reasons even though the two are not the same thing. Sometimes proportionalist views have been associated with consequentialist moral theories, or more broadly, with instrumentalist views of rationality.[14] As our formulation of it reveals, however, proportionalism

[12] On some varieties of supervenience relevant to practical reasoning see R. M. Hare, 'Supervenience', in Hare, *Essays in Ethical Theory* (Oxford: Clarendon Press, 1989), or John McDowell, 'Non-Cognitivism and Rule-Following', in McDowell, *Mind, Value and Reality* (Cambridge, Mass.: Harvard University Press, 1998).

[13] We say 'or' because the direction of definition typically depends on which of the two ideas the readership is deemed already to understand. In *What We Owe to Each Other* (Cambridge, Mass.: Harvard University Press, 1998) T. M. Scanlon 'passes the buck' from the concept of value to that of reason. Others may regard it as more perspicuous to 'pass the buck' in the other direction. We doubt whether this buck should be passed at all, not because there can be no valid interdefinition of values and reasons, but because neither of the two concepts really is any easier to understand than the other.

[14] See John Finnis, *Fundamentals of Ethics* (Oxford: Clarendon Press, 1983), 85–6. We think that what we call proportionalism is the same thing that Finnis calls by that name.

need not be such a parochial creed. A proportionalist may believe that reasons track values or that values track reasons. The latter possibility is the one associated with deontological moral views, views according to which, in the Rawlsian idiom, the right is prior to the good.[15] So long as the values in question are held to track the reasons consistently, or in other words so long as actions are held to be good just to the extent that they are right, such deontological moral views are fully compatible with proportionalism.

Nevertheless many people do take issue with proportionalism. Their common anxiety tends to be this one. Surely, they say, values are impersonal things, whereas reasons are (or can be) personal.[16] I can have my reasons and you can have your quite different reasons, without any implication of rivalry. But my values and your quite different values, the thinking goes, can only be rivals. If reasons are personal and values are impersonal, it is concluded, then reasons cannot possibly correspond to values. They must vary somewhat independently of each other. The variations could be in either direction. There could be reasons that do not correspond to values. There could also be values that do not correspond to reasons. Different critics of proportionalism emphasize one or other of these possible asymmetries. But are any of these critics right? Are there any genuine counter-examples to proportionalism?

3.1 Reasons without Values

One attack on proportionalism cites the possibility of there being reasons that do not correspond to values. The operative components of those reasons, it is said, do not, strictly speaking, imply corresponding positive evaluations of the actions for which they are reasons. The most common suggestion, and the one that we will emphasize, is this. Desires as well as values can constitute reasons for action.[17] Perhaps so, the

[15] Rawls in fact divides deontological moral views into two types. A deontological theory 'either does not specify the good independently from the right, or does not interpret the right as maximizing the good': *A Theory of Justice*, rev. edn. (Oxford: Oxford University Press, 1999), 26. Possibly deontological theories of Rawls's second type do defy proportionalist interpretation, although, for reasons that will emerge in Sects. 5 and 6 below, the matter is not straightforward.

[16] For a survey and exemplification of this anxiety see David McNaughton and Piers Rawling, 'On Defending Deontology', *Ratio*, 11 (1998), 37.

[17] A different kind of counter-example to the view that all reasons correspond to values might be thought to arise in the law. Legal reasons are source-based rather than merit-based. In other words, if asked for a legal reason for doing something the correct response is always to cite some authority rather than some value. But this is no counter-example. Whenever a legal authority creates a legal reason to do something, doing that thing is claimed by the authority to be of value. Does this mean that sometimes reasons correspond only to *claimed* rather than actual values? It does not, for to the extent that the values are only claimed rather than actual the legal reasons are only claimed to be reasons, that is, they are only reasons from the legal point of view. For one explanation of this phenomenon see John Gardner, 'Law as a Leap of Faith', in Peter Oliver, Sionaidh Douglas-Scott, and Victor Tadros (eds.), *Faith in Law*, (Oxford: Hart Publishing, 2000).

proportionalist could respond, but even if desires figure in reasoning they need not be severable from values in order to do so. First, the fact that something is desired could itself be one of the things that lends value to its pursuit. Secondly, desires themselves could answer to values, in which case the appearance that a desire is a reason could be explained away by pointing to the values that support the desire. Either way the introduction of desires into our picture of reasons would drive no wedge between reasons and values.

Are either of these suggestions about the role of desires in rationality tenable? Could there be value in the fact that desires are satisfied? Or could desires answer to values? We think that both suggestions are tenable, but that they are interlocked, so that the first possibility depends on the second. When desires are sufficiently supported by reasons they are themselves capable of becoming further reasons. When that condition is met, they are capable of becoming our *goals*, and goals do not merely reflect reasons but also constitute them.

Think about a case in which the condition is not met. Suppose that a man, call him *E*, checks to make sure that he has locked his front door before leaving for the office. Having checked the door he starts down his front path, only to turn at the gate and check the door again, this time pushing against it heavily several times. Having checked the door a second time he walks down his front path and gains the street, only to turn and check the door yet again. And so on, over and over, so that it takes him ten minutes to leave the house finally, still looking over his shoulder as he turns the corner of the road. Is his desire to check the door on each successive occasion a reason to check the door on that occasion? We can discount the reason to check the door so as to avoid the anxiety that he may otherwise feel during the course of the day as the result of his desire remaining unsatisfied. This reason corresponds to a value, the value of having a day that is free from anxiety, for a day of anxiety is a day when other valuable things could have been achieved, as well as a day of negative experiences. *E* might cite his desire as the reason here but if he did he would be suppressing the operative premiss, namely, that nagging desires drain value from one's day. The fact that *E* has the desire is the auxiliary premiss of this reason. Our question is whether the desire to check the door on each successive occasion is any reason to check the door once the removal of anxiety has been subtracted from the story. Is the desire ever operative, and so a reason in its own right?

The case is a variant on that of *A*, whose action was based on a pathological belief and who did not have the reason that he thought he had to jump from the bridge. *E*'s action is based on a pathological desire, which is in turn based on a pathological belief that he has left the door unlocked. Is there any more reason to check the door than to jump from the bridge? *E* is unlikely to say that he just felt like checking the door, without giving a further reason. Even if he would say such a thing it would make him doubly crazy. Who just feels like checking a door, that they know full well to be locked, in order to make sure that it is locked? What *E* is more likely to say is that he was unsure whether the door was locked, that he could not remember whether he had locked it, that he had been robbed once as the result of leaving his door open and wanted to be sure not to leave the door open again, or something like that. All these would be good reasons to check the door, and to want to check the door, were E not so palpably deluded in his belief that he had left the door unlocked.

E is likely to offer such an explanation just because he recognizes that desire, like action, answers to reason. Where desire is unsupported by reason, as the inadequacy of E's explanations shows that it was in his case, desire is itself no reason to do what would satisfy it. As E recognizes, his desire would only be a reason for action if it were either a valuable desire (i.e., if it really did contribute to reducing the risk of his door being unlocked), or if it were rendered rationally significant by the value of avoiding the frustration or anxiety that would come of its non-satisfaction (in which case it would be auxiliary to that operative premiss). Either way it would fail to disrupt the proportionate relationship between reason and value.

Perhaps, as in A's case, the problem here is that the desire is a pathological one. Perhaps more compelling counter-examples could be gleaned from consideration of the apparently paradoxical cases in which people deliberately set themselves, or claim to set themselves, against the pursuit of value. These cases divide into three types. First there is the simple case of people who set themselves against the pursuit of value without realizing what they are doing, for they mistakenly hold to be valuable that which is not, and not valuable that which is. Such people call for no reassessment of the relations between reason and value. Their situation is akin to that of B. In so far as they are mistaken about value, they are likewise mistaken about the reasons for action that apply to them. In so far as they are nevertheless rational this is because they nevertheless have reason to believe what they mistakenly believe. At best they are excused rather than justified in what they do on the strength of such a belief.

The second type of case is more problematic. It is that of *akrasia*, or weakness of will. This is often thought to pose the greatest challenge to rational accounts of human agency, for it is a case in which desires for one action overcome the reasons that the agent is aware would lend more support to the performance of another.[18] But this characterization itself makes clear why *akrasia* poses no challenge to proportionalism, for in so far as the agent knowingly acts against reason she knowingly acts against value. Or at any rate there is nothing in *akrasia* to suggest otherwise. In effect it is another, albeit less dramatic and more everyday, case of the pathological. It is less dramatic because in general *akratic* people have a reason to do what they do, and correspondingly there is value in it. The problem is only that in the light of the alternatives they do not have *enough* reason, *enough* value, to justify what they do, as well they know.

[18] The *locus classicus* is Donald Davidson's 'How is Weakness of the Will Possible?' in his *Essays on Actions and Events*, n. 10 above.

This leaves us with the third type of case. This is the type of case in which the agent *literally* sets himself against the pursuit of value. What he aims at is evil *qua* evil.[19] There is of course no need for us to show that this character has reasons for what he does. Perhaps he is irrational. But how is it even intelligible that he thinks as he does? How could he imagine, if proportionalism is true, that he could have reason to pursue evil without pursuing it under the description of countervailing good? Must we conclude that proportionalism is false, that there are things other than values that could conceivably count as reasons? Not so. In so far as this character is intelligible he does indeed secretly pursue (what he regards as) evil under the heading of good. As the ridiculous pursuits of Satanists the world over demonstrate, the description evil is a kind of code-word for what is covertly regarded by its pursuer as a good thing. Perhaps it is the value of membership in a group sharing the *frisson* of forbiddenness, or perhaps it is just the value of contrariness. One should not deny that there may be real value in these things. Of course this real value, in so far as it is a value at all, may not be enough to justify the pursuits in question when set against their genuinely bad features. But this only goes to show that proportionalists have nothing to be afraid of in this kind of example. The question of what would justify these pursuits is indeed a question of their value, for one has no other reasons to cite in defence of them than those which correspond to actual values that they have.

It is tempting to conclude from this that desires drop right out of the rational picture, that they do not add to the case for doing anything, but provide people at best with motivational fortification (and at worst with motivational obstacles) in doing what there is in any case reason for them to do. But this would be an overly hasty conclusion. When one's desires are sufficiently supported by reasons the fact that one has these desires can give one further reasons to do as one desires. These further reasons represent the value of one's being personally engaged, via one's desires, in what are in any case valuable pursuits. Can this explain the idea, flagged earlier, that reasons for action are somehow personal things, that I have my reasons and you have yours?

It does not yet provide a full explanation. One's engagement is valuable, and this value, like other value, is in principle there for all to pursue. There is no suggestion in what we have said so far that the value of personal engagement is an agent-relative value, one that figures especially in the life of the engager and is thus especially relevant to his or her practical reasoning.[20] In so far as it yields reasons it yields reasons

---

[19] Sometimes deliberate infliction of pain or suffering is thought to fit this anomic profile, but in most cases it does not. Normally it is thought to be deserved, or justified for the greater good, and valuable under that heading. The view we offer on these matters is akin to that of Warren Quinn in 'Putting Rationality in its Place', in Quinn, *Morality and Action* (Cambridge: Cambridge University Press, 1993).

[20] The distinction between the agent-relative and the agent-neutral was introduced by Thomas Nagel in *The Possibility of Altruism* (Oxford: Clarendon Press, 1970), 90–5 and named in these terms in his 'The Limits of Objectivity', in Sterling McMurrin (ed.), *The Tanner Lectures on Human Values, Volume 1* (Salt Lake City: University of Utah Press, 1980), 79, at 102. The term 'agent-relative' has often been used in looser ways, for example to denote special responsibilities. However in the strict sense special

not only for each to be personally engaged but also for all to contribute to that personal engagement. Thus if there is a sense in which some practical reasons are personal ones, this remains to be explained.

3.2 Values without Reasons

We conclude that if there is a case against proportionalism it does not lie in the existence of reasons that do not correspond to values, for there are none. Does it lie in the converse possibility? Are there values that do not correspond to reasons? Take the case of two friends who haven't been getting along with one another recently. Recognizing the threat to their friendship they agree to go out for the day to see if they can mend matters. One of them, overly anxious about the situation, does everything he can to please the other, much to the other's annoyance. A brief argument between them ensues and the anxious friend, call him F, promises not to try to please his companion further. Of course, if he keeps this promise, part of the value of his doing so will be that it pleases his friend. Yet if F acts *in order to* please his friend, if that value is operative in his reasoning, he will break his promise. It follows that the value of pleasing his friend gives F no reason to keep his promise, despite the fact that this value is part of the value of keeping the promise. F has every other reason to keep his promise, but not this one.

The explanation of this phenomenon lies in the fact that it is part of the nature of a reason that it must be logically possible to do as that reason would have one do *by acting for that reason*. The problem in F's case is that if he tries to keep his promise in order to please his friend he necessarily breaks his promise. It would be logically self-defeating for him to act for that reason. It follows that he does not have that reason to act, even though his action has the corresponding value, that is, the value that would correspond to the reason if he had it.

It does not follow that this value gives *nobody* any reason to act. Suppose that F has another friend G, who is aware of the promise and of how much it matters to F's friendship with the promisee. G also knows that F is a very anxious person, and that it will not take much, perhaps only a comment on the promisee's dark mood, to restore F's self-defeating eagerness to please. In order to save F from breaking his promise in this way, G, who has joined the two friends for lunch, keeps silent when he might otherwise have spoken. G's reason for his silence is to forestall the promisee's displeasure at the breaking of the promise. He has no wish to make the promisee's mood any darker. There is nothing logically self-defeating about G's acting for this reason. He can contribute to F's keeping his promise for a reason which is not a reason for F to keep that promise himself, even though it corresponds to part of the value of F's keeping the promise. To

responsibilities are agent-neutral if there are reasons not only for A to fulfil them but also for B, C, D etc. to contribute to A's fulfilment of them.

treat the fact that the promise-breaking will displease the promisee as a reason for F's promise-keeping is logically self-defeating for F, but not for G.

We doubt whether any value-bearing facts are free of rational significance for everyone. Their lack of rational significance is always relative to particular people and particular actions by those people. The most common situation is that the first party, the one whose action will carry the value in question, is the one for whom that value is no reason, whereas third parties, those who can contribute to the performance of the value-bearing action by the first party (e.g. by scheming, cajoling, compelling), have rational access to that value. They can scheme, cajole, or compel for that reason even though the first party cannot perform the action for that reason.

We called this the most common situation but some will say that the situation we are describing is not common at all. Some will say that our example was an unusual and contrived one, not far from the paradoxical case of a promise not to keep one's promises. We think, on the contrary, that our case is far removed from this paradoxical case. Ours is a promise of an intelligible, valid, and we think fairly common type. More important, our promise brings into sharp relief a feature of practical life that may also arise even without the intervention of any promise, command, request, or similar content-independent device for creating reasons.

Consider a friendless soul, call her H, who hears everyone talking about the great value of having friends. Never having participated in this unfamiliar value she sets out to do so. She is an extremely good mimic. She quickly gets the hang of acting towards people in seemingly friendly ways and quickly picks up what she takes to be a circle of friends. Not only that, but these people also regard her as part of their circle. All the time, however, her eye is only on the value of having friends. She never thinks about her so-called friends in the way that friends do. Their joys and sorrows are never her joys and sorrows, their passions are merely embarrassments to her, and so on. She thinks about them as beings who satisfy her need to have friends. What she does not realize is that this way of thinking about them, this way of reacting to them, is itself incompatible with her having friends. She has no friends while she aims, in her relations with her pseudo-friends, at having them as friends. Imagine H being asked, by an outsider to the circle, why she is friends with members of the circle. She says that it is in order to have friends. This only shows that she is not friends with them at all. Her pursuit of the value of having friends is logically self-defeating. Of course, H's basic problem is that she misunderstands the value of having friends. Some will say that this example is one of evaluative error rather than self-defeat in the pursuit of genuine value. But our point is that H's evaluative error lies precisely in her thinking that one can have friends in order to have friends. It is true that having friends is part of the value of friendship. But that is not a reason for performing any of the constituent acts of friendship.[21]

---

[21] Notice again that this inhibition does not carry over to third parties. It is open to G to take action for the sake of F's having friends, albeit misunderstanding that value exactly as H does. This is not logical anathema to G's helping to forge fine new friendships for F.

In our view, the example can be replicated. There are other values that one cannot in logic bring to one's actions by pursuing them. We think, for example, that the intrinsic values of some or all of the moral virtues are among these values. We suspect that there is no courage in actions performed in order to display courage, no compassion in actions performed for the sake of being compassionate, and so on. These are tricky cases and we cannot develop them here. But the cases that we did develop already show that proportionalism is an oversimplified doctrine. Many writers have tried to cast doubt on the doctrine by showing that some reasons do not correspond to values. We rejected this critique but endorsed the less widely supported critique that, relative to some agents and some actions, some values do not correspond to reasons. Some values that would lie in those agents performing those actions do not correspond to reasons for those agents to perform those actions, even though they may well yield reasons for others to contribute to such performance.

4 Reasons and Persons

We have started to see, through studying the relationship between reasons and values, how reasons could be more personal than values. Given one value which both F and G could serve through their actions, namely the value of pleasing the promisee, G (the third party) had a reason corresponding to that value but F (the promisor) did not. But so far this seems to be an asymmetry in the wrong direction. One would have expected the value of personal engagement to be such that in respect of his own promise F had reasons that G did not. The only glimpse of agent-relativity in reasons that we have seen so far seems, perversely, to shift the rational burden of each person's activities onto others.

But return to the story of F's promise and G's contribution to his keeping it. Consider a possible complication. Having noticed the promisee's bad mood over lunch G might be tempted to warn F to keep the promisee sweet by, for example, not breaking his promise. F's pleasing the promisee is a reason for G to contribute to that pleasing, after all, and what contribution would come more naturally than a word of friendly advice about the promisee's mood? But in the case of C and her parcel bomb we drew attention to a special feature of warnings and advice. To warn or advise someone is to draw their attention to reasons that already apply to them. We already know that pleasing the promisee is no reason for F to keep his promise. It follows that G, knowing what F promised, cannot warn F to keep his promise for this reason. That would not be a contribution to F's keeping his promise at all. Rather it would be a contribution to his violation of it. This is another case of self-defeating action. What makes it self-defeating is not the reason for which G performs his action, but rather the action that he performs for that reason. He has the reason to act, unlike *F*, but the reason is not a reason to perform this tempting action, for the reason is a reason to contribute and this would not be a contribution.

This is just a special case of a very widespread phenomenon. We already drew the distinction between doing as a reason would have one do and doing it for that reason. In the last section we claimed that nothing is a reason for anyone to do anything that that reason would have them do unless it is logically possible for them to do it for that reason. Now we add a further point. Sometimes people perform actions for reasons which do not in fact support their performing those actions but which support their performing other actions instead. They have those reasons, for it would be logically possible for them to do, for those reasons, as those reasons would have them do. Unfortunately, what they actually do for those reasons is something else. For instance, they have a reason to contribute to someone else's actions but what they do for that reason is far from a contribution. It is actually a hindrance. This is an important kind of rational mistake. It differs subtly from the mistakes made by *A* and *B*, which were mistakes about which reasons apply to them *tout court*. This, by contrast, is a mistake about which actions are supported by reasons that admittedly apply.[22]

Among the most common mistakes of this kind are mistakes by third parties that ignore the value of personal engagement. This value, as we said, is an agent-neutral one like all others. Everybody's personal engagement with valuable activities is in principle everybody's business. This way of putting the point raises the spectre of a world of nosy parkers, intruding into each other's lives at every turn. It reminds one of the familiar objection to utilitarianism that it gives everyone one and the same goal of serving everyone's goals.[23] But notice that this image ignores the fact that many contributions that people might be tempted to make to other people's pursuit of their goals will not be contributions at all, for they will detract from rather than adding to the personal engagement that the very idea of pursuing a goal implies. Rather than there being more personal engagement in the world, thanks to these nosy parkers there will be less. The reason they have to contribute to other people's personal engagements are not, therefore, reasons to perform these pseudo-contributory actions.

This is the main thing that gives people the impression that reasons are somehow more personal than values.[24] The reality is that the reasons in question are as agent-

---

[22] The difference is subtle because arguably in each case the mistake lies in the auxiliary premiss. However there is a sense in which reasons apply to *G* and do not apply to *A* and *B*. *G* has reason to be frustrated if he discovers that there is nothing he can do to help *F*, whereas *A* and *B* have no reason to be frustrated (although they think they have) if they find they have no means of escape.

[23] The objection is Bernard Williams's famous integrity objection in 'A Critique of Utilitarianism', in J. J. C. Smart and Bernard Williams, *Utilitarianism: For and Against* (Cambridge: Cambridge University Press, 1973), 116–17. The point is further developed by Peter Railton in 'Alienation, Consequentalism, and the Demands of Morality', in *Philosophy and Public Affairs*, 13 (1984), 134.

[24] We here build on Joseph Raz, *The Morality of Freedom* (Oxford: Oxford University Press, 1986), ch. 12. Our conclusions go beyond those that Raz defends.

neutral as the values (barring the special cases we dealt with in the last part of the previous section). They are as much reasons for third parties as for first parties. The point is, however, that third parties only have it in their power to make limited contributions to first-party conformity with those reasons. Thus the reasons as applied to the third parties are reasons for a more restricted and less exciting range of interventions than they may be tempted to suppose. In the face of this there may be some value in people thinking agent-relatively about other people's roles and pursuits.[25] Of course this too can get out of hand, and can descend into an absurd egoism. Nevertheless, within limits, adopting an agent-relative perspective in our practical reasoning may help us, from day to day, in resisting the temptation to get so involved in other people's personal engagements that they stop being other people's personal engagements, and their value as such is destroyed by our well-intentioned but self-defeating meddling.

5 REASONS AND REASONING

The previous section introduced examples that illustrated the value of indirect reasoning. In these examples one had a reason to do something but in acting for that reason one was apt to do the wrong thing. Having a reason to help (say that one's friend is having trouble achieving his goals), and acting for that reason, one was apt to interfere to the point of hindering rather than helping. In such cases it is *contingently* self-defeating to act for a certain reason.[26] It is not logically self-defeating, because it is logically possible that when one intends to help one helps. Nevertheless features of oneself or one's predicament may impede one's success. There may be distractions, or temptations, or other complications which make it likely that in aiming to help one only hinders. This is the vice of the much maligned 'do-gooder', who realizes that she has reason to help others but doesn't know when to stop. She doesn't notice that at a certain point her eagerness that others should reach their goals, and consequent insistence on participating in their doing so, is precisely what gets in the way of their reaching their goals. For at a certain point *her* participation dilutes *their* participation, the very personal engagement that is part of the value of their having

[25] For a strong agent-neutral case for limited agent-relativism see Derek Parfit, *Reasons and Persons*, n. 4 above, part one.

[26] Parfit's *Reasons and Persons* (previous note) begins with a study of self-defeatingness. His contrast between what is directly self-defeating and what is indirectly self-defeating is close but not identical to our contrast between what is contingently and what is logically self-defeating. Parfit also emphasizes what we ignore, namely, that self-defeatingness is exacerbated by many-person activities. This is the source of familiar rational difficulties in co-ordination problems and prisoners' dilemmas.

and pursuing goals. At this point she has a reason not to try to help. It does not follow that she has no reason to help. This would follow only if acting for the sake of helping were logically self-defeating, which in this case it is not. Nor does it follow that she has a reason not to help. What she has is a reason not to act for a certain reason, namely, for the reason of helping. Such reasons not to act for a reason have become known, following Raz, as *exclusionary reasons*.[27]

Sometimes, obviously, it makes sense to act for the sake of protecting one's children. Getting one's children to wear their seat-belts does help to protect them from some injuries, and in the case of most people there is nothing that would be distracting or complicating in getting children to wear their seat-belts for that very reason. But other operations regarding the safety of one's children are more complex.

Consider a parent, call him *J*, who forbids his children to go out and play in the street in order to protect them from heavy traffic and malevolent strangers. In the short term he succeeds. But soon things start to go wrong. The older child grows up obedient but timid. When he at last finds himself alone in the streets as a young adult he is ill equipped to cope with traffic and strangers. He is unsure how to gauge the speed of approaching traffic and is no judge of character. The younger child, on the other hand, grows up rebellious and reckless. She crosses the road without regard to traffic and is utterly undiscriminating in her choice of company. As they enter adulthood both children are vulnerable to dangers that they would not have been as vulnerable to had their father *J* not set so much store by their safety and so forbidden them to play in the street in their teenage years. *J*'s setting so much store by their safety, and his consequent protective action for the sake of that safety, is contingently self-defeating (assuming that it is his children's long-term safety, safety into adulthood, that he is setting store by). To do as that reason would have him do, that is, to make his children safer, it would be better for *J* not to have so often acted for that reason, in other words, not to have been so protective. As with so many parents, the reason tempted him into the vice of over-protectiveness. In view of that temptation he had, on at least some occasions during their upbringing, a reason not to act for that reason: an exclusionary reason.

Some people have doubted the very possibility that there can be exclusionary reasons.[28] One explanation for their doubt is that they misinterpret the proposition about reasons that we introduced in Section 3, namely, that nothing is a reason unless it is logically possible to do as that reason would have one do by acting for that reason. According to the misinterpretation nothing is a reason unless it is possible *in the circumstances* to do as that reason would have one do by acting for that reason. This misinterpretation gives rise to two myths, which we will call the rationalist myths. The combination of these two myths yields the conclusion that there are fewer reasons for

[27] Joseph Raz, *Practical Reason and Norms*, n. 11 above, 39.

[28] See e.g. Michael S. Moore, 'Authority, Law and Razian Reasons', *Southern California Law Review*, 62 (1989), 829 at 859 ff. This example is interesting because of its explicit subscription to the rationalist myths described below.

action than might have been supposed but that those reasons offer greater security against error for their faithful followers.

The first is the myth often captured in the slogan 'ought implies can'. As this slogan is used by those in the thrall of the rationalist myths, it means that people who have attenuated capacities or attenuated opportunities also have, by that token, fewer reasons for action. They lack the reasons for action to do whatever they lack the capacity or the opportunity to do. We will not directly tackle that myth here.[29] Our main interest lies in the second rationalist myth. According to this myth it is in the nature of a reason that there can be no better way of doing what any reason would have one do than by acting for that reason. Reasons, the thinking goes, are for following. How is it compatible with this truism, ask subscribers to the second rationalist myth, that sometimes it is better, even so far as the reason itself is concerned, not to follow that reason? How can there ever be a reason not to follow a reason? How are exclusionary reasons possible?

One prominent development of the second myth in modern moral philosophy sees it invoked as a principle for coping with a variety of conflicting reasons. According to the second myth, recall, there is no better way of doing what any reason would have one do than by acting for that reason. For some it is a short step from this proposition to the proposition that there is no better way to act as the *balance* of reasons would have one act than by *balancing* those reasons, that is, by *deliberating* about the pros and cons of the various actions that are open to one in the circumstances.

Yet one need not introduce the idea of an exclusionary reason to show that this short step is a step in the wrong direction. Deliberating about what to do is itself something one does. It is an action (or activity) preliminary to other actions (or activities). As such there are ordinary reasons in favour of and against engaging in it. It follows that deliberating about what to do is not always the best way to do as the reasons that figure in one's deliberation would have one do, for that equation would eliminate the reasons for and against deliberation itself. To put it tersely, there are some values that are badly served by deliberate action but that are well served by spontaneous action.[30] Most obviously there is the value of spontaneity itself, which is

[29] What we will say, however, is that one particular class of reasons is capped by capacity. These are interest-based reasons (or reasons of well-being). Something is in your interests (serves your well-being) if firstly, it is valuable, and secondly, you have the capacity to participate in its value. You still have reason to pursue things that do not pass the second test, but their value will not increase your well-being. The same thing goes for the well-being of other people. You will not increase other people's well-being by pursuing value in which those people cannot participate. The view that reasons are all capped by capacities may come of an unholy alliance of two false assumptions, one, that reasons are all reasons of well-being, and two, that all reasons of well-being are agent-relative. For further discussion of these and related points see Timothy Macklem, 'Choice and Value', *Legal Theory*, 6 (2000), 1, and John Gardner, 'The Mysterious Case of the Reasonable Person', *University of Toronto Law Journal*, 51 (2001), 273.

[30] This is one interpretation of Bernard Williams's famous 'one thought too many' argument in 'Persons, Character and Morality', Williams, *Moral Luck* (Cambridge: Cambridge University Press, 1981) at 18. However another way to read that argument would make it a rendition of our argument in Sect. 2 above, to the effect that certain supposed operative premisses are in fact redundant and so not operative at all.

a constituent of many valuable relationships. But there is also, more prosaically, the value of the time saved by not stopping to deliberate. These values yield reasons against deliberating about whether to perform the actions that one has reason to perform. So the suggestion that the best way to do as reasons would have one do is necessarily to count or weigh up those reasons fails. This failure has nothing to do with exclusionary reasons. Exclusionary reasons are not reasons against deliberating, or against including certain reasons in one's deliberations, but reasons against acting for certain reasons, whether one's action involves deliberation or not.

Much confusion in contemporary moral, political, and legal philosophy comes of the assumption that our rational faculties are our deliberative faculties. There is a sense in which, since deliberation is a rational power, action is less rational if not deliberate. But it is only in one respect less rational. In other respects it may be more so.

Somebody who reacts instinctively to save his life does not exhibit all of his rational faculties. Most obviously, he does not exhibit his capacity for deliberation. But all things considered he is more rational than somebody who exhibits her capacity for deliberation but, thanks to the time wasted in deliberating, dies as she exhibits it. The master capacity that goes under the heading of rationality is the capacity to act for reasons, and this the instinctive self-preserver exhibits *par excellence*, better than his more deliberative counterpart. After all, he jumps out of the way of the speeding juggernaut while she stays fatally in its path, working out what to do. He is driven by raw fear. This shows the fallacy of the widely touted contrast between reason and emotion. Our fear or anger, so long as it is justified fear or anger, is rationality's friend. One is justified in being afraid or angry just in case one's fear or anger is grounded in facts which are such that if they make one afraid or angry one is thereby more likely to react to them in a measured way than if one measured the way for oneself. Naturally, as we already mentioned in Section 1, it is possible to perform an unjustified action out of justified fear or anger. Nevertheless the justification of one's fear or anger lies in the likelihood that one will not perform such an action.[31] Like all justification the justification is rational. If asked why one was fearful or angry one gives one's reasons.

So the issue of deliberation is a distraction. Exclusionary reasons are reasons that regulate the reasons for which one acts. The sense that they are paradoxical does not come of the thought that *deliberately* doing what reasons would have us do is ratio-

---

[31] Naturally in determining whether the action that one performs out of emotion is justified one must take account of the value of expressing that emotion. One should not assume that an emotion is justified only if it tends towards the performance of actions that would be justified *apart from* the value of expressing that emotion. The test is whether the actions would be justified *taking account of* the value of expressing the emotion. Thus our view of the justification of emotion is not reduced to a purely instrumentalist one. However some emotions are more instrumental than others. The justification of actions expressing grief or guilt, for example, is typically heavily affected by expressive value, whereas fearful or disgusted actions typically take more of their justification from facts other than the fact that they express fear and disgust, making those latter emotions more purely instrumental in their rational role.

nally superior to doing the same thing *intentionally but without thought.* Rather it comes of the thought that *intentionally* doing what reasons would have us do (whether with or without thought) is rationally superior to *accidentally* doing what reasons would have us do, where this means doing as those reasons would have one do but for some *other* reason. The question raised by the second rationalist myth is whether there is something fishy about accidentally doing as a reason would have one do. Is this not to defy or betray one's own rationality?[32]

To see why not one has to understand the true sense in which reasons are there to be followed, and the true sense in which rationality would have one act on the balance of reasons. What rationality strictly speaking asks is that one always act for an *undefeated* reason. The balance metaphor that is in common use focuses attention on cases in which reasons are defeated in ordinary conflicts with ordinary reasons for rival actions. In other words they are outweighed. But reasons that are excluded by exclusionary reasons are also defeated reasons. When rationality asks that one act on the balance of reasons, accordingly, it asks that one act for a reason that has neither been outweighed nor excluded. This formulation reveals that the reality is a kind of *tertium quid* between accident and intention. There is nothing wrong with doing as a reason would have one do but not for that reason (in other words, accidentally doing as the reason would have one do), so long as one does do it for *some* undefeated reason (and in that sense intentionally engages with reasons). This sharpens the test of justification that we proposed in Section 1. In Section 1 we said that to show that one's action was justified one must show that reasons did indeed support the course of action that one engaged in and that one acted for one of those supporting reasons. Now we state this biconditional test more technically but also more tersely. To show that one's action was justified is to show that one performed it for an undefeated reason. (And by the same token, to show that one's belief is justified is to show that one held it for an undefeated reason, to show that one's fear is justified is to show that one felt it for an undefeated reason, and so on.)

It may be objected that our talk of defeated reasons illicitly glosses over a major difference between reasons that are outweighed and those that are excluded. When a reason is outweighed, that actually makes a difference to what one ought to do. The correct action is the one supported by the outweighing reasons and vainly resisted by the outweighed ones. On the other hand, the objection goes, an excluded reason is, by our own testimony, merely one for which one ought not to act. The device of exclusion is simply an indirect device for making it the case that one does what one ought to do anyway, given the weighing of ordinary reasons. So understood, exclusionary reasons belong to the philosophy of means rather than ends.[33]

[32] This is the basis of Robert Paul Wolff's attack on authority in *In Defense of Anarchism*, 2nd edn. (Berkeley: University of California Press, 1998), ch. 1. Raz replies, in defence of exclusionary reasons and hence in defence of authority, in *The Authority of Law* (Oxford: Clarendon Press, 1979), ch. 1.

[33] This contrast between the philosophy of means and the philosophy of ends has dogged the so-called 'rule utilitarian' approach to moral reasoning. The great insight of rule utilitarians such as Mill

But the contrast here is a false one. The fact that a reason is defeated, whether by outweighing or by excluding, is entirely irrelevant to the question of whether it would be better to do as that reason would have one do. It would *always* be better to do as every reason would have one do, defeated or otherwise, thanks to the fact that every reason corresponds to a value. In a situation of rational conflict reasons pull one in two or more incompatible directions. Given the incompatibility it is not possible to realize the value in both actions. Tautologously, it is best to act for the best, or in other words, not to perform an action that realizes less value than some other action that one might have performed. But of course it would be better still if by some miraculous change in circumstances, as well as doing what the undefeated reasons would have one do, one also did as the defeated reasons would have one do. This applies as much to outweighed as to excluded reasons. Outweighed reasons do not lose their rational force in the sense of being any the less reasons for action, or in the sense that there is any less appeal than there would otherwise be to doing as they would have one do. The only effect of their being outweighed, like the effect of their being excluded, is to eliminate the rationality of acting for them.

6 THE FORCE OF REASONS

We introduced the category of exclusionary reasons by concentrating on cases in which by acting for a certain reason one risked failing to do as that very reason would have one do. In such cases the role of exclusionary reasons is to control counter-productivity. But not all exclusionary reasons exist to serve this purpose. Some are there to make it more likely that one will do what a certain reason would have one do, not by excluding *that* reason but by excluding some *other* reason, often but not always a conflicting reason. Once at the restaurant it is better not to tailor your choices from the menu according to price, for to do so is to miss out on the spirit of the evening. Likewise it is best not to give one's friends financial advice with a view to one's own profit, since in the process one betrays one's friendship. Examples of this type

---

and Sidgwick was that rules cannot be regarded as mere means to the fulfilment of some independently specified end. What one ought to do given the rule was not necessarily what one ought to do apart from the rule. But deep errors of the kind exposed in the next paragraph led to this insight being underestimated and to rule utilitarianism coming to be regarded as a kind of faint-hearted and untrustworthy variant on act utilitarianism. In reality, of the many things that are wrong with rule utilitarianism, most are owed to act utilitarianism. Rule utilitarianism's one great triumph was its breaking free in the respect just identified from its act utilitarian parentage. The issue is famously explored in John Rawls, 'Two Concepts of Rules', *Philosophical Review*, 64 (1955), 3. A refreshing recent reminder of the triumph is Brad Hooker's *Ideal Code, Real World* (Oxford: Clarendon Press, 2000).

abound. They differ from cases in which reasons are merely outweighed. Naturally one may have other reasons to try what happens to be the cheapest item on the menu, or to advise one's friend to make the investment that will also, as it happens, be to one's own profit. These reasons may outweigh the reasons to do the opposite. The point is that when this is the case one has other undefeated reasons to do as the excluded reasons would have one do. But one also has exclusionary reasons not to do it for the excluded reasons, in other words not to do it because of the cheapness or the profit as the case may be.

The classic case in which exclusionary reasons perform this function of fortifying reasons against their opponents is the case of *duty* (also known as obligation). To have a duty to do something is to have a reason to do it that, (i) does not depend for its existence on one's goals at the time, and (ii) is also a reason not to act for certain conflicting reasons. The first feature gives duties their *categorical* character. Categorical reasons are those that are not hostage to the prevailing personal goals of the agent to whom they apply. One's reasons to promise are often dependent on what one wants to achieve, but once one has promised the reason created by the promise does not bend to the changing winds of one's ambitions. But for our purposes it is the second feature that is more important. A reason to do something that is also a reason not to act for certain countervailing reasons is a special kind of reason that is labelled by Raz a *protected* reason. A protected reason is not merely the coincidental conjunction of a reason to act and an exclusionary reason not to act for certain countervailing reasons. The point is that the very same fact that is one's reason to act is also one's reason not to act for certain countervailing reasons. The very fact that one promised is both a reason to do what one promised and a reason not to be moved by the fact that doing it is now more inconvenient than it was when one promised. When a reason has this special protected structure we feel its force as *mandatory* force. We are *required* to do what the reason would have us do. Reasons can be categorical but not mandatory and mandatory but not categorical. Duties are the special and important case of reasons that are both (i) categorical and (ii) mandatory.

Imagine, for example, that a keen follower of the arts is offered the opportunity to stay in a friend's flat in Edinburgh during the Festival. It is a plum opportunity. Although he lives not far away in the Glasgow suburbs he has rarely had the opportunity to get to the Festival, let alone the chance to stay for several days. There are no strings attached and the keys will be left for him with a neighbour. The case for going strikes him as overwhelming. But alas our culture vulture, call him K, finds that his car won't start on the morning that he is due to set off and the local mechanic says that it will take a week to repair. It looks as if he will have to haul himself into town by bus in order to take the train to Edinburgh. All this hassle has only added to the stress that he was beginning to feel at the prospect of being away from work during a week when, as it turns out, a lot of important clients plan to come in. All things considered the whole idea is becoming more trouble than it is worth. There is no way he will enjoy the Festival under such stressful conditions. His enthusiasm for the arts is waning by the minute. So far so good. *K*'s reasons for seizing the opportunity may now be defeated. But things would be different if he had agreed to look after the flat in his friend's absence and because of this his friend, nervous of leaving his flat empty during Festival season, had not hired a paid house-sitter. In that case *K* is under an obligation to go to Edinburgh as he said he would. What this means is that he has a reason to go to Edinburgh, namely, that he agreed that he would, and this reason has two special features. Unlike his love of the arts, it is a reason which does not ebb and flow with his changing ambitions and moods and enthusiasms. That is to say, it is a categorical reason. What is more, it is not only a reason to go to Edinburgh but also a reason not to stay at home for the reason that going to Edinburgh would now be more awkward or disruptive than he imagined it would be at the time when he agreed. In other words, the reason is also mandatory.

Let us put the categorical character of duties or obligations on one side for a moment. It affects the conditions under which duties exist rather than the force that they have when they do exist. Our focus will be on their force. The force of duties has two dimensions. To put it another way, duties attack their opponents (the reasons for action with which they conflict) on two levels. First of all they have their ordinary weight as reasons for action. Secondly, they have a special, built-in exclusionary force that protects them against conflicting reasons for action, irrespective of the ordinary weight that either they or their opponents have. It might be thought that the second aspect renders the first redundant. Since duties exclude, what is there for them to outweigh? Since their opponents are already defeated why do they need to be defeated again? The simple answer is that the exclusionary force of duties need not be absolute. Typically, the fact that doing something is one's duty means that one cannot plead certain objections to doing it. Often one cannot plead inconvenience or irritation for example. In *K*'s case, where the obligation is assumed by agreement, *K* cannot plead the everyday inconveniences and irritations that he had reason to take account of at the time when he made the agreement. Yet other reasons against performance of the duty remain available to be acted upon. For instance, if *K*'s house was burgled on his first day in Edinburgh that might well be an unexcluded reason to return home. And if that other reason is weighty enough it may well justify him in abandoning the Edinburgh flat, thereby breaching his duty to his friend.

At this point everything depends on the weight of the reasons left in play, including the weight of the duty itself, now conceived as an ordinary reason for action. It should not be assumed that this reason wields a particularly great weight. Reasons can be mandatory yet trivial. They can be good at defeating by exclusion but poor at defeating by weight. One has a mandatory but not particularly weighty reason to thank one's hosts at the end of a party. The fact that one was tired at the end of the evening is no reason not to thank them, for that reason is certainly excluded. Yet a whole host of reasons, ranging from the fact that one's baby-sitter has just made an anxious call to the fact that one's host was deep in conversation, may well be sufficient to justify breach of the duty.

This creates an interesting linguistic ambiguity. In one sense of 'wrong', actions are regarded as wrong if and only if they are unjustified. The fact that there can be justified breaches of duty introduces, however, a different nuance of the word wrong. There can be actions that are wrong although justified and that create a special pressure for justification precisely because they are wrong. They are things which, all things considered, it was right for one to do and yet in doing them one did something wrong. In the latter inflection 'wrong' just means 'in violation of a requirement', leaving the question of justification open.[34]

It is often thought that wrongdoing in this latter sense is of special importance because of the traces it leaves on one's life. The point cannot be denied and yet it can be overstated. Every time one does not do what *any* reason would have one do, be that reason mandatory or otherwise, a trace is left on one's life. This is always in principle a matter of regret, for as we saw reasons do not lose their force as reasons merely because they are defeated.[35] Where ordinary reasons are concerned, however, this enduring force, like the original force of the reasons in question, is merely *advisory*. It may weigh heavily, but all the many and well-known reasons not to regret also weigh heavily and often justify one in getting on with one's life regardless.

Where one fails to do as a mandatory reason would have one do, however, the enduring force of the reason is different. It continues to be a mandatory reason even after one's failure. Just as some reasons not to perform the required action were excluded by virtue of the fact that the action was required, so some reasons to forget all about one's non-performance of the action afterwards are excluded. In other words, it is not so easy to brush aside the failure to do as a mandatory reason would have one do. It cannot just be a matter of pointing out that one would have a better life if one stopped crying over spilt milk. This is true *a fortiori* where the mandatory reason is also categorical, for here changes in one's goals do nothing to eliminate the reason's application, and this is true no less when the time for performance is past. One cannot escape the blemish on one's life by a simple change of direction. The rational pressure that this creates is the familiar pressure for various remedial and purgatory reactions, such as apology, payment of compensation, penance or punishment.[36] The

---

[34] Some people like to follow W. D. Ross, *The Right and the Good* (Oxford: Clarendon Press, 1930) in deploying the label 'prima-facie wrong' for actions that are wrong in the latter sense. Similarly they may speak of prima-facie duties, prima-facie reasons, and so on. This usage is misleading. Prima-facie reasons are just reasons, prima-facie duties are just duties, and correspondingly, prima-facie wrongs are just wrongs. For trenchant criticism of Ross's expression see John Searle, 'Prima Facie Obligations', in Joseph Raz (ed.), *Practical Reasoning* (Oxford: Oxford University Press, 1978).

[35] Bernard Williams's long flirtation with the view that reasons are 'internal' rather than 'external', leading him away from the position we adopted in Sects. 1–3 above, came primarily of the thought that the position we adopted leaves no room for regret. We hope to have demonstrated the opposite. See Williams, 'Ethical Consistency', in Williams, *Problems of the Self* (Cambridge: Cambridge University Press, 1973).

[36] The same forces create the rational pressure for retrospective emotions such as guilt, shame and regret. The moral importance of these emotions demonstrates the importance of the point made about the expressive (as well as instrumental) value of emotion in n. 31 above.

appropriateness of each of these reactions is, of course, subject to further conditions. Some, like punishment, may be unjustified if the action to which they are responses is a justified action. But be that as it may, all require violation of a duty.

We just spoke of ordinary (unprotected) reasons for action as having a merely advisory force as opposed to a mandatory force. Notice that this is not the same as saying that they are permissive. To be sure, there are some reasons which are such that it is permissible not to do what they would have one do, and supererogatory (or 'beyond the call of duty') to act for them. These represent another special type of reason involving exclusionary elements. They are not merely unprotected reasons but positively *exposed* reasons. We cannot explore their logical structure here, which is more complex still than that of a protected reason.[37] But it is worth mentioning them simply to warn against the familiar tendency to think that reason has only two voices, namely the raised voice of requirement and the conspiratorial whisper of permission. This legalistic contrast unfortunately misses out rationality's normal speaking voice. Normally reasons are simply our counsel and guide. All special exclusionary components apart, a reason merely supports the action (or belief, emotion, etc.) that it supports. In the absence of any exclusionary force, a reason to perform that action makes that action advisable. If there are conflicting reasons, the fact that one action is supported by weightier reasons than any of the others simply makes it the most advisable action. Perhaps I do a better job of my shopping if I go early on a Saturday, ahead of the crowds, rather than later in the day. And perhaps all else is equal: I am not inclined to have a lie-in, I have nothing else planned for either part of the day, and so on. If I go later I clearly do the less advisable thing. Rationally speaking, I err. I do the wrong thing in the first sense we mentioned. But I do nothing wrong in the second sense. It is not mandatory for me to go shopping at the most advisable time. For, so far as the story goes, I have no protected reason to do so.

A common assumption, we suspect, is that in cases like this a protected reason automatically swings into action at the final hurdle. Our conclusion, clearly, is that it is not rational for me to defer my shopping. So surely going shopping early is my only option *except on pain of irrationality*? I may be under no requirement to go shopping now if my reason to do so is defeated, but since it is undefeated and every conflicting reason is defeated, doesn't the general requirement to be rational, the general requirement to act for an undefeated reason, swing in and turn this into a mandatory reason at the end?

We doubt whether there is any such general requirement to be rational. Some people in some special roles, such as judges and other bureaucratic officials, are under duties to be rational in those roles. Moreover we all do have various duties connected with respect for our own rationality and that of others. Yet it is a long way from this to the conclusion that rationality itself is required of us across the board. But even if it is, notice, this claim confirms rather than denies the most important point we

---

[37] See Raz, 'Permission and Supererogation', *American Philosophical Quarterly*, 12 (1975), 161.

made in this section. To understand the idea of a general requirement to be rational one would need to understand what a requirement is that distinguishes it from an ordinary reason for action. It is tautologous to claim that we have reasons to be rational. But it is not tautologous to claim that we are subject to a *requirement* to be rational, or (what is more) that this is our *duty*. Since these claims are not tautologous there must be something more to requirements and duties than there is to ordinary reasons. This section explained what that 'something more' is. Requirements (or mandatory reasons) are protected reasons, meaning that they are reasons for action that are also reasons not to act for certain reasons that militate against that action. Duties (or obligations) are exactly the same, but with the extra feature that they are also categorical, meaning that they are not hostage to the prevailing personal goals of those who are subject to them.

One explanation of why people have been anxious about conceding the fundamental agent-neutrality of reasons has been the thought that if one person's reasons to act automatically yield reasons for everyone else to contribute to the first person's acting as those reasons would have her act, then our horizons are filled with extremely demanding duties.[38] After all, the thought goes, reasons are mandatory, and reasons to serve the goals of others depend on *their* goals, not on our own goals, and so appear to be categorical. Is there any room left, the question arises again, for me to have goals of my own?

We provided a partial response to this anxiety in Section 4. We said that there are limits to the extent to which it is possible for one person to contribute to another's pursuit of her goals, and that possibly, in view of the likelihood of overenthusiastic intervention, people should adopt, within limits, an agent-relative approach to life. Now we add another point. Even if one could do a lot to help another achieve her goals, it does not follow that one has a *duty* to do so. In fact there is no reason to think that even if another has a duty, whatever one can do to help them perform their duty is one's own duty.

The fact that one person's having a reason automatically gives all people reasons to contribute to the first person's doing as the reason would have him do does not entail that, if the first person's reason is a categorical mandatory reason, the reasons of all others involved are categorical and mandatory as well.[39] To establish that they are, one would need to show that relative to each person there are reasons not to act on certain countervailing reasons, including those that relate to that person's goals. This is very often a tall order. *A fortiori* it is a tall order to show that one has duties to contribute to everyone else's fulfilment of their goals. Naturally this does not mean that

[38] For powerful expression and critique of this anxiety see Samuel Scheffler, *Human Morality* (New York: Oxford University Press, 1992).

[39] Technically: One has reason to do whatever is sufficient to contribute to the satisfaction of any (other) reason, whether or not it be necessary. However one does not necessarily have a duty to do whatever is sufficient to contribute to the performance of any (other) duty. On these aspects of the logic of practical reasoning see Anthony Kenny, *Will, Freedom and Power* (Oxford: Blackwell, 1975), ch. 5. Throughout this paper we have broadly sided with Kenny's conclusions.

one never has such duties. It just means that the existence of all such duties depends on the arguments that support the existence of that particular duty, in other words, that support one person's contributing to the pursuit of another person's goals independently of her own and irrespective of at least some of the price that has to be paid.

7 THE ROLE OF CHOICE

So in two ways, we have discovered so far, rationality hems us in less than some have been accustomed to think. But so far we have neglected a third, and some may say more important, way in which rationality leaves our options open. We have said nothing of the role of incommensurability. Leaving aside for a moment the complicating effect of exclusionary reasons, two alternative actions are incommensurable if neither is supported by weightier reasons than the other and yet the reasons on the two sides are not equal in weight either.[40]

Suppose that a young woman, call her L, has two alternative activities before her this afternoon. She can go to a matinee screening of *Casablanca* with her aged father or she can have a game of tennis with her brother. Both are valuable pursuits. They will make different members of her family happy in different ways, will provide her with different kinds of relaxation, and will each contribute differently to her pursuit of her own goals, for she is both a film buff and an avid tennis player. Neither outing can be postponed, for *Casablanca* is being screened for one afternoon only and her brother can only get this afternoon off from work. What is she to do? It is not as if one alternative will bring greater pleasure than the other, or will make more interesting demands than the other, or will meet anyone's needs more than the other. There seems to be nothing to choose between them. L may conclude that the two alternatives are equally supported by reasons.

But this is not the only possible conclusion. If they are equally supported by reasons then any little extra reason on one side or the other will make it the case that that alternative is rationally superior. Suppose that L's father rings to tell her that *Casablanca* is to be screened in a new print. Assuming that the quality of the new print strengthens her reasons to see the film, albeit ever so slightly, L should presumably regard her father's call as settling the matter. She was previously unaware of one of the reasons that militated in favour of the film, and in her ignorance of that reason had calculated that all the other reasons were evenly balanced. Assuming she does not now regard that calculation as having been mistaken in any other way, she now knows that it was mistaken in one way, namely that one reason was omitted. If without that

---

[40] Raz, *The Morality of Freedom*, n. 24 above, at 322.

reason the two alternatives were equal in respect of rational support they cannot possibly be equal with that reason added.[41] Yet L may conclude that there is still nothing to choose between the alternatives. If she is right so to conclude, both before and after she is furnished with the extra information, the case is one of incommensurability. The reasons to go to the film with her father neither outweigh nor are outweighed by the reasons to play tennis with her brother. And yet they are not of equal weight either.

Reasons of equal weight are of little day-to-day importance in practical reasoning, for the necessary small adjustment to eliminate the equality almost always lies close at hand. Typically one can strengthen one's reasons to perform one action rather than the other simply by adjusting one's goals, so adjusting the value of personal engagement, which promptly tips the balance. At this point the reasons on the other side are defeated by weight. But things are different where the reasons on the two sides are not equal but incommensurable in weight. In cases of incommensurability adjustments to the reasons on one side of the argument do not necessarily lead to reason favouring that side. This means that incommensurability of reasons has far more day-to-day importance than equality of reasons, for the small adjustments that one can call upon to resolve the latter do nothing to resolve the former. That being so, the principle of rationality that commends action for an undefeated reason does not adjudicate as between the two alternatives. Still assuming no exclusionary complications, both actions are supported by undefeated reasons. Yet there is no point in trying to tip the balance for there is no balance to tip.

Some people offer what they take to be an alternative interpretation of L's predicament. They say that if the new, admittedly rationally relevant information (that the print of *Casablanca* is a fresh one) fails to tip the balance in favour of the film, then that shows that the two alternatives before L, while possibly not equal, were and remain *roughly* equal.[42] But what does this mean? We think that it probably means that L is somewhat uncertain of the weight to be attached to some or all of the various reasons involved, so that her conclusion before her father calls (that the reasons were equally balanced) was necessarily an approximation.[43] Yet, the story must continue, the additional reason provided by her father does not exhaust the margin of error in the original approximation, and therefore provides no reason for her to revise it. The alternatives remain roughly equal.

It may be that there are some cases like this.[44] But if so they are different from cases of incommensurability. The notion of rough equality belongs to the realm of indirect reasoning strategies, for it is a strategy (one may doubt whether it is a good one)

---

[41] This point (relied upon by Raz) is owed to John Mackie, 'The Third Theory of Law', *Philosophy and Public Affairs*, 7 (1978), 1, at 9.

[42] e.g. Derek Parfit, *Reasons and Persons*, n. 4 above, 430–2; James Griffin, *Well-Being* (Oxford: Clarendon Press, 1986) 80–1.

[43] For another possible explanation of what some writers may mean by rough equality, see Macklem, 'Choice and Value', n. 29 above, where the position outlined in the text is also further explored.

[44] We say 'it may be' because we disagree with each other here.

designed to cope with uncertainty about the weight of reasons. Given the uncertainty, so the story goes, one has an exclusionary reason not to act for very small additional reasons in favour of one side. But in cases of incommensurability there is no reason not to act for the very small additional reasons that may be brought to bear in the vain hope of resolving the conflict by rational means. One may act for these reasons to one's heart's content but one will still be no closer to a decisive rational direction. The rival paths will still both be supported by undefeated reasons and it will still be impeccably rational to take either.

Although we are both believers in the pervasive role of incommensurabilities in rational life this is not the place to defend that belief. However it is important to appreciate its significance. One may ask why the thought of incommensurability makes people so edgy. Even among those who have a duty to be rational, or in other words, a duty to act for an undefeated reason, it is not clear why any should be thought to have a duty, or even a reason, never to act *against* an undefeated reason.[45] Perhaps the feeling that people have such a reason is a further reflection of the perniciousness of the rationalist myths that we referred to in Section 5. These myths were the work of those who read into rationality a promise of security against chance, luck, arbitrariness. The will is regarded as an arbitrary factor in need of rational control. But the will is not arbitrary in any worrying sense so long as it always responds to undefeated reasons. This condition is amply met in normal cases of incommensurability in which reasons on both sides are undefeated. Rationality led one as far as it promised to do by leading one to this situation. It promised no more. It was merely a bizarre unfounded expectation of those frightened by the human condition that it would lead one further and tell one which way to choose given that both choices were already *ex hypothesi* rationally defensible.

It could be replied that the role of choice is already amply accommodated by the considerations we adduced earlier. We already made space for people to have their different goals and for this to affect what they ought to do. But the role of will that we introduce here is more radical. It explains not only how we bring our goals to bear on what we ought to do but how we are ever set free enough to acquire those goals in the first place. So far as the earlier arguments were concerned our goals exerted rational pressure on us, justifying some courses of action that would not have been justified without them and correspondingly withdrawing justification from others. But in the normal situations of incommensurability mentioned in this section both alternatives are *ex hypothesi* justified, and one's choices do not tip the rational balance. Rather they send one in one direction rather than the other without making it a matter of *rational* determination that one went that way.

---

[45] Much work in jurisprudence, asserting or denying the existence of 'right answers in hard cases', has been based on the assumption that judges do have such a reason, or even such a duty. Occasionally public expectation may generate such a reason, but by and large, in our view, judges have nothing to fear in the fact that they did not defeat the reasons against their decision, so long as they gave undefeated reasons for their decision.

We just spoke of 'normal situations of incommensurability' as opening up our options. This was to leave space for a special class of cases in which the effect of incommensurability is, disturbingly, reversed. Rather than offering us more than one justified way forward, incommensurability here denies us any justified way forward and relegates us to the situation in which the best we can hope for is an excuse. The situation we have in mind is a special case in which the conflict of incommensurables is a conflict between two or more *protected* reasons. The basic problem is that the reasons are protected against each other. Each excludes the other from consideration. When this happens the normal effect is that the conflict is decided by the weight of the reasons *qua* exclusionary. The question is: which of the two reasons not to act for a reason is the weightier? But suppose the two exclusionary reasons are themselves incommensurable. In that case neither defeats the other. Thus neither prevents the other from exerting its exclusionary force. Thus both of the reasons for action are defeated by being excluded. Thus there is no way to act for an undefeated reason. This is the core case of what is colloquially known as a moral dilemma. Many things referred to as moral dilemmas do not quite reach this pitch of tragedy. But all carry intimations of it. All remind us that the supposed security of rationality is not only compromised in the direction of giving us all elbow room to follow our wills, but occasionally is also compromised in the direction of locking us into a situation in which, whatever our virtues, we are doomed to act against the basic maxims of rationality.[46]

When the concentration camp guard offered Sophie the choice between sending both of her children to their deaths and choosing which child to save, his scheme was to imperil her rationality in just the way that we have described. He hoped that by facing her with two conflicting and mutually exclusionary incommensurable duties towards her children, namely, the duty to protect them and the duty not to display more love for one than for the other, he would leave her in the situation of having no justified alternative before her, and hence with her rationality demeaned (in addition to all the other horrors that she will experience). Most readers of *Sophie's Choice* believe that the guard failed in his plan. Sophie was justified in saving one child while condemning the other to death. Either this was not a display of more love for the saved child, most readers think, or the duty not to display more love for one child than the other was outweighed by the duty to protect. Of course this leaves Sophie in the rational predicament that we described in Section 6. She still was in breach of one of her duties and the scars of this remain with her.[47] You may say that this is bad enough. But it falls short of the moral destruction that the guard aspired to. He aimed

---

[46] We suspect that these are the cases that Williams means to label 'tragic' in 'Conflicts of Values', in Williams, *Moral Luck*, n. 30 above, at 74, although his remarks are open to more than one interpretation.

[47] Some hold that the very presence of such scars, if they are rational, must reflect the presence of some incommensurability. For excellent discussion which brings out both the element of truth and the element of falsity in this view, see Jonathan Dancy, *Moral Reasons* (Oxford: Blackwell, 1993) 120 ff.

not only to damage Sophie as a parent but to damage her as a rational human being by putting her in a situation in which nothing she could do would be justified.

8 THE STANDARD OF REASONABLENESS

A number of contemporary moral philosophers distinguish rationality from something else called reasonableness.[48] As they describe it, the standard of reasonableness is more accommodating than rationality, for it leaves latitude for differences of opinion, for rival views of what it is that rationality demands. It must be said that by and large it is obscure in these views what it is about rationality that the more accommodating test of reasonableness is needed in order to escape. All too often it seems that these views rely on a parody of rationality, in which the rational person is one who has developed just one aspect of her rational functioning at the expense of all others. On this picture the rational person is a single-minded deliberator about everything, or a pure instrumentalist who uncritically takes the value of her goals for granted and pursues them ruthlessly, or a high-minded person of principle who scrupulously abandons all partiality. We agree that it is possible to use the word rational to pick out these narrow and limited abilities, but the abilities so picked out are indeed narrow and limited and the mastery of one at the expense of the others is not rationality in any sense in which that could constitute a valid complete ideal for human agents. Properly understood, rationality is just what we have described in this chapter. It is exactly the same as reasonableness. As we have urged, it is simply the capacity and propensity to act (think, feel, etc.) only and always for undefeated reasons. As an ideal the reasonable person, or the rational person (as she might just as well be called) is the person who fully exemplifies this capacity and propensity, and does so in her beliefs, emotions, attitudes, actions, and so on. Wherever there are reasons, she does not defy their force.

On this view 'reasonable' means much the same as 'justified'. A reasonable action is a justified action, a reasonable belief is a justified belief, a reasonable emotion is a justified emotion, and so on. By the same token, a reasonable person is no less and no more than a person who is justified in whatever aspects of her life call for justification. In the law, the standard of the reasonable person is sometimes used to test beliefs, and the test of reasonableness is then the test of justification. It is true, as we said in Section 1, that acting on the strength of a justified belief is not the same thing as acting justifiably where that belief is false. Such an action is not justified but excused. It

---

[48] John Rawls, 'Kantian Constructivism in Moral Theory', in *Journal of Philosophy*, 77 (1980), 515; Scanlon, *What We Owe to Each Other*, n. 13 above, 22–33.

may be that the idea that an excused action is nevertheless the action of a reasonable person is what has given credence to the idea that a standard of reasonableness offers greater latitude than the standard of rationality. It may be that this has led some to conclude that rationality is what justifies while reasonableness excuses. Yet this is a mistake. The only thing that can excuse is a justification. That is to say, the justification of one human response, for example, a belief or emotion, is what excuses another human response, normally an action. The standard of the reasonable person is one of justification throughout. It is the standard of rationality, a standard that one meets if one has undefeated reasons and responds to those reasons, be it in one's beliefs, or emotions, or attitudes, or actions, as the case may be.

CHAPTER 12

RIGHTS

F. M. KAMM

RIGHTS are most often thought of as claims to something or alternatively as protected options to act. By 'claim', I do not mean that anyone does (or even is permitted to) engage in the act of claiming; only that someone is entitled to something. That someone has a right can provide a unique reason for action on the part of the rightholder or others. For example, that someone has a right to something can be a reason for according it to him independent of other reasons, such as that it would produce good or satisfy a preference. Furthermore, this reason seems to function as an exclusionary or silencing reason. That is, it excludes our considering certain other factors that would ordinarily be reasons. For example, if someone has a right to something, that someone else would get some pleasure from having it is irrelevant, not merely outweighed. It is because rights silence many other prima facie reasons that they come close to putting an end to an argument about what to do. However, if not all considerations are silenced by rights, they need not be bottomlines.[1] In addition, a right is a distinctive reason that has correlated with it (or even gives rise to) a duty in someone. (By contrast, if a someone will suffer if I do not help him, that is a distinctive reason to help, but it may not give rise to a duty.) Importantly, this duty is owed *to* the rightholder in particular. Not all duties we have are owed to particular people. Individual persons who are conscious agents are typical bearers of rights. However, infants are not agents and yet they are commonly thought to have rights. Possibly, groups which are not agents also have rights.[2] Moral rights are said to exist indepen-

---

[1] For the idea of exclusionary reasons see Joseph Raz's *The Morality of Freedom* (*MF*) (Oxford: Oxford University Press, 1986).

[2] Consider the following case as possible intuitive support for such group rights: suppose members of a group (who identified with the group) have been killed unjustly because they were members of the group. They have no direct family descendants. Had they or their descendants lived on, they would have

dent of any legal system; one shows they exist by moral argument. A certain class of these, human rights, tell us what is owed to human persons just in virtue of their being human persons. Legal rights depend on the legal system, but may, in some way, be related to moral rights. In this article, I shall first consider certain conceptual aspects of rights (both moral and legal) and then move to more substantive issues about the ground of rights, conflict between rights and promoting goods, and conflict among rights.

1 CONCEPTUAL BASICS

The most famous conceptual scheme of rights is due to Hohfeld.[3] His typology includes four types of rights. The first is a claim-right held by person *A* against another person *B*. It is (on Hohfeld's view) equivalent to (i.e. it exists if and only if) *B* has a duty to *A* in respect of the content of the claim, for example, that he be off *A*'s property. The claim-right can be negative (to non-interference) or positive (to some contribution). The right is directional, that is, directed towards someone (possibly many people), and entails that the latter have a correlative and directional duty to the rightholder. Hence, if *B* owes something to *A* and *B* fails in his duty, he may not merely act wrongly, he may *wrong A*. No one else may have any duty to *A*, for example, to see to it that *B* performs his duty to *A*, or even not to interfere with what *A* has from *B*. In virtue of this, a claim-right that *A* has need *not* involve what is known as a restriction (or constraint) on interference by (any) others with that to which *A* has a claim.

As Joel Feinberg notes,[4] in a world without rights held by people, there could still be duties; not all duties to do something for *A* are duties (owed) to *A* correlative to rights held by *A*. (Instead, I might have a duty correlative to God's right that I do something for *A*.) If I fail in this duty, I may have done something wrong. I may even have treated *A* incorrectly in the light of his properties, affecting him badly. But I could do all this without wronging *A* (even if he is the object of the duty), because it is not to him that I owed performance of the duty. The right in *A* adds the idea of

had a right to compensation for persecution. Would it be unreasonable to argue that the group to which they belonged has a right to receive the compensation (just as familial descendants would have) and a duty to use it for other group members? This is a case in which the compensation is owed to the group, it is not merely a matter of its being just that they get a fair share of money. For the group might be very well off, having more than its share of goods. Indeed, if they did not have a right to the money, it would be morally wrong to give it to them, since the money would be better spent on others.

  [3] In *Fundamental Legal Conceptions* (New Haven, Conn.: Yale University Press, 1923).
  [4] In 'The Nature and Value of Rights', *Journal of Value Inquiry*, 4 (1970).

owing something to A (though it may add more than this); A's holding the debt of B in some way.[5] This, I shall say, makes A the subject of the duty as well.

As Judith Thomson emphasizes,[6] it is possible that B ought not carry out his duty x to A (correlative to A's right), in virtue, for example, of his having more important duties to others.[7] Further, the truth of this need not be a reason to believe that B has no duty x to A in the circumstances, and A has no correlative right. That is, we need not think of A's 'right to x from B' as a specified 'right to x from B, except when m, n, o, . . .'. Instead, A's general right to x may be *non-absolute*, and so infringeable, but it is because he still has this right in circumstances m, n, o that he may be owed compensation if the right is infringed. Hence, it is not that one has a right only if someone ought to grant it.[8]

Thomson takes the view that if we may infringe someone's right, we have not wronged her. It is only in violating a right (i.e. not granting it when we ought to) that we have wronged someone. But is it not possible to wrong someone in the course of doing what we ought to do? For example, suppose A has a right that I not lie to him, but I ought to in order to save B's life. It seems to me that I have wronged A, though I infringe and do not violate his right. This suggests that it may be possible to permissibly wrong someone.

In part in virtue of their infringeability, Thomson suggests, it is conceptually part of the idea of a right that it implies subsidiary duties besides the duty strictly correlative to it: if one does not carry out the correlative duty, one has a duty to either seek release from the rightholder or provide compensation to him. These three are not equally good alternatives, however, as the performance of the duty strictly correlative has pride of place.[9] It is also possible (given, for example, conflicts with other overriding rights or duties) that one also ought not carry out any of the subsidiary duties. In sum, there is no necessary conceptual connection between there being a right and its being true that, as a bottom line, something ought to be done in respect of the rightholder.

[5] Doctors were very willing to think of themselves as having duties and their patients as being the object of the duty. However, they resisted the idea of patients having claim-rights against them, and this implies they resisted the idea of having a duty (owed) to the patient.

[6] In *The Realm of Rights* (Cambridge, Mass.: Harvard University Press, 1990).

[7] Duties correlative to rights might also be overridden by supererogatory acts. On this, see my 'Supererogation and Obligation', *Journal of Philosophy* (Mar. 1985), and below.

[8] Judith Thomson distinguished between infringing a right (permissible) and violating a right (impermissible). I shall also distinguish between permissibly transgressing a right (infringing) and impermissibly transgressing a right (violating). So 'transgressing' is neutral as between the permissible and the impermissible. Also note that violating a right is different from violating a person. The latter is some sort of physical intrusion, permissible or impermissible. For Thomson's distinction, see 'Ruminations on Right', reprinted in the collection of her essays, *Rights, Restitution and Risk: Essays in Moral Theory*, ed. W. A. Parent (Cambridge, Mass.: Harvard University Press, 1986) and also in her *The Realm of Rights*.

[9] Given that this is Thomson's view (e.g. p. 94 n. 7), it is odd that she claims (p. 96) in *The Realm of Rights* that if one pays compensation, it is inappropriate to feel guilt at not having carried out the duty strictly correlative to the right. Might not guilt be appropriate because one has not carried out that part of the right whose fulfilment has pride of place?

Rights might be nonabsolute and still be so-called trumps over utility, if they are overridden by factors other than utility.[10] But I doubt that all rights—rather than just the most important human rights—are not overrideable by utility considerations sometimes. And even the most important human rights may have utility thresholds that are just extremely high. If so, many rights will not be trumps over utility as well as being nonabsolute for other reasons.

Hohfeld's second class of rights are the privileges. *A* has a privilege relative to *B* with respect to *x*, if he has no duty to *B* with respect to *x*. So he is at liberty relative to *B* with respect to *x*; this is usually understood as involving a bilateral option, a choice to do or not do something with respect to *x*. (While Hohfeld did not speak of 'liberty to do', it is common to extend the notion of a bilateral option so that it applies to actions *per se*.) But *A*'s liberty does not entail a duty on the part of anyone not to interfere with his actions with respect to *x*. (Liberties may be the Hobbesian conception of rights.) A liberty to do, in the sense that involves a bilateral choice and some claim to non-interference with either choice, would be what Thomson refers to as a 'cluster right.' Hart notes[11] that the claims often associated with liberties to do do not entail duties strictly correlative to the object of the liberty. I may be at liberty to look at you, but you have no duty to let me look at you if you may permissibly put up a screen in front of you. The duty you have related to my liberty is one you may also have apart from my liberty, for example, not to knock out my eyes (as a way of interfering with my liberty to look at you).

Is the idea of a liberty right also the idea behind what moral philosophers refer to as 'prerogatives?' (For example, Samuel Scheffler[12] speaks of having a prerogative not to promote the good that is *not*, however, accompanied by a constraint on anyone from forcing one to promote the good.) Not quite, for notice that such a prerogative implies that it is morally permissible to (i.e. it is not morally wrong to) not promote the good. By contrast, the idea of having a liberty right (or a claim-right) is not so strong, as there may be moral or legal rights to do what is morally wrong That is, while I have no duty to you to do something, it would still be wrong of me not to do it.

Finally, in Hohfeld's scheme, there are the rights that are powers to alter the rights of oneself and others, and the rights that are immunities from the powers of others to alter one's rights. Hence, these are meta rights.

---

[10] I owe this point to David Enoch.

[11] In 'Bentham on Legal Rights', *Oxford Essays in Jurisprudence: Second Series*, ed. A. W. B. Simpson (Oxford: Oxford University Press, 1973).

[12] In Samuel Scheffler, *The Rejection of Consequentialism* (Oxford: Oxford University Press, 1986).

2 THEORIES OF RIGHTS AND CORRELATED DUTIES

Are rights prior in any sense to their correlative duties so that they are the ground of duties? Hohfeld's view is that a claim-right is equivalent to a directed duty. This 'if and only if' relation is still compatible with rights giving rise to duties. On Thomson's view, a claim-right just *is* a directed duty, and this involves the denial of a priority relation. Suppose either of these views were true. Then, if one had duties to oneself, one would have a right against oneself. But this is implausible. Does not the fact that duties to oneself are at least possible but rights against oneself are not, argue against equating duties owed to A with A's rights? (One possible way to respond to this challenge is to analyse duties *to* oneself as really duties that *are proper responses to* the characteristics one has, for example, rational humanity. Only in that sense are they 'owed' to oneself. By contrast, my owing to another person is owing to *him* (not merely owing a response to his characteristics, even if it is in virtue of these that I owe something to him). Hence, he can hold the debt against me in a way I cannot hold a debt against myself when I have a duty to myself.) Even if duties to oneself without rights were directed to the person in the right way, they would not show that rights are prior to and give rise to directed duties.

Perhaps the following thought experiment will help with this issue. Imagine a one-person world with A in it. It would make sense, I think, to say that A had rights, in the sense that the characteristics he has make it the case that if someone else, B, existed, B would have a duty to A not to treat him in certain ways. Though we conceptualize the right as involving a potential directed duty, its source in characteristics of A leads us to think of A's right as prior. Further, in a one-person world with A as a rightbearer, it would not make sense to say that anyone *actually* had duties to A. Suppose duties owed to C were based not on characteristics of C but rather on characteristics of the dutyholder D. For example, suppose D is a criminal and his punishment is to obey the next perfect stranger who appears (not his victim). Hence, if C were the next person to exist, he would have a right against D that stems from D's characteristics that give him a directed duty.[13] In this case, I think it makes sense to think of the directed duty giving rise to the right, because it is properties of the dutyholder that give rise to the duty/right pair. In the world without C, does D have a duty? I do not think so. So there is a sense in which rights can exist without anyone actually having the directed duties to which they give rise, and though directed duties can give rise to rights, they will not exist if an actual rightbearer does not.[14]

[13] Raz says rights give rise to duties; duties do not give rise to rights. But in this case, a duty does seem to give rise to a right.

[14] In addition, if a general right is connected with several directed duties (each of which involves a particular correlated right), then at least the general right seems prior to the duties. That rights can give rise to new duties, Joseph Raz sees as the dynamic character of rights. See *MF*, 171.

If one thinks that rights involve (at least potentially, even if they are not reducible to) duties owed to someone, then there is essential reference to someone other than the agent of the duty in the duty. This other person is the rightholder. Some theories of rights focus on some characteristic of the rightholder (e.g. his interests) that gives rise to the specific right/duty set. Other theories of rights focus on a power—either to choose or to make claims—that the rightholder is said to have in addition to his being the subject of a directed duty. Let us briefly consider some of these theories.

2.1 Beneficiary and Choice Theories

According to Bentham, to have a right is to be the intended *beneficiary* of a duty.[15] Hart famously raised the third-party beneficiary cases as an objection to this view. For example, I can have a right that you take care of my mother. My mother is the intended beneficiary, but I have the right against you, and you owe the duty (whose object is my mother) to me. (I am the subject.)[16] The mark of my having the right, Hart says, is that my choice is a valid ground for determining whether you should give the aid to my mother; for example, I can waive the right and release you from the duty. The mark of my having the right is not that I will be benefited by its being carried out. Herein lies the origin of Hart's Choice Theory of Rights.

It is worth noting several things about the third-party beneficiary case. (1) We can agree that the mother can *set the condition* on being aided. That is, if she does not wish to be aided, the person who owes it to me to aid her may not do so. This, however, is consistent with her not having the right; it is not the same as her waiving or cancelling the right. Hence her setting the condition on aid is not enough to show that my mother, not I, has the right to her being cared for. Yet, when Hart discusses welfare rights,[17] he locates a right in the recipient of the welfare simply because the recipient sets the conditions for the receipt of welfare, that is, he must petition to have the right acted on, even though he cannot cancel the right. But if power to set the conditions were sufficient evidence of having a right, my mother would have one, too, in the third-party case. It seems that in the case of the welfare rights, those who do not claim the welfare do not merely set conditions on others granting the right. They waive their right. But they do not thereby alienate it, should they choose to exercise it on another occasion. (2) Important evidence that it is not my mother who has the right is that if I decide to release the agent from his duty, my mother has no power to stand in the way of his being released. However, what if my mother got only a derivative right contingent on my right? My waiver would give me a power to revoke her right

---

[15] This obviously must presuppose something other than an act-utilitarian theory of duties.
[16] In 'Bentham on Legal Rights'.
[17] 'Bentham on Legal Rights'.

and so would be the dominant right. Yet it would not be the only right. But if she had such a right, why is she unable to singlehandedly waive the right (as I can) rather than merely set conditions for its being acted on? (3) It might be said that I too am an intended beneficiary—not just an unintended beneficiary—of the right. This is because my *interest* (in the sense of what is in my interest) in being able to make contracts so that I get what I want is in question. (This interest can be at stake and satisfied, even if this means that other interests of mine are thereby set back.) Still, since my mother's interests are also aimed at, how can an intended beneficiary theory decide whether I or my mother is the rightholder? At the very least, being an intended beneficiary is not sufficient for saying who has a right, unless we both have rights. But if we both have rights, we should again consider why my waiver alone (and only my waiver) is sufficient to release the agent from his duty. (4) If I am also an intended beneficiary, this might be used to help show that it is my right, not my mother's. Suppose my desire for my mother's welfare is weak, I don't want it very much. Then it is only weakly in my interest that a contract backing a weak desire be fulfilled. Suppose my mother's interest in her welfare, by contrast, is strong as her life is at stake in getting the aid. Suppose the right that she be aided comes in conflict with a quite strong, unrelated right or with a quite significant good. Intuitively, I believe, given the facts of the case, the right could be easily overridden. This is likely to be true only if the stringency of the right reflects my weak interests rather than her strong interest. (But suppose whose interest is reflected in the right's stringency does not always signal whose right it is, so that I could have a strong right because of someone else's strong interests. Could it be that my weak interest gives my mother a weak right when her interest is strong?)

More generally, Hart's Choice Theory raises several questions. (*a*) He believes that inalienable rights present a problem for his theory and will have to be dealt with as immunities from the power of others to change one's status, not as protected choices of the rightholder to waive or demand fulfilment of his right. But it is possible to *waive* even an inalienable right.[18] For example, I may waive, on a given occasion, my right to speak even if I cannot alienate my right to speak. So perhaps inalienable rights are not really a problem for Hart, though non-waivable ones might be. (*b*) A third party, not I, may have the power to relieve someone of his duty to me. But that does not show that the duty is not owed *to me* but rather is owed to the third party who can release him.[19] (*c*) Perhaps it is the power to 'claim' in the sense of 'insist on' the right, rather than the power to waive it, that is crucial. Joel Feinberg emphasizes such an activity of claiming.[20] But claiming (like waiving) is a separate act; it is possible that I might have a right and correlatively someone owes me something, and yet I have no right to insist on getting it.

---

[18] See Joel Feinberg, 'Euthanasia and the Inalienable Right to Life', *Philosophy & Public Affairs*, 7 (1978).

[19] This point was raised by Peter Graham.

[20] In 'The Nature and Value of Rights'.

2.2 Interest Theory and Status-as-a-Person Theory

1. Joseph Raz offers an Interest Theory of Rights. In one account of it, he says some entity has a right if and only if some interest (i.e. aspect of the well-being) of the entity (which is capable of being a rightholder) is sufficient to ground a duty.[21] (Raz contends that a right based on an aspect of someone's well-being need not contribute to his overall well-being. Also, he says, it is possible that the interest that gives rise to the right is not represented in that to which someone specifically has a right. So, for example, I may have a right to my shirt because it is in my interest to have personal property, even if my interest in having my shirt specifically is not strong enough to generate a right to it. The right to the shirt is then a derivative right from a more general right to property.) Raz also offers a second, slightly different account of rights: there is a right if and only if some interest (i.e., aspect of well-being) of some entity capable of being a rightholder is sufficient to ground a duty *to care for and promote the interest in a significant way*.[22]

The first and second accounts have different implications. For example, suppose I see that you have a very high level of well-being. That may be sufficient to ground a duty in me to see that your well-being does not improve further (for reasons of equality with others, or because you do not deserve so much well-being). On the first (but not the second) account of rights, you would have a right that I carry out this duty, but that hardly seems true. The first account differs from Bentham's in that Bentham requires that the rightholder be a 'beneficiary'. Only Raz's second account incorporates this element.

The second account, however, implies that if you are very sick, and this is sufficient to give me a duty to help you in some significant way, you have a right that I help you. But, some might suggest that I have a duty to help you—I morally must help you—without your having a right that I do so. Then there would be a duty grounded in your interest alone, and yet you would have no right. For example, if I have a duty to help you by praying for your recovery, you might still not have a right that I relate to God in this particular way. Indeed, we may agree that *I have a duty* to save someone from drowning and this is merely because it would be greatly in her interest to be saved. But to say she has a right to be saved says more than this: it implies that I have *a duty to her* (as subject). In the absence of a correlative right, the person who drowns loses out because I did not do my duty, but she has no more (or less) ground for complaint

[21] *MF*, 166. Raz affiliates himself with a broadly Benthamite theory of rights. However, note that Bentham's theory does not require that an interest in the beneficiary be sufficient for a duty in order that there be a right even if the right is lodged in the beneficiary. Bentham's theory leaves it open that *A*'s directive that *B* promote *C*'s interest is necessary—in addition to *C*'s interest—to give rise to *C*'s right (on the assumption the theory is not wrong to locate the right in *C*). So Raz's theory seems to ignore the possibility that an agent can, in virtue of having a certain power, endow someone with a right, assuming the recipient has the properties which make him capable of being a rightholder at all. Another contrast with Bentham will be noted in the text.

[22] *MF*, 183.

against my failure to respond than anyone else has. We might say that a right would give someone in particular a moral entitlement to the aid being given. The fact that someone has a duty stemming from another's interest gives no one in particular a moral entitlement to his fulfilling the duty.

These problems arise, I believe, because in both accounts of rights that Raz offers the duty is not described as a directed duty owed to the person with the right. (Even the second account does not say we owe promotion of someone's interest *to him*.) When Raz (and also Feinberg) claim that a right is more than a correlative duty, neither, unlike Hohfeld and Thomson, has in mind a *directed* duty, one owed to someone. (Indeed, when Feinberg contrasts a right with a duty, he contrasts a duty that *is* owed to someone with other duties.[23] His defence of the view that rights are prior to correlative duties is weak, therefore.)

Raz can offer additional reasons for thinking that a right is more than even a directed duty based on an interest in the rightholder. He points to what he thinks is the dynamic character of rights, that is, they can give rise to new duties that do not now exist though we know the right exists. For example, if someone has a right to education, this may give rise, he thinks, to many duties (not just one) correlative to it; which ones it does give rise to may vary with time and place. Rights can be dynamic in this way when the object of the right is more general than the specific duties it generates. (This is connected to Raz's point that not all ways in which the interest can be promoted give rise to duties.) But notice that when the general right gives rise to these duties, it seems it will simultaneously give rise to subsidiary rights that *are* strictly correlative to (and, for all that the dynamic character of rights implies, may be no more than) the directed duties.

2. I have suggested that there might be duties that your interest is sufficient to give rise to in me without your thereby having a right. It is also possible, I think, for there to be rights in someone where there is no interest (aspect of well-being) of his sufficient to give rise to a duty (even derivatively). If I simply endow you with the right to some of my money, your interest in having the money played no role, let alone a sufficient role, in my now having a duty to give you my money. (This leaves it open, that it may be in my interest to have the power to endow you with a right, but it is not an interest of yours which the right I endow you with serves, even indirectly in the way a right to your shirt serves your interest in personal property generally.) This is consistent with it being in your interest to have a right (though the interest in having a right also played no role in generating your right). It is even consistent with the possibility that you could have no right that was not in some way in your interest. Yet, in fact, I do not believe it is true that you could have no right that was not in your interest in some way. I might endow you with a right to do something (a privilege relative to me plus a claim against me to non-interference), though it serves no interest of yours to have it. For example, I give you a nontransferable right to set off a nuclear

---

[23] 'The Nature and Value of Rights'.

weapon when you are angry. Here are other examples of rights that do not arise from the interest of the rightholder (even if, as a side-effect, they serve his interests): a parent might have a right to obedience from his child, a priest may have a right to respect from his followers.

Raz himself says that the stringency of a right can outdistance the importance of the interest that it most directly protects. In some cases, he thinks this is because the interests which give rise to a right or which determine the stringency of the right are not necessarily the interests of the person whom the right specifically protects. He says:[24] 'The main reason for the mismatch between the importance of the right and its contribution to the rightholder's well-being is the fact that part of the justifying reason for the right is its contribution to the common good'. An example is the importance of a journalist's right to speech, which is mostly, he thinks, a function of the interests of his audience.

It is not clear that his account of the importance of a right outstripping the interest it directly protects in the case of the journalist is consistent with his two accounts of the relation between rights and interests. They say that a right is present when an interest of the rightholder is *sufficient* to give rise to a duty. But if the satisfaction of interests of others is the reason why the journalist gets a right to have his interest protected, his interest is *not sufficient* to give rise to the duty of non-interference with his speech. Possibly the journalist's interest in writing is sufficient to give rise to a weak right, but the great stringency of the right is not a function of the interest which gives rise to it. But Raz speaks of the interests of others (in a case like the journalist) as 'part of the justifying reason' for the right (not just for its stringency). A Razian might instead argue that an interest in the person whose right it is gives rise to the right and some other factor accounts for the stringency of the right.[25] I shall not explore this possibility since I am concerned to argue that rights and their stringency could reflect something other than interests.

In the case of many legal rights, someone's having a right may arise entirely because this serves the interests of others rather than his interests. For example, it is theoretically possible for a policeman to have a right to use a gun in defence of everyone except himself. An intelligent being may have the (legal and moral) right to protect animals simply out of concern for the animals' interests not his own.

Could some rights be justified completely independently of serving any being's interests, let alone the interests of the rightholder? The example of the priest who has a right to respect might be one. Persons might have a right to treatment as equals—an essentially comparative right—without our duty to them being based on their interests. Rather, I would say, this right is based on their nature as persons not necessarily related to any aspect of their well-being. Even if it turns out to be in their interest to have this nature, the right derives from their nature not their interest in having

---

[24] In 'Rights and Individual Well-Being', *Ethics in the Public Domain* (New York: Oxford University Press, 1994), 55.
[25] David Enoch's suggestion.

it. A person's right to treatment as an equal may even lead to levelling down (i.e. taking away from some without giving to others) against anyone's well-being. If there were an independent 'dignitary interest' in being treated as an equal (i.e. because it promotes some aspect of psychological well-being), it is not because this treatment serves that interest that a person has a right to it. It may simply be fitting to treat a person no differently from anyone else. As another example, the right to punish, in a retributive theory, is justified independently of concern for anyone's interest: it may be a burden to punish others, it is a burden to them to be punished, and it may not be expected to do society good. Yet, we may have a right to see to it that someone receives what he deserves, as a way of taking human agency seriously.[26]

Finally, in this vein, consider another example Raz gives that involves an ordinary citizen's right to free speech. He claims it is more important than her interest in speaking freely that it protects. His account of this is that she (not another) has a strong interest in benefiting from the free speech of others. Indeed, Raz claims that his own interests would be better served by living in a society where others have a right to free speech and he lacks it than in a society where he has the right and others lack it. In this case, it is not as producer of speech but as beneficiary of it that one's interests are most important. An implication of this view is that a given person has the strong right to speak only because it would not be possible to deny it to him without denying it to others as well. The Interest Theory requires the non-separable allocation of a strong right of free speech in order to account for its strength in any given person. For if they were separable, the really strong right would be the right to have others be free to speak.[27]

By contrast, if we do not remain wedded to an interest theory of rights, we can recognize that any given person's interest in speaking freely is not great, and yet still argue that he has a strong right to free speech, even when its strength is independent of any other interest of his or anyone else's that it (directly or indirectly) serves. The right to speak may simply be the only appropriate way to treat people with minds of their own and the capacity to use means to express it. Even if their interests would be set back only slightly by interfering with their free speech, the permissibility of doing so (i.e. the absence of their having a right that it not be done) would imply that they were beings of a quite different sort.[28] It fails to respect people not to give them the option of speaking. Someone may waive (or perhaps even alienate) the right in order to promote his greater interests. But to say that any given person is not entitled to the strong right to free speech is implicitly to say that no person is so entitled non-instrumentally. That is, it is a way of saying that certain crucial features of human nature are not sufficient to generate the right in anyone. And this seems to be a mis-

[26] This example is Larry Temkin's.

[27] Presumably, one does not have a right to their actually speaking—though this is what is really in any given person's strongest interest on Raz's analysis—since then others would have a duty to speak.

[28] Thomas Nagel presents a similar argument in 'Personal Rights and Public Space', *Philosophy & Public Affairs*, 24/2 (spring 1995).

take. On the alternative account I am offering of why the importance of a right can outstrip any interest it protects, we might say that some rights are a response to the good (worth, importance, dignity) of the person and/or his sovereignty over himself, rather than a response to what is good *for* the person (what is in his interests).[29] If it is in a person's interest to be a being of such importance, the right is still not a response to his interest in being important, but simply to his importance. (The interest gets protected as a side-effect, not as the point, of the right.) The strength of the right is not a mark of the strength of the interest it protects, but a mark of the fact that the right is a response to a characteristic of persons that makes persons important. Hence, it is a response to a characteristic that may itself be a necessary presupposition of the importance of protecting their interests.[30]

[29] The rights that are due to the worth of the person and his sovereignty over himself are presumably rights that all persons have and are (at least) fundamental human rights. I shall not in this chapter broach the question in detail of what these human rights are, but it may be useful to raise certain warning flags. When some point to a person's capacity for agency in the light of reasons, they derive a fundamental human right to free agency, including perhaps rights to conditions for the maintenance of that agency. Perhaps this is a correct move, but we must be careful how we interpret it. I have already suggested that a fundamental right to free agency need not derive from such agency being a good for the person. Now notice that if we remove someone's kidney against his will or interfere with his actions on several occasions, we do not yet interfere with his being a free agent or with the conditions for his being a free agent. (James Griffin has pointed this out in unpublished material.) But it is a mistake to think that it is permissible to do whatever leaves someone still able to be a free agent even when this interferes with particular decisions he makes as a free agent. Respect for someone as a free agent requires respect for the particular expressions of his agency. However, his decisions as an agent to exert control over things need only be respected when they concern what he has a right to control (or at least to try to control). So if he makes a decision to give up his own kidney, his decision should be respected. When he decides to donate your kidney, his decision need not be respected. This suggests that in addition to any fundamental right to free agency, there will be fundamental rights to those things that make one a separate person (e.g. one's body parts), whether or not those things are necessary conditions for being a free agent. This is what I mean by referring to a person's sovereignty over himself.

[30] I shall have more to say (in Section 3.2) about how a right and its stringency may not be a function of the interest it protects. The points I have made about the possible independence of rights from interests also bear on the theses of Louis Kaplow and Steven Shavell in their manuscript *Principles of Fairness versus Human Welfare*. They assume that satisfaction of preferences is of fundamental importance, rather than satisfaction of interests. But they do not see rights as ways to satisfy preferences; rather they criticize rights for interfering with the satisfaction of preferences. When a right would interfere with the satisfaction of every person's preference, the right is irrational they claim. Yet, I have suggested that the right to punish if exercised may interfere with the satisfaction of everyone's preference and yet not be irrational. Furthermore, how can we assume that the satisfaction of preferences is of fundamental importance? The objects of some preferences are worthless, not representing true interests or values. Even when this is not a problem, we may wonder whether the satisfaction of the preferences (or interests) of some creatures matters unless they matter. And perhaps certain rights reflect the worth of certain creatures (persons versus penguins), a necessary presupposition of the importance of satisfying their preferences. (And an argument against satisfying preferences that interfere with continuing respect for what gives the creatures their worth.)

3 Rights and Conflicts

Even the Interest Theory does not imply that a right which protects an interest thereby promotes interests overall within the life of one person or overall among people. Hence, there may be conflicts between respecting rights and maximizing interests satisfied. (I shall refer for the time being to maximizing interests satisfied as producing the greater good). This should be no surprise, since to say that someone has a right to something is ordinarily a way of excluding the calculation of overall goods and evils in deciding how to treat him. (Hence, the right is referred to as one type of 'exclusionary reason'.) Suppose the balance of good over evil recommends that A get x. In an act-consequentialist system that maximizes the good produced, this will mean that someone has a duty to provide A with x. If the balance of good shifts even a bit in another direction, A should not have x. The idea that A had a right to his life in this system would be redundant for 'produces most good for A to have his life' or 'it is right that A has his life'. But the idea of a right is meant to contrast with such ideas.[31] Under the act-consequentialist view, if we could save two lives by taking another person's life, he would have no right to his life. That his right appears and disappears in this way makes the idea of a special sovereignty over his life (the usual notion of a right to life) misplaced. Except for the fact that his interests are given equal weight with others in the calculation of what is overall good, he is treated as a resource for promoting the good.[32] However, a notion of a right that is not redundant in this way could be given by a rule-consequentialist system: overall, according rights and not balancing goods and evils on each occasion will maximize the good brought about. This is a theory of rights as instruments for promoting the maximal satisfaction of interests.

Non-consequentialists, by contrast, try to justify a system of rights that has noninstrumental value and that may conflict with bringing about the greatest good overall even eventually. Further, even if this greatest good is sensitive to the distribution of goods among people, so that priority is given to the interests of the worst off, non-consequentialists will insist that a right may stand in the way of producing this fair distribution. (For example, the worth of each individual may imply that each has rights to bodily integrity and these can interfere (overall and in the long run) with the

---

[31] So if Bentham's theory of rights says that having a right makes one the beneficiary of a duty, this could only be a necessary, not a sufficient, condition for having a right.

[32] When we must decide whether to use our resources to aid one person or two others, I think it is correct to save the greater number. We can use a Balancing Argument that tells us that what each person is owed is to be weighed against the equal opposite person with the remaining person deciding the issue. But when saving the two people requires us to use the other person (not our resources), the fact that he has a claim to control his own life rules out using the Balancing Argument. (On the Balancing Argument, see my *Morality, Mortality, vol. i: Death and Whom to Save from It* (New York: Oxford University Press, 1993).

distribution of bodily organs so that years lived by all people are maximal and fairly distributed.)

However, the concept of a right need not imply that when respecting the right conflicts with producing more good, respecting the right will always take precedence over the good (either at the act or rule level). Rights need not be absolute but rather may have thresholds beyond which calculation of goods and evils is reintroduced. I may have a right that you give me something, but if a great good is possible only by transgressing my right, this may be permitted. Then the right will have been infringed rather than violated. The more good we must sacrifice rather than transgress the right, the more *stringent* is the right. It has been claimed that some fundamental human rights are stringent enough to stand in the way of even great goods whose achievement they prevent. This may be because they represent the worth of the person which is the presupposition of the importance of promoting her interests. But rights can also conflict with the personal interests of agents who have to act in accord with them. For example, someone's right to be saved by his bodyguard may give the bodyguard a duty even to give up his life for his employer. There are then at least two measures of the stringency of a right: (1) how much good is needed to override it, and (2) how much an agent must do to fulfil the duty associated with it. As we shall see, these two measures need not always coincide. This will be true, for example, if a right which someone must do a great deal to accord does not require much good to override it (perhaps less good than another right which one need not do a great deal to accord).

Rights may also conflict with other rights. (The two measures of stringency may not coincide here either, if a right one must do a great deal to accord (and so is very stringent in that sense) should be overridden by another right (which is more stringent in that sense) that one need not do as much to accord.[33]) Rights that protect interests may even conflict with maximizing, *ex ante*, the protection of the very interest the right directly protects of the very person whose right it is. We shall now consider each of these types of conflicts and ways of measuring the stringency of rights.

3.1 Conflicts of Rights and Goods

1. Consider first the conflict between rights (both positive and negative) and great goods *not* protected by rights.[34] Can the good override the right if it is produced by aggregating small goods over many people, or must someone among those who will lose out on a good face being worse off than the rightholder would be if his right is not

---

[33] I first discussed this issue in 'Supererogation and Obligation', and further in chapter 12 of *Morality, Mortality, vol. ii: Rights, Duties, and Status* (New York: Oxford University Press, 1996).

[34] Under 'goods', I include both benefits and the avoidance of harm.

respected? The latter view (which involves what is known as 'pairwise comparison' of individuals one at a time) seems more plausible than the former. So, one reason why rights can trump goods is that the total good is not distributed over persons in the right way. (But it is still possible that the aggregate loss to many people, each of whom will lose out on as much but no more good than the rightholder would lose provide a reason to override the right. We will consider below whether goods distributed in this way may still not override rights.)

Ronald Dworkin tried to explain why some rights trump great goods, in the sense that they must not be transgressed for the sake of producing the great goods, even if we take utilitarianism as a background theory. He argued that external preferences of some people whose object involves denying the equal weight of the preferences of others should not be counted in a utilitarian calculation to determine how much good is at stake if we do not act. He thought this is true, even if individual people will suffer more (through lack of satisfaction of their external preferences) if we do not act than the people whose interests we would act against would suffer. Rights that trump aggregated utility may be, in his view, heuristic devices that represent the elimination of such external preferences from a social calculus without our actually having to do this calculation on each occasion.[35] This explanation, how-ever, does not explain why anyone should have a right that trumps aggregated pref-erences that are not inappropriately external. For example, why does one person have a trump right not to be killed when we could save the lives of five people by killing him, and each person prefers to survive? (Dworkin's explanation of rights as trumps in terms of eliminating external preferences also does not specifically call for pairwise comparison to see how much each individual will lose; it allows us to consider an aggregate of nonexternal preferences, each of which is a preference for a small good.)

Judith Thomson offers an account of why some rights must never be transgressed, even to achieve great goods *not* involving inappropriate external preferences, even when each person would suffer as great a loss as the rightholder if the great good is fore-gone. Her view is, in a sense, that there is not enough *morally relevant* good in the world to override some maximally stringent rights. This is because, she argues, in deciding whether to transgress a right, we must consider not aggregate good but rather do pair-wise comparison to see how badly off each individual whose goods compose the aggre-gate good would be if we do not transgress the right. Sometimes it will not be possible for any one person to suffer a fate *sufficiently* worse than the rightholder would suffer if his right is transgressed and only that would justify transgression. For example, we must not violate the right not to be killed of one person to save ten from drowning through natural causes even more painfully, because no one of the ten will suffer a fate *sufficiently* worse than the rightholder would. Thomson's account allows that there are

---

[35] Dworkin, 'Rights as Trumps', in *Theories of Rights*, ed. J. Waldron (Oxford: Oxford University Press, 1984).

rights such that someone could suffer a sufficiently greater loss than the rightholder and then the right might be permissibly infringed. Her view, I think, also implies that an increasing number of people who will suffer such a sufficiently worse fate does not add to the justification for infringing the right beyond what we had with one. (Why should the sufficiently worse fate aggregate in a morally relevant way when equally bad fates do not in her view?)[36] Her view also seems to ignore the possibility that there are rights whose stringency is not a function of the interest at stake, and so even if someone will suffer a much worse fate than the rightholder would, the right is not infringeable. For example, someone's fate may be much worse if another person's freedom to read pornography is not limited than the reader's fate would be if it is limited, and yet it could be wrong to limit his freedom to read.

Yet another proposal as to why a right may take precedence over a great good is that the violation of a right always produces a worse outcome than the absence of the great good (perhaps, for example, because it is worse to die of a rights violation than to die of natural causes). This proposal seems extremely implausible, in part because it would imply that we never have a reason based on considerations of good to override a right. The implausibility can be brought home by considering the following hypothetical. Suppose I could either prevent A's right not to have his arm removed from being violated or else save the lives of twenty other people drowning in an accident involving no rights violations. I cannot do both. I believe I should save the twenty. Yet, if the rights violation resulted in the worse outcome, I would have strong reason to prevent it instead. The deep error in this view is to think that the right someone has that others not treat him in a certain way is a reflection of our view about how bad a state of affairs will exist if he is treated in that way. If that were true, five people's being treated in that way would be an even worse state of affairs, and it would then be permissible to kill one person to save five from being killed, but that is wrong.

Thomas Nagel thinks that this error results from trying to explain an agent-relative requirement (that applies to each agent, that he not *do* something to someone) by what has agent-neutral value, that is, a bad state of affairs involving rights violations that anyone has a duty to prevent.[37] Those who treat rights violations as new types of negative values that are used to evaluate how bad an outcome will be are rights-consequentialists. The alternative view is that rights are side constraints;[38] they can tell us not to do something to a person, even if its being done would stop the same thing being done to a greater number of other people.

Some have interpreted the view of rights as agent-relative requirements in such a way that it is *my* transgressing the right in order to produce a great good that

---

[36] Thomson is careful to distinguish her view about what to do when a right conflicts with goods from what should be done when goods to one person conflict with goods to many. In the latter case, it is permissible, on her view, to aggregate (at least) the numbers who will suffer equally bad fates and who can be aided equally. So, in the absence of rights, one should save ten people rather than save one person.

[37] See Nagel, 'Personal Rights and Public Space'.

[38] The term is Robert Nozick's. See *Anarchy, State and Utopia* (New York: Basic Books, 1973).

produces the worse state of affairs (at least from my perspective) relative to absence of the great good. On this view, I must not do something because it will bring about the worse state of affairs from my perspective. Here an agent-relative evaluation of the *outcome* is fitted into a consequentialist perspective, so that to avoid the worst outcome I should not transgress the right.[39] The agent's concern with himself might also be put in a non-consequentialist framework: one's responsibility to not transgress a right is greater than any duty one has to produce the best outcome because one must not be the sort of agent who does certain types of acts. The emphasis in these accounts seems to shift from the significance of the right of the potential victim (that implies I should not do something to him) to the importance of a particular agent's not being a certain sort of agent. This suggests that if another agent were to transgress the right for the sake of greater good, one would have no reason to stop him. So, for example, suppose B will violate A's right not to have his arm removed in order to save many other lives. Do I have a reason (even if not a duty) to put aside my activities to stop the violation, rather than let it be the cause of the greater good? I think I do.[40] On the other hand, if it were most important that I not be involved in acts of a certain type, should I reduce the number of such acts I am involved in? May I kill one person now to stop a threat I started yesterday that will soon kill five people? I think not. These cases suggest that it is a mistake to interpret agent-relativity as essentially *my* concern with myself that leads me not to violate a right. Rather it is because the right I would come up against should not be violated to achieve the greater good that I must not transgress it, even though its being violated by me is not the worst state of affairs either from my perspective or anyone else's.

Indeed, the existence of rights has the following seemingly paradoxical implication in cases of conflict with producing greater goods. Suppose B will violate A's right not to have his arm removed, in order to save many other lives in an accident. However, there is only a ninety per cent chance that A's losing his arm will succeed in saving the others. It is certain, however, that I can save the others. Hence, I go to save them though this will not stop B violating A's right. (I have a reason to stop him but I have even more reason to save many lives.) Now, suppose my route to saving the others becomes blocked; there is nothing I can do to help them. It is consistent for me, as someone who would have tried to save the lives of many, to now act on the reason I have to stop B from violating A's right, even if this means the many will not be saved.

My suggestion for understanding how respect for rights can entail this is that the right not to be harmed that cannot be overridden expresses a degree of inviolability

---

[39] See e.g. Amartya Sen, 'Rights and Agency', *Philosophy & Public Affairs*, 11 (1981).

[40] And this is not because I would otherwise be intending the act by another's hand, for I need not be intending it. For example, I may be a very busy person and making some effort so that transgressions do not occur is an imposition I would like to avoid, yet I have a reason to make the effort.

of the person.[41] (High inviolability can serve one's interests in life, but one might have a non-overridable right not to be harmed by A, even if one will otherwise be similarly harmed by B. In this case, one's interest in life will not be protected by the right against A, nevertheless the right may exist.) Inviolability is a status—a description of what it is not permissible to do to a person, and it does not depend on what *happens* to a person. Even if one is violated impermissibly, one does not lose one's inviolability. The permissibility of my leaving A who will have his right transgressed, so that I can go and save others, does not involve morality endorsing (making it permissible) that A be harmed. However, if there were no reason to stop his being harmed to save others, this would involve morality endorsing his being harmed to save others and hence endorsing a less inviolable status for the person. So, in so far as respecting a right not to be harmed involves respecting a status of inviolability, whether one has succeeded in respecting a right does not depend on whether the person has been violated or his interests set back.

Carrying this account of rights further, we can see that in the conflict between rights and the greater good, it is possible to offer an account of why an agent should not transgress a right that is, in a certain way, good-based. To do this, however, we need to expand the idea of the good to include more than promoting interests. We also need to move beyond the consequentialist idea of *producing* (causally) the good. That is, there may be a type of good that already exists but that would not exist if it were permissible to transgress the right of one person to save many lives. This is the good of being someone whose worth is such that it makes him highly inviolable, makes it improper to treat him in certain ways. This good does imply that certain of one's interests should not be sacrificed, but inviolability counts not merely because it instrumentally serves those interests. (Overall and *ex ante*, it might not even serve those interests, as the impermissibility of taking off someone's arm to save many others in an accident will actually reduce *ex ante* every individual person's chances of survival.) Inviolability is a reflection of the worth of the person. On this account, it is impermissible for me to harm the person to save many in the accident, because doing so is inconsistent with his having this status; if I harmed him, it would, of course, be my act that did so, but that it would be mine is not what gives me most reason to avoid it. I should avoid it because it is inconsistent with his status.

Furthermore, inviolability is a status that every person has only if it is impermissible to transgress any given person's rights. Each person who dies because it is impermissible to harm a person to save them in an accident also has the high inviolability, but only because it is indeed impermissible to harm that other person. If the properties that a person has *qua* person were not sufficient to give rise to high inviolability

---

[41] I have discussed this approach in 'Harming Some to Aid Others', *Philosophical Studies* (Nov. 1989), 'Nonconsequentialism, the Person as an End-in-Itself, and the Significance of Status', *Philosophy & Public Affairs* (1992), and in *Morality, Mortality*, ii. What I say about the inviolability of persons is meant to apply only to innocent, nonthreatening bystanders. Nothing I say denies that it is permissible to violate aggressors, threats, etc.

in one person, they would not do so in others. This means that if it were permissible to harm the one to save the others, no one would have the sort of value that is expressed by high inviolability. So the good approved by each person's being inviolable is, in a sense, overriding the good of their being alive to those who will perish.[42]

It is important to distinguish the good *of* the person which may give rise to his inviolability from its being good for the person to be a person of such worth and, hence, inviolable. Even if it is in his interest, this is not the source of the rights associated with his being inviolable. He must have a certain nature, rather than an interest, in order to be worthy of inviolability. Furthermore, any interest he had in *being* the sort of entity who is inviolable would also be distinct from any interest he has in *being recognized* as this sort of a being. (This is what is sometimes called a dignitary interest.) His interest in this recognition could not be the fundamental reason why he has the right that is to be recognized. Indeed, his having the right could be the mark of his being the sort of entity whose interests and desires (e.g. to have his rights recognized) should be given serious consideration.

Inviolability need not be absolute. The *degree* of inviolability could correlate with how bad the fates of others must be before we may override the right or possibly with how many people will suffer bad fates. Unlike Thomson's view which I described above, the position I am describing now does not seem committed to non-aggregation of individual fates whose badness equals that which the rightholder would suffer if his right were transgressed. That is, it does not seem committed to the view that increasing the numbers of people whose fates would be comparable to the rightholder's is irrelevant to whether we may transgress the right. It is just that one of the goods it counts *against* the rights transgression is the good of each person being someone whose status involves inviolability.

The distinction between the aggregative and non-aggregative proposals for measuring the degree of inviolability (and hence, the stringency of the right) is, I believe, worth exploring further. In order to do this, let us consider what I call the $5 Case: each of twenty people will lose his $5 bill as a result of a gust of wind coming and blowing it away. The only thing that will get the money back to each is taking away A's $5 bill which alone survives the storm and investing it to recoup the lost

---

[42] Note that I have not here explained why the worth of a person expresses itself in high inviolability rather than a status of high 'saveability', so that we must sacrifice one to save many from natural death. But, in this connection, I believe the following point is important: The status of persons qua persons is a function of what is true of any one person. If you should be saved simply because you are in a group with more people, that does not indicate that you or the others as individuals have higher saveability, only that the numbers of people could affect what we should do. Strictly speaking, a status of high saveability would have to show up as a duty to do a great deal to save any *one* person. (It would be paradoxical to say that it showed up in the permissibility of killing one to save one from less than death, for then the one who would be killed is the one who should most be saved.) This point—that status is determined person by person and is not affected by numbers—may be related to Thomson's position that numbers do not count in deciding whether to transgress a right for a great good (even if they count when transgressing a right is *not* at issue or in conflicts between rights of the same type).

$100. Unfortunately, *A* will soon be gone and will not be able to benefit.[43] It is indeed wrong, I think, to take *A*'s $5 to prevent a permanent loss to each of the others which is no greater than the one he will suffer. It is true that if it were permissible to take his $5 for this purpose, the claim of any person, including those who benefit, to his $5 would be a weaker claim. It is only if it is impermissible to take *A*'s $5 that each of the others would have a stronger right to keep his $5 (if he had it). (This is all analogous to what was said above about inviolability of one person and all persons.) However, even if all this is true, no one thinks that the right to keep one's $5 is highly inviolable. The test of its *low inviolability* is the fact that if one other person were to lose a really important good unless we took $5 from A, it might well be permissible to do so.

I have tried to show that we can generate the same argument for the impermissibility of taking *A*'s $5 to save twenty other people's $5 bills as we can generate for the impermissibility of taking *A*'s life to save twenty lives. That is, if it were permissible to do so, it would be true of every person that he and his right are not as inviolable. I do not deny this is true, but what, I ask, is implied by its being true in *both* types of cases? Possibly that the ability of a right to 'stand up' to the aggregation of losses to many people is *not* a measure of the degree of inviolability, but rather an indication (as Thomson's view suggests) that we have made an error in the logic of rights by considering the numbers of people who would benefit when deciding whether to infringe it. In the $5 Case, it seems not so much that we wish how we act to reflect a certain degree of inviolability of anyone's possession of $5; it is more that we think it is in some way illogical to count the equal losses of the many people.[44]

To summarize: in Section 2.2, I questioned the Interest Theory of Rights on the basis of Raz's claim that the strength of a right often seemed greater than the weight of the interest it protects. I suggested that this might be because it represents the worth of the person, not his interests. More recently, I have discussed why sometimes the most important interests of a person (e.g. to not die) seem to be given greater weight than the comparable interests (e.g. to not die) of many others. One answer I have considered to why this is so is, again, that the worth of each person is implicated in the impermissibility of violating one of them, and this worth of each of the people is taking precedence over the interests of some in not dying. I suggest that the strength of the right can outdistance even the interest it protects because it expresses something true of all people that surpasses the interests of any. Without denying this view, I have also raised a question about whether not allowing aggregated losses to count against a right shows the stringency of the right (and degree of inviolability of the person) or is rather a reflection of the fact that counting aggregated losses would evince a deep logical error in understanding rights.

---

[43] I first presented this sort of case in *Morality, Mortality*, ii, ch. 11.
[44] I shall return to this issue once more below.

2. Now I wish to consider another aspect of inviolability: the quantitative degree of inviolability is not all that matters. The *way* in which it is permissible and impermissible to transgress a person and his rights is also of significance. This fact, I believe, helps us argue against an interest theory of rights. Raz observes that interests may not give rise to *all* the rights that might protect them. I do not believe that he adequately explains why this is so, and that an explanation is inconsistent with an interest theory.

Someone might have the same quantitative degree of inviolability if it were (1) permissible to transgress only in way x and not in way y, as if it were (2) permissible to transgress only in way y and not in way x. Yet, the former might be the correct and the latter the incorrect way to treat a person. I believe that the fact that the same interest can go unprotected in one way and yet be protected in another indicates that it is at least more than the presence of an interest in a creature capable of having rights that generates the right; it is also the manner of treatment of the person that would be involved in affecting his interests that is crucial to whether a right exists.

In discussing conflicts between rights and goods, we have so far seen one example of this—even if we may not harm (e.g. kill), it could be permissible to allow harm (e.g. let die). The most obvious interest at stake (living) is the same in both cases. However, when we kill we can deprive someone of the life he would be caused to have independently of us; when we let die, someone loses life he would have had only by making use of our services. His sovereignty over his life is only at stake when we kill, the aider's sovereignty over her life is at stake when the question arises for her of whether or not to let die. This, rather than interests alone, helps account for the presence or absence of rights. Might we say that it is in one's interest *per se* to be sovereign over one's life, as distinct from its being in one's interest to be alive? But we have also seen that one could leave someone who is being deprived of his sovereignty (when someone else is killing him) to do something else. Hence, sovereignty's being in one's interest could give rise to a right not to be killed but not a right to be aided. Why? The interests affected are the same. (Note that sacrifices we would physically have to make rather than kill or rather than let die could be the same, so the difference in cost to agents need not account for the presence or absence of the rights.) No doubt if it were permissible to kill, morality would endorse the transgression of sovereignty but need not do so if it is permissible to allow a transgression (still considered impermissible). But we still need an explanation of why letting the transgression occur can be endorsed when its effects on the victim's interests are the same.

The importance of the different *ways* in which interests can be protected for the generation of rights is at stake in the very interpretation of the claim that rights trump goods. Those who speak in this way want to insist that the deliberate transgression of a right is not permitted in order to bring about certain goods; but the cases we have considered above show that this does not commit them to the claim that we should always sacrifice the same goods in order to prevent the deliberate transgression of a right. (It was permissible to go to save the many from natural disaster rather than go to rescue the one person from being killed to save them.)

Even talk of the impermissibility of the deliberate transgression of a right is not sufficiently precise. Let us hold constant both the interest in, for example, life and the interest in sovereignty of the rightholder, as well as the interests involved in promoting the greater good. It is still true that there are some ways in which a person has a right not to be deliberately interfered with and other ways in which a person does not have the right not to be deliberately interfered with to achieve these same goods. A case that philosophers discuss, called the Trolley Problem, illustrates this. Suppose a trolley is out of control (due to natural disaster) and headed to killing five. We could save the five by redirecting it onto a side track, but we foresee it will thereby hit and kill a single person. It is said to be permissible to do this; we would not incorrectly transgress a right if we did so. However, it would not be permissible to throw a bystander into the trolley—a right would be incorrectly transgressed— if this were necessary to stop it from killing five. This suggests that the strength of a right not to be killed is not solely a function of the interest it most obviously protects (i.e. life for everybody in all these cases) but of the manner in which the interest is affected. (This assumes that there is no other reason why it is permissible or impermissible to kill besides the rights involved.) Of course, in order to support these judgments about cases we need a general account of when and why someone has a right not to be deliberately killed in one way but not in another. I believe the correct account will say something about how greater goods should be *causally related* to such lesser evils as harm to people, and this will not represent a concern merely for the interests of potential victims.[45] Nor will it, I believe, reflect a concern for interests of agents. (For example, the permissibility of turning the trolley but the impermissibility of throwing someone into a trolley is not a function of the difficulty for the agent of doing each. In any case, if difficulty to the agent were crucial, this would give an agent only an *option* not to throw someone into a trolley, not a duty not to.)

3.2 Conflicts of Rights and Personal Interests

So far, I have considered how rights might withstand or be overridden by greater goods. But if a right may be overridden by a greater good, that does not settle the question of what we must do. Suppose, for example, that A has a right that B meet him for lunch, but on his way to lunch, B sees C in need of a kidney transplant. It would do such a great deal of good to help C that we would think it *permissible* for B to fail in his duty to A. But presumably we think B is not required to give his kidney to bring so much good about. Hence, it is supererogatory for him to do so; he has no

---

[45] For specifics on this, see 'Toward the Essence of Nonconsequentialism', in *Fact and Value: Essays in Ethics and Metaphysics for Judith Jarvis Thomson*, eds. Byrne, *et al.* (Cambridge, Mass.: MIT Press, 2001).

duty to do it. However, if he wishes to do so, he may; he would be mistaken to think that A's right could only be overridden if he had a duty to save C at the cost of a kidney. Supererogatory acts may, therefore, come into conflict with rights and override them.[46]

In this case, A will lose so little if his right is overridden, we might think he should waive it. But suppose D has a right against his bodyguard, E, to have his life saved, even at great personal expense to E. E now faces a choice between saving D or saving ten thousand strangers. I do not think that D is obligated to waive his right to E's services. Yet, I believe, it is permissible for E to abandon D to save the ten thousand. This is so even if he would not be willing to sacrifice as much personally to save the ten thousand as D will lose if he is not helped, or as E would have been willing conscientiously to lose had it been necessary to carry out his duty to D. Hence, it is permissible, in order that the ten thousand can be saved, for E to let D suffer more than E would be willing to suffer for the ten thousand. If he is willing to do this, he ought to. Hence, his duty is not what E necessarily ought to do. Indeed, if the cost to E of saving the ten thousand is small (and, hence, not supererogatory), he ought to do this straightforwardly and ought not to honour D's right to have him save his life.

So far, we have seen that (1) the greater good may take precedence over a right just in so far as we compare those two factors, but (2) whether we are required to do what brings about the greater good can depend on how this impacts on we who would have to bring it about. This is because considering the two factors of personal good and greater good, it is often supererogatory to produce the greater good. Let 'P' stand for 'personal good', 'GG' for 'greater good', 'D' for 'duty correlative to a right', and '$>$' for 'may take precedence over'. Then we can represent these two claims as $P > GG$, and $GG > D$. Can we conclude, by transitivity, that $P > D$? This would imply that if someone is not obligated to make great efforts to bring about the greater good, he would not be obligated to make such great efforts in order to accord someone his right. But this is wrong. Even if E is not obligated to give up his life to save the ten thousand, and he may save the ten thousand instead of D, he could be obligated to give up his life to save D when doing this did not interfere with his saving the ten thousand.[47] Here we have an example of how D's right is stringent relative to E's efforts, while the greater good is not stringent relative to E's efforts. But D's right is not so stringent relative to the greater good. So, if the efforts needed to bring about the greater good are small, E ought to bring it about rather than accord the right, even though according the right could require big efforts from E but producing the greater good could not.

This, of course, does not imply that every right could require maximal efforts from the person who is duty bound. If there is no specific contract to the contrary, for

---

[46] This case, those that follow, and the discussion of them repeat what I first said in my 'Supererogation and Obligation'.

[47] For more detail on explaining the intransitivity, see 'Supererogation and Obligation', and ch. 12 of my *Morality, Mortality*, ii.

example, your obligation to meet someone for lunch could be overridden by the fact that the cost to you of doing so is paralysis.

Suppose that, in the circumstances, *E* knows that if he were to accord *D* his right, he would actually suffer the loss of his life that he is obligated to suffer to fulfil his duty to *D*. Suppose further that this same loss is physically required in order to save the ten thousand, if *E* does that alternative act. Does the loss of his life, ordinarily supererogatory for purposes of saving the ten thousand, now become obligatory for that purpose since the loss is no greater than what *E* will wind up actually suffering in any case if he does his duty? I do not think so; someone might raise a moral objection to being obligated to do for the sake of one end (greater good) something he will conscientiously do for another end. Someone may refuse to suffer the large loss for the sake of the greater good *per se*. However, this does not mean that *E* is never obligated to give his life as a means of saving the ten thousand. Suppose that *E* can save the ten thousand at small cost to himself if he abandons *D*. Alternatively, if he takes a more dangerous route costing him his life, he can save both the ten thousand and *D*. If he really owes his life to satisfy *D*'s right, then if he wishes to save the ten thousand, he must choose the more dangerous route. The fact that he would produce a great good that could override *D*'s right will not excuse him from the fulfilling duty to *D* at the maximal obligatory cost. In this case, *E* gives his life only indirectly for saving the ten thousand; given his choice to save them, he must do so in a way which fulfils his duty to *D*, given this is possible. (Of course, when *E* sees that the cost to him of saving *D* will have to rise above what it would otherwise be if he also saves the ten thousand, he may decide not to do so.)

3.3 Conflicts of Rights[48]

1. *Types of Conflicts.* If rights can conflict among themselves, this would imply that even when a right cannot be granted, it was nevertheless a real right, not just a factor that had to be considered in determining what right there is. It has been claimed that rights conflict only because the duties to which they give rise conflict.[49] However, suppose two people have been granted rights to medicine but there is only one indivisible portion available. It seems the rights conflict, but no one need have a duty that conflicts with any other duty. The conflict arises because each grantee is at liberty to use the medicine, and yet each has a duty to abstain from its use (correlative to the right each has to exclude the other). These duties to abstain are not in conflict; rather the liberty and the duty that each has are in conflict.

[48] For more detailed discussion of this issue see my 'Conflicts of Rights: Typology, Methodology, and Nonconsequentialism', in *Legal Theory*, 7 (2001), 239–54.

[49] Waldron, in 'Rights in Conflict', *Liberal Rights* (Cambridge and New York: Cambridge University Press, 1993), to which all subsequent notes also refer.

When rights conflict because duties correlative to them do, the *duties can be in one agent* who cannot fulfil them both. We can call this our 'agent-relative conflict'. There can be such conflicts of *negative with negative rights* when one agent, for example, in charge of a runaway trolley must decide how to direct it—towards killing *A* or towards killing *B*.[50] There can be conflicts of *negative and positive rights*, as when an agent must decide whether to harm someone in order to fulfil an obligation to aid someone else. There can be conflicts of *positive and positive rights*, as when an agent owes aid to ten different people and can only help one.

We can also understand rights as conflicting when different agents are responsible for fulfilling correlative duties. We can call this an 'agent-neutral conflict'. One agent will either meet the requirement of the rightholder to whom he is obligated (by way of negative or positive rights) or another agent will meet the requirement of the rightholder to whom he is obligated, but each will not simultaneously satisfy the claim of his rightholder. A particular type of agent-neutral conflict arises when an agent transgresses a negative right to prevent another agent violating negative rights. (In this case, the second agent will fail to do his part in satisfying a right no matter what happens, but his rightholder will not suffer the violation of his right if the first agent intervenes.) Notice that, in this case, from the agent-relative perspective, the first agent faces a conflict between fulfilling a negative duty and *helping* someone else avoid the violation of his negative right. If this is covered by a positive right for help, from the agent-relative point of view there is a conflict between a negative right and a positive right, even while it is a conflict between negative and negative at the agent-neutral level.

All these types of conflicts can occur between rights involving the same interests or involving different interests, for example, less and more important interests.

2. *Conflicts and Stringency.* How should we resolve the conflicts? It might be claimed that we decide on the basis, first, of the stringency of the rights involved (whichever right is stronger takes precedence) and then, given stringency is the same, on the number of rights that will not be fulfilled. Again, we are asked to measure the stringency of rights. Thomson[51] suggests that the stringency of rights is a function of the importance of the interest they protect[52] and when we face a conflict of rights, at least in an *agent-relative conflict*, we should accord the one that would involve the more important interest and where interests are the same, the greater number.

---

[50] Waldron (ibid.) suggests in an agent-relative system of only negative rights there cannot be conflicts, but this seems wrong. A slightly different case involves an agent who has a choice between (*a*) defusing a threat he started in the past to one person that is about to come to fruition now and (*b*) starting a threat now to someone else. In this case, the agent will become the violator of negative rights whichever he does, but at the present time he faces a conflict between a negative right and a positive duty to aid his potential victim of a negative rights violation.

[51] In *The Realm of Rights*.

[52] Above, I described one sense of stringency as a function of how much good is needed to permissibly override a right. Connecting these two ideas says that amount of good necessary to permissibly override is a function of the significance of the interest protected.

But it has already been argued above that one should reject the view that rights arise solely from the interests they protect and that one should accept that the stringency of a right may be out of proportion to the importance of the interest it protects. So, for example, suppose a negative right not to have his arm cut off protects person A against everyone and a positive right to assistance from her bodyguard protects the life of B. If interests were the only measure of the stringency of rights (even if not a full account of the origin of rights), it would be permissible for the bodyguard to take off A's arm if this were the only way to fulfil his duty to save B's life. But this is impermissible. Indeed, Thomson makes use of the impermissibility of doing this to argue that there are no positive rights to assistance.[53] But it seems clear that there can at least be contractual positive rights between a bodyguard and his client. So, I think one must conclude from this case that the stringency of rights is not only a function of the interests at stake but of the type of right and the way in which its non-fulfilment would treat the person.

Still, it would oversimplify to say that negative rights are more stringent than the positive, especially when the importance of interests is held constant. For example, a bodyguard might have a positive duty to redirect an out-of-control trolley from killing five of his clients toward killing one other person instead.[54]

Similarly, in a case that seems to involve a conflict of negative rights, the stringency of rights is not merely a function of the interest it protects. Suppose we could stop a runaway trolley from killing five people either (a) by redirecting it onto a track where it will kill one person or (b) by throwing one person in the way of the trolley when we know this will (only) paralyse him. Even though the interest at stake in the latter case is less than that in the former, it may be permissible to do the former and not the latter.

Finally, it seems possible that right A could come with *explicit assurances* that it will not be overridden even if the agent faces a conflict between according it and according right B that protects a weightier interest than does right A. Here again, the right involving the lesser interest should be accorded.

In *agent-relative conflicts*, it seems that even if we should choose to accord the most stringent right, this will not necessarily be the one protecting the most important interest. In agent-neutral conflicts, it seems clearly incorrect that we should resolve conflicts by according the most stringent right. For this would imply that we should take off someone's arm in order to stop one person (or several people) from being killed. Here the relative stringency of the rights may not be in dispute—the right not to be killed may be stronger than the right not to have one's arm removed—and yet we should not decide what to do on this basis.

---

[53] Thomson, *The Realm of Rights*.

[54] Aggregation of rights should not always decide matters. For suppose A on Island A has a contractual right to have his life saved and so does B on Island B, but we can only go in one direction. On Island B is also to be found C, who has a contractual right to have his sore throat cured, which we could do as well if we went to help B. I think it would be wrong to let the far less significant right of C decide which one of A or B gets his important right satisfied. For more on these issues, see my *Morality, Mortality*, i.

Without telling us what gives rise to the stringency of a right, Waldron suggests a method for measuring rights' stringency in agent-neutral conflicts. He takes it that we might measure the strength of the right not to be tortured relative to the right to free speech by noting that we would not torture someone no matter how much free speech would be lost if we did not. This is evidence that the right not to be tortured is much stronger than the right to free speech, he thinks. There are, I believe, significant problems with this procedure for measuring the strength of rights. We cannot compare the strength of two rights, R_1 and R_2 *per se*, by comparing (a) the strength of the prohibition on intentionally causing the transgression of R_1 with (b) the foreseen, unintended letting happen of transgression of R_2 (if we do not infringe R_1). The variation in the contextual features associated with R_1 and R_2 (intended versus foreseen, causing versus letting happen) may account for the impermissibility of transgressing R_1 to stop transgressions of R_2. (We noted above that the permissibility of torturing would involve morality endorsing a less inviolable status for persons; the permissibility of allowing free speech to be violated does not endorse the violability of people's free speech.) So with these different contextual factors, we would not be measuring the weight of R_1 versus R_2 *per se*. Yet this is how the procedure Waldron uses works. Using this procedure, one could even prove that *R_1 is stronger than R_1*, for it may be impermissible to intentionally transgress one person's right not to be tortured in order stop any number of other people from being tortured. Yet, it is clear that R_1 cannot be stronger than itself. The procedure could also 'show' that R_1 is stronger than R_2 and R_2 is stronger than R_1. For one may have a right not to be tortured to death (R_1) to save people from having their right not to be killed without being tortured (R_2) violated and one may also have a right not to be killed without torture (R_2) to save people from having their right not to be tortured to death (R_1) violated. But it would entail a contradiction to say R_1 is stronger than R_2 and R_2 is stronger than R_1.

The correct way, I think, to test for the relative stringency of R_1 and R_2 is to test them in cases that equalize all factors in the contexts of the two rights. Here are some tests—all in agent-relative conflict contexts— that at least satisfy this principle of equalization: (1) The Choice Test. If the only way to achieve a certain goal is to transgress R_1 or to transgress R_2, which would one sooner do, given that one had to do one of them? (This test allows that we do something wrong whatever we do.) The suggestion is, one would sooner transgress the weaker right when all other things are equal. (2) The Goal Test. How important a goal must one have for it to be permissible to intentionally transgress R_1? To intentionally transgress R_2? The suggestion is that transgressing the stronger right requires a more important goal, when all other things are equal.[55] (This test corresponds to the test discussed above: how great a good is necessary to override a right.) (3) The Effort Test. How much effort would one

[55] Alon Harel argues that free speech could be infringed for the sake of preventing insult but not to win a war, though the latter is a more important goal. But here all things are not equal; free speech plays an important role in seeing to it that the war is justified and pursued correctly.

have to make (or loss would one have to suffer) (*a*) to avoid foreseeably transgressing the right, (*b*) to accord the right, or (*c*) to compensate or undo the effects of transgression? ((*b*) in this test corresponds to the test discussed above: how much must someone do to fulfil the duty correlated with the right.) The suggestion is that the stronger right will require more effort. The Choice Test is in one way more revealing than the other two, because two rights may differ in strength and yet the weaker one be so strong that maximal efforts are needed to avoid transgressing it and maximally important goals are needed to justify infringing it. (Remember, however, that at least in agent-neutral contexts, the measure of strength of the rights *per se* does not determine what to do.)

There are at least three problems with these tests. First, the Effort Test and the Choice Test may give conflicting answers. For example, a bodyguard may be required to make a much greater sacrifice to save the life of his client than he would be obliged to make to avoid doing what will cost some stranger his arm. Yet, it might be impermissible for him to do what will save his client's life by means that foreseeably cost a stranger his arm. Secondly, the Effort Test and the Goal Test may give conflicting answers (as we saw above). A bodyguard may be required to make a much greater sacrifice to save his client's life than he would be required to make to fulfil the right of another employer, service to whom will save ten thousand lives. Yet the goal of saving five thousand lives could override the client's right but not override the right of the other employer to his service saving ten thousand lives.[56]

The third problem is that the use of these tests to measure the stringency of rights depends on an assumption of transitivity: if R_1 stands up to loss x and R_2 does not, then R_1 will stand up to R_2. It is always possible, due to a particular interaction between R_1 and R_2, that this is not so. Hence, these tests are at most prima-facie indications of the stringency of rights in comparison to other rights. For example, suppose person A has a right to assistance to degree x, but person B has such a right only to degree $x - n$. Even if we can say that the claim of A is more important than the claim of B, it is possible that when the two are in conflict, we should grant B his right because B is the parent of A and children should never be served before parents.[57]

In using these tests (or others like them), it is important to realize that just because R_1 and R_2 yield the same result in some cases, this does not mean that they are *per se* as strong. We cannot prove a universal truth that R_1 is as strong as R_2 by showing for *some* equalized contexts that we must spend the same amount, for example, to avoid transgressing each. For as the cost of not transgressing goes up, R_1 may require it and

[56] The Effort and Choice Test could also diverge when the conflict is between a supererogatory act and a duty. One might do more to accomplish a supererogatory act than one was required to do to meet a duty, and yet one should not violate the duty to accomplish the supererogatory act. (In 'Supererogation and Obligation', I described different conflicts between the Choice and Effort Test: one might be required to make a great effort to do a duty but not for a supererogatory act, and yet the supererogatory act could be chosen instead of the duty.)

[57] For discussion of these sorts of intransitivities, see my 'Supererogation and Obligation', *Morality, Mortality* (ii, ch. 12).

R_2 not. But if R_1 yields a different result from R_2 in even one case and R_2 offers no comparable different result from R_1, then we have evidence that R_1 differs in strength from R_2 *per se*. (Only one negative is needed to deny a universal truth.)[58]

Waldron offers another way to determine the relative strength of rights. He says that if we take a right seriously, we must take it to generate associated duties, in addition to the primary duty not to violate it (e.g. not to torture). For example, the duty to punish torturers, the duty to educate against torturing, and so on. But surely, he says, all the duties associated with the right not to be tortured are not stronger than any duties associated with free speech. For example, duties to punish violations of free speech might be stronger than the duties to educate against torture (as measured, let us say, by how many resources we should spend on each). But if some duties associated with the stronger right can be outweighed by some duties associated with the weaker right, then, he suggests, the stronger right is not so strong after all, and might, after all, be outweighed by sufficiently important considerations stemming from the weaker right. (Here he moves backward from the weakness of some duties associated with it to the weakness of the original right. The argument has a reductio form. That is, if we assume a right has great strength, we can show it does not have such great strength.)

I do not think this argument is correct, though one of its points seems correct. Does taking rights seriously imply taking associated duties—aside from the primary one of not intentionally transgressing the right—seriously? (Is that an indication the original right is very strong?) When Ronald Dworkin said that some rights were trumps over utility, could he have meant to imply that we must suffer that same loss of utility in order to prevent someone from intentionally violating those rights (or to facilitate the exercise of the right) as we must suffer rather than intentionally violate those rights?[59] If he did, the claim that rights are trumps would be implausible.[60] It is a merit in Waldron's discussion that he denies that all duties associated with a right are equally strong.[61]

[58] The issues here are similar to those in discussion of whether the duty not to kill is more stringent than the duty not to let die. See my discussion of that issue in *Morality, Morality*, ii.

[59] The formulation does not speak to whether rights trump other rights. See 'Rights as Trumps'.

[60] It may be possible that some arguments in public policy that call for action to prevent violation of rights use the rights-as-trumps argument incorrectly.

[61] Note also that while Waldron is quite right to recognize that a fourth-ranked duty associated with torture may be outweighed by a second-ranked duty associated with free speech, this still does not show that the n-ranked duty associated with R_1 would not outrank the n-ranked duty associated with R_2. Evidence for even this additional claim might be provided by the fact that while not torturing to death is more important than not intentionally killing (without torture), this alone does not imply that rescuing victims from attempts at death-by-torture is more important than rescuing victims of ordinary attempted killings. Here is an account (that I do not necessarily endorse) of why this could be so. Torturing mistreats someone in a way that is even more inconsistent with his nature as a person than killing him. But when we have to decide whom to leave to his sad fate, we would not endorse this inappropriate treatment. Therefore, only the loss each person would suffer might be relevant and we should not allow an additional loss (from torture) that is small in comparison to the loss each could be saved from (death) to decide whom we help.

As I noted above, I think this point gives us reason to deny that a right is present because an interest in a creature capable of having rights is sufficient to give rise to a duty. For example, if the right not to be tortured arose completely from the interest in not being tortured, then one would have a right that any manner of treatment which had a high probability of resulting in torture be equally prohibited (given the same cost of doing so), including not helping prevent torture. But if the right not to be tortured is also about whether morality rules out the treatment of persons in a certain particular manner leading to torture, then we could account for why there would be a very strong right not to be tortured that trumps foreseen loss of utility and not as strong a right that tortures be prevented. One may even have a right against an act aimed at torturing which is known to have a low probability of success and not have as strong a right to aid that has a high probability of preventing certain-to-occur torture. This is just the thesis of non-consequentialism—that the state of affairs resulting (e.g. interests affected) can be the same and one way of its coming about is permissible and another not—applied to rights violation.[62]

However, it is a mistake in Waldron's argument to conclude from the fact that duties associated with a supposedly strong right can be weak and also outweighed by some duties associated with a supposedly weaker right, that the strong right isn't so strong after all. And even that preventing some violation of the weaker right could, after all, outweigh intentionally transgressing the stronger one. If the manner in which the interest is affected is important, the direct intentional infringement might not be outweighed, either in agent-relative or agent-neutral conflicts, even if other ways of affecting the interest can be outweighed.

For example, A's right not to be intentionally pushed in harm's way when this will cost him his leg may be weaker than B's right not to be intentionally killed. But in discussing the Trolley Problem, we have seen that the former right is stronger than B's right not to be killed *as a consequence of* turning the trolley to try and save a greater number. Though the interest in being alive is stronger than the interest in not losing a leg, the different manners of treatment help determine the strength or even existence of the respective rights. This does not show that we may intentionally kill B in order to prevent A from being put in harm's way when this will cost him his leg.[63]

---

[62] Dworkin himself makes use of a non-consequentialist distinction in his defence of a right to request physician-assisted suicide. He considers the objection that such a right (and associated right of a doctor to act on it) may lead to more violations of the right not to be killed against one's will through mistaken exercise of the right. While he grants that a sufficient number of such foreseen mistakes might weigh against the right, he insists that the government's *intending* to deny someone's right to assisted suicide must be contrasted with its foreseeing (but not intending) those mistakes. See 'The Philosophers' Brief to the U.S. Supreme Court', *The New York Review of Books* (27 Mar. 1997), 41–7.

[63] This issue is related to my discussion of Peter Unger's views in *Living High and Letting Die* (New York: Oxford University Press, 1998). See my 'Rescue and Harm', *Legal Theory*, 5/1 (Mar. 1999). I hope to add (on this issue) to those comments in the future. Of course, this does not mean that if we face a conflict between (*a*) A's being killed as a consequence of turning a trolley to save a greater number or (*b*) A's having his leg intentionally taken off to save a greater number, we must choose (*a*). We may do what

I conclude that we will need some argument besides these of Waldron's to show that a right is not strong enough to trump the protection of different rights.

3. *Applications.* Let us consider in some detail how the considerations which I have highlighted in discussing conflicts of rights might play out in a much-discussed type of case involving conflicts from the agent-neutral perspective between negative rights. We can imagine that unless agent1 kills Joe, agent2 will kill Jim and Susan. Waldron claims[64] that if we have an interest-derived theory of rights and we are concerned about rights, then this sort of conflict of negative rights should lead agent1 to consider killing Joe. (This is so, even if concern for rights would not imply that someone should kill Joe in order to save Susan and Jim from a fatal natural disaster. Some have even claimed that it is paradoxical, irrational not to kill Joe if one is concerned with rights.) He says if agent1 must not kill Joe despite what the other agent will do, this will be because we have a duty-based rather than a rights-based theory (or at least rather than a rights-based theory derived from interests). The theory will be duty-based, he says, because we focus on the significance for an agent of killing and see it as something he must not do; we do not focus on the interests of the potential victims protected by rights.

This model attempts to derive a constraint on the agent from 'inside (the agent) out (to the victim)' rather than from 'outside (the agent in the victim's right) in (to the agent)'.[65] I think it is wrong. First, note that it is not clear that a duty-based account that focuses on what it means for an agent to kill would always tell agent1 not to kill when (intuitively) he should not. For if agent1 had (or will) set a bomb that will kill Jim and Susan unless he now kills Joe, an agent's concern for his not killing might recommend that he prevent more of his killings by killing Joe. Yet it seems impermissible for him to do so.

Secondly, consider the Art Works Case: if someone loves art, he will be disposed to preserve and not destroy art works. What should this person do if he must destroy one art work to stop someone else destroying five equally good ones? Presumably it is permissible for him to destroy one to save the five. This suggests that the constraint on harming persons is not derived from inside the agent out, but from *outside* her in, since the constraint reflects the kind of entity she would act on—a person, not a work of art.

Thirdly, there are, I believe, agent-focused views that focus on the quality of an agent's act or state of mind rather than on a victim's right, but they do not take note of the 'agent's mark' on the act, victim, or outcome. For example, the quality of the act or state of mind in which an agent must engage if he kills the one person is found

would be impermissible (take his leg off) if done on its own, as a substitute for what it is permissible to do if this is in the interest of *A*. I call this the Principle of Secondary Permissibility.

[64] In his introduction to *Theories of Rights*.

[65] As in Stephen Darwall's 'Agent-Centered Restrictions from the Inside Out', *Philosophical Studies* (1982), and Elizabeth Anderson's *Ethics and Economics* (Cambridge: Cambridge University Press, 1993).

repellent. The act would be the agent's if he did it, but it is not essentially its being *his* rather than someone else's, but what it is in itself, that repels him. Advocates of this view might claim it explains why someone should not kill one person now to save a greater number of people even from her *own* past or future bad acts. However, notice that the explanatory structure of *this* duty-based constraint would be essentially the same as a rights-based constraint. In both, one instance of either an act-type or right-type stands in the way of minimizing misconduct involving many instances of the same act-type or right-type. If the logic of concern for the duty does not require that we minimize its transgression but simply not transgress it, why should the logic of the concern for the right require that we minimize its transgression?

I believe that a rights-based theory that focuses on the right-bearing potential victims of rights transgression could require agent1 not to kill Joe. It is, at minimum, not irrational or paradoxical to be concerned about rights and yet not minimize rights violations by transgressing rights. The argument for this involves a variation on what was said above in discussing conflicts of rights and goods. If it were permissible for agent1 to kill Joe to save Jim and Susan, this would have to mean that Joe has a weaker negative right not to be killed than if it were impermissible to kill him. (This will be true even if we were infringing and not violating his right; one that could not be permissibly transgressed would be stronger.) Since what is true of him is true of everyone else—as we must universalize moral properties—Jim and Susan also would have weaker negative rights. To be protected by weaker negative rights indicates that one is less inviolable and, I think, this indicates that one is a being of less intrinsic worth. The stronger one's negative right, the more inviolable one is. This inviolability is a *status* (that is, it tells us what it is impermissible to do to a person); it has nothing necessarily to do with what *happens* to a person. If Jim and Susan are left to be killed because Joe is not killed, they are violated but they are no less inviolable than Joe. This is because morality did not endorse (that is, did not imply that it is permissible) to kill them; they are wrongfully killed. By contrast, if it had been permissible to kill Joe to save them, morality would endorse a form of killing and hence endorse reduced inviolability for everyone, expressing (I think) the view that each individual is a less important type of being. Concern for a right can rationally be expressed not by acting as though the right everyone had is weaker so that it is permissible to minimize the violation of this weaker right, but by acting in accord with the strength of the right. It is important to emphasize that it is difference in permissibility of killing that would reduce the status, not any actual killings. Furthermore, what it is impermissible to do and the associated degree of inviolability is not legislated by our choosing any given morality: we do not make people violable. They either do or do not deserve to be inviolable. If they do, we should act in accord with this.

If there is a strong negative right, agent1 could be required not to kill Joe, not for an essentially agent-focused reason, such as that he should be more concerned with his agency than with the agency of others (or more concerned with his agency *now* than with his earlier or future agency). Rather he will be required not to kill Joe for an agent-neutral reason (i.e. a reason each agent must be concerned about), the high inviolability of any person he comes up against expressed by a strong negative right protecting persons. Agent1 should be stopped by the right of any person he would kill, but not because there is anything special about that person (its being *his* victim) or because there is anything special for the agent in its being his act that kills.[66]

This justification for not minimizing rights violations *focuses on the distinction between a person's status (what it is permissible to do to him, expressing what sort of being he really is) and what happens to a person rather than on the distinction between what one agent does and what another agent does.* If there are beings with the elevated status of inviolability, this can mean that more violations will happen. I believe that this analysis implies that, at a higher level, the agent-neutral conflict between the rights not to be killed of Joe and the same rights of Jim and Susan disappears to some extent. Suppose it were significant for each one of them (whether they thought so or not) that he or she is a being worthy of high inviolability. Then Jim and Susan are the 'beneficiaries' of the impermissibility of killing Jim. Of course, they will not benefit in being alive (or in having their right enforced and recognized by people), as he does. And 'being alive' (and secondarily, the interest in the enforcement and recognition of rights) is presumably the interest which the interest theory of rights sees the negative right as protecting. The conflict in rights disappears to some extent at a higher level, consistent with an interest theory of rights, only if it is in a person's interest to simply be someone who is worthy of inviolable status, to be the sort of entity who truly merits this status.

But we may reject even this attenuated form of an Interest Theory. An alternative account of the right (and other fundamental human rights) is that the status to which it gives rise expresses a good that is not so much in a person's interests as it is a good in him that makes his interests worth protecting. It may make the world a better place to have in it entities who deserve this status; it may be an honour to those who have the status to have it. But the status is not important primarily because it is the interest of the person to have it or because it serves the other interests of the person, if it does. Fundamental human rights, at least, are not concerned with protecting a person's interests, but with expressing his nature as a being of a certain sort, one whose interests are worth protecting. They express the *worth of the person* rather than the *worth of what is in the interests of that person*, and it is not unimaginable that it will be harder to protect the other interests of a person just because of the worth of his

[66] When no interests at all are at stake if rights are protected, it becomes especially clear that a concern for rights alone does not necessarily lead to minimization of rights violations. Consider the Priest Case. Each priest has a right that I bow to him, simply as a mark of respect. One priest is coming down the road, so I should bow. But behind him are coming five priests. They will have passed beyond the point where I can bow to them, if I bow to the first one. In addition, someone else will fail to bow to them, and I could prevent this by not bowing to the first priest. It seems clear that I should fulfil the right of the first priest whom I come across. This case suggests that it might make more sense (even if it would not be right) to transgress a right to protect interests rather than out of concern for minimizing violations of the right. For more on this see my *Morality, Mortality*, ii.

person.[67] It is still true that at a high level, the conflict between the rights, so conceived, of Joe and the tandem of Jim and Susan disappears to some extent—the two of them could not have this right, this status, if Joe did not and this is separate from their having the right enforced.

Another way of putting this point is in terms of what rights exclude as reasons for overriding them. If people have high inviolability in certain respects, then the rights expressing that inviolability will specifically exclude certain factors as reasons for infringing the rights. For example, a right expressing high inviolability of life could say (or imply) 'the person's right not to be killed will not be overridden even for the sake of saving many more people from being killed'. This is what Joseph Raz would call a right functioning as an exclusionary reason. Suppose Jim, Joe, and Susan each has this right, but Jim and Susan will have their right violated. To violate Jim for the sake of the right they all share—that is, to count numbers at all—would be self-defeating. It would be self-defeating for it to be permissible to maximize *protection of the right* by violating Joe for the sake of Jim and Susan, since the right specifically says not to do this. We could not protect the right by making it permissible to do what in essence denies that it is a right each has. This would be a futilitarianism of rights. (This analysis succeeds, I think, in bringing together (1) the view that minimization of transgression would wind up defending only a weaker right with (2) the view that there is something logically incoherent with counting the numbers of rights violations or sufferers of comparable losses. As such, this analysis seems to bring together the two different approaches (discussed above pp. 494–5) to explaining why a good may not override a right, one approach ruling out aggregation in principle, the other possibly permitting it. But is the sense of incoherence the same?)[68]

The analysis I have provided here of negative versus negative right conflicts can be applied to other rights (e.g. the right to free speech) when transgressing the right in one person would prevent its transgression in others. Indeed, we can see a contrast in the outcome this analysis yields from the outcome of the analysis Waldron provides of conflicts of free speech.[69] Waldron considers the case of a conflict in the rights of free speech of the Nazis and the Communists. The Nazis want to speak freely with the effect that the Communists will lose their right to speak freely. May we interfere with Nazi free speech *for the sake of the right of free speech itself*? Waldron gives three reasons for saying yes: (1) the speeches they claim the right to make would bring an end to the form of life (i.e. all having free speech) in which the idea of free speech is conceived; (2) the content and tendency of the speech is incompatible with the very

<hr/>

[67] Here we might recollect Mill's view that one could prefer to be Socrates dissatisfied than a fool satisfied.

[68] It might be argued that the best state of affairs is one in which it is true that people have the inviolable status but someone acts impermissibly to violate one person in order to save more from being violated. But this only shows that our aim should not be to produce the best state of affairs, but rather to act in accord with the values (such as inviolability of persons) that exist.

[69] In 'Rights in Conflict'.

right asserted; and (3) to count as a genuine instance of free speech, a person's contribution must be related to his opponent in a way that makes room for both.

Waldron's views, it seems to me, yield a weaker form of the right to free speech that is required if we are to achieve a goal of maintaining some free speech overall. If each had a stronger right to free speech, it could, on the model I presented above, exclude as a reason to limit it protection of free speech itself. That is, the strong right can encapsulate a *status* that each has as a free-speaker, even if respect for this status results in some people (who still have the very same status) not speaking freely because they improperly have their right violated. While it might be wrong to exercise this right to stop others' free speech—there is a well-worn distinction between exercising a right and doing the right thing—and while we might infringe (permissibly transgress) the right for the sake of a particular good, namely more people actually exercising a right to speak, this is not the same as justifying transgressions of the right out of concern for the stronger right to free speech itself. If we infringe this strong right for the good of people speaking freely, all I am claiming is that we are not thereby acting out of concern for and protecting the stronger right.

4. **Ex Ante *Perspectives.*** Cases which are taken to represent conflicts of rights (or interests) among individuals can, from a sufficiently *ex ante* perspective, be made to seem like cases in which individuals, by agreement, waive their strong rights in order to promote *their own interests.* So consider again the case of killing one (in a way that is ordinarily considered a violation of a right) for the sake of saving five from being killed. There are (at least) two types of *ex ante* perspectives we can take on this. From either one, any person considers that he might be either the person who will be sacrificed or one of the five who will be saved by the sacrifice. In *ex ante* (1), each has a (subjective) probability of being an actual person who *never* had any chance of being one of those to be saved but only the certainty of being the one sacrificed. In *ex ante* (2), each is an actual person, who has both a smaller (subjective) probability of being the one sacrificed and a greater (subjective) probability of being one of the five benefited. I think the *ex ante* (2) perspective offers a stronger ground for arguing that we should think of rights as having been waived. It is more difficult to impose a loss on a person who in his actual (not hypothetical) life never himself had a chance of benefiting from an arrangement that now costs him something, even if he had a chance of being a different person who actually stood a chance of benefiting (as in *ex ante* (1)).

From each of the *ex ante* perspectives, there are two attitudes to take to the different positions that might be occupied (i.e. the sacrificed or the saved). In the first, each person can conceive of the position of the sacrificed as one that *he* has a smaller probability of falling into. This way of thinking allows each to imagine that no one will actually fall into the position. However, in fact we know that someone will definitely fall into that position. So each should rather take the second attitude: each should think of that position as not only one he runs a risk of being in, but as a position that some person will actually occupy. Indeed, perhaps he should consider only that it is a position that some person will actually occupy.[70]

How should each of us conceive of that actually unlucky person if there were an agreement to kill him to save five? As someone who (in *ex ante* 2) was himself willing to run a risk of being killed (at a time when he would be unwilling to be killed) in order to maximize his own chances of not being killed (as he has a higher chance of being killed if he is not willing to run this risk). People take risks of death all the time to increase their probability of survival, as well as for other lesser goods. For example, some people take a risk of dying from a side-effect by taking a drug which has a much higher probability of saving their life. But in our case, unlike this case, the death is imposed deliberately at a time when we know it can no longer be in the interest of the person to risk it. It was just in his interest *ex ante* to run the risk of being put in this position later.

How might we defend rights against such *ex ante* waiver reasoning—really a form of alienation of a right-at-a-later-time? One approach is to invalidate the relevance of *ex ante* reasoning for moral conclusions as a whole. On this view, we must decide how to treat a person simply by considering what we shall do to him relative to needs and effects on others. The fact that each person had the same probability of being that person and that each maximizes his chance of satisfying his interests by the ability to treat another in that way has no bearing on deciding if that form of treatment is morally appropriate.[71] Another (related) approach is to argue that the right to some forms of treatment is not alienable *ex ante*, even for the sake of maximizing one's own interests, presumably because the right against such treatment expresses the worth of the person which is the ground of the importance of promoting his interests to begin with. That it was *ex ante* in one's interests to risk being treated in a certain (otherwise impermissible) way does not show that it is permissible to be treated in that way. (This may leave it open that it is permissible, at the time the loss is to be imposed (or the nearest conscious time to it) to willingly allow oneself to be sacrificed for the sake of *others* (rather than as a final step in having maximized one's own interests *ex ante*) or to willingly allow oneself to be sacrificed at a time when it is still for the sake of one's own interests that this happens. This is more appropriately described as waiving rather than alienating the right.)[72]

There is at least one problem with designating some rights as inalienable in this way. One can show, I believe, that the very same right which is not alienable *ex ante* for one reason may be alienable for another. And it seems that whether it is alienable or not is a function not of how many people would suffer a loss comparable to the person sacrificed, but rather how much worse would be the fate of the people who

[70] Thomas Scanlon emphasized the distinction between these two attitudes in 'Utilitarianism and Contractualism', *Utilitarianism and Beyond* (Cambridge: Cambridge University Press, 1982).

[71] I believe Thomas Scanlon holds such a position. See *What We Owe to Each Other* (Cambridge, Mass.: Harvard University Press, 1998).

[72] See Feinberg, 'Euthanasia and the Inalienable Right to Life'.

will benefit from one's sacrifice. (I take this as additional support for Thomson's view (described above), that aggregation has no role in the permissibility of infringing rights but preventing a sufficiently worse fate does.)[73]

Consider, for example, that it might be wrong to agree *ex ante* to cut off someone's arm at a time he is not willing to give it in order to save the arm of each of five people, even though such an agreement would maximize his chances of keeping an arm. Does this mean the right not to have one's arm cut off to help others is inalienable *ex ante*? In the Two Diseases Case,[74] there are two diseases in a community. One, the Arm Disease, causes one and only one arm per person to fall off, and is very prevalent among a part of the population whose members we can identify beforehand. The second, the Death Disease, is very rare in a *different* part of the population that we can identify as susceptible to it. The only thing that cures the Arm Disease is a serum made by taking the finger of a person who was subject to the Death Disease but did not get it, and the only cure for the Death Disease is a serum made by taking the arm of a person subject to the Arm Disease who did not get it.

I believe it would be in the interest, *ex ante*, of all involved to make an agreement to provide the resources necessary to make the serums at the time they are needed, and that enforcement of this agreement would not be morally wrong. This is so even though this is an *ex ante* (1) type agreement, since actual people know the diseases to which they are subject. There is a high incidence of the Arm Disease, so there is a high probability that the people once susceptible to the Death Disease lose a finger in exchange for avoiding the small risk of a big loss to them, that is, death. There is a low incidence of the Death Disease, so there is low probability that a person once susceptible to the Arm Disease will lose an arm (ultimately), in order to lower a high probability of his suffering the loss of an arm.

This is a case in which an Arm person would have to pay with the *very item* he had attempted to increase his probability of keeping (his arm) at a time when it is known it is no longer in his interest to do so (for he no longer faces the threat of the Arm Disease), having received only the benefits of increased probability of protection from the Arm Disease. In this case, the arm would be sacrificed to prevent an even greater loss (death) to another person. That is, what the person who is sacrificed loses is significantly less than what the person who is saved would lose if he were not saved.

Finally, note that the manner in which a harm would occur seems crucial to whether or not a mere greater number being saved from the same loss can justify the harm. In this regard, consider the Ambulance Cases. In Ambulance Case 1,[75] a community has to decide whether to have an ambulance. If it does, it will save many lives that would otherwise be lost, but a small number of people who otherwise would not

---

[73] Though, in a suitably described Trolley Case, Thomson is herself willing to make use of *ex ante* alienation to justify killing some to save a greater number of others (roughly) when this decreases each person's *ex ante* subjective probability of losing what is important to him. See *The Realm of Rights*.

[74] I first discussed this case, as well as the Ambulance Cases that follow, in *Morality, Mortality*, ii

[75] Suggested by Ronald Dworkin.

have died prematurely will be hit by the ambulance as it races to the hospital. Indeed, we may imagine that (for some reason) it is known to be only people who would not need the ambulance to save their lives who will be hit by it. At the time of the agreement, no one knows whether he or she is such a person. This is an *ex ante* (1) type of case. Is it permissible to have the ambulance? Perhaps so, and even more certainly, it would be permissible in *ex ante* (2) type cases. Hence the mere numbers of equally great loss that will occur do seem morally relevant here.

Now consider Ambulance Case 2. The same community is deciding the rules for the performance of the ambulance. More lives overall will be saved if it is agreed that when the ambulance is on its way to the hospital with many people whose lives are to be saved, it will not stop—even though it could—to keep from running over someone in its way. Should the community agree to this? Another possibility in Case 3 is for the community to agree to install new brakes that make it impossible for the ambulance to stop before hitting someone whenever more people are in the ambulance who could be saved than would be hit in the road. These agreements seem impermissible.

People's right not to be killed could be presented as a reason for not introducing vehicles that might kill them, if no benefit would come from having such vehicles. But in Case 1, the benefit coupled with the fact that no one does anything deliberately— aside from having the vehicles at all for the sake of their benefit—to harm seems to defeat an objection based on a right not to be killed. In Case 2, by contrast, we deliberately do what we know will kill someone when we could easily avoid it (albeit at the opportunity cost of saving more lives). This manner of causing the death makes the objection from the right not to be killed appropriate, and the greater number of those who will die is insufficient to override it. In Case 3, deliberately making it impossible for us to easily avoid killing someone is similarly ruled out by the right not to be killed.[76]

---

[76] I think there is some similarity between my use of the ambulance cases and Thomas Scanlon's discussion of cases in his section on the relevance of probability of harm in his *What We Owe To Each Other* (Cambridge, Mass.: Harvard University Press, 1998), 206–9.

CHAPTER 13

LAW AND OBLIGATIONS

LESLIE GREEN

LAW is a realm of obligation and duty.[1] It may require us to fight wars, to refrain from assault, to pay taxes, to keep agreements, to take care, to report crimes, to protect the environment, and to take its judgments as binding and final. Creating, varying, and enforcing such obligations is not the only business of law. It also secures rights, confers powers, defines terms, and so forth. While it would be wrong to suggest that these can somehow be reduced to obligations, it is none the less true that they can only be fully understood with reference to them. To grasp the significance of the power to contract, for example, one must understand that it gives rise to duties to perform or pay damages. To understand the right to free speech, one must see that it grounds in others a duty not to silence. To understand the definition of a 'minor' one must understand the obligations from which such persons are exempt, and those they are powerless to create or change.

The obligatory character of law is central for another reason. Legal obligations may conflict, not merely with narrow self-interest, but with many other important obligations. The duty of military service may conflict with the duty to care for one's family, the duty to send one's children to school with one's religious duty to promote the faith. The law's own attitude to such conflicts is clear: its requirements are to take priority, except where it permits otherwise. But should *we* accede to this peremptory attitude, and on what grounds? Obviously enough, particular legal obligations may require things that on their merits ought to be done anyway: they are demanded by morality, efficiency, courtesy, and so forth. But some want to add another argument. They say that, in addition to any such considerations, we also have a moral obligation to do any and all of these things *because* they are required by law, at least when the

---

[1] For present purposes I use these terms interchangeably.

legal system is reasonably just. That is, they appeal to what the western philosophical tradition calls a doctrine of 'political obligation'. Whether such a reason exists is of both philosophical and practical importance, for the law's own view about the content and exigency of its obligations is enforced, as Locke said, by any penalties up to and including death. Nowhere are the stakes higher.

The tradition was confident of the existence of political obligation and doubtful only about which of two main grounds justify it. Voluntarist theories find their most influential expression in the writings of John Locke, who holds that we have duty to obey the law when, but only when, we consent to its rule. The competing approach, defended by Locke's critic David Hume, maintains that our voluntary acts are here irrelevant, and that the obligation to obey is sufficiently justified by the value of government under law. Of course, these two alternatives were not universally endorsed, but until recently serious doubts were entertained only by anarchists and others who reject the rule of law. The contemporary emergence, and perhaps even dominance, of a third position is therefore of great interest. A number of legal and political philosophers who do value government under law have become sceptical, and reject both the Lockean and Humean traditions in favour of the view that there simply is no general obligation to obey the law as traditionally conceived.[2] Here, I explore the grounds of such scepticism and gauge its implications for legal theory.

1 Obligation and the Nature of Law

The ordinary concept of law comes to us, as Donald Regan puts it, wearing a 'halo',[3] on prominent display in the familiar contrast between the rule of man and the rule of law. Perhaps then there is an intimate connection between the obligation-imposing character of law and its positive valence? Could the explanation for the halo simply lie in the fact that law's requirements are also *morally* obligatory? If so, this might suggest a constraint on legal theory. Philip Soper once held that, 'actual obligation is one of the phenomena of legal systems for which theory must account'.[4] And Ronald

---

[2] See M. B. E. Smith, 'Is There a Prima Facie Obligation to Obey the Law?', *Yale Law Journal*, 82 (1973), 950–76; J. Raz, *The Authority of Law* (Oxford: Clarendon Press, 1979); A. J. Simmons, *Moral Principles and Political Obligations* (Princeton, NJ: Princeton University Press, 1979); J. Feinberg, 'Civil Disobedience in the Modern World', *Humanities in Society*, 2 (1979), 37–60; R. Sartorius, 'Political Authority and Political Obligation', *Virginia Law Review*, 67 (1981), 3–17; L. Green, *The Authority of the State* (Oxford: Clarendon Press, 1988).

[3] Donald H. Regan, 'Law's Halo', in Jules Coleman and Ellen Frankel Paul (eds.), *Philosophy and Law* (Oxford: Blackwell, 1987), 15–30.

[4] Philip Soper, *A Theory of Law* (Cambridge, Mass.: Harvard University Press, 1984), 4. Soper modifies his view in 'Law's Normative Claims', in Robert P. George (ed.), *The Autonomy of Law: Essays on Legal Positivism* (Oxford: Clarendon Press, 1996), 215–47.

Dworkin still maintains that, 'A conception of law must explain how what it takes to be law provides a general justification for the exercise of coercive power by the state, a justification that holds except in special cases when some competing argument is specially powerful'.[5] From there it may seem a short step to Lon Fuller's conclusion that law cannot be what the positivists think it is, for how could there be 'an amoral datum called law, which has the peculiar quality of creating a moral duty to obey it?'[6]

In fact such views misrepresent the constraint that the obligatory character of law places on legal theory, for they elide three different questions. First, how should we understand the *normativity* of law—the pervasive use of normative terms, including 'obligation' and 'duty', in stating and describing the law? Secondly, what could give the law *legitimacy*—what might justify its rule, including its ultimate use of coercive force? And finally, the question of *obligation*: should the law's subjects take its requirements as morally binding? Though often confused, or at any rate fused, these are different and partly independent problems for jurisprudence.

1.1 Normativity

A theory of law should explain the character and meaning of statements like the following: 'The statutes of Canada must be published in French and English', 'Citizens of Georgia have an obligation to abstain from sodomy'. But to say that these are simply moral obligations is to say both too much and too little. It is too much since it is notorious that people make such statements without taking the requirements in question as stating any valid moral reason and even while regarding them as quite wrong. It is too little, because it assumes rather than explains what it is to have a moral obligation in the first place.

To have an obligation is to have a reason to act or to refrain from acting—a reason with which one is in some sense *bound* to conform. But in what sense? The exigency of legal obligations is plainly not to be found in their weight or importance: it is as certain that I have a legal obligation not to destroy your junk mail misdelivered to me as it is that this is a trivial matter. On the other hand, courts have extremely weighty reasons not to introduce conflicting rules into the law, yet they have no legal obligation to refrain from doing so. Obligations thus display what H. L. A. Hart called '*content-independence*': their existence does not depend on the nature or significance of the actions they require or prohibit.[7] But if the exigency of obligations is not a

5 Ronald Dworkin, *Law's Empire* (Cambridge, Mass.: Harvard University Press, 1986), 90.

6 Lon L. Fuller, 'Positivism and Fidelity to Law—A Reply to Professor Hart', *Harvard Law Review*, 71 (1958), 630, repr. in Joel Feinberg and Jules Coleman (eds.), *Philosophy of Law*, 6th edn. (Belmont, Calif.: Wadsworth, 2000), 100.

7 For Hart's first statement of this idea, see 'Legal and Moral Obligation', in A. I. Melden (ed.), *Essays in Moral Philosophy* (Seattle: University of Washington Press, 1958), 82–107. His position is later refined in 'Commands and Authoritative Legal Reasons', in his *Essays on Bentham* (Oxford: Clarendon Press, 1982), 243–68

function of their content, then what is it? Three theories have been especially influential.

On *sanction-based* accounts, to be under an obligation is for it to be likely, or ordered, or justified, that one will suffer a sanction for acting or failing to act in a certain way.[8] Advanced by Hobbes, Bentham, Austin, J. S. Mill, O. W. Holmes and Kelsen, sanction theories are now nearly friendless. The difficulties are well known.[9] First, all versions depend on an implausibly wide notion of a sanction, including not only punishments but also civil remedies as such compensation and even mere nullity. Secondly, legal duties do not leave it to the option of the subject whether to comply. 'You have an obligation not to steal' cannot merely mean 'If you steal you will be punished', for judges are not indifferent between people, on the one hand, stealing and being jailed, and on the other hand not stealing at all. Thirdly, legal duties are not bounded by the probability of detection and we refer to obligations when it is certain that no sanction will follow and even when there is no provision for sanction of any kind, as when we say that the highest courts have a duty to apply the law. Finally, while sanctions do provide reasons for acting, they are reasons of the wrong kind. The reason for avoiding a sanction is the disvalue of the sanction discounted by the probability of suffering it. But this variable quantity depends on both the content of the sanction and on the goals of the agent, whereas duties are independent of both.

Such considerations led Hart to suggest that while sanctions might figure in a partial analysis of 'being obliged' to do something, they cannot explain 'having an obligation'. Sanctions are important because they are one of the most dramatic expressions of law's power, its most important technique of reinforcing the duties it imposes—not because they explain what it is to have a duty. Instead, Hart defends a *rule-based* theory according to which we have obligations only when we are subject to social practice-rules of a certain sort. A practice rule exists only when there is regularity of behaviour, deviations from which are criticized, such criticism is regarded as legitimate, and at least some people treat the regularity as a standard for guiding and appraising behaviour and thus use characteristically normative language in referring to it. Not all practice rules are obligation-imposing, however; most are just ordinary customs and conventions. Hart claims that obligations require the presence of three further features: the required behaviour is enforced by serious or insistent pressure to conform; it is believed important to social life or to some valued aspect of it; and it may conflict with the interests and goals of the subject.[10] Since these beliefs and

[8] A helpful discussion of these variants, and objections thereto, is P. M. S. Hacker, 'Sanction Theories of Duty', in A. W. B. Simpson (ed.), *Oxford Essays in Jurisprudence: Second Series* (Oxford: Clarendon Press, 1973), 131–70. For Hart's reply to Hacker, see his 'Legal Duty and Obligation', in *Essays on Bentham*. However, it is not possible to bring everything Hart says about obligation in this essay into a consistent relationship with his other writings. See in particular his puzzling endorsement of something like a sanction theory at p. 160.

[9] See H. L. A. Hart, *The Concept of Law*, 2nd edn., ed. P. A. Bulloch and J. Raz (Oxford: Clarendon Press, 1994), 26–49, 82–91.

[10] ibid., pp. 85–8.

practices may have as their objects any standards of conduct whatever, the content-independent character of obligations is preserved. The practice theory thus proposes a general account of legal, moral and conventional obligations: *what it is* for an act to be obligatory is the same in each context, though the criteria that determine *which acts are* obligatory vary.

While the practice theory avoids most of the pitfalls of sanction-based accounts, it is in the end no more acceptable.[11] People speak of obligations when they are well aware that there are no relevant social practices, as might a lone vegetarian in a meat eating society. The practice conditions may be satisfied in cases where there is no obligation but only generally applicable reasons, as when victims are regularly urged to yield their wallets to a mugger. Most important, the fact that there is an obligation to φ is a reason for φ-ing; yet outside certain special cases the fact that there is a general practice of φ-ing is not a reason for doing as that practice requires. Hart's last writings therefore restrict the scope of the practice theory to the realm of conventional obligations, where the fact of common practice is a non-redundant part of the reason for conforming to it. But not all legal obligations can be understood as merely conventional—many reinforce behaviour that would be mandatory even in the absence of customary conformity, such as the obligation to abstain from rape.[12]

A more plausible account is *justification-based*. On this view, obligations are characterized by the sort of justifications that they purport to offer: content-independent and binding reasons for action. Their bindingness combines two features. First, obligations are *categorical* in force; they apply to the norm-subject independently of his own interests or goals. In view of the use Kantians make of this notion, it is worth emphasizing that there is nothing intrinsically moral in the idea of a categorical reason for acting: 'Shut up!' is a categorical imperative. The second feature is noticed by Hobbes and Locke in their discussions of the nature of political authority.[13] Obligations require that the subject set aside his own view of the merits of acting and comply none the less. The best elaborated and most persuasive account of this feature is due to Joseph Raz.[14] Obligations are categorical reasons that are protected by *exclusionary* reasons not to act on some of the competing reasons to the contrary. They are reasons for acting, together with 'second-order' reasons *not* to act on some other

---

[11] Ronald Dworkin, *Taking Rights Seriously* (Cambridge, Mass.: Harvard University Press, 1978), 48–58; Joseph Raz, *Practical Reason and Norms*, rev. edn. (Princeton: Princeton University Press, 1990), 53–8.

[12] Even with respect to conventional obligations, the practice theory ultimately fails, for conventional rules provide only ordinary reasons for acting, not binding ones. I explore various aspects of this issue in the following papers: 'Law, Co-ordination, and the Common Good', *Oxford Journal of Legal Studies*, 3 (1983), 299–324; 'Authority and Convention', *Philosophical Quarterly*, 35 (1985), 329–46; and 'Positivism and Conventionalism', *Canadian Journal of Law and Jurisprudence*, 12 (1999), 35–52.

[13] Thomas Hobbes, *Leviathan*, ed. C. B. Macpherson (Harmondsworth: Penguin, 1968), pt. II, ch. 25: 303; John Locke, *Two Treatises of Government*, ed. P. Laslett (Cambridge: Cambridge University Press, 1963), II, s. 87: 367.

[14] See Joseph Raz, 'Promises and Obligations', in P. M. S. Hacker and J. Raz. (eds.), *Law, Morality and Society: Essays in Honour of H. L. A. Hart* (Oxford: Clarendon Press, 1977), 210–28; and Joseph Raz, *Practical Reason and Norms*, 35–84.

reasons. Two cautions should be noticed. First, the excluded reasons must be presumptively valid; if a certain fact in itself provides no justification for doing something, then one needs no special reason not to act on it. Exclusion rules in the law of evidence, for example, direct one not to rely on certain considerations that would otherwise be relevant; one does not appeal to them to explain why we should not draw inferences from irrelevant or invalid considerations. Secondly, obligations exclude *some* contrary reasons—typically at least reasons of convenience and ordinary preference—but they do not normally exclude all. An exclusionary reason therefore is not a reason of absolute weight, but a reason of a different order. The binding character of obligations thus depends not only on the power of the justifications it offers for doing something, but also on its power to exclude from consideration competing contrary considerations.

A justificatory account of obligation is not free of controversy, and it is subject to refinement, but it makes good on the deficits of the sanction-based and rule-based theories. It accounts for some familiar features of obligations, and it gives a credible picture of the practical conflicts referred to at the outset—we can think of these as practical assessments made from different viewpoints, distinguished by the sorts of considerations they permit or exclude. As we might put it, '*legally speaking* there is an obligation to φ' means that from the point of view of the law there are binding reasons to φ and exclusionary reasons not to act on some of the reasons to the contrary. But this might not represent all relevant reasons from the moral point of view—perhaps some of the reasons that law purports to exclude are precisely the most morally salient reasons. To say that something is taken as, or put to us as, a binding, content-independent reason is not to say that it is one, so there is no commitment to the unacceptable thesis that all legal obligations are of their nature moral obligations though, as with the practice theory, there is a unified explanation of obligations in these different realms.

1.2 Allegiance

The normativity of law thus involves questions about how law presents itself to us. Questions of allegiance, which have dominated Western political philosophy at least since the seventeenth century, bear on how the law's subjects should respond. But what exactly is the issue of allegiance? Hume, to whom that term is due, refers indifferently to the 'moral obligation to submit to government', the duty to accept 'the authority of the rulers', the rulers' right to punish, and the 'blind submission' owed by subjects.[15] He treats these as roughly equivalent ideas and draws no distinctions among them. Certainly they all find a place in ordinary moral reflection about the

---

[15] David Hume, *A Treatise of Human Nature*, ed. L. A. Selby-Bigge (Oxford: Clarendon Press, 1967), 547, 548, 554.

law; but are they really interchangeable? Other philosophers do not make that assumption. Locke, for example, holds that one may be entitled to coerce others without any positive authority over them, at least where this is licensed by the 'executive power of the law of nature'.[16] Hobbes maintains that the state is entitled to coerce people who have no duty to submit, since the necessity for self-preservation voids all positive obligations.[17] Those possibilities suggest that we should at least distinguish the question of what justifies the rule of government—the problem of *legitimacy*—from the question of what justifies the duty to obey—the problem of *obligation*.[18]

Questions of legitimacy bear on both the scope and the location of authority: by what right does the law make and enforce its requirements? By what right does *this* legal system, among all actual or possible claimants, do so over *these* subjects? Questions of obligation involve the moral justification for taking law at its word and rendering the obedience it demands: treating it, as explained above, as a categorical and binding reason to act, not only thinking, but also acting, from the legal point of view. It is important to see that obedience is therefore more than a willingness to 'support and comply with' the law, in Rawls's phrase. One may comply with the law by doing what it in fact requires, without knowing that there is law or what it requires. Such a coincidence between law and behaviour is both common and desirable, since a reasonably just legal system should often require us and motivate us to do what we have independent reason to do. While it is true that compliance without obedience is usually sufficient to avoid sanctions, one obeys the law only if one is actually guided by it.

Whether there is an obligation of obedience is thus a matter of whether we should act from the legal point of view and obey the law as it claims to be obeyed.[19] What it claims is supreme power to determine our rights, obligations, powers, and liberties, and to have our compliance independent of our individual assessment of the merits of what is required. This obligation lapses if the regime is fundamentally illegitimate, but it is supposed to survive at least minor and occasional injustices of its laws. That there is such an obligation is assumed or at least avowed by officials, though the extent to which they share views about its grounds is hard to discern.[20] Judges speak and act as if those subject to the law have a duty to obey it, unless they are exempted by some other legal or legally recognized principle, and they treat sanctions as reinforcing motivation and not as an option.[21] As Donaldson MR put it, 'The right to

---

[16] Locke, *Two Treatises*, II, ss. 8–9: 312–13.   [17] Hobbes, *Leviathan*, pt. II, ch. 14: 199.

[18] On the distinction see especially Kent Greenawalt, *Conflicts of Law and Morality* (New York: Oxford University Press, 1987), 47–61, and William A. Edmundson, *Three Anarchical Fallacies: An Essay on Political Authority* (Cambridge: Cambridge University Press, 1998), 7–70.

[19] Joseph Raz, *Authority of Law*, 233–49.

[20] See Mark Hall and George Klosko, 'Political Obligation in the United States Supreme Court', *Journal of Politics*, 60 (1998), 462–80.

[21] *U.S.v Macintosh*, 283 U.S. 605 (1931), at 623. See discussion of this material in Hall and Klosko, 'Political Obligation in the United States Supreme Court'.

disobey the law is not obtainable by the payment of a penalty or a licence fee. It is not obtainable at all in a parliamentary democracy . . . '.[22]

The official point of view is significant, for it is one of the main sources for evidence about the content of political obligation, the other being traditions of argument within the community. Identifying and understanding these is a crucial task for descriptive legal theory. And since every description of an object is a selection from among all possible facts about it, every description displays evaluative considerations in determining which facts are salient.[23] At the same time, however, it is not a matter of first-order moral or political argument. When we ask the moral question how we should respond to law's requirements, we are concerned not with how it might be desirable for law to address us, but with how it does.

The most insistent critic of this view is Dworkin. He rejects the descriptive enterprise and with it the ordinary concept of obligation, suggesting instead that law is binding only in some 'more relaxed way'.[24] One can get a feeling for just how relaxed this is from his view that understanding the law is *never* a matter of trying to grasp what it requires of us, but rather a matter of 'Each citizen . . . trying to discover his own intention in maintaining and participating in that practice'.[25] Obedience does not involve a citizen's response to the law demands, but rather a 'a conversation with himself', and thus 'Political obligation is . . . a more protestant idea: fidelity to a scheme of principle each citizen has a responsibility to identify, ultimately for himself, as his community's scheme'.[26] While it is not possible here to explore these ideas fully, a few remarks are in order. While it is true that whenever I interpret something I am the interpreter, that hardly makes me the hero of every story. That my interpretative ambitions are mine does not show that *content* of my interpretation is an attempt to discover my intentions in participating in that practice. We often interpret practices in which we do not participate, and what it might mean for an ordinary citizen to 'maintain' the practice of law is obscure. Even in a democracy that effectively guarantees political participation, ordinary citizens are *law-takers* in much the way that consumers in a competitive market-place are price-takers: each is confronted by legal requirements that respond to his will, if at all, only in concert with the will of others. Thus, each individual subject no more decides to maintain the practice of law than each individual speaker decides to maintain the meaning of words. To identify the law's requirements with what each individual would do well to imagine it requiring, were the matter up to him, is to give a misleading picture of the structure and depth of the moral conflicts referred to at the outset of this chapter. Like some

[22] *Francome v Mirror Group Newspapers Ltd.* [1984] 2 All ER 408 at 412.

[23] I follow Amartya Sen, 'Description as Choice', in his *Choice, Welfare and Measurement* (Oxford: Blackwell, 1982). For a contrary view about the role of evaluation in description see John Finnis, *Natural Law and Natural Rights* (Oxford: Clarendon Press, 1980), 3–19.

[24] Dworkin, *Law's Empire*, 429 n. 3.   [25] ibid. 58.

[26] ibid. 413. For criticism on this point see G. J. Postema, ' "Protestant" Interpretation and Social Practices', *Law and Philosophy*, 6 (1987), 283.

Hegelians, Dworkin does not actually confront the problem of obedience; he avoids it.

Having distinguished legitimacy and obligation, the question arises what the relationship is between the two. There is clearly no moral obligation to obey an illegitimate legal system—not even an explicit promise would bind one in a Nazi or Stalinist regime. (Though one may have moral reasons for compliance with particular edicts.) But while legitimacy is thus necessary for obligation, the converse is not true.[27] I am justified in resisting unlawful arrest, but have no authority over the offending officer. The Allies were justified in coercing the Nazis and enforcing the Nuremberg judgments, but had no right to command German citizens. Dworkin disagrees. 'No state should enforce all of a citizen's obligations', he writes,

But though obligation is not a sufficient condition for coercion, it is close to a necessary one. A state may have good grounds in some special circumstances for coercing those who have no duty to obey. But no general policy of upholding the law with steel could be justified if the law were not, in general, a source of genuine obligations.[28]

One of these claims is not controversial: there are moral obligations that law should not enforce, for example, ordinary promises, fidelity to one's lover, and so on. If the law were sufficiently invasive in such matters it would lose its legitimacy. The other points however are doubtful. Dworkin supposes law should be enforced only if it is a source of valid obligations. But that condition is surely too narrow, for it is also a proper function of law to secure conformity with weighty moral reasons, whether or not they are independent obligations, and coercive sanctions are sometimes the best way to do that. One may believe that law should protect the environment and punish polluters without thinking this is a matter of prior moral obligation: it may not be obligatory at all—it may be an ordinary moral reason of great weight—or its obligatory character may be a consequence of rather than a reason for law's intervention.[29] In any case, these points—that coercive law must be legitimate and must be justified by moral reasons—are quite different from the idea that legitimate coercion must rest on a prior obligation *to obey* and, in the face of the Lockean objection, they lend nothing to its credibility. States properly coerce members of other states over whom they neither claim nor exercise any authority. That being so, there must be something like a prior moral right to enforce the requirements of justice. It does not matter whether we follow Locke as far as thinking this a natural right to *punish*—perhaps the concept of punishment is too closely bound up with the idea of positive authority to be disentangled.[30] But the essential point remains: within a general theory of allegiance, legitimacy and obedience are different issues.

[27] See further, Green, *The Authority of the State*, 71–5, 149–53, 242–3.

[28] Dworkin, *Law's Empire*, 191.

[29] On the capacity of law to create moral wrongs, see Tony Honoré, 'The Dependence of Morality on Law', *Oxford Journal of Legal Studies*, 13 (1993), 1–17.

[30] Thomas D. Senor, 'What if There are No Political Obligations?', *Philosophy and Public Affairs*, vol. 16, 260–8.

1.3 Justification

Law's claims are therefore substantial and invite moral scrutiny. Unless the obligation of obedience is supposed to be primitive,[31] we should be able to ground it in some familiar moral principles. But law is not the only social institution that claims obedience, and the plausibility of its claims cannot be assessed without considering further its nature. Are we therefore dependent on an adequate theory of the nature of law before we can assess the validity of a duty to obey?

Soper once held that 'the idea about what law is already entails the conclusion about the obligation to obey[32] and, as we have seen, Fuller thinks that an 'amoral datum' cannot create a duty to obey. That, however, is too simple. Even if law is austerely a matter of fact, that tells us nothing about whether there is an obligation to obey the law as determined by such facts. After all, whether or not someone has promised, and what he has promised to do, are also matters of fact determined by what he has said and done and by the conventions about such words and commitments. But promises generate obligations to perform. There is no reason why the same might not be true of law as positivists conceive of it. Contrariwise, the existence or content of law may depend on morality and yet this might not entail a general duty of obedience. Even if there is a necessary connection between law and morality, that might only mean that every true legal system is necessarily legitimate or, more weakly, has systemic value. None the less, the Fuller–Soper position points to an important truth. Although political obligation is not entailed by law's nature, it is constrained by it. As we have already seen, recognizing an obligation of obedience involves more than paying careful attention to law, or treating it as food for thought, or as valuable advice. But we cannot know whether there is a duty to obey *the law* unless we know something about law and the role it plays in human life. So aren't we back in Soper's bind? Not exactly, for there are significant features that are recognized by any plausible theory of the nature of law, but which stop short of determining such a theory.

First, law is *institutionalized*: it is the product not only of human thought and action and in that sense a social construction; it is more significantly the product of institutionalized thought and action. Nothing is law that is not in some way connected with the activities of institutions such as legislatures, courts, administrators, police, and so on. Neither ideal social norms nor general social customs, but only an institutionally relevant subset of these, count as law. Institutionalization is a matter of degree; the highly centralized and differentiated institutions of modern legal systems are but one possibility. Nor need we suppose that law is exhausted by

---

[31] E. F. Carritt maintained, 'all attempts to explain this recognition of political obligation in terms of something else lead to confusion, self-contradiction, and the evident misdescription of facts which we cannot doubt'. *Morals and Politics* (Oxford: Clarendon Press, 1935), 2. But even a basic obligation can be non-reductively illuminated.

[32] Soper, *A Theory of Law*, 8–9.

institutional facts. Those are matters in dispute among legal theories—Hart says that law is just those standards that courts are bound to apply in accord with their own customary practices; Dworkin holds that it includes any moral reason that is good ground for a court's decision. But on the general idea of the institutional character of law, positivists and modern natural lawyers are in agreement.

Secondly, law has a *wide scope*. It is a significant part of our concept of law that it is not limited to the affairs of a small group, such as a club, nor does it only attend to one restricted domain of life, such as baseball. Law governs high-stakes, open-ended domains, and is capable of regulating the affairs not only of small 'face-to-face' societies but large, dispersed, loosely structured organizations of many millions of people. Whether law chooses to exercise as much authority as it can is another question. Most modern legal systems, and all legitimate ones, are legally limited, but we should have no illusions about their power or importance: they not only claim power to regulate but *actually* regulate the most vital interests of all within their territory.

Thirdly, law is *morally fallible*.[33] It may require behaviour that is iniquitous, such as fighting in immoral wars. It may proscribe behaviour that is innocent, such as homosexual activity. It may fail to impose obligations that we all should bear, such as a duty of easy rescue. And it may do morally desirable things, such as taxation for public goods, in unjust ways. Morality always stands in appraisal of law, and not the other way around. Again, this is neutral between positivism and natural law. No one claims that law is morally infallible, and even if there is some necessary connection between law and morality, this is not it. The explanation for the fallibility of law may take competing forms, but the general idea is another of the deepest features of law for which any competent theory must account.

These three features do not specify a theory of law—they do not even suffice to distinguish law from all other forms of social order. They are jointly compatible with the most stringent legal positivism or the most capacious natural law. But together with the analysis of obligations, they help anchor an account of allegiance to law and release us from Soper's bind. From the fact that we are considering a moral obligation of obedience, it follows that we are seeking a binding and content-independent moral reason for compliance, one that is universal in the sense of covering all subjects of the law and all occasions on which their compliance is required. From the fact that it is obedience to *law*, we know that these requirements are broad-ranging, morally fallible, and are connected with institutions that are in some way distinct from the ordinary flow of social life. One last constraint follows from the doctrine of legitimacy. Legitimacy is a necessary condition for obligation, and legitimacy is a matter of both the scope and the location of authority. Although Swedish law may be sufficiently legitimate, Canadians have no obligation to obey it—not even if it should address itself to them. The obligation of obedience is thus understood to bind individuals to

---

[33] H. L. A. Hart, *Law, Liberty and Morality* (Stanford, Calif.: Stanford University Press, 1963), 3–4; and David Lyons, *Ethics and the Rule of Law* (Cambridge: Cambridge University Press, 1985), 66–8.

a *particular* legal system, the one of which they are citizens or subjects.[34] 'Particularity', as it is often called, does not presuppose or entail that reasons for obedience are agent-relative in character; it may be a consequence of the local urgency or efficacy of agent-neutral considerations, for example, the duty of beneficence or justice. Particularity seeks to reflect the common understanding that there is a special relationship between individuals and their legal systems, one that will tell in case of conflict between the requirements of their own system and any other. How can law which is institutionalized, wide-ranging, and morally fallible generate universal, particular, and binding reasons to act? That is the problem of political obligation. As we shall see, it is a very difficult problem.

2 VOLUNTARY OBLIGATIONS

2.1 Consent

A distinctive theme of Western political thought is the idea that political obligation is justified only by the consent of the governed.[35] In Hobbes, Locke, Rousseau, and Kant we find many variations on the claim that our duties to law are determined by some form of individual agreement, whether express or tacit. Promises, contracts, oaths, and vows all fall into this general area. In its core meaning, consent of these sorts is not only voluntary, it is performative: it is given with the intention of changing the rights, duties, powers, or liabilities of another, and it succeeds in part because it is known to be done with that intention.[36]

Allowing that consent may bind, it does not automatically follow that it does so in this context, for there are limits to what even competent adults can commit themselves to. This is the core of Locke's argument in the *Second Treatise*. If there are promissory powers we necessarily lack then we can never be held to have validly exercised them. On any plausible view, the capacity to enslave oneself is such a power. Thus, absolute governments are always illegitimate. Locke's argument suggests a more general worry, however, for there are other boundaries to our normative powers, including defeating conditions such as mistake, coercion, or duress. Precisely because law has a wide scope and is morally fallible, the promise to obey may seem

[34] It is of course possible to owe particular obligations to more than one legal system. For discussion and defence of the particularity requirement see Simmons, *Moral Principles and Political Obligations*, 31–5, and Green, *The Authority of the State*, 227–8.

[35] For helpful discussion of the voluntarist tradition see Patrick Riley, *Will and Political Legitimacy* (Cambridge, Mass.: Harvard University Press, 1982).

[36] Cf. Raz, *The Morality of Freedom* (Oxford: Clarendon Press, 1986), 80–2.

fatally open-ended and, if irrevocable, hazardous. Perhaps then its validity is limited to situations with further safeguards, including periodic reaffirmations of consent, if not Renan's *plébiscite de tous les jours*. And what should we say about duress? It is notorious that loyalty oaths tend to proliferate in the very circumstances in which they are invalid. The extorted professions of loyalty in seventeenth-century England or in the McCarthy years in the United States bound no one, and the same is true now of those demanded of refugee immigrants or military conscripts. Some have argued, following Hume, that such problems are endemic because people rarely have any choice but to live under their law. While that may be a sound objection to the idea that continued residence itself counts as consent, it does not show that express consent never binds. As Harry Beran argues, those who freely assume full membership of their political community when there is a right to exit and secession and space for internal dissidents cannot be said to be forced to remain.[37] And we must not conflate the correct idea that most people have no effective choice but to stay in their country with the suggestion that they have no effective choice but to acknowledge an obligation to obey it. Mere compliance with the law is normally sufficient to avoid coercive pressure.

To show that political consent is not inevitably defeated does not, however, show that it is valid. We also need to explain why we should want a power to bind ourselves to government in the first place. Hume challenges the Lockean to account for the moral obligation to obey the law:

> Your answer is, *because we should keep our word.* (. . .) I say, you find yourself embarrassed, when it is asked, *why are we bound to keep our word?* Nor can you give any answer, but what would, immediately, without any circuit, have accounted for our obligation to allegiance.[38]

Contrary to what Hume here implies, however, Locke does have a non-redundant theory about this.[39] It is not conspicuous in the *Second Treatise* because it is not necessary there, where the central question is about the limits of any possible promise, and not the justification for keeping promises in general. But Hume's objection is of interest for what it reveals about his view of consent. He thinks promising is solely a matter of 'public utility', by which he means the 'apparent interests and necessities of human society'.[40] We must keep our promises only because promising is an instrumentally useful institution; but in complex societies the very same is true of government, which cannot exist without the 'exact obedience' of its subjects.[41] We therefore have a duty to obey whether or not we have consented. Both of these artificial virtues 'stand precisely on the same foundation' and 'being of like force and authority, we gain nothing by resolving the one into the other'.[42]

---

[37] Harry Beran, *The Consent Theory of Political Obligation* (London: Croom Helm, 1987).

[38] David Hume, 'Of the Original Contract', in *Essays, Moral Political, and Literary*, ed. E. F. Miller (Indianapolis: Liberty Classics, 1985), 481.

[39] See *Essays on the Law of Nature*, ed. W. von Leyden (Oxford: Clarendon Press, 1958), 183.

[40] Hume, 'Original Contract', 481.   [41] ibid. 480.

[42] Hume, *Treatise of Human Nature*, 481, 'Original Contract', 481.

Though this argument seems to have persuaded many, it is fundamentally flawed. Hume's quarrel with a rationalistic meta-ethics here obstructs his understanding of the substantive morality. To defend the necessity of consent one does *not* need to show that promising is natural or primary, but only that it has special value in the circumstances. The fact that two normative practices have ultimate foundations of the same type does not prove that one is not necessary for the validity of the other, any more than the fact that two rooms rest on the foundations of one house proves that one can enter the second without passing through the first. In defending consent, theorists appeal to two different sorts of considerations. First, there are instrumental reasons for wanting deliberate control over our duties. When their incidence depends on the will of those who bear them, there is generally less chance that they will be harmed. That is admittedly not the only way to protect subjects, but it is a good one when the stakes are as high as they are in the case of allegiance to law. It is true that the requirement of legitimacy also does some of this work—however, legitimate governments are still imperfect governments, and consent enables individuals to limit their commitments if they need to. It also empowers those who wish to change their allegiance from one legitimate government to another to do so forthwith, without awaiting the slow growth of other sorts of moral ties.

But this is not the whole story. Such instrumental considerations do not explain the role of promising in all contexts. To require that people can marry only with their own consent, for example, obviously has instrumental benefits; but the exchange of promises has a further role as constitutive of a valued relationship and as a solemn expression of its beginning. Hume's instrumentalism conceals these functions, but perhaps we see them at work in Locke's suggestion that while almost any receipt of law's benefits will count as 'tacit' consent to obey, only actual explicit consent will make people 'members' of a commonwealth.[43]

Those are the main reasons for thinking that consent, if given, could bind. But *is* it given? It is by many officials, by voluntary immigrants, and by others in special cases; but many do nothing that can properly be counted as consent. The career of consent theory in the face of its evident failure of universality is a history of its extension, dilution, and ultimately subversion. Consider only the two most famous salvage attempts to produce 'tacit' consent on the part of those who apparently do no such thing. Continued residence was suggested already in the *Crito* and famously and fatally elaborated by Locke:

every man that hath any Possession or Enjoyment, of any part of the Dominions of any Government, doth thereby give his *Tacit Consent* (...) whether this his Possession be of Land, to him and his Heirs for ever, or a Lodging only for a Week, or whether it be barely travelling freely on the Highway.[44]

---

[43] Locke, *Two Treatises*, II, s. 122: 394. For commentary see A. John Simmons, '"Denisons" and "Aliens": Locke's Problem of Political Consent', *Social Theory and Practice*, 24 (1998), 161–82.

[44] Locke, *Two Treatises*, II, s. 119: 392.

This fails because performative consent is tied to certain conventions: it must be *recognized* that φ-ing in circumstances *C* counts as consenting, and the individual must φ intentionally or at least knowingly invoke that convention. One cannot consent by accident. Owning property or benefiting from the rule of law notoriously does not mean that the subject thereby undertakes a duty of obedience, so if it generates any duty to obey it cannot be by a voluntary route. Esoteric arguments to the effect that it *ought* to bear this meaning simply concede the point. Participation in politics, the other main candidate, fares no better. Not only is participation itself nowhere near universal, no one—certainly not the police or courts—thinks those who do not vote have no, or even weaker, obligations to obey. Thus the common analogies between participation and promissory estoppel are misguided.[45] It may be that in ordering a meal I induce a restaurateur to serve me in the expectation of payment, but it is also crucially true that those who do not order, or who order while announcing that they will not pay, do not get served. In politics, in contrast, the responses and expectations of others are not correlated to one's degree or kind of participation. Whether or not one has voted, run for office, or served on a jury, one is met with the very same demands for and expectations of obedience.

Consent to a legitimate government thus provides exactly the sort of reason the tradition has in mind: it generates a content-independent, binding reason to comply and it establishes a special relationship with a particular legal system. Perhaps that is why Hume, who thinks consent both improbable and unnecessary, none the less concedes that among the possible foundations for obligation consent is 'the best and most sacred of any'.[46] That it cannot yield a duty of anything like the right scope sets legal theory off on the search for an alternative.

2.2 Expressive Theories

Even if the obligation to obey must be voluntary, it does not follow that it must be the result of a performative act intended to assume an obligation. It may be enough that obligation is in some way a necessary consequence of a contingent relationship voluntarily created.

What I shall call 'expressive theories' adapt the second function of promising to a non-performative context. The most popular model here is friendship.[47] While people usually choose their friends, they do not do so in order to have people to owe duties to. Indeed, such a reason for making friends is incompatible with true friendship. But once one has friends, one has obligations to them—obligations of support, honesty, and reciprocity. Whatever other reasons one might have for fulfilling these obligations, doing so also expresses and is known to express loyalty to one's friends.

---

[45] e.g. Peter Singer, *Democracy and Disobedience* (New York: Oxford University Press, 1974), 45–59.

[46] Hume, 'Original Contract', 474.

[47] Raz, *Authority of Law*, 250–61.

Expressive theories offer the most plausible non-reductive interpretation of the traditional arguments from gratitude or community.[48] On such views we are bound to obey because that is an appropriate expression of emotions that we have good reason to feel: gratitude to the law for all that it gives us, respect for its good-faith efforts to guide us, or a sense of belonging to a community under law. Joseph Raz suggests, 'A person identifying himself with his society, feeling that it is his and that he belongs to it, is loyal to his society. His loyalty may express itself, among other ways, in respect for the law of the community.'[49] When such an attitude is permissible—when the law is legitimate—and when it flourishes it is a genuine source of obligations.

Although expressive obligations are sometimes valid, they none the less fail to justify the duty to obey the law. They leave unexplained why *obedience* fittingly expresses gratitude or loyalty to law. It is not enough to say 'it just does', as we might to one who asks why the word 'dog' refers to dogs. In addition to any conventional aspects, certain relationships have internal necessities that make expressive behaviour appropriate or inappropriate, and these necessities depend on the nature and purposes of the relationships in question. Consider Locke's objection to attempts to ground the duty of obedience in such notions as the biblical injunction to honour one's parents:

> A Man may owe *honour* and respect to an ancient, or wise Man; defence to his Child or Friend; relief and support to the Distressed; and gratitude to a Benefactor, to such a degree, that all he has, all he can do, cannot sufficiently pay it: But all these give no Authority, no right to any one of making Laws over him from whom they are owing.[50]

Locke's claim that one should *thank* a benefactor, *respect* the wise, or *defend* a friend are not claims about what is conventional, but about what is fitting in view of the nature of the relationship in question; that is why they do not call for the kind of authority and obedience we see in law. For Locke, obedience *is* fitting in other contexts, for example, the relationship of parent and child, or creator and created. Children do not choose their parents, nor creatures their creators, and they owe them obedience, if they do, on grounds that have nothing to do with voluntarism.

Moreover, even where there are conventional aspects to the expression of gratitude, respect, or loyalty to the law, and where obedience is a possible expression of those feelings, it does not follow that obedience is the only or best way to show it, as Raz acknowledges. Our idea of the appropriate expression of gratitude is not determined by the subject–state relationship. Only in rare and highly ritualized cases is there a mandatory way to express respect, such as in prescribed forms of dress or address in court. In our cultures, the conventional meaning of obedience is actually more complex, for our moral heritage is not only Hebrew but also Greek. Alongside

---

[48] See A. D. M. Walker, 'Political Obligation and the Argument from Gratitude', *Philosophy and Public Affairs*, 17 (1988), 191–211, and G. Klosko, 'Political Obligation and Gratitude', *Philosophy and Public Affairs*, 18 (1989), 352–8.

[49] Raz, *Authority of Law*, 259. See see also his 'Government by Consent', in J. R. Pennock and J. W. Chapman (eds.), *Authority Revisited: Nomos XXIX* (New York: New York University Press, 1987), 76.

[50] Locke, *Two Treatises*, II, s. 70: 356.

the idea that obedience to law is a proper expression of the devotion of a people, we have also inherited the idea that it displays a servility inappropriate in a city of free and equal citizens. These conflicting meanings typically leave the individual considerable latitude as to how to express the attitudes in question.

Finally, feelings of gratitude, loyalty, and respect are most at home in the personal contexts that form the paradigms for expressivism. Their extension to the institutionalized and bureaucratic realm of law is generally far-fetched. We must remember Hart's lesson that the alienation of law and life is a standing risk in modern society, that the law is precisely *not* a smoothly fitting part of *Sittlichkeit*, or the soul of a nation, and this flows not from corruption or injustice but simply from the estrangement of law and people that is inevitable when law is bureaucratized, technical, and arcane.[51] For all of these reasons, expressivism seems destined to fare little better than performative consent in grounding obligations to obey.

2.3 Fairness

The last significant move within the voluntarist tradition abandons the claim that obedience depends on either performative or expressive acts, and retreats to the position that it flows from a mere willingness to benefit from the reciprocal compliance of others. The element of will thus remains, though in an attenuated form compatible with the bureaucratic and alienated nature typical of legal cultures. Perhaps the most influential contemporary theory of obligation, the theory of fairness or fair play was defended by Hart[52] and most influentially elaborated by Rawls thus:

Suppose there is a mutually beneficial and just scheme of social cooperation and that the advantages it yields can only be obtained if everyone, or nearly everyone, cooperates. Suppose further that cooperation requires a certain sacrifice from each person, or at least involves a certain restriction of his liberty. Suppose finally that the benefits produced by cooperation are, up to a certain point, free: that is, the scheme of cooperation is unstable in the sense that if any one person knows that all (or nearly all) of the others will continue to do their part, he will still be able to share a gain from the scheme even if he does not do his part. Under these conditions a person who has accepted the benefits of the scheme is bound by a duty of fair play to do his part and not to take advantage of the free benefits by not cooperating.[53]

The validity of that general moral principle has sometimes been doubted. Robert Nozick, for example, offers a variety of counterexamples intended to show that without consent the receipt of benefits cannot bring an obligation to reciprocate: 'If each day a different person on your street sweeps the entire street, must you do so when

[51] Hart, *Concept of Law*, 117.

[52] H. L. A. Hart, 'Are There Any Natural Rights?', *Philosophical Review*, 64 (1955), 175–91.

[53] John Rawls, 'Legal Obligation and the Duty of Fair Play', in S. Hook (ed.), *Law and Philosophy* (New York: New York University Press, 1964), 9–10.

your time comes? Even if you don't care that much about a clean street? Must you imagine dirt as you traverse the street, so as not to benefit as a free rider?'[54] He invites similar scepticism about a duty to help provide music through a public address system, or to pay for books that someone has thrust on you. In fact, such cases do not meet the Hart–Rawls conditions: they are mere externalities, or independent of co-operation, or unjust in their distribution of benefits and burdens.[55] Most important, however, in none of them can the beneficiaries plausibly be said to 'accept' the benefits. Admittedly, Rawls never specifies what that condition requires, but Simmons's proposal that they must either try to get the benefits and succeed, or take them knowingly and willingly seems broadly consistent with the spirit of the principle.[56]

The role of the acceptance condition is controversial,[57] but it is common ground that without it fairness does not create voluntary obligations. (We shall see below, in Sect. 3.2, where it actually leads.) Acceptance does not, of course, *reduce* fairness to consent: those who jump subway turnstiles accept the benefits of public transportation without intending to assume any obligation to pay their fair share. But the acceptance condition none the less renders fairness vulnerable to the very same objection as the consent principle: not enough people perform the relevant action. Many benefits, including law and order, national security, public health and so on, are what Simmons calls 'open benefits' that could be avoided only by extraordinary changes in one's life style, by internal exile in a remote part of the country, or by emigration (which will only take one to another country and another set of compulsory benefits). This is not to deny that some people willingly accept the benefits of co-operation and are therefore bound in fairness to do their part. Some immigrate in search of them, or assume roles and positions calculated to yield them. And even if a minimum package of benefits is standard and unavoidable, many actively pursue more—their children enjoy compulsory schooling but also clamour for places in public universities. Although the basic moral principle is valid and relevant in such cases, it simply does not carry the obligation to obey as far as law reaches.

Finally, unlike both consent-based and expressivist theories, fairness is insufficiently particularized, for such benefits as people do willingly accept do not always respect the boundaries of legal systems. Americans tune in to the Canadian Broadcasting Corporation, Canadians to National Public Radio, and everyone uses the internet. With greater transnational communication and co-operation, such benefits are only likely to expand. No doubt some particularization of our duties can be explained by the fact that many systems of co-operation are local; but this rough and ready truth does not track the claims of law.

[54] Robert Nozick, *Anarchy, State and Utopia*, (New York: Basic Books, 1974), 94
[55] See Simmons, *Moral Principles and Political Obligations*, 118–36.   [56] ibid. 106–8.
[57] Richard J. Arneson, 'The Principle of Fairness and Free-Rider Problems', *Ethics*, 92 (1982), 616–33.

3 Non-voluntary Theories

While other variations on voluntarism are no doubt possible, it is difficult to see how any such theory can survive the objections to consent, expressivism, and fairness, for these flow from a common problem. It is of the essence of voluntarism that it is rooted in the wilfulness of political arrangements, and the jurisdiction claimed by law seems bound to overreach the contingent relations established by individual choice. To Hume, that suggests an obvious conclusion:

> [I]t being certain, that there is a moral obligation to submit to government, because everyone thinks so; it must be as certain, that this obligation arises not from a promise; since no one, whose judgment has not been led astray by too strict adherence to a system of philosophy, has ever dreamt of ascribing it to that origin. Neither magistrates nor subjects have form'd this idea of our civil duties.[58]

Hume's objection to consent may be generalized, for all voluntary obligations depend on the beliefs of the subject. One cannot promise by accident—'no man can either give a promise or be restrain'd by its sanction and obligation unknown to himself'[59]—but neither can one unwittingly express an attitude or accept a benefit. So Hume is right to say that lack of the relevant belief negatives a voluntary obligation of obedience. But Hume also claims that there must be an obligation because 'everyone thinks so'. Notice that this second appeal to belief is of logically different status from the first. *Absence* of the first-person belief that one has performed the relevant voluntary act negates the claim that one has a voluntary obligation. But the *presence* of a belief that there is a non-voluntary obligation does not validate it. The fact, if it be one, that 'everyone thinks so' may suggest that *there is* an obligation to be justified, but it cannot itself be a *ground* of that obligation. Because non-voluntary obligations are belief-independent, common opinion is not decisive one way or another. What we therefore need is some moral principle that applies in these circumstances and is capable of generating obligations of obedience to law. The most influential candidates are of two types.

3.1 Associative Obligations

The smallest departure from voluntarism retains one of its main features: the contingency of social relations. For the voluntarist, this is explained by the fact that such relations are created if not deliberately then at least willingly. For the associationist, these are merely special cases. Following the philosophical idealists through the lush overgrowth of organic metaphor, they emphasize the gradual growth and

---

[58] Hume, *Treatise of Human Nature*, 547.   [59] ibid. 549.

development of significant relationships like family, religion, and community. Common moral thought holds that family, for example, owe each other special duties of loyalty, respect, and support that partly constitute their relationship but which do not, or at any rate need not, arise from agreement. There is an important truth here, for we are often less engaged in choosing, pursuing, and revising our goals than we are in adapting and accommodating ourselves to the contingencies the world throws up—for example, even those who choose parenthood do not choose their particular children with their unique constitutions and temperaments.[60] A theory of allegiance to law ought surely to find some way to accommodate this reality.

Like communitarian theories of justice, with which they have certain affinities, associationist doctrines of obligation are often vague, asserting that people in organic associations feel obligated by their membership, but without articulating any moral reasons that might ground those feelings.[61] One version focuses on the obligations attached to social roles. There are two problems about role obligations, and they are often poorly distinguished.[62] First, there is the question of validity: what establishes that the duties attached to a station are binding even when one is conscripted into it? Most associationist theories overemphasize this issue and treat the problem of role obligations as if it were a matter of explaining why non-voluntary duties ever bind. But that is a false problem. Anyone who recognizes that there are voluntary obligations must also recognize non-voluntary ones, for the duty to keep agreements cannot itself be founded on agreement. Moreover, there may not be any general obligation to perform the duties of one's station; these may be justified piecemeal by different considerations in different cases. The apparent general duty may simply be an intermediate conclusion summarizing a range of unrelated reasons, including the dependence of others on one's performance.

The second problem is about content. Why should we acknowledge a role consisting of just *these* duties? Associationists sometimes argue as if in explaining how non-voluntary obligations are possible we have automatically explained why their scope and content should be determined by social roles, but that plainly does not follow. Dworkin ventures an answer to this question. He says that we have 'a duty to honour our responsibilities under social practices that define groups and attach special responsibilities to membership . . . '.[63] These duties are not consent-based; their content and liability depends on group practice rather than on individual agreement, and practice not only identifies but in some way also justifies the duties, provided that certain conditions hold. First, every true community must be a bare community

[60] See Charles Larmore, 'The Idea of a Life Plan', *Social Philosophy and Policy*, 16 (1999), 96–112.

[61] A. J. Simmons, 'Associative Political Obligations', *Ethics*, 106 (1996). C. H. Wellman, 'Associative Allegiances and Political Obligations', *Social Theory and Practice*, 23 (1997), 181–204.

[62] Cf. Michael O. Hardimon, 'Role Obligations', *Journal of Philosophy*, 91 (1994), 333–63.

[63] Dworkin, *Law's Empire*, 198. I discuss Dworkin's account in greater detail in 'Associative Obligations and the State', in Allen Hutchinson and Leslie Green (eds.), *Law and the Community: The End of Individualism?* (Toronto: Carswell, 1989), 93–118, and draw on that argument here.

satisfying the minimal conditions for group life as defined by social practice.[64] Next, its members must think that their obligations are special, personal, and derive from some good-faith interpretation of equal concern for the well-being of all members. These conditions are said to justify associative obligations as such: 'If the conditions are met, people in the bare community have the obligations of a true community whether or not they want them . . . '.[65]

No doubt political associations bear certain similarities to other non-voluntary relationships: people rarely choose their states, they do not agree with all their laws, nationality structures their identities, political relationships grow organically, and membership in a state may in some cases have intrinsic value. But there are also significant disanalogies. Once again, the institutional nature of law militates against any secure fit between legal order and social life. If parenthood or neighbourhood are associations, they are so in a sense that brings them closer to the desires and needs of their occupants. Subjects of the legal system do not normally stand to those institutions as neighbours stand to their neighbourhood. Then there is the matter of scope. In the paradigmatic cases of associative obligations there is a degree of social intimacy that cannot be expected in law. As Rousseau puts it, 'The more the social bond is stretched, the slacker it becomes'.[66] Should that not give us pause?

Dworkin's account avoids this problem. He denies that the conditions for associative obligation involve actual beliefs or desires of members of the association, or even of anyone at all. They are 'interpretive properties': 'practices that people with the right level of concern would adopt—not a psychological property of some fixed number of the actual members'.[67] That is to say, a bare community becomes a true community if a certain complex argument holds true, irrespective of its members' attitudes. Dworkin's rhetoric aside, this is obviously at some remove from associative obligations and the organic view of social life that inspires them. Such obligations seek to explain the moral force of the contingent and accidental; when they fall out of a necessary interpretative imputation that no one may actually endorse, detached from the lives of its subjects, it is plain that we have left associative obligations far behind.

Nor is it clear how the problem of content is to be resolved. Dworkin's paradigm for associative ties is the non-voluntary association of siblings—fraternity is the exemplar that he has in mind. But the content of fraternal or sororal obligations lies in the neighbourhood of mutual aid or respect, not obedience. That is why the usual associative model for obedience relations is not in fact the horizontal association among siblings but the vertical hierarchy of parent and child. However, the normal arguments for parental authority have nothing to do with communal association: they are instrumental or expressive. Perhaps there is an expressive element in Dworkin's theory, for he requires that as a condition of legitimacy a community

[64] Dworkin, *Law's Empire*, 207–8.   [65] ibid. 201.
[66] *The Social Contract*, bk. II, ch. 9, trans. M. Cranston (Harmondsworth: Penguin, 1968), at 90.
[67] Dworkin, *Law's Empire*, 201.

display the virtue he calls 'integrity': a principled coherence expressing a doctrine of equal concern for its members. That virtue may be admirable; it may contribute to legitimacy. But while someone's having integrity may win them our respect, admiration, and emulation, it does not follow that it is wrong for us to interfere with their projects and ambitions, nor does it give them any claim to our obedience.

It is a final worry for any associationist view that it is liable to generate conflicting communal obligations, as it perhaps did for Antigone, caught between her sisterly and religious duty to bury her brother and her ruler's command forbidding it. As subjects are often also sisters and patriots parishioners, associative obligations are endemically competing.[68] These conflicts, unresolvable from the point of view of each association, suggest why communitarianism is, as Dunn rightly says, a feeble and sentimental solution to the problem of political obligation:

> Religious and social solidarity, so far from being the solution to the problems of political instability, are virtually the source of that instability. The point of political obligation was precisely to contain, to bring under rational and humane control, the diffuse but vivid menace which these wider imaginative binds represented.[69]

3.2 Necessary Institutions

In all accounts canvassed thus far there is a pressure in the direction of arguing that political obligation is somehow inevitable or necessary. The final theory overtly embraces this idea. In Hume, but also at points in Hobbes or Kant, we find the view that law is a necessary institution without which the most prized things of life would just be impossible, and that an obligation of obedience is a necessary condition for the existence of law. That thought pulls us away not only from every form of voluntarism, but from contingency itself. The fundamental argument is stated by Elizabeth Anscombe: 'If something is necessary, if it is, for example, a necessary task in human life, then a right arises in those whose task it is, to have what belongs to the performance of the task'.[70]

There is a forensic problem of identifying the necessary institutions. Hobbes and his successors propose a rationalistic method: an institution is necessary if suitably motivated and situated people would agree to adopt it. If sound, such an argument identifies what we have reason to believe, want, or do; it does not of course show that we actually believe, want, or have done it. In contrast to an actual contract theory which is a species of consent, hypothetical contractarianism lies wholly in the realm

---

[68] The importance of obligations to secondary associations is emphasized by Michael Walzer, *Obligations: Essays on Disobedience, War, and Citizenship* (Cambridge, Mass.: Harvard University Press, 1970), 4–23.

[69] John Dunn, 'Political Obligation', in David Held (ed.), *Political Theory Today* (Stanford, Calif.: Stanford University Press, 1991), 29.

[70] Elizabeth Anscombe, 'On the Source of the Authority of the State', *Ratio*, 20 (1978), 17.

of the rational (though, in its most influential versions, a thin and even foolish view of rationality).[71] Others follow Hume's empiricism:

A small degree of experience and observation suffices to teach us that society cannot possibly be maintained without the authority of magistrates, and that this authority must soon fall into contempt, where exact obedience is not paid to it. The observation of these general and obvious interests is the source of all allegiance, and of that moral obligation, which we attribute to it.[72]

And here we may also include the speculative teleologies of Aristotelian theories according to which political activity is necessary to the full development of human nature.

Though there are therefore different ways of identifying the necessary institutions, with somewhat different results, most accounts share certain features. One well-developed representative is due to George Klosko.[73] Although he wants to ground obligation in reciprocity, he rejects as too stringent the idea that the benefits of law must be accepted, or even flow from some scheme of co-operation. His idea is rather that there are certain 'presumptively beneficial public goods', goods that anyone would want and which require social co-operation to produce. Now Klosko appears to treat this in a Hobbesian or Humean way, as defined by reference to the wants of the subjects; but a generalization of his approach could adopt an objective theory of benefit, grounded in reasons that apply to everyone rather than reasons of which they are aware. And thus not only self-interest or personal needs, but also security for the interests of others or the public may be among the presumptively beneficial effects of law.

There is no doubt that some of what law does is in this way essential—above all, it saves us from the parlous circumstances of a state of nature. But law's ambitions are more expansive than that. It also does things that are permissible but not necessary: it prohibits cruel treatment of animals, enacts residential zoning, declares official languages, establishes national holidays, supports education and the arts, creates honours, and promotes exploration of the heavens. And in the service of what is mandated by necessity, law draws lines and distinctions that are themselves merely permissible—it defines an age of consent, an acceptable level of risk imposition, formalities for wills and marriages, and so on. It is important to notice that neither the vast range of permissible state activity, nor the permissible determinations, to use Aquinas's term, of necessary activities are fixed by the requirements of legitimacy.

What then is the connection between the necessary and the permissible? Klosko's view is that the state must provide the necessary goods, and if it does that, it may also provide discretionary ones provided that it does so fairly. But that is not exactly the

---

[71] See Amartya Sen, 'Rational Fools', in his *Choice, Welfare, and Measurement*.

[72] Hume, 'Original Contract', 480.

[73] George Klosko, *The Principle of Fairness and Political Obligation* (Lanham, Md.: Rowman and Littlefield, 1992).

issue: the question is not whether it is legitimate to provide optional goods, but whether there is the same obligation of reciprocity to contribute to their provision as there is to the necessary ones. One cannot argue that the optional goods are all essential for the necessary ones: it is hard to see how space exploration is necessary to airline safety. But there is a more fundamental objection here. Even where there are instrumental relationships between the two kinds, they do not transmit obligations from ends to means. If A has an obligation to φ and χ-ing is a necessary, or even highly desirable means to φ-ing, it does not follow that A has an obligation to χ. If I have an obligation to pay you five dollars tomorrow, and the only way I could pay is to give you the five silver dollars my mother gave me as a present, it does not follow that I have any obligation to pay you in silver. Obligation imposing reasons are not transitive across ideal, or even necessary, means to their fulfilment.

What's more, it is unclear what *is* necessary for law to fulfil its socially necessary functions. It is sometimes alleged that law needs exactly what it demands. As Creon puts it in *Antigone*: 'Whoever is chosen to govern should be obeyed I must be obeyed, in all things, great and small I just and unjust', failing which there is only anarchy: 'This is why cities tumble and the great houses rain down I this is what scatters armies'.[74] Hume similarly holds that the authority of the magistrate cannot survive without 'exact obedience'. But all such claims founder on the fact that what is actual must be possible. Law does not in fact enjoy exact obedience, and disobedience in certain small or unjust things does not bring cities to ruin. It is obviously possible for legal systems to withstand certain kinds and quantities of disobedience, and when that brings more good than harm there can be no objection on grounds of necessity.

This is wholly consistent with the thought that legitimate government is a necessary and beneficial institution. The only issue is whether a policy of general obedience is a necessary policy. In many areas of life we need an efficacious common policy, and no such settlement can survive if everyone should pick and choose when to comply. All of that is true. But an argument that *some* policy is needed is not an argument in favour of a *particular* policy. And the policy that we are considering here, that of taking all of the law's requirements as binding, is but one of the options. There is no reason to think that in all legitimate states, at all times, and for all people it is always the optimal one. The state's own view is something like *actual-rule* utilitarianism: the thesis that obeying the actually existing set of legal obligations is always best. Where law is both institutionalized and morally fallible, this is the least plausible form of consequentialism going.

I mentioned above that although Klosko sees his doctrine of presumptive public goods as an elaboration of fairness, its logic actually pulls away from that theory. Let us pursue this idea further. If law's benefits really are so important then we should not remain indifferent to their provision. If there are things that everyone desperately

---

[74] Sophocles, *Antigone*, trans. Dudley Fitts and Robert Fitzgerald (New York: Harcourt, Brace and Co., 1940), 46.

needs, and if co-operation is needed to provide them, then surely it is wrong to fail to provide them. While the principle of fairness prohibits free-riding, it does not show that one must enter any given scheme of co-operation in the first place. Those who jump turnstiles are free-riders and violate the obligation to pay their share; but those who walk instead of taking the subway do not. Klosko's argument for the crucial importance of presumptive goods—goods that are the very foundation of social life—thus has little in common with a fairness-based theory. In fact, it leads in the direction of Rawls's mature thought, which abandons fairness in favour of an obligation based on the natural duty of justice:

This duty requires us to support and comply with just institutions that exist and apply to us. It also constrains us to further just arrangements not yet established, at least when this can be done without too much cost to ourselves. Thus if the basic structure of society is just, or as just as it is reasonable to expect in the circumstances, everyone has a natural duty to do his part in the existing scheme. Each is bound to these institutions independent of his voluntary acts, performative or otherwise.[75]

This is about as far as one can plausibly move from voluntarism. Yet the duty to comply with just institutions may not always counsel obedience. Even in a reasonably just state, and even with respect to those laws that are, from the point of view of justice, non-optional, there may be cases in which disobedience is licensed by natural duty. Reasonably just legal systems may have local and occasional injustices, provided these are not too severe. What would be wrong with complying with these laws only as far as such compliance is necessary to ensure respect for the administration of justice?

Moreover, the idea that we must comply with just institutions that 'apply to us' seems unacceptably broad. John Simmons argues convincingly that an institution can apply to me and be just and yet fail to bind me to comply with its rules. An Institute for the Advancement of Philosophers cannot benefit me, however justly, and then demand that I pay its dues.[76] He concludes that Rawls fails to distinguish a weak, purely descriptive, sense of 'application', meaning that one falls within the scope of an institution, and a stronger normative sense according to which the institutional duties are not merely addressed to me, but are binding for me. As a voluntarist he thinks that could only result from my agreement or at least acceptance of its benefits.

This seems plausible if we are thinking of purely optional benefits. But according to Jeremy Waldron,[77] the example reveals an ambiguity between two senses of 'just'. Although the Institute *operates justly*—it fairly distributes the benefits it provides, it does not discriminate, and so on—it is not an institution whose activities are *required by justice*. On the contrary, it is clearly optional from that point of view. But, asks

75 John Rawls, *A Theory of Justice* (Cambridge, Mass.: Harvard University Press, 1971), 115
76 Simmons, *Moral Principles and Political Obligations*, 148.
77 Jeremy Waldron, 'Special Ties and Natural Duties', *Philosophy and Public Affairs*, 22 (1993), 1–30.

Waldron, if the aim of the Institute were to give aid to the homeless, and if this were required by justice rather than charity, and if that institution were an efficacious means of doing this, would we not have a duty to assist it, irrespective of any agreement or benefit on our own part? If Hobbes or Kant are right that the rule of law itself is not an optional extra but a matter of the direst necessity, and if we suppose that this necessity is most urgent with respect to those with whom we regularly interact—our neighbours—might there not be a 'range-limited' duty to obey any institution able to secure it?[78]

Although the distinction between an institution that behaves justly and an institution that achieves justice is important, so too is the distinction between an institution that does justice and an institution that *only* does justice. As I argued above, it is false to suppose that all of a reasonably just state's activity can be accounted for in this way. Thus, natural duty and necessity arguments both fall to the same objection: the conditions of legitimacy set the boundary of the *permissible* in law, not the *mandatory*. To show, against libertarian partisans of minimal government, that there is nothing wrong with state-subsidized moon-landings, national parks, or art galleries is not to show that these are required by justice. A natural duty argument will thus only ground a narrow obligation to obey the law—an obligation to obey those laws that are intimately connected with the requirements and administration of justice.

All necessity arguments thus suffer from an underlying problem: they try to get the theory of legitimacy to do too much work, a tendency that stems, strange as it may sound, from overvaluing justice. Despite the recent consensus that justice is the 'first virtue of social institutions', political institutions also have other virtues and are liable to other vices. The fact that we have a notion of tolerable injustice—one worth putting up with for the sake of other benefits—suggests that justice should sometimes take a back seat to other ideals. Law should indeed do justice, but it should also protect animals and the environment, maintain aesthetic ideals, encourage excellence of character, and promote the general conditions for human flourishing. Law's capacity to do such things is limited—some can only be promoted indirectly—and how it goes about it is constrained by the conditions of legitimacy. But within those limits law may properly set obligations for us, and here the natural duty of justice is ill placed to follow.

4 SCEPTICISM AND ITS SIGNIFICANCE

The accumulated failures of all voluntary and non-voluntary theories strongly suggest that there is no obligation to obey the law. How can legal theory tolerate such

[78] ibid. 14–16.

scepticism? Hume writes, 'nothing is a clearer proof, that a theory of this kind is erroneous, than to find, that it leads to paradoxes repugnant to the common sentiments of mankind, and to the practice and opinion of all nations and ages'.[79] Klosko too thinks this is among our deepest intuitions: 'the existence of strong general feelings that we have political obligations . . . is supported by our most basic feelings about politics. I take it as obviously true that most people believe they have obligations to their governments'.[80]

Does this suggest that scepticism about obligation must fail to achieve a 'reflective equilibrium' between our considered judgments about cases and a systematizing normative theory?[81] Shouldn't we accept our most basic pre-theoretical judgments, what Rawls calls our 'provisional fixed points' in argument: fixed because we are not to abandon them lightly, but provisional because they might, in principle, yield to a sufficiently persuasive theory? Perhaps. But the Rawlsian problem of coherence is not really in play here.[82] The 'fixed point' that these philosophers detect is not a judgment about a *case*—as it is when we demand that utilitarian theories explain why we should not punish the innocent. On the contrary, what feels fixed is a *theory*, namely, the theory of political obligation. No one argues that the sceptic's theory cannot be brought into equilibrium with casuistic judgments about when the law should be obeyed. There is no suggestion that a sceptic cannot explain why we should sometimes obey a law that is pointless or unjust; it is understood that in such cases he may appeal to content-dependent considerations, such as the risk of setting a bad example, upsetting expectations, or causing unfairness. The sceptic's claim is simply that such considerations do not generalize to a content-independent, universal obligation to obey. What scepticism actually conflicts with is the theory that everyone has such an obligation—but that is no more relevant than the fact that utilitarian theories of punishment conflict with retributivism. Agreeing with one's competitors is not a condition of reflective equilibrium.

A Humean *reductio* cannot therefore be justified in this way; it must instead rest on confidence in the method of common opinion in moral philosophy. The cogency of such arguments cannot be addressed here. Luckily, we do not need to, for there is in fact no convincing evidence to show that a belief in a general duty to obey is part of common, as opposed to official, moral consciousness.[83] Of course, subjects generally do have pro-attitudes towards their legal systems, but we should be careful in pronouncing about their content. In some general remarks on philosophical method, Thomas Nagel writes, 'Given a knockdown argument for an intuitively unacceptable

[79] Hume, 'Original Contract', 486.

[80] Klosko, *The Principle of Fairness and Political Obligation*, 22, see also 68.

[81] Rawls, *Theory of Justice*, 19–21, 46–53, 578–86. Cf. N. Daniels, 'Wide Reflective Equilibrium and Theory Acceptance in Ethics', *Journal of Philosophy*, 76 (1979), 256–82.

[82] I argue this point more fully in 'Who Believes in Political Obligation?', in W. A. Edmundson (ed.), *The Duty to Obey the Law* (Lanham: Rowman and Littlefield, 1999), 301–17.

[83] The best study is T. R. Tyler, *Why People Obey the Law* (New Haven: Yale University Press, 1990). I argue that it fails in 'Who Believes in Political Obligation?'.

conclusion, one should assume there is probably something wrong with the argument that one cannot detect—though it is also possible that the source of the intuition has been misidentified'.[84] Sceptical arguments about political obligation fall into the second alternative. The most plausible source of the intuition is three more general theses, all sound, and all consistent with scepticism:

T1. There is normally good reason to do what law requires.

T2. Some people have moral obligations to obey the law.

T3. There are some laws that everyone has a moral obligation to obey.

What is false is only:

T4. Everyone has a moral obligation to obey all the laws.

Denying T4 denies what some subjects take to be true, and what officials put it about as true: that there is always a binding, content-independent moral reason to do as the law requires of us. This will, in appropriate cases, make a difference to our practical reasoning, and it will make an even more significant difference to our understanding of the relationship between the individual and the law. Chaim Gans doubts this. He thinks sceptics deny that there is a general obligation to obey on the basis of trivial or esoteric examples—'jaywalking at three o'clock in the morning'—whereas these are not cases in which anyone ever cites the obligation to obey to begin with.[85] Rather, we see it at work when bad laws should none the less be obeyed, or when civil disobedients acknowledge that political obligation establishes a special justificatory burden. Yet here, Gans complains, the sceptic actually *agrees* on the outcome—he insists, as I did above, that in such cases there may be special reasons to comply with law. '[I]t would seem preferable to interpret people's views on practical issues in the way which best supports their practical implications, rather than rejecting these views and then resurrecting all their significant practical ramifications, in the manner of the anarchists.'[86]

This is, however, a misunderstanding. First, the theories are not extensionally equivalent: the sceptic insists on considering countervailing reasons that the believer in political obligation excludes and that will make a difference at the margin in a variety of cases. Secondly, the esoteric cases do matter, for they are the crucial tests. Where obedience is pointless, where there is reason to disobey and no content-dependent reason to obey, there we should expect to see the force of political obligation. These test cases are different from the crazy hypotheticals put forward in some other areas of philosophy, for instance, those that invite us to speculate about what we would 'intuitively' say about personal identity after teleportation. There is no science fiction in speed signs in the desert. We have experience of them; we know what we

[84] Thomas Nagel, *Mortal Questions* (Cambridge: Cambridge University Press, 1979), p. x.

[85] Chaim Gans, *Philosophical Anarchism and Political Disobedience* (Cambridge: Cambridge University Press, 1992), 90.

[86] ibid. 90–1.

would say; and anyone not in the grips of a theory will see that it strongly suggests that there is no general obligation of obedience.

It is also doubtful that the significance of political obligation is displayed in real cases of civil disobedience. It is striking that, as far as one can tell, every significant theorist who defends the obligation of obedience thinks his own jurisdiction is sufficiently just to trigger it. Locke wrote to make good William's claim; Hume wanted to include even China and Persia. It is clear that contemporary philosophers who defend political obligation have in mind their own countries, or countries very much like them. (One is reminded here of Kelsen's remark about the ideological drift of natural law theories: everyone who believes there are moral requirements for the validity of law also believes that his own legal system, properly understood, satisfies them.)[87] The idea that political obligation is normally thought to erect a significant moral hurdle against disobedience is puzzling. David Lyons rightly asks, 'how could philosophers of good will have assumed that moral justification was required to disobey laws supporting chattel slavery, racist colonialism, or Jim Crow?'[88] Indeed, it is unhistorical to think that Thoreau, Gandhi, or King thought their societies reasonably just and that disobedience called for special justification. But it is equally true in our day that the Greenham Common women, or ACT-UP, or the Seattle protestors, thought their societies radically defective and denied any moral inhibition to disobedience beyond establishing the justice of their cause. Political obligation seems as idle here as it does elsewhere.

The answer to Fuller's question is therefore clear. How does it come to be that law has the unusual quality of creating an obligation to obey it? It doesn't—there is no such obligation. To the different question of how law seems obligatory and what its halo consists in we have other answers. Our theory of normativity will give us some interpretation of the obligation-statements that are so central to law, and our theory of legitimacy will explain how and when law is justified in enforcing its rule. Beyond this, however, the general problem of an obligation to obey will just drop out.

Soper wonders whether that is coherent. He asks, 'How could it be that the practice of law, in the claims it makes, is so out of step (and presumably has always been out of step as long as states have existed) with moral philosophy?'[89] Perhaps the practice of law is not so deferential to philosophy, or perhaps statements of legal obligation are not always made with their full force. The fact that law must be put forth as morally obligatory does not entail that it must *be* morally obligatory. Compare the case of papal authority. Suppose a sceptical argument to the conclusion that popes lack the infallibility they claim—suppose that atheists or the reformed Christian churches are right in thinking this an unjustifiable pretence. Would this in any way

---

[87] Hans Kelsen, 'Law and Morality', in his *Essays in Legal and Moral Philosophy*, ed. O. Weinberger (Dordrecht: D. Reidel, 1973), 92.

[88] David Lyons, 'Moral Judgment, Historical Reality, and Civil Disobedience', *Philosophy and Public Affairs*, 27 (1998), 48.

[89] Philip Soper, 'Law's Normative Claims', 231.

undermine our confidence in the *character* of the claim? Would it suggest that the pope doesn't really claim any such authority after all? That is implausible. It is a familiar feature of many social institutions and roles that their nature is determined by what their occupants say and do, rather than by the validity or plausibility of those claims.

At this point there may be a temptation to acquiesce in the failure of the theories while resisting its significance. Jonathan Wolff is among those who succumb: 'I do not think that it is a flaw in a theory of political obligation if it has the consequence that some people are left without political obligations. To see this we should start by asking why universal political obligation was thought so desirable in the first place.'[90] The error here is simply that it is not a question of what is desirable, but of what it is. When we are attempting to understand deep features of our institutions, conceptual reformism is out of place. This is not to deny that our concepts may change. Popes did not always claim infallibility—that was a nineteenth-century innovation—and they may someday abandon it. There are, however, limits to how far an institution can change while retaining its identity. (Could a pope abandon the doctrine of apostolic succession?) Perhaps law will cease to claim authority, judges will no longer insist on the duty to obey, and we will all treat it as a price system. But in that case law itself will have changed, and our interest in its obligations will simply fade out.

5 THE PLACE OF OBLIGATION

How then should we respond to law's claims? In some circumstances, we may endorse Thoreau's robust rigorism: 'It is not desirable to cultivate a respect for the law, so much as for the right. (. . .) Law never made men a whit more just; and, by means of their respect for it, even the well-disposed are daily made the instruments of injustice.'[91] That is the right answer in an unjust regime. In more benign circumstances, however, the mixed policy indicated by T3 would be justifiable: there may be core areas and issues with respect to which one should accept an obligation of obedience and others that demand watchful attention. This is not a 'pick and choose' strategy, but neither is it political obligation, although depending on the scope and content of the core, it may approach it (this may have been Hart's view).[92]

[90] Jonathan Wolff, 'Political Obligation, Fairness, and Independence', *Ratio* (n.s.) 8 (1995), 97.

[91] Henry David Thoreau, *Walden and 'Civil Disobedience'* (New York: New American Library, 1960), 223.

[92] 'The recognition of an obligation to obey *the law* must as a minimum imply that there is at least some area of conduct regulated by law in which we are not free to judge the moral merits of particular laws and to make our obedience conditional on this judgment. In a modern state it seems most

Beyond this, we should acknowledge that good citizenship under law is a complex ideal. It involves obligations, but also of virtues, supererogations, and ideals. Does that suggest that the problem of political obligation is ill-posed? Bikhu Parekh claims that 'political obligation properly so-called has little to do with the obligation to obey the law' but is better understood as 'an obligation to take an active interest and to participate in the conduct of public affairs, to keep a critical eye on the activities of government, to speak up against the injustices of their society, to stand up for those too demoralized, confused and powerless to fight for themselves, and in general to help create a rich and lively community'.[93]

It is pointless to quarrel over words. The standard term for the duty of obedience is 'political obligation', though John Dunn may be on the mark in calling that 'a nineteenth-century name for a typically seventeenth-century problem'.[94] It is certainly not a theory of civic virtue, nor does it exhaust the obligations that conscientious citizens owe their law. But broadening the scope of 'political obligation' to include these other virtues and duties will not answer the sceptic, for on no plausible theory does political obligation not *include* the duty to obey the law. Without the central duty of obedience, a more comprehensive theory of political obligation is simply unmotivated.

We might, however, draw a different lesson from Parekh's observation: it may be that a single-minded focus on political obligation has occluded other important relationships to the law. Some desirable actions, traits and dispositions are not obligatory at all. Reflecting on his fellow Scots' tepid and sometimes tentative allegiance to the Hanovers, James Boswell wrote:

However convinced I am of the justice of that principle, which holds allegiance and protection to be reciprocal, I do however acknowledge, that I am not satisfied with the cold sentiment which would confine the exertions of the subject within the strict line of duty. I would have every breast animated with the *fervour* of loyalty; with that generous attachment which delights in doing somewhat more than is required, makes 'service perfect freedom'.[95]

That aspiration is laudable. Good citizenship aims for more than the calculating rigour of duty. It also seeks the virtues of civility, including tolerance where intolerance would be permitted, and the supererogatory acts that Boswell so admires. But beyond obedience and beyond civic virtue, there may still be other obligations in play.[96] Consider an analogy. A thriving market economy cannot survive merely on the punctilious observation of the obligations of property and contract; it requires

---

plausible to suggest that this area is that which includes matters of defense and economic welfare but excludes, say, matters of religion or esthetic taste.' Hart, 'Legal and Moral Obligation', 82–107.

[93] Bikhu Parekh, 'A Misconceived Discourse of Political Obligation', *Political Studies*, 41 (1993), 243.

[94] John Dunn, 'Political Obligation', 24.

[95] James Boswell, *A Journal of a Tour to the Hebrides with Samuel Johnson* (London: J. M. Dent, 1901), 189.

[96] In *Authority of the State* I mistakenly assumed that what is not an obligation of obedience must be a matter of virtue only.

also customary practices that cannot be provided by law or the market—what Durkheim calls the non-contractual foundations of contract. Many of these lie in the realm of political culture, and establishing them afresh is very difficult, as post-Soviet Europe has taught us. But there are also other exigencies of civil society: we must be open to dealing with strangers, we must deal in good faith, and we must not exploit inevitable loopholes in our agreements. It is not too much to regard these as social obligations antecedent to the market. Law does what it can to support and reinforce them, but it is helpless to create them *ex nihilo*.

Much the same holds true of the rule of law. The excessive focus on obedience has concealed at least three other sorts of obligations that underpin legal order.

1. *The obligation to facilitate the rule of law.* Natural duty theorists are correct to emphasize this, and wrong only to treat it as the foundation for obedience. Law itself supports the obligation to facilitate the rule of law, by imposing duties to report crimes, or to refrain from obstructing the police, or to avoid contempt of court, or to serve as a juror or witness. But there are many more occasions on which we can further or hinder the rule of law than there are occasions when we can obey. What's more, we can undermine the rule of law *without* disobeying. In the anti-poll tax days, the Scottish Labour Party mounted a 'Stop It' campaign, urging people not to withhold payment but to return their forms querying everything possible in an effort to make the tax unadministrable.[97] While some frivolous or vexatious queries may be prohibited by law, the administrability of any tax scheme counts on a considerable degree not only of voluntary compliance, but also limiting questions and objections that one is legally entitled to make.

There is a temptation to equate the rule of law with a system in which there is both willing compliance and, when that fails, rigorous and fair-minded enforcement. But, paradoxical as it seems, from the perspective of the rule of law there can be not only too little compliance, but also too much. Officials undermine it when they over-police areas in which it is proper to prohibit but wrong aggressively to enforce: indecency offences, jay-walking, drug use. Subjects undermine it when they obey when they should resist. Obedience is part of the rule of law, but not the whole, and not always the most important part.

2. *The obligation to know the law.* A second neglected obligation is logically prior to obedience. One cannot be guided by a law that one does not know. Of course, many legal systems disallow (for good reason) the defence of ignorance of the law and in that sense presuppose that subjects know it. But I have in mind something deeper— a basic acquaintance with the most significant legal institutions and traditions of one's own state. This is not necessary for the existence of law—as Hart argues, all that is needed from ordinary subjects is general compliance. Nor is it necessary for human

---

[97] See Richard Bellamy, 'The Anti-Poll Tax Non-Payment Campaign and Liberal Concepts of Political Obligation', *Government and Opposition*, vol. 29 (1994), 27.

perfection: it is permissible to take little interest in the law, and to tend one's own garden. But the rule of law cannot flourish where everyone withdraws in that way, even if each has some valid reason for so doing.

In spite of all the discussion of the arbitrary and even inconsistent[98] character of Holmes's suggestion that we understand law from the point of view of the 'bad man', little has been said about why the instrumentally motivated merit the criticism implied in his term 'bad'. If law really were a price system, this would make no sense. To explain it, we need to account for the importance of law's subjects being properly motivated by the law. There is nothing wrong with most people having no grasp of interstate trucking regulations or the requirements for certifying a class-action lawsuit—if they need to know they can ask their lawyers. But there is surely a moral deficiency in a society committed to the presumption of innocence, to proof beyond reasonable doubt in a criminal trial, to due process of law, or to the obligation not to discriminate and in which many people have no idea that these principles animate their legal system, what they involve, or how they are justified. And if that suggests that there is an obligation to know the law, then law must be knowable and we must strive to make it so, as Bentham continually insisted.

3. *The obligation to develop the law.* Finally, most discussions of the duty to obey proceed as if law were static. But law is dynamic and, as Kelsen says, it regulates its own creation. All the considerations about the necessity and value of the rule of law suggest that it should be also adapted to fulfil those values in changing circumstances. In such cases, valid reasons for stability in legal institutions, including ease of administrability and protection of expectations, are to be excluded in favour of the substantive values that the law should pursue.

The obligation to develop the law bears on citizens generally, but it is addressed most urgently to legislative and adjudicative officials. It is sometimes doubted that it applies to the courts. Fuller writes, 'Surely moral confusion reaches its height when a court refuses to apply something it admits to be law . . .'.[99] But this is an oversimplification. Courts have the power not only to apply law but to change it. They may do so intentionally, through the exercise of their equitable jurisdiction, their powers to overrule or distinguish cases, and by applying the doctrine of desuetude. They may also do so unintentionally through the gradual crystallization of new legal rules. The silence on these matters among students of legal obligation may be due to simplistic views about the judicial role and crude theories of the separations of powers, but it is

[98] Inconsistent, because such a point of view can give no principled reason for focusing on legal institutions—prediction of the activities of the courts—as against any other social power-holders, and in this case we cannot do what Holmes says we should do: understand law as a matter with 'well defined limits' ('The Path of the Law', *Harvard Law Review*, 10 (1897), 457, repr. in J. Feinberg and J. Coleman (eds.), *The Philosophy of Law*, 174). Predictions about the interference of the powerful do not respect these limits.

[99] Fuller, 'Positivism and Fidelity to Law', 86.

impossible to doubt that it is also a result of the continuing domination of the prob-lem of obedience.

That is only a sketch of some important obligations that are too little discussed; it does not purport to establish their foundation or draw their limits. But perhaps it suggests that we have been too concerned with the obligation of obedience, and that it is time to think more broadly about what we owe the law. One benefit of scepticism about political obligation is that it may release our thinking from that familiar har-ness, and encourage exploration of these, and other, obligations to the law.

CHAPTER 14

RESPONSIBILITY

CHRISTOPHER KUTZ

1 INTRODUCTION

CLAIMS of responsibility are notoriously multifarious. H. L. A. Hart's tale of the drunken captain, here adapted slightly, still shows this best:

(1) As captain of the ship, Smith was responsible for the safety of his passengers and crew. (2) But he drank himself into a stupor on his last voyage and was responsible for the loss of the ship and many of its passengers. (3) The doctors initially thought his drinking might have been the product of a paralytic depression, but later concluded that he had, in fact, been fully responsible at the time he became drunk. Smith initially maintained that the exceptional winter storms were responsible for the loss of the ship, but at trial, (4) after he was found criminally responsible for his negligent conduct and sentenced to ten years imprisonment, (5) he declared that no legal penalty could alleviate his guilt, for which he sought to atone. (6) Some of the survivors of the wreck, however, declared that they wished to put their nightmare behind them, and forgave Smith. (7, 8) Meanwhile, the president of the cruise line issued the following statement: 'Although the company must accept its legal responsibility for the loss of life and property, we bear no culpability for the disaster, since Smith fraudulently concealed from us his earlier employment problems, and our alcohol screens turned up no evidence of his drinking.'[1]

    I am grateful to Michael Green and Meir Dan-Cohen for their comments and criticism, as well as to students and colleagues in the Jurisprudence and Social Policy Program, to whom I have presented many of these ideas in different form. I am also grateful to Cambridge University Press for permission to re-use passages also appearing in my *Complicity: Ethics and Law for a Collective Age* (New York: Cambridge University Press, 2000).

[1] H. L. A. Hart, 'Postscript: Responsibility and Retribution', in *Punishment and Responsibility* (New York: Oxford University Press, 1968), 210–37, 211.

The story rehearses different uses of 'responsibility' in our everyday social, moral, and legal discourse; the numbers distinguish either different senses of responsibility, or different exemplary contexts in which someone takes responsibility or is held responsible. Here is Hart's catalogue: First is a claim of *role* responsibility: Smith, in virtue of his position as captain, had specific obligations to safeguard his ship and his passengers. A claim of role responsibility states the expectations of an agent's conduct towards some charge. Second is a claim of *causal* responsibility: the captain's insobriety is cited as the cause of the vessel's loss. Causal responsibility might be better thought of as a species of explanatory responsibility, causation being typically the best explanation of an event.[2] Third is a claim of *capacity* responsibility: the captain's decision to drink was not the product of a pathology, or some other non-deliberative causal process, but rather reflected his exercise of a power of rational self-determination. Being responsible, in this sense, simply is a matter of having the competency of self-government. Four, five, six, and seven relate to claims of different kinds of individual *liability* responsibility, respectively accountability to the demands of the criminal law, tort law, and morality. Finally, eight involves a claim of *collective* responsibility, a claim whose distinguishing feature is that the responsible subject involves a plurality of individuals.

Much of the modern literature involves attempts to refine, reduce, and compare elements of Hart's taxonomy—to show, for example, why moral and criminal liability share a common foundation, why role responsibility is the foundation for liability responsibility, or why collective responsibility cannot be reconciled with individual responsibility. R. A. Duff, for example, distinguishes causal, prospective, and retrospective responsibility, making claims of causal responsibility factual and the other two normative. Prospective responsibility (what I have called role responsibility) is defined by norms governing conduct, and retrospective responsibility is accountability for failure to meet those norms. Capacity responsibility is then defined derivatively, in terms of whether an individual is an appropriate candidate for prospective or retrospective responsibility; only responsible agents can be held responsible.[3] T. M. Scanlon similarly distinguishes between judgments of substantive and attributive responsibility. Judgments of substantive responsibility involve claims about what people are required to do for one another, and judgments of attributive responsibility are judgments that some act or event is a proper basis of moral appraisal.[4] Finally, Stephen Perry, following Tony Honoré, makes a distinction within the field of attributive responsibility, between act and outcome responsibility.[5]

However we slice the idea of responsibility, it is apparent that we need considerable information to deploy the term. First, we need to know the *object* of the agent's

---

[2] I ignore the question whether omissions can be, strictly speaking, causes.

[3] R. A. Duff, 'Responsibility', in E. J. Craig (ed.), *Routledge Encyclopedia of Philosophy* (New York: Routledge, 1998), R: 290–4.

[4] T. M. Scanlon, *What We Owe to Each Other* (Cambridge, Mass.: Harvard University Press, 1998), 248.

[5] Stephen Perry, 'Responsibility for Outcomes, Risk, and the Law of Torts', in Gerald Postema, ed., *Philosophy and the Law of Torts* (Cambridge: Cambridge University Press, 2001), 72–130.

putative responsibility. Is it a task, a status, someone's well-being, conduct, or an event? Secondly, we need the *ground* for demanding this responsibility—that he performed some act, caused the event, was invested with duties of a specific sort. His having or lacking a capacity for responsibility enters as a precondition of his responsibility, but being responsible includes the nature of his relation to the act, state, or outcome, whether he did it, caused it, manifested it, and so on.

In other words, we need to know whether the agent accepted the role, performed the act, caused the harm; and whether the agent did so consensually or involuntarily, intentionally or accidentally, sanely or madly. The idea that attributions of responsibility rest solely on facts about agents and their relations to certain harmful (or favourable) events or states is familiar and attractive. To give this idea a name, let us call it *retributivism*. The fundamental idea of retributivism is that responsibility is a moral property of agents that consists in or supervenes upon underlying facts of agency and upon agents' connections to the world. Such facts uniquely determine the moral desert of the agent; it is then a primary job of our moral and legal institutions to mete out to agents the response they deserve. On the simple retributivist picture, responsibility is a moral fact, pertaining to a relation between an agent and an object of assessment.

The retributive conception of responsibility is not wrong. It is radically incomplete. For claims of responsibility are more elliptical than I have so far indicated, in two ways. First, beyond the facts of agency, capacity, and causation, we need to know the *response* demanded of and to the agent, and conditions of *warrant* for that response: is it (among the range of possibilities) contrition, or civil liability, or criminal punishment, and what are the criteria for appropriate application of each? The truth of a claim of responsibility depends on the mode of demanded response. Smith, for example, may be justly liable in tort but not in criminal law. If his fault is minimal or non-existent, then resentment by his victims may be unwarranted, even though he himself must properly regard the accident with great regret.

Attributions of responsibility occur not in a juridical vacuum, but in specific interpersonal and circumstantial contexts. Such attributions are fundamentally *relational*: they depend upon the character of moral, legal, and social relations among the actor, the victim, and the evaluator. Consequently, we need to know what I will call the *position*, or identity, of the respondent to the agent, as well as the relation between them. The justification for demanding a given response depends on the position and the relation of the respondent to the agent. Is the respondent a victim, a court, the agent himself or herself, a bystander? Smith, arguably, owes his victims but not the state an apology; and the state, but not his victims, has a right to punishment after a fair trial. At that, Smith may only be justly punished by the state with the appropriate jurisdictional relationship to him—even a scrupulous adjudication of the merits of his conduct by an alien court would be irrelevant to the justice of his punishment.

Relational and positional dependence reflect a number of deep facts about responsibility claims. First, the complex set of practices involved in taking responsibility,

projecting responsibilities, and finding and holding persons and collectives responsible can only be made sense of against the background set of social, political, and legal
relationships and their constitutive norms. Secondly, the contextual and relation-
dependent nature of responsibility claims means that, fundamentally, responsibility
is a social practice and not the neutral registration of independent moral facts.
Claims of responsibility are things *we do*, revelations of our agency. Thus, thirdly,
making responsibility claims, of ourselves or others both constitutes and transforms
our agency and our relations to one another. Consequently, judgments of responsibility must be understood in terms of the ideals of agency and community that they
reflect and effect.

The fundamentally relational character of responsibility is reflected in a recent
efflorescence of philosophical work on moral and legal responsibility, including the
works mentioned above. This literature has demonstrated, sometimes merely implicitly and sometimes despite itself, that the traditional chestnuts of the topic—such as
the problem of psychological determinism, the legitimacy of strict liability, or the distinction between tort and criminal responsibility—will be cracked not with a priori
arguments but instead with examinations of the relationships and expectations that
give point and structure to our responsibility practices. Indeed, shifts and divisions
within recent philosophical literature make sense only with the realization that different theories reflect different conceptions of the background relations. The shift in
contemporary moral and legal thinking, away from the systemic view of consequentialism and towards a deontology focusing on individual responsibility, manifests the
central social and political dilemma of late modernity: reconciling individual meaning and autonomy within the increasingly consolidated social world.

The subject of responsibility could clearly consume much of the subject-matter of
law, including many matters treated elsewhere in this volume. This chapter will not
pretend to be a complete treatment of the idea, but rather is a sketch of some important sub-themes within the topic. Section 2 discusses moral responsibility. Moral
responsibility serves as a template for more institutionalized forms of responsibility,
thus the capacities it presupposes and its criteria of liability can illuminate other
forms. Section 3 takes up criminal responsibility, notably the problems of finding an
adequate theory of criminal legislation, appropriate response, and criteria of responsibility. I will try to show that the periodic oscillations between managerial and retributive approaches to punishment reflect a deeper debate about the nature of
state–social relations. In Section 4 I treat the exemplary case of tort liability, focusing
on the debate in tort theory between instrumentalist and corrective justice views.
Again, my aim is to show how a relational understanding of responsibility clarifies
the debates within tort theory.

Thus, I leave several topics for further exploration. In particular, I do not discuss
the question of what Ronald Dworkin has called 'political responsibility', that is,
the responsibility on the part of the state generally or state officials particularly to
justify their conduct—a responsibility particularly at issue in jurisprudence and

administrative law.[6] Although political responsibility might be thought of as a version of role responsibility (at least in many instances), I have omitted its discussion because it belongs properly to jurisprudence, discussed extensively in this volume, and to political theory more broadly. Engaging those questions would force too great a digression from the central focus of this chapter on individual responsibility. For similar reasons I will not treat, except in passing, the subject of 'social responsibility', as it relates to the social welfare obligations of individuals or other entities. Finally, my discussion of legal responsibility in private law is limited to tort law, although the subject of responsibility in contract law also raises interesting philosophical questions, for example, about the relation between promise and contract, and the justification of promissory estoppel and unconscionability principles.[7] For the most part, however, the relevant issues of agency and repair, and the social ideals they presuppose, are aired in the tort law discussion.

2 MORAL RESPONSIBILITY

Moral responsibility names a set of practices, and our conduct, consequences, and character are the objects of those practices. We hold ourselves and each other morally responsible for how we act, what we bring about, and who we are. This is an entirely unremarkable claim, and would seem a natural starting-point for discussions of moral responsibility. But philosophical discussions of moral responsibility have instead often been waylaid by the challenge of reconciling a conception of responsibility with a naturalistic understanding of human deliberation and action. The philosophical problem of responsibility arises from two powerful ideas. On the one hand, it seems that we do not morally praise or blame others for acts not somehow the products of their choices; and even when the acts are the products of their choices, we will withdraw blame if we discover that, for some reason, the person could not have chosen other than as he or she did. Had the ship been sunk by an unnoticeable iceberg, Captain Smith would have been off the hook, as he would also have been had his drinking been the product of a disease (though he might have been responded to in some other way, e.g. therapeutically). This observation is then transformed into the metaphysically more ambitious claim that moral responsibility for an act (or the consequences of an act) requires both that the agent could have done otherwise, and

---

[6] Ronald Dworkin, 'Hard Cases', in *Taking Rights Seriously* (Cambridge, Mass.: Harvard University Press, 1975), 88. See also Thomas Nagel, 'Ruthlessness in Public Life', in *Mortal Questions* (Cambridge: Cambridge University Press, 1979), 75–90.

[7] See, in this volume, ch. 21. See also the essays collected in Peter Benson (ed.), *The Theory of Contract Law: New Essays* (New York: Cambridge University Press, 2001).

that the agent is responsible because his or her choice was the cause of the act. On the other hand, any plausible conception of humanity's place in nature must make room for the idea that our choices and actions are as subsumed under natural laws as all other phenomena.

The conjunction of a naturalistic understanding of human action, thus subsumed, and the conception of responsibility in terms of a capacity to choose freely among a range of options generates the metaphysical free will problem. For a naturalistic understanding of human action suggests either that choices are the determinate products of antecedent events, or that they are the products of pure indeterminacy. Either way, the conception of responsibility as capacity to do otherwise is undermined.[8] Moral responsibility, extrapolated from this argument, is a fundamental aspect of our social lives, and yet it seems to require a kind of freedom unavailable in the world we inhabit.

There are two things to notice about the genesis of this problem, both related to the concept of responsibility from which it arises. First, the problem arises from an underspecified understanding of responsibility: the putative requirement of free choice is taken roughly as an intuitive axiom. The result has been to interpret the notion of free choice in terms of counterfactual possibilities, and then to compare that interpretation against claims about physical necessity. Secondly, the understanding of responsibility is basically *solipsistic*, in that only facts about the agent, his choice, and his acts, are relevant to the ascription of responsibility; relations to other agents are irrelevant. The result is that the metaphysical notion of being responsible is taken as primary, and the notions of holding or taking responsibility are derivative. One is morally responsible in general if one possesses the relevant capacity for free choice, and morally responsible for a particular act or event if that act or event resulted from such a choice.

The metaphysical problem of free will has inspired much difficult and interesting work.[9] But the mere capacity conception of responsibility, coupled with the disregard for the social relations in which ascriptions of responsibility are embedded, has meant that the metaphysical debates tended to reveal little about the underlying notion. The social and psychological meaning of responsibility was neglected. This all changed with Peter Strawson's seminal 'Freedom and Resentment', an article that

[8] This discussion is obviously greatly simplified and abbreviated. See John Martin Fischer, 'Introduction' to *Moral Responsibility*, ed. John Martin Fischer (Ithaca: Cornell University Press, 1986); Fischer and Mark Ravizza, *Responsibility and Control* (Cambridge: Cambridge University Press,: 1998); Fischer, 'Recent Work on Moral Responsibility', *Ethics*, 110 (1999), 93–139; Bernard Williams, 'How Free does the Will Need to Be?', in *Making Sense of Humanity* (Cambridge: Cambridge University Press, 1995), 3–21; Gary Watson, 'Free Action and Free Will', *Mind*, 96 (1987), 145–72. Fischer and Watson include extensive bibliographies.

[9] For some especially valuable work, see Peter van Inwagen, *An Essay on Free Will* (New York: Oxford University Press; the work by Fischer mentioned in n. 8; Hilary Bok, *Freedom and Responsibility* (Princeton: Princeton University Press, 1999); and Susan Wolf, *Freedom within Reason* (New York: Oxford University Press, 1990).

aimed to reverse the traditional direction of explanation. Rather than explain the notion of holding someone responsible in terms of a capacity for responsibility, Strawson suggested taking the idea of holding responsible as primary, and then understanding the capacity sense of responsibility in terms of the liability sense of responsibility. The result is to ground the abstract notion of moral responsibility in a set of social practices of holding ourselves and one another responsible, not in a metaphysical conception of free choice. Obversely, Strawson extracts the incapacity for responsibility from our social practices of excuse. The hope, then, is that the metaphysical free will problem can be disarmed by showing that the social practices of excuse do not generalize under the threat of causal determinism but are, rather, context-specific.[10]

What Strawson noticed was that ascriptions of responsibility have a crucial affective dimension. Our practices of accountability are made up of natural patterns of emotional reaction, or 'reactive attitudes', to the welcome and unwelcome attitudes of others manifested in their conduct towards us.[11] When I blame you for slapping me on the back of the neck, I am venting my resentment at the hostility implicit in your act; and when I am grateful to you for courteously holding the door for me, I am expressing my delight at the goodwill you demonstrate. My responses to your actions flow principally from my assumptions about the sentiments expressed by your conduct, not the consequences produced by it. Thus, when I discover that the attitude to which I am reacting is absent or different than I had supposed, my reaction naturally transforms. If I discover that you slapped my neck in order to swat away a bee, then I will no longer resent the action as an attack upon me. Or, if I discover that you have been merely careless in swinging your hand around, I may revise my resentment to focus upon your disregard rather than your hostility. My reactions similarly shift when the attitude is present, but has a suspect aetiology—perhaps an effect of your paranoid delusions. Now I do not resent your hostility, but try to understand it, because it no longer expresses your considered sentiments, but only the state of your mental health.

There are two points to notice here. First is that the capacities and incapacities presupposed by our reactive attitudes are straightforwardly psychological, not metaphysical. 'Will' thus names an item accessible to naturalistic investigation. Since there is no evident reason to think that the truth or falsehood of determinism bears on the nature or exercise of these capacities, the psychological concept of responsibility can be unyoked from the metaphysical concept. Once the two are unyoked, it is difficult to see the motivation for the metaphysical problem our ordinary responses, as distinct from the intrinsic philosophical interest in whether our behaviour has ultimate external causes. The test for this claim is whether, if we really believed determinism

---

[10] See R. Jay Wallace, *Responsibility and the Moral Sentiments* (Cambridge, Mass.: Harvard University Press, 1994), for a deep exploration of Strawson's argument.

[11] Peter Strawson, 'Freedom and Resentment', reprinted in *Free Will*, ed. Gary Watson (New York: Oxford University Press, 1982), 59–80, 62.

was true, our ordinary responses would erode. But that test is pragmatic, not logical, and cannot be resolved by theoretical discussion. Strawson's view thus opens up conceptual space for an independent investigation of the norms internal to the practices of responsibility, norms whose content can be divorced—in great part even if not entirely—from metaphysics.

Secondly, and relatedly, our disinclination to express reactive attitudes to partly or wholly non-responsible agents is explained not merely by the quality of their wills, but by the nature of our relations with them. Thus, the norms governing our practices of responsibility are in part *social* norms, deriving from and governing our relations with others. Though children and the insane do indeed manifest attitudes of hostility and goodwill, we tend to take what Strawson calls an 'objective' rather than a 'participant's' view of their attitudes. Instead of attempting to define the quality that responsible agents' wills have and non-responsible agents' wills lack, Strawson emphasizes the way that our awareness of cognitive and affective limitations in non-responsible agents naturally precludes them from participating in the relationships characteristic of adult society.[12] We see them not as accountable subjects but as the objects of understanding, treatment, or education—that is, as quasi-participants in therapeutic relationships.

It should be clear from this brief description that a Strawsonian view does not insist that we must have these reactive attitudes in every case in which they might be warranted. To borrow an example from Jay Wallace, a rogue might act in a way that would warrant recrimination, but be so charming that we cannot work up the indignation.[13] Moral responsibility is, in any event, a normative rather than descriptive concept: someone's being responsible is a matter of being warranted by the relevant social norms in having certain attitudes towards them. Just as I may form unwarranted attitudes towards someone whom I mistakenly take to be responsible, so I may fail to form warranted attitudes. Studies of the moral emotions by such writers as Patricia Greenspan, Jean Hampton, Michael Moore, Herbert Morris, Jeffrie Murphy, Samuel Scheffler, Gabriele Taylor, Bernard Williams, and Richard Wollheim, have also contributed to a normative understanding of our emotional responses.[14] We may also extend the notion of a warranted response from affect alone to acts of contrition, punishment, gratitude, and reward. In its most general sense, to be responsible is for certain responses to be warranted, in virtue of what one has done and why one has done it.

---

[12] Strawson, 'Resentment', 66.   [13] Wallace, *Moral Sentiments*, 76.

[14] See P. S. Greenspan, *Practical Guilt: Moral Dilemmas, Emotions and Social Norms* (New York: Oxford University Press, 1995); Michael S. Moore, *Placing Blame* (New York: Oxford University Press, 1997) (esp. 'The Moral Worth of Retribution'); Herbert Morris, *On Guilt and Innocence* (Los Angeles: University of California Press, 1976); Jeffrie G. Murphy and Jean Hampton, *Forgiveness and Mercy* (Cambridge: Cambridge University Press, 1988); Samuel Scheffler, *Human Morality* (New York: Oxford University Press, 1993); Gabriele Taylor, *Pride, Shame and Guilt* (New York: Oxford University Press, 1985); Bernard Williams, *Shame and Necessity* (Berkeley: University of California Press, 1993); and Richard Wollheim, *The Sheep and the Ceremony* (Cambridge: Cambridge University Press, 1979).

The claim that responses are warranted by governing social norms necessarily implies some social relativism. Relativity to social norms can arise in at least two innocuous ways: social norms define the nature of the act in question and they regulate the appropriate response. A remark that is a mild tease in one society (or social subgroup) can be a grave insult in another; and an insult that demands redress in one place may permit a cheek-turning in another. But anchoring responsibility in local norms may seem to imply as well a less palatable, more thoroughgoing relativism, leaving no room to criticize quaint local traditions such as scapegoating or ritual sacrifice. Moreover, social norms conflict and are frequently indeterminate in their demands even when they do not conflict. Thus, the Strawsonian approach may well lead to questions of responsibility that can receive only partial and limited answers.

There are, however, a couple of responses to these worries. First, social norms are rooted in a collection of human needs, wants, and dispositions that are only semi-plastic—influenced but not fully determined by physical and social environments. The Strawsonian account recognizes local variation, to its considerable advantage; but the degree of that variation should not be overestimated. In every culture where accidents and injuries happen—which is to say in every culture—the responsibility practices that arise will persist only if they cohere with other normative and explanatory concepts. Practices bearing too little relation to such basic considerations as causality and proportionality, for example, are unlikely to flourish over time, for they will fail to cohere with other basic cultural and scientific institutions. While pockets of magical thinking will surely persist in any culture, they are unlikely to remain the bedrock of responsibility practices. There thus will be room in any culture with a notion of causality (which is to say every practically feasible culture) for criticism of pure scapegoating. Moreover, nothing in the Strawsonian account precludes grounding (or criticizing) some set of responsibility practices in terms of some non-relative ethical standards (for example, standards of fairness or equal treatment). Warrant can emerge from local context, or from absolute ethical standards (if they exist), or both; no deep relativism is implied.

The second point concerns indeterminacy. It is a consequence of the Strawsonian view that when responsibility norms conflict (either local or absolute norms), there will be no clear answer what response is warranted, despite disagreement among the participants in the debate. But 'underdeterminacy' is the better term for this state of affairs, not 'indeterminacy', for it is not the case that no response is warranted, but rather that the set of applicable norms is insufficient to warrant any unique response. And it seems a virtue of the Strawsonian account to imply such underdeterminacy, for underdeterminacy is surely also a feature of the moral (and legal) lives the account aims to reflect. Moreover, underdeterminacy, unlike indeterminacy, makes room for argument, as participants contest the relative weight or priority of different potential norms, for example when the spirit of a rule is best honoured by an exception, or when mercy's place must be subordinated to collective security.

So Strawson's suggestion is helpful, not just for the way in which it allows us to avoid metaphysical thickets, but by making room for the relational and positional character of responsibility. It should now be clear that the attitudes and expressions of agents only warrant response given a certain understanding of the nature of the relationship between agent and respondent. In Strawson's very rough division, the relationship must be either participatory or potentially participatory: the agent to whom we respond must be someone with whom we will or could co-operate in social life. Our attitudes and expressions both indicate and constitute the nature of a participatory relationship. In general, we care about our relationships with others in virtue of the ways they can make our lives good (or bad), both in themselves, and as vehicles for promoting our interests. So the responses characteristic of accountability are warranted by the point and demands of the relationship. What we take responsibility and hold each other responsible for are deviations between our actual conduct and the norms constitutive of the relevant relationship.

Acknowledging relationality entails, as Strawson acknowledges, a necessary variability in warranted responses depending upon the nature of the relationship in question: what might constitute callous indifference between friends or lovers is simply good manners between commercial transactors.[15] For example, if I carelessly break a neighbour's vase at a party while dancing on his grand piano, my neighbour is warranted in resenting my carelessness and asking for an apology, though not in, say, smashing my glasses. Reciprocally, an apology or restitution is warranted on my part (and perhaps even obligatory). But my responsibility does not end with a simple interaction between my neighbour and myself. There are countless other positions from which other agents may respond to my act. For example, other guests at the party may also feel indignant at having their pleasant evening disrupted by my loutish behaviour, and they may expect a public display of contrition for their sake, though they could not appropriately feel personally aggrieved in the same way as my neighbour. Perhaps some of the guests are relatives of my neighbour, however, and they may take the event more personally than friends and acquaintances present. I may also be accountable to my own family for the harm, since they will now be embarrassed before the neighbour, and I may owe them a promise to take more care in the future. Finally, to and from the public at large only very constrained responses are warranted. While anyone who heard about my accident could consider me a fool, and say so, a more direct response to me personally would be thought self-righteous and nosy; and it would be self-abasing of me to confess my shame to a random person met in the street.

This essential and obvious fact of responsibility, its relational and positional dependence, is unexplained on the retributive, desert-based model. The retributivists' exclusive focus upon an agent's intentional state and actions dictates that all warranted responses flow from a single constant value: what the agent deserves. The response warranted by desert is thus univocal, dependent upon facts about the agent rather than the agent's relations to others. One could object that the variability of warranted responses can be made consistent with the retributive model: an agent

---

15 Strawson, 'Resentment', 71.

'deserves' multiple and varied responses from different people. On this interpretation, 'desert' just means that some response (or set of responses) is warranted on some ground. While there is nothing objectionable about this use, it falls well short of the traditional ambitions of the desert model, namely itself to provide a justification for hard treatment and prescribe the upper and lower limits of that treatment.

Strawson's own account works best where the form of background participatory relationship that grounds and warrants response is most conspicuous, that is, in the domain that I have called social accountability. His account is less helpful in explaining the special character of our moral responses to agents with whom we share no particular set of relationships—for example, my reaction upon reading in the paper that an employer has exploited its workers. Here I am outraged, towards the employer and on behalf of the workers, though I cannot in any deep sense identify myself with either of their positions. Strawson says that the relationship among moral respondents in such cases is simply a 'generalized' form of the claim to goodwill made by members of participatory social relationships. He does so in order to explain what he calls the 'vicarious' nature of moral reactions: responses like moral indignation are 'essentially capable' of being directed at others' attitudes towards others as well as at attitudes directed towards ourselves.[16] Strawson says these vicarious reactions are 'humanly connected' with participant reactions, though he does not explain the nature of this connection.[17] Strawson is surely right to suggest that it is a deeply rooted fact that humans—or at least members of minimally cohesive societies—have a propensity to pass judgment generally on others' compliance with social norms.[18] Indeed, it is hard to imagine how a society could maintain its normative structure if its members were not disposed to monitor and censure each other for non-compliance. It is in this propensity, layered and modified through cultural forms, that the institutions of judgment, punishment, and repair find their ground.

Sometimes responses to agents are not motivated by the attitudes those agents manifest, nor by their failure to conform their conduct to appropriate norms. Sometimes an agent's mere causal linkage with a harm may warrant a response from others. The responses characteristic of accountability for consequences can also only be understood in terms of the moral and social relationships among the parties, and their different positions with respect to the harm. The striking asymmetry in accountability for consequences between the responses of agents themselves, on the one hand, and victims and onlookers, on the other, has not been fully appreciated. In particular, agents can reproach themselves for faultless conduct that causes a harm, even when their victims, and onlookers, do not reproach them. This asymmetry of responses to

[16] Strawson, 'Resentment', 71.   [17] ibid. at 72.
[18] David Hume makes such a claim in his *Enquiry*, though he grounds the disposition in a notion of self-interest generously expanded by our capacities of sympathetic identification. David Hume, *An Enquiry Concerning the Principles of Morals*, ed. J. B. Schneewind (Indianapolis: Hackett Publishing, 1983; 1st pub. 1777), § 5, pt. I.

consequences reflects the deep role that causal relations have for agents in structuring their understanding of (or relationship to) themselves. Those affected by the agent, in contrast, care less about causal relations in the absence of faulty conduct.

While conduct-based responses are warranted by the way that agents' behaviour manifests attitudes of respect, contempt, or indifference regardless of whether that conduct causes harm, consequence-based responses are warranted by the fact of a harm regardless of whether the conduct was faulty. Causality, in isolation from conduct, indicates nothing about how agents have previously viewed their relations with others. The ready-to-hand example of the significance of causality is Oedipus. Despite their initial strangeness, the characters' reactions in *Oedipus Rex* can be intelligible to modern readers once the magical elements of fatalism and pollution are stripped away. Reasons of consequence explain these reactions: 'incest', after all, describes a situation, not a content of will, or an attitude. Oedipus has, by his own actions, brought on (and engaged in) this situation, and this contingent, causal connection grounds his horror and self-reproach.[19]

Oedipus' response to the fact of his causal role is what Bernard Williams calls 'agent-regret': regret that a state of affairs obtains whose occurrence involved one's own agency.[20] Agent-regret rests on no sense of wrongdoing, and is compatible with impeccable conduct, even conduct so recognized by the agent.[21] However, it seems a mistake to distinguish agent-regret fully from guilt, for although an awareness of wrongful acting is a typical part of guilt, awareness of having done something awful, even if unwittingly, can suffice.[22] Oedipus' response was partly shame at his incestuous disgrace. But his horrible self-mutilation can only be explained by something else, something that we can recognize as a form of guilt: a gesture at repaying a wrong he has done. The causal relation itself need not be entirely direct to trigger guilt. If, while tending a friend's cat, it slips outdoors despite my protections and gets hit by a car, I will feel not merely sorry for my friend but guilty towards her. Although the death is not my fault, I have provided for its occasion, and so my relations to her differ from those of any other sympathetic friend. Indeed, because of the friend's trust in me, I am likely to feel even worse than the driver who, also let us assume faultlessly, actually killed the cat.[23]

These examples bring out a striking feature of consequential accountability: where conduct is not at issue, there is an especially radical asymmetry in response among

[19] See Bernard Williams' discussion of the Oedipus example, in Bernard Williams, *Shame and Necessity* (Berkeley: University of California Press, 1993), 56–60.

[20] Bernard Williams, 'Moral Luck', in *Moral Luck* (Cambridge: Cambridge University Press, 1981), 20–39.

[21] As Williams notes, one of the roles played by other moral agents may be to insist upon the rightness of conduct in order to erase the significance of an agent's connection to the harm. Williams, 'Moral Luck', 28.

[22] Taylor, *Pride*, 91.

[23] Of course, the driver him- or herself also now stands in a special normative relation to my friend, the cat's owner, owing her at least the courtesy of informing her that the cat is dead.

the various positions that the harm itself creates. My friend is unlikely to resent me, even though I feel guilty. More precisely, if the accident is not my fault, then my friend would be unwarranted in resenting my role, since I will not have acted badly, while my feelings will be warranted by my causal role and our prior relationship, as well as by the protective role I assumed towards his cat.[24] Likewise, Oedipus' compatriots more pity than despise him for his crime. The principal reason for this asymmetry is that agents' causal relations necessarily inform their conceptions of themselves, of who they are. For victims, by contrast, the significance of the harm consists largely in the mere fact of its occurrence, and not its causal link to a particular agent.

The relation between agents and their effects is one of identity, in a certain sense. What an agent has caused is an important part of that agent's history and life, as important as what that agent has intentionally done, believed, and hoped for. The regret signals the fundamental unluckiness of the causal connection between this agent and those consequences. Because regret for faultless accidents maps the agent's actual (as opposed to idealized) course through the world, the general absence of such regret is found primarily among children and extreme Kantians, for whom the fantasy or ideal world is more salient than the real. As H. L. A. Hart and Tony Honoré have suggested, it is through claims of causal authorship that '[i]ndividuals come to understand themselves as distinct persons, to whatever extent they do, and to acquire a sense of self-respect . . .'.[25] It is important to note, however, that 'what I have done' does not name a naturally limited universe of events: agents are causally related to infinitely many events, under infinitely many descriptions, and only some of those events, under some descriptions, will be salient. The concept of what an agent has done is given itself by our practices of accountability and conception of causation. Beyond bodily movements themselves, the extension of an agent's field of causal influence is given by a complex and deeply rooted normative conception.[26]

The shape of that conception—what causal relations are picked out as warranting a response—is the subject of an enormous literature. Although some writers have attempted to locate normative considerations in a metaphysical conception of causation, most have instead adopted a non-normative, context-neutral conception, then

---

[24] This is not to say that I would be morally wrong not to feel at all guilty, but only lacking a full grasp of the relevant moral norms. And self-laceration is clearly out of place.

[25] H. L. A. Hart and Tony Honoré, *Causation in the Law*, 2nd edn. (New York: Oxford University Press, 1985), p. lxxx. See also Honoré's discussion of 'outcome-responsibility' and its relationship to identity in Tony Honoré, 'The Morality of Tort Law—Questions and Answers', in *Philosophical Foundations of Tort Law*, ed. David G. Owen (New York: Oxford University Press, 1995), 73–95, 81–3.

[26] This is consistent with a certain understanding of Donald Davidson's claim that 'We never do more than move our bodies; the rest is up to nature'. Donald Davidson, 'Agency', in *Essays on Actions and Events* (New York: Oxford University Press, 1981), 43–62, 59. The 'accordion effect' that licences further ascriptions of events to my agency relies on causal relations external to me, but the particular relations singled out are, as Davidson would acknowledge, deeply dependent upon our normative concerns. See also Joel Feinberg, 'Action and Responsibility', in *Doing and Deserving* (Princeton: Princeton University Press, 1970), 119–51.

relied on pragmatics to explain ordinary usage.[27] According to generic conceptions, a person's act is typically one item among enormously many causally relevant events and conditions that are jointly sufficient for an event's occurrence. As many philosophers have argued, whether that act is highlighted as noteworthy ('*the* cause'), by the agent or another, depends in part upon its relation to stable background conditions, its role in durable structures of events, its susceptibility to intervention or control, and so on.[28] The relevance of the agent's intervention in the cat and Oedipal cases is obvious. But I want to suggest that, in more difficult cases, agents' social and moral relations to others are especially important to agents' seeing their acts as causally connected to harms. This is particularly true of omissions, as when my failure to bring a sick child promptly to the doctor results in suffering: the nature of my accountability will depend upon my relation to the child. But my seeing myself as the positive cause of another's misery also depends upon my understanding of the structure of our mutual relations. If we are competitors in business and my low prices unintentionally drive you into bankruptcy, I may see your failure to meet my prices, rather than my own act, as the cause of your demise.[29] In contrast, if we are friends and my unintentional act results in your suffering, I am likely to reproach myself for my causal role and do what I can to make amends.

My gesture of repair as an agent is, in these cases, more complicated than just the reaffirming or re-establishing of the character of a relationship between agent and victim. When I see myself as accountable for a harm I merely cause, and when repair of that harm is at least possible in part, my gesture of repair is directed at myself as well as at my victim. It is directed at the victim in so far as it is an attempt to compensate for a burden I have imposed. And it is directed at myself in so far as it provides a way for me to transform my trajectory through the world, eliminating what is unfortunate about what I have done. Here we see a further asymmetry in the responsive positions of agent and victim, particularly in cases of faultless wrongdoing: while my victim may be indifferent to the source of compensation, I may feel that it must, in symbolic part at least, come from me.[30] And even if neither I nor my victim feels it

[27] Hart and Honoré's *Causation in the Law* is still the leading work on the morally relevant notion of causation. But see also Joel Feinberg, *Harm to Others* (New York: Oxford University Press, 1984); and Richard Wright, 'Causation in Tort Law', *California Law Review*, 73 (1985), 1775–98. For other important accounts of a generic conception of causation, see also J. L. Mackie, *The Cement of the Universe* (New York: Oxford University Press, 1974); and David Lewis, 'Causation & Postscript', in *Philosophical Papers* (New York: Oxford University Press, 1984), 159–213. Michael Moore began a project of demonstrating that the ordinary language of degrees of causation and intervening causation reflects the actual metaphysics of causation. See Moore, 'Causation and Responsibility', *Social Philosophy & Policy*, 16 (1999), 1–51; and cf. 'The Metaphysics of Causal Intervention', *California Law Review*, 88 (2000), 827–77, 876–7.

[28] Lewis, 'Causation'.

[29] That I will see it this way says much about my view of what constitutes appropriate relations among competitors.

[30] Williams makes a similar point, in 'Moral Luck', 28–9. I do not mean to claim that agents usually will feel this way, except in the most tragic of circumstances.

necessary that I provide the compensation, an apology or other gesture of repair may also be called for, and that can come only from me.

This account of causation as a source of reasons warranting response may seem circular, for if merely singling out a causally relevant factor as the cause depends upon a prior conception of appropriate relations between the parties, then the relevant notion of causation is doing no independent normative work.[31] The notion of cause and warranted response are indeed interdependent and so, in a sense, functionally circular, but the circularity is not vicious. We make our causal contributions in social as well as physical space; the norms and interests that define that social space inevitably play a role in helping to delineate the causal relations we perceive. Once we have identified a given act as the cause of some harm, on the basis of background expectations of appropriate behaviour, then we are led to modify our conception of that background, and so alter our future perceptions of what is a cause and what a mere condition. My friend forgives me this time for letting the cat out; either the driver or the cat itself may be regarded as the cause of its death. But if several more cats die while in my care, my friend's perceptions of my causal role in the harms, and so her responses to me, will undoubtedly change.

As I have said, the position of victims, and the responses warranted by their relations to the harm, differ dramatically from the agents' own responses, particularly in cases of faultless causation; and these responses also depend upon the way victims view their relations to agents and onlookers. For agents, their causal relation to a harm warrants feelings of self-reproach. But because the agents manifested no ill conduct or will, victims' resentment on that basis is unwarranted. No prior moral or social relationship has been devalued by the harm, but only a distribution of goods distorted. As a result, the victim's response is more likely to be a demand for compensation unaccompanied by reproach. Whether this claim for compensation is seen as having normative force, by victim or agent, is itself a product of the relationships among the parties and society at large. 'It wasn't my fault', when true, is a perfect excuse from accountability for conduct, but it bears no direct relationship to the moral question of compensation. Given a certain understanding of social and moral relationships, 'that you caused it' can sufficiently warrant a claim for compensation. (The embedding of compensatory demand in the relationships constituted by a legal system, in the form of tort law, is the subject of Section 4.)

So far my discussion has concerned the event-paradigm of greatest traditional interest to moral philosophers, when one person injures another directly. But it is worth noting that many of the harms and miseries of modern life fall outside the paradigm of direct action. Think of buying a table made of tropical wood that comes from a defoliated rain forest, or using a CFC-based air-conditioner, along with

---

[31] This charge of circularity is the standard criticism of tort lawyers' use of the notion of 'proximate cause': to say of a party's conduct that it was the proximate cause of the harm is virtually to foreclose the question of liability. Much of *Causation in the Law* can be seen as an attempt to give independent content to the notion of proximate cause. Section 4 takes up the issue of causation in tort law.

10,000,000 others, and so jointly putting a hole in the ozone layer; being a citizen of a nation that bombs another country's factories in a reckless attack on terrorists; or inhabiting a region seized long ago from its aboriginal occupants; helping to design an automobile that the manufacturer knowingly sells with a dangerously defective fuel system, or working in a health-care bureaucracy that carelessly allows the distribution of HIV-contaminated blood. All of these examples are instances of a mediated relation to harm, where injury is brought about through the actions of others. And many of them are cases where what any one individual does makes no difference; only together do individuals cause harm.

These mediated relations to harm are the domain of *complicity*. Just as purely consequential responsibility tests will-oriented models of responsibility, so complicitous accountability puts pressure on consequence-oriented models. For it is a familiar fact of our moral and legal practices that we blame, punish, and demand compensation from complicitous agents even though what they did made no difference. The bank would have been robbed regardless, the ozone hole formed, the battle fought. The puzzle arises because, if causal contribution is necessary to responsibility, then no one is responsible, for no one makes a difference. And even when an individual difference is made, say when one person acts as lookout during a robbery, our practices of blame and rules of punishment go far beyond the causal contribution. What complicitous responsibility centrally challenges is an appealing, intuitive, principle of responsibility, that someone can only be responsible for events over which he had control. Call this the 'control principle'.[32] An account of responsibility that aims to reveal rather than replace these pervasive practices of responsibility will have to show how responsibility can outrun both causation and control, without becoming simply a free-form virtual guilt shared by all.

In other work I have tried to do this.[33] Briefly, I argue that once we have in hand an analytical understanding of co-operation, a normative account of complicity follows suit. Individuals who cooperate share what I call 'participatory intentions', that is, intentions to do their parts of some collective act. Participatory intentions ground our basic practice of action- and outcome-ascription in co-operative contexts, so that, for example, when two of us together write an opera, you writing the music and I the book, each of us can truly say, 'we wrote the opera'. Each of us should be regarded as an author of the opera, albeit an inclusive author, in virtue of our individual collective participation in its creation. Responsibility for it—praise or blame—then tracks the ascription of authorship. This is because the will of each can be deemed manifest in the collective product.

[32] The 'control principle' is endorsed, in varying forms, by Douglas Husak, *Philosophy of Criminal Law* (Totowa, NJ: Rowman & Littlefield, 1987), 98; and by Stephen Perry, 'Responsibility for Outcomes, 82.

[33] I treat this subject at length in Christopher Kutz, *Complicity: Ethics and Law for a Collective Age* (Cambridge: Cambridge University Press, 2000).

Now, differences in particular causal contributions change the responses warranted to particular individuals; it is reasonable to celebrate Mozart more than his librettist, Da Ponte. And there is a truth in the control principle: individuals who cannot control *whether* they participate at all (hostages or dupes, for example) cannot be held responsible for the collective harm.[34] But in cases of full overdetermination, when no individual really does make a causal difference, blame (or praise) may still fairly lie. Derek Parfit's famous 'harmless torturers', each of whom gives a torture victim an individually imperceptible but aggregatively awful electrical jolt, provides a stark example of the problem.[35] Parfit himself struggles to accommodate consequentialist ethics to a form of responsibility that seems, on its face, precisely independent of individual consequence. Others have attempted to develop a theory of causation that makes sense of such cases.[36] I am sceptical, myself, whether these approaches work, even on their own terms. Whatever the ultimate account of complicitous responsibility, however, it will have to go at least partly by way of the participatory intentions of the agents—their will, independent of its effects, to join in a collective act that does injury. For in the absence of any salient individual causal contribution, surely it is the co-operation itself that explains responsibility. Implication follows participation.

3 Criminal Responsibility

A working theory of criminal responsibility presupposes an answer to one question, and must answer two more questions. It presupposes an answer to the question of what norms should define the domain of criminal law. And it must provide answers to the following questions: first, what counts as a violation of those norms; and secondly, what responses are warranted by their violation? Clearly, these questions must be answered together if they are to be answered intelligibly. If the criminal norms aim primarily at conduct as opposed to consequence, then the criteria of responsibility will emphasize causation over quality of will. If the norms protect very great or vulnerable interests, then more serious responses are likely to be deemed warranted.

---

[34] More difficult questions arise concerning those who control their initial participation, but not its ultimate extent—those who get taken on a ride, so to speak. Presumably they are accountable by reference to the risk they run in participating in a potentially injurious enterprise.

[35] Derek Parfit, *Reasons and Persons* (New York: Oxford University Press, 1984), 80. If the example is too surreal, consider the huge bombing fleet that burned Dresden in World War II. No one plane made a difference, but each contributed to a collective horror. I discuss the Dresden case extensively in *Complicity*, ch. 4.

[36] See Alvin I. Goldman, 'Why Citizens Should Vote: A Causal Responsibility Approach', *Social Philosophy and Policy*, 16 (1999), 201–17.

And if the responses deemed warranted for violation are very severe, then the criteria of responsibility ought to be narrow—assuming some background political principles against the infliction of suffering or favouring the retention of individual liberty. This is not to say that a theory of one of these subjects determines answers to the other two, but only the more modest point that the criminal norms, criteria of responsibility, and responsive practices must hang together in reflective equilibrium.

Criminal norms have traditionally protected the most important interests in life, security of body, and security of possession. By protecting these interests from malicious incursion, criminal law makes social life possible by making social trust possible. Relying on state power to quell each other's urges to act selfishly or viciously, we can forge the co-operative relations that make our lives good.[37] It is true that the reach of criminal norms in modern times has extended beyond these core interests into many regulatory domains. These regulatory domains often use only weak criteria of responsibility, forgoing requirements of knowledge and intent. The extended reach of criminal norms provokes worry even when the actual sanctions are not severe, because the expressive, condemnatory aspect of criminal norms carries over from the core concerns.[38] But what determines whether a given interest will be expressed and protected through criminal law is only in part a function of its intrinsic importance. It is also a function of the special responsive position of the state as the expressive and enforcement agency, as well as of the state's relations to other social institutions. Demands for a moralized criminal law—a law punishing private, consensual behaviour on grounds of its immorality—reflect in their proponents not just a concern to maintain a (probably illusory) normative status quo, but also a deep insecurity about the capacity of non-coercive social institutions to govern behaviour. 'There oughtta be a law!' is spoken not by the discoverer of a new norm, but by someone unhappy about an old norm's current efficacy. A similar point holds for the criminalization of regulatory matters: the choice to rely upon sanctions, as opposed to tax- or market-based approaches, often reflects both an articulated judgment about the efficacy of different means to the same result, as well as more inchoate beliefs about the need for state authority to supplement private forms of social ordering.

Just as contested ideals of state–civil society relations explain debates about the allocation of authority between criminal and other norms, so they also explain debates about the proper response to violations of those norms and criteria of responsibility.

---

[37] Tort and contract law have similar functions, also stabilizing co-operation. Richard Posner's economic analysis of criminal law, according to which the purpose of criminal norms is to prevent intentional bypass of market transactions, can be expressed less crassly in terms of making consensual, co-operative relations possible.

[38] See, famously, *United States v. Dotterweich*, 320 US 277 (1943) (president of pharmaceutical company convicted of interstate shipping of misbranded and adulterated drugs, despite lack of knowledge or intent).

Discussions of warranted response have typically come in the form of different theories of punishment. Theories of punishment divide into two groups. On the one hand, there are true theories of punishment, which attempt to offer a justification for the intentional and condemnatory hard treatment of violators of criminal norms. In this group there is some discussion of the proper sort of hard treatment, whether it includes physical pain, execution, incarceration, or shaming penalties. But discussion primarily focuses on how to justify a treatment whose unpleasantness is assumed—whether it is to be justified in retributivist or expressive terms.[39] The second group consists not in theories of punishment *per se*, but in theories of the proper treatment of offenders, where the proper treatment may not involve state-inflicted suffering at all. All such theories are, self-evidently, instrumentalist, and utilitarian theories are the most obvious examples. Hard treatment will be justified, if it is, through its role in deterring other crime or in subordinating the offender to social authority. Gentler, rehabilitative and educative theories also fall into this group, as do reparative theories—that is, approaches to offence that attempt to mend the social ties severed by the criminal offence.[40] Finally come theories that represent a hybrid of instrumental and intrinsic concerns. Hart's theory of punishment, further developed by Mackie and Scanlon, takes this form: a system of punishment whose infliction is sensitive to offenders' wills is justified both as a means of maintaining civil order against a background of general liberty, and as a system peculiarly appropriate to beings who value the ability to determine by choice whether they will come into conflict with the state.[41]

Contrast criminal responsibility with moral responsibility. Within morality's broad limits, variety reigns. Friends and family members can reproach each other for minor defects of character as social acquaintances cannot. The fury and rage expressed by lovers at betrayal, well-warranted though it may be, would be wholly out of place even between friends. Likewise, the poignant guilt properly felt at the betrayal of a friend might well be considered self-lacerating if it were directed at all moral transgressions. Social morality is effective precisely because there is room for

[39] See Moore, 'Moral Worth of Retribution'; Morris, 'Persons and Punishment', in *On Guilt and Innocence* (Berkeley: University of California Press, 1976); Joel Feinberg, 'The Expressive Theory of Punishment', in *Doing and Deserving* (Princeton: Princeton University Press, 1970).

[40] See e.g. Barbara Wootton, *Social Science and Social Pathology* (London: Allen & Unwin, 1959); Jean Hampton, 'The Moral Education Theory of Punishment', *Philosophy and Public Affairs*, 13 (1984), 208–38; Geoffrey Sayre-McCord, 'Criminal Justice and Legal Reparations as an Alternative to Punishment', forthcoming in *Philosophical Topics*, ed. Ernest Sosa and Enrique Villanueva (New York: Blackwells); Steven Garvey, 'Punishment as Atonement', *University of California Law Review*, 46 (1999), 1801–58.

[41] See H. L. A. Hart, 'Legal Responsibility and the Excuses', in *Punishment and Responsibility*, 28–53, J. L. Mackie, 'The Grounds of Responsibility', in *Law, Morality, and Society*, ed. P. M. S. Hacker and Joseph Raz (Oxford: Oxford University Press, 1977); T. M. Scanlon, 'The Significance of Choice', reprinted in *Equal Freedom* (Ann Arbor: University of Michigan Press, 1995), 39–104. See also Alan Brudner, 'Agency and Welfare in the Penal Law', in Stephen Shute, John Gardner, and Jeremy Horder (eds.), *Action and Value in Criminal Law* (New York: Oxford University Press, 1993), 21–53.

play in its joints. Though the norms governing warranted response have shifted enormously through time and across cultures, and depended crucially upon the state's eagerness and capacity to keep the civil peace, there have always been limits to appropriate response, even if those responses have greatly transgressed the generally pacific borders of contemporary Western elite social morality. I will stipulate here, however, that absent circumstances of self-defence, the limits of moral response are the limits of language and feeling. Physically violent or coercive responses to individuals are only morally permitted to the state.

Legal systems protect the interests that morality protects, centrally the means and liberties necessary to live well as a rational and reflective, project-centred agent. To the extent that legal systems do anything more than simply express (vehemently) these norms, then it is necessary to conceive law instrumentally to some extent, judging systems better or worse in their capacity to secure these interests. But this need not be a crassly functionalist conception of law any more than of morality, which also performs a function of protecting the interests and relationships that make our lives good. Law is good because the interests it protects are valuable; and legal responses are warranted by the importance of those interests. If liberties and well-being are values within the law, then legal responses that compromise those values are suspect. While the restrictions upon moral wrongdoing and free-riding that legal institutions dictate are not themselves objectionable compromises to agents' interests, the use of threats and application of sanctions to guarantee those restrictions do compromise autonomy.

It follows that if coercive measures by the state are warranted at all, they are warranted because no non-coercive measures are adequate to protect social interests once moral and legal forms of accountability have failed. Unlike social and moral responses, whose verbal or emotional nature is only of concern to those for whom the relationships they protect have value, coercive responses are of concern to any self-interested agent. While legal systems may depend primarily, as Mackie suggests, upon the efficacy of an adverse legal characterization of certain acts, coercive threats play an essentially ancillary role in motivating those unswayed by a desire to maintain morally appropriate relations.[42]

The interests justifying legal responses themselves limit those responses. If, as under liberal regimes, legal systems aim to protect meaningful forms of individual autonomy and social co-operation in general, then individuals' autonomy interests will be of concern as well in the administration of legal sanctions. As Hart (and Scanlon following him) has argued, this concern for autonomy, rather than a concern for rectifying moral wrongs, can best explain the general restriction of penal sanctions to cases of voluntary conduct.[43] By making the infliction of those legal sanctions that severely infringe individual autonomy depend upon the choices

---

[42] Mackie, 'Grounds of Responsibility', 187–8.
[43] Hart, 'Legal Responsibility and the Excuses'; Scanlon, 'Significance of Choice.'

individuals make, the state has done what it can to ensure the autonomy of each citizen. Due process considerations also serve to protect individual autonomy from undue state interference. The concern for autonomy also helps to explain the criminal law's 'act requirement', that only voluntary attempts and commissions are punishable, and not inchoate plans or involuntary movements.[44] Because who an agent is and what an agent causes are far less sensitive to choice, criminal punishment on these bases is far more restricted.[45]

The debates among theories of punishment have famously tended to stress an ideal of the person, enhanced or compromised by the relevant punitive practice. Immanuel Kant famously denounced the 'serpent-windings of utilitarianism' on the grounds that it uses the offender simply as a means of general social control, thus failing to respect him as a rational agent meriting concern for his own ends.[46] By contrast, critics of the retributivist ideal preferred by Kant, according to which it is intrinsically good or right to ensure that wrongdoers suffer, have worried that talk of the rightfulness of punishment served mainly to mask the punisher's desire to humiliate, a desire coming from a sense of resentment not justice. As Nietzsche put it (with characteristic exaggeration), Kant's 'categorical imperative reeks of cruelty'.[47]

Disputed ideals of the person do drive the debate over punishment, but to focus only on the person punished involves a kind of ethical solipsism. Equally important is an ideal not of the individual but of social and political relations. Different theories of punishment implicate, and are implied by, different conceptions of the proper relation of the individual to the community. What must strike anyone working in the area of punishment theory is the way in which different theories have come to dominate or recede, it seems, as a matter of shifts in broader political views. When Hart began writing on punishment, for example, the philosophical status quo was reformist and rehabilitative, not retributive. Along with other writers, he rejected rehabilitative theories out of a concern about the reduction of the offender to a psychological system to be manipulated by the state.[48] Hart rejected retributivist theories of punishment as well, partly on the familiar conceptual ground that they

[44] With the important and largely deplorable exception of Anglo-American conspiracy law, according to which liability can be incurred at a very early stage of planning.

[45] It is worth noting that criminal sentencing is heavily characterological, especially in death penalty proceedings. Punishment is aggravated or mitigated in proportion to the moral worth of the convicted.

[46] Immanuel Kant, 'Doctrine of Right', in *The Metaphysics of Morals*, ed. and trans. Mary Gregor (Cambridge: Cambridge University Press, 1991), 331–3.

[47] Friedrich Nietzsche, *On the Genealogy of Morals*, ed. and trans. Walter Kaufmann (New York: Vintage, 1967; 1st pub. 1887), book II, § 6 (my translation). Nietzsche's own preferred alternative to punishment, at least in the moral realm, was a kind of confident forgetting exemplified by Mirabeau. *Genealogy*, book I, ¶ 10, p. 39.

[48] The most famous statement rejecting the rehabilitative ideal is in C. S. Lewis, 'The Humanitarian Theory of Punishment', *Res Judicatae*, 6 (1953), 224–30; see also the essays collected in Sanford Kadish, *Blame and Punishment* (New York: MacMillan, 1987). Isaiah Berlin's objections to a politics grounded in a notion of 'positive liberty' also echo concerns about the manipulative state. See his 'Two Concepts of Liberty', in *Four Essays on Liberty* (New York: Oxford University Press, 1970), 118–72 .

depended upon a 'mysterious piece of moral alchemy' that made two ordinarily impermissible acts amount to justice.[49] But his conceptual argument (or observation—he hardly took retributivist theories seriously enough to argue against them) can be fairly seen as a product of a general sentiment that retributivism in punishment was faintly barbaric, as compared with enlightened utilitarian social policy. By the 1980s, however, retributivist theories had come to flourish, propelled in significant part by the work of Michael Moore and Andrew von Hirsch.[50] It seems hardly coincidental that fashion in philosophical theories of punishment has tracked fashion in political practice (or vice versa), as particularly US penal policy has shifted from rehabilitative to fiercely punitive practice and increasing emphasis on individual rather than social responsibility.[51]

This sociology of recent theorizing is meant to do more than point out the obvious fact that philosophers too are creatures and creators of the *Zeitgeist*. It also demonstrates the analytical point that theories of warranted response must be interpreted in terms of the background conception of social relations they presume. I have already mentioned how rejection of rehabilitative theories was early driven by worries about the therapeutic politics they presumed.[52] The rejection of utilitarian theories has as much to do with their treatment of individuals as means, as with the more general, managerial conception they hold of the state. In utilitarian political theory of a crude but familiar kind, the state is conceived as an expert at social engineering, attempting to maximize net social satisfaction.[53] Doubts about utilitarian political theory, related both to its implicit dependence on expertise and to its failure to see individual members of society as co-operating agents, not just joint consumers, have led to its displacement in the field of distributive justice.[54] A theory of punishment resting on a conception of the state as social manager is equally undermined by these doubts. Retributivist theories, with their emphasis on individual dignity, point up the defects of utilitarian views. But retributivists have thus far failed to come up with a conception of the state that makes the infliction of just punitive deserts a legitimate objective

[49] Hart, 'Postscript', 234.

[50] See Moore, *Placing Blame*; and Andrew von Hirsch, *Doing Justice* (New York: Hill and Wang, 1976).

[51] The public shift is easily seen in California's politics, usually a harbinger of national trends, a politics that resulted in such successful ballot initiatives as, in 1994, a 'Three Strikes' law that incarcerates a wide range of recidivists for life (codified as Cal. Penal Code § 1170.12); and, in February 2000, Proposition 21, a ballot measure that greatly expanded the reach of prosecutorial authority over the young. It passed overwhelmingly. For a general discussion of changes in criminological practice, see David Garland, *Punishment and Modern Society: A Study in Social Theory* (Chicago: University of Chicago Press, 1993).

[52] Doubts—possibly mistaken—about the effectiveness of rehabilitative measures probably contributed more to their loss of public support.

[53] This is, roughly, Henry Sidgwick's view, see Sidgwick, *Methods of Ethics* (Indianapolis: Hackett Publishing, 1981; 1st pub. 1874). It is this view of utilitarianism that John Rawls criticizes in *A Theory of Justice* (Cambridge, Mass.: Harvard University Press, rev. edn. 1999), § 5.

[54] Although co-operative models of utilitarianism are available; see Donald Regan, *Utilitarianism and Cooperation* (New York: Oxford University Press, 1980).

of the state.⁵⁵ It certainly is possible to conceive of the state as the people's agent in delivering deserts, both retributive and distributive; but this conception is hardly uncontroversial, resting as it does on a metaphysically robust and pre-institutional understanding of desert.⁵⁶ The reparative justice theories now emerging reflect a more communitarian ideal of social relations in their focus on reconciling individuals with their societies. Unless there is reason to think that some particular political conception will come to hold sway—and I see no such reason—the relationality of responsibility means that debates among punishment theories will go unresolved.

The concomitant of the relationality of criminal responsibility is its positionality. It is not merely a legal conceit that while the prosecutor represents 'the people', the court represents impartial justice. For the position of justice taken by the law is very special and circumscribed. When legal institutions assume the partisan position of the victim and the posture of resentment, the rights and liberties of defendants are severely compromised, situations for which the sedition trials of the twentieth century are the best exemplars.⁵⁷ The warranted response of victims to hostile behaviour is resentment; but resentment is wholly inappropriate from the institutions of justice. The position the criminal law represents is not simply an integration over all social and moral positions, and legal responses do not represent whole, overall responses to wrongs. Instead, legal responses are ideally made from a particular position, that of the state, and represent one form of response among many. Regardless of what individuals deserve, the state's responses flow from the relations that tie each individual to one another, agent and victim alike, and are limited by the claims internal to those relationships.

Reminding ourselves of the special position of the state is particularly helpful in getting a handle on the old chestnut of theories of punishment, why unsuccessful attempts should be punished less severely than successfully completed crimes. On one side is the view that the proper basis of punitive, as opposed to compensatory, responsibility is either the social danger of the defendant's conduct, the contempt for legal norms evinced by that conduct, or both, and that these bases are the same for unsuccessful and successful attempters alike.⁵⁸ Since the basis of responsibility is the same, there is no reason to punish differently. Adjusting punishment to actual harm, on this view, simply confuses punitive and compensatory responses. Proponents of

⁵⁵ This criticism is made by Jeffrie Murphy in 'Retributivism, Moral Education, and the Liberal State', *Criminal Justice Ethics*, 4 (1985), 3–11.

⁵⁶ For response, see Moore, 'Moral Worth of Retribution', 150–1; for the controversy, see Scanlon, 'Significance of Choice'; and Samuel Scheffler, 'Liberalism, Desert, and Reactive Attitudes', *Philosophy and Public Affairs*, 21 (1992), 299–323.

⁵⁷ Even when the state is apparently the victim, as in tax fraud or treason, we must keep in mind that it has no tax or security interests of its own, but only those of its citizens. This derivative status renders its position, normatively at least, wholly unlike the positions of unmediated victimhood.

⁵⁸ For representative statements of this view, see Sanford Kadish, 'Luck of the Draw', in *Blame and Punishment*; J. Feinberg, 'Equal Punishment for Failed Attempts', *Arizona Law Review*, 37 (1995), 117–34; Stephen Schulhofer, 'Harm and Punishment: A Critique of the Emphasis on the Results of Conduct in the Criminal Law', *University of Pennsylvania Law Review*, 122 (1974), 1497.

differentiated punishment, by contrast, observe that our moral responses as a matter of fact track the harm we do. We blame ourselves more when misjudgment results in real harm; and we resent more the malevolent acts of others, simply because those acts cause us harm.[59] The connection between this bit of moral phenomenology and state punishment is a retributive theory of punishment, according to which the state's role is to administer a (univocal) moral desert.

The relation between luck and responsibility is deeply vexed, and it is unclear, to say the least, whether our practices of responsibility can be fully regimented or ratio-nalized in terms of specific bases of response.[60] Reconciling responsibility with luck is a deep problem, perhaps an insoluble one, for moral theory. But it must only be solved for the theory of punishment if state punishment ought genuinely to mimic interpersonal moral response and resentment—whether it really is to be Sidgwickian 'resentment universalized'.[61] If the argument for distinguishing successful from unsuccessful attempts can be given no firmer basis than coherence with interper-sonal moral practice, then there is no good case to adding actual harm as a factor in calculating punishment, independent of social danger and antisocial will. To do otherwise is to confuse the particular purposes of the criminal responsibility system with the more general expressive and constitutive functions played by our practices of moral responsibility.

The second main point of intersection between criminal law and philosophical interest concerns the criteria of responsibility. In Anglo-American law, the criteria of criminal responsibility converge with the criteria of moral responsibility: where moral claims are warranted, so generally is legal sanction; and where there is moral excuse or justification, so too there is legal excuse or justification. While the expres-sive function of criminal law makes overlap between moral blame and criminal guilt likely, the very high degree of convergence in modern doctrine and statute is the product of the concerted effort by a number of criminal scholars, notably Hart, Sanford Kadish, Herbert Wechsler, and Glanville Williams, to limit the encroach-ment of strict liability doctrines.[62] That said, any specifically legal conception of cul-pability must recognize that legal authority is always exercised in doubt. Criminal law presents the most serious epistemic problems, given its focus upon individual inten-tions. Intentions are inferred from scatterings of circumstance, causal explanations

[59] See Moore, 'The Independent Moral Significance of Wrongdoing', in *Placing Blame*, 191–248; Leo Katz, 'Why the Successful Assassin is More Wicked than the Unsuccessful One', *California Law Review*, 88 (2000), 791–812.

[60] For the deeper philosophical discussion of moral luck, see Thomas Nagel, 'Moral Luck', in *Mortal Questions* (New York: Cambridge University Press, 1979), 24–38; and Williams, 'Moral Luck'.

[61] See Sidgwick, *Methods of Ethics*, 280–1.

[62] The American Legal Institute's Model Penal Code is Wechsler's lasting legacy; for Williams see his *Criminal Law: The General Part* (London: Stevens and Sons, 2nd edn. 1961).

Where strict liability still obtains, in the regulatory domain mentioned above, or in specific doctrines of, for example, publicans' vicarious liability, the penalties are generally comparatively mild, and liability can often be tied, through the exercise of prosecutorial discretion, to some failure of role respon-sibility.

are shaped by the interests of the contesting parties. Unfortunately, just resolution of cases requires good information; and good information is generally expensive and difficult to obtain. No individual accused of a crime can be expected, practically or normatively, to divulge a culpable state of mind. The distinction between premeditated and spontaneous homicide, for example, can be the difference between execution and incarceration. Premeditated homicide can be proven by evidence of advance planning. However, the most subjectively inclined courts have held that killing can count as premeditated in the absence of planning, so long as the accused has the opportunity to reflect on the decision to kill.[63] Since obviously no killer will admit to premeditation, and since there is rarely a surviving witness to the crime, the judge or jury's decision often teeters upon a scaffolding of circumstantial evidence and psychological inference.

Despite pervasive doubt and uncertainty, decisions must be made and distinctions drawn, whether in the name of retributive justice or credible deterrence. It is therefore no wonder that evidentiary matters play a central role in the criminal process. Some of the restrictions upon the evidence that can be procured by the state and brought to bear in the courtroom, such as the requirement of a duly authorized warrant for a comprehensive search, stem from a generalized concern about the limits of police intrusion. But other restrictions reflect fundamentally epistemic concerns, such as the exclusion of evidence of a defendant's prior criminal history, or of hearsay reports of the defendant's statements. Although prior criminal history is clearly relevant to the proof of crime in question, such evidence is rightly excluded in many cases on the grounds that its effect upon juries is more prejudicial than probative.[64] Without these protective evidentiary rules, a system of criminal responsibility could not possibly be applied in justice.

Contrast the circumstances of criminal justice with those of moral theory. Although moral philosophers since Kant have warned of the inscrutability of individual intention in the first as well as third-personal cases, most moral theories ignore these epistemic problems, including Kant's own moral theory.[65] Deontologists focus on agents' underlying intentions and self-conceptions; and utilitarians resort to the idealized fiction of fully informed, 'ethical' preferences in order

---

[63] See *Sandoval v People*, 117 Colo. 558, 192 P. 2d 423 (1948) ('it matters not how short the interval between the determination to kill and infliction of the mortal wound, if the time was sufficient for one thought to follow another').

[64] See e.g. *Brinegar v United States*, 338 US 160 (1949) ('[M]uch evidence of real and substantial probative value goes out on considerations irrelevant to its probative weight but relevant to possible misunderstanding or misuse by the jury'). Note that evidence of a defendant's criminal history is often brought in after conviction, at the sentencing stage, as an aggravating factor.

[65] See Immanuel Kant, *Groundwork of the Metaphysics of Morals*, trans. Mary Gregor (Cambridge: Cambridge University Press, 1998; 1st pub. 1785), ch. 2, 407: 'We are pleased to flatter ourselves with the false claim to a nobler motive, but in fact we can never, even by the most strenuous self-examination, get to the bottom of our secret impulses; for when moral value is in question, we are concerned, not with the actions which we see, but with their inner principles, which we cannot see.' That said, Kant's mechanism of evaluating potential maxims does seem to presuppose a large amount of self-knowledge.

to justify their criterion of right action.⁶⁶ Whether agents have acted wrongly and are accountable for so acting thus depends upon deep facts about their deliberative and motivational capacities, fine-grained attributions of intentional content, unequivo-cal motivation, and empirically adequate predictions of future consequences.

In general, the moral judgments we make and the responses we offer may be wildly out of line with the evidence necessary to support their application. The jerk who cuts me off on the highway may be distracted by great personal loss. But this possi-bility is unlikely to stop me from thinking him a jerk. Moral theory and practice can live by idealized epistemic standards because the stakes in the moral game are low in any particular case. The relationships that social morality plays the dominant role in protecting can usually be repaired through apology and understanding. I may unfairly resent your failure to meet me, not realizing that you had a sick child to take care of. When you have a chance to explain, or when I otherwise discover the reason for your absence, all is again put right between us.

By contrast, the belated acquittal of someone unjustly convicted puts little right, for nothing can repair the violence done to one's sense of autonomy and worth by unjust punishment. To be imprisoned, publicly despised, and stripped of elementary civil rights is to have one's political, social, and moral identity undermined or lost: it is to become an object of the state's authority, rather than a subject who authorizes the state's exercise of that power.⁶⁷ Freedom and compensation may be valid claims stemming from unjust process or sentence, but they are not a full means of repair. Given the moral and human costs of wrongful conviction, it surely follows that a nec-essary condition of a just penal institution is that it make very few mistakes. Legal judgments have little point unless actually applied and enforced; they are worthless merely as indicators of moral norms. But in order to be legitimate, legal judgments must be well-rooted in both fact and political morality. Legal theorists and moral philosophers who distinguish sharply between normative and evidentiary issues run the risk of ignoring the social space, with its costs and limitations, in which legal rules are necessarily embedded.⁶⁸ The problem is that an awareness of the law's epistemic constraints can quickly become licence for a cavalier cynicism about alibi and excuse. To the extent that exculpatory considerations are narrowed because of difficulties of proof, so broadens the scope of legal intrusion.

⁶⁶ See e.g. Barbara Herman, 'Moral Deliberation and the Derivation of Duties', in *The Practice of Moral Judgment* (Cambridge, Mass.: Harvard University Press, 1993), 132–58; Richard Brandt, *A Theory of the Good and the Right* (New York: Oxford University Press, 1979); and John Harsanyi, 'Rule Utilitarianism and Decision Theory', *Erkenntnis*, 11 (1977), 25–53.

⁶⁷ One can, of course, take on a new identity as a result of imprisonment, just or unjust. My point is that one cannot return naïvely to the normal positions of an equal citizen. One becomes either an anti-social rebel, or a sentimental citizen.

⁶⁸ Douglas Husak is an example of a legal theorist who may distinguish too sharply between the two. He argues that questions of the difficulty of proving *mens rea* do not bear upon the justice of a *mens rea* requirement. Husak, *Philosophy of Criminal Law*, 59–60. Although I agree with Husak that intentional-ity requirements should not easily be compromised for the sake of easing the burden of proof, I do not think the position generalizes to the autonomy of liability rules from epistemic questions.

Within these epistemic constraints, two different kinds of criteria are generally relevant to criminal responsibility: criteria of capacity, and criteria of intentionality.
The capacity demanded for criminal liability is, roughly, that demanded for moral
responsibility: a capacity to govern oneself by practical reason, responsive to the
moral and factual considerations that obtain. The requisite capacity for practical
rationality evidently incorporates a number of different components: a perceptual
component, for establishing the nature of one's environment; a conative component,
through which one finds some possibilities of action desirable as goals and others
undesirable; an evaluative-cognitive component, for weighing the reasons for and
against the potential goals; an instrumental-cognitive component, for determining
how to realize those goals; and a volitional component, through which one actually
acts on the desired goals.[69] Note that there is nothing about the having or exercise of
this capacity that is incompatible with causal determinism.[70] This is not meant to beg
the free will problem, but only to point out that the metaphysical capacity to act
otherwise demanded by incompatibilists is a further requirement, going beyond the
core practical capacity.[71] And even if compatibilist understandings of moral responsibility are not, finally, acceptable, it is plausible to argue that here is one point where
legal and moral criteria of responsibility may reliably diverge. For the moral notion
may well be thought to import a theologically or metaphysically ambitious conception of responsibility, related to divine judgment or existential meaningfulness. The
sublunary ambitions of law, meanwhile, might be satisfied with a conception of fair
attributability for which the practical reason capacity suffices.[72]

Metaphysical debates notwithstanding, those persons without the capacity to reason practically are manifestly to be treated or incapacitated, not punished. It remains
a vexed question in law and philosophy what sort of rational incapacities fatally
undermine culpability.[73] The traditional M'Naghten requirement is that the defen-

---

[69] For a more thorough examination of the relevant self-governing capacity, see Fischer and Ravizza,
Responsibility and Control; and Moore, 'The Legal View of Persons', in *Law and Psychiatry* (Cambridge:
Cambridge University Press, 1984), 44–112.

[70] Since it demands that one's actions flow from a process of reasoned action, it does seem incompatible with any notion of physical indeterminacy that would make action or decision essentially random.

[71] For discussion see Fischer and Ravizza, *Responsibility and Control*, 44–51; Stephen J. Morse,
'Diminished Capacity', in Shute, *Action and Value*, 239–78; Scanlon, 'Significance of Choice', 61–4.

[72] This is again to emphasize the special responsive position of the state, and to deny, contra Moore,
that it should take the role played by God in a godless world.

[73] Another small philosophical literature has emerged concerning the 'actual' blameworthiness of
corporate actors, where this question is usually approached through the metaphysical question whether
corporations are moral persons. See, e.g., Peter French, *Collective and Corporate Responsibility* (New
York: Columbia University Press, 1984); and Larry May, *The Morality of Groups* (Notre Dame, Indiana:
Notre Dame University Press, 1987). The metaphysical discussion seems to me largely to miss the genuinely central question. Given that all groups are groups of people, what are individuals' responsibilities
for what their groups do? Examining complicity seems to me the better way to approach the problem,
than to inquire in what sense General Motors can be properly blamed. Of course, there are important
questions about the *effectiveness* of different measures directed at corporate groups. For an excellent

dant will only be excused from responsibility if he does not 'know the nature or the quality of the act he was doing; or if he did know it, that he did not know what he was doing was wrong'.[74] This is obviously an extremely restrictive definition, according to which a defendant who understood the wrongness of his act, but was compelled to do so by Satanic voices in his head, would not be excused. The purely cognitive definition was therefore expanded by the American Legal Institute into the requirement that the defendant be able to 'appreciate the criminality of his conduct' and 'to conform his conduct to the requirements of law'.[75] Other definitions have been put forward as well, notably the short-lived but famous definition offered by the federal court of appeals for the D.C. Circuit, that a defendant be deemed non-responsible if his unlawful act was 'the product of mental disease or mental defect'.[76]

None of these definitions fully captures the idea of incapacity that juries almost certainly operate with, but all indicate the general scope of the questions surrounding criteria of responsibility.[77] The genuinely difficult questions come at the margins of capacity, for example, with agents who suffer delusions but who know that they do so (as with many schizophrenics), or with agents who recognize the wrongness of their acts but who seem completely to lack ordinary concern for wrongness.[78] Given the general lack of knowledge about the nature of mental illness and the inhospitability of legal proceedings to nuanced discussion, epistemic constraints are tightest in this domain. This is mainly a problem for retributivists, who may find that any operationizable criteria of mental capacity will err, either by demanding treatment for those who ought be punished, or by demanding punishment for those demanding treatment. For instrumentalists, the choice between incapacitating and punitive responses is less significant.[79]

Moral responsibility hinged on conduct, in the sense of intentional activity, and causation. The most serious moral responses, such as blame and recrimination, fall where conduct and causation run together: when the agent causes harm with a will that evinces lack of respect for another's interests. Criminal responsibility follows suit. Liability for most crimes is based upon a combination of criteria regarding the defendant's bodily acts and their consequences, and the intentions, knowledge, or awareness with which those acts were done and their consequences produced. The terms 'subjective' and 'objective' are used, respectively, for the intentional and the

discussion, see Brent Fisse and John Braithwaite, *Corporations, Crime, and Accountability* (Cambridge: Cambride University Press, 1993).

[74] *Regina v M'Naghten*, 8 Eng. Rep 718 (1843).   [75] Model Penal Code § 4.01.
[76] *Durham v United States*, 214 F.2d 845, 862 (D.C. Cir. 1954).
[77] See Moore, 'The Legal Concept of Insanity', 245, for this surely correct observation.
[78] See John Deigh, 'Empathy and Universalizability', *Ethics*, 105 (1995), 743–63; see also Fischer and Ravizza, *Responsibility and Control*, 76–81.
[79] There would be a problem for instrumentalists if defendants could easily demonstrate insanity, then simulate a quick recovery, thus avoiding both punishment and lengthy incapacitation; the deterrence system would clearly be undermined. For better or worse, this does not seem an actual problem, as confinement of the criminally insane is notoriously lengthy.

conduct, circumstance, and consequence criteria, often also called the *mens rea* and *actus reus* elements of a crime.

Unfortunately, 'subjective' and 'objective' are also used for a wholly different contrast in criminal law, to distinguish between individualized and normalized standards. In this sense, subjective criteria predicate liability upon the actual capacities and beliefs of the agent, while objective criteria predicate liability upon the capacities and beliefs that could reasonably be expected of a generally competent rational agent.[80] At the risk of departing somewhat from standard legal usage, I will use the terms 'individualized' and 'normalized' for this sense of 'subjective' and 'objective' criteria. Philosophical questions arise about both sorts of criteria.

Standardly, criminal liability requires that a single agent perform the specified acts or cause the specified harms, with or because of a specified mental state or states. First-degree murder, for example, requires the subjective element of a premeditated intention to kill, as well, of course, as the 'objective' result that the agent has caused another's death in acting upon that very intention. Second-degree, or 'depraved-heart' homicide, does not require killing as an aim, but does require that the defendant believe killing a likely consequence of his actions. For some crimes, the defendant's mental state must be highly determinate: larceny requires not only the objective taking of another's property, but a subjective intent to deprive the other permanently of that property. And there are many crimes that can be committed with a still culpable but not intentional mental state, such as recklessness or gross negligence. The defendant must be engaged in some activity intentionally (e.g. driving), but need not be driving with an intent to kill to be found guilty of vehicular homicide. It suffices if the defendant's objective conduct consists of driving, that conduct causes a death, and, for recklessness, that he is aware of the risks his driving presents. Crimes committed negligently must be handled differently, for the question is not whether the defendant had any particular mental state, but whether he lacked a state he should have had, namely attention to the relevant risks.[81] Clearly, subjective and objective criteria interpenetrate, for the objective conduct component is itself intentional—for example, the taking of property, or the killing of another—and may merely be accompanied rather than caused by the relevant subjective state. The subjective component is not, therefore, generally an explanation of the conduct, but rather a mental state relevant to the assessment of the defendant's moral culpability.[82]

[80] See e.g. Hart, 'Legal Responsibility'.

[81] Both recklessness and negligence raise questions of individualized versus normalized standards, questions I treat shortly.

[82] This description, in fact, only works for the individual-actor paradigm. In cases of complicity, the accomplice has a culpable *mens rea*, namely an intention to further the principal's criminal objective, but his actions fall well short of the *actus reus* component of the offence. For a superb discussion, see Sanford H. Kadish, 'Complicity, Cause, and Blame: A Study in Doctrine', *California Law Review*, 73 (1985), 323–410. As with the harmless torturers mentioned above, the justification in liability has to be grounded almost entirely in the accomplice's participatory intention, not in his causal contribution. See my *Complicity*, 220–36.

The subjective and objective criteria of responsibility invoke the traditional analytical philosophical problems of giving an account of intentional action, including the problems of relating intention to bodily movement, individuating acts, and intentional omissions; and writers in criminal legal theory have pursued these philosophical problems.[83] But it is unclear that a legal theory needs a deep philosophical account of these problems. Take the problem of act-individuation: a defendant throws down a match, thus setting fire to a house and killing the inhabitants. There is a philosophical dispute between so-called fine-grained individuators, such as Alvin Goldman, who argue that the defendant performs many different acts (throwing down the match, burning down the house, and killing the inhabitants), and coarse-grained individuators, such as Donald Davidson, who argue that the defendant performs but one act, the bodily movement of throwing down the match, which act can be described in many different ways, as a house-burning, inhabitant-killing, and so on.[84] The relevant questions of criminal responsibility are, however, neutral between these issues in action theory. These questions include whether, for example, the burning or the killing can be traced causally to the match throwing; whether the defendant intended the burning or the killing, or was reckless towards those consequences; and whether the burning and the killing merit independent, cumulative punishments. They are not purely metaphysical questions or problems of action theory. They are, rather, normative, and will be answered instead by reference to a theory of punishment. The terms of these theories are the folk or commonsensical notions of deliberation, foresight, intention, and action; the normative challenge lies in relating these terms to a scale of culpability.[85] Even the difficult questions raised by automatism and mind control must be answered in terms of a normative theory of responsibility and the criteria of self-governance, theories which need only presuppose and not analyse the basic idea of doing something for a reason.

More difficult philosophical questions about responsibility arise regarding the question whether the punishment system should deploy individualized or normalized criteria of responsibility. Claims of specific (not general incapacity) excuse from responsibility or justification are the main place issues of individualized and normalized criteria and arise, typically when the defendant unreasonably believes that justifying or excusing circumstances obtain. A defendant who commits a crime under the unreasonable belief that his life is being threatened might plead duress or self-defence. But these issues also arise with crimes defined partly in terms of results, such as homicide. Return to the arsonist, and suppose that anyone reasonably intelligent

[83] See e.g. Michael Moore, *Act and Crime* (New York: Oxford University Press, 1993); and Antony Duff, *Intention, Agency, and Criminal Liability* (New York: Oxford University Press, 1990).

[84] Alvin I. Goldman, 'Action and Crime: A Fine-Grained Approach', *University of Pennsylvania Law Review*, 142 (1994), 1563–86; Donald Davidson, 'Agency', in *Essays on Actions and Events* (New York: Oxford University Press, 1980), 43–61.

[85] For discussion of this point, see Ripstein, *Equality, Responsibility, and the Law* (New York: Cambridge University Press, 1999), 14; and Jennifer Hornsby, 'On What's Intentionally Done', in Shute, *Action and Value*, 55–74.

would have realized there was a substantial chance people might be sleeping in this house.[86] But this defendant was in fact so addled or unintelligent that she was not in fact aware of the risk. Should she be punished for reckless homicide, none the less— that is, causing death not intentionally but with a conscious disregard of the relevant risks—on the grounds that any reasonable person would have been aware of those risks, even if she was not? The case for an individualized standard, which would acquit in this instance, is that however indefensible her conduct, she must evince the particular culpable mental state which the law targets. If the justification for punishing someone with that mental state depends on the wickedness of agents with that state, then punishment is morally unjustified; and if the punishment's justification is deterring agents from acting recklessly, then it also misses its target, since she was not, by her own lights, acting recklessly. Similarly in the excuse and justification contexts, there is a strong moral case for individualized standards: the defendant simply did not have the ill will targeted by the criminal norm. Nor is the failure of deterrence in these cases worrisome since, in the excuse case, the norm is not expected to deter in such circumstances, and in the justification case, the norm should not deter.[87]

Now, these considerations only reach so far. Even if she was not specially deterred by the punishment, others might generally be, and might also be dissuaded from acting recklessly with the hope of being acquitted on erroneous individualized grounds. Secondly, at most these considerations show that punishing her for reckless killing is unwarranted; punishment for negligent killing might still be warranted; and there is no obvious reason to distinguish sharply between the punishment schedules for each. Thirdly, the epistemic limitations of the criminal process may suggest that a fairer process will be one that deploys normalized standards rather than one that is likely to fail if it attempts to discern individual beliefs. These are largely pragmatic considerations. But some, most recently Arthur Ripstein, have tried to make a positive, principled case for normalized standards.[88] Criminal norms are devices for allocating autonomy, where 'autonomy' means control over person and property—as I put it before, they define a minimum normative content for social and moral relations. In a liberal state, a legitimate system of criminal norms allocates autonomy

[86] These facts are loosely taken from *R. v Hyam* [1973] Q.B. 99 (C.A) (defendant set fire to house hoping to frighten romantic rival, killing the rival's two daughters). Similar issues are raised by crimes that make specific beliefs part of the definition, notably rape, which in some formulations makes the defendant's belief that the victim does not consent, an element of the crime. In the notorious English *Morgan* case, it was held that a defendant's unreasonable but sincere belief that a woman had consented to intercourse could be a complete defence to the rape charge; now, it is often held that the defendant's belief about consent must be reasonable. *R. v Morgan* [1976] A.C. 182. (The defendants in question were supposedly persuaded by Morgan that his wife enjoyed intercourse under duress.)

[87] The relation between deterrence and the excuses raises the important distinction between conduct rules, addressed to citizens, and decision rules, addressed to adjudicators. Excuse rules are arguably decision rules alone, and should not play a role in citizens' deliberations. See Meir Dan-Cohen, 'Conduct Rules and Decision Rules: On Acoustic Separation in Criminal Law', *Harvard Law Review*, 97 (1984), 625–77.

[88] See Ripstein, *Equality*, 163–70. Ripstein's argument is much subtler and more complex than I show here.

equally, giving each citizen the same measure of protection and control. The defendant here failed to take the interests of others into account, not by acting badly in the face of awareness of the relevant risks to potential victims, but by failing to consider the risks at all. If she is acquitted, the victims will, in effect, have been deprived of the measure of autonomy to which state norms entitle them. One need not think of punishment as compensation to the victims to think they have a claim on state punishment here. Given the necessarily expressive dimension of punishment, an acquittal may be thought to signal that the state condones the way in which the defendant failed to give due regard to the victims' interests. As Ripstein puts it, the state would otherwise condone the defendant's substitution of private rationality for public reasonableness. Nor does there appear to be unfairness towards the defendant. Assuming she had the capacity to advert to the risks, the norm under which she is punished is a reasonable constraint on her behaviour, and so she has not received less protection to her own autonomy than to which she is entitled.[89] After all, she could have avoided punishment altogether simply by not torching the house.

Of course, this argument, like the argument for subjectivism, might be taken instead to support the more limited point, that there be some state response to the particular flaw in the defendant's conduct, namely, that she caused harm through unreasonably failing to advert to the relevant risks. What the argument shows is that there should be a criminal norm prohibiting negligence. Punishment for negligence still incorporates normalized standards of conduct into the criminal law, but by establishing a separate criminal norm. Declining to integrate normalized standards into particular offences, however, may well serve purposes of analytical clarity, as well as focusing attention on the normative question of what response is appropriate for the particular kind of conduct engaged in by the defendant. The same point holds true for claims of excuse or justification founded in unreasonable beliefs: there is clearly a justifiable (and often taken) middle path of treating these as cases of 'imperfect defences', and mitigating but not eliminating punishment.

What the dispute between individualized and normalized standards ultimately reveals is, again, how important it is to see criminal law's criteria of responsibility as constitutive of interpersonal normative relations. The debate cannot be settled without an account of the conduct citizens owe one another, the specific meaning and response demanded by failure to meet that standard of conduct, and the role of the state in creating, expressing and defending that standard. The impulse towards individualized standards comes from a view of the state as principally responsible for denouncing or punishing failures to meet that standard; the impulse towards normalized standards from a view of the state as principally responsible for ensuring a fair allocation of autonomy among citizens. Hart famously argued that the law of excuse should be understood not to conceal a particular moral conception of responsible agency, but rather as a way of maximizing citizens' liberty against the

---

[89] Compare Scanlon, 'Significance of Choice', 89–96.

background of a deterrence system, by maximizing citizens' ability to control the incidence of coercive force.[90] Hart's view offers a healthy reminder of the importance of understanding the distinctive relation between the state and citizens in a liberal order, by relating it to the political value of autonomy instead of moral values implicated by retribution. But it is too narrow a view, for we also expect the state to express the moral force of the conduct norms we set for ourselves. We must not complicate our understanding of the state's functions, and so complicate our understanding of the criteria of criminal responsibility, when we realize that these criteria define both our relations to one another as well as our relations to the state.

4 LEGAL RESPONSIBILITY FOR ACCIDENTS

In contemporary legal theory, criminal law concerns responsibility for acts and tort law, responsibility for outcomes. As we have seen, this theoretical contrast can mislead, since one can be criminally responsible for the consequences of one's conduct (e.g. murder), and one can be responsible in tort on the basis of one's conduct (e.g. an intentional injury). What chiefly distinguishes tort from criminal law is the nature of the warranted response: tort law governs the state creation of a compensatory response from the agent towards the victim, while criminal law, at least conventionally, solely involves a response from the state towards the agent.[91] Tort and criminal law should thus be understood as complements, not necessarily treating different objects of responsibility, but as involving different responses. The complementary nature of criminal and tort liability is worth bearing in mind even in those instances where only one form could lie, as when someone violates a criminal norm without causing any harm (e.g. a failed attempt), or causes harm without transgressing a criminal norm. The latter is the domain of accident, when ordinarily permissible activities go awry and cause harm.

If tort law is defined as the legal norms governing compensatory responses from injurers to victims, then it is apparent that tort law is only one of many possible systems treating responsibility for accidents. Rather than dictate or enforce responses between injurers and victims, the state could, for example, simply ensure victim

---

[90] Hart, 'Legal Responsibility'.

[91] As I mentioned above, the practice of criminal law might come to include a reparative or restitutionary elements, through which the state oversees a response from agent to victim. The pure restitutionary model, such as that suggested by Randy Barnett in *The Architecture of Freedom* (New York: Oxford University Press, 1998), simply replaces criminal with tort law; it ignores the reasons to repair other relations sundered by criminal acts, including relations to the state.

compensation through a mandatory insurance fund, as in New Zealand.[92] Or the state could make injury an occasion for punishment, leaving victims with only the moral compensation of seeing justice done. But the system on which most of the world has converged takes as a central feature the linking of injurers and victims through the enforcement of private compensatory response. Accordingly, the task modern legal theorists have set for themselves is a defence of the legal practice of accountability for accidents.

The range and depth of modern theories of tort is great, and interested readers should turn to Arthur Ripstein's chapter in this volume for a survey. What I will do instead is indicate some of the general patterns of theorizing and to show how the choice among them mainly turns on the ideal of interpersonal and political relations they presuppose. One major division runs through modern theorizing, between what can be called *allocative* and *attributive* theories of responsibility, each side of the division reflecting a different conception of the relation among individuals and between them and the state.[93] Allocative theories of responsibility treat accidental harm as an incident of communal life, to be handled collectively in the first instance, with individuals bearing liability only if that serves the collective interest. Attributive theories, by contrast, treat harms as problems for individuals; the task of a legal system is to recognize and enforce the reparative obligations individuals have towards one another.

Consequentialist theories, of which the economic models are the most thoroughly worked out, typify the allocative approach. A normative goal is posited, for example, utility or wealth maximization, and then various principles are defended on the grounds that when accident costs are so allocated, utility will indeed be maximized, through readjustment of incentives, spreading effects, and so forth.[94] It becomes an empirical question whether, say, a fault principle best achieves the normative goal. Moreover, pursuit of the consequentialist goal may dictate principles that depart very far from ordinary tort practice, such as simply allocating the costs of the accident among the wealthiest. It will thus be purely contingent whether the legal principles of tort reflect anything like the common-sense moral paradigm of injurer-repair. But non-consequentialist approaches may also have an allocative structure, such as Jules Coleman's earlier 'annulment theory' of tort. According to the annulment theory, the purpose of tort law is to ensure the rectification of wrongful losses and wrongful

---

[92] For a recent reassessment of New Zealand's alternative to a tort system, see Bryce Wilkinson, 'New Zealand's Failed Experiment with State Monopoly Accident Insurance', *Green Bag*, 2d 2 (1998), 45–55.

[93] I borrow these terms, along with much else in my discussion, from Jules Coleman; see his 'Second Thoughts and Other First Impressions', in Brian Bix (ed.), *Analyzing Law* (New York: Oxford University Press, 1998), 257–322, 301–6. But borrowing so much from Coleman is merely to keep company with much of the rest of tort theory in the last two decades.

[94] See e.g. Guido Calabresi, *The Costs of Accidents* (New Haven: Yale University Press, 1970); William N. Landes and Richard A. Posner, *The Economic Structure of Tort Law* (Cambridge, Mass.: Harvard University Press, 1987); and Steven Shavell, *Economic Analysis of Accident Law* (Cambridge, Mass.: Harvard University Press, 1987).

gains, where 'wrongful' is determined by reference to the norms governing legitimate transfer of holdings and liberties.[95] On this view, the function of tort law is to maintain the allocation of holdings provided by the prevailing scheme of distributive justice. Still other allocative approaches are suggested by egalitarian theories, for example, following the principle that accident costs ought to be distributed in such a way that both preserves an equal initial distribution of resources and demands a display of equal concern by individuals.[96]

Alternatively, the costs of accidents might be allocated so as to maximize individual autonomy, with autonomy conceived broadly in terms of individuals' capacity to engage in effective planning.[97] All these allocative principles might generate the same set of operational principles—fault-based injurer liability, no-fault social insurance, strict liability—but the emergence of those principles would be in each instance grounded in a collective responsibility for the costs of accidents. Allocations of responsibility to individuals are derivative.

Attributive theories of tort law, by contrast, make individual ascriptions of responsibility primary. The theory of individual responsibility may be moral, in the sense of being prior to political institutions, or it may be political; but the task of a system of legal responsibility is to give effect to the underlying claims and duties of individual responsibility. So-called libertarian theories of tort law exemplify the attributive approach.[98] On a libertarian view generally, agents are regarded as entitled, as a matter of pre-political, natural right, to the profits of their causal interventions. Costs would then be treated symmetrically, as also the entitlement, albeit unwanted, of productive agency. It is a further consideration on the libertarian view that injury diminishes the legitimate entitlements of the victim, depriving him of (some of) the value of his holdings in a way inconsistent with the norms of legitimate transfer.[99] But the central concept is one of responsibility for one's accidents, where responsibility is understood in terms of causation.

[95] See Coleman, 'Tort Law and the Demands of Corrective Justice', *Indiana Law Journal*, 67 (1992), 349–79.

[96] Such an approach is suggested by Ronald Dworkin in *Law's Empire* (Cambridge, Mass.: Harvard University Press, 1986), 276–312. In his 'What is Equality? Part 2: Equality of Resources', *Philosophy and Public Affairs*, 10 (1981), 283–345, Dworkin lays the ground for an alternative approach, according to which accident costs should allocated to individuals when those costs reflect, in a specified sense, choices of those individuals; and otherwise should be allocated so as to preserve an egalitarian distribution of resources. This approach is further developed in Eric Rakowski, *Equal Justice* (New York: Oxford University Press, 1991), 227–43.

[97] This approach is suggested by Hart's theory of criminal liability, discussed above.

[98] Richard Epstein's early view, in 'A Theory of Strict Liability', *Journal of Legal Studies*, 2 (1973), 151–204, is still taken as exemplary of libertarian theories of tort. While Epstein still considers himself a libertarian, his more recent work, in *Simple Rules for a Complex World* (Cambridge, Mass.: Harvard University Press, 1995), seeks a utilitarian foundation for tort law. Whether or not Epstein can reconcile libertarianism with utilitarianism, his newer view is clearly allocative—which may reduce actually held, genuinely libertarian theories of tort to a null set.

[99] As a corollary, if no agent is responsible for the victim's loss, finding compensation in a mandatory insurance pool would be an illegitimate taking.

Now, theories grounding responsibility on causation suffer from a crippling defect, familiar already from my discussion of moral responsibility: in a metaphysical sense, a broad variety of conditions and events count equally as causes of a given harm; only pragmatic, normative criteria can distinguish them. As Ronald Coase pointed out, most accidental injuries arise from an interaction between plaintiffs and defendants—one walking while the other is driving, one using a product while the other is producing it, and so forth.[100] Indeed, in the modern world of mass torts and mass production, causal criteria hardly exclude anyone from liability. Take the Bhopal disaster of 1984, when a pesticide plant leaked poisonous gas, killing thousands of nearby residents. The disaster seems to have been the product of lax supervisory and maintenance standards at the plant, under-trained employees, understaffing as a result of low profits, the absence of effective regulatory authority within the relevant Indian ministries, inadequate monitoring by US headquarters, much less by Union Carbide shareholders; coupled with the decision by residents to move to or remain near an industrial facility whose central product was highly toxic.[101] Clearly, different causally implicated parties bear very different levels of responsibility for the tragedy. So causal criteria at best determine a range of liability candidates. Only by reference to further, normative criteria can one party be designated 'the cause', or one 'injurer' and the other 'victim', terms that load a direction of causation and not merely a description of harm.

Others have offered attributive theories of legal responsibility grounded in a richer notion of moral responsibility than mere causation. Ernest Weinrib, for example, treats tort liability as simply the reflection of individuals' moral responsibilities to remedy the rights they infringe. Moral compensatory responsibility rests, in turn, on a basically Kantian understanding of the requirements of practical reason. A rational agent who wills an act must perforce accept responsibility for the consequences of that act; to impose the costs of one's act on others willy-nilly is to fail to respect the demand that one act only in accordance with principles that all might follow.[102] Compensatory responsibility is self-attributed, in the sense that it follows from the exercise of practical reason.[103] Jules Coleman's intermediate work, *Risks and Wrongs*, similarly ties legal reparative obligations to moral claims of compensation, claims grounded in a normative conception of individual agency.[104] Unlike his earlier,

[100] Ronald Coase, 'The Problem of Social Cost', *Journal of Law & Economics*, 3 (1960). For a rich development of this point, see Stephen Perry, 'The Impossibility of General Strict Liability', *Canadian Journal of Law & Jurisprudence*, 1 (1988), 147–71.

[101] See the comprehensive *New York Times* series of reports on the disaster, 'The Bhopal Disaster: How it Happened', in the 28, 29, and 31 Jan. 1994 issues, all p. A1. The Bhopal plant was operated by Union Carbide India, whose shares were 50.9% owned by Union Carbide Co. (US), 22% directly by the Government of India, and the remainder among 23,000 Indian citizens.

[102] Ernest Weinrib, *A Theory of Private Law* (Cambridge, Mass.: Harvard University Press, 1995).

[103] For a suggestive development of a Kantian view of tort liability, see Barbara Herman, 'What Happens to the Consequences?', in *Practice of Moral Judgment*, 94–112.

[104] Jules Coleman, *Risks and Wrongs* (Cambridge: Cambridge University Press, 1992), 314–18.

purely allocative, 'annulment theory' of tort which focused on the general claim of victims that their wrongful losses be remedied, Coleman's newer agency-centred theory aims to show the special moral obligations agents have 'to repair the wrongful losses for which they are responsible'.[105] This principle of corrective justice, Coleman suggests, is simply immanent in our particular and contingent social practices.[106] However, the extension of this moral principle to legal responsibility is indirect. A legal system *may* implement the corrective justice principle directly, through the sort of enforceable, individualized reparative obligations characteristic of the tort system. Or it may not implement corrective justice, and instead implement some sort of purely allocative scheme in which individual reparative obligations do not directly figure.[107]

Finally, there are theories combining both allocative and attributive aspects. Stephen Perry, building on Tony Honoré's notion of 'outcome-responsibility', offers a theory of tort liability grounded independently in agents' moral responsibility for the outcomes they produce and over which they have control.[108] This claim of responsibility, not yet rising to a compensatory duty, flows from the phenomenology of agency, as I discussed above in reference to moral responsibility: our self-understanding as persisting, embedded agents depends, in part, upon our seeing ourselves as marking the world.[109] As Perry realizes, the interactive contexts that dogged libertarian theories pose a challenge for him as well, for injuries arising from intersecting activities will typically reflect the agency and control of all parties. (Though you hit me with your car, I might have chosen not to go for a walk, and so I equally controlled the outcome.) Thus Perry supplements the notion of outcome-responsibility, which limits prima-facie candidacy for liability, with an allocative principle according to which accident costs ought to lie with those at fault, or who otherwise impose unusual risks on others. Similarly, Coleman, with Arthur Ripstein, has recently put forth a conception fusing allocative and attributive considerations.[110] On their view, corrective justice is still a matter of instantiating the attribu-

[105] Coleman, *Risks*, 324.

[106] Coleman, 'The Practice of Corrective Justice', in Owen (ed.), *Philosophical Foundations*, 63, 53–72. To say that the principle of corrective justice is contingent, however, is not to say that it is merely contingent, in any sense of 'merely' beyond the metaphysical. For the principle that agents have special reason to repair their wrongs resonates throughout a set of ideals of agency, concern for others, and personhood. The principle, in other words, depends on a broad set of relational practices. Echoes of Strawson are strong.

[107] Coleman, *Risks*, 386–406. The state may not do justifiably nothing, at least if it has a defensible ideal of distributive justice.

[108] See Perry, 'Responsibility for Outcomes'; Perry, 'The Moral Foundations of Tort Law', *Iowa Law Review*, 77 (1992), 449–513; Tony Honoré, 'Responsibility and Luck', *The Law Quarterly Review* (1988), 530–53.

[109] Perry, 'Moral Foundations', 498. Perry suggests that outcome-responsibility is grounded only in one's responses to one's own outcomes. But, being the social beings we are, surely our reactions to what others do, and theirs to us, contribute to the phenomenological importance of causation and control.

[110] See Jules Coleman and Arthur Ripstein, 'Mischief and Misfortune', *McGill Law Journal*, 41 (1995), 91–130; see also Ripstein's independent exploration in Ripstein, *Equality, Responsibility*.

tive principle that individuals must bear the costs of their own conduct. This principle is immanent in a contingent set of social practices and not, as with Perry, derived from a moral theory of agency. But the question of which costs individuals 'own' should not be understood simply as a matter of social convention. The question of cost ownership must, rather, be answered by reference to a political theory concerning the proper allocation of risk and responsibility.[111] In short, Coleman and Ripstein make a political, allocative principle primary and then attribute specific reparative duties on the basis of the liability criteria it specifies, while Perry makes a moral, attributive principle primary, and then deploys a political, allocative one.[112]

The debate among tort theorists partly reflects different descriptive concerns: some theorists, such as Epstein and Calabresi, meant their contributions to be largely revisionary, while others, such as Perry, Coleman, and Posner, have claimed to be providing accounts sensitive to the actual content of doctrine, albeit accounts that aim to justify that doctrine. But, as with debates about criminal responsibility, what is really at stake are the distinctive ideals of social relations the views manifest. Further attention to this point by theorists might obviate the pressure to find a basically a priori argument for a moral or political principle justifying reparative obligations.[113] I argued in Section 2 that some notion of responsibility is clearly rooted in the experience of agency itself, as well as demanded by the facts of communal, conflicting life. But the responses specific to that notion, in other words the *content* of responsibility, will inevitably be a product of specific institutional arrangements and social life. It is, of course, a task for historians to document the emergence and transformation of the principles structuring tort law—as has been done, for instance, for the fault principle in Anglo-American law, showing its subsequent limitation in workplace and product contexts as a response to economic, social, and intellectual pressures.[114] The philosophical point is not to reject tort theory in favour of history,

[111] In the version of liberal political theory Coleman and Ripstein defend, the proper allocation is one that ensures an equal allocation of security, thus deploying normalized standards of liability, and reflects a deliberate ranking of the relative value of different activities. Coleman and Ripstein, 'Mischief', 126–9.

[112] Since Coleman and Ripstein make attribution subsidiary to allocation, their argument may seem to threaten to collapse corrective justice into distributive justice, as Perry argues. Perry, 'Mischief', 154. But if corrective justice is distinguished from distributive justice by its generation of agent-specific obligations, then Coleman and Ripstein have indeed put forth a corrective justice view, albeit one rooted in distributive justice. Alternatively, they could be read as showing that distributive justice must be understood in terms of both agent-general and agent-specific reasons. See Coleman, 'Second Thoughts', 312–16.

[113] It would be equally a mistake to rely on a Strawsonian invocation of 'natural' patterns of response, the 'natural' being clearly a product of the social.

[114] The English case *Holmes v Mather* [1875] 10 Ex. 21 contains the first prominent claim that negligent or wilful misconduct is a necessary element in a legal claim for compensation. Morton Horwitz argues that the move to negligence in American law expressed a deliberate social policy of subsidizing emerging industries. He notes also, however, that jurists focused on fault as a useful tool for determining liability in cases of joint collision, of which there were suddenly many. Morton Horwitz, *The Transformation of American Law: 1780–1860* (Cambridge: Mass., Harvard University Press, 1977), 85–99. See also Lawrence M. Friedman, *A History of American Law*, 2nd edn. (New York: Simon & Schuster, 1985).

but rather to recognize the central place that contingent social norms must play in even a philosophical account.

Return to the central debate between purely allocative, economic theories and purely attributive, corrective justice theories. Even assuming that a purely attributive theory can deal with the problem of interaction, the choice between theories depends primarily on a normative conception of the social arrangements to be regulated under the appropriate regime. With highly regularized domains of activity, such as automobile driving, industrial employment, and perhaps mass production and consumption, the systemic, managerial model of social relations presupposed by an economic approach seems both appropriate and attractive.[115] These are, in other words, the domains in which a public regulatory response seems correct: they present a collective problem of managing, spreading, and reducing costs, arising out of a generally valued and common activity, and in which the state can legitimately and effectively exercise authority. Within such a specified domain, the anti-individualism and cross-individual trade-offs that characterize the economic approach can be cabined, unthreatening to more general political ideals of individualism. By contrast, an untrammelled extension of an allocative approach to the general run of activity may indeed threaten those social and moral ideals. But much depends on the degree to which legal forms of responsibility are understood to reflect moral forms; and this too will surely vary with the relevant domain of activity, and with the particular social understanding of the relation between law and social morality. In the absence of a conception of such relations, the idea that an agent has a duty to pay compensation is empty. In some social conditions, ideals of personal responsibility and individual autonomy may indeed be threatened by tort doctrine.[116] In other conditions, the subsumption under allocative principles of even quite a broad range of activities may simply reflect an underlying collectivist ethos.

Again, my point is not that philosophical reflection on legal responsibility is beholden to particular cultural practice. An especially valuable form of philosophical activity is to point to alternative, more desirable social and political ideals, whether or not these are actually instantiated in legal practice, or are otherwise internal to the culture. I do not, above all, mean to endorse a blanket relativism towards social and legal practice; they are, of course, open to any manner of rational, critical treatment that one's meta-ethics provide. Another task is to engage in philosophy's traditional task of conceptual clarification, attempting to render perspicuous the principles and ideals animating a given legal culture, as well as showing what those ideals logically entail. What I mean to point out is simply that a relational under-

---

[115] See e.g. Justice Roger Traynor's famous concurrence in the products liability case *Escola v Coca Cola Bottling Co.*, 24 Cal. 2d 453, 461, 150 P.2d 436, 440 (1944), in which he defends enterprise liability in terms of insurance and incentive effects.

[116] The social transformation may come to be viewed generally positively, as is arguably the case in the domain of industrial accidents, with the shift from no employer liability without fault, to no-fault workers' compensation.

standing of tort law brings out the relevant dependence on social and moral ideals, and properly focuses attention on the normative crux of theoretical debates.[117]

5 CONCLUSION

I began with a catalogue of the many uses of responsibility, but this chapter has generally sought a unity within the subject. I have emphasized the way claims of responsibility can only be understood as specific social practices, responsive to a background set of social, moral, and political relations and ideals. This basically Strawsonian path through the thickets of responsibility seems to me independently correct, as a way of illuminating important features of claims and responses of responsibility. But it also casts a useful light on a set of debates within legal theory, between retributivists and utilitarians in criminal law, for example, and between allocationists and attributivists in tort. These debates seem currently at a philosophical standstill, though they shift from one decade to the next. But the general turn in moral and legal theorizing about responsibility, towards a relational conception, gives reason to hope that these debates may begin to move ahead, as their adherents confront and attempt to justify the ideals their accounts presuppose. And reconstructing responsibility has importance beyond what it shows about philosophical debate. For it is in understanding responsibility that we see ourselves as actors, creators, empathizers, and sufferers. It is in understanding responsibility, in short, that we know ourselves as persons.

[117] Coleman and Ripstein are, as I have noted, particularly conscious of this dimension of tort theory.

CHAPTER 15

PHILOSOPHY OF THE COMMON LAW

GERALD J. POSTEMA

1 INTRODUCTION

COMMON law is judge-made law. Every student of Anglo-American law knows that. By virtue of the doctrine of *stare decisis*, judicial decisions are held to be binding not only on the parties in the case before the court, but also on future courts in the jurisdiction deciding similar cases and thus binding on all those to whom the judge-made rules in question are addressed. In novel cases, where law arguably is silent, judges fill the silence with new binding precedents. Of course, *stare decisis* allows courts to 'distinguish' the cases they face from what might first appear to be relevant and binding precedents, and allows courts to 'extend' precedents beyond their explicit four corners by analogy. The doctrine, reluctantly and within narrow limits, even allows judges to overrule precedents when judges find them to be especially troubling. In this way, common law courts massage precedents and in the process make new law. There is nothing puzzling in this familiar tale. It poses no especially interesting challenge to existing theories of law and fits very comfortably into a variety of positivist accounts. (We might also be able without too much difficulty to square it with rival natural theories.) Law is essentially the product of lawmaking—the only major difference between common law and other forms of law lies in the institution doing the legislating.

Well, it may be just a little puzzling. After all, it appears that judicial *legislating* is done in the course of *adjudicating*. Legal rules are made in the course of applying the rules to the very case that called for the rulemaking. This is enough to convince Fred Schauer at least that common law is 'uncommonly puzzling' (Schauer 1989: 455). And Bentham attacked it relentlessly for confusing these two very different functions, resulting in radical uncertainty and a mask for judicial abuse of power (Bentham 1970: 184–95). We expect judges to follow rules, but it appears that in common law practice rules follow the judges. Common law becomes even a little more puzzling when we look into the history of English law. In a *Yearbook* report of a fifteenth-century case we find it argued, 'precedents and usages do not rule the law, but the law rules them' (Tubbs 2000: 45). Legal historians widely agree that before the eighteenth century there was no firm doctrine of *stare decisis* in English common law (Simpson 1973: 77; Gray 1992: 157–8). Indeed, it may not have been established until sometime in the nineteenth century. It is not entirely a coincidence that the positivist under-standing of common law as strictly *judge-made* law emerged at the time of the hard-ening of the doctrine of precedent in English common law. Indeed, it was Bentham who first used the term 'judge-made law', hurling it against English law as a term of contempt and abuse. The fact that it seems so innocent, and even descriptively appropriate, to us in the contemporary common law world is testimony to the dis-tance we have travelled from the jurisprudential world of classical common lawyers—a journey launched by Bentham's withering critique of eighteenth-century common law and John Austin's recasting of common law understanding to make it fit classical positivist jurisprudence.[1]

But if historians are correct, English common law functioned well enough for over 500 years without the one thing that, according to current orthodoxy, held the prac-tice together as a form of law. Moreover, it was this common law practice in its seven-teenth-century form, understood as seventeenth-century common lawyers understood it, that spread with English colonialism to the New World and beyond. Thus, current practice and historical evidence pose a challenge to familiar views about the common law. Common law, and widely shared conceptualizations of it, may have been (and may continue to be) considerably more complex than our com-mon knowledge admits. What we have taken for common knowledge about com-mon law may not be knowledge at all. We should take a closer look. Its characteristic mode of functioning may raise important issues for our philosophical understand-ing of the nature of law and legal reasoning.

How, then, are we to understand common law? This question appears to be unwieldy, especially if one expects a survey of common law jurisprudence from its birth in the twelfth century to its modern manifestations around the world. To make the task a bit more manageable I propose to look at common law jurisprudence in the seventeenth century, a very critical point in its development. By the seventeenth cen-tury common law practice had matured and there had emerged a group of reflective

---

[1] Bentham (1970: 152–5, 184–95, 1977: 188–273, 1998: 123–40); Austin 1885: ii. 525–33, 620–60); Postema (1986, ch. 8).

common lawyers who sought to articulate, albeit in a piecemeal, occasional, and sometimes partisan political fashion, a coherent understanding of the law they practised. They were engaged participants in the legal practice of their day: lawyers, judges, royal counsellors and parliamentarians, not philosophers. Hence, they never articulated a full-fledged philosophical theory of law. Yet, they shaped a distinctive perspective on questions about the nature of law and legal reasoning, and the normative authority of law, questions that are still at the center of philosophical reflection on law. In Section 2, I outline key themes and broad notions of common law jurisprudence; in Section 3 I translate them into a contemporary philosophical idiom and explore arguments that might be given in support of them.

2 CLASSICAL COMMON LAW JURISPRUDENCE

To classical common lawyers, law was not something laid down either by will or nature; rather, it was something taken up,[2] used in deliberation and argument, and followed in practice: 'the only method of proving, that this or that maxim is a rule of the common law', Blackstone wrote in the mid-eighteenth century, 'is by shewing that it hath been always the custom to observe it' (Blackstone 1765: i. 68). Law was regarded not as a structured set of authoritatively posited, explicit norms, but as rules and ways implicit in a body of practices and patterns of practical thinking all 'handed down by tradition, use, [and] experience' (Blackstone 1765: i. 17). These rules were the product of a process of a common practice of deliberative reasoning, and constituted the basic raw materials used in it. Common law was *reasonable usage* (Hedley 1610: 175), observed and confirmed in a public process of reasoning in which practical problems of daily social life were addressed. 'Custom' and 'reason' were the twin foci of this conception of law. These two notions were complementary, mutually enhancing and supporting, and mutually qualifying.

2.1 Common Law as Custom of the Realm

All general discussions of the common law started with the claim that common law was common custom of the whole realm (Hedley 1610: 175; Hale 1971: 17, 30; Blackstone 1765: I, 67). This was 'general custom' (as opposed to local custom of manor or shire) that was 'immemorial', existing from 'time out of mind'. For some

---

[2] I am indebted to James Murphy for this apt phrase.

common lawyers this was sufficient proof of its wisdom. Hedley argued, for example, that common law is common reason 'tried by time', the 'trier of truth [and] author of all human wisdom' (Hedley 1610: 175; see Coke 1628: 97b). Other seventeenth-century writers more modestly held that long usage fitted the law to the nature of the English people (Hale 1971: 30). There was also some disagreement over what it meant to claim that common law was immemorial. Coke claimed that most of the key doctrines and rules of common law remained essentially unchanged since Roman times (Coke 1793, *Second Reports*, preface), but in this he was no doubt eccentric. Matthew Hale expressed a more moderate and common view when he wrote in the last third of the seventeenth century, 'the strength and obligation, and the formal nature of a law, is not upon account that the Danes, or the Saxons, or the Normans, brought it in with them, but [rather that] they became laws, and binding in this kingdom by virtue of their being received and approved here' (Hale 1971: 43).[3] Not to be taken literally, the image of ancient origin, according to Hale, stood for three other key features of common law.

First, the common law was characterized by historical continuity. It may have gone through vast changes over its history, but through these changes it maintained its integrity as a single, coherent body of law. Despite the variations over the centuries, we can say it is the same law, just as the Argonauts' ship was the same when it returned home as when it departed, even though during its long voyage it had been repaired so often that it was made up of scarcely any of the original materials (Hale 1971: 40). And nothing of this ship of law was immune to change.

Secondly, continuity depended on integration of each part into the whole. To claim that common law existed 'time out of mind' meant that the validity and binding force of any rule of law depended not on who made it or when, but on its being 'received and approved' in the kingdom. This 'reception' was manifested in their integration into the body of doctrines and practices that makes up the common law. *Integration*, not *origin*, was the key (Hale 1971: 3, 6, 8). This integration of custom, statute, or judicial decision is not simply a matter of logical consistency or coherence. It is a practical and historical matter: *practical*, because it is a matter of whether the rule is 'taken up', practised, and used (by its subjects and by officials who must assess their actions in light of the law); and hence, *historical* because only time can tell whether a rule, however it happened to be introduced, is thus integrated and becomes part of the common law.

Finally, for Hale, and many of his contemporaries, integration involved accommodating the rule or maxim to the nature of the nation, 'such as by a long experience and use is as it were incorporated into their very temperament, and, in a manner, become the complexion and constitution of the English Commonwealth' (Hale 1971: 30; see Davies 1615: ii. 252, 255). The common law was said to be the 'constitution' of the nation—its basic normative structure and the root of its collective health. The

---

[3] Note: throughout this chapter I have silently modernized spelling, capitalization, and punctuation.

constitution Hale had in mind was not limited to the constitution of government; it was the constitution of *the people*. Also, the process of accommodation worked two ways. The rules of law, at first rough and clumsy, are refined over time, softened to fit the contours of the community's daily life. Simultaneously, following the rules and practices shapes the dispositions, beliefs, and expectations of the people. Thus, what they took to be reasonable and practicable solutions to the problems of social inter-action depended on a sense of continuity of present practice with the past; but also, what counted as continuous with the past depended heavily on what were regarded by participants as reasonable projections from the arrangements and practices of the past to present conditions and problems. This also explains Hale's claim that com-mon law was 'received and approved' in the kingdom. This was not a matter of mere expression of consent, but rather acceptance of it in virtue of and manifested in the law's integration into their lives.

Yet, for Hale, like all common lawyers, custom always had its status as law in and through the activities of the courts. But this raises the important question about *whose* custom is the custom of the common law, that of the people or that of the courts? There is no doubt that already by the sixteenth century, common law had become highly technical and no longer, if it had ever been, merely a reflection of cus-toms of the land. So, surely, common law was, as Bentham later called it, custom *in foro* rather than custom *in pays* (Bentham 1977: 182–4, 217–18). Classical common lawyers did not deny this, but they insisted nevertheless on a fundamental link between the two. The groundwork for articulating this link was laid by St German in the sixteenth century. He distinguished clearly between *general customs*, which were diffused throughout the realm and known to lawyers and lay people alike, and *max-ims*, which were the specialized rules of law known only in the king's courts (St German 1974: 59). Maxims had their 'strength and warrant' in, and 'take their effect by', the general customs of the realm. At the same time, they were rooted in a shared sense of their reasonableness, that is, of their suitability in, and their contribution to the coherence of, the rest of the common law and the practices of which it consists (ibid.). Thus, although lawyer's law might have seemed arcane to the ordinary Englishman, nevertheless, its claim to validity was thought to rest on the fact that it was congruent with the customs that were second nature to the people, and with the body of the common law as a whole refined by its distinctive discipline of reasoning. Thus, common law was not to be equated with custom of the realm, but the latter was the radical source of its validity, not literally by derivation, but by source and con-gruence.

2.2 Common Law as Common Reason

Common reason and natural law. The mantra of classical common lawyers was: 'the common law is no other than common reason' (Coke 1628: 97b, 183b; Hedley 1610:

175; Finch 1759: 75; Doddridge 1631: 242). However, despite the echoes of ancient natural law doctrine,[4] common law writers had something quite different in mind. They piously granted that natural law was the ultimate ground of all law, but rarely sought to bring this ground into their workaday world. Natural law was too abstract and theoretical for their pragmatic, concretely focused minds; it was too often silent, or contested, or simply out of touch with concrete human affairs (Hale 1956: 502–4). '[R]eason is the life of the law, nay the common law itself is nothing else but reason', Coke famously wrote, but he rushed to add that by this he meant not 'natural reason' but the 'artificial reason' of the trained common lawyer, 'an artificial perfection of reason gotten by long study, observation, and experience, and not every man's natural reason . . .' (Coke 1628: 97b). Similarly, in typical common law fashion, Hale insisted that the reason of the common law was the embodied prudence and deliberative judgment of the judge who, through his emersion in the concrete details of common law is fluent in the common language of human affairs, and thus best able to articulate notions of the 'just and fit . . . common to all men of reason'—better than philosophers or theologians who seek to do so 'transported from the ordinary measures of right and wrong' and cut off from 'the common staple of humane conversations' (Hale 1956: 502, 503).

This 'artificial reason' of common law differs in at least two respects from natural law as commonly understood. First, it was not thought of in terms of broad general principles, and by itself provided no contentful tests by which to assess the legitimacy of a given legal rule or doctrine. It was regarded, rather, as *disciplined practice* of reasoning. If 'reason' legitimated some doctrine, this was only because that doctrine survives critical scrutiny in a *process of reasoning and disputation.* Secondly, when the clear and uncontested law (what we now call 'black-letter law') yielded no unambiguous solution to a legal problem, the tendency of the common lawyer was not to consult extra-legal moral sources, as a natural lawyer might do, but rather to look deeper and longer into the accumulated fund of experience and example provided by the common law. Common lawyers put their faith in the ability of a trained reasoning capacity, immersed in the vast resources of experience supplied by law to yield reasonable and sound solutions in even the most difficult or apparently novel cases.

Artificial reason. Several features characterize 'artificial reason' as conceived by classical common law jurisprudence. First, it was *pragmatic,* focused on practical problem solving. It addressed concrete situations and problems and sought to forge solutions from the materials that were ready to hand. It measured success in terms of whether the proposed solution works; and the measure of its 'working' was whether it was 'taken up' in further cases.

---

[4] Cicero captured the Stoic doctrine, later elaborated in Thomist natural law theory, when he wrote, 'law is the highest reason . . . when firmly established and completed in the human mind' (*De Legibus,* i. 6.18).

Secondly, artificial reason was a *contextual* competence. '[M]en are not born common lawyers', Hale remarked, 'neither can the bare exercise of the faculty of reason give a man a sufficient knowledge of it, but it must be gained by the habituating and accustoming and exercising that faculty by reading, study, and observation to give a man a complete knowledge thereof' (Hale 1956: 505). The problem-solving typical of the common law judge was seldom merely a matter of looking up a relevant rule and applying it to the facts of the case before him. Typical common law reasoning was neither deductive nor inductive, but *analogical*, arguing from one case to the next on the basis of perceived likenesses and differences and the location of the instant case in the landscape of common experience painted by the judge or lawyer in command of the full resources of the common law.

Thirdly, artificial reason was self-consciously *nonsystematic*. Not hostile to theoretical reflection—it was far too practical for that, willing to use whatever tools lay ready to hand—but it was decidedly not a theoretical or systematic turn of mind. At the same time, it was not strictly particularistic in the current philosophical sense of that term. Common lawyers were not opposed to thinking in terms of universalizable reasons, and they were keen to secure coherence of their judgments with other solutions and parts of the law. Still, they typically sought *local* coherence. Overall coherence of moral or practical vision was less important to common lawyers than concrete workability. Thus, classical common law resisted reduction to a system of axioms or first principles from which its constituent maxims, rules, and decisions could (at least in principle) be inferred. Several prominent common lawyers sought to identify especially important general principles running through much of the law, but these collections were manifestly *unsystematic*. Bacon, for example, clearly meant his collection of maxims to be an aid for the student of the common law, but it was important, he thought, not to give the student the mistaken idea that the common law was to be found in these general principles or maxims (Bacon 1630: B3).

Fourthly, the artificial reason of common law was essentially *discursive*,[5] that is, a matter of deliberative reasoning and argument between interlocutors. The unwritten common law was deposited in the experience and memory of practitioners, Doddridge wrote, 'thence to be deduced by deceptation and discourse of reason: and that when occasion should be offered and not before'. Common law, he added, is reason 'tried and sifted upon disputation and argument'.[6] Coke made explicit a point that is clear but still implicit in Doddridge's thought: the disputation they have in mind is specifically *forensic*. In difficult cases, Coke argued, no individual alone and outside a court of justice, could ever discover the right reason of a rule of common

[5] This word is now obsolete, but it was current in the seventeenth century, and it nicely captures the interlocutory as well as the strictly discursive aspect of common law reason (*OED*).

[6] Doddridge (1631: 241, 242). 'Deceptation', or 'disceptation', is an archaic term meaning 'disputation, debate, or discussion'; 'to discept' is to dispute, debate, express disagreement or difference of opinion (*OED*). I am grateful to Michael Lobban for this reference and generally for deepening my understanding of classical common law jurisprudence. His work on seventeenth-century common law will appear in vol. 10 of Pattaro, Postema, and Stein (forthcoming).

law. For it is only in the process of argument, regarding concrete cases, in open court subject to reasoned challenge, that law is to be found and forged (Coke 1793, *Ninth Reports*, preface).

Finally, then, the reason of common law is itself *common* or *shared*. It is not 'natural' in the sense of being a merely individual capacity. It is an intellectual competence, a discursive faculty that is learned through participation in a practice of public forensic argument, situated in and moving about in a world of recorded experience of 'human affairs and conversation'. The philosopher and theologian are not suited for this task, Hale argued, for it is not an enterprise of discovery of general practical principles through the exercise of abstract reason, but rather an enterprise of judging particular cases through grasp of concrete relations and arrangements woven into the fabric of common life (Hale 1956: 502–3). In his *History*, Hale traces the process by which a judge seeks a rule of decision in a particular case. He goes first, says Hale, to the settled common law and custom of the realm, then to authorities and decisions in past cases, and finally to 'the common reason of the thing' (Hale 1971: 46). This, of course, is not the Hobbesian idea that once the sources of law run out the judge must appeal to his natural reason, or the civilian view (adopted by English equity practice) that the judge must appeal to conscience. Rather, Hale's judge goes back again to the cases and the 'human conversations' in which they are rooted and by sensitive judgment aided by analogy to other relevantly similar cases finds a solution. It is the *common* reason of the thing that the judge seeks.

This explains in part the willingness of a common law judge to seek only local coherence, rather than broad theoretical coherence of a single moral vision or systematic rationality. The aim of this artificial reason is convergence of judgment on common solutions, thereby securing effective practical guidance. Larger theoretical coherence, when it does not serve the end of convergence of judgment, was regarded as, at best, a luxury, and more typically an obstacle to achieving the end. But law, common lawyers maintained, is not concerned with the moral vision of any individual, however soundly argued it may seem to be, but rather with the convergence of the views and judgments of the larger community, and forging and maintaining a common sense of reasonableness. Salience, not vision, and pragmatic convergence, not theoretical coherence, were its fundamental aims.

2.3 Precedent and Statute in Classical Common Law Jurisprudence

Precedent. Already in the fifteenth century orthodox common law judges could write, 'precedents and usages do not rule the law, but the law rules them.... Precedents are not in all cases binding upon the courts' (*Long Quinto*, M.f. 110, quoted in Tubbs 2000: 45). Of course, this was not meant to deny absolutely the legal relevance of judicial decisions, but rather to undermine the claim of particular judicial decisions to binding authority. The general legal significance of a case, in the eyes of a common lawyer, lay in the nature and quality of the argument for the decision. The gradual appearance of more sophisticated recording techniques in the seventeenth century did not fundamentally alter this underlying doctrine. Vaughn, CJ in *Bole v Horton* wrote, 'If a court give judgment judicially, another court is not bound to give like judgment, unless it think that judgment first given was according to law' (Tubbs 2000: 182). Similarly, Hale maintained that judicial decisions, while they bind 'as a law between the parties thereto, as to the particular case in question, 'till revers'd by error or attaint, yet they do not make a law properly so called' (Hale 1971: 45). A century later Blackstone echoed Hale and Vaughn: '*the law* and the *opinion of the judge*, are not convertible terms, or one and the same thing; since it may happen that the judge may *mistake* the law' (Blackstone 1765: i. 71; emphasis in the original). Hedley added,

if a judgment once given should be peremptory and trench in succession to bind and conclude all future judges from examining the law in that point or to vary from it, then the common law could never have been said to be tried reason . . . for it should then be grounded merely upon the reason or opinion of 3 or 4 judges . . . [Therefore no] judgment should be so sacred or firm that it may not be touched or changed. (Hedley 1610: 178–9)

Thus, no single judicial ruling has the authority of law (beyond *res judicata* for the parties) just in virtue of the judge's having decided it, and future judges are free to test a prior court's formulation of a rule or doctrine of common law in light of the legal community's shared sense of reasonableness. Only in so far as the decision can be integrated into the body of the law—made consistent and reasonably coherent (at least within its local context)—*and* is taken up in the deliberation and argument of the legal community, is it to be given legal credit. If a judicial ruling is entrenched and regarded as peremptory, thereby blocking all subsequent assessment of its reasonableness and coherence with the whole (in the forensic context of 'deceptation'), just by virtue of a judge's decision alone, the common law in general could no longer claim authority.

Still, Hale hastened to add that, although judicial decisions fail to make law properly so called, 'they have a great weight and authority in expounding, declaring, and publishing what the law of this kingdom is', they are the best *evidence* of the law (Hale 1971: 45). A century later Mansfield wrote in the same vein, 'precedent, though it be evidence of law, is not law itself, much less the whole of the law'.[7] Classical common law jurisprudence resolutely resisted the theoretical pressure to identify law with canonically formulated, discrete rules of law. Law, on this view, is not a set of rules or laws, but a practised framework of practical reasoning, and this practised framework provides a form of social ordering. Its rules and norms can be formulated, perhaps, but no such formulation is conclusively authoritative. In *De Augmentis,* Bacon

---

[7] *Jones v Randall* (1774) Lofft 383, 385, quoted in Lieberman (1989: 126); see also Coke (1628: 254a) and Blackstone (1765: i. 69).

counselled 'not to take the law from the rules, but to make the rule from the existing law [that is, the body of argued opinions and decisions]. For the point is not to be sought from the words of the rule, as if it were the text of the law. The rule, like the magnetic needle, points at the law, but does not settle it' (Bacon 2000, Book 8, aphorism, 85, Bacon 1858: v, 106). Moreover, each formulation of a rule is in principle vulnerable to challenge and revision in the course of reasoned argument and dispute in the public context of litigation.

Is it possible, then, to say that common law jurisprudence recognized binding precedent? The answer is yes, although it differs rather sharply from the more familiar view inspired by classical positivism. The view has three salient features. First, past judicial decisions claim judicial respect and attention not in virtue of merely having been decided—laid down or posited—but in virtue of having been taken up by subsequent courts and thereby having found a place within that body of common experience. They have this place because they were products of a process of discoursive reasoning and contextually situated reflective judgment. Secondly, while individual cases are not regarded as establishing authoritative rules, they are taken to illustrate the operation of proper legal reasoning, to exemplify the process of reasoning within the body of experience. Thirdly, past cases do not preclude deliberation and reasoning in subsequent cases, but rather they invite and focus that reasoning. The prior court's formulation of the issues, and the reasons for resolving them as it did, and the rule on which it rested its decision, are not regarded as final. It is always open to judges in future to test any precedent court's formulation of the rule of its decision. Hence, subsequent courts participate with the precedent court in reasoning about issues raised by the case and extend that reasoning to the case before them. Yet, judicial formulations of the issues and the rules are due respect, because the prior court has claim to expert authority.

Statutes. The attitude of common lawyers towards statutes was complex and conflicted, especially in the heyday of classical common law jurisprudence. By the seventeenth century, it was no longer possible to deny the legislative power of Parliament. This forced common law jurisprudence to address directly the place of the products of parliamentary legislation in the common law of England. Hale articulated a subtle account of the relationship between enacted and common law that remained influential until Blackstone and still deserves attention.[8]

Recall that Hale argued that debates over the antiquity of common law were wrongheaded. It was impossible to deny that the common law over its long history had been subject to a great deal of change (some of the most dramatic changes resulting from royal legislation). No part of the law, including laws authorizing lawmaking, had been immune to change; yet, the common law, like the Argonauts' ship, maintained its identity. Continuity, he insisted, not antiquity, was the key. The 'formal and

---

[8] I have defended this reading of Hale's view of the validity of statutes in Postema (1986: 19–27). I summarize conclusions of that argument here.

obliging force' of common law lay not in its origin but the reasonable conviction that the laws fitted well together and fitted the common life of the English people.

Hale distinguished between written and unwritten law. As he understood them, these terms did not refer to two kinds of laws, but rather to two modes of existence of law (or, as we might say, forms of legal validity). Some laws were valid in virtue of having been explicitly made by an authorized lawmaker; other laws were valid in virtue of incorporation into the common law. The class to which a given law was assigned was not determined solely by the way it came into being, but by its present mode of validity. The validity of written law was a function of its having been enacted according to established formal, constitutional rules. Unwritten law, regardless of its origin, drew its authority from its present incorporation into the use and practice of common law. The process of incorporation or integration worked on precedent and statute alike. Only through continual use, exposition, interpretation, and extension—through being *taken up* and appropriated by practitioners of the common law—was a novel rule or doctrine made part of the common law. Through 'contrary usage' the opposite effect was also possible: the doctrine could be narrowly limited, for example, precedent may be 'distinguished' to the point of extinction of its general legal effect. The same might happen to laws initially introduced by legislative act. The statute might not be taken up and incorporated into common law practice, but rather it might be narrowly interpreted, limiting its scope and legal significance. While the laws authorizing its creation exist the statutes remain valid law, but they do not enjoy deep or wide impact on the law without incorporation. Moreover, statutes that are not eventually incorporated are vulnerable to changes of constitutional or lawmaking authority. This, Hale speculates, is probably what happened to many ancient statutes that did not survive in memory. The continuity of law, on this view, is guaranteed not by some posited norm according to which a validly enacted rule remains valid until repealed,[9] but rather on the more strenuous test of incorporation into the use and practice of common law judges and lawyers, and more fundamentally (and more indirectly) into the use and practice of the people. The common law and its custom, Hale insisted, was 'the great substratum' of the law (Hale 1971: 46).

Thus, on Hale's view, the status of statutory law, which may initially have greater claim to treatment as valid law than precedent, can change—indeed, he suggests that if it is ultimately to survive it must change—from resting on formal rules of authorized lawmaking to incorporation into the normative family of common law. This represents a shift from formal to substantive validity, from dependence on what are

---

[9] Hart (1983: 16) endorses this explanation of the continuity of law, relying on Finnis (1973: 61–5). Note that for both Hart and Finnis this norm is an explanatory postulate. They attribute it to courts (judges 'must tacitly accept' it, Hart says) in order to explain why courts freely accord validity to statutes even after the 'parent laws' authorizing their enactment go out of existence. Hale offers an alternative explanation. It has the virtue, apparently lacking in Hart's proposal, of being falsifiable. To test his hypothesis, one would merely have to determine whether courts tend to endorse as valid orphaned statutes even though the courts regard the statute as failing the 'incorporation' standard.

now called 'content independent' criteria of validity to substantive integration into the law and the life of community to which it gives structure.

2.4 Common Law Jurisprudence as a Theory of Law

This, in brief outline, is the classical common law conception of law. We might even call it a *theory* of law, but we would have to add immediately that *qua* theory it was relatively modest. It sought to capture general and fundamental structural features of law, but its focus was largely local. Its account was not meant to apply to law anywhere, at any time, but in the first instance at least only to the common law they practised. It did not strive to contribute to universal jurisprudence, the enterprise that seeks to articulate conceptually necessary features of law wherever it is alleged to exist. This is not to say that the conception, if coherent and plausible as an account of the defining features of common law, would have no implications for universal jurisprudence, but only that those implications would be largely limiting and negative—in the way that a counter-example forces revision of a universal thesis.

Thus, the theoretical ambitions of common law jurists were very different from those typical in the natural law tradition. This may explain in part why common law thinkers were willing to rely rather uncritically on broad natural law concepts when they, albeit rarely, did venture to make universal pronouncements about the nature of law. They did so, confident that their own local conception of law was broadly consistent with natural law orthodoxy, but they could not be bothered to set out the grounds for their confidence. Their lack of theoretical persistence was partly due to the fact that they were, in almost every case, not philosophers and theoreticians but active practitioners, and there was not any immediate practical need to work out the theoretical details. It may also have been due to the fact, perhaps only vaguely evident to them, that were they to find that they could not borrow freely from the natural law tradition, they would have no publicly recognized framework for presenting their conception and would have to work one out systematically on their own. This was, perhaps, an issue best left unaddressed, since they lacked the resources to battle on the broader theoretical front.

Thus, we are left the task of considering how to fit the common law conception of law into the long tradition, or rather overlapping traditions, of philosophical reflection about the nature of law. The common law conception, I think, represents a view of law that is in important respects incompatible with both orthodox natural law thought and with orthodox legal positivism. It represents a distinctive approach to understanding the nature of law and legal reasoning, a third way of conceptualizing the phenomena of modern law. It is too early to rule out rapprochement with one or the other of the dominant jurisprudential traditions, but we benefit from an appreciation of insights we might gain from approaching the theoretical explanation of legal phenomena from the distinctive starting-point that classical common law theory provides. Keeping in mind the modesty of its theoretical pretensions, I propose to develop some themes of classical common law jurisprudence in the idiom of contemporary jurisprudence and to try to make a case for the plausibility of its most important theses.

3 COMMON LAW CONVENTIONALISM

3.1 Positivist vs. Common Law Conventionalism

The emphasis of common law jurisprudence on the customary nature and foundations of common law suggests a possible liaison with mainstream positivism. Like contemporary positivism, common law jurisprudence conceives of law as a kind of institutionalized convention, or complex set of conventions. So, in what follows I will refer to the contemporary articulation of this theory as 'common law conventionalism'. Yet, it differs in important ways from Hart's positivist conventionalism (Hart 1994) and alternative accounts of law inspired by Hart's theory (e.g. Coleman 1998, 2001; Marmor 1998; Waluchow 1994). It departs from positivist conventionalism at two crucial points.

First, it rejects the model of laws that many positivist theories adopt.[10] On that model, law is understood as a set or systems of rule-like directives. The existence, validity, and content of these directives is said to be determinable by appeal to content-independent criteria. The set as a whole, also, has its unity largely in terms of relations among the directives external to their content. Moreover, according to this model, these directives guide action by providing law subjects with reasons for action that pre-empt their action-directing deliberation on potentially competing reasons they may have.

However, as we have seen, the common law conception of precedent, at least one recognized source of law, is strictly inconsistent with this model. Lon Fuller, perhaps the most important contemporary common law theorist, wrote in his unjustly neglected work, *The Anatomy of Law,* 'a judicial decision is always an explained thing' (Fuller 1968: 90). Perhaps to be more accurate, he should have said, 'a judicial deci-

---

[10] Some positivists may not be wedded to this model, for example, those who adopt an 'inclusivist' view of the conventional practice at the foundations of law (Coleman 1998; Waluchow 1994). They might find common law conventionalism's account of laws and legal reasoning (to some degree) congenial, but they are committed to a version of what I will call Hart's 'formal conventionalist' account of the foundations of law. I should add that positivists are not the only theorists attracted to the model of laws that common law conventionalism decisively rejects. There is a long and important line of theorists within the natural law tradition, especially active in the seventeenth century, who also embraced it (see Postema 2001).

sion is reasoned thing', but his point is clear. In common law the normative force and authority of a judicial decision extends beyond the facts and the parties litigating in the particular case, yet that precedential force does not depend solely on the authoritative utterance of a general rule in the body of the judge's opinion. The judge in a prior case does not unilaterally and finally fix the scope or meaning of a rule through his or her decision, regardless of how carefully crafted the language of the opinion is. In the end, it is the quality and force of the reasoning, not the public utterance of it, that lends authority to a court's rationale (Chapman 1994: 43). Common law conventionalism shifts theoretical attention from laws—the authoritative directives produced by lawmaking institutions—to the process of practical reasoning with and within law. Law, on this view, is a matter of convention, but it is a convention of a special sort, namely a practised discipline of practical reasoning. This departs decisively from the model familiar in positivist jurisprudence.

Secondly, common law conventionalism offers a distinct alternative to Hart's account of the conventional foundations of law. According to Hart's theory legal rules exist not as socially practised conventions but as systemically valid rules, and systemic validity is a matter of being a member of a set of rules identified by a common rule of recognition. The rule of recognition is not itself a valid legal rule, but an entirely different kind of rule, a convention constituted by the practice of law-applying officials. The rule of recognition is a social fact, a fact about the regular practice of officials. Yet, it is a rule; its normativity depends on its being treated as such by those who practise it. The rule of recognition guarantees the unity and continuity of the legal system. (Actually, Hart's main argument for the rule of recognition is that it alone can explain the more immediate and theoretically fundamental facts of the persistence and unity of law.)

Thus, necessarily, at the foundation of any legal system is this recognition convention consisting in the convergent behaviour and appropriate attitudes of law-applying officials and their professional associates. The existence of such a rule is a conceptually necessary condition of the existence of law in a given time and place. As a matter of conceptually contingent but 'natural' necessity, and a condition of the efficacy of law, law subjects must generally behave in ways consistent with the laws identified by the rule of recognition. It is not at all necessary, however, and may even be rare, that citizens themselves will take an 'internal attitude' towards the law, and it is very unlikely that they will grasp, let alone endorse, the governing rule of recognition. Hence, on this view, the scope of the convention on which law in any society is founded will, by a combination of conceptual and natural necessity, be limited uniformly to the practice of law-applying officials and (some) lawyers.

I will call this 'formal conventionalism' to contrast it with the 'material conventionalism' regarding the foundations of law endorsed by common law conventionalism. By 'formal' I do not mean to imply that it is committed to the view that the criteria of recognition practised by officials in any given legal system necessarily concern only matters of non-evaluative social facts, facts about the sources of the laws.

Some conventionalists following Hart—so-called 'inclusivists' (Coleman 1998; Waluchow 1994; and even Hart 1994: 248–9)—argue that it is an open question, to be determined by contingent facts about the practice of law-applying officials in actual legal systems, whether their rule of recognition includes only source-based criteria, or also includes moral tests of some sort. Hart-inspired conventionalism is 'formal', rather, because its locates the conventional foundations of law in a narrow, structural, proto-constitutional feature of a legal system, namely, the criteria practised largely just by law-applying officials by which valid rules of law are distinguished from invalid ones. In contrast, common law conventionalism insists that, as a conceptual matter, a structure of control could not operate *as law* unless it were built on a broader conventional base, that is, unless there is a substantial degree of congruence in substance, and continuity of modes of practical reasoning, between formal, institutional elements of law and wider social practice.

Thus, the contemporary version of common law jurisprudence insists that law is conventional in two respects, in both of which it decisively departs from key positivist doctrines: (1) law is a special kind of convention, a practised discipline of practical reasoning, and (2) it depends for its existence on substantial congruence and continuity with broader practices in the community. In what follows, I shall attempt to explain more fully and make plausible these two key theses.

3.2 Convention of Common Reasoning

The deliberative discipline of common law. Classical common lawyers held that common law was common yet 'artificial' reason. Although Coke was inclined at times to dress this notion in mystery and legal mysticism, more sober common lawyers used this phrase to capture the pragmatic, non-systematic, contextual, and essentially discoursive nature of common law. Common law conventionalism follows the lead of Coke's sober colleagues. It maintains that law, in the jurisdictions in which common law is dominant, offers ordinary practical reasoning a multi-layered, practised discipline of deliberating and reasoning together regarding public matters. Common law conventionalism reorients thinking about the nature of law dominated by positivist and natural law conceptions. Its theoretical point of departure is not a set of norms, prescriptions, or propositions of law, but rather a practice of common practical reasoning. Rather than a metaphysical thesis, it urges a methodological thesis, a point about order of explanation and understanding, not an ontological point about the ultimate order of being.

Common law conventionalism calls attention to a number of key ways in which law disciplines practical reasoning. First, the *pragmatic* spirit of common law forces deliberation and argument about practical matters—matters that can touch large issues of political morality and pervasive aspects of social life—to focus on concrete situations, and the relatively specific problems that arise in them. It focuses on the matters at hand, mindful of implications that go well beyond the case, but allowing the specific circumstances and problems to orient deliberations. Secondly, legal practical reasoning is *historical*: it anchors deliberation and what classical common lawyers call 'deception' to past decisions and actions taken by or on behalf of the community—decisions which, for that reason, are understood to be prima-facie normative for the community and its members. Explicit lawmaking activities (and the constitutions, statutes, and regulations they produce), as well as precedent-setting decisions and actions (primarily of officials, but also in some cases of ordinary citizens) direct their deliberation and provide the resources with which participants in this practice build their arguments. Thirdly, while the discipline makes use of all appropriate and valid forms of reasoning and argument, its central and distinctive technique is *analogical* thinking. Fourthly, this discursive process is essentially *collaborative*: it is a practice of thinking, arguing, deliberating, and deciding in common. Finally, this essentially collaborative enterprise is formally institutionalized in a public forum. This provides a public focus, forum, and exemplar for a practice with the potential for wide participation in society.

This sketch of the discipline of common law reasoning needs to be developed at each of its key points, but within the limits of this chapter I will focus only on the third and fourth, which I think most need elaboration and explanation.

Analogical thinking. The distinctive technique of the common law discipline is analogical thinking,[11] which consists of two analytically distinct intellectual processes: *analogical reasoning* and *reflective assessment*. They typically work in tandem in particular instances of common law reasoning, but in many cases the second may be tacit.[12] Consider first analogical reasoning proper.

There is no formal logic of analogical argument. Deductive logic governs arguments—ordered structures of premises leading to conclusions—and so it is appropriate to speak of deductive *arguments*, but there is no deductive *reasoning*. Reasoning often uses, but cannot be restricted to deductive argument. Deductive logic regiments our thinking as it moves from one proposition to another, but it is

[11] For more extensive discussions see Chapman (1994: 64–106), Sunstein (1993), Brewer (1996), Levenbook (2000), and Postema (unpublished).

[12] Brewer (1996) distinguishes three stages of analogical reasoning, the first two of which bear some similarity to the two components I identify. This is not the place to work out in detail the differences between my account of analogical thinking and Brewer's analysis of 'exemplary reasoning'. However, it may help understanding of the account sketched in the text to note a few of the more important differences. (1) Although I agree that the intellectual processes are components or stages of analogical *thinking*, unlike Brewer, I think distinctively *analogical reasoning* goes on only at the first stage. The intellectual processes at work in the stage of reflective assessment (Brewer: 'confirmation stage') are of a different nature. (2) Brewer regards the process I call analogical reasoning proper as a matter of abductive reasoning. I do not think this captures adequately the nature of the reasoning or the kind of intellectual capacities involved in analogical reasoning. Chapman (1994: 64–106) sketches a more promising alternative account consonant with classical common law jurisprudence. (3) Brewer gives more prominence to construction of rules in analogical reasoning than in my view is warranted. I say a few words about this issue in the text.

powerless to do more. It cannot compel, even in a normative sense, a reasoning person to accept a proposition as true. For that we need *reasoning,* for it is an exercise of reasoning, with the help of rules of deductive logic of course, that brings us to accept a conclusion, feeling the force of the argument for it, rather than, for example, abandoning one of its premises. Analogical thinking involves a form of reasoning in this sense. There is no analogical argument in the strict sense in which there is deductive argument—there are no formal rules of inference, either *sui generis* or derived from deductive logic. Nevertheless, it is a form of reasoning, not mere feeling or particularistic intuition. While it boasts no rules akin to those of deductive logic, analogical reasoning has a general structure and is subject to important constraints—this is especially true of its use in law—and in virtue of them it displays a recognizable, indeed indispensable, form of reasonableness.

Analogical reasoning is reasoning by or from example, *a similibus ad similia,* from like to like. It moves from particular to particular without relying in any fundamental way on articulated prior rules (Aristotle, *Nicomachean Ethics,* bk. II, ch. 24). The process is familiar. First, one or more past cases (decisions and the factual circumstances they addressed) are brought into a frame with a more or less detailed narrative of the facts of the case to be decided, and relevant similarities and differences are noticed. A tentative comparison class is constructed on the basis of rough assessments of relevant similarities. At work already here is a sense of relevance—call it *threshold relevance.* In typical instances of analogical reasoning in law, these two movements are mutually referential and mutually dependent. While the facts of the case lead one to retrieve a collection of cases to serve as the rough comparison class, the narrative of the facts is influenced by familiarity with the cases and the categories they exemplify. As Llewellyn once said, judges 'have been law-conditioned. . . . [T]hey see significances . . . through law-spectacles' (Llewellyn 1960: 19).

Next, a more *robust* sense of relevance groups together some of the cases falling in the comparison class into a class of 'like cases', while it distinguishes others. A pattern takes shape that makes sense of treating some of the cases in the same way; an intelligible guide for action is identified, although it may not be possible to articulate it completely. Rational pressure giving shape to the emerging sense of the likeness of these cases comes from *all* parts of the initial rough comparison class: cases judged similar to the instant case, those judged dissimilar and 'distinguished', and the instant case itself. The construction of the class of like cases is the result of a kind of triangulation among these focal points.

Note that even the process of distinguishing presupposes some degree of (threshold) relevant similarity. Distinguished cases are members of the initial rough comparison class; otherwise they would not present an intellectual challenge to the deliberator. It is in virtue of this initial relevance that distinguished cases exert pressure on the shape of the class of 'like cases'. The present case also exerts its share of pressure. It can urge reconsideration of received views of the salience or importance of facts of previous cases and thereby of the reasons on which their decisions rest.

This is one reason why rules of law may seem to change as they are applied (Levi 1949: 3 f.) and why common lawyers regard each formulation of a 'rule' of past cases as corrigible, vulnerable to revision.

This process can yield a determinate result, an understanding sufficient to ground a decision in the present case that is consonant with precedent and fit to guide future decisions and actions. Success is not guaranteed, however. In some cases analogical reasoning will substantially narrow the range of alternatives for dealing with the problem facing the court without uniquely determining a solution. At other times, the guidance will be largely unhelpful. In these cases, analogical thinking is forced to move to the stage of reflective evaluation to which we will turn presently.

The process of constructing the rough comparison class (based on a sense of threshold relevance) raises interesting theoretical questions, but assessments of *robust relevance* are the most puzzling to students of analogical reasoning in law. It is the deliberators' sense of robust relevance and absence of it that leads them to bring the present case into a family of like cases including only some members of the initial comparison class, and on the basis of this classification decide the present case. The details of this process deserve more extensive treatment than can be given them here, but we need to comment on a few important features of the process.

First, while judgments of similarity and dissimilarity in analogical reasoning presuppose, or rather manifest, a sense of relevance, it would be a mistake to claim that such judgments presuppose *a rule* in terms of which relevance is defined. It is the existence of some facts in common that brings the general rule into play (Levi 1949: 3). The point, however, is not that the judgment of relevance is logically particularistic. *Repeatable* properties of the analogues and disanalogues are selected from an uncountable host of other facts and features of the compared cases, and the family that is constructed must make sense as a pattern for future action, in ways I will mention presently. The force of the analogical reasoning is a function of how normatively compelling the pattern is. So, it is possible for judges to express their conclusions of analogical reasoning in terms of a rule, or at least a rule-like pattern. However, the rule is not an input into the reasoning process, but part of its output (Chapman 1994: 67–8), and not the most important part at that. In analogical reasoning, no rules of fixed and determinate scope are in play as inputs.

Explicitly formulated rules purport to offer complete and mature normative categories, but examples offer something more open ended and partial: normative categories that are incomplete, not fully articulated, and still capable of growing (Levenbook 2000: 202–5). It may be useful to try to formulate the rule implicit in a range of cases, but common law judges are always sensitive to the tentative and vulnerable nature of that enterprise. Understanding of the topography and termination point of the path of a legal doctrine is often imperfect and always subject to reconsideration in light of further cases. This rather cautious and conservative point is what underlies Levi's otherwise radical-sounding claim that it is not the intention of the prior judge that fixes the meaning of a precedent decision but what the present judge, attempting to see the law as a fairly consistent whole, thinks it should be (Levi 1949: 3).

Secondly, the assessments of robust relevance on which analogical reasoning depend are not the results of more general theoretical reflection, moral or otherwise. It is a mistake to treat these assessments as the outcome of attempts to locate the examples in the comparison class under some moral (or other practical) principles that purport to justify them. Locating and assessing such principles is part of analogical *thinking*, but not of analogical reasoning proper. As we shall see, this further intellectual process presupposes results of analogical reasoning. The two must be distinguished because the 'meaning' or content of a precedent example is not strictly determined by the justification of complying with it (Levenbook 2000: 192–6).

Thirdly, analogical reasoning in law is in aid of *practical* deliberation; it serves the *normative* purpose of guiding actions. Thus, the class of like cases must not only be interesting, suggestive, or evocative, as an apt metaphor might be, but it must also be practically intelligible. That is, it must project an intelligible pattern that can be followed, not only by the decision-maker, but also by the community governed and directed by it. Thus, the pattern must make normative sense to those who are expected to follow it and to those expected to accept its application as vindication of a decision based on it.

In this respect, common law reasoning stands like Janus at the gate between the past and the future, looking to decide the case at hand while looking both backward to the field of examples and commitments from which we have come and forward to the field of the future into which deliberators and those who depend on them are passing. It looks to the past not only for help and guidance, but for normative direction, for commitments undertaken that have implications for decisions for cases at hand and for actions and decisions in the future. This is not merely an aspiration; it is also a significant constraint on common law reasoning.

Fourthly, because it seeks to provide normative guidance, leads to and purports to ground a decision of the community on a matter of public importance, and claims to be binding, analogical reasoning in law proceeds in the service, and within the constraints, of a concept of (a species of) justice, sometimes misleadingly called 'formal justice' (Chapman 1994: 67). Levi puts the structuring question of analogical deliberation this way: 'When will it be just to treat different cases as though they were the same?' (Levi 1949: 3). This notion is indispensable (albeit not sufficient, see Postema 1997) to an explanation of whatever normative force precedent and analogues extending from them purport to have, but it is not an easy notion to understand. It is perhaps easier to say what it is not than to capture its positive content. On the one hand, it cannot be a generic or conclusive notion of justice. While it may have some prima-facie and defeasible moral force, it is likely to fall well short of full-dress moral justification, or even such justification in the name of justice. On the other hand, we cannot equate it with a purely formal notion of consistency, or treating like cases alike according to some rule (i.e. according to some rule or other). Understood in this way, the notion is entirely empty (Westen 1990, ch. 9). Any case is 'like' any other case in some respect and the likeness can be expressed in the form of a rule. The problem with this empty notion is not that its guidance is utterly indeterminate; but rather that it is utterly indiscriminate: it fails to capture a notion of *justice* relevant to analogical reasoning. Since anything goes as far as this notion is concerned, it follows that it cannot be a notion *of justice*; for if justice does anything morally important, it discriminates, it leads us away from some courses and leads us to others. Thus, the normative notion involved must impose a substantive constraint. It cannot, in the name of justice, simply require that like cases be treated alike however 'like' is determined, for it helps us assess likeness and unlikeness. How are we to characterize the substantive idea of justice involved in our assessments of robust relevance in analogical reasoning in law? I doubt whether anyone has been able to say with any confidence. But the fact that we do not yet have an adequate account of this notion should not lead us to conclude that it is not at work at an inarticulate level in these assessments. Any attempt to theorize the operation of justice in this context will be answerable to our intuitive capacity to make such assessments. The important point to keep in mind here is that a sense of justice is indispensable to the assessments of robust relevance in analogical reasoning in law.

Finally, the collaborative nature of common law reasoning (Fuller 1968: 93) exerts additional pressure on our assessments of robust relevance in analogical reasoning. While it is always individuals who participate in analogical reasoning in law, they proceed with a keen sense that they deliberate, as Hart put it, not each for his own part only (Hart 1994: 116), but as members of a larger whole. They regiment their perceptions and judgments to a common point of view, just as we adjust our judgments of size of objects in our visual field for distortions of light and perspective. This capacity for reflective judgment is a social capacity, the ability to reason from a body of supposed shared experiences to solutions to new practical problems, to judge what one has good reason to believe others in the community would also regard as reasonable and fitting. These judgments can be made with confidence, not because one is a good predictor of others' behaviour, but because one understands at a concrete level the common life in which they all participate. To become fluent in the language of 'human affairs and conversation' is to acquire the social capacity to make judgments that even in novel cases one can be confident will elicit recognition and acceptance as appropriate in one's community. This capacity is rooted not in shared general beliefs or values, but rather in living, working, and especially talking together, in the concrete activities of ordinary life, making the adjustments of action and perspective necessary to achieve understanding of our common world and acting intelligently and purposefully in it.

The reflective component of analogical thinking. Often analogical reasoning of the form we have just sketched will be sufficient practically speaking to ground a decision of law. Decision-makers will legitimately feel no need to raise further questions regarding the results of the process. The decisions will appear to the decision-makers and those depending on their decisions as reasonably coherent with the existing law and intelligible enough to give relatively determinate guidance for the future. However, in other cases the results may not be as happy. The process may yield troublingly indeterminate results (*practically*, not merely logically, indeterminate), and decision-makers may be forced to make a principled choice among the alternatives produced. Or the practically determinate result may be compelling when considering the instant case with its nearest analogical neighbours, but out of phase with law viewed more broadly. This apparent lack of more global coherence may have a merely technical legal focus, or it may cast its eye even more broadly on important matters of moral concern. In these cases, those involved in analogical thinking may feel pressure to reflect more broadly on the results of the prior process.

The methodology of this reflective process has been described in various ways, but Dworkin's 'interpretive' account of legal reasoning (Dworkin 1986: chs. 2, 3, 7), while the target of criticism from many quarters, may be the best available characterization of the intellectual process at this level. Briefly stated, the methodology requires that the deliberator seek that set of general principles (theory) that makes the best overall sense of law, such that the principles not only imply the more specific rules or decisions under review but also show them to be justified (for this the principles must approximate true or rationally warranted principles of morality). Alternative principles are ranked according to the extent to which they 'fit' the legal data and 'appeal' from a moral point of view.

There is much to be said for Dworkin's characterization of this process as an account of an important part of common law reasoning. Even severe critics of Dworkin's theory of law admit that the process he described is 'the dominant methodology in both the practice of law and legal scholarship' (Alexander and Kress 1995: 288). However, common law conventionalism insists that this process of reflective evaluation of the results of analogical reasoning is subject to constraints Dworkin himself did not recognize. First, the *pragmatism* of analogical thinking significantly reins in the urge to achieve global systematic coherence. As we have seen, common law is more concerned with workability on the ground, than with coherence of broad moral vision. While it cannot accept blatant incoherence of a result with other fundamental parts of the law that tend to undermine the legitimacy of large parts of the law, it is tolerant of incompleteness of vision and a degree of lack of overall systematic coherence. It is more concerned with coherence of legal doctrine with the activities, practices, and lives of the citizens whose interactions it seeks to guide than with more abstract theoretical coherence of legal doctrine. It is willing to sacrifice some theoretical coherence for substantial resonance of the law in the community it serves. Hence, while there is pressure at the reflective stage to achieve systemic and moral coherence, even this part of analogical thinking tends towards relatively local rather than more global coherence, coherence of practice rather than of theory.

Secondly, the essentially collaborative, public dimension of common law reasoning reinforces this tendency. Sound analogical thinking will tend to seek out doctrines arising from past decisions that other players, officials and citizens alike, can anticipate or at least recognize and find intelligible. Thus, Dworkin's mythical superhuman judge 'Hercules' is not a hero of common law reasoning. His theoretical successes, if they fail to take fully into account their dependency on intelligibility to others in a context of public justification, fail as grounds for assessing rules or patterns arising from past decisions.[13]

3.3 Material Conventionalism

Classical common law jurisprudence insisted on the conventional (customary) foundations of law. Critics from Bentham (1977) to the present (Waldron 1998) have challenged this claim. Yet, classical common lawyers would have regarded these criticisms as misplaced. As we have seen, they were the first to deny that common law is nothing more than social custom. They were keenly aware of the difference, indeed the distance, between practice of the courts and social mores and practices. Nevertheless, taking a cue from St German, they held the subtler view that the force and validity of law were rooted in broad social practice. But it was integration of the law into the life of the community, congruence of practice and continuity of modes of practical reasoning, that they stressed, not identity of law and social norms. It is this subtler, but not uncontroversial view, 'material conventionalism', that I will now try to articulate and defend.

Hart's formal conventionalism theory reduced the necessary role of conventions in law to an absolute minimum: law is fundamentally conventional, but only because, like an inverted pyramid, it balances the entire normative weight of the legal system on the single point of official practice. It is formal, because the conventions on which law rests are concerned with structural features of law, not with the internal coherence of its doctrines and their congruence with the lives of citizens. Material conventionalism maintains that law can exist and function properly only when law institutionally identified and applied sinks its roots into the soil of broader social practice. Continuity of reasoning practice and congruence of substantive standards is necessary for law. This is not a claim about the role that extra-legal 'social norms' typically play in legal reasoning (Eisenberg 1988), neither is it a claim about necessary conditions of good or effective law; rather, it is a claim about the conditions that must obtain if a set of rules and institutions, and the coercive machinery it directs, is to

[13] For a striking example of the pressures on courts to achieve collectively coherent decision even when individual members of the court are drawn to very different individual theories of the relevant law, see the discussion of the so-called 'doctrinal paradox' in Kornhauser and Sager 1993.

operate *as law*, whether good or bad law. These contrasts suggest a point from which an argument for material conventionalism can begin.

The argument for the congruence thesis at the heart of material conventionalism rests on two key premises.[14] The first ('normative guidance') premise is, in brief, that law by its nature seeks to provide wholesale normative guidance to rational, self-directing agents. The second ('interdependency') premise concerns the social environment in which the agents to which law's norms are addressed find themselves. This social environment is characterized by complex interdependence of actions; it is a vast network of webs of interactions. Before we proceed we need to clarify these two premises.

Normative guidance and interdependency. We should notice, first, that the normative guidance premise takes no position on the issue of the fundamental tasks or functions of law. It merely holds that law by nature and design seeks to guide action. Normative guidance is not a function of law; it is, rather, a defining technique or instrumentality that may be put to many different uses. Normative guidance is a defining feature of law, not its function or purpose. Secondly, the normative guidance premise maintains that law as such *seeks* to guide action, or purports to guide action, not that it always or necessarily does so successfully.

Thirdly, we need to explore briefly the notion of normative guidance. Following Shapiro, we should distinguish normative guidance from normative governance (Shapiro 1998: 472–3). Let us call the agent whose action falls within the scope of a norm the norm agent with respect to it. Norms *govern* behaviour when they are valid and actions of their norm agents fall within their scope. They provide a basis for evaluating the actions, and may encourage the evaluator to act in certain ways in response to them. Thus, they may provide secondary guidance even when they do not guide their primary norm agents. Norms *guide* the actions of their norm agents when they function as rules or norms in the practical reasoning of their norm agents leading to the formulation of intentions and actions on them. Norms that govern action typically are designed also to guide those actions, but this is not always the case.

We can distinguish further two kinds of norm governance. For *mere norm governance* it is sufficient that the norm is valid and applies to the norm agent's action. Norm governance is *robust* when, in addition, the norm shapes the way in which the norm agents publicly present and justify their actions to themselves and others. Thus, it is possible for agents to be governed by a norm, and to acknowledge that governance implicitly by using it in good faith to justify or vindicate their actions taken (or seek to justify or excuse violations of the norm), even though they did not use the norm in deliberations that led to their actions. They may be, but need not be, insincere in such cases. Insincerity does not disqualify it as robust norm guidance in the eyes of the law, since law is inclined only to look on behaviour not on motivation.

---

[14] The argument developed here elaborates and extends an argument familiar to readers of Lon Fuller's work (Fuller 1969, 1981). Fuller's argument is sketched in Postema (1994: 368–80).

Following Shapiro again, we can also distinguish two forms of normative guidance (Shapiro 1998: 489–92). A norm offers *epistemic guidance* if the norm agent learns what she must do—what her duties and responsibilities, or her rights, are, how she is to proceed in order to achieve a desired legal result—from the norm. The norm can guide epistemically, even if the norm agent is motivated to comply by considerations independent of the norm. It offers *motivational guidance* if the norm agent is motivated, at least in part, to comply with the norm by the fact that the norm governs the agent's conduct in the circumstances. Typically, agents that are motivationally guided by a norm will also be epistemically guided by it. To be motivated by a norm is to regard it as legitimate and to act at least in part on that assessment. In both forms of normative guidance, the norms play a role in the norm agent's practical reasoning, but the roles are different. The most robust form of normative guidance is motivational (or motivational-cum-epistemic) guidance.

Fourthly, it is distinctive of law to seek to provide normative guidance *wholesale*, as it were. That is, it seeks to guide not by issuing directives to individual norm agents in the specific circumstances in which they find themselves case by case, but rather by promulgating norms that are relatively general both with respect to norm agents and to circumstances. Moreover, the normative guidance premise makes a claim about a legal system in general, not about every component (every rule or norm) of the system. Law seeks to guide action through the instrumentality of its component laws, but not through them alone, for the way the laws are linked together can also play a role in practical guidance. This takes some of the burden off any specific rule or norm. Law as a whole may succeed in guiding without every single component doing so or even making pretence of doing so. These two features imply that normative guidance is a matter of degree. It is a matter of degree how general its norms are, how widespread in a community the law's normative guidance is, and how much of the legal system succeeds in offering normative guidance. Thus, the claim that by its nature law seeks to guide action involves a scalar measure. If some attempt to exercise control of social behaviour fails *as law*, presumably this is because its normative guidance potential falls below some minimal threshold.

Before we proceed we should note two important implications of the normative guidance premise. First, it presupposes that norm agents are intelligent, rational, self-directing agents. That is, they are able to understand themselves, their natural and practical environment, and the actions available to them in their environment, and they have the capacity to direct their actions in accord with the norms or reasons that apply to them in that environment. If officials are to undertake to guide or robustly govern action in a legal manner, they must do so in ways that acknowledge and engage these capacities of rational self-direction. It must *address* rational, self-directing agents. Secondly, the normative guidance premise places limits on the kinds of behaviour and modes of communication and of control that law can enlist in the project of normative guidance. Interventions that trigger action without *addressing* norms or rules or reasons or normative examples *to them* may achieve compliance but fail to do so *as law*. Thus, bulk compliance with its norms (*pace* Hart) is not enough for the existence of law in a community, for it may be entirely epiphenomenal, or it may achieve compliance exclusively through means that do not even attempt to address its subjects as rational, self-directing agents.

The second, 'interdependency', premise holds that the social environment in which rational, self-directing agents typically act is characterized by complex interdependence, that is, it is a vast network of webs of interactions. This is a pervasive, fundamental fact about the environment in which rational self-directing agents find themselves. Unlike the first premise, this premise does not express a conceptual truth about law. But it is in certain respects like a conceptual truth. It has the same status as the circumstances of justice have with regard to the nature and shape of justice according to Hume (Hume 1975: 183–92). That is to say, not only is it generally true that the agents whom law seeks to guide find themselves in this environment, but further, that outside of this environment, law and its distinctive technique lack intelligible point or purpose. This is not to say that we can derive from this premise a thesis about the necessary task or function of law, but only that whatever that task may be, if there is one, it must take this environment into account. Law cannot ignore this fact without utterly silencing its normative voice.

So, we have arrived at the following point. We know that law as such seeks to provide wholesale normative guidance and the resources for robust normative governance, that this presupposes that citizens (and officials), the norm agents of law, are self-directing rational agents, engaged in webs of interdependent actions. And thus to achieve normative guidance laws must be addressed to citizens and must be of such a nature that self-directing agents can understand them and appreciate their practical force, and on this basis apply the norms to their own actions. The conclusion material conventionalism needs to establish is the following: wholesale normative guidance and robust normative governance of rationally self-directing and complexly interacting agents is possible in this environment only if law is congruent with background social practices and widespread public understandings of them. Congruence, like normative guidance, is a matter of degree. What needs to be shown is not that law must be maximally congruent, but only that if it falls below some threshold it ceases to function as law. This argument does not define the threshold. It seeks to establish a foothold for material conventionalism against its rival, formal conventionalism, which denies the relevance of congruence and settles for a 'bulk compliance' condition. So, it is sufficient if it can show that a substantial degree of congruence is necessary for law to function without defining the threshold.

Congruence is not merely a condition of the *existence* of law. It is also an *aspiration* of law. Addressing norms to rational self-directing agents is not merely something law as such seeks to do, but it is also something we demand as a condition of respect for those individuals and as a condition of their liberty. It is no surprise, then, that lovers of liberty have often thought law to be an ally. The rule of law ideally extends the demands for congruence well beyond the minimum necessary for the bare existence and minimal functioning of law as such. However, it is a mistake to conclude from this natural link to the ideal of the rule of law that the congruence thesis is *merely* a thesis about an ideal for law (or ideal *of law*). It is first of all a condition of something's existing and functioning as law. On the other hand, it is also a mistake to conclude that ideally there should be no discontinuity between law and social practices. For part of what makes it possible for law to do useful things in society is its formality and institutionality, its resolute focus on details, its commitment to keeping present to mind the normative past of the community, and its introduction of finality into discussion of matters that see no present prospect for closure. These matters are not always on the minds, nor do they always deeply inform the practices, of people in the community. Part of law's value lies also in its distance from practice and from the values and systems of belief of the people it seeks to guide.

Argument for the congruence thesis. The argument proceeds by counter-position. Suppose legal norms as a system were largely incongruent with ordinary social practice. To provide normative guidance for those it purports to govern it must promulgate its norms in such a way that norm agents can both understand their meaning—that is, understand what is involved in complying with them—and grasp their practical point or force—that is, see why someone might think she has at least a prima-facie reason to comply with them. Moreover, because the norms operate wholesale and are addressed to rational self-directing agents whose actions are woven into thick networks of interdependence, the meaning and practical force must be publicly accessible. That is, it must be possible for people to have a rough idea how others with whom they interact read the norms. Without substantial congruence this is simply not possible. Let us see why.

First, understanding the meaning of a rule or example (knowing what one is to do) cannot be separated from grasping its practical point (knowing why, i.e., what reasons someone might have to do it). The *what* and the *why* are interdependent. It is easy to see how the why depends on the what: one has a reasonably determinate, intelligible reason to do something only when there is something sufficiently determinate to do. More importantly, in contexts of social interaction, the practical force (the why) of rules often depends heavily on reasonable expectations of how others on whom one's actions depend are likely to act, and that, in turn, depends on how they understand what the rule requires. Equally, the what depends on the why: norms, whether they are explicit rules or informal examples, lay out patterns of actions over time and different circumstances. To understand the meaning of a norm is to grasp what is involved in following it. This understanding depends on its practical point. Intelligibility is not merely a function of understanding words in a language, but understanding how those words connect with the range of actions available to one, and this latter understanding requires a capacity to give the words practical significance. That, in turn, requires that one be able to see some point in carving up the world of action in some ways rather than others. Grasping the practical point of a norm is essential to understanding what is involved in following it. And this requires that the norm agent be able to set the language of the norm, or the example of an action or decision, into a practical context that makes intelligible, practical sense to her.

Secondly, cut off from ordinary daily life and social practices, law cannot hope to make its meaning accessible to norm agents. If the law as a system is largely incongruent with ordinary social practice, then lawmakers cannot rely on understandings that already inform their daily lives to help norm agents understand the meaning or grasp the practical force of the law's directives. For example, precedents would not have the rich environment of similar examples and patterns of interacting necessary for them to have meaning. It would be hard for individual agents not only to determine how to generalize beyond specific decisions, but also even to determine what a case 'on all fours' with the precedent might be. The same is true for explicitly made, carefully articulated, and publicly announced rules. They, too, have meaning only when norm agents know how to apply the general categories they define to specific cases, only when they can identify with confidence a specific case as an instance of the rule. This is never merely a function of the linguistic meaning of the rules. For it is as normative guides for behaviour, with a certain texture, in contexts of action and interaction, that the words of the explicitly made rules must be grasped. As Kant recognized, this requires a special exercise of judgment—he called it 'Mutterwitz' (common sense)—and that in turn requires a grasp of a context of application. Cut off from that context, the rule is a fish out of water.

Note that a regime of sanction-backed commands or authoritative directives (content-independent and peremptory rules) cannot succeed. The problems they both face are rooted in the fact that they seek practical force for the commands or directives entirely external to their content. Sanctions and authority provide reasons that are designed precisely to operate entirely independently of the norms they underwrite. They are all-purpose motivational means. They are no respecters of content. Moreover the command or exercise of authority is intended to have a peremptory effect in the practical reasoning of norm agents. Thus, no guidance regarding the meaning of the directives can be expected from the sources of their practical force. This is thought to be the point of relying on commands and authoritative directives. But, then, all the weight in determining the content of the norms must fall on the linguistic resources of fixed meaning as elaborated by consideration of the lawmakers' intentions. Without sinking their roots deeply into the soil of ordinary daily life, however, the efforts of the lawmakers will be utterly ineffectual. Their intentions for the shape, scope, and meaning of the rules cannot be determined apart from considering how law subjects will take up the promulgated rules. Unless they are willing to tailor norms to the situations of each law subject, they will have to depend on the same resources as we have considered above.

The importance of a sustaining environment of social understandings is amplified by the need for individual agents to anticipate the understandings of those with whom they regularly interact. Legal norms must have publicly accessible meaning and practical force. Even if it were feasible for governing officials to communicate clearly to citizens individually the norms by which they were expected to guide their actions, the officials would fail—or at least fail to *govern by law*—because the individuals addressed in this way could not count on other agents, on whose actions they depend, to understand the norms in the same way. The routines, customs, conventions, and practices of ordinary daily life—the affairs and conversations of common social life, as Hale would put it—provide a common context in which to locate public understandings of the examples and rules of law. Cut off from this context, law's attempt to provide normative guidance could not hope to succeed. Robust normative governance would suffer the same fate, since the legal norms could not provide resources with which individuals might seek publicly to justify their actions to others.

This argument does not assume that citizens must accept or endorse or commit themselves to the norms. Neither does it depend on background consensus in society on basic values or general principles, let alone consensus on what Rawls calls comprehensive moral, religious, or philosophical doctrines. What it requires, rather, are understandings on the ground, i.e. common or overlapping activities and practices that have practical meaning and force for those who participate in them. Material conventionalism maintains that it is necessary that law be incorporated into the *ordinary social life* of the community it seeks to govern, while it will always be different and to a degree distant from it. For this, it is not necessary that legal norms be incorporated into any general theory or comprehensive doctrine about that social life or its underlying principles. Providing the soil into which law must sink its roots are 'conversations' not creeds, practices not principles, ordinary affairs and activities not theories and doctrines. These resources give practical life to law's norms. Entirely without them, law's normative guidance and robust normative governance would be rootless.

Of course, this is not to say that it is unfeasible to seek to control social behaviour without deference to ordinary social life. It is to say, rather, that if minimal conditions of congruity of substance and continuity of reasoning are not met, any attempts at social control will have to be massively intrusive, dependent on direct coercion and on situation-by-situation, narrowly formulated commands. If a legal system were to lose its balance and topple into this condition, people subject to its increasingly arbitrary twists and turns (as they would inevitably perceive it), would at some point find themselves in a large-scale version of scorer's discretion (Hart 1994: 141–7). No longer would it be possible to regard the administrators of control as playing by the same rules as the people they sought to control, but rather by some other rules or no rules at all. The game of law would have been transformed into a game of administrators' discretion. There would be no point in trying to understand the rules in order to use them as guides, even epistemic guides, to action. All attention would turn rather on the decisions, instance-by-instance of the administrators. Subjects would become entirely dependent on the wills of the administrators. The problem with that is not that it is costly, or unfeasible, or morally abhorrent, but, rather, that it is unrecognizable as functioning (even badly functioning) law. Whatever is at work, it is not law, for it does not manifest the defining feature of seeking to provide wholesale normative guidance. Thus, law as such can function only if it is congruent to a substantial degree with the social life of the community it seeks to govern.

We can now draw implications of this argument for the contest between Hart's formal conventionalism and material conventionalism. Formal conventionalism holds that at its foundations, law rests on a narrow convention, the practice of law-applying officials with respect to identifying valid legal norms, requiring in addition only the bare fact of bulk compliance of law subjects with the norms they identify and seek to apply. This, we now see, is insufficient. On the contrary, what is necessary rather is incorporation of the formal, institutionalized system of law into the life of the community it seeks to govern at least to the extent required by the congruence thesis defended above. Moreover, the validity of legal norms depends at least as much on their substantive incorporation into the body of the law as on their conformity to external criteria whether purely factual or moral. This twofold incorporation explains at least as well the persistence of law over time, and offers a more compelling explanation of the unity of the legal system than Hart's rule of recognition hypothesis.

3.4 Authority and Authorities in Common Law Conventionalism

'It is not Wisdom, but Authority that makes a Law', Hobbes argued in his *Dialogue*, adding even more pointedly against Coke, 'Statutes [i.e. proper law] are not Philosophy as is the Common-Law, and other disputable Arts, but are Commands, or Prohibitions' (Hobbes 1971: 55, 69). Bentham carried this challenge further in the next century, charging that common law is nothing but a matter of 'unauthoritative jurisprudence' (Bentham 1970: 153). Necessarily, law is a matter of general rules, he argued, yet on orthodox common law assumptions these rules were not set out publicly in judicial decisions, but were to be constructed from them, and no judicial formulation was authoritative. But, then, he charged, this treats legal rules as nothing more than 'inferential entities', fictitious constructions. 'From a set of *data* like these [namely, a set of judicial decisions] a law is to be extracted by every man who can fancy that he is able; by each man perhaps a different law: and these are the *monades* which meeting together constitute the rules . . . of common or customary law' (Bentham 1970: 192). The alleged rules of common law exist, not as publicly accessible general prescriptions, but as private conjectures, personal inferences—not as law, Hobbes would say, but as 'philosophy'. Thus, common law jurisprudence fails as an intelligible coherent account of law. Whatever the alleged rules of common law are, they cannot be rules of law. Common law is 'a thing merely imaginary' (Bentham 1977: 119).

This critique suggests an important challenge to common law conventionalism, not to its endorsement of the convergence thesis we have just considered, but to its model of law and its role in practical reasoning. The challenge might go like this. Law seeks to provide public normative guidance, but it does so in a distinctive way, namely, by addressing authoritative directives to citizens whom it seeks to govern and guide. These directives are able to make a difference in the practical reasoning of norm agents because their status as rules of law is determined by content-independent criteria and they function in a pre-emptive fashion in the practical reasoning of citizens. That is, the content and scope of the directives can be determined by strictly non-evaluative forms of investigation and reasoning. If they are indeed authoritative, they offer reasons to act and reasons for not considering potentially competing moral or practical considerations. In this way, legal authorities secure finality with respect to those issues law is deployed to address. Common law conventionalism cannot account for the normative guidance that law as such seeks to provide, because identification of its prescriptions depends on substantive, content-related deliberations, the results of which are said to be constantly open to reassessment. Thus, it cannot account for the distinctive authority of laws or the role of institutionalized authorities in the legal system. It cannot hope to provide normative guidance in precisely those contexts in which, by its own admission, law is most concerned to address, namely, complex social interaction calling for public standards that enable citizens to coordinate their interaction. Authoritative directives, in contrast, eliminate the need for agents to engage in evaluative deliberation about the appropriate courses of conduct open to them. They can appeal, rather, to publicly accessible rules, the validity and content of which can be determined by non-evaluative marks of their authoritative sources.

This challenge can be refined and developed in various respects, but it may suffice for present purposes, since my aim here is merely to indicate in broad strokes how common law conventionalism might try to defend itself against a challenge coming from this quarter. Note, first, that common law conventionalism, like its seventeenth-century ancestor, was as unhappy as Hobbes was with philosophy as a model for law, but it likewise resists the model of command (or its refined cousin, authoritative directives). It seeks to shift the weight of attention from the directive aspects of law to its deliberative aspects. Common law conventionalism and its critics start from the same premise: law as such seeks to provide public normative guidance. But common law conventionalism refuses to equate law's normative guidance exclusively with the kind of difference that authoritative directives are said to make in practical reasoning. Its conception of normative guidance is broader, including within it a role for authorities and their authoritative directives.

Common law conventionalism denies that authorities and authoritative directives are theoretically central to law. It is useful in this regard to recall the familiar debate over the role of coercion in the law. Legal theorists have long been tempted to explain the distinctive manner of law's functioning in terms of coercive sanctions. Critics of sanction theories correctly charge that this strategy promotes an undeniably salient and important aspect of law to an undeserved position of theoretical prominence, treating what is of secondary importance as core with the result that we are blinded to important features of law. For example, reasoning about legal obligations is reduced to predictions of official coercion, nullity of an attempted exercise of a legal power is treated as punitive, rules of law are treated as external impositions from above, and the complex way in which laws seek to guide actions is obscured. The solution, critics argue, is not to deny that coercion has a role in law, but rather to find an account of law and normative guidance that makes room for, but does not reduce to, the operation of coercive sanctions. We run the same risk, common law conventionalism argues, if we equate law with discrete legal rules regarded as authoritative directives. Again undeniably salient and important but secondary features of law that are treated as core, with the result that important aspects of law and its distinctive mode of operating are obscured or mischaracterized. Making law's authoritative directives central to our understanding of law highlights its role in giving finality to issues that threaten otherwise to disrupt or confuse social interaction. But to focus on it exclusively blinds us to the fact that law not only institutionalizes the execution of deliberation, but also institutionalizes deliberation itself. It also distorts our understanding of the normative guidance that law seeks to provide. It encourages us, for example, to think of precedent in terms of rules, as ill-drafted statutes, rather than as examples, and to think of analogical reasoning as a form of discovery of official rules, the content and scope of which is already fixed by prior decisions. It also forces us to think of judicial decision-making as a kind of unauthorized and shadowy lawmaking and the law arising from common law decisions as judicial legislation. At the same time, it obscures the collaborative aspects of the common law deliberation and the discipline to which law subjects this deliberation.

Common law conventionalism's notion of normative guidance is wider than that captured by the notion of authority. Rather than regarding looking (exclusively) to discrete rules or norms of the legal system as the primary guiders of action, common law conventionalism looks to resources in the system of law as a whole, to its process and not just its product, to provide normative guidance. As a result, the kind of guidance offered is not limited to supplying to a class of agents specific reasons for the actions represented in a general rule, reasons for acting in a certain way and reasons precluding deliberation on other reasons the agent might consider. Rather, law is seen to provide a framework for common deliberation about courses of action and reasons for them. Law situates the practical reasoning and deliberation of individual rational, self-directing agents in a three-part framework: (1) a disciplined practice of practical deliberation exemplified in, but not restricted to, the activities of legal officials, (2) a body of examples that enables agents to define the practical problems they face and work towards a solution of them, and (3) an institutionalized public forum in which the practice is carried on, one that models a form of public, collaborative reasoning and which is open to active and passive participation by citizens. As part of this institutionalized process, the decisional conclusions of this deliberation are in certain respects and for certain purposes regarded as final and congeal into authoritative directives. Thus, this broad strategy for normative guidance gives authority an important role to play, but it does not take the lead. The aim of this wider kind of normative guidance is not to provide a surrogate for individual deliberation leading to action in public social contexts, but rather to redirect and provide a discipline and a body of resources for such deliberation.

Is law construed in this way utterly unable to provide guidance to rational self-directing agents where it is needed most, namely, in negotiating the complex webs of social interaction they face day-to-day? There are reasons to think it does not. First, we must keep in mind that the question is not whether law as modelled by common law conventionalism does the best job possible in providing normative guidance for social interaction. Common law conventionalism only claims that the normative guidance law offers takes this form; whether it is greatly successful in providing such guidance or even whether its claim to provide such guidance is generally warranted in any particular case is not at issue (any more than the alternative view holds that law always has the authority it necessarily claims). The issue is whether its claim to do so is practically intelligible. It would not be practically intelligible if it were obvious on the surface that it could not in any likely social circumstances perform as it promises, or if certain structural features systematically undermined its ability minimally to so do. It is true that the practical deliberation of isolated individuals, viewing parametrically the social world they face, and without any anchors of common experience or common judgment, would probably fail to meet this minimum standard. But that is not the kind of disciplined practice of practical deliberation institutionalized in law as conceived by common law conventionalism.

Secondly, to the extent that this broader form of normative guidance makes judicious use of authority, it shares whatever success it can hope to achieve. Of course, it is conceivable that by locating authoritative directives in this larger context of institutionalized deliberation all the advantages of the former are lost, but that surely is not clear at this point. Moreover, the most plausible versions of the view that identifies law with authoritative directives do not deny that judges and courts regularly and legitimately engage in deliberation with wide latitude (using, but not restricted to, reasoning with fixed legal rules), but they regard such activities as falling outside the purview of a theory of law (Raz 1995, ch. 13). Whatever the general merits of such a view might be, it is even more vulnerable to this worry about undermining the public coordination potential of law, should the worry prove to be serious. Indeed, common law conventionalism may have an advantage since it has an account of how law seeks to discipline deliberation in a way that arguably enhances its public normative guidance.

Finally, a more fundamental question is what should count as successful public normative guidance as viewed not from a moral-political view, but from the point of view of the aims of law in any particular community. Suppose it turns out that a more

Hobbesian conception, precluding as far as feasible individual practical deliberation, promises more tranquil social interaction, a more orderly public life. It does not follow, obviously, either that this is what law as such must seek. We may demand with Hume that law 'cut off all occasion of discord and contention', but what reason have we to think that this demand is built into the nature of law itself. Indeed, we may ask more of law and of ourselves as participants in the public life governed by law. We may ask, for example, that it help us as a community to seek greater justice for our life together, even though we disagree in deep and important ways about what justice requires.[15] An institutionalized practice of public argument and deliberation that enables an enterprise of this sort does not lose its status as law just because it risks being somewhat less orderly than the Hobbesian ideal. Neither is its claim to provide normative guidance thereby proved practically unintelligible. According to the *Iliad*, the god Hephaestus made a shield for Achilles depicting a city of war and a city of peace. The city of peace was represented by a wedding and a trial. Orderly and effective normative guidance may be evident not in the absence of tension, conflict, or dissension, but in the presence of a framework in which the conflicts can be articulated and resolution of them can be sought deliberatively in public. Normative guidance so construed has a certain moral appeal, but for present purposes that is not the important point. It is not the appeal but the intelligibility of the conception that was challenged. So far, we do not seem to have reason to doubt its intelligibility.

Conclusion. Taking a cue from seventeenth-century common law jurisprudence, we have sketched a theory of law that departs in important ways from familiar natural law theories in stressing the conventional foundations of law and from familiar positivist accounts in taking a convention of a special sort, a practised discipline of public practical reasoning, as a defining feature of law. Bentham took common law jurisprudence seriously enough to spend a large part of his life trying to refute it and undermine its grip on lawyers in England and abroad. While his refutation failed, he was right to spend his philosophical energies on this conception of law. It is time again to enter it—or its descendant, common law conventionalism—in the jurisprudential sweepstakes alongside its more familiar rivals, positivism and natural law theory, and give it a run for its money.

REFERENCES

Alexander, Larry, and Kress, Kenneth (1995), 'Against Legal Principles', in Andrei Marmor (ed.), *Law and Interpretation* (Oxford: Clarendon Press), 279–327.

[15] Developing an idea familiar from Dworkin's work, albeit in a direction he may not endorse, I have called this enterprise the search for 'integrity', which I argue is the pursuit of the public virtue of justice in circumstances in which justice is broadly in dispute (Postema 1997).

Austin, John (1885), *Lectures on Jurisprudence*, 2 vols. (London: John Murray).

Bacon, Francis (1630), *Elements of the Common Laws of England* (London; (repr. New York: Garland Publishing Company, 1978).

—— (1858), *On the Dignity and Advancement of Learning* (1605), in *Works*, 7 vols., eds. James Spedding, Robert Leslie Ellis, and Douglas Denon Heath (London: Longman).

Bentham, Jeremy (1970), *Of Laws in General*, ed. H. L. A. Hart (London: Athlone Press).

—— (1977), *A Comment on the Commentaries and A Fragment on Government*, ed. J. H. Burns and H. L. A. Hart (London: Athlone Press).

—— (1998), *Legislator of the World: Writings on Codification, Law, and Education*, ed. Philip Schofield and Jonathan Harris (Oxford: Clarendon Press).

Blackstone, William (1765), *Commentaries on the Laws of England*, 4 vols. (Oxford: Clarendon Press, 1765–9).

Brewer, Scott (1996), 'Exemplary Reasoning: Semantics, Pragmatics, and the Rational Force of Legal Argument by Analogy', *Harvard Law Review*, 109: 923–1028.

Chapman, Bruce (1994), 'The Rational and the Reasonable: Social Choice Theory and Adjudication', *University of Chicago Law Review*, 61: 41–122.

Cicero (1928), *De Legibus*, tr. Clinton Walter Keyes (Cambridge, Mass., Harvard University Press, Loeb Classical Library).

Coke, Edward (1628), *First Institute of the Laws of England* (rep. New York: Garland Publishing Company, 1979).

—— (1793), *The Reports of Sir Edward Coke, in Thirteen Parts*, 7 vols. (Dublin: J. Moore).

Coleman, Jules (1998), 'Incorporationism, Conventionality, and the Practical Difference Thesis', *Legal Theory*, 4: 381–425.

—— (2001), *The Practice of Principle* (Oxford: Oxford University Press).

Davies, John (1615), *Irish Reports*, in Alexander Grosart (ed.), *The Works . . . of John Davies*, 2 vols. (Edinburgh, 1876).

Doddridge, John (1631), *The English Lawyer* (London: Assignees of I. More).

Dworkin, Ronald (1986), *Law's Empire* (Cambridge, Mass.: Harvard University Press).

Eisenberg, Melvin A. (1988), *The Nature of the Common Law* (Cambridge, Mass.: Harvard University Press).

Finch, Henry (1759), *Law, or a Discourse Thereof* (repr. New York: Augustus M. Kelly Publishers, 1969; 1st pub. London 1627).

Finnis, John (1973), 'Revolutions and the Continuity of Law', in A. W. B. Simpson (ed.), *Oxford Essays in Jurisprudence* (Oxford: Clarendon Press), 44–76.

Fuller, Lon L. (1968), *The Anatomy of Law* (New York: F. A. Praeger).

—— (1969), *The Morality of Law*, 2nd edn. (New Haven: Yale University Press).

—— (1981), 'Human Interaction and the Law', in Lon L. Fuller, *The Principles of Social Order*, ed. Kenneth Winston (Durham, NC: Duke University Press), 211–46.

Gray, Charles M. (1992), 'Parliament, Liberty and the Law', in J. H. Hexter (ed.), *Parliament and Liberty from the Reign of Elizabeth to the English Civil War* (Stanford, Calif.: Stanford University Press, 1992), 155–200.

Hale, Matthew (1956), 'Reflections by the Lrd. Chiefe Justice Hale on Mr. Hobbes His Dialogue of the Lawe', in William Holdsworth, *A History of English Law*, 7th edn., 17 vols. (London: Methuen, 1956; 1st pub. 1670s?).

—— (1971), *A History of the Common Law of England*, ed. Charles M. Gray (Chicago: University of Chicago Press).

Hart, H. L. A. (1983), *Essays in Jurisprudence and Philosophy* (Oxford: Clarendon Press).

Hart, H. L. A. (1994), *The Concept of Law*, 2nd edn. (Oxford: Clarendon Press).

Hedley, Thomas (1610), Speech in Parliament on Royal impositions, in Elizabeth Read Foster (ed.), *Proceedings in Parliament 1610* (New Haven: Yale University Press, 1968).

Hobbes, Thomas (1971), *Dialogue Between a Philosopher and a Student of the Common Laws of England*, ed. Joseph Cropsey (Chicago: University of Chicago Press).

Hume, David (1975), *An Enquiry Concerning the Principles of Morals*, ed. L. A. Selby-Bigge, 3rd ed., rev. by P. H. Nidditch (Oxford: Clarendon Press).

Kornhauser, Lewis A., and Sager, Lawrence G. (1993), 'The One and the Many: Adjudication in Collegial Courts', *California Law Review*, 81: 1–59.

Levenbook, Barbara Baum (2000), 'The Meaning of Precedent', *Legal Theory*, 6: 185–240.

Levi, Edward (1949), *An Introduction to Legal Reasoning* (Chicago: University of Chicago Press).

——(1965), 'The Nature of Judicial Reasoning', *University of Chicago Law Review*, 32: 395–409.

Lieberman, David (1989), *The Province of Legislation Determined* (Cambridge: Cambridge University Press).

Llewellyn, Karl N. (1960), *The Common Law Tradition: Deciding Appeals* (Boston: Little, Brown Publishers).

Marmor, Andrei (1998), 'Legal Conventionalism', *Legal Theory*, 4, 509–31.

Pattaro, Enrico, Gerald J. Postema, and Peter Stein (eds.) (forthcoming), *A Treatise of Legal Philosophy and General Jurisprudence*, 12 vols. (Dordrecht: Kluwer Academic Publishers).

Postema, Gerald J. (1986), *Bentham and the Common Law Tradition* (Oxford: Clarendon Press).

——(1994), 'Implicit Law', *Law and Philosophy*, 13: 361–87.

——(1997), 'Integrity: Justice in Workclothes', *Iowa Law Review*, 82: 821–55.

——(2001), 'Law as Command: The Model of Command in Modern Jurisprudence', *Nous, Philosophical Issues*, 11: 470–501.

——(unpublished), 'If this keeps up . . . : Analogical Thinking in Law'.

Raz, Joseph (1995), *Ethics in the Public Domain* (Oxford: Clarendon Press).

St German, Christopher (1974), *Doctor and Student* , ed. T. F. T. Plucknett and J. L. Barton (London: Selden Society; 1st pub. 1523, 1530).

Schauer, Fred (1989), 'Is the Common Law Law?' *California Law Review*, 77: 455–71.

Shapiro, Scott (1998), 'On Hart's Way Out', *Legal Theory*, 4: 469–507.

——(2000), 'Law, Morality, and the Guidance of Conduct', *Legal Theory*, 6: 127–70

Simpson, A. W. B. (1973), 'The Common Law and Legal Theory', in A. W. B. Simpson (ed.), *Oxford Essays in Jurisprudence* (Oxford: Clarendon Press), 77–99.

Sunstein, Cass (1993), 'On Analogical Reasoning', *Harvard Law Review*, 106: 741–91.

Tubbs, J. W. (2000), *The Common Law Mind: Medieval and Early Modern Conceptions* (Baltimore: The Johns Hopkins University Press).

Waldron, Jeremy (1998), 'Custom Redeemed by Statute', in M. D. A. Freeman (ed.), *Current Legal Problems 1998: Legal Theory at the End of the Millennium* (Oxford: Oxford University Press), 93–114.

Waluchow, W. J. (1994), *Inclusive Legal Positivism* (Oxford: Clarendon Press).

Westen, Peter (1990), *Speaking of Equality* (Princeton: Princeton University Press).

CHAPTER 16

PHILOSOPHY OF PRIVATE LAW

BENJAMIN C. ZIPURSKY

1 INTRODUCTION

WHY does the private law impose liability on those who commit legal wrongs? Contemporary legal theorists tend to focus on one of two types of explanation. Deterrence theorists, particularly proponents of the law and economics movement, emphasize that when the law imposes liability, it sends an incentive to potential wrongdoers which has the effect of decreasing wrongdoing—socially harmful conduct.[1] Corrective justice theorists employ a framework that is deontological, explaining that the imposition of liability is predicated on the recognition that defendants who have wronged plaintiffs owe it to them to make them whole.[2] The debate

I am grateful to Jules Coleman and Scott Shapiro for their comments, discussion, edits, encouragement and patience. I am also grateful to John Goldberg for helpful comments, and particularly for turning me to Blackstone as a font of recourse theory within the tradition of liberal political theory.

[1] See e.g. William M. Landes and Richard A. Posner, *The Economic Structure of Tort Law* (1987). See also Guido Calabresi, *The Costs of Accidents* (1970); Steven Shavell, *Economic Analysis of Accident Law* (1987); Guido Calabresi and Douglas Melamed, 'Property Rules, Liability Rules, and Inalienability: One View of the Cathedral', *Harvard Law Review*, 85 (1972), 1089; Ronald Coase, 'The Problem of Social Cost', *Journal of Law and Economics*, 3 (1960), 1.

[2] See e.g. Jules L. Coleman, *Risks and Wrongs* (1992); Ernest J. Weinrib, *The Idea of Private Law* (1995). See also Arthur Ripstein, *Equality, Responsibility and The Law* (1998); Richard A. Epstein, 'A Theory of Strict Liability', *Journal of Legal Studies*, 2 (1973), 151; George P. Fletcher, 'Fairness and Utility in Tort Theory', *Harvard Law Review*, 85 (1972), 537; Stephen R. Perry, 'The Moral Foundations of Tort Law', *Iowa Law Review*, 77 (1992), 449.

between these historically rooted approaches continues within the legal and philosophical academy today.

I shall suggest, in what follows, that both sides of the debate have erred by omitting a fundamental legal concept, the concept of a private right of action. The oversight traces back to the framing of the question itself: why does the law impose civil liability on those who commit legal wrongs? *The law* does not *impose* civil liability. The law *empowers* private parties to have other private parties held liable to them, *if they choose*. The study of liability under the private law should, in the first instance, focus on why certain individuals are *empowered and permitted* by the law to act in certain ways, not on why certain persons are required to be sanctioned or held liable.

A focus on private rights of action is salutary both in explaining liability under the private law, and in locating private law liability within the structure of the legal system more broadly. As to the former, it will lead us to recognize a fundamental family of principles at the core of private law litigation; individuals who have been legally wronged by others are entitled to an avenue of civil recourse against those who have wronged them.[3] But from a broader point of view, it will permit us to revitalize the nearly dormant idea of the distinction between private and public law. Once we clearly grasp the idea of a private right of action, we will be in a position to credit the role of the state in all law, while simultaneously recognizing distinctive doctrinal, jurisprudential, and political features of private law.

2 LEADING THEORETICAL MODELS OF PRIVATE LAW

2.1 Law and Economics Approaches

According to the law-and-economics views that are most prevalent in private law scholarship today, such as those of Richard Posner or Steven Shavell, a court that enters a judgment for damages against a defendant in civil litigation is imposing the equivalent of a fine upon that defendant. Hence, a rational reconstruction of the legal rules and principles that determine when courts are supposed to enter such judgments will be a rational reconstruction of a system of fines or penalties that the state imposes under certain circumstances. These theorists recognize, of course, that our system is set up so that private parties initiate the proceedings that culminate in this imposition of a fine, and they are the recipients of the payment of these fines, which

---

[3] I introduced the idea of civil recourse in an earlier article devoted entirely to torts. See Benjamin C. Zipursky, 'Rights, Wrongs and Recourse in the Law of Torts', *Vanderbilt Law Review*, 51 (1998), 1.

are entitled 'damages' awards. But these are contingent facts of our system. The fundamental fact is that an imposition of a monetary fine is attached to either: the non-compliance with certain rules of conduct; the non-compliance with a contractual agreement; the imposition of an injury; or the infringement of a property right.

The economic deterrence model of private law is committed to several interesting points on basic questions about private law. First, it treats the private law as fundamentally a regulatory enterprise of the state. The rules of private law are aimed at influencing individual conduct so as to facilitate desirable outcomes—typically, efficient allocation of resources. This regulatory aspect of private law applies whether tort or contract or property or some other form of private law is under analysis.

Secondly, and relatedly, the norms of private law are purely instrumental, in at least two respects, one pertaining to *value*, the other to *content*. The value of particular norms of private law is entirely a matter of the value of the outcomes achieved through these norms, and, relatedly, the value of compliance with the norms is entirely derivative of the values such norms achieve in the long run. Moreover, for a wide variety of putatively deontic vocabulary used in these norms—terms such as 'right' and 'duty', for example—the content of these terms within the norms is explicable only in terms of a reductive model that ultimately ties to the values instrumentally aimed at by these norms.

Thirdly, the plaintiff-driven structure of private litigation is a contingent feature of private law, on this view. It is often the case that the persons who suffer injuries as a result of the violation of liability rules are the most efficient sources of evidence with regard to the violation. Hence, there is value in providing such persons with an incentive to attempt to enforce the liability rule. The prospect of being the recipient of the defendant's liability provides this incentive. That is the primary reason why, at least in torts, victims are permitted to sue.

It is tempting to say that, on the economic view, the subjects traditionally referred to as 'private law' are really only special cases of public law: rules laid down by the state in order to further state interest in an efficient allocation of resources, which operate by informing individuals of the prices that will be attached to certain forms of conduct. Of course, traditionally 'private' law areas such as tort, contract, and property, tend to involve conduct that has a greater particularized impact on a private individual, and tend to involve individual entitlements more centrally. But in content, both areas of law are alike in being public.

There are, I believe, numerous leading theorists whose views roughly speaking conform to the above; Posner and Shavell are good examples, but there are numerous others. Before moving on, however, it should be noted that the economic view can be understood to underline a rather different view of private and public law, one which begins with the private and explains the public in terms of it. On this view, most famously articulated by Calabresi and Melamed, the point of law is to structure and to protect a system of private entitlements in a manner that will lead to efficient allocation of resources. Liability rules and property rules are wholly and partially private means of doing so. However, there are many reasons why society needs some norms of conduct set down in a command-and-control style, as inalienability rules in criminal law, as well as a background system within which all the rules can be made. On this view, public law may be understood as the limit case, and backdrop, for private regulation of entitlements.

The economic model of private law has numerous strengths and weaknesses. Its conceptual clarity, its capacity to accommodate numerous areas of private law, its provision of a powerful methodological framework that permits quantitative analysis, are all appealing features; moreover, a great deal of its attractiveness stems from its ability to account for a variety of peculiar features of legal structure that differentiate, say, tort from contract and both from property. Nevertheless, as a general approach to understanding private law, the economic approach appears to suffer from several significant shortcomings, which have been pointed out by a number of scholars. In its reflexive reductivism, it drains the private law of numerous layers of doctrinal structure. Its emphasis on efficiency, which even its exponents have now conceded is plainly inadequate from a normative point of view, is also entirely incredible from an interpretive point of view. In so far as the private law has goals, they are more various and constrained than efficiency.

More generally, the private law of tort, contract, and property presents itself as a distinctive system of private right, and the economic model cannot accommodate this deontic idea. It is not simply that the economic model rejects the idea of private law from a normative point of view. It is that there is no room to articulate what this idea even means, so that it can be confronted as part of our law and then rejected. To be sure, the idea of an individual entitlement and the idea of individual preferences play an important role here, but the law protecting these entitlements and satisfying these preferences is aimed at doing so only in so far as these are components of a larger social welfare function which the law is aimed at maximizing. It is the public interest in maximizing efficiency that underlies the private law, just as it underlies public law.

With this interpretive shortcoming come two others. The distinction between private law, within our legal system, and public law, relates in part to a distinction in normative orientation. The intuitive understanding of private law as a domain of private right contrasts with the domain of public law as one of public good, public benefit, or public right. The law of private property and contract, for example, is about realizing justice between private parties, and about respecting individual right and duty, whereas the criminal law or immigration law or welfare law, for example, is about serving public needs or goods. The economic model loses this distinction. While it is perhaps somewhat tendentious to describe this loss as a shortcoming (it might be viewed as a vital insight), I am inclined to suggest that the loss of the interpretive and analytical apparatus for understanding the distinction is a shortcoming, even if one should not want to treat such a distinction as warranted.

Finally, and relatedly, the economic model leaves little room to understand the distinctive institutional role played by common law courts interpreting the private law.

On the instrumentalist model favoured by the economic approach, courts crafting rules for new cases are essentially crafting a piece of legislation that is aimed to achieve public ends, albeit with an awareness of the role of *stare decisis* and the particularity of the parties before them. This view misses a set of special features that adjudication in private law is often taken to have. Courts deciding whether a plaintiff in a certain kind of putative fact pattern has a right of action are not deciding what rule to make up. Rather, even if it is a new case, they are deciding whether the fabric of law that already exists is such that plaintiff is entitled to relief from the court. The rules of private law are not generalities laid out ahead of time by courts cum legislatures. They are the accretion of cases decided by courts on the basis of who, among the private parties, is entitled to use the courts against the other.

These criticisms have been developed by numerous scholars in both interpretive and prescriptive garb. From a prescriptive point of view, the family of criticisms aims to show the value and bindingness of a system of law that hinges upon concepts of right, and the tenuity or unjustifiability of the price-setting system envisioned by the economist. Put in interpretive terms, the criticisms point out that the subjects traditionally regarded as Anglo-American private law are animated by the concepts and principles spelled out above; whether justifiable or not, any effort to capture what the law is misses the boat if it fails to leave room for these concepts and ideas. This chapter's criticisms are put forward from an interpretive point of view.

2.2 Corrective Justice Theories

Corrective justice theorists, most particularly Jules Coleman and Ernest Weinrib, have rightly emphasized a particular line of doctrinal and structural shortcoming in economic views, at least from an interpretive perspective. They have criticized the economic accounts for their failure to recognize the essential role of the private plaintiff in private law. A defendant is not fined, but held liable to a plaintiff. The relational nature of the liability distinguishes it from a fine. More broadly put, the fact that it is liability to a plaintiff, rather than simply a requirement that defendant pay something, is said to undercut the plausibility of a pure deterrence model. Our system is not indifferent—as it would be on the pure deterrence model—to the identity of the beneficiary of a fine. Rather, it is insistent, within private law, that the liability is to the plaintiff. Instrumental explanations of this private aspect of private law have been found plausible by some economists, but powerful arguments have been offered from philosophical and non-philosophical quarters that these explanations are not adequate.

Coleman's interpretation of tort law depicts it as a domain of responsibility for losses. When one individual injures another by wronging her or by invading her rights, and when the injury is the injurer's fault, then the injurer is responsible for that loss. The idea of corrective justice is that one who is responsible for another's injury has an obligation of repair running to the victim. Tort law enforces such obligations of repair, built upon legally recognized definitions of wrong, right, and fault. The private law is private because it involves relations between private parties, obligations to the victim from the injurer, not obligations to the state from the injurer or obligations from the state to the victim. Tort law involves the notion of right either centrally, or correlative to the wrongs that it involves. The role of the court is central, for it enforces obligations of repair that it recognizes as a matter of principle, given the principles that are implicitly or explicitly embedded in the common law. Its enforcement of duties of repair is backward-looking, not forward-looking.

Weinrib's account differs from Coleman's in several respects, three of which are particularly relevant to his account of private law as such. First, the privacy of private law stems from the nature of the duties and rights within it. These duties and rights are intrinsically relational: duties to persons or classes of persons, and rights against persons and classes of persons. Drawing upon Kantian themes, Weinrib suggests that freedom and equality are possible within a framework of right and duty that situates individuals with regard to one another, and constitutes a domain of possible individual action. The privacy of private law consists in its articulation of a juridical domain of individual right and duty among private parties. Secondly, the rectification, or corrective justice achieved within private law, is not merely a matter of taking responsibility for an injury, and therefore restoring a factual equilibrium. It is a matter of restoring a normative equilibrium, not a factual equilibrium. Thirdly, the role of courts in private law is quite different from the role of legislatures in public law. Courts are not making law, they are simply giving legal effect to the domain of juridical rights and duties among private parties that the formal conceptual framework of the private law provides.

As efforts to capture the concepts central to private law, Coleman's and Weinrib's theories improve upon instrumentalist approaches in numerous respects. First, they begin to explain why areas of private law, such as torts, are less public than other areas, such as constitutional or criminal law. The duties and rights run to other private parties, not to the state, on corrective justice views. Secondly, and relatedly, they begin to capture the doctrinal structure of at least some areas of private law—especially torts—better than the economic views. Thirdly, by limiting themselves to an interpretive project, and by casting a wide explanatory net around the idea of rectification and corrective justice, they create room within which we can understand how judicial decisions might be thought to grow out of a set of principles internal to some area of law, rather than being imposed by courts acting like legislators. For all of these reasons, corrective justice theory has both deepened our understanding of private law and broadened jurisprudential horizons considerably. Nevertheless, there are more than enough reasons to be sceptical about the capacity of corrective justice theory to provide an adequate explanatory framework in private law.[4]

---

[4] One further caveat: while Coleman has not even claimed for corrective justice theory the capacity to cover private law more generally (his account is aimed only at tort, and he offers a different model for understanding contract), Weinrib's project purports to cover the very idea of private law.

First, private law is diverse. This is not simply because many important areas of private law—for example, trusts and estates, corporations, and partnerships, involve lawyer's work that is not primarily litigation. It is because, even within litigation, the tort model of taking responsibility for losses or repairing injuries is inadequate. Contract is pivotal to private law but actions for breach of contract are often not about repairing injury, but about, compelling performance or payment of its equivalent (expectation). Property is essential to private law but property litigation pertains to redress for interference with right, and does not require that any damage whatsoever has been done.

Secondly, neither the concept of factual equilibrium nor that of normative equilibrium generates a concept of rectification sufficient to explain the workings of private law. As several scholars have pointed out, including Coleman and Weinrib, it is not possible to take Aristotle's notion of rectification literally, if one is aiming to capture private law with it. In tort, for example, an accident victim's loss is not in any non-question-begging sense the injurer's gain. In some relatively simple cases involving restitution and property law, it is possible that such a model would work, but that is overwhelmingly the exception. Hence, one moves to a picture in which rectification means restoring the victim (but not necessarily by return of a gain). However, restoration of the victim is highly over-inclusive, for there are many cases of injury that do not generate liability (and even many cases in which fault plus injury do not generate liability). For these reasons, theorists like Coleman, Perry, and Ripstein move to a notion of responsibility for injury, rather than rectification in articulating a corrective justice theory, but this underlines their inability to move beyond tort. Weinrib, by contrast, moves from rectification as a concept pertaining to factual equilibrium, to rectification as a concept pertaining to normative equilibrium. This move is problematic for numerous reasons, however. It is notoriously difficult to make clear what this Hegelian/Kantian/Aristotelian synthesis means. To the extent that it breaks ties with the notion of equilibrium as making whole, it compromises its original strength, of capturing the making-whole remedy as a part of private law. But to the extent that it adheres to this notion of equilibrium, it leaves unaccounted for huge areas of private law that permit a variety of remedies (e.g. punitive damages, injunctive relief). More importantly, the notion of normative equilibrium presupposes a teleology for private law which, as discussed below, is highly problematic.

Thirdly, the privacy of private law cannot lie in the relationality of rights and duties it enforces. The fundamental rights and duties of a great deal of criminal law are also relational in the same sense, and yet criminal law is quintessentially public law. The rights not to be battered, raped, murdered, robbed, defrauded, or eavesdropped upon, and the right not to have one's property converted or damaged are all rights protected by the criminal law. Moreover, the norms of the criminal law impose duties upon each person not to treat others in the aforementioned ways. This is a domain of relational rights and duties, yet it is not private law. More generally, in so far as individual freedom depends upon a framework that recognizes a juridically enforceable domain of publicly articulated liberty and security, it is not clear why this could not be done through public law.

Finally, private law, on the corrective justice view, does not provide the stark contrast it claims to provide, to the instrumentalism of the economist. That is because corrective justice theory ultimately provides quite a teleological account of private law. Private law, on the Aristotelean view and the neo-Aristotelean view of Weinrib, facilitates the realization of normative equilibrium. On Coleman's view, tort law sees to it that legal responsibility is laid on the doorstep of whomever is at fault. Put more broadly, on both views, private law serves to transfer a loss to the party who ought to be bearing the loss. Now this teleological aspect of private law does not make it instrumentalist, for it remains open to recognize constitutive value in the system; its value does not merely lie in the state of affairs restored. However, this teleological aspect of private law does raise three problems. First, it erases or at least blunts the distinction between public law and private law, for that distinction is most illuminatingly characterized by the difference between a domain whose point is to seek public goals and one in which that is not the point. Yet if private law is said to aim towards the realization of a sort of equilibrium, then it seems to be aiming for a public goal, ultimately. Additionally, while the recognition of a telos does not entail pure instrumentalism, it opens the door to questions about whether ours is the best system for reaching the telos, all considered. However, as Weinrib, Coleman, Ripstein, and other corrective justice theorists have argued, the domain of reasons in private law appears to be resilient to incursions of a more consequentialist sort. Moreover, corrective justice theorists—particularly Weinrib—have emphasized the possibility of adjudication without politics. Finally, since Aristotle, a signal feature of the concept of corrective justice has been its distinctness from distributive justice, and yet it is difficult to get a grip on the idea of an equilibrium of entitlements that ought to be restored, without assessing the justice of that equilibrium from a broader point of view that includes distributive justice. More pointedly, regarding the legitimacy of private law even partially in terms of its capacity to realize a just equilibrium, seems like a recipe for undercutting the private law, because there are powerful reasons to doubt that the status quo is just from a distributive point of view.

Of course, these descriptions of law and economics and corrective justice are overbroad, and many important qualifications and possible responses have been left unspoken. But it is enough to see the outline of a general problem in the contemporary theory of private law. One choice—currently the favourite of the legal academy—is to regard the distinction between private and public law as artificial in the pejorative sense of that term, since all law is simply a set of devices designed to cause private actors to modify their activities in a manner that will be most socially beneficial. The problem with this view is akin to the problems of the radical consequentialist in moral theory: at least from an interpretive point of view, it entirely omits a world of concepts that make sense to lawyers and citizens and have played a role in structuring our system. In law (perhaps unlike morality, perhaps not) the interpretive project is of great importance, because stability and lawfulness depend, in part, on continuity with the law *as it has been understood*. There is therefore ample reason to search for a way of understanding private law that is more open to a public/private distinction, and more receptive to the structure of private law, than law and economic approaches are.

Corrective justice theorists—particularly Ernest Weinrib—have promised new routes into thinking about private law, but we have seen several grounds for scepticism about them. It is doubtful whether they will span all of private law, indeed, anything beyond tort; it is unclear whether the notion of an equilibrium can be made cogent; the concept of private law as a domain of relational rights and duties sweeps too broadly, and pulls in much of public law, and the teleology of corrective justice itself presents several problems. With these concerns in mind, I shall point down a different path for thinking through the nature of private law, and the significance of the distinction between private law and public law.

2.3 A Fundamental Problem of Both Approaches

Both of these views neglect the essential role of private rights of action in the private law. They differ in their analysis of the requirement that defendant pay damages; the law-and-economics scholar understanding the requirement as a fine, the corrective justice theorist as an obligation. On both sorts of view, the role of a plaintiff in bringing an action is, essentially, to trigger a process in which the state inquires whether the stated requirement applies to the defendant: whether defendant should be fined, or whether defendant owes plaintiff damages. People who perform acts such-and-such should incur a fine: people who perform acts such-and-such and injure or infringe some right are obligated to compensate the injured party.

Civil liability to private parties works very differently from this, however. The state does not answer the question: should conduct of this sort be fined? Nor does it answer the question: does a defendant in this position have an obligation to provide the plaintiff with what she seeks? Rather, the court asks the question: in light of what defendant has done, should plaintiff's demand for damages from the defendant be enforced? A court that decides to enforce the demand a plaintiff has put forward is not necessarily deciding that conduct of the sort in question should be fined. Nor is it necessarily deciding that defendant has an obligation to pay damages, or any other remedy, to the plaintiff. It is deciding that the plaintiff is entitled to have her or his demand for some relief granted. To be sure, one possible basis for such a decision is that a regulatory system has authorized and empowered plaintiffs to be paid enforcers under certain circumstances, and another possible basis is that the defendant owes plaintiff the remedy requested, and that the law ought to enforce such obligations. In this sense, both an economic account and a corrective justice account could be used to provide explanations of why our law grants plaintiffs rights of action. But these possibilities indicate that a more fundamental analytical level has been overlooked. The phenomenon to be analysed and described, in the first instance, is the right plaintiffs enjoy to have certain demands enforced providing that they prove certain facts.

While the first theme of this chapter concerns the analytical structure of private rights of action, the second concerns how best to interpret their normative basis. I shall argue that, in paradigmatic private law cases, the availability of private rights of action depends upon a principle of civil recourse: a person who has been civilly wronged in certain ways is entitled to an avenue of recourse, through the state, against the one who committed the wrong. Drawing from Blackstone and Locke, I offer a basis within social contract theory for grasping the normative appeal of this principle. In a nutshell, I argue that private rights of action in private law represent a domain within which individuals may pursue a state-created avenue of self-help.

3 PRIVATE RIGHTS OF ACTION

3.1 Rights of Action as Conditioned Legal Powers

Several features of private rights of action are significant. First, in Hohfeldian and Hartian terms, it is a legal power (albeit conditioned and mediated) to act in certain ways. An individual who brings a tort or contract suit, if successful in obtaining a judgment, will alter the legal relation between herself and the defendant. The ability to alter legal relations is a form of legal power.[4a]

Secondly, and closely related, the legal rules that recognize private plaintiffs as having rights of action are, in Hartian terms, power-conferring rules.[5] (Nothing is meant to be packed in to the term 'rules' here—as opposed to 'principles').Thus, the rule that a property owner who is able to prove a nuisance is entitled to have an injunction against the nuisance entered against a defendant is a rule that confers upon property owners the power to put the defendant under an injunction against engaging in certain activity. The rule that a tort plaintiff who obtains a damages verdict is entitled to a judgment against the defendant confers upon persons a power to render a defendant legally in debt to them.

Thirdly, the power conferred is conditioned. Individuals do not have the power simply to cause another person to have a new debt to them, if they so wish. The

---

[4a] Wesley Newcomb Hohfeld, 'Some Fundamental Legal Concepts As Applied in Judicial Reasoning', 23 *Yale Law Journal* 16 (1913).

[5] H. L. A. Hart, *The Concept of Law*, 2nd edn. (1992).

changing of the legal relation is something one can do only if one is able to satisfy certain conditions: typically, crossing certain procedural thresholds and meeting certain evidentiary standards to the satisfaction of a factfinder, regarding whether the defendant has acted in certain ways and the plaintiff has been or will be affected in certain ways.

Fourthly, the power conferred is mediated, rather than direct. The plaintiff's right of action is a power to have the state alter the legal relations between the parties. If the above-mentioned conditions are satisfied, then *the court* will enter a judgment or grant an injunction, for example. It is only by virtue of the acts of a third party—the state—that the legal relations are altered. However, the plaintiff with a right of action has the legal power to have the state change these legal relations: it is almost as if the state acts as an agent of the plaintiff, once the plaintiff is determined to have satisfied the requisite conditions. In this way, a right of action is a mediated power.

3.2 Rights of Actions and Courts

Whether a private right of action exists in a particular case depends on courts in at least two ways. As indicated, the power is mediated by a court's grant of relief, in any particular case. However, courts are entrusted to determine whether the conditions which the power-conferring rules set out have been satisfied. Moreover, the very phenomenon of this legal power depends for its existence on the existence of institutions that enforce (mediate) and the existence of institutions that adjudicate.

Secondly, a rule conferring a private right of action under certain conditions providing a certain remedy is itself a legal norm, which must have authority if the private right of action is to exist as a legal right of action in a particular case. However, this is not to say what sort of norm this must be, or what its provenance must consist in (at least so far as the concept of a private right of action goes). Thus, for example, the federal eavesdropping law in the United States, Title III, creates a private right of action for a damages award against one whom the plaintiff is able to prove has electronically eavesdropped on her. Here, the norm comes from an explicit statement of the United States Congress. By contrast, a Californian will have a private right of action against a person who unreasonably intrudes upon her seclusion, but this will be in virtue of appellate courts in California having committed themselves to a rule that a person who suffers this sort of invasion has a right to compensatory and (perhaps) punitive damages against the intruder. Note that where the legal norm in virtue of which the right of action in a particular case exists is one that owes its authority to the judiciary (rather than the legislature or some other source), the judiciary plays at least three roles *vis-à-vis* right of action: creator of authority for rule, adjudicator of conditions, enforcer of remedy.

3.3   Action and Private Rights of Action

The private right of action is a power to act against certain others. In this sense, it is
(*a*) a power to act in certain ways; (*b*) intrinsically relational. The question is whether
plaintiff has the power to act against the defendant, by changing the defendant's legal
status in relation to the plaintiff. That a private right of action is a right to *act* in certain ways is obvious from its name, and equally obvious from the ongoing nature of
public discussion about litigiousness in America. The prevailing sentiment is that a
culture of litigation is unpleasant, in part because it involves constant antagonism,
people constantly acting *against one another* in the courts. For better or worse, the
phrase 'private right of action' reminds us of this absolutely central feature of torts.

3.4   The Privacy of Private Rights of Action

The private right of action is *private* in that it is a power of a party other than the state.
In some areas of the law—criminal law and immigration law, for example—the state
is empowered to alter the legal status of individuals by acting (through courts). In
private law, by contrast, it is a private party who has this power. Conversely, the power
that is enjoyed by the state is a power of creator, adjudicator, and enforcer, but not the
power of prime actor. Of course, the courts are not prime actors in criminal law or
regulatory law either, but the *state* is a prime actor, *qua* plaintiff in those areas, but not
in private law.

3.5   Private Rights of Action as a Species of Rights

The private right of action has a feature often deemed to be an important attribute of
rights—whether to assert it or not normally lies within the discretion of the person
whose right of action it is. It is interesting to note the many ways in which this feature
of private rights of action has been varied and weakened over the past decades—in
each case, however, with both deliberateness and a recognition that something of
fundamental importance to the nature of the right of action is being compromised.
Hence, for example, a class action must be safeguarded in so far as it involves a non-
right-holder's assertion of a plaintiff's right of action. A subrogation agreement with
an insurer must specifically not take from the insured the right to sue, but only
assume the residual right to recover such proceeds or sue absent the plaintiff's suit.

Private rights of action often enjoy another attribute that suits them well for the
label 'rights'. One who has a private right of action is often said to be *entitled* to obtain
a judgment or a remedy against the defendant. When a court recognizes someone as
having a private right of action, it is often recognizing not only that they do have the

legal power in question, but also that they are entitled to have that power. In this sense, a private right of action possessed by a genuine holder is somewhat like the right to vote of an enfranchised citizen; it is not only a power, it not only lies within the discretion of the holder, but it is regarded by our system as something to which the plaintiff is entitled.

This is not an essential feature of a private right of action. Where a legislature decides, for example, to empower certain private persons to litigate against certain criminal defendants in order to enhance the prosecution of the crime in question, and adds a 'bounty' payment for such private attorneys general, an argument can be made that this is a private right of action. Of course, once the statutory scheme is in place, there is a sense in which the private plaintiff is entitled to compensation or entitled to the right of action. But this is nothing like what courts mean when they say that a person who is defamed by being called a child molester has a *right* of action, or is *entitled* to act, against the defamer. The assertion that the plaintiff is entitled to an action against the defendant is in part an assertion that there is such an entitlement in plaintiff in light of what defendant did. It is not simply an assimilation of the facts of the case to a broader power-conferring rule for defamation cases. On the contrary, the power-conferring rule is in a sense an entrenched and general version of a principle that such plaintiffs are entitled to have the power to act against the defendant.

The assertion of a private right of action involves an assertion of an entitlement *against the state*. The plaintiff makes a claim against the state that she or he is entitled to this affirmative assistance from the state. A power-conferring rule, if it has the status of a rule, entitles the possessor of the private right of action to conduct by the state that would render the plaintiff's actions ways of acting against the defendant.

The notion that a plaintiff is entitled to a right of action is, I shall argue, centrally important to the idea of a private law. Instrumentalists and formalists alike often argue that private law purports to be about non-public reasons for holding defendants liable to plaintiffs; instrumentalists decry such ideas as incoherent. I shall argue in subsequent sections of this chapter that the notion of a private right of action as an entitlement to use the courts to obtain a remedy is indeed central to the notion of private rights of action, and, to some extent, private law.

3.6 The Triangularity of Private Rights of Action

A private right of action involves a triangle of relationships. A plaintiff has a claim against the state to its assistance in changing the legal relations of the defendant. Note that the claim for affirmative assistance from the state is a claim aimed at generating an ability to act against the defendant (by altering its legal status). The question of *against whom the power to act exists*, is answered by saying it is a right of action against the defendant. It is therefore natural to assume that the right of action is correlative to a duty on the part of the defendant to pay. That would be a mistake. As indicated, the right is, in the first instance, a power to act through the state (albeit, against the defendant). Being the holder of a private right of action against a defendant for a damages remedy to be paid to oneself is different from being the legally designated beneficiary of an obligation of a defendant. This is because a legal power to act so as to alter a third party's legal status so that it becomes obligated to pay a certain person or to act for the benefit of a certain person is distinct from the status of being the beneficiary of the changed legal relation. This is so even if the status of the beneficiary and the status of the power-holder overlap. Indeed, being a beneficiary of a damages remedy or an injunctive remedy is neither a necessary nor a sufficient condition of a private right of action, as a conceptual matter.

3.7   The Sense in which Private Rights of Action are like Privileges

In an important practical sense, a right of action is a privilege to act against another. Considered as a means of acting against another, and held against the backdrop of a political and legal culture that prohibits the coercion of behaviour or the non-consensual transfer of property, the right of action provides an exception to the prohibition of private action against others. A person may not privately coerce another to perform a contract, but she may obtain an injunction: a person may not privately take land or money from another, but she may obtain a judgment and/or a lien. If we look at private rights of action against the backdrop of this prohibition, it is a privilege to act against third parties in certain ways.

Uses of the phrase 'private right of action' are, in practice (as opposed to philosophical analysis), attached to a further phrase that indicates the nature of the defendant's legal misdeed or violation that gives rise to the private right of action. Thus, courts speak of a 'private right of action for invasion of privacy' (a tort) or a 'private right of action for securities fraud' (predicated on violation of a statute). It is part of the concept of a private right of action as it is deployed in the law that it is always conceived of in relation to a particular act of the defendant who is being sued, where that act is being characterized as to its legal status (e.g. invasion of privacy, violation of section 10b–5).

4 A Contractarian Model of Private Rights of Action in Private Law

Just as punishment cuts across the criminal law, so private rights of action cut across the civil law. One part of criminal law theory goes to the question of why crimes as diverse as homicide and grave desecration are both considered crimes; another part goes to the nature and normative basis of punishment. Similarly, private law theory includes questions about the nature and interrelationship of areas such as torts, contracts, and property; another goes to the nature and normative basis of private rights of action, which exist in all three. This part of the chapter addresses the latter question, via an exploration of Lockian and Blackstonian ideas.

4.1 Locke on Redress

While contemporary theorists have tended to focus on either utilitarian, Aristotelian, or Kantian explanations of the structure of private law, I think an explicit and illuminating social contract theory account is suggested by an underdeveloped aspect of Locke's theory in the *Second Treatise*. A much-discussed component of Locke's theory focuses on the natural right to punish wrongdoers, and the ceding of that right to the state, in return for the state's undertaking to enforce the criminal law through punishment. But Locke also asserted—equally confidently, but significantly less popularly, that individuals have a natural right to redress wrongs done to them, in particular.

Besides the crime which consists in violating the law and varying from the right rule of reason, whereby a man so far becomes degenerate and declares himself to quit the principles of human nature and to be a noxious creature, there is commonly injury done to some person or other, and some other man receives damage by his transgression; in which case he who has received any damage has, besides the right of punishment common to him with other men, a particular right to seek reparation from him that has done it . . .[6]

On Locke's view, this liberty to seek redress must be ceded in entering a political society.

Man, being born, as has been proved, with a title to perfect freedom and uncontrolled enjoyment of all the rights and privileges of the law of nature equally with any other man or number of men in the world, *has by nature a power not only to preserve his property—that is, his life liberty, and estate—against the injuries and attempts of other men*, but to judge of and punish the breaches of that law in others as he is persuaded the offense deserves, . . . But because no political society can be or subsist, without having in itself the power to preserve the property

---

[6] John Locke, *The Second Treatise of Government*, ed. Thomas P. Peardon (1952; 1st pub. 1694), 7–8.

and, in order thereunto, punish the offenses of all those of that society, there and there only is political society where every one of the members has quitted his natural power, resigned it up into the hands of the community in all cases that exclude him not from appealing for protection to the law established by it. [emphasis added][7]

Just as the individual right to punish was replaced by a system of criminal law administered by the state, so the individual right to redress wrongs was replaced by a system of civil law, in which the state, through judges, saw to it that injuries were redressed by the injurer.

But though every man who has entered into civil society has thereby quitted his power to punish offenses against the law of nature in prosecution of his own private judgment, yet, with the judgment of offenses which he has given up to the legislative in all cases where he can appeal to the magistrate, he has given a right to the commonwealth to employ his force for the execution of the judgments of the commonwealth, . . . Whenever, therefore, any number of men are so united into one society as to quit every one his executive power of the law of nature and to resign it to the public, there and there only is a political or civil society. . . . And this puts men out of a state of nature into that of a commonwealth by setting up a judge on earth, with authority to determine all the controversies and *redress the injuries that may happen to any member of the* commonwealth.[8]

Locke's suggestion that civil law is a means of redressing wrongs is on solid ground, as is his contrast between redress and punishment. Locke insightfully recognized that, in so far as the state acts under the civil law, it is acting on behalf of an individual victim, whereas, in so far as the state acts in the criminal law, it is prototypically acting on behalf of all members of the community. Moreover, he rightly insisted that the state is *acting* in both the private law and the criminal law, both in providing redress and in punishing.

Yet Locke appears to have missed a feature of enormous importance in the civil law, in many ways setting the stage for our legal tradition's neglect of the concept of a private right of action. The passage immediately above suggests that Locke viewed judges as redressing injuries, rather than viewing judges as permitting private parties to obtain redress by bringing their injurers to court. He recognized in the case of punishment, however, that the executive was actually the enforcer of the laws, and that the courts stood to adjudicate disputes between the executive and the individual. It is not clear from the *Second Treatise* whether Locke (mistakenly) believed that the executive played the initiating role in this enforcement in the case of injuries, but appears that he (rightly) regarded the magistrate as the only organ of state power that played a role in individual litigation under the private law. Nevertheless, there is no indication that Locke recognized that litigation to redress injuries is privately instigated and privately prosecuted, unlike litigation seeking punishment. It is therefore easy to read the *Second Treatise* as contemplating a system in which the state undertakes to punish when appropriate and to seek compensation for those injured, when appropriate.

---

[7] John Locke, *The Second Treatise of Government*, at 48–9.   [8] ibid. at 49–50 (emphasis added).

And because it is a work concerning what sort of political and legal system would be justifiable (rather than accurately portraying the extant system in England), it is possible that Locke was justified in defending such a system.

Locke's view of crime and punishment under the social contract was, of course, a distinctive contribution to the social contract tradition emanating out of Hobbes. As against Hobbes's views that the need for a state arises out of the absence of natural right, Locke argued that, even assuming there to be a natural right and wrong that normal persons were typically capable of ascertaining, there would still be a need for a state because the individual inclination to punish wrongdoers would precipitate chaos absent an authority. Having postulated a natural power and inclination to punish, however, Locke created for himself the need to explain how a state could justifiably forbid such private punishment. Locke's answer is a breakthrough of liberal political theory: the state's prohibition of private punishment and the state's use of its own power to punish are really two sides of the same coin: the state's prerogative to punish exists as an entrustment, by its citizens, of their own natural power to punish. It is only because the state undertakes to act on behalf of its citizens to punish those who commit wrongdoings that it: (i) justifiably prohibits individuals from exercising their individual right to punish; (ii) justifiably punishes, as the state. The power of the state to punish is therefore entirely derivative; the obligation of the individual not to engage in private punishment is conditional on the state's having undertaken that role.

Although there is limited evidence on this point, it seems likely that Locke held an analogous view as to the right to seek compensation for individual injuries. There is a natural right and power to seek compensation for an injury done to one. However, if each person acted on what he or she perceived to be an injury caused by another, and engaged in self-help remedies, this would lead to chaos. But the problem will be solved if each entrusts to the state the power to ascertain whether such an infringement occurred, and the power to redress the injury by requiring the injurer to compensate the injured party. The state has the power to do this because individuals have entrusted it to the state; individuals are justifiably prohibited from doing this because the state will be doing it on their behalf.

Regardless of whether this was in fact Locke's view, it seems clear that such a view is possible. In exploring private rights of action, this Lockian view is interesting for several reasons. First, it locates the justification for private law in the private rights of response of individuals who have been injured or wronged. The justifiability of a system of remedies through courts in civil law is derivative, on this view, of the right of an individual to seek redress. Secondly, the natural right to seek redress is private, and it is the right only of the person who is injured. Thirdly, as crystallized in the social contract metaphor, Locke recognized that individuals do not in fact, and should not (from a normative point of view), actually have a broad right of self-help when injured. To the contrary, the natural right is conceded in place of the state's assuming the power to force persons to redress injuries or wrongs that they have caused.

Abstracting from the metaphor, we may say that there is a private right, according to Locke, to have the state (which forbids broad self-help remedies) to assume and to exercise the power to seek redress for the victim, in light of the state's prohibiting self-help. Fourthly, and relatedly, the state's forbidding of private self-help carries with it an obligation to seek redress for one who has been victimized by the wrong of another. In all of these ways, the right to redress as Locke understood it resembles the private right of action in our system: it is private, it is personal to the one who was victimized, it exists in conjunction with a general prohibition by the state against private self-help, and the concept is a concept of a right, against the state, to this remedy. Moreover, the state has a duty to provide this to the victim.

Interestingly, however, the Lockian picture does not match the law we actually have. In the actual Anglo-American legal system, the state typically plays no executive role in seeking compensation for those injured.[9] The system of private law does not involve the state as the criminal law involves the prosecutor. The actor, in private law, is in fact the private party who was injured. That party is not, as Locke seems to have envisioned, merely the beneficiary of the redress obtained by the court. Indeed, the party is the one who 'prosecutes' the private action. Moreover, the plaintiff's bringing a case to court is not merely a matter of a request for action by the court. Rather, the private party must prosecute the action at every step. Even if plaintiff obtains a judgment from the court, the judgment itself is not redress; the judgment creates a debt of the defendant to the plaintiff. It will still be plaintiff's job to enforce the payment of the debt. Hence, the picture of the state as *sua sponte* ordering wrongdoers to pay their victims is entirely incorrect. Courts judge that certain demands by plaintiffs shall be granted, and accede to those demands.

In Lockian terms, our legal system strikes a different legal bargain between the individual and the state than Locke himself imagined. Injured individuals do give up the right to engage in violent actions of self-help, but they get something in return that is different than Locke imagined. In return, individuals receive a private right of action. As explained above, this is a private power to act, through the state, to change the legal status of the defendant, on condition that one prove certain things about the defendant's conduct. Within the Lockian social contract framework, the private right of action might be understood as follows. Rather than forbidding individual victims from acting against the wrongdoer and acting in their behalf to obtain redress, our system has selected a more nuanced alternative. The victim is permitted to act against the wrongdoer to obtain redress, but only through a particular, artificial framework of civil law. The civilizing transformation of this private aggression is the earmark of the private right of action.

---

[9] Of course, during early stages of English law, actions for damages were sometimes publicly prosecuted. See, e.g., David J. Seipp, 'The Distinction Between Crime and Tort in the Early Common Law', 76 *B.U.L. Rev.* 59 (1996).

4.2 Blackstone on Redress for Private Wrongs

These quasi-Lockian musings are not idiosyncratic; on the contrary, a similar analysis of private rights of action is found in the most authoritative and exhaustive analysis of the common law—Blackstone's *Commentaries*. In the third book, entitled 'Private Wrongs', Blackstone wrote that courts are instituted precisely to provide private parties with an avenue of recourse to victims of private wrongs:

The more effectually to accomplish the redress of private injuries, courts of justice are instituted in every civilized society, in order to protect the weak from the insults of the stronger, by expounding and enforcing those laws, by which rights are defined, and wrongs prohibited. This remedy is, therefore, principally to be sought by application to these courts of justice; that is, by *suit* or *action* in nature.[10]

Blackstone explicitly treated *redress through the courts* as one of three different species of remedy. A more primitive form of redress is obtained by the action of a party himself, as when one defends oneself or one's family against an aggressor, or one removes a nuisance from one's land. Blackstone contrasted this basic self-help with purely legal forms of remedy—'redress by the mere operation of law', such as when an unpaid creditor automatically retains part of a debtor's estate because he has been made an executor of the estate, or when a proprietary interest reverts to the wronged party under certain circumstances. Synthesizing aspects of each of these two opposites, Blackstone wrote:

The next, and principal, object of our inquiries is the redress of injuries by *suit in courts*: where in the act of the parties and the act of law co-operate; the act of parties being necessary to set the law in motion, and the process of the law being in general the only instrument, by which parties are enabled to procure a certain and adequate redress. (22)

An overriding precept is the familiar statement, 'wherever the common law gives a right or prohibits an injury, it also gives a remedy by action; and, therefore, wherever a new injury is done, a new method of remedy must be pursued' (122). The bulk of Book Three describes the many different courts, the wrongs for which one may seek redress in each of these courts, and the writs one must use to seek various kinds of redress for various wrongs in each of these courts. In short, Blackstone's survey of the kinds of rights to go to court corresponds roughly to his survey of the variety of private wrongs. Throughout Book Three, we learn that where there is a right of which an individual has been deprived or a wrong that has been committed upon the individual, there is a way to go to court and have the court provide a remedy.

[10] William Blackstone, *Blackstone's Commentaries* (St. George Tucker, ed. 1803) (reprinted with Introduction by Paul Finkelmand and David Cobin 1996), Vol. IV, Book Three, Chapter 1, p. 2.

4.3 A Locke/Blackstone Synthesis on Redress in our Actual Private Law

Blackstone's putatively descriptive (but partially normative) statement that there is a remedy for every private wrong calls to mind Locke's insistence, within the social contract model, that the state is obligated to punish and to provide redress for injuries. Yet Blackstone correctly recognizes that remedies within the civil law are not a product of the state, acting in executive fashion, but rather an entitlement of a wronged party who has begun to act—who has sued in court—to have his requested remedy granted. The synthesis of Locke and Blackstone which this suggests is the view that the power to alter a defendant's legal status through having a judgment entered against him—the private right of action—is something a private party who has been wronged is entitled to from the state. Conversely, the state—having deprived individuals of other means of self-help—is obligated to empower individuals with an avenue of civil recourse through the courts. Courts that recognize a private right of action as a matter of right to a party who has been wronged are applying precisely this sort of Lockian principle.

The Lockian social contract metaphor cannot take much pressure, as sympathetic critics from Hume to Rawls have pointed out. The metaphor is often taken as a placeholder for a broader argument based on the existence of reasons for members of a group of persons within a state to regard a state bounded by certain norms as legitimate and authoritative and to act as members of it, reasons conditioned on the likeminded acceptance of other persons in the state. This is not the place to undertake the project of unpacking the metaphor; a vast contractarian and anti-contractarian literature exists on this topic. But assuming it is not incoherent generally to try to unpack contractarian arguments in this manner, it is worth looking at what it would mean in the context of private rights of action. Within the Lockian framework, the statement was that a natural right to seek redress existed, and that the concession of this right was returned by the state's taking on the role of providing redress through law. With Blackstonian adjustments, the assertion is that the natural right to seek redress is conceded in return for a right of civil redress, a private right of action. In terms of reasons, and abstracted from natural rights and the social contract, the view appears as follows: in light of the fact that we each have instincts to redress wrongs done to us that the state prohibits us from acting upon, and that such a framework of raw liberty to redress wrongs would be of some value to the person who was wronged in terms of self-preservation and self-restoration, the state is obligated to provide to someone who has been wronged an avenue of civil recourse, a civil right to redress, through the courts, against the wrongdoer. That is a 'private right of action', and it is the essence of the private law.

4.4 The Idea of Civil Recourse

The framework derived from Blackstone and Locke can be generalized and abstracted from these historical connections. At the basis of our system of private law is a principle that, under a variety of different circumstances, individuals are *entitled* to act against other private parties in a variety of ways. Most plainly, our system judges that one who has been wronged by another *is entitled* to an avenue of recourse against that other—is entitled to *respond* to the way he has been treated by the other.

It is a critical aspect of political society that *avenging a perceived wrong or rights invasion or injury is not a sufficient justification for aggressive action against another.* Therefore, a civil political society has prohibitions on violent conduct against others, and those prohibitions sweep broadly enough to include—to outlaw—responsive aggressive action. Hence, a punch in the nose does not justify a punch in the nose; a (past) infringement of property rights does not justify battery or conversion; a careless injury does not justify the forcible seizure of assets to compensate, or the parallel responsive infliction of injury. The breaking of a promise does not justify an angry punishment of the promisor, or a private coercion of performance. Under our law these are all prohibited. And under our conception of a civil political society, private action is not permitted in these circumstances. Indeed, although the notion *lex talionis*—an eye for an eye—retains appeal to some criminal law theorists, who theorize about the state's capacity to seek retribution, the notion of *lex talionis* as a principle of private retaliation is widely rejected, and its rejection is treated as the first step towards a tolerably civil notion of political society.

It is a common misconception of thinkers as diverse as Aristotle, Locke, and Holmes, that the rejection of crude notions of private retaliation entails an utter rejection of notions of private *response* to wrongdoing. The civility of our civil law does indeed reside in its rejection of the permissibility of private aggression. But, as Blackstone saw, while the rejection of private aggression is replaced by the aggrandizement of public aggression, in the case of punishment, that is only part of the story. In the case of *redressing wrongs* personal to an individual, *the rejection of purely private aggression is replaced by the empowerment of private parties to alter the legal status of wrongdoers, through a civil process that includes the state.* Individuals are prohibited from responding non-civilly to a variety of wrongs to them, but they are simultaneously empowered to respond civilly. A private right of action for a remedy is what individuals are empowered with.

Let us return now to our question of the place of private rights of action in our actual common law. We are only a short step from a possible answer. The social contract model suggests that the state's obligation to empower plaintiff civilly derives from the state's having prohibited the wronged individual from responding to the wrongdoing in any other way. Having been deprived, by the state, of the liberty to strike back and to take back aggressively, the wronged individual is entitled to receive from the state *some* avenue of recourse against the defendant. Conversely, having deprived the individual of the liberty to take back when wronged, the state is obligated to provide some avenue of recourse to the wronged individual against the wrongdoer. By empowering individuals with a private right of action, the state dispatches this obligation. Because providing an adequate avenue of recourse is an obligation of the state to the individual who is wronged but deprived of the liberty to respond aggressively, the private right of action is something to which the individual is entitled. The principle that the individual is so entitled is therefore the basis of a recognition of a private right of action. The idea of an entitlement to a private right of action thus finds support within a liberal individualistic conception that extends beyond a proprietary, or 'holdings'-based notion of rights against others, into a notion that conceives of individuals as possessing both rights against being treated a certain way, and an ability to act responsively in order to protect and vindicate oneself.

We gain greater insight into the principle of recourse by seeing what would be lost in a world with a punishment-and-compensation system, but no private rights of action. It is tempting to view rights of action as merely instruments for attaining compensation. On this view, what one is entitled to is one's holdings, as well as a certain degree of deterrence and punishment of those who violate the law. Criminal law handles the punishment and some of the deterrence. Private law is an instrument for restoring holdings and adding to the deterrence. What is missing in this picture, however, is the private individual's own entitlement to *force* others legally into acting, to *choose* a remedy, and to *vindicate* her own rights. We have a complete dependency upon the enforcement and discretion of the state. Moreover, the degree of protection one has is entirely dependent upon whether one believes that the concept of 'holdings' can accommodate all of the ways in which individuals attempt to vindicate their interests.

5 REVISITING PROBLEMS IN PRIVATE LAW

Using the analytical structure of private rights of action, and the normative idea of civil recourse as pillars, we are now in a position to point towards a resolution of several fundamental problems in the theory of private law.

5.1 The Variety of Private Rights of Action

An appealing feature of law and economics approaches, as Jules Coleman has pointed out, is its ability to unify apparently diverse fields of law. Thus, for example, tort, contract, and property—traditionally key fields of private law—can be understood as designed in different ways to achieve the same end: efficient allocation of resources. Corrective justice theories, while to some extent rescuing the distinction between private and public law, did so at the cost of providing an overarching framework for the diverse areas of private law. An emphasis on civil recourse, private rights of action, and private powers, permits us both to distinguish private from public law, and to offer a broader account of the unity of private law.

This section unifies private law, at least in connection with litigation, by pointing out that in torts, contracts, property, a distinctive feature is that individuals have private rights of action. In each area, moreover, courts recognize plaintiffs as entitled to private rights of action because of the defendant's conduct towards them. However, the trigger of a private right of action, and more deeply, the basis of the right to an avenue of civil recourse, differs in the three cases. In tort, a private right of action is generated by the defendant having wronged the plaintiff, under a legally recognized relational norm that obligates defendant to refrain from treating persons a certain way. In contract, the private right of action is generated by the defendant having bound herself or himself to a private agreement. In property, it is the defendant's actual or anticipated invasion of a property right that generates a private right of action.

5.1.1 *Tort*

The notion of a private right of action based on a defendant's tort is easily grasped. A tort is an act that the common law treats as a wrong. Thus, for example, a plaintiff who is battered, defamed, defrauded, falsely imprisoned, or maliciously prosecuted has a private right of action against the batterer, defamer, defrauder, false imprisoner, or malicious prosecutor. Similarly, a plaintiff who has been injured by a negligent driver or hurt by her doctor's medical malpractice, or her lawyer's legal malpractice, will have a private right of action against a negligent driver, doctor, or lawyer. In all of these cases, there is a norm embedded in the common law enjoining persons from treating others a certain way, and thereby designating a certain manner of treating others as a wrong, a breach of a civil obligation to treat others a certain way. Once a court decides that the plaintiff has established that the defendant committed a tort against her, the court recognizes in plaintiff a private right of action. The court is, in effect, deciding that plaintiff is entitled to have her demand for a judgment of damages (or injunctive relief) against the defendant enforced, in light of the fact that defendant treated her that way. But note that the court begins with a demand by plaintiff that a damages award be entered against the defendant. The question faced by the court is not: should defendant be forced to pay plaintiff? The question is: should plaintiff's demand that defendant have a judgment entered against her be granted? Defendant's commission of a tort serves as a reason for empowering plaintiff, for permitting plaintiff's demand for a judgment to be granted.

There are, then, mid-level principles found throughout tort law, recognizing that a plaintiff who has been treated in a certain manner is entitled to a private right of action—for example, a person who has been defamed is entitled to a private right of action against the defamer. Each of these principles can be understood, in part, in terms of the idea of civil recourse. Each combines recognition of a certain act as a form of wrong that the law is willing to recognize as a wrong, on the one hand, with recognition of an entitlement to an avenue of recourse for the wrong. This culminates in the recognition that plaintiff is entitled to a power to act against the defendant through the state. At a practical level, the court in fact recognizes in plaintiff this power by accepting and acting upon the plaintiff's demand to alter defendant's legal status.

5.1.2 *Contract*

The condition of a private right of action in the common law of contracts is typically that the plaintiff prove that the defendant breached a contractual obligation to her to perform. The state has no free-ranging power, however, to require parties to a contract to perform. Rather, the state enjoins a promisor to perform only where the promisee has asserted a private right of action for specific performance. The availability of courts in which a disappointed promisee is able to compel specific performance is, in a sense, an affirmative right of citizens to a means of securing compliance with promises made to them.

The private right of action in contract for specific performance can also be understood in terms of the idea of civil recourse. Having entered a contract, and given consideration for it, a private party should not be required to endure the breach of that contract passively. Yet in civil society, aggressive or violent self-help is prohibited. Our system solved this problem, traditionally, by permitting a promisee to act civilly through the state to compel performance of a promise. A private right of action in contract for specific performance is plainly a power to render a promisee legally compelled to perform on pain of a possible contempt sanction by the state. Again, the explanation of the court's affording this relief is not simply the defendant's obligation to perform; it is the plaintiff's right to have the defendant perform, in light of the defendant's promise to her.

Contemporary Anglo-American contract law disfavours specific performance as a remedy, offering only a damages remedy in most actions for breach of contract. However, the typical measure of damages is expectation, which arguably manifests the specific performance conception. A plaintiff's role as promisee who has provided consideration is what entitles plaintiff to the power to compel the promisor to provide the equivalent of performance (expectation).

Interestingly, courts in the twentieth century became increasingly enamoured of a conception of breach of contract as a form of wrong. Moreover, plaintiffs frequently seek damages awards as compensation for an injury inflicted by the breach. In this sense, breach of contract is sometimes seen as a form of tort. Plaintiffs are able to seek redress for the wrongful injury that was inflicted upon them. Note that a private right of action to render a wrongful breacher indebted to the plaintiff in an amount geared to make plaintiff whole is quite a different concept than a private right of action to coerce performance, or equivalent, to one to whom performance is owed. A contemporary understanding (and probably a historical one as well) will certainly require an understanding of both of these conceptions of rights of action in contract.

Whichever model or paradigm of contract is deemed dominant (and I would still maintain that the first is dominant), the notion of private rights of action is pivotally important. Courts that enforce specific performance or that impose expectation or reliance damages are doing so out of recognition of a private right of action. They are recognizing promisees (or injured parties) as entitled to a power to alter defendant's legal relations to plaintiff, through the state. The entitlement is inferred from what the defendant has and has not done to the plaintiff, and how the plaintiff has been affected, and how the plaintiff has interacted with defendant. The right to enter and enforce contracts is a fundamental form of legal power citizens are granted within a liberal political system.

5.1.3 *Property*

The right to the exclusive control, and the use and enjoyment of one's property, are fundamental liberal rights as well. A party whose property rights have been infringed (by trespass or nuisance) is entitled to a private right of action against the infringer. Indeed, a private right of action can be seen as a civilized limit case of a variety of remedies of self-help that exist in the law of property (including a privilege of defence of property, recapture of chattel, etc.) A landowner whose property is being trespassed upon or who is enduring a nuisance is entitled to an injunction against the infringer. The private right of action for an injunction is a power to have the state enjoin defendant from engaging in interference with plaintiff's property right, on pain of civil contempt.

Why is the plaintiff entitled to a right of action for an injunction? Arguably, the right to the state's aid in protecting against property infringements is implicit in the notion of a property right as a right of exclusive control over the property. The bundle of rights that constitutes a property right includes the right to require others to refrain from interfering with one's rights. But note that there are limits to the rights of self-help in protecting one's property. One may not exceed what is proportional. There is no reason to believe that the limits to non-civil, aggressive self-help will be sufficient to protect one's property. This will be particularly problematic where the infringer is stronger than the property owner. But if the plaintiff is the property owner, then by definition the plaintiff is entitled to be free of these interferences. A state's recognition of a private right of action, its recognition of the entitlement to a power, gives substance to the more abstract entitlement to be free of such interferences, just as the recognition of a power to act through the state for specific performance (or expectation) gives flesh to the more abstract entitlement to be paid (or to enjoy the benefits of performance).

5.1.4 *Criminal Statutes*

Certain areas of statutory law dramatically illustrate an entirely different meaning to private rights of action. An excellent example is the standing a private person enjoys in a *qui tam* action seeking to impose liability on a government contractor who has defrauded the government. There are statutes permitting private actions to be commenced against a defendant who has defrauded the government.[11] The statutes were placed there by the legislature, on the ground that permitting private plaintiffs to sue might well increase the level of deterrence and the level of responsibility. No one thinks that a private right of action in a *qui tam* action is recognized by courts as a matter of principle. No one thinks it is about a plaintiff's entitlement to a power against defendant who has treated him or her in a certain way or infringed her right.

An interesting contrast is found in federal eavesdropping law. Title III, for example, prohibits the use of electronic devices to listen into telephone calls.[12] It contains criminal enforcement mechanisms, as well as procedures for law enforcement officials to seek warrants. But it also contains a private right of action, by statute. Although the statute is a creation of the legislature, and although the legislature plainly wants to deter eavesdropping and to recognize the need for compensation, this is not to say that there is no entitlement within this statute. It is entirely plausible to assert that the inclusion of a private right of action for civil damages reflects a legislative judgment that persons who are eavesdropped upon surreptitiously are *entitled* to a right of action against the eavesdropper. Similarly, New York Civil Rights Law section 51 permits a private right of action for injunctive relief or damages to any person whose name, portrait, picture, or voice was misappropriated without consent for purposes of trade or advertising. The New York Assembly also made such conduct a criminally sanctionable misdemeanour. The point of the civil provision is to respect the entitlement of persons whose likeness was misappropriated to redress the misappropriation privately.

American federal antitrust and racketeering laws represent a hybrid of the *qui tam* idea and the private entitlement idea. Antitrust laws criminalize restraint of trade, empower the United States to seek criminal punishment (through prosecution), empower the Federal Trade Commission to seek various remedies. But they also

[11] See generally, Jill E. Fisch, 'Class Action Reform, Qui Tam. and the Role of the Plaintiff', 60-*Aut Law and Contemporary Problems*, 167 (1997).

[12] 18 U.S.C. §2510, et seq.

empower private parties to seek injunctive relief and to seek damages. Notably, private parties can receive triple damages. The triple damages provision was intended to encourage private parties to bring actions. A major goal of antitrust law is the protection of the interests of consumers. Because conspiracies in trade are difficult to ferret out, it is often private parties who will be in a good position to identify and assert that a violation of the antitrust laws has occurred. To this extent, the statutory provision affording plaintiffs a private right of action should be interpreted as aimed at enhancing enforcement for the benefit of the public in general. On the other hand, unlike *qui tam* actions, and like tort and privacy actions, antitrust plaintiffs are typically asserting that they personally were the victims of unfair competitive acts (such as conspiracies to boycott them, conspiracies to fix prices), and the recognition of a right of action in the victim of the wrong (and not other parties) reflects the operation of a principle of recourse in the legislative intent as well.

Whether an express private right of action under a statute should be understood as a reflection of an idea of deputizing private plaintiffs (as in *qui tam*), as principally a matter of private entitlement (eavesdropping), or as a hybrid (antitrust) is a matter of interpretation. In any case, however, a principal basis of entitlement is rule-based, because these are express statutory provisions directly authorizing the empowerment of persons situated in a particular way. This is to be contrasted with the realm of the common law, in which the entitlement is inferred as a matter of principle by courts from the facts proved by the plaintiff about the interactions between plaintiff and defendant.

5.2 How is Private Law Different From Public Law?

A fundamental difference between public and private litigation is that public litigation—most obviously, criminal prosecution—involves a state's effort to exercise its power to act against a defendant, whereas in private litigation, it is a private party who attempts to exercise her power against the defendant. Many salient features of the public/private distinction follow from this more basic point. This obvious, and salient distinction has been discarded in recent years by legal scholars because it appears to presuppose a naïve understanding of private law as self-executing. Private law only succeeds, of course, if the courts act, and the courts are arms of the state. Hence, some form of state action is as necessary to a tort or property suit as it is to a criminal prosecution, as famous opinions like that in *Shelley v Kraemer* indicated.[13] This seems to imply that the state's action in criminal litigation or public law more generally cannot be what distinguishes it from private law.

---

[13]   334 U.S. 1 (1948).

The prior analysis of private rights of action and civil recourse points to a more sophisticated response to these observations. The state acts in private litigation, but its action is quite different than in public law, where it is initiating the action against the defendant, and it is acting in its executive capacity. The nature of a court's decision to permit a private right of action, I have argued, is a decision to empower, to facilitate, and to permit action by a private individual. The state is acting, but responsively; it is not initiating action. Moreover, it is not acting in its executive capacity. This does not mean that the state has no responsibility for its action, or that norms on state action could not possibly reach to the state's judicial action in private law. It means that the decision to assign responsibility to the state for this type of action is on a different moral and political footing than the decision to assign responsibility to the state when it is the author of the actions, and acting in an executive capacity. More specifically, it is not enough to conclude that the action of the plaintiff against the defendant ought not to be chosen (although it might be enough in public law), because the state is not this actor. The state is making a decision that a plaintiff is entitled to act this way, and is empowering and permitting this action. In the legal and political setting, as in the non-legal, there is sometimes a gap between what one ought to do oneself, and what one ought to permit or facilitate others' doing, if they so choose. Conversely, in both domains, there are classes of cases in which the objectionability of the underlying action destroys the individual plaintiff's claim to have any right to the state's empowerment or permission to do it.

Thus, for example, a court's decision, as in *Shelley*, to permit enforcement of a racial covenant may indeed implicate constitutional concerns, but those are constitutional concerns about empowering and privileging individuals to enforce racial covenants. This leaves open the possibility that there are many cases where enforcement of private rights of action leads to undesirable or even unjust outcomes, yet the state is not necessarily responsible for those outcomes. Conversely, under the public law—and specifically under criminal law—it is the state's responsibility to make discretionary judgments about the appropriateness of the exercise of the power of the state to enforce the law.

The distinction between the state's executive power in public law and the lack thereof in private law also promises to explain a variety of other basic distinctions between criminal and tort law. Most obviously, the nature of the acts that will generate civil liability is quite different than the nature of an act that will generate criminal liability. This is obviously an enormously broad topic, but a basic insight is generated by the model above. The gravamen of a criminal wrong is an act that will generate in the state a power and privilege of the state to act, an entitlement, one might argue, to a public avenue of recourse. Hence, an offence against the state is what is called for, and (generally) an offence whose gravity is sufficient to generate an entitlement to a particular form of remedy—the remedy of punishment. This typically carries with it a fairly high level of moral opprobrium, but need not be individualized to a victim: hence, both inchoate offences and victimless offences are candidates for criminal liability.

Contrast this with the sort of act that will qualify to generate civil liability. It is essential that if an individual is to have a right of action, the act in question must be an invasion of his or her rights: it must be targeted and it may not be inchoate. On the other hand, there need not be any moral opprobrium associated with an actor who performs the act (at least for some branches of civil liability, and some remedies). For large ranges of private law, particularly tort, the range of remedies is ample, and the nature of the act generating liability is that it produces an injury, and implicates, to some degree, the notion of an individualized wrong.

Finally, there are obvious procedural differences in criminal and civil liability, and these differences are illuminated by the distinction between public and private rights of action. Most plainly, and implicit in much of the early discussion of this chapter, private rights of action are entitlements of the victim, not of the state. The victim's choice is a necessary condition of the existence of an action, in the civil law. The opposite is true in public law. The victim's choice is neither necessary nor sufficient. The right to prosecute criminally is a power of the state.

More generally, civil liability contains far fewer procedural protections against liability. This is not, as is commonly said, because civil law concerns who among private parties shall bear a loss. It is because a scheme of individual vulnerability to private right of action implicitly carries with it a scheme of individual powers to act against others. The vulnerability to private action by others is reciprocal to the entitlement to act against others. An ample scheme of privileges and entitlements to act against others is, I have suggested, intrinsic to a social contract model in which we forgo all natural liberties of responsive action.

By contrast, individuals under our constitutional scheme, and even the common law constitutional scheme from which it arose, are provided with far greater protections against the actions of the state as criminal prosecutor. This is not simply because of the power and might of the state, as prosecutor, nor is it simply because of the gravity of the particular punishments it seeks to impose. It is because the concept of punishment by the state occupies an entirely different role in the relation between individuals and the state than the concept of civil liability. The state, *qua* executive, is not being provided with a right of action in order to equilibrate the state's own power, which has been diminished by the scheme of restraint that comes with civil society; that is the civil case. On the contrary, as my discussion of Locke indicated, the very point of the state as *punisher* bespeaks its role as above-and-beyond the realm of reciprocal rights to act against one another. The state possesses the power to punish that has been acquiesced by the people, and it is a power to punish as the ultimate authority. The procedural protections—for example, the need to prove guilt beyond a reasonable doubt—are conditions on the power to punish, and their effect is to constrain and diminish the enormous vulnerability of individuals to the state's power. The diminution of this vulnerability does not carry with it a diminution of individual powers, because vulnerabilities are not correlative to powers in the realm of public rights of action.

5.3   Are The Traditional Subjects of Private Law Parts of a Unified Domain?

This chapter has largely centred around private rights of action and the areas of private law in which those private rights of action are recognized. A great deal of what is typically considered 'private law', however, does not involve litigation (at least not directly). Hence, the law of trusts and estates, for example, is prototypically considered private law, but this classification does not refer to private rights of action. The same is true, for example, of much of the law of business associations, intellectual property, property, and other areas. A theory of private law that is purely litigation-based is therefore, at a minimum, incomplete. I suggest, however, that insights regarding private rights of action give rise to a more general way of understanding private law.

Recall that legal norms recognizing private rights of action are, in effect, rules conferring upon individuals conditioned powers to act against others through the state; they are a form of power-conferring rule, applicable to private parties. Non-litigation based areas of legal practice—such as trusts and estates—confer legal powers upon private parties to alter the legal relations of third parties. Thus, for example, the laws concerning private property create powers in property owners to convey certain bundles of rights to others; the laws concerning wills create powers in persons to bequest property to others; similarly for the laws concerning trusts. Contract law in part empowers persons to bind themselves and others to contract; corporate law empowers certain private enterprises to function with legal status, and obviously conditions and regulates that functioning in innumerable ways. Private law thus contains myriad rules vesting in private persons (and entities) a variety of legal powers.

Public law goes beyond criminal and regulatory litigation, just as private law goes beyond private rights of action. State and federal constitutional law empowers certain legal entities—municipalities, Congress, the Executive—with a variety of legal powers. It also restricts those powers in various ways, for example, by putting certain civil liberties beyond the range of conduct that government entities are empowered to invade. It also designates persons (e.g. judges, mayors, tax assessors) as public officers and thereby clothes them with enormous legal powers. Beyond these power-conferring rules, public law evidently includes a wide array of duty-imposing rules, rules requiring persons and artificial entities to conduct themselves in various ways, and to treat others in various ways. Whether the violation of such a rule will give rise to a public right of action, or a private right of action (or both) is determined by the public and private power-conferring rules.

5.4 Anti-instrumentalism in Private Law Adjudication

A dramatic feature of Ernest Weinrib's *The Idea of Private Law* is its assertion that adjudication in private law need not be understood instrumentally, in terms of decisions about what will promote publicly oriented goals. On the contrary, Weinrib asserts that private law adjudication involves a pattern of internally connected reasons that are independent of assertions about the public good. Two central theses of the Realist and Critical Legal Studies critique of private law concern the nature of adjudication in the traditional private law subjects, such as torts, contract, and property. According to these critiques, private law jurisprudence on the traditional model maintains that adjudication of issues in private law is *determinate* and that it is *apolitical*. Realists and Crits reject both of these claims.[14] I will not comment here on the determinacy thesis, but assume for the purposes of argument that any particular strong version of a determinacy thesis is either untrue or not demonstrable, and that, therefore, it should be assumed that adjudication involves an element of choice that is not wholly foreordained or bound by precedent. I suggest, however, that the understanding of private law in terms of private rights of action and civil recourse lends insight into the debate on the role of politics and morality in private law adjudication.

The standard criticism of private law neutrality claims is that: (1) there is always a selection or choice among alternative options; and (2) this choice always involves a view or endorsement of the public good, and that, therefore (3) adjudication in private law inevitably requires a view or endorsement of the public good. The foregoing analysis of private rights of action and civil recourse suggests that (2) may not be precisely correct. Even if there is a choice among options, and even if this choice is evaluative, it does not follow that the choice involves a view or endorsement of the public good. For the question, in many areas of private law, is whether a plaintiff is entitled to be empowered to act against the defendant in a certain manner. Now of course this is an evaluative choice in many respects, and it surely contemplates a broader normative scheme, perhaps one along the social contract lines articulated earlier. Moreover, it typically involves an acceptance of an underlying set of norms of conduct (as in tort). And it involves the court's willingness, or permissiveness, in facilitating the realization of certain distributive schemes in particular cases, as well as more broadly. In all of these significant respects, it is true that political and moral neutrality are not maintained.

It may be that some influential views of the neutrality of adjudication in private law are undercut by the forgoing concessions. However, it remains open to say that there is an important sense in which some forms of adjudication in private law may be distinctive, and distinctively non-public in their orientation. As I have argued at length above, the recognition of a power need not be premised on a view as to the appropriateness of the plaintiff exercising that power, or of the outcome of the

---

[14] See, e.g. Mark Kelman, *A Guide to Critical Legal Studies* (1987), and sources cited therein.

exercise of that power. It is true that the state's action and facilitation are necessary in order for the private law to operate. But the court is committing itself only to the entitlement to the power, not to its exercise or the outcome of that exercise. The state is no more endorsing the exercise or the outcome than it is endorsing exercises of the right to self-defence. It is permitting (and facilitating) a liberty (and power) whose value is justified by the general concession of a broader liberty of aggressive action.

Taken out of the social contract metaphor, the point about adjudication in private law is as follows. Choices courts make about when individuals are entitled to prevail in private law are not necessarily, or even fundamentally, choices about which outcomes are best. They are choices that recognize a domain of private redress, as part and parcel of living in a society in which courts function as a civil means of sidestepping private aggression. The courts doing private law therefore do not necessarily see themselves as conduits to a better state of affairs or a better society, and candour does not demand that they see themselves in such a light. Rather, they may see themselves as constituting an artificial and civil means through which individuals may act against one another. Whether the results of this action against one another are independently valuable or promote the values the court wishes to promote is quite a different question. Hence, even if one concedes (as in (1) above) that private law adjudication requires choice, and choice of a normative character, it does not follow that private law adjudication is best understood in terms of choices of values the court wishes to promote. Hence, while this adjudication is surely not value-neutral in every important sense of that term, this is not to say that adjudication even in private law necessarily aims towards states of affairs that courts wish to achieve. Appropriately qualified, then, there is a certain sense in which private law adjudication may be neutral with respect to the attainment of certain sorts of public goals.

6 CONCLUSION

A cornerstone of twentieth-century legal theory is that law is political through and through. Subjects traditionally classified as 'private law', including torts, contracts, and property, have been appropriately included under this slogan, for these are parts of law, and importantly political parts of law at that. However, a wide range of theorists have wrongly inferred that there is nothing especially private about these parts of law, and that adjudication in these areas involves choices among social goals just as it does in incontrovertibly public areas of law. With this inference, the entire distinction between private and public law has been banished as a relic of reactionary nineteenth-century regimes.

I have argued above that the realists and instrumentalists who have depicted private law areas as idiosyncratic forums in which public goals such as efficiency are sought have missed a great deal that is special both in doctrine and in jurisprudence. However, their chief antagonists today, corrective justice theorists, have offered far too narrow a framework for understanding private law, and have too quickly assumed that by replacing brash instrumentalism with deontology, they will recapture private law.

Ironically, the recapture of private law begins with the recognition that the state *is* essentially involved in private adjudication, but it purports to take a distinctive type of role. Private law is essentially driven by private rights of action. This means that the fundamental decisions made by the state are decisions about empowerment and privilege. Courts treat individuals who have been wronged, or whose property or contractual rights have been invaded, as entitled to act against other private parties. It is not that justice is done if such powers are created. It is that our entire public system that concentrates the power of aggression in the state makes private law available as a civilized channel through which private parties may act against one other. We regard individuals as entitled to engage in such action against one another.

The ideas of civil recourse, private rights of action, and private legal powers more generally, invite us to begin exploring the idea of private law in an entirely new light; one which offers an opportunity to see the public/private distinction while recognizing the state's role in both; which captures the doctrinal subtleties within different areas of private law; which usefully contrasts litigation with non-litigation areas in both public and private law; and which offers an understanding of how we could recognize that, even if our system justly recognizes powers in individuals, that is not a sufficient reason to believe that what it accomplishes is, all considered, just.

CHAPTER 17

PHILOSOPHY OF TORT LAW

ARTHUR RIPSTEIN

TORT law answers two of the most fundamental questions faced by any society: 'how should people treat each other?' and 'whose problem is it when things go wrong?' There are many ways in which such questions might be resolved—criminal law and administrative regulation place limits on the ways in which people treat each other, the informal norms of morality still others. Schemes of social insurance and public welfare provide other ways of dealing with losses, private charity others yet again, and simply leaving losses where they fall another.

Tort law is striking because it supposes that the question of how people treat each other and the question of whose problem it is when things go wrong are at bottom the same question. If plaintiff is to recover from defendant, defendant must have breached a norm of conduct that governs the ways in which he may treat her, rather than some other norm concerning the ways in which some *other* person may be treated. That principle is itself an expression of the way in which tort law subordinates questions about who must deal with some problem to questions about how people treat each other. As Cardozo puts it, plaintiff does not recover as the 'vicarious beneficiary' of a wrong done to another. Instead, she must establish a wrong 'personal to her'.[1]

An earlier version of this chapter was presented at the Oxford–Toronto legal philosophy conference, in February 2001, where Tony Honoré provided instructive comments. I am also grateful to Lisa Austin, Dennis Klimchuk, Sophia Reibetanz, Benjamin Zipursky, and an anonymous reader for comments on earlier drafts.

[1] *Palsgraf v Long Island Railroad*, 169 NE 99 (NY CA 1928).

Tort liability is not always predicated on a defendant's faul—liability is sometimes 'strict', for example, in the case of using explosives, or keeping wild animals. In such cases, whether defendant exercised reasonable, or even heroic, precautions is irrelevant to liability. But even in these cases, plaintiff can rightly complain of what defendant did to her, because it was something which she was entitled to be free of. The standards of tort law govern the things people do to each other, not simply the ways in which they behave.

The same two questions could be combined in other ways as well. For example, Elisabeth Anscombe, in her essay 'Modern Moral Philosophy', suggests that a person is responsible for the bad consequences of anything bad that he does. Hegel takes a similar view. On this view, a person is responsible for the bad consequences of violating a norm. Tort law combines the questions differently. If you violate the norm that specifies a level of conduct you owe to another person, you are responsible for the injury that the norm told you not to impose. The differences between these two ways of combining the questions are significant: the way in which tort law combines them, but not the Anscombe–Hegel way, builds limits on the scope of responsibility into the basis of responsibility. This difference is important, because the consequences for which tort law holds persons responsible are not unlimited.

The connection between the two questions is mirrored in the structure of a tort action. Tort law articulates norms of conduct and resolves conflicts in the context of disputes between private parties. Plaintiff is entitled to a remedy against defendant only if her injury can be described as a matter of defendant wronging plaintiff. Plaintiff does not come before the court and say 'defendant did something dreadful, and look what happened to me as a result'. Instead, plaintiff's complaint takes the form 'defendant is not allowed to do that to me'. The phrase 'to me' is crucial; the plaintiff is not saying that defendant is not allowed to do something *simpliciter*; if defendant behaved badly, but plaintiff was not injured, or if her injury is the result of a wrong done to another person, she is not entitled to a remedy.[2]

As between the parties before it, the court must decide whose problem the unwelcome situation is—is the plaintiff simply out of luck that he finds his neighbour's

---

[2] Both contract and restitution also involve private rights of action, and so both can be thought out as subordinating questions about who bears which costs to questions about how people treat each other. In a contract action, plaintiff's allegation has the form of 'that's mine. Give it back!' That is, plaintiff asserts a right to the terms of a bargain. In a tort action, plaintiff's allegation is of the form 'defendant isn't allowed to do that to me'. The plaintiff asserts a right to be free of defendant's conduct. The remedy sought by the plaintiff reflects this difference; in a tort action plaintiff wants the wrongful deed undone, while in a contract action plaintiff wants the promised deed to be done. Aristotle, in the *Nicomachean Ethics* says that corrective justice restores the equality of the parties, but his examples suggest that the equality is restored by one party giving something back to another. Although we can usefully represent tort damages as returning the injury to the injurer to whom it rightly belongs, the point of returning it is to make it as though the parties had interacted on appropriate terms, that is, to make it as though the wrong had never occurred. If defendant has wronged plaintiff, treating the resulting injury as defendant's problem is just a way of making it as though they had not interacted, and defendant had simply injured himself.

activities annoying, or is the defendant committing an enjoinable nuisance? Is the plaintiff's injury hers to deal with, or is it one for which defendant is responsible and so liable in damages? In each case, the question of remedy may be foremost in the minds of the parties. The court addresses the question of remedy—the question of whose problem it is—by asking the seemingly distinct question of the acceptable limits of behaviour. The entire proceeding is structured by questions of whether defendant behaved unacceptably towards plaintiff, and whether plaintiff's injury is appropriately related to defendant's mistreatment of her. The structure of a tort action thus expresses the way in which it answers questions about whose problem it is when things go wrong by considering the ways in which people treat each other.

My aim in this chapter is to explain the way tort law brings the two questions together. The main task in doing so is to explain the sense in which tort law predicates liability on responsibility. Defendant must pay plaintiff if, but only if, she is responsible for plaintiff's injury The relevant notion of responsibility depends on norms of conduct, and much of the chapter will be taken up with developing that notion and explaining why it has features that are strikingly different from other familiar conceptions. I will focus largely on responsibility in negligence, in large part because I think the relevant conception of responsibility is most striking there. I will explain why questions of foreseeability figure prominently in questions of responsibility, why the standard by which such foreseeability is judged is, with two prominent exceptions, the abilities of a reasonable person of ordinary prudence, and why not all foreseeable injuries attract liability.

Before turning to negligence, however, I should say a few words about its relation to other areas of tort law. As I said above, liability in tort is sometimes 'strict', and so does not depend upon the degree of care exercised by defendant. Liability for 'abnormally dangerous' activities is strict, as is liability in nuisance, as well as liability for the use of another person's property. This may seem an odd grouping of areas, and it probably is. That's because the basis for liability being strict is so different in the three heads of liability. Without going into the details of each, I will simply assert that what they all share is the plaintiff's entitlement to have defendant act differently. Liability for other torts, such as fraud and battery, is intentional, that is, requires that defendant have intended harm to plaintiff. Here too it is clear that plaintiff's claim to a remedy depends upon her right that defendant not treat her as he did.

Some have been tempted by the thought that negligence occupies a sort of middle ground between strict liability and intentional torts. I will not pursue that line of thought here. Instead, I want to suggest that negligence is central in a different sense of that term, that it is central because it illustrates the way in which our two questions come together in a particularly clear way. Beginning with negligence will enable us to see how liability could sometimes be strict, and also why liability for intentional wrongdoing—wrongdoing the morality of which is relatively uncontroversial— would be limited in ways strikingly different from the ways in which the Hegel–Anscombe model would suggest.

I also focus on negligence because so many people find it puzzling, both in its general structure and its particular doctrines. Much of this puzzlement comes from a failure to appreciate the way in which its conception of responsibility depends upon norms of conduct, and indeed, perplexity about what those norms of conduct are. One consequence of such puzzlement is close to a century of calls for the replacement of negligence liability (or some part of it) with some other kind of compensation scheme. Many critics of tort liability object that it is arbitrary, because it makes too much depend on luck—either because liability depends on actual harm caused, or because compensation depends upon the defendant's conduct, not that of the victim.[3] And sometimes the charge is that negligence liability is wasteful, because accidents could be reduced more effectively, and victims compensated more cheaply, if talk about responsibility were abandoned. Two decades ago, mandatory social insurance was usually the recommended replacement; the more recent recommendation is that people insure themselves against whatever misfortunes might befall them.

The criticisms of negligence liability sometimes reflect impatience with its distributive consequences, or the belief that tort liability is a particularly inept way of realizing some set of social purposes, such as deterrence, compensation, or retribution. Yet such interpretations of negligence law get much of their currency from the apparent difficulty of understanding it in terms of norms regulating the ways in which people treat each other.

The idea that when one person mistreats another, the injurer must deal with the consequences of that mistreatment is familiar and compelling in other departments of private law. In those areas of the law, the fact that different people fare differently gives rise to neither objection nor perplexity. In cases of intentional wrongdoing, for example, the relation between the relevant norms of conduct and the damages sought is clear—the aggrieved plaintiff wants defendant to pay the costs of the wrong he has inflicted on her. Nobody has seriously entertained the possibility that insurance, either social or private, should replace tort liability for such intentional torts as defamation, battery, or false imprisonment. As a result, nobody has said that people should insure themselves against the prospect of those wrongs. Nor is anyone likely to suggest that it is unfair that victims of those torts recover, while people who suffer similar losses in other ways do not, or that successful batterers pay more in damages than unsuccessful ones.[4] Again, those who suggest that society must help out those who suffer losses through crimes do so supposing that the criminal will lack sufficient resources so that plaintiffs will be left with their losses,

---

[3] See e.g. Atiyah, *The Damages Lottery* (Oxford: Hart Publishing, 1997), and Christopher Schroeder, 'Corrective Justice, Liability for Risks, and Tort Law', *University of California Law Review*, 38 (1990), 143.

[4] Some people have suggested that completed crimes should not attract more severe *punishment* than failed attempts. But those arguments are invariably framed in terms of a contrast between punishment and compensation, taking it for granted that compensation should depend on consequences. See e.g. J. C. Smith, 'The Element of Chance in Criminal Liability', *Criminal Law Review*, 63 (1971).

not that it is unfair or arbitrary to make criminals bear the costs they create if they can afford to.[5]

The same can be said for other bases of liability in private law. So far as I know, nobody has suggested a scheme of social insurance to protect those who have suffered losses through breach of contract, even where the breach was not intentional. Nor have there been suggestions that people who suffer similar losses in other ways be compensated. Here too, the absence of such suggestions reflects the clarity of the relation between the norms of conduct specified in a contract and the damages sought for its breach. Plaintiff's demand that defendant make her 'whole' is the obvious response to the fact that she is less than whole because of the way in which defendant wronged her. The same applies to liability for conversion of property, for which defendant is liable to plaintiff because the thing taken was *hers*. Because the relation between the remedy and norms of property are clear, nobody has suggested that those who take property by mistake be allowed to keep that property, and the original owners be left to insure themselves against such a possibility. Instead, the person who takes another's property is expected to set things right by returning the property owner to the situation he was in, and remained entitled to be in. The same point can be made in cases of restitution for mistaken payments. Worries about compensating those who lose through such mistakes do not arise, because there is so obviously an appropriate party to make up the losses.

Critics claim that negligence liability is arbitrary because they fail to see the connection between norms of conduct and liability in negligence. As I will show, it is just as tight as in the other examples I have mentioned. To show that it is, I will explain the sense in which plaintiff's complaint is that her injury properly belongs to defendant because defendant has breached a duty that he owed to her. Tort law articulates distinctive conceptions of responsibility and fairness between persons. Taken together, they provide a way of understanding both how people can interact on grounds of justice, and why those who fail to interact on those terms must answer for the problems that result.

To begin, I will say something about the two basic normative principles that tort law incorporates. They are basic in the sense that more specific norms of conduct and repair provide concrete interpretations of them.[6] The first is a basic norm of conduct, or rather a norm about norms of conduct: tort law demands that people accept reciprocal limits on their freedom. Nineteenth-century nuisance cases fill out this idea in terms of the slogan 'live and let live'. I will formulate the same point as the principle

---

[5] In *Lamb v London Borough of Camden* [1981] QB 625 (CA) Lord Denning objects to *Chomentowski v Red Garter Restaurants* (1970) WN (NSW) 1070, in which a crime victim sought to recover from his employer, pointing out that the criminal injuries compensation board is charged with compensating victims of violent crimes. It is difficult to believe that even Denning would point to the existence of the board as a reason against holding the *criminal* liable for the victim's loss.

[6] They are also basic in the sense that they require qualification in cases of special relationships, in which parties are asymmetrically situated, such as those between professionals and their clients. I do not consider those in any detail here.

that one party may not set the terms of interaction unilaterally. However it is formulated, the principle requires filling out if it is to say anything about particular ways in which people might interact; the abstract formulations require only that *any* standards of conduct apply to all equally, on the basis of interests that all can be supposed to share. But it does not tell us which interests count, nor how they can be counted. None the less, the abstract formulations are illuminating, because they turn out to constrain both the ways in which norms of conduct are formulated, and the ways in which interests are described. The relevant interests in both liberty and security are described in terms of the type of interest that is at stake, rather than its magnitude on a particular occasion. As a result, whether one person needs to take account of another's interest depends on whether all persons need to take account of the interest of others, not on the importance of the competing interests to the particular parties.

The notion of reciprocity at work here needs some filling out. You might wonder, for example, whether *any* principle, consistently applied, would generate reciprocal norms of conduct. Although there may be a sense of 'reciprocity', in which this is true, that is not the sense intended here. The sort of reciprocity I have in mind grows out of an idea of private persons pursuing their separate ends, and supposes that standards of conduct are reciprocal just in case they enable each person to pursue his or her ends as much as is compatible with others pursuing their own ends. Plaintiff's complaint about her injury appeals to norms governing how people are allowed to treat each other.

The principle that one party may not set the terms of interaction unilaterally also provides the basis of the second principle, which requires that people bear the costs their conduct imposes on others. That requirement sounds good in the abstract, but can only provide guidance taken together with some way of determining where costs lie. Provided people treat others as they should, any losses that result are simply the problem of those they befall (although public law may provide a way in which some larger group can hold them in common). But if one person wrongs another, the latter's loss becomes the former's to deal with.

This connection between wrongdoing and loss, and so between the two principles, can be put in economic terms—one person should not displace the costs of his activities onto others—or in terms of people taking responsibility for their actions. However it is put, if it is to have application in particular cases, it requires some way of determining which messes belong to which people, or which costs accompany which activities, or what people are responsible for. Described in terms of displaced costs, tort law's norms of conduct determine what counts as a cost of which activity. In the idiom of responsibility, norms of conduct mark the line between what a person has done and what is (merely) a by-product of her action. Tort law combines the principles by letting injuries lie where they fall unless they come about through one person's wronging another, where wrongdoing consists in setting the terms of interaction unilaterally in the primary sense. The second principle, then, can be thought of as a special case of the first: to allow one person to place costs on others that they cannot place on her is to let her determine the costs of interaction unilaterally.

I think both principles are attractive, but my purpose here is less to defend them than to articulate their role in tort law. At any rate, a necessary first step towards assessing or defending them is to see how particular institutions might make them determinate. Without institutional embodiment, neither principle has much to say for or against anything anyone might do. A requirement that people treat each other in the same ways that they will be treated tells us that any standards of conduct must protect people equally from each other, but does not, on its own, tell us what losses people should be protected against, or what degree of forbearance on the part of others such protection requires. To guide conduct while protecting people equally, standards must abstract away from some differences between the situations in which people find themselves, focusing on some features of those situations while treating others as irrelevant. Again, the idea that people must bear the costs of their own activities requires some way of assigning particular costs to particular activities; tort law answers that question by considering norms of conduct.[7]

RISKS AND NORMS

The law of negligence sets limits on the risks that people may impose on each other. Not all risk imposition is inappropriate. As Lord Reid remarked in *Bolton v Stone*, 'In the crowded conditions of modern life, even the most careful person cannot avoid creating some risks and accepting others'.[8] Where a risk is inappropriate, the person who imposes it does so at his own risk. That is, should the risk ripen into an injury, the result is the injurer's to deal with. If a risk is not inappropriate, however, its costs

---

[7] At the same time, the institutions themselves can only be justified by articulating and defending the principles they express. If the pattern of norms and remedies imposed by tort law can be seen to hang together in light virtue of intuitively appealing principles, then that very pattern can be vindicated. There may well be other reasons for keeping an institution of tort law, ranging from the spreading of accident costs or the promotion of economic efficiency to the symbolic importance of allowing individuals a day in court or a taste for decentralized processes. The justification in terms of underlying principles enjoys a certain primacy, if only because it offers reasons for the specific pattern of decisions that is at issue.

Because those duties are owed to others, their satisfaction is inherently vulnerable to factors beyond an individual's control. The possibility of this is less puzzling than some seem to suppose. If I owe you 100 dollars, the possibility of my meeting my obligation is vulnerable in the same way. Such vulnerability does not entail that I really only owe you an attempt, or perhaps repeated attempts, to repay you. Instead, it means that I am answerable for consequences not wholly within my control. In the same way, tort duties make me answerable for consequences not wholly in my control.

[8] *Bolton v. Stone* [1951] AC 850 (HL) per Lord Reid.

simply lie where they fall; it is one of the risks of ordinary life, as opposed to a risk that one person imposes on another. This point is sometimes made in terms of an idea of risk allocation. It is certainly the effect of negligence law to allocate risks in the sense that it determines who will bear their costs. It is also in some sense its purpose to do so, because it determines which risks people are allowed to impose on each other. Talk of risk allocation is potentially misleading, however, because risks are allocated in a particular principled way, the point of which is to protect people from each other.

The boundary between appropriate and inappropriate risks is set by a system of norms of equal freedom. All are allowed an equal liberty to pursue their ends, subject to the requirement that they not interfere with the ability of others to pursue theirs. The requirement that the class of plaintiffs and type of injuries be foreseeable reflects the law's role in articulating standards of conduct. Those standards can only guide conduct if they tell people what to do, and no standard can tell a person to avoid an unforeseeable consequence. That those standards are meant to protect people equally from each other explains the objectivity of the standard of care.

The common law's standard of reasonable care, and the familiar figure of the reasonable person through which that standard is expressed, provide a way of striking the appropriate balance between liberty and security. The reasonable person is neither the typical person nor the rational person who adopts the best means in pursuit of his or her ends. Instead, the reasonable person is the one who exercises appropriate restraint in light of the interests of others. The reasonable person is a construct to strike a balance between different interests. To do so we need to decide how much weight to attach to which interests. Decisions about such matters invariably import substantive judgments about what is important to a person's ability to lead a self-directing life. Such matters will occasionally be controversial, though most such interests—freedom of action and association on the one hand, and bodily security and security of possession on the other—will not. Still, the point of the reasonable person standard is to balance such interests in a way that is fair to all concerned. Rather than aggregating them across actual persons, so that one person's loss is made up for by another's gain, we construct a representative reasonable person, who has interests in both liberty and security. A standard of reasonable care protects people equally from each other, allowing each equal liberty to pursue his or her ends, and equal security against the unwanted effects of others pursuing their ends.

The purpose of appealing to what would be done by a reasonable person is to generate reciprocal norms of conduct. That purpose gives shape to the interests that it can protect. It might be thought, for example, that people have a general interest in security, as opposed to the narrower interest in security against injury by others that the law of negligence protects. But because the law of negligence articulates norms of conduct, it can only take account of interests that can be protected through norms that can guide behaviour. One person could not owe another a duty to prevent another person suffering a particular type of injury (say, property damage) in general, because a particular type of injury can come about in too many different ways.

As a result, there is no course of action that one person could follow to protect another (or herself for that matter) against a type of injury. One person can only owe another a duty to avoid bringing about a particular type of injury in a particular way. As a result, the law of negligence protects those interests against certain kinds of invasions, rather than protecting them *per se* in the way that, for example, a distributive or social insurance scheme might aim to minister to them. Distributive schemes can, though need not, focus on particular needs apart from any questions about how they came about. Thus a health insurance programme can treat people solely on the basis of their medical need. Tort law cannot take account of need as such. Because it aims to direct people's conduct, it can only look to interests that it can ask people to take account of. The possibility of directing conduct is essential to its central doctrines.

FORESIGHT

It is a commonplace of the law of negligence that a defendant is only liable to plaintiffs who, and for injuries which, are foreseeable. Foreseeability enters into questions of duty—one does not have a duty to avoid unforeseeable injuries—and into questions of proximity and remoteness—as a matter of law, unforeseeable types of injury are too remote, even if they are caused by the breach of a duty.[9] On one plausible understanding of this requirement, foreseeability operates as an independent constraint on liability. The intuitive idea is straightforward: you are only answerable for, and so potentially liable for, the consequences of your acts if it makes sense to include those consequences among your deeds. But any act has indefinitely many consequences, only some of which count as your deeds in any interesting sense. That class is selected by the concept of control: if you could have foreseen, and so could have avoided, an outcome, it counts as something that you have done. Otherwise it counts only as something that happened as a result of something that you did, because control is not exercised with respect to unforeseeable consequences. On this understanding, then, the relation between agents and outcomes is prior to, and independent of, any norms of conduct. Indeed, on this view, the connection goes in the other direction: norms can only apply to outcomes to which agents are directly related, and for which a person is responsible in the prenormative sense. You can only be liable for foreseeable injuries because you can only be responsible for them. Liability is predicated on responsibility, which can be

---

[9] I don't mean to deny that there are some questions of remoteness that are not addressed by considerations of foreseeability. I say more about this issue below.

ascribed without considering any general norms of conduct. I will call this the 'independent constraint view'.[10]

The independent constraint view has considerable moral appeal, because it expresses the idea that a person is only liable for something if he is responsible for it. It does less well as an account of tort liability, because an account of tort liability must not depart too much from settled tort doctrine. Perhaps a legal system that answered to the independent constraint model would be desirable in so far as it would make tort law somewhat more continuous with other aspects of morality. But if we want to understand the way in which tort law conceives of responsibility, and the nature of the moral claim it asserts, the independent constraint model is the wrong place to begin. In particular, it faces two serious difficulties. First, the requirement of control that accounts for its moral appeal is most plausible when the control is actually exercised—when, for example, defendant considered the risk in question, and decided to ignore it. Yet the law of negligence not only does not require that defendant consider the risk, it does not require that the particular defendant be capable of considering that particular risk. Instead, the law asks what account a reasonable person, with ordinary capacities of foresight and prudence, would have taken of the risk. While it is not impossible to claim that this more abstract specification of the requisite capacities serves as an independent constraint on attributions of responsibility, it is rather more difficult to see the motivation for treating it as a constraint. If the particular defendant did not, or could not, foresee the risk, why suppose that the consequence in question is only attributable to her if somebody else would have foreseen it, or if she herself would have foreseen it, had she been less tired, or more attentive?

Part of the difficulty comes from the fact that talk about what a person 'could' have done is notoriously slippery. Tony Honoré and Stephen Perry have both argued that the relevant notion of 'could' should be understood as referring to the agent's general capacities, whether or not those capacities were exercised on a particular occasion.[11] Unfortunately, the notion of general capacity is considerably more opaque than the notion of duty it is supposed to constrain: if I drive carelessly because tired, is the relevant general capacity the one I have while well-rested, or the one I have while tired? Looking at questions of duty provides a straightforward way of deciding what someone should have avoided—he should have avoided the very injury that plaintiff was entitled to be free of. If we eschew questions of duty in favour of some question about what the defendant could have done by exercising his ordinary capacities, we need some principled way of deciding which capacities are to count.

The other difficulty for the independent constraint model comes with the law's distinction between type and extent of injury. If a defendant is liable for an injury of

[10] Stephen Perry has done the most to develop this line of thought. See his 'The Moral Foundations of Tort Law', *Iowa Law Review*, 77 (1992), 494 and 'Responsibility for Outcomes and the Law of Torts', *Philosophy and Tort Law*, ed. G. Postema (Cambridge: Cambridge University Press, 2001).

[11] Stephen R. Perry, 'Moral Foundations'; Tony Honore, *Fault and Responsibility* (Oxford: Hart Publishing, 1999).

a particular type, he is liable for its full extent, even if that extent could not be foreseen. If plaintiff has an 'eggshell skull' and so suffers terribly from what others would have experienced as a minor injury, defendant is liable for his full losses, just as defendant must make up any lost earnings of an injured plaintiff, even if he could not have known that plaintiff would have earned so much. While the distinction is not always easy to draw in particular cases, disagreements about how to draw it presuppose its significance. Yet the independent constraint model makes this distinction puzzling. If avoidability or control serves to connect a person to a consequence, an agent who could not have foreseen a specific consequence cannot be responsible for it, even if he was responsible for another, similar consequence.

The two problems have a common root. Questions about whether someone could have avoided some consequence are clear enough when applied to a particular person avoiding a particular consequence. The law predicates liability on the answer to a different question: could a reasonable person have foreseen this type of injury to persons in plaintiff's class? The further we abstract from the particular person and the particular injury, the more strained the concept of control becomes.[12] Some of that strain can be relieved by supposing that foreseeability, control, and capacity must all be relativized to a particular description of the risk. Indeed, I will suggest that the duty account explains why a particular description of the risk would be appropriate. But supposing that action takes place 'under a description', merely displaces the problem for the independent constraint model, because we need to decide which

[12] Nor can the foreseeability requirement plausibly be explained as an expression of a more general precondition of agency or responsibility, as is suggested by Jules Coleman in *The Practice of Principle* (Oxford: Oxford University Press, 2001). Although a being with no capacities for foresight could not be a responsible agent, either agency or responsibility requires the ability to foresee or avoid a *particular* consequence for which one is responsible. There is a familiar sense in which a careful driver is responsible for running over an unforeseeable pedestrian. The driver regrets the fact that *she* was the one who ran over the pedestrian, and so wishes that she had taken a different route or started out earlier. Some norms of repair may follow from this sort of responsibility—perhaps she has a special obligation to call for help, or stay with the victim until help arrives, in a way that someone who witnessed the accident does not. But such moral obligations as she has do not arise from the fact that she violated a norm of conduct, because she did not violate any such norm. The pedestrian cannot complain that the driver should have been more careful.

Again, In *Dooley v Cammell Laird & Co., Ltd.* [1951] 1 Lloyd's Rep 271, the plaintiff crane operator suffered nervous shock when a negligently inspected cable on the crane he was operating snapped, dropping his load where he thought his fellow workers were standing. (His view was obstructed. As it turns out, nobody was hurt below). Nobody has any difficulty understanding his reaction, and the ways in which it exceeded the reaction we would expect from someone who witnessed the accident. The plaintiff was implicated in the accident, even though he was under no duty to inspect the cable.

The transparency and familiarity of this conception of responsibility goes some way to explaining the law's periodic attraction to the idea of directness in addressing questions of remoteness. Directness forms part of a familiar and important conception of agency and responsibility. That conception is in tension with the law's primary interest in guiding conduct. In so far as directness matters to responsibility, it matters independently of any concerns about duties, and cannot be reconciled with an approach that makes them central. Where injury is direct, but not of a kind against which defendant could be asked to take precautions, plaintiff cannot complain that defendant should not be allowed to do that to him, because there is no candidate for a norm that plaintiff might invoke.

description to apply in assessing whether defendant had control in the appropriate sense. Do we apply the description defendant actually had in mind, if any? Or do we choose some other description, perhaps based upon norms that ought to have governed defendant's conduct? The latter course is the one the law has elected to follow. But that is because it accepts a duty conception of responsibility, rather than the independent constraint model. That is, it subordinates questions of responsibility to questions of entitlement.

These criticisms of the independent constraint model are not meant to be conclusive, but rather to set the stage for an alternative account. On what I will call the 'duty account' foreseeability is required for liability in negligence because the norms of negligence law enjoin people to avoid certain consequences. Such norms can only apply to conduct they can govern. That is, they can only proscribe such conduct as they can guide. So a norm cannot say 'do not do x' unless the person to whom it applies has some way of bringing his or her conduct into conformity with the norm. If he or she is to do so, there must be some way of telling whether or not one is doing x, or making x more likely. Where x is unforeseeable, the prospect of it cannot serve to guide conduct, because, being unforeseeable, nothing in particular counts as avoiding it. Because no norms can apply to such injuries, those who suffer them cannot complain of inappropriate treatment by the defendant. The duty account lies at the heart of Cardozo's opinion in the *Palsgraf* case. As Cardozo puts it, 'A different conclusion will involve us, and swiftly, too, in a maze of contradictions. . . . Life will have to be made over, and human nature transformed, before prevision so extravagant can be accepted as the norm of conduct, the customary standard to which behaviour must conform.'[13] The contradiction Cardozo speaks of does not concern the central holding in the case, which is that liability requires the breach of a duty owed to plaintiff. It may be unjust, but it is not contradictory to impose liability without the breach of a duty. What *would* be contradictory is the imposition of a duty to avoid unforeseeable consequences. The plaintiff's case fails because defendant violated no norm of conduct, not because no norm happened to regulate such conduct, but because no norm *could* regulate the consequence in question. The law could not ask defendant to avoid that sort of conduct, because there was no course of action defendant could have adopted that would count as avoiding it. So nobody could owe anyone else a duty with respect to that consequence. As a result, plaintiff cannot complain that defendant isn't allowed to injure her in that way, because defendant's conduct could not be prohibited. In order for a norm to govern conduct, there must be something that counts as satisfying that norm. The point of the foreseeability requirement, then, is not that an unforeseeable consequence fails to be connected to the defendant's agency in the right way. This may or may not be true; certainly a person can feel implicated in an injury he could have done nothing to avoid.

---

[13] *Palsgraf v Long Island Railroad* 169 NE 99 (NY CA 1928).

The duty account thus offers an independent explanation of the importance of foreseeability. Taken together with the idea that the specific norms of negligence law serve to protect people equally from each other, it also allows us to understand the two features that the independent constraint account was unable to accommodate. First, it explains why the relevant capacity for foresight is that of the reasonable person, rather than that of the particular defendant. It also explains the two exceptions to this rule, namely children and persons with physical disabilities. Secondly, it explains why injuries are categorized by their type rather than their extent.

Unforeseeable injuries set an outer boundary for a norm-based conception of responsibility, because where an injury is unforeseeable, the possibility of that type of injury cannot provide a potential injurer with any reason to take precautions, because avoiding it cannot provide anyone with a reason to do anything. As a result, such injuries will always be deemed too remote for the injured person to recover. Sometimes precautions are impossible because a risk is pervasive, so that nothing in particular counts as taking precautions against it. For example, if one ship carelessly damages another, the owner of the first is liable for both the damage and any profits lost because of the time required for repairs, but not for any further damage that is sustained because, as a result of those delays, the ship encounters a storm it would otherwise have missed. The risk of storms is faced by those who travel by ship, and no course of action was open to the defendant which would change the likelihood of plaintiff being caught in a storm.[14] Although there is one sense of the word 'foreseeable' in which the subsequent storm could be foreseen—that is, it is not a possibility one could rule out—that is not the sense that is of concern here. Instead, a type of injury is foreseeable only if it could provide a reason for pursuing one course of action rather than another. In this latter sense, the storm is not foreseeable, because the initial injury is just as likely to enable the ship to avoid a storm as it is to expose it to one. At other times an injury depends on a 'freakish' concatenation of events, or a risk that depends on a combination of events which is not freakish, but has never been encountered before. In each class of cases, the possibility of the injury could have provided no guidance to the injurer. Plaintiff cannot complain that defendant should have taken account of the hazard, because in each case, thinking of it in advance could not have made any difference to the injurer's conduct. As a result, the injurer is not responsible for plaintiff's loss.[15]

---

[14] For the same reason, defendant is not entitled to offset damages owed even if he could show conclusively that plaintiff would have encountered a more severe storm if not for defendant's negligence.

[15] The concept of foreseeability functions slightly differently in addressing some 'duty' questions. Ordinarily, if an injury was unforeseeable, there could not have been a duty, and so there could not have been a breach of that duty. In some cases, questions arise whether a specific class of persons owes a duty to some other class of persons, over and above the duties that all persons owe to each other. For example, in *Tarasoff v Regents of the University of California* 551 P. 2d 334 (1976), the question arose whether a therapist has a duty to warn people who might be attacked by her patients. Foreseeability is among the factors to be considered in deciding whether such a duty is owed, because unless such attacks are foreseeable—that is, unless therapeutic assessments are reliable, psychiatrists cannot be required to act on

Where a peril can be anticipated in advance, it can provide the basis for a norm of conduct, even where its likelihood is small. The chance that a rescuer will intervene to save someone who is endangered provides a reason to take precautions, even where other factors would make the precautions unnecessary. If the primary victim of negligence does not have a cause of action against a tortfeasor, perhaps because the rescuer's intervention prevented it, a third party who was injured while attempting a rescue can still recover, because the danger to potential rescuers provides an independent reason to take precautions. Where someone has assumed the risk of injury, the danger to third parties who may seek to save him can be considered. Although private law enforces no affirmative duty to aid others, it is not up to the defendant to create a dangerous situation and insist that anyone aiding those in the peril he has created do so at their own risk.[16]

I suggested that the concept of foreseeability plays a central role in addressing questions of remoteness. I did not mean to suggest that all such questions can be resolved by appeal to it. Where consequences of a single type extend continuously, there may be some point at which a 'line must be drawn'. The duty conception explains why such line-drawing exercises do not arise in every case: plaintiff's entitlement to be free of defendant's in affliction of a particular type of injury in a particular way is prerequisite to liability.

In other cases, however, injuries are alike in type, but different plaintiffs are injured by a single deed which is a wrong against the first plaintiff. The classic example of this is fire. Here some courts have developed tests for limiting the scope of liability, despite the fact that both the type of injury—burning—and the class of plaintiffs—those within the range of the fire's spread—are foreseeable. In *Ryan v N.Y. Central Railway*, the court drew a bright line—defendant is only liable for the first building that burns. The same court modified the rule in *Rome* to include the first neighbouring property that burned. The first rule seems silly; if a fire consumes several buildings belonging to defendant before spreading to plaintiff's property, plaintiff is out of luck. But the second acknowledges that defendant owes his neighbours a duty to contain fire on his land. Why draw the line at the first neighbour?

In one sense, the line is arbitrary, and any way of drawing it must depend on something other than the equal rights of the parties. The *Ryan* court remarks on the availability of first-party property insurance in explaining its decision, but those

them. Although whether the injury was foreseeable enters into answering a question of law, it still is ultimately a factual inquiry which serves as a constraint in the same way in these cases: whatever other considerations go into determining whether one class of person owes a duty to another class of persons, no person can have a duty to look out for injuries that they cannot look out for.

[16] *Harrison v British Railways Board* [1981] 3 All E.R. 679. Rescuers of property are not normally protected in the same way. But in some cases they clearly would be, despite the fact that there is no duty to protect one's own property. I can demolish my house, even if others enjoy its shade. But I must do so in a way such that others will not reasonably believe that they should intervene. If I set fire to it in the night, my act is negligent because of the risk that someone might believe that there are people trapped inside, and so run the risk of injury.

comments do not distinguish the first building burned from any other; the same point might provide the basis for eliminating all liability for property damage. The fact that someone is able to insure against a wrong by another does not relieve the wrongdoer of responsibility; the real question in *Ryan* concerns who is wronged by a negligently caused fire. On that issue, the court gets closer to the point, suggesting that the spread of fire is always in some sense the result of negligence. While this way of putting it perhaps overstates the matter, there is a key insight underlying it, namely that the risk of fire spreading is one of the 'background' risks that we all face, just as the risk of crime is a background risk we all must face (*vis-à-vis* public authorities). So some line must be drawn between the risk I impose through my action and the risk that others already bear. The *Rome* court characterized as too remote those consequences which depend upon a concurrence of accidental and varying circumstances, over which the negligent party has no control. To fail to protect anyone from a neighbouring fire is unacceptable; to protect everyone from a neighbouring fire is not even a candidate for a norm of conduct.

In some respects, the example of the spread of fire is distinctive because the question of remoteness is purely quantitative. Any place where the line might be drawn will be numerically distinguishable, but qualitatively indistinguishable from the next possible place where it might be drawn. At some point, whether and how the fire spreads depends in part on the condition of the property of the intermediate property owners, against which the person who caused the fire can normally take no further precautions. Plaintiff cannot complain that she would have taken greater precautions; if a fire spreads through enough intervening properties, plaintiff's complaint could only be that she should not be left with the cost of a fire that is not her fault. Yet she already faced that risk; were she to say she would have conducted herself differently had she known, the question naturally arises as to how she would have conducted herself, given that the particular defendant's starting a fire that would endanger her was one of an enormous number of potential sources of the very same risk, not all of which she had even potential indemnity against.

The indeterminacy, if we are to call it that, which arises because there is no principled way of drawing the line at some particular number of injuries, is a familiar but untroubling feature of many line-drawing exercises in the law. To determine whether goods, such as a shipment of wheat, have been received 'in good condition' a court faces a similar problem.[17] One bad grain is not a problem, and there is no specific number of grains that marks a clear cut-off between good and bad condition. As a result, the court must draw an arbitrary line. None the less, neither of the parties can complain of injustice, because neither can complain that that precise number was not what he had agreed to.

---

[17] See the excellent discussion of this type of example in Timothy Endicott, "Objectivity, Subjectivity, and Incomplete Agreements', *Oxford Essays in Jurisprudence*, 4th ser., ed. Jeremy Horder (Oxford: Oxford University Press, 2000).

The Objective Standard

The standard of care in negligence—how careful one has to be in relation to the risk of injury—is objective. That is, it does not depend upon the abilities of the particular defendant. All are expected to rise to a common standard of foresight, even those who have limited abilities. This objectivity follows directly from the law's aim to protect people equally from each other. If all are entitled to equal liberty and equal security, then neither plaintiffs with special susceptibilities nor defendants with limited abilities can ask for special accommodations from others. The person with unusual susceptibilities cannot impose extra duties on others, because to impose such duties would violate the requirement of reciprocity; one person would be able to bind others more than they were able to bind him. For symmetrical reasons, the person who has difficulty coming up to the standard of conduct he owes to others cannot demand that others simply accept their injuries. To make one person's good faith efforts at safety the measure of another's security would be to allow that person to set the terms of interaction unilaterally. Instead, all are held to a common standard. That has been the law at least since *Vaughan v Menlove*.[18] As a result, whether a norm applies on a particular occasion need not depend on whether the person could have done otherwise.[19] The norm applies if it is part of a system of norms that is justified.

The sense in which a person can be answerable for failing to do his duty even though he did his best is familiar in other contexts. Suppose, for example, that I owe you a bicycle, or $100, perhaps because you have performed your part of a contract and I must now perform mine, or because I have borrowed, or found, your bicycle or money and must return it. The difficulty I face in giving it to you may be relevant to what you make of my failure to deliver it in a timely fashion. But such difficulties as I face do not serve to cancel my duty to you. I continue to owe you the bicycle or the money, even if my failure to return either is perfectly understandable. Tort duties are similar, in that they are owed to particular persons, and are not discharged merely by good faith efforts to discharge them. My duty to return your bicycle or money may have been voluntarily undertaken in ways that the duties imposed by tort law are not. Then again, I may have undertaken it without having foreseen the difficulties I now face. None the less, I still owe you the bicycle or the money; I do not get to keep either just because I failed to foresee how circumstances might change. Moreover, how I came to have the duty and whether I am responsible for my failure to satisfy it are separate issues. However I come to have the duty, I am answerable for my failure to comply with it.

---

[18] (1837) 132 ER 490 (CP).

[19] Nor does it depend, as another strand in the free will literature would suggest, on whether the act in question expressed the agent's own reasons. The duty not to injure others applies to the person who does not identify with or endorse the reasons or desires he is acting on.

Despite its clear connection to a norm of reciprocity, the objective standard of care has remained a source of puzzlement and controversy, in a way that the law's indifference to the plight of people with unusual sensitivities has not. The line of thought goes something like this: if a defendant is not liable for an unforeseeable injury because the prospect of it could not guide anyone's conduct, how can he be answerable for injuries the prospect of which could not have guided *his* conduct in particular? The puzzle is deepened, I think, by the fact that certain defendants, notably children and those with physical disabilities, are held to a lower standard. Holmes famously remarked[20] that the slips of the hasty and awkward person are 'no less troublesome to his neighbours than if they sprang from guilty neglect'. Yet the same could be said of the slips of children and persons with disabilities. Why the difference?

The beginning of an answer can be found by remembering that tort law specifies norms of conduct. Standard treatments of negligence distinguish between duty of care and standard of care, reserving the former for questions of whether the plaintiff is in the class of persons for whose interests one must look out, and the latter the question of whether defendant was sufficiently careful of those interests. But both issues turn on norms of conduct. The 'duty' question turns on whether defendant should have foreseen the possibility of injury to plaintiff. The 'standard' question sharpens that inquiry further, by asking whether defendant should have taken a particular precaution, and answers that question by asking whether the peril to the plaintiff was sufficient to justify taking it. Both questions are objective in the sense that both depend on the degree of care people are entitled to expect from each other. The duty account explains this double objectivity—people are entitled to have others look out for security, and to have them take the necessary steps to protect it.

Consider first the situation of the person of ordinary capacities who fails to foresee a foreseeable injury. Suppose further that he was doing as well as he could in the circumstances. The injured plaintiff can complain that 'he's not allowed to do that to me.' He can also say 'you should have thought of that'. It isn't open to defendant to argue that no norm applied to him because he was trying his best. He cannot so argue because the question of whether or not a norm applies doesn't depend on defendant alone. His efforts may well be relevant to what we make of his failure—the person who fails because indifferent is in important respects worse than the person who fails because clumsy, tired, or confused. But his failure is still a failure in a duty he owed to plaintiff.

When someone fails to take precautions against foreseeable injuries, the injured plaintiff can say 'you should have thought of that'. The person whose attention is diverted is no different than any other person who is negligent—he has failed to accord to others the weight to which their interests are entitled. The person who was too tired to notice the risk, or too unfamiliar with the tools he was using, fails his neighbours, and they can rightly complain that he ought to have been more careful.

---

[20]   *The Common Law* (Boston: Little Brown, 1881), 79.

Again, the person who, like the defendant in *Vaughan v Menlove*, tried his best to avert a risk is best described as mistaken about the consequences of his deeds. Although his mistake may be honest, it is still his mistake.

The real puzzle for the objective standard is the person whose attention is somehow *always* diverted—he either cannot foresee that others might be injured by his conduct, or can foresee it but somehow cannot be guided by that realization. This brings me to the first exception to the objective standard. Very young children certainly fall into the category of persons whose attention is almost always diverted, not in the sense that they can never pay attention to anything, but in the sense that they can easily be distracted from the things to which they should attend. Not surprisingly, they are exempt from liability because they are exempt from any duties to take care. Courts often point to the ways in which children are either impulsive or prone to complete absorption in whatever they are doing. Part of the difficulty is a lack of foresight, which prevents children from appreciating the dangers they pose. Because they cannot foresee certain perils, any duty to take account of them cannot apply to them. Another part is the lack of what courts sometimes call 'prudence', the ability to attach appropriate weight to factors that they are, in some sense, able to grasp. Slightly older children may have no difficulty understanding why, for example, they should not run with scissors—someone might lose an eye. Their difficulty comes in acting on that realization—while excited, they systematically fail to attach appropriate weight to the peril.[21] As children mature, they are held to higher standards, both because they are capable of foreseeing a broader range of risks and because they are capable of conforming their behaviour to a broader range of duties. The ability of children at a particular stage of development to act on particular duties is at bottom a question of fact rather than norm: is it realistic to expect a child at this level of development to conform his or her behaviour to this particular requirement? Like so many factual questions, it is bound to be controversial, and there is a danger that prejudices and stereotypes will shape the answer it receives in any particular case. Such controversy is unfortunate, but probably unavoidable, in addressing questions concerning the limit of the law's ability to direct conduct.

Such a description of the limited capacities of children may seem to restate rather than resolve the puzzle. Why is the person whose capacities for foresight and prudence are no better than those of a child held to the standard of a reasonable adult of ordinary prudence? Such a person, we might imagine, could be treated as having only reached an arrested stage of development. Yet the law is resolute in its refusal to hold such a person to a lower standard.

---

[21] Some of the leading cases on child defendants, such as *McHale v Watson* (1966) 115 CLR 199 (Aust. HC) seem to me to draw the right line, but in the wrong place. In particular, they take it for granted that boys are more easily allured by risks than girls. The 12-year-old defendant in *McHale* responded to what Kitto, J. called 'the natural affinity between a spike and a piece of wood' and so overlooked the danger his spike posed to the plaintiff. I do not mean to defend such stereotypes. But I do think my account explains why, if they are accepted, they lead to the results they do in ways that are not at odds with the law's underlying structure.

But the puzzle rests on a misunderstanding of the way in which the capacities characteristic of a particular developmental stage are relevant to the standard to which a child is held. The law of negligence does not hold children to a lower standard than adults only because their capacities are limited. Instead, the law must hold them to a lower standard in order to avoid results at odds with its core commitments; once the standard is lowered, it must be graduated on the basis of the capacities characteristic of a child of that developmental stage. A newborn infant or toddler is entirely beyond the law's reach in all respects. No standard of conduct could be guiding its actions. A fully grown adult is presumed to be able to bring his or her behaviour into conformity with the law's requirements. Between these two extremes, there is no sharp dividing line. Instead, once we have the extremes in view, we have no choice but to treat stages intermediate between them as lying along a continuum. Since that is a continuum of ability to conform to the law, various places along that continuum are treated as various degrees to which one can bring one's conduct into conformity with the law. As a result, in dealing with children, the degree of foresight and prudence to be expected of a child at that developmental stage is relevant to any assessment of a particular child's ability to bring his or her conduct into conformity with the law's requirements. The adult who never developed powers of foresight and prudence beyond those characteristic of an adolescent is not held to a lower standard, because no question arises of where to place such a person on that continuum between infants and adults. Such a continuum presupposes the idea that all adults, including this one, belong at one end of that continuum. So we reach the conclusion that capacities are relevant in the case of children not because capacities are always relevant to the duties one person owes another, but because children are an intermediate case between infants who can owe no duties, and adults who owe each other reciprocal duties.

Now consider the second category of people who are exempt from liability, namely those with physical disabilities. Here too, the primary exemption is not from liability, but from duties to avoid injuring others in particular ways, and the reason is the same: certain physical incapacities make it impossible for a person to conform to particular norms. It makes no sense to say 'you should have thought of that earlier' to a person whose physical disability prevents her from doing what the law requires, because thinking of it would not have made a difference to her conduct. Like the person who is physically restrained, the person who is physically disabled is beyond the reach of any norms of conduct. To say to the blind person that she should have seen the danger, is not just insulting, though it is certainly that. It is also pointless, because the advice in question could not have made a difference to her conduct. There are exceptions. If a blind person operates a motor vehicle, it does make sense so say that she should have thought of the peril earlier, because there is a particular thing she should have considered at a particular time, namely, the need for vision in order to avoid endangering others while operating a motor vehicle.

People with specific disabilities are thus exempt from liability because they are exempted from specific duties, the appreciation of which cannot direct their behaviour. Adults with limited intelligence or self-control are not so exempt because the law only takes account of the very specific incapacities characteristic of disabilities. The only place a general incapacity is relevant is in the case of children, for whom special treatment is appropriate precisely because adults are held to a common standard. The clumsy person can be told that she should have been more careful on a particular occasion, even if, being clumsy, she has difficulty being more careful in general. And the rash person can be told that he should have thought before acting on a particular occasion, even though he has difficulty resisting his impulses. Supposing that the clumsy person can sometimes take precautions, advice to take particular precautions is always to the point, even if there will be occasions on which he is unable to take them. And it is always to the point to tell the rash person to be more careful. For competent adults, the ability to conduct an activity safely does not usually require self-consciously thinking about safety. Instead, competent drivers drive safely, and are able to recognize circumstances in which extra attention is required. More generally, competent adults conduct themselves safely, that is, they take appropriate precautions when engaged in familiar activities, and are able to recognize when unfamiliar activities require special attention. That is a general ability, which the law supposes that all adults are entitled to expect of each other. The person who is hasty or awkward is expected to recognize his or her own limitations. As a result, the law supposes that, in the case of an adult, there is no difference between defendant's inability to be guided and his simply having failed to be guided on a particular occasion. Because the advice is not pointless in the way that the imagined advice to the blind person was, norms can require the clumsy person to be careful, or the rash person to think before acting.

Recall again the structure of a tort action: an aggrieved plaintiff comes before a court seeking recourse against a defendant who (she alleges) has wronged her. The plaintiff's complaint takes the form: defendant is not allowed to do that to me. As we've seen, where the plaintiff was unforeseeable, or the injury too remote, defendant can reply that no norm of conduct could prohibit his action. The examples of persons with physical disabilities show that a norm of conduct can also fail to apply to a particular person because consideration of it could not have made a difference to what that person would have done. The blind person, or the person who cannot reach a switch provide examples, as does the person who has a first and unexpected epileptic seizure. Nothing could direct him to behave differently than he did.

The child or disabled person is no less of a bother to his neighbours than is the awkward or hasty adult. But given his limited capacity to conform his behaviour to the law, he is not subject to all of its norms. As a result, the plaintiff's complaint—that defendant is not allowed to do that—fails because no binding norm prohibits it.

Cases in which an adult defendant's lack of foresight or prudence prevent him attaching appropriate weight to dangers to others are different. In those cases, the law supposes that defendant would have been guided if he had thought through the likely consequences of his deeds, or attached appropriate weight to the interests of others.

Of course, he wasn't so guided, either because he did not consider the risk, or because he didn't attach sufficient importance to it. But that much is true of the person who is inattentive, tired, or indifferent. In such cases, the law did not make a difference on the particular occasion. But its inability to make a difference on that occasion is the same regardless of why foresight or prudence are limited on that occasion. The law can only impose duties that could guide conduct, assuming that those guided by them take appropriate precautions and have appropriate concern. But it does not condition liability on whether someone was in fact so guided. To so condition it would hold one person's security hostage to another person's efforts, and so fail to protect them equally from each other.

To sum up, the law recognizes no difference between the failure to foresee a particular consequence and the inability to foresee it on that occasion, and no difference between the failure to be guided by the prospect of injury one has foreseen and the inability to be so guided on that occasion. If someone were never able to foresee a certain type of injury, they would be treated differently, as people with perceptual disabilities are treated. And if someone were never able to be guided by the prospect of injury, they would be treated differently, as young children and the mentally ill are treated.

It is worth emphasizing that this way of understanding the exceptions to the objective standard do not rest on any idea of the law offering special accommodation to those in difficult circumstances. To be accommodating in this way would violate the basic principle of reciprocity, because it would put the costs of accommodation on the security of others. On grounds of symmetry, such accommodation would also require that special account be taken of the unusual sensitivities of plaintiffs. The rationale for the exceptions lies instead in the fact that the norms of conduct in question cannot be enforced. Of course, they can be enforced in the sense that those who violate them can be made to pay. But they cannot be enforced in the sense that coercion can be used to guarantee or even encourage compliance with them. In this respect, the exceptions occupy a position analogous to the criminal law's defence of duress, at least on one understanding of that defence. The person who commits a crime in the attempt to save his own life lies beyond the criminal law's ability to shape his conduct, since as Kant observes, the prospect of future punishment will never be as vivid in his mind as the prospect of immediate death. You can lock such a person up, or hang him, but doing so will fail as a punishment.

In the same way, a child can be fully aware of the danger posed by running with scissors, yet unable to resist temptation when excited. Indeed, that is why children can be allured, and so are not contributorily negligent in circumstances in which an adult would be: a child who can appreciate the danger of fire or swimming pools can be overcome by his curiosity.[22] As a result, the norm cannot direct his conduct.[23] In

[22] See e.g. *Hughes v. Lord Advocate* [1963] AC 837 (HL).
[23] Are these claims about children true? My purpose in mentioning them is not to defend them, but to show how they operate in carving out the exception. If boys are more easily tempted than girls, that too is relevant to whether they can bring their behaviour into conformity with the law.

cases in which consideration of a norm cannot change the way people behave, the law is incapable of demanding compliance with it. The most it could do is impose liability even though no norms governed defendant's conduct. That it does not do so reflects the subordination of questions of liability to questions about norms of conduct.

Confusion about the pointlessness of liability in such cases is easy, since any case in which it is pointless to hold someone responsible is also unfair. But the converse does not follow. The difference between these two claims brings the difference between norms of conduct and liability rules into sharper focus. It would not be pointless to make children and people with physical disabilities liable for the harm they cause, that is, to treat them as the insurers of those who others could foresee they might injure, just as it would not be pointless, from the point of view of deterrence, to punish people acting in conditions of necessity. But any such punishment would fail to address the wrong.

TYPE AND EXTENT OF INJURY

I now turn to the law's distinction between type and extent of injury. Norms of conduct direct people to look out for dangers their conduct poses for others. As we've seen, they can only direct people to look out for types of injury that are foreseeable. If injury is a foreseeable consequence of some action, steps must be taken to make it safer by making it less likely to cause injuries of that type.

I should emphasize that preventing injuries based on their type is not the only possible norm of conduct. That is, the duty account requires that liability in negligence be limited to foreseeable injuries, but it does not, on its own, require the distinction between type and extent of damage. There are other possible norms of conduct that could serve to guide action, but are rejected by the law of negligence because they fail to satisfy our other criterion, that of objectivity, which, as we saw, requires that the relevant norms protect people equally from each other.

One particular candidate for a norm of conduct would have us look not to the types of interests that are at stake, but rather to their extent on a particular occasion. In particular, one could factor in both the expected costs of safety precautions on a particular occasion, and the probable extent of injury if those precautions are not taken, in deciding whether precautions are merited in a particular case. This is not just a hypothetical example offered by way of contrast, but a serious proposal in torts scholarship. Some proponents of economic approaches to negligence law, most prominently Richard Posner, suggest that questions of liability in negligence are, and should be, answered in just those terms.[24]

The intuitive idea is familiar from decisions that people make about their own safety. Despite the high priority we attach to safety, any investment in safety requires forgoing other things that are themselves valuable. As a result, there are limits on how much it makes sense to spend. Those limits are arguably a function of three things: the cost or inconvenience of the precaution, the type or seriousness of damage I am seeking to avoid, and the likelihood of that damage occurring. Suppose I am deciding whether or not to purchase a new ladder for changing light bulbs. Whether or not the expenditure makes sense depends on the cost of the ladder, the harm it would help me to avoid, and the likelihood of that harm ensuing. Consider two scenarios. Perhaps the only alternative to the ladder is for me to stand on tiptoes on the top edge of an old and unstable ladder. The extra expenditure makes sense because of the likelihood and the seriousness of the harm that might result—a broken arm or back if I fall. But if I am unusually agile, perhaps the injury is unlikely, and so the expenditure is unnecessary. Alternatively, perhaps the old ladder is just as stable as the new one, but the new one has a special hole for holding light bulbs, so that I am less likely to drop one if I get the new ladder. Since light bulbs are inexpensive, it does not make sense for me to get the new ladder, because the expected cost it is supposed to avoid is lower than the cost of the precaution. Put in Hand's own terms

[T]he . . . duty to provide against resulting injuries is a function of three variables: (1) the probability . . . (2) the gravity of resulting injuries . . . (3) the burden of adequate precautions. Possibly it serves to bring this notion into relief to state it in algebraic terms: if the probability is called P; the injury L: and the burden of precautions B; liability depends on whether B is less than L multiplied by P: i.e. whether $B < PL$.[25]

As a way of looking out for one's own safety, the Hand test captures an important idea: prudent people will neither overinvest nor underinvest in safety. Instead, they should take such precautions as are appropriate, in light of the importance to them, avoiding injury and avoiding the expense and inconvenience of precautions. In so far as those factors can be monetized, it makes sense to do so, because the extent of precaution that is appropriate is a linear function of the three factors.

But the Hand test is meant to capture more than that, for it is also supposed to show how careful one person should be with the safety of *another*. The reasoning is the same: what it is reasonable for me to do is what it is rational for me to do, and it is only rational for me to take such precautions as are justified by the balance of benefits over costs. Here its apparent advantages turn out to be illusory. The fact that some sort of cost-benefit analysis is appropriate in deciding what measures to take to promote one's own safety does not, on its own, show that it is appropriate in deciding

[24] Posner first made this point in 'A Theory of Negligence', *Journal of Legal Studies*, 1 (1972), 29, and has defended it, both as a positive and normative account of the law in various places since.

[25] *United States v Carroll Towing Co.* 159 F. 2d 169, 173 (2d Cir. 1947).

what measures are appropriate for another's safety. The point here is analytical as well as normative: in order to understand what tort law is trying to do, we must look to its broad structural features, and explain those features, rather than dismissing them whenever they fail to match one's preferred theory, be it normative or explanatory. The Hand test misses out on important structural features of negligence liability; moreover, it does so because it is at odds with the core idea that one party may not set the terms of interaction unilaterally.

We have already encountered one example of negligence law's objectivity, in its refusal to consider a particular defendant's abilities to comply with a norm. The law's refusal to take account of the special needs of ultrasensitive plaintiffs provides another example. In each of those cases, one party's liberty or security is entirely hostage to idiosyncratic features of the other. The Hand test might be thought to provide an alternative approach, since the equation 'B < PL' takes account of the interests of both plaintiff and defendant. But although it takes account of both, it does so in a way that treats both as idiosyncratic, and so cannot explain important features of tort doctrine.

First consider the situation of a potential defendant deciding how much care to take in order to avoid an injury of a certain probability and magnitude. Whether or not an extra investment in care is justified depends on the cost (Hand's 'B'). But the size of B will in turn depend on its opportunity cost: the advantage defendant will have to forgo in order to make the extra investment in safety. Thinking of precautions in terms of opportunity cost is necessary to avoid overinvestment in safety. To return to the example of the ladder, if I will need to store it somewhere and thus leave myself with insufficient room to store something else of value, that needs to be factored into my decision. Again, if I am transporting something valuable but perishable—perhaps I need to get sushi-quality tuna to the airport before today's flight leaves, or else it will be worthless—it makes sense for me to be less careful with the safety of my other property than if I am transporting something that will retain its value, and the only cost of delay is the time I lose.

The Hand test transplants this sort of reasoning to the case in which someone else's safety is at stake. So if I am transporting something expensive and perishable, it makes sense to take more risks with the safety of others than if I am transporting something less valuable. That is, the burden of precautions (Hand's 'B') depends on what else is at stake for me. I set the terms of interaction unilaterally in so far as the security of others is hostage to the amount I stand to gain by forgoing precautions.[26]

[26] Strictly speaking, if the Hand test is to be economically efficient, it also requires defendants to take account of the perils to them that result from failing to take precautions. In our sushi example, the risk of losing the cargo in a road accident needs to be factored into calculating Hand's 'L'. In a recent article Robert Cooter and Ariel Porat have emphasized this dimension of the Hand test. See Cooter and Porat, 'Does Risk to Oneself Increase the Care Owed to Others? Law and Economics in Conflict', *Journal of Legal Studies*, 24 (2000), 19. Cooter and Porat argue that considerations of self-injury would make the test more defensible; in my view it makes the concern about unilateral setting of terms of interaction more, rather than less, serious.

Now consider the situation of the plaintiff. In deciding how much care is required, defendant needs to weigh against potential avoidance costs to him the costs the injury is likely to impose on plaintiff. We've already seen that this means that he must consider the particular costs he will face. He must also consider the particular costs that will be faced by the plaintiff. Whether particular precautions are justified by their costs depends on who is likely to be injured, because some people are more expensive to injure than others. Among the standard heads of damages are loss of income. So the defendant must consider the likely income of those who might be injured by his action. Should the class of potential plaintiffs be high income earners, then, other things being equal, Hand's 'L' will be larger, and defendant must take additional precautions. Should they be low income earners, the result is different. To take an example, someone driving through a retirement community would, other things being equal, need to exercise less by way of precautions than someone driving through an area where the people who might be injured were young or gainfully employed. Perhaps residents of retirement communities are less able to avoid injuries because of their decreased mobility. But if so, that comes under Hand's 'P' rather than 'L', and so does not change the fact that, other things being equal, those who can be injured inexpensively are entitled to less by way of precautions. Driving examples make the point vividly, but other examples are no more difficult to construct. Less care is required in the discharging of toxic wastes near poor neighbourhoods than near rich ones. Press reports suggest, depressingly, that less care is likely to be exercised when poor people are likely to be injured than wealthy ones. The Hand test suggests, surprisingly, that they are *entitled* to less care. Thus on the Hand test potential plaintiffs, as well as potential defendants, are able to set the standard of care to which they are entitled unilaterally.

If both parties can set the terms of interaction unilaterally, why doesn't this count as a version of reciprocity on the grounds that two unilateral acts cancel each other out, so to speak? The difficulty is that the degree of care to which each person is entitled is a function of the assets and priorities of the particular people with whom they happen to be interacting. It might be thought that a person would just as soon have the degree of care to which he is entitled depend on the features of those with whom he is interacting as to have it depend on the protected interests of a hypothetical reasonable person. But the law does not give people whatever level of care they would most wish for. Instead, it seeks to protect them equally from each other. To do so requires that my interest in bodily security, or security of property, counts the same as yours, regardless of their relative economic value.

The law does not use the Hand standard to assess liability.[27] Rather, the three factors that Hand mentions are all relevant to setting the standard of care. But all are set

---

[27] Even Hand arguably meant something quite different; in the pair of cases in which he offered the test, his concern was with the degree of care that parties could be expected to take with their own safety. In one of those cases, *Conway v O'Brien,* 111 F. 2d 611 (2d Cir. 1940) he notes that the factors do not admit of quantitative assessment 'even theoretically'.

in terms of the representative reasonable person—that is, the importance of particular interests in both liberty and security. Those interests matter, because all people have an interest in being able to pursue their ends free from the interference of others, and all have an interest in security in their persons and property. Protecting those interests does not lead to an efficient level of safety—protected interests can be important enough to justify precautions that exceed their dollar value in a particular case.[28]

Even if the law does not use the Hand test, some might suppose that this is a failure that should be remedied.[29] Although I said at the outset that my aim was to articulate the organizing principles of tort law rather than to defend them, I will permit myself a few words of defence here: the idea of reciprocity at work in tort law captures an important understanding of fairness, one that both requires that people interact on fair terms and demands that wrongs be righted when they fail to so interact. My aim in developing and explicating them is, as I said, to explain tort doctrine. But if explaining a practice in terms of normative ideas that are familiar and powerful is not sufficient to justify it, it goes some way towards doing so. In particular, it shows that the practice is not arbitrary, and so that its failures to comport with some competing normative standards—say of economic efficiency—need not be taken to show it to be irrational or immoral.

[28] It might be thought that the Hand test can be reformulated so that it does not incorporate these idiosyncrasies. Rather than looking at the specific defendant's potential gains and actual class of plaintiffs put at risk, we might look instead to the gains and losses that typically follow from the failure to take a particular precaution. The difficulty with such a proposal is that it would undermine the putative rationale of the Hand test, namely economic efficiency. Consider the example in which injurer and victim are the same person in this light. In deciding whether to take a precaution with my own safety, it is rational for me to consider the costs and benefit to me, not whether that precaution would be worthwhile for some other person with different assets and priorities. Again, in deciding whether or not to invest in something for the sake of something other than safety—an automatic espresso maker for convenience, say, or a bottle of champagne to consume—I need to consider the details of my own budget and the benefits I expect, what Wilfredo Pareto called my 'tastes and obstacles'. I choose irrationally if I decide based on what someone else, with tastes and means different from my own, would choose. As a result, a system that required people to exercise care based on the average gains and losses would lead to overinvestment in safety in some cases, and underinvestment in others. There is no reason to think that these over- and underinvestments would average out, any more than there is reason to think that efficient outcomes can be achieved in the economy as a whole by distributing a bundle of goods based on what most people want, rather than allowing people to make their own choices based on their own priorities. Overinvestment amounts to a deadweight loss in terms of efficiency, and underinvestment will, over the long run, lead to injuries greater than it would have cost to prevent them. This sort of composite Hand test does come close to the standard that courts enforce. But it fails the test of efficiency that putatively rationalizes liability.

[29] In recent years, prominent defenders of economic analysis have shifted the focus of their inquiry from explaining tort doctrine to outlining what it should be. See e.g. Louis Kaplow and Steven Shavell, 'Principles of Fairness versus Human Welfare: On the Evaluation of Legal Policy' (http://www.law.harvard.edu/programs/olin_center/). Such a shift in focus is a clear testament to its explanatory failures. The attempt to revive it as a normative enterprise strikes me as a classic case of what economists sometimes call the strategy of 'too much invested to quit'—an attempt to redeem all of the work that has gone into it by using it for some other purpose.

LIBERTY AND SECURITY

Negligence law's requirement of foreseeability and the exceptions to the objective standard of care can both be explained solely in terms of the ability of norms to govern conduct. No norm of conduct could ask people to take account of things of which no account can be taken, and no norm can require a person to do things that she is unable to do. The objectivity of the standard of care, and its focus on type rather than extent of injury, are both explained in terms of the idea of reciprocity. A subjective standard would allow one person to set the terms of interaction unilaterally; a standard that considered competing interests quantitatively would hold each person's liberty and security hostage to the particular wealth and priorities of those with whom they happened to interact.

Other features of negligence law rest on more specific assessments of the importance of particular interests in liberty and security. Standards of conduct could be limited to foreseeable consequences, thereby honouring the requirement that they guide conduct, and imposed uniformly, thus honouring the reciprocity constraint, but would burden either liberty or security too greatly. Examples of standards that are too lax because they place too great a burden on security are easy to think of: everyone could be allowed to engage in a dangerous activity, such as high-speed driving. Provided that all were able to engage in them, allowing such activities would not violate reciprocity, but it would put an important security risk in peril for the sake of a comparatively unimportant liberty interest.

Examples of standards that could apply to all, but which burden liberty too much are also easy to construct: requiring people to drive at 2 m.p.h. would make automobiles much safer, but would place too great a burden on people's ability to come and go as they pleased.

I now want to suggest that other familiar features of tort doctrine can be explained in the same way. Consider the bar to recovery in negligence for pure economic loss. The prospect of economic loss to others provides the basis for a possible norm of conduct: someone towing a barge in fog can take account of the fact that a variety of people rely on the bridge that he might hit; someone leaving a fire unattended can take account of the losses faced by people who depend in various ways on the buildings that might burn down. Moreover, such a norm need not violate the condition of reciprocity, because a norm requiring that each person take account of all possible effects on others could be applied to all equally. But although such a norm is possible, it would be too demanding. That is why the law supposes that the fact that people depend on other people, and on the continued availability of things in various ways, provides no reason to take extra precautions.

If we focus on the plaintiff's complaint about the defendant's conduct, the reason for excluding pure economic loss becomes clear. To bring it into focus, consider an analogy with the duty owed to rescuers. A rescuer is entitled to recover from the person who created the peril, even if the primary victim of that peril is barred from recovery, on some grounds such as assumption of risk or contributory negligence. The rescuer can also recover if he acts pre-emptively, for example, by pushing someone out of the path of an oncoming train, and is injured although the person rescued was not. In these cases, the rescuer recovers because she can complain because the initial injurer drew her into the situation. This is evident where the defendant has put herself in the peril to which the rescuer responds, but it is just as true in other cases as well.

Contrast this with the case of pure economic loss. If my restaurant thrives because of customers from your nearby hotel, I cannot recover my lost profits from you if you close it, or from the arsonist who burns it down. If my factory closes down because your barge destroys the public bridge that provides the only access to the island on which it is located, I cannot recover my losses from you, even though you could have foreseen the harm that befell me, and even though you would have been liable for those losses had I owned the bridge you destroyed. The reason you escape liability is that, although the possibility of my losing something on which I have come to rely could be the basis of a norm of conduct, it would place too great a burden on your liberty to be asked to take account of such things. The possibility of others relying on things going a certain way is so pervasive that to require people to take account of it would narrow the range of freedom to almost nothing. Instead, those who depend on the availability of things they do not own do so at their own risk.[30]

These examples may seem to be an incoherent grouping: destroying a bridge is an unreasonable act with the foreseeable consequences that third parties will be inconvenienced. Closing my hotel, by contrast, has foreseeable consequences, but is not unreasonable. In fact, that is the very issue: the foreseeable impact of one's deeds on others only gives rise to a duty in cases in which persons more generally could owe such a duty to each other. If you do not have a right to the continued presence of my hotel, you have no such right, whether you lose the hotel's presence through my decision to demolish it, through an arsonist's intentional deed, or through someone's carelessness. Nobody has a duty to take account of your use of it, even if they are prohibited on independent grounds from doing the very same deed that deprives you of it. You still cannot say 'he's not allowed to do that *to me*', even if he is not allowed to do that. The law cannot require people to take account of all of the ways in which their actions might affect others. Because it does not require them to take account of those

---

[30] Where someone relies on the continued availability of their spouse, or a family member, they do have a cause of action for wrongful death. In such cases, their rights in relation to that person are what Kant calls 'a right to a person akin to a right to a thing', in the sense that it is a right against the entire world, rather than a contractual right against a particular person. The law can protect certain relationships in that way. Which relationships it so protects depends on substantive views about social life. In Kant's example, and through the nineteenth century in the common law, domestic servants were so regarded.

effects, it also cannot hold them answerable if they bring about those effects, even if they do so through conduct that is prohibited on other grounds.

There are two points here. The first is that although a norm requiring people to take account of all of the foreseeable ways in which one person depends on another provides the basis of a possible norm of conduct, such a norm would be too demanding, because almost anything one does runs the risk of disappointing the expectations of others. If I own a hotel and you own a nearby restaurant that draws customers from among my guests, you have no cause of action against me in tort if I close my hotel or open a competing restaurant. To impose such a duty on me would burden my liberty too greatly. For just the same reason, imposing a duty on third parties to protect your dependence on the availability of my hotel would place too great a burden on their liberty. The damage to the hotel itself provides a basis for a duty owed to me to avoid burning it down. Although a further duty for your benefit would not constrain his conduct any more than it is already constrained in the particular instance, to make your vulnerabilities the basis of a duty would limit his freedom, for what he was allowed to do would always depend on its effects on you.

Again, the important point here is that negligence law subordinates questions of liability to norms of conduct. The person who damages the bridge could be made to pay for the damage he causes to the businesses stranded as a result, but he could not have a duty to see to it that those businesses retain access to the bridge. Such a duty could only be spelled out in ways that are so expansive as to make everyone responsible for the impacts of their conduct on others. To impose liability without the breach of a norm would be at odds with the overall structure of negligence law; to enforce a norm requiring so much would leave people no freedom.

Secondly, it might be thought instead, that the appropriate norm should only prohibit such interferences where the loss was likely to be severe or substantial; it would fail to protect people equally from each other, because it would make the care to which people are entitled depend on the extent, rather than type, of injury that they might suffer. But such a norm would face all of the difficulties we already saw with the Learned Hand test.

The fact that other people depend on the availability of various objects that they do not own, and various persons with whom they have no special legal relationships, cannot provide a reason to limit one's activities because if it did, one's activities would be eliminated. Almost anything anyone might do can run the risk of disappointing the settled expectations of third parties. The problem is that the only non-negligent act would be sitting quietly in one's room. A norm of conduct that says 'do not do anything that will foreseeably deprive others of persons or objects upon which they rely' precludes almost anything anyone might do. Nor can the same purported duty be saved by stating it more narrowly, saying, for example, 'do not damage bridges because people cross them'. To see why, consider another example: suppose that defendant has an independent defence to a negligence action for damaging the bridge—perhaps it is his own bridge,[31] or perhaps the bridge was made vulnerable by its owner's negligence in constructing it, so that exposing it to the risk is the only way in which defendant can safely navigate the river. Or perhaps the bridge suffers no real damage from the collision, but is closed for inspection. Defendant does not owe bridge users a duty of care when he does not owe one to the bridge owner. As a result, he does not owe a duty of care to the bridge users. The situation is thus very different from those situations in which a defendant is answerable for the injuries of rescuers. In such cases, the duty owed is direct.

Commentators sometimes suggest that the reason there is no liability in negligence for pure economic loss is that to allow it would lead to liability out of all proportion to the seriousness of wrongdoing. Courts frequently acknowledge the financial implications of their judgments, but just as frequently refuse to be guided by them. Moreover, as we have seen, the distinction between type and extent of liability means that a small wrong can lead to massive liability if it leads to massive loss. So one needs to be cautious in supposing that such factors are pivotal. Instead, the real difficulty with liability in such cases is that the only possible norm of conduct on which it would depend would either be so demanding as to leave almost nothing outside its reach, or else limited in ways that made norms of conduct depend upon the magnitude of the interests at stake. So the core problem is not one of unlimited liability, but of liability that is not tied to the violation of a defensible norm of conduct.

Conclusion

I said at the outset that my main examples would be drawn from the tort of negligence. I also suggested that negligence provided a clear illustration of the ways in which tort law subordinates questions of liability to questions about norms of conduct, and sought to explain some of the broad structural features of the norms of conduct imposed by the law of negligence. In this closing section, I will, too briefly, gesture in the direction of one other area of tort liability, and explain how the analysis developed here can be extended to it. In particular, I want to suggest that such an analysis can be extended to explain the role of norms of conduct which can be invoked in cases in which liability is strict.

In cases in which liability is strict, such as the use of explosives, or the keeping of wild animals, it might be thought that no norms are at work, since the dangerous activity in question is legal, even though the person engaged in this is liable for the

---

[31] A property owner does not owe a duty to third parties to protect his own property against damage (unless he accepted such a duty via contract). *Moorgate Mercantile v Twitchings* [1977] A.C. 890.

harm it causes. But as our discussion of negligence indicates, carelessness as such is not prohibited. Instead, defendant's duty is to avoid injuring plaintiff in the ways that plaintiff is entitled to be free of. So I may not cause you to break your leg through my carelessness. In the same way, I must not knock down your house through my blasting, or allow my elephant to trample your garden. The ease or difficulty, or indeed, the near impossibility, of my discharging this duty while blasting or keeping wild animals does not undermine your entitlement to be free of those injuries, anymore then your entitlement to be free of negligent injuries depends upon the ease or difficulty I have in driving safely while tired. The law does not prohibit driving while tired; nor does it say 'you are free to do so provided you pay for any harm you cause'. Instead, it says 'don't injure others through careless driving', and empowers those who are injured through the violation of that norm to recover damages because they have been wronged. In just the same way, the law neither prohibits blasting nor conditions its legality on readiness to pay for harm caused. Instead, it says 'don't injure others through your blasting' and empowers those who have been injured through the violation of that norm to recover damages because they have been wronged. The duty to avoid injuring others through blasting provides a genuine guide to conduct, even though it does not tell someone how to blast without liability.

In all such cases—whether liability is conditioned on intention, negligence, or is strict—plaintiff can recover damages just in case she can establish that defendant was not allowed to do that to her. Tort law decides whose problem something is by looking at how people are allowed to treat each other.

CHAPTER 18

PHILOSOPHY OF CONTRACT LAW

JODY S. KRAUS

THE turn of the twenty-first century has marked a renaissance of scholarship exploring the philosophical foundations of the economic analysis of law. This renaissance reflects the increasing efforts within particular disciplines to understand the relationship between philosophical and economic theories of law. These efforts are nowhere more evident than in contemporary contracts scholarship. As in private law scholarship generally, economic analysis is the dominant paradigm in contemporary contracts scholarship. But alongside the vast body of economic contracts scholarship produced over the last thirty years, a core body of philosophical contracts scholarship has steadily developed in relative obscurity. Although these two bodies of scholarship have largely passed each other like ships in the night, they have begun to take occasional notice of one another over the last ten years. Two well-known economic analysts of contract law have undertaken the most extensive efforts to engage the philosophical contracts scholarship. In his recent book, Michael Trebilcock assesses the compatibility of two prominent theoretical approaches found in contemporary contract scholarship.[1] Most philosophical contract theories are grounded on some

I thank Barry Adler, Jules Coleman, John Goldberg, Steve Hetcher, Chris Kutz, Stephen Perry, Bob Rasmussen, Alan Schwartz, Bob Scott, and Scott Shapiro for helpful comments. I also thank participants in workshops held at the University of California at Berkeley's Boalt Hall (GALA seminar), the George Mason University Law School, Vanderbilt University Law School, the University of Virginia Law School, and the Sixth Annual Analytic Legal Philosophy Conference at the University of Chicago Law School.

[1] Michael Trebilcock, *The Limits of Freedom of Contract* (Cambridge, Mass.: Harvard University Press, 1993) (hereinafter *Limits*). I follow Trebilcock in focusing almost exclusively on single-value, or

notion of autonomy. Economic contract theories are grounded on some notion of efficiency. According to the 'convergence thesis', contract law 'simultaneously promotes individual autonomy and advances social welfare'.[2] Therefore, autonomy and welfare theories will converge in their recommendations for the substantive content of contract law, even though their bases for those recommendations may be incompatible.[3] If true, the convergence thesis obviates the need to adjudicate between autonomy and welfare contract theories. Either perspective will yield the same results. Trebilcock carefully assesses and rejects the convergence thesis. If Trebilcock is right, we can no longer believe these two ships are travelling different routes to the same destination. One of them is heading in the wrong direction.

In a highly influential article, Richard Craswell argues that autonomy theories of contract are deficient because they have no implications for the content of contract default rules.[4] As Craswell construes them, the most prominent autonomy theories of contract are at least loosely based on a philosophical analysis of promising. Because Craswell believes that economic theories do address the content of default rules, the implication of his thesis is that most autonomy contract theories are seriously deficient compared to economic theories. Taken together, Trebilcock's and Craswell's theses set an agenda for contemporary contracts scholarship by raising anew the question of the relationship between autonomy and economic theories of contract law. Trebilcock's thesis argues for assessing the relative merits of each approach in order to adjudicate the contest between them.[5] Craswell's thesis constitutes an opening salvo in that contest. His thesis suggests that autonomy contract theories are inferior to economic contract theories in so far as they cannot provide answers to many of the central questions of contract law. A third possibility is that

'monistic', contract theories, and do not consider multiple-value, or 'pluralistic', contract theories. Pluralistic contract theories advert to autonomy, efficiency, morality, social norms, policy, experience, and other values to explain and justify contract doctrines. Trebilcock ultimately endorses this approach, as does Melvin Eisenberg. The challenge for these theories, like the challenge for pluralistic normative theories in general, is to explain how their explanations and justifications can be defended in the absence of a master principle for ordering the competing values they invoke. The theories I consider here purport to provide explanations and justifications derived from the single value of either autonomy or welfare, however defined. They therefore purport to explain and justify contract law by rendering it coherent under a single explanatory/justificatory principle.

[2] ibid. at 22. Trebilcock's principal source for the claim is Milton Friedman's famous statement that '[t]he possibility of coordination through voluntary cooperation rests on the elementary—yet frequently denied—proposition that both parties to an economic transaction benefit from it, *provided the transaction is bilaterally voluntary and informed*'. Milton Friedman, *Capitalism and Freedom* (Chicago: University of Chicago Press, 1962), 13.

[3] In the philosopher's parlance, the convergence holds that autonomy and welfare theories of contract are intentionally incompatible but extensionally equivalent.

[4] Richard Craswell, 'Contract Law, Default Rules, and the Philosophy of Promising', *Michigan Law Review*, 88 (1989), 395 (hereinafter 'Default Rules').

[5] However, Trebilcock claims both deontic and consequentialist theories are 'valid in their own right'. Because he lacks a 'meta-theory that weights and ranks these various values', he argues that both values should be pursued in various social and legal institutions according to those institutions' relative competency. Trebilcock, *Limits*, above n. 1, at 248.

both kinds of theories might be combined to produce an overall theory that takes advantage of the strengths, and avoids the weaknesses, of each kind of theory.[6] But in order to judge the relative strengths and weaknesses of autonomy and economic contract theories, these theories must share the same objectives. To the extent they do not, neither theory is to be preferred over the other. They are, in effect, theories about different things. One theory can be judged superior to another only to the extent both are attempting to answer the same questions and share similar methodological commitments.

In this chapter, I identify a set of methodological commitments that help explain why autonomy theorists (to whom I shall also refer as 'deontic' theorists), and economic theorists (whom I shall also refer to as 'consequentialist' theorists) often find themselves at cross purposes. I examine the theories of Charles Fried and Peter Benson, two of the most extensively developed autonomy theories of contract law.[7] Based on an analysis of these theories, I argue that autonomy theories tend to treat the doctrinal statements as the principal legal data for contract theory to explain and justify, accord primacy to the normative task of contract theory, and require that contract theory explain and justify the conceptual distinctiveness of contract law. In contrast, economic theories tend to treat the outcomes of cases as the principal legal data for contract theory to explain and justify, accord primacy to the explanatory task of contract theory, and aspire to explain away, rather than explain, the conceptual distinctiveness of contract law. I argue that apparently first-order conflicts between autonomy and economic contract theories in fact are implicit, second-order conflicts over legal methodology. As a result of these methodological differences, adjudicating supposed first-order disputes between autonomy and economic contract theories is sometimes tantamount to an 'apples–oranges' comparison: the theories are making different kinds of claims about different things.

Craswell's objection that autonomy theories cannot provide a theory of contract default rules appears to point to an additional difference in the methodological commitments of autonomy and economic contract theories. In Craswell's view, autonomy theories are committed to the *ex post* perspective in adjudication because they

[6] I outline the structure such a theoretical effort might take in Jody S. Kraus, 'Reconciling Autonomy and Efficiency in Contract Law: The Vertical Integration Strategy', *Philosophical Theory*, suppl. to *Nous* (forthcoming 2001); Jody S. Kraus, 'Legal Theory and Contract Law: Groundwork for the Reconciliation of Autonomy and Efficiency', *Journal of Social, Political, and Legal Philosophy* (forthcoming 2002). For attempts to provide a limited Rawlsian justification for choosing efficient rules in particular legal contexts, see also Daniel A. Farber, 'Economic Efficiency and the Ex Ante Perspective', *The Jurisprudence of Corporate and Commercial Law*, ed. Jody S. Kraus and Steven D. Walt (Cambridge [England]; New York: Cambridge University Press, 2000); Alan Schwartz, 'Proposals for Products Liability Reform: A Theoretical Synthesis', *Yale Law Journal*, 97 (1988), 353, 357–67.

[7] Randy Barnett also has a well-developed theory of contract law, but as it has developed it no longer clearly qualifies as a purely deontic theory. I explain Barnett's views and assess the extent to which it evidences the methodological commitments discussed here, in 'Theories of Contract' to appear in E. Zalta (ed.), *The Stanford Encyclopedia of Philosophy* (on-line), ed. L. Murphy and J. Raz, sections on philosophy of law (forthcoming, 2002).

claim that the resolution of contract disputes must be derived from the parties' agreement. But by definition, the resolution of a contract dispute that falls within a contractual gap cannot be decided based on the parties' agreement. Thus, Craswell concludes that the autonomy theories cannot address the problem of contractual gaps because of their commitment to the *ex post* perspective in adjudication. Because economic theories are committed to the *ex ante* perspective in adjudication, they have no difficulty in addressing the problem of contractual gaps. Surprisingly, however, the commitment of autonomy theories to the *ex post* perspective in adjudication need not disable them from addressing the problem of contractual gaps. Whether it does depends on their understanding of the moral basis of autonomy, their views on the nature of law, and their understanding of the scope of contract law. Thus, I will argue that Fried's theory provides a perfectly coherent approach to filling contractual gaps, while Benson's theory does not. In Fried's case, the deontic commitment to the *ex post* perspective is not nearly so wooden as to constitute a structural impediment to gap-filling. Rather than reflecting incompatible views on the permissibility of the *ex ante* perspective, the dispute between Fried's autonomy theory and Craswell's economic approach on the question of gap-filling turns out to be a disagreement over the kind and weight of evidence necessary to justify ordinary interpretations of intent. I therefore argue that opposing methodological perspectives in adjudication only sometimes account for the first-order disagreements between deontic and economic contract theories.

The methodological differences between autonomy and economic contract theories in part are grounded in opposing views about the nature of law and legal theory. Thus, I conclude that contract theory cannot avoid the larger questions of jurisprudence that confront all legal theories. In debates between contract theories that have the same methodological commitments, the explanation and justification of contract law is genuinely at stake. But in debates between contract theories that endorse opposing methodological commitments, it is the methodological commitments themselves, rather than contract law, that are at stake. At the very least, this suggests that genuine advances in explaining and justifying contract law will require contract theorists to uncover and make explicit the second-order positions their theories implicitly endorse. A complete theory of contract law, however, would not only articulate but also defend its jurisprudential foundations.

can the deontic approach be understood modally?
-- more specifically, Lewis' counterfactuals
    as conditionals that are world-relative
duties arise via such conditionals, given the
world-making work that contracts do

1 Four Methodological Issues in Contract Theory

In this section, I present the four methodological issues that divide contemporary autonomy and economic theories of contract. Although I believe the opposing methodological positions associated with each kind of theory can plausibly be viewed as natural developments within the different intellectual histories of each perspective, I take no position on whether any of them are contingent or necessary features of deontic or economic theories.[8] My present purpose is to demonstrate that the autonomy and efficiency theories I consider do in fact evidence the methodological tendencies I describe, and that by attending to them, apparently first-order disputes can be revealed to be second-order disputes.

1.1 Doctrine as Legal Theories versus Doctrine as Legal Data

Contemporary economic and deontic legal theories can be viewed as alternative responses to the doctrinal scepticism of legal realism and the doctrinal cynicism of critical legal studies. Broadly understood, legal realism views the legal doctrines and arguments in opinions as obscuring more than they reveal about the real grounds of decision, though realists themselves differ about what those real grounds are: psychological idiosyncrasies of the judges, policy preferences, and uncodified commercial norms are all factors different Realists emphasize.[9] Critical legal studies share the sceptical view of legal doctrines and arguments, but reduce all judicial decision-making to 'pure politics', ignoring the other factors that the Realists emphasized. Both economic and deontic legal theory take doctrine seriously. They hold that legal doctrine can be explained and justified by a theory that makes it coherent. Indeed, both implicitly acknowledge that demonstrating the coherence and intelligibility of legal doctrine is a precondition for its justification. And each claims to provide an account that accomplishes both tasks. It is therefore tempting to conclude that these theories differ only with respect to the substantive explanatory and normative

---

[8] Ironically, it is the association of the *ex post* perspective in adjudication with deontological theories, and the *ex ante* perspective in adjudication with economic theories, that holds out the most promise as being logically compelled by each theory's foundational principle. Yet this is the one methodological opposition that, upon analysis, turns out to explain the substantive disagreements between autonomy and economic theories of contract only for particular kinds of autonomy theories, such as Benson's. Economic objections to the first order claims of the more prevalent kind of autonomy theories, such as Fried's, cannot be traced to the conflict between the *ex post* and *ex ante* perspectives in adjudication.

[9] See Brian Leiter, 'Rethinking Legal Realism: Toward a Naturalized Jurisprudence', *Texas Law Review*, 76 (1997), 267.

principle each employs. To explain and justify legal doctrine, economic theory relies on a principle of efficiency, while deontic theory relies on a principle of autonomy. But while both kinds of theories agree on the importance of legal doctrine, they disagree over the nature of legal doctrine.

The common law method requires judges to interpret the law based on the rationales and outcomes of past judicial decisions. The dispute between deontic and economic theories concerns the ultimate relationship between law, judicial statements of legal doctrine, and case outcomes. Both doctrinal statements and case outcomes appear to be co-equal sources of law. Indeed, the relationship between stated doctrine and case outcomes appears to be circular: doctrinal statements are distillations of principles derived from previous cases' outcomes, and case outcomes are ostensibly determined by the application of these distilled principles. The common law seems to consist in this dynamic itself, rather than either the doctrinal statements or outcomes alone. Yet particularly in hard cases, the question of which has priority over the other seems to be forced. Which is the legal wheat to the other's legal chaff?

Economic theory takes the view that the law consists in the best principled account of case outcomes, whether or not that account constitutes a plausible interpretation of doctrinal statements.[10] The implicit assumption underlying this view is that the ultimate touchstone for legal interpretation is case outcomes, rather than doctrinal statements distilled from them. Like legal realism and Critical Legal Studies (CLS), economic analysis does not take the doctrinal invocations and restatements as legal data to be explained. Instead, it treats doctrines as mere *theories* of case outcomes. Therefore, in hard cases, which make up the bulk of appellate court decisions, economic analysis takes one of two interpretive approaches. First, if the semantic content of the relevant doctrinal statement seems to under-determine the result because its essential terms are vague, economic analysis claims to interpret the meaning of these terms by using economic principles to systematize ordinary intuitions about their use. For example, some economic theories claim that common intuitions about whether reliance on a promise is reasonable are generated by an inchoate and unarticulated analysis of whether the promisee's decision to rely was based on an accurate discount of the probability of the promisor's performance. Secondly, if the semantic content of the doctrinal statement is inconsistent with the efficiency account of the cases decided under the doctrine, economic theory simply ignores the semantic

[10] In this respect, economic analysis shares the view of law that Dennis Patterson attributes to Langdell: that 'the state of the law could be divined from underlying principles'. Dennis Patterson, 'Symposium on Taking Legal Argument Seriously: Taking Commercial Law Seriously: From Jurisprudence to Pedagogy', *Chicago-Kent Law Review*, 74 (1999), 625, 626 . However, although this view underwrote Langdell's first attempt to identify (or perhaps impose) the set of principles defining contract law, the success of his attempt had the effect of canonizing those principles into doctrines that came to be regarded as the law itself. Thus, even while Langdell subordinated doctrinal statements to outcomes in divining the law of contracts, the very act of stating the underlying principles serves to subordinate subsequent outcomes (and prior inconsistent outcomes) even as it grounds its own claim to authority in case outcomes, rather than doctrinal statements.

content of the doctrinal statement entirely, substituting the economic principle in its place.[11] Economic theory therefore treats the process of adjudication as a 'black box' and views legal theory as offering explanations of what's inside the black box.[12] On this view, law consists in whatever principles best explain the outcomes, not the express reasoning, in judicial decisions. Doctrinal statements are mere evidence of the law, rather than constitutive elements of law itself. Because the law is constituted by case outcomes, the legal theorist's job is to provide the best-available principled account of those outcomes, without regard to the doctrinal statements judges offer in defence of their decisions.[13]

In contrast, deontic theory rejects the view that the law consists in whatever principle best unifies case outcomes, irrespective of the express reasoning offered by the judges who decide them. Instead, deontic theory treats doctrinal justifications offered by judges as constitutive elements of the law. Outcomes serve as constraints on plausible interpretations of these doctrinal statements, but do not in themselves have independent legal significance. This view draws support from Dworkin's approach to jurisprudence and Rawls's approach to political philosophy. According to Dworkin, judges properly decide hard cases by interpreting the law in the best light possible, subject to the constraint of fit with the reasoning of past judicial decisions.[14] For Rawls, one of the formal requirements for the justification of state coercion is that the justifying reasons be publicly available. No matter how compelling otherwise, those reasons cannot justify state coercion unless the state publicly offers them as its ground for coercion.[15] Thus, deontic theories take doctrinal statements seriously as sources of law, rather than as mere evidence. Instead of viewing them as failed, naive

[11] Thus, under the first approach, economic analysts can plausibly claim that their interpretations provide a rigorous and operational, but still faithful, account of what most people would take those terms to mean. But under the second approach, economic analysts provide analyses of cases that simply cannot qualify as plausible interpretations of the plain meaning of the doctrine language. A clear example of such an analysis is the economic interpretation of the bargain theory of consideration, discussed in the next section. The economic theory interprets the requirement that consideration be actually bargained for as a requirement that the promise be made in a 'bargain context', even if no actual bargain takes place.

[12] As one deontic theorist puts the point, 'I submit, without taking the time to prove it, that most legal economists have little or no theoretical regard for common-law reasoning. For most, the common law is a black box producing grist for the efficiency mill. The fact that common-law rules so often appear to be efficient remains a mystery and one that economists have long since given up trying to explain'. Randy E. Barnett, '. . . And Contractual Consent', *Southern California Interdisciplinary Law Journal*, 3 (1993), 421, 437.

[13] Economic analysis does use doctrinal statements as devices for sorting factually similar case outcomes into categories of cases that are likely to share the same principled explanation. This view was sometimes expressed by Karl Llewellyn, the principal drafter for Article 2 of the UCC, who praised Article 2 for its usefulness as '*an easy and effective filing system*' for cases. Karl Llewellyn, 'Why We Need the Uniform Commercial Code', *University of Florida Law Review*, 10 (1957), 367 at 369.

[14] Ronald Dworkin, *Law's Empire* (New York: Columbia University Press, 1986).

[15] See John Rawls, *Political Liberalism* (1993) (hereinafter *Political Liberalism*). Of course, the idea of public justification and public reason is much richer than this. The core of the idea is that public justifications can invoke only those normative claims with which all reasonable people agree. See ibid., ch. VI.

theories of case outcomes in need of reconstruction, deontic theories typically seek to identify the deeper philosophical principles that underwrite them.[16] Thus, unlike economic theory, deontic theory treats doctrinal statements as constitutive of the law even when their plain meaning fails to determine a result in a particular case. Deontic theorists either accept such legal indeterminacy or undertake interpretive strategies that reveal a more determinate meaning. But unlike economic theorists, deontic theorists will never adopt a view of the law that is inconsistent with the plain meaning interpretation of doctrinal statements, even if that view provides the best-available, principled explanation of case outcomes. Thus, the criterion of fit with outcomes provides the dispositive constraint on legal interpretation for economic analysts, whereas the criterion of fit with stated judicial reasoning provides the dispositive constraint for deontic theorists. As a result of their disparate jurisprudential views about the status of doctrines and outcomes, deontic and economic theorists regard each other's theories as mistaking legal chaff for legal wheat.

1.2 Normative versus Explanatory Primacy

Legal theory is both a normative and explanatory enterprise. Most contemporary contract theories at least implicitly pursue both enterprises simultaneously. Deontic theorists routinely take themselves to be providing both an explanation and a justification of contract doctrines (although they do not typically take themselves to be providing explanations of case outcomes). Economic theories are also most naturally construed as offering both an explanation and a justification of contract law, where contract law is conceived as those principles that best unify and predict case outcomes (whether or not they constitute plausible interpretations of stated contract doctrines). Indeed, as an analytic matter, if an explanation is prerequisite to understanding, then explanation is logically prior to justification. How could a theorist justify a doctrine without first understanding it? Thus, deontic theorists must explain contract doctrines before they can justify them. And the economic theorist's explanatory project can be viewed as logically the first step in providing a justification of case outcomes, whether or not the economic theorist ultimately undertakes the second step of providing a justification of outcomes she has explained.

Some economic theorists, however, disavow either the explanatory or normative enterprise of contract theory. Traditional economic analysis makes no explicit claim to provide self-sufficient justifications of case outcomes, but instead claims only to identify an efficiency principle that renders case outcomes coherent and provides a

---

[16] However, a deontic theorist could reject the legal significance of disembodied outcomes without embracing a plain-meaning interpretation of doctrines. Although most deontic theorists implicitly endorse a plain-meaning interpretation of doctrine, the essence of their disagreement with economic theories lies in their rejection of the legal significance of disembodied outcomes and their view that law consists in the doctrines invoked in judicial opinions, however interpreted.

basis for predicting how courts will rule in future cases.[17] By disavowing the normative enterprise, these theories avoid confronting the well-known philosophical objections to consequentialist justifications generally, and efficiency justifications in particular. Conversely, much of contemporary economic contract theory claims solely to be identifying efficient solutions to traditional problems in contract law, rather than explaining and normatively assessing existing contract doctrines. By disavowing the explanatory enterprise, these theories avoid the need to reconcile their abstract efficiency analyses with the inconvenient twists and turns of contract doctrine as applied in actual cases. Some of the theorists who present economic analyses in this way embrace consequentialism, and reject deontology, as the correct normative principle.[18] Others simply remain silent, and therefore agnostic, on the normative force of efficiency principles. But even these theorists would argue that efficiency analyses must be at least relevant to the overall normative assessment of legal rules.

However, even the economic theories that claim to be either purely explanatory or purely normative have at least implicit explanatory and normative implications. These theories try to explain judicial decisions, and judges at least implicitly claim to be exercising justified state coercion. Unless judges are in bad faith or systematically mistaken about the justification of their decisions, by explaining their decisions as efforts to promote efficiency the economic theorist implies that the goal of efficiency is at least a plausible basis for justifying the exercise of state coercion. Thus, although the traditional economic theorist disavows the normative enterprise to avoid the need to defend the normative credentials of efficiency principles, it is fair to assume she finds the goal of efficiency a normatively plausible ground for the exercise of state coercion. Similarly, although some contemporary economic theorists disavow the explanatory enterprise, their normative enterprise inevitably presupposes an explanation and normative assessment of existing contract law. The problems for which they propose efficient solutions are framed in terms of existing doctrines, and by implication their proposed solutions constitute a critique of existing doctrinal solutions. For example, contemporary economic contract theorists have written extensively on the problem of identifying the most efficient remedies for breach of contract. Although these theorists often make no express claim to have explained existing contract doctrines, their project presupposes some explanation of the

[17] Richard Posner's presentation of the economic analysis of law provides a classic example of its explanatory priority: 'In contrast to the heavily normative emphasis of most writing, both legal and economic, on law, the book emphasizes positive analysis: the use of economics to shed light on the principles of the legal system rather than to change the system'. Richard Posner, *Economic Analysis of Law*, 3rd edn. (Boston: Little, Brown, 1986).

[18] A notable recent example is Lewis Kaplow and Steven Shavell's recent effort to defend a purely normative economic analysis of law, including contract law. *See* Lewis Kaplow and Steven Shavell, 'Principles of Fairness Versus Human Welfare: On the Evaluation of Legal Policy', *Harvard Law Review*, 114 (2001), 961. For an assessment of their project, see Jules L. Coleman and Jody S. Kraus, 'Review of Kaplow and Shavell's *Principles of Fairness Versus Human Welfare: On the Evaluation of Legal Policy*' (manuscript) (forthcoming, 2002).

doctrines defining contractual obligation and breach. Because they endorse the goal of efficiency as the correct one for the law to pursue, by demonstrating the unique efficiency of a proposed new doctrine they necessarily criticize the existing doctrine. Indeed, many contemporary economic analyses begin by demonstrating why existing doctrinal solutions are inefficient and then proceed to design a more efficient doctrine to replace them.

The fundamental difference between deontic and economic contract theories is not that one is exclusively normative and the other exclusively explanatory. Despite strategic efforts to disavow one or the other enterprise, all contract theories at least implicitly make both normative and explanatory claims. Instead, the crucial second-order disagreement between deontic and economic theories is over the relative priority between explanation and justification, as well as the contest between stated doctrine and case outcomes as sources of law. Deontic theories not only take doctrines to be their principal object of inquiry, but also accord priority to justifying these doctrines. The primary goal of deontic theories is to demonstrate that contract law is a morally and politically legitimate institution, rather than to explain how contract law determines outcomes in particular cases. In contrast, economic theories are principally concerned to explain how contract law determines outcomes in particular cases. Both kinds of theorists acknowledge the importance of both justification and explanation. But deontic theorists are methodologically committed to undertaking the justificatory task first, and explaining particular cases later, while economic theorists are methodologically committed to undertaking the explanatory task first, and justifying the existence of contract law later.[19] Therefore, deontic theorists reject economic theories because they endorse the principle of efficiency, which deontic theorists regard as an implausible normative principle. For the deontic theorist, there is no point in explaining law with a principle that holds out no hope of justifying it. Similarly, economic theorists reject deontic theories because they employ autonomy principles, which economic analysts regard as wholly inadequate to explain case outcomes. For the economic theorist, there is no point in justifying law with a principle that holds out no hope of explaining it.[20]

---

[19] Economic analysts typically explain and justify the distinctions between different areas of law on grounds of comparative institutional competence. For a superb overview of this kind of analysis, see Neil Komesar, *Imperfect Alternatives: Choosing Institutions in Law, Economics, and Public Policy* (Chicago: University of Chicago Press, 1994).

[20] It is worth noting as well that economic analysts are often sceptical that the autonomy principle has normative power in contract law because the vast majority of transactors are corporations rather than individuals. The autonomy stakes in corporate transactions are, at a minimum, less direct in contracts between people acting as agents for corporations than in contracts between people acting in their individual capacity. But this is not to say that autonomy values are not at stake when corporations act. Both the autonomy of the agents and of the individuals represented by the corporations may be at stake. None the less, deontic theorists bear the burden of explaining how autonomy principles apply in contracts between corporations.

1.3 The Origins of Methodological Disagreement

The dispute over the relative priority of the normative and explanatory enterprises of contract theory may simply reflect the different theoretical goals of deontic and economic theorists. Deontic theorists tend to be philosophers who find normative questions inherently interesting. The tools they bring to bear in legal analysis are most naturally suited to the normative enterprise. Deontic theorists therefore may prize justification over explanation in legal theory.[21] Economic analysts, however, tend not to be philosophers and instead find explanatory questions inherently interesting. The tools they bring to bear in legal analysis are most naturally suited to the explanatory enterprise. Moreover, many non-economist lawyers have been attracted to the economic analysis of law precisely because it attempts to provide fine-grained explanations of case law. Some lawyers might have a passing interest in understanding the moral or political justification of legal institutions. But all lawyers (and most law professors) have a professional obligation to understand particular case outcomes. The economic analysis of law has thus been fuelled both by its instrumental value to lawyers and law professors in understanding case outcomes as well as by its inherent interest to economist lawyers.

These intellectual origins may explain not only the different priorities of deontic and economic contract theories, but their different conceptions of legal explanation and justification as well. For example, economic analysts typically seek explanations of decided cases that yield predictions for undecided cases. Such explanations would therefore be falsifiable. Deontic theorists, however, typically do not attempt to explain outcomes in particular cases, much less to predict outcomes in undecided cases. But they insist they have explanations of cases none the less. Consider a contracts case in which a court applies the doctrine of promissory estoppel to allow one party to recover. A deontic theorist might explain the court's decision by asserting that the court found the promisor to have acted wrongfully by making and breaking a promise on which the promisee reasonably relied. Given that finding, the principle of corrective justice supports recovery because it requires wrongdoers to compensate their victims for the harm they wrongfully cause. This deontic explanation of the case holds that the court's ruling is based on its attempt to pursue corrective justice, and in so far as the court succeeds in that task, this explanation constitutes a justification as well.

---

[21] Deontic theorists uniformly accord priority to the normative enterprise of contract theory. That enterprise is to assess whether contract law is justified. In principle, this enterprise is neutral on the question of whether contract law is justified. However, most well-developed deontic theories of contract law engage this normative enterprise by setting out an affirmative argument for the justification of contract law. For example, both Fried and Benson provide an affirmative justification for contract law. But in itself, the priority of the normative enterprise of contract theory has no necessary stake in demonstrating that contract law is in fact justified. The normative enterprise simply seeks the correct answer to the question of whether contract law is justified.

But the economic analyst would find this explanation insufficient because it fails to identify any criteria, let alone operational criteria, for determining when a promisor acts wrongfully by breaking a promise and when a promisee's reliance is reasonable. Because the deontic explanation of the case leaves the critical concepts of wrongful conduct and reasonable reliance unanalysed, it cannot explain why the court deemed the promisor to have acted wrongfully and the promisee to have relied reasonably. It therefore does not provide an explanation of why the promisee prevailed in that case but the promisee in another promissory estoppel case did not. The deontic explanation would simply hold that although both courts were pursuing corrective justice, one court found wrongful conduct and reasonable reliance and the other did not. The deontic theory's claim is therefore conditional: if the court's judgment on these critical questions is correct, then its ruling is justified by the principle of corrective justice. Thus, state coercion enforcing the court's ruling is justified provided the state is justified in pursuing corrective justice. In contrast, the economic analyst of contract law might explain why the promisee in one promissory estoppel case prevailed and the other did not by 'reconstructing' in economic terms the courts' findings on wrongful conduct and reasonable reliance. For example, economic analysts, such as Charles Goetz and Robert Scott, have argued that in winning promissory estoppel cases the promise was made in a bargain context, while in losing cases the promise was made in a non-bargain context.[22] A bargain context is one in which the promisor would have made the promise even if it were clear to her that the promise would be legally enforced. The underlying economic theory predicts courts will enforce promises in the former but not in the latter contexts, and claims that by doing so, courts maximize overall net beneficial reliance on promises in society. Enforcing promises in bargain contexts increases beneficial reliance without significantly reducing the underlying activity level of promising itself. In contrast, enforcing promises in non-bargain contexts, such as typical intra-familial contexts, decreases net beneficial reliance. Promises made in non-bargain contexts are typically so reliable that there is little to gain by making them legally enforceable, and legal enforcement will significantly reduce the underlying activity level of promising in these contexts. Although this economic account explains the case outcomes, the deontic theorist will find it wanting for at least two reasons. First, the principle it relies on does not in itself provide a basis for justifying the exercise of state coercion. Secondly, it explains the case outcome by explaining away the court's own express justification for its ruling. As we have seen, deontic theorists are concerned to explain the court's express basis for its ruling rather than particular case outcomes.

Both deontic and economic contract theorists implicitly believe they are putting first things first. Since the deontic theorist seeks justification, the first task is to select a plausible justificatory principle. The second task is to determine the extent to which

---

[22] See Charles J. Goetz and Robert E. Scott, 'Enforcing Promises: An Examination of the Basis of Contract', *Yale Law Journal*, 89 (1980), 1261 (hereinafter 'Enforcing Promises').

contract law can be understood as justified by that principle. Since the economic analyst seeks explanation, the first task is to generate a theory that parses case outcomes. That in turn will reveal the genuine reasons courts implicitly use to decide cases. Only after these genuine reasons are discovered can the question of whether these rulings are justified be raised. If we don't understand the true bases of contract case outcomes, then we cannot assess whether those outcomes are justified. But the deontic theorists will respond that their theory does identify the genuine reasons courts use to decide cases and, unlike economic theories, corresponds to what courts say they are doing. They will argue that not all reasons can be given operational definitions that facilitate falsifiable predictions. In some cases, they argue that the content of these reasons—for example, the semantic content of the terms 'wrongful conduct' and 'reasonable reliance'—is *developed* through the practice of the common law and cannot be determined in advance.

Thus, the implicit disagreements between deontic and economic contract theories over the status of doctrinal statements and outcomes, and the relative priority of the normative and explanatory enterprises of legal theory, reflect deep controversies surrounding the nature of legal explanation and justification. This divide helps explain why each kind of theory typically regards the other as seriously deficient, if not pointless.

1.4 The Distinctiveness of Doctrinal Areas

For the same reasons that economic analysis does not take the semantic content of doctrines seriously, it also rejects the significance of traditional distinctions between apparently different bodies of law. Similarly, because deontic theory takes doctrinal distinctions seriously, it takes the differences between areas of law seriously and therefore seeks to explain them. Thus, although both economic and deontic theories seek to unify the legal doctrines within a given area of law, economic theories seek to unify apparently diverse areas of law under the same principle of efficiency, while deontic theories often seek to explain and preserve the distinctiveness of apparently different areas of law by emphasizing how different principles are required to explain, and therefore to justify, different areas of law. The deontic theorist's concern to provide an account of the distinctiveness of an area of law often derives from the view that any adequate explanation of the law must take seriously the terms in which the law itself is cast. If private law doctrines are at pains to distinguish between claims arising in contract and those arising in tort, then an adequate explanation of the law governing contract and tort must provide a principled account for the distinction between contract and tort. If stated legal doctrine presents that distinction as essential, then an adequate explanation of those areas of law must identify a principle according to which these areas of law are essentially different.

In addition, the tendency of deontic contract theories to seek to identify principles distinctive to contract law may, as a historical matter, stem from the formalist doctrinal origins of contract law. The central organizing doctrines of modern contract law were in large measure conceived—really pre-conceived—by Christopher Columbus Langdell and his followers. In organizing the first law school casebook, Langdell sought to impose order on the chaos of cases on contract law. Langdell imposed that order by culling through thousands of cases and selecting the ones that provided the best evidence of what appears to be an a priori, formalist theory of contract far from self-evident in the case law itself. According to Gilmore's stylized account, that theory 'seems to have been dedicated to the proposition that, ideally, no one should be liable to anyone for anything. Since the ideal was unattainable, the compromise solution was to restrict liability within the narrowest possible limits.'[23] Holmes then developed Langdell's anti-liability concept further by confining the scope of consideration using the bargain theory,[24] and Williston subsequently subordinated the subjective to the objective theory of intent.[25] Despite Corbin's later success in adding the doctrine of promissory estoppel to the otherwise unified and coherent doctrinal edifice built by Langdell, Holmes, and Williston, contemporary contract doctrine still invites a formalist explanation and justification. Its apparent internal doctrinal unity and coherence, together with the centrality of anti-liability doctrines, suggest the possibility of a singular, principled, individualist account implicit in the law itself. Philosophers with training in the theories of Kant and Hegel would naturally be drawn to formalist bodies of law that lend themselves to moral and political justification derived from first principles based on autonomy and liberty.[26] The modern, quasi-scientific approach to law favoured by economic analysts, in contrast, dismisses formalistic doctrinal language in favour of cold hard facts, like case outcomes. And like all scientific theories, economic analysis seeks the broadest account of the data possible. An a priori restriction of an explanation's domain to the historically arbitrary boundaries of doctrinal categories is anathema to the scientific self-conception of economic analysis.[27]

[23] Grant Gilmore, *The Death of Contract*, 2nd edn. (Columbus: Ohio State University Press, 1995), 15. Gilmore may be a bit tongue-in-cheek here.

[24] ibid. at 22–3.

[25] ibid. at 47–9.

[26] The suggestion that proponents of deontological moral theories might have been attracted to contract law because of contract law's origins in Langdellian formalism is not meant to suggest, however, that deontological contract theorists would accept the particular formalist features Langdell ascribed to contract law. For example, Fried, a Kantian contract theorist, rejects the consideration doctrine even though it is a central pillar in Langdell's formalist edifice of contract law. It is the aspiration to formal, internal coherence that might invite the application of the deontological formalist normative systems, not necessarily all of the particular formalist features contract law has acquired.

[27] For a discussion of the scientific self-conception of economic analysis, see Brian Leiter, 'Holmes, Economics, and Classical Realism', in *The Path of the Law and Its Influence: The Legacy of Oliver Wendell Holmes, Jr.*, ed. S. J. Burton (Cambridge, New York: Cambridge University Press, 2000), 285–325 (with a reply by Jody S. Kraus at 326–32).

Thus, because of their opposing views on the nature of legal explanation and their divergent intellectual histories, deontic and economic theories each embrace a criterion of success that the other regards as a criterion of failure.

1.5 The *Ex Ante* and *Ex Post* Perspectives in the Context of Adjudication

The contemporary divide between deontic and economic theories of contract law is thought to reflect a fundamental difference in their conception of private law adjudication. It is natural to align deontic theories with the *ex post* perspective, and economic theories with the *ex ante* perspective in adjudication. The argument parallels the debate in analytical jurisprudence over how judges should decide cases. Everyone agrees that judges should take an *ex post* perspective when deciding easy cases. But in hard cases, the views seem to differ. Deontic theory regards common law adjudication as properly confined to deciding disputes exclusively on the basis of pre-existing rights and duties. Therefore, even in hard cases, deontic theories take an *ex post* perspective on the legal rules at stake in common law adjudication. The adjudication is guided by considering the retrospective effect of the decision on the pre-existing rights of parties. Economic theorists believe judges must decide hard cases by establishing new rules that create prospective rights and duties.[28] Since litigants in hard cases have incurred sunk costs, no efficiency objective can be served by focusing on them. Thus, economic theory treats common law adjudication, especially of hard cases, as the effective equivalent of legislating new legal rules. It therefore analyses the legal rules at stake in common law adjudication from an *ex ante* perspective by focusing exclusively on the prospective effects of judicial decisions. The deontic theorist rejects the economic theorist's *ex ante* approach as violative of individual rights and the basic Kantian maxim to treat persons as ends in themselves and not as mere means: to decide a dispute between two litigants by selecting the decision rule with the most desirable prospective effects is to use the litigants solely as means to the collective ends of society, not as ends in themselves.

[28] The classic debate between these positions took place twenty years ago, when Richard Posner confronted Ronald Dworkin. Posner argued that judges should decide hard cases by creating a rule that would be in most parties' best interest going forward. Dworkin argued that such a rule was unfair because it failed to respect the rights of the litigants. Dworkin's objection was, in essence, Kant's objection to treating persons as mere means rather than ends in themselves. Dworkin conceded that Posner's position was perfectly defensible in the context of legislation, which has prospective effects only. But because the purpose of adjudication is to resolve disputes, its effects are, first and foremost, retrospective. See e.g., Ronald Dworkin, 'Is Wealth a Value?', *Journal of Legal Studies*, 9 (1980), 191; Ronald Dworkin, 'Why Efficiency?', *Hofstra Law Review*, 8 (1980), 563; Richard Posner, 'The Ethical and Political Basis of the Efficiency Norm in Common Law Adjudication', *Hofstra Law Review*, 8 (1980), 487; Richard Posner, 'Utilitarianism, Economics, and Legal Theory', *Journal of Legal Studies*, 8 (1980), 191.

On this view, the nub of the disagreement between deontic and economic approaches to the common law adjudication of hard cases lies in their different conceptions of law and the lawmaking process. In its simplest form, the dispute is whether there are right answers in hard cases. Dworkin famously answers this question in the affirmative. Indeed, Dworkin's interpretive theory of law requires that judicial reasoning in hard cases is best explained as an effort to identify what the law already requires, rather than what the law should require in the future. Of course, the right answer thesis is controversial. Positivists among others have argued forcefully against it. If Dworkin is right, however, the *ex ante* perspective urged by the economic analyst directly conflicts with respect for individual legal rights. The *ex ante* perspective would countenance rights violations any time adoption of the most desirable rule going forward would yield a result contrary to the existing rights of one of the parties. Indeed, Dworkin has argued as much. But if Dworkin is wrong, and there is no right answer in genuinely hard cases, then no decision in the case could be violative of the parties' pre-existing legal rights. On this view, it would presumably no longer be cogent to object to the economic analyst's *ex ante* perspective on the ground that it might yield results violative of the litigants' pre-existing legal rights.

Of course, this is a grossly oversimplified simple account of the jurisprudential foundations underlying the dispute between *ex ante* and *ex post* perspectives on adjudication. Even positivists who reject Dworkin's right answer thesis and his interpretive theory of law may have powerful objections to the *ex ante* perspective in common law adjudication, depending on exactly how that perspective is defined. But the point is that these general debates in analytic jurisprudence seem to fuel the perception that deontic and economic contract theories are subject to the same methodological divide. Deontic contract theory is supposed to object to the ex ante perspective because it holds that the function of courts is to vindicate individual rights, rather than to create them. For the economic analysts, the deontic objection is based on a naive and unsustainable conception of legal rights and the process of adjudication. The common law process in hard cases is and must be a substitute for legislation. Thus, the conflict between economic and deontic theories of contract law is perceived to derive from the inherent tension between the *ex ante* and *ex post* perspectives in the common law process of adjudication.

The *ex post/ex ante* divide in analytic jurisprudence is genuine, and it does seem to explain the first-order disagreements between economic theories and Benson's contract theory. But despite the claims that this divide provides the grounds for mutual criticism of deontic and economic contract theories generally, disputes typically attributed to this divide turn out to be disputes not over fundamental jurisprudential questions but rather ordinary questions of contract interpretation. As consideration of Fried's theory reveals, the deontic commitment to the *ex post* perspective in adjudication is fully consistent with allowing *ex ante* concerns to enter under proper circumstances. Those circumstances depend on how one understands the nature of moral and legal rights, and their relationship to the social conventions that underwrite our ordinary expectations.[29]

The remainder of this chapter presents the contract theories of Charles Fried and Peter Benson. My objective is neither to defend these theories, nor even to identify the principal substantive objections against them. Rather, I present the essential and representative features of each theory in order to identify their underlying methodological commitments, and to illustrate how these commitments can provide systematic explanations for many of the apparently substantive disagreements between autonomy and economic theories of contract law.

2 CHARLES FRIED'S *CONTRACT AS PROMISE*

Contemporary deontic contract theory begins with Charles Fried's *Contract as Promise*. Fried's analysis ranges over a wide spectrum of contract doctrines. An examination of selected doctrinal discussions in Fried's book illustrates how this classic example of a systematically developed deontic theory of contract law (1) accords primacy to the normative rather than explanatory project of contract theory, (2) is designed principally to establish the distinctiveness of contract law, (3) views doctrine as the legal data to be explained and does not seek to explain case outcomes, and (4) accords primacy to the *ex post* over the *ex ante* perspective, but none the less accommodates many of the same kinds of *ex ante* considerations central to the economic analysis of contract law. The first three of these methodological commitments are integrated features of Fried's theory.

2.1 Normative Primacy, Distinctiveness, and Doctrinal Statements as Data

Fried's theory constitutes an explicit defence of the claim that contract law provides a ground of legal obligation distinct from any other area of law.[30] He states that he is defending the 'classical view of contract proposed by the will theory'[31] against critics

---

[29] See below, Sect. 2.4.

[30] 'I begin with a statement of the central conception of contract as promise. This is my version of the classical view of contract proposed by the will theory and implicit in the assertion that contract offers a distinct and compelling ground of obligation.' Charles Fried, *Contract as Promise* (Cambridge, Mass.: Harvard University Press, 1981), 5–6.

[31] ibid. at 6.

who deny that the will theory, or any theory based on one principle alone, can unify contract law and establish its distinctiveness from other private law areas.[32] Fried's central argument for contract law's distinctiveness is that it is the only body of law devoted exclusively to enforcing promissory obligations.[33] At times, Fried seems to advance the distinctiveness thesis out of sheer conviction, based on his reading of contracts case law, that the formidable array of his contemporaries were wrong to deny it. But it is clear that Fried's principal motivation for advancing the distinctiveness thesis is to support his normative claim that contract law is morally justified because it legally enforces the moral obligation to keep promises.[34] The legal enforcement of the moral obligation to keep promises, in Fried's view, is essential to vindicating the idea of rights central to liberal individualism.[35] Fried's strategy for

[32] Fried is quite clear that his theory is, first and foremost, a response to three kinds of extended attacks on the internal coherence and distinctiveness of contract law then current in the contracts literature (the attacks are by Atiyah, Friedman, Gilmore, Horwitz, Kennedy, Kronman, and Macneil). Indeed, at the outset of his project Fried writes, 'I shall just set out [the main thrust of these critics' views] so that my readers may be clear what I am reacting against' (ibid. at 3). Each attack denies that contract law can be rendered both distinct and internally coherent by any principle, including the will theory's principle of self-imposed obligation. The first attack relies on historical analysis to demonstrate both distant and recent history of collective control over a large range of issues that should be free from such control according to the will theory of contract. Fried responds to this attack by defending the normative, rather than explanatory, credentials of contract as promise. He asserts the ancient ancestry not of contract as promise but of the promise principle itself. He then argues that historical and contemporary vacillation in the social acceptance of the promise principle has no bearing on its moral validity. The second attack rejects the will theory because it cannot explain contractual recovery based on reliance or past benefit. Fried responds by relegating cases based on reliance or past benefit to areas other than contract law, such as tort law. The third attack argues that the notion of a self-imposed obligation is itself incoherent. Fried defends the coherence of the principle of self-imposed obligation by endorsing a Kantian rights theory based on the moral significance of trust (ibid. at 83–91). Each of Fried's responses reflects his view that contract law can and should be conceived as an internally coherent and distinct area of law exclusively devoted to vindicating the moral obligations generated by the promise principle.

[33] Fried variously claims to be providing an explanation of particular contract doctrines (e.g. Fried writes that contract as promise 'generates the structure and accounts for the complexities of contract doctrine', ibid. at 6), supplying a moral justification for contract law (e.g. Fried claims the promise principle is 'the moral basis of contract law', ibid. at 1), and offering solutions 'to perennial conundrums' in contract law (ibid. at 132). But his central claim is that contract as promise explains contract law's 'essential unity' (ibid. at 6), and 'that contract offers a distinct and compelling ground of obligation' (ibid.). See also Peter Benson, 'Contract', in A Companion to Philosophy of Law and Legal Theory, ed. Dennis Patterson (Cambridge, Mass.: Blackwell Publishers, 1996), 24, at 37 ('Fried's central aim is to vindicate the distinctive character of contract and the primacy of the expectation interest').

[34] Fried's thesis holds that contract law, and only contract law, enforces the moral obligation to keep promises. It is therefore properly a form of the distinctiveness thesis. But for the normative purpose that motivates Fried, he need advance only the claim that contract law enforces the moral obligation to keep promises. An adequate defence of the claim that contract law is justified by the promise principle does not necessarily require that no other bodies of law also enforce the promise principle. Fried none the less asserts the full distinctiveness thesis.

[35] The first sentence in Fried's book states his intention to argue that the promise principle is 'the moral basis of contract' (ibid. at 1). Fried claims that '[t]he regime of contract law, which respects the dispositions individuals make of their rights, carries to its natural conclusion the liberal premise that individuals have rights. And the will theory of contract, which sees contractual obligations as essentially self-imposed, is a fair implication of liberal individualism' (ibid. at 2).

justifying contract law is first to explicate and defend the moral promise principle,[36] and then to demonstrate that the obligations recognized and enforced by contract law are moral obligations arising out of the moral promise principle. Fried therefore devotes the bulk of his second chapter to explicating and defending the moral promise principle before turning exclusively to his defence of the distinctiveness thesis in the remaining chapters. Thus, although the central preoccupation of Fried's book is to defend the distinctiveness thesis, that defence is in service of his overall normative project of justifying contract law on the basis of the moral promise principle that he believes underwrites liberal individualism.[37]

Although Fried clearly accords priority to the normative task of contract theory, that commitment requires him to devote the vast bulk of his efforts to providing an explanatory contract theory. Yet unlike the explanations of economic contract theories, Fried's explanations do not attempt to explain case outcomes. In order to prove that contract law is justified by the promise principle, Fried must examine sources of contract law—contract cases, the Restatement (Second) of Contracts (hereafter R2d.), and Article 2 of the Uniform Commercial Code (hereafter UCC)—to demonstrate that they are best explained as efforts to enforce promises. Typically, Fried proceeds by considering a series of stylized vignettes of classic contract cases to determine whether they constitute counter-examples to his thesis. For each example he considers, Fried implicitly sorts it into one of three categories. The first category consists of cases he claims were properly decided on the basis of contract law. Those are cases in which the contract doctrine invoked is best understood as enforcing the moral obligation to keep promises. The second category consists of cases he claims were not properly decided on the basis of contract law. Those are cases in which the doctrine invoked cannot be understood as enforcing the moral obligation to keep promises, but rather are best explained based on normative principles underwriting other areas of law, such as tort law. The third category consists of cases Fried claims were decided on the basis of incoherent contract law. Those are cases in which the doctrine invoked cannot be understood as enforcing the moral obligation to keep

---

[36] Fried casts his argument as a defence of the will theory. According to Fried, the will theory 'sees contractual obligations as essentially self-imposed' (ibid. at 2). His version of the will theory claims that 'the promise principle' is 'the moral basis of contract law'. The promise principle is 'the principle by which persons may impose on themselves obligations where none existed before' (ibid. at 1). Fried's defence of the will theory proceeds first by explaining how promising is possible. He argues that promising is made possible by the existence of a social convention that defines the practice of promising. According to Fried, such a practice enhances autonomy by allowing individuals to transform morally optional activity into morally mandatory activity. Fried explains the moral force of such a convention by arguing that breaking a promise constitutes a breach of trust: 'There exists a convention that defines the practice of promising and its entailments. This convention provides a way that a person may create expectations in others. By virtue of the basic Kantian principles of trust and respect, it is wrong to invoke that convention in order to make a promise, and then to break it' (ibid. at 17).

[37] For a lucid presentation of Fried's account of the moral obligation to keep promises, see Benson, 'Abstract Right and the Possibility of a Nondistributive Conception of Contract: Hegel and Contemporary Contract Theory', Cardozo Law Review, 10 (1989), 1077, at 1098–1103. For his trenchant criticism that Fried's conception of autonomy is at bottom teleological, see ibid. 1103–17.

promises and cannot be reinterpreted as cases decided under a defensible principle operating in non-contract law. In sum, Fried's claim is that all and only those cases decided on the basis of a doctrine supportable by the promise principle qualify as genuine contracts cases. If they can't be supported by the promise principle, they are either defensible as non-contract cases, or indefensible because incoherent.[38]

Despite its normative priority, Fried's theory therefore offers an extensive explanation of contract law. Yet unlike economic contract theories, his theory offers no explanation of case outcomes. Two reasons explain why. First, Fried focuses exclusively on defending the distinctiveness thesis. His sole goal in examining contract doctrines is to defuse doctrines that constitute potential counter-examples to his claim that contract is based exclusively on promise. Once Fried has demonstrated that a given doctrine can be understood as giving effect to the promise principle, or can instead be relegated to another body of law, that doctrine no longer constitutes a potential counter-example to his contract-as-promise thesis: it is either a contract doctrine that satisfies the promise principle or it is not a contract doctrine at all. Thus, the potential counter-example doctrine is defused. Fried has no reason to proceed further to offer an explanation of how the doctrine applies to particular cases. Similarly, if the promise principle cannot explain a given contract doctrine, and that doctrine cannot readily be assimilated to another body of law, Fried's sole concern is to defuse the potential significance of that doctrine as a counter-example. In this case, he deems the doctrine indefensible because incoherent. If a contract doctrine is incoherent, no theory can explain it. It therefore does not constitute a counter-example to his theory. Again, because Fried's sole objective is to defend the distinctiveness claim, his job is done once the counter-example doctrine is explained or explained away. No reason remains for explaining the cases decided under that doctrine.

The second reason Fried's theory fails to explain case outcomes is that he is implicitly committed to views on the status and interpretation of doctrine that reject the realist and CLS critique of legal doctrine, and therefore reject case outcomes as stand-alone sources of law. Fried implicitly treats contract doctrines, rather than contract

[38] So described, Fried's defence of the distinctiveness claim is analytic: by virtue of his stipulative definition, any case that cannot be plausibly interpreted as enforcing the promise principle does not qualify as a genuine contracts case. Fried a priori rules out the possibility of a genuine counter-example by argumentative fiat. The only way for Fried to avoid vicious circularity in defending his distinctiveness claim would be to settle in advance on *theory-independent* criteria for determining whether a case, and the doctrine under which it was decided, are genuinely part of contract law. But Fried could avoid this problem by redescribing his project. Instead of following his contemporaries in debating the 'true' nature of contract law, Fried could instead simply assert that the promise principle is available to explain and therefore justify a great deal of what is normally considered contract law. Little seems to be at stake in deciding whether those cases and doctrines that cannot be so explained and justified none the less constitute 'genuine' contract law. Fried's fundamental claim, after all, is that liberal individualism, and its attendant promise principle, requires and therefore justifies much of modern contract law, even though it cannot similarly justify some of what is (rightly or wrongly) regarded as contract law. This redescription of Fried's explanatory project frees him from the burden of justifying uninteresting conceptual claims about the true nature of contract law.

case outcomes, as the primary source of contract law, and likewise implicitly limits the permissible interpretations of doctrines to their plain meaning. These views explain the reasoning underlying Fried's conclusion that if contract doctrines cannot be explained by the promise principle or by non-contract law, they must be incoherent. According to the economic contract theorist, a contract doctrine is not necessarily incoherent simply because neither the promise principle nor principles explicit in non-contract law can explain it. The economic contract theorist would claim that some other principle, such as a principle of efficiency, might explain the cases decided under that doctrine and thereby render the doctrine coherent. But if the primary source of contract law is contract doctrine, and the acceptable interpretations of contract doctrine must be based on their plain meaning, then theories that do not provide plausible interpretations of the plain meaning of a contract doctrine are ruled out. Even if an efficiency principle can make sense of the case outcomes reached under a particular contract doctrine, that principle would not qualify as an explanation of contract law because it does not provide a plausible interpretation of the doctrine under which those cases were decided. And if the doctrine is the primary source of contract law, a theory that focuses exclusively on case outcomes, and completely disregards the doctrine's plain meaning, cannot constitute an explanation of the contract law applied in those cases. On this view, simply rendering case outcomes coherent under a principle, by itself, does not qualify as an interpretation of the law applied in those cases. On Fried's implicit view, case outcomes are results, rather than sources, of law. The law itself is contained in the doctrines courts use to explain case outcomes. Case outcomes therefore cannot be used to explain away the plain meaning of doctrines. Thus, Fried's view rejects, and the economic analyst's view presupposes, the interpretive legacy of the realist and CLS critiques of doctrine.

2.2 Illustrations: The Enforcement Doctrines

These methodological commitments are illustrated in Fried's discussion of contract law enforcement doctrines. According to Fried's theory, virtually all promises not intended to be legally unenforceable, including gift promises, should be enforced by contract law.[39] Yet American contract law does not enforce all such promises. The

[39] Fried's position is that all promises, including gift promises, should be enforced, provided they are intended by the parties to be legally enforced, they are voluntary, rational and deliberate, and they do not create illegitimate third party effects: 'Allowing people to *make* gifts (let us assume freely, deliberately, reasonably) serves social utility by serving individual liberty. Given the preceding chapter's analysis of promise, there simply are no grounds for not extending that conclusion to *promises* to make gifts.... My conclusion is . . . that the doctrine of consideration offers no coherent alternative basis for the force of contracts, while still treating promise as necessary to it.... Along the way to this conclusion I have made or implied a number of qualifications to my thesis. The promise must be freely made and not unfair.... It must also have been made rationally, deliberately. The promisor must have been serious enough that subsequent legal enforcement was an aspect of what he should have contemplated at the time he

doctrines of consideration, promissory estoppel, and past material benefit, for example, are routinely used to deny certain promises legal enforcement.[40] Each of these doctrines therefore represents a potential counter-example to Fried's distinctiveness claim that contract law enforces the moral obligation to keep promises. Under each of these doctrines, courts sometimes hold that although a promise was unequivocally made, it is none the less not legally enforceable. Fried addresses each of these doctrines separately. He first considers the standard doctrine of consideration. Ordinarily, contract law will not enforce promises that are not supported by consideration. Fried begins his analysis of this doctrine by paraphrasing the 'bargain theory' of consideration as stated in two critical sections of the Restatement (Second) of Contracts that define and circumscribe the requirement of consideration.[41] He then argues that the bargain theory, interpreted in light of its plain meaning, cannot provide a coherent explanation for the patterns of enforcement in ten representative cases decided under the consideration doctrine:

The bargain theory of consideration not only fails to explain why this pattern of decisions is just; it does not offer *any* consistent set of principles from which all of these decisions would flow. These cases particularly cannot be accounted for by the two guiding premises of the doctrine of consideration: (A) that only promises given as part of a bargain are enforceable; (B) that whether there is a bargain or not is a formal question only.[42]

Fried ultimately concludes that 'the standard doctrine of consideration . . . does not pose a challenge to my conception of contract law as rooted in promise, for the simple reason that that doctrine is too internally inconsistent to offer an alternative at all.'[43]

Fried's discussion of the consideration doctrine clearly illustrates the three methodological commitments discussed above. First, as his final conclusion reveals,

promised. Finally certain promises, particularly those affecting the situation and expectations of various family members, may require substantive regulation because of the legitimate interests of third parties.' *Contract as Promise*, above n. 30, at 37–8.

[40] Fried concedes that his theory cannot explain the patterns of enforcement in American contract law: 'I conclude that the life of contract is indeed promise, but this conclusion is not exactly a statement of positive law. There are too many gaps in the common law enforcement of promises to permit so bold a statement. My conclusion is rather that the doctrine of consideration offers no coherent alternative basis for the force of contracts, while still treating promise as necessary to it' (ibid. at 38).

[41] Fried identifies the consideration doctrine with two propositions: '(A) The consideration that in law promotes a mere promise into a contractual obligation is something, or the promise of something, given in exchange for the promise. (B) The law is not at all interested in the adequacy of the consideration. The goodness of the exchange is for the parties alone to judge—the law is concerned only that there *be* an exchange' (ibid. at 29). The first proposition paraphrases R2d. §71(1) and (2): '(1) To constitute consideration, a performance or a return promise must be bargained for. (2) A performance or return promise is bargained for it if is sought by the promisor in exchange for his promise and is given by the promisee in exchange for that promise'. The second proposition paraphrases R2d. §79: 'If the requirement of consideration is met, there is no additional requirement of (a) a gain, advantage, or benefit to the promisor or a loss, disadvantage, or detriment to the promisee; or (b) equivalence in the values exchanged; or (c) "mutuality of obligation"'.

[42] *Contract as Promise*, above n. 30, at 33.   [43] ibid. at 35.

Fried's sole motivation for analysing the doctrine of consideration is to disarm it as a threat to the distinctiveness thesis. Fried concedes that the promise principle cannot explain the bargain theory of consideration. But instead of acknowledging this failure as a limit to his explanatory theory, Fried argues that the consideration doctrine is inexplicable in principle. Secondly, the argument Fried presents implicitly relies on the view that contract law consists in the plain meaning interpretation of contract doctrines rather than other principles that might provide a coherent account of contract case outcomes. For Fried, an explanation of the consideration doctrine requires an explanation of how the bargain theory, interpreted in light of its plain meaning, explains the outcomes in the classic consideration cases. Fried thus begins by arguing that the doctrinal propositions A and B are inconsistent: 'The matrix of inconsistency is just the conjunction of the propositions A and B. Proposition B affirms the liberal principle that the free arrangements of rational persons should be respected. Proposition A, by limiting the class of arrangements to bargains, holds that individual self-determination is not a sufficient ground of legal obligation . . . '.[44] Assuming Fried is right to conclude these two propositions are inconsistent, the plain meaning of the consideration doctrine cannot be given a coherent interpretation. In his view, the promise principle explains proposition B, presumably because proposition B asserts that the enforcement of promises turns solely on the parties' intent and not on a third party's judgment of the adequacy of the parties' exchange. But like any principle that explains proposition B, it is necessarily contradicted by proposition A. Presumably, proposition A's bargain requirement, in Fried's view, implies that the enforcement of promises will turn on a third party's substantive judgment of the adequacy of the parties' exchange.[45] Thus, since the law consists in propositions A and B, and those propositions are inconsistent when interpreted according to their plain meaning, the law itself is incoherent. Once Fried takes himself to have demonstrated the incoherence of the bargain theory, his task of defending his theory is complete. The promise principle fails to explain the bargain theory of consideration because no principle can explain it. In Fried's view, so much the worse for the consideration doctrine, not the promise principle. Given that his exclusive concern is to defend the distinctiveness thesis, there is no point in considering whether the consideration doctrine could be rendered coherent by a principle that explains many of the outcomes of the consideration cases but ignores the plain meaning of the bargain theory.[46]

Fried's failure to consider alternative explanations of consideration case outcomes is explained in the first instance by his single-minded focus on defending the

[44] ibid.

[45] For present purposes, the accuracy of Fried's interpretation of propositions A and B (his paraphrased versions of R2d. §§ 71 and 79) is not relevant.

[46] Significantly, Fried concludes that '[*the bargain theory*] does not offer *any* consistent set of principles from which all of these decisions would flow', ibid. at 33. He does not claim that no theory offers a consistent set of principles to explain these cases.

distinctiveness thesis.[47] But Fried's resistance to non-promissory alternative accounts of the consideration doctrine can be explained, in part, by his implicit methodological view of the status and interpretation of contract doctrine. Fried's inference from the incoherence of the plain meaning interpretation of the bargain theory to the incoherence of the consideration doctrine itself implicitly presupposes that contract law consists in the plain meaning of its doctrines, rather than in whatever principles render coherent the set of cases decided under particular doctrinal rubrics within contract. In Fried's view, if the plain meaning of the bargain theory cannot be given a coherent interpretation, the consideration doctrine and the cases decided under it are necessarily incoherent. For the economic contract theorist, like the realists and CLS theorists before them, the failure of the bargain theory to provide a coherent explanation of consideration case outcomes merely demonstrates that the bargain theory itself, construed according to its plain meaning, constitutes a bad theory of the considerations cases. The bargain theory does not itself constitute the consideration doctrine. The true semantic content of the consideration doctrine, for the economic analyst, is provided by the principle that best explains the consideration case outcomes. Thus, for the economic contract theorists, the true semantic content of all contract doctrines is provided by the principles that explain contract case outcomes, whether or not they happen to correspond to the plain meaning of doctrinal formulations.

Thus, when Fried discusses the so-called moral consideration cases (decided under the material benefit rule (R2d. §86)),[48] the modification cases (R2d. §89), and the debt revival cases (decided under R2d. §§82 and 83),[49] he does not conclude that no principle can make sense of these cases. Rather, he claims that because these cases cannot be explained by the plain meaning of the bargain theory, the doctrine of consideration is incoherent. He does not allow for the possibility that the content of the consideration doctrine might be provided by some principle that makes sense of the consideration cases but rejects the plain meaning interpretation of the bargain theory. Consider Fried's discussion of two representative debt revival cases. In the first, a widow promises to repay the debt of her deceased husband. In the second, a

---

[47]   Indeed, Fried sometimes appears to beg the question outright: 'My conclusion is . . . that the doctrine of consideration offers no coherent alternative basis for the force of contracts, *while still treating promise as necessary to it*' (ibid. at 38; emphasis added). Of course, if Fried's contract-as-promise theory is not presumed to be true in the first instance, there is no reason to rule out the possibility that an alternative theory will provide a coherent basis for the force of contract without treating promise as necessary to it. As I discuss below, rather than relying on circular reasoning, Fried's preference for the promissory account of contract law can be explained, at least in part, by his methodological views about the status and interpretation of contract doctrine.

[48]   §86. Promise for Benefit Received (1) A promise made in recognition of a benefit previously received by the promisor from the promisee is binding to the extent necessary to prevent injustice. (2) A promise is not binding under Subsection (1): (a) if the promisee conferred the benefit as a gift or for other reasons the promisor has not been unjustly enriched; or (b) to the extent that its value is disproportionate to the benefit.

[49]   These are cases IV–X in *Contract as Promise*, above n. 30, at 31–3.

contractor makes a written promise to repay a debt discharged in bankruptcy and barred by the statute of limitations. Under the consideration doctrine, the court refused to enforce the former promise because the bank gave the widow nothing of value. In the latter, the court enforced the promise on the ground that the contractor's prior obligation supported his later promise. Fried regards these two cases as irreconcilable under the consideration doctrine:

Whatever the substantive merit of allowing recovery in such cases, the stated explanation is obviously gibberish. To be consistent the courts would have to find that in such cases there was no bargain, any more than in the case of the widow, since one does not bargain for what one already has: the repentant contractor has already got clear of all obligation the money that he subsequently promises to pay.[50]

Because he believes the bargain theory of consideration is gibberish, Fried rejects the consideration doctrine itself as gibberish. For him, the courts' stated rationale *is* the doctrine of consideration. If it can't be explained, the *law* of the cases simply can't be explained.

Economic analysts would agree with Fried that the *stated* rationale under which consideration cases are decided is gibberish. But for them, the point of legal theory is to supply coherent rationales in place of the stated gibberish that makes up the plain meaning of contract doctrines invoked by courts to explain their decisions. For example, Charles Goetz and Robert Scott argue that most contract enforcement doctrine outcomes can be explained by viewing enforcement cases as occasions for maximizing net beneficial reliance.[51] For example, they would hold that the widow's promise should not be legally enforceable because doing so in this class of cases would be likely to decrease net beneficial reliance overall.[52] In all probability, a widow's promise to pay her husband's debt is motivated by moral or religious convictions. It is therefore likely to be very reliable. Little is to be gained by making it legally enforceable. In addition, making it legally enforceable would be likely to deter widows from making such promises in the future. Had her husband's creditor sought to compel her to make a legally enforceable promise, she would probably have refused. Because she is likely to view her promise as a morally supererogatory act, she would not view legal enforcement as appropriate. Enforcing her promise would be likely to deter similarly situated parties from making similar promises in the future.[53] Thus, legal enforcement of promises in this kind of context would lead to a relatively small increase in the reliability of such promises but a relatively large decrease in the quality and quantity of such promises in the future. Enforcement therefore would be

[50] ibid. at 32.   [51] See Goetz and Scott, above n. 22.

[52] This and other applications of Goetz and Scott's net beneficial reliance theory of contractual enforcement is based on 'Enforcing Promises', above n. 22, and its further elaboration in *Contract Law and Theory*, 3rd edn., ed. Robert E. Scott and Jody S. Kraus (Newark; San Francisco; Charlottesville: Lexis, forthcoming).

[53] Or alternatively, require such parties to incur the costs of 'opting out' of the default enforcement rule by expressly stating that she does not intend her promise to be given legal effect.

likely to decrease overall expected net beneficial reliance. In contrast, the contractor's promise, while reliable, is not likely to be as reliable as the widow's promise. It is likely to be made solely out of self-interest. The contractor has a professional motivation to honour his discharged business debts. By doing so, he provides reassurance to potential future creditors on whom his future success depends. If he decides to abandon his business, or his self-interest otherwise conflicts with his promise, he is less likely to keep it. Thus, there is more to be gained by enforcing his promise than the widow's promise. And unlike legal enforcement of the widow's promise, legal enforcement of the contractor's promise is not likely to deter similarly situated parties from making the same quality and quantity of promises in the future. If his past creditor had insisted that he make a legally enforceable promise to repay his debt, it would have been in the contractor's self-interest to agree. His refusal to agree to make his promise legally binding would substantially undermine the likely point of making his promise—to reassure his future creditors of his bona fides. Thus, legal enforcement of the contractor's promise will increase the reliability of such promises without decreasing the quality and quantity of such promises in the future. Legal enforcement of promises in the contractor's context therefore maximizes overall expected net beneficial reliance.

In sum, the economic analyst agrees with Fried that the bargain theory fails to explain the consideration cases, but unlike Fried, treats the bargain theory as a failed theory of consideration that needs to be replaced by a better theory. Goetz and Scott's theory explains the consideration doctrine by interpreting it as just one device among others that courts use in contracts cases to maximize overall expected net beneficial reliance. Goetz and Scott's theory is just one of a number of economic theories that can allow the economic analyst to explain why courts do not enforce promises like the widow's but do enforce promises like the contractor's. Thus, Fried uses cases to test the coherence of the plain meaning of the doctrines courts use to decide them. If the plain meaning of a doctrine fails this coherence test, Fried rejects that doctrine *and the cases decided under it.* Economic analysts also use cases to test the coherence of the plain meaning of doctrines. But if the plain meaning of a doctrine fails this coherence test, the economic analysts reject only that interpretation of the doctrine but not necessarily the cases decided under it. In the economic analyst's view, when Fried rejects the cases along with the plain meaning interpretation of the doctrine, he is throwing out the baby with the bath water.

Ultimately, then, the most fundamental disagreement between economic analysts and deontic theorists like Fried is about sources of law. Both agree that doctrinal formulations are useful as a theoretical point of departure for analysing the law. For the economic analyst, doctrinal formulations are useful because they provide salient and convenient categories for organizing case outcomes that presumptively can be explained by the same set of principles. In addition, the plain meaning interpretations of doctrinal formulations provide an initial theory of the law applied in the cases decided under them. But for the economic analyst, the plain meaning interpretation of a doctrine is just a theory. Like any theory, it can be disconfirmed by the legal data it purports to explain. Since doctrines purport to explain case outcomes, those outcomes are the data of legal theory. Thus, for economic analysts, case outcomes, not the plain meaning interpretations of doctrine, are sources of law in themselves.[54] In contrast, Fried regards doctrines as more than merely devices for categorizing case outcomes and prima-facie theories of the law that decided them. For Fried, case outcomes are mere results of the application of law, not sources of law in themselves. The legal significance of a case outcome is, for Fried, entirely derivative of the legal significance of the doctrinal reasoning the court used to justify it. If the doctrinal reasoning applied in a case is not coherent, then the case outcome standing alone, disembodied from the reasoning the court used to justify it, has no theoretical significance and no status as law.

Fried's discussion of promissory estoppel provides stark confirmation of his exclusive focus on defending the distinctiveness thesis and confirms the view that he assigns no legal significance to case outcomes in themselves.[55] Fried's explanation of promissory estoppel is limited to his claim that it constitutes a 'belated attempt to plug a gap in the general regime of enforcement of promises, a gap left by the artificial and unfortunate doctrine of consideration'.[56] With almost no analysis of promissory estoppel case law, Fried asserts that promissory estoppel should be understood as a natural, if inadequate, institutional response to the problem of promissory under-enforcement created by the consideration doctrine. Fried considers promissory estoppel, therefore, only to buttress his claim that the consideration doctrine is anomalous.[57] His suggestion is that the emergence of promissory estoppel provides evidence that contract law itself has begun to reject the doctrine of consideration because it runs contrary to the requirements of the promise principle which otherwise animates contract law. Apart from the merits of his claim, Fried's discussion of promissory estoppel illustrates his exclusive focus on defending the distinctiveness thesis and his lack of interest in explaining case outcomes.[58] He makes no effort to

[54] To be sure, no theory, including economic theories of contract law, explain all the data. Economic analysts will reject some case outcomes as inconsistent with their explanatory theory. But economic analysts will resist wholesale rejection of central doctrines on the ground that their ostensible rationale fails to explain them. Instead, they will seek to identify alternative principles that explain most, or the most important, case outcomes decided under that doctrine.

[55] §90. Promise Reasonably Inducing Action or Forbearance (1) A promise which the promisor should reasonably expect to induce action or forbearance on the part of the promisee or a third person and which does induce such action or forbearance is binding if injustice can be avoided only by enforcement of the promise. The remedy granted for breach may be limited as justice requires. (2) A charitable subscription or a marriage settlement is binding under Subsection (1) without proof that the promise induced action or forbearance.

[56] *Contract as Promise*, above n. 30 at 25.

[57] 'The anomalous character of the doctrine of consideration has been widely recognized. A variety of statutes abrogate some of its more annoying manifestations . . .' (ibid. at 35.

[58] As a general proposition, Fried is surely right that promissory estoppel evolved to 'fill gaps' in enforcement created by the consideration doctrine. But his claim that it evolved to enforce the promises that would be enforced under the promise principle but are not enforced under the consideration

explain, under the promise principle or any other principle, which promises are enforced under section 90.[59] Once he conceives of promissory estoppel as a counter-measure against the consideration doctrine, and thus a doctrine designed to bring contract law in alignment with the promise principle, it is no longer a threat to the distinctiveness thesis. An explanation of which promises are enforced under section 90 is beside the point.[60]

The only promissory estoppel case Fried discusses is *Hoffman v Red Owl Stores*.[61] In *Hoffman*, the plaintiff, Hoffman, engages in preliminary negotiations with the defendant to obtain a supermarket franchise. In the course of extended negotiations, Hoffman relies on defendant's assurances that he will be granted a franchise if he meets their stated conditions. But when he meets them, defendants change the conditions and do not award the franchise. The court finds for Hoffman on a theory of promissory estoppel and awards reliance damages. Even at the time Fried was writing, there was a substantial body of scholarship discussing *Hoffman* and the application of promissory estoppel in preliminary negotiation cases.[62] That scholarship attempted to explain when courts do or should allow recovery for reliance on

doctrine is less plausible. If this claim were true, then promissory estoppel should provide recovery for any promisee that detrimentally relies on a promise. But under the reasonableness test of §90, recovery is routinely denied to promisees who have detrimentally relied. Thus, if he ignored the historic development of contract doctrine, Fried could just as well interpret the consideration doctrine as an institutional response to the under-enforcement problem created by promissory estoppel.

Fried also seems implicitly to be advancing the normative claim that promissory estoppel is justified as a corrective to the problem of under-enforcement created by the consideration doctrine. This claim appears to be circular. Fried's direct critique rejects the consideration doctrine because it is incoherent, not because it leads to promissory under-enforcement. His claim that the consideration doctrine leads to under-enforcement of promises *presupposes* that contract law ought to conform to the promise principle. Unless the claim that contract law *ought* to conform to the promise principle has already been established, there is no force to the objection that the consideration doctrine fails to enforce all the promises the promise principle would enforce. His objection to the consideration doctrine therefore applies with equal force to promissory estoppel: both doctrines prohibit enforcement of some promises the promise principle would enforce.

[59] He does suggest that 'principles of tort' can be used to impose liability in the absence of a promise when one party gives 'vague assurances that cause foreseeable harm to others'. *Contract as Promise*, above n. 30, at 24. Although he does not, Fried could conceivably rely on such tort principles to try to account for the cases decided under promissory estoppel. But the vague invocation of 'tort principles' hardly provides a coherent account of promissory estoppel.

[60] If Fried had acknowledged the numerous cases in which recovery is denied under §90 to promisees who detrimentally rely on promises, he might have felt compelled to examine these cases to explain either why the promise principle does not support recovery in those cases or why they are unsupportable.

[61] 133 N.W.2d 267 (1965).

[62] See e.g. 'Recent Developments: Contracts—Expanded Application of Promissory Estoppel in Restatement of Contracts Section 90—Hoffman v. Red Owl Stores, Inc.', *Michigan Law Review*, 65 (Dec. 1966), 351; Bruce A. Coggeshall, 'Note: Contracts: Reliance Losses: Promissory Estoppel as a Basis of Recovery for Breach of Agreement to Agree: Hoffman v. Red Owl Stores, Inc., 26 Wis. 2d 683, 133 N.W.2d 267 (1965)', *Cornell Law Quarterly*, 51 (1966), 351; Charles L. Knapp, 'Symposium on the Restatement (Second) of Contracts. Reliance in the Revised Restatement: The Proliferation of Promissory Estoppel', *Columbia Law Review*, 81 (1981), 52.

representations made during preliminary negotiations. Fried's discussion of *Hoffman*, however, is limited to the sole purpose of defending the distinctiveness thesis. Fried introduces the case only to refute the claim that it constitutes a counter-example to the distinctiveness thesis. Fried introduces *Hoffman* after he has taken the position that contract-as-promise requires an expectancy remedy for breach of contract. Since *Hoffman* awards reliance damages for defendant's failure to keep its promise,[63] Fried's critics might argue it demonstrates that contract law is not based on the promise principle. Fried's response is that *Hoffman* should be understood not as a contracts case but as a torts case instead.[64] Fried thus defuses *Hoffman* as a threat to the distinctiveness thesis by reclassifying it as a tort law case, which is consistent with an award of reliance damages, rather than a contracts case, which requires, on Fried's view, an expectancy award. Once he has defused *Hoffman*, however, Fried makes no effort to explain when promissory estoppel will lie in a preliminary negotiation (or any other) case. His only point is that when it does lie, and reliance damages are awarded, it sounds in tort rather than contract.[65] The economic analyst, however, has no interest in whether the case sounds in tort or contract, but is exclusively concerned with explaining when recovery will be allowed under promissory estoppel.[66]

2.3 The *Ex Post* Perspective in Adjudication

In his highly influential critique of deontic contract theories, Richard Craswell argues that deontic theories such as Fried's are seriously deficient because they fail to provide any guidance in understanding how courts do or should decide cases in which the relevant issue falls within a contractual gap.[67] For Craswell, contractual gaps exist whenever contractual parties either attempt but fail to resolve an issue

---

[63] Because the court believes defendant's assurances fell short of a 'definite' and detailed promise, it avoids describing defendant's conduct as 'breach of contract' and concludes simply that 'injustice would result here if plaintiffs were not granted some relief because of the failure of defendants to keep their promises which induced plaintiffs to act to their detriment' (*Hoffman v. Red Owl Stores, Inc.*, 133 N.W.2d 267, 275 (1965)).

[64] 'Promissory obligation is not the only basis for liability; principles of tort are sufficient to provide that people who give vague assurances that cause foreseeable harm to others should make compensation' (*Contract as Promise*, above n. 30, at 24).

[65] Fried's argument is not intended to presuppose that recovery in promissory estoppel cases is limited to reliance damages. As a matter of law, it is clear that this is not the case. Fried's point is simply that when reliance damages are awarded, liability cannot be based on contract. *Hoffman* is of interest to Fried solely because the court awarded reliance damages. Since contract as promise, in Fried's view, requires expectancy damages for breach of contract, Fried must argue that liability in *Hoffman* is not contractual.

[66] See e.g. Avery Katz, 'When Should an Offer Stick? The Economics of Promissory Estoppel in Preliminary Negotiations', *Yale Law Journal*, 105 (1996), 1249; 'Enforcing Promises', above n. 22, at 1317–19.

[67] See above n. 4.

unambiguously, or fail even to consider an issue.[68] He argues that 'creative interpretation' is required to resolve any contractual disputes over issues falling within a
contractual gap.[69] His central point is that deontic theories such as Fried's cannot
explain or guide the interpretation necessary to fill contractual gaps. Fried's theory
holds that courts in contract cases do and should hold the promisor to the content of
his promise. But in gap cases the promise has no unambiguous content bearing on
the relevant issue. As Craswell notes, the vast majority of contractual disputes require
courts to settle issues not provided for by the express terms of a promise.[70] To name
just a few, parties often fail to specify the proper remedy for breach, the conditions
under which performance is excused, the information, if any, each party must dis-
close to the other, which party should bear the risk of loss of goods in transit, and
which warranties, if any, the promisor is providing to the promisee. In short, the
express terms of an agreement always radically under-determine its content. An adequate descriptive and normative contract theory would provide a set of background
rules for contract law to explain how courts do and should interpret such agreements. These background rules include both so-called 'default rules', which impute
terms into all agreements in the absence of parties specifying otherwise, and 'mandatory' rules, which impute terms that cannot be avoided into all agreements. Craswell
argues that deontic theories such as Fried's lack the resources necessary to identify
and evaluate contract background rules because they are 'content neutral. They give
reasons why an individual who has promised to do φ thereby incurs some form of
obligation to do φ, regardless of how φ is filled in.'[71] As a result, deontic contract theories must be supplemented with independent theories that 'do virtually all of the
work involved in fulfilling the needs of contract law'.[72]

Craswell's critique provides a vivid context for examining the extent to which
deontic theories are limited to the *ex post* perspective. If deontic contract theories
hold that the sole ground for liability in contract is the parties' past agreement, then
deontic theories appear committed to an *ex post* perspective. Yet whenever an agreement fails to provide grounds for resolving a contract dispute, the *ex post* perspective
runs out. Whether the problem is to recommend the content of legislated default
rules, such as those found in article 2 of the UCC, or to describe or assess common law
default rules, the *ex post* perspective of deontic theories appears to disable them from
providing answers. Fried would, in large measure, agree with this part of Craswell's
critique, although he would not regard it as a criticism of his theory. As Craswell

[68] 'While it is perhaps more common to speak of "interpretation" in cases where parties attempt to
resolve an issue but do so with insufficient clarity, and to speak of applying default rules in cases where
the parties made no attempt to address an issue, the principle is much the same in either case' (ibid. at
505).
[69] ibid. at 504–5.
[70] As Craswell puts the point, 'some method must be found to *interpret* the parties' agreement, to
provide rules governing any topic *not explicitly settled* by the parties' (ibid. at 504–5; second emphasis
added).
[71] ibid. at 515–16.   [72] ibid. at 508.

notes, Fried explicitly disavows the claim that the promise principle has implications for gap-filling. He readily admits that other principles, external to the parties and their agreement, must come into play to fill these gaps. Fried's sole objective is to demonstrate the absolute priority of the promise principle *within its domain*. Where that principle has no application, Fried has 'no dog in the fight'. As we have seen, Fried defines contract law as that body of law that can be explained and justified by the promise principle. In his view, contract law by definition runs out wherever contracts run out. For Fried, contract law and theory answer questions regarding matters addressed by contracts. Questions regarding matters not addressed by contracts can be addressed, of course, only by non-contract law and theory.

Thus, by conceptual *ipse dixit*, Fried removes the question of default rules from the arena of contract theory. This much is enough to demonstrate why economic analysts might find Fried's theory of limited interest. Fried is interested in defining and defending a version of contract law whose domain is circumscribed by the promise principle. Economic analysts of contract law are interested in explaining and justifying contract law. There can be no question that the problem of contractual default rules is fundamental and important to contract law. By apparently bowing out of the debate, Fried concedes the irrelevancy of his theory for much of interest to contract scholars. But to make matters worse (to the considerable distress of economic analysts like Craswell), Fried refuses to leave the stage after his swan song. Indeed, Craswell makes the point that Fried's theory is irrelevant to the default rule debate, not by showing that Fried fails to endorse any default rules, but instead by demonstrating that Fried endorses a host of default rules his theory cannot justify. For each default rule Fried supports, Craswell argues Fried's theory's *ex post* perspective disables it from describing or evaluating the default rule. Instead, Craswell argues that Fried helps himself to a jumble of arguments that appear to have no relationship to promise, autonomy, or each other. Craswell thus writes: 'Sometimes Fried relies on people's existing expectations; sometimes he uses economic arguments; sometimes he rests on principles of "fault" or "altruism"; and sometimes . . . he advances no justification at all. Such a scattershot approach to the selection of default rules does little to advance our understanding of contract law.'[73]

Craswell's central claim is that the *ex post* perspective of deontic contract theories structurally disables them from identifying and evaluating contract background rules. Unfortunately, his illustrative critique of Fried proceeds on the basis of a conflation between two fundamentally different kinds of default rules. Once this distinction is taken into account, Craswell's criticisms no longer appear to establish a generalized structural limitation of deontic theories. Instead, they reveal a simple disagreement over the sufficiency of different kinds of evidence for establishing whether contractual parties have formed subjective intentions on particular issues. Thus, even if Craswell's criticisms are sound, at most they establish that Fried's

[73] ibid. at 523.

theory is currently irrelevant to determining the content of the particular default rules he discusses. But Fried's theory remains potentially relevant to all default rules, and may currently have direct implications for the content of default rules Craswell does not discuss. The relevancy of Fried's theory for default rules turns out to be a matter of contingent empirical fact, rather than a priori structural incapacity.

The key to understanding Fried's position is that his theory requires a strict distinction between interpreting the meaning of contract terms, and filling in gaps not governed by contract terms. Craswell lumps these problems together in his definition of default rules.[74] But for Fried, the constraints on a theory of contractual interpretation are quite different than those governing gap-filling. Fried reserves the term 'interpretation' for the task of determining the subjectively intended meaning of a term. Thus, someone who has assigned a particular meaning to an agreement should regard herself as having *interpreted* the agreement only if she believes the parties to the agreement subjectively intended their agreement to have that meaning. By proposing an interpretation of a term, the interpreter implicitly asserts that the meaning ascribed to the term by the interpretation represents the subjectively intended meaning of the parties. Fried contrasts interpretation with 'interpolation'. An interpolation describes the task of adding semantic content to terms, or imputing entirely new terms in agreements, that the parties did not subjectively intend when they entered into their agreement.[75] Thus, someone who has assigned a particular meaning to an agreement should regard herself as having *interpolated* (from) the agreement only if she believes the parties to the agreement did not subjectively intend the assigned meaning. The distinction between interpreting and interpolating agreements is crucial to Fried's theory because it marks the boundary between contract and non-contract law. The task of interpreting a term falls squarely within contract law and theory, as they are conceived by contract-as-promise. Contract-as-promise requires fidelity to the content of promises and interpretations describe that content. The task of interpolating a term or agreement arises only if an interpretation is impossible because the parties formed no subjective intent relevant to resolving the issue in question. Interpolation is required only if a determination is made that the disputed issue falls within a genuine gap in the parties' subjective intentions. Thus, interpolations necessarily will be guided by non-contract law and theory.

Craswell's conflation of the distinction between interpretation and interpolation helps to explain why he is puzzled by Fried's insistence that the promise principle must explain some default rules, while it need not—indeed cannot—explain other default rules. For example, Craswell cannot understand why Fried asserts that the

---

[74] 'While it is perhaps more common to speak of "interpretation" in cases where parties attempt to resolve an issue but do so with insufficient clarity, and to speak of applying default rules in cases where the parties made no attempt to address an issue, the principle is much the same in either case' (ibid. at 505).

[75] 'In contract law, there is a vaguely marked boundary between interpreting what was agreed to and interpolating terms to which the parties in all probability would have agreed but did not' (*Contract as Promise*, above n. 30, at 60.

expectancy damage remedy for breach is a default rule compelled by the promise principle, but the default rules governing impracticability and mistake are not.[76] The short answer is that Fried believes that parties who form contracts that do not provide an explicit remedy term subjectively intend the expectancy remedy.[77] But he believes that parties who form contracts that do not provide an explicit term governing excuse and mistake failed to consider those issues and so had no relevant subjective intentions at all. In the former case, the promise principle requires courts to interpret the agreement in order to respect their autonomy and enforce their moral obligations. In the latter case, courts must interpolate by using non-promissory principles.[78] The promise principle (and thus contract law) has no bearing on matters on which parties failed to come to an agreement. Of course, the plausibility of Fried's specific conclusions about these particular default rules turns entirely on his basis for deciding that all parties not expressly stating otherwise subjectively intend their agreements to be governed by expectancy damages, while parties not expressly stating otherwise have formed no subjective intention concerning excuse and mistake.[79]

[76] 'Default Rules', above n. 4, at 523.

[77] Admittedly, Fried's justification of the expectancy damage rule is far from clear on this point. Fried simply asserts that 'If I make a promise to you, I should do as I promise; and if I fail to keep my promise, it is fair that I should be made to hand over the equivalent of the promised performance. In contract doctrine this proposition appears as the expectation measure of damages for breach. The expectation standard gives the victim of a breach no more or less than he would have had had there been no breach—in other words, he gets the benefit of his bargain' (*Contract as Promise*, above n. 30, at 17). My claim is that this justification presupposes that the parties subjectively intended their agreement to include the expectancy damage option for the promisee. Thus, Fried's claim that the expectancy rule follows from the principle that 'the promisor should do as [he] promised', and that 'he gets the benefit of his bargain' makes sense if we presume that the parties subjectively intended to provide the expectancy damage remedy as an option for the non-breacher. Others have argued that if specific performance is not available, expectancy damages are the logically or conceptually entailed remedy for breach of promise. See e.g. Thomas Scanlon, 'Promises and Contracts', in *The Theory of Contract Law*, ed. Peter Benson (Cambridge; New York: Cambridge University Press, 2001), and Peter Benson, 'The Idea of a Public Basis of Justification for Contract', *Osgoode Hall Law Journal*, 33 (1995), 273. See below Sect. 3.2 for my argument that this view is non-responsive to Craswell's questions because it makes expectancy damages analytic, and simply raises the question of the appropriate remedy at one level removed.

[78] 'As we have seen in the discussion of mistake and impossibility, interpretation may fail to locate a core of agreement, and so at some point we must admit that the contract gives out. In such a case we have nothing to do but to reach for other principles of resolution than promise' (*Contract as Promise*, above n. 30, at 89).

[79] A similar analysis applies for the other default rules Craswell considers. For example, Fried argues that, absent the parties specifying otherwise, all promisees should have the right to rescind the contract: 'Parties bind themselves reciprocally. If one party treats himself as not bound, the other may also treat himself as not bound. By breaking his contract, a contractual partner not only opens himself up to claims for damages but releases his opposite number' (ibid. at 117). Craswell views the question of rescission as just another default rule. As he sees it, we need some basis for choosing whether to interpret contracts as granting the right of rescission unless otherwise specified, or not granting that right unless otherwise specified. In Craswell's view, Fried's promise principle has no bearing on this question: 'While a system of promising with that default rule would certainly expand a promisor's freedom, so too would an institution of promising with any other rule as its default rule. The quoted passage merely asserts that our system of promising contains rescission as one of its default remedies, without doing anything to justify

Unfortunately, Fried does not explain his basis for making these determinations. Nor does he offer a general theory about how such determinations should be made. Nevertheless, Fried's argument refutes Craswell's claim that his theory has no *potential* relevance for any default rules. Fried's theory is directly relevant to determining the content of default rules for *interpreting* contracts. When there is persuasive evidence that the parties formed the relevant subjective intent, Fried's theory requires courts to interpret contracts in accordance with that intent, provided there is also persuasive evidence of its content. Craswell is surely justified in demanding that Fried justify his fac-

that rule' ('Default Rules', above n. 4, at 520). Craswell is thus mystified to find that Fried not only endorses the rescission default rule, but does so on the ground that it is a 'corollary of the binding force of promising' (ibid. at 520). Craswell is further confused when he discovers Fried acknowledging that, with respect to recission, '[t]here is no obvious a priori reason for one or the other response' (ibid. at 521) (quoting Fried). But Fried's position is perfectly coherent. His justification for the rescission default rule is that '[a]ny other outcome would disturb the expectations on which contractual terms are usually established' (*Contract as Promise*, above n. 30, 118). Fried's claim is that most people subjectively intend their agreements to be governed by the rescission remedy option, and that this fact provides sufficient grounds for inferring such a mutual subjective intention in any case in which the parties fail to specify otherwise. *On the assumption that these premises are correct*, it follows that contract-as-promise requires contracts to be held to include the rescission remedy option. Given the truth of these premises, Fried's theory must treat the question of whether a contract is governed by the rescission remedy option as a matter of *interpretation*, not *interpolation*. In his view, there is no contractual gap to fill in agreements that fail to specify whether promisees are entitled to the rescission remedy. Rather, contract law must respect the actual subjective intent of the parties on this question, which requires interpreting agreements as providing the rescission remedy option. This analysis is consistent with Fried's claim that there is no a priori reason for one rule or the other. Fried's argument instead rests on an a posteriori reason for favouring the rescission default rule: most parties in fact subjectively intend their agreements to include the rescission remedy option.

Thus, in the end, Craswell's objection is not that Fried's theory cannot possibly be relevant to justifying the contract default rule governing rescission. If Fried's factual premises are correct, his theory does provide a justification for choosing a rescission default rule (though Fried would claim it is an interpretive default rule rather than a gap-filling default rule). Craswell's real objection is that Fried's argument does not yet convincingly demonstrate that Fried's theory is *in fact* relevant to this default rule. Craswell's complaint is that Fried hasn't demonstrated the truth of his factual premises. He has two objections to Fried's grounds for inferring an actual subjective intention to include the rescission remedy in any given contract: 'Fried cites no sociological data to support this claim' ('Default Rules', above n. 4 at 521 n. 77); and 'Fried says nothing to explain why the expectations of most people in the community should necessarily be dispositive in any individual case' (ibid. at 521). Both of these complaints constitute objections to the truth of the premises in Fried's argument, not the validity of his argument. None of these criticisms demonstrates that Fried's theory has no potential implications for the rescission default rule. The first objection rightly demands that Fried support a factual assertion, which may or may not be true. If the assertion is false, then Fried's theory in fact has no relevance for this particular default rule. But this fact in no way undermines the potential relevancy of Fried's theory for any other default rule. Its relevancy for any particular default rule will be purely contingent on people's subjective expectations. The second objection can easily be met by arguing that subjective intentions in particular cases can be reasonably inferred from true generalizations about the frequency of such subjective intentions in the general population (absent particularized evidence to the contrary). Finally, Craswell alleges Fried's argument contradicts other positions Fried has taken because 'at other points in his analysis Fried seems to view the enforcement of community expectations as the realm of tort' (ibid. at 521). Fried would argue, consistently, that community expectations provide the *standards of conduct* governing tort law, while community expectations are relevant to contract law only in so far as they provide a *basis for inferring subjective contractual intent*.

tual inferences about parties' subjective intent on various issues, such as contract remedies and excuses. But a demonstration that Fried fails to provide such a justification provides absolutely no support for the claim that Fried's theory is *necessarily* irrelevant to explaining or justifying the content of any default rules. It merely undermines Fried's case for the relevancy of his theory to the particular default rules he discusses. The relevancy of Fried's theory for determining the content of any particular default rule will turn on whether or not the issue in question is one governed by the actual subjective intent of the parties. That determination may be difficult to make, but Fried's theory requires it to be made. Craswell's critique points out the need for Fried to develop a systematic and defensible theory for how this determination should be made without begging the question. But this is a problem necessarily faced by *any* contract theory. The very idea of background rules presupposes a metaphysically firm, if evidentially soft, distinction between matters within and outside the scope of an agreement. Indeed, at the outset of his article, Craswell makes precisely this distinction when he defines the domain of background rules as those rules required to settle disputes about topics not 'explicitly settled' by the parties. Thus, before we can decide whether any background rule is required to settle a dispute, we must first determine whether the parties' agreement explicitly settled the issue in question. Like Fried, Craswell offers no theory for how this determination should be made.

Thus, Craswell's arguments do not, in fact, support his contention that Fried's theory is necessarily irrelevant for identifying and evaluating default rules. Both Craswell and Fried agree that, in Fried's terms, Fried's theory is relevant for interpreting contracts but irrelevant to interpolating them. Since Craswell includes both exercises under the rubric of 'default rules', we can say that Fried's theory is relevant to determining the content of interpretive default rules but irrelevant to determining the content of interpolative default rules. Craswell's criticism is that Fried employs an unarticulated and undefended theory for deciding whether parties shared the relevant subjective intent in any given dispute. Craswell's claim is that we need a default rule to tell us what to do when we don't know whether deciding a case requires us, in Fried's terms, to interpret or interpolate. For Craswell, the gap case is one in which either we know the parties did not form the relevant mutual intent or we don't know what mutual intent they formed. In either case, the court has to decide without adverting to the parties' intent. Fried would treat such cases as true gap cases that require the court to interpolate. As a practical matter, it would be impossible for the court to justify its decision on the basis of the promise principle because, by hypothesis, it has insufficient evidence of the relevant content of the promise.

But I suspect Craswell's real complaint here is that Fried's principal source for evidence of subjective intent is 'background conventions and understandings' that create expectations,[80] as well as 'inchoate meanings'.[81] When 'plain meaning' runs out,

---

[80] *Contract as Promise*, above n. 30 at 84–5.

[81] 'It is a truism in the philosophy of language that in interpreting a person's words we are not guessing at the hidden but determined content of some list in the speaker's head. Rather, our concerns

Craswell sees indeterminacy of subjective intent and the concomitant need for a true gap-filler. Although it is possible to fill the resulting gaps by adverting to background conventions, we need a theory of gap-filling default rules to tell us whether we should. For Fried, however, the subjectively intended meaning of terms is necessarily informed by background conventions. So when the surface meaning of a term does not resolve an issue, Fried adverts to background conventions to determine whether subjective intent is likely to extend beyond the surface meaning to resolve the issue.[82] If in his judgment it does, then there is no need for a true gap-filler—standard contract interpretation does the job on its own and the case is therefore governed by contract law.[83] A true gap-filling default rule is required only if Fried believes the background conventions do not provide persuasive evidence of subjective agreement. Then courts must go beyond the agreement, and therefore beyond contract law, to resolve the dispute.[84] Thus, the true disagreement between Craswell and Fried is over the status of background conventions as evidence of subjectively intended meaning, not the potential relevance of contract-as-promise for interpretive gap-filling default rules. Their disagreement is over the familiar, albeit complex, question

particularize, render concrete, inchoate meanings. (So when a person refers to all the even numbers between 10 and 1000, he intends to refer also to the number 946, though that number may not figure explicitly on some list in his head)' (ibid. at 60).

[82] Here Fried forays into a brief discussion of the relationship between philosophy of language, semantics, and contractual interpretation. His view, informed by Lon Fuller's discussion of Wittgenstein, is that all meaning is necessarily contextually determined by a system of background expectations. Thus, '[p]romises, like every human expression, are made against an unexpressed background of shared purposes, experiences, and even a shared theory of the world. Without such a common background communication would be impossible' (ibid. at 88). He claims that the system of background conventions is not 'susceptible to a factual, cognitively identifiable specification' in advance of all possible circumstances, but is nonetheless knowable: 'It is possible to call something a matter of understanding, even though its actual results cannot have been specified beforehand in terms of necessary and sufficient conditions. . . . The fact that we cannot, for example, be said to know beforehand all instances of what counts as cruel behavior does not mean that our designation of a novel instance as true cruelty is an arbitrary decision. There is an element of understanding, and the concept of cruelty itself determines our decision, though we cannot fully know that determination beforehand' (ibid. at 87–8). Thus, on Fried's view, a court *ex post* can make a determination that the parties' subjectively intended a given meaning for a term in their agreement even though, at the time of their agreement, the parties could not have known this precise meaning was part of their intention.

[83] Fried takes the standard good faith interpretation of contracts to provide a clear example of judicial interpretation, rather than interpolation: 'In each case a reasonable interpretation of the parties' agreement, of their original intentions, against the background of normal practices and understandings in that kind of transaction, would be quite sufficient to provide a satisfactory resolution' (ibid. at 86).

[84] Fried claims that in cases in which parties think they have agreed but actually have not, '[t]he one basis on which these cases cannot be resolved is on the basis of the agreement—that is, of contract as promise. The court cannot enforce the will of the parties because there are no concordant wills. Judgment must therefore be based on principles external to the will of the parties' (ibid. at 60). Thus, he claims '[t]he further courts are from the boundary between interpretation and interpolation, the further they are from the moral basis of the promise principle and the more palpably are they imposing an agreement' (ibid. at 61).

of the relationship between semantic theory, conventions, and interpretation, rather than the deep structure of deontic theory and its potential relevance for default rules.[85]

Craswell's failure to take into account Fried's views on meaning and contractual interpretation is typical of the literature discussing Fried's theory. For example, a failure to appreciate Fried's interpretive views also leads Randy Barnett to the misleading conclusion that Fried's account of the objective theory of liability conflicts with his theory's claim that contractual liability cannot be imposed on unwilling parties.[86] The objective theory of contract treats parties as legally bound solely on the basis of their manifestations of intention, irrespective of their subjective intentions. Fried's theory clearly requires that contractual obligation be based on shared subjective intentions, and therefore rejects the objective theory of contract because it imposes contractual liability in the absence of such intentions. Fried argues that the objective theory of contract originated in a misguided attempt by classical contract law proponents to disguise the truly non-contractual nature of liability imposed in the absence

[85] Craswell has since written on the subject at length. See Richard Craswell, 'Do Trade Customs Exist?', in *The Jurisprudence of Corporate and Commercial Law*, ed. Jody S. Kraus and Steven D. Walt (Cambridge; New York: Cambridge University Press, 2000). For my response, see Jody S. Kraus and Steven D. Walt, 'In Defense of the Incorporation Strategy' (ibid. at 193).

[86] Barnett claims that '[s]ome will theorists uneasily resolve [the conflict between subjective understanding and objectively manifested behaviour] by acknowledging that other "interests"—for example, reliance—may take priority over the will [citing *Contract as Promise*, above n. 30 at 58–63]. By permitting individuals to be bound by promises never intended by them to be enforceable, such a concession deprives a will theory of much of its force. Requiring the promisor's subjective will to yield always, or almost always, to the promisee's reliance on the promisor's objective manifestation of assent undermines the claim that contractual obligation is grounded in the individual's will and bolsters the view that contractual obligations may be imposed rightfully on unwilling parties' (Randy E. Barnett, 'A Consent Theory of Contract', *Columbia Law Review*, 86 (1986), 269 (hereinafter 'Consent'), at 273–4. But Fried's view does not 'bolster the view that contractual obligations may be imposed rightfully on unwilling parties'. Quite the opposite. It takes the view that *non-contractual* obligations may be imposed rightfully on unwilling parties. Nor is Fried's theory embarrassed by 'acknowledging that other "interests" . . . may take priority over the will'. When an individual objectively promises and causes another to justifiably rely, Fried holds that the state may be justified in protecting the objective promisee's reliance, even though the promisor did not subjectively intend to promise. This view is perfectly consistent with Fried's contract as promise. Such liability is justified by non-promissory, non-contractual principles. The will theory asserts only that promissory liability may be imposed if and only if the promisor subjectively intended to promise. Nothing about contract as promise prevents Fried or any other will theorist from holding that there are circumstances under which state coercion can justifiably be brought to bear against the will of individuals. For example, will theorists are not, and need not be, opposed to imposing criminal liability even though the source of the justification of such liability is not the will of the criminal. See also 'Consent' at 300–1 ('[A] theory that bases contractual obligation on the existence of a "will to be bound" is hard pressed to justify contractual obligation in the absence of an actual exercise of will. It is difficult to see how one is legally or morally committed to perform an agreement that one did not actually intend to commit oneself to and still hew to a theory that based the commitment on its willful quality'). Again, Barnett misinterprets Fried's theory as being committed to the proposition that liability *of any sort* cannot be imposed on individuals in the absence of their will. The promise principle is intended to explain and justify contractual liability, not all liability.

of subjective agreement yet under the rubric of contract law.[87] But Fried does not reject the objective theory of liability generally. His claim is that when liability is imposed on the basis of what an ordinary person would have intended, the resulting liability can be characterized as genuinely contractual only if the hypothetical intentions of the ordinary person provide sufficient grounds for inferring the actual subjective intentions of the parties. In that case, the objective manifestations of intent serve merely as persuasive evidence of the presence of the subjective intent necessary for genuinely contractual liability (i.e. liability justified by the promise principle), rather than as alternative, non-promissory grounds for imposing liability. Thus, if the hypothetical intentions of the ordinary person do not provide adequate evidence of the parties' subjective intent, the imposition of liability based on objective (and decidedly not subjective) intent is non-promissory and therefore non-contractual.[88] Yet Fried has no objection to deciding such cases on this basis. Indeed, Fried readily admits that there are good reasons why courts should not allow individuals to escape liability on the ground that they did not subjectively intend what they objectively manifested. First, such claims might justifiably be disbelieved. But even if believed, a court should impose liability anyway in order to protect the reasonable expectations of the promisee for which the promisor is responsible, or to safeguard the efficacy of contract law by ensuring that parties will be able effectively to communicate subjective intent accurately in the future. The first ground for liability is based on the deontic value of preventing or compensating wrongful or negligent harm. The second ground is based on the consequentialist value of enhancing opportunities to incur contractual liability for future individuals. In Fried's view, both of these justifications for liability are justified, but neither of them grounds *contractual* liability. Therefore, Fried supports liability based on the objective theory of intent as justified instances of non-contractual obligation. However, if a court believes that neither party subjectively intended what they objectively manifested, it should not impose liability unless this would undermine confidence in objective meaning. By undermining confidence

---

[87] 'Another of classical law's evasions of the inevitability of using noncontractual principles to resolve failures of agreement is recourse to the so-called objective standard of interpretation. In the face of a claim of divergent intentions, the court imagines that it is respecting the will of the parties by asking what somebody else, say the ordinary person, would have intended by such words of agreement. This may be a reasonable resolution in some situations, but it palpably involves imposing an external standard on the parties' (*Contract as Promise*, above n. 30 at 61).

[88] Fried could have made this point far clearer than he did. Recall Fried's claim that '[i]n the face of a claim of divergent intentions, the court imagines that it is respecting the will of the parties by asking what somebody else, say the ordinary person, would have intended by such words of agreement. This . . . palpably involves imposing an external standard on the parties' (ibid. at 61). Put this way, it is puzzling why Fried automatically rejects the court's claim that it is respecting the will of the parties. It is possible that the parties did subjectively intend what the ordinary person would have intended even though there is a *claim* of divergent intentions. Parties make false, self-serving claims all the time. The argument makes sense, however, if we modify Fried's sentence to read, 'in the face of a *credible* claim of divergent intentions'. If a court believes that both parties did *not* subjectively agree on the relevant issue, but none the less resolves that issue, then the decision is not properly a matter of genuine contract law, as Fried conceives it. It would be false to assert that the decision is based on the will of the parties.

in objective meaning, the decision would jeopardize the institution of contract law and the conception of autonomy and liberty it advances. Again, the question of whether to impose liability in this case depends on a balance of competing concerns external to the parties' (subjective) agreement. Fried's only point is that imposition of liability in this case would not be contractual, even though it might or might not be justified.[89] Thus, Fried's only concern here is to defend his conception of contract as promise against the claim that the objective theory proves contractual liability is non-contractual. As we have seen, Fried's standard response relies on conceptual stipulation: all contractual liability is based on promise, therefore any liability not based on promise is non-contractual. In a nutshell, Fried just wants it to be clear that decisions imposing liability for so-called 'objective agreements' do not demonstrate that contract is not based on promise, but rather demonstrate that such decisions are not based on contract. Fried endorses the objective theory of liability, but rejects the objective theory of contract.

Craswell's critique therefore does not undermine the relevancy of contract-as-promise for interpretive default rules. But Craswell's other complaints stand. First, as Fried concedes, contract-as-promise has no bearing on default rules for interpolating agreements (true gap-filling). That this concession is no embarrassment to Fried demonstrates a fundamental difference between his objectives for contract theory and those of the economic analyst. His project is to explain and defend the distinctiveness of contract law, not to explain all 'non-contract' law that may be relevant to enforcing agreements. Economic analysts of contract have no interest in the distinctiveness thesis. Their exclusive goal is to explain all legal doctrines relevant to enforcing agreements, whether or not those agreements qualify as 'contracts' according to Fried's theory. This alone surely explains why economic analysts find Fried's theory of little use. Secondly, Fried none the less opines on how such gaps should be filled by suggesting a variety of considerations for filling different kinds of gaps. For example, Fried invokes considerations of fairness to justify a gap-filling default rule requiring sharing in cases of impracticability and mistake,[90] but relies on considerations of

[89] 'Perhaps a promisor should not be allowed to claim that she did not mean by a term what is generally implied by that term. But if she is not allowed to excuse herself by showing this private, special intention, it is not because we doubt that sometimes people truly have such special intentions. Rather we may bar such a claim as a matter of fairness to the other party or as a matter of practical convenience. We rather suspect either (1) that the claimant did mean what is usually meant, took her chances, and is now trying to get out of what has turned into a bad deal; or (2) that though *she* didn't mean it, her opposite number did, and reasonably assumed that *she* did mean it, so that it would be unfair to disappoint the opposite party's expectations now by urging some surprising, unexpected, secret intention. . . . These are perfectly reasonable, practical grounds for administering a system that in general seeks to effectuate the true intentions of the parties. Where we really can be confident that neither party intended to cover this particular case, and where we can reach that conclusion without fearing a spreading disintegration of confidence in contractual obligations generally, no reason remains for enforcing this contract' (ibid. at 66–7). To be perfectly clear, the last sentence should have read, '. . . no reason remains for enforcing this *agreement*', because, on Fried's view, the only ground for enforcing that case is based on non-contract law.

[90] ibid. at 57–73.

'convenience' to justify the 'mailbox' default rule governing offer and acceptance.[91] As Craswell points out, Fried appears to offer no reason why fairness is not invoked to govern offer and acceptance, or why convenience is not relevant to the rules governing mistake and impracticability.[92] Clearly, Fried cannot generate these conclusions by drawing on contract as promise because the rules are, by hypothesis, non-promissory cases. What is the basis for Fried's justification of these rules, and how in particular can Fried reconcile his use of consequentialist principles, such as future convenience for prospective contracting parties, with the deontic foundations of his theory?

The answer to both of these questions lies in Fried's broader jurisprudential views about the nature of law and adjudication.[93] Fried subscribes to Dworkin's theory of law and adjudication, as Dworkin had developed it at the time Fried was writing. Fried believes that judges have no discretion in deciding hard cases because there is a right answer for every possible legal question. As Fried understands Dworkin's view, law provides a uniquely right answer in every case because it necessarily incorporates morality. The law consists in a 'reasoned elaboration of principles, including moral principles',[94] which together are, in principle, sufficient to generate a uniquely correct result in every case. Thus, the parties in adjudication have pre-existing legal rights which courts are bound to vindicate. In this respect, Fried sees a parallel between his general jurisprudential views and his theory of contract. The adjudication of contract disputes must be based exclusively on the prior subjective intentions of the parties. On this view, the parties' prior subjective agreement creates moral rights and obligations the court is bound to enforce. Thus, the adjudication of contract disputes requires judges to take an exclusively *ex post* perspective. Similarly, on the Dworkinian view to which Fried subscribes, even in non-contractual disputes, decisions must be based on the litigants' pre-existing legal rights. All disputes require judges to identify and vindicate the pre-existing legal rights of the litigants. Thus, the adjudication of all disputes requires judges to take an exclusively *ex post* perspective. So while Fried views contract law as enforcing moral rights, he shares Dworkin's view that law itself incorporates morality. When judges decide cases, they are necessarily called on to enforce morality. In this respect, the deontic character of Fried's theory of contract is embedded in the deontic foundation of Dworkin's rights-based jurisprudential theory.

But Fried is at pains to emphasize that contract law, and the promise principle that justifies it, provides no constraints whatsoever on decisions that cannot be based on the litigants' subjective intentions. The constraints that apply to gap-filling default rules (for interpolation), therefore, are generated by the deontic character of

[91] ibid. at 52.

[92] 'Default Rules', above n. 4 at 522–3.

[93] For his discussion of jurisprudence and its relevance for his contract theory, see *Contract as Promise*, above n. 30 at 67–9.

[94] ibid. at 68.

adjudication. Gaps are to be filled, according to Fried, by 'residual principles of law', which include moral principles.[95] On this Dworkinian view, all adjudication is constrained by the obligation of judges to respect the pre-existing legal rights of the litigants. Fried argues that the very idea that individuals have rights entails that individuals cannot be sacrificed to collective goals such as efficiency, redistribution, or altruism. Rights derive from the inherent value of autonomy—they enable individuals to plan, consider, and pursue their own ends. Because individuals make these plans against society's background conventions, respect for individual rights prohibits courts from undermining these expectations without providing fair notice. Such a right is basic for securing individual autonomy. Without it, individuals would be unable to plan and pursue their ends. Any change in the content of the law must therefore be made prospectively only, either through legislation or judicial rulings with a purely prospective effect.[96] Thus, although Fried's theory does not prohibit change in gap-filling default rules, it constrains the rate of change and provides no direct guidance for the direction of change. Fried's underlying jurisprudential commitments therefore build in a normative bias in favour of the status quo for gap-filling default rules.

The litigants in gap cases have the right to have their legitimate expectations respected, and those expectations are based on society's background conventions.[97] These are the same background conventions that sometimes provide sufficient evidence of parties' actual subjective intent. But in gap cases these conventions both guide and constrain adjudication, not because they provide evidence of the parties' subjective intent, but because they form the basis of the parties' legitimate and therefore legally protected expectations. Thus, the deontic constraints of adjudication prohibit courts from taking an *ex ante* perspective by ignoring the parties' legitimate expectations. To do so would be contrary to the individual rights of litigants. Courts cannot simply pursue efficiency or any other value without regard to the rights of the

---

[95] '[W]e know perfectly well how to fill the gaps in a contract. There is no bare flesh showing, as it were, when relations between persons are not covered by contractual clothing. These relations take place under the general mantle of the law. Indeed, the very absence of gaps in the law makes it easy to admit that there may be gaps in contract. For when relations between parties are not governed by the actual promises they have made, they are governed by residual general principles of law' (ibid. at 69).

[96] 'Conventions . . . define expectations, permit planning, and constrain the court's pursuit of either efficiency or altruism in the particular case. For if efficiency or altruism were our sole concern, there would be no a priori reason why they might not be better served if courts sometimes took it upon themselves to decide particular cases on an ad hoc basis, free of the constraints of preexisting convention. But courts generally do not operate on such an ad hoc basis, and they rarely admit it if they do. . . . Efficiency, redistribution, and altruism are certainly among the law's many goals. By pursuing those goals according, but only according, to established conventions—including conventions established prospectively or gradually by courts—the collectivity acknowledges that individuals have rights and cannot just be sacrificed to collective goals. The recourse to prior conventions permits individuals to plan, to consider and pursue their own ends. And once they have made and embarked on plans against this background it would be unjust to change the rules in midcourse . . . . Changes should be prospective only' (ibid. at 85).

[97] Presumably, for Fried an expectation would not be legitimate if not grounded in good reason. Background conventions constitute one source of good reasons for forming expectations.

parties, but must instead respect expectations based on background understand-ings.[98] However, because the rights of litigants are determined, in part, by their legit-imate expectations, which in turn are determined by background conventions, if the background conventions *themselves* allow an *ex ante* perspective, then courts can *to that extent* take an *ex ante* perspective as well. Indeed, in such cases, the litigants not only lack grounds for complaint, but are affirmatively entitled to the court taking that perspective by virtue of their legal right not to have their legitimate expectations undermined. Here, their legitimate expectation is that in adjudicating their dispute courts will take into account certain prospective effects of its decision on others. Thus, background social conventions that permit consequentialist considerations to be brought to bear in resolving certain kinds of issues permit, indeed require, courts to take such considerations into account when adjudicating disputes. In sum, Fried's deontic contract and jurisprudential views commit him to the *ex post* perspective in adjudication. But that perspective simply requires judges to vindicate the parties' pre-existing rights. Parties in adjudication have the right not to have their legitimate expectations upset. But if their legitimate expectations are based on background con-ventions that permit prospective effects to be taken into account in resolving the issue they are litigating, then respect for their rights is consistent with resolving their dis-pute using an *ex ante* perspective. Fried thus provides a deontic justification for the possibility of the *ex ante* perspective in adjudication by demonstrating how the *ex post* perspective itself might require a shift to the *ex ante* perspective.

In the end, then, Fried's theory contemplates that both interpretation and inter-polation will be informed by background conventions. When background conven-tions provide the basis for interpreting an agreement being adjudicated, the state coercion used to enforce the judgment is justified because it enforces a party's moral obligation to keep a promise. The conception of autonomy foundational to Fried's liberal theory requires that individuals have the power to incur this obligation. When background conventions provide the basis for interpolating an agreement being adjudicated, the state coercion used to enforce the judgment is justified because it respects the individuals' rights not to have their legitimate expectations upset. Coercion is justified because the prevailing party has a pre-existing legal right to have his legitimate expectations protected. That right in turn is a corollary of the individ-ual right to form, revise, and pursue a system of ends that is part of the conception of autonomy at the foundation of Fried's liberal theory. Thus, although the use of back-ground conventions in both interpretation and interpolation is ultimately justified by the foundational value of autonomy, autonomy is mediated by the idea of volun-tary obligation in the former, and the ideas of fair notice and planning in the latter. In both interpretation and interpolation, background conventions are relevant only if

---

[98] 'A court . . . must inquire into the background understandings (including those established by prior decisions) of a particular case. For those who have not patience with anything but forward-looking policies of social betterment, this inquiry will seem a vain, even foolish exercise—as would scrupulous adherence to one's promises' (ibid. at 85).

they are consistent with the parties' subjective intentions. In interpretation, the various background conventions will be either displaced or implicitly invoked by the parties' subjective intentions. In interpolation, the background conventions will govern disputes between the parties not otherwise governed by their subjective intentions. Thus, Craswell's charge that, on this interpretation of Fried's theory, 'sociology is doing all the work involved in fulfilling the needs of contract law'[99] rings hollow. Given the necessary relevance of context to any interpretive enterprise, all contract theories must ultimately rely on a combination of sociology, other allied disciplines, and ordinary intuition. Craswell's charge instead must be that Fried's theory is somehow objectionably over-reliant on background conventions for interpretation. But in the absence of an argument for why and how a theory of contract interpretation should avoid or minimize its reliance on expectations, there is no basis for this claim. And in any event, it is clear that in Fried's theory, whatever work sociology is doing, it is hardly doing *all* the work. In fact, sociology does *none* of the normative work. Sociology is relevant to contract law only because, on Fried's jurisprudential view, the individual rights that liberal individualism requires courts to respect in contract cases are sometimes informed by society's background conventions.

Fried's view, so understood, still faces Craswell's practical question of how these background conventions are to be determined, especially by courts, and the normative question of how such a theory provides a basis for criticizing and recommending prospective changes in current default rules.[100] But our concern is not with the practical viability and theoretical breadth of Fried's approach to default rules, but the question of whether and how his theory has any implications for default rules. Fried has coherent arguments for his claim that both interpretive and interpolative default rules informed by background conventions are justified. Craswell claimed to demonstrate that Fried's theory necessarily is irrelevant because it necessarily takes an *ex post* perspective in adjudication. Craswell is right that Fried's *contract* theory has no implications for true gap-filling default rules and, in a sense, he is right that Fried's theory necessarily takes an *ex post* perspective in adjudication. But he is wrong that Fried's contract theory has no implications for interpretive default rules, and that Fried has no coherent *non-contract-theory* defence of the gap-filling default rules he supports. In both cases, Fried has a coherent argument for using background conventions as default rules. Fried's contract theory supports his claim for interpretive default rules, and his jurisprudential views support his claim for interpolative default rules. In addition, Fried has a coherent account of how both theories might allow a court to take both an *ex post* and an *ex ante* perspective in adjudicating agreements. And that account explains why Fried believes courts are sometimes justified in settling disputes over agreements by taking into account various consequentialist considerations. In the final analysis, Craswell's claim fails to reveal a fundamental feature of deontic theories that puts default rules and *ex ante* considerations beyond their

---

99 'Default Rules', above n. 4 at 508.   100 ibid. at 505–8.

reach. Instead, it reveals that contract interpretation implicates serious philosophical and pragmatic issues that transcend the differences in methodologies between deontic and economic contract theories.

2.4 Summary

The methodological commitments of Fried's deontic theory of contract explain why economic analysts of contract generally ignore or reject it. Fried accords theoretical priority to the twin objectives of justifying contract law and demonstrating its conceptual distinctiveness from other bodies of law. These lead him to dismiss or ignore, rather than explain, important contract doctrines that cannot be explained and therefore justified by the promise principle. His conceptualism also fuels his view that the law consists in the plain meaning of its doctrinal formulations and that case outcomes have no theoretical significance divorced from the reasoning offered in their support. Economic analysts of contract law, however, are principally interested in explaining case outcomes, not the doctrinal formulations that purport to justify them. And they have no interest in preserving the distinctiveness of contract law from other areas of law. Indeed, given that their objective is to explain case outcomes, the theory with greatest explanatory power, in their view, will be one that provides an explanation of case outcomes across apparently distinct areas of law, thereby demonstrating the underlying unity, rather than distinctiveness, of apparently diverse areas of law such as contract and tort. Rather than seeking to explain the distinctiveness of contract law, economic analysts want to explain its distinctiveness away.

Finally, Fried's distinctiveness thesis, his subtle view about the relationship between contract theory and jurisprudence, and his insufficiently articulated views about semantics and interpretation invite misinterpretation and misunderstanding. Fried's concession that his contract theory does not speak to gap-filling default rules appears to confirm the economic analysts' view that deontic theories are irrelevant to this important debate. But as we have seen, Fried's contract theory has direct implications for interpretive default rules, and his general jurisprudential views about law and individual rights have equally direct implications for interpolative default rules. Misunderstandings of Fried's views about semantics and interpretation lead economic analysts and others to conclude his explanations of doctrines are inconsistent, arbitrary, or question-begging. In fact, his accounts reflect a consistent application of his interpretive methodology and jurisprudential views. In each kind of case, he first determines whether the context is sufficient to indicate the parties to a dispute are likely to have had a subjective intent relevant to resolving the question at issue. Then, he determines which background expectations are relevant either to interpreting the meaning of their agreement or filling in the gaps left open by their agreement. The diverse and apparently inconsistent results reflect the underlying diversity of the background expectations that, on Fried's jurisprudential view, necessarily inform individual rights and thus constrain and guide adjudication.

2.5 Conclusion

To be sure, Fried's theory rests on many controversial premises and its presentation is unquestionably obscure. It is constructed on the shaky ground of several deep and complex debates of Fried's time: the classic death-of-contract debate in contract law, the CLS and emerging communitarian attacks on liberal individualism, opposing theories of semantics in the philosophy of language, and the jurisprudential debate between Dworkinian rights-theorists and Hartian legal positivists. Inevitably, Fried sometimes misjudges the plate tectonics of these shifting continents and his theory falls through the cracks. But it is the first sustained effort to align contemporary contract law with a normative theory that enjoys both wide intuitive appeal and deep philosophical credentials. Indeed, the most common objections to Fried's normative argument are based not on difficulties with its underlying Kantian conception of autonomy, but with its unreflective embrace of naive legal moralism: the inference that the state is justified in coercively enforcing all moral obligations.[101] Deontic contract theorists in Fried's tradition, therefore, often find little of interest in economic contract theory. Those theories are grounded on consequentialist principles which are widely regarded as counter-intuitive and philosophically objectionable. Although no one denies the relevance of consequentialist reasoning for moral, political, and legal theory, only recently have serious academics begun to revive the claim that consequentialism can provide an adequate normative foundation for any of these enterprises. In addition, because deontic theorists accord priority to the normative project of legal theory, they take seriously the question of whether the law as it is written provides an adequate justification for the decisions reached under the law. Especially in light of recent theory emphasizing the importance that political justification be available for public inspection and debate, deontic theorists are dubious of theories that purport to explain judicial decisions on the basis of hidden reasons that dismiss the plain meaning of the justifications offered in the decisions themselves.[102]

---

[101] Peter Benson is the only critic who argues that Fried's conception of autonomy itself is seriously defective. But Benson's ground for objecting to Fried's theory—that it is ultimately a teleological rather than deontological conception—leads him also to reject every contemporary contract theory but his own. Moreover, rather than questioning the viability of autonomy justifications of contract law, however, Benson's claim is that contemporary autonomy contract theories must be rejected because they do not remain sufficiently true to the deep philosophical arguments that explain the normative significance of autonomy. Benson therefore endorses a Hegelian theory of contract that rests on a thoroughly deontological conception of autonomy.

[102] For example, in Political Liberalism, Rawls argues that state coercion can be justified only by making available public justifications that draw on shared ideas in the public political culture. Peter Benson applies this idea to the justification of contract law. See 'Public Basis', above n. 77.

Explanations of case outcomes divorced from their ostensible justifications may be useful for practising attorneys, law professors organizing cases in casebooks, and even judges trying to take account of otherwise irreconcilable precedents that bind them. But they may have no inherent interest for deontic theorists seeking genuine normative justifications for the political coercion exercised through the rule of law. In the end, the most fundamental methodological difference between deontic and economic contract theorists is not only their differing respective priorities in the normative and explanatory projects of legal theory, but their differing conceptions of the objectives of legal explanation itself.

3 PETER BENSON

In Peter Benson's first major contribution to contract theory, he accords primacy to the normative project of justifying contract law and grounds that justification on the idea of consent as a transfer of entitlement.[103] Benson claims that the major doctrines of contract law conform to this conception of contract. Benson also argues that the entitlement theory of contract rests on a purely Hegelian conception of autonomy, and that only such a conception can provide an adequate normative justification of contract law. Benson's central thesis is that all contemporary contract theories except his, including ostensibly autonomy-based theories such as Fried's, provide a teleo-logical justification of contract law. As such, their justifications do not derive from a genuinely deontic conception of autonomy in which individuals have free will. Each of these justifications, therefore, at most explains how contract generates a morally conditional obligation. Only a Hegelian justification of contract can explain how and why contractual obligation is morally unconditional. Moreover, Benson argues that the central doctrines and animating principles of contract law can be explained and justified only by this deontic conception of autonomy. Thus, even if the teleological arguments of contemporary contract theory could provide an adequate normative foundation for some legal institutions, they cannot justify the institution of contemporary contract law.[104]

---

[103] See Peter Benson, 'Abstract Right', above n. 37.

[104] Benson rejects in their entirety every contemporary contract theory other than Randy Barnett's, including ostensibly autonomy-based theories such as Fried's and Kronman's, on the ground that they ultimately rest on teleological principles inconsistent with respect for the free will of autonomous persons and are therefore unable to explain or justify contract law. Benson rejects the contemporary autonomy-based theories of Charles Fried (see 'Abstract Right', above n. 37 at 1092–117; 'Contract', above n. 33 at 37–40; 'Public Basis', above n. 77 at 288–93) and Joseph Raz (see 'Contract' at 33–7), the welfare-based theories of Anthony Kronman (see 'Abstract Right' at 1119–45; 'Public Basis' at 302–5; 'Contract' at 45–8)

However, Benson's more recent scholarship suggests he no longer views the Hegelian conception of autonomy as justifying contract law in its own right. Instead, Benson argues that the justification of contract law should proceed analogously to the justification of Rawlsian political liberalism. Rawls argues that a political conception of justice can be justified only by constructing principles of justice out of the fundamental ideas in the public political culture. The resulting justification does not presuppose the truth of any particular comprehensive moral view, but instead accommodates all reasonable comprehensive views, each of which, by definition, endorses political liberalism from its own point of view.[105] Similarly, Benson argues that the justification of contract law must be constructed from what he calls the basic normative ideas present in our public *legal* culture in general, and from the principles and doctrines of contract law in particular.[106] The possibility of such a 'public juridical justification' presupposes that 'there is present in the common law—in judicial decisions—a set of normative ideas that implicitly contain a whole theory of contract and, furthermore, that this theory is able to settle the very questions which the law must answer to adjudicate contract disputes'.[107] Benson's claim, therefore, is that this set of ideas provides the normative foundation for the justification of contract law. Although Hegelian autonomy may indeed provide a true moral justification for contract law, its truth is irrelevant for purposes of providing the public justification that is 'essential to making the coercive operation of the law legitimate' on a liberal conception of justice.[108] Instead, the Hegelian concept of contract simply provides a heuristic conceptual framework for unifying the otherwise diverse set of basic normative ideas implicit in the common law of contracts.[109] Hegelian moral and political theory, then, plays no foundationally normative role in the public justification of

and Charles Goetz and Robert Scott (see 'Public Basis' at 299–302; 'Contract' at 50–4), the corrective justice theory of James Gordley (see 'Contract' at 43–5), the mixed autonomy-and-welfare theories of Michael Sandel (see 'Abstract Right' at 1092, 1117–19) and Michael Trebilcock (see 'Public Basis' at 312–15), and the reductivist theories of Lon Fuller (see 'Contract' at 25–9) and Patrick Atiyah (see 'Contract' at 29–33), which subsume contract law under general tort principles. Benson presents and criticizes Barnett's theory in 'Public Basis' at 293–9 and 'Contract' at 40–3.

[105] See *Political Liberalism*, above n. 15. For an explanation of the idea of political justification and the criticism that it need not and cannot remain neutral on its own truth, see Jody S. Kraus, 'Political Liberalism and Truth', *Legal Theory*, 5 (1999), 45.

[106] Benson, 'Public Basis', above n. 77, at 305.   [107] ibid. at 306.   [108] ibid. at 306.

[109] Benson argues that the conception of contract underlying and unifying the common law of contract 'has been developed with great rigour and completeness in the long tradition of legal philosophy that stretches from Aristotle to Hegel.... While the work of Kant and Hegel, where this idea is most fully elaborated, supposes a philosophically deep conception of practical reason, their arguments can be presented and understood on the basis of widely-shared everyday notions of legal accountability and obligation.... In other words, the leading ideas and claims in their accounts of contract can be presented in a way that stands apart from their deeper philosophical elaboration. Moreover, while the philosophical tradition elucidates the form and content of this conception of contract at a high level of abstraction, it can provide guidance in the endeavour to exhibit the coherence and the unity of conception in the well-established doctrines of contract law, because after all, philosophy too begins—and can only begin—with ordinary moral experience' (ibid. at 321).

contract law, except in so far as it is derived from, or provides a fair representation of, the normatively fundamental ideas in the public legal culture of contract law.

By adopting a Rawlsian approach to the justification of contract law, Benson in effect converts the justificatory project of contract theory into an explanatory project. Benson's initial project is to justify contract law by defending the Hegelian concept of autonomy and demonstrating how that concept explains and therefore justifies contract law.[110] But his current approach no longer requires him to defend the Hegelian concept of autonomy. Instead, he must independently identify the normatively fundamental ideas implicit in the public legal culture of contract law, and then construct from these ideas a coherent theory of contract law to serve as the basis for arbitrating all contractual disputes. Unsurprisingly, Benson claims the Hegelian concept of contract is the best theory of contract that can be constructed out of the fundamental ideas in the public legal culture of contract law. But on this Rawlsian approach to justification, the normative force of the Hegelian concept of contract law derives entirely from its claim to be embedded in the normatively fundamental ideas of the common law of contract. The claim that the Hegelian theory of contract derives from the Hegelian concept of autonomy, and thereby vindicates a metaphysically deep conception of free will, has no bearing on its justificatory force.

Benson begins his sketch of a public justification of contract law by identifying three normative ideas fundamental to the private law, and one provisionally fixed point of contract law. The three normative ideas are found in the principle that there can be liability for misfeasance, but no liability for mere nonfeasance,[111] the 'juridical conception' of persons, defined independently of their abilities to pursue the good and as having a capacity to have, acquire, and exercise rightful possession for and by themselves as free and equal,[112] and the idea of private transactions between two per-

---

[110] Rather, the burden on Benson's theory would be to defend the Hegelian conception of autonomy and contract, as well as establish that it explains and justifies contract law. All of Benson's writings on contract theory, however, simply presuppose the truth of Hegel's views. Indeed, in the principal article in which he presents his Hegelian theory of contract law, Benson repeatedly prefaces his conclusions with the phrase, 'If Hegel is right', as he does in the final paragraph of the article. Benson, 'Abstract Right', above n. 37 at 1198. Instead of defending Hegel's views directly, Benson defends the claim that all autonomy-based contract theorists purport to ground their theories on an ideal of autonomy that can be vindicated only by Hegel's (and perhaps Kant's) conception of autonomy, and not the conceptions they endorse in their own theories. Thus, his argument is directed at those who already acknowledge the normative force of the Hegelian ideal of autonomy, but do not realize that their non-Hegelian conceptions of autonomy ultimately fail to ground that ideal adequately.

[111] Benson makes this claim throughout his scholarship: 'At common law there is one fundamental principle that provides a basic point of view from which the rights and duties that can arise between parties in private transactions are construed and elaborated. I am referring to . . . the principle that there can be no liability for nonfeasance, with the severely limited idea of responsibility which this entails. This principle pervades, and is often explicitly recognized as regulative, in all areas of private law. Indeed, it is taken as an essential and distinctive feature of private law. Offhand, it therefore appears well-suited to serve as an organizing principle for a public basis of justification of contract' ('Public Basis', above n. 77 at 315).

[112] ibid. at 316.

sons: that through their interactions, one party either acquires rightful possession of something from the other or, alternatively, suffers an interference with his or her rightful possession by the other.[113] The provisionally fixed point of contract law is that the law should, in principle, protect the plaintiff's expectation interest.[114] Benson does not purport to justify these normative ideas or the provisionally fixed point of contract law. Instead, his claim is that they constitute widely shared, natural, and appropriate starting-points from which to build a theory of contract law. Thus, they are presented as facts about the public legal culture of contract law, rather than as defensible ideas or features of contract law. Any theory of contract law must begin by trying to take account of them. Presumably, the theory of contract is built, just as Rawls builds the principles of justice, by using the process of reflective equilibrium. The justificatory task requires the contract theorist to attempt to comprehend the normatively fundamental ideas and fixed points of contract law within one coherent theory. Each normatively fundamental idea and provisionally fixed point of contract law can be rejected only if it cannot be rendered consistent with the maximally consistent theory available. Benson's claim is that Hegelian theory provides the best-available theory to explain the coherence and unity of these fundamental normative ideas and the provisionally fixed point of contract law.

Thus, Benson's original theory of contract rests on the plausibility of Hegel's theory of autonomy and contract, and the success of Benson's efforts to demonstrate a substantial alignment between Hegel's conception of contract and the central principles and doctrines of contemporary contract law. Benson's new approach, however, constitutes a creative and original synthesis of Rawlsian political theory and Hegelian autonomy and contract theory. Its ultimate defensibility will turn, in large measure, on the defensibility of applying Rawlsian political justification to a specific legal institution and its 'public legal culture', as well as the success of Benson's effort to demonstrate a substantial alignment of contract principles and doctrine with the Hegelian contract ideal. The present purpose of examining Benson's theory, however, is not to assess its merits, but rather to identify the extent to which it evidences the methodological commitments I have argued are associated with deontic theories of contract.

3.1 Normative Primacy, Distinctiveness, and Doctrine as Data

Benson's project is devoted, first and foremost, to establishing the moral and political justification of contract law. He begins by rejecting Fried's equation of moral and legal obligation, and grounds legal obligation in consent rather than promise. Benson's initial theory justifies contract law as morally necessary to vindicate the Hegelian conception of autonomy and free will. Benson argues that a mere promise, without offer and acceptance, generates what Kant calls a 'duty of virtue'. Duties of

[113] ibid. at 317.   [114] ibid. at 317–18.

virtue are genuine moral obligations, but they are not owed to anyone in particular. Such moral obligations cannot explain or justify the use of state coercion to require compensation to a disappointed promisee because they fail to confer on the promisee a correlative moral right to the promisor's performance. But when an offeror makes an offer that is accepted, the acceptance gives rise both to the promisor's moral obligation to perform and to the promisee's correlative moral right to the promised performance. Kant calls moral obligations which generate correlative rights 'juridical'.[115] For Kant and Hegel, promises made as part of an offer effectively transfer to the promisee the moral right to the promised performance upon acceptance. Benson argues that this right constitutes ownership in whatever is promised. State coercion to enforce juridical obligations is therefore justified to protect individual ownership. Failure to perform a promise made as part of an accepted offer constitutes a refusal to respect a transfer of ownership (of the promised performance) that was effective upon acceptance. On Benson's Hegelian theory, the moral right of ownership is entailed by the Hegelian conception of autonomy and free will, and as such, is inalienable.[116] Therefore, state coercion to enforce juridical obligations created by accepted offers is morally justified (indeed morally required) in order to protect the inalienable moral rights possessed by individuals conceived as having genuinely (metaphysically undetermined) free will.[117] And as we have seen, even on the Rawlsian version of Benson's theory, this Hegelian framework for understanding autonomy plays a crucial role in the justification of contract law. It provides the unifying theory that explains how the normatively fundamental ideas of contract law cohere with one another and the expectancy remedy, the provisionally fixed point of contract law. In other words, Benson's view is that the most basic normative ideas and elements of contract law are best viewed as entailments of Hegelian autonomy theory.

Benson's explanatory agenda, then, is entirely in service of his claim that the common law of contracts embeds the Hegelian concept of contract law. The Hegelian

---

[115] For the distinction between 'duties of virtue' and 'juridical' obligation, see Benson, 'Contract', above n. 33 at 40. For further elaboration and defence of the distinction, see Benson, 'Grotius' Contribution to the Natural Law of Contract', *Canadian Journal of Netherlandic Studies*, 1 (1985), 1. See also 'Public Basis', above n. 77 at 293 ('[Contract doctrines] suppose a distinction between promises that create correlative rights and duties which are coercible, and promises that may only give rise to an ethical duty of fidelity)' (ibid. at 297) (criticizing Barnett's theory because promises made with an intent to be bound may not create 'a relation of correlative rights and duties which can be coercively enforced').

[116] According to Benson, Hegel claims that '[t]he essential first condition of the possibility of free will is that its activity be conceived as independent from determination by inclination or, more generally, by anything given to it' ('Abstract Right', above n. 37 at 1157). Further, 'the first way in which self-determination is actualized must be as a person having a capacity to own external things' (Ibid. at 1157). Thus, Hegel claims the moral capacity to own is 'inalienable' (ibid. at 1165).

[117] 'What abstract right entails is an account of the intelligibility of contractual obligation that can be realized by a positive legal order consistently with the Idea of freedom. Moreover, it implies that a person's individual capacity to own and therefore to acquire or to alienate by contract can never be denied outright, whether by the state or by another individual' (ibid. at 1188).

concept of contract law rests on clear distinctions between public law and the private law, and within the private law, between property, tort, and contract. Thus, like Fried's project, Benson's Hegelian project leads him to defend the distinctiveness thesis.[118] Benson argues that contract law is distinct from other bodies of law because of its unique place in the private law. The private law itself, Benson argues, is founded on the principle of no liability for mere nonfeasance.[119] That principle marks the private law as the exclusive domain of autonomy. In the private law, the sole basis for legal liability is respect for autonomy. The law of property respects autonomy by vindicating the moral right of ownership through initial acquisition entailed by autonomy. The law of torts respects autonomy by requiring compensation for wrongful harm to others' property (which includes their bodies). And the law of contract respects autonomy by facilitating and enforcing the voluntary transfer of property ownership. All legal liability in the private law is imposed in order to vindicate and protect individual autonomy by vindicating and protecting the individual right to own and transfer property. Outside of the private law, justice may require that individuals come to the aid of others and otherwise take into account the interests, desires, and needs of others. But inside the private law, '[n]o one is accountable for failing to minister to another's needs, wishes, or purposes. One need not assist others to acquire or preserve rightful possession of anything. What a person must not do is to interfere with, injure, or adversely affect another's rightful possession, whether innate or acquired. The principle of no liability for nonfeasance stipulates only prohibitions.'[120] This principle of limited liability, which Benson characterizes as the 'moral point of view' of the private law,[121] constitutes the first of the three normatively fundamental ideas of the private law.

---

[118] Benson explicitly endorses the distinctiveness thesis throughout his work. See e.g. Benson, 'Contract', above n. 33 at 29 (rejecting Fuller's theory on the ground that it 'does not attempt to justify the normal rule of contract damages on a basis that is consistent with the distinctive character of private law') (ibid. at 36) (rejecting Raz's theory of contract on the ground that it does not 'seem to account for the central and distinctive feature of contract').

[119] '[C]ontract law reflects a basic principle of private law that there can be no liability for mere nonfeasance' ('Abstract Right', above n. 37, at 1083); 'By "nonfeasance", I mean the failure to confer an advantage upon another, in contrast to misfeasance, which is the failure to respect what *already* rightfully belongs to another' (ibid. at n. 8); 'At common law there is one fundamental principle that provides a basic point of view from which the rights and duties that can arise between parties in private transactions are construed and elaborated. I am referring to the . . . principle that there can be no liability for nonfeasance, with the severely limited idea of responsibility which this entails. This principle pervades, and is often explicitly recognized as regulative, in all areas of private law. Indeed, it is taken as an essential and distinctive feature of private law, in contrast to public law. . . . According to the principle of no liability for nonfeasance, a right always has the form of being a claim against someone else who is under a corresponding or correlative duty, and the content of the right always has to do with rightful possession of something that can be owned . . . *Unless* and *until* one has rightful possession of something, others cannot be under a corresponding duty. Duties are thus obligations owed to persons with respect to something that is their own' ('Public Basis', above n. 77, at 315).

[120] ibid. at 315.   [121] ibid. at 317.

The second normatively fundamental idea of the private law is 'the juridical concept of the person'. Benson claims the private law presupposes that 'individuals are to be viewed as, and *only* as, subjects with a capacity to have, acquire, and exercise rightful possession for and by themselves. Their personal characteristics and activities are normatively significant only insofar as they can be construed in terms of this central and defining feature.'[122] Further, individuals are conceived as free and equal, in the sense that every individual is equally entitled to the ownership rights safeguarded by the private law.[123] The third normatively fundamental idea of the private law is the idea of a private transaction between two persons. In the private law, liability is assigned solely on the ground 'that through their interaction, one party either acquires rightful possession of something from the other or, alternatively, suffers an interference with his or her rightful possession by the other. Only insofar as interaction has this feature does it count as a transaction.'[124] Thus, Benson claims the principle of no liability for nonfeasance, the juridical concept of the person, and the idea of a transaction together form a unified and coherent theory of moral responsibility that underwrites liability in the private law, and distinguishes the private law from all other areas of law.

Contract law, in turn, is distinguished from property and tort by virtue of the kind of liability it imposes. Whereas property law simply assigns rights of exclusive possession, and tort law protects those rights from wrongful injury, contract law assigns liability for expectation damages to protect individuals' ownership rights. While tort liability is for wrongful injury to property, contract liability requires no wrongful injury. Indeed, an expectancy award can be given even in the absence of any reliance by the promisee. The expectancy award, unique in the private law, demonstrates that liability in contract is premised on the view that the promisor transfers rightful ownership at the time his offer is accepted, rather than at the time he actually performs. On this view, performance does not itself effect a transfer of ownership. Rather, performance is required in order to respect the ownership rights *previously* transferred to the promisee at the time the promisor's offer was accepted. Thus, a showing of detrimental reliance on a promise is no more relevant to contractual liability than a showing of injury would be relevant in a conversion action for theft. In both cases, the plaintiff's recovery requires that he receive the value of what was already his. Just as the thief wrongfully interferes with the owner's right of exclusive use of his personal property, the breaching offeror wrongfully interferes with the promisee's right to the promised performance.[125]

[122] 'Public Basis', above n. 77, at 316.   [123] ibid.   [124] ibid. at 317.
[125] '[A]t the moment of formation, and therefore prior to and independent of performance, the plaintiff must be represented in legal contemplation as having acquired from the defendant actual rightful possession of something that is interfered with by breach and restored by an award of expectation damages at the remedy stage. In protecting the expectation interest, the law supposes that the plaintiff ought to have received the defendant's promised performance. We may infer from this that what, in legal contemplation, the plaintiff must be deemed to have acquired at formation is, therefore, rightful or juridical possession of this performance. Only if contract can be construed in this way will a breach constitute the kind of wrong that comes under misfeasance' (ibid. at 319).

Benson thus vindicates the distinctiveness thesis by engaging in abstract analysis of general principles, and demonstrating the conceptual coherence between the expectation remedy and the Hegelian concept of contract. His explanation of offer and acceptance doctrine is abstract as well, never descending to the level of doctrinal detail (for example, he never attempts to explain or justify the details of offer and acceptance, such as the mailbox rule). Moreover, Benson's theory virtually never purports to explain how doctrines apply to generate particular outcomes in cases. Benson's theory is premised on the idea that an explanation of contract law must explain the language and concepts of contract law, not merely the outcomes of contract cases. Both his initial Hegelian theory, and his subsequent Rawlsian–Hegelian theory, take the plain meaning of doctrine at face value and seek a theory that unifies and justifies those doctrines in their own terms. In particular, Benson's view is that an area of law, such as contract law, must be explained from the point of view of the law itself as evidenced in the plain meaning of doctrinal language.[126] Indeed, Benson quite explicitly rejects as a non-theory of contract any theory that purports merely to explain outcomes of contract cases, divorced from the plain meaning of the doctrines used by courts to decide them. This is, in fact, one of Benson's central criticisms of economic theories of contract law:

At no point does economic analysis make the legal point of view with its normative ideas the immediate object of its analysis. . . . Instead, it begins with interests and preferences and its sole normative principle is welfare-maximization. At most, economic analysis applies this framework directly *to the bare conclusions of contract doctrine detached from the normative ideas which give them life and meaning from a legal point of view.* It hopes to show that these conclusions coincide with what economics requires *from its own standpoint.* Even if economic analysis were to become complete in its own terms, it is doubtful that it could legitimately claim to be a theory of contract law as opposed to an economics of transactions.[127]

---

[126] Benson writes that '[theories of contract law must] preserve the essential character of contract *from a legal point of view*' ('Contract', above n. 33, at 37; emphasis added); he describes autonomy theories as trying 'to account for *the legal point of view*' (ibid. at 33; emphasis added); he argues that Goetz and Scott's and Kronman's theories fail to take 'the retrospective orientation of *the legal point of view* in settling the rights and duties of parties' (ibid. at 52; emphasis added); he claims that '*contract law presents itself as a point of view* constituted by a set of principles and categories that articulate certain basic normative ideas' (ibid. at 54; emphasis added); he argues that contemporary contract theories presuppose a distributive theory of fairness that 'the positive law does *not* frame in distributive terms and *which appear on their face* to embody the values of individual autonomy and liberty' ('Abstract Right', above n. 37, at 1081–2; emphasis added); he claims that '*on their face,* these legal doctrines suppose a distinction between promises that create correlative rights and duties which are coercible, and promises that may only give rise to an ethical duty of fidelity' ('Public Basis', above n. 77 at 293; emphasis added); he claims a public justification of contract 'would mean that there *is present in the common law—in judicial decisions*—a set of normative ideas that implicitly contain a whole theory of contract' (ibid. at 306; emphasis added).

[127] 'Contract', above n. 33, at 54 (first emphasis added). Benson also writes that '[i]n general, discussions of wealth-maximization, either as an explanation of the law or as a normative goal for the law, focus on whether the *conclusions* of legal doctrine and judicial decisions are, in fact, explicable on the basis of wealth-maximization' ('Public Basis', above n. 77 at 307).

Benson's failure to consider case outcomes reflects his methodological commitment to taking doctrinal language and concepts seriously as sources of law. On this view, outcomes are simply results whose explanation consists in elaborating the plain meaning of doctrine. Benson evidences no aspiration to explain how the doctrines he discusses apply to generate definite outcomes in specific factual settings. This is seen in his accounts of offer and acceptance, consideration, and the objective theory of intent.[128] In each case, his sole concern is to explain how the plain meaning of these doctrines coheres with the Hegelian concept of contract. No effort is made to explain, for example, why courts have found consideration in certain cases but not others. In general, Benson's view appears to be that once the plain meaning of contract doctrines has been unified under a Hegelian rubric, the heavy lifting of contract theory is done. There is the suggestion that a theory which provides a complete public justification of contract law would contain within it all the resources necessary to adjudicate any contract dispute.[129] But Benson's extensive theoretical efforts so far have yet to yield explanations of contracts case outcomes.

Benson's concern to vindicate the distinctiveness thesis derives from his view that contract law consists in the plain meaning of doctrine. For Benson, the task of both an explanatory and normative theory of contract law is to provide a normative principle that *inherently limits* liability to voluntary transfers. Thus, one of Benson's primary criticisms of economic theories of contract law is that the normative principle they endorse is 'inherently expansionary': it alone cannot explain the doctrinal limits of liability essential to contract law.[130] For example, the principle of welfare maximization cannot on its own explain why it would be impermissible to force involuntary transfers that maximized expected welfare. Economic analysts typically explain the voluntariness requirement of contract law as the best-available institutional mechanism for ensuring that property transfers maximize expected welfare

---

[128] See e.g. 'Public Basis', above n. 77 at 307, 326. See also Peter Benson, 'The Unity of Contract Law', in *The Theory of Contract Law: New Essays*, ed. Peter Benson (Cambridge; New York: Cambridge University Press, 2001), 118. (This article was not available in time to be incorporated in the present analysis of Benson's work. However, its treatment of the doctrines of offer and acceptance, consideration, and unconscionability illustrate Benson's interest in explaining how the structural features of these doctrines conform to his conception of contract, rather than how doctrinal formulations determine particular outcomes in individual cases.)

[129] 'A public justification attempts to show that the public legal culture contains, even implicitly, a coherent and definite conception of contract informed by principles that can settle most, if not all, issues of justice that arise in contractual relations' ('Public Basis', above n. 77 at 321). But Benson continues, 'Such a justification, if successful, will undoubtedly guide the application of these principles to particular facts, but it will not be determinative. Inevitably, judgment must be brought to bear to decide the significance, weight, and appropriate application of the favoured principles in particular, always individual, circumstances, thus making inescapable a range of different possible assessments, all reasonable' (ibid.). Although he does not mention it, perhaps the most persistent cause of epistemic, if not metaphysical, indeterminacy in contracts stems from the problem of interpreting the content of agreements, rather than the difficulties of balancing various normative principles.

[130] This is also the central, systematic criticism advanced against economic theories of tort and contract in Ernest Weinrib, *The Idea of Private Law* (Cambridge, Mass.: Harvard University Press, 1995).

given the contingent, empirical difficulties of identifying welfare-enhancing transfers absent consent. But the welfare principle itself carries with it no inherent prohibition against forced transfers. In contrast, the deontological Hegelian conception of
autonomy which Benson endorses explains why the voluntariness requirement is a
morally necessary, rather than empirically contingent, feature of contract law.[131]

Benson's rejection of the economic explanation and justification of the voluntariness requirement reflects two methodological commitments. The first is that only a
deontological conception of autonomy can provide an adequate justification of state
coercion. Thus, demonstrating how contract law is just one institutional variant
among others for advancing the goal of maximizing expected welfare provides, in his
view, no justification at all. The goal of maximizing expected welfare is not normatively defensible as a foundation principle for justifying state coercion.[132] Secondly,
an adequacy condition on any explanation of contract law is that the explanatory
principle demonstrates why the essential features of contract law are essential to contract law. Economic theories explain why the essential features of contract law are
contingently justified, while genuinely deontological explanations, such as Benson's,
explain why those essential features are necessarily justified. Benson's view is that
only this sort of explanation and justification of contract law explains the concept of
contractual liability that is both implicit and explicit in the plain meaning interpretation of contract doctrines. An adequate explanation and justification of contract law, therefore, must explain why contract liability is essentially, not merely
contingently, different than tort liability, and why liability in the private law generally
is essentially, not merely contingently, different than liability outside of the private
law. The principle of welfare maximization provides precisely the opposite kind of
explanation and justification. It explains how conceptually distinct areas of law can
be explained and justified as institutional variants devoted to the maximization of
expected welfare. For economic analysts, the 'inherently expansionary' nature of the
principle of welfare maximization is a virtue that affirms its explanatory power. For
Benson, the economic view of the boundaries of conceptually distinct areas of law as
contingently, rather than necessarily, justified demonstrates its manifest failure to
provide an adequate explanation of the body of law it purports to explain. In short,
deontic theories explain, and economic theories explain away, the apparent distinctiveness of contract law.

Benson's criticism of economic contract theories that rely on the notions of Pareto
and Kaldor–Hicks efficiency also illustrate how disagreements between deontic and
economic contract theorists often stem from the different priorities each assigns to
the normative and explanatory goals of contract theory. Benson argues that the

[131] Or on the Rawlsian version of Benson's theory, the Hegelian concept of autonomy constitutes the
deepest moral conception embedded in the public legal culture of contract law.

[132] Or on the Rawlsian version of Benson's theory, Benson's criticisms would be that the principle of
welfare maximization is inconsistent with the deep moral conception of the person embedded in the
public legal culture of contract law.

concepts of Pareto and Kaldor–Hicks efficiency are inherently inadequate explanatory tools because both can be applied to assess the efficiency of a transaction *ex ante* or *ex post*.[133] For example, a transaction that is Pareto efficient *ex ante*, because each party prefers the exchange at the time he agrees to it, may not be *ex post* Pareto efficient, at the time of performance. Pareto efficiency itself cannot explain why the *ex ante* Pareto result that argues for enforcing the agreement should be privileged over the *ex post* Pareto result that argues against enforcing the agreement. Some normatively prior principle is necessary to justify indexing the Pareto inquiry to the *ex ante* or *ex post* perspective. Efficiency theories that rely on the Pareto criterion are therefore normatively incomplete. Yet efficiency theorists typically privilege the *ex ante* Pareto result without defence, and proceed to demonstrate how various legal doctrines can be explained by viewing them as advancing *ex ante* Pareto efficient transactions. Such economic analysts are content to stipulate the primacy of the *ex ante* Pareto result simply because by doing so they are able to explain case outcomes. They have little interest in defending the Pareto criterion itself, let alone the normative primacy of the *ex ante* Pareto result. Deontic theorists such as Benson reject the Pareto criterion as normatively inadequate from the start, and so evidence no interest in testing its explanatory powers. For them, there is no point in such an exercise because it will not advance understanding of the normative justification of contract law. For economic theorists concerned to explain contract outcomes, the proof is in the pudding (or perhaps, any port in a storm will do). The Pareto criterion is attractive if and only if it can explain and predict case outcomes. A demonstration of how the (*ex ante*) Pareto principle can unify a set of outcomes that otherwise appear arbitrary is useful for lawyers. Further, it potentially contributes to the justification of contract law because it demonstrates that contract case outcomes can be rendered coherent and mutually consistent. Presumably, this much will be required of any minimally adequate justification of contract law.

Benson's theory is far more philosophically sophisticated than Fried's. His chief objective is to demonstrate how all contemporary contract theories, even those ostensibly based on autonomy, are ultimately teleological in character, and therefore cannot vindicate the concept of autonomy as the exercise of free will. He rejects Fried's theory as teleological because it ultimately grounds the moral obligation to keep a promise on the contingent desire to maximize individual freedom.[134] And he effectively demonstrates how every other contemporary contract theory ultimately rests contractual liability on teleological grounds.[135] In their stead, he presents

---

[133] Benson's criticism is based on similar criticism made by Jules Coleman and Michael Trebilcock. See 'Public Basis', above n. 77, at 284–8.

[134] Benson, 'Abstract Right', above n. 37, at 1103–17.

[135] Benson demonstrates both the teleological character of contemporary contract theories, and how they fail to cohere with the normatively fundamental ideas underlying the private law and the distinctive features of contract law, such as expectancy damages. Although his demonstration of their ultimately teleological character is convincing, his characterization of some economic theories of contract is not always equally convincing. For example, Benson subscribes to Trebilcock's claim that Goetz and

Hegel's theory as a truly deontological theory of contract. Hegel's theory provides an express argument for the moral necessity of contract law as the embodiment of autonomy and the vindication of truly undetermined, free will. Although Benson's grasp of the normative foundations of contemporary contract theory is firm, and his Hegelian critique quite effective, it is simply not his ambition to explain how contract doctrine yields particular outcomes in particular cases. Just as it is equally and manifestly not the ambition of economic theories to provide a genuinely deontic explanation and justification of the plain meaning of contract doctrine.

3.2 The *Ex Post* Perspective

Benson argues that the private law in general, and contract law in particular, evidences the 'retrospective orientation of the legal point of view in settling the rights and duties of parties to a particular past transaction now before a court'.[136] As we have seen, Craswell claims this retrospective orientation disables autonomy theories from resolving disputes concerning contractual gaps.[137] Recall that Fried allows gap-filling to take prospective effects into account because gap-filling falls outside the domain of contract law and is governed by general principles of non-contract law. Thus, Fried argues that the goal of facilitating future contracting qualifies as an acceptable rationale for adopting a particular gap-filling rule. Benson, however, appears categorically to reject any teleological reasoning in contract law, and so rejects all justifications of judicial decisions in contract cases based on its prospective effects. Thus, Benson rejects Fried's and Barnett's argument that contractual gaps should be filled according to rules that will decrease the expected costs of contracting by decreasing the expected frequency of gaps in future contracts. Such reasoning is teleological in character and therefore inconsistent with Benson's account of contractual obligation.

Scott's net beneficial reliance theory supports imposition of contractual liability in the absence of the parties' consent to be legally bound. He therefore rejects their theory as inconsistent with the normatively fundamental principle of no liability for nonfeasance ('Public Basis', above n. 77 at 300–3). But Goetz and Scott's theory does not countenance the imposition of liability in the absence of consent to be bound, and indeed rejects liability in such circumstances. Rather, their theory in effect provides an interpretive rule for implying such consent. They argue for enforcement in bargain contexts, in which an intent to be legally bound is more likely than not, and against enforcement in non-bargain contexts, in which an intent to be legally bound is less likely than not, absent special circumstances. Their theory simply provides an 'interpretive' default rule for deciding whether to enforce promises absent clear evidence of the parties' intent to be bound.

[136] 'Contract', above n. 33 at 52.

[137] Trebilcock also raises Craswell's objection against autonomy theories. Benson puts Trebilcock's claim as follows: 'We should not forget that the rules are elaborated in the context of adjudication. Thus, the rules will be imposed on at least one set of litigants as the proper resolution of their dispute, even though they will have had no opportunity to contract around them. This, however, violates their autonomy, making the tension between welfare and autonomy values inescapable' ('Public Basis', above n. 77 at 283).

Benson therefore must either deny the existence of contractual gaps, or explain how courts should fill them based solely on *ex post* considerations of autonomy.

Benson's first strategy is to argue, like Fried, that the cases Craswell believes constitute contractual gaps are not in fact true gap cases. Benson claims that Craswell generates gap cases only by invoking a widely discredited theory that limits interpretation to express meaning and does not consider meaning implied from context.[138] For example, Benson argues that once implied contextual meaning is taken into account, the doctrines of non-disclosure, mistake, and frustration can be justified on grounds of actual consent, and therefore do not, as Craswell claims, constitute gap-filling background rules.[139] Benson claims that each of these doctrines applies when 'one party seeks to be released from her duty to perform on the basis that she would not have made the agreement had she known at that time what she now knows'.[140] Whether they should be released depends, in Benson's view, on whether their contract explicitly or implicitly excuses performance under the relevant circumstances. In the absence of express language addressing a particular excusing condition, Benson argues the parties should be regarded as having implicitly consented to the general principles underlying contractual obligation. In particular, the parties should be regarded to have implicitly (but none the less actually) consented to the principle of no liability for nonfeasance. Because the parties tacitly agree to the background principles of contract law when they intentionally undertake contractual liability, and the principle of no liability for nonfeasance is one of those background principles, all contractual parties should, prima facie, be interpreted as having 'assumed the risk of such losses'.[141] This prima-facie interpretation can be defeated by evidence that one of the parties expressly or implicitly made the other's contractual rights and duties 'in effect conditional upon the absence of certain information imperfections'.[142]

[138] '[T]he public justification does not limit the kind of act of will that can generate a contractual obligation to the express words of the parties. Conduct or words of any kind may provide a basis for inferring manifestations of will that can reasonably be construed as mutually-related voluntary acts . . . Moreover, like any meaningful act or utterance, such conduct and words must be viewed and interpreted in a given particular context' (ibid. at 323).

[139] '[T]he public justification roots the allocation of risks in the parties' actual consent . . . Actual consent can be express or implied. The central idea is that the analysis turns entirely on what the parties did. In this way, it is thoroughly retrospective and indifferent to dynamic considerations' (ibid. at 328–9).

[140] ibid. at 329. Benson continues: 'In the cases of non-disclosure, the complaint is that the party with the information should have disclosed it to the party now asking release. Where there has been mistake or frustration, typically neither party possessed the information at the time of entering the agreement' (ibid.).

[141] ibid.

[142] ibid. at 330. Benson continues: 'The parties' common intention to make performance conditional may be inferred, not only from the parties' express words, but also from the 'substance, words, and circumstances' of their transaction. In short, this common intention may also be found to be implicit in their agreement as interpreted in its particular context. In both instances—express and implicit—it should be emphasized that this determination is arrived at by inferring from what the parties have actually done' (ibid. at 330–1).

How should courts determine whether the parties implicitly agreed that a particular non-disclosure, mistake, or frustration of purpose would constitute an excuse for performance? Benson argues that a court must determine

the parties' common intention retrospectively on the basis of their manifested acts or will, reasonably construed in accordance with an objective standard. The test is: looking at the terms and subject matter of a contract in light of its surrounding circumstances, can we infer that the parties considered, or ought to have considered, as reasonable people, the duty to perform as so obviously dependent on the non-occurrence of a contingency that, had the contingency been brought to their attention, they would have thought it unnecessary to provide for it explicitly in their agreement? If yes, a court is justified in finding an implicit condition that makes that duty to perform dependent on the absence of the contingency.[143]

Benson's analysis in effect treats the principle of no liability for nonfeasance as an 'interpretive' background rule against which parties' intentions will be construed absent evidence to the contrary. His claim is that this principle is publicly known and therefore constitutes an objective source for interpreting the meaning of contracts. The failure of contractual parties to manifest an intention to the contrary justifies the inference that they intended the background understanding to govern. Unless contextual evidence establishes a contrary intent, all parties actually, though implicitly, consent to being legally bound to perform irrespective of any non-disclosure, mistake, or frustration of purpose. Thus, Benson's theory, like Fried's, relies on the distinction between interpretive ambiguity and genuine contractual gaps, the difference between Fried's interpretation and interpolation. Benson claims that every case of excuse for non-disclosure, mistake, and frustration can be resolved by mere interpretation, rather than interpolation, because parties always implicitly intend to be bound to perform unless express terms or context indicates otherwise, in which case they implicitly intend performance to be conditioned. Either way, the question is one of determining contractual intent, not filling in a gap where no contractual intent exists. Benson's contract theory can therefore resolve questions of non-disclosure, mistake, and frustration without taking an *ex ante* perspective that takes prospective effects into account. These cases all turn, instead, exclusively on an *ex post* inquiry into the parties' contractual intent, albeit implied or tacit. Thus, these doctrines do not require Benson's theory to sacrifice its exclusively teleological character.

Now economic analysts like Craswell would likely find this response unsatisfactory for two reasons. First, although this view of these doctrines does demonstrate how these disputes can be resolved using the *ex post* perspective, Benson provides no guidance for determining the circumstances under which courts will or will not allow these excuses. On Benson's view, it depends on the court's determination of the parties' actual intent, which in turn is discovered by answering the hypothetical question of whether the parties would have agreed to the excuse had it been brought to their attention. Benson provides no account of the circumstances under which courts will

---

[143] ibid. at 332–3.

answer this hypothetical in the negative or affirmative. In contrast, economic analyses of these doctrines purport to identify structural features of the parties' circumstances that will lead a court to excuse or require performance. Because some of these economic accounts begin by asking precisely the same hypothetical Benson asks, it might be possible to combine Benson's view with the more detailed explanations economic analysis provides. The economic analyses often hold that courts find excuses in the particular circumstances they identify because those are the circumstances under which the parties would have agreed to those excuses had they considered them. But economic analysis does not make the further claim that this hypothetical agreement provides compelling evidence that the parties in fact actually, although implicitly, agreed to such an excuse. It justifies the practice of excusing performance in those circumstances on the ground that doing so is likely to allow parties to maximize the expected joint value of contracts in the future. But Benson would claim these are the circumstances under which the parties in the dispute actually did agree that performance would be excused. For economic analysts, this inference is unnecessary, so Benson's analysis adds nothing of value to the explanatory enterprise. For Benson, however, the inference to actual intent is critical to maintaining the impermissibility of *ex ante* considerations in contract adjudication.

The second reason economic analysts are likely to find Benson's account unsatisfactory is that it stipulates, rather than demonstrates, that all parties actually intend their contracts to contain no excuses, absent express or contextual evidence to the contrary. Craswell's intuition is that, at least in some cases, parties simply do not consider, tacitly or otherwise, the question of whether performance should be excused by a particular condition. Benson asserts that the principle of no liability for nonfeasance is basic to contract law and that therefore, all else equal, all parties tacitly consent to it. But Benson's inference from the principle of no liability for nonfeasance to a presumption against excuse begs the question. The distinction between nonfeasance and misfeasance presupposes a logically prior determination of a party's obligations. Whether a party's conduct constitutes misfeasance or nonfeasance depends entirely on what that party is obligated to do. If a contract contains an excuse, then failure to perform constitutes nonfeasance, not misfeasance. By definition, if a party's performance is excused, he has no obligation to perform. Excusing performance is therefore perfectly consistent with the principle of no liability for nonfeasance. Indeed, the imposition of liability in the face of a valid excuse would itself violate the principle of no liability for nonfeasance. However, if a contract does not contain an excuse, then, by definition, failure to perform constitutes misfeasance, rather than nonfeasance. The imposition of liability in the case of unexcused performance is therefore also consistent with the principle of no liability for nonfeasance. The principle of no liability for nonfeasance, therefore, makes the imposition of liability turn on a logically prior and independent determination of the parties' obligations. The principle itself can be applied only if the parties' obligations have already been determined. It is therefore logically irrelevant to making that determination in the first instance. Thus, Benson's assertion that parties tacitly intend their contracts to contain no excuses for performance relies on a question-begging argument. Given that the principle of no liability for nonfeasance provides no grounds for inferring actual intent on questions of excuse, Benson's claim boils down to a mere assertion based at most on an intuition Craswell does not share.

Unsurprisingly, Benson's argument fails to demonstrate the logical impossibility of a contractual gap. Even if there were some reason to believe most parties tacitly agree that performance will not be excused, it is still possible that under some circumstances, parties might not agree either way (as a matter of subjective or objective intent). Fried emphasizes that actual consent, even merely tacit or implied consent, can only go so far. In his view, contractual gaps will always be possible in principle. Benson avoids putting his deontic commitment to the test by denying the possibility of contractual gaps. But his argument for that claim does not succeed. Benson could claim that there are other basic principles in the public legal culture of contract law to which parties tacitly consent and thereby avoid contractual gaps. This approach is reminiscent of Fried's strategy of falling back on general principles of law to fill contractual gaps. But because Fried acknowledges contractual gaps, he claims these principles are not part of contract law and so avoids the need to claim that parties tacitly consent to them. Because Benson is committed to finding such principles within contract law, and yet rejects teleological justifications within contract law, he is forced to argue that everyone necessarily gives their tacit consent to all the principles underlying contract law. Fried resists the claim that consent can be stretched that far. By asserting that claim, Benson risks diluting the normative significance of consent.

Benson's discussion of expectancy damages illustrates the same tendency to dodge the question of contractual gaps by defining them away. Craswell argues that the question of what remedy a party is entitled to for breach is often unaddressed in contracts and therefore constitutes a gap that must be filled. Benson claims that expectancy damages, like the principle of no liability for nonfeasance, is simply a constituent part of contract law. But unlike his analysis of mistake, disclosure, and frustration doctrines, Benson does not suggest that the expectancy rule therefore constitutes an 'interpretive' background rule that creates a prima-facie case for expectancy damages absent the parties' contrary manifestation of intent. Instead, he appears to argue that the best public justification for contract law will necessarily include expectancy damages in all contracts because it is the only remedy consistent with the normatively fundamental ideas underlying contract law. On this view, expectancy damages are indispensable for maintaining and explaining the distinctive structure of contract law because any other remedy would be inconsistent with the uniquely contractual idea that a transfer of ownership takes place at formation, rather than at performance.[144] Benson's defence of the expectancy measure of

[144] 'The idea that the formation of a contract entails a transfer of non-physical possession at the moment of agreement implies, in turn, a general entitlement in principle to expectation damages for breach of contract. Expectation damages, I have suggested, fit with and are implied by this conception of

damages amounts to the claim that the promisee who accepted an offer is necessarily entitled to the promised performance or its equivalent. Benson's claim, therefore, is that Craswell misconstrues the question of contractual remedy as a contractual gap, not because parties implicitly agree to the expectancy remedy, but because the right to expectancy damages is analytic: the very idea of a contract entails it. But rather than avoiding Craswell's question, by construing the expectancy remedy as analytic, Benson just raises it again at one level removed.

Benson's claim is that when A promises B 'to do X', that promise entails B's right to A's performance of X or its equivalent. Any other remedy would be inconsistent with the idea that contract transfers from A to B at the time of formation the entitlement to A's performance of X. But Craswell's question can be recast in Benson's analytic framework. Craswell's question is how to interpret A's promise to B. It is possible that A's promise is 'to do X', subject to the implicit qualification that in the event he fails to do X, his sole obligation will be to reimburse B for any harm suffered because of B's detrimental reliance on A's promise. Alternatively, it is also possible that A made his promise without considering whether B should be entitled to expectancy or to reliance damages for his failure to do X. In both of these cases, Benson's claim that expectancy damages are analytic provides no purchase on what amount A must pay B in the event of breach. If a court determines that A's promise was 'to do X or pay reliance damages', then, in Benson's terms, a court awards expectancy damages by requiring A to pay B's reliance damages, not B's expectancy (i.e. the value B would have received if A had done X). If a court determines that A simply did not consider, tacitly or otherwise, the proper remedy for his failure to do X, then requiring A to pay B's expectancy cannot be justified on the ground that expectancy is analytic to contract. So defined, expectancy merely requires that the promisor give the promisee his expectancy. But the promisee's expectancy turns on what was promised. In a true gap case, the promise is silent on what remedy was promised, so the expectancy remedy, as Benson conceives it, can provide no guidance as to what A should be required to pay B. Expectancy simply requires A to pay B the value of his promise, but it provides no assistance in determining the content of A's promise. Thus, the problem with Benson's expectancy analysis is precisely the same as the problem with his analysis of non-disclosure, mistake, and frustration. In both cases, the principles he invokes presuppose the answer to the question he uses them to answer. Just as the principle of no liability for nonfeasance presupposes, and therefore cannot determine, a prior deter-

contract, consistent with the principle of no liability for nonfeasance. . . . If the plaintiff were limited to reliance damages, a contract could not be viewed as conferring any possession different from or in addition to what the plaintiff already had *prior* to the transaction. Contract could not be conceived as a mode of acquisition, and the defendant's duty to perform would apply to something that the plaintiff possessed prior to and independent of the defendant's promise. The action for breach would be indistinguishable from a claim in tort against a defendant for failing to use due care in the making and the performance of a voluntary undertaking. But then there would be no need for the further legal requirements of offer and acceptance or consideration. We could not account for the legal point of view' (ibid. at 324–5).

mination of the parties' obligations, the analytic conception of expectancy on which Benson relies presupposes, a prior determination of, and so cannot determine, the content of the promise. Because promises can contain a term governing the obligation of the promisor upon failure to perform, the award of an expectancy remedy, as Benson conceives it, requires a prior determination of the promised remedy to which the promisee is entitled. In short, Benson's analytic conception of expectancy is content free. It directs a court to enforce the parties' agreement, but it provides no guidance for interpreting the content of that agreement. And it is precisely that determination that leads Craswell to search for an interpretive default rule. Benson avoids that search only by stipulating a vacuous, analytic definition of expectancy that assumes away the problem of a genuine contractual gap.

Thus, Benson's response to Craswell's critique insists on maintaining the *ex post* perspective, but does so by failing to explain case outcomes and neglecting to explain how courts do or should resolve genuine contractual gaps. Unlike Fried, however, Benson is unable to avail himself of the various teleological justifications for adopting gap-filling rules. Presumably, Benson feels compelled to reject Fried's rationale for gap-filling, such as maximizing individual freedom, and the analogous goal of minimizing the gap between subjective and objective intent for future parties, as both impermissibly teleological. Once it is conceded that genuine contractual gaps are possible, and cannot be defined out of existence through analytic techniques, Benson faces the same crossroads that Fried faced by ceding ground to teleological arguments. But once he concedes the possibility of genuine contractual gaps, it is difficult to see how he can take the position that (unlike Fried's view), gap-filling must take place within contract law and that no teleological arguments can be used to justify gap-filling rules. If consent runs out, something else must replace it. Yet it is not readily apparent what other facts about the parties and their transaction would be relevant to fill a gap from an *ex post* perspective in adjudication. Unless Benson ultimately agrees with Fried that genuine gaps fall outside the domain of the private law, his theory's commitment to the *ex post* perspective appears to disable it from addressing the problem of contractual gaps.

4 Conclusion

Contemporary contract theories share the ambition of discovering an internal coherence and consistency in the law of contracts. Such a discovery advances both the pragmatic goals of lawyering, legal design, and adjudication, and the normative goal of justifying the coercion exercised through contract law. Despite this shared ambition, economic and deontic contract theories appear to disagree at every turn.

Many of the apparently first-order disagreements between economic and deontic contract theories in fact reflect implicit second-order disagreements over the status as law of doctrinal statements and pure case outcomes, the relative priorities of the normative and explanatory enterprises of contract theory, and the importance and nature of explanations of the conceptual boundaries between contract law, the other areas of the private law, and public law. I have suggested that deontic contract theories tend to treat the doctrinal statements, rather than case outcomes, as the essence of contract law, accord primacy to the normative project of contract theory, and relatedly, regard the necessary distinctiveness of contract law from other bodies of law to be an essential feature of contract law that any adequate contract theory must explain. In contrast, economic theories of contract tend to treat bare case outcomes as the essence of contract law, accord primacy to the explanatory project of contract theory, and attempt affirmatively to explain away, rather than to explain, the apparently necessary conceptual distinctiveness of contract law.

I have not argued, however, that any of these methodological tendencies are themselves necessary commitments of either deontic or economic contract theories. My claim is that the best developed theories of each kind evidence these tendencies, and that attending to them helps to understand why deontic and economic theorists are often at cross purposes, rather than at loggerheads. Surprisingly, the one methodological issue that appears most likely to entail logically opposing commitments in deontic and economic contract theories turns out not to account for any systematic differences between these approaches. Thus, the strong association between deontic theories and the *ex post* perspective, and economic theories and the *ex ante* perspective, does not account for the different normative and explanatory positions these theories advance. While Benson professes a deontological commitment against gap-filling, because he relies on unsuccessful arguments to deny the possibility of contractual gaps, it is unclear he has a sustainable *ex post* position on contractual gaps. He may eventually be forced to allow teleological considerations to enter by, for example, following Fried and relegating gaps to non-contract law. But it is clear that for Fried, what appear to be deep second-order disagreements over which of these perspectives is most appropriate to adjudication turn out, in most instances, to be good faith first-order disagreements over how particular contracts should be interpreted. Deontic theorists tend to be content to leave interpretation to the vagaries of context and 'shared background understandings', while economists tend to demand firmer, more operational, criteria for contract interpretation. In this respect, both enterprises would be well served by efforts to clarify the meaning of express terms as well as the particular background understandings in various common business contexts. The difference between deontic and economic theorists on this count is probably best explained by the historical aspiration of economic analysis of law to be a quasi-empirical science, and the historical development of deontic theories of law as straightforward applications of purely philosophical theory. It is therefore easy to understand why economic analysts would strive to replace vague interpretive inquiries with predictively valid operational tests, while deontic theorists, familiar and comfortable with the perennial questions of philosophy of language, would see no reason or way to avoid conclusions that leave the law subject to the deep complexity and ultimate indeterminacy of meaning.

The methodological commitments underlying the analyses of contemporary contract theory may not be logically compelled, but they are systematically in evidence, to various degrees, in the major theories I have considered. By attending to these differences, contract theorists can replace pointless debates with more fruitful inquiries over the genuine points of disagreement, and begin to evaluate each other's theories on the criteria most appropriate to them. Ultimately, the hope is that by exposing these methodological differences, a more complete contract theory can be developed that clearly articulates and defends its methodological commitments and provides a more comprehensive explanation and justification for the law of contract.

the philosophy of language running through this field is very odd; I bet there's one source for Wittgenstein (Dworkin?) and everyone else is cutting and pasting...
this would all work better starting with Davidsonian semantics (or maybe Lewis's)

also, there's no reason for the economists to be squeamish about that, once they see that there's no normative content to philosophical semantics

this is a great big target; I can hit it.

CHAPTER 19

PHILOSOPHY OF PROPERTY LAW

PETER BENSON

1 INTRODUCTION

THIS chapter examines the right of property as one part of the theory of private law. On the whole, recent work in the theory of property has taken as given that its fundamental question concerns, and must concern, the justice of private property as one among several main institutions of society that distribute the benefits and burdens which arise through social co-operation.[1] Private property is to be evaluated from the standpoint of political, that is, distributive, justice, and it is to be compared with alternative ways of distributing holdings, viewing it always as one part of a complex system of social, economic, and political institutions. If a society permits private

I wish to thank Daniel Batista, Joshua Getzler, Katie Sykes, Sophia Reibetanz, and the anonymous reader for this volume for their helpful suggestions on earlier versions of this chapter. I am particularly grateful to Jim Harris and James Penner for their careful written comments and instructive conversations from which I benefited while presenting the paper at Oxford University as part of the Oxford–University of Toronto Jurisprudence Conference in February 2001.

[1] This is true of J. Waldron, *The Right to Private Property* (Oxford: Clarendon Press, 1988), S. R. Munzer, *A Theory of Property* (New York: Cambridge University Press, 1990), and J. Christman, *The Myth of Property* (New York: Oxford University Press, 1994). Two notable exceptions are J. W. Harris, *Property and Justice* (Oxford: Clarendon Press, 1996) and J. Penner, *The Idea of Property in Law* (Oxford: Clarendon Press, 1996). The difference between these last two works and the present effort is that this chapter makes explicit a definite normative conception of private law and considers what the right of property consists in when it is viewed strictly and solely within the parameters of this conception.

property, a primary question is how much, if any, inequality in property holdings should be allowed.[2] Moreover, the theory must determine which sorts of things (for example, natural resources, the means of production, and so on) can be privately owned or transferred and the limits or provisos to which this is subject, all in light of the end of realizing social and political justice.

This preoccupation with distribution in holdings contrasts strikingly with the intrinsic orientation of the principles of ownership and acquisition in private law which, on their face, seem indifferent toward just such concerns. Indeed, the merest familiarity with how these principles are understood and applied within private law suggests that the question of distribution is not even raised as a relevant consideration. However urgent and central this issue may be from the standpoint of political and social justice, the principles of acquisition and ownership operate as if it did not exist. It would seem, then, that a theory of property must first of all concern itself with the apparently non-distributive conception of property in private law. It is this that, in the first instance, calls for an explanation. And it is precisely this that contemporary theoretical efforts do not address. Such explanation is all the more needful given that for centuries, and across the major developed legal traditions, it has been standard to view the right of property not only as a fundamental and essential element of private law but also as receiving its purest and original expression in private law, for which it provides the organizing idiom. In addition, the evaluation of property regimes and the determination of reasonable limits thereon in light of the requirements of distributive justice presuppose that it is morally possible for individuals to own things exclusively of others and to dispose of things in a way that gives rise to individual rights and obligations. The exploration of these questions is necessary in its own right and is preliminary to any examination from the standpoint of distributive justice.

Our topic, then, is the idea of property in private law. And the normative justification that I propose will have as its subject matter property just as it belongs to and functions within private law. I shall suppose, even if only provisionally, that private law can be suitably analysed in its own terms as a distinct ensemble of principles, doctrines, and considerations. It has a normative character and integrity of its own. On this view, private law sets its own definite requirements of pertinence, reasonableness, and fairness—requirements that may not necessarily be identical with those of political and distributive justice. While private law is, and ultimately must be analysed as, just one part of a legal system that includes much more than it, the present inquiry is not immediately concerned with the relations between private law and those other parts. To establish that the private law of property, despite its apparent indifference to distributional concerns, can indeed be part of a liberal system of

---

[2] This formulation is taken from Munzer, *Theory of Property*, at 191–2. By way of an answer to this question about distributive equity, as he calls it, Munzer proposes a pluralist justification that integrates distinct norms of utility and efficiency, justice and equality, and finally labour and desert. See chs. 8, 9, and 10.

justice, it will be necessary to bring out the notion of reasonableness that animates this non-distributive idea and to show that it expresses conceptions of freedom and equality that are suitably liberal in character. I shall try to do this by sketching a justification that aims to be on a public basis, in Rawls's sense of the term.[3] By way of introduction, let me indicate in summary form the conception of 'private law' that I shall suppose throughout and the sense in which I take a justification to be 'public'.

Private law, as I understand it, is characterized by a specific, and indeed a distinctive, conception of rights that I shall call 'juridical'. I present this conception at the start of the chapter in order to orient the discussion. It should not, however, be taken as an a priori foundation or explanatory principle for what follows. Rather the conception is intended to articulate at a high level of generality pervasive features and requirements that characterize the most basic doctrines of the different parts of private law, as these have been largely settled across most common law jurisdictions. In this chapter, I shall try to show in some detail how the juridical conception is reflected in the right of property.[4] For purposes of this introductory statement, I identify three essential features of the juridical conception of rights.

First, this juridical conception presupposes that, in order to establish a valid claim *vis-à-vis* the defendant, the plaintiff must, independently of and prior to the defendant's wrong, have something that comes under his or her right exclusively as against the defendant. We abstract this feature from the fact that in tort or contract, for example, the law views an award of damages or specific relief for breach of the plaintiff's rights as a matter of compensation, owed by the defendant to the plaintiff, and that, in giving such remedies, the law seeks to place the plaintiff in the position that he or she was in prior to the defendant's wrong. Because in legal contemplation, the

---

[3] See J. Rawls, *Political Liberalism* (New York: Columbia University Press, 1993) and 'The Idea of Public Reason Revisited', in *Collected Essays*, ed. S. Freeman (Cambridge, Mass.: Harvard University Press, 1999). I believe that the way I have construed the idea of a public basis of justification in the present chapter conforms with Rawls's understanding. Of course, some may disagree with this claim as a matter of interpretation. In any case, the approach that I have taken must stand on its own feet—or not at all. Here I should note that, perhaps alone among recent contributions to the theory of property, Harris's *Property and Justice*, above n. 1, ch. 10, explores the possibility of a public basis of justification for property, although he does not call it this. He evaluates the legitimacy of the institution of property in light of a minimalist conception of just human association which, he says, is designed for public debate about social and political institutions. It is a conception that is, he claims, 'in fact assented to by the public culture of the modern world', ibid. at p. 180. This is to approach the question of justification on a public basis. As I see it, the main difference between our respective justifications is that the one I formulate is framed solely in terms that are internal and specific to juridical conception of rights, hence to private law understood as a distinctive normative domain, whereas Harris's is not so limited.

[4] In previous articles, I have tried to show how this juridical conception is reflected in the doctrines and principles of contract law and tort. See, P. Benson, 'The Unity of Contract Law', in P. Benson (ed.), *The Theory of Contract: New Essays* (New York: Cambridge University Press, 2001), 118–205 (hereinafter *Contract Law*), and P. Benson, 'The Basis for Excluding Liability for Economic Loss in Tort Law', in D. Owen (ed.), *The Philosophical Foundations of Tort Law: A Collection of Essays* (New York: Oxford University Press, 1995) (hereinafter 'Excluding Liability in Tort').

remedy is understood as repairing loss and not as bestowing upon the plaintiff some-thing new, the law must suppose that prior to and independently of the wrong, the plaintiff *already has something* that is by rights his or her own (*suum*), with which the defendant is duty-bound not to interfere. Moreover, since the remedy is owed by the defendant to the plaintiff, the latter must have something that comes under his or her rights exclusively *as against the defendant*: an ownership interest of some kind. So far as the juridical conception is concerned, an individual's 'protected interests' are, and must be, characterized just in this way. Unless and until one has such an owner-ship interest, one lacks a basis, within the juridical conception of rights, to make a valid claim against others. Consequently, the fact that one may want or need some-thing does not, as such, give one any valid claim against others. In this respect, the notion of protected interest in the juridical conception of rights differs sharply from the parallel idea in, say, a political conception, which typically takes legitimate needs to be an appropriate basis for making claims *vis-à-vis* others. Absent the requisite ownership interest, the juridical conception does not recognize any relation of right and duty between individuals and so no possibility of liability or wrong. It follows that a defendant is subject only to a *prohibition against injuring what already comes under the plaintiff's right of ownership*: in the formulation of the common law, there is no liability for nonfeasance.[5]

Secondly, the juridical conception supposes that this protected ownership interest, and hence the plaintiff's right, is of such a kind that the *only* way it can be injured is just through an *external interaction* between the parties. And this supposes in turn that what the plaintiff has is something that can be affected externally by the defen-dant's externally manifested choice. The object of this interest, we suppose for now, can be either bodily integrity or something that may be reasonably viewed as external to the plaintiff.[6] The sole relevant question is whether the defendant's choice (act or

---

[5] The distinction between misfeasance and nonfeasance is a fundamental, and indeed an organizing, feature of private law. As Francis Bohlen said, 'no distinction [is] more deeply rooted in the common law and more fundamental'. See F. Bohlen, 'The Moral Duty to Aid Others as a Basis of Tort Liability', *University of Pennsylvania Law Review*, 56 (1908), 217 at 219. To prevent misunderstanding, I should emphasize that the distinction between misfeasance and nonfeasance, as I think it is best understood, is *not* the same as the difference between acts and omissions; nor does it turn on the presence or absence of factual causation. An omission (such as a failure to perform in breach of contract) may be misfeasance and an act (such as intercepting the flow of percolating water) may be nonfeasance. Moreover, my fail-ure to rescue you in the absence of a special relationship between us—a case of nonfeasance—may, by the 'but-for' test, be a cause of resulting injury to you. There is nonfeasance whenever the defendant's act or omission interferes with or otherwise affects something that does *not* come under the plaintiff's exclu-sive rights as against the defendant. If the defendant refrains from doing this, it amounts, in legal con-templation, to the conferral of a benefit upon the plaintiff. By contrast, misfeasance is an act or omission that *does* injure something that is legally the plaintiff's, exclusive as against the defendant. Clear and helpful judicial presentations of this distinction, are found in Lord Diplock's influential speech in *Home Office v Dorset Yacht*, [1970] A.C. 1004 at 1027 (Eng. H.L.) and Chief Judge Cardozo's decision in *H. R. Moch Co. v Rensselaer Water Co.*, 159 N.E. 896 (N.Y. 1928).

[6] At this point in the argument, I simply assume that the object of the external interest must be either one's body or some external thing. I explicate this view in the rest of the chapter. I should add that even

omission), as exercised in relation to the plaintiff, can count as a voluntary interference with the latter's protected external interest, irrespectively of the defendant's particular purposes or inward intention and independently of the impact that the choice may have on the plaintiff's needs, wishes or advantage. This quite radical indifference toward need is, I have already said, a hallmark of the juridical, as distinguished from a political, conception of rights. And it fits with the common law principle of no liability for nonfeasance. There cannot be a general duty of rescue, for this would suppose that even where a defendant has done nothing to injure the plaintiff's protected external interests, the latter's needs can be the basis of claims against the former. But this is incompatible with the juridical conception.

Thirdly and finally, the juridical conception of rights supposes that, from within its own standpoint, determinations of liability can be complete and self-sufficient when made just on the basis of the above-mentioned normative considerations; that is, when limited to considerations that are intrinsic to external interactions between parties that affect their protected (ownership) external interests, without assessing what the general welfare or common good may require. In so restricting its purview, the law purports to articulate terms that are fair and reasonable *as between the parties*, in light of their particular interaction and treating them throughout as free and equal persons.

Starting from the widely shared view that property, in contrast to the right of bodily integrity, is *acquired* by action of the requisite kind, and further that, in contrast to contractual rights, it is *in rem*, we are looking for a common law idea of property that reflects the main features of the juridical conception of rights, as just set out. Thus, it must be an idea that stipulates a mode of acquisition the character of which is appropriately external and consonant with a transactional analysis, as contemplated by the juridical conception of rights. Supposing that we have found a principle that specifies the necessary and sufficient conditions for such acquisition, the next question is whether it can be reasonably justified from a normative point of view. More particularly, how might it be compatible with the freedom and equality of persons that one of them is entitled to exclude others from something—possibly by his or her unilateral act and without their prior assent—when previous to the acquisition, those excluded had equal standing to make the thing their own? This brings me to the idea of a public basis of justification, which guides the entire argument of the chapter. The following brief remarks, abstract and incomplete as they must be, will have to suffice.

What, first of all, makes a justification 'public'? A justification's being public refers to the immediate source of the subject-matter that is to be justified and to the terms

here I do not suppose that one 'owns' one's body in the very same way that one owns an external thing. As the chapter elaborates, these two rights are in certain respects qualitatively different. I should also alert the reader to the fact that throughout the chapter, I distinguish between *ownership* on the one hand and *property* on the other. As I will explain in due course, the right of property is just one specific instance of ownership or, more precisely, one specific way of acquiring ownership. Contract is another. Ownership is pervasively presupposed by the whole of private law, of which property is but one part.

of this justification. Thus a public justification *starts* with principles, doctrines, and values that are pervasive and settled in different parts of the legal and political culture of a given society—for example, in the principles, doctrines, and historically author-itative writings that make up its private and public law.[7] It takes these publicly avail-able ideas as provisionally fixed starting points for further reflection.

This further reflection explores whether, and, if so, how, these publicly available principles and values fit together to form a whole that is at once intelligible and rea-sonable. Because the starting-point for a public justification is the public legal and political culture itself, there is no criterion or standard extrinsic to this culture from which the justification can proceed or upon which it can build. The path of justifica-tion must be wholly immanent to the public culture. Thus a public justification tries to relate doctrines and principles to some organizing conception that is internal to them and to show how, when viewed in relation to this conception, they are severally necessary to its full articulation as well as mutually supportive. The sort of fit that we are seeking is conceptual and normative.

In order to bring out the unity and reasonableness of a given ensemble of doctrines and principles as fully as can be done on a public basis, the justification takes a fur-ther step and, moving to a higher level of abstraction, it makes explicit certain funda-mental normative ideas that are implicitly supposed in the public understanding of those principles and doctrines. Fundamental normative ideas, we shall see, can include conceptions of the person, of social relations, and so forth. These ideas pro-vide a framework, which is presented as latent in the public legal and political culture, that enables us to see more clearly and fully the normative import and the coherence of the principles and values of that culture. In the public legal and political culture of a liberal democracy, a normative conception of persons as free and equal will play a pivotal role within this framework. So long as the framework offers individuals a shared and reasoned basis for settling the claims and questions of justice that arise in their various legal and political relations, the public justification has realized its prin-cipal aim. It leaves to philosophy the further and deeper task of ascertaining the ulti-mate truth of the normative ideas that it employs.

Precisely because a public basis of justification takes seriously the reasoning that animates the public understanding of the doctrines, principles, and considerations of the different domains of the legal and political culture, it must be attentive to the way that culture makes distinctions among its many legal and political relations.

---

[7] Thus the notion of 'public' in this sort of justification does not refer to public, as opposed to private, law. There can be a public basis of justification for private law as well as for public law, with the justifica-tions reflecting the distinctive character of the principles, doctrines, and values that make up the domain that is the subject of justification in each case. Rawls has worked out a public justification for the domain of the political—for the assignment of rights and duties and the division of the benefits and burdens of social co-operation as these pertain to what he calls 'the basic structure of society', above n. 3. I have dis-cussed the character of a public basis of justification as it might apply to private law in 'The Idea of a Public Justification for Contract', *Osgoode Hall Law Journal*, 33 (1995), 273 at 305–34 and have tried to elaborate in detail such a justification for the law of contract in 'Contract Law', above, n. 4.

Thus, the argument in this chapter will centrally depend upon the cogency of a series of qualitative contrasts which, I claim, the public culture itself draws, including that between private and public law and, within private law, between property and contract as well as between property and liability. The guiding idea is that unless we are careful to take stock of the distinctive features and limits of each category we will not achieve a clear and satisfactory understanding of our subject-matter nor provide a suitable justification for it, at least not from a public point of view.

In keeping with this idea of a public basis of justification, then, we shall begin our inquiry by looking to the public legal culture itself, and more specifically to the settled doctrines and principles of the common law, to see whether they contain an idea of property that might plausibly be the sort that we are seeking: an idea of property that is strictly intrinsic to private law, with its juridical conception of rights. If the common law does indeed present us with a well-settled principle that seems on its face to satisfy this criterion, we shall begin with it. The burden of the next two sections is to argue that there is such a principle and that this principle is distinct from, but at the same time integrated with, the two other basic categories that fill out the juridical conception, namely, contract and liability. This principle, I shall claim, embodies, and indeed represents, the idea of property in private law. In the fourth and final section, I try to complete the justification by sketching an argument for the intrinsic reasonableness of this idea. The aim is to show that it reflects the liberal ideal of the freedom and equality of persons.

To prevent misunderstanding, there is a final point that I should make concerning the relation between the subject matter of this chapter and the law of property as a topic of legal study.[8] It might be thought that with an idea of property that purports to be intrinsic to private law, one should be able to apply it directly to, and thereby to account for, the many aspects of acquiring, transferring, fragmenting, and forfeiting the different sorts of items (land, goods, intangible movables, money, funds, and so forth) that are ordinarily viewed as coming under 'property law', whether as practised in modern societies or as analysed in the standard textbooks. Otherwise, one might ask, how can it be *the* idea of property that is intrinsic and fundamental to private law? Now while it is certainly the case that, within reasonable limits, a theory of property should be able to provide an account of many of these facets of the law of property, it does not, and should not, attempt to do this in the first instance. Rather, the theory's first task must be to identify and clarify the most basic and the most pervasive presuppositions (an example being the contrast between rights *in rem* and *in personam*) without which we cannot identify something as pertaining to a distinct legal relation that we may reasonably call 'property'; and the theory should elucidate the conception that holds these presuppositions together as an integrated whole. This, I claim, is what the idea of property accomplishes. Here it is particularly important to

---

[8] As set out in such standard works as F. H. Lawson and B. Rudden, *The Law of Property*, 2nd edn. (Oxford: Clarendon Press, 1982).

keep in mind that many of the topics standardly discussed in property textbooks represent complex or, in James Penner's term,[9] 'hybrid' legal institutions that combine features of more than one elementary kind of legal relation; for example, property and contract. Moreover, the principles, instruments, and regimes discussed may incorporate considerations that go beyond the juridical conception of rights and that embody social and economic imperatives that can be legitimately pursued only via legislative enactment. But, as I have tried to emphasize, the public legal culture itself requires that we be attentive to the distinctive characters of the various legal relations. If a theory of property is to be suitably applicable to anything at all, it must therefore first take this requirement to heart. The result of doing so is, I argue, the idea of property intrinsic to private law.

2 A PRIVATE LAW PRINCIPLE OF PROPERTY

The main object of this section is to argue that the principle of first occupancy meets the criteria of a right of property that is intrinsic to private law. To this end, I first try to clarify the essential character of this principle by bringing out its prima-facie fit with the juridical conception of rights. Having done this, I identify and elucidate the essential 'incidents of property' that specify the right acquired through first occupancy. Against the 'bundle of rights' view, I argue that, although each of these incidents is distinct from the others, they are mutually integrated as individually necessary expressions of a single underlying idea of property right that reflects the juridical conception. My claim is that these, and *only* these, incidents are intrinsic to the right established by first occupancy. Moreover, each of these incidents instantiates this right as such. Yet, without any one of them, my contention is that the underlying conception of property is incompletely fulfilled. What, in my opinion, distinguishes this account of the incidents of property is that it attempts to remain strictly within the parameters of a view that takes property to be a principle of acquisition, construed in accordance with the juridical conception of rights. Indeed, my view is that the apparent difficulty in explaining and justifying the incidents of property as they have been traditionally understood is due to a failure to consider them in this light. To bring out this point, I contrast the proposed approach with that of A. M. Honoré,[10] who has provided the leading contemporary analysis of the incidents of ownership. Already in this section, it will be apparent to the reader that I sharply

[9] Above, n. 1 at 93–7.
[10] A. M. Honoré, 'Ownership' in A. G. Guest (ed.), *Oxford Essays in Jurisprudence* (Oxford: Clarendon Press, 1961).

distinguish the right of property from both contract and liability principles. Because this contrast is pivotal to my characterization of the right of property, I shall pursue it in the third section through an explicit and more detailed discussion of how property, contract, and liability are genuinely distinct categories, yet at the same time fully integrated and mutually interconnected under the juridical conception of rights. Through that discussion, I hope to show not only that first occupancy embodies an idea of property that is intrinsic to private law, but, even more, that it is the *only* principle that has this character. It represents the idea of property in private law. And it will be via this understanding of first occupancy that I shall explore its reasonableness in the fourth and final section.

To see how the common law understands the principle of first occupancy, a natural starting point is the leading case of *Pierson v Post*.[11] The facts were that Post was pursuing with his hounds a fox across an uninhabited and unowned stretch of land when Pierson, well knowing that the fox was being hunted and chased, intervened from nowhere and captured it. The simple question before the court was whether Post, by the pursuit with his hounds in the manner alleged, had acquired such a right to, or property in, the fox as would sustain an action against Pierson for killing and taking it away.

At stake is the elementary and fundamental issue of who, as between two persons, owns a previously unowned thing. Both the court and the dissent assume that in order to become the owner of a previously unowned thing, one must *do* something. Property in a previously unowned thing is acquired, not innate. By implication, it is not enough merely to want or need something or to think of one's being in a certain relation with it. The fact that one may be more deserving than another if measured against any given standard—whether of excellence, need, contribution to the common good, and so forth—does not as such give one a better claim to the thing. Independently of and prior to action, everyone is in the same juridical position *vis-à-vis* the thing: it belongs to no one and may be taken by anyone. What act, then, must a person perform to acquire property in it? To this question, however, the court and dissent give different responses.

The dissent derives the requisite act as a means toward the goal of promoting the destruction of 'pernicious and incorrigible' beasts such as foxes, to the great advantage of 'our husbandmen, the most useful of men in any community'.[12] To encourage

---

[11] 3 Cai R. 175; 2 Am. Dec. 264; 1805 WL 781 (N.Y. Sup.) (N.Y. 1805). See also the well-known English case of *Young v Hichens*, 6 Q.B. 606. Among the many contemporary theoretical discussions of the principle, I mention Harris, above n. 1, at 213–20 in particular but more generally the whole of Part II; R. Epstein, 'Possession as the Root of Title', *Georgia Law Review*, 13 (1979), 1221; Waldron, above n. 1 at 284–90, 386–9; and S. R. Munzer, 'The Acquisition of Property Rights', *Notre Dame Law Review*, 66 (1991), 661. The seminal discussion is still that of Holmes in *The Common Law*, ed. M. DeWolfe Howe (Boston: Little, Brown, and Company, 1963), lecture VI. Holmes's analysis of possession is an indispensable source for conceptualizing the principle of first occupancy as part of a public basis of justification.

[12] Above, n 11 (per Livingstone, J.).

and support this good, the dissent would give the property in the animal to the one who, having discovered it and being engaged in the pursuit of it, has a reasonable prospect of taking it. Property vests even before the animal is actually subdued and captured. If a person's skill and labour in finding and pursuing the animal can be brought to nothing by the chance, last moment intervention of a 'saucy intruder' who, benefiting from the first person's efforts, finds himself in a position to capture it, 'who', asks the dissent, 'would keep a pack of hounds or . . . at the sound of the horn and at peep of day . . . mount his steed and for hours together . . . pursue the windings of this wily quadruped . . . ?'[13] Accordingly, one who satisfies the criterion of pursuit with prospect of imminent capture has the property as against anyone else who comes after.

In contrast to the dissent, the majority does not posit any substantive purpose to be advanced or any common good to be served, save that whatever rule is adopted must conduce towards certainty and order in society. Instead, it presents the prerequisites for gaining property as free-standing reasonable requirements: property is acquired by one who 'manifests an unequivocal intention of appropriating the animal to his individual use, has deprived him of his natural liberty, and brought him within his certain control'.[14] But while Post's pursuit of the fox undoubtedly manifested an intention to take the animal for his individual use, it did not, as such, deprive it of its independence and bring it under his certain control. For this reason, the majority concludes, Post's pursuit fell short of what is necessary to gain the property in the fox, with the consequence that his action against Pierson for killing and taking it away must fail.

Does the principle of first occupancy, as understood by the majority in *Pierson*, reflect the juridical conception of rights? To provide an answer, we must examine more carefully the character, content, and implications of the right which first occupancy establishes.

To begin, first occupancy emphasizes the external aspect of rights that is central to the juridical conception. Let me elaborate.

First occupancy applies to things that are 'external' in the sense of being initially independent of the purposes of those who would appropriate them.[15] The fact that one wishes, desires, or needs to have possession of an object is not, in itself, sufficient: as already noted, one must *do* something. More specifically the requirement of occupancy is that one do something with or to the object that can be reasonably construed as presently and effectively bringing it under one's own purposes—that it is oneself,

---

[13] ibid.   [14] ibid. (per Tompkins, J.).

[15] For the purposes of the following discussion and, indeed, for the treatment of the right of property in this chapter, I consider property only in external *corporeal* things. This is a simplifying device. The way corporeal objects come under the principle of first occupancy is clear, relatively to the case of, say, intangibles. If we cannot provide a suitable and coherent account of property in corporeal objects, we cannot hope to do so for other more difficult instances, such as intellectual property. The latter raises a particular set of questions that must be addressed in their own right and which I cannot discuss within the parameters of this chapter.

and not others, who control it. Whether one has actually brought an external object under one's control is decided by how one's act reasonably would appear to others. And this in turn will depend upon the contingent particular features of the thing, its physical relation to the person, and so forth. In the case of wild animals, such as Pierson's fox, occupancy can be achieved only if the animal is deprived of its freedom of movement. Where the object is inanimate or incapable of escape, it may be sufficient to grasp or mark it, to bring it onto one's property, and so on, depending upon the object's particular characteristics and its physical relation to oneself and others. In all instances, one treats the thing as subordinate to one's purposive capacity by affecting it in some way—by, as it were, touching it *ab extra* and imposing upon it a contingent condition that is by no means native or necessary to it.

In discussing the requirement of occupancy, I have assumed that it consists in a *purposive* subjection of something to one's certain control and power. If, for reasons of analysis, we insist on distinguishing the 'physical' dimension of the subordinating act from its intentional side, often referred to as the requirement of '*animus possidendi*', we should view the first element as the purely physical impingement upon the thing that deprives it of its independence in the manner just discussed, and the intentional element as the existence of manifested purposiveness in so affecting it or, in other words, as the purposive subjection of the thing to one's control. But, to prevent misapprehension here, it should also be borne in mind that these two elements are not two separate things; each of them is juridically relevant *only* in union with the other. Thus, it is crucial that the requisite *animus* should not be equated with the need, wish, desire, or intention to appropriate what one does not yet have. Rather, it makes explicit the purposive character of the present and completed act that deprives the thing of its independence and that imposes upon it effects that manifest this subordination.

Unless and until one subordinates the object in this way, one's relation to the object must be put in terms of, and must, therefore, give standing to, one's needs, desires, or intentions. It cannot be external in a manner that reflects the juridical conception of rights. To clarify, suppose that one is in hot pursuit of a fox but that one has not yet mortally wounded it, ensnared it, or otherwise rendered escape impossible. While one may want, need, or intend to have the fox, it continues to be independent exactly as it was before. And what one manifests to others by so pursuing, but not subduing, the animal is *just* that one *wants, needs, or intends* to take it. One's 'relation' to the fox must make essential reference to these inward factors and must therefore be rooted in the pursuer alone. This will be true of any act that falls short of depriving the animal of its independence.[16] By contrast, once one has actually subdued the fox and

---

[16] Locke takes the view that pursuit is sufficient to give the pursuer private property in the animal, the reason being that 'whoever has imploy'd so much *labour* about any of that kind, as to find and pursue her, has thereby removed her from the state of Nature, wherein she was common . . .'. J. Locke, *Two Treatises of Government*, book II (New York: Cambridge University Press, 1988) at 290. From the standpoint of the juridical conception of rights, however, the fact that one has expended one's effort and

brought it under one's present and effective control, there *is* an actual relation between person and fox that can make reference to the fox as an object without rooting this in the person's inner disposition as such. In other words, the requirement that there be an act that cancels the animal's independence is essential to the possibility of there being a relation between person and animal that is 'external' in the sense of not being a reflection of the person's inner states.

If the mere pursuit of the fox can, at most, manifest the pursuer's inner states, what about the act of subduing the animal? By depriving the fox of its independence and bringing it under one's present and effective control, one has *already* subjected it to one's purposes, or, more exactly, to one's purposive capacity. Occupancy, that is, the purposive subordination of an external object, establishes the immediately necessary and sufficient conditions of putting an object to use. In other words, by occupying something, one has already and presently treated it as usable. Indeed, inasmuch as use may be said to consist in putting something to one's purposes, occupancy itself may be viewed as making use of the thing. For this reason, what occupying something in the requisite way manifests is an unequivocal intention to use it, where the use is not just a wished-for or needed outcome but something which one is presently accomplishing through putting the object to one's purposes.

While acquisition by first occupancy occurs without the participation of others, the requisite intention must be such as can be reasonably apparent to them. The inference of such intention to use is, moreover, one that others, indeed that *any* other person, may reasonably draw from the external, indeed physical character of the act of occupancy. It is a conclusion that in principle can reasonably hold against others in general. In this way, the act required for acquisition by first occupancy is *public* as against any and everyone in the very way that we ordinarily conceive a right *in rem* to be.

If we suppose that, as a general matter, the juridical conception views publicity as an essential requirement of justice in the establishment of rights, it is important to point out that the particular way in which first occupancy satisfies this requirement—namely, that the intent must be reasonably manifest to anyone in general—reflects the crucial fact that first occupancy makes the *unilateral* act of a single person, alone and without the participation or consent of others, the necessary and sufficient basis for acquisition. Because interaction with others plays no necessary role in the establishment of this right, the intention to use can only be manifest to others in a way that does not depend upon or reflect interaction with any given individual. Thus the intention to use must be reasonably manifest to anyone in general just on the basis of what the occupier has done with or to the thing.

labour is relevant *only* inasmuch as this entails the subordination of the object in the requisite way. In other words, what counts is, not that one has laboured as such, but rather that one has done something that brings the object under an external relation with oneself. That Post laboured to find and then to pursue the fox and that Pierson benefited from Post's effort and perhaps would not have captured the fox without it are, in and of themselves, juridically irrelevant considerations. So far as the juridical conception is concerned, labour either counts merely as an external act of the requisite sort or it is nothing at all.

It should be emphasized, however, that the right is exclusive as against other individuals *qua* separate and distinct.[17] The quality of being *in rem* reflects the fact that the publicness of occupancy is *vis-à-vis* anyone and everyone in general rather than in relation to someone in particular. But this does not do away with the separateness and singularity of individuals. Because the principle of first occupancy holds that it is the plaintiff's unilateral act alone, without the participation or concurrence of others and irrespective of any good to be achieved, which establishes a right of property, it views individuals as separate from and independent of each other and recognizes them, in Rawls's terms, as 'self-authenticating sources of valid claims'[18] *vis-à-vis* others. Individuals are regarded as having a capacity to make claims against others that have weight of their own apart from being derived in any way from the rights or claims of others, from duties owed to society, or from considerations and requirements of the common good, however conceived. The source of the validity of the claims lies *in the persons themselves* who posit the necessary acts. When subordinating things to their purposes, then, individuals are deemed to be acting in accordance with their own ends without having to justify those ends by reference to the purposes of others, whether individually or collectively.

The requirement that one must manifest an intent to put the thing to one's individual use does not mean that the use must be 'selfish'. Rather, the principle of first occupancy is *indifferent* as to whether a given use is selfish or altruistic: it makes no difference in principle whether the plaintiff's ends are for his benefit alone or for the good of another or even whether, in putting a thing to a given purpose, the plaintiff acts in fulfilment of a duty *vis-à-vis* a third party. The purpose, the choice are still his. What is necessary, then, is only that it be a purpose which reasonably appears to be the plaintiff's, that is, which is reasonably attributable to the plaintiff as a separate and independent person. And just because it qualifies as a purpose of a person so viewed, it constitutes an intent to exclude others. At least, any stipulation[19] that the plaintiff manifests 'an intent to exclude others' does not require more than this.

It is, moreover, just because acquisition via first occupancy is established by individuals in their capacity as self-authenticating sources of claims that the property so acquired must count, in legal contemplation, as *private* property, with the content and exercise of the right of property being attributed to an individual's own determinations, irrespective of the wishes or purposes of others. Indeed, unless something is such that it can be occupied by a single individual to the exclusion of others, it cannot become the property of anyone in particular.[20] What, more exactly, is the content of

---

[17] This point is not sufficiently recognized by Penner in his criticism of Hohfeld's view of the *in rem–in personam* distinction. Above n. 1, at 25–8.

[18] See, Rawls, *Political Liberalism*, above n. 3 at 32–3.   [19] See Holmes, above n. 11 at 174–8.

[20] For example, in English law it has been held that underground percolating waters in undefined channels is not the property of anyone precisely because it cannot be occupied in the requisite way. See *Mayor of Bradford v Pickles* [1895] A.C. 587 (Eng. H.L.). Earlier writers standardly make this point and give examples. See e.g. A. Smith, *Lectures on Jurisprudence* (Oxford: Clarendon Press, 1978) at 25;

this right of private property? This brings us to the important task of determining and elucidating the 'incidents' of the right of property under the principle of first occupancy.

First, one who has occupied something in the requisite manner has the exclusive right to possess it. More precisely, he has the exclusive right to have the object under his physical control and to take it into his physical control at any time. We derive this in the following way. On the one hand, we must view occupancy as an act that establishes the right of property. One can exercise this right only with respect to something that one has made one's own. Yet the act through which property is acquired must itself be rightful and must itself be compatible with the change that the acquisition of property makes to the legal relations between the occupier and others. Thus, the act that, from one point of view, establishes the right of property, must, at the same time, be *itself* an exercise of the right of property. But this is just to say that the content of the requisite act and the content of the right so acquired are one and the same. Now the act of occupancy that establishes property in something necessarily entails taking possession of it. Accordingly, the right of property is specified as the right to possess an external object, to the exclusion of others. And since the right-creating act may be viewed as simply a taking possession of the thing, the right to possess is identical with the right of property as such.

Further, the entire juridical significance of the right to possess lies in the fact that it is *exclusive* as against others in the sense that others are placed under a correlative legal (as opposed to factual) *disability vis-à-vis* the right-holder: they can no longer bring about, through their unilateral acts, the juridical effect of making the thing their own. More specifically, those who come after one who has already occupied something no longer have the legal power to bring it under their control or purposes, thereby changing the existing juridical relation between the occupier and themselves with respect to the thing, nor have they the legal power to do anything unilaterally that can extinguish or even limit his property in it. This disability applies to them, however, only in so far as the other acts *as the proprietor* of the thing; that is, only if he externally manifests in action (by exercising one of the incidents of property ownership) the present intent to subject it to his purposes. And, correspondingly, it is the fact that the person first in occupancy does this that places others under this disability. Within these parameters, we may speak of the owner having a right or protected interest in the thing that is correlative to the disability imposed on others. Since the meaning and scope of this right and disability are correlative, the right to possess does not encompass an assurance that the right-holder's personal circumstances and condition or the surrounding external circumstances will be such that he can in fact take the thing into possession at will. And it is wholly indifferent as to whether the right-holder's preferences, desires, needs, and so on are satisfied if he is

W. Blackstone, *Commentaries on the Laws of England, Book the Second: Of the Rights of Things* (Chicago: University of Chicago Press, 1979) ch. I at 14; and G. W. F. Hegel, *Philosophy of Right*, trans. T. M. Knox (Oxford: Oxford University Press, 1952) at para. 52.

able to do so. All it does is to guarantee that others are excluded from the thing under the legal disability of not being able, as a matter of rights, to make it their own.

Note that, at this point in my argument, I have characterized the immediate correlative of the right as a disability rather than as a duty.[21] The right–disability relation is definitive of first occupancy. The sole question is one of *acquisition*, that is, whether someone, through his or her unilateral act, has or has not acquired exclusive property in something. The significance of being under a disability with respect to a thing, is, to repeat, simply that one *no longer has the power to acquire property in it* through one's unilateral act. As I will try to explain more fully in the next section, a right-*duty* relation pertains to a different juridical category, that of liability. While the latter sort of relation presupposes and is, I shall argue, fully integrated with the right–disability

[21] This characterization of the relation does not, I acknowledge, fit with Hohfeld's classification inasmuch as he holds that the correlative of a disability is an immunity, not a right (whose proper correlative is a duty). Putting the analysis I propose in Hohfeld's terms, my taking possession first represents the exercise of a power (correlative to a liability in others) that brings them under a disability (correlative to an immunity in me). Prima facie, each of us has this power with respect to any external thing. However, once one of us has exercised it, this extinguishes the power in others so far as the exercise of the latter would be incompatible with the act of the first.

This being said, I do not think it is inapposite to construe the property relation as a right-disability relation, if 'right' is understood in a wider sense. (Hohfeld himself distinguishes between two uses of 'right', one that is narrow or strict and that has duty as its correlative and another that is broad or generic and that presumably can have something other than duty as its correlative. See W. N. Hohfeld, *Fundamental Legal Conceptions as Applied in Judicial Reasoning* (Westport, Conn.: Greenwood Press Publishers, 1923) at 36–8.) Referring to one side of the relation as a 'right' brings out the fundamental point that my acts with regard to external things can be the object of a requirement of respect which I may claim against others and which is owed me by them. The use of 'right' captures the crucial point that the exercise of any of the incidents of property is never the exercise of a mere liberty in Hohfeld's sense but always something more, since, whether or not one is in actual physical possession of one's thing, others cannot rightfully make it their own. This requirement of respect is given specificity in the following ways. In the first instance—under the heading of property and acquisition—the requirement takes the particular form of a disability on the part of others that denies them the power to make my thing legally their own by their unilateral acts. I shall argue in the next section that a further instance of this requirement—considered under the heading of liability—is that others cannot do anything that injures or wrongs me as proprietor. In both instances, the proprietor has a right (claim) against others to such respect which, correlatively, is owed to him by them. On the other hand, I have chosen to use disability rather than duty because the notion of duty in any meaningful sense implies that one should or should not do something (non-compliance being morally blameworthy or at least wrongful), whereas in the case of the right to property under first occupancy, there is strictly speaking no act required or prohibited but simply a denial of right-producing character to the unilateral actions of non-proprietors. It is therefore less appropriate to speak here of duty even in a large sense. Moreover, the right and disability are correlative in the sense (which may diverge somewhat from, but is arguably compatible with, Hohfeld's) that the operative facts which establish the right simultaneously and necessarily establish the disability, and vice versa; that the right is to be understood only in relation to the disability, and vice versa; and finally, that if one specifies the content of the right, one necessarily and equally determines the content of the disability, and vice versa. On this view, right and disability are but two sides of the same specification of the requirement of respect. For all these reasons, I have chosen the right-disability characterization of the legal relation of property. I thank Jim Harris for suggesting to me the need to discuss the relation between my characterization of the property relation and Hohfeld's important classification.

relation, it is nevertheless distinct. These two forms of relation are not just two distinct standpoints from which to analyse the facts; they are also differently constituted with different criteria of what is relevant and necessary and they are framed to address different juridical questions, so that they single out different ensembles of facts as pertinent and necessary. The right–duty relation has to do with more than just the question of acquisition. The issue that liability addresses is not whether the defendant has acquired something—the inquiry assumes that he has not and cannot because he is subject to the disability—but whether the defendant has *injured* something that already belongs to another. It specifies reasonable terms for *interaction* between two parties where one of them has acted in a way that affects something that comes under the other's exclusive proprietary right.

Now it is certainly possible that a given instance of taking possession may involve *nothing more* than merely grasping the object. If such is the case, occupancy—and with it the right and correlative disability—are coeval with physical possession of the thing and cease the instant one no longer has it in such possession. While this perfectly satisfies the definition and requirement of taking possession, it is nevertheless categorically ambiguous, from a legal point of view. Because others are excluded only in so far as one is physically connected with the thing, they cannot touch it without affecting in some way one's bodily integrity. Thus, the exclusion can be viewed as rooted in the right of bodily integrity; it is unnecessary to refer it to a right to an external thing, that is, to something that can be separable and different from one's body. Yet if there is to be a right of property that is irreducibly distinct from the right of bodily integrity, it must be necessary to so refer it. Consequently, it is essential to the very existence of a distinct juridical category of property that it be possible to view individuals as having possession of something in a way that satisfies the definition and requirement of first occupancy *even when they are no longer in actual physical possession of it*.[22] Where taking possession consists in merely grasping the thing, this point is not brought out and remains purely implicit. Yet it is perfectly possible to take possession in a way (e.g. by marking it) that reasonably exhibits to others that one has put, and that one is continuing to put, something to one's purposes even when the object is not in one's present physical possession. In these instances, the occupancy that establishes the right can continue in time despite an interruption in present physical possession; a first occupier does not automatically cease to have the right of possession just because he or she no longer has the object in actual physical possession.[23] Taking possession is accomplished in a way that makes explicit the fundamental point that it *must* be possible to be in *rightful possession of an external thing* without having it in one's physical possession.

[22] This point was first made by Kant. See I. Kant, *Metaphysics of Morals: The Doctrine of Right*, part I, ch. I, in *Practical Philosophy*, trans. M. Gregor (Cambridge: Cambridge University Press, 1996), 401–4 (6: 245–50) (hereinafter *Doctrine of Right*).

[23] 'Everyone agrees that it is not necessary to have always a present power over the thing, otherwise one could only possess what was under his hand. . . .When certain facts have once been made manifest which confer a right, there is no general ground on which the law need hold the right at an end except the manifestation of some fact inconsistent with its continuance . . .'. Holmes, above n. 11 at 186.

More generally, as long as an intent to use the object may be reasonably inferred by others on the basis of what has been done with or to the object, others must take that intent as continuing in existence. Because the juridically relevant intent is objective, the continuance of the necessary intent requires nothing more than the continuance of certain external, that is, publicly available, facts, whatever may be the actual inner intent of the right-holder. Here we see clearly that, although it is a fundamental feature of first occupancy that the right is acquired through a single individual's act alone, what this act is and whether it can count as the requisite act are determined by how it reasonably appears to others in general. Indeed, it is because, as it were, the very being of the act is in relation to others that one can be deemed to be in present and continuing possession of something when one does not have it in one's physical possession. In relation to oneself, the physical trace of one's act of taking possession represents only something that one *has* done and that, depending upon one's future decision, one *may* renew.

If the right to physical possession is the first 'incident' of the right of property acquired by first occupancy, the second is the exclusive right to use; that is, the right to determine what purposes the thing will be put to and actually to put it to these purposes. From one standpoint, occupying something may be viewed as subordinating it to one's purposive capacity and as constituting the immediately necessary step towards putting the thing to a particular purpose, making occupancy the condition of use but not use itself. At the same time, occupancy may also be regarded as itself an instance of use, inasmuch as it affects the thing in order to realize one's purposes. For use is in general any activity that treats something as an object in the pursuit of, or as a means towards the realization of, one's ends. Since the act that establishes the right of property is itself necessarily a making use of the thing, the right of property is further specified as the right to use one's thing, to the exclusion of others.[24] And since the right-creating act may be viewed as simply a determination of the thing's use, this right to use is identical with the right of property as such.

Similarly to the right to possess, the right to use does not ensure that the right-holder will in fact be able to use the thing or that, in using it, his or her preferences and purposes will be satisfied. The whole meaning of the right is contained in the idea that it is an *exclusive right to determine* the uses to which the thing is put. What the right ensures is just that the locus for determining use cannot be in someone other than the right-holder. The immediate correlative of the right to use is that others are placed under a *legal* disability: they cannot unilaterally do anything that represents a rightful use of the thing or that causes the first occupant to lose his or her right to use it. And this legal disability can be imposed upon others in general because the act that establishes the property is public in the requisite way.

---

[24] The argument here takes the same form as that made to show that the right to possess is an incident of the right of property. See p. 765, above.

Once the right to use is viewed in this light, it must be construed as open-ended, in a particularly strong way. To prevent misunderstanding here, it is crucial to bear in mind that, on the view that I am taking, the only question that is relevant when the right of property is at stake is whether someone has done something which manifests to others the requisite intent to use. This intent is pertinent only in so far as it relates to the issue of acquisition and its bearing upon others is merely that they may be under the legal disability of no longer having the legal power to determine how a thing is to be used. Now *any* use of something qualifies as bringing it under one's purposes and therefore as manifesting the requisite intent. But so far as the person's relation to the thing goes, a thing, by definition, has no standing to constrain the particular uses to which it will be put. And because the only juridical dimension of the relation between the occupier and others concerns the point that the occupier *alone*[25] has the right to determine uses—the others being under a disability in this regard—they also have no standing to decide the particular purposes to which it will be put. Accordingly, the right of property so acquired is not intrinsically limited to any particular use or particular set of uses but rather comprises the potential for an undetermined or open-ended multiplicity of uses. The validity of acquisition by first occupancy does not depend upon whether the plaintiff is pursuing a particular purpose or not. Neither the pursuit of nor the failure to pursue any particular use or particular set of uses can affect the plaintiff's capacity to acquire something (which, of course, must be unowned) or, once having gained it, to continue to have it.

Moreover, the right of use does not entail any built-in prohibition against wasteful uses:[26] one can spoil or destroy one's things. The fact that others may need one's thing is, as such, irrelevant because, in keeping with the juridical conception of rights, need is not a basis upon which one can found proprietary claims against others. Even one who uses his or her property in a way that violates the rights of another (say, by constituting a nuisance) does not thereby and as a matter of the right of property cease to be owner of it. For the right can be lost only by abandonment or, alternatively, by transfer to another through a mutually consented transaction. But a use that violates the rights of others can be construed as neither. Rather, by using it in this way, the owner becomes subject to the distinct though connected idea of liability, as I have already discussed very briefly and will explain more fully in the next section.

A third incident of the right of property acquired by first occupancy is the right to alienate. Just as the principle of first occupancy does not suppose that individuals are obligated to bring anything under their power in the first place—the decision to do

[25] It should be mentioned here that the right to determine the uses of one's property does *not* preclude one's being influenced by others, or indeed one's treating others as authorities to be followed in deciding how to use it. The right does not suppose that right-holders view themselves as the best equipped, or even as morally authorized, to make this decision on their own. It does not regard them as atomistic, unsituated selves. Rather, even where one voluntarily submits to another's authority, say, on religious or moral grounds, this submission is deemed *in law* to be the expression of one's own decision and choice.

[26] As it does in Locke's account, above n. 16 at 290.

so or not is wholly at their option—so the principle does not oblige them, once having initially occupied the thing in the requisite way, to continue to occupy it. The relation between first occupier and thing imposes no obligation whatsoever upon the former. So, in taking something under my control and possession, I can do something with or to it that manifests the present intent of divesting myself of possession or of restoring the thing to its condition of being independent of me, thereby extinguishing the correlative disability that was imposed upon others with respect to possession and use. It is only as one who is in rightful possession of something that one can do something with or to it that is intelligible as an alienation of it; and, of course, it is only a thing that can be alienated. Occupancy may thus be specifically expressed either positively, by putting a thing to a chosen use, or negatively, by returning the thing to its condition of being independent. In each instance, the first occupier is doing something that manifests the subordination of the thing to his or her purposes. Analysed in this way, alienation is itself a specification of occupancy and so the right to alienate is a further determination of the right of property. Indeed, given that alienation is the full and complete occupancy of the thing, the right to alienate is identical with the right of property as such. This right to alienate is exclusive in the sense that others are under the correlative disability of no longer having the legal power to make the thing ownerless; they can unilaterally do nothing that restores the thing's independence, thereby divesting the right-holder of rightful possession. Just as it is the latter's act alone that establishes the property, so it is equally his or her act alone that can divest it.

Here it is important to underline that the only immediate and necessary consequence of alienation, so far as the right of property is concerned, is just that the one who alienates ceases to have property in the thing. In other words, the thing becomes ownerless. This is *all* that alienation produces. If the thing, being unowned, is to become again the property of anyone, someone must initiate the acts required by first occupancy and take it into his or her possession. The acquisition that would result therefrom would arise through an operative fact that, juridically speaking, is entirely distinct and separate from the preceding alienation. Alienation here is just a unilateral abandonment of the property in the thing and the extinction of the corresponding disability in others; it neither creates nor even contributes to the creation of any new rights. In this regard, as I will try to make clear in the next section, there is a basic, qualitative difference between alienation under the principle of first occupancy and transfer (including the power to transfer) rights. Whereas alienation is a unilateral act by a single person that makes the thing ownerless, a transfer of rights, of which contract is the chief example, is constituted by the combined acts of two persons which ensure that the thing never ceases to be in the rightful possession of one of them.[27]

---

[27] I discuss this further in Section 3 at pp. 778–90, below.

It is widely supposed by contemporary scholars that the appropriate way to construe the incidents of property is as a 'bundle' of rights, liberties, powers, immunities, and so forth.[28] This view rests on two assumptions. First, at a formal level, the image of a bundle suggests that the incidents are joined together *ab extra* rather than intrinsically interconnected; there is no internal necessity to their being together and they are not expressions of a single idea. Presumably, one can in principle add incidents to, or subtract them from, the bundle. Secondly, substantively, the bundle view presupposes that the right of property is normatively heterogeneous in that it includes a variety of distinct fundamental juridical conceptions and relations—not just rights but liberties, powers, liabilities, and immunities as well.

In my view, both assumptions are mistaken. The three incidents or specifications, as I would characterize them, of the right of property under first occupancy—namely, the right to possess, the right to use, and the right to alienate—are fully integrated and mutually interconnected, albeit distinct, expressions of the very same conception of property: in acquiring property by first occupancy, one does not, and cannot, acquire anything less or more than all three of these incidents. Moreover, while these incidents are mutually distinguishable, they are, in fundamental juridical terms, all rights. While one may certainly specify aspects of the right of property as liberties, powers, and so forth, these are all rooted in and derivative from the three rights of possession, use, and alienation. In this section, I will challenge the first premise of the bundle view by suggesting briefly how the three incidents are both severally distinguishable and yet fully integrated aspects of the same idea of property[29]—and that there are no other basic incidents besides these three. For the time being, I shall continue to suppose that these incidents take the form of rights. In the last two sections, I will try to show more fully why it is both possible and reasonable to view the incidents as rights only.

I have suggested that when the three incidents of the right of property—namely, the right to possess, use, and alienate—are viewed at a high level of abstraction, each of them is simply a mode of unilaterally subordinating something to one's purposes. This unilateral subordination is external in a way that reflects the juridical conception of rights. From this angle, the three incidents reflect the very same idea and are indistinguishable. As such, each of these incidents may be said to be intrinsic to the right of property that is acquired by first occupancy.

But furthermore, they express this idea in qualitatively distinct ways. Taking possession and use may be distinguished inasmuch as the former unilaterally subordi-

[28] A helpful and thorough recent discussion of this view is found in J. E. Penner, 'The "Bundle of Rights" Picture of Property', *University of California Law Review* 43 (1996), 711. Among the more influential statements of the view are Hohfeld, above n. 21 at 96–7, in particular; and Honoré, 'Ownership', above n. 10.

[29] One of the few recent efforts to construe the incidents of property as core elements of a coherent idea of ownership is the instructive discussion by Richard Epstein in *Takings: Private Property and the Power of Eminent Domain* (Cambridge, Mass.: Harvard University Press, 1985) at 58–62.

nates something to one's power, hence one's purposive capacity, whereas the latter consists in its unilateral subordination to a determinate purpose. Use manifests an intention that carries through taking possession in the choice of a particular purpose to which the possessed object is put. As for alienation, it is true that in one sense it can be regarded as a kind of use of one's thing that consists in purposively doing something in particular to or with it—it is not a mere absence of physical possession because this would not necessarily be incompatible with the continuation of rightful possession and use. Nevertheless, alienation is a unilateral purposive subordination of the thing that is distinct from taking possession and use inasmuch as it manifests the intent precisely to place the thing beyond one's possession and use.

The final point is that the three incidents are conceptually integrated in a way that assures completeness. The starting-point must be taking possession. For given the juridical conception of rights, it is only through an initial act of this kind that the requisite external relation can be established between person and (unowned) thing. Taking possession brings something under a person's purposive power and capacity. Thus, it is conceptually prior to use and establishes the possibility of use, since it is only something that is under one's power that one can put to a particular use. For its part, use is essentially an act that completes taking possession in the form of explicitly putting the thing to a particular purpose. Use is therefore second in the conceptual sequence. Now, use represents the merely positive realization of taking possession—a purely positive connection between person and thing via the imposition of a particular purpose—inasmuch as it does not bring out explicitly the fact that, even as an owner, one is not required to appropriate anything at all so that it is not in the least necessary that one continue to possess the thing. Alienation represents a kind of use of one's thing that makes this fundamental point explicit. On the one hand, alienation incorporates the prior incidents of taking possession and use, because, to be intelligible as alienation, the act must be done with or to something that is in one's possession and must entail the purposive imposition of effects upon it. But by representing a purposive dealing with one's thing that manifests the fact that one *need not* be in possession, alienation completes use. It integrates taking possession and use in a way that expresses the fundamental character of the external relation between person and thing in the juridical conception of rights: individuals are under no requirement to appropriate things, to enter into contractual relations with others, and so on. Of the three incidents, alienation is an exercise of the right of property—for, as I have emphasized, it is as an owner of something that one alienates it— that exhibits most fully and explicitly the distinctive character of this right under the juridical conception.

I conclude that the three rights of possession, use, and alienation exhaust the possible fundamental incidents that are intrinsic to acquisition by first occupancy. Possession, use, and alienation represent at the highest level of abstraction all the possible qualitatively distinct modes of unilaterally subjecting a thing to one's purposes, supposing that we begin with the condition of the thing being *not yet* property and end with the condition of its being *no longer* property. Alienation leaves off precisely where taking possession begins—with an unowned thing; the circle, and hence the conceptual sequence of the forms of occupancy, is complete. This conclusion is in accordance with the traditional view taken by both the common law and the civil law, going back to the three-part Roman law division of *ius possendi, ius utendi,* and *ius abutendi.*

At this point in the argument, my contention has been that the rights to possession, use, and alienation exhaust the fundamental incidents intrinsic to acquisition by first occupation. In Section 3, I shall take the further step of arguing that first occupancy is the only elementary category of private law that qualifies as a right of property. So the view that I shall ultimately defend is that these, and *only* these, rights are the fundamental incidents of the right of property in private law. This view contrasts with that taken by scholars who have suggested a more extensive list of incidents. The difference stems, I believe, from the fact that whereas the approach taken in this chapter views property as a specific mode of acquisition within the juridical conception of rights that is distinct from both contract and liability, the more extensive lists represent amalgams of *qualitatively different* juridical categories and relations that are arrived at by empirically gathering together the various rights, liberties, duties, immunities, liabilities, and so forth that apply to property owners in their many diverse legal relations in a modern legal system. However, in keeping with the legal point of view, a public basis of justification requires that, in specifying the incidents of property or, say, the essential features of contract, we be attentive precisely to the characteristic differences among such relations. If I am correct, it must be the case that incidents other than the rights to possess, use, and alienate are reducible to one of these three or, in the alternative, are extrinsic to the principle of first occupancy as such and bring into play other kinds of legal relations. To illustrate this point, I will now briefly discuss what is widely considered the most influential contemporary account of the incidents of ownership, namely, that of A. M. Honoré.[30]

Honoré identifies eleven standard incidents of ownership which he regards as 'necessary ingredients in the notion of ownership, in the sense that, if a system did not admit them, and did not provide for them to be united in a single person, we would conclude that it did not know the liberal concept of ownership'.[31] These incidents comprise the right to possess, the right to use, the right to manage, the right to the income of the thing, the right to the capital, the right to security, the right or incidents of transmissibility and absence of term, the prohibition of harmful use, liability to execution, and the incident of residuarity. Now certain of these incidents are indeed irreducibly fundamental and intrinsic to acquisition by first occupancy; others are reducible to or are specifications of such incidents; and still others presuppose legal relations (belonging to contract, principles of liability, public law, and so on) that, I shall argue, go beyond this concept of acquisition, thereby making his account of incidents over-inclusive.

[30] Above n. 10.   [31] ibid. 112.

For example, the right to possess, which Honoré defines as the right to be put in, and to remain in, exclusive control of a thing, coincides essentially with the right to possess discussed above. It is a fundamental intrinsic incident, which Honoré notes, is the foundation of the whole superstructure of ownership.[32] Similarly, subject to an important qualification, Honoré's right to use, right to manage, and right to the income together comprise the right to use as analysed above. Although he differenti-ates these rights, Honoré himself points out that on a wide interpretation, 'use' can incorporate both management and income.[33] The qualification is that by including in the content of the right to income such items as rents and profits derived from allowing others to use one's thing, Honoré goes beyond the parameters of the con-cept of property that is strictly entailed by acquisition through first occupancy. This is reflected in the fact, noted by Honoré, that the rights to rent and profits are claims *in personam*, not *in rem*. As I will argue in the next section, such rights presuppose a notion of acquisition that is effected via a transfer between two parties, not through the unilateral act of a single party. As such, they have their source in contract rather than first occupancy.

The same remark applies to the fifth incident, the right to the capital. This right consists in the power to alienate one's thing and to consume, waste, or destroy the whole or part of it. The right of use that is intrinsic to acquisition by first occupancy certainly comprises the right to consume or destroy the thing. Beyond this, first occu-pancy comprises the further intrinsic incident of the right to alienate which essen-tially consists just in the right to abandon. By contrast, the power to transfer one's thing during life or on death and by way of gift, sale, mortgage, bequest, and so forth, goes beyond this right to alienate since it has to do with a transaction by which the thing is acquired by another rather than with a unilateral abandonment that simply and only makes the thing ownerless.

Honoré's sixth incident, the right to security which consists in an ordinary immu-nity from expropriation by other individuals, is logically entailed by the three funda-mental incidents. This immunity simply reflects the fact that it is the right-holder alone who, by his or her externally manifested choices, has the right to determine the duration of the property interest. Whether liability to expropriation by the state or by public authorities is consistent with the recognition of the right of property acquired by first occupancy and if so, what the fair terms of such expropriation might be are matters that must be analysed, not from within the standpoint of the juridical con-ception of rights taken by itself, but from a quite different perspective that specifies the appropriate relation between the right of property on the one hand and the right of the state on the other. Once again, therefore, these questions take us beyond the determination of the intrinsic nature and character of the right of property in first occupancy.

---

[32] ibid. 113.   [33] ibid. 114.

The incidents of transmissibility, absence of term, and residuary character[34] reflect the three standard incidents of right to possession, use, and alienation. To the extent that they are not reducible to one of these, they bring into play juridical relations that do not belong originally or intrinsically to the concept of property in first occupancy: for instance, they suppose relations of transfer, whereby another acquires a full or limited ownership interest from the right-holder. Thus, the residuary character of ownership simply signifies that, despite the fragmentation of ownership, there is one—the owner—in whom the right to take possession continues to vest as against all others: 'in the end', ownership must reside in this person, for only in this way can it be a right that is exclusive against the others.[35]

The last two incidents enumerated by Honoré, namely, the prohibition of harmful use and liability to execution, also go beyond the right established by first occupancy—but for a different reason. Starting with the prohibition of harmful use, there is the preliminary point, rightly noted by J. W. Harris,[36] that this prohibition does not depend upon whether one owns the instrument that poses a risk of harm to others. But even supposing that one *does* own the instrument of potential harm, the question of whether and in what way one's use is to be limited so as to comply with the rights of others is distinct from the sole fundamental issue that first occupancy addresses: what are the necessary and sufficient conditions of acquiring (or losing) property in an unowned thing? On this analysis, the correlative of the right is the legal disability placed upon others. As I have already mentioned but will explain more fully in the next section, I distinguish between the idea of a correlative disability on the one hand and that of a correlative duty not to interfere or injure on the other hand. While the harm and rectification principles certainly suppose that the plaintiff has a right of ownership in the object of the protected interest—the absence of which right will result in the plaintiff's being non-suited—they postulate a relation of right and correlative duty, not merely correlative disability.

By way of illustration, consider the law of nuisance. Nuisance law settles conflicting claims of land usage as between two or more individual landowners.[37] Let us suppose that each landowner has acquired his or her right through first occupancy. Now while it is necessary for a plaintiff to establish that the defendant is interfering with a use or interest that comes under his or her exclusive right of property, this is not a sufficient condition for a successful action. The court must also decide whether the parties' uses are ordinary or extraordinary as determined by the so-called 'local community standard' and it is only if the plaintiff's use is ordinary and the defendant's is not that the action will succeed. But even on a purely rights-based inter-

[34] In Honoré's account, these are respectively the seventh, eighth, and eleventh incidents and are discussed at ibid. 120–2 and 126–8.

[35] Honoré notes that '[i]n the end, it turns out that residuarity is merely one of the standard incidents of ownership'. Ibid. 128.

[36] Above n. 1, at 32–3.

[37] By 'landowner' I mean anyone who has the minimally required proprietary or possessory interest in land.

pretation of this standard that attempts to frame it in terms of a notion of equality that is independent of considerations of general welfare, the standard requires an analysis of 'ordinary usage' that crystallizes a notion of equality for property-users in interaction with each other. This goes beyond the question of who, as between two parties, has the valid claim to a single thing. The aim of the nuisance analysis is to determine, not whether the defendant has, or has acquired, a proprietary interest of some kind, such as an easement, in the plaintiff's land but rather whether the defendant's use of his or her own property has injured the plaintiff's proprietary right.

The same general point applies to an action in negligence. To show that the standard of care has been violated, it is not enough—although it is essential—for the plaintiff to put forward an exclusive proprietary right as against the defendant. The plaintiff must also establish that the defendant did not act reasonably in the circumstances. And this requires a determination of the fair and reasonable terms to govern an interaction consisting of *two* sides: the plaintiff's exclusive proprietary right in something versus the defendant's own distinct interest in his or her freedom of action. While it may be the case that fairness and reasonableness require that the defendant refrains from activity that foreseeably imposes a substantial and non-ordinary risk on the object of the plaintiff's proprietary right irrespective of the costs to the defendant of so refraining,[38] this conclusion rests on something more than a principle of acquisition. The defendant's assertion of a right of action is not a competing claim to have the property in the damaged thing. A principle of acquisition, whether first occupancy or something else, determines who, as between two persons, has the exclusive property in something and thus settles the conflicting claims of two persons with respect to *one* thing only. By contrast, liability principles in nuisance and negligence law settle conflicting claims over the appropriate boundaries between two things. In contrast to first occupancy, the operative facts that give rise to liability necessarily include interaction between two parties.[39]

The foregoing discussion of the incidents of property ownership highlights the conceptual parameters of the idea of property which, I contend, is reflected in the principle of first occupancy. A basic premise of the argument is that this right of property is purely a principle of acquisition and that it must be strictly understood as such. Even granting that this is a correct presentation of the principle of first occupancy, there is still the important question of whether, so far as private law is concerned, the right of property is properly viewed as restricted to *just* what this principle entails. Why isn't it arbitrary to limit the right to just this? What has emerged from the discussion of the incidents of the right of first occupancy is that there may be a difference between acquisition by first occupancy on the one hand and both a transfer of ownership and principles of liability on the other. For my argument to succeed, it must be the case that: (1) within private law, the categories of first occu-

---

[38] This is arguably the standard which English and Commonwealth courts apply and which is set out most influentially in the leading case of *Bolton v Stone* [1951] A.C. 850 (Eng. H.L.) (per Lord Reid).

[39] I further discuss the idea of liability as a distinct juridical category in Section 3 at pp. 791–9.

pancy, transfer, and liability are genuinely distinct and completely exhaust its basic structure; and (2) the right of property falls solely in the category of first occupancy and not in transfer or in liability. While I cannot hope to set out fully the needed argument in the compass of this essay, I wish to try to sketch how these categories should be understood and explain why the resulting threefold classification is complete and exhaustive, with first occupancy alone representing the idea of property in private law. The next section explores these matters.

3 Property, Contract, and Liability: Distinct but Integrated

My first task in this section is to show that first occupancy and contract are both modes of acquiring ownership of things but, at the same time, that they are qualitatively distinct as modes of acquisition. First occupancy and contract, I shall claim, are the two fundamental modes of acquiring ownership. Moreover, I will argue that the idea of property in private law, as distinguished from ownership, is properly identified with first occupancy, not contract. I will then go on to elucidate briefly the idea of liability in private law and indicate its relation to property and contract. My contention, for which I can only sketch the kind of detailed and full argument that would be essential, is that property, contract, and liability exhaust the fundamental categories or elements of private law, taking the latter to embody the juridical conception of rights.

Before I discuss the relation between first occupancy and contract, however, there is a point of clarification that should be made concerning the scope and import of first occupancy. It might be thought that this principle applies only where the thing to be acquired is *res nullis*—that is, not yet owned by anyone at all. But this is not the case. Rather, any time an individual claims to have acquired something in relation to another on the ground that he or she *took possession of it before the other*, the principle of first occupancy is invoked. This is true whether or not the thing is *res nullis* absolutely speaking. What counts is just whether, *relative to another*, one person has taken possession *prior in time* to the other. It is worth noting here that the fact that my right may be relative in the sense of being against one person but not another (who has, we suppose, a better claim under first occupancy than I) does not alter its character as *in rem*.[40] On the view that I am suggesting and will shortly fill out in a little more detail, it is *in rem* because, given that my mode of appropriating the thing is

---

[40] Penner, above n. 1 at 147–9, emphasizes this point.

public *vis-à-vis* everyone, the one who is placed under the correlative disability counts as anyone in general. And, as I tried to explain in the previous section, it is public in this way because appropriation is by my unilateral act, without the participation or concurrence of others.

So far as contractual rights are concerned, it is relatively well settled that they are *in personam*; that is, that they are in their very conception relative as between the parties to the contract. As well, the objective test for contract formation holds that the meaning and import of one party's acts is decided by how they reasonably appear, not to anyone in general, but to the other party in the context of their particular interaction situated in its surrounding circumstances. In the following discussion of the relation between contract and first occupancy, I shall treat these settled features of the law as provisionally fixed points.

By contrast, there is a further view about the character of contractual rights that I will challenge. According to this view, the *in personam* right that is acquired at contract formation and prior to performance is not a full and genuine right of ownership, despite the fact that it is acquired, is exclusive as against another, and is fully protected by the principle of liability in private law. On this view, it is only with performance that a party obtains an ownership right in a thing. The right *in personam* is inherently transient, passing into the right *in rem*, which represents its conclusion and stable stopping point. The right *in personam* must therefore be brought under the rubric of some notion other than the acquisition of ownership, such as the morality of promising, and the right must be construed as a right to performance in contrast to an ownership right in a thing. The fact that, upon performance, the transferee owns the thing promised is explained consistently with this understanding as the outcome of an initial unilateral abandonment by the transferor followed in time by a similarly unilateral appropriation by the transferee: no new principle is invoked other than that of first occupancy. The 'transaction' consists of two separate instances of exercises of the right of first occupancy. On this approach, then, acquisition by first occupancy is the sole mode of acquiring ownership of things. Rights *in rem*, and not those *in personam*, are genuine ownership rights.

On its face, however, the notion that contract can be understood as entailing a right that can be acquired and vindicated by general private law principles of liability but which nevertheless is irreducible to an ownership right over a thing is unintelligible from the standpoint of the juridical conception of rights. Moreover, as I will discuss in more detail, if contractual acquisition may only be analysed in terms of two separate acts each of which comes under the principle of first occupancy, it is difficult if not impossible to account for basic, undisputed doctrines and features of the law of contract. I shall argue for a different analysis. Rather than exhausting the ways in which ownership may be acquired, first occupancy is just one of two qualitatively different modes of acquiring ownership, with contract (or any form of transfer from one party to another) constituting the second. Indeed, contrary to the above view, I shall try to explain why contractual rights *in personam* in fact represent most fully and completely the idea of ownership in private law, thereby fulfilling the juridical import of first occupancy. We begin by trying to think through how the basic character of contract might, and even must, be understood if it is to be intelligible as a mode of acquiring ownership that is categorically distinct from first occupancy.

Now, as a general matter, there may be acquisition of something that is unowned or, alternatively, already owned by another. This division is both fundamental and exhaustive. In the case of an unowned object, acquisition is and must be by the principle of first occupancy. If there is to be a second, genuinely distinct mode of acquiring ownership, it must be contained, therefore, in an analysis of how acquisition of something already owned differs from the acquisition of something unowned. This second mode of acquisition must take to heart the crucial fact that the thing is already owned by another. It must intrinsically make reference to this fact. Understanding the acquisition of something already owned in terms of two separate unilateral acts, where one party abandons the thing and the other appropriates it, does not, however, do this. The act of abandonment makes the thing ownerless and available to anyone; the act of appropriation takes up the thing in the condition of being simply unowned (by anyone) and the resulting right is indifferently the same as against the original owner and anyone else who has not already taken possession of it. The acquisition cannot be construed as appropriation by one *from the other*. There is, in short, *nothing* in this form of acquisition that intrinsically and necessarily refers to the other party's initial ownership. Clearly, to think through a mode of acquisition that does incorporate this fact we must be able to conceive of a form of acquisition in which the thing is acquired by one *in the condition of being owned by another*; in other words, it must be possible to construe the thing, at the moment of appropriation, as *still* the other's. Only then will the thing be appropriated in a condition other than that of being unowned. Let us now see more particularly what such acquisition would have to entail.

First, such acquisition must be effected by *two* acts of will: there must be alienation by the owner—or else the second party will continue to be subject to a legal disability—*and* there must be appropriation by the second party—otherwise there can at most be an abandonment, and not a new acquisition of ownership. However, merely by stipulating a requirement that there be two acts, we have not yet categorically distinguished this form of acquisition from taking possession following a prior abandonment, which does not require that we go beyond the principle of first occupancy. To ensure that the acquisition is from another and irreducible to first occupancy in any circumstance, there is a further requirement: the two acts must be *mutually related* in the following way.

Acquisition from another requires that the acts of alienation and appropriation be two sides of a single relation, such that neither side can be defined nor have legal effect except in combination with the other. Thus, the act of alienation must manifest the intent that it counts as alienation if, but only if, there is appropriation by the other, and vice versa: each side is defined only in relation to the other.[41] So understood, these acts are already distinguishable from abandonment (which makes the thing ownerless and available to anyone) followed by taking possession (which is a purely unilateral act that does not directly involve the participation or concurrence of anyone else).

More particularly, it must be possible to construe the mutually related acts of the parties under two distinct aspects, each of which is necessary to the complete elucidation of acquisition from another. First, if the appropriation by one is to be compatible with the other's right of ownership, it must be with the latter's consent and must therefore be in response to and after the latter's externally manifested and unreserved decision to alienate. The two acts must be in a temporal sequence, with the first act inviting the second which, in turn, follows and responds to it. Secondly, it must, however, also be possible to construe the relation between the acts such that there is *no gap whatsoever* between them: there must not be a time when the thing has ceased to be the first party's but has not yet become the second party's. For if there were such a gap, however small, during that interval the thing would become ownerless and the second party would appropriate it in this condition—and therefore in accordance with the principle of first occupancy. We must, in short, be able to construe the mutually related acts as absolutely co-present and simultaneous.[42] If there is to be a second mode of acquisition that is conceptually irreducible to acquisition by first occupancy, it must be possible, therefore, to view the first party *as being and remaining an owner* of his thing even while he alienates and the second party appropriates it, and, similarly, the second party as an owner even while he appropriates and the first party alienates it. Paradoxically, each party must be represented as remaining an owner while ceasing to be or while becoming one. It is only on this condition that there can be a conceptually gapless transfer between them.

Acquisition from another—let us call it 'derivative acquisition'—seems, then, by its very terms to be distinct from and irreducible to acquisition by first occupancy. The fundamental difference between them is this: whereas the operative fact that satisfies the principle of first occupancy is the unilateral act of a single party, the operative fact in the case of derivative acquisition is a union of acts of two parties. It takes but one person to do everything that is necessary and sufficient to establish a right under first occupancy; derivative acquisition is possible only through the united wills of two.

[41] In Hegel's words, 'my will as alienated is at the same time another's will'. Above n. 20, para. 73.

[42] It was Kant who first specified this requirement of simultaneity—which he called the 'principle of continuity'—as essential to the possibility of acquisition from another. See his *Doctrine of Right*, above n. 22, part I, ch. II, sect. II at 424 (6: 274). Hegel's formulation of this idea is found in *The Philosophy of Right*, above n. 20, para. 72.

It is, however, precisely because first occupancy arises through the unilateral act of a single person that there is a tension within this principle that is not fully resolved by it. The whole juridical meaning of the right of property lies, after all, in its being *exclusive as against others*: the other-relatedness of property is not a contingent or secondary aspect, but is rather necessary and intrinsic to the right of property as such. It is true that the other-relatedness of property is reflected in the requirement that the unilateral act must be one that is publicly recognizable in the requisite way. Still, it is by their unilateral and isolated acts without the participation or concurrence of others that individuals acquire property by first occupancy. Moreover, while the idea of acquisition of external things, in contrast to the right of bodily integrity, necessarily postulates, we saw, the possibility of one's being in rightful possession of something without having it in one's physical possession, first occupancy requires an initial act of taking the thing into one's physical possession; and where occupancy is achieved through grasping (as opposed to marking, forming, or using) it, one's possession is coeval with physical possession, ceasing the instant one no longer has it within one's physical grasp. That there must be an initial act of physical occupancy follows, I argued, precisely from the fact that one appropriates the thing through one's unilateral act independently of the participation of others. Thus, the operative fact that satisfies first occupancy does not exhibit on its face, as it were, the very feature, namely, relation to another, that is essential to its being a proprietary right.

There is a further tension within the principle of first occupancy stemming from the character of the operative fact that satisfies it. Taking the full and complete operation of the principle in any particular instance, one person acquires something to the exclusion of everyone else: with respect to the appropriated thing, the one who has a right is under no disability whereas everyone else is *just* under a disability with no right as against the first in possession. Yet it is implicit in our understanding of the principle that any one of those barred *could*, as a matter of rights, have acquired the very same thing under different circumstances.[43] That every person has an equal capacity in law for acquisition is a basic premise of the interpretation of this principle in the public legal culture. At the most fundamental level this premise consists in an idea of reciprocity that one is subject to constraints *vis-à-vis* another only in so far as one also has rights as against the other, and vice versa. Yet the operation of first occupancy does not expressly make reciprocity part of the operative facts giving rise to the right.

Because derivative acquisition requires mutually related acts of choice as indicated above, it is not subject to these tensions. In derivative acquisition, and in contrast to first occupancy, the acts that establish the legal relation exhibit on their face the character of that relation. One example of derivative acquisition that immediately comes

---

[43] I am grateful to Daniel Batista for this formulation.

to mind is the present, fully executed transfer of ownership. But, as I have argued else-where, the instance of derivative acquisition that brings out most fully and explicitly the distinctive character and features of such acquisition is contract.[44] Here, I will briefly highlight certain fundamental points about the common law of contract in order to show how contract completely fulfils the juridical character of the right acquired by first occupancy, making contract distinct from, yet continuous with, first occupancy. One notion of ownership informs both.

The first point is that the law itself suggests that contract is, and must be viewed as, a mode of acquisition; and, more specifically, that although the right acquired by contract is *in personam*, this right is nevertheless a right of ownership, in the sense of entailing rightful possession of a thing exclusively as against another. Let me explain.

In case of breach of contract, a plaintiff is entitled to expectation damages or, where these are not adequate, to specific performance. In giving such remedies, the intention of the law is to put the plaintiff in the position that he or she would have occupied had the defendant performed as promised. The law views this as a ruling and a just principle of compensation. Now if expectation damages and specific per-formance are compensatory in character, as the law supposes they are, it must be the case that, prior to the breach, the plaintiff has a right, exclusive as against the defen-dant, in the thing that is vindicated by the remedy. In legal contemplation, the breach represents, not a failure either to confer a benefit upon the plaintiff or to fulfil the plaintiff's needs and expectations, but rather an injury to the plaintiff's protected interest: it deprives the plaintiff of physical possession of something that is already his or hers by right at contract formation, even before the agreed-upon time for perfor-mance. Breach of contract is misfeasance, not nonfeasance. Because the source of this protected interest can only be the contractual agreement itself, it must be possible to view the plaintiff as acquiring something from the defendant at the moment of, and through, contract formation. In light of the availability of the expectation remedy construed as a form of compensation, contract is properly construed as a mode of derivative acquisition.

Moreover, although the right acquired by contract is often characterized as a right to another's performance, this right, in the final analysis, is a right of ownership.[45] *What* the plaintiff acquires is reflected in the content of the remedy, in keeping with the idea that the remedy aims to place the plaintiff in the position he would have occupied had his right been respected. Expectation damages give the plaintiff money which represents the full value of the contracted-for thing (whether an object or a

---

[44] For a more detailed discussion of this point, see 'The Unity of Contract Law', above n. 6, at 132 ff. I should note here that the question of whether the right of bequest, like contract, comes under the idea of derivative acquisition and transfer (as Harris and Kant suggest) or whether it should be viewed as a crea-ture of social and family policy (as Hegel argues) is a matter that I cannot discuss in this chapter. I do not, however, believe that my analysis of property, contract, and liability would be affected either way. For Harris's view, see above n. 1 at 249 ff.; for Kant, above n. 22 at 440–1 (6: 294–5); and Hegel, above n. 20, para. 80.

[45] I discuss this question more fully in 'The Unity of Contract Law', above n. 6 at 134–7.

service) at the time performance was due. In addition, such damages provide the plaintiff with the means to purchase an equivalent of the thing on the market and thereby to obtain physical possession of it. Where no such equivalent is obtainable, money damages cannot fulfil this dual function and so will be deemed 'inadequate'. In such case, only specific performance can accomplish these ends and is, in principle, the appropriate remedy. The contractual right which vests in the plaintiff at contract formation therefore includes the right to the physical possession and the value[46] of the contracted-for thing. And correlatively, at contract formation, the defendant has no such right to the thing as against the plaintiff.[47] But a right to the exclusive physical possession and the value of an object or service is proprietary in character, belonging to him or her who is its owner. As between these two parties, therefore, the plaintiff is owner of the thing contracted for.

The second point is that acquisition by contract is accomplished by mutually related acts of will, in this way displaying its character as derivative acquisition. We see this in the fundamental doctrines of contract formation. Thus, there must be offer *and* acceptance—*two* expressions of will. By itself, an offer confers, not a right at all, but merely a power of acceptance. Unless and until the offer is met by acceptance, contract formation does not occur. The contractual relation is irreducibly two-sided. Furthermore, as noted earlier, the meaning of each side is identical with how it reasonably appears to the other party. In other words, the assents that bring about contract formation—and therefore the acquisition of rights—must be public *as between the parties.* It is these externally manifested assents, in and of themselves and not as indicators of or surrogates for actual inner assent, that directly bring about formation. Similarly to the doctrine of offer and acceptance, the doctrine of consideration ensures that there are two sides, not one. This is reflected in the fundamental requirement of quid pro quo: to be enforceable, a promise must be made in return for the promise or the doing of something else, with the thing promised and the substance of the return consideration being two *qualitatively different* things. Since each side must give up something useful in return for the receipt of something else that is useful—this is clearly the case with the bilateral contract but it is also true of the unilateral contract—each side may be viewed as both alienating and acquiring things in which they can have an ownership interest.

This two-sidedness of contract is further reflected in the common law principle of unconscionability, which itself may be viewed as a doctrine that pertains to contract

[46] As I explain shortly, the analysis of contractual acquisition shows that value is the substance of what one owns when one owns something.

[47] I suppose throughout this discussion of contract *as a mode of acquisition* that contract formation establishes a new right-disability relation between the parties with respect to external things, one that did not exist before. Analysed under the idea of liability, however, contract is viewed under the rubric of a right–duty relation. A breach can therefore be characterized in two ways: first, it does *not* give the defendant a right to the thing he has promised the plaintiff nor does it deprive the plaintiff of his right, which remains vested in him from the moment of formation; it is also a wrong that interferes with the plaintiff's rightful possession of the thing, as this has been established by the terms of their agreement.

formation. While not free from controversy, a widely accepted interpretation of unconscionability judges contracts against a baseline of equality in exchange.[48] Each party has, prima facie, the right to receive from the other equal value for what he or she alienates. At the same time, no one is obliged to receive equal value. So by their words and actions reasonably construed, parties may manifest an intent to enrich each other or to assume the risk of the corresponding loss, thereby, in effect, waiving the right to an equivalence. Where, however, an inequality of values appears to result from a party's impaired bargaining power, this will ordinarily negative the existence of donative intent or assumption of risk. In this way, the giving and receiving of equal value is a supreme regulative principle that provides the baseline for assessing the validity of any contract.

Now, on the one hand, *value* is necessarily and explicitly relational or two-sided: the value of something is expressed in relation to something else, where the things compared are qualitatively different in terms of their respective particular features and uses. So long as the standpoint is just that of first occupancy and the exercise of the right to use by a single person, we may speak of the usefulness to that person of something compared to something else, but not its value. Things have value when they can be thought of as exchangeable and therefore as owned by two different persons who choose to treat them as commensurable. On the other hand, value is the identity that subsists in this difference: under the aspect of value, qualitative differences between things are a matter of indifference; as expressions of value, each represents (some quantum) of the same thing. And in so far as each party is entitled, though not obliged, to receive *equal* value from the other, the content that each acquires from the other is absolutely identical with what he or she alienates and with what the other acquires in turn. In alienating my thing (i.e. its value), I continue to have the same thing; and similarly, you appropriate only what you already have. Thus, each of us remains owner of the same thing even as we alienate or appropriate—as must be supposed, I noted earlier, if there is to be a gapless transfer from one person to another in keeping with the idea of derivative acquisition.

The third point is that contract exhibits on its face the possibility of the acquisition of non-physical, but nevertheless fully effective and rightful, possession. In contract, rightful possession can be acquired independently of physical possession of the objects of those rights. Indeed, unless this is the case, the idea of an enforceable but purely executory contract becomes instantly impossible. This is because it is *at contract formation*, that is, independently of and prior to parties' obtaining physical possession of what they have been promised, that the parties' rights are fully and completely established. It is these—and *only* these—rights that are vindicated by

---

[48] For a recent survey and thoughtful discussion of different conceptions of unconscionability, see S. M. Waddams, 'Unconscionable Contracts: Competing Perspectives', *Saskatchewan Law Review*, 62 (1999), 1. A leading Anglo-Commonwealth decision that reflects the view set out in the above text is Lord Denning's concurring opinion in *Lloyds Bank v Bundy* [1975] 1 Q.B. 326 (Eng. C.A.). I discuss unconscionability in more detail in 'The Unity of Contract Law', above n. 6 at 184–201.

expectation damages or specific performance in case of breach. Performance itself does not confer any new contractual rights: by performing, a party merely gives—or, more precisely, does not withhold from—the other party physical possession of what is already rightfully the other's from the moment of contract formation. The moment of physical possession is completely subordinated to and follows rightful possession; contract formation comes first and establishes the contractual relation, with performance being reduced to a mere sequel.

Acquisition in complete independence of having physical possession is possible in virtue of the two-sidedness of contractual acquisition. Contract presupposes that the thing promised is already in the rightful exclusive possession of one of the parties. As between them, ownership can be transferred just by the decision of the first to alienate in relation to the decision of the second to appropriate. So long as these decisions represent, as between the parties, fully crystallized and externally manifested choices, this is sufficient. As we saw, the reason an unowned thing must be initially taken into one's physical possession is that it is only in this manner that a present and effective appropriation can be externally manifest to others when their participation is irrelevant. This is no longer the case with contractual acquisition. In both first occupancy and contract, the source of rights is in the *externally manifested choices* of individuals, in keeping with the juridical conception of rights.

The fifth point concerns the explication of the *in rem* and *in personam* distinction and the relation between these two categories of rights. Starting with the fundamental idea that rights with respect to external things (that is, things other than one's body) are *acquired* and not innate, the difference between real and personal rights reflects the difference in the sorts of *acts* through which they are acquired. The right *in rem* is established by the unilateral act of a single person with respect to an unowned thing without the participation or concurrence of others.[49] The fact that *no one else* participates translates into a publicity requirement that must hold *vis-à-vis any*one in general: a right that may therefore be 'against the world'. Moreover, the ways in which the right is exercised are determined by the single individual's choices alone, as these are reasonably manifested to others in general. As long as the individual continues to do this, the exercise of the right *in rem* is intrinsically unlimited with respect to duration and to the content of use.

By contrast, rights *in personam* are established through the combined acts of two individuals. Reflecting the fact that personal rights are acquired by acts that are public *only as between the parties to the transaction*, such rights hold only as against another definite individual. Further, the content of the right is determined not by either of the parties taken in isolation from the other but rather in and through their

---

[49] The right of bodily integrity, although not a right with respect to an external thing, is *in rem*, seeing that it is against others in general. The negative feature that it and a proprietary right *in rem* share is that the necessary and sufficient conditions of neither involve the participation of others. In the case of bodily integrity, this is assured by the right being innate; in the case of property, by the right being acquired through the unilateral act of a single person.

interaction. In contrast to rights *in rem*, personal rights have a character that is thoroughly transactional in nature. Thus, the content of the right may, within limits, be shaped (and therefore restricted) by the parties' agreement. For example, whether the plaintiff has acquired as against the defendant a right to use the contracted-for thing for a given particular purpose is decided by whether the purpose is of a kind that was reasonably contemplated by the parties at the time of contract formation, given the terms of their agreement reasonably construed in the context of its surrounding circumstances.[50] Similarly, the modalities under which the plaintiff is to obtain physical possession are determined by the contractual terms. The fact that the plaintiff may not be entitled to obtain physical possession of the thing contracted for until a certain time after formation and even then only in a certain way simply represents the contractually determined manner in which the plaintiff is to take physical possession and initially to exercise his or her right thereto.[51] The transactional determination of the right does not disqualify it as a right of ownership but rather frames the way it is such. And in spite of the limited scope which the right may (but need not) have, so long as the plaintiff has the right to take possession of *some*thing and has, albeit within limits, the right to determine its use—and this is assured *both* parties by the requirement of consideration—the proprietary character of the right is preserved.

On the foregoing analysis, personal rights, no less than real rights, are rights of ownership. They differ, however, in the particular manner in which they determine the content of ownership. Ordinarily, I have already noted, real rights are taken to be more fully proprietary than personal rights: the paradigm case of ownership, it is assumed, is a right to a thing that holds against the world. At most, personal rights are partial and incomplete ownership rights, being *merely* against a definite individual and achieving completion through the acquisition of a real right to the promised thing via actual performance. The analysis that I have proposed reverses this characterization.

Personal rights, not real rights, represent the fullest expression of the right of ownership. What makes a right *in personam* as opposed to *in rem* is just the fact that the operative facts giving rise to the right are transactional. But the *juridical* dimension

[50] This idea is enshrined in the analysis of liability for breach of contract under the principle enunciated in *Hadley v Baxendale* (1854) 9 Ex. 341. *Hadley* holds that in determining the scope of the defendant's liability for loss arising through wrongful interference with the purposes to which the plaintiff intended to put the promised thing, it is necessary for the plaintiff to show that the loss was of a type that was reasonably contemplated by the parties at the time of contract formation.

[51] Thus, whether it is incompatible with the plaintiff's rights for the defendant to profit on the occasion of his breach by selling the thing to a third party is determined by their contract: if the right under the contract is just to be put in possession of the thing at a certain time, then the value of this possession to the plaintiff, and not the defendant's savings or profits, is the relevant measure of the right. While this conclusion coincides with that reached by the efficient breach theory, the reasoning that leads to it draws only on the juridical conception of rights.

in the right of ownership is not the relation between person and thing as such, but the relation of exclusion between one person and another with respect to the thing. Hence personal rights, and not real rights, arise through acts that fully reflect the very dimension in ownership that is juridical.

Moreover, in light of the transactional character of personal rights and, more particularly, the doctrine of consideration's requirement of quid pro quo, both parties alienate and appropriate something, with the consequence that one party can appropriate only in so far as the other does as well. The exercise of the equal capacity for acquisition by both parties is a necessary condition for the acquisition by each: parties have rights only in so far as they are also subject to disabilities, and vice versa. Indeed, given the right to equal value under the doctrine of unconscionability, each party can appropriate the very same thing (*qua* equal value) as what he or she alienates and consequently from what he or she is excluded. The fact that persons have the legal capacity to acquire the very thing from which they are excluded, which, as stated above, is presupposed by but not realized in the operation of the principle of first occupancy, is here made an express condition of the validity of acquisition. Keeping in mind that even under the principle of first occupancy, rights and legal disabilities are attributed to individuals in their capacity as distinct and separate persons—so that a *right–disability relation as between two individuals* fully and completely instantiates the legal relation in property—it may be readily seen that acquisition by contract (or by some other kind of derivative acquisition entailing the participation of two persons) represents the mode of acquisition that expresses the legal relation in first occupancy, but in a way that shows the parties to be equals. The fact that the contractual relation, and therefore, the right *in personam*, is as between just two persons reflects nothing more or less than the essential form that the legal relation has in property and, more generally, in the juridical conception of rights. If we are to express the equal capacity for ownership of persons in their legal relations *inter se*, it must be via a form of acquisition that is effected by the mutually related *acts of just two persons*, and therefore by a single, unified interaction wherein each of them both alienates and appropriates the same thing. In this way also, personal rights are continuous with and complete real rights.

Finally, we also saw that if the acquisition of external things is to be a basis of rights that is distinct from bodily integrity, the possibility of non-physical, though rightful and fully effective, possession must be supposed. But it is only when acquisition is transactional that it can be effected independently of having physical possession. The fact that the parties' rights and corresponding legal disabilities are fully and completely established at contract formation and that this is separated from the moment of performance means that, here also, contractual, that is, personal, rights fully reflect the very thing that must be supposed but that can be only partially realized in the acquisition of real rights.

The contrary prevailing assumption that real rights are more extensive and complete than personal rights may seem plausible if we take the view, argued most influentially by Hohfeld,[52] that, intrinsically considered, the two sorts of rights have the same general character, the difference between them being merely quantitative: there are simply *more* relations of right in the case of a right *in rem* than in that of a right *in personam*. I have tried to show, however, that they do not have the same character but rather are qualitatively distinct categories of rights. The fact that one category is against (indeterminately) anyone whereas the other is as against (a determinate) someone is just a reflection of the difference in the respective modes of acquisition.[53]

It is important here, even at the risk of some repetition, to settle the *juridical* significance of the fact that first occupancy can establish multiple right-disability relations, in contrast to a contract's one such relation. Although each of the *in rem* relations is identical because founded upon the very same unilateral act which is public *vis-à-vis* anyone in general, each is, at the same time, a *distinct* relation which, taken by itself, is whole and complete. The occupier's right is fully instantiated in each such relation. From a legal point of view, it would be simply unintelligible to say that the more such relations there are, the greater or more fully realized is the occupier's right. The value of the right remains constant irrespective of the number of relations because it is fully realized in any given relation and every relation is a whole unto itself. It is mistaken to construe the *in rem* relation as consisting of a right on one side with multiple corresponding disabilities (or duties) on the other side. As I have tried to emphasize throughout this discussion, under the juridical conception of rights, the legal relation is always individuated and always obtains between two, and only two, persons. That is why a right-holder can limit his or her right relative to another without affecting in any way the disabilities to which others continue to be subject. That is also why, strictly speaking, any claim of *in rem* right is always relative to another individual. Now if each real right is individuated and is complete and wholly realized as such, it makes no intrinsic difference, from a legal point of view, *how many* relations of this kind there may be in given circumstances. Thus, the fact that contract consists of *one* right–disability relation between two persons cannot in itself be viewed as a diminishment or as an incomplete realization of the right *in rem*. To the contrary, because the features of relation-to-another, purely non-physical appropriation, and the equal capacity for rights can only, I have argued, be realized in acquisi-

---

[52] Above n. 21 at 77.

[53] Because Hohfeld does not restrict the application of the *in rem–in personam* distinction to legal relations viewed under the aspect of acquisition but applies it as a purely formal quantitative distinction to any legal relation, he is compelled to take the view that a real right should 'regarding its character as such be carefully differentiated from the [personal] secondary right or claim . . . arising from a violation of the former'. See n. 21 above at 101. This is necessary in order to avoid 'confusions of thought' that would otherwise follow from the widely shared assumption that there must be some basic identity between the characterization of the primary right on the one hand and that of the analysis of liability and of the appropriate remedy for violation of this right on the other hand. Ibid. at 102 ff. My contention that the *in rem–in personam* distinction is illuminating when taken as reflecting differences in modes of acquisition avoids possible confusion while upholding, as I shall explain shortly in the discussion of liability, the idea that there is an underlying identity in the nature of the right, liability, and remedy.

tion that requires the participation of more than one person, personal rights, which reflect this mode of acquisition, are intrinsically and in a qualitative sense the more satisfactory expression of the right–disability ownership relation.

Further, if the view that personal rights are completed by and fulfilled in real rights is correct, it should follow that performance, by which the plaintiff obtains physical possession of the thing contracted for, transforms the plaintiff's initially personal right as against the other contracting party into something more or different. But it does not. The fact that the plaintiff has physical possession of the thing does allow the principle of first occupancy to operate *as against third parties*. If we suppose that third parties did not have property in the thing prior to and including the moment when the plaintiff gained physical possession of it via the other contracting party's perfor-mance, the plaintiff is first in possession relative to the third parties. As against the latter, the plaintiff has acquired the exclusive property in the thing on the basis of first occupancy. *Vis-à-vis* the other contracting party, however, first occupancy cannot apply because at no point does he unconditionally abandon what was initially his, thereby rendering it ownerless. The source of this party's exclusion from the plain-tiff's thing (now physically possessed) must be the fact that he has transferred it at contract formation; only this can block his claim to retake it. The exclusion of this party and the establishment of the plaintiff's right against him are fixed at formation and remain unchanged up to and including the moment when the plaintiff obtains physical possession upon the other's performance.[54]

I have argued that first occupancy and contract are two modes of acquiring own-ership. By making relation to another and the independence of rights from continu-ous physical possession explicit and necessary features of acquisition, contract may be viewed as continuous with and as completing acquisition by first occupancy. Put in other terms, contract fills out the idea of ownership in first occupancy such that it exhibits on its face the very features that define an exclusive right to an external thing. The point that contract completes first occupancy, while juridical and conceptual, is not metaphysical. There is nothing mysterious about it. It is reflected, for example, in the trite proposition that one who has the property in something also owns its value. Value is treated as the substantive content of any proprietary right despite the fact that, as I explained, it is elucidated in connection with contract and not with first occupancy. Value can be read back into the right of property acquired by first occu-pancy only because value is implicit in it (more particularly, in the content of the right to use) and because contract is continuous with it (by constituting this content as part of a two-sided relation).

[54] This analysis of rights *in personam* and *in rem* also applies to present transfers of property that do not involve the performance of contractual obligations. The basic difference between such transactions and contract is that, in the latter but not the former, the acquisition of the right *in personam* is made explicit by the division of the transaction into the two moments of contract formation and performance. However, even in the case of non-contractual transfers of property, the transferee's right against the transferor flows from the latter's act of alienation and so is against the transferor on a basis that does not hold against third parties.

First occupancy and contract (or, in general, derivative acquisition) exhaust the elementary modes of acquiring ownership in private law. We begin with first occupancy because, independently of legislative, customary, or statutory provisions and rules, it enunciates the principle applicable to any and every acquisition of something that, as between any two individuals, is a presently *unowned* thing. Contract builds upon this by articulating the principle of acquisition applicable to something that, as between two individuals, is *already owned*. So far as the *basic forms of acquisition* go, these must be the two—and *only* two—modes of acquiring ownership of things as between individuals.[55] Now of these two categories, only first occupancy gives rise to rights *in rem* and these are qualitatively distinct in character from the rights *in personam* of contract.[56] Accordingly, if we suppose that rights of property must be real rights, first occupancy is the only elementary form of acquisition of ownership in private law that can count as acquisition of property. This is the sense in which I claim that it represents the principle of property intrinsic to private law. What, then, is the basic idea of property right that is reflected in first occupancy? It is the idea of a right *with respect to a thing* which can be *acquired* by an individual's *unilateral act* without the participation of others and which can be exclusive *against anyone else in general* who does not have a prior right to possess it. This is the idea that must be supposed if, from a juridical point of view, a legal relation is to qualify as proprietary. And, to repeat, for this idea to apply, it is not necessary that the unowned thing be a *res nullius* in absolute terms; rather, the requirement is merely that it be presently unowned as between any two parties. The conception of being unowned, like that of ownership itself, is relative as between individuals.

Having discussed the differences as well as the continuity between property and contract, I now want to extend the comparison to encompass principles of liability. The following brief account of liability as a third distinct yet connected category of private law completes the analysis of the juridical conception of rights for the purposes of this chapter.

[55] This seems to have been Holmes's view. He suggests that possession and contract are the 'chief' special relations out of which special rights and duties arise. Above n. 11, at 130. Kant argues that there is a third category of acquisition which he characterizes as a right to a person akin to a right to a thing and which gives one a right to the possession (though not the use) of *another person* as a thing. According to Kant, one acquires the status of the other person, more specifically, of one's spouse, children, or servants. See above n. 22 at part I, ch. II, sect. III. In the text above, my claim is that property and contract exhaust the modes of acquiring external *things*. Discussion of Kant's third category is beyond the scope of this chapter although it should be noted that there is evidence that contemporary private law views the idea of possessing another's status as problematic. This is reflected in its reluctance to recognize or to expand negligence actions for economic loss or for loss of consortium arising out of injury to one's spouse or servant. For example, see *Best v Samuel Fox & Co., Ltd.*, 2 All E.R. 394 (Eng. H.L.).

[56] I should emphasize that throughout this chapter, the analysis is from the standpoint of pure private law (i.e. the juridical conception of rights) and therefore supposes only those principles of right that apply as a matter of reasonableness to individuals in their mutual interactions, apart from legal formalities and legislative provisions. My contention is that, viewed in these terms, first occupancy and contract must give rise, respectively, to rights *in rem* and rights *in personam*.

The idea of *liability* in private law, such as it is reflected in the various substantive grounds of liability,[57] is a distinct juridical category, different from both property and contract, in virtue of the fact that it applies only to an involuntary interaction between two parties and implies a legal relation of right and correlative duty, not right and mere legal disability. I will discuss the idea of liability in general terms, with references to intentional tort and negligence by way of illustration.

As a preliminary to the analysis of the necessary and sufficient conditions of liability, the law requires an affirmative answer to the question: does the plaintiff have a right of ownership *as against the defendant* in the very thing which the defendant has in some way affected? Unless the requisite proprietary right can be shown, the liability analysis never gets off the ground: any loss suffered would sound in nonfeasance, not misfeasance.[58] Clearly, if the plaintiff has a right of ownership *in rem*, it can be a right against the defendant in particular. Note, however, that by requiring that the plaintiff has a right of ownership as against a definite individual (viewed as independent and separate), the liability analysis is continuous with the way in which rights are explicitly presented in contract. Keeping in mind that any rights, including those *in rem*, are, and can only be, fully vindicated, and therefore fully recognized, under the idea of liability, the fact that the latter postulates rights in the form that they have in contract further suggests that this form represents the true and final form of right under the juridical conception. In addition, it is consistent with the way in which, I have argued, the relation between real and personal rights is appropriately conceived.

However, an affirmative answer to the ownership question does not address, let alone answer, the central issues of liability which are: has someone acted in a way that is incompatible with the plaintiff's right of ownership and, if so, what is the appropriate juridical response in these circumstances? It is no longer a question of deciding who has a right of ownership but rather of determining which sort of acts are prohibited by the right because they are incompatible with it. While this takes us beyond the issue of acquisition, whether in property or contract, the answer, we shall see, is continuous with the previous analysis.

I have argued that the immediate correlative of the establishment of a property right in something is the imposition of a disability upon any and everyone else who does not already have property in it. This disability exists from the instant the prerequisites of first occupancy are satisfied, whether or not others have yet come on the scene. It simply means that because the thing occupied is no longer available to others for acquisition, quite literally *nothing* that others might do can modify the rightholder's property in it. It does not matter what they do: *whatever* it is, it cannot

---

[57] In this chapter, I assume that there are three main distinct grounds of liability at common law, namely, unjust enrichment, tort, and breach of contract. I also distinguish between civil wrong and criminal wrong and focus my remarks upon the former.

[58] I have tried to show in detail elsewhere that this is the problem that confronts plaintiffs in situations of negligently caused pure economic loss where the common law has traditionally denied recovery. See P. Benson, ' Excluding Liability in Tort', above n. 4. For further discussion of this fundamental distinction, see my remarks in n. 5, above.

possibly be rights-establishing with respect to the thing, because the thing is simply no longer available to them for appropriation. The disability does not, therefore, specify what sort of act would be incompatible with the owner's right. Just as the right–disability analysis does not identify any determinate act on the defendant's part that is, or would be, incompatible with the plaintiff's right, so it represents the plaintiff's right in terms similarly indeterminate, as a pure potentiality: it says only that it is the plaintiff, not the defendant, who may rightly take possession of, use, or alienate the thing and does not specify when the plaintiff has been able *to realize* his or her right *vis-à-vis* the defendant. And, in light of the fundamental idea of no liability for nonfeasance, this further specification reduces to the question of when an actual exercise of the plaintiff's right via determinate acts (which is the only way it can be realized) has been thwarted or interfered with by another. While the *establishment* of the right–disability relation, whether by first occupancy or by contract, requires that there be actual determinate acts (entailing the exercise of one or more of the three incidents of ownership) by one or both parties, the analysis in terms of right and disability does not carry through this requirement in its treatment of the *enjoyment* of the right. But unless a right can be exercised, realized, and enjoyed as against others (within the parameters of the purely external character of rights in the juridical conception), it is no right at all. The determination of the acts of both parties with respect to this further aspect is therefore necessary. Moreover, in keeping with the correlativity of right that has been explicitly brought out in the analysis of contractual acquisition, this further specification of acts on each side of the legal relation must be accomplished in a way that simultaneously engages *both* sides of the relation. The definition of the prohibited acts of the defendant must therefore be specified in terms that simultaneously determine the content and scope of the exercise and enjoyment of the plaintiff's right, and vice-versa. As I shall now explain, this is done under the rubric of the idea of liability, which is both distinct from and continuous with the analysis of acquisition in property and contract.

Like contract, the idea of liability, I have said, postulates an interaction between two parties as essential to the establishment of the pertinent legal relation between them. Beginning with the side of the defendant, there must be a manifestation of choice (which I shall refer to as an 'act') of a certain kind. The sort of act that is necessary is specified by drawing upon the analysis of right in property and contract. First, it must be an externally manifested exercise of choice. More particularly, it must consist in effectively and actually bringing the plaintiff's thing[59] under the defendant's purposes: the defendant must do something to or with it that is recognizably purposive. Whether there is a manifested subordination of the thing by the defendant is determined in accordance with an objective test in the circumstances of the parties' interaction, namely, by how the act would reasonably appear to a reasonable

---

[59] For the purposes of simplicity of presentation, I refer here only to the plaintiff's things and not his or her person (i.e. his or her body). The proposed interpretation of liability applies to both.

person in the plaintiff's position. The wrongful conduct must mirror the kind of act that is necessary to establish the right of property. It is wrongful, however, because it is unilateral.[60]

The purposive character of the defendant's subordination of the plaintiff's thing may be of two kinds. In the first, the defendant intends to subordinate it to the exclusion of the plaintiff, knowing that it belongs to the plaintiff or at least to someone other than himself. In a sense, the defendant manifests the full *animus possidendi* that is requisite to property acquisition but with the difference that the intended subject of exclusion is the rightful owner. Here, the defendant intends to assert control over the thing in the face of the plaintiff's right of ownership. It is an intended unilateral taking and gives rise to *criminal or malicious* wrong. In the second kind, which gives rise to *civil* wrong, the defendant does something to or with the plaintiff's thing in the pursuit of his own purposes but, in contrast to the previous situation, he does not manifest an intent to control it in the face of the plaintiff's right or the right of anyone else. Here it is crucial that the defendant does not actually know that the thing

---

[60] In the law of negligence, the requirement of fault ensures that there can be no liability unless the defendant externally manifests choice that reasonably appears as an imposition of purposes over the plaintiff's thing, in circumstances where the defendant should reasonably take the thing to belong to someone other than himself. Unless, at the moment of action, the defendant is able reasonably to foresee the risk of the effects that he imposes on the plaintiff's thing, these effects, and the resulting damage, cannot be viewed as avoidable by him or as the outcome of choice. In the absence of reasonable foreseeability, the imposition of effects cannot possibly be purposive and so incompatible with the owner's right of property. Strict liability is inconsistent with the idea of property in private law. This conclusion goes against the seemingly plausible view that strict liability may be justified precisely on the ground that if something is my property, then you are excluded from it, and if, without my consent, you do anything to it (foreseeable or not) which impairs my ability to possess, use, or alienate it, this violates my right of ownership. Strict liability, it is argued, takes the right of ownership seriously. The argument is mistaken, however, because it elides the difference between the analysis of acquisition and that of liability. While it is true that, from the standpoint of acquisition, nothing you do can give you property in my thing, it does not follow that anything you do to it is also a wrong. The right of property, which requires an external manifestation of choice for its establishment, can only be infringed by an external manifestation of choice with respect to the effects that constrain the plaintiff's exercise of ownership rights. In this way, the analysis of liability, like that of contract, expressly treats the parties as equals and, in contrast to the acquisition of property, it makes an actual interaction the foundation of the pertinent legal relation. Moreover, because of the interactional basis of liability, the standard of fault in negligence, like the standard of contract interpretation and formation, is objective: a defendant will be imputed with foresight of just those kinds of risks that another, in the circumstances of their interaction, could reasonably presume him to have. And finally, in making the distinction between the reasonable and unreasonable imposition of risks, the fault standard cannot, consistently with the juridical conception of rights, give standing to considerations of need, talent, particular purpose, or welfare. Thus, in and of itself, the fact that the defendant has to incur costs to avoid imposing foreseeable risk should not affect the prohibition. And this is indeed the view widely taken in Anglo-Commonwealth jurisdictions. These jurisdictions do, however, take into account such general facts as that, in living together in the crowded conditions of modern life, we cannot avoid creating or accepting certain risks. These are risks that exist because of a social fact for which no one individual is responsible. Everyone is deemed to have accepted these background risks, the imposition of which is not unreasonable. See Lord Reid's influential speech in the leading case of *Boulton v Stone* [1951] A.C. 850 at 867. I should add that a similar distinction is drawn in nuisance law where it takes the form of a contrast between ordinary and extraordinary use of land, as determined in light of a local community standard.

belongs to another. There is no express disregard shown for the plaintiff's right. In this kind of wrong, at the highest, the defendant, as a reasonable person, *should have known* in the particular circumstances that it belonged to another.[61] On the view that I take, the category of civil wrong comprises, more particularly, unjust enrichment, negligence, intentional tort, and breach of contract (which together constitute a conceptual and ordered sequence that expresses the character of civil wrong with ever greater explicitness and completeness). In the following brief discussion of liability, I will focus my remarks on civil wrong and, within this category, on negligence, while here and there relating the latter to the other instances of civil wrong.

Thus, for example, circumstances giving rise to negligence paradigmatically consist in a defendant doing something in pursuit of his own independent purposes that imposes effects upon the plaintiff's thing, thereby diminishing its value or otherwise interfering with the plaintiff's use of it. A distinguishing feature of negligence, in contrast with intentional torts, say, trespass or conversion, is that the defendant does not directly take physical possession of the plaintiff's thing[62] but imposes effects upon the thing, with the consequences just noted. In the case of intentional tort, the defendant brings the plaintiff's thing under his power to the exclusion of others in circumstances where he should reasonably (but does not actually) know that the thing belongs to another. The 'intentional' aspect of the tort, in so far as it is a civil wrong, is just this factor of purposive conduct that entails a taking into possession. By contrast, in negligence, the defendant implicitly subordinates the plaintiff's thing to his purposes, thereby, in effect, making use of it. But here it is only a matter of making use 'in effect' and 'implicitly' since there has been no taking into possession and so no *animus possidendi*, unlike the conduct constituting an intentional tort. In negligence, then, the defendant's manifestation of choice has juridical significance under the aspect of liability, not because it explicitly expresses the sort of intent that would be a prerequisite for acquisition. It is enough that it does so in effect. It is an act, amounting to an implicit making use of the plaintiff's thing, that interferes with the plaintiff's exercise of ownership with respect to it. As we move through the civil wrong

---

[61] To be exact, in tort and breach of contract, it is necessary that the defendant should reasonably know that the thing which he affects belongs to another. By contrast, liability for unjust enrichment supposes that the defendant could *not* reasonably have known this. In the case of unjust enrichment, the law requires that the defendant does not acquire the plaintiff's thing (which gives rise to the defendant's enrichment) either from the plaintiff by way of gift or on some other legally recognized basis. This ensures that the issue as between the parties is not 'who is the owner of the thing?'—the plaintiff is—but rather 'what requirements apply when the defendant has a value that results from having, using, or alienating the plaintiff's thing, where the defendant cannot reasonably know that it belongs to the plaintiff?' This is a question of liability that applies to a particular form of interaction between the parties.

[62] It is *just* this fact that negligence does *not* involve the defendant directly taking possession of the plaintiff's thing that distinguishes it from intentional tort and breach of contract. Thus the difference between intentional tort and negligence is not that the former requires a manifestation of intent to interfere with the plaintiff's rights. An intent to injure another—in this particular case, an intent to exclude the owner from his thing when one knows that he is the owner—makes the wrong criminal and punishable rather than civil.

categories of intentional tort and breach of contract, and culminate with the idea of criminal wrong, the act that constitutes the wrong comes to manifest ever more expressly and completely the character of intent that is necessary to the establishment of ownership.

If the defendant's act is to constitute a civil wrong that is incompatible with the plaintiff's ownership under the juridical conception of rights, it must impose effects that *interfere with the external manifestation* of that right. Just as it is only through external acts that the right is established and exercised, so it is only by an act that interferes with the external manifestation of the right that the right can be injured externally. The idea of an external injury is the notion of injury that fits with the juridical conception of rights, which has to do *just* with the *externality* of interaction between two parties. Now, the external expression of the right of property is not the bare thing itself—for this would disregard the fact that the thing has been acquired and is therefore presently subsumed under the owner's externally manifested will—but rather the plaintiff's rightful capacity to possess, use, or alienate it. There is an injury to the right's external aspect if the effects which the defendant's unilateral action imposes upon the thing constrain what the plaintiff would otherwise have done with or to it in the exercise of one of these three incidents of ownership.[63] And any such limit or constraint, when measured, is *loss*.

The requirement of loss is continuous with and reflects the juridical fact that unless one has something that comes under one's exclusive rights as against others, one does not have any claims against them. It completes the fundamental premise of the juridical conception that there is liability for misfeasance but not for nonfeasance. Unless I have something, I have no claim; and unless another affects my having it, there is no wrong. For this reason, loss is also the *only* consequence of the defendant's act that is relevant. The defendant's act and the plaintiff's loss thus constitute the two sides of an interaction that gives rise to liability. Indeed, neither side has juridical significance except in so far as it is tied to the other. Unless the defendant's act causes loss, it is merely a purposive manifestation of choice that has no proprietary significance, positively or negatively; and the same is true where the plaintiff's ability to put his or her thing to purposes is constrained by something that is not an act or that imposes the constraint without affecting the thing. In both cases,

---

[63] According to Austin, the right of property consists of two distinct and inherently separable elements: first, a right of indefinite use that excludes others from disturbing the owner's acts of user and, secondly, a right to exclude others from using the object themselves. See J. Austin, *Lectures on Jurisprudence*, ii, 4th edn. (London: John Murray Publisher, 1879) at 836–7. To the extent that there is a distinction here, it is, put in the terms of the present chapter, one between property viewed as a mode of acquisition with the correlative of the right being a disability (Austin's second element) and property viewed under the aspect of liability, with the correlative of the right being a duty of non-interference (Austin's first element). It is necessary to emphasize, however, that unless the defendant's unilateral use affects the plaintiff's ability to use, there is no wrong, no external injury—no violation of right. In short, the one element cannot be conceived without the other, so far as the complete articulation of the juridical conception of rights goes.

there is not the kind of interaction that is needed for there to be an external injury to the right of ownership under the juridical conception.

Understood in this way, loss is necessary for there to be a wrong. If there is no loss, there is no wrong. On the view that I have taken, wherever there is a violation of rights of ownership, there is, and must be, loss: 'every injury imports damage in the nature of it'.[64] If we wish to characterize infringements of the right of ownership as 'normative' and loss as 'material', then liability supposes the inseparability of both dimensions, in this way reflecting the inseparability of the normative and the material in the analysis of ownership itself. This is so even if the wrong produces no determinable quantum of damage, as where the defendant interferes with the plaintiff's rightful possession but in a way that does not affect the thing's value or the uses to which the plaintiff intends to put it: 'if no *other* damage is established, the party injured is entitled to a verdict of nominal damages'.[65] And because loss represents the impact of the defendant's act on the plaintiff's ability to possess, use, or alienate his thing—that is, on something that must reside in the plaintiff as a person separate and independent from the defendant, it is a consequence of the defendant's act that refers exclusively to the plaintiff, reflecting the two-sidedness of the juridical relation.

The common law says that damage must be proved to sustain an action in negligence, unlike actions for intentional tort and breach of contract. How might this be explained by the approach that I have suggested? In the case of negligence, the wrong does not consist in a taking (into possession) of the plaintiff's thing but, at most, in an implicit unilateral making use of it. This is how it must reasonably appear to someone in the plaintiff's position if there is to be liability. However, in circumstances of negligence, there is, *ex hypothesis*, no agreement between the parties to regulate and interpret their interaction and the defendant counts as anyone who might be under the disability that is correlative to the plaintiff's property-right. Accordingly, the only basis on which the plaintiff may reasonably infer that the defendant has implicitly made use of his thing is if the defendant has physically impinged upon it in a way that negatively affects its use or value. While the resulting injury may limit the plaintiff's ability to take possession of his thing, any such interference with possession will be inseparable from the adverse impact upon use or value which is the gravamen of the action. By contrast, in cases of intentional tort and breach of contract where the wrong *can* consist in a unilateral taking into possession, it is possible for there to be an interference with the right of possession as such, quite apart from the effects of the wrong upon use and value. The fact that nominal damages are available for intentional tort and breach of contract but not for negligence may be explained on this basis. I should add that while intentional tort, unlike negligence, may consist in a

64   *Webb v Portland Manufacturing Co.* (1838), 3 Sumner's Rep. 189 at 192 (per Story, J.) (hereinafter 'Webb'). Statements to the same effect are pervasive in the decisions, one of the earliest being Chief Justice Holt's seminal opinion in the case of *Ashby v White* (1703) 2 Ld. Raym. 938. A variety of such statements are referred to in *Constantine v Imperial London Hotels, Ltd.* [1944] 2 All E.R. 171 (K.B. Eng).

65   *Webb*, at 192 (emphasis added).

wrongful taking possession, such taking, like the injury in negligence, can occur only through the defendant *physically* affecting the thing. In this respect, both species of tort differ from breach of contract where a mere omission to perform, whether or not the defendant has actual physical possession of the thing promised, is *per se* an interference with the plaintiff's rightful possession, quite apart from its impact on use or value. In the terms of the proposed analysis, the mere failure to perform may reasonably be viewed as a wrongful retention of the thing, that is, as a wrongful taking possession of it. It is the existence of an agreement that allows the plaintiff reasonably to construe the omission as a wrongful retention by the defendant of what is owed him, and this interpretation holds from the moment of contract formation, prior to and independently of performance. Hence, the fact that the analysis of contractual liability reflects the explicitly transactional character of contractual acquisition and its independence from the moment of physical appropriation enables breach of contract to be *per se* a wrong for which nominal damages are available.

Vis-à-vis the one who has property in something, others are under a correlative *duty* not to do something that reasonably appears to be a unilateral and external imposition of purpose upon it. And note that, in contrast with ethical duties of virtue and benevolence, the duty here is simply a prohibition. Here, for the first time in the analysis of the juridical conception of rights, we have the hallmark of private law: a legal relation of right and correlative duty.[66] Thus, the full meaning of the exclusivity of the right of ownership is expressed, not merely in the imposition upon others of a disability, but in this prohibition of a certain kind of interaction. The juridical conception of property is fully expressed in terms of this right–duty relation and each of the three incidents of property is itself elucidated in these terms. At the same time, it should be emphasized that even the property that is correlative to the disability is a right and not a mere liberty: it imposes conditions of respect upon others that limit what they can accomplish from a legal point of view.[67]

---

[66] The clearest and most carefully articulated judicial statement of the correlative character of this relation is still that of Chief Judge Cardozo in *Palsgraf v Long Island R.R.*, 162 N.E. 99 (N.Y. 1928).

[67] Contrary to the view taken by Hohfeld, I am suggesting therefore that property is originally and necessarily a right only and not even in part a liberty, except in so far as this is already implied by the notion of right. Thus, by having a right to take, use, or alienate something exclusively of others, one also and necessarily has the liberty (i.e. the permission correlative to the disability in others) to do so. Moreover, contra Hohfeld, right and liberty are not coeval; liberty is not, like right, a fundamental juridical relation. The category of mere liberty can seem fundamental in so far as it applies to any situation where no rights of others are at stake. But, in and of itself, a pure absence of rights is a non-juridical situation. It is only because individuals can and do have rights and because the baseline which is supposed in juridical thought is the possibility of rights that liberty, in the sense of being correlative to an absence of right, is a meaningful juridical category. Otherwise, we would have to say that natural forces are, juridically, at liberty to affect other things. Rights are conceptually supposed by, and prior to, liberties. Of course, by limiting his right of ownership exclusive as against another, a proprietor can give the other a permission (that is, a liberty) to possess or use his thing without conferring upon the other any right to exclude him. (Hohfeld gives this possibility as proof that rights and liberties are distinct, equally fundamental legal relations. See, above n. 21 at 41.) However, the liberty that arises in this way also presupposes the pre-existence of the right of ownership *as a right* and so is not equally fundamental with it.

The defendant's act and the plaintiff's loss are, I have said, the two sides of an external interaction, which is the form of social relation that is ordered by the juridical conception of rights. Being two distinct yet intrinsically connected sides, they can be compared in terms of value. Value, we saw, is the mode in which property is conceived when its social character is fully realized. Under the idea of liability, the loss embodies and sets the *value* of the act, viewed as an external injury to the plaintiff's right.[68] What the defendant has wrongfully done has this value and the value constitutes his or her 'gain'. This value is attributed to the act, not because the act has such value in the eyes of the defendant nor because it represents a certain usefulness to the defendant which can then be compared to the usefulness which the plaintiff's protected interest has for the plaintiff, but simply for the reason that this value represents the character of the act solely in terms of its impact on the juridically protected interests of the plaintiff: external relation to another is the exclusive aspect under which it is considered. We have also seen in the discussion of unconscionability that, in legal contemplation, no one is presumed to give away his or her thing for nothing; to the contrary, the norm of strict equality of value applies. The defendant's gain, being wrongful and therefore at the expense of the plaintiff, must be brought under the standard of right, that is, it must be brought into line with the equality of value. This gives rise to the so-called secondary right to compensation.

By redressing the loss through compensation, the law explicitly represents the wrongful act and the loss as equivalent:[69] they are the same thing viewed from different sides of the legal relation. This is the true meaning and the final expression of the correlativity that is distinctive of the juridical point of view. Through it, both what counts as the exercise and the enjoyment of the right of ownership as well as the conduct that is excluded by that right are simultaneously specified in determinate terms. This completes the elaboration of the fundamental categories of the juridical. The fact that the analysis of liability makes central the aspects of interaction (entailing a legal relation between two persons) and of value (entailing an identity between two things) demonstrates its continuity with contract. It also confirms the earlier account given of the relation between real and personal rights. While the category of value first comes into play in contract and not property, one is taken to be an owner of value for the purposes of redressing violations of one's property in things. Liability understands property in the terms of contract. The requirement to compensate supposes that the juridical meaning of real rights is completed by that of personal rights. Note,

---

[68] 'At any rate, when what was suffered has been measured, one part is called the loss and the other the profit.' Aristotle, *Nichomachean Ethics*, trans. T. Irwin (Indianapolis: Hackett Publishing Company, 1985), at 126.

[69] I should make clear that the claim made in the text about the significance of loss—that the aim of the law must be to repair loss—does not mean that the law may never make reference to the savings or profit that defendants obtain by breaching their obligations. To the contrary, it may do so if, in given circumstances, this is an appropriate way to measure the value of the plaintiff's loss. See, for example, the determination of loss in *Livingstone* v. *Rawyards Coal*, 5 App. Cas. 25 (1880). But even here, the aim of the law is to compensate for loss, not to redress gains as such.

finally, that the rationale which I have tried to sketch for the requirement to compensate reflects the basic character of the juridical conception of right and so does not refer to considerations of individual or social welfare. On the proposed approach, compensation for loss is the *juridically* necessary and appropriate response to civil wrong. Where, as is the case in civil wrong, the defendant does not manifest an intent to injure the plaintiff's rights, the defendant *ex hypothesis* views his activity *solely* in terms of the realization *of his own independent ends*, without reference one way or another to the plaintiff's rights. In response to such civil wrong, the requirement to repair loss brings out explicitly the other-related import of the defendant's negligent conduct which is imposed as a constraint upon or an interference with it. It establishes boundaries that reflect the idea that acting incompatibly with another's rights is prohibited, not licensed.[70]

4 THE REASONABLENESS OF THE RIGHT OF PROPERTY

In the preceding sections, I have tried to show that first occupancy is a principle of property—and indeed the only such basic principle—that fits with private law's juridical conception of rights and, further, that property, contract, and liability are conceptually interconnected parts of this conception. First occupancy is not merely a principle; it may also be viewed as the most elementary and pervasive idea of property in private law. To show this fit between first occupancy and the juridical conception of rights is a principal task of a public basis of justification. But there is a further step that must be taken. There is the question: is the principle reasonable? As others have already observed, the decisions—and in this respect *Pierson*[71] is typical—simply assume the reasonableness of a principle that gives the property to one who occupies something first in time. The issues they address are rather what occupancy consists in and what conditions must exist to satisfy it. When the question of reasonableness is

---

[70] I should emphasize that this conclusion applies only to civil, *not* criminal, wrongs. It is only where the defendant has not manifested an intent to injure the plaintiff in his or her rights that a requirement to repair loss brings out explicitly the other-related import of the defendant's conduct and represents a constraint upon it. In the case of criminal wrong, the defendant's conduct is already expressly other-related in a negative sense and a requirement merely to compensate for loss would set the terms of a licence to injure rather than represent compulsion exercised against the defendant's culpable intent. It would force an exchange upon the plaintiff rather than express a prohibition against the defendant's wrong. The juridical response to such wrong must therefore be punishment that interferes directly with the wrongdoer's exercise of his capacity to pursue his ends, not just a requirement to compensate.

[71] Above n. 11.

taken up in scholarly writing, most contemporary writers have concluded that the case for its reasonableness is doubtful—or at most that first occupancy may be legitimate, not on account of its own intrinsic moral acceptability, but because it is workable when subordinated to other principles that ensure a certain measure of fair equality of opportunity and equality of goods. Richard Epstein, a proponent of the principle, suggests that the grounds for embracing it are institutional and historical: given that we have adopted it in the past and that it has become the 'organizing principle of most social institutions' as well as the basis of titles, a very considerable burden of persuasion lies, he argues, on those who would favour another principle to show why this displacement is necessary and reasonable.[72]

For the purposes of a justification that addresses a liberal public political and legal culture, however, we hope that something more may be said in its favour. We want to see whether first occupancy—and the idea of property which it embodies—are *inherently* suited to be part of a legal and political order that honours individuals as free and equal persons. The question is whether the principle is intrinsically reasonable in the sense of articulating norms that are consonant with, and indeed expressive of, this view of individuals. Although, in trying to answer this question, we must go beyond what the judicial decisions expressly discuss, we should be careful to avoid introducing into our answer considerations that are foreign to the manner in which the principle is judicially presented. To be public in the appropriate way, the justification must ideally be continuous with the public legal presentation of the principle and must complete it. To sketch such a justification is the task of this final section.

A public basis of justification, then, initially focuses on the principle of first occupancy, taken by itself and understood in its own distinctive terms, and asks whether, viewed as such, these terms plausibly reflect respect for the equality and freedom of all who come under its operation. In a public basis of justification, it is the principle of first occupancy itself that provisionally sets what it is that must be justified as well as the sorts of considerations that can or cannot be part of the justification. Now this principle supposes that, through one's *unilateral* act *alone*, one can rightfully place everyone else, *without* their consent, under a legal disability that did not exist before. How can this be compatible with the freedom and equality of those who are so affected? This is the first and most fundamental question for a public basis of justification.

To appreciate fully the challenge that this question poses, we should recall here that the principle of first occupancy is applied without regard to its impact on the wellbeing, needs, purposes, or moral qualifications of those whom it excludes. It is not tempered by ensuring, through a Lockean proviso for example, that other, equally good, opportunities for acquisition exist for those excluded.[73] It does not contain or

---

[72] Epstein, above n. 11 at 1241–3.

[73] According to Sidgwick, first occupancy as a principle of acquisition may be directly justified on a utilitarian basis only 'provided that other men's opportunities of obtaining similar things are not thereby materially diminished'. The inclusion of this proviso, which makes explicit reference to

require any compensatory or offsetting measures at all. Nor does the principle constrain its operation in a way that brings outcomes into line with any conception of equality in distribution. To the contrary, chance, circumstance, and, in general, morally undeserved advantages, are given relatively free play to determine outcomes. First occupancy cannot plausibly be viewed as a principle of desert. It should be emphasized here that the principle applies *completely and finally in a single case* and therefore requires in any such instance a final and complete outcome in which possibly one person's welfare is enhanced (by acquiring the property) only by making others worse off (through the imposition of a disability that did not exist before). In any given instance, the claims of need, interest, talent, comparative resources or moral desert *of those excluded* (by virtue of the disability imposed upon them) will count for nothing. How can such a principle be reasonable in the sense of treating those excluded as free and equal persons on a par with the proprietor?

To see whether first occupancy is compatible with respect for equality and freedom, it will be necessary to formulate an appropriate normative conception of the person as free and equal. Where principles of justice and fairness of any kind are at stake, the requirement of respect is always owed to individuals. We must, as Rawls has said,[74] be fair to persons, not to their conceptions of the good. We make this point theoretically explicit by formulating an appropriate conception of the person which highlights in what respect individuals are owed justice. In keeping with the idea of a public justification, however, we are looking for a specification of freedom and equality that fits with the basic character of the principle to be justified. While all norms and principles that belong to a liberal political and legal order ideally articulate one general conception of freedom and equality, they may do so in different ways. In the case of first occupancy, the notion of freedom and equality cannot make reference to the satisfaction of needs or equality of resources as normatively relevant considerations. If first occupancy is to be justified on a public basis, it will have to be in terms of a *specific* conception of the person as free and equal—one which, even if reasonable in its own terms, need not be appropriate when other principles and normative issues, for example those arising from within political and distributive justice, are in question. In case of the latter, following Rawls, persons are viewed as having an interest in obtaining certain specified social goods that enable them to exercise and realize their powers as free and equal citizens. The political conception of the person as free and equal citizens incorporates a notion of legitimate needs. This will not be true of the juridical conception of freedom and equality and the corresponding conception of the person will reflect this.

To prevent misunderstanding, it is important to emphasize from the start the limits of the present effort at justification. The main aim is to see whether the idea of

considerations of welfare and opportunity, disqualifies a direct utilitarian justification of the principle of first occupancy as a *public* basis of justification. H. Sidgwick, *The Elements of Politics*, 4th edn. (London: Macmillan, 1919), at 71.

[74] J. Rawls, 'From Fairness to Goodness', in *Collected Essays*, above n. 3, at 285.

property in private law expresses, in and of itself, a notion of reasonableness that is consonant with our liberal public legal and political culture. If it does not reflect a morally plausible conception of freedom and equality, it cannot, even prima facie, belong to a liberal legal order. But the justification does not attempt to go further than establishing that it can so belong. The contention is *not* that the right of property and indeed the juridical conception of rights are by themselves sufficient to realize social and political justice. To the contrary, the justification clearly suggests that the juridical conception can at most constitute a part and not the whole of justice. For example, the indifference towards need is not only the hallmark of the juridical conception; it also represents its limit from the standpoint of any reasonable complete theory of liberal justice. Nor does the argument for the intrinsic reasonableness of the juridical conception attribute to it absolute value. The argument does not exclude the possibility that, within a complete theory of justice, the juridical conception, and more particularly the principles of acquisition and liability, will be subordinated to principles of social justice that ensure fair equality of opportunity and a fair distribution of the benefits and burdens of social co-operation. Indeed, it may reasonably be assumed that this must be the case. The following discussion of the reasonableness of first occupancy does not, therefore, seek to settle the appropriate relation between the juridical conception and the other parts of justice. It merely attempts to show how the private law idea of property may be given, to borrow J. W. Harris's term, a prima-facie justification as one part of the system of liberal legal and political values.[75]

My argument for the reasonableness of the right of property proceeds in two stages. In the first, we ask whether the right is reasonable when viewed from within the juridical conception. More specifically, we determine whether property can be accounted for in terms that are consonant with the moral basis of other, relatively undisputed, rights within the juridical conception. We provisionally suppose the validity of these other rights and see whether they and property share the same normative basis. I shall consider the right of property in relation to, first, the right of bodily integrity and, secondly, what I shall call 'the narrow conception of property' in which the right to use things free from interference continues only so long as one has them in one's physical possession. The recognition of the latter rights—in particular the right of bodily integrity—is settled beyond doubt in the public legal and political culture. I hope to show that, viewed from within the juridical conception of rights, the right of property has the same normative basis as these other, comparatively uncontroverted, rights. Within the juridical conception, there is no reason to accept the latter but not the former. Throughout this part of the argument, I take as given the juridical conception's indifference to need, well-being, and interest. Indeed, my con-

---

[75] Above n. 1, ch. 13. As Harris correctly observes, this is also how Hegel views the sort of justification he gives property in 'Abstract Right', the first section of the *Philosophy of Right*.

tention is that it is only within a normative framework of this kind that the right of property can be justified in the way that I have suggested.

In the second stage of the argument, I no longer merely assume this framework but ask whether the juridical conception's indifference to need is consonant with respecting persons as free and equal. The inquiry moves from a consideration of the moral fit of the right of property within the juridical conception to an evaluation of the juridical conception itself as a plausible instantiation of the liberal ideals of freedom and equality. It is at this point that I shall, even if briefly, make reference to the juridical conception of the person—or 'juridical personality'—and discuss its relation to the political conception of the person. Here again, my aim is to bring out the intrinsic reasonableness of the juridical conception of the person while at the same time noting its limits from a more complete point of view.

Starting with the settled conviction that individuals have an innate right in their bodies that is exclusive as against the world, can we show that, within the juridical conception of rights, a right to acquire exclusive property in external things through one's unilateral acts rests on the same moral basis as the right of bodily integrity? To answer this question, we must first clarify the essential character and basis of the right of bodily integrity in the juridical conception.

The right of bodily integrity is, first of all, a *right*, that is, it refers to the fact that each individual has the rightful exclusive possession and use of his or her own body as against everyone else. This right implies that others are under the legal disability of not having the power to acquire rightful possession or use of my body. Moreover, as in the case of a property right in an external thing, this exclusion is the basis of a principle of liability that prohibits others from acting in a way that subjects my body to their purposes. It is important to note another respect in which the right of bodily integrity is identical in character to the right of property: it is *just* exclusive, so that the right of bodily integrity does not oblige others to assist, preserve, or otherwise to enhance the condition or circumstances of my bodily existence. There is no general duty to rescue. What others must not do is purposively to affect my body in a way that either interferes with my exclusive possession of it or limits the uses to which I can put it. The liability rule is negative and prohibitive in character, in keeping with the juridical conception's organizing idea of no liability for nonfeasance.

There is, however, a basic way in which the right of bodily integrity differs from the right of property in external things: the former right is everywhere taken to be innate; individuals are recognized as having it independently of and prior to doing anything. While it is true that I 'take possession' of myself and make my body an instrument for my use by developing my mental and physical powers, yet, just in so far as I am a living being, I am and must be taken to be in my body—at least this is how others must reasonably view me. Being in my body, I have an external existence that immediately distinguishes me from that of others; and inasmuch as my body is something that can be directly or indirectly affected by the external choices of others, it is something external within the meaning of the juridical conception of rights. Nevertheless, it must be emphasized that my body is *not* an external thing which is *res nullius* until appropriated: it is always in my rightful possession independently of and prior to my acts. It is not something that can be appropriated or alienated at all. Being innate, my right in my body is also inalienable, in contrast to all acquired proprietary rights.

In a liberal democratic public culture, the most firmly settled and the absolutely pivotal moral belief is the intrinsic wrongfulness of slavery. Human persons must never be treated as mere objects of use for others; that is, they must never be unilaterally subordinated to their ends. If this is not right and binding, nothing is. The conviction that slavery is an offence against the person necessarily supposes that person and body are not to be viewed as separate entities from the standpoint of rights, however one may understand the relation between them from a religious, philosophical, or other point of view. So I cannot say to you: in mistreating your body, I am touching something merely external to you, not you yourself. Indeed, it is *only* by touching something that is external but that at the same time embodies you, that I can wrong you. So far as one's *inner* freedom is concerned, it is untouchable by others: in chains we can still be free. Persons can make claims against others only in so far as they are embodied in or related to something external in the requisite way.[76]

The fact that my body is untouchable so far as others are concerned and that mistreatment of my body is an offence *against me* (and not against some master who has a legally protected interest in me) is the first and most fundamental manifestation of the fact that I am recognized as a self-authenticating source of valid claims. Individuals are so regarded, it will be recalled, when they are taken as having a capacity to make claims against others that have weight of their own apart from being derived in any way from the rights or claims of others, from duties owed to society, or from considerations and requirements of the common good, however conceived. The source of the validity of the claims lies *in the persons themselves* who make them. The slave, by contrast, is a human being who is not recognized as a source of valid claims *at all*.[77] In the case of the right of bodily integrity, the fact that I am alive, in and of itself, provides the content for a valid claim against others: being alive in my body, I exist in a way that individuates me externally *vis-à-vis* others and, as such, it can be the object of a claim that has its source in me as an independent and separate person.

Now the right of bodily integrity is one side of a contrast that is also universally recognized in the public legal culture: the difference between *persons*, who, morally

---

[76] We need not view this conclusion as metaphysical. It is implied by the most firmly held basic beliefs underpinning the public legal culture. An influential non-philosophical statement of this idea is found in Blackstone's *Commentaries*, above n. 20, at bk. I, ch. 1, 125: 'Because as there is no other known method of compulsion, or of abridging man's natural free will, but by an infringement or diminution of one or other of these important rights [namely, the rights of bodily integrity and private property], the preservation of these, inviolate, may justly be said to include the preservation of our civil immunities in their largest and most extensive sense'. For a philosophical elucidation of the same idea, see Hegel, *Philosophy of Right*, above n. 20, paras. 90–8.

[77] This formulation, as well as the characterization of persons as self-authenticating sources of claims, are taken from Rawls. See *Political Liberalism*, above n. 3, at 33.

speaking, can never be mere objects of use, and *things*, which *can*. Things do not possess legal personality and standing—they cannot have rights or duties and they are not sources of valid claims against others. There is nothing in the normative characterization of things that precludes their being put to purposes of any and every sort. Of course, the thing–person distinction does not settle which entities are or are not things, and in certain instances there may be uncertainty or disagreement in the public legal culture about the appropriate classification. This said, there is wide and undisputed agreement about the appropriate classification in the great majority of cases, which suffices for the purposes of the present discussion. With respect to these instances, the public legal culture holds that there is a categorical and irreducible difference between persons and things and, further, that something must definitely belong to only one of these two categories and not the other.

The fact that the non-usability of human persons goes hand in hand with the usability of things is a crucial point that must be kept firmly in mind in treating the relation between the right of bodily integrity and the right of property. Indeed, I will now argue, it provides the conceptual linkage between them and the way of transition from the first to the second. My contention is that if individuals are recognized as having a right of bodily integrity, they cannot be under a general prohibition against subordinating and using external things. The right of bodily integrity and the *permissibility* of such possession and use go hand in hand. Keeping in mind that, in the juridical conception of rights, needs, preferences, merit, or distributional considerations neither establish nor rule out interpersonal claims, this permissibility follows from the usability of things, just discussed, coupled with the fact that, starting from the right of bodily integrity within the framework of the juridical conception, it cannot possibly be a wrong against others for individuals to use things, as I will now explain.

Through their bodies, individuals are inevitably situated in time and space. Always and independently of our so choosing, we must be somewhere and in interaction with some things. This is the only mode in which we exist. Unless the right of personal integrity is to be illusory, it must include the right to be somewhere in interaction with some external things for some time. Or, more exactly, in so being, we do not do others any wrong and in their dealings with us, others must take us as they find us—which means: as here in some place and affecting some things. Moreover, in protecting bodily integrity, we necessarily protect the capacity of individuals to exercise and to develop their mental and physical powers and with this their ability to choose. These powers, both as potential and developed, come under their exclusive rights as against others. With the protected exercise and development of their powers, individuals are somewhere and interact with external things as a result of choice and purpose. However, the fact that I have *chosen* to be somewhere or to make use of something (supposing of course that I have not done so in a way that interferes with the bodily integrity of others) cannot, in and of itself, change the permissible character of my being there or my affecting the thing and does not relieve others of the necessity of taking me as I am in these circumstances in their interactions with me.

I cannot abstract from my capacity to choose or, in other words, cannot choose not to choose: this is the given condition in which I find myself. If others have to take me as they find me, they must take me as a choosing, purposive agent.

The fact that our purposively affecting external things is not only not prohibited by the right of bodily integrity but is also the inevitable result of the exercise of those capacities which come under its protection, does not, however, give us property in these things exclusively as against others. As far as our physical relation to external things (which here includes the land upon which we exist and move) is concerned, the outermost parameters of the right of bodily integrity is the right to be somewhere for some time: that is, others cannot say that it is wrongful for us to be where we happen to be at any given point in time or that in removing us by affecting our bodily integrity, they do not violate our rights.[78] But it is only in so far as we are actually touched or affected in our bodies that the right is engaged. If others can use the things with which we are in contact without affecting our bodies, they can do so permissibly. The crucial point is that while the right of bodily integrity does not prohibit the purposive subordination and use of things, neither does it validate it *as an act of choice* that is distinct from one's bodily existence. It does not recognize the exercise of choice *as itself* a possible basis of valid claims against others and as an expression of our status as self-authenticating sources of claims. Thus, because the categories of taking possession, use, and alienation are externally manifested *exercises of choice* with respect to external things, they do not have juridical existence under the rubric of bodily integrity. If, however, these ways of affecting external things can be understood as expressing our status as self-authenticating sources of claims when articulated as a right that goes beyond the right of bodily integrity, there is nothing in the latter that a priori precludes this; on the contrary, it would be arbitrary to deny that such acts can have intrinsic normative significance when the right of bodily integrity ensures their very possibility. Being compatible with the right of bodily integrity, this extension could represent the continuation and the further realization of the very conception of ourselves that underlies it.

This is precisely the character of the right of first occupancy. By this principle, an individual's acts are recognized as being potentially decisive in establishing interpersonal claims. These acts can have *any* content whatsoever so long as they reasonably appear to others as one of the three modes of subordinating external things to an individual's purposes. By specifying the acts in this way, the principle of first occupancy carries through the distinction between person and thing at the highest level of generality: these are the distinct though conceptually interconnected modes of *treat-*

---

[78] The fact that my being on the earth' surface is not wrongful plays a crucial role, as Kant emphasizes, in the analysis of first occupancy. When I appropriate something that is on the ground, no one else can claim that I cannot have acquired the thing because I did not already possess the ground on which the thing is situated, leaving it open to him or her to take possession of both ground and thing. Everyone has the same innate right to be anywhere (where chance or unavoidable choice has placed him) and each of us is necessarily occupying the land where he or she happens to be. For Kant's view, see above n. 22, above at part I, ch. II, sect. I at 414–15.

ing things as usable objects. Any and every act that a person accomplishes, however complex or developed, may be construed in these terms alone. Moreover, the definitions of both the requisite acts and the objects of these acts are external in keeping with the juridical conception of rights. The act is defined by how it reasonably appears to others and the object of the act is something that can be affected by anyone, hence by others. Since it must be possible to construe the acts as possible modes of treating things as usable objects, the unity or integration of act and object under an external aspect is essential to what the act is, from the juridical point of view. This same integration is reflected in the fact that the act can have any content, so long as it counts as a purposive subordination of a thing. The content-neutrality and open-endedness of the act corresponds to the unqualified usability of things: given their inherent normative status as usable, things have no standing to resist being made subject to *any* purpose whatsoever.

By viewing such acts as necessary and sufficient to establish claims against others, the law recognizes individuals as self-authenticating sources of valid claims. We saw that in the case of the right of bodily integrity, an individual's body, being an external mode of individuation relative to others, is a vehicle for expressing the person's status as a self-authenticating source of claims. The same is true of that individual's acts: so far as others are concerned, it is only I who can accomplish my acts and it is only I who am immediately present in them.[79] And because these acts are defined with respect to particular external things that can be appropriated in their singularity—for only thus can their possession, use, or alienation be exclusive to a given individual—the acts are through and through modes of expressing the individuality of agents as self-authenticating sources of claims. Note, finally, that while this view of the right of property treats acts (similarly to bodies) as vehicles of individuation, it does not invoke any notions of merit or desert.[80] Reference to need, preference, merit, individual and social well-being, or distributional considerations would be incompatible with the very possibility of a juridical justification of first occupancy on a public basis.

The right of property views each and every individual as having the capacity to establish claims in relation to others through his or her acts. To express the fact that

---

[79] This significance of acts is brought out by Alexandre Kojève in his important work *Esquisse d'une phenomenologie du droit* (Paris: Editions Gallimard, 1981) at 477: 'It is in and through his *acts* that *A* differs from all the members of society since it is his acts that *actualize* his power of being [sa puissance d'être] by transforming it into a here and now, by definition different from all others' (my translation).

[80] The focus on acts in the view that I am proposing should not therefore be taken as reflecting a labour theory of property, which, as commonly understood, invokes notions of desert and reliance. In my opinion, labour theories that purport to be rights-based have been correctly criticized as fundamentally unsound. For an older yet, I think, decisive criticism, see Kant's discussion in *The Doctrine of Right*, n. 22, above at part I, ch. II, sect. I, p. 413 and for a more recent critical discussion, see Epstein, n. 11, above at 1225–30. Sidgwick, above n. 74, proposes a utilitarian-based labour theory which, in its own terms, is not vulnerable to these criticisms. For present purposes, the difficulty with Sidgwick's approach is, as I noted earlier, that it cannot serve as a public basis of justification While I cannot discuss the matter further here, I think that Locke's account, or at least a certain strand of it, can plausibly be interpreted along the lines that I have suggested in the text.

individuals are *self*-authenticating sources of claims, these acts are, and originally can only be, purely unilateral: they come from and are performed by single selves viewed as separate and distinct. And just as one's right of bodily integrity continues at least as long as one is alive, so the right of property continues at least as long as one can reasonably be viewed by others as acting in a way that manifests the requisite intent. The intrinsically unlimited character of the right of property reflects, once again, the fact that, through it, we are viewed as self-originating sources of claims. If we fail to respect the exclusivity of property claims, we fail to recognize the possibility that individuals can express their status as self-authenticating sources of claims through their actions.

If this is so, and in light of the public recognition of the right of bodily integrity, it must be arbitrary to deny the possibility or legitimacy of some kind[81] of right of property in external things. We saw that the right of bodily integrity itself protects the capacity for action. By representing the conceptually most basic and general way that acts, as distinct from mere states of being, can be the basis of claims by one person in relation to others, the right of property integrates the exercise of this capacity into the same moral framework. Indeed, viewed as modes of individuation, the difference between body and act is merely that between a power and its actualization. From the perspective of the public legal culture, the reason the human body is viewed as a protected interest is that it belongs to a being who has a capacity for action. For it is only a being with a capacity for purposive action that is imputed with responsibility and is subject to duty; and it is only a being that has at least the potential to be a unit of responsibility that is recognized by the public legal culture as having a capacity for rights. But unless the capacity for action can be fulfilled through its exercise under definite conditions, it is no real potentiality. Accordingly, if there is something intrinsic to a person's exercise of his or her capacity for purposive action such that it cannot be, in its own right, a source of claims, then neither can the fact that a person has a body be the basis of rights against others. Not only does the right of property, viewed in this way, complete the right of bodily integrity; both rights stand or fall together.

The fact that those excluded from something that has been brought under another's right can no longer unilaterally exercise their capacity for action with respect to that thing is not incompatible with their equality, any more than is the right of bodily integrity inconsistent with the equality of those whom it excludes. In both instances, the limitation need not represent an injury to their rights, at least from a certain moral point of view. While everyone has the equal capacity to establish claims through their acts, they do not have a claim against anyone unless and until they accomplish the necessary act in the requisite way. For the right of property to apply, there must be an already completed act in the very same way that the right of bodily

---

[81] The qualification in the text 'some kind' of property right is necessary at this point. It signals that I have yet to argue for the full-blown conception of property that is reflected in the principle of first occupancy as against what I call the 'narrow conception' of property right. I address this further comparison at pp. 809–11 below.

integrity applies only to an already existing body. Neither right, it must be emphasized, ensures that individuals will in fact have, or will in fact have the opportunity to
obtain, the interest it protects. If the purely unilateral exercise of one's capacity to
establish claims through one's acts is to be consistent with the equality of others, all
that is necessary is that it must be exercised only with respect to things that have not
already been acquired by them. I conclude, then, that those barred from acquiring
something because it has already been appropriated in accordance with first occupancy cannot claim, *as a matter of private right within the meaning of the juridical conception*, that any injury has been done them. Moreover, once again from within this
framework, any distribution of property on the basis of some other norm would have
to be consented to by those already in rightful exclusive possession of the property
and would have to be accomplished through a series of agreements in conformity
with the principles of contract.

Analysed as a mode of acquisition, the right of property reflects the immediate
normative implications of the thing–person contrast as realized in relations between
individuals who are viewed as self-authenticating sources of valid claims, when considerations of need, well-being, and particular interest are matters of indifference.
Granting this conclusion, it might nevertheless be objected that the argument does
not settle the question of what, more precisely, is the character of the right of property that may be justified on this basis. Perhaps the most that can be justified is a right
of property that is coextensive with actual physical possession. While there is controversy over the reasonableness of a full-blown right of property which can continue
even when the owner does not have actual physical possession, few reject the narrower conception which entails a right to use things transiently and to be free just
from interference with actual use.[82] According to this narrow view, as soon as one no
longer has physical possession of the thing, others are entitled to take possession of it.
I want to suggest that the narrow view must in fact give way to the unrestricted conception of property right that is recognized in first occupancy. It is not the case that
the prior argument for a right in external things as an extension and completion of
the right of bodily integrity leaves the character of the former right undetermined. As
I shall now explain, it is the unrestricted conception, not the narrow view, that unambiguously and fully reflects the idea of a private right of property in external things
which is continuous with, but at the same time genuinely distinct from, the right of
bodily integrity.

Consider, first, the character of the right of property in the narrow view. Like
the principle of first occupancy, the narrow view presupposes that one can make

---

[82] This is Sidgwick's characterization. See n. 73, above, at 67. Adam Smith presents the narrow conception as the first stage in the recognition of property. See above n. 20, at 18–23. By contrast, Kant, correctly in my view, does not regard it as a conception of property right at all. According to him, the fact
that one's right is coterminus with one's having physical possession of the thing shows that the right is
only apparently proprietary and is in fact indistinguishable from the right of bodily integrity. See Kant,
n. 22, above at pt. I, ch. I, sect. 6. The argument that follows in the text is, I believe, basically Kant's.

something one's own and can impose a legal disability upon others simply by *doing* something with or to it which reasonably appears to others as manifesting an intent to subordinate it to one's power. The act counts as that individual's own act—it is not imputed to anyone else—and the thing is deemed to be wholly subsumed under it— the thing has no separate standing once subordinated. Even the narrow conception of the right of property may be viewed as taking individuals to be self-authenticating sources of valid claims, who can establish claims through acts which are imputable to them as distinct and separate persons. And just as my act is 'my own' and not 'yours', so the thing that is wholly subsumed by the right of property under this act is 'mine' and not 'yours'. This view of ourselves is suggested by the exclusionary character of even the narrow conception of the right of property and holds so far as we are taking a juridical point of view. The fact that one is barred from using something that is already in another's physical possession is not, therefore, taken as a limit upon one's equal right to own things. The equal right consists just in a capacity to establish valid claims against others and one does not have any such claims *unless and until* one posits certain acts—acts which are imputable to oneself as a distinct and separate person. Accordingly, the mere fact that first occupancy extends the legal disability upon others by applying the exclusion where the owner does not have physical possession, does not necessarily conflict with the equal right which even the narrow conception presup- poses. It depends upon whether first occupancy construes the act requirement in a way that is consistent with its role and significance in the narrow view.

Now although it may be reasonable to require some sort of physical taking to estab- lish property in an unowned thing as against the world—for this is the only kind of act that will satisfy the requirement of publicity in these circumstances—it does not fol- low from this that the right can continue only so long as the right-holder continues to have it in his actual physical possession. Having recognized the possibility of making claims against others via unilateral acts that subordinate unowned things to one's pur- poses, the only thing necessary is that it be *reasonably apparent to others* that the thing continues to be subject to one's power, whether or not one is in actual physical pos- session of it at any given moment. But this, I argued earlier, is certainly possible in many instances—for example, when one takes possession by marking or imposing some form on the thing. Moreover, from one's own standpoint, why should one agree to rule out *ab initio*, as ever possibly establishing claims against others, modes of using things which originate in oneself and which express the range of one's rational and practical powers, even though they may not require continuous physical possession? Once the publicly manifest and purposive subordination of something is seen as not necessarily requiring continuous physical possession, the equal right to acquire may be viewed as exercised even where such continuous physical possession is lacking. The resulting imposition of a more extensive disability upon others is not therefore incompatible with their rights just because of the more expansive definition of the acts that must be respected. The more expansive definition simply fills out the content of acts that have the requisite character to establish proprietary claims against others.

The fact that the resulting disability imposed upon others is greater than in the case of the narrow view does not make it problematic so far as the juridical conception of rights is concerned. Of course, the additional disability may be problematic when considerations of need, particular purpose, merit, comparative resources, or general welfare are taken into account.[83] But, as I have emphasized, the whole discussion thus far has been undertaken from within the juridical conception of rights. In evaluating both the narrow and the full-blown conceptions of property right, we suppose, even if provisionally, that such considerations are irrelevant.

The unrestricted conception of property in first occupancy represents the idea of property that the narrow conception implicitly presupposes but only ambiguously realizes.[84] If the right of property is to qualify as a genuinely distinct yet basic juridical category, it must depend upon necessary and sufficient conditions that set it apart from the right of bodily integrity. The fact that property is a right in an *external thing*, that is, in something that is distinct from one's body, is obviously crucial to its being a juridical category of its own. At the same time, both sorts of rights presuppose possession of the requisite kind: one must be in possession of one's body or of the external thing if one is to have a claim *vis-à-vis* others with respect to them. It is through my being in possession that I am so connected with the object that I can be affected by another's touching it. If property in external things is to be a distinct category of rights, it must be possible to represent my being in possession of the thing in a way that is separate from my possession of my body. If, however, it is necessary that I be in physical possession of the thing in order to be affected by your touching it, my right to exclude will be only as against acts that can affect my right of bodily integrity. Thus the only sort of possession that is fully and unambiguously independent from possession of my body is *non-physical* possession of the thing: it must be possible to represent me as having it in my possession even though it is not in my actual physical possession. Non-physical possession of the thing is possession of it *as an external thing*. If the narrow conception of property is adopted, possession of the thing cannot be represented as possession of an external thing and so, neither fully nor unambiguously, as a right of property at all. The narrow conception of property is untenable on the very premises that it must presuppose if it is to qualify as a distinct category of right.

This completes my argument for the reasonableness of the right of property from the standpoint of—that is, from within—the juridical conception of rights. Thus far, the entire argument rests, then, on the assumption of the normative irrelevance of need, merit, individual or social well-being, and so forth. It is important to be clear as to the meaning of the assumption. It is not merely that one's *arbitrary* desires or needs cannot be the basis of claims against others. Nor is it just that one is expected to be able to subordinate one's desires to the requirements of right. This weak version of the irrelevance of desire and need must be presupposed by *any* normative

[83] This is of concern to a direct utilitarian justification and is addressed by the inclusion of a Lockean proviso or some other qualifying principle. See Sidgwick, above n. 73, at 70 ff.

[84] The argument in this paragraph was first stated by Kant, as I have already noted in n. 82 above.

conception whatsoever. The juridical conception, as a specific normative idea, sup-poses the much stronger premise that needs, desires, considerations of well-being, and so forth of *any kind* are not, as such, the basis of claims against others and play no role in determining their content. The juridical conception, unlike, for instance, a political conception of justice, has no place even for a notion of legitimate needs. In face of the objection that this extreme indifference to need must be unreasonable, it is not enough to show the reasonableness of any principle or norm from within the juridical conception. We must take the further step of seeing whether the juridical conception itself may be compatible with a view of individuals as free and equal per-sons. More particularly, we must identify the moral power or powers attributed to them as such persons that would make this indifference to need morally plausible.

We have seen that the right of property views individuals as having and exercising a capacity for choice through which they are self-authenticating sources of valid claims against others. Now if individuals are taken to be *self-authenticating* sources of valid claims, they are attributed a capacity to make claims the validity of which does not depend upon their satisfying any prior particular purpose or consideration: individu-als are recognized as having standing and value just in and of themselves, not through others nor on account of the desires, purposes, conception of the good, or characteris-tics that they happen to have. In other words, they can make claims that have weight without supposing the antecedent validity of any particular factor that is given to them, independently of their choice, from within or from without. Indeed we may say that if one is viewed as a self-authenticating source of valid claims *at all*, one is taken to have the capacity to dissipate the hold that anything, from which one can distinguish one-self, has over oneself. Only thus is one regarded as doing something that has its source *in oneself alone*. Accordingly, by recognizing individuals as self-authenticating sources of valid claims, we ascribe to them *a moral power to think of themselves as distinguished from and unlimited by any particular factor* that might be viewed as an antecedent source—and thus the real 'owner'—of their claims. It follows that recognizing indi-viduals as sources of claims entails regarding them as not inevitably tied to their needs, preferences, and so forth but rather as *choosing* to adopt or refuse them in the forma-tion and execution of their ends. And this points to a second moral power: individuals are recognized as having a capacity to set and to realize ends—that is, as having and exercising a capacity to choose something—in a way and with a content that reflects the fact that the ends are theirs alone and are not imputable (for the purpose of assign-ing rights or duties) to anything or anyone else. Individuals have, we may say, a *legiti-mate interest* in exercising these moral powers in their actions and anything that fulfils this interest can be made the basis of valid claims against others.

In the public legal culture, having these two moral powers is at least a sufficient basis for recognizing individuals as possessing moral personality (with the absolutely equal standing to make claims that this entails) as well as for imputing to individuals the effects that they produce through their actions, in so far as they affect the claims of others. Once again, the conception of moral powers is normative rather than metaphysical.[85] In our judgments, both everyday and juridical, we make reference to these powers, or at least implicitly suppose them, when we require that individuals be viewed as accountable for their acts, even in the face of the strength of their strongest impulses, the weight of their personal history and circumstances, or the fact that others may have approved or even ordered their actions. We cannot make sense of our public legal culture unless we view, and are entitled to view, ourselves in this way.

Now although it is perfectly reasonable within a liberal political conception of justice to suppose that individuals have needs for external things, the satisfaction of which enables them to develop and exercise their moral powers, and that, on this basis, they can make claims against others to a fair division of the necessary goods, we cannot begin straightaway with such need-based claims. If there is to be a conception of needs that is appropriate for individuals as self-authenticating sources of claims, it must be consonant with their absolute independence as such persons. In order to arrive at this conception of needs, we must *first* specify a relation between persons with respect to the external world that can give rise to claims that are *not* based upon needs of any kind. This first step must consist in, therefore, an exercise of the two moral powers that is intrinsically defined with respect to the external world, yet that preserves the independence of persons *vis-à-vis* it. And this step constitutes a conceptually distinct expression of freedom and equality. By treating needs of any kind—and indeed any particular feature to which one may respond—as not yet a basis for interpersonal claims, this first step represents individuals *just* as persons without qualification or any further determinations. Each is identical to everyone else for the simple reason that all are defined solely in terms of a capacity for the two moral powers without reference to any factor or consideration that might differentiate them. The equality of individuals consists in their absolute identity as self-authenticating sources of claims.

This conceptually basic view of individuals as free and equal is the juridical conception of the person ('juridical personality') and is reflected in the right of property. What distinguishes property, and more generally the juridical conception of rights, as a *specific* normative conception is that the only legitimate interest which it attributes to individuals is in the exercise of their moral powers via acts that deal with *purely external* things; that is, with things that form no part of their status as self-authenticating sources of valid claims and that count merely as usable. Thus, on the one hand, it must be emphasized that individuals are and remain self-authenticating sources of claims whether or not they appropriate anything. In the juridical conception, persons are *not* viewed as having an interest in exercising their moral powers *because* they need external things in order to be free and equal. They are sacrosanct and untouchable in themselves, irrespective of what they do in the external world. At the same time, however, *as persons*, they are taken to

[85] I note here that diverse, indeed opposing, philosophical accounts recognize these moral powers as at least provisionally valid, from a moral point of view. This is obviously true of Kant and Hegel. But it also holds for Sidgwick. See, H. Sidgwick, *The Methods of Ethics*, 7th edn. (Indianapolis: Hackett Publishing Company, 1981; 1st pub. 1907), bk. I, ch. V. sect. 3 at 65–70.

have, at least as a potentiality, the power for choice and the capacity to realize self-chosen purposes in the world. It would therefore be arbitrary and unreasonable to hold that persons are sacrosanct and untouchable *only* in so far as they have *not* yet exercised this power and capacity. They must be recognized as such in their actions as well. Now *ex hypothesis* things are simply what may be used and persons are authorized to use them. Everyone has the same authorization to put things to their chosen purposes. When they bring things under their purposes (via acts of appropriation, use, or alienation), this manifestation of purpose in the world is to be accorded the respect owed to persons as such. This is to respect persons in their actions. The fact, however, that it is not until they actually subordinate things to their purposes that individuals have valid claims against others reflects the independence of persons from things: precisely because we are viewed as not needing anything, there is, as it were, no original connection between us and things—no intrinsic reference to things as part of our being free—save the general authorization to use things. We must therefore do something that brings about an individuated relation with things that can be the basis of claims against others. When the moral point of view is framed solely and exhaustively in terms of the fundamental contrast between independent persons and usable things, this must necessarily, and can only, be accomplished via acts of appropriation, use, or alienation. The right of property, in other words, may reasonably be viewed as an extension of the moral idea underlying the prohibition against slavery to mutual relations among persons respecting their purposive dealings with external things.

When an individual appropriates something to the exclusion of others, he does not count in the particular or in any way that differentiates him from others but only *as a person*. The fact therefore that it is this individual rather than that who is owner is a matter of complete indifference. Ownership represents the exercise of the moral powers that are shared identically by all. The exclusivity of the right merely reflects the fact that ownership is a complete exercise of these powers in any given instance. Each instance of ownership represents, as it were, the complete embodiment of juridical personality. If every such instance need not be respected by others, no one can reasonably claim such recognition in any instance. The normative significance of the exclusive right is that the juridical personality which is identical in everyone has been accorded respect in a way that exhibits the fact that the general and equal authorization to use things can be a basis for interpersonal claims. The fact that one individual's need is satisfied whereas another's is not can be wrong and unfair only when freedom consists in something more than our capacity to express in the external world our bare independence from need. But, to repeat, such indifference towards need is conceptually basic in our understanding of freedom and must be presupposed if we are to arrive at a view, such as a political conception of the person, that specifies a notion of legitimate needs as a basis for claims against others. Understood in this way, the right of property is a doctrine that can belong to a liberalism of freedom.[86]

[86] I take this beautiful phrase from Rawls's lectures on Hegel in *Lectures on the History of Moral Philosophy*, ed. B. Herman (Cambridge, Mass.: Harvard University Press, 2000), at 330.

CHAPTER 20

THE PHILOSOPHY OF CRIMINAL LAW

LARRY ALEXANDER

THERE are many possible points of entry into, and organizational formats appropriate for, the subject of the philosophical underpinnings of criminal law. Mine may appear overly idiosyncratic, but I hope the reader will find the following map of the terrain of criminal law illuminates the major philosophical issues within it and their relationships to each other.

My point of entry into the topic is legal punishment, which I choose because legal punishment defines the domain of criminal law. Legal punishment is some treatment, meant to be unwelcome, that is imposed by legal authorities for violations of legal prohibitions. The basic question that I shall use to organize the materials is: what acts (or other things) justify legal punishment?

There are, of course, many possible points of entry and organizational schemes appropriate to a topic as vast and controversial as the philosophy of criminal law. None the less, I believe that my point of entry—in virtue of what is someone justifiably punished?—and the organizational scheme that follows naturally therefrom are the most perspicuous. The answer that I give to my point-of-entry question—one is justifiably punished if one deserves punishment, and one deserves punishment in virtue of acting (or, in some cases, failing to act) with insufficient concern for the interests of others for which one is obligated to act with concern—is developed naturally in three stages. In the first stage, Theories of Punishment, I relate the justification of punishment to desert. In the second stage—Criminal Law: The General Part—I take up the general features of acting with insufficient concern. In the third stage—Criminal Law: The Special Part—I ask what are the interests of others for which we must show concern in acting on pain of deserving punishment, and which reasons override what risks to those interests. Because the third stage leads inevitably into the vast territory of general normative theory, I shall deal with it rather cursorily. The core of the philosophy of criminal law as a distinctive subject lies in the first two stages, theories of punishment and the general part of the criminal law.

1 THEORIES OF PUNISHMENT

My basic question leads first to the topic of theories of punishment. Theories of punishment take up the question of in virtue of what is punishment for violations of legal prohibitions justified. I shall divide theories of punishment into retributive, consequentialist, and threat-based.

1.1 Retributive Theories

1.1.1 *Types of Retributive Theories*

All retributive theories justify punishment on the ground that persons who culpably commit or attempt acts and omissions that are morally wrong deserve punishment. Retributive theorists differ among themselves over whether deservingness of punishment is a sufficient or only a necessary condition for justified punishment. 'Weak retributivists' believe that negative desert is a necessary but not a sufficient condition for justified punishment, and that another necessary condition is that punishment bring about good consequences, such as deterrence of crime or the reform or incapacitation of criminals.[1] In other words, for weak retributivists, the violator's negative desert sets a ceiling on the amount of punishment that may justifiably be imposed on him; but no punishment may justifiably be imposed if it is not expected to bring about good consequences.

'Strong retributivists', on the other hand, hold that negative desert by itself provides a justification for punishment, and that punishment of wrongdoers to the extent of their negative desert is permissible in the absence of any predicted good consequences. Strong retributivists differ in the strength of their retributivism. Some believe that negative desert permits but does not require punishment, whereas others

---

[1] Those whom I label 'weak retributivists', others call 'mixed theorists' (referring to their mixture of consequentialist and retributive concerns). See e.g. Michael S. Moore, *Placing Blame* (1997), 92–4; H. L. A. Hart, *Punishment and Responsibility* (1968).

believe that there is a moral duty to see that those who deserve punishment receive it. The latter in turn differ over the strength of the moral duty to punish the deserving, or, put differently, over the strength of countervailing moral considerations necessary to override the duty. No one believes that the duty to punish those who deserve punishment is so strong as to require the investment of all social resources in its fulfilment.

1.1.2 *The Ground of Negative Desert*

Retributivists differ not only over the strength of the duty to punish the (negatively) deserving, but also over a number of other issues. One issue is whether negative desert is a function of culpable acts themselves, or whether, instead, it is a function of the character of the actors that the culpable acts reveal. In other words, is the basic ground of negative desert choice or character-revealed-in-choice? More on this when we take up both culpability conditions and excusing conditions.

1.1.3 *Moral Responsibility*

On either ground for negative desert, the retributivist must confront the free will/determinism issue as it bears on moral responsibility. If our choices—including character-forming choices—are caused by our unchosen character, and our unchosen character is caused by our genes and environment, is moral responsibility and hence negative desert undermined? Obviously, this philosophical problem transcends criminal law and is a field unto itself.

1.1.4 *Personal Identity*

Another issue for retributivists is that of personal identity through time. Sometimes in the course of lengthy imprisonment, and perhaps occasionally even in the time between his committing a crime and standing trial for it, the criminal undergoes such a radical change of values and character that he no longer can identify with the prior 'self' who committed the crime. Does the 'new man' still deserve the punishment that the prior self served?[2]

1.1.5 *Measurement of Desert*

Issues of more practical importance for retributivists concern the measurement of negative desert. There is actually a whole nest of issues here.

Comparative Versus Non-comparative Justice

First, is negative desert essentially comparative or noncomparative in nature? In other words, is the punishment an offender deserves a function solely of how much

---

[2] See e.g. Rebecca Dresser, 'Personal Identity and Punishment', *Boston University Law Review*, 70 (1990), 395.

similar offenders are punished, or is there a specific amount of punishment that each offender deserves irrespective of how much others are punished?

Suppose we take the latter position, and suppose we conclude that the non-comparative ('cosmic') negative desert is ten years imprisonment.[3] Then if for a given act of armed robbery by A, A is given ten years imprisonment and armed robber B, who differs in no morally relevant respects, is given five years imprisonment, has A been treated unjustly? He has received his cosmic desert, though he has been treated comparatively (with B) unjustly. If, alternatively, both A and B receive a punishment of five years imprisonment, both will have been treated comparatively justly but non-comparatively unjustly. Is the non-comparative injustice an injustice *to* anyone? And how is it to be gauged? (How much punishment does, say, armed robbery non-comparatively—cosmically—deserve?)

On the other hand, if we reject the existence of non-comparative justice, we can presumably impose *any* punishment on A and B so long as it is the same for both of them and so long as it is less than the punishment that more culpable wrongdoers received—that is, so long as punishments are *proportional* to negative desert.

Of course, if we are required not only to punish the equally deserving equally, but also to punish the more culpable wrongdoers more than the less culpable wrongdoers, we might end up in a position close to that of the proponents of non-comparative justice. For if we require not only proportionality of punishment to wrongdoing, but also proportionality between how wrongdoers are treated and how the innocent and virtuous are treated, comparative justice may leave us with no more discretion in setting punishments than does non-comparative justice.

Retributive versus Distributive Justice

A related issue is how the negative desert with which retributivists are concerned fits into a more general scheme of *distributive* justice. If one believed that everything—benefits as well as harms—should be distributed according to desert, positive as well as negative, then retributive punishment would just be an aspect of a more general scheme of distribution according to desert. On the other hand, if goods generally are distributed by some metric other than desert, the question arises how retributive punishment is to be meshed with distributive justice. For example, suppose A and B each commit similar crimes and deserve similar punishments. A, however, is much wealthier than B—and not just monetarily—due solely to good fortune, not positive desert. Is the just punishment for A one that will leave him just as miserable as B—in which case it may have to be harsher than B's—or is it one that is equally as harsh as B's, even if it leaves A better off than B? Looked at another way, should B's harsh life or the prior injustices he has suffered reduce his punishment as a matter of retributive justice? Or is the just amount of punishment impervious to past misfortunes and

---

[3] Obviously, how non-comparative desert is fixed for any particular culpable act is an enormously difficult problem. For a good survey of the difficulties, which the author concludes are insurmountable, see Russ Shafer-Landau, 'Retributivism and Desert', *Pacific Philosophical Quarterly*, 81 (2000), 189.

injustices and to present circumstances? These questions can be capsulized in this vignette: *A* commits an armed robbery and thereby deserves to suffer *X* amount of pain as punishment. As *A* leaves the scene, he is struck by lightning and suffers *X* amount of pain as a consequence. Should the lightning strike affect and perhaps reduce to zero the amount of punishment imposed for the crime?[4]

A related problem arises whenever one posits deontological constraints in addition to the retributivist ones. For example, if *A* is protected by a deontological constraint, expressed in the criminal law, against being compelled to lift a finger or spend a penny to save *B*'s life, what is *C*'s retributive desert if *C* violates the deontological constraint and its criminal law expression and forces *A* to expend a modest amount of effort or uses *A*'s property without *A*'s consent *in order to save B's life*? Does *C* deserve punishment, and if so, how much? He has violated serious prohibition(s) of the criminal law, which in this case we are assuming mirrors morality. But is *C* deserving of serious (or any) punishment?

1.1.6 *The Strength of the Retributivist Constraints*

For weak retributivists, who view negative desert as merely a side-constraint or ceiling on punishment, which punishment is otherwise to be justified by the good consequence it produces, the principal wrong to be averted in punishment is knowingly punishing or taking an unjustifiably high risk of punishing an innocent person, or punishing a guilty person more than he deserves, in order to bring about good consequences. In other words, the weak retributivist's desert-measured side-constraint on punishment is directed only at knowing or reckless violations, not unintended, non-reckless ones. No human system of punishment can avoid the possibility of punishing the innocent and punishing the guilty more than they deserve.[5] The question is how great a risk of doing so is permissible? The burden of proof placed on the state to prove a defendant's guilt will affect how many people innocent of the charge (or guilty of a lesser offence than charged) will be punished more than they deserve. So, too, will how crimes and defences are statutorily defined. If the state must prove only a low level of culpability—or no culpability whatsoever—for the crime as a whole, or for particular elements thereof, then the less culpable or the totally innocent will predictably be punished as much as the more culpable. This would appear to violate retributive justice whenever the judge is aware or believes it likely that the criminal defendant deserves less punishment than the crime of which he is convicted carries. It is less certain whether retributive justice is violated by setting a particular

---

[4] For a useful discussion of some (but not all) of these matters, see Douglas N. Husak, 'Already Punished Enough', *Philosophical Topics*, 18 (1990), 79.

[5] For a much fuller discussion of this issue, see Larry Alexander, 'Retributivism and the Inadvertent Killing of the Innocent', *Law & Philosophy*, 2 (1983), 233; David Dolinko, 'Some Thoughts about Retributivism', *Ethics*, 101 (1991), 537; David Dolinko, 'Three Mistakes of Retributivism', *University of California at Los Angeles Law Review*, 39 (1992), 1623; David Dolinko, 'Retributivism, Consequentialism, and the Intrinsic Goodness of Punishment', *Law & Philosophy*, 16 (1997), 507.

burden of proof or defining the culpability required for particular elements of crimes in a way that creates a high risk in individual cases—and a virtual certainty over an array of cases—of punishment greater than deserved.[6]

With respect to strong retributivism, the question is what considerations override the *permission* to punish (for 'weak' strong retributivists) or the *duty* to punish (for 'strong' strong retributivists). Detecting, convicting, and punishing the guilty to the extent they deserve are costly. They consume scarce resources. They harm the family and friends of those convicted. In some cases they deprive society of the productive talents of the convicted. At what point do such costs override the duty or permission to give offenders their negative deserts?[7]

Finally, although retributivists normally view matching punishment to negative desert as either a side-constraint or as a duty, it is possible to view it as neither but as instead a goal. Thus, it might be the case that punishing some people more than they deserve and others less will over time result in more people receiving the punishment they deserve than if punishment equal to desert is pursued in each case. More plausibly, if we take victimization by criminals as well as punishment greater than desert to be instances of *undeserved harm*, then the goal of minimizing undeserved harm might require punishing more than is deserved in some cases. Obviously, this form of retributivism is more consonant with a consequentialism that takes desert as a basis of distribution than it is with any moral view that takes desert to be a deontological side-constraint.

1.2 Consequentialist Theories

I am going to give consequentialist theories of punishment very short shrift in these pages. The reason is this: consequentialist theories of punishment are part of consequentialist moral systems in which all acts, motives, rules, and institutions are judged by the consequences they produce. Utilitarians judge the criminal law and punishments for crimes by whether they maximize the relevant maximand, such as happi-

---

[6] A related problem is the rule-like form of criminal prohibitions. Often, crimes are intentionally defined in a rule-like manner that makes them over and underinclusive with respect to culpable acts but which makes them less susceptible to good and bad faith claims of ignorance of law or to irregular administration of the law. An example might be the legal prohibition on assisted suicide, an act which may not itself be culpable in many circumstances, but which, if legalized, may usher in all kinds of abuses and mistakes. For retributivists, the problem of rule-like form, which is justified by its consequences, is structurally similar to the problems of burdens of proof, resource allocations to proving and defending criminal charges, and so forth. See generally Larry Alexander and Emily Sherwin, *The Rule of Rules: Morality, Rules, and the Dilemmas of Law* (2001), ch. 4.

[7] See generally Louis Kaplow and Steven Shavell, 'Fairness versus Welfare', *Harvard Law Review*, 114 (2001), 961, 1225–304; David Dolinko, 'Retributivism, Consequentialism, and the Intrinsic Goodness of Punishment', *Law & Philosophy*, 16 (1997), 507; Douglas N. Husak, 'Why Punish the Deserving?', *Nous*, 26 (1992), 447.

ness or welfare. Egalitarian-consequentialists judge criminal law and punishment by whether they produce an equal distribution of welfare, or opportunity for welfare, or capabilities, and so forth. It is solely a contingent matter whether any given definition of a crime or defence, any stringency or allocation of the burden of proof, and any punishment for a given crime—or even, conceivably, a reward for refraining from a given crime—will produce the relevant consequences and distribution thereof. Although consequentialists have many things to say about how crimes should be defined, proved, and punished, in the end, criminal law and punishment are not distinctive aspects of consequentialist theories.[8] Consequentialism has very little to offer wholesale to criminal law theory aside from such common-sense consequentialist nostrums as (1) other things being equal, a greater punishment will deter crimes more than a lesser one (except for masochists and martyrs); (2) some kinds of punishment—for example, execution and imprisonment—will reduce crime through incapacitating would-be criminals; (3) some kinds of punishment will reduce crime through reformation of criminals; (4) the costs of crime itself, of crime detection, prosecution, and punishment, and of deterrencce of innocent and valuable activity are a function of, *inter alia*, the definitions of crimes and defences, the levels of punishment prescribed, the allocation and stringency of burdens of proof, and the technology of crime detection.

1.3 Threat-Based Theories of Punishment

Recently, some have advanced what they regard as a theory of punishment that is premised neither on the negative desert of the criminal nor on the general social consequences of punishment. The theory begins from the premise that individuals have various rights, and that having rights entails a permission to threaten those who would wrongfully violate those rights. It is then argued, more controversially, that the right to threaten entails the right to make good on the threat if the rights-violation occurs. From this it is concluded that criminal punishment is justified by virtue of its threat being justified.[9]

This theory departs from retributivism in two respects. First, some who deserve punishment according to retributivism—because they acted culpably—would not be justifiably punished under this theory because they had not first been threatened with punishment in the relevant way. Secondly, some who might deserve little punishment under retributivism because their culpability was minor would suffer severe punishment under the threat-based theory because they were threatened with severe punishment and failed to heed the threat.

---

[8] See e.g. Kaplow and Shavell, 'Fairness Versus Welfare', 1225–304.

[9] See e.g. Daniel Farrell, 'The Justification of Deterrent Violence', *Ethics*, 100 (1990), 301; Warren Quinn, 'The Right to Threaten and the Right to Punish', *Philosophy & Public Affairs*, 14 (1985), 327.

It is this latter departure from retributivism that makes threat-based theories controversial. For it seems that it licenses potentially Draconian punishments for even minor crimes so long as the criminal has been threatened prior to the crime's commission. This departure from retributivism draws support from the widely held intuition that we can do things to make committing even minor crimes quite dangerous, so long, at least, as the criminal is warned of the danger (and so long as the danger to innocent people is sufficiently low). If I own Mt. Everest, presumably I can place my jewellery on its peak in order to make theft of the jewellery obviously dangerous and thus unlikely to be attempted. Likewise, to prevent unauthorized picking of my prize roses, I can presumably surround them with a crocodile-filled moat, at least so long as I post signs and loudspeakers broadcasting in all languages that crossing the moat is likely to be fatal.[10]

The only difference between these examples of making minor crimes obviously dangerous and threat-based Draconian punishments is that the latter require that someone choose to make good on the threat after the criminal ignores it. In the cases of Mt. Everest and the crocodiles, once the criminal ignores the threat, his fate is out of the hands of the threatener. Whether this difference is of moral significance is, of course, the important issue for threat-based theories.[11] For if we may threaten *but never impose* punishment greater than that deserved by retributive lights, the distinctiveness of threat-based theories dissolves.

2 CRIMINAL LAW: THE GENERAL PART

I shall assume from here on that desert is the key to justifying legal punishment, which leads to the question of in virtue of what do people deserve punishment. I shall follow tradition and divide the answer to that question into two parts. The first part, which is known as the general part of the criminal law, deals with those things, *aside from the type of harm caused or risked*, that are material to a person's deservingness of punishment. The second part of the answer to the question of in virtue of what is punishment deserved, which is known as the special part of the criminal law, deals with identifying those harms or wrongs that justify punishment of those who cause, attempt, or risk them. In this section, I take up the issues of the general part of the criminal law, leaving for Section 3 the issues of the special part.

[10] See generally Larry Alexander, 'Self-Defense, Punishment, and Proportionality', *Law & Philosophy*, 10 (1991), 323; Larry Alexander, 'Consent, Punishment, and Proportionality', *Philosophy & Public Affairs*, 15 (1986), 178; Larry Alexander, 'The Doomsday Machine: Proportionality, Prevention and Punishment', *The Monist*, 68 (1980), 199.

[11] See ibid.

2.1 Legality and Retroactivity

It is well established in American criminal law that no one can be criminally punished if the crime of which he is guilty has not been enacted by statute, as opposed to having been developed judicially.[12] It is also the case that as a matter of federal constitutional law, no one may be punished for conduct that was not deemed criminal at the time it occurred but was only criminally prohibited at a later time.[13] These two principles—the principle of 'legality', requiring that criminal prohibitions be statutory, and the principle against retroactivity (no *ex post facto* criminal laws)—are closely related and are designed to ensure that the criminality of conduct is known before the fact to those who might engage in it so that they can be influenced by that knowledge.

Are legality and prospectivity necessary conditions for criminal desert? Many people believe so, which is why the Nuremberg trials of Nazi leaders after World War II was quite troubling to those who believed that the laws that the Nuremberg defendants were charged with violating were created after the fact. But if Nuremberg is instructive, it is so because it shows that legality and prospectivity are not necessary conditions for deservingness of punishment. The absence of a criminal statute prohibiting genocide is immaterial to the negative desert of those who commit it because it is sufficient for such desert that one understand the wrong-making characteristics of genocide, which do not depend on its legality. For the most serious crimes—homicide, battery, rape, theft, and so on—the wrong-making characteristics are obvious to almost everyone. The absence of a prior statutorily enacted prohibition does not eliminate or even mitigate deservingness of punishment, even if, as a matter of positive law, it constitutionally bars it.[14]

2.2 The Requirement of a Voluntary Act

It is orthodoxy that in general there can be no crime that does not have as an element a voluntary act.[15] A voluntary act is a willed bodily movement—or a willed attempt

---

[12] See Joshua Dressler, *Understanding Criminal Law*, 2nd edn. (1995), 20, 29–35.

[13] US Constitution, Art. I, §§ 9, 10.

[14] The converse is true in this sense: criminal prohibition of an act is not sufficient to establish that one who violates the prohibition deserves punishment. The act must be wrongful, and illegality is not by itself sufficient for wrongfulness, as the historical record of pernicious criminal laws makes obvious. However, an act that is otherwise not wrongful can become so by criminal prohibition if the prohibition is part of a programme to specify and coordinate individual contributions to bring about a morally obligatory state of affairs. Thus, although I do not have a pre-existing moral obligation to pay precisely 37 per cent of my income to the government, I do have an obligation to do my fair share; and the tax code and the criminal laws that enforce it are means of specifying and coordinating our fair shares. After the tax code is enacted, I *do* have an obligation to pay 37 per cent, and it would be morally wrong for me to fail to do so.

[15] See Joshua Dressler, *Understanding Criminal Law*, 2nd edn. (1995), 71–4; Model Penal Code, § 2.01(1).

to move one's body (a mental act)—by someone who is otherwise in control of his willings.[16] Thus it is said that there can be no punishment for mere thoughts or even for bare intentions. The former are not subject to the will, and neither thoughts nor intentions involve bodily movements.[17] Nor can there be punishment for a mere status, at least so long as the status is not coupled with a voluntary act.[18]

The major issues surrounding the voluntary act requirement are what kinds of conditions defeat voluntariness; is the voluntary act requirement completely subsumed within the requirement of culpability; and when, why, and how can one be liable for omissions rather than acts. The topic of omissions is best dealt with under the special part of the criminal law because it is really just an aspect of what kinds of duties fall within the legitimate scope of the criminal law and underpin judgments of negative desert. If there is a duty to act that is appropriately enforced through the criminal law, the fact that liability turns on a failure to act rather than an act (a willed bodily movement) is immaterial so long as the conditions that defeat the voluntariness of a bodily movement are not present. In other words, the same factors that negate criminal liability by showing that no voluntary act occurred also defeat liability premised on a failure to act when the criminal law rightfully imposes a duty to act. When the criminal law does so is discussed in Section 3 (the special part of the criminal law).

Turning to the first question—what conditions defeat voluntariness—the answer usually consists of some form of altered consciousness, such as somnambulance, hypnotic trance, or automatism.[19] In theory, the actor in an altered state of consciousness is not morally responsible either because he cannot access fully his reasons for action or because he is not fully in control of his willings.[20] (Bodily movements that are not conscious at all, or that are completely reflexive, are not 'acts' at all, much less voluntary acts.) On the other hand, acts done out of habit, even though not fully conscious, are considered voluntary, on the ground that the actor can control the acts by engaging his attention.[21]

Impulsiveness so extreme that the normal mechanisms of agent control are bypassed would also seem to defeat the voluntary act requirement. Such a pathology

[16] See generally Michael S. Moore, *Act and Crime* (1993). On mental acts, see ibid. at 95–112.
I am tempted by the mental act view for the following reason: I can imagine one who wills a bodily movement in a circumstance in which willing that movement is culpable, but whose body fails to respond. (Imagine someone with his thumb on a bomb's detonator who wills that he depress the detonator but whose thumb does not move.) Such a person would be guilty of an attempt to commit a wrongful act, which, as I argue below in Section 2.5.1, is all that matters for negative desert.

[17] See Douglas N. Husak, *Philosophy of Criminal Law* (1987), 93.
[18] See Dressler, *Understanding Criminal Law*, 80; *Robinson v California*, 370 US 660 (1962).
[19] See Robert F. Schopp, *Automatism, Insanity, and the Psychology of Criminal Responsibility* (1991), 71–5, 132–59; Model Penal Code, § 2.01(2).
[20] See generally Schopp, *Automatism, Insanity, and the Psychology of Criminal Responsibility*.
[21] See Model Penal Code, § 2.01(2)(d). I believe that acts done out of habit are best analysed in conjunction with the notion of 'opaque recklessness'. See text at n. 32 below; Kimberly Kessler Ferzan, 'Opaque Recklessness', *Journal of Criminal Law and Criminology*, 91 (2001), 1, 46–7.

is ordinarily relegated to the insanity defence, where it must be conjoined with the presence of a mental disease or defect.[22] There is no reason, however, why evidence of extreme impulsiveness might not be used to negate the voluntary act element and thus the crime rather than merely to raise a defence to it.[23]

On the other hand, circumstances that make options other than commission of a crime extremely difficult for the actor to choose, although they may relieve the actor of moral responsibility and excuse his crime, ordinarily do not defeat the voluntariness of his choice to commit the crime in the sense with which the voluntary act requirement is concerned. The actor's prudential or agent-relative moral reasons (such as a threat to his child) in favour of committing the crime so dominate his moral reasons against committing it that we cannot deem him deserving of punishment for his choice, even though the choice reflects his rational agency. These circumstances are appropriately considered as possible defences to, not denials of, criminal charges.

Underlying these 'defeaters' of the voluntary act requirement—altered states of consciousness and impulsiveness—is the idea that no one is blameworthy for his acts if his rational agency is sufficiently impaired at the time. The impairment might affect his will, so that he is not enough in control of what he does to be morally responsible therefor. Or it might affect his rationality, depriving him of access to the ordinary reasons he has for and against particular acts.[24] Either way, he is not sufficiently in control to be deemed to be a voluntary actor.

This gets us to our second question, namely, whether the voluntary act requirement can be separated from the requirement of culpability. I believe that it cannot be. In order to be a culpable act, an act must be voluntary; and every condition that negates a voluntary act perforce negates culpability. If that were not the case—if, for example, sleepwalkers were culpable for what they did while sleepwalking—there would be no reason to exempt them from criminal liability. A separate requirement that a voluntary act be proved is included within the requirement that a culpable act be proved.

Moreover, there is a good reason for folding the voluntary act considerations into the culpability inquiry and eliminating the separate element of a voluntary act.[25] Every would-be crime will include voluntary acts by the 'criminal' as part of its story.

---

[22] See Model Penal Code, § 4.01(1).

[23] Because I would argue that the prosecution must prove all factors necessary for defendant's act to be deemed culpable—including the absence of justification or excuse—it is irrelevant as a practical matter whether extreme impulsiveness negates the voluntariness of defendant's act or excuses it. (The defendant would, of course, have the burden of *producing* evidence on matters such as excuse, justification, and conditions, such as somnambulance, automatism, or hypnotism, that defeat voluntariness.) Therefore, I am indifferent to whether, as a practical matter, impulsiveness negates or only excuses voluntary action.

[24] See generally Schopp, *Automatism, Insanity, and the Psychology of Criminal Responsibility*.

[25] See generally Larry Alexander, 'Voluntary Acts: The Child/Davidson Trilemma', *Criminal Justice Ethics*, 11 (1993), 98; Larry Alexander, 'Reconsidering the Relationship Among Voluntary Acts, Strict Liability, and Negligence in Criminal Law', *Social Philosophy & Policy*, 7 (1990), 84.

The hypnotized defendant perhaps voluntarily placed himself in the presence of the hypnotist. The sleepwalking defendant voluntarily went to bed without locking herself in her bedroom. The automobile driver suffering an epileptic seizure got behind the wheel while seizure-free. The driver of the car with a stuck accelerator voluntarily drove the car. In all these cases we can tell the story of the crime such that the crime contained a voluntary act. Of course, the act may have been a completely innocent one, and that is the point. If there is a culpable act present, that is all that is needed for deservingness of punishment. And if there is not, the presence of voluntary but non-culpable acts will not justify punishment.

Therefore, the central question should be which of the various factors that are supposed to bear on whether the voluntary act requirement is satisfied affect culpability. For example, can one be culpable for one's thoughts? Surely there might be some kinds of *thinking*—mental *acts*—that are at least culpability-eligible. If it were somehow harmful to others for me to attempt to calculate the first one hundred prime numbers, but I nevertheless do so, I can surely be deemed blameworthy and perhaps deserving of punishment. On the other hand, I am probably not culpable merely because a particular thought entered my mind. The latter, unlike mental calculations, is out of my direct control (though it may be the product of some other act over which I do have direct control and which could therefore be culpable).

If bare thoughts cannot be the basis of desert, how about intentions? Is intending an act over which I exercise control? I shall defer dealing with this issue until I take up incomplete attempts.

The other factors that bear on the voluntariness of acts bear on culpability for precisely the same reasons—they undermine access to reason and control. Arguably, therefore, those who act in ways that would otherwise be culpable but who do so in altered states of consciousness are non-culpable. So, too, are those who cannot control their impulses. The culpability inquiry includes everything the voluntary act inquiry does without remainder.

2.3 Criminal Culpability

Criminal culpability is standardly broken down into the three culpable mental states of purpose, knowledge, and recklessness and the two non-mental states of negligence and strict liability.[26] When the relevant element of the crime is bringing about a particular result, such as a death, the culpable mental state of purpose is defined as having the conscious object of causing that result.[27] Thus, a purposeful homicide would be an act causing the death of a person undertaken by the actor with the conscious object of causing death. When the relevant element of the crime is merely some cir-

---

[26] See e.g. Model Penal Code, §§ 2.02(1); 2.05(1)(b).
[27] See Model Penal Code, § 2.02(2)(a)(i).

cumstance accompanying the act—for example, the circumstance that the victim of the homicide is a police officer, or the place of the burglary is a residence—purpose with respect to such an element is usually synonymous with belief in its existence.[28] Thus, one who kills a victim believing him to be a police officer has 'purposely' killed a police officer even if it was not his desire that his victim be a police officer. (Of course, one could have a circumstance element that required purpose in the sense of conscious object, though it would be an unusual crime that did so.) Likewise, where the element of the crime concerns the nature of the criminal's conduct, as opposed to the result of that conduct or its accompanying circumstances, 'purposely' engaging in that conduct usually amounts to nothing more than intending that conduct aware of its nature. Thus, where purposely stating a falsehood is a crime (as in the crime of perjury), one satisfies this conduct element by intending to state what one knows to be false.

The culpable mental state of knowledge refers to a belief that the criminal element exists or, where the element is the result brought about by the actor's conduct, a belief to a practical certainty that the result would occur.[29] Knowledge does not require any particular attitude towards conduct, result, or circumstance. Purpose, on the other hand, at least where it requires that the element be the actor's 'conscious object', is all about the actor's attitude rather than his beliefs. One can act purposely with respect to an element even if one believes it highly unlikely that the element exists or will be brought about if the element is one's conscious object. (One does have to believe, however, that one's conduct has increased the likelihood of the element's existence, even if only slightly.)

Neither purpose nor knowledge takes account of the reasons the actor has for acting that he believes justify his action. Recklessness, however, builds the actor's reasons for acting into the culpable mental state. The actor who is reckless with respect to an element of a crime acts with a conscious disregard of a substantial and unjustifiable risk that the element characterizes, accompanies, or will be caused by his conduct.[30] That is, the reckless actor must be aware of a risk of an element that is both a substantial risk and an unjustifiable risk.

There are many issues that swirl around the culpable mental state of recklessness.[31] One set of issues concerns just how subjective is recklessness. It is clear, for example, that if an actor takes what he believes is an 80 per cent risk of killing someone merely in order to get home in time to watch his favourite TV show, whether *he* would characterize that risk as either 'substantial' or 'unjustifiable' is immaterial. Those characterizations are surely an objective matter of law.

[28] See Model Penal Code, § 2.02(2)(a)(ii).
[29] See Model Penal Code, § 2.02(b)(i), (ii).
[30] See Model Penal Code, § 2.02(c).
[31] For a lengthy discussion of the issues regarding recklessness that follow, see Larry Alexander, 'Insufficient Concern: A Unified Conception of Criminal Culpability', *California Law Review*, 88 (2000), 931.

On the other hand, what if the actor believes he is creating a risk because he is mistaken about some fact? (He believes he is driving at an unsafe speed, but his speedometer is broken and he is really driving much more slowly and safely.) Is such an actor reckless (assuming his reasons do not justify creating the risk that he believes he is creating)? Or is such an actor only attempting to be reckless?

The better answer to this question is that such an actor should be deemed 'reckless'. First, if one believes, as I do, that one is as negatively deserving for attempted crimes as for successful ones—an issue I address in Section 2.5—then 'attempted recklessness' and 'recklessness' would merit equal treatment. Secondly, the distinction between 'recklessness' and 'attempted recklessness' depends upon a distinction between the risks the actor estimates and the 'real' risks created by his conduct. But the notion of a 'real' risk, as opposed to some person's assessment of risk, is confused. Risk is an epistemic rather than an ontic notion, and it is always assessed from a particular informational perspective. Only God, who knows everything, knows the 'real' risks of conduct, which are, for any outcome, either one or zero. Therefore, attempted recklessness, which relies on a notion of risk that is neither God's nor the actor's, will only be definable arbitrarily.

Another issue regarding the subjectivity of recklessness is whether the actor must consciously advert to either the specific dangers his conduct is creating or the exact magnitude of the risk he believes he is taking. If, for example, the actor jumps a red light, he may think to himself 'This is dangerous', but he may not think 'This creates a 10 per cent chance of death, a 20 per cent chance of bodily injury, a 40 per cent chance of property damage', and so forth. Is the actor who only thinks 'This is dangerous' reckless, and, if so, with regard to which outcomes? I raise this issue but cannot deal with it here.[32]

A final issue regarding the subjectivity of recklessness is whether the requirement that the risk that the actor believes he is taking be substantial is independent of the requirement that it be unjustifiable. I believe that it is not, and that all the work is done by the latter requirement. If someone subjects another to even a tiny risk for callous or malicious reasons, the former is surely reckless. Consider playing Russian Roulette on another without his consent and just for thrills with a gun containing a million chambers and one live round. Surely this one-in-a-million risk is recklessly imposed, even though it is quite small, and lower than many other risks that are non-culpably imposed. It is the actor's reasons in light of the magnitude of the risk that do all the work. No particular threshold of magnitude is required.

I believe that these three culpable mental states—purpose, knowledge, and recklessness—all exhibit the single moral failing of insufficient concern for the interests of others.[33] When one has as one's conscious object that those interests be damaged

[32] See ibid. at 954 n. 62. See also Kimberly Kessler Ferzan, 'Opaque Recklessness', *Journal of Criminal Law and Crimology*, 91 (2001), 1.

[33] See generally Larry Alexander, 'Insufficient Concern: A Unified Conception of Criminal Culpability', *California Law Review*, 88 (2000), 931; Dan M. Kahan, 'Two Liberal Fallacies in the Hate Crimes Debate', *Law and Philosophy*, 20 (2001), 175, 180–2. Although insufficient concern does denote a

(purpose) or believes to a practical certainty that they will be damaged (knowledge), insufficient concern is presumptively established. If the actor has reasons for acting that in fact justify his action and rebut the charge of insufficient concern, he should have to raise these reasons as defences.

With respect to risks to others' interests short of practical certainty and reasons for action other than the desire to harm, the presence or absence of insufficient concern is a matter of the actor's justifying reasons. This is why absence of justification is internal to recklessness but external to purpose and knowledge. Logically, however, given that acts with either purpose or knowledge can be justified, all three culpable mental states can be viewed as aspects of the single moral failing of imposing risks to others' interests for reasons that do not justify that level of risk-imposition.

This unified conception of criminal culpability is theoretically expedient for several reasons.[34] It allows us to make sense of some otherwise anomalous forms of culpability, such as 'wilful blindness'. Wilful blindness refers to cases where the actor has reason to believe that an element of a crime exists but deliberately refrains from investigating further because he wants to preserve his ignorance. Some instances of wilful blindness are treated by courts as equivalent to 'knowledge', though that is a fiction. The actor has refrained from acquiring knowledge, which is inconsistent with his having it. None the less, he is culpable for taking an unjustified risk that the element exists, which means he is technically reckless rather than knowing. But in many situations he may be more culpable than the ordinary reckless actor, which is why courts are tempted to call him knowing. Once we see that knowledge and recklessness are parts of a unified conception of criminal culpability, however, we can be relieved of the necessity of pigeonholing wilful blindness as either knowledge or recklessness.

If purpose, knowledge, and recklessness are just components of a single conception of culpability, namely, insufficient concern, negligence is not. First, and uncontroversially, the negligent actor has no particular mental state at the time of the conduct in question. Negligence is defined by failure to advert to a substantial and unjustifiable risk, which means that the actor could be adverting to anything else.[35]

---

defect of character, that does not mean that retributive desert, which is culpability-based, is, at a foundational level, character-based. For the character defects that are revealed by choices expressing insufficient concern are just that—character defects—*as-revealed-in-choices*. Character defects not so revealed should not be the basis of retributive responses. See Heidi M. Hurd, 'Why Liberals Should Hate "Hate Crimes Legislation"', *Law and Philosophy*, 20 (2001), 215, 224–32.

I should also point out that in some instances, when criminal prohibitions reflect deontological constraints (for example, preventing the killing of one innocent person to save ten), or are deliberately overbroad for consequentialist reasons (for example, preventing morally justifiable mercy killings), insufficient concern and legal culpability may come apart. See Larry Alexander and Emily Sherwin, *The Rule of Rules: Morality, Rules, and the Dilemmas of Law* (2001), ch. 4.

[34] See generally Larry Alexander, 'Insufficient Concern: A Unified Conception of Criminal Culpability', *California Law Review*, 88 (2000), 931.

[35] See Model Penal Code, § 2.02(d).

Secondly, and quite controversially, the negligent actor is, I believe, not culpable for failing to advert and does not deserve punishment for his negligence.[36] There are two related reasons for this conclusion. First, as mentioned previously with regard to 'attempted recklessness', there is no non-arbitrary way of specifying the risk of causing an element of a crime that the actor is creating if we jettison both the actor's estimate and God's (which is always one or zero). The negligent actor is supposed to be failing to perceive the 'real risk'—the risk the 'reasonable actor' would perceive—yet the reasonable actor is not God. Rather, the reasonable actor, from whose vantage 'real risk' is assessed, is a construct who has some of the epistemic limitations of the actual actor but not others. But the construct can take an infinite number of forms, and there is no good reason to choose any one of them.

Secondly, no one is culpable for failing to advert because no one has control over adverting to matters to which he or she is not already adverting. Of course, a failure to advert at the relevant time may be caused by an earlier culpable choice in which the actor chose to risk, for insufficient reasons, that he would later fail to notice or comprehend a risk. In other words, an earlier choice reflecting insufficient concern may cause inadvertence. Inadvertence itself, however, does not reflect insufficient concern and is therefore not culpable. Nor is insufficient concern by itself culpable, even if it causes inadvertence to risks to others, if it does not cause inadvertence through a choice that exhibits it.

Finally, strict liability denotes the absence of a requirement of culpability regarding an element of a crime.[37] Without culpability regarding the element, the mere presence of the element does not show that the actor deserves punishment or the enhancement of punishment therefor.

Therefore, negligence and strict liability, which are not culpable mental states and do not evidence negative desert, cannot themselves provide justifications for punishment. Of course, punishment for negligence and strict liability, by not requiring proof that the actor adverted to a risk that he had inadequate reasons for taking, make convictions of the truly culpable—those who *do* act with insufficient concern—easier to obtain. The strong retributivist's duty to punish the guilty will thus be more easily fulfilled, though at the cost of violating the injunction to avoid punishing more than is deserved.

Punishment based on negligence or strict liability, of course, does promote consequentialist goals. Not only does it make conviction less costly and more certain, but it deters those truly culpable actors who would otherwise act with insufficient concern believing that they will avoid conviction because proof of their insufficient concern will fail. Of course, punishment based on negligence or strict liability produces negative consequences as well, such as overdeterrence (deterrence of innocent, socially valuable activities). Because actors cannot control whether they will be

[36] See generally Larry Alexander, 'Insufficient Concern', 949–53; Larry Alexander, 'Reconsidering the Relationship'.
[37] See Dressler, *Understanding Criminal Law*, 125.

negligent or strictly liable, if risk averse they will stay far away from activities, even socially valuable ones displaying proper concern for others' interests, that might result in their punishment. For example, if selling mislabelled drugs is a crime even if the seller has acted non-culpably, sellers might take more than reasonable care—that is, excessively costly precautions—to avoid selling mislabelled drugs, with the result that beneficial drugs become more expensive or unavailable.

However the consequentialist calculus turns out, criminal liability premised on negligence or strict liability is going to result in the punishment of those whom authorities believe are truly non-culpable and thus not deserving of punishment. Unlike the occasional innocent defendants who are convicted of crimes by judges and jurors who believe they are guilty, defendants punished for negligence or strict liability will often be thought to have acted with proper concern for others and thus non-culpably. The judges and jurors will thus be knowingly punishing these defendants more than they deserve to be punished.

2.4 Exculpatory Mistakes of Fact and Law

The treatment of exculpatory mistakes of fact and law is for the most part merely a logical corollary of the analysis of criminal culpability in the previous subsection. If a crime requires as an element that the actor act *knowing* that fact *F* exists, or *knowing* that his act has legal status *L*, then an actor who mistakenly believes not-*F* or not-*L* has not committed the crime.[38] Therefore, for the most part, a claim of exculpatory mistake of fact or law will be intensionally and extensionally equivalent to a denial that one possessed the culpable mental state alleged.

The one point worth discussing is mistakes regarding the content of the criminal law itself. How should we regard those who claim 'I didn't know it was a crime to *X*'?

For almost all crimes, awareness of or even negligence regarding the existence of the crime is not an element of the crime.[39] And that is surely justifiable for conduct that evidences moral culpability apart from its illegality, for reasons discussed above regarding the principle of legality. One is culpable and deserving of punishment for purposely, knowingly, or recklessly killing, injuring, raping, or taking the property of another, at least in the absence of a good excuse or justification, even if one is unaware that such conduct is legally proscribed.

On the other hand, much conduct that is criminal is immoral only because it has been legally proscribed. Although it may be morally wrong for me not to pay my fair

---

[38] One can, of course, act purposely with respect to *F* or *L*, even if one mistakenly believes that one's act will not produce *F* or *L*, if it is one's conscious object in acting that *F* or *L* be produced, and one also believes that one is increasing the chance that *F* or *L* will be produced, though obviously not to greater than 50 per cent. And recklessness only requires belief in a risk of sufficient magnitude to be unjustifiable, not that the belief regarding magnitude be correct.

[39] See Model Penal Code, § 2.02(9).

share of taxes to the federal government, it is not morally wrong for me not to pay 37 per cent of my marginal income to the federal government in taxes except in so far as that has been made the tax rate by law. Likewise, it may be morally wrong for me to harm the environment in adding on to my house; but it is only morally wrong for me not to file an environmental impact statement if such a statement is legally required as part of a coordinated effort to protect the environment.

In cases in which the moral wrongness of conduct depends on its having been legally prohibited, those who are non-culpably ignorant of the legal prohibition do not evidence culpability and hence negative desert by such conduct. Criminal law doctrine, therefore, which generally refuses to recognize ignorance of criminal law as defeating criminal liability unless awareness of the law is explicitly made an element of the crime, must therefore be reformed for many crimes if punishment for their violation is to be deserved.

One final note about mistakes. Sometimes proof of a mistake will show that the accused did not culpably commit the crime for which he is charged, but, had things been as he believed them to be, he would have culpably committed a different crime. If a hunter, believing he is hunting deer out of season, shoots at and kills what he believes to be a deer, but what turns out to be a human being, he may not have committed a culpable homicide, but he may have *attempted* to violate the law regulating the deer-hunting season. In other words, his *exculpatory mistake* regarding homicide may turn out to be an *inculpatory mistake* regarding attempted hunting out of season. And it is to the topic of attempts that I now turn.

2.5 The Completed Attempt as the Sole Touchstone of Negative Desert

A completed attempt to commit a crime occurs either when the actor, acting with the purpose (conscious object) that a forbidden result occur, engages in conduct that he believes will make that result more likely to occur without further conduct on his part; when the actor believes that a forbidden result will almost certainly result from his conduct; or when the actor believes that the conduct he believes he is engaging in is forbidden. Put more succinctly, one commits a completed attempt when one engages in conduct such that, if the facts are as one believes them to be or as one hopes them to be, one will have committed a crime.[40] A completed attempt is distinguished from a successful crime by virtue of the failure of the intended or contemplated result to occur or a mistake regarding the forbidden nature of the conduct. If defendant fires a bullet at victim, desiring to kill him, he has committed murder if the victim dies but a completed attempted murder if the victim lives. If defendant puts what he

---

[40] See e.g. Model Penal Code, § 5.01(1)(a), (b).

believes is a fatal dose of arsenic in victim's drink and leaves the scene, expecting the victim to consume the drink, then whether or not he desires victim's death, he has committed an attempted knowing homicide if the substance is not arsenic but something harmless. And if defendant steals what he believes is a $10,000 painting from victim, but the painting is only worth $100, defendant has attempted grand theft but only successfully committed petty theft.

In all cases of completed attempts, the defendant has acted culpably. Whether or not he intends to go further than he has gone, he has surely gone far enough to be culpable. Indeed, because he will already be fully culpable for a successful crime if the result he hopes for occurs, or if his beliefs about the nature of his conduct, its effects, and the surrounding circumstances turn out to be correct, *and since success at this point is out of his control and cannot therefore affect his culpability*, he is perforce culpable for his completed attempt.

What is true of completed attempts is also true of reckless acts. The culpability of reckless acts is exhausted in the commission of them. It is unaffected by whether the culpable level of risk that defendant believes he is taking turns out to be lower than the actual risk of one—in those cases where the act results in a forbidden harm—or higher than the actual risk of zero—in those cases where the reckless act causes no harm.

Having defined a completed attempt, I turn now to four theoretical issues that arise from the centrality I have given it. First, does one deserve more punishment for a successful crime than from the completed attempt alone? Secondly, do *incomplete* attempts deserve punishment, and if not, how should various inchoate crimes be dealt with? (Such crimes include conspiracy, solicitation, and crimes defined in terms of 'committing crime *A* with the intent to commit crime *B*'.) And relatedly, how should complicity in others' crimes be defined if incomplete attempts are not culpable?

Thirdly, how should we regard those whose completed attempt involves a criminal prohibition that is the product of their imagination—what is usually termed a 'legally impossible' attempt? And fourthly, if successful crimes *do* merit greater punishment than completed attempts, what kinds of theoretical issues must be confronted that are otherwise obviated by equating the desert of attempts and successes?

2.5.1 *Should Success Matter to Punishment?*

Completed attempts as opposed to successful crimes involve a divergence between what the actor subjectively believes or hopes is the case and what objectively occurs. Some attempt theorists quarrel with making attempts so subjective, so dependent on what the actor believes he is doing rather than what he is actually doing. I hold, however, that 'objective' theories of attempts —those that require that the criminality of the attempt be somehow 'manifest' apart from the actor's state of mind—are incoherent and incapable of non-arbitrary articulation.[41]

---

[41] See Larry Alexander, 'Inculpatory and Exculpatory Mistakes and the Fact/Law Distinction: An Essay in Memory of Myke Bayles', *Law & Philosophy*, 12 (1993), 33, 65–7.

The other great divide among criminal law theorists is over whether successful crimes deserve more punishment than attempted crimes. Just as I have stated, against those who favour an objective account of attempts, that I believe all completed attempts, as I have defined them, display culpability meriting punishment—and just as I shall argue below that *only* completed attempts, and not incomplete ones, should be punished[42]—I argue that completed attempts are all that should be punished in the sense that they should not be punished less than the completed crimes they attempt.

The argument for this position is straightforward.[43] The result of one's completed attempts—whether it turns out to be a successful crime—is out of one's control once one has completed the attempt. The distinction between a completed attempt and a successful crime is therefore a matter of luck. Luck cannot affect culpability. And culpability is all that affects negative desert.

Two identical defendants, D_1 and D_2, fire at two victims, V_1 and V_2, intending to kill them. V_1 has, unbeknownst to D_1, a Bible in his pocket that absorbs the bullet, or a very strong constitution, whereas V_2 does not. V_1 lives, and V_2 dies. The distinction between D_1's attempt and D_2's success is one of resulting luck, not culpability. The same is the case where both D_1 and D_2 believe they are exceeding the speed limit, but D_1's speedometer is broken while D_2's is not, and only D_2 is actually exceeding the speed limit. Again, the difference between D_1 and D_2 is solely a matter of luck, not culpability.

Those who believe that successful crimes should be punished more than completed attempts, at least if they believe successful crimes *deserve* more punishment, do not deny that successful crimes and completed attempts are equally culpable. Rather, they argue that wrongdoing itself, in addition to culpability, bears on negative desert. They admit that wrongdoing in the absence of culpability (a non-culpable accident, for example) is inert regarding desert. But when culpability is present, they argue, wrongdoing (success) increases negative desert.

As far as I can see, however, they have only two arguments for this, one positive and one negative. The positive argument is that morality enjoins us not to *do* wrong rather than not to *try* to do wrong, or not to act *thinking* that we are doing wrong. So only wrong*doing* violates moral maxims.

I believe that this argument is ultimately irrelevant even if true. For it is admitted that wrongdoing does not merit punishment in the absence of culpability. And our culpability reflects all that we can control regarding compliance with the maxims of morality. If wrongdoing is inert in terms of desert in the absence of culpability, it is a mystery how it is energized if, through luck, it coexists with culpability.

The negative argument is that even if wrongdoing is a matter of luck, so too is culpability. The actor's character, that disposes him to attempt a crime, may be due to his

42 See Sect. 2.5.2 below.
43 The discussion in this section draws heavily on Larry Alexander, 'Crime and Culpability', *Journal of Contemporary Legal Issues*, 5 (1994), 1.

(constitutive) luck in terms of genetics and environment. Likewise, the actor's finding himself in a situation that triggers his criminal dispositions may be a matter of (circumstantial) luck, as when one would-be thief finds himself penniless and in the presence of another's jewellery, while another would-be thief wins the lottery and is never tempted to steal.

It is true that one's character and circumstances are in significant part matters of luck. There is a difference, however, between constitutive and circumstantial luck on the one hand and the result luck that distinguishes attempts and successes on the other. The premise of culpability is that, within limits, one can control and is morally responsible for resisting the dispositions of one's character and the temptations of one's circumstances. Of course, this topic is at the core of the free will/determinism debates. But short of rejecting moral responsibility and hence culpability and negative desert altogether, the retributivist's assumption is that inborn character and circumstances are not destiny, and that even if choices are generally predictable, one can choose against character and temptation and is appropriately deemed morally responsible therefor.

Result luck is a different matter. Because it is not a matter of what we choose to do, but a matter of whether our choices succeed, it is beyond our control in a way our choices are not.

2.5.2 Incomplete Attempts and Inchoate Crimes[44]

An incomplete attempt occurs when an actor intends to commit a completed attempt in the future and has taken some steps short of, but in the direction of, committing that completed attempt. Those steps may or may not be completed crimes in themselves. Thus, someone who lies in wait for a victim, intending to assault or kill him, has committed an incomplete attempt of assault or homicide. Someone who enters a dwelling without consent, intending to steal its contents, has committed an incomplete attempt of theft. In the latter case, but not the former, the act committed (unauthorized entry of the building) is itself a crime (trespass). Moreover, the combination of that crime and the incomplete attempt is deemed to be a distinct crime (burglary). Everything I have to say against criminalizing incomplete attempts applies full force to crimes like burglary which are of the form 'commits crime A with the intent to commit crime B'.

My case against incomplete attempts as culpable acts deserving of punishment is this. Forming an intention to commit a culpable act, even when coupled with taking steps in that direction, although it frequently reflects a character flaw, is not itself a culpable act. It seems to be much closer to an evil thought, over which one has no control, than to a culpable act, over which one does. It may be formed with varying degrees of resolve. It may be conditioned, either explicitly or implicitly, on various

---

[44] The discussion in this section draws heavily on Larry Alexander and Kimberly D. Kessler, 'Mens Rea and Inchoate Crimes', *Journal of Criminal Law and Criminology*, 87 (1997), 1138.

circumstances being present at the time of execution that may range from highly probable to highly improbable. ('I will not rob the bank tomorrow if I win the lottery tonight'; 'If I discover my spouse to be unfaithful, I will beat her up'; etc.) And there is always the possibility that between the time the intention is formed and the time it is to be executed, one will renounce the intent. Until the time the incomplete attempt becomes a completed one, the actor is in complete control and has not (and does not believe he has) increased the risk of harm to the victim (though he believes that he *will* do so in the future).

A related point is that the circumstances that will obtain at the time of the completed attempt are opaque at the time of the incomplete attempt. Suppose Adam intends to have sex with Lolita, who, unbeknownst to Adam, is under age. Suppose Adam takes Lolita to a motel, and suppose taking her to the motel with the intent to have sex with her is a sufficient step to count as an incomplete attempt to have sex with her. Has Adam committed an attempted statutory rape of Lolita? It is possible that he would not have discovered her age between the time at which he entered the motel and the time at which he would have had sex with her (or completed an attempt to have sex). On the other hand, it is possible that Adam would have discovered her age in that time period, in which event he might have decided against sex or else decided to commit statutory rape. At the point of the supposed incomplete attempt, at which point he could be arrested, how this will play out is uncertain. And the same is true of all incomplete attempts, including the intended crimes that are part of such incomplete attempt crimes as burglary. (Suppose Adam breaks into Lolita's house intending to have forcible sex with her if she is wearing a red dress, and intending to steal any Picassos she possesses, though he thinks it unlikely she possesses any.)

Perhaps the opacity problem can be averted if we require that the actor who commits an incomplete attempt exhibit insufficient concern at the time of the incomplete attempt. Nevertheless, because the intent to commit a crime in the future is hard to distinguish from a mere desire, the existence of which is not subject to the actor's control; because it is backed by varying degrees of resolve; because it is conditioned on facts that may be of any degree of likelihood; because it is opaque to the circumstances that will obtain at the time of execution; and most of all, because its execution remains subject to the control of the agent, I believe that incomplete attempts are not themselves culpable acts. (If incomplete attempts were culpable acts, they, unlike completed attempts, *would* merit less punishment than successes.) Incomplete attempts should not be crimes. And crimes such as burglary that have incomplete attempts as part of their definition should likewise be abolished.

For similar reasons, crimes or forms of criminality that involve the acts of others—solicitation, conspiracy, and complicity—which usually rest on the actor's intent that others commit a crime in the future,[45] should be rethought.[46] If someone else's crime

---

[45] See Model Penal Code, §§ 2.06(3)(a); 5.02(1); 5.03(1).
[46] See Larry Alexander, 'Insufficient Concern', 944–7.

is involved—as it always is in solicitation and complicity, and as it sometimes is in conspiracy—the basis for the actor's criminal liability is the recklessness of creating an unjustified risk that the other person will commit a crime.[47] His purpose that such a crime be committed, which is usually required under current law, is only evidence that the risk created is unjustifiable for lack of a justifying reason. Given the opacity of the circumstances in which the future crime will be committed, the actor should be deemed reckless based on his assessment of the likelihood of various crimes he has fostered. His liability should not be dependent upon what the others in fact do, but should be complete at the point he gives aid or encouragement. At that point, he has completed his recklessness. (Legitimate merchants who suspect their customers of intending to commit crimes with the merchandise or services provided might nevertheless be deemed not to be reckless as a matter of law.)

If the plan in a conspiracy is that the actor himself will carry out the agreed upon crime, the actor should not be liable at that point. The actor has not increased the risk of his own future criminality because he retains full control over it, unlike the case where he induces another to commit the crime.

2.5.3 *Legally Impossible Attempts*[48]

I have defined completed attempts, which I regard as the bases of all negative desert, as conduct in which if things were as the actor believes or hopes them to be, he will have committed a successful crime or created a wrongful risk. What if, however, the actor's mistake that prevents the successful crime is a mistake of positive law?

I should just state that many mistakes of positive law pose no difficulty. Suppose the actor makes a mistake of property law and takes a piece of property that is legally abandoned but that the actor believes is still the property of its former owner. The actor has committed a completed crime of theft despite his mistake of law. When the mistake concerns the law other than the criminal law under which the actor is being prosecuted for attempt, it does not negate the attempt.

The problem of legal impossibility is best illustrated by the chestnut hypothetical of two hunters who go deer hunting on 15 October, the first day of the deer-hunting season. Mr Fact knows that the deer-hunting season begins on 15 October, but he believes he is hunting out of season because he has misread the calendar and believes that today is 14 October. Mr Law, on the other hand, knows that today is 15 October but believes the hunting season begins on 16 October. Both believe that they are violating the law. But orthodoxy has it that only Mr Fact can be convicted of an attempt.

The problem is that if we punish Mr Law, we are apparently allowing him not only to imagine that he is violating a law but also to imagine the law that he is violating. But

---

[47] See ibid.; Sanford H. Kadish, 'Reckless Complicity', *Journal of Criminal Law & Criminology*, 87 (1997), 369.

[48] The discussion in this section draws heavily on Larry Alexander, 'Inculpatory and Exculpatory Mistakes', 43–70.

if we do that, what culpability shall we attach to his act? Is violating a hypothetical 16 October hunting season as culpable as violating the actual 15 October hunting season? And what if someone believes, erroneously, that it is a crime to dance on Sundays and proceeds to do so. How culpable is such a person? Can he be deemed to have committed 'attempted illegal dancing' when there is no crime of illegal dancing and no punishment prescribed therefor?

We can see why the legally impossible attempt is deemed unpunishable. On the other hand, Mr Law surely appears to be as culpable as Mr Fact. Moreover, because mistakes of law can be translated into mistakes of fact—mistakes about those facts that constitute the law, such as what words the statute contains, what those words mean, and so forth—the line between mistakes of law and mistakes of fact can be effaced. Suppose, for example, that the hunting law is that one may hunt deer any day that a green flag is flown from the fish and game headquarters, and one may not hunt deer any day a red flag is flown. Mr Fact—or is it Mr Law?—is colour-blind and perceives the green flag as red. He none the less goes hunting, believing that he is acting illegally. Is his attempt legally impossible or only factually impossible? Or consider that every mistake of fact can be translated into one of law. Mr Fact believes (mistakenly) that 'it is *illegal* to hunt *today*'. The person who believes he is firing a loaded gun at someone, when in fact the gun is unloaded, believes (mistakenly) 'it is *illegal* to do what I am doing'. And so for every attempt.

There is a deep puzzle here. On the one hand, we do not want to say that anyone who mistakenly believes he is violating a law that is the product of his imagination has committed an attempt. On the other, all attempts involve mistakes that can be cast as mistakes of law. And surely the Mr Laws of the world can be as culpable and hence deserving of punishment as the Mr Facts.

Perhaps what distinguishes our hypothetical would-be scoff-law who dances on Sunday from Mr Law is that in the latter case there *is* a law ('no deer hunting until 15 October') that is in the 'neighbourhood' of the law that Mr Law imagines ('no deer hunting until 16 October'). That is not a very robust distinction, being one only of degree and not kind. But it may be the best we can do if we wish to preserve the tie between culpability for attempting *mala prohibita* crimes and the actual existence of those crimes.

My colleague Michael Moore disagrees strenuously with all this.[49] Moore distinguishes those facts that go to the meaning of the law from those facts that go to its extension. If one makes an inculpatory mistake regarding a meaning fact, there is no attempt liability. The act-type that one believes one is committing is not illegal, even though one believes—because of mistakes of fact that bear on the law's meaning—that it is illegal. The act-type that Mr Fact believes he is committing—hunting on 14 October—is illegal. That of Mr Law—hunting on 15 October—is not, *even though*

[49] The following is based on conversations with Michael Moore.

what led Mr Law to believe that it was illegal was a mistake of fact (e.g. that the number 5 in the statute's date of 15 October was a 6).

Moore's argument rests heavily on the ability to distinguish facts that go to the law's meaning from those that go to its extension. Moore would, for example, in my green flag v. red flag hypothetical, describe the mistake—perceiving a green flag to be red and then believing that one was hunting illegally—as one regarding extension, and the act-type—hunting on a day with a red flag—as illegal. But could not the law be characterized as 'it's illegal to hunt today' and the mistake regarding the flag's colour as a meaning mistake rather than an extension mistake? And could not the act-type that the hunter believes he is committing be described as 'hunting on a no-hunting day'?

Consider the analogous case of *Larkin v Grendel's Den, Inc.*,[50] in which the law effectively delegated to churches the power to proscribe bars locating within a certain distance of their premises. Suppose an establishment owner believes erroneously that a church next door has objected to his opening a bar, but he does so anyway. Has he made a mistake of law (it's illegal to open a bar next to this church) or only one of extension? Does the law consist of only the facts regarding what the legislature enacted, or does it include the facts regarding what its delegate, the church, has declared? Is the relevant act-type 'opening a bar near this church' (not illegal) or 'opening a bar near a church that has objected' (illegal), given that the bar owner could describe his act both ways?

Finally, Moore's approach requires a theory of individuating laws, even though most would consider individuation to be a matter of perspicuous elaboration rather than one with substantive implications. Consider a case that is the converse of *Regina v Smith (David)*.[51] In the original case, the defendant, enraged at his landlord, stripped his apartment of panelling that he had earlier installed. Charged with wilful destruction of his landlord's property, he defended successfully on the ground that he had not known the law of fixtures that made the panelling the property of the landlord and thus believed he was destroying his own property. Suppose we convert the case from one of exculpatory mistake to one of inculpatory mistake. The defendant believes the panelling *is* the landlord's (he studied fixtures in Property class). But, unbeknownst to him, the jurisdiction has changed that law, and the panelling is now regarded as his property, not his landlord's. So he has not committed the successful crime that he intended of destroying his landlord's property. Has he committed an attempt?

On Moore's account, the defendant could describe his act-type as 'destroying the property of another' (illegal) or 'destroying property installed on the property of another' (not illegal, but believed to be so because of another mistake regarding the law's meaning). Is his a mistake of the criminal law's meaning or only its extension? Does the criminal law of theft include the law of property or does it not? And why should that matter?

---

[50] 495 U.S. 116 (1982).   [51] 2 Q.B. 354 (1974).

2.5.4 *Rejecting the Equation of Attempts and Successes and the Problem of Proximate Causation*[52]

I have taken the position that culpability is all that matters for gauging retributive desert, and that the criminal law should only be concerned with attempts and subjectively reckless acts, not with whether those acts are objectively wrong or cause harm. If that position is rejected, as it is by all criminal codes and by some criminal law theorists, then those who reject it must confront the problem of proximate causation. That is, once success and not just culpability is deemed a factor in retributive desert, one must distinguish among those whose culpable acts cause prohibited results and ask which of them caused the results in the manner that adds to their negative desert.

What is usually denominated cause-in-fact is not a major theoretical issue. The cause-in-fact inquiry asks merely whether the prohibited result would have ensued had the culpable actor not acted as he did. The answer is usually quite straightforward, except in cases of overdetermination, where it is usually deemed sufficient for extra negative desert that defendant's act be a sufficient cause of the result. (Why being a sufficient cause rather than a necessary one adds to one's negative desert is usually not explained, however.)

The proximate cause inquiry asks who among those culpable actors who have caused the prohibited result in fact should none the less not be deemed to have caused it in the sense that merits negative desert. The latter are those who have not 'proximately caused' the result because the causal chain from their culpable act to the result is of the wrong type to hold them responsible for the result.

There are two principal types of causal chains that raise the issue of proximate causation. One is the deviant causal chain. Here is an illustration. Ed wants to kill Edna and replaces the water in her bedside glass with poison. Edna is awakened by thunder, which also shakes the nightstand, causing the poison to spill. Edna jumps out of bed, slips on the wet spot caused by the spill, hits her head, and dies. Here is another illustration. Ed shoots at Edna, intending to kill her. The bullet misses, ricochets into a chandelier, which falls on Edna and kills her. Or, frightened by the missed shot, Edna rushes from the house and into the street, where she is hit by a car and killed. Or the bullet severely wounds her, and years later she succumbs to an infection that would not have killed her but for her weakened condition.

The other causal chain that raises proximate cause problems is one involving the unplanned intervention of other wrongdoers. Ed shoots at Edna, intending to kill her, and leaves her for dead in a dangerous part of town. She is not in fact dead, but

---

[52] The causation issues that I bypass because of my equation of attempts and successes for purposes of assessing negative desert are discussed usefully and at great length in *Placing Blame*. See also Michael S. Moore, 'Causation and Responsibility', *Social Philosophy & Policy*, 16 (1999), 1. Moore, of course, believes that successes increase negative desert relative to the underlying attempts. Causation, therefore, is a puzzle that he, unlike me, must resolve.

she is later killed by one of the many savage criminals in the neighbourhood where Ed left her, or by the negligence of an employee at the hospital where she is taken.

I do not believe that there is any way satisfactorily to resolve these questions regarding when the actor does or does not merit greater negative desert because of results he has brought about. All answers have the ring of arbitrary *ipse dixits*. And the reason is that the questions are wrongheaded. Results cannot add to culpability, and culpability is all that is material to desert, for the reasons given in the previous discussion of the attempt/success distinction. Because results *cannot* affect desert, it is pointless to ask whether the result is a product of a causal claim so deviant, or so influenced by other factors that it *should not* affect desert.

2.6 The Individuation of Crimes

I have argued that the key to negative desert is the culpable act, whether or not it is objectively wrongful or causes harm. Consider, however, the following examples. Al wants to kill Bob and fires a shot at him on Monday. He misses. On Tuesday, he fires another shot, which also misses. And so on through Saturday. Al has committed six attempted murders. Compare Al with Carl, who attempting to kill Dan, fires all the bullets in his six-shooter in rapid succession. Has Carl committed six attempted murders or only one?

Or consider Ed, who forces sexual intercourse on Fran on Monday, forces fellatio on Felicia on Tuesday, and on. Ed has committed several sex crimes. Suppose, however, that he abducts Fran and then forces her to perform several different sex acts within a short period of time. Has he committed several sex crimes or only one?

Finally, consider George, who every day for ten days removes a $20 bill from Harry's billfold. He has committed ten thefts. Suppose, however, that he removes $200 in one grasp. One $200 theft or ten $20 thefts? Would it matter if he removed the $200 one $20 bill at a time but all within a few seconds?

These examples raise the problem of individuating culpable acts.[53] If we ask how many willed bodily movements have occurred, we find that both Al and Carl have committed six attempted homicides, Ed has committed several sex crimes regardless of the amount of time between them or the number of victims, and George has committed ten thefts if he removes the bills one at a time, whether over ten days or a few seconds, but only one theft if he removes them all at once.

If we think that Al deserves more punishment than Carl, that Ed deserves more punishment if he acts over several days with several victims, and that George deserves more punishment if he acts over several days but not if he removes the money one bill at a time within a few seconds, what explains our intuition? Do we believe that

---

[53] For a useful discussion of crime-individuation premised on act-individuation, see Moore, *Act and Crime*, 305–90.

culpability and hence negative desert are subject to a 'volume discount'?[54] If so, why? Do we perhaps believe that the real basis of desert is character, and that culpable acts are merely evidence of the traits that desert tracks? That might explain why, for example, Carl's firing six shots at once does not seem to be six times as bad as Al's firing one shot.

I believe that the problem of individuation of culpable acts is one that presents difficulties for someone like me, who takes culpable acts to be the basis for negative desert, and who rejects character as the desert basis except in so far as it is manifest in culpable acts. I offer no solution to it here, but invite those who have roughly the same outlook on punishment as I to try their hand at solving it.

2.7 Justification

Scholars and courts have debated a number of issues concerning justification defences: what marks the distinction between a justification and an excuse? When he commits what is otherwise a crime, what mental state must the defendant have regarding a justification in order to be able to claim it? Is (the absence of) justification just part of the definition of a crime, or are justifications best conceptualized as distinct from the crimes they override? What are the moral bases of such justifications as 'lesser evils' and self-defence?

I am going to offer some answers to these questions, although without all the necessary supporting arguments. I hope that the coherence and clarity my answers provide will be weighty enough to make up for the argumentative shortfall.

First, I think it is most perspicuous to view justifications as merely exceptions to crimes. In other words, one can think of a crime on the model of 'do not do X unless either Y or Z'. Y and Z qualify the general injunction to refrain from X. Exception Y might refer to circumstances in which the normal harm associated with X is not present. Exception Z, on the other hand, might refer to circumstances in which the harm associated with X exists but is less than the harm of refraining from X. Although both Y and Z are exceptions to the crime of Xing, Z-type exceptions are the ones we think of as 'justifications'. None the less, like exceptions of type Y, justifications (type Z) can be written into the criminal law as qualifying exceptions and often are. Even when they are separately expressed, they are functionally equivalent to exceptions written into the criminal prohibitions themselves.[55]

Secondly, when one commits what is otherwise a crime in circumstances in which a justification is present, one has committed no wrong and caused no prohibited

---

[54] I owe this characterization to Leo Katz.

[55] For this reason, I concur in the Model Penal Code's decision to treat (absence of) justification as a matter that the prosecution must prove beyond a reasonable doubt and on which the defendant merely has the burden of producing evidence. See Model Penal Code, §§ 1.12(2)(a); 1.13(9)(c), (10). See also n. 23 above.

result. If one acted unaware of the presence of the justification, then one has in effect attempted a crime but has not succeeded in committing one, any more than would be the case if one were unaware of an excepting circumstance that rendered one's normally harmful act harmless.[56] Moreover, because attempts and successes, being equally culpable, merit equal retributive desert, nothing turns on the question whether the unknowingly justified actor should be deemed to have committed only an attempt. (I suspect that the intractable nature of the argument over whether the unknowingly justified actor has committed a successful crime or only an attempt is due in part to the fact that there *is* a harm, albeit not a net harm, and in part to the view that successes and attempts should receive different punishments.) And the actor who is aware of the justifying circumstances but unmotivated by them—he would have committed the crime in the absence of the justification—should be deemed not to have committed (or attempted) the crime. He has had the good (from his viewpoint) circumstantial luck of being able to do what he would normally be prohibited from doing. And just like the billionaire who has the character of a thief but who has the good luck to be able to make money without stealing, or the person who enjoys killing and who gets the job of executioner, the justified actor who would have acted without the justification or who takes advantage of the justification in order to act on disreputable reasons does not commit a culpable act, no matter how unsavoury his character.

Thirdly, because justifications are exceptions to crimes—functionally built into the definitions of crimes—one who mistakenly but non-culpably believes he is justified has not committed the crime, but only because he lacks the *mens rea*.[57] Because, however, he has engaged in the prohibited conduct or caused the prohibited result, he is *not* a *justified* actor. Rather, he is on a par with the actor who has an excuse. This is important as a theoretical matter because it precludes a clash of justified actors. A justified actor might clash with an excused or otherwise non-culpable actor, but not with another justified actor.

Fourthly, unlike justifications, excuses are not exceptions to crimes. Rather, they undermine culpability, either by showing that the actor is not a rational agent and thus not morally responsible, or by showing that the actor's personal reasons for acting, though inadequate to justify his act from an impartial perspective, none the less diminish his culpability therefor because ordinary actors would find those reasons

---

[56] For a sample of the debate over the unknowingly justified actor, see Heidi M. Hurd, 'Justification and Excuse, Wrongdoing and Culpability', *Notre Dame Law Review*, 74 (1999), 1551; Paul H. Robinson, 'Competing Theories of Justification: Deeds vs. Reasons', in *Harm and Culpability*, ed. A. P. Simester and A. T. H. Smith (1996); Paul H. Robinson, 'A Theory of Justification: Societal Harm as a Prerequisite for Criminal Liability', *University of California at Los Angeles Law Review*, 23 (1975), 266; George Fletcher, 'The Right Deed for the Wrong Reason: A Reply to Mr. Robinson', *University of California at Los Angeles Law Review*, 23 (1974), 1269.

[57] That is, a non-culpable mistake that the factual grounds exist for a justification negates *mens rea*. A mistake regarding whether those grounds are legally sufficient to justify violation is tantamount to a mistake of law.

compelling. Obviously, the factors that determine excuses are personal to each actor and can shield only that actor from liability. On the other hand, if an act is justified, it is not a crime for anyone.

Fifthly, the substantive reasons that justify crimes are on a par with the substantive reasons for the prohibitions they qualify. Because the latter belong to the special part of the criminal law, justifying reasons also should be considered under the special part rather than the general part. None the less, I shall here consider two basic justifications, one that qualifies all crimes—the lesser evils defence—and one that qualifies the crimes of battery and homicide—the defence of self, others, and property against aggressors.

2.7.1 *The Lesser Evils Defence*

The lesser evils defence is a free-floating, residual justification that attaches to every crime (although in some jurisdictions, not to homicide). If the harm sought to be avoided by the criminal act is greater than the harm the act would cause, the actor is permitted to choose the criminal act (or what would otherwise be the criminal act).[58] (The justifications are always permissions to do what is otherwise criminal, not requirements to do so. This is in keeping with the criminal law's general refusal to punish omissions.)

What counts as a 'lesser evil' is not legislatively specified but is left for case by case development. There are two aspects of the defence, however, that are interesting as a theoretical matter. First, despite its phrasing, the lesser evils defence does not necessarily embody a utilitarian social philosophy in which averting a greater harm always justifies committing a lesser one. The defence is perfectly consistent with deontological constraints that place emphasis on how a greater harm is averted. Thus, take the classic pair of hypotheticals in which the taking of one life can save five—the Trolley problem and the Surgeon problem. In the Trolley problem, someone can divert a runaway trolley from the main track, on which five workers, oblivious to the trolley, are working, to a siding on which one worker is working. The general consensus, even among deontologists, is that it is permissible to divert the trolley. In the Surgeon problem, a surgeon can harvest five organs from a healthy and unsuspecting patient and transplant them to five patients who will otherwise die. Deontologists deny that the surgeon may do so. The difference between the two cases for the deontologist is that in Surgeon, but not in Trolley, the one victim is being 'used' to save the five.[59]

Now the lesser evils defence is surely consistent with this deontological distinction. All one has to say is that in Surgeon, the killing of the patient is not in the appropriate sense a 'lesser evil' than the death of the five, even though it is a 'lesser harm'.

The second interesting theoretical point about the lesser evils defence is that as it is usually formulated, it does not apply if it is clear that the legislature, in prohibiting

---

[58] See e.g. Model Penal Code, § 3.02(1).
[59] See generally F. M. Kamm, *Morality, Mortality*, ii (1996), 143–71.

the conduct in question, considered the type of harm that violating the prohibition might prevent and rejected an exception for that type of harm.[60] Thus, if the legislature has considered the Trolley exception to the prohibition of homicide and explicitly or implicitly rejected it, then one who diverts the trolley cannot invoke the defence.

The notion of an implicit rejection of an exception is more problematic than it may appear. The prohibitions of the criminal law are rules, and like all rules, they are blunt—over and underinclusive relative to their background justifications. When a legislature promulgates the rule 'Do not kill', it presumably is aware that the rule is or may be over and underinclusive. When a defendant, therefore, invokes the lesser evils defence and claims the rule would be overinclusive in his case, is it open to argue that by issuing a blunt rule, the legislature has implicitly rejected such an exception as he is claiming? There is a deep philosophical issue here regarding the compatibility of rules and implicit exceptions based on background morality.[61]

2.7.2 Defence of Self, Others, and Property Against Aggressors

It is a universal defence to battery that one was defending one's property against a thief. And it is a universal defence to homicide that one was defending one's person or that of another against seriously violent aggression.

The philosophically interesting aspects of these defensive force defences are, first, to what extent they should be hemmed in by requirements of retreat, proportional force, and imminence of danger, and, secondly, to what extent they should be viewed as justifications rather than excuses.[62]

Although I cannot spell out the complete argument here, I believe these two philosophical puzzles are interdependent. Put succinctly, in cases where the aggressor is not culpable—lacks *mens rea*, has an excuse, is an infant, and so forth—defensive force should be conceptualized as an excuse and assimilated into the general excuse of duress. Moreover, in order to be excused, the defendant must not have been able to retreat or otherwise cede a right protecting a lesser interest than the aggressor loses if defendant employs defensive force. For it is not a lesser evil—the paradigm for all true justifications—that a non-culpable aggressor suffer a harm in order to avert a lesser harm to the one employing defensive force (or to someone he is protecting). And even when the defender has no alternative but to take the life of the non-culpable aggressor in order to save his own, this is not a case of choosing the lesser evil. Rather, it is an excusable tragic choice.

---

[60] See Model Penal Code, § 3.02(1)(c).

[61] See Larry Alexander and Emily Sherwin, *The Rule of Rules: Morality, Rules, and the Dilemmas of Law* (Durham: Duke University Press, 2001), ch. 4.

[62] The issues in this section are discussed extensively in Larry Alexander, 'A Unified Defense of Preemptive Self-Protection', *Notre Dame Law Review*, 74 (1999), 1475, 1476–86, 1494–505; Larry Alexander, 'Self-Defense, Justification, and Excuse', *Philosophy & Public Affairs*, 22 (1993), 53.

On the other hand, when the aggressor is culpable—and even if the aggressors out-number the defenders—the notion that harming or killing the aggressor(s) is a lesser evil seems more palatable. Indeed, in cases of culpable aggression, what is controversial is not whether one is justified in using force to defend oneself or others. Instead, what is controversial are the standard requirements for employing justified defensive force: retreat must be impossible and, what is equivalent, the force employed be pro-portional to the harm threatened. (These are equivalent because both retreat and proportional force require the defender to cede his rights: if the defender retreats, he cedes the right to remain where he was; if he must use the energy and suffer the pain of bare knuckles rather than spare both with a gun, he cedes the right not to be com-pelled to expend energy and suffer pain; and if proportional force will be unavailing, he must cede the right the aggressor is violating. Typical examples of the latter are thefts and trespasses at some distance from the owner, who can only prevent them with a gun, or minor batteries inflicted by, say, a large man on a small woman, who likewise can prevent them only with deadly force.) Where the aggressor is a culpable aggressor, these limitations on defensive use of force are questionable. Surely it would be permissible to make even minor crimes extremely dangerous for culpable actors—for example, by surrounding one's apple tree with a shark-filled moat, with appropriate warnings posted. With non-culpable aggressors, however, the use of force to resist is not a 'lesser evil' than suffering the harm, retreating, or employing only proportional force, and appears to be at best excusable rather than justifiable.[63]

I should point out that my reference to 'culpable aggressors' is in tension with, if not contradictory of, what I said regarding incomplete attempts. I deemed the latter to be non-culpable because the actor has not yet created a danger to others' interests and is still in control over whether such danger is created. Although the actor's pre-sent state of mind may exhibit 'insufficient concern', his actions as yet have not (as least as he understands his action and their risks to others).

All defensive force, however, is pre-emptive: it occurs *before* the act to which it is an anticipatory response. Therefore, the 'aggressor' at which it is aimed will at most have committed an incomplete attempt. (If he has committed a completed attempt, then the use of force against him is not defensive.)

So in what sense is a culpable aggressor 'culpable' if he has not committed a com-pleted attempt, and if incomplete attempts are not culpable acts? He may have a bad character, and he may intend harm, but he is not a culpable *actor*.

If forced to choose between changing my position on incomplete attempts and changing my position on responses to 'culpable aggressors', I would change the latter and treat all pre-emptive defensive force as excusable rather than as justifiable. On the other hand, one could attempt to reconcile the positions by arguing that the culpable

---

[63] These arguments about defensive force do, of course, turn on substantive values and thus might be considered more appropriately discussed in the context of the Special Part of the criminal law. I take them up here only because self-defence is usually discussed under the General Part. I owe this point to Mitchell Berman.

aggressor *is* a culpable actor, *not with respect to the crime he is intending, but with respect to unjustifiably creating in his victims or their defenders a fear of attack.*

Finally, *when* the attack by the aggressor will occur if not pre-empted by defensive attack is relevant only in so far as it bears on the probability of the attack and on avenues of retreat and alternative modes of defence. The imminence of the attack has no independent relevance.

2.8 Excuse

One who claims an excuse for what would otherwise be culpable conduct may be asserting either that he is not a rational actor and thus not morally responsible, or that the choice to refrain from a crime or attempt was difficult in a sense that lessens or eliminates his culpability therefor. The three main excuse defences that I shall examine are insanity, intoxication, and duress. A fourth, infancy, is similar to insanity in that it amounts to a claim that the offender is not a morally responsible actor because of a condition—here, immaturity—that impairs his assessment of reasons or his volitional control.

2.8.1 *Insanity*

The insanity defence usually requires that the offender prove that at the time he acted, he had a mental disease or defect that affected either his ability to understand the nature of his conduct or his volitional control of it.[64] The central questions regarding the defence are whether the cognitive prong of the defence adds anything to the ordinary *mens rea* requirement (especially if negligence is omitted) and whether the volitional prong refers to anything real—that is, whether there are 'irresistible impulses'.[65]

The first question is, can one possess the mental states of purpose, knowledge, or recklessness—what I have unified as 'insufficient concern'—and yet because of mental disease fail to appreciate the nature of his conduct in a way that renders him non-culpable?[66] If not, then the cognitive prong of the insanity defence is superfluous given the *mens rea* requirement. I take no stand on this question other than to point out that even if it is possible to act with *mens rea* but be non-culpable for cognitive reasons, the requirement that those cognitive reasons be tied to mental disease seems gratuitous. Even if all such cognitive impairments will be so tied, why make that a requirement? Perhaps the mental disease serves as evidence that the claim of

---

[64] See e.g. Model Penal Code, § 4.01(1).

[65] See Stephen J. Morse, 'Rationality and Responsibility', *Southern California Law Review*, 74 (2000), 251, 256–8.

[66] See Schopp, *Automatism, Insanity, and the Psychology of Criminal Responsibility*, 27–70.

cognitive impairment is not bogus, and the absence of mental disease triggers a con-clusive presumption that there was no impairment.

Similar questions can be asked about the volitional prong. Are there in fact actors who are so impulsive that they cannot be deemed responsible and hence culpable? And if so, what does the requirement of mental disease add except evidence to but-tress the impulsivity claim?

Finally, because the presence of a voluntary culpable act is normally part of the prosecution's burden of proof (beyond a reasonable doubt), why should insanity be a defence at all rather than merely a denial of the charge?[67] Although we would expect a defendant who suffers from a mental disease that undermines his culpability to produce affirmative evidence of that fact—we do not expect prosecutors to *disprove* unraised claims like insanity—this 'burden of production' is different from the bur-den of proof. The latter is on the prosecution with respect to all elements of crimes, and a culpable act should be an element of all crimes (in my view, really the only ele-ment).

A final issue best dealt with in connection with the insanity defence is whether psy-chopaths, who in one sense understand perfectly well the nature of their criminal acts and have an otherwise normal ability to control their impulses, should none the less be regarded as not morally responsible.[68] The basis for such a conclusion would be that psychopaths do not understand moral reasons *qua* moral reasons, and that such understanding is essential to culpability. The proponents of this position must not only show that psychopaths lack such understanding, and that such understanding is necessary for culpability. They must also show that psychopaths differ in kind rather than degree from ordinary culpable actors, or that failure to understand a moral rea-son as a distinctive type of reason is different from the failure to understand the *weights* of moral reasons relative to other reasons. I leave it to others whether those claims can be vindicated.

2.8.2 *Intoxication*

I shall be quite brief here. Although intoxication is traditionally listed as an exculpa-tory excuse, it is not. Rather, intoxication functions in the criminal law as an *in*culpa-tory factor, not an exculpatory one. Involuntary intoxication is immaterial to culpability itself, though it may result in an actor's being unaware that he is creating an unjustifiable risk and thus will explain the actor's lack of culpability.

Voluntary intoxication, on the other hand, can only increase criminal liability, not decrease it. Ordinarily, if an actor commits an act unaware that he is thereby imposing an unjustifiable risk of harm or wrongdoing, and the cause of his being thus unaware is voluntary intoxication, the law deems him to be guilty of reckless

---

[67] See n. 55 above.
[68] See e.g. Peter Arenella, 'Convicting the Morally Blameless: Reassessing the Relationship between Legal and Moral Accountability', *University of California at Los Angeles Law Review*, 39 (1992), 1511.

harming or wrongdoing. In other words, his becoming voluntarily intoxicated, although not punishable when it leads to no further harm, substitutes for the actual mental state of recklessness when it does lead to further harm or wrongdoing.[69]

A theoretically preferable course for those like me who would detach desert from results would be to deem voluntary intoxication to be a minor crime in some circumstances (those most likely to lead to further harmful conduct). That might present some insurmountable practical difficulties, but it would at least get rid of the current system in which intoxication may or may not be criminal depending on the luck of the consequences. (The same approach should be taken to those who take actions that they realize create unjustifiable risks that they will later cause harm non-culpably—those who undergo hypnosis by evil hypnotists, drive cars knowing of their susceptibility to seizures, or put themselves in circumstances they know can trigger uncontrollable impulses to harm.)

2.8.3 *Duress*

The insanity excuse looks at impairments of the actor that undermine moral responsibility. The excuse of duress, on the other hand, looks at the actor's circumstances and asks whether they rendered the choice to avoid otherwise criminal conduct so difficult for him that his culpability for choosing the criminal conduct is diminished partially or entirely. In cases of duress, the actor's circumstances do not *justify* his otherwise criminal choice. The choice is not of a lesser evil, at least not from an impartial standpoint. (If it were, the lesser evils justification would cover it.) Rather, the choice, although not of a lesser evil when everyone's interests are considered impartially (or when everyone's deontological rights are taken into account), *is* of a lesser evil from the standpoint of the actor. The actor gives his life and limb and those of his family more weight relative to the interests of others than they would be given from an impartial point of view. The excuse of duress excuses some actors who show others' interests insufficient concern because their giving their own interests greater concern is understandable and non-culpable.

One philosophical issue for duress is what personal interests of the actor are sufficiently weighty from the personal point of view that they excuse the actor's failure to act on the balance of moral reasons. A clear case in favour of the excuse would be one where the actor violates a deontological constraint but imposes a small harm relative to the one he would otherwise have suffered. Thus, an actor faced with a threat of imminent death unless he steals medicine from a druggist would undoubtedly be afforded the defence. (Whether the threat of death comes from another person, as the defence currently requires, or from natural causes should be irrelevant, a point many critics have made.) Perhaps even Surgeon should be entitled to the defence if the five dying patients he saves are his children.

---

[69] See e.g. Model Penal Code, § 2.08(2).

Another type of case covered by the excuse is one where there are no deontological constraints, the harm the actor imposes on the victim is greater than the threatened harm to the actor or his family that he averts by harming the victim, but the latter harm is none the less of such magnitude that we do not expect anyone except the heroic to submit to it. If, threatened with death by either persons or natural causes, the actor to avert this threat must steer his car in the direction of two innocent children, we expect him to do so even though it is not the morally correct choice. We do not deem him culpable for choosing wrongly in such circumstances.

As I argued above, I believe that all cases of defensive force against unjustified but non-culpable aggressors—whatever the reason they are non-culpable—to the extent such defensive force is itself non-culpable, should be characterized as excusable rather than as justifiable.[70] (I am assuming the lesser evil justification to be unavailable.) Indeed, I think such uses of force fit the paradigm of duress.[71] The person who believes he is going to be shot by gun-toting children who are too young to be morally responsible, by lunatics, or by those who lack *mens rea* (say, because they have been misinformed that the defender is about to blow up a building) is surely facing a threat that makes his use of force excusable, but from an impartial standpoint, the death of the attacker or attackers is not a lesser evil than the actor's injury or death.

The requirements that force the defender to cede certain lesser interests to avoid employing force or deadly force—the retreat and proportionality requirements—work as limitations on the excuse of duress in cases of non-culpable aggression though they ill-fit the use of defensive force against culpable aggressors. Because the defender is not justified, but only excused, in harming the aggressor, he should be faced with a loss as dire as the one he is imposing.

Finally, as I have portrayed it, the defence of duress focuses on rational, not psychological, compulsion. That is, committing the crime under duress is a highly rational choice even if not the morally correct choice; it is not an impulse made irresistible by the circumstances. Some, however, do view duress as tantamount to a claim of irresistible impulse, where the normative issue is whether the defendant's inability to resist the impulse to commit the crime shows a character defect for which he can be blamed (e.g. excessive cowardice). Those who take this view of duress obviously take a character rather than culpable choice approach to negative desert. For those like me who take a culpable choice approach to desert, a truly irresistible impulse, whether or not reflective of a bad character trait (excessive cowardice or greed), is not culpable, although it may reflect, like non-culpable harms committed because of intoxication, prior culpable acts that predictably led to the inability to control the impulse in question.

---

[70] See text following n. 62.   [71] See Larry Alexander, 'A Unified Defense', 1494–8.

3 Criminal Law: The Special Part

This section will be brief relative to the previous one. The special part of the criminal law asks which interests of others are such that one who shows those interests insufficient concern in his acts deserves punishment. And answering *that* question requires doing general normative theory, which is beyond the scope of this entry. There are a few things that can be said about the shape such a normative theory must have to be consistent with the account of the criminal law above.

3.1 Desert-Sensitivity

If a normative theory has no place for desert—as is true, for example, of a thoroughgoing welfarist theory—then it cannot be meshed with an account of the criminal law that takes negative desert as its central organizing feature. In other words, if, as I have argued, criminal law is distinguished by its focus on negative desert, then the normative theory that tells us which interests the criminal law should protect in its special part must be compatible with desert-based punishment. And that is a significant limitation on the range of normative theories available for a theory of the special part.

3.2 Liberal Versus Perfectionist Theories of the Special Part

Perhaps the single most important attempt in the last century to develop a theory of the special part of the criminal law is Joel Feinberg's magisterial four-volume work, *The Moral Limits of the Criminal Law*.[72] Feinberg believes that the criminal law can only legitimately be applied to conduct that causes harm or that causes serious offence. (More on serious offence below.) 'Harm' for this purpose 'refers to those states of set-back interest that are the consequence of wrongful acts or omissions by others'.[73] Thus, 'transitory disappointments, minor physical and mental "hurts", and a miscellany of disliked states of mind', although evils, are not harms for Feinberg because they do not involve setbacks of interests.[74] Nor are setbacks of interests caused by conduct that is morally permissible (such as business competition or legitimate self-defence), or that is consented to by the person whose interests are set

---

[72] Joel Feinberg, *The Moral Limits of the Criminal Law: iv: Harmless Wrongdoing* (1988); Joel Feinberg, *The Moral Limits of the Criminal Law: iii: Harm to Self* (1986); Joel Feinberg, *The Moral Limits of the Criminal Law: ii: Offense to Others* (1985); Joel Feinberg, *The Moral Limits of the Criminal Law: i: Harm to Others* (1984).

[73] Feinberg, *The Moral Limits of the Criminal Law*, i: 215.   [74] ibid. at 215–16.

back.[75] On the other hand, acts that unjustifiably risk harm do fall within the harm principle and can be legitimately punished, as can otherwise harmless acts that cause harm when aggregated.[76]

Not all harms caused by wrongful conduct justify criminal punishment. For example, harms caused by imitative conduct should not be imputed to the conduct imitated for purposes of criminal punishment in the absence of extreme culpability.[77] Moreover, even the harmfulness of conduct is not sufficient for its criminalization: criminalization itself causes harm and cannot be justified unless the harm it causes is less than the harms caused by the conduct criminalized.[78]

Feinberg appears to accept the necessity of immorality for (criminal) illegality. He generally rejects criminal proscription of conduct that is harmful only to those who voluntarily engage in it (legal paternalism) (because they are not wronged).[79] But he rejects the sufficiency of immorality for criminal punishment. If the immoral conduct causes no harm to others, or causes harm to others too minuscule to justify the harms caused by criminal punishment, then it may not legitimately be punished through the criminal law.[80] Feinberg's position is thus consistent with weak but not strong retributivism.

Feinberg's position on the legal enforcement of morality is, of course, quite controversial. Many find problematic his denial that conduct that causes harm through imitation by others should be considered harmful in the sense that would justify criminal proscription, at least in the absence of a very high degree of culpability. (Feinberg does, however, allow criminal punishment of those who 'incite' others to engage in harmful conduct;[81] and he appears to approve of civil liability even for those whose conduct is harmfully imitated by others.) Just as controversially, Feinberg denies that the deleterious effects of immoral conduct on the actor's character should count as a harm justifying criminal punishment, even if acquiring a vicious character is bad for the actor herself, even if the actor wishes to prevent her acquiring such a character (self-paternalism), and even if one with a vicious character is more likely wrongfully to harm others.[82] (Feinberg appears not to reject as a matter of principle criminalizing conduct that causes harm to others only by causing vicious character traits; but he is quite sceptical of the efficacy of the criminal law in that endeavour.)[83] And, similarly, Feinberg denies that the coarsening effects of harmless immoralities on the public culture should count as harms to others justifying criminal intervention.[84] Finally, he rejects the view, associated with Patrick Devlin in his debate with H. L. A. Hart, that a community may legitimately criminalize otherwise harmless immoral conduct on the ground that unpunished immoral

[75] Feinberg, *The Moral Limits of the Criminal Law*, i: 215.   [76] ibid. at 216.

[77] ibid. at 244–5.   [78] ibid. at 217.

[79] Feinberg, *The Moral Limits of the Criminal Law*, iii.

[80] Feinberg, *The Moral Limits of the Criminal Law*, iv.

[81] Feinberg, *The Moral Limits of the Criminal Law*, i: 240.

[82] Feinberg, *The Moral Limits of the Criminal Law*, iv: 285.   [83] ibid. at 132.

[84] ibid. at 128.

acts undermine the moral code that defines the community and thus threatens the community's existence *qua* community.[85]

Feinberg sets forth a fairly capacious notion of immorality, one that includes conduct that does not cause harm to others in Feinberg's sense of causing harm, conduct such as the depraved and degraded. The harm principle he adumbrates does not define immoral conduct but rather limits its legitimate regulation through the criminal law. That leaves several avenues available for attacking Feinberg's position.

First, one might accept both Feinberg's broad conception of immoral conduct and the harm principle but reject Feinberg's restrictive view of the latter. Thus, one might have a more capacious view of harm and thus for the scope of the criminal law. Or one might take a more generous view than Feinberg's of how immoral conduct *causes* harm to others. Thus, one might join Devlin in claiming that destruction of a community-defining moral code should count as a harm justifying criminal punishment. Or one could claim that the coarsening effects on public culture is such a harm, or that the causal links between immorality, vicious character formation, and harm to others are sufficiently strong to warrant criminal proscription of immorality.

Alternatively, one can accept the philosophical position Feinberg rejects—legal moralism, the position that immorality is sufficient for criminalization—but come to conclusions similar to Feinberg's by rejecting Feinberg's broad view of what counts as immoral. For example, Ronald Dworkin, in his contribution to the debate against Devlin's position on criminalization, argued not against Devlin's legal moralism, but rather against Devlin's rather uncritical view of what counted as immoral.[86] Dworkin's position was that something very much like Feinberg's or Mill's harm principle functions not as an external constraint on what kinds of immoral conduct can be legitimately criminalized, but rather as an internal constraint on defining conduct as 'immoral'. Similarly, Michael Moore endorses legal moralism and its principle that those who do wrong deserve to be punished.[87] None the less, Moore's conception of what counts as 'wrong' is far less capacious than Devlin's and operationally much closer to the conduct Feinberg's harm principle would permit to be punished.[88]

Finally, one could, like Feinberg, hold that the class of immoral conduct includes much that is not harm-causing in Feinberg's sense, but reject Feinberg's harm principle altogether. For such a person—the pure legal moralist—acts that are immoral and degrading may be criminally punished, even if they are harmful in no other way.

Feinberg's rich discussion of the contours of harm to others that justifies criminal punishment covers topics that, although quite important in their own right, are

---

[85] ibid. at 133–40. John Kekes has recently argued that this is a misinterpretation of Devlin's position, and that Devlin was only arguing for the enforcement of that portion of the moral code essential to protect minimally good lives—perhaps the very portion of the moral code Feinberg would enforce. John Kekes, 'The Enforcement of Morality', *American Philosophical Quarterly*, 37 (2000), 23, 27–8.

[86] Ronald Dworkin, *Taking Rights Seriously* (1977), 248–53.

[87] Moore, *Placing Blame*, 68–78.   [88] ibid. at ch. 18.

peripheral to our concern in this chapter. Among those topics are whether people can be wrongfully harmed posthumously; whether exploitation counts as a wrongful harm; whether failures to prevent harm can be wrongful harms; whether other-regarding interests can be the basis of wrongful harm (not if they are malicious or sadistic, according to Feinberg); whether foetuses and infants, the severely retarded and senile, and animals can be wrongfully harmed; and whether one can be wrong-fully harmed by an act necessary for one's existence (i.e. the status of Derek Parfit's 'person-affecting' principle). (The question whether failures to prevent harm can be wrongful harms—whether, that is, bad Samaritans can be punished under Feinberg's harm principle, which Feinberg answers affirmatively[89]—is dealt with below under the topic of Omissions.)[90] For our purposes here, however, what are most important are Feinberg's rejection of moral paternalism— the position that the criminal law can legitimately be employed to protect people from harming their own moral charac-ter—and his rejection of legal moralism, which deems immorality to be sufficient for criminal enforcement even if it is 'harmless'. Moral paternalism is best considered as part of the broader topic of paternalism generally. For the core philosophical issue in moral paternalism is not whether the *immorality* of self-corrupting behaviour justi-fies its criminalization, but is instead whether the harm to oneself that might justify criminal punishment for one who otherwise accepts paternalistic justifications for criminal laws includes harms to one's moral character in addition to harms such as death, physical injury, and penury. That is why Feinberg's rejection of moral pater-nalism—as opposed to his rejection of legal moralism—is best considered under the general topic of paternalism and will not be further taken up here.[91] So we shall turn now to consider the case for and against legal moralism.

Before turning to legal moralism, it is important to examine a category of conduct that Feinberg excludes from the purview of the harm principle but not from the legit-imate authority of the criminal law. The category is that of conduct that causes pro-found offence to others. Feinberg devotes an entire volume to the concept of offence.[92] He concludes that offence, no matter how serious, does not count as a harm as Feinberg defines it in *Harm to Others*. None the less, Feinberg concludes that conduct that is profoundly offensive can legitimately be criminalized (the Offence Principle).[93] Examples of profoundly offensive conduct in our culture are public for-nication and masturbation, public bestiality, public handling of excrement, and pub-lic desecration of corpses.[94]

Feinberg would restrict the profound offence exception to the harm principle to conduct that occurs in public. Bare knowledge that such conduct is occurring in

[89] Feinberg, *The Moral Limits of the Criminal Law*, i: ch. 4.   [90] See Sect. 3.3 below.
[91] I should point out that if one deserved punishment for highly imprudent acts, the punishment would increase the imprudence. Would that then increase negative desert, and therefore punishment, and therefore negative desert, *ad infinitum*?
[92] Feinberg, *The Moral Limits of the Criminal Law*, ii.   [93] ibid. at 1.
[94] ibid. at 10–13.

private, no matter how disturbing, cannot justify criminalizing its private occurrence.[95] Otherwise, as Feinberg recognizes, criminalizing offensive conduct would likely collapse into legal moralism. (Whether Feinberg's restriction of criminalization to public offensive conduct is defensible, and thus whether Feinberg can avoid legal moralism while embracing punishment of offensive conduct, is a matter I shall take up below.)

Turning now to legal moralism, it is important to get some sense of the type of conduct the legal moralist would punish but that 'liberals' like Feinberg would exempt from punishment as a matter of principle. The conduct would, of course, have to be immoral. At the same time, however, it would not wrongfully set back the interests of others (else it would fall within Feinberg's harm principle), nor would it be publicly engaged in (else it might profoundly offend others and be legitimately criminalized on that ground).

Here are some examples of conduct that might be deemed immoral but not harmful: bestiality (sex with animals); exploitation (taking advantage of another's dire straits to extract most of the contractual surplus from transacting with him); producing and consuming hard-core pornography that appeals to lurid and sadistic impulses; and putting on and attending gladiatorial contests in which contestants voluntarily fight to the death as a spectator sport, an example contributed by Irving Kristol.[96] Bestiality may not fall within the harm principle, even if animals come within the protection of the principle because they have interests that can be set back, if bestiality does not in fact set back those interests. Exploitation may not fall within the harm principle because the 'victim' is not harmed but is inadequately benefited. Pornography may not fall within the harm principle unless it 'causes' its consumers to harm others.[97] And gladiatorial contests may not fall within the harm principle for the same reason. Yet arguably, each of these types of conduct is immoral.

Feinberg accepts the immorality of the conduct in these examples, but he denies that the conduct can be legitimately criminally punished in the absence of harm or offence. He is somewhat equivocal about the gladiatorial example, in part because he has doubts about whether gladiatorial contests could avoid harm to others—for example, whether they could avoid attracting gladiators whose 'consent' was not truly voluntary,[98] or whether they could avoid so coarsening their audience that they cause an increase in violent crimes.[99] In the final analysis, however, Feinberg appears to concede that preventing evils other than harms to others may be a legitimate reason for criminalization, just one that is almost always outweighed by the harms of criminalization, but perhaps not outweighed in the case of gladiatorial contests.

---

[95] ibid. at 60–71.
[96] Irving Kristol, 'Pornography, Obscenity, and the Case for Censorship', *The New York Times Magazine* (28 March 1971).
[97] Feinberg, *The Moral Limits of the Criminal Law*, iv: 22, 132.   [98] ibid. at 330–1.
[99] ibid. at 132, 329–31.

What would Feinberg's rejection of legal moralism entail for 'victimless crimes' such as prostitution, gambling, and drug use? The answer is not at all clear. Open solicitation of prostitution might fall within the principle permitting criminalization of acts that are profoundly offensive. Acts within any of these categories might involve harm to others (e.g. adultery, use of joint funds without consent). And particular instances of gambling and drug use might involve the wrongful risking of harm to others, as when one is likely to lose the family's milk money, drive while impaired, or become too addicted to fulfil one's legal obligations. Therefore, Feinberg, despite his rejection of legal moralism, might endorse criminalization of at least some instances of these activities.

Aside from conjuring up powerful examples like Kristol's gladiatorial contests that weaken the conviction of anti-legal moralists like Feinberg, what can be said more systematically on behalf of legal moralism? One approach for the legal moralist is that taken by Michael Moore.

Moore argues that the point of criminal law is to see that wrongdoing (and culpable attempts and risks of wrongdoing) is punished.[100] And wrongdoing includes not only those wrongful acts that fall within Mill's or Feinberg's harm and offence principles. For Moore, if an act is morally wrong, there is always a reason to prosecute and punish it through the criminal law.

Despite his legal moralism, however, Moore would probably reach conclusions on punishability very similar to Feinberg's. For Moore holds that while the immorality of conduct is always a reason for its proscription, the reach of the criminal law is tempered by three countervailing moral concerns. First, like Dworkin, Moore refuses to equate what *is* immoral with what a legislative majority, or a majority of the populace, *believes* to be immoral. A criminal statute is legitimate for Moore only if the conduct it forbids is truly immoral; and whether conduct is truly immoral is a matter of moral reality, not moral belief.[101] For example, Moore himself believes that most consensual sexual activity, including homosexuality, is not immoral and therefore should not be criminalized, regardless of the views of democratic majorities.[102]

Secondly, Moore believes that the costs of criminalizing conduct—costs in terms of resources, erroneous convictions, loss of privacy, corruption, and disrespect for law—are reasons that weigh against criminalization and in many cases dictate that immorality go unpunished.[103] Additionally, there is what Moore deems the 'presumption of liberty' that treats the criminal law's reduction of autonomy and acting from virtue as a moral bad that weighs against criminalization.[104] Surely many minor immoralities—for example, promise-breakings—should go unpunished because the moral costs of criminalization outweigh the retributive principle that immorality should be punished.

---

[100] Moore, *Placing Blame*, 70.   [101] ibid. at 662–3.   [102] ibid. at 756.
[103] ibid. at 663–5.   [104] ibid. at 76–8, 747–8.

Thirdly, Moore endorses a right to liberty, a right that immunizes from punishment many types of immoral conduct.[105] Moore rejects Mill's and Feinberg's harm principle as the basis for the right and instead characterizes the right as protecting a sphere of 'self-defining choices'.[106] The self-defining choices that are protected by the right to liberty include choices that are immoral and otherwise legitimately subject to criminal proscription and punishment. Thus, Moore endorses a 'right to do wrong'.

Moore applies his right to liberty to the question of criminalizing drug use.[107] He canvasses various arguments to the effect that drug use is immoral—it contravenes the ideal of asceticism; it creates the risk of wrongdoing; it reduces productivity; it impedes flourishing; and it can lead to the destruction of the self. Moore rejects any moral obligation to be as productive as possible, to attain a human ideal, or to flourish.[108] Moore does believe, however, that in some cases, conduct is immoral because it risks injuring others without an intervening culpable act. But drug use risks injury through increasing the likelihood of the drug user's future culpable wrongdoing, and Moore rejects deeming the drug use a proxy for the immoral conduct it might make more likely.[109]

Moore does accept, however, a moral obligation to refrain from destroying our capacity to act as moral agents.[110] At this point, Moore's right to liberty kicks in because the self-destruction is a self-defining choice. So although it is morally wrong to take drugs to the point of self-destruction, it would also be morally wrong for the state to punish such wrongdoing.[111]

Joseph Raz, like Feinberg, believes that there are morally repugnant actions that do not harm others in Feinberg's sense of harm.[112] He also denies, contrary to many liberals, that respect for autonomy requires toleration of all non-harmful choices.[113] Autonomous choices have value, argues Raz, only when they are directed at ends that are truly morally valuable.[114] Therefore, eliminating morally base choices as options does not impair the value of autonomy.[115]

Despite his finding no value in autonomous choices directed towards morally base (though harmless) ends, Raz none the less endorses something like Feinberg's harm principle to exclude criminal punishment of harmless immoralities.[116] Raz sharply distinguishes between criminal proscriptions of harmless immoral conduct and use of less coercive measures like taxes and subsidies to encourage the morally good and discourage the morally bad. Coercion through the criminal law, says Raz, is 'an indiscriminate invasion of autonomy'.[117] That is because 'imprisoning a person prevents him from almost all autonomous pursuits'.[118]

So Raz rejects enforcement of morality through the criminal law, if not through less coercive legal means. But as many critics of Raz have pointed out, the overall

---

[105] ibid. at 763–77.
[106] ibid. at 775.
[107] ibid. at 779–95.
[108] ibid. at 780–1, 783–7.
[109] ibid. at 782–4.
[110] ibid. at 787–8.
[111] ibid. at 792–5.
[112] Joseph Raz, *The Morality of Freedom* (1986), 397.
[113] ibid. at 380–1.
[114] ibid. at 380, 412.
[115] ibid. at 380–1, 410–12.
[116] ibid. at 418–22.
[117] ibid. at 418.
[118] ibid.

thrust of his arguments about the value of autonomy appears to favour legal moralism. After all, the threat to autonomy in punishing those who engage in harmless immorality lies not in the form of punishment, such as imprisonment, but in the practical preclusion of the immoral option. For imprisonment is only one historical form of criminal punishment. Fines are another, yet they leave those subject to them with every bit as much autonomy as those who are taxed. Similarly, if the punishment for harmless immorality were electric shocks or whippings, people would be deterred from immoral choices by the threat of such punishments, but the punishments themselves would not impede autonomy. And Raz appears to deny that making unworthy choices unattractive or even unavailable in any way impairs the value of autonomy, given that the value of autonomy is realized only through worthy choices.

Thus, Raz has provided a powerful argument for legal moralism and against Feinberg's harm principle, despite his endorsement of that principle. If there are harmless immoralities, the choice of which is valueless no matter how autonomous, then Raz should endorse their criminalization in the absence of excessive costs in doing so.

Let us turn now to the question whether support for criminalization of profoundly offensive conduct is consistent with rejection of legal moralism, as Feinberg maintains. There are strong reasons to doubt that it is.

Because Feinberg and Legal Moralists would endorse criminalizing those harmless immoralities that offend—the former because of the offence, the latter because of the immorality—and because many (most?) harmless immoralities will offend those aware of them, what room is left for operation of Feinberg's injunction against Legal Moralism? One area is where harmless immoralities fail to offend seriously enough to warrant their criminalization. A Legal Moralist might reach exactly the same anticriminalization conclusion as Feinberg for these cases. This is because there will be interests of the actor that will be set back by criminalization that may well outweigh the interest in punishing immorality in cases where the immorality is so minor that it will not cause serious offence. Although it is not clear exactly how the Legal Moralist will weigh the abstract value of punishing immorality against the various more concrete interests that will be set back by criminalization, there is no reason to think she will ignore or heavily discount the latter.

The area where Feinberg and the Legal Moralist clearly part company is that of offensive and immoral conduct that occurs in private. This is what Feinberg calls the 'bare knowledge problem'.[119] Suppose Alfred is profoundly offended as a result of merely knowing of Betty and Clara's lesbian relationship, the intimate practices of which occur behind closed doors in their apartment. Suppose Alfred is not abnormal in his offence and that offence at lesbian practices is widespread and serious. And suppose, merely for the sake of argument, that lesbian practices *are* immoral, though

---

[119]   Feinberg, *The Moral Limits of the Criminal Law*, ii: 61–71.

harmless. Will Feinberg's Offence Principle then legitimate for liberals the criminal prohibition of lesbian practices?

Feinberg wants to deny that it will. He draws a bright line between offensive criminal practices that Alfred perceives directly in public places and those that Alfred knows of other than through direct perception. It is here that the notion of wrongdoing plays a role under the Offence Principle as it does under the Harm Principle. To be punishable, conduct must not only offend; it must also wrong its victims. This requires, says Feinberg, that the victims' grievances be personal. Alfred cannot claim that *he* is wronged by Betty and Clara's immoral conduct, despite his being offended by the thought of it.

At an earlier point in his argument, Feinberg claims that one can suffer lower order, non-'profound', offences, such as revolting or disgusting or boring sights and smells, only if one directly perceives them rather than merely learns of them.[120] When one *does* perceive them, and thereby suffers the offence, the grievance one feels is felt to be personal, a wrong to the perceiver.

The offence one suffers because of violations of moral norms—in Feinberg's terms, 'profound' offence—does not depend upon my perceiving as opposed to knowing about the violations. Alfred suffers profound offence whether or not he witnesses Betty and Clara in their lesbian intimacies or merely knows of them. *But where he does not witness the conduct, but merely knows of it, his grievance is not a personal one because he cannot claim the conduct is a wrong to him.* And if the conduct, because unwitnessed, wrongs no one, it cannot be prohibited under the Offence Principle.

I agree entirely with Feinberg's analysis of profound offence, except for the conclusion he draws from it.[121] There are two horses Feinberg might ride here, and neither one will get him where he wants to go. One is the distinction between perceived conduct and known conduct. The other is the distinction between conduct that offends because it violates norms and conduct that violates norms because it offends. Let us take up each of these distinctions in turn.

Feinberg rests his position on the distinction between perceived and known conduct. He wants to say that if Alfred were to be unwillingly forced to view Betty and Clara's lovemaking, *then even with respect to his profound offence* (the offence he suffers as a result of the violation of the moral norm), he has a personal grievance eligible for protection under the Offence Principle. If Alfred merely knows of Betty and Clara's conduct, however, then he lacks a personal grievance.

What are the grounds for Feinberg's distinction between perception and knowledge? There are two possibilities. One possibility is that there is a different quality to offences that are perceived as opposed to offences that are merely known about. The other possibility is that perception, but not knowledge, individuates the harm of

---

[120] ibid. at 57–8.

[121] See Larry Alexander, 'Harm, Offense, and Morality', *The Canadian Journal of Law and Jurisprudence*, 7 (1994), 199.

860 THE PHILOSOPHY OF CRIMINAL LAW

offence in a way that makes the resulting grievances capable of characterization as wrongs to particular people.

The first possibility overlooks the fact that we are dealing here with profound offence, offence responsive to the fact that moral norms have been violated. Whether Alfred directly perceives Betty and Clara or merely knows about them, that part of his offence that is profound offence would be constant. At least Feinberg gives no argument that it would not be. Alfred's direct perception is just one way for him to know about Betty and Clara's profoundly offensive conduct. In all cases it is his knowledge that moral norms are being violated that causes his offence.

Consider Agnes, who believes that extra-marital sex, including heavy petting, is immoral (but harmless). She has learned that Barbara and Charles, unmarried, are having an affair, and she is profoundly offended. At a dance she observes another couple, Bill and Candy, engaging in rather heavy petting. At first she believes they are married, and she is not offended by their behaviour, even though it is indiscreet. When she is informed that they are not married, she suffers profound offence. Clearly her offence in both cases is a product of her knowledge that moral norms are being violated. Perception in the second case merely provides her with evidence of the violation.

The other possible basis for Feinberg's distinction between perceived and known immoral conduct is that perception but not knowledge somehow personalizes the offence in a way that allows us to identify specific persons who have been wronged. This, too, is problematic. Consider two cases of immoral conduct, one that is perceived by thousands of people, and one that occurs in private but that is learned of by a few people. There is no conceptual bar to claiming that the few have been wronged. ('If you act immorally, and others find out, you have wronged them: this is a risk you take whenever you act immorally.') Nor is there a conceptual bar to claiming that thousands have each been personally wronged in the first case. Mere numbers are irrelevant, though if they were relevant, they would cut in favour of, not against, mere knowledge.

I conclude that Feinberg has not offered a convincing rationale for distinguishing between cases of profound offence that involve direct perception of offending conduct and cases of profound offence that involve bare knowledge of offending conduct.

Moreover, Feinberg in some sense trivializes his liberal freedom from moralistic criminal prohibitions by forcing those who would engage in harmless immoralities to do so behind closed doors. Because he has already discounted their interests in engaging in such conduct as sordid and wicked, if they are not attempting to communicate ideas, they will lose out in the balancing under the Offence Principle unless they retreat from the public realm. But why if we are to bar Legal Moralism through the front door should we allow it in through the back door in the form of protecting against profound offence, a protection that makes the immoralist a second-class citizen who cannot engage in his favourite pastimes out of doors?

If, in the case of profound offence, we reject Feinberg's distinction between perceived and merely known immoral conduct, we are left with another possible distinction that might prevent the Offence Principle from collapsing into Legal Moralism: the distinction between conduct that violates moral norms because it offends and conduct that offends because it violates moral norms. Although Feinberg does not ultimately rely on this distinction in making his case against criminalizing immoral conduct that occurs in private, it is useful to consider the implications of employing such a distinction. After all, the distinction appears much more closely related to the rejection of Legal Moralism than does the distinction between perceived and merely known conduct.

Feinberg acknowledges the distinction between conduct that is immoral because it offends and conduct that offends because it is immoral, and at one point he even appears to be drawing the boundary between the Offence Principle and Legal Moralism on the basis of it. Ultimately, however, he countenances prohibition of conduct that offends because it is immoral so long as the conduct occurs in public.

But suppose he were to reject this and demand that conduct be offensive independently of immorality before it may be prohibited under the Offence Principle. Would this get him where he wants to be? Surely not. If we eliminate from the application of the Offence Principle all conduct that offends because violative of norms (as opposed to conduct which violates norms because it offends), the Offence Principle will be eviscerated. It will apply perhaps to conduct the sight, smell, or sound of which would be offensive in all cultures—perhaps the smell of sulphuric acid or the sound of chalk screeching on a blackboard. But most of the offensive conduct that Feinberg wishes to criminalize as profoundly offensive would not be eligible for prohibition under the Offence Principle.[122]

Most of the conduct that offends us does so by virtue of its flouting of norms. This is obviously true of such things as belching in public. It is probably also true of public bulimic or coprophagic conduct, since there may very well be cultures that do not find such conduct revolting. And it is true of such conduct as public nudity or public fornication.

[122] It is an interesting question, one that space precludes taking up here, whether aesthetic regulations fall on the offensive sight, smell, or sound side of the line or the offensive-because-norm-violative side of the line. Judgments of ugliness do seem phenomenologically different from judgments of offensiveness due to norm violations; but it is possible that the former ultimately rest on social norms that have been buried in the subconscious.

In private correspondence, Mitch Berman has suggested a distinction between two ways that norm violations might cause offence. He writes, 'I wonder whether Feinberg might have some success were he to respond by drawing the distinction (roughly) in terms of whether belief that the conduct violates a norm functions in the cognitive process of experiencing offence. So, for example, the offence of viewing public defecation might be culture-specific but does not seem to depend upon a conscious sense of its norm-violatingness in the way that Agnes's offence at adultery does. Put another way, perhaps even if most of the conduct that offends us does so by virtue of its flouting of norms, only some of it offends us *qua* flouting of norms.' E-mail from Mitchell Berman, 9 May 2001.

Feinberg appears at some points to believe otherwise. He points out that we are offended by public nudity or fornication but not by private nudity or fornication.[123] Therefore, it is our perception of the conduct, not its violation of norms, that causes our offence. The norms against public nudity and fornication are the only norms they violate, and they do not explain, but are explained by, the offence caused.

This analysis of such norms is incorrect. Public nudity and fornication do not everywhere and at all times offend. They offend when they violate norms about public behaviour, norms that are in no sense universal.

It is correct, of course, that nudity and fornication in private do not violate our norms and do not offend us. And it is, therefore, also correct that it is something about their being public that leads to our condemning public nudity and fornication. But it is incorrect to conclude that bare perception (no pun intended) rather than norm transgression is the source of our offence in such cases. There are norms about proper conduct in public that are sources of offence when violated but that do not protect against offence that pre-exists the norms themselves. Eliminate the norms and you eliminate the offence.

Consider in this connection the following example. Bill and Candy engage in public fornication before an enthusiastic crowd of twenty onlookers. No one present is offended because no one endorses the norm against public fornication. Alfred, however, who was not present but who would have been offended had he been present—he subscribes to the norm against public fornication—hears about Bill and Candy. Will he be offended by what they did, and if so, why?

I believe that Alfred may very well be offended (in the profound sense) even though no one present was. And the source of such offence will not necessarily be his imaginings of what Bill and Candy looked like at the time. Alfred may be offended just by the fact that Bill and Candy violated a norm to which Alfred subscribes, at least if we assume that the norm does not admit of an exception when the onlookers will not be offended. (The norm against public fornication might indeed not admit of such an exception: we may think that public fornication is improper even if no one present minds it.)

Feinberg must admit that many offence-giving public acts are so because they violate norms that are prior to offence. That admission, coupled with the prior argument that the perception/knowledge distinction is irrelevant in the case of offence caused by norm violations (profound offence), threatens either to collapse the Offence Principle into Legal Moralism almost completely or, alternatively, to rescue the Offence Principle by reducing its application to the small number of cases of universally revolting sights, smells, and sounds.

To save a more robust Offence Principle and yet avoid Legal Moralism, Feinberg might resort to the following argument. It is true, he might say, that most of the cases of offence that I would allow to be punished involve norm violation as the source of

123 Feinberg, *The Moral Limits of the Criminal Law*, iv: 15–16.

the offence. But the norms in question, as opposed to the norms with which my rejection of Legal Moralism is concerned, are understood as culturally relative conventions about proper behaviour in public and thus about how to show respect (and disrespect) to those present. Every culture needs conventions of this kind because in every culture people need to know whether they are being shown disrespect (and should therefore feel offended). The content of these norms can be quite variable, since their content is relatively unimportant. That is, their content is relatively unimportant in the same way the content of the norm about which side of the road to drive on is relatively unimportant.

There surely are norms that fit this description. Their public violation causes offence to those present (at least if they subscribe to the norm). Their private violation does not cause offence because they cannot be privately violated. (They only apply to conduct in others' presence; and those present must endorse the norms as appropriate vehicles for demonstrating respect.)

This argumentative strategy is problematic for several reasons. First, it oddly privileges purely conventional norms over norms believed to be universal. The former can be enforced through the criminal law under the Offence Principle; the latter are legally unenforceable (at least through criminal sanctions).

Secondly, many of the acts that a Feinberg liberal would presumably find punishably offensive consist of publicly flouting norms that are believed to be universal moral norms, not conventional norms of the respect/offence-giving kind. Consider homosexual embracing and kissing in public. The strategy in question would apparently rule out punishment for this, even if the offence it caused (by its direct perception) were serious, widespread, and so forth, and not outweighed by free speech or other interests of the actors. For unless there were a conventional norm deeming homosexual kissing in public to be disrespectful of those present—as opposed to a moral norm condemning homosexual behaviour generally—the offence felt by the witnesses would be of the profound variety and no different, or so I have argued, than the offence they would feel if they merely learned of this conduct but did not see it.

Of course, there might be a conventional meta-norm that deems publicly flouting moral norms to be disrespectful of those present, and violation of this conventional meta-norm might then legitimate punishment, even if violation of the underlying moral norm would not. But this tack for legitimating punishment exposes a third and I believe quite devastating weakness in the strategy I am describing. The weakness is this. There is nothing in principle that keeps us from having norms governing how to demonstrate respect (and give offence) that deem as disrespectful all public flouting of nonconventional moral norms. Whenever, therefore, we wish to criminalize public immoral conduct, it will be unclear even to ourselves whether we are criminalizing it because it is immoral (Legal Moralism) or because it violates our norms regarding offence. Moreover, there is nothing in principle that prevents us from regarding *private* immoral conduct as disrespectful to anyone who learns about it, at least if we jettison the distinction between perceiving and merely knowing about conduct. (If no one ever learns about private immoral conduct, it will not be punished anyway, even under Legal Moralism.) And given that private immoral conduct *will* cause profound offence among those who learn of it, we may in fact deem it disrespectful of those whom it offends. In that case, the line between the Offence Principle and Legal Moralism is all but obliterated. In any event, under the argumentative strategy we are considering, private immoral conduct is always hostage to the content of conventional norms regarding how respect and offence are shown.

In the end, once the perception/knowledge distinction is dropped, the fact that those offences which Feinberg would punish are more often than not products of norm violations leads to the result that the Offence Principle covers most of the territory that Legal Moralism might otherwise occupy. Feinberg cannot want this result, but neither can he avoid it, unless he eliminates norm violations as legitimate sources of punishable offence. His choice, then, is between a denatured liberalism, one that through the Offence Principle embraces most if not all of what the Legal Moralist wants, and an anaemic Offence Principle, one that covers only universally noxious sights, sounds, and smells.

3.3 Omissions

The final topic I shall take up under the special part of the criminal law is that of criminal liability for omissions. Despite the topic's ordinary placement in the general part of the criminal law, I relegate omissions to the special part because what is distinctive about them is whether and when, as a matter of normative theory, one has an enforceable moral duty to aid such that omitting to aid makes one deserving of punishment. If one does have a duty to aid, the implications for the general part are quite spare.

Let me take up the last point first. If one does have a duty under the criminal law to aid someone in peril, then if one fails to render that aid, one is potentially criminally liable. Whether one is actually criminally liable depends on several factors. One factor is whether one possessed *mens rea* with respect to whether the victim was in peril, whether one's aid was necessary to remove the peril, the degree of effort and risk required to remove the peril, and the grounds for the duty to aid in addition to the victim's peril (discussed below). Thus, if one did not realize that there was a high probability that the victim was in peril (and one did not desire that he be), that one could effectively rescue him, that others would or could not, that the rescue would be safe and easy, or that the other grounds for the duty were present, one would not be culpable for omitting to aid and would not deserve punishment. Likewise, if one did realize that these factors were present, but could not act because of a paralysing fear, because of a threat of death if one attempted the rescue (duress), or because the rescue would imperil several others (lesser evils), one again would not be culpable for omitting to aid.

Conversely, if one mistakenly believed all the conditions for the duty to aid existed, and without excuse or justification one failed to aid, one would be culpable for attempting a criminal omission. And as I argued above, one's criminal desert should be the same whether one commits a criminal omission or only attempts one. Therefore, on my view, just as one need not worry about whether an attempt (or reckless act) 'proximately caused' a harm, one need not worry about the metaphysics of how omissions cause harms. Culpable failures to act are all that criminal desert depends upon.[124]

So much for how the general part considerations bear on omissions. As I said, omissions are nothing special in so far as the general part is concerned. What makes omissions significant is their relation to the special part. Under what circumstances should one have a duty to aid such that a failure to fulfil that duty deserves punishment?

Anglo-American criminal law in this regard reflects a normative theory that is libertarian accented. For in general Anglo-American criminal law does not impose a duty to aid, no matter how great the peril the victim faces, no matter how numerous the victims, and no matter how easy and safe the aid required to remove the peril.[125] In the absence of one of the conditions mentioned below, one is not required to save ten infants from drowning, even though one would need very little effort to do so and would face virtually no risk to one's safety, even though one is fully aware of the peril and the necessity, ease, and safety of the rescue, and even though one has no excuse or justification for not rescuing. (In this case, a libertarian might be tempted to say, not that one who fails to rescue does not *deserve* punishment, but only that others are bound by a deontological constraint on *imposing* punishment. In other words, this may be one of those areas in which retributive desert does not mesh well with a libertarian normative theory.)

Anglo-American criminal law does recognize a duty to aid in three types of circumstances.[126] First, there is a duty to aid where one has caused the victim's peril. Secondly, there is a duty to aid where one has voluntarily undertaken to do so. And thirdly, there is a duty to aid where one has a status obligation to the victim, as when the victim is one's child or spouse. I shall take up these in order.

Causation of peril is a relatively non-problematic ground for a duty to aid when the causation is physical. Thus, when A knocks B into a pond, A has a duty to rescue B (assuming, of course, no excuses or justifications and that the rescue will be easy and safe). The only controversial issue here is whether A's physically causing B's peril must itself be culpable, or whether instead A has a duty to rescue B even if A knocked

[124] It should be obvious that application of the 'voluntary act' requirement to omissions is unproblematic. If one realizes that the grounds for a duty to act are present or likely so, and one nonetheless refrains from willing the act required, one has voluntarily omitted to act in the sense relevant to the voluntary act requirement.

[125] See Dressler, *Understanding Criminal Law*, 86.

[126] See generally Larry Alexander, 'Criminal Liability for Omissions: An Inventory of Issues' (forthcoming in British anthology, 2001).

B in the pond non-culpably.[127] (The weight of authority points to a duty to rescue even in the absence of culpability.)

More problematic are those cases where A has caused B's peril through non-physical means. Usually these are cases where either B placed himself in peril in reliance on his belief in A's willingness to rescue him—and A is aware of this—or B is in peril and others are refraining from rescuing him because *they* are relying on A to rescue (and A is aware of this). Causation of peril by inducing reliance (in various ways) is a daunting topic within normative theory and worthy of much more treatment than I can give it here.

Voluntary undertakings to rescue are quite unproblematic. The real issue here is whether voluntary undertakings to rescue by themselves result in duties enforceable by the criminal law, or whether they do so only when the victim or others have relied on the voluntary undertaking and thereby imperilled the victim. In other words, the issue is whether voluntary undertakings are a separate ground for a duty to rescue or whether they are merely included within the ground of causation of peril.

Status obligations are notoriously difficult to account for within a thoroughgoing libertarian normative theory. Thus, it is no surprise that the status exception to the general absence of a duty to rescue is hard to define, particularly if those obligations cannot be reduced to voluntary undertakings or imperilling by reliance. As we move from the statuses of spouse and parent to such brave new statuses as sperm donor, gestating mother, and so forth, the need for a satisfactory theoretical account of this exception will become painfully obvious.

A final point about criminal liability for omissions. Even where the law imposes a duty to rescue, the duty is limited to rescues that are safe and easy. In other words, even when one has caused the victim's peril or undertaken to rescue him, one is not required to expend great effort or resources or to face great risks of injury or death, even if the peril to the victim discounted by its probability is greater than the peril/sacrifice of the rescuer discounted by its probability.

There is both a theoretical and a practical problem here. The theoretical problem is how to account for any limit on the duty to rescue short of one that would minimize total losses.[128] The problem is virtually identical to the problem faced by those libertarian deontologists who would impose a duty to rescue if the number of victims or the danger they face reaches the point of 'moral catastrophe' but would not impose a duty short of that point—the problem of specifying the 'deontological threshold'.[129]

The practical problem is that without a theoretical account of what demarcates an 'easy rescue', defendants lack clear notice of the extent of their duties under the

---

[127] There is also an issue regarding how deviant or remote the causal chain from the actor's conduct to the victim's peril can be.

[128] See generally Larry Alexander, 'Affirmative Duties and the Limits of Self-Sacrifice', *Law & Philosophy*, 15 (1996), 65.

[129] See generally Larry Alexander, 'Deontology at the Threshold', *San Diego Law Review*, 37 (2000), 893.

criminal law. And although I have downplayed the importance of notice with respect to such core criminal duties as those to refrain from killing, battering, raping, and stealing, the scope of the duty to rescue is different. For if a court determines that the limit on the defendant's duty to rescue a drowning victim is, say, a 10 per cent risk of the defendant's drowning, can we say that a defendant who thought the limit was 9 per cent is fully culpable for his mistake, especially if the court cannot give a theoretical justification for the determination?

CHAPTER 21

PHILOSOPHY OF INTERNATIONAL LAW

ALLEN BUCHANAN
DAVID GOLOVE

1 CURIOUS NEGLECT

CONTEMPORARY political philosophers tend to neglect international relations. Contemporary philosophers of law usually have even less to say about the philosophy of international law. Rawls's work has dominated political philosophy for more than a quarter of a century, but only recently has he extended his theory to the international sphere, and then only in a rather skeletal fashion.[1] The major contemporary philosophers of law largely proceed as if there were no international legal system to be theorized about.[2]

---

[1] John Rawls, *Law of Peoples* (Cambridge, Mass.: Harvard University Press, 1999). This book is not, and does not purport to be, a comprehensive philosophy of international law.

[2] In *The Concept of Law* Hart includes one chapter on international law, but addresses only the analytical question 'Is what is called international law really law?', without developing or even mentioning the subject-matter of a moral theory of international law. Hart does not provide a normative theory of domestic law either; he only addresses the analytic questions. See H. L. A. Hart, *The Concept of Law* (Oxford: Clarendon Press, 1961). Nor do Ronald Dworkin or Joseph Raz extend their theories to international law.

There are some notable and quite recent exceptions to this general neglect. In contemporary political philosophy, there are important discussions of international distributive justice, but for the most part the principles offered are at best only tenuously connected with institutions, including institutions of international law.[3] Yet how proposed principles are to be institutionalized can make a difference; principles that look plausible for making one-off decisions may be unsuitable as institutional rules.

Even when the importance of institutions in achieving international distributive justice is acknowledged, little is said as to what distinctive role, if any, international law should play.[4] In contrast, there has been an outpouring of valuable work in the positive liberal theory of international relations, including significant explorations of the role of international law in the overall international system.[5] But there has been little explicit connection between positive and normative theorizing. Positive liberal theorists of international relations and international law, quite understandably, have concentrated on developing an explanatory framework that challenges the dominant Realist paradigm in international relations and, as social scientists, cannot be faulted for refraining from developing a normative theory. More problematically, the minority of political philosophers who attempt to extend their normative views to the international arena have, for the most part, not been very explicit about the role of positive theory in their enterprise.[6] We shall argue later that once the weakness of at least the

[3] Onora O'Neill, 'Justice, Gender, and International Boundaries', in *The Quality of Life,* ed. Martha Nussbaum and Amartya Sen (New York: Oxford University Press, 1993) and Charles Beitz, 'International Liberalism and Distributive Justice: A Survey of Recent Thought', *World Politics,* 51 (1999), 269–98.

[4] See Darrel Moellendorf, 'Constructing the Law of Peoples', *Pacific Philosophical Quarterly,* 772 (1996), 132–54; Liam B. Murphy, 'Institutions and the Demands of Justice', *Philosophy and Public Affairs,* 274 (1998), 251–91; Thomas Pogge, *Realizing Rawls* (Ithaca, NY: Cornell University Press, 1989); 'An Egalitarian Law of Peoples', *Philosophy and Public Affairs,* 23 (1994), 195–224; Henry Shue, *Basic Rights: Subsistence, Affluence, and U.S. Foreign Policy,* 2nd edn. (Princeton: Princeton University Press, 1996); Charles Beitz, *Political Theory and International Relations* (Princeton: Princeton University Press, 1979); and Review Essay of *Law of Peoples,* by John Rawls, *Ethics,* 110 (2000), 669–98.

[5] See Thomas Risse, Stephen C. Ropp, and Kathryn Sikkink (eds.), *The Power of Human Rights: International Norms and Domestic Change* (New York: Cambridge University Press, 1999); Andrew Moravcsik, 'Taking Preferences Seriously: A Liberal Theory of International Politics', *International Organization,* 51 (1997), 513–54; Anne Marie Slaughter, 'International Law in a World of Liberal States', *European Journal of International Law,* 6 (1995), 503–38; 'International Law and International Relations Theory: A Dual Agenda', *American Journal of International Law,* 87 (1993), 205–39; 'The Liberal Agenda for Peace: International Relations Theory and the Future of the United Nations', *Transnational and Contemporary Problems,* 4 (1995), 377-420. Positive liberal theory of international relations, which is discussed at greater length below, maintains that states have preferences other than merely for the maximization of their power, that state preferences are shaped both by internal constituencies that are themselves in some cases linked to international and transnational groups and actors, that state preferences differ depending upon the kind of society in which the state is embedded, and that there are significant, stable patterns of genuinely co-operative interaction in international relations.

[6] Charles Beitz is an exception to this observation. See Beitz, *Political Theory and International Relations,* 11–66. See also Allen Buchanan, 'Recognitional Legitimacy and the State System', *Philosophy and Public Affairs,* 28 (1999), 46–78. Another body of literature in which normative and positive concerns are more closely linked is that concerning the democratic peace hypothesis (that developed democracies

more extreme forms of the Realist theory of international relations is appreciated, the way is clear for engaging in the enterprise of a moral theory of international law.

There is also a rich and burgeoning normative literature on self-determination, secession, and group rights—topics which, as we will show, are central to the philosophy of international law.[7] However, with only a few exceptions, works in these areas fail to draw any institutional implications from the moral principles they enunciate or, when they do, focus only on domestic institutions. Even those few theorists who suggest that their views on secession and self-determination might be incorporated into international law tend to assume that the moral reasoning they use to support their favoured principles need not take into account the fact that these principles are to be implemented through international legal institutions. Most remarkably, views on self-determination and secession are usually developed without reference to existing international legal doctrine and practice and in the absence of a consideration of how the moral principles that are offered might be incorporated into the international legal system.

The relatively underdeveloped state of the philosophy of international law may be attributed to at least three factors. First, it is only one instance of a more general failing in contemporary moral and political philosophy: the neglect of *institutional* moral theorizing. Too often it is assumed that the effects of attempting to institutionalize those principles, or even to act on them effectively given existing institutional constraints, are wholly irrelevant to the task of justifying them. The result of this way of proceeding is that principles are endorsed which are not suitable for institutionalization, because they are inconsistent with existing institutional arrangements whose abandonment would be morally prohibitive even if possible, or because institutionalizing them would generate incentives that undermine the realization of other important principles.

tend not to make war on one another). See Michael Doyle, 'Kant, Liberal Legacies, and Foreign Affairs, Parts 1 and 2', *Philosophy & Public Affairs*, 12 (1983), 205–35, 323–53.

[7] See Harry Beran, *The Consent Theory of Obligation* (New York: Croom Helm, 1987); 'A Liberal Theory of Secession', *Political Studies*, 32 (1984), 21–31; Lea Brilmayer, 'Secession and Self-Determination: A Territorial Interpretation'. *Yale Journal of International Law*, 16 (1991), 177–202; Allen Buchanan, *Secession: The Morality of Political Divorce from Fort Sumter to Lithuania and Quebec* (Boulder, Colo.: Westview Press, 1991); 'Theories of Secession', *Philosophy & Public Affairs*, 261 (1997), 31–61; 'Federalism, Secession, and the Morality of Inclusion', *Arizona Law Review*, 37 (1995), 53–63; Jocelyne Couture, Kai Nielsen, and Michel Seymour (eds.), *Rethinking Nationalism* (Calgary: University of Calgary Press, 1998); Hurst Hannum, *Autonomy, Sovereignty, and Self-Determination: The Accommodation of Conflicting Rights* (Philadelphia: University of Pennsylvania Press, 1996; 'Rethinking Self-Determination', *Virginia Journal of International Law*, 34 (1993), 1–69; Chandran Kukathas, 'Are There Any Cultural Rights?', *Political Theory*, 20 (1992), 105–40; William Kymlicka (ed.), *The Rights of Minority Cultures* (New York: Oxford University Press, 1995); Robert McKim and Jefferson McMahan (eds.), *The Morality of Nationalism* (New York: Oxford University Press, 1997); Margaret Moore (ed.), *National Self-Determination and Secession* (New York: Oxford University Press, 1998); and Wayne Norman, 'The Ethics of Secession as the Regulation of Secessionist Politics', in *Self-Determination and Secession*, ed. Margaret Moore (New York: Oxford University Press, 1998).

Secondly, until recently the Realist theory of international relations has been dominant, and according to it moral theorizing about international relations and hence about international law is futile. Although in recent years Realism has been vigorously challenged by piecemeal criticism of its key assumptions and more systematically by positive liberal theory, its pessimistic implications for the normative enterprise may persist—especially among political philosophers and philosophers of law who are not familiar with the serious weaknesses of the Realist view.[8] Thirdly, many take a rather disparaging view of international law, regarding it as at best a pale shadow of what we ordinarily think of as a legal system. Thus one commentator has stated that 'international law is to law as professional wrestling is to wrestling'—the implication being that international law is largely pomp and posturing, and that the outcomes are more or less scripted by dominant states.[9] The most extreme form of this view—Legal Nihilism—denies that what is called international law is law.

The importance of institutional moral reasoning will be emphasized at a number of points in this chapter, as we proceed with the task of framing some of the central issues of the philosophy of international law. But since we believe that the failure to take institutions seriously is ubiquitous in contemporary moral theorizing and not at all peculiar to the philosophy of international law (or the relative lack thereof), we will concentrate chiefly on the Realist challenge and on the Legal Nihilist's denial that there is a subject-matter for a philosophy of international law.

An important limitation of our discussion should be emphasized. This chapter addresses the normative dimension of international law—the moral theory of international legal doctrine and institutions—not what Hart would call the analytic dimension (what makes a norm a part of international law, what is international law?), and not the epistemology of international law (what are the ways of knowing legal facts of international law?). After responding to the Realist and Legal Nihilist challenges to the enterprise of normative philosophy of international law, we (1) develop a conception of the relationship between normative theorizing about international law and the realities of the current state-centred international system and (2) articulate most of the main issues a normative theory of international law must address, indicating the key choices which a theorist faces, and thereby suggesting an agenda for further research. One important area in the domain of a moral theory of international law will not be dealt with explicitly, solely for reasons of space: the theory of just war. Traditionally, just war theory includes two components: an account of the justifications for going to war and a set of constraints on how war may be conducted. Although we will not deal with either of these issues explicitly, what we

---

[8] For some leading works of positive liberal theory that explicitly criticize Realism, see the following. Moravcsik, 'Taking Preferences Seriously'; Slaughter, 'International Law in a World of Liberal States'; 'International Law and International Relations Theory'; 'The Liberal Agenda for Peace'.

[9] Gerhard Von Glahn, *Law among Nations: An Introduction to Public International Law* (New York: Macmillan, 1986), 2. Von Glahn attributes this description of international law to Stephen Budiansky, *U.S. News & World Report*, 20 Sept. 1993, 8.

have to say about human rights, humanitarian intervention, and the conditions for the legitimacy of governments will have direct and fairly obvious implications for them.[10]

2 The Realist Challenge and the Competing Liberal Paradigm

According to Realism, the nature of international relations precludes morality in that sphere. And because morality is not operative in the international sphere, a moral theory of international law is an exercise in futility.[11] There are several variations on the Realist theme, and in some cases it is not clear what exactly is meant by the thesis that morality is not operative in international relations. This could mean either that (i) moral 'oughts' do not apply to international relations—that there are no true or justified statements about what anyone ought (morally) to do; or that (ii) no one in fact acts morally in international relations (nor will do so in the future), or that (iii) moral behaviour in international relations is fundamentally irrational and therefore infrequent (assuming that parties in this arena do not often act in fundamentally irrational ways). On any of these interpretations, Realism leaves no room for a moral theory of international law. If interpretation (i) is correct, then there can be no true or justified moral theory of international law; if (ii) is correct, then a moral theory of international law will be practically irrelevant because no one will ever attempt to implement it; and if (iii) is correct, then a moral theory of international relations will be relevant only for fundamentally irrational agents (who, it is assumed, will constitute a minority of international actors).

The last of these arguments is the most commonly held view among Realists today. Typically, the Realist characterizes international relations as a Hobbesian state of nature, with the following features: (a) There is no global sovereign, no supreme arbiter capable of enforcing rules of peaceful co-operation. (b) There is (approximate) equality of power, such that no one state can permanently dominate all others. (c) The fundamental preference of states is to survive. (d) Given conditions (a) and (b), what is rational for each state to do is to strive by all means to dominate others in

[10] Michael Walzer, *Just and Unjust Wars* (New York: Basic Books, 1977).

[11] George F. Kennan, *American Diplomacy, 1900–1951* (Chicago: University of Chicago Press, 1951); Thucydides, *History of the Peloponnesian War*, trans. John H. Finley, Jr. (New York: Modern Library, 1951; 1st pub. *c*.400 BC); Kenneth Waltz, *Man, the State, and War: A Theoretical Analysis* (New York: Columbia Press, 1959); and *Theory of International Politics* (Reading, Mass.: Addison-Wesley Pub. Co., 1979).

order to avoid being dominated (to rely on what Hobbes calls 'the principle of antic-ipation'). (*e*) In a situation in which each party rationally anticipates that it is ratio-nal for others to dominate, without constraints on the means they use to do so, moral principles are inapplicable.[12]

In its purely positive variant, Realism is a descriptive-explanatory account of the nature of international relations. As we have noted, however, Realists typically draw a meta-ethical implication from their descriptive-explanatory theory: broadly, that morality is inapplicable to international relations. Most who subscribe to the Realist's descriptive-explanatory account do, however, draw one important moral implication, even while denying the application of moral principles to international relations generally—the principle that state leaders ought to act in the interests of their states without regard for moral constraint. It is useful, therefore, to distinguish between Positive Realism, which describes international relations as a Hobbesian state of war, and what might be called Fiduciary Realism. According to the latter, responsible state officials, reflecting on the (Hobbesian) nature of international rela-tions, should act only so as to maximize the survival prospects of their states, without regard for any moral constraints.[13] Fiduciary Realists are not moral nihilists or scep-tics: they believe that state leaders do have moral obligations to their own peoples, but they believe that fulfilling these obligations requires rejecting any moral constraints on behaviour towards other states. Fiduciary Realists disregard other moral prin-ciples for the sake of acting on one overriding moral obligation: to serve the interests of their states.[14]

Fiduciary Realism should be distinguished from what may be called Legal Nihilism. The Legal Nihilist contends that there is no subject-matter for a normative theory of international law—because there is no such thing as international *law*. In support of the assertion that there is no international law, the Legal Nihilist notes that the so-called international legal system lacks (i) an enforcement mechanism for its rules, (ii) an international legislature, (iii) courts with compulsory jurisdiction, and (iv) what Hart calls a rule of recognition—a definitive criterion for determining what is law in the system.[15] In addition, some who deny the existence of international law do so on the ground that the very concept of state sovereignty is incompatible with the idea of a law that binds states: to be sovereign is to be the ultimate maker of law

[12] See Charles Beitz, 'Justice and International Relations', *Philosophy & Public Affairs*, 4 (1975), 360–89 and Lea Brilmayer, *American Hegemony: Political Morality in a One-Superpower World* (New Haven: Yale University Press, 1994).

[13] See Edward H. Carr, *The Twenty Years' Crisis, 1919–1939: An Introduction to the Study of International Relations* (New York: Harper & Row, 1964); George F. Kennan, *American Diplomacy, 1900–1951* (Chicago: University of Chicago Press, 1951); and Hans J. Morgenthau, *Politics among Nations: The Struggle for Power and Peace*, 6th edn., rev. by Kenneth W. Thompson (New York: Knopf, 1985).

[14] Hans Morgenthau holds an interesting variant of the Fiduciary Realist view: he asserts that even if there are moral principles that apply to international relations in principle, it is best for state leaders exclusively to pursue the interests of their own states, because attempts to produce good for mankind generally lead to great human suffering. See Morgenthau, *Politics among Nations*.

[15] See Hart, *The Concept of Law*.

and hence not to be subject to any higher law. Underlying most versions of Legal Nihilism is the claim that what is called international law is not law because it lacks the effectiveness that is a necessary condition for a system of norms to be law.

As popular and entrenched as the Realist and Legal Nihilist views are, they do not pose insuperable obstacles to the enterprise of a moral theory of international law. Positive Realism consists of a set of dubious empirical generalizations about the international sphere, while Fiduciary Realism, presupposing the truth of these empirical generalizations, concludes that given this state of affairs the responsible state official will disregard moral constraints in the pursuit of his state's interests. Legal Nihilism assumes an indefensibly simplistic conception of what is necessary for the existence of a legal system, exaggerates the differences between domestic and international law, and radically misconstrues the concept of state sovereignty.

First consider the sweeping empirical generalizations that constitute the core of Realism. Much of the most interesting work in international relations in the past two decades indicates that international relations is not in fact a Hobbesian war of each against all. According to many recent studies, there are stable patterns of peaceful co-operation and effective supranational regimes, some bilateral, some regional, and some genuinely global in scope—including defensive military alliances, financial regimes, trade agreements, structures for scientific co-operation, environmental accords, and international support for human rights, economic development, and disaster relief. Moreover, the ability to make credible commitments for peaceful co-operation is a valuable asset for states as it is for individuals, and techniques for building trust are varied and ubiquitous.[16] Survival is not an issue, much less the only issue, in many contexts of state interaction (consider, for example, relations between Britain and the United States over at least the past 120 years or relations among most Western European states over the last fifty years). Nor are states even roughly equal in power and hence in vulnerability. Powerful states can afford to take risks in efforts to build co-operation. They also face lesser risks when acting co-operatively because the costs to others of betraying their trust may be very great.

Perhaps most importantly, contrary to the Realist, liberal internationalist theorists have argued that state preferences are neither fixed nor uniform among states. The (positive) liberal theory of international relations marshals substantial evidence for the thesis that state preferences (more precisely, the preferences expressed by state leaders in official policy) vary, depending upon the internal character of the state, and change over time as a function of the activities of various groups within states, particularly as these interact with transnational and international governmental and non-governmental entities.[17] Finally, according to one important strand of liberal

---

[16] Robert H. Frank, *Passions Within Reason: The Strategic Role of the Emotions* (New York: Norton, 1988).

[17] Moravcsik, 'Taking Preferences Seriously'; Slaughter, 'International Law in a World of Liberal States'; 'International Law and International Relations Theory'; 'The Liberal Agenda for Peace'; and Risse *et al.*, *The Power of Human Rights*.

theory, democratization promises to expand the sphere of peaceful, co-operative interaction while at the same time more fully implementing human rights principles, because developed democracies do not make war on each other and because democracy provides the most reliable assurance that basic human rights will be respected.[18] In sum, Positive Realism has been vigorously attacked for denying the existence of international co-operation and for assuming without sufficient justification that the extent of co-operation does not and never will provide space for ethical behaviour and hence for a moral theory of international law. Now that the Realist theory has been seriously challenged, the enterprise of developing a moral theory of international law, as an element of a broader moral theory of international relations, is seen to be feasible. At minimum, the moral theorist need no longer feel compelled to undertake a systematic effort to counter the premises of Positive Realism in order to proceed with moral theorizing.

Moral Minimalism. There is a related view which, while not denying the possibility of a normative theory of international law, implies that any such theory must be of very limited scope. According to what might be called Moral Minimalism, an essential and distinguishing feature of international law is that it is a system of rules for the interaction of entities that do not share ends.[19] The implication is that the lack of shared ends severely limits the normative content of international law and hence the scope of a moral theory of international law. There are several difficulties with this view, however. First, in at least some versions, the underlying premise of the argument seems to be that moral claims can be justified only on the basis of a consensus among those to whom the rules apply. Although we cannot address this point here, this meta-ethical premise is itself highly controversial.

Secondly, even if we accept this meta-ethical premise, at least most of the societies that make up the international community do share some ends: peace and the creation and maintenance of a stable, predictable framework of interaction. It may also be said that any state that makes a plausible claim to legitimacy must also share the end of realizing domestic justice and that there is some evidence of an expanding consensus on some of the substance of justice, for example, through resolutions and treaties that give increasingly specific content to the most basic human rights. Thus, the Moral Minimalist must deny the scope of this expanding consensus and deny as well the possibility that the international community will come to share more robust ends in the future. At the very least, the Moral Minimalist must specify the ends that are shared and those that are not before we can assess how constraining the absence of shared ends is on the enterprise of moral theorizing about international law.

---

[18] See Doyle, 'Kant, Liberal Legacies, and Foreign Affairs'; Bruce M. Russett, *Grasping the Democratic Peace: Principles for a Post-Cold War World* (Princeton: Princeton University Press, 1993); and Amartya Sen, *Poverty and Famines: An Essay on Entitlement and Deprivation* (New York: Oxford University Press, 1981).

[19] Terry Nardin, *Law, Morality, and the Relations of States* (Princeton: Princeton University Press, 1980).

This last problem is particularly acute because Moral Minimalism asserts that what distinguishes international law from domestic law is that the latter consists of a framework of rules for those who share ends while the former does not. However, it is usually said of a liberal domestic society that its public order does *not* rest upon shared ends—other than those of security and justice. Hence to make a case that there is little scope for moral theorizing about international law, the Moral Minimalist must either reject the broad distinction she tries to draw between the nature of international law and the nature of domestic law or spell out exactly why it is that the lack of shared substantive ends precludes significant normative theorizing for international law but not for domestic liberal legal institutions.

Rawls's theory, as developed in *Political Liberalism* and *The Law of Peoples*, can be seen as providing an answer to this latter question: although the members of liberal societies do not share substantive ends, they do share a core conception of justice, the idea of society as a fair system of co-operation among free and equal persons, while the international order contains societies that do not share this conception.[20] This shared core conception of justice in liberal societies provides the foundation for a more morally robust system of law; its absence implies that the moral content of international law, at least as it pertains to human rights, must be minimal. Notice that the 'must' in the last sentence is ambiguous: it could mean that without a globally shared core conception of justice a morally robust system of international law cannot be effective or it could mean that it cannot be morally justified. The former is a claim about feasibility; the latter, at least for Rawls, is a claim about legitimacy—about the conditions under which it is morally justifiable to enforce principles. On Rawls's view, it is not morally justifiable to force others to comply with principles that they can, from the standpoint of their own (reasonable) conceptions of justice or of the good, reasonably reject. For the Rawlsian Moral Minimalist, the fact that people in non-liberal societies do not share the basic conception of society as a fair system of co-operation among free and equal persons implies that they can reasonably reject the sorts of substantive principles that can be included in a liberal legal system. Similarly, the legal systems of non-liberal societies can justifiably include substantive moral principles that it would be illegitimate to impose on a liberal society—principles that liberals could reasonably reject, given their shared conception of justice or their shared substantive ends. Therefore, the lack of a globally shared core conception of justice implies that the content of international law, which is to bind all societies, liberal and non-liberal, must be minimal.

The assertion that there is no core conception of justice capable of providing the foundation for a morally robust theory of international law is an empirical claim about the extent of moral disagreement across state boundaries. It can be argued, however, that there is in fact an expanding global culture of human rights that reflects a growing consensus on a conception of justice based upon recognition of the equal-

20 Rawls, *Law of Peoples* and *Political Liberalism* (New York: Columbia University Press, 1993).

ity and freedom of all persons. (For example, Article 1 of the Universal Declaration of Human Rights states that 'All human beings are born free and equal in dignity and rights'.)[21] According to this view, the notion of equality and freedom expressed in the major human rights conventions may provide the basis for the development of a moral theory of international law whose content is substantial.

Finally, the Moral Minimalist puts the cart before the horse. Whether or not a consensus on substantive ends is possible in the international community may depend in part upon how international law evolves and whether a moral theory of international law can be articulated in such a way as to gain widespread support. It is probably true that international society currently lacks the institutional resources for bringing about the degree of agreement on substantive ends that many (though certainly not all) domestic societies enjoy. But the possibility that this may change cannot be ruled out.

Indeed, the international legal system already includes principles, practices, and institutions that are contributing to the emergence of wider consensus on the content of human rights norms. For example, the multiple processes by which human rights compliance is monitored, including the functioning of the International Human Rights Committee in responding to complaints about violations, do not leave our understandings of the content of human rights norms unchanged. Instead, these processes contribute to the formation of more determinate shared beliefs about what the various human rights are.

One cannot assume, of course, that the existing resources of international law are sufficient for achieving a morally defensible, determinate content for international legal norms concerning human rights, nor for producing a system of norms that as a whole is coherent enough and powerful enough to address all the issues. Moral theorizing has its own contribution to make, by articulating basic principles and providing a rationale for developing new institutional resources. In the end the best way to determine the scope of a moral theory of international law is to engage in the process of constructing a theory and then see whether or not it provides practical guidance for improving the system.

Legal Nihilism. There are two ways the Legal Nihilist view can be understood: as an analytic claim about the features a system of rules must have if it is to constitute a legal system, paired with the assertion that what we call international law does not satisfy those conditions; or as a claim that a system of rules is not a legal system unless its rules effectively constrain or determine the behaviour of those to whom the rules are directed, along with the assertion that international law is not effective. Both of these understandings of Legal Nihilism raise fundamental questions about the nature of law that cannot be thoroughly addressed here. Instead, we only briefly address the analytic claim in so far as it seeks to pose a challenge to the possibility, or coherence, of a normative theory of international law.

---

[21] Burns H. Weston, Richard A. Falk, and Anthony A. D'Amato (eds.), *Basic Documents in International Law and World Order* (St Paul, Minn.: West Publishing Co., 1980), 161.

Understood as an analytic claim about the nature of law, Legal Nihilism is beside the point. The Nihilist points to the lack of a recognized agent with a monopoly on the legitimate use of force to enforce the norms of the system, the lack of a legislative body with the capacity to legislate new norms, and the lack of a system of courts with compulsory jurisdiction to resolve disputes. The Nihilist may also claim that international law lacks a rule of recognition in H. L. A. Hart's sense. But whether these features of domestic legal systems are a necessary part of the concept of law or not, and whether the Nihilist has correctly understood the character of the international legal system, is largely irrelevant to the normative dimension of international relations. For even if it were true that what we call the international legal system is not a legal system strictly speaking, it certainly has strong affinities with what are undoubtedly systems of law. Moreover, because this system claims supremacy in its domain and includes provisions for sanctions, and even the use of force, to compel compliance with its norms, it is as suitable a subject for moral theorizing as what the Nihilist deems a legal system properly speaking.

The Legal Nihilist's focus on the effectiveness of the international legal system is even more problematic. The features of the international system to which the Nihilist points may well be defects which limit the degree to which international law can effectively guide the conduct of states and other actors. But for the reasons we have already explained in discussing Realism, notwithstanding these defects, existing international institutions have in fact proved effective in supporting peaceful, rule-guided co-operation in many areas. Even in the difficult area of human rights, where international law has often been violated, human rights norms have nevertheless had important effects on oppressive governments. For example, the very fact that there are human rights covenants signed by the great majority of states exerts pressure on oppressive states to deny that they are violating human rights even when they in fact do so, equips forces within and outside the oppressive state with powerful mechanisms for exerting pressure on them, and influences the character of normative discourse in international fora. More important, there are many areas of international law in which compliance is quite impressive, for example, with regard to trade agreements, the law of the sea, diplomatic immunity, treaties governing outer space and the Antarctic, international postal and communications regulations, and many others. Moreover, there is no reason to rule out the possibility that the capacity of these institutions will grow over time—indeed, that they may take on one or more of the features whose absence disturbs the Nihilist. In rejecting this possibility, the Nihilist reveals that his view is largely parasitic on Realism. Because international relations is a Hobbesian state of nature afflicted by a massive assurance problem, the Nihilist might argue, states will never allow the emergence of a system that would have the features (including an enforcement mechanism, courts of compulsory jurisdiction, etc.) that would genuinely bind them. If, however, Realism can no longer be taken for granted as we have argued, then the Legal Nihilist position becomes much less compelling. Like the Realist challenge, it does not pose an insuperable obstacle to a normative theory of international law.

Some Legal Nihilists make another sort of conceptual claim. They argue that there can be no international law because the sovereignty of states precludes their being bound by any law. But, as Hart persuasively argued, this claim fails to understand that the powers, rights, and immunities that constitute sovereignty are defined by international law. The concept of a sovereign state is a relational, institutional concept—to be sovereign is to be a member of a system of entities defined by and subject to international law.[22] The powers of sovereignty as defined by international law have changed and will presumably change again in the future. For example, it is a distinctive feature of international law since at least 1945 that sovereign states no longer have the right to violate the human rights of their citizens or to engage in aggressive war.[23]

Our purpose here is not to provide a conclusive refutation of the various Legal Nihilist analytic claims about what law is. For as we have already argued, to engage the analytic debate seriously is to concede too much to the Legal Nihilist. Even if it were true that what we call the international legal system is not a legal system strictly speaking, it certainly has strong affinities with what are undoubtedly systems of law. Moreover, because this system claims supremacy in its domain and includes provisions for the use of force to compel compliance with its norms, it is as suitable a subject for moral theorizing as what the Nihilist deems a legal system properly speaking.

The moral legitimacy of the state system. One last challenge to the enterprise of normative theorizing about international law is worth considering. International law consists primarily of rules for the interaction of states. Hence a normative theory of international law must assume the existence of states. But states are institutionally defined within the state system as having unique privileges *vis-à-vis* any other actors. To that extent normative theorizing about international law would seem to assume the legitimacy of the state system and with it the ascendancy of the state. However, by assuming the legitimacy and ascendancy of the state, normative theorizing about international law helps to legitimate the state system and thereby to perpetuate the capacity of states to commit great moral evils and to impede moral progress.[24] It is states, after all, who engage in wars, the most destructive of human conflicts, and who

[22] Hart, *The Concept of Law*.

[23] Charter of the United Nations, adopted 26 June 1945, entered into force 24 Oct. 1945: repr. in *International Law: Selected Documents* (Boston: Little, Brown and Company, 1995), 1–28; Universal Declaration of Human Rights, adopted by the United Nations General Assembly 10 Dec. 1948: repr. in *International Law: Selected Documents*, 381–6; International Covenant on Civil and Political Rights, adopted by the United Nations General Assembly 16 Dec. 1966, entered into force 23 Mar. 1976: repr in *International Law: Selected Documents*, 387–403; International Covenant on Economic, Social and Cultural Rights, adopted by the United Nations General Assembly 16 Dec. 1966, entered into force 3 Jan. 1976: repr. in *International Law: Selected Documents*, 410–18; Convention on the Prevention and Punishment of the Crime of Genocide, adopted by the United Nations General Assembly 9 Dec. 1948, entered into force 12 Jan. 1951: repr. in *International Law: Selected Documents*, 419–21.

[24] Brilmayer, *American Hegemony*, 177.

are the most frequent and egregious violators of human rights. Furthermore, the control over resources that the state system accords to states as an element of sovereignty is perhaps the single greatest impediment to eradicating the most grievous distributive injustices in our world.

This objection wrongly assumes that moral theorizing about international law is necessarily conservative with regard to the state-centred character of the existing international system. To engage in moral theorizing about international law without acknowledging that the existing system is still to a large degree a state-centred system, could only result in a theory of little practical relevance. However, by taking the state-centred character of the system as a provisional given, the normative theorists need not endorse the legitimacy of existing states or of the state system.[25] Here a familiar distinction between ideal and non-ideal theory is relevant. Ideal theory specifies the ultimate moral optimum, under the assumption that the principles it articulates will enjoy full compliance. Non-ideal theory articulates principles for conditions in which there is serious non-compliance, including principles designed to help bring about the transition to circumstances in which the principles of ideal theory can be fully implemented.[26]

Whether or not the most comprehensive and defensible ideal moral theory of international law would include a prominent role for states as we now know them is a complex question—and one that probably cannot be answered until we have much more developed examples of moral theories than we now possess. But what is clear is that a non-ideal theory with practical import for our world must take the existence and current prominence of states seriously.

There are, in fact, several reasons to think that even ideal normative theory will presuppose something like states, though perhaps with considerably reduced powers in certain dimensions of sovereignty. First, a plurality of territorially based units each having considerable powers of self-government is presumably needed to avoid both the inefficiencies and injustices to which a world government would be prone.[27] Secondly, assigning primary responsibility for portions of the globe to different political entities provides them with incentives for conserving resources, reducing the risk of a global 'tragedy of the commons'.[28] Thirdly, according to some political philosophies, an irreducible pluralism regarding conceptions of public order or of social justice speaks in favour of a plurality of political units, within which different values can find effective expression.[29] (Note that there is no inconsistency between this argument and the rejection of Moral Minimalism: pluralism might be sufficiently deep to make it attractive to have a plurality of territorially based political societies with some of the

---

[25] Allen Buchanan, 'Recognitional Legitimacy and the State System', *Philosophy and Public Affairs*, 28 (1999), 46–78.

[26] For further discussion of the contrast between ideal and non-ideal theory, see John Rawls, *A Theory of Justice* (Cambridge, Mass.: Belknap Press of Harvard University, 1971), 8–11, 245–51.

[27] Immanuel Kant, *Perpetual Peace*, trans. and ed. by Lewis White Beck (Indianapolis: Bobbs-Merril Educational Publishing, 1957; 1st pub. 1795) and Rawls, *Law of Peoples*.

[28] Rawls, *Law of Peoples*, 39.   [29] Walzer, *Just and Unjust Wars*.

powers of self-government we now ascribe to states, without being so deep as to preclude any substantial moral content for international law.) Fourthly, it can be argued that there are limits to the scale of the political units in which democracy can flourish and that a truly democratic global state is not feasible. For all of these reasons, a division of the world's area into something resembling states may be morally defensible and even attractive, quite apart from the fact that for the foreseeable future we are likely to be stuck with a system in which states are prominent constituents.[30]

A moral theory of international law ought to provide a critical account not only of what the scope and limits of state sovereignty should be but also of the conditions under which the state system itself is legitimate. Because the normative enterprise conceived in this way does not assume either that states or the state system itself are morally legitimate, it cannot be viewed as inherently conservative.

Suppose, for example, that the best moral theory of international law turned out to support the following conclusions: (1) current international law is too restrictive regarding the right to secede; a more morally defensible international legal system would recognize a unilateral right to secede in many more instances than is now the case; (2) international law should be transformed so as to include international mandates for instituting autonomy regimes for certain groups (e.g. indigenous peoples) within existing states, and should impose on the international community clear obligations to monitor and enforce such arrangements. Suppose, further, that the best moral theory also concluded (3) that intervention to prevent systematic violations of fundamental human rights was not only permissible but obligatory in certain cases; (4) that states are under robust obligations to redistribute resources to benefit the global poor; and (5) that for the international legal and institutional system to be legitimate it would have to be much more democratic than it currently is—that the disproportionate influence that a small number of powerful states have in shaping and applying international law robs the system of legitimacy. A moral theory having these five features would pose a very serious challenge to the state system as we have known it; yet it could begin by taking the state-centred character of the existing system as a provisional given.

3 THE NATURE OF A MORAL THEORY OF INTERNATIONAL LAW

Structure. The fundamental structure of a normative theory of international law, as ideal theory, would consist of the following elements: (1) an account of the moral

---

[30] This paragraph draws on Buchanan, 'Recognitional Legitimacy'.

point, or goals of the institution of international law, the most fundamental moral values it ought to serve, (2) an articulation of the moral reasons for supporting the institution of international law as a means of achieving those goals or serving those values, (3) a specification of the conditions under which the international legal system would be legitimate, at least in the sense of there being an adequate justification for the processes of creating and enforcing the rules of the system,[31] (4) a statement of and justification for the most fundamental substantive principles of the system (including principles specifying the scope and limits of human rights, minority rights, and rights of self-determination, principles governing the use of force on the part of states and international organizations (just war and humanitarian intervention), principles specifying criteria for recognition of entities as members of the system, and principles governing trade relations, the distribution of global resources, environmental protection, and international financial regimes). The needed justification would consist chiefly in showing how the implementation of these principles would further the basic moral goals or fundamental values of the system and that they would do so in morally acceptable ways.

To convey just how fundamentally contentious moral theorizing about international law is, we merely note that there is disagreement as to the first item—the nature of the goals or values that the system of international law is to help achieve or serve. Until very recently, the predominant view has been that the overriding goal of the system is peace or, rather, the even more limited goal of peace *among states* (which is compatible with much violence within states)—and that justice is a legitimate aim only in so far as its pursuit would not threaten to undermine peace. A more ambitious moral theory—and one that we believe is ultimately more plausible—takes the chief goals of the international legal system to be peace (not just among, but within states) and justice.[32]

In the next two sections we structure the most basic issues that a normative theory of international law would have to address by relying on a distinction between two types of principles, those of transnational and of international justice. Transnational justice concerns those rights and duties that obtain between members of the same state or between the government of a state and its members which ought to be recog-

---

[31] 'Legitimate' in this minimal sense is to be contrasted with 'legitimate' in the 'right to be obeyed' sense commonly employed in political philosophy. The right to be obeyed (also sometimes called political authority) implies a correlative obligation to obey the government; legitimacy in the justified enforcement sense does not.

[32] David Luban, 'Just War and Human Rights', *Philosophy and Public Affairs*, 9 (1980), 160–81 and Buchanan, 'Recognitional Legitimacy'. The notion that peace among states was the predominant principle of the international legal system was reflected in widely held understandings of the United Nations Charter, with its emphasis on maintaining international peace and security and its seemingly absolute prohibition on 'the threat or use of force against the territorial integrity or political independence of any state'. UN Charter, art. 2(4). More recent trends have challenged this understanding, for example, NATO's intervention to prevent genocide in Kosovo. There is now a lively debate over the legality of 'humanitarian intervention'. Independent International Commission on Kosovo, *Kosovo Report* (New York: Oxford University Press, 2000).

nized by international law as being universal, that is, as applicable to all states. In other words, transnational justice principles articulate the principles of justice that the international community ought to insist are met by all states in their internal affairs. International justice concerns the rights and duties of the subjects of international law so far as they are not members of the same state and do not stand in the relationship of government to governed within a state. International justice includes the rights and duties of states to one another, but also more than this. It also encompasses the rights and obligations of global corporations, non-governmental organizations such as environmental and human rights groups, and international financial institutions and trade regimes. Finally, international justice also includes principles specifying the permissibility and/or obligatoriness of intervention across state borders in support of principles of transnational justice.

The distinction between transnational and international justice applies to both ideal and non-ideal theory, at least if it can be assumed that ideal theory will include a plurality of primary, territorially based political entities—something like what we now call states. In Section 4 we identify some of the main issues that the two types of principles would have to address, both in ideal and non-ideal theory. Here we consider briefly some of the distinctive features of non-ideal theory, mainly to clarify the practical function of moral theorizing about international law.

A proper realism: setting moral targets under the constraint of moral accessibility. Non-ideal theory must steer a course between a futile utopianism that is oblivious to the limitations of current international institutions and to the nature of international law as it now exists, on the one hand, and a craven capitulation to existing injustices that offers no direction for significant reform, on the other. The task of ideal theory is to set moral targets for the future that can provide useful guidance for action here and now, while at the same time providing standards for morally evaluating current international law and legal process.

Here a distinction between *feasibility*, *accessibility*, and *moral accessibility* is useful. An ideal normative theory is feasible if and only if the effective implementation of its principles is compatible with human psychology, the laws of nature, and the limits of natural resources available to human beings. Clearly, a theory that failed to meet the requirement of feasibility would be of little or no practical value. In addition to being feasible, an ideal theory should be accessible. A theory is accessible if it is not only feasible but in addition if there is a practicable route from where we are now to at least a reasonable approximation of the state of affairs that satisfies its principles. In other words, if ideal theory is to be useful for us, the ideal it specifies must be accessible to us, not just compatible with human psychology, the laws of nature, and the limitations of natural resources. This is an important distinction because not all states of affairs that are feasible are accessible. For example, the historical path we have already taken might preclude us from achieving some things that are accessible to human beings with different histories.

Finally, it can be argued that ideal theorizing should be subject to a further constraint: *moral* accessibility. Other things being equal, a theory should not only specify an ideal state of affairs that can be reached from where we are (though perhaps only after a laborious and extended process of change), but also the transition from where we are to the ideal state of affairs should be achievable without unacceptable moral costs. A requirement of moral accessibility is designed to signal that non-ideal theory should make a case that the corresponding ideal theory's principles can be satisfied through a process that begins with the institutions we now have and that does not involve unacceptable moral wrongs in the process of transition. Whether or not the moral costs of transition are acceptable will depend, in part, upon how defective the current state of affairs is (and upon the probability that efforts of reform will in fact succeed in escaping them without substituting other, comparable evils): other things being equal, greater costs are acceptable if needed to escape great evils. Yet according to some moral theories, there are limits on what we may do to bring about morally desirable ends. Part of a non-ideal theory's task is to provide an account of when the moral costs of transition are unacceptable.[33]

Finally, we want to caution against the overly simplistic notion that the conclusions of ideal or even of non-ideal theory yield principles that can be directly translated into actual legal prescriptions. Even when we have the most solidly founded moral principles on hand, there always remain complex practical questions about their implementation into legal norms. The goal of political philosophy is to provide aims that can and should help guide the lawmaker, but political philosophy's comparative advantage sharply diminishes when it comes to assessing how to implement those aims into any actual code of law. Here, familiarity with other disciplines, appreciation of systemic dynamics at all levels, knowledge of the political and legal culture, and a sense of political timing are, among many other considerations, of crucial importance.

The morality of transition. It would far exceed the bounds of this chapter to explore in any detail the complexities of what might be called the morality of transition as an essential element of non-ideal theory. However, we will mention briefly one feature of the international legal system as it now exists which may complicate the problem of the morality of transition: the international legal system currently possesses very limited resources for achieving large-scale moral reform without illegality. Illegal acts sometimes may be necessary to achieve significant moral improvement in the content of international law, due to the peculiarities of how international law is made and how the way it is made limits the possibilities for changing it.[34]

---

[33] We owe the distinction between feasibility and accessibility to Joshua Cohen. It is not clear to us whether his notion of accessibility amounts to our notion of moral accessibility, that is, accessibility without excessive moral costs.

[34] Allen Buchanan, 'From Nuremberg to Kosovo: The Morality of Illegal International Legal Reform', *Ethics* (forthcoming).

The two most important sources of international law are treaty and custom. Achieving a significant moral reform by treaty may be an extremely difficult and lengthy process if the system is sufficiently corrupt—if a substantial number of states are perpetrators of the very wrongs the reform is designed to eliminate. Hence reform may appear more likely by the establishment of a new, more enlightened norm of customary international law. However, the first actions that begin the process of constituting a new customary norm will constitute violations of existing customary norms, and hence be illegal.[35] This is a distinctive feature of customary systems which lack a legislature. Three examples will illustrate the nature of the problem, which we call the paradox of customary law.

In the nineteenth century the British government used the unrivalled power of the British Navy systematically and deliberately to destroy the international slave trade. Foreign ships were forcibly boarded and their human cargoes confiscated and freed, in some cases in the absence of bilateral treaties authorizing such actions. The destruction of the international slave trade, along with various activities of abolitionist groups in the United States and Britain and the victory of the North in the American Civil War, contributed to the eventual eradication of slavery and to the beginnings of the modern human rights movement. At the time, however, many claimed that some of the actions of the British Navy were violations of international law. (The British government argued that slavers were pirates and that the international law of piracy made the Navy's acts legally permissible, but not everyone, then, or now, found this line of argument to be convincing.)[36] Similarly, the Nuremberg War Crimes Tribunal undoubtedly played an important role in establishing both human rights norms and the prohibition of aggressive war—both impressive reforms of the international legal system—yet many would argue that some of the punishments meted out by the Tribunal were in fact illegal acts. Finally, the recent NATO intervention in Kosovo may prove to be the beginning of movement towards a new norm of international customary law permitting intervention in internal conflicts involving ethnocide or genocide in the absence of UN authorization, so long as the intervention is conducted by a regional collective security organization. Yet a strong case can be made that regardless of the morality of the NATO intervention, it was illegal.

The possibility that it may be necessary to commit illegalities for the sake of moral progress is not unique to the international legal system. Civil disobedients deliberately commit illegal acts to stimulate moral reforms in existing law. However, the frequency and gravity of such conflicts between legality and morality may be greater in

---

[35] The process of achieving a new norm of customary international law may not be any less difficult than the treaty process. In principle, customary international law requires the support, or at least the acquiescence, of the whole community of states. On the other hand, it may be that the less formal customary law process makes it easier for some states that would not sign on to a treaty nevertheless to acquiesce in a new norm of customary law.

[36] James A. Rawley, *The Transatlantic Slave Trade* (New York: Norton, 1981) and Alfred P. Rubin, *Ethics and Authority in International Law* (New York: Cambridge University Press, 1997).

the international legal system because the international system lacks mechanisms for fundamental legal reform (such as provisions for constitutional amendment) that are available in developed domestic systems. If, as many would affirm, international law is a relatively undeveloped system, with severe limits on its capacity for legal reform, and if at the same time it is also a very deficient system from the standpoint of morality, then one would expect that the problem of illegal action for the sake of legal reform would not be uncommon.

Describing the paradox of customary law as a conflict between legality and morality is misleading, however. The conflict is between a commitment to achieving a change in the law that makes the law morally better and honouring the moral commitment to support the rule of law by fidelity to the law as it is. A non-ideal moral theory of international law ought to illuminate this problem as an important element of its account of the morality of transition.

It is worth noting that there is an important asymmetry between the actions of the British Navy against slave traders or of the victorious allies at Nuremberg or NATO in Kosovo, on the one hand, and the typical case of civil disobedience, on the other. The civil disobedient can expect to pay and is willing to pay a penalty for violating existing law for the sake of creating morally better law. But what is peculiar to the three international cases cited is that those committing the illegal act were able to commit it with impunity. Especially when it comes to creating new, more enlightened customary norms by acting contrary to existing customary norms, the engine of moral reform in the international system is often hegemony or at least a gross inequality in power among states. Later we will consider the proposal that to be legitimate the international system itself would have to be much more democratic than it currently is—that the moral justification for enforcing international law is seriously compromised by the glaring political inequality among the members of the community of states. If this is so, then there is an added complexity to non-ideal theory's engagement with the morality of transition: the possibility that the effort to make the system more legitimate by achieving greater equality of power among states regarding the creation and enforcement of international law may in some cases undercut the conditions for illegal, but morally productive change, by reducing the asymmetry of power that is sometimes required for successful reform. The fact that the conscientious reformer may face this dilemma indicates a need for meta-reform—for enriching the system's capacity for lawful improvement.

4 Transnational Justice

Principles of transnational justice specify those requirements of justice applicable to relations *within* states that are the proper concern of international legal regulation. This formulation does not assume that transnational justice includes all requirements of justice that may be valid within a particular state. Beyond the domain of transnational principles of justice other principles of justice may apply to relations within states. Nor does it preclude the possibility of a significant degree of irreducible pluralism with respect to justice: once the requirements of transnational justice are met, what justice requires within one state may differ from what it requires in another. Transnational justice consists only of those principles that are valid for all states with regard to their internal affairs.[37]

The theory of transnational justice encompasses at least the following major issues. (1) What are human rights, which rights are human rights, and how are assertions about human rights to be justified? (2) Are principles specifying individual human rights sufficient to capture the full content of transnational justice, or are principles for group rights (e.g. rights of self-determination) for certain sorts of groups within the state such as national minorities or indigenous peoples also needed?

It is perhaps not much of an exaggeration to say that from the mid-nineteenth century until the adoption of the UN Charter in 1945, international law consisted mainly of principles in the category of international justice. State sovereignty, in its internal dimension, was conceived of as virtually unlimited, with the consequence that there was little space in international law for principles of transnational justice. Some of the most significant moral progress in international law in the past half-century has consisted in the expansion of the domain of transnational justice, chiefly through the development of individual human rights norms.

As will become clearer in Section 6, human rights play a fundamental role in both transnational and international justice. First, according to some normative views, including Rawls's in *The Law of Peoples*, only those states that meet the requirements of transnational justice, understood as respect for individual human rights, are entitled to enjoy the rights and privileges of members in good standing of the international community. In this type of theory, the requirements of transnational justice limit the rights of sovereignty conferred by principles of international justice and at the same time specify the conditions for membership in the system of states by providing criteria for recognition.[38] The idea that only entities that satisfy the most basic principles of transnational justice ought to be accorded the full rights, privileges, and

---

[37] We are grateful to Scott Shapiro for suggesting the general distinction between transnational and international justice.

[38] See Buchanan, 'Recognitional Legitimacy and the State System'.

immunities that comprise sovereignty is attractive in part because such a normatively demanding practice of recognition would provide incentives for just behaviour. However, an adequate defence of such a practice would have to address the
problem of negative externalities: penalizing a government by withholding recognition may have the unwanted effect of depriving its citizens of international representation, even though they are not to blame for the bad behaviour of their government.
And contrariwise, denying unjust states the ability to participate in international
institutions may in some cases so seriously disrupt co-operative relations among
states as to threaten important values for the international community as a whole. To
what extent these problems can be ameliorated by the creation of international institutions able to provide an independent voice for citizens of such states is uncertain.
As a result, as a matter of non-ideal theory, it may prove necessary to limit the disabilities imposed on unjust states to discrete areas where non-recognition will be
most effective in promoting internal justice.

Secondly, human rights play a central role in specifying principles governing the
use of force across state borders, in the theory of humanitarian aid, humanitarian
intervention, and just war theory, all of which are important elements of international justice. According to some views, intervention is justified only to stop serious violations of human rights. The doctrine of human rights can also provide
grounds for bilateral or multilateral obligations of aid, understood as obligations of
justice rather than as duties of charity. Finally, appeals to human rights provide the
rationale for constraints on the means by which war may be conducted, the treatment of non-combatants, and so on.

The nature of human rights. By definition, human rights are those moral entitlements that accrue to all persons, regardless of whether they are members of this or
that particular polity, race, ethnicity, religion, or other social grouping. Human
rights are understood to be claim-rights: they entail obligations on others. In the earlier phases of the human rights movement, governments were assumed to be the primary or even the sole others upon whom the obligation fell, since governments were
thought of as the chief potential violators of human rights. Increasingly, however, it
is recognized that non-governmental actors, including private 'death squads', global
corporations, and abusive parents and spouses, can and do violate human rights.
And with this recognition has come an acknowledgement that governments are
responsible, not only for refraining from violating their citizens' human rights, but
also for ensuring that others do not violate them.[39]

Justifications for human rights. Several distinct justifications for assertions about
individual human rights have been offered. Although the moral foundations from

---

[39] Jack Donnelly, *Universal Human Rights in Theory and Practice* (Ithaca, NY: Cornell University
Press, 1989); *The Concept of Human Rights* (London: Croom Helm, 1985); *International Human Rights*
(Boulder, Colo.: Westview Press, 1998); and Rhoda E. Howard, *Human Rights and the Search for
Community* (Boulder, Colo.: Westview Press, 1995).

which these justifications are developed may in some cases be inconsistent, in most cases the justifications converge on roughly the same list of human rights, or at least on lists with considerable overlap. Here we can only sketch in broad strokes some of the more prominent justifications, to convey an appreciation both for their diversity and for the tendency toward convergence. Individual human rights are presented as (1) principles whose effective institutionalization maximizes overall utility,[40] (2) as required for the effectiveness of other important rights,[41] (3) as needed to satisfy basic needs that are universal to all human beings, (4) as needed to nurture fundamental human capacities that constitute or are instrumentally valuable for well-being or human flourishing,[42] (5) as required by respect for human dignity,[43] (6) as the institutional embodiment of a 'common good conception of justice' according to which each member of society's good counts,[44] (7) as required by the most fundamental principle of morality, the principle of equal concern and respect for persons,[45] (8) as principles that would be chosen by parties representing individuals in a 'global original position' behind a 'veil of ignorance',[46] and (9) as necessary conditions for the intersubjective justification of political principles and hence as a requirement for political legitimacy.[47]

Different justifications may yield differences as to the inclusion or exclusion of some items on the list of individual human rights. Yet it can be argued that all these justifications support *at least* a core set including the rights to life (understood as freedom from arbitrary killing or injury, without due process of law, etc.), to liberty (understood as at least including freedom from slavery, involuntary servitude, and forced occupations), to freedom of conscience (understood as at least including freedom from religious persecution), and to subsistence (satisfaction of basic material needs).

The societal ethical relativist challenge to human rights. Societal ethical relativism is the view that ethical principles can be justified only by reference to the concrete social practices and traditions of a particular society. Accordingly, there are no human rights—no rights that all persons have simply because they are persons. Instead, all

[40] R. M. Hare, *Morality: Its Levels, Method and Point* (New York: Oxford University Press, 1981).

[41] Shue, *Basic Rights*.

[42] Amartya Sen, 'Well-Being, Agency and Freedom', *The Journal of Philosophy*, 82 (1985), 169–221, 200–21; *Inequality Reexamined* (Cambridge, Mass.: Harvard University Press, 1992), 39–42, 49; *Commodities and Capabilities* (New York: Oxford University Press, 1999); Martha Nussbaum, *Women and Human Development* (Cambridge: Cambridge University Press, 2000); and 'Aristotle, Politics, and Human Capabilities: A Response to Antony, Arneson, Charlsworth, and Mulgan', *Ethics*, 111 (2000), 102–42.

[43] Donnelly, *Universal Human Rights*; *The Concept of Human Rights*; *International Human Rights*.

[44] Rawls, *Law of Peoples*.

[45] Ronald Dworkin, *Taking Rights Seriously* (Cambridge, Mass.: Harvard University Press, 1977), 180–3.

[46] Beitz, 'Justice and International Relations'; Moellendorf, 'Constructing the Law of Peoples'; and Fernando R. Téson, *A Philosophy of International Law* (Boulder, Colo.: Westview Press, 1998).

[47] Joshua Cohen and Joel Rogers, *On Democracy* (New York: Penguin Books, 1983).

rights (and obligations) accrue to persons only by virtue of the distinctive, concrete relations they enter into with other members of their particular society. And if there are no human rights, then one cannot argue from the assumption that there are human rights to their inclusion in principles of transnational justice.

If any of the various justifications listed above ((1)–(9)) is sound, then there are some human rights, and the most extreme form of societal ethical relativism is false. To our knowledge, however, extreme societal ethical relativism has few if any takers in discussions of the normative theory of international law, or in real world political debates about human rights. Instead, the dispute tends to focus not on whether there are any human rights, but upon which rights are to be included in the list of human rights. For example, it is sometimes said that the right to democratic governance is not a human right, but at most a right that is appropriate for certain kinds of (liberal, Western) societies. Or, some complain that the right against gender discrimination, at least as it is understood in Western legal systems, is not a human right, because it is not appropriate for societies in which there are pronounced differences in the roles of men and women.

Notice that even if extreme societal ethical relativism were true, it is not clear that it would have such radical implications for the moral philosophy of international law as many would suppose. First of all, even if there are no human rights, there might turn out to be a set of rights that happen to be recognized by virtually all societies, and these could supply the substance of transnational justice.[48] (Our society might support international legal institutions for the enforcement of transnational justice in order to ensure that we comply effectively with the principles to which we are committed, using human rights treaties as 'self-binding mechanisms' and to ensure that other states live up to what we believe are genuine human rights principles.) Secondly, extreme societal ethical relativism is compatible with there being one set of principles of justice that is appropriate for embodiment in international law if the international community is, or is becoming, a single society in the relevant sense. And here we arrive at a severe limitation on the practical import of societal ethical relativism in both its extreme and more limited forms: if ethical principles are societally relative, what counts as a society? How socially integrated does a group of persons have to be to have a morality that is in some significant sense distinctive to and only appropriate for that group?

Even if it is true that at present there is sufficient societal diversity in our world that some particular putative human rights, such as the right to democratic governance, are not now plausible candidates for inclusion in the domain of transnational justice, that may not be true in the future if the phrase 'global society' becomes an accurate description. In fact there is already much interpenetration of values and beliefs among societies. Nor is there anything approaching unanimity on values *within*

---

[48] Michael Walzer, *Thick and Thin: Moral Argument at Home and Abroad* (Notre Dame: Notre Dame University Press, 1994).

societies; in that sense to speak of a society's values is already a gross oversimplification. Moreover, international law is one tool (among many others) for helping to build a global society. Indeed when human rights advocates appeal to international human rights standards in the domestic courts of their own societies, they help foster a domestic consensus on basic values where it is presently lacking.

Often what appears to be a denial that something is a human right is better understood as something quite different: either an admonition to avoid insensitive moral condemnation of persons in other societies or a rejection of intervention (or more violent modes of intervention) to enforce the right in question. For example, it is sometimes said that persons from Western societies have no right to condemn the practice of clitoridectomy practised in some African and Middle-Eastern states. This could be merely an appropriate warning to abstain from self-righteous rhetoric that fails to distinguish between human rights violations that involve deliberate and vicious wrongdoing, such as a government's torturing of dissidents, and violations that are deeply rooted in cultural practices that do not involve deliberate wrongdoing. Or it could be a warning against what would probably be extremely counterproductive efforts to intervene forcibly to end the practice in question. It is very important to distinguish, however, between (1) whether something is a human rights violation and whether persons are justified in identifying it as such, (2) whether those involved in the practices that constitute the violations are morally culpable, and (3) whether intervention to stop the violations is appropriate.

The difficulty is that loose talk about the diversity of human societies often runs all of these together. Whether clitoridectomy is a human rights violation depends upon whether the best justification (or set of justifications) for human rights claims implies that this practice violates a human right. If clitoridectomy is a human rights violation, then the fact that it would be callous and self-righteous of Westerners (or anyone else) to lump together those who participate in this practice with deliberate evil-doers (such as Nazi death camp commandants or dictators who order political murders) does not change the fact that clitoridectomy is a human rights violation. Similarly, the fact that intervention to abolish such a deep-rooted cultural practice would probably be both unsuccessful and destructive, does not count against the claim that clitoridectomy is a human rights violation, but only illustrates that the theory of humanitarian intervention does not consist of the simple assertion that intervention is justified whenever human rights are violated.

The charge of cultural imperialism. Societal ethical relativism also ought to be distinguished from yet another objection to attempts to rely on the concept of human rights as a foundation for a normative theory of international law. It is sometimes said that appeal to individual human rights serves to consolidate and extend the dominance of Western states in international relations. The chief problem with this charge of cultural imperialism is not that it is false, but that it is at best a half-truth. No doubt Western states (and non-Western ones as well) sometimes accuse other states of human rights violations to further their own agendas, and no doubt power-ful states (most but not all of which are Western states) sometimes exercise morally indefensible selectivity as to the targets of their accusations. It is also true, however, that there are many cases in which non-Western groups have successfully used the concept of human rights to advance their interests in conflicts with Western states.[49] The issue here, however, is not whether there are human rights, or whether human rights doctrine can play an important role in shaping international law. Instead, the real issue is that of *legitimacy*—the legitimacy or lack thereof of the ways in which human rights are formulated, invoked, and applied in international law and politics.

When a handful of states exerts disproportionate influence on the formulation of human rights norms, on the monitoring of human rights, and above all on the appli-cation of sanctions to states that are accused of violating human rights, the legitimacy of the entire system is called into question. The proper response, however, is not to confuse questions concerning the legitimacy of these processes or of the system as a whole with the issue of whether there are human rights or which rights are human rights. In Section 6 we take up the issue of system legitimacy.

Group rights. During the League of Nations period, between the two world wars, international law included provisions for group rights, chiefly in the form of cultural rights for certain national minorities, but lacked clear norms specifying individual human rights. Partly because of the League's failure to stem Fascist aggression and partly because the concept of national minority rights was discredited by Hitler's use of the alleged abuse of ethnic Germans in Czechoslovakia and Poland as a pretext for invasion, minority rights were accorded at best a minor role in the new international legal order forged by the United Nations after 1945.[50] Instead, the domain of transna-tional justice in the UN Charter era consisted almost exclusively of individual human rights, combined with recognition of a 'right of self-determination of peoples' that has been restricted to the case of decolonization. There is some indication, however, that greater attention to rights of minorities is emerging, especially in the area of indigenous peoples' rights.[51]

The chief issue for a moral theory of international law is whether the Charter era's near exclusive focus on individual rights is defensible, or whether transnational just-ice should also include a prominent place for group rights in addition to the limited right to self-determination invoked in the context of decolonization—and if so, how the relationship between these types of rights should be conceived. More specifically,

[49] Hannum, *Autonomy, Sovereignty, and Self-Determination*; and Risse *et al.*, *The Power of Human Rights*.

[50] Patrick Thornberry, *International Law and the Rights of Minorities* (Oxford: Clarendon Press, 1991) and John Packer and Kristian Myntii (eds.), *The Protection of Ethnic and Linguistic Minorities in Europe* (Abo/Turku: Abo Akademi University Press, 1993).

[51] S. James Anaya, *Indigenous Peoples in International Law* (New York: Oxford University Press, 1996); Hannum, *Autonomy, Sovereignty, and Self-Determination*; and Benedict Kingsbury, 'Sovereignty and Inequality', *European Journal of International Law*, 9 (1998), 599–625.

if group rights are included in international law, should they be understood as coordinate with individual human rights, and therefore conceptually basic, or as being in some way derivative?

A preliminary difficulty is the ambiguity of the term 'group rights'. To sort out the items that sometimes go under the heading 'group rights', we begin with the contrasting term. Individual rights are rights that are attributed to individuals and which individuals can wield (that is, waive, exercise, make claims on the basis of) as individuals, on their own behalf. Group rights, in what we will call the strong sense of the term, are rights that *cannot* be invoked by individuals as such, but only by persons or sets of persons representing groups. (There is a weaker sense of 'group rights' which might be called dual-standing rights: these rights can be invoked by individuals as individuals (so long as they are members of the appropriate group) but also by the group or by its representatives.)[52] Group rights in the strong sense are the most controversial: they include rights to land and other natural resources or rights to a share of control over development of land, various rights of self-government or self-administration for groups, rights over the conduct of various cultural activities including the teaching of languages, rights to restrict the use of other languages than that of the group in question at least in certain contexts, and rights to subsidies for the teaching of language or for other cultural activities.[53]

Certain national minorities, as well as many indigenous peoples groups, claim that individual human rights are insufficient—that the effective protection of their legitimate interests requires various group rights (in the strong sense). In some cases, the groups in question have been adamant that 'mere minority cultural rights'—which include the freedom to speak the minority language and to engage in its distinctive cultural practices and also perhaps rights to state subsidies for preservation of the minority culture—are not enough. They insist that rights of self-government are required, ranging from autonomy arrangements within states to full independence.

Whether a right is a group right (in the strong sense) is a matter of who is entitled to wield the right—group rights (in the strong sense) are wielded by groups or their representatives on behalf of them, individual rights are wielded by individuals as such, on their own behalf. This characterization of group rights (in the strong sense) leaves open the question of the *grounds* for the right, which may be either individualist or collectivist. Individualist justifications for group rights (in the strong sense) appeal to the value such rights have for individuals. Collectivist justifications appeal to benefits for the group that cannot be reduced to benefits for the individuals who comprise the group.

---

[52] Allen Buchanan, 'Liberalism and Group Rights', in *In Harm's Way: Essays in Honor of Joel Feinberg*, ed. Jules L. Coleman and Allen Buchanan (New York: Cambridge University Press, 1994); Will Kymlicka, *Liberalism, Community, and Culture* (New York: Oxford University Press, 1989); *The Rights of Minority Cultures*; and Margaret Moore (ed.), Introduction to *National Self-Determination and Secession* (New York: Oxford University Press, 1998).

[53] Kymlicka, *The Rights of Minority Cultures*.

Some have assumed that group rights (in the strong sense) are incompatible with the individualism that is essential to liberal political theory. If 'individualism' means justificatory individualism, this is clearly not the case. It is not necessary to appeal to the good of the group, as an irreducible value, to justify group rights (in the strong sense). Instead, one can ground a group right (in the strong sense) in the benefit which the group right confers on individuals, for example, (1) by affording them better protection of their individual human rights or (2) as mechanisms for ameliorating the ongoing effects of past discrimination on individuals. Rights to self-government for certain groups can perform both of these functions. Understood in this way, group rights (in the strong sense) are institutional back-ups for individual rights, not challenges to liberal individualism.

Much of the territory covered by minority cultural rights (as distinct from rights to self-government) could in principle be encompassed by better enforcement of some of the most fundamental individual human rights—in particular, the right to freedom of religion and conscience and the right to freedom from discrimination on grounds of race, ethnicity, or religion. Indeed, these individual human rights were originally invoked largely to provide protection for minority groups, especially religious minorities. However, as a practical matter, there may be situations in which the most effective way to protect the individual rights of a minority group may be to recognize certain group rights for it, including limited rights of self-government. In some cases the scope of these rights of self-government will include control over cultural activities, including the teaching of the minority language; in other cases, it may extend to local policing functions and control over land use and development, as with many indigenous groups in the United States and Canada. Which rights of self-government are appropriate will depend upon what is needed to protect the individual rights of group members.

So far we have only considered the role of group rights (in the strong sense) in protecting individual rights or ameliorating the continuing effects of past violations of individual rights. There are two additional grounds for rights of self-government for indigenous peoples. First, in many cases indigenous groups formerly enjoyed their own governments, which were destroyed by acts of injustice perpetrated in the process of colonization. In these cases, recognizing indigenous self-government rights is simply the restoration of self-government. Secondly, indigenous peoples often have suffered the unjust taking of their lands, sometimes through the breaking of treaty commitments made by the state or by imperial powers. In some cases, the appropriate initial remedial response will be to restore the lands or some comparable territory or to provide monetary compensation to the group, and to ensure that the group has the requisite powers of self-government to decide upon the ultimate disposition of the land or money that is awarded.[54]

---

[54] Anaya, *Indigenous Peoples in International Law*; Allen Buchanan, 'The Role of Collective Rights in a Theory of Indigenous Peoples' Rights', *Transnational Law & Contemporary Problems*, 3 (1993), 89–108;

These two justifications for group rights (in the strong sense) do not argue that group rights are the proper response to violations of individual rights or the continuing ill-effects of past violations of individual rights. They appeal instead to the need to rectify past violations of group rights (in the strong sense), either rights of self-government or collective rights over territory. The individual human rights listed in the major human rights conventions, at least as ordinarily interpreted, may not provide adequate mechanisms for addressing either the injustice of the destruction of indigenous self-government or the unjust taking of lands. Again, however, this analysis does not entail that these group rights must have a collectivist rather than an individualist justification. The rights to self-government and collective control over territory may themselves be derived from considerations pertaining to the interests of individuals.

The case of indigenous peoples perhaps provides the clearest indication that the non-ideal theory of transnational justice must include group rights; in other words, that the international legal order should in some cases require states to recognize group rights (in the strong sense) for some groups within them. But there are other minority groups within states, not usually identified as indigenous, who have also suffered systematic discrimination, unjust taking of their territory, and destruction of their self-government, and who continue to suffer the effects of these injustices. The fact that other groups have experienced some of the same problems as indigenous peoples raises the question of whether, at the deepest level of theory, indigenous peoples' rights form a distinctive category of rights. Without pretending to answer this complex issue, this much can be said: the proper response here is to steer a course between pretending that all of the most serious grievances of indigenous peoples are utterly unique, on the one hand, and assuming that the proper remedial response to injustices must always be the same, regardless of the particularities of the case, on the other.

Some critics have held that the conventional individual human rights are inadequate because they fail to acknowledge the importance to individuals of group membership. This diagnosis misses the mark. Some of the most central individual human rights, such as the rights to freedom of religion and association and the right to freedom from discrimination on the basis of race or religion, are valuable chiefly to individuals as members of groups. Rather, the chief limitation of individual human rights as they are typically understood is not that they fail to acknowledge the importance to individuals of group membership, but that they are oriented exclusively towards the present and the future; they are not designed to address the problems of past unjust takings of lands, violations of treaties between groups, or the restoration of self-government. Nor—as the case for affirmative action demonstrates—can one assume that the *present* implementation of individual human rights principles will in

David Lyons, 'The New Indian Claims and Original Rights to Land', *Social Theory and Practice*, 4 (1977), 249–72; and Douglas Sanders, 'The Re-Emergence of Indigenous Questions in International Law', *Canadian Human Rights Yearbook*, 3 (1983), 12–30.

every case adequately counter the continuing effects of massive past violations of individual human rights. For all of these reasons, at least one type of group right (in the strong sense), rights of self-government, will play a significant role in the non-ideal theory of justice, at least in the case of indigenous peoples or of other groups for whom similar issues of remedial and restorative justice arise.

The critics' claim, however, can be reformulated to raise a more fundamental challenge to the exclusion of group rights (in the strong sense) from the ideal theory of transnational justice. Here, the claim is not that individual rights fail to acknowledge the importance to individuals of group membership, but, rather, that they fail adequately to secure those interests. Thus, an adequate normative theory of international law must determine whether various alleged group rights should enjoy the same fundamental status in ideal theory as individual human rights presumably do, or whether they are properly located only in non-ideal theory, as institutional remedies whose appropriateness will depend upon various contingencies.

Sometimes those opposed to rights of self-government (or other group rights in the strong sense) for indigenous peoples or other minorities mistakenly assume that such arrangements are anti-individualistic simply because they are proposals for group rights, with the implication that group rights are somehow inherently problematic. But this response is fundamentally confused: all rights of all governments, from the state to the local level, are group rights in the strong sense: they are rights that cannot be wielded by individuals as individuals, but only by groups or by representatives of groups. Thus any liberal-individual theory of justice that acknowledges the legitimacy of any political units whatsoever, of any scale, already thereby concedes that there are group rights, namely, rights of self-government. The current state-centred system of international law *is* a system of group rights; it assigns great, though no longer unlimited rights of self-government to what we call states, with the result that non-state groups (such as national minorities and indigenous peoples) face severe obstacles in gaining international support for their efforts to achieve rights of self-government.

In that sense, the question for ideal theory is not whether there are group rights—there are as long as there are to be any self-governing entities—but rather: what sorts of entities, under which circumstances, should international law recognize as having which sorts of rights of self-government? The aspirations of indigenous peoples and other minority groups within states for rights of self-government are not an attempt to replace a system that only acknowledges individual rights with one that includes group rights; it is an attempt to modify the existing system of individual and group rights.

The issue of rights of self-government for minorities within states puts considerable pressure on the division between transnational and international justice. To the extent that rights of self-government and other group rights are justified as being remedies for shortfalls in the protection of individual human rights, it is appropriate to include them in transnational justice, assuming that the protection of human rights is at the core of the latter category. However, the second type of argument we have suggested in support of rights of self-government for indigenous peoples—that these rights are sometimes required to restore unjustly destroyed institutions of indigenous self-government or as part of a process for remedying the unjust taking of lands—appeals to the fact that the relations between indigenous groups and colonizing entities are or were similar to those between states. (In many cases European settler state officials made treaties with indigenous groups and in some cases appeared to recognize them as sovereign states.) To the extent that this is so, it could be argued that rights of self-government for indigenous peoples ought to be regarded as falling under the heading of international justice. The discourse of tribal sovereignty that is becoming so prominent in the United States endorses this conceptual shift.

Distributive justice as a human right. Historically, the most disputed issue concerning the scope of individual human rights concerns the status of so-called economic rights or rights of distributive justice, especially those that go beyond the right to subsistence. In the field of human rights activism, as opposed to the realm of theory, a recent strategy has been to argue that recognition of the right of freedom of association, coupled with international labour standards for health and safety, may be a more effective route toward improving the material well-being of the world's worst-off people, than insistence on a utopian egalitarian human right to a share of society's or of the world's wealth.[55] In the theory of human rights, however, there are fundamental disagreements concerning rights of distributive justice.

Much of the dispute has concerned whether rights of distributive justice are properly part of the domain of transnational justice; that is, whether international law should require states to meet certain standards in their internal distributive relations. This was a major question at issue in Cold-War debates as to whether human rights conventions should include so-called social and economic rights as well as civil and political rights. Beginning roughly in the 1970s, however, issues of international distributive justice have become more prominent, chiefly in the discourse of regional inequality, especially as between the Northern and Southern Hemispheres, or more generally in discourse that includes claims about what the more developed countries owe those that are less developed. In the remainder of this section, we examine the major theoretical stances on *transnational* distributive justice; in the next section we consider distributive justice as one element of the broader domain of *international* justice.

Doubts about transnational distributive justice. There are at least three distinct positions that have led many theorists to be sceptical about a significant role for transnational distributive justice in international law: Deep Distributive Pluralism

---

[55] See e.g. David Montgomery, 'Labor Rights and Human Rights: A Historical Perspective', in *Human Rights, Labor Rights, and International Trade*, ed. Lance A. Compa and Stephen F. Diamond (Philadelphia: University of Pennsylvania Press, 1996).

(according to which inter-societal disagreements about distributive justice are so basic and intractable as to make broad-based support for principles of transnational distributive justice impossible), Societal Distributive Autonomy (according to which distinct societies should be free to develop their own principles of distributive justice), and the Institutional Incapacity View (according to which international institutions are currently incapable of replacing the individual state as the authoritative arbiter and enforcer of distributive justice). Each will be considered in turn.[56]

Deep Distributive Pluralism. This is a variant of the Moral Minimalist position encountered earlier, focused specifically on distributive justice rather than on moral principles generally. According to Deep Distributive Pluralism, disagreements among societies about how resources are to be distributed within the state are so basic and intractable that substantive principles of transnational distributive justice cannot gain sufficiently broad support to function as elements of international law. The most obvious difficulty with Deep Distributive Pluralism, as a reason to deny a significant role for transnational distributive justice in international law, is that it seems premature to conclude that inter-societal disputes about distributive justice are uniquely and permanently unresolvable. Once we give up the unrealistic picture of societal cultures as social billiard balls that are both internally homogeneous and impervious to external influences, why should we assume that values concerning distributive justice (unlike those concerning other human rights) are immune to revision in the direction of greater inter-societal consensus? Moreover, much will depend upon how demanding proposed standards of transnational distributive justice are. Agreement on minimal standards that guarantee every citizen a right to some 'decent minimum' or 'adequate level' of resources may be considerably easier to obtain than agreement on more generous or more egalitarian standards. In fact there is already evidence of a broad consensus that there is at least a right to subsistence among the human rights.[57] In the end, whether or not disputes about distributive justice are significantly more recalcitrant to rational resolution or at least convergence of opinion

---

[56] We will not consider here the more general view that there are no 'positive' rights of any kind among the human rights because rights by their nature are purely negative, consisting only of constraints on the behaviour of others towards the right-holder, rather than any obligations to act. For a critique of this view see Kristen Hessler and Allen Buchanan, 'Specifying the Human Right to Health Care', in *Care and Social Justice*, ed. Margaret Battin, Rosalind Rhodes, and Anita Silvers (New York: Oxford University Press, forthcoming).

[57] Charter of the United Nations, adopted 26 June 1945, entered into force 24 Oct. 1945: repr. in *International Law: Selected Documents*, 1–28; Universal Declaration of Human Rights, adopted by the United Nations General Assembly 10 Dec. 1948: repr. in *International Law: Selected Documents*, 381–6; International Covenant on Civil and Political Rights, adopted by the United Nations General Assembly 16 Dec. 1966, entered into force 23 Mar. 1976: repr. in *International Law: Selected Documents*, 387–403; International Covenant on Economic, Social and Cultural Rights, adopted by the United Nations General Assembly 16 Dec. 1966, entered into force 3 Jan. 1976: repr. in *International Law: Selected Documents*, 410–18; Convention on the Prevention and Punishment of the Crime of Genocide, adopted by the United Nations General Assembly 9 Dec. 1948, entered into force 12 Jan. 1951: repr. in *International Law: Selected Documents*, 419–21.

than disputes about human rights generally is a question of fact, to be answered by cross-cultural empirical research or by the success or failure of efforts to forge a global consensus.

At present, agnosticism is the more reasonable stance. Given that the interpenetration of cultures through the development of a global economy and through an evolving transnational civil society is such a recent and as yet incomplete phenomenon, and given that serious systematic theorizing about distributive justice is in its infancy, the assertion that inter-societal disputes about distributive justice are permanently unresolvable is premature. To put this issue in perspective: only ninety years ago the idea that states would agree to an outright prohibition on aggressive war would have been greeted with derision; little more than fifty years ago anyone familiar with international affairs would have thought it naïve to believe that states would ever publicly agree to the limitations on their internal sovereignty imposed by human rights conventions.

A different source of scepticism about the possibility of a significant role in international law for transnational distributive justice is the perceived indifference of the international legal system to the whole domain of distributive injustice. Some critiques of the international legal system point to the unfairness it tolerates and even facilitates and then conclude that there is little reason to think that distributive justice will ever be accorded a prominent role in it. Yet a closer look at the full range of international law reveals that fairness discourse, and in some cases explicit appeals to distributive justice, are far from absent. In a masterful treatise entitled *Fairness in International Law and Institutions,* Thomas M. Franck provides a systematic overview of the various areas of recent international law in which considerations of distributive justice play a significant role. Especially striking instances include (1) multilateral compensatory financing (e.g. treaty-based commitments of wealthier states to compensate poorer trading partners for detrimental fluctuations in prices of commodities the latter export), (2) multilateral lending institutions that provide subsidized loans and credits for economic growth and the reduction of poverty in the worst-off countries, (3) international judicial interpretations of treaties governing exploitation of continental shelves, seabeds and their subsoils that appeal to the notion that the allocation of resources should be determined by considerations of equity where this is understood as giving special weight to the interests of the poorer states, (4) treaties concerning outer space and Antarctica that recognize them as a 'common heritage' from which all mankind is to benefit, and (5) environmental agreements that impose obligations on states to conserve resources for mankind generally, including future generations.[58]

The upshot of Franck's analysis is that there is a growing consensus, concretely manifested in the substance of international law and legal discourse in a number of

---

[58] Thomas M. Franck, *Fairness in International Law and Institutions* (New York: Oxford University Press, 1998).

distinct areas, not only that distributive justice matters, but also that some policies and institutional arrangements are unacceptably unjust. Although it is impossible to predict how much consensus on substantive standards of distributive justice in any of these areas will emerge and how effective efforts to secure compliance with agreed-upon principles will be, these developments at least call into question the assumption that the character of the international legal system is irremediably hostile to considerations of distributive justice.

Franck's examples for the most part pertain to international, not transnational distributive justice. It seems unlikely, however, that considerable consensus on the former should be emerging, and yet significant consensus on the latter be impossible. Efforts to give special weight to the needs of the worst off through special provisions in trade agreements or compensatory financing for poorer countries that are heavily dependent on exporting commodities presumably reflect a more general concern about the needs of worse-off individuals, rather than lower revenues for states. It may well be that for purely practical reasons the domain of international justice has been more hospitable to considerations of distributive justice rather than has that of transnational justice. Given current institutional capacity, securing agreement on and compliance with principles of transnational distributive justice may be more difficult, in part because transnational justice presents a more direct challenge to state sovereignty over resources than the sorts of international distributive arrangements described by Franck.

Societal Distributive Autonomy. According to this view, which is found in the works of Michael Walzer, there is no room for transnational distributive justice in international law because states ought to determine their own internal distributive arrangements.[59] According to Walzer, each distinct society is engaged in an ongoing process of developing and revising shared social meanings that ground distinctive principles of distributive justice, and the identity and well-being of individuals depends upon their participation in this cultural project. The benefits that individuals derive from the process depend upon its integrity, and this in turn requires that their shared meanings be worked out among themselves without standards being imposed from outside. Thus, the whole enterprise of transnational distributive justice is illegitimate, because it is an attempt to impose an external conception of distributive justice, with the result that the integrity of the indigenous process will be undermined.

There are several serious difficulties with this position. First, and most obviously, existing state borders and the memberships of distinct societies do not always, or even usually, coincide: most states encompass a plurality of distinct groups, so that Walzer's picture of a single process of developing shared meanings for a single people within the borders of the state is extremely inaccurate.

---

[59] Walzer, *Just and Unjust Wars* and *Spheres of Justice: A Defense of Pluralism and Equality* (New York: Basic Books, 1983).

Secondly, given the fact of the global economy and communications, the process of developing shared meanings is already and unavoidably subject to substantial external influences. If these far less controlled influences do not involve destructive interference with the process of developing shared social meanings, the same may well be true of the adoption of minimal global standards for domestic distributive justice. Everything will depend upon the content of the principles of transnational distributive justice and how they are developed and applied.

Thirdly, in many states some individuals (and in some cases the majority) are barred from meaningful participation in the process of articulating shared social meanings concerning justice, and sometimes they are barred precisely because they lack the material resources to participate, or even to achieve the minimal health and longevity required for participation. In many cases minority groups are so deprived of resources that they can neither participate meaningfully in the larger cultural processes of the state nor maintain their own distinctive culture and participate in its own meaning-generating processes. Minimal standards of transnational distributive justice, which would assure every individual a share of resources, would in such cases facilitate the very benefits that Walzer assumes would be endangered by them. Walzer's emphasis on cultural integrity and the goods it brings to individuals is a valuable insight, but it is better seen as a caution against cultural insensitivity in setting global standards than as a conclusive reason not to include principles of transnational distributive justice in a system of international law.

Institutional Incapacity. This view, unlike the previous two, does not rule out minimum requirements of transnational distributive justice *in principle.* Instead, it argues that under current conditions and for the foreseeable future the international legal system lacks the institutional resources to serve as the primary agent to determine what obligations of distributive justice obtain among those within the state and to ensure compliance with these determinations.[60] Instead, only individual states have the institutional capacity for being the primary arbiters and enforcers of distributive justice within states.

The needed institutional capacity does not consist solely in the inability to enforce principles of transnational distributive justice. Just as important is the capacity to make authoritative judgments about what distributive justice within the state requires and to adjudicate the application of these requirements.[61]

Unless one is willing to take the radical stance that the whole thrust of the institutionalization of human rights is misguided, the advocate of this view must make the case that the current institutional resources of international law are better fitted to articulate and enforce rights against genocide, torture, and religious discrimination, and other basic civil and political rights, than to specify and enforce principles of transnational distributive justice. Otherwise, the Institutional Incapacity View rules

60 Thomas Christiano, 'Democracy and Distributive Justice', *Arizona Law Review,* 37 (1995), 65–72.
61 ibid.

out not only transnational distributive justice but any significant role for inter-national institutions for securing justice of any sort.

In order to make a persuasive case that institutional incapacity rules out trans-national *distributive* justice without ruling out protection of other human rights, one could argue that the task of monitoring compliance with principles of distributive justice within states is exceptionally daunting, if only because judgments about dis-tributive justice, when made about societies as a whole, require very complex eco-nomic data and detailed knowledge about the workings of institutions. Determining whether a particular government engaged in more than fifty instances of torture in the past year, or that it jailed members of the opposition press, may be much simpler. The international legal order has only recently begun to develop these relatively sim-pler institutional structures for monitoring compliance with basic civil and political rights; it is very far from being able to determine whether comprehensive principles of transnational distributive justice are being effectively implemented.

On the other hand, the plausibility of the Institutional Capacity View may depend upon the content of the relevant principles of distributive justice. Thus, for example, a principle that required only that all members of society have sufficient resources to live at a subsistence level might not be as subject to the kind of objections which the Institutional Capacity View raises as would be a more robust principle.

The Institutional Capacity View, unlike Deep Distributive Pluralism and Societal Distributive Autonomy, allows for the possibility that principles of transnational dis-tributive justice may eventually come to occupy an important role in international law. It thus acknowledges that reasoning about principles of transnational distribu-tive justice is a legitimate part of the *ideal* moral theory of international law (while at the same time acknowledging that for the present at least transnational distributive justice will not play a prominent role in non-ideal theory). Just as important, the Institutional Incapacity View, again unlike Deep Distributive Pluralism and Societal Distributive Autonomy, is compatible with a commitment to trying to build the institutional capacity needed for making transnational distributive justice a reality.

In the next section we explore the main theoretical choices available in the domain of *international* justice, which concerns the principles of justice that are applicable to relations among states. These include principles of distributive justice, but also other types of principles, including those that determine which entities ought to be recog-nized as states and those that specify the obligatoriness or permissibility of humani-tarian intervention to help ensure that states comply with the requirements of transnational justice in their treatment of their own citizens.

5 INTERNATIONAL JUSTICE

International distributive justice. We noted earlier that issues of distributive justice must be considered under each of the two major divisions of the normative theory of international law, transnational justice and international justice. Transnational distributive justice concerns the rightful distribution of resources among members of the same state, so far as this is a proper concern of international law; international distributive justice concerns the rightful distribution of resources among states, or among persons or groups living in different states. The issues of international distributive justice can be illuminated by a distinction between two different ways of grounding obligations of international distributive justice.

The distinction is between theories of international distributive justice that ground obligations in the fact of interaction across state boundaries and those that do not. According to Interactionism, obligations of distributive justice only obtain among those who are engaged in co-operation with one another.[62] So there can be principles of international distributive justice between states only because, as a matter of fact, there are co-operative interactions across state boundaries.

A variant of Interactionism focuses not only on the idea that there is co-operation across state boundaries but that this co-operation occurs within a global basic structure, the international analogue of what Rawls calls the basic structure of a single society.[63] The global basic structure must be regulated by principles of distributive justice for the same reason that Rawls says the basic structure of the individual state must: because its effects on the prospects of individuals and groups are pervasive, profound, enduring, and to a significant degree not a matter of choice. Interactionists who emphasize the existence of a global basic structure contend that the most basic principles of distributive justice must include principles to regulate the global basic structure, or, in Rawlsian terms, that the global basic structure is a primary subject of justice. Just as principles to guide individual conduct would be insufficient to achieve distributive justice in the case of the single state because the effects of the basic structure are profound and systematic, so international distributive justice requires principles to regulate the global basic structure.

The Non-interactionist view, in contrast, holds that international distributive obligations would exist even if there were no interactions across state borders. The most obvious basis for the Non-interactionist view of the domain of justice is a robust version of what Rawls calls the Natural Duty of Justice: a general moral obligation to work to ensure that all persons have access to just institutions. If there is such an obligation and if just institutions include the implementation of principles of distributive justice, then international distributive justice does not depend upon the fact of co-operative interaction or upon the existence of a global basic structure.

---

[62] Beitz, 'International Liberalism and Distributive Justice'.   [63] Rawls, *A Theory of Justice*.

The Robust Natural Duty of Justice, presumably, is based on something more fundamental: a principle of equal consideration for persons. The intuitive idea is that equal consideration requires not only that we refrain from violating persons' rights, but that we do something to help ensure that all persons have access to institutions that will protect their rights.[64] All liberal theories other than strict libertarianism hold that equal consideration for persons requires that all persons have access to at least a modicum of resources required for the meaningful choice or for the effective exercise of their basic rights. If this is the case, then the Robust Natural Duty of Justice obligates us to help create the institutions needed to achieve distributive justice for all. Whether doing this is best achieved by international support for transnational distributive justice or by institutions of international distributive justice will depend in part upon whether or not it is assumed that the individual state is to remain the primary agent of distributive justice. If states are assumed to be the primary agents of distributive justice and if it turns out that some states have insufficient resources to satisfy the principles of transnational distributive justice, then the Robust Natural Duty of Justice will require the establishment of institutions to redistribute resources from richer to poorer states—in other words to create a regime of international distributive justice.

Charles Beitz's view combines Interactionist and Non-interactionist components. Although he emphasizes that the existing extent of global interaction is sufficient to ground duties of distributive justice across borders, he also believes that justice would require international redistribution even in the absence of interaction, to ameliorate inequalities in resources among individuals in different states. It should be noted, however, that while Beitz clearly believes that there are obligations of distributive justice that do not depend upon co-operative interaction, he is perhaps less clear regarding his endorsement of the Robust Natural Duty of Justice. However, unless something like the Robust Natural Duty of Justice is assumed, it is hard to see what the basis is for obligations of justice in the absence of co-operative interaction.

Another variant of Interactionism ought to be distinguished. Thomas Pogge grounds obligations of distributive justice not on the fact of interaction or the existence of a global basic structure *per se* but upon the obligation not to harm.[65] According to this view, the existence of a global basic structure is noteworthy from the standpoint of international justice only because it creates opportunities for harming others through our participation in it.

Pogge apparently believes that grounding international justice in this manner is preferable because the obligation to prevent harm is a stricter or more obviously valid duty than the duty to benefit others. This choice of argumentative strategies comes at

---

[64] For a defence of the Robust Natural Duty of Justice, see Allen Buchanan, 'The Morality of Inclusion', *Social Philosophy and Policy*, 10 (1993), 233–57 and 'Justice, Charity, and the Idea of Moral Progress', in *Giving: Western Ideas of Philanthropy*, ed. J. B. Schneewind (Bloomington, Ind.: Indiana University Press, 1996).

[65] Pogge, *Realizing Rawls* and 'An Egalitarian Law of Peoples'.

a price, however. The first difficulty with it is that the global basic structure is so exceedingly complex that the sense in which we can be said to be 'interacting' with all other persons around the world is correspondingly attenuated. And because 'participation' in the global basic structure is so attenuated, the attribution of harm becomes correspondingly problematic. So even if it can be shown that particular individuals are being harmed by the operation of the global structure, it may be far more difficult to show that any given individual is responsible for the harms that others suffer as a result of the myriad complex interactions that take place within the global basic structure. In some cases, it may be plausible to attribute causation of harm to persons in positions of great power in the global structure, such as the leaders of the most powerful states or of global financial institutions such as the World Bank or of multilateral corporations, but it would be much more difficult to argue that ordinary persons cause harm to others through their participation in the global basic structure. Secondly, to the extent that the existing global basic structure is the 'only game in town', it may be misleading to say that our participation in it is voluntary; yet it would seem that voluntariness is a condition for responsibility. Thirdly, if the obligations of distributive justice are purely negative—the duty not to harm—then presumably the scope of distributive obligations is quite limited. At most, the well-off are obliged to ensure that the worse off are not made any worse off than they would otherwise be in the absence of any participation in the global basic structure.[66]

One final difficulty with Pogge's view is worth noting. In any co-operative scheme, no matter how just, some individuals will be harmed. For example, simply due to bad luck or to poor judgment on my part or to the fluctuations of market demand, I may suffer a setback to my economic interests because I choose the wrong profession or buy the wrong stocks, or I may lose my job to a better qualified person. But not all such harms are injustices (or wrongs). Pogge's attempt to base international distributive justice on the obligation not to harm therefore is fatally incomplete unless an account of unjust harms can be supplied. However, to distinguish between unjust harms and harms that do not constitute wrongs, one needs a theory of justice, including, presumably an account of what people are entitled to as a matter of just distribution. The question then arises: if such an account of distributive justice is available, why not appeal directly to it rather than to the rather problematic notion of causing harms through participation in the basic structure?

The Non-interactionist view, which grounds international distributive obligations in the Robust Natural Duty of Justice, avoids these difficulties. It requires neither a theory of participation capable of showing that all humans are in some meaningful sense co-participants in a global scheme of co-operation that generates obligations of distributive justice of each towards all, nor an account of responsibility for harm that grounds distributive obligations of individuals in extremely

[66] See Liam B. Murphy, 'Institutions and the Demands of Justice', *Philosophy and Public Affairs*, 274 (1998), 251–91.

complex, indirect patterns of interaction among billions of individuals. The crucial task for the Non-interactionist, rather, is to make a convincing case that equal consideration for persons requires not only refraining from violating their rights but also working to ensure that all persons have access to institutions which will ensure that their rights are protected. Underlying this view is the claim that there is a deep incoherence in asserting that equal regard for persons requires refraining from violating their rights even if this comes at great cost, while denying that equal regard requires any efforts whatsoever to ensure that persons' rights are protected from violations by others.

Perhaps the more difficult task for the Non-interactionist approach to international distributive justice is to provide a convincing account of the *scope* of the Robust Natural Duty of Justice in order to articulate its concrete implications. In particular, much must be said about what the individual is required to do—what costs she must bear—in order to co-operate with her fellow citizens in the multi-generational project of building international institutions of distributive justice. In the absence of domestic and international institutions that specify and fairly distribute the burdens of providing access to just institutions for all, it may be impossible to determine with any specificity the scope of the natural duty. What any given individual ought to do in this regard will depend in part upon what can be done, and what can be done will depend upon existing institutional resources. If one is extremely pessimistic regarding the prospects for developing effective institutions of international distributive justice, one might conclude that for the foreseeable future the Robust Natural Duty of Justice does not apply at the international level, at least so far as distributive justice is concerned. One might conclude instead that the best way to honour the principle of equal regard for persons on which the Robust Natural Duty of Justice rests is to attempt to alleviate the condition of (some of) the world's poorest by private donation.

Secession and self-determination. Earlier we argued that at least with regard to indigenous peoples, there is a case for international support for rights of self-government, when these rights are needed to restore unjustly destroyed institutions of self-government, to help rectify past unjust takings of lands, to prevent violations of individual human rights, or to reduce the ongoing deleterious effects of past violations of individual human rights. In its most extreme form, self-government means independent statehood. One of the most basic and difficult issues for a moral theory of international law concerns what the legal status of secession should be. If the international community recognizes the legitimacy of a group's secession from an existing state, the secessionist entity is accorded the status of a full-fledged member of the state system, with all the distinctive rights, privileges, and obligations characteristic of states, and as being entitled to engage in equal relations with other states. Hence the international legal response to secession raises the most fundamental issues of the second main division of the moral theory of international law, international justice—those principles of justice that specify the rights and obligations that obtain between persons or entities by virtue of their being members of different states and that ought to be recognized in international law.

The status of secession in existing international law. According to the preponderance of opinion among international legal scholars, there is at present no international legal right to secede except in two rather specific circumstances: (1) what might be called classic cases of colonization (as when an overseas colony liberates itself from metropolitan control), and (perhaps) (2) reclaiming of sovereign territory that was subjected to military occupation by a foreign power through an act of aggression.[67] Some might add a third condition: where a racial (or perhaps religious) group is denied meaningful access to and participation in government. By a 'right' here is meant a claim-right: to say that a group has the right to secede implies (i) that it is permissible for them to attempt to establish their own independent state out of a portion of the territory of the state in which they are now located, and (ii) that others, including the state in question, are obligated not to interfere with this attempt.

It is important to observe here that this view about the status of secession in international law concerns only what might be called unilateral (or non-consensual) secession. Nothing in international law renders impermissible freely negotiated agreements to allow secession between the secessionists and the state, as occurred with the secession of Norway from Sweden in 1905. Nor does international law preclude secession by constitutional provision.[68]

Some legal scholars have recently argued that international law, while only including a (claim-)right to secession in the narrow circumstances described above, does not include any clear prohibition of secession either. They have further argued that since what is not forbidden is permissible in international law, secession is permissible, that is, that there is what Hohfeld called a liberty-right (though not a claim-right) to secede.[69] From this it would follow that if the state resists secession it would not be violating any requirement of international law even though international law does not prohibit the secessionists from attempting to secede.

The ambiguity or silence of international law on cases of secession other than those involving classic decolonization or military occupation is not merely a theoretical

---

[67] Antonio Cassese, *Self-Determination of Peoples: A Legal Reappraisal* (New York: Cambridge University Press, 1995) and Hannum, *Autonomy, Sovereignty, and Self-Determination.*

[68] See Constitution of the Federal Democratic Republic of Ethiopia, 1994. The Federal Democratic Republic of Ethiopia. In: http://www.ethiopar.net/English/cnstiotn/consttn.htm; ICL 2000 Constitution of the Former Soviet Union, 1977. Wuerzburg University and Charter 88. In: http://www. uni-wuerzburg.de/law/r100000_.html; Political Database of the Americas 1999 Saint Kitts and Nevis Constitution, 1983. Georgetown University and the Organization of American States. In: http://www.georgetown.edu/LatAmerPolitical/Constitutions/Kitts/stkitts-nevis.html. It is important to distinguish between secession by explicit constitutional provision, secession compatible with constitution, and secession by constitutional amendment (as suggested by a recent Canadian Supreme Court Reference Ruling). See *Reference re Secession of Quebec*, 1998. 2 S.C.R.

[69] Franck, *Fairness in International Law and Institutions.*

deficiency. The confused and ineffectual international response to the break-up of Yugoslavia and, more recently to the wars of Chechen secession, shows not only a lack of political will but a lack of consensus on principles. In the case of Yugoslavia the Western powers vacillated between proclaiming the conflict to be an internal dispute protected from intervention by the veil of state sovereignty and attempting to constrain what appeared to be the inevitable process of dissolution by applying the international legal principle of *uti possidetis*, rather implausibly, to a situation quite different from the one in which the principle had previously been recognized. The principle of *uti possidetis*, according to which borders may only be changed by agreement, provides the foundation in international law for the territorial integrity of existing states. This principle was invoked in the processes of decolonization in South America and later affirmed by the Organization of African Unity during the period of African decolonization in the 1960s and 1970s. In the case of Yugoslavia, the principle was applied, not to the borders of colonial states but to the internal borders of a self-governing federation.[70]

The title of an outstanding book on the dissolution of Yugoslavia describes the international response as a 'triumph of the failure of will' and this is no doubt true.[71] However, a will guided by sound principles, and more important, principles for which good reasons can be given, may be more constant, other things being equal.

In the past decade there has been a remarkable growth in the normative literature on secession.[72] For the most part this work focuses on the right to secede as a unilateral moral claim-right, rather than upon specifying the conditions under which special rights to secede might be generated through agreement or created by constitutional provisions.[73] In most cases the implications for international law are left wholly unclear.[74]

---

[70] Misha Glenny, *The Fall of Yugoslavia: The Third Balkan War* (New York: Penguin, 1992); James Gow, *Triumph of the Lack of Will: International Diplomacy and the Yugoslav War* (London: Hurst, 1997); and Susan L. Woodward, *Balkan Tragedy: Chaos and Dissolution after the Cold War* (Washington, D.C.: Brookings Institution, 1995).

[71] Gow, *Triumph of the Lack of Will*.

[72] Beran, *The Consent Theory of Obligation*; 'A Liberal Theory of Secession'; Buchanan, *Secession*; 'Theories of Secession'; David Copp, 'Do Nations Have the Right of Self-Determination?' in *Philosophers Look at Canadian Confederation*, ed. Stanley French (Montreal: Canadian Philosophical Association, 1979); Couture *et al.*, *Rethinking Nationalism*; Omar Dahbour and Micheline R. Ishay (eds.), *The Nationalism Reader* (Atlantic Highlands, NJ: Humanities Press International, Inc., 1995); McKim and McMahan, *The Morality of Nationalism*; Moore, *National Self-Determination and Secession*; David Philpott, 'In Defense of Self-Determination', *Ethics*, 1052 (1995), 352–85; Yael Tamir, *Liberal Nationalism* (Princeton: Princeton University Press, 1993); and Christopher Wellman, 'A Defense of Secession and Political Self-Determination', *Philosophy and Public Affairs*, 24 (1995), 357–72.

[73] Buchanan, 'Theories of Secession'; Norman Wayne, 'Secession and Constitutional Democracy', in *Democracy and National Pluralism*, ed. F. Requejo (New York: Routledge, forthcoming); and Cass Sunstein, 'Constitutionalism and Secession', *University of Chicago Law Review*, 58 (1991), 633–70.

[74] Buchheit is an earlier exception, but his view mainly concerned with what the law is, does not provide a systematic moral analysis. See Lee C. Buchheit, *Secession: The Legitimacy of Self-Determination* (New Haven: Yale University Press, 1978).

Theories of secession. Moral theories of (unilateral) secession can be divided into two main types: Remedial Right Only Theories and Primary Right Theories.[75] Remedial Right Only theories conceive of the right to secede as analogous to the right to revolution, as the latter is understood in the mainstream of liberal theories of revolution: as a remedy of last resort for persistent and grave injustices. Revolution aims at overthrow of the government; secession aims at severing a portion of the state's territory from its control. What is common to the Remedial Right Only Theory of the (unilateral) right to secede and the mainstream liberal account of the right to revolution is that in both cases the right only exists under conditions of serious injustice. Different Remedial Right Only theories of secession provide different accounts of the sorts of injustice for which secession is the appropriate remedy. One major division along these lines is between theories that recognize only genocide or massive violations of the most fundamental human rights as being sufficient to justify secession (in addition to classic colonization and unjust military occupation or annexation) and those that also recognize the state's violation of internal autonomy arrangements for national minorities or indigenous groups or the state's failure to acknowledge valid claims to internal autonomy.

It is important to note that Remedial Right Only Theories only concern the conditions under which there is a right to *unilateral* secession. They are compatible with a very permissive stance on negotiated or constitutional secession. In that sense, Remedial Right Only Theories are not as conservative as might first appear.

Primary Right Theories, in contrast, have a more permissive view of the (unilateral) right to secede. What different Primary Right Theories have in common is that they reject the thesis that the unilateral right to secede exists only as a remedy for injustice. Primary Right Theories divide into two main types: Ascriptivist Theories and Plebiscitary Theories. The former hold that certain groups whose memberships are defined by what are sometimes called ascriptive characteristics have the (unilateral) right to secede, simply because they are such groups. Ascriptive characteristics include being of the same nation or ethnicity or being a 'distinct people'. (Such characteristics are called ascriptive because they are ascribed to individuals independently of their choice.) The most common form of Ascriptivist theory is the view that nations have a right of self-determination that includes the (unilateral) right to secede.[76]

Plebiscitary (or voluntarist or associative-group) theories in contrast assert that a region may secede if a majority of persons residing in it choose to secede, regardless of whether they are unified by any characteristics other than this desire for independence,

---

[75] See Buchanan, 'Theories of Secession'. For a similar distinction with different terminology see Moore, *National Self-Determination and Secession* and Norman, 'Secession and Constitutional Democracy'.

[76] Couture *et al.*, *Rethinking Nationalism*; Moore, *National Self-Determination and Secession*; Percy B. Lehning (ed.), *Theories of Secession* (New York: Routledge, 1998); and McKim and McMahan, *The Morality of Nationalism*.

including any ascriptive characteristics. What Ascriptivist and Plebiscitary theories have in common is that they do not require injustice as a necessary condition for the unilateral right to secede. However, both types of Primary Right Theories allow the possibility that injustice provides one type of justification for unilateral secession as well. Primary Right Theories are not Primary Right *Only* theories; they allow secession as a remedy.

No comprehensive comparative evaluation of the major types of theories of the moral right to secede can be attempted here.[77] Instead, we will only attempt to identify some of the major strengths and weaknesses of the two types of theories, proceeding on the assumption that these theories are supposed to provide guidance for how international legal institutions should respond to secession and in particular that they are supposed to provide answers to the question 'Under what conditions should the international community recognize a secessionist entity as a new state?' In other words, we will evaluate Remedial Right Only and Primary Right Theories as normative accounts of how the international legal order ought to respond to secession, on the assumption that the principles they recommend are to be institutionalized within a system of principles constituting a comprehensive normative theory of international law.

As Lea Brilmayer has rightly stressed, secession is not simply the formation of a new political association among individuals, it is the taking of territory, accompanied by a claim to be entitled to sovereignty over that territory.[78] Accordingly, rival theories of secession should be seen as providing alternative accounts of what it takes for a group to come to have a claim of sovereignty over territory that is at the time included in the territory of an existing state. As we shall see, some of the most serious objections to Primary Right Theories question the cogency of their accounts of exactly what it is that gives an intra-state group title to sovereignty over part of the state's territory.

Remedial Right Only Theories. This approach recognizes at least two ways a secessionist group can have the requisite claim to territory: (*a*) by reclaiming territory over which they were sovereign but which was unjustly taken from them (as with the Baltic Republics' secession from the Soviet Union in 1991); or (*b*) by coming to have a claim to sovereignty over the territory as a result of availing themselves of a last resort remedy against serious and persisting injustices (such as human rights violations or violations of agreements by which the state accorded the group some form of autonomy within the state). In the former case the basis of the claim to territory is straightforward: the secessionists are simply claiming what was theirs and what was recognized as theirs under international law. The issue becomes more complicated, however, when two questions are considered: (1) was the sovereignty of the entity in

[77] Allen Buchanan, 1998 'The International Institutional Dimension of Secession', in *Theories of Secession*, ed. Lehning and Moore, Introduction to *National Self-Determination and Secession*.

[78] Brilmayer, 'Secession and Self-Determination'.

question disputed at the time of its annexation (if so, then the claim to recover lost territory is to that extent problematic, given the lack of an authoritative international judicial body to adjudicate the issue)? (2) Do legitimate interests in stability argue for a statute of limitations on unjust takings of sovereign territories, and if so, how is its duration to be determined?

In the latter case, the Remedial Right Only Theory begins with a presumption that existing states have valid claims to their territory but then argues that such claims to territory must be subordinated in the face of persistent patterns of serious injustices towards a group within a state that cannot be remedied short of secession. The intuitive idea is that international justice imposes upon the state an overriding duty to protect the basic human rights of all its citizens and that even its claim to its own territory may be subject to defeasance if the state is incapable of, or unwilling to, carry out this obligation.[79] Thus, the validity of the state's claim to territory cannot be sustained when the only remedy which can assure that the fundamental human rights of a persecuted group within the state's territory will be respected is secession.[80]

The Remedial Right Only approach makes a basic distinction between the state and the government. If a government violates the fundamental human rights of a group of its citizens living in a portion of the state's territory, then that group may, as a remedy of last resort, secede. But this only means that the government's profound injustice towards the group can void the state's claim to that portion of its territory. The government's unjust behaviour does not void the state's claim to the rest of its territory. This way of understanding the basis of the secessionists' claim to territory is attractive because it avoids the unacceptable implication that a bad government's actions undermine the legitimacy of the state. Such a view is implausible because it would impose an unjust penalty upon the people as a whole—even when they oppose the government's unjust policies. The loss of the seceding territory is a loss to the people of the state as a whole, but it is justified on the grounds that the secession is the remedy of last resort for those who have suffered a serious injustice. The right of the injured group to avail themselves of this remedy does not affect the state's claim to the remainder of its territory.

Given the tendency for secession to provoke massive violence and cause severe political instability, the strength of the Remedial Right Only approach is that it places a significant constraint on unilateral secession—the requirement of a serious and persistent grievance on the part of the secessionists. To that extent it captures the intuition that non-consensual state-breaking, like revolution, is a serious affair, requiring a weighty justification. Another strength of the Remedial Right Only approach is that it appears to provide the right incentives: states that are just are immune to legally permitted unilateral secession and entitled to international support in maintaining the full extent of their territorial integrity against secessionist

79 Buchanan, 'Recognitional Legitimacy and the State System'.
80 Note that another qualification is needed: the state must meet minimal standards of justice in its external relations as well. Ibid.

threats. On the other hand, if, as the theory dictates, international law recognized a unilateral right to secede as a remedy for serious and persistent injustices, this would give states an incentive to act more justly.

However, some critics have complained that the Remedial Right Only Theory assumes a bias in favour of the status quo by requiring secessionists to establish a grievance in order to justify unilateral secession. This objection can be answered if Remedial Right Only Theory can be made to cohere with a cogent account of what gives the state a valid claim to territory in the first place.[81]

Other critics have complained that Remedial Right Only Theories are disturbingly irrelevant to the concerns of most groups seeking self-determination—for in most cases, it is nationalism that fuels the quest for self-determination, not grievances of injustice *per se*.[82] The key to responding to this objection is to notice that the Remedial Right Only Theory of secession is only a theory of the (unilateral) right to secede, not a comprehensive theory of self-determination. Secession is only the most extreme form of self-determination. Short of independent statehood there is a very broad range of self-determination arrangements, with varying degrees and dimensions of autonomy. In the end, the plausibility of the Remedial Right Only Theory of secession depends upon its being integrated into a comprehensive theory of self-determination, and one which gives the claims of nationality their due.

In our view, the most plausible attempt to achieve this integration would involve uncoupling the right to secede from issues of intra-state autonomy. This approach might be dubbed the 'isolate and proliferate strategy': The unilateral right to secede is isolated as a rather constrained right, understood as a remedy of last resort for persistent violations of basic rights, while a much more permissive and supportive stance is to be adopted by international law towards proliferating a variety of intra-state autonomy regimes, tailored to the exigencies of different problems.[83] According to the isolate and proliferate strategy, talk about *the* right of self-determination is misleading and not constructive, partly because it encourages the view that if a group is entitled to some form or other of self-determination then it thereby also has the right to opt for self-determination in its most extreme form, independent statehood.

Uncoupling the right to secede from the legitimate interests that groups may have in various forms of autonomy within the state can be liberating. For one thing, it may allow the groups in question to get what they need without the risks involved in secession. For another, it may make states more receptive to legitimate claims to autonomy if they believe they can respond to these without implicitly endorsing the right to secede.

[81] For an attempt to provide the needed account of the valid claim to territory, see Buchanan, 'Recognitional Legitimacy and the State System'.

[82] Moore, Introduction to *National Self-Determination and Secession*.

[83] Buchanan, *Secession*; Morton H. Halperin, David Scheffer, and Patricia L. Small, *Self-Determination in the New World Order* (Washington: Carnegie Endowment for International Peace, 1992); Hannum, *Autonomy, Sovereignty, and Self-Determination* and 'Rethinking Self-Determination'.

The Remedial Right Only approach need not reject claims to independence on the part of nations; it only rejects the much stronger claim that nations *as such* have a unilateral right to secede. In many cases the groups that have suffered the most serious and persistent injustices are in fact nations and would be accorded the right to secede by the Remedial Right Only Theory. To that extent it is inaccurate to say that the Remedial Right Only Theory ignores the realities of nationalist self-determination movements. But perhaps more importantly, the Remedial Right Only Theory, when suitably integrated into the isolate and proliferate strategy, would provide principled support for various modes of national self-determination short of secession. If this could be achieved, the Remedial Right Only Theory would avoid one of the major objections to Ascriptivist Theories—the fact that they would most likely require unacceptable costs due to the violence that would most likely be unleashed by legitimizing the principle that every nation has a right to its own state. At present, however, no theory is available that both limits the right to unilateral secession to remedial cases and also provides a comprehensive, principled account of when various groups, including those that qualify as nations, ought to be recognized under international law as having rights to autonomy short of secession. Only if it can be successfully integrated with such a theory will a Remedial Right Only Theory of the unilateral right to secede be able to answer in a fully satisfactory way the charge that it ignores the nationalistic character of many actual secessionist movements.

Plebiscitary (Primary Right) Theories. The appeal of Plebiscitary Theories is that they appear to make the determination of boundaries a matter of choice, or, more accurately of majority rule; to that extent they bask in the popularity of the idea of democracy. However, given what is at stake in unilateral secession, it is far from clear that the mere fact that a majority of persons residing in a portion of the state desire independence should be sufficient to give them a unilateral right to secede, in the absence of any grievances. More specifically, why should one assume that the mere fact of residing in a portion of the territory of a state authorizes persons to decide by majority vote not only to change their own citizenship, but also to deprive others (the non-secessionists) of their current citizenship and to remove a part of the territory of the state without the consent of any of that state's citizens who happen to live outside the area in question?

According to the doctrine of popular sovereignty, which lies at the core of the liberal-democratic conception of the state, the state's territory is properly conceived of as the territory of the people as a whole, not just those who at a particular time happen to reside in a portion of it. But if this is so, then it is hard to understand how the mere fact that a majority of citizens in a certain portion of the people's territory desire their own state could confer on them the right unilaterally to appropriate that territory for themselves, in the absence of any grievances. The weakness of the Plebiscitary Theory, then, is its account of what grounds the secessionists' right to territory. That this is a serious flaw becomes more evident when one recalls that according to the

Plebiscitary Theory the state from which secession occurs may be perfectly just. As a general account of what grounds valid claims to territory, the Plebiscitary Theory looks implausible indeed: claims to territory would come and go as majorities come and go. But quite apart from the obvious problem that this conception makes state boundaries liable to extraordinary instability, why the desire of certain people who happen to be in the majority in a region of an existing state should generate a title to territory remains a mystery.

Another objection to plebiscitary versions of Primary Right Theory has been raised by Allen Buchanan and Donald Horowitz among others. International legal support for a plebiscitary right of unilateral secession would most likely thwart strategies for reducing intrastate conflicts through decentralization, including various forms of federalism and consociationalism. If state leaders know that secession will be considered a right under international law for any group that can muster a majority in favour of secession in any portion of their state, they will not be likely to be receptive towards proposals for decentralization. They will view decentralization as the first step towards secession, because the creation of internal political units will provide the basis for future plebiscites on secession.[84] In addition, acknowledgement of a plebiscitary unilateral right to secede would create perverse incentives regarding immigration. States that did not wish to risk losing part of their territory (which includes most if not all states) would have a strong reason for limiting immigration (or internal migration) that might result in the formation of a secessionist majority in a portion of the state's territory.

We noted earlier that some find Plebiscitary (Primary Right) Theories attractive because they seem to embody a principle of democracy.[85] However, it is a mistake to think that the commitment to democracy requires acceptance of the Plebiscitary Theory.[86] The *justifications* for democratic governance within given political boundaries do not in fact support the thesis that boundaries may be redrawn simply by majority vote. There are two chief justifications for democratic government. The first is that democracy is intrinsically valuable from the standpoint of equal respect for persons or equal consideration of persons' interests. The core idea is that the basic moral equality of persons requires that they have an equal say in the most important decisions that determine the character of their polity.[87] Yet clearly this justification for democracy does not imply that the decision whether to secede should be determined unilaterally by a majority in favour of secession in a portion of the territory of an existing state as opposed to being determined by a majority of all citizens.

[84] Buchanan, 'Theories of Secession'; 'Federalism, Secession, and the Morality of Inclusion'; and Donald L. Horowitz, 'Self-Determination: Politics, Philosophy, and Law', *Nomos*, 39 (1997), 421–63.

[85] Philpott, 'In Defense of Self-Determination'.

[86] The remainder of this paragraph and the next are drawn from Buchanan, 'Democracy and Secession'.

[87] Harry Brighouse, 'Against Nationalism', in *Rethinking Nationalism*, ed. Couture *et al.*; and Thomas Christiano, *Rule of the Many: Fundamental Issues in Democratic Theory* (Boulder, Colo.: Westview Press, 1996).

The first chief justification for democracy tells us that all who are members of a particular polity—all who must live under a system of rules that determine the fundamental character of social life—should have an equal say in deciding what those rules are. But the principle of democratic rule cannot tell us what the boundaries of the polity should be, because in order to implement democratic rule we must have already fixed the boundaries of the polity. The right to democratic governance is a principle that specifies a relation of equality among members of the same polity, not a right to determine the membership of polities or their boundaries.

The second chief justification for democracy is instrumental: it holds that democratic governance tends to promote important goods, including peace, freedom, and well-being. Once again, the force of the justification for democracy depends largely upon the assumption that what is being justified is a process of decision-making for a polity—the use of majoritarian procedures for determining the fundamental rules for the polity. In particular, the claim is that citizen well-being will be best served if all citizens are allowed to express their preferences, at least on fundamental matters that affect all. This argument clearly cannot support the claim that only some citizens (those in a particular portion of the polity) ought to be able unilaterally to decide a matter that will affect all citizens of the polity. Hence it cannot support the Plebiscitary Theory of the (unilateral) right to secede.

More important, as some commentators have pointed out, recognition of a plebiscitary right to (unilateral) secession could actually undermine democracy and thereby undercut the very goods that provide its instrumental justification.[88] The very idea of constitutional democracy emphasizes that democratic decision-making is not appropriate for all types of decisions; constitutional provisions (including entrenched rights, judicial review, etc.) demarcate the proper domain of democratic decision-making. One important goal of constitutional design is to help ensure that citizens will engage in genuine democratic deliberation, that public debate leading to voting decisions will consist as far as possible in principled dialogue, with a minimum of strategic behaviour and unprincipled manipulation.[89] Just as important, constitutional provisions can help ensure that citizens have incentives to invest in the hard labour of deliberative democracy. However, if 'exit' from the state can be achieved unilaterally, by a geographically concentrated minority through a majority vote, in the absence of grievances, the temptations to engage in strategic behaviour and to avoid the hard work of convincing others by principled dialogue may be overpowering. A dissatisfied minority may evade the demanding task of constructively 'voicing' their discontents by simply unilaterally redrawing the political boundaries

[88] Buchanan, 'Theories of Secession'; and Sunstein, 'Constitutionalism and Secession'.

[89] Joshua Cohen, 'Deliberation and Democratic Legitimacy', in *The Good Polity*, ed. Alan Hamlin and Phillip Petit (London: Blackwell, 1989); 'Procedure and Substance in Deliberative Democracy', in *Democracy and Difference: Changing Boundaries of the Political*, ed. Seyla Benhabib (Princeton: Princeton University Press, 1996). Review of *Political Liberalism*, by John Rawls, *Michigan Law Review*, 92 (1994), 1503–46; and Amy Gutmann and Dennis Thompson, *Democracy and Disagreement* (Cambridge, Mass.: Belknap Press of Harvard University, 1996).

to exclude those with whom they disagree. Or, they may use the threat of 'exit' as a strategic bargaining tool to nullify the majority's decisions. Implementation of the Plebiscitary Theory of the right of unilateral secession, rather than being an application of the principle of democracy, might under some circumstances undermine the practice of democracy.

Whether or not such constitutionalist arguments show that a plebiscitary right to (unilateral) secession is incompatible with deliberative democracy is not clear. They do seem to establish, however, that justifying the Plebiscitary Theory will require much more than a simple appeal to democracy.

Ascriptivist (Primary Right) Theories.[90] This approach to unilateral secession has a long pedigree, reaching back at least to nineteenth-century nationalists such as Mazzini, who proclaimed that every nation should have its own state. Critics of the Ascriptivist variant of Primary Right Theory have argued that it would legitimize virtually unlimited unilateral, forcible border changes because it confers an entitlement to its own state on every nation (or 'people' or distinct society). Those who advocate this theory have replied that it does not *require* every nation (or distinct people) to exercise its unilateral right to secede and have conjectured that were the Ascriptivist Theory accepted as international law not every group upon which it confers this entitlement would choose to secede. Nevertheless, given the historical record of ethno-nationalist conflict, the worry remains that institutionalizing the principle that every nation is entitled to its own state would exacerbate ethno-national violence, along with the human rights violations it inevitably entails. Thus the moral costs of incorporating the Ascriptivist version of Primary Right Theory into international law may appear prohibitive—especially if there are less risky ways to accommodate the legitimate interests of ascriptivist groups, such as better compliance with human rights norms and recourse to intrastate autonomy arrangements. From the standpoint of non-ideal theory, which must take the moral costs of transition into account, this is a significant consideration.

There are variants of Ascriptivist Theory that go some distance towards allaying the worry that acceptance of the theory would add fuel to the fires of ethno-national conflict by qualifying the unilateral right of secession for nations (or distinct peoples) in various ways. For example, the Ascriptivist may hold that there is a presumption in favour of each nation or distinct people having a right to its own state if it so desires, or a prima-facie unilateral right to secede for all such groups, but the international legal system is justified in requiring some groups to settle for autonomy arrangements short of full independence to avoid dangerous instability or to accommodate similar claims by other groups to the same territory. This way of responding to the worry about adding fuel to ethno-national conflicts comes at a price: what was orig-

---

[90] For more detailed characterizations of the Ascriptivist view, as well as more comprehensive criticisms of it, see Harry Brighouse, 'Against Nationalism' and Allen Buchanan, 'What's So Special About Nations?', both in Couture *et al.*, *Rethinking Nationalism*.

inally billed as a unilateral right of every nation as such to its own state now looks more like a highly defeasible presumption in favour of independence for nations. And unless a fairly concrete account of the conditions under which the presumption is not defeated is provided, it is hard to know what the practical implications of this qualified Ascriptivist view are.

Earlier we noted that critics of the Ascriptivist version of Primary Right Theory tend to focus on the potential costs in terms of exacerbated ethno-national conflict of incorporating the view into international law. However, it is not enough to note the potential costs of acceptance of the Ascriptivist Theory and its incorporation into international law. It is also necessary to understand the putative benefits of having a system in which the rights of nations to their own states is acknowledged. David Miller has usefully distinguished two ways in which Ascriptivist theories can be supported: by arguments to show that nations need states or by arguments to show that states need to be mono-national.[91] The first type of argument has two variants: one can argue that nations need to have their own states, either (1) in order to be able to protect themselves from destruction or from forces that threaten their distinctive character, or (2) in order for co-nationals to have the institutional resources to be able to fulfil the special obligations they owe to one another as members of an 'ethical community'. Both of these considerations can, under certain circumstances, weigh in favour of some form of political self-determination for nations, but it is not clear that either is sufficient to ground a general right of all nations to full independence and hence a unilateral right to secede. Indeed Miller marshals them in support of a much weaker conclusion: that nations have a 'strong claim' to self-determination.

Moreover, how important it is for a nation to have its own state will depend upon how important states are, and how effective institutions of transnational justice are in providing protections for individuals and groups that do not make them so dependent upon having a state of their own. Interestingly, to our knowledge, advocates of the Ascriptivist view that nations need their own states have not considered the extent to which that view depends upon statist assumptions. This is yet another example of the failure to distinguish between ideal and non-ideal theory and to take a diachronic view of the international system that allows for the possibility that states may not always be as important as they now are. In a world in which there are manifold forms of self-determination, the distinction between having and not having one's own state may be not only less significant, but even difficult to draw. An analogy here with property rights may be useful: some libertarian political theorists have mistakenly thought that there is a natural right to property that has a determinate content; what they have failed to understand is that property rights are simply bundles of forms of control over things. Some combinations of forms of control are generally superior to others on grounds of efficiency and/or fairness, but which particular combination is optimal may vary from situation to situation. Similarly,

---

[91] David L. Miller, *On Nationality* (New York: Clarendon Press, 1995).

sovereignty, the bundle of rights, liberties, and privileges that define independent statehood, can be 'unbundled'. Realizing that the only options are not the whole traditional bundle or nothing at all can be liberating, but it also makes the flat assertion that nations as such are entitled to their own state look less plausible.

The second type of justification for the view that nations are entitled to their own states also has two variants: the first, which dates back at least to John Stuart Mill's work *Considerations on Representative Government*,[92] asserts that democracy can only flourish in mononational states, because states in which there is more than one nation will be lacking in the solidarity, trust, or shared sentiments and values that democracy requires. The second, advanced by David Miller, asserts that states need to be mononational in order to achieve distributive justice, because distributive justice requires significant redistribution of wealth among citizens and the better off will only be willing to share their wealth with their less fortunate fellow citizens if they see them as co-nationals.[93] Both forms of the 'states need to be mononational' argument raise very interesting questions about the motivational conditions necessary if crucial state functions are to be successfully performed.

Mill apparently based his judgment that multi-nation states are incompatible with democracy on historical experience. However, some would argue that there are cases of multinational democratic states: Canada, Belgium, and perhaps Switzerland (depending upon whether one regards the latter as multinational or merely multi-ethnic). One might also add the United States, since most Indian tribes have a legal status that approaches sovereignty. Of course modern proponents of Mill's argument would be quick to point out that the continued existence of Belgium and Canada are in doubt due to nationalist secession movements. On the other hand, it could be argued that Mill's generalization is prematurely pessimistic: genuine democracies are a very recent phenomenon and until even more recently there have been almost no serious attempts, even on the part of democratic states, to recognize the claims of nations within states, through various forms of autonomy arrangements.[94] So as a justification for institutionalizing a principle of independent statehood for all nations, with the risk of instability and violence this might entail, Mill's pessimism about multinational democracies may seem to some to be premature.

The second version of the 'states need to be mononational' argument also faces serious objections. First, whether or not nationalism will facilitate or instead block large-scale redistribution of wealth will depend upon the character of the nationalism in question. Nationalist solidarity may not extend to willingness to redistribute wealth. As socialists from Marx onward have observed, the privileged minority has often been quite adept at appealing to nationalism to counteract the redistributive impulse. Secondly, even in cases where nationalist sentiment facilitates redistribu-

---

[92] John Stuart Mill, *Considerations on Representative Government* (Buffalo, NY: Prometheus Books, 1991; 1st pub. 1861).
[93] Miller, *On Nationality*.
[94] This and the next paragraph draw on Buchanan, 'What's So Special About Nations?'

tion, one must ask: what else does it facilitate? Miller appears to argue from the fact that a morally pristine, highly idealized nationalism would facilitate distributive justice (or democracy) to the conclusion that nations *as such* are entitled to their own states or at least to a presumption thereof. But there are many historical instances in which the national unity that Miller assumes will be harnessed for the pursuit of distributive justice has been ferociously directed towards conquest and against non-nationals and dissenting members of the nation itself. In addition, one might well question a view that makes the motivation to achieve distributive justice depend upon recognition of co-nationality. The price of arguing that the better off will only be willing to share their wealth with those they recognize as co-nationals is that it seems to preclude any significant redistribution across borders. Indeed, if Miller's hypothesis about redistributive motivation is correct, then a system in which states were mononational might actually be an impediment to international distributive justice. An international system designed on the assumption that only co-nationals will be motivated to share wealth is not likely to foster motivational support for international distributive justice.

One final doubt about the distributive justice version of the 'states need to be mononational' argument is worth considering. One should be suspicious about large generalizations about the limitations of concern for others, including the willingness to share wealth with them, that do not take into account the effects of institutional arrangements on such motivation. Whether or not nationalist solidarity is the only, or even the most effective, motivation for redistribution of wealth, may depend not only upon the concrete character of the nationalism in question, but upon the sorts of institutions within which nationalism exists. Rousseau's proposal to take human beings as they are and describe institutions as they ought to be is of little help if we do not know where the boundary between human nature and institutional effects lies. One danger of Miller's redistributive solidarity argument is that it proceeds as if there is a particular limitation on motivation that is natural and therefore permanent and then concludes that institutional design—in particular the division of the world into states—should acknowledge that limitation, without asking whether different institutional arrangements might affect the motivational limitation.

Our discussion of theories of self-determination and secession is inevitably incomplete; the literature on these topics is proliferating so rapidly that we are not able to do justice to the full range of positions in a brief discussion. Our aim, rather, has been to introduce some useful structure into the debate and to indicate the major strengths and weaknesses of the main alternative theories.

Humanitarian intervention. Humanitarian intervention is to be distinguished from humanitarian aid. Humanitarian aid is external assistance provided to relieve human suffering with the consent or at least not against the wishes of the state within whose territory the aid is delivered. Humanitarian intervention is generally understood to mean incursions into what would ordinarily be the protected domain of state

sovereignty, without the state's consent, chiefly for the sake of preventing the violation of human rights.

Clearly, this conception of humanitarian intervention grounds the normative
theory of intervention in the doctrine of human rights. Hence the theory of humanitarian intervention presupposes a specification of which rights are human rights, to
articulate (1) the necessary conditions for justifiable intervention (the actual or
threatened violation of human rights), (2) the goal of intervention (the protection of
human rights), and (3) the constraints on the means of intervention that may be
employed. The theory of human rights therefore plays a role in both of the main divisions of the moral theory of international law: as we have already seen, in specifying
the core of transnational justice, the principles that states are obligated by international law to satisfy in their internal affairs; and, under the heading of international
justice, in specifying the conditions under which states may intervene (or are obligated to intervene) across state borders.

The issue of humanitarian intervention is as complex as it is morally urgent. Here
we can only indicate some of the main choices a theorist of intervention must make
in response to the most central issues. An adequate theory of intervention would have
to (1) specify the sorts of human rights violations that are necessary for justified intervention, (2) determine whether other conditions than the violation of human
rights—such as the violation of intra-state autonomy agreements—can count
towards justifying intervention, (3) articulate what other conditions must be satisfied
before intervention is justified, all things considered (such as a reasonable expectation that the intervention will be effective, the likelihood that intervention will not
produce worse rights violations, effects on systemic stability, etc.), (4) determine
whether and if so when (and under what institutional structures) international law
should make humanitarian intervention obligatory, as opposed to merely permissible, and (5) provide a principled account of which sorts of entities if any have the
primary right to intervene and which entities may only intervene if properly authorized to do so by the former.

Grounds for intervention. Theories of humanitarian intervention may be distinguished according to which sorts of human rights are relevant to the justification of
intervention.[95] Conservative (or 'grave breach') theories count only on the most
severe violations as reasons for intervening—in the extreme case holding that intervention is justified only if needed to prevent or halt genocide or other large-scale
killings. Liberal theories allow that less extreme conditions, such as persistent religious persecution or violations of the right to democratic governance, can also justify
intervention. The basis of the disagreement between conservative and liberal theories of humanitarian intervention is often not clear, however. In some cases, the

---

[95] Walzer, *Just and Unjust Wars*; and Randall Forsberg, 'Creating a Cooperative Security System:
Randall Forsberg in debate with Hayward Alker, Jonathan Dean, Carl Kaysen, Joanne Landy, Steven
Miller, and Stephen Van Evera', *Boston Review*, 17 (1992), 6–12.

conservative may insist that only the most extreme human rights violations should count as justifications for intervention chiefly for purely practical reasons—because she surmises that any less demanding criteria would be too likely to be abused, serving as a pretext for interventions that are anything but humanitarian in their motivation, or because of the risk that even sincere humanitarian intervention will produce worse consequences than those it is designed to prevent or will simply be ineffective. Other conservatives, however, may have more deeply principled reasons for requiring extreme human rights violations as a necessary condition for intervention: they may be value pluralists or societal ethical relativists whose list of genuine human rights is highly restricted.[96] Finally, some who take a conservative stance on intervention may do so because they place a high value on political self-determination, believing that it is extremely important to allow states to work through their own difficulties and tread their own path towards justice, even if this means not interfering with any but the most egregious human rights violations. One variant of the view that respect for political self-determination requires a conservative stance on intervention would restrict this respect to democratic states. The idea would be that proper respect for democratic processes means allowing certain mistakes to be made, so long as they do not reach the level of 'grave breaches' of the most basic human rights, such as mass killings or genocide.

To the extent that the disagreement between conservatives and liberals is simply a difference as to the practical consequences of adopting a leaner or a more extensive list of human rights violations to serve as necessary conditions for intervention, rather than a dispute about which rights are really human rights, the issue is empirical. However, when the dispute is about practicality rather than basic principle, it is rare for either party to this dispute to shoulder the formidable burden of providing the needed empirical evidence for her position. To the extent that the disagreement is about the value of self-determination, and the concern that intervention necessarily disrupts the natural process of moral-political development in a society, one potential difficulty is that conservatives pay too little heed to the actual conditions in which 'self-determination' is exercised in many societies. While writers such as Michael Walzer seem to suppose that all members of society are participants in the process of communal identity formation and that they are rightly seen as endorsing the ultimate outcomes reached through these processes or at least the processes themselves, in fact this is often not the case. More attention needs to be paid to the conditions under which all or even most individuals could be said to be participating in the process. The mere absence of genocide or mass killings—which is compatible with violations of other important human rights—seems insufficient to afford much prospect of successful indigenous moral-political development, much less for the meaningful participation of all citizens in it. But if this is so, then the argument that intervention should be undertaken only when there are mass killings or genocide in

[96] Walzer, *Thick and Thin*.

order to avoid disrupting indigenous processes of moral-political development seems considerably weaker.

It is also important to note that if the point is to reduce the risk of abusive or inept interventions, making genocide or mass killings a necessary condition for intervention is not the only way of doing this. For example, a theory of intervention that recognized other human rights violations as prima-facie grounds for intervening, but required a higher threshold of evidence that intervention would be effective, or would not produce even worse human rights violations, might turn out to be functionally equivalent to a 'grave breaches' theory. Similarly, abuses and ineptitude might be minimized by requiring a complex procedure of collective authorization for intervenors. Nevertheless, there is more than a grain of truth in the Walzer–Mill view: those who advocate intervention often tend to underestimate the level of ongoing commitment that would be needed to bring about anything more than a temporary interruption of human rights violations in a state. Building rights-respecting institutions requires more than disarming rights violators. It also requires changes in the political culture, and this is not likely to be achieved quickly or by coercive methods. This way of formulating the Walzer–Mill view has an advantage: it does not assume that if left alone states in which large-scale human rights violations are occurring will successfully negotiate the path of moral-political development; instead, it emphasizes that the changes in political culture that are needed to sustain rights-respecting institutions are generally *more likely* to come about through internal forces than by the sort of intervention that is likely to occur, given, among other things, the level of commitment that intervention is likely to exhibit. This version of the conservative argument may be compatible with moving to more permissive conditions for intervention if and when a greater commitment to sustained efforts to build just institutions in other states develops.

Intervention in support of group rights. Another crucial question for the theory of humanitarian intervention is whether violations of certain *group* rights can justify intervention in the absence of violations of individual human rights. If, as some have suggested, the state's adherence to an internal autonomy agreement that grants rights of self-government to an ethnic, religious, national, or indigenous minority is properly a matter of international legal concern, then arguably the theory of humanitarian intervention should be expanded accordingly. Perhaps the strongest argument in favour of doing so is that when states violate internal autonomy agreements violent secessionist conflicts often develop, with massive violations of individual human rights.[97] A theory that allows or requires intervention to preserve intra-state autonomy agreements for *this* reason would still be founded on respect for individual human rights, but would not require actual or imminent violations of individual human rights as triggers for intervening.

[97] This has in fact occurred in a number of cases including Sudan, Iraq (the Kurds in the North), Eritrea, and Kosovo.

Expanding the grounds for humanitarian intervention to include violations of intra-state autonomy agreements might be justified as an important element of the 'isolate and proliferate' strategy sketched earlier in our discussion of self-determination. In particular, it could be argued that only if the international community is willing to support intra-state autonomy agreements in this way would it be reasonable to expect dissatisfied minorities to settle for limited self-government rather than full independence. The case for intervention in support of intra-state autonomy agreements would be most compelling in cases in which autonomy for the group in question was justified as a remedy for serious past injustices and to ameliorate their ongoing effects.

On the other hand, it is worth pointing out that recognition of a right (or duty) of intervention on such a pre-emptive theory could substantially expand the number of situations in which intervention would be justified. For example, some have argued that non-democratic states are more likely than democratic states to be aggressive externally and to violate human rights internally. A pre-emptive theory might, then, justify intervention against a non-democratic regime on the basis of what it might do, rather than what it currently is doing or is threatening to do imminently. Such a permissive rule, however, would perhaps create an unacceptably high risk of abusive interventions.

Constraints on intervention. Earlier, in our discussion of the cultural imperialist challenge to human rights, we made a triple distinction that is crucial for the theory of humanitarian intervention: whether practices within a state are violations of human rights, whether those participating in the rights violating practices are morally culpable, and whether intervention to halt human rights violations is justified. Each of these three questions poses its own distinctive issues. Accordingly, any reasonable theory of humanitarian intervention must acknowledge that even if certain rights violations are necessary for justified intervention, other conditions must be satisfied before intervention is justified all things considered. Most obviously, some interpretation of a principle of proportionality is required: intervention should not produce even more serious violations of human rights. In addition, the timing and means of intervention should be chosen so as to support or at least not to damage indigenous efforts to reform the rights violating practices or to develop more enlightened political institutions generally. Both of these requirements are common-sensical and uncontroversial (at least so long as they are left at the level of abstract principle), yet each has been frequently violated in the name of humanity, usually with disastrous results. A developed theory of humanitarian intervention would have to articulate these principles more precisely, illustrating them and supporting them by application to concrete situations in which the question of humanitarian intervention actually arises or should arise.

Authorized versus unauthorized interventions. Normative views on humanitarian intervention are sometimes divided into those that require intervention to be collective and those that allow unilateral intervention. The more fundamental distinctions, however, are between internationally authorized and unauthorized interventions, whether unilateral or multilateral, and between systems that have a public authority for deciding when to intervene and a public agent of enforcement and those which have only the former but must rely upon private enforcement agents, whether single or collective. A system lacking its own enforcement agent (an international military force) may none the less include institutions for authorizing other agents (the military forces of a single state or of a coalition of states) to intervene. The contrast between private and public enforcement is therefore too blunt. There is a great difference between what might be called discretionary, extra-institutional private enforcement and publicly authorized, institutionally constrained private enforcement. In the former, a private entity (whether an individual state or group of states) has broad discretion to enforce rules. In the latter, a private entity may only enforce rules if it is authorized to do so by the public authority and operates within the framework of well-crafted international legal institutions for formulating rules, adjudicating their application, and providing constraints within which publicly authorized private enforcers can operate. At present the international legal system is very far from satisfying these conditions for public authorization of private enforcement.

A fundamental issue, then, is whether enforcement activities that are not authorized by an international public authority ought ever to be permissible under international law. Clearly, the case for unauthorized enforcement is strongest when the most fundamental human rights are being violated on a large scale and when the existing system of collective authorization is ineffective. Those who supported the NATO intervention in Kosovo argued that these two conditions were satisfied in that instance: Serbian forces were engaged in ethnic cleansing and massive human rights violations against Kosovar Albanians, and two permanent members of the UN Security Council, Russia and China, would not support authorization for intervention.

This sort of argument for unauthorized intervention is incomplete, however. One must also consider whether such unauthorized interventions will further weaken an admittedly deficient system and also whether they will contribute to the emergence of a pattern of the use of force that has worse consequences for human rights (and other important values) than the inefficacy of the existing system of authorization.[98] In the case of the international legal system, the temptation to engage in unauthorized and hence illegal acts of intervention may be especially strong, not just because the existing system of authorization is ineffectual, but because in some areas international law has only very limited resources for lawful reform of its own institutions. Thus, for example, the same five members of the United Nations Security Council that each have the power to veto any resolution of the Security Council that would

---

[98] Buchanan, 'From Nuremberg to Kosovo'.

authorize an action like the intervention in Kosovo likewise have the power to block any amendment to the United Nations Charter that would limit or remove the veto power. A comprehensive moral theory of international law would include an account of the conditions, if any, under which illegal acts of humanitarian intervention are morally justified and of what the international legal response to such illegal acts should be when they occur.

System legitimacy. We noted in Section 3 that sometimes what first appear to be rejections of the content of particular international legal norms, especially those concerning human rights, are better understood as challenges to the legitimacy of the system in which those norms are formulated, applied, and enforced. The legitimacy of the international legal system can be coherently questioned just as can the legitimacy of a domestic legal system. It is important to be very clear, however, about what is meant by 'legitimacy' in this context. First, our question concerns the conditions the international legal system would have to satisfy if it were to be *correctly* regarded to be legitimate, not with the conditions under which it is in fact *perceived* to be legitimate. In other words, the task for the moral theorist is to develop a normative theory of legitimacy, not a psychosocial one.[99] Secondly, as with domestic legal systems, stronger and weaker notions of legitimacy ought to be distinguished. In particular, one should distinguish legitimacy in what we will call the strong sense, perhaps better called political authority, from a weaker sense. According to the strong, or political authority sense of 'legitimacy', a legal system is legitimate if and only if two conditions are satisfied. (1) its processes for making, applying, and enforcing laws are morally justifiable, that is, the officers of the system are morally justified in attempting in good faith to carry out the functions those processes assign to them (legislation, adjudication, enforcement, etc.); and (2) those to whom the laws generated by the system apply have an obligation to the public power constituted by the system to obey it. The second, much weaker notion of legitimacy includes only (1). For clarity, we will refer to the more demanding notion consisting of conditions (1) and (2) as political authority and the weaker notion, consisting only of (1), as legitimacy.

In the normative theory of the individual state, some contemporary political philosophers have focused on the question of whether the state, or a certain kind of state, has political authority. Their main preoccupation has been with determining whether the second condition can be satisfied—the requirement that those upon whom the laws are imposed are obligated to the government to obey it—and it is fair to say that this quest has not been successful.[100] It is not altogether clear, however, why showing that citizens are obligated to the government to comply with its laws and policies should be assumed to be the *sine qua non* of political philosophy. For one thing, the most basic moral question for political philosophy would seem to be

[99] Franck, *Fairness in International Law and Institutions.*
[100] A. John Simmons, *Moral Principles and Political Obligations* (Princeton: Princeton University Press, 1979).

whether the making, application, and enforcement of rules is morally justifiable. For
another, even if those upon whom the officers of a legal system attempt to impose
rules have no obligation to obey the public power as such, they may none the less have
weighty prudential and moral reasons to comply with the laws, if the laws are not only
consistent with but help to further the observance of important moral principles,
and if the processes by which the laws are framed, applied, and enforced meet appropriate moral standards. Finally, it is crucial to understand that legitimacy in the
weaker, morally justifiable lawmaking and enforcement sense, does not require that
those to whom the laws are applied have an obligation to obey the public power. This
fact has perhaps been overlooked because of the perennial attraction of consent theories of political authority and obligation, especially as developed in the social contract tradition. For according to these theories, both the moral justification for
making, applying, and enforcing laws and the obligation to obey the public power
have the same source, namely, the consent of the governed. But given the well-known
difficulties with consent theories, which we will not rehearse here, there is all the
more reason to explore the possibility that a normative theory of legitimacy should
focus on the weaker, not the stronger sense of legitimacy. Accordingly, in what follows we will mean by 'legitimacy' only legitimacy in the weaker sense. Our question,
then, is under what conditions is it morally justifiable for system-authorized agents
to make international law, apply it, and enforce it.

Surprisingly, there is little available by way of explicit, systematic theorizing about
the conditions of legitimacy for the international legal system. There is a considerable literature that points out deficiencies in the system—such as the disparity of
political power among states despite their formal equality—and then assumes more
than argues that these deficiencies impugn the legitimacy of the system. However,
the assumption that these deficiencies delegitimize the system is less than convincing in the absence of an explicit account of system legitimacy. Indeed, it is rare to find
a clear statement of system legitimacy as a normative concept. Instead, attention has
focused primarily on two other question: (1) under what conditions is the international legal system as a whole, or particular norms within it, *perceived* to be legitimate, and (2) what makes international law binding? The former question, as we
have already emphasized, is descriptive, not normative. The latter focuses on the
reasons the subjects of international law have for complying with it, rather than
upon what makes the exercise of political power within the system morally justifiable.

There is, of course, the traditional view according to which state consent is both
necessary and sufficient for the legitimacy of norms within the international legal
system. Some theorists apparently assume that this state consent theory of the legitimacy of norms yields an adequate theory of the legitimacy of the system when combined with the assumption that the legitimacy of the system is reducible to the
legitimacy of the norms it contains. On this view, adherence to the state-consent
supernorm is necessary and sufficient for system legitimacy.

The idea that adherence to the state-consent supernorm is *sufficient* for system legitimacy is dubious for several reasons, especially if it is supposed to provide a basis for saying that the international legal system as it is or is likely to be in the foreseeable future is legitimate. First, the state-consent supernorm, as it actually operates in the international legal system, is too morally anaemic to confer legitimacy, either on individual norms or on the system as a whole. What counts as consent in the system is not qualified by any requirement of voluntariness that would give what is called consent normative punch. International law simply pays no attention to the background conditions—for example, limits on inequalities in bargaining power—which would be necessary before a state's 'consent' could be deemed normatively significant. To hold that such an unmediated conception of 'consent' itself bestows legitimacy (understood as the moral justifiability of enforcement) would be to adopt an unjustifiable libertarian view, all the more problematic in light of the gross inequalities that actually exist within the international system.

Secondly, it is inaccurate to characterize the current system as one in which the state-consent supernorm is satisfied for all norms. In the domain of customary law, it is not the case that norms enjoy the consent of all states, unless one is willing to stretch the notion of consent to the point at which it is so normatively inconsequential as to provide no connection with the moral justification for wielding political power. Stronger states have disproportionate influence on the creation and revision of customary international law and weaker states must, for the most part, play by the customary rules. Opting out—publicly and persistently dissenting from customary norms—is simply not a viable option for weaker states. So it is hardly more plausible to say that the existence of a customary norm proves that it satisfies the state-consent supernorm than it is to say that by remaining within the boundaries of a state, the individual has given her tacit consent.

Thirdly, to assume that state consent to norms confers legitimacy in a system in which many states do not represent the interests or preferences of their citizens is to indulge in the now thoroughly discredited view that Charles Beitz calls the Autonomy of States—the error of treating states as if they were moral persons in their own right, rather than merely being institutional resources for their citizens.[101] Until all or at least most states become genuinely legitimate representatives of their members, state consent cannot by itself serve to legitimate particular norms or the system as a whole, even in cases where consent is truly voluntary. For all of these reasons, state consent to the norms of the system does not appear to be sufficient for the legitimacy of the system.

The claim that state consent to norms is a necessary condition for system legitimacy is also highly problematic, if only because as we have seen what passes for consent in the system is morally anaemic. There are, however, at least two arguments in favour of the claim that state consent is necessary for system legitimacy worth

---

[101] Beitz, *Political Theory and International Relations.*

considering. According to the Moral Minimalist Argument, state consent is required for legitimacy because it is the only thing that can make the enforcement of norms across borders morally justifiable in the absence of a globally shared set of substantive ends or a shared core conception of justice. According to the Predation Prevention (for Instrumentalist) Argument, state consent is a necessary condition for system legitimacy because it reduces the risk that stronger states will prey on weaker ones.

The Moral Minimalist position, which we encountered earlier as an objection to the very enterprise of developing a contentful moral theory of international law (Sect. 1), assumes a meta-ethical view according to which moral principles are only valid, or at least are only justifiably enforced, upon those who share the values that those principles express. In the present context the Moral Minimalist holds that the members of the so-called international community are in fact moral strangers—that there are no (or perhaps only a limited number of) shared values that can ground enforceable principles that are to be applied across borders. The next step in the Moral Minimalist argument is the assertion that in the absence of shared values, adherence to the state-consent supernorm is the appropriate second-best mode of securing legitimacy for norms (and that if the norms of the system are legitimate, then the system is also).

We need not rehearse in detail all the objections that can be advanced against Moral Minimalism. The most serious are these two. First, it can be argued that the expanding global culture of human rights, which is partly though imperfectly institutionalized in international law, is evidence that a core conception of justice is becoming more and more widely shared. The Universal Declaration of Human Rights, as well as other central human rights conventions, explicitly endorses the idea that the inherent dignity of free and equal persons entitles them to be treated in certain ways, and this supports the claim that there is or may be an evolving shared core conception of justice. But even if there is as yet no shared set of values capable of providing the basis for justifying the enforcement of international legal norms, the global culture of human rights is evidence that one may be emerging. Secondly, the Moral Minimalist exaggerates the homogeneity of values within society. Deep disagreements about the substance of justice exist within as well as across state borders. Yet few would accept the meta-ethical premise of the Moral Minimalist that the consent of each citizen is required if the enforcement of laws is to be morally justifiable.

The Moral Minimalist position is typically invoked by traditionalists who regard the existing system as legitimate but who are disturbed by the thought of departures from strict adherence to the state-consent supernorm. Notice, however, that if the problem of gaining global consensus on values turns out to be as severe and intractable as the Moral Minimalist assumes, and if it is true that in the absence of consensus nothing but state consent could render the system legitimate, it does not follow that the system is or is likely to become legitimate. Instead, given the fact that the existing system contains many norms to which some states have not in any meaningful sense consented, and given that the system does not ensure the background conditions under which consent can be normatively potent, the proper conclusion to draw is that the system is illegitimate. Furthermore, given the morally anaemic notion of consent that operates in the system, there is no reason to believe that if the system were so transformed that all its norms actually did enjoy state consent this would be sufficient for legitimacy. The Moral Minimalist view, therefore, cannot be invoked to support the traditionalist assumption that the existing system is legitimate because it is based on consent. On the contrary, if Moral Minimalism were true, one would simply have to admit that the existing international legal system is illegitimate. Such a result would hardly be palatable to those who invoke Moral Minimalism to try to show, for example, that humanitarian intervention is illegitimate because it violates the state-consent supernorm and thereby threatens to undermine the legitimacy of the system. Moral Minimalism, when combined with a sober recognition both of the extent to which the existing system is not consensual and of the normative impotence of what passes for consent in the system, implies that there is no legitimacy to be undermined.

The second, instrumentalist argument for the conclusion that state consent to norms is necessary for system legitimacy can be outlined as followed. (1) To be legitimate the international legal system must provide a minimum of protection to weaker states from predation by the stronger ones. (2) The requirement of state consent to norms is a necessary element, for now and for the foreseeable future, of minimally adequate constraints on predation by stronger states on weaker ones. (3) Therefore, state consent to norms is a necessary condition (for now and in the foreseeable future) of the legitimacy of the international legal system.

The instrumentalist argument is clearly located in non-ideal theory. As such, it presents a major challenge to those who argue for piecemeal reform of the international legal system that would further subordinate the requirement of state consent without providing other mechanisms to prevent predation. At the same time, however, even as a matter of non-ideal theory, it is not clear that adequate constraints on predation can *only* be achieved by adherence to the state-consent supernorm. Here an analogy with domestic constitutions may be illuminating. The risk that more powerful citizens will prey on weaker ones can be reduced by an entrenched system of basic rights, and by institutional arrangements designed to approximate the ideal of equal protection under the law, without giving each citizen a veto right over public policy. Similarly, how important strict adherence to the state-consent supernorm is will depend upon whether the international system includes other effective constitutional constraints on the abuse of power. For example, if the UN General Assembly were accorded a genuine legislative function over some significant domain of issues, this might provide some protection against some forms of predatory behaviour by stronger states, due to the fact that weaker states are in the majority in that body.

Furthermore, the costs of achieving constraints on predation by adherence to the state-consent supernorm may be exorbitant. The requirement of state consent—

which is in effect a veto right for every state—provides a formidable obstacle to improving a system whose greatest defects lie in the behaviour of some of the very states whose consent is required in order to create and enforce norms that would prohibit their wrongful behaviour. So even if protection of weaker states from predation by more powerful ones is a necessary condition of system legitimacy, and even if adherence to the state-consent supernorm helps to provide protection to weaker states, it does not follow that the system can only be legitimate if there is adherence to the state-consent supernorm. That conclusion would follow only if state consent were the only way, or the least costly effective way, to achieve adequate protection for weak states. Whether that is the case remains to be seen. The state-consent supernorm is one possible constitutional provision among others for protecting weaker states against predation. It is a complex question of constitutional design as to whether it is the best way to achieve this end, given the present institutional resources of the international legal system. But even if it is the best instrument for reducing the risk of predation given current institutional resources, it does not follow that it is the ideal arrangement. The question remains open as to whether it may be possible and desirable to develop existing institutional resources so that the state-consent norm might be replaced by other, superior constitutional provisions.

A quite different approach to the question of system legitimacy than the insistence on strict adherence to the state-consent supernorm is to argue that the system would be more legitimate were it more democratic. However, the notion of 'democratizing' the international legal system is ambiguous. Democratizing the system could mean any of the following: (i) increasing the scope and importance of decision-making through majoritarian voting by states (augmenting state-majoritarianism); (ii) making states more democratic, so that their governments actually function as agents of their citizens; or (iii) making international institutions more representative by increasing the influence of various non-state actors on the making, application, and enforcement of international law. (Non-state actors here include individuals acting on their own behalf, as well as various transnational civil society groups, including human rights organizations, indigenous peoples' rights organizations, etc.)

Consider first the assertion that a larger role for state-majoritarian decision-making is required for system legitimacy, or at least that this would make the existing system *more* legitimate. Presumably the appeal of this proposal for reform lies in the perception that the current system is unfairly dominated by powerful states. Democratization, understood as state-majoritarianism, is proposed as an obvious mechanism for diminishing the morally arbitrary inequality of power among states, and thereby enhancing the legitimacy of the system.

But expanding the role of state-majoritarianism in the making, application, and enforcement of norms is only one way of reducing the political inequality of states. Again, the issue is one of constitutional design, and it would be rash to pronounce that the only practicable and morally defensible constitution for the international legal system must include a rule requiring that all (or even most) decisions concerning the making, application, and enforcement of law are to be made by state-majoritarian voting. State-majoritarianism is not the same as the political equality of states; it is only one possible constitutional arrangement for achieving political equality. So even if it is assumed that greater political equality among states is a necessary condition for system legitimacy, whether state-majoritarianism is a necessary condition for legitimacy will depend upon whether there are other, less costly but sufficiently effective constitutional arrangements for decreasing political inequality among states.

There is another reason to temper enthusiasm for state-majoritarianism as a mechanism for increasing system legitimacy: there is no direct connection between democratic representation of individuals and state-majoritarianism because states contain vastly different sized populations. A system in which all important international legal determinations are made by a majority vote among states, under the ideal condition that states accurately represent the preferences of their citizens, would give unequal weight to the preferences of some individuals, namely, those who are members of states with small populations. Thus, for example, a state-majoritarian system would accord Slovenia the same number of votes as China, a result hardly compatible with an appeal to the equality of persons. At a minimum, state-majoritarianism would have to be replaced by a system that weighted voting more closely to population. Perhaps, something like a two-chamber system familiar from federal systems would provide a model.

The attraction of the proposal to democratize the system by adopting state-majoritarianism lies in the fact that the current system encompasses extreme inequalities of political power among states, in spite of the formal equality of states. However, to some extent the preoccupation with inequalities among states (rather than among individuals) may be due to the unquestioned traditionalist assumption that international law is (and will remain) exclusively the law of states. Once we acknowledge that international law now encompasses subjects and actors other than states and that the sovereign powers of states have been successively constrained by changes in international law over the last fifty years, it is no longer clear that equality of *states* should be the overriding desideratum so far as system legitimacy is concerned. Much will depend upon how successful democratization in the second and third senses is: unless states are more democratic, and unless the system empowers non-state actors, increasing the political equality of states may do little to enhance system legitimacy. Yet if the system continues to make progress in empowering individuals and groups to help shape international law without being so dependent upon representation by their states, then the political inequality of states becomes to that extent less problematic. Consequently, how cogent a proposal for increasing the role of state-majoritarian decision making is will depend upon very complex predictions about what the institutional resources of the system are and are likely to be.

Liberal individualism and the legitimacy of a state-centred system. Lea Brilmayer has suggested that the fact that the international legal system accords such a fundamental status to states in the making, application, and enforcement of law poses a special problem for a liberal account of system legitimacy.[102] For liberalism, she correctly observes, assumes moral individualism—the position that the justification of moral principles must be grounded ultimately in appeals to the welfare and freedom of individuals. But if one embraces moral individualism, how can one justify a system that assigns such a dominating role to states? Our analysis of the choices facing the moral theorist of international law sheds considerable light on this problem. Whether or not a moral theory of international law is sufficiently individualistic to be called liberal in this sense will depend upon a number of factors. Consider a theory that includes the following features: (1) principles of transnational justice that require entities to protect the basic individual human rights of their populations and subjects them to intervention in the case of grave breaches; and (2) a cosmopolitan conception of distributive justice, according to which states as such have no claims to resources, but have derivative claims due to their functioning as the most effective agents currently available for ensuring the distributive dimension of transnational justice, that is, for securing the rights of their citizens to distributive shares; and (3) a set of rules and procedures that allow for the legitimate break-up of states through secession as a remedy of last resort for persistent violations of individual human rights of minorities concentrated in a portion of the state's territory. Such a theory could hardly be called statist in a derogatory sense, since it clearly makes the privileged status of states wholly conditional upon how and whether they serve the welfare and freedom of individuals. Yet a system that satisfied the theory's requirements might still accurately be characterized as one which privileges states, so far as it assigns to states a preponderant role in the making, application, and enforcement of international law.

This conclusion reinforces our earlier conjecture, in Section 1, that a moral theory of international law that takes the privileged position of states as provisionally given need not be unacceptably conservative. The question, remains, however, as to what sorts of conditions the theory should require the system to satisfy if the system is to be legitimate. Here we can only briefly consider one suggestion for how to begin the task of developing a theory of system legitimacy. Most of what we say about the conditions of legitimacy for an international legal system would apply to a domestic legal system; in that sense there is little that is novel in our suggestions. A key question for further research on this topic is the extent to which the domestic analogy holds. In our rebuttal of the Realist and Legal Nihilist challenges in Section 1, we argued that the differences between domestic and international legal institutions are often exaggerated by those who are very sceptical of the whole enterprise of normative theorizing about international law. If that is correct, then there is at least some reason to begin by pushing the domestic analogy as far as it will go.

---

[102] Brilmayer, *American Hegemony*.

The question, recall, is this: under what conditions are the authorized agents of the international legal system morally justified in making laws, applying them, and enforcing them? From the case of domestic legal systems, we would presumably conclude that consent to particular laws is not required, either on the part of states or individuals. But we have also noted that consent to the system as a whole, understood as being manifested in joining the club of states and thereby acceding to its existing rules, is also not a plausible candidate for conferring legitimacy. Here, too, the domestic analogy supports our conclusion: whether or not the authorities of the state are justified in enforcing the laws on me surely does not depend upon whether I have chosen to join the state. And I may have conclusive moral, religious, or prudential reasons for complying with the laws, without having consented to them or to the system as a whole.

Given the problems we noted earlier with the view that state consent is either necessary or sufficient for system legitimacy, consider, instead, a conception of legitimacy that does not rely on consent. Suppose that the international legal system met these criteria: (i) the norms of transnational justice include the requirement that all states respect the basic human rights of all those within their borders, (ii) principles of international justice, including the rules for the conduct of war, the prohibition on aggressive war, and those that specify the conditions for humanitarian intervention, also reflect a commitment to securing basic human rights for all persons, (iii) the processes by which international legal rules are framed, applied, and enforced satisfy a requirement of democratic equality among states, so that more powerful states do not wield disproportionate power in those processes; and (iv) the system approximates the chief formal criteria for the rule of law: legal rules are appropriately general, legal change is sufficiently slow and predictable that the law can serve as a relatively stable framework for the expectations of persons as rational planners, rights of due process approximate the ideal of equality before the law, and there is strong presumption against retroactive criminal sanctions. Any legal system that met all of these requirements could surely make a strong claim to legitimacy in the weak sense: agents who made, applied, and enforced laws within an institutional framework that met these conditions could make a credible claim to be morally justified in doing so. Such a conception of system legitimacy might more accurately be characterized as 'justice-based' rather than 'consent-based'. However, among the constitutional provisions of a system that satisfied its conditions, state consent, at least for certain kinds of decisions, might play an important role. The point, however, is that the legitimacy of the system would not be defined in terms of state consent.

To summarize: our suggestion is that the sorts of conditions that count towards the legitimacy of a domestic legal system have analogues in the case of the legitimacy of the international legal system. In our view, the real difficulty is not so much how to specify the ideal conditions that would be sufficient for legitimacy, but rather how to specify legitimacy under non-ideal conditions. Each of the requirements listed above can be satisfied to a lesser or greater extent. The problem, then, is to determine how closely a system must approximate the ideal in order to be legitimate. One suggestion worth considering is this: there is no general answer to this question; at least so long as it is reasonable to expect that the system can be improved towards a closer approximation of the ideal criteria, whether the system-authorized agents of a legal system are justified in making, applying, and enforcing laws in the system will depend in part on what the alternatives to supporting the system are. In circumstances in which the choice is between a condition of lawlessness in which massive human rights violations are virtually inevitable and support for an admittedly defective but improvable system, the standards for legitimacy—the degree to which the ideal criteria must be satisfied—will be correspondingly lower.

6 Conclusion

This chapter has not been an attempt to formulate even a sizeable fragment of a moral theory of international law. Instead, our aim has been to impose some structure on the numerous, complex, and interrelated issues that a moral theory of international law would have to address and to indicate some of the main choices open to those who would attempt to develop a comprehensive theory. Because the moral theory of international law is so underdeveloped, we are acutely aware of the limitations of our discussion. We will have achieved some measure of success, however, if our analysis helps focus attention on this neglected and exciting area.

CHAPTER 22

LAW AND LANGUAGE

TIMOTHY A. O. ENDICOTT

Our polity consists of words.
(Demosthenes XIX.184)

. . . the power of words can damage the city.
(Demosthenes, *First Proemium* 1. 3)

DEMOSTHENES was the first lawyer we know of to preoccupy himself with language. He knew that not only the constitution but much of the public life of a community is made up of the utterances of its citizens. And he knew and he deployed the power of language to charm a legislature, and to subvert justice. In the speeches he wrote for private litigants, he used his expertise with words to manipulate the jury; and he always accused his clients' opponents of using words to manipulate the jury.

Words are tools that lawyers (advocates and judges and legislators) use for their good or bad or indifferent purposes. But that is not a special feature of law. Words are tools that we all use for similar purposes. Is there anything distinctive to be said about law and language? It is true that English legal language has special features. But those complex features have roots in English legal history and culture, and not in the nature of law. Demosthenes went out of his way to use the language of his audience (a jury of hundreds). Every 30-year-old Athenian citizen could be a jury member in any law-suit, and so the language of the courts was part of the language of every citizen. Even in English-speaking countries today, many lawyers try to use language that non-lawyers understand—and they often succeed. Lawyers need to use language, and they

936   LAW AND LANGUAGE

use it in interesting ways, but that does not mean that an understanding of the nature of language will help us to understand law. Biochemists need to use language, and they use language in interesting ways, but there is nothing about biochemistry that can best be said by saying something about language. Does an understanding of the nature of language have anything more to offer to jurisprudence, than it has to offer to biochemistry?

In this chapter, I will address that basic jurisprudential question. How, if at all, is the nature of law related to the nature of language? I will not reach many of the ways in which people might be interested in language and in law at the same time. There are various focuses of interest in language and law.[1] I will only be concerned with some of the ways in which people have claimed that an understanding of language will help to solve problems of jurisprudence. In fact, I will need to limit attention to just a few of those ways, and the introductory section aims to explain how. I will argue that, in order to understand the nature of law, legal philosophers need to understand the nature of language. But the point is not as obvious as it might sound, and it needs argument.

1   Introduction

There certainly *are* gains to be made by paying attention to language, if only because an understanding of language can help us to clear up the misconceptions that important legal philosophers have built upon distorted understandings of language. There are few uncontroversial points in jurisprudence, but this must be one: anyone who has paid attention to what legal philosophers have said about language will have a vivid sense that some of it is basically misguided. And it is an important point, because understanding other people's mistakes is a crucial task for legal theorists. Even the most original have gained by identifying misconceptions. But, of course, any attempt to say *which* conceptions are misconceptions will be very controversial. This chapter attempts to identify some of the most interesting and important mistakes that legal philosophers have made about language.

Is that all? Do legal philosophers need to pay attention to language only to avoid pitfalls? Joseph Raz has recently suggested that view:

... possibly philosophy of language and semantics can help primarily by providing clarifications where misunderstanding of language or its use may lead to an error. By and large, as long as in one's deliberation about the nature of law and its central institutions one uses language

---

[1]   See the Further Reading at the end of this chapter.

without mistake there is little that philosophy of language can do to advance one's under-standing.[2]

That view may seem odd, because language is so important to law that it seems obvi-ous that the study of language can illuminate the nature of law. But we should not take it for granted. We should ask the following question: *Is there anything worth understanding about law that can best be said by saying something about language?* I think that the answer is 'yes'. There are three reasons why understanding language might be useful:

1. *Law uses language.* Jurisprudence is different from biochemistry, because law is made by means of linguistic utterances. We could probably imagine communities in which law is made without any use of language: for example, a system in which a binding precedent is set by the outcome a judge gives in cases whose facts everyone knows. There is nothing essentially linguistic about precedent-based decision-making. But, in fact, every common law system I know of today has a developed industry for the reporting of cases, and a doctrine that gives legal force to the *ratio* that the precedent-setting court expressed. Legislation using language is, as far as I know, a universal feature of legal systems. So law is typically made by linguistic utter-ances. Lawyers do not just use language like biochemists; law is made by means of lan-guage. Without understanding how language works, we cannot understand the nature of law. But the question remains whether philosophy of language has anything to say that is helpful in jurisprudential debates—anything that is pertinent and not banal.

2. *Law is like language.* Languages and legal systems are the most common and the most sophisticated systems of social rules that human communities have. Language and law are also the two most common and sophisticated co-ordination schemes in human communities. That is, they provide solutions to problems that face people who need to co-operate, and who share a limited understanding of each other and limited good will. And they provide techniques for providing new solutions to new problems.

Beyond these unhelpful abstract comments it is difficult to see what to do about the similarities between a language and a legal system. The differences are stark and the similarities may seem unilluminating. And even the abstract comments are con-troversial—it is controversial whether either language or law is a rule-governed activ-ity, and it is not clear whether these are two controversies or aspects of a single controversy.

---

[2] 'Two views of the Nature of the Theory of Law', *Legal Theory*, 4 (1998), 249 at 254. H. L. A. Hart made a similar statement in 1983: *Essays in Jurisprudence and Philosophy* (Oxford: Clarendon Press, 1983), 5. But Hart's statement is rather obscure, and not clearly consistent with the claims he was still making for the usefulness of linguistic philosophy to jurisprudence.

3. *Legal theorists must use language.* Part of the task of the legal theorist is to under-stand (and to communicate an understanding of) the terms in which the subject matter is to be described. It became clear in twentieth-century jurisprudence that fashioning useful terminological tools is not just a preliminary exercise (as it might be if we were doing, e.g., physical geography), but is one of the central challenges of the discipline.

Of these three reasons to think that the study of law ought to be related to the study of language, the first is reflected in work on the role of the language of the law in legal reasoning and adjudication. The third has played an important role in discussions of method in jurisprudence. The second offers a rather more obscure promise: that philosophy of language can help with the legal theorist's problems of understanding rules and systems of rules. All three concerns are addressed in the work of H. L. A. Hart, who stands out for his deliberate attempts to put philosophy of language to work in jurisprudence.

I will set out to describe and to assess a tradition of talking about language that is centred on Hart. I will start with Jeremy Bentham. The philosophical innovations that served Bentham's political agenda included the invention of a form of linguistic philosophy. Hart was Bentham's sympathetic critic, and Hart's views deserve atten-tion in their own right and as a background to understanding the work of his own critics, Joseph Raz, John Finnis, and Ronald Dworkin.

My discussion will aim to point out some misconceptions and insights that can be identified in the work of those five writers. They all use remarks about language to argue that other people have misconceived the nature of law. Reviewing their work helps to see how an understanding of the nature of language can expose muddles, and to see whether philosophy of law needs philosophy of language for any other purpose.

I simplify the task by omitting a survey of scepticisms about law that find support in views about language. That is a major omission. If the language of law is bunk used to mystify people, we can use the study of language as a tool for demystification and debunking. Many legal scholars have argued that law is a form of oppression that dis-sembles itself in words. I should explain why I will not survey those attempts.

Legal language has certainly been used to mystify, deceive, and swindle. Lawyers and judges and other officials have often abused their rhetorical power, and obscurity is ingrained in the styles of expression that students learn at law school. They learn more in the first months of legal practice, once teachers stop telling them to be clear. As George Orwell said, 'When there is a gap between one's real and one's declared aims, one turns as it were instinctively to long words and exhausted idioms, like a cut-tlefish squirting out ink'.[3]

---

[3] 'Politics and the English Language', in *Shooting an Elephant and Other Essays* (London: Secker & Warburg, 1950).

It is important to keep in mind that lawyers are not unique in this tendency. Orwell was actually talking about politicians. Lawyers do the same as other people, but with the self-assured sophistication that you get by joining an ancient, learned profession. To Charles Dickens, legal language was like 'that kindred mystery, the street mud, which is made of nobody knows what, and collects about us nobody knows whence or how, we only knowing in general that when there is too much of it, we find it necessary to shovel it away . . .'.[4]

There are two sceptical views about legal language: (1) that it is a tool fashioned for ruling the oppressed, and (2) that it is meaningless (either specially meaningless, or because language in general is meaningless), so that it cannot be used to rule anything. Both views converge in the idea that it is a tool for oppression because it hides its own meaninglessness in rhetoric that disguises the abuse of power.

I will not discuss the support that legal sceptics seek in views about language, partly because the area has been much surveyed.[5] More importantly, I think that sceptical attacks get no support from the abuses and deceits of lawyers. That is, the language of the law may or may not be used to oppress and to deceive. It is in the nature of language that it is apt for such uses, but there is nothing in the nature of language that makes law a tool of corruption or deceit. Lawyers and lawmakers can use language either to abuse people or to serve them.

So I will not survey sceptical views of language and law. Except for the remarkable sceptical views of Jeremy Bentham. His appeals to language provide a useful background to Hart—and Bentham's misconceptions are so extraordinary that they ought to be more widely known.

2 BENTHAM AND THE NONSENSE DOCTRINE

> Only with reference to language can the attribute denoted by the word universal be with propriety attributed to the subject of *law*.[6]

---

[4] *Bleak House* (1853).

[5] See Kent Greenawalt, *Law and Objectivity* (Oxford: Oxford University Press, 1992), esp. chs. 2–5; Endicott, 'Linguistic Indeterminacy', *Oxford Journal of Legal Studies*, 16 (1996), 667–97; Lawrence B. Solum, 'Indeterminacy', in *A Companion to Philosophy of Law and Legal Theory* (Oxford: Blackwell, 1996), 488–502; Ken Kress, 'Legal Indeterminacy', *California Law Review*, 77 (1989), 283; Brian Bix, *Law, Language and Legal Determinacy* (Oxford: Clarendon Press, 1993).

[6] Jeremy Bentham, *Pannomial Fragments*, in J. Bowring (ed.), *The Works of Jeremy Bentham* (Edinburgh: Wm. Tait, 1843), vol. III, ch. III 'Expositions', p. 217.

It is no exaggeration to call Bentham the first linguistic philosopher—although his remarks on language owed much to his reading of John Locke.[7] Philosophers had been paying attention to the meaning of words since Plato and Aristotle, but Bentham assigned central importance to the characteristic technique of linguistic philosophy: he tried to solve philosophical problems by claiming that people will make disastrous blunders unless they understand how language works.

Some of the results are bizarre and misguided. It is absurd, for example, to say that the study of law is only general (or 'universal') when it is restricted to a study of language. Bentham thought that general descriptive jurisprudence 'must confine itself to terminology'.[8]

Yet it is not as absurd a view as it sounds. The language, the terminology that Bentham had in mind includes terms such as *power, right, obligation, liberty*, and of course, *law*.[9] If we could account for the meaning of those terms, we could deal with some of the most important questions that philosophers of law have addressed, because we would know how to make sense of the characteristic legal claims that people make. The absurdity in Bentham's claim about jurisprudence is the idea that such an account could 'confine itself to terminology'. His own account of the meaning of those terms is part of an account of what rights, obligations, laws, and so on are. So in his attention to the corresponding terms, Bentham does not *confine* himself to terminology, and no one could seriously do so.

His general jurisprudence was certainly a theory of law, and not just of the meaning of the word *law*. But Bentham constructed his theory of law with claims about language. In his tirades against Blackstone, his bitterest complaint was not that Blackstone was reactionary and smug about the common law, but that his doctrine was '*unmeaning*'.[10] Bentham claimed that, in order to say anything clear and meaningful, a theorist had to be able to 'expound' theoretical terms, by reference to 'simple' terms[11]—that is, 'terms calculated to raise images either of substances perceived, or of emotions; sources, one or other of which every idea must be drawn from, to be a clear one'.[12] Substances, or 'real entities' are physical, and emotions are 'sensible' characteristics of physical objects. Only physical objects and their sensible characteristics are clearly comprehensible, and only physical and psychological terms have a

---

[7] Locke viewed modern philosophy as attempting to 'speak intelligibly'. See *An Essay Concerning Human Understanding* (Glasgow: Collins, 1977; 1st pub. 1690), book three 'Of Words', and esp. ch. IV, 'Of the Names of Simple Ideas'.

[8] *The Principles of Morals and Legislation* (1781), 323.

[9] I will mark linguistic expressions (words, phrases, sentences) with italics, and actual or hypothetical utterances with quotation marks.

[10] *A Fragment on Government* (1776), ed. J. H. Burns and H. L. A. Hart (Cambridge: Cambridge University Press, 1988), 113.

[11] The notion of simple terms was one of Bentham's borrowings from Locke (see n. 7 above).

[12] *Fragment*, 108 n. Cf. *Of Laws in General* (1782), ed. Hart (London: Athlone Press, 1970) (hereafter *OLG*), 283 n.: '. . . abstract phraseology must on many occasions be tolerated . . . but on no occasion can it be clearly understood unless it can be translated into such expressions as have a direct reference to the sensible objects that are in question'.

clear meaning. *Pain* and *pleasure* were Bentham's favourite simple terms—he reckoned that there is nothing more sensible than pain and pleasure. So we can comprehend them clearly enough to say something meaningful with their names. '*Pain* and *pleasure* at least, are words which a man has no need, we may hope, to go to a Lawyer to know the meaning of'.[13]

Three distinctively Benthamite features of this technique of exposition deserve attention: the way in which it exposes duties (etc.) as fictitious entities, the idea of the 'proper sense' of a word, and the notion of the expression of emotion as an alternative to the use of words to refer to sensible entities.

2.1 Paraphrasis, Fictitious Entities, and Sensible Objects

There are no 'simple terms' that are equivalent to the central legal terms. So Bentham invented a special method of expounding abstract theoretical terms, which he called 'paraphrasis'.[14] He thought that concrete terms could be expounded by definitions, but that abstract terms needed his new technique: instead of translating a term like *duty* into other words, he proposed to translate sentences containing the word *duty* into other sentences.

Paraphrasis frees the theorist from a fruitless search for a set of words to substitute for the term being defined. And it reminds the theorist not to seek an object for which the word acts like a label. And it solves a problem that Bentham had identified with definition *per genus et differentiam*.[15] But its chief attraction to Bentham was that paraphrasis is extremely useful for debunking notions such as duty. If you define *duty*, it sounds as if you are saying what duty is. But if you translate *I have a duty* into another sentence, it sounds as if you are saying what someone really means when they use the word *duty*. Paraphrasis lets the theorist replace the duty. So Bentham's exposition of the term *duty* was as follows: 'That is my *duty* to do, which I am liable to be *punished*, according to law, if I do not do: this is the original, ordinary, and proper sense of the word *duty*'.[16]

The debunking facility offered by paraphrasis was important to Bentham because he thought that words are 'fallacious coverings'[17] for ideas. Words like *right* and *duty*

---

[13] *Fragment*, 28.   [14] *Fragment*, 108 n., *OLG*, 294–5.
[15] The problem being that no *genus* is available for some terms that a theorist might need to define. *Fragment*, 108 n.
[16] *Fragment*, 109; cf. Austin, *The Province of Jurisprudence Determined* (1832), ed. Hart (London: Weidenfeld & Nicolson, 1954), 14. Note that Bentham's exposition of *duty* is not a paraphrasis. But it provides a formulation that may be substituted not for the word *duty*, but for clauses using the word (and then by paraphrasis, a sentence such as *It is my duty to look after my children*, can be paraphrased as *If I do not look after my children, I am liable to be punished according to law*). In Bentham's method there is actually nothing essential about the role of sentences, or their 'translation'.
[17] *OLG*, 144.

are 'phantastic denominations'[18]—frauds that look as if they stood for something—but there is no such thing! The only meaningful words are 'names of real entities or of the sensible affections of determinable real entities'.[19] Other terms cannot be *defined*, because they have no real reference. But the technique of paraphrasis lets Bentham expound them by pointing out their relation to real entities such as pain and pleasure.

A word may be said to be expounded by *paraphrasis*, when not that *word* alone is translated into other *words*, but some whole *sentence* of which it forms a part is translated into another *sentence*; the words of which latter are expressive of such ideas as are *simple*, or are more immediately resolvable into simple ones than those of the former.[20]

Abstract words are pseudo-names for fictitious entities, but in the context of a sentence they can be translated into expressions that have a direct reference to sensible objects.

Bentham thought that *jurisprudence* is an example of a pseudo-name for a fictitious entity. How awkward for someone engaged in jurisprudence! His solution to this quandary was bizarre and trivial. He wrote that the word *jurisprudence* has no meaning except when placed 'in company with some word that shall be significative of a real entity'.[21] But the word *book* was enough! He thought that talk of *jurisprudence* is unintelligible, but that it was intelligible to talk about a book of jurisprudence.

Unlike jurisprudence, according to Bentham, a law is a real entity.[22] The phrase *a law*, at least, could be expounded by definition rather than paraphrasis. A law is a sensible expression of will communicated by a sovereign, and backed by a threat of pain.[23] Bentham thought it a great advance to keep attention focused on the pain and the pleasure that accompany law (in its various forms, at various times, and in various communities).

Bentham's definition of *law* is deeply flawed, and his expositions of *duty* and *right* seem to me to replace right and duty with different relations: liability to pain, and power to inflict pain. Many people have objected to Bentham on those grounds. Yet Bentham thought that his exposition was right as a matter of the meaning of words. How could Bentham think that he was right about duty because of the original, ordinary and proper sense of the word *duty*?

---

[18] *OLG*, 251.   [19] ibid. 252.   [20] *Fragment*, 108 n.
[21] *Introduction to the Principles of Morals and Legislation* (1780), ed. Burns and Hart (1970), 323 (hereafter *IPML*).
[22] But 'the fictitious entity called *law*' is drawn by abstraction from the real entities called *laws*. *OLG*, 16.
[23] See *OLG*, 1.

2.2 The Veil of Mystery and the 'Proper Sense' of Words

The implication of Bentham's linguistic approach is that no one who disagrees with his theory of duty knows the meaning of the word *duty*. That would be absurd, even if his theory were right. The explanation of this absurdity is that while Bentham was a linguistic philosopher, he was not an ordinary language philosopher—that is, he did not try to resolve philosophical problems by pointing out the ways in which words are ordinarily used. He thought that the language in which people had tried to express their understanding of law was partly meaningless, and partly ill-fashioned (because of its 'poverty and unsettled state')[24] for analytical work.

The ingenuity of the first authors of language . . . has thrown a kind of veil of mystery over the face of every science, and over none a thicker than over that of jurisprudence. . . . We must however have learned upon every occasion how to pierce through it at pleasure before we can obtain a clear perception of the real state of things.[25]

Language is important to jurisprudence because people use it in such misconceived ways that a jurist needs to work out what is really going on—and what it is proper to call *a law*.

Bentham's follower, John Austin, adopted his notion of the proper sense of words, and used the phrase 'properly so called'[26] as a central methodological placeholder in his theory of law. Austin gives only a fragment of an explanation of the notion. He says that a term is used 'properly' when it is applied to something that has 'all the properties which belong universally to the class'. When something possesses 'only some of the properties which belong universally to the class', the name denotes it 'improperly or analogically'.[27] This explanation purports to show what makes the proposed use of a term 'proper', but it flagrantly begs the question. The phrase 'the class' assumes the conclusion that needs to be justified: that there is a class, all members of which share all the same relevant characteristics, to which it is (exclusively) proper to apply the term. That gap in the foundations of Benthamite jurisprudence could have been filled, however. Bentham and Austin could have explained what 'properly so called' meant. In fact, what they say only makes sense on the assumption that the importance of pain and pleasure makes it proper to use *law* in the way they propose. Then what is wrong in their theory is (1) their evaluation of the principles on which people act and ought to act, and (2) their vitriolic prejudice that use of terms by people who do not share their evaluation is meaningless babble.

A more complete Benthamite account of the proper sense of words might run as follows: it is proper to apply a term to a class if doing so will give the term a clear sense by reference to sensible objects, and will accommodate the utilitarian conception of

---

[24] *IPML*, 98.   [25] *OLG*, 251.

[26] Throughout *The Province of Jurisprudence Determined*; see e.g. 122–4.

[27] *The Province of Jurisprudence Determined*, 120. Cf. Bentham: 'a *declaratory* law . . . is not properly speaking a law', *IPML*, 330.

value. If it is not possible to do that for an expression, then the expression *has no proper sense*.

Bentham had an explanation for the use of expressions that have no proper sense.

2.3 Expressive Uses of Words

We have seen that Bentham thought that terms for real entities (like *a law*) can be expounded by definition. Abstract terms (like *duty*), which do not name sensible objects, are only related to real entities. By pointing out the relations, we can expound them by paraphrasis. So *right* and *duty* can be expounded by paraphrasis insofar as they refer to *legal* rights and duties. The sovereign's threat to inflict pain gives them an intelligible relation to real entities.

Only so much can be done, however. If no such relation can be found, the theorist must expose a term as nonsense. So, to take one famous example, Bentham said that 'natural rights is simple nonsense: natural and imprescriptible rights, rhetorical nonsense; nonsense upon stilts'.[28] The stilts are imprescriptibility; the nonsense is the lack of an intelligible relation to pain, pleasure, or any other emotion or physical substance. Natural rights do not even have a relation to sensible objects, so the term *natural right* cannot be expounded—and that means that the very notion is nonsense. Sentences using the words *natural rights* cannot be translated into intelligible sentences. Bentham's explanation for the use of such nonsense was as follows:

If I say a man has a natural right to the coat or the land—all that it can mean, if it mean any thing and mean true, is, that I am of opinion he ought to have a political right to it; that by the appropriate services rendered upon occasion to him by the appropriate functionaries of government, he ought to be protected and secured in the use of it: he ought to be so—that is to say, the idea of his being so is pleasing to me—the idea of the opposite result displeasing.[29]

Consider the following:

1. He has a natural right to the coat.
2. The idea of his having a political right to the coat is pleasing to me.

Bentham is wrong, if only because (1) cannot mean the same as (2). At least, (1) cannot mean the same as (2) in the sense in which language means something. (2) can be the force of an utterance of (1)—what pleases me might be evident from the fact that I uttered (1).

It seems that Bentham considers pure normative statements (as to what ought to be done, all things considered), to be uses of *meaningless* sentences to express what

[28] *Anarchical Fallacies*, in J. Bowring (ed.), *The Works of Jeremy Bentham* (Edinburgh: Wm. Tait, 1843), vol. II, art. II, p. 501.

[29] *Pannomial Fragments*, in J. Bowring (ed.), *The Works of Jeremy Bentham* (Edinburgh: Wm. Tait, 1843), p. 218. Cf. *Fragment*, 110 n., where he calls the assertion of the speaker's 'internal sentiment' a separate, improper 'sense' of normative language.

pleases the speaker. Yet Bentham equivocates between expressivism and utilitarianism: he says that it makes sense to say that an action *ought* to be done, or is *right*, or is not *wrong*, if what is meant is that it is 'conformable to the principle of utility'. 'When thus interpreted, the words *ought*, and *right* and *wrong*, and others of that stamp, have a meaning: when otherwise, they have none.'[30] So the word *ought* can be given a meaning, but only by relation to sensible objects—to pain and pleasure. Non-utilitarian theories are not just false, they are nonsense that we use to express our feelings of pain and pleasure or to seek pleasure.

Bentham foreshadowed twentieth-century linguistic philosophy. Paraphrasis anticipated twentieth-century methods of analysis. His notion of the proper sense of a word was an inarticulate anticipation of twentieth-century methodology in jurisprudence. And his expressive theory of meaning for pure normative statements (though it was not consistent) anticipated twentieth-century attempts to use language to explain the normativity of law. All of these innovations are developed in the work of Hart; the last innovation is the most important mistake in the interesting history of law and language.

Scorn and contempt were Bentham's characteristic attitudes to law and to language—blinding contempt for the common law, and contempt for William Blackstone, and scorn for the language of the law. Yet he felt scorn too, for anyone who was not interested in law and language—anyone 'in whose estimation the benefit of understanding clearly what he is speaking of, is not worth the labour'.[31]

3 HART ON THE USES OF WORDS

> In this field of study it is particularly true that we may use, as Professor J. L. Austin said, 'a sharpened awareness of words to sharpen our perception of the phenomena'.[32]

Hart unearthed and illuminated Bentham's contributions to jurisprudence. But he did not fall for Bentham's extravagant mistakes. He did not share Bentham's scorn for the language of the law, and he took a very different approach to it. Where Bentham wanted to expound legal language in a way that debunked the self-conceptions of lawyers, Hart wanted to resolve jurisprudential problems by shedding light on those self-conceptions. *Elucidate* was Hart's favourite word. He adopted an approach to

---

[30] *Introduction*, 4.   [31] *Fragment*, 108 n.
[32] *The Concept of Law* (hereafter *CL*), 2nd edn. (Oxford: Clarendon Press, 1994), p. v.

language that was quite opposed to that of Bentham, for all that they shared. We can call it 'the face-value principle': it is the view that we can understand people's practices (and resolve philosophical puzzles about them) if we understand the language that people use from their own point of view. 'What is needed', said Hart, 'is a "hermeneutic" method which involves portraying rule-governed behaviour as it appears to its participants.'[33]

What fruit did Hart's preoccupation bear? In his inaugural lecture at Oxford University, Hart made some enthusiastic but obscure comments about language.[34] In his work as a whole I think we can identify four important insights into the nature of language with which Hart sought to elucidate the nature of law. I will refer to them as (1) *the context principle*, (2) *the diversity principle*, (3) *vagueness*, and (4) *performative uses of language*. Principles (1) and (4) were pioneered by Bentham; (3) was not especially important to Bentham, and his theory is undermined by his failure to attend to principle (2).[35]

The first three principles are important to legal theory, but it is a dangerous mistake to think that the fourth is important. I will start by describing each, and I will discuss criticisms by Dworkin, Finnis, and Raz of the way in which Hart used each. Wittgenstein discussed each of these four insights in provocative ways, and Hart wanted to put his work to use; in fact, we can introduce each principle with a remark of Wittgenstein's.

3.1 The Context Principle

> We may say: *nothing* has so far been done, when a thing has been named. It has not even *got* a name except in the language-game. This was what Frege meant too, when he said that a word had meaning only as part of a sentence.[36]

> (Wittgenstein)

That is Wittgenstein's formulation of the principle first pointed out by Bentham, and endorsed by Gottlob Frege.[37] This principle was important to Frege for his ground-breaking association of meaning with the truth-value of propositions; to

---

[33] *Essays in Jurisprudence and Philosophy* (Oxford: Clarendon Press, 1983), 15.

[34] 'Definition and Theory in Jurisprudence', ch. 1 in *Essays in Jurisprudence and Philosophy*.

[35] It would no doubt be possible to identify other features of language that Hart appeals to at various points. They include some more particular points such as the distinction between 'extensional objects' and 'intensional objects' that he used in discussing the law of criminal attempts (*Essays in Jurisprudence and Philosophy*, ch. 17). In that case and others, I think that Hart uses terminology and ideas from 'philosophical semantics' to make points that a lawyer with Hart's common sense could have made without ever mentioning language.

[36] *Philosophical Investigations* (Oxford: Blackwell, 1953), sect. 49.

[37] See Michael Beaney (ed.), *The Frege Reader* (Oxford: Blackwell, 1997), 15–20 and 108–10.

Wittgenstein it was important for his view of uses of words as moves in various language-games, and his association of meaning with use.

Frege's formulation of the principle is false. Supermarket shelves and phonebooks are packed with examples of words used meaningfully without any sentences. But what gives those words meaning in those contexts is what makes them useful for saying things—and the context principle should be interpreted as pointing that out. The meaning of a word is what makes it useful for forming the sentences with which people make utterances; if a word were useless for that purpose, it would be meaningless. Bentham and Frege exaggerated the importance of sentences. It is the context of an *utterance* that gives a word meaning. A word has meaning only in so far as it can be used in utterances, and to remind ourselves of the meaning of a word (or to explain it to someone) it is generally helpful to point out utterances or types of utterances in which it is characteristically used.

A word cannot be understood without understanding what is and can be done with it. The word *prune* can be a noun meaning *dried plum*, or a verb meaning *trim*. Since the origins of each are different, and the meanings are so different, and they are not even the same part of speech, we should say that there are two different words, *prune* and *prune,* which are mere homonyms (i.e. the same in sound and spelling, and the same in no other way). Yet here is a sentence which does not differentiate: *Prune!* You cannot understand the meaning of the sentence unless you understand the context of the utterance—that will typically tell you whether someone is demanding a dried plum or telling someone to trim. As J. L. Austin put it, 'The total speech act in the total speech situation is the *only actual* phenomenon which, in the last resort, we are engaged in elucidating'. The meaning of an utterance depends in a variety of ways on context: on the situation of the speaker and of any listener. And words have no meaning except in so far as they are useful to speakers and listeners.

We saw the importance of the context principle to Bentham—it supported his technique of paraphrasis, and he used it to debunk the notion of natural rights, and to debunk any theory of law that did not define all the multitude of terms for juridical pseudo-entities by translating sentences using them into sentences using terms for 'real entities'. Hart, too, used it for expounding the meaning of juridical terms. But in Hart's work it turns into a form of the face-value principle: look at the statements that people use some problematic term to make; if we can make sense of those statements, we will have a clear view of the meaning of the term. This technique is borrowed from ordinary language philosophy but has survived it. And it explains how Hart used the context principle to develop a view of language contrary to Bentham's.

Hart offered a common-sense view of the personality of corporations. He claimed that it was a mistake to focus on the word *corporation,* and to wonder what sort of thing it stood for. He drew an analogy to the term *trick* in games such as bridge and euchre. Suppose you find yourself puzzled about what a trick *is,* and you can only think that it must be a weird sort of entity. Just ask when it is true to say that someone has taken a trick, and ask the consequences of taking a trick. Then you will know what *trick* means, because you will have a clear view of its use.

The basic misconception that Hart aims at is the notion that the meaning of a word (or at least the meaning of a noun) must be an object, for which the word is a label. *Apple* is a label for apples, on this view, and *right* is a label for rights; but rights have no colour and they cannot be peeled or bitten, so they must exist on a different plane from apples. Hart thought that it was an important mistake to put rights or corporations on such a plane. And he thought it was an easy mistake to make because of 'the great anomaly of legal language—our inability to define its crucial words in terms of ordinary factual counterparts'.[38]

It was a bizarre slip for Hart to call that an anomaly of legal language. I think it reflects inattention rather than a deep misconception, because he illustrated the trait with the word *trick*. The trait does not distinguish legal language, and it is not an anomaly in any sense. It is not even a peculiarity of the language of rule-governed activities.[39] Every abstract noun has the same trait: think of *trick* in the senses it has outside games. Think of more abstract words such as *ability*, *suspicion*, or *love*. But concrete nouns have the same trait too: think of the word *plate*.[40] There are plates of various kinds (dinner plate, gold plate, book plate, tectonic plate . . .) but they are not 'factual counterparts' for the word *plate*. The notion of a factual counterpart suggests that the word is a label—as if, when I ask you for a plate, you have nothing to do but to find what bears the label. In fact, to fulfil my request, you need to make evaluative judgments of relevance to the present situation of the different ways in which different objects may properly be called 'plates'. Those judgments may be very straightforward, in some contexts, but it is always badly misleading to think of the word *plate* as a label for plates. Perhaps *all* concrete nouns have the same feature: even *apple* is not a label for apples, although the same thing that makes the word useful in various utterances also makes it useful for making labels. The meaning of a word is not an object for which it stands, but is a way (or a variety of ways) to use it. So the context principle is not an anomalous feature of legal language, but it points out a very important feature of words as diverse as *right*, *trick*, *love*, *plate*, and *apple*.

How important is the context principle for legal theory? It *can* be useful for clearing up misconceptions—the later Wittgenstein, for example, used it as part of his attack on misconceptions about language that afflicted the early Wittgenstein. But a limitation on Hart's approach is that although the reasoning behind the context principle is sound, it may be superfluous. It is not just that you may find you do not need

[38] 'Definition and Theory', 25.
[39] While he was trying to understand the notion of rules, Hart was simultaneously working on the notion of systems of rules; he had a tendency to treat the context of a system of rules as critically important for the meaning of legal terms: 'attention to the diverse and complex ways in which words work in conjunction with legal rules of different types would serve to dispel confusion, such as [fiction theories of rights]', *Essays in Jurisprudence and Philosophy*, 3; cf. 276.
[40] For a discussion of the word *plate* and the notion of family resemblances see B. Rundle, *Wittgenstein and Contemporary Philosophy of Language* (Oxford: Blackwell, 1990), 60–3.

to think about the nature of corporations. Even if you do, you may not start by suffering from the misconception that the word *corporation* must stand for some sort of object that differs from apples in spooky respects.

How important in legal theory are the misconceptions that Wittgenstein needed to clear up? Hart says that, in spite of Bentham's leap forward, 'jurists have continued to hammer away at single words',[41] but he does not identify the culprits. The context principle would be useful if we found someone who thought that, for example, *law* is a label for a thing like an apple only not crispy and red. I do not know of any such people, although it may be that some writers on the personality of corporations have suffered from the analogous malady.[42]

Ironically, the most important use to which we can put the context principle is against people like Bentham. Bentham did not think that, for example, *jurisprudence* stood for a strange object. He thought that *because* it does not stand for a sensible object, it stands for a fictitious object, and is therefore meaningless unless it can be attached to a meaningful word like *book*. And the word *right* is meaningless outside the legal systems that give it an intelligible relation to the pain and pleasure that follow the use of force. Hart, by contrast, points out that a word is not meaningless just because it does not stand for a sensible object. Where Bentham held that abstract juridical terms are meaningless because there are no objects for which they are labels, Hart followed Wittgenstein in thinking that words are not labels. Their meaning is determined by rules for their use, and not by their being pinned to objects. So Hart, for example, had no fiction theory of rights, because he did not think that a word like right must stand for either a sensible object or a fictitious object.

Perhaps the context principle is only useful for clearing up misconceptions. But they are important misconceptions, in legal practice as well as in legal theory. The context principle is crucial for lawyers. If they flout it, they are capable of making a hash of the words used in legislation, or in the expression of the *ratio* in a precedent, or in a legal instrument. And adjudication sometimes offers a court a word on a plate, in a fashion that may encourage a judge to ignore the context. Every sensible technique of legal interpretation includes a version of the context principle.[43] Context

---

[41] ibid. 26.

[42] 'Metaphysical realists' and 'semantic realists' are often thought to suffer from this malady. Perhaps some have done so, but the philosophical debates between 'realism' and 'anti-realism' are much too complex for realists to be generally viewed as suffering from the malady of ignoring the context principle. See David O. Brink, 'Semantics and Legal Interpretation (Further Thoughts)', *Canadian Journal of Law and Jurisprudence*, 2, (1989), 181; Michael Moore, 'The Semantics of Judging', *Southern California Law Review*, 54 (1981), 151, and 'A Natural Law Theory of Interpretation', *Southern California Law Review*, 58 (1985), 277; and Nicos Stavropoulos, *Objectivity in Law* (Oxford: Clarendon Press, 1996).

[43] So e.g. English techniques of statutory interpretation became more sensible when the House of Lords held, in the *Prince of Hanover* case, that the context needs to be considered not only when the ordinary meaning of the words is unclear, but in order to identify the ordinary meaning of the words: *Attorney-General v Prince Ernest Augustus of Hanover* [1957] AC 436. In *Arbuthnott v Fagan* [1996] LRLR 135, Steyn LJ drew on the *Hanover* case to support the proposition that, in the interpretation of a contract, 'The meaning of words cannot be ascertained divorced from their context'.

can even tell when someone like Mrs Malaprop meant something other than what she said.[44]

The principle is also crucial for theorists who are trying to make something useful of their own theoretical terms. It is a principle that need not be expressed—it simply must not be flouted. But it is so important that it is worth stating. The role it ought to play in understanding theoretical terms is very closely linked to the role of the diversity principle, and it will be worth discussing them together.

3.2 The Diversity Principle

> ... if you look at [games] you will not see something that is common to all, but similarities, relationships, and a whole series of them at that ... we see a complicated network of similarities overlapping and criss-crossing: sometimes overall similarities, sometimes similarities of detail.[45]

(Wittgenstein)

Hart said that it was dogmatic to think that there must be one common feature or set of features that something must have if a term is to apply to it,[46] and he drew both on Wittgenstein's remark about games, and on the suggestive term 'family resemblances', which Wittgenstein used for the similarities that hold among instances of a term like *game*, or *language*. Those instances may have a variety of characteristics which support the application of the term in different ways, rather than a closed set of characteristics, all of which they alone share.

Diversity of grounds of application of words is inextricably linked to the context principle: variations in contexts make it appropriate to extend the application of a word in diverse ways because of diverse similarities. The context in which a word is used may make it clear which considerations are relevant (or particularly relevant) to its application in a particular context. A word may have a single, clear ground of application that varies with the context (e.g. *tall*), or there may be a variety of considerations that are relevant in different contexts to the application of a word. *Parent* as

[44] Lord Hoffmann in *Mannai Investment Co. Ltd. v Eagle Star Life Assurance Co.Ltd.* [1997] 3 All ER 352 at 375.

[45] *Philosophical Investigations*, sect. 66, *CL*, 280. Cf. 'Think of the tools in a tool-box: there is a hammer, pliers, a saw, a screw-driver, a rule, a glue-pot, glue, nails and screws.—The functions of words are as diverse as the functions of these objects. (And in both cases there are similarities.)' *Philosophical Investigations*, sect. 11.

[46] *CL*, 15–16; see also *EJP*, 277, rejecting 'the old idea that when a general term or concept is applied to many different instances all the instances must share a single set of common properties. This is a dogma; there are many different ways in which the several instances of a general term are linked together, besides this simple way; and an understanding of these many different ways is plainly of particular importance in the case of legal terms.'

used in a school prospectus will apply to anyone with care and control of a child, and will not apply to a biological father or mother who has no care and control; as used in a genetics text, *parent* will apply just to the biological mother and father.[47] We might say that, in the standard case, a parent is the biological father or mother and also has care and control. Biological parenthood and care and control of children are two different grounds of application of *parent*; the central case of a parent unifies those grounds.

It seems that there must be some intelligible unity to the grounds of application of a word. Otherwise, there is not one word, but two mere homonyms, like *prune* and *prune*. We must be able to ascribe unity to the grounds of application of a word, if we are to account for the notion that, for example, *parent* is one word (with various senses), while *prune* is two. Let's use the term *sense* for an aspect of the meaning of a word; I will call a term 'univocal' if there is a unifying pattern to its senses (so that they are aspects of a single meaning). The notion of univocality is vague, because there is a variety of ways in which similarities among instances of a term might unify its senses, more or less. The senses of *prune* are unrelated; the senses of *bank* are related, but so remotely that we should say that it is equivocal; I do not know about, for example, the senses of *trick*. But *game* and *parent* are clearly univocal.[48]

Wittgenstein suggested that there is no unifying rationale for the network of similarities among games.[49] But in that case, how can we conceive of *game* as univocal (like *parent*), rather than equivocal (like *prune*)? I think we should say that it is possible to give an account of a pattern to the similarities.[50] There are principles to the extension of the term. In so far as Wittgenstein's remarks on family resemblances suggested that there are no such principles, they lose sight of a point that Wittgenstein of all people ought to accept: that we can make sense of the ways in which people use words and explain their meaning.

What place should the diversity principle have in legal theory? Hart used the principle in his remarks on interpretation and adjudication, and also (more deliberately) in discussing method in jurisprudence. The diversity of grounds of application of terms needs to be kept in mind if we are to understand the way in which legislation creates rights and duties, and if we are to make sense of adjudication. The paramount legal example of the diversity principle is the word *reasonable*, and Hart mentions its use to create a 'variable standard', the content of which can be specified by courts if there is a doctrine of precedent.[51] In any area in which legal doctrines impose a standard of reasonableness, a variety of considerations will be relevant to the reasonableness of forms of conduct; the standard varies with the context, but in any particular

[47] So said Butler-Sloss LJ, in a statement of the context principle in *Re C*, [1993] 3 All ER 313 at 317–18 (CA).

[48] Although *game* has different, related senses when used to refer (1) to chess, rugby, etc., and (2) to pheasant, venison, etc. It is univocal in its various applications in either of these senses.

[49] *Philosophical Investigations*, sect. 66.

[50] As Joseph Raz did in *Practical Reason and Norms* (London: Hutchinson, 1975), 122–3.

[51] *CL*, 132.

context, the question of whether someone has acted reasonably is likely to turn on a variety of considerations. The unity in the concept of reasonableness is nothing less abstract than the notion that, in some context, a practical consideration might demand attention. But the diversity principle is important not only in the case of such extreme abstractions. Like the context principle, the diversity principle is crucial for legal interpretation, and almost any interesting case on the interpretation of words offers an example.

Hart also thought that the diversity principle was crucial to method in jurisprudence—because it applies to jurisprudential terms as well as to terms used in the law. In attempting to elucidate the concept of law, he resisted an urge to which Austin, Bentham and Kelsen allegedly succumbed: the urge to find 'the common qualities which are . . . held to be the *only* respectable reason for using the same word of many different things'.[52] Instead, Hart recommended that the theorist identify a particular puzzle about law that might trouble someone, and then point out those features of central cases of law that we need to remind ourselves of, in order to resolve the puzzle. John Finnis has offered an important elaboration of Hart's 'central cases' method.

Finnis—The Systematic Multi-significance of Theoretical Terms

Wittgenstein was not the first to point out the variety of similarities among the instances of general terms. He applied to language in general a point that Aristotle had made about terms that were to him both ordinary words and philosophical terms, such as *friendship* and *health*. Aristotle pointed out that such words do not apply by *mere* homonymy (like *prune*); their instances are homonymous by reason of various relations of analogy among the grounds on which the word is applied to each.[53] Finnis drew on Aristotle's remarks to elaborate Hart's 'central cases' method in a way that requires an account of the diversity of grounds of application of a term like *law*, and a justification of the theorist's technique for 'selecting concepts'.[54] He argued that a theorist could make something useful out of theoretical terms such as *law* only by paying attention to ways in which its application might be accounted for by relations of analogy: in its 'focal meaning', the term applies to 'central cases'; the theorist's job is to uncover 'the "principle or rationale" on which the general term ("constitution", "friend", "law" . . .) is extended from the central to the more or less borderline cases, from its focal to its secondary meanings'.[55] The aim is then to 'exploit the systematic multi-significance of one's theoretical terms', by giving a full account of the central cases that allows one to understand peripheral cases *as* peripheral.

Two features of this approach are important to understanding the role that Finnis proposes for language in legal theory: (1) the dangerous metaphors of *central* cases

[52] *CL*, 279. On Hart's 'central cases' method, see esp. *CL*, 81.
[53] See e.g. Aristotle's discussion of friendship, or love, in *Eudemian Ethics* H2, 1236a16–23.
[54] *CL*, ch. I.   [55] *Natural Law and Natural Rights* (Oxford: Clarendon Press, 1980), 11.

and *focal* meaning, and (2) the associated claim that all judgments as to the explanation and application of theoretical terms are based on evaluative judgments.

(1) *Central Cases and the Context Principle*

Finnis's emphasis on focal meaning elaborates the diversity principle in a way that is helpful for the purpose he shared with Hart: avoiding the paralysing search for 'one thing common'. Yet the approach seems to seek 'one thing common', in the characteristics of one central case. Finnis approves a remark of Hart's, that 'the extension of the general terms of any serious discipline is never without its principle or rationale'.[56] But *extension* is ambiguous between the general and the particular: Hart may have been saying either (i) that for every theoretical term, there is a principle that unites everything to which it applies, or (ii) that there is always a principle to an extension of a term to any particular state of affairs. In the context it seems that Hart meant (ii), and that is certainly the more cautious claim; (i) takes it for granted that the term is univocal. The 'central' and 'focal' metaphors suggest that there *is* one thing common: a relation (closer or more distant) to a single paradigm whose features define what is characteristic. Finnis seems to suggest that, to understand a term, you must identify one instance (or one type of instance) as paradigmatic, and identify anything that is significantly different as only peripherally an instance of the term. Yet, for example, chess and rugby are both games, and are very different in important respects, and yet neither is more centrally a game than the other.

Consider the term *parent*. There are certainly contexts in which the central case of a parent is both a biological mother or father, and has care and control of a child—and in those contexts, a stepfather, or a biological mother with no care and control, is a parent only in a peripheral sense. And the different senses of *parent* are obviously unified by the importance in so many contexts of the fact that biological parents characteristically have care and control. Yet, in genetics, there is nothing *more central* about the parent with care and control. And although there are good reasons to say that, in the *abstract*, the central case of a parent is a biological parent *and* has care and control of the child, there is no central case, in that sense, of a game.

So in order to make any judgment as to what cases are central and what cases are peripheral, a theorist needs to appreciate the context in which the question is asked. And the theorist should not assume that it is possible to give a general, principled account of the extension of a term ((i) above), nor suggest, like Wittgenstein, that it is not possible. It is an open question in a study of the use of words by theorists and by people in ordinary discourse. We need to remind ourselves of the fact that underlies Aristotle's insights: that language use is creative, not only because it allows us to speak metaphorically and allegorically, but because people give meaning to terms (even non-figurative meaning), on account of similarities in the characteristics of the things that they talk about. Because of that characteristic form of creativity in the use

[56] *CL*, 210.

of language, what is being said by means of a form of words may depend on relations of resemblance among things a word is used (and can be used) to refer to.

As for theorists, their use of theoretical terms is one instance of the creative use of language, and they have a certain freedom: they can 'select their concepts', as Finnis puts it. In fact, they need to do so. For them, identifying a principle that unites the instances of their theoretical terms is a goal to pursue. They must 'select concepts' not because, as Bentham thought, the abstract words of ordinary language are mostly nonsense, but because those words have their application on the ground of such a diverse network of analogies of different kinds, that it takes careful critical judgment to discern which ways of extending the term are useful for the purposes of the theorist. John Austin thought that analogical uses of theoretical terms are improper uses; Finnis adopts Aristotle's view that analogical extensions of terms are a basic part of the proper meaning of terms—so that the question of which analogies ground the proper application of a term is a central question for the theorist.

It is not inconsistent with anything in Finnis's work to say that the diversity principle relies on the context principle. Perhaps it is implicit in his account of the importance of the theorist's selection of point of view. That account assigns a critical role to evaluative judgments in legal theory.

(2) *Evaluation and the Meaning of Theoretical Terms*

Finnis concludes that the meaning that theorists give to their theoretical terms presupposes value judgments. Here too we can say the same about the language of the law, and the language of legal theory.

If I have some of the characteristics of a parent and not others, a court cannot decide whether I have some right or duty that the law gives to 'parents', without asking the purpose of the enactment. In a manner of speaking I am a parent, and in a manner of speaking I am not. The court cannot simply ask 'Is he the child's parent?' without asking what sense of *parent* is relevant to the purposes of the law, because that question has a variety of answers that correspond to the diversity of characteristics of parents. No good outcome can be reached in such a case without judging the reasons why, in that area of the law, rights and duties should be ascribed to parents. A court determined not to change the standards, but only to give them effect, still needs to decide what view of the purposes of the law would best make sense of the sources of law.

Similarly in the use of theoretical terms, the theorist needs to evaluate the subject-matter to judge how the terms of a theory make it possible to draw important distinctions and not to draw misleading distinctions. Finnis objects to the methods of Bentham and Austin more starkly than Hart does; he says that they offered no justification for their definitions. In that simple form, the charge looks unfair: the materials for a justification are here and there in Bentham's untidy work. He would have been eager to respond to Finnis's methodological requirement of 'attention to practical point': he considered that his definitions and paraphrases expounded his theoretical terms in their 'proper sense', because it was proper for the theorist (i) to restrict attention to sensible objects, in order to say something clear, and (ii) to focus attention on pain and pleasure, in order to account for what matters. Finnis's objection (as his work shows) ought to be that Bentham's empiricist notion of clarity is incoherent, and that his utilitarian conception of value takes fragments of what matters to human beings, and distorts them.

Aside from those objections to Bentham's evaluations, however, there is also reason to think that the very requirement of evaluation by the theorist is fatal for Bentham's view of jurisprudence. The meaning of ordinary and theoretical terms relies on evaluative presuppositions as to which similarities among particulars *deserve* to be treated as justifying the application of a term. That means that even a philosophy that expounds the meaning of all terms by reference to names of real entities will rest on the evaluative judgments presupposed by the use of terms for real entities. Bentham's methodological requirement of clarity only obscures the role of the evaluative judgments that give content to the clearest and most sensible of terms.

3.3 Vagueness

> For how is the concept of a game bounded? What still counts as a game and what no longer does? Can you give the boundary? No. You can *draw* one; for none has so far been drawn. (But that never troubled you before when you used the word 'game'.)[57]

> (Wittgenstein)

It is important that Wittgenstein used the word *game* to illustrate both vagueness and what he called 'family resemblances'. The two are linked. A word is vague if there are cases in which it is not clear (even when we know the meaning of the word and the facts of the situation) whether the word applies or not. Even when we know how old a person is, it may not be clear whether it is true to say that he or she is a child. The word *game* is vague, in part, because there are a variety of ways in which activities may be more or less like games—various considerations are relevant to the question whether some activity is a game or not (just as there is a variety of considerations relevant to the question whether some person is a child). The picture of vagueness as a fringe of fuzziness is misleading because it may be unclear not only:

- how closely some activity resembles some paradigm game in some particular respect,

but also

---

[57] *Philosophical Investigations*, 68.

- what activities are paradigm games, what sorts of resemblances are relevant, and how those resemblances relate to each other.

As a result, it is misleading to think of vagueness as unclarity as to where a dividing point lies on a spectrum. Hart spoke of vagueness as the trait of words whose application is clear in some cases (in what Hart called the 'core') and unclear in others (the 'penumbra').[58] Uneasy with that metaphor, he used another, 'open texture', which we should view as Hart's jargon for vagueness.[59]

Hart pointed out the vagueness of law to bolster his account of the law of a country as a system of rules, by defusing the scepticism that points out that rules do not always determine an outcome. His remarks on open texture were his main contribution to the theory of adjudication.[60] And here, at least, the importance to jurisprudence of an understanding of language is straightforward and undeniable—if Hart is right about language. He thought that law offers a framework of guidance on a great range of questions of behaviour, but that it also leaves a great deal open. And he considered that to be an important fact about law (and not just about e.g. English law in 1962).

In every legal system a large and important field is left open for the exercise of discretion by courts and other officials in rendering initially vague standards determinate, in resolving the uncertainties of statutes, or in developing and qualifying rules only broadly communicated by authoritative precedents.[61]

Ronald Dworkin's theory of law and adjudication has strenuously opposed that view. The debate raises an important question about law and language: what is the relationship between the language in which law is formulated, and the rights and duties that the legal system affords and imposes?

Dworkin on Vagueness

Dworkin objected to the notion that the legal position of litigants may be at the discretion of judges. Hart thought that when a judge exercises the 'discretion thus left to him by language . . . , the conclusion, even though it may not be arbitrary or irrational, is in effect a choice'.[62] In Dworkin's view, judges should not have a choice—they should identify the rights of the parties and enforce them. He argued that Hart's view gives an *unattractive* picture of the law, because if judges decide people's rights on non-legal grounds, they are not taking the parties' rights seriously.[63] They are undemocratically and retrospectively ordering the threat or use of state coercion in a way not licensed by law.

---

[58] For a discussion of the core and penumbra metaphors (which Hart did not invent) see Endicott ,'Linguistic Indeterminacy', *Oxford Journal of Legal Studies*, 16 (1996), 667 at 668.

[59] *CL*, ch. VII.1; *Essays in Jurisprudence and Philosophy*, 274. See the Appendix to this chapter, on open texture.

[60] Adjudication was not a primary concern in *The Concept of Law*, but see also 204–6, and sects. 3, 4, and 6 of the 'Postscript'.

[61] *CL*, 136.   [62] *CL*, 127.   [63] See *Taking Rights Seriously*, rev. edn. (1978), chs. 2 and 4.

Dworkin also argued that Hart gives an *inaccurate* picture of the role of language in law: we need 'to discriminate between the fact and the consequences of vagueness'. Rules of construction could eliminate vagueness by, for example, requiring that the rule be applied only to cases in 'the indisputable core of the language'.[64] In this form, Dworkin's argument against Hart's view fails. First, there may or may not be such rules. Such rules are common in some areas of criminal law, but there are none that apply to, for example, most doctrines of reasonableness in private law. Secondly, such rules of interpretation might reduce judicial discretion, but they cannot eliminate it. They could only achieve Dworkin's purpose if there were sharp boundaries between the clear cases of the application of vague terms, and the borderline cases. But, as Joseph Raz first pointed out, even 'the indisputable core of the language' is vague.[65] That is, there is no sharp boundary between the clear cases and the unclear cases of the application of vague language. We may use a precise blood-alcohol limit to *replace* a rule against driving while intoxicated, but we cannot eliminate judicial discretion by saying that a rule against driving while intoxicated is only to be applied in clear cases.

Beyond Words

This debate about the vagueness of language may seem unsatisfying and beside the point, because we want to say that there is more to the law than the mere application of words. If that is so, then perhaps vagueness is a defect in language that need not lead to indeterminacies in the law. Dworkin takes that view, and he is not alone. One of Hart's concessions about *The Concept of Law* might seem to support it:

... the question whether a *rule* applies or does not apply to some particular situation of fact is not the same as the question whether according to the settled conventions of language this is determined or left open by the words of that rule. For a legal system often has other resources besides the words used in the formulations of its rules which serve to determine their content or meaning in particular cases.[66]

The suggestion is that *The Concept of Law* took a naïve view of the relation between the conventions of language and the requirements of legal rules. But Hart does not withdraw the basic claim that the open texture of language leads to indeterminacies in the law. And we could read his concession simply as admitting that his book had not explained why, for example, a rule prohibiting vehicles from the park does not necessarily prohibit an ambulance, even though the word 'vehicle' applies to the ambulance by the settled conventions of language.

---

[64] Ronald Dworkin, 'No Right Answer?' in P. M. S. Hacker and Joseph Raz (eds.), *Law, Morality and Society* (Oxford: Clarendon Press, 1977), 58 at 67–9.

[65] *The Authority of Law* (Oxford: Clarendon Press, 1979), 73–4. See also Brian Bix, *Law, Language and Legal Determinacy* (Oxford: Clarendon Press, 1993), 31–2, and T. A. O. Endicott, 'Vagueness and Legal Theory', *Legal Theory*, 3 (1997), 37–63.

[66] Hart, *Essays in Jurisprudence and Philosophy*, 'Introduction', 7–8.

But once Hart admits the distinction between the application of the *words* of a rule and the application of the *rule*, he seems to have conceded what Dworkin claims. Given that distinction, it seems that *no* claim about indeterminacy in the law follows from the vagueness of the language of the law. Linguistic indeterminacy does not entail legal indeterminacy.

Of course, it is true that a judge applying a vague rule (against e.g. 'driving while intoxicated') would have a great variety of resources as a guide. There might be a rule of interpretation requiring strict construction of penal legislation, so that only clearly drunk people are prohibited from driving. There will be other relevant considerations—such as the principles of the legal protection of liberty on the one hand and of public safety and order on the other, principles of strict construction of criminal legislation, analogies with the ways in which tort law holds people responsible for creating risks to others, analogies with driving licence laws, laws prohibiting minors from driving, and so on. It will be an important part of the judge's task to take such considerations into account. The use of similar resources is a pervasive feature of legal practice, as are legal duties to use such resources. Perhaps legal systems *always* have such resources.

As Dworkin might put it, the question whether those resources yield a determinate answer in any case is not a *linguistic* question, but a *substantive* question. It would take an internal, interpretive argument to support the claim that the judge has a choice—an interpretive argument which has no *general* grounds for that claim, but has to compete, case by case, with the view that any particular defendant has a legal right to be acquitted, and with the view that the defendant ought (legally) to be convicted.

But there are two reasons to conclude that the interpretive considerations relevant to the decisions do not answer all questions of what counts as drunk driving. The fact that the law has 'other resources besides the words' does not distinguish law from other uses of language, and there is reason to claim that the resources of the law are generally not precise.

Hart's notion of what is determined by 'the settled conventions of language' suggests that a *word* might apply to an object by those conventions, but a rule *using* such a word might not apply because of the resources of the law. But what does it mean to say, for example, that the word 'vehicle' applies to ambulances by the settled conventions of language? It cannot mean that a police officer is talking nonsense if he says, 'We must keep all vehicles away from the accident scene so that the ambulances can get through'. If that is not nonsense, then ordinary conversational uses of language do not lack 'resources besides the words'. Hart's concession simply forgets the context principle, which is a reminder that whether an ambulance counts as a vehicle depends on the context in which the word *vehicle* is used—and there is nothing in the context principle that is at war with the settled conventions of language. Any notion of linguistic conventions needs to comport with that principle.

If there are indeterminate cases for the application of a vague word such as *intoxicated*, they are not eliminated by the resources of communication that accompany *all* uses of language. If that is right, the fact that law has 'other resources besides the words' does not offer to eliminate indeterminacies that arise outside the law.

The second reason for thinking that interpretation cannot eliminate the indeterminacies that arise from vagueness has to do with the nature of the law's resources. It may seem that we can only say that those resources may or may not eradicate indeterminacies. It is certainly *conceivable* that the interpretive resources of the law might yield precise requirements when a lawmaker uses vague language. If a highway code prohibits driving automobiles while intoxicated, it might conceivably be right for a court to interpret the law to prohibit driving automobiles just when the driver's blood alcohol limit is above the precise level set for bus drivers. But I think that there are general reasons to conclude that the resources of the law do not eradicate indeterminacy. We can say three things: (i) those resources are generally considerations of principle; (ii) they will only eliminate indeterminacies if they have a *special structural feature*—precision; and (iii) considerations of principle generally lack that feature.

Think of the considerations mentioned above, which might bear on the interpretation of a vague enactment: strict construction, protection of liberty, analogies with other departments of the law, and so on. None of them is precise.[67] What is more, the reasons why they are imprecise give reason to generalize about the resources of the law. General principles of consistency with other areas of the law are vague, because they are forms of analogical reasoning, and the operative notions of sufficiency and relevance of similarities are vague. Principles of protecting liberty are vague, because they need to account for the interests with which freedom of action is in tension. That is not to say that there could be no precise technique for protecting liberty. But such a technique would not be a principle—a starting-point for reasoning that could have general application to the treatment of a variety of behaviour. Among the arguments of principle that Dworkin has discussed throughout his work, there is none that is not vague. And there is no reason to think that a consideration of all of his vague arguments of principle would yield a precise view of the requirements of the law.

It seems that a good theory of interpretation will not include the claim that there are no indeterminacies in the legal effect of vague enactments. But it is important to see that the point is not just a point about language, or about legislation. Vagueness in the application of words like *game* and *child* and *intoxicated* only helps us to see an important point about the general principles that theories like Dworkin's insist are part of the law. Those standards are not sharply bounded in their effect, any more than mere vague words are sharply bounded in their application. Even if a theory of law includes Dworkin's claim that the law of a country is the set of principles that its

---

[67] General principles of promoting the common good, or other values or interests, are also vague. Note that, for present purposes, we do not need to identify the limits of the law. The problem of vagueness is not just that judges must take into account non-legal considerations; it is that legal and non-legal considerations will not ordinarily give the law a precise content.

courts ought to act on, it should not include his claim that there is a single right answer to (virtually) every legal dispute.

This controversial claim, if correct, demands an answer to Dworkin's claim that Hart's picture of adjudication is unattractive. That is, if courts must commonly make decisions that are not determined by the law, we need to say whether that activity is undemocratic and contrary to the rule of law, as Dworkin suggests. We must portray much adjudication as a necessary evil, or else develop a picture of the creative role of courts as a potentially valuable feature of the rule of law.[68]

3.4 Performative Uses of Language

Worte sind Taten.[69]

(Wittgenstein)

Hart pointed out that people use language to do things other than making statements, and he claimed that this insight is important for jurisprudence.[70] It is an insight that Hart got from J. L. Austin, who thought it meant a 'revolution in philosophy'.[71] Austin had much in common with Hart, including a yen for 'elucidating' the use of language.[72] Austin thought it important that words are not used merely to make statements of fact. But the first stage of the philosophers' response to that insight had been to dismiss other sorts of utterance as pseudo-statements, as Bentham and A. J. Ayer[73] had done. Those philosophers adopted the nonsense doctrine. Austin saw that response as 'unfortunate dogmatism', and he offered an alternative: 'Yet we, that is, even philosophers, set some limits to the amount of nonsense that we are prepared to admit we talk: so that it was natural to go on to ask, as a second stage, whether many apparent pseudo-statements really set out to be "statements" at all'.[74] To avoid saying that we talk nonsense with our 'apparent pseudo-statements', Austin said that many such utterances are 'performatives'—utterances such as 'I apologize' that are not true or false, but are meant and understood to do

---

[68] For one such account see Endicott, 'The Impossibility of the Rule of Law', *Oxford Journal of Legal Studies*, 19 (1999), 1.

[69] Wittgenstein, *Philosophische Bemerkungen* (1933), in the Wittgenstein Archive, http://www.hit.uib.no/wab/sample/vw115-ad.htm#92, Item 115 Verso Page 33.

[70] See Hart, *Essays in Jurisprudence and Philosophy*, 275: 'Wittgenstein said somewhere that words are also deeds ("Wörter sind auch Taten")'.

[71] *How to Do Things with Words* (Oxford: Clarendon Press, 1962), 3. In a passage typical of Austin's style he went on to say, 'If anyone wishes to call it the greatest and most salutary in its history, this is not, if you come to think of it, a large claim.' (ibid.)

[72] e.g. ibid. 147.

[73] See *Language Truth and Logic*, rev. edn. (London: Gollancz, 1950), 22: '... since the expression of a value judgment is not a proposition, the question of truth or falsehood does not here arise.' And see ch. VI, 'Critique of Ethics and Theology'.

[74] *How to Do Things with Words*, 2.

something other than make an assertion (and in the right circumstances they really do it). Such an utterance has an 'illocutionary force' that is not constative (i.e. directed to making a true or false statement), but performative.[75]

Austin made tantalizing suggestions that, by paying attention to what people do with words, we can resolve philosophical problems about morality and value without the dogmatism of the nonsense doctrine. In an echo of Bentham, he said that ' "ethical propositions" are perhaps intended, solely or partly, to evince emotion or to prescribe conduct or to influence it in special ways'.[76] I will briefly discuss that suggestion and its role in moral philosophy, because it provides a background to Hart's use of performatives in legal philosophy.

Performatives and Morality

Concerning evaluation, Austin hinted that philosophers interested in the word *good* are well advised to 'take the line of considering what we use it to do'. If they take that line, they have their work cut out for them:

But we shall not get really clear about this word 'good' and what we use it to do until, ideally, we have a complete list of those illocutionary acts of which commending, grading, etc., are isolated specimens—until we know how many such acts there are and what are their relationships and inter-connexions.[77]

This remark offers philosophers a twofold way of dodging the need for a philosophical account of value. First, Austin won't ask what *good* means, or what counts as good. He leaves out of the picture any account of what is good or bad (or what is right or wrong), by recommending that we think instead about the varieties of approving or disapproving actions that people perform. Secondly, he sets *that* task aside indefinitely by saying that it would take 'a complete list of those illocutionary acts'. He puts aside the question of what is good and what is right for a different pursuit, which he then defers.

It seems to me that the best alternative to the nonsense doctrine is to say that the 'apparent pseudo-statements' that we make with normative and evaluative language are statements. The sentence *I apologize* is not ordinarily used to make a statement; the sentence *I ought to apologize* is ordinarily used to make a statement (which can be used to perform various speech acts, including the speech act of apologizing). This view of moral statements lends itself to the view that they can be true.[78] By contrast, an understanding of value and normativity debunks its subject-matter if it confines itself to pointing out the performative functions of words. Of course, many philosophers have set out to debunk value and normativity, moved by Bentham's

---

[75] You perform an act when you make an utterance of the kind that Austin called 'constative', but I will follow his use of the term 'performative' for utterances that perform other acts.

[76] ibid. 2–3.   [77] ibid. 162.

[78] But it does not entail such a view: the people who make moral statements may be systematically mistaken, as J. L. Mackie argued: *Ethics: Inventing Right and Wrong* (Harmondsworth: Penguin, 1977).

empiricist impulse, or by a naturalizing impulse. Their theories have been labelled non-cognitivist, subjectivist, non-realist, quasi-realist, emotivist, prescriptivist, projectivist, and so on. This is no place to assess those theories, but I propose that such efforts should constrain their method: they should not start, in the way Austin suggests, from an unexplained focus on the illocutionary forces with which evaluative and normative statements can be uttered. Moral questions are questions of how to live, and those questions are not questions of the meaning of the word *to*, or of the illocutionary force with which someone might utter it. Moral philosophy has little to gain and everything to lose from a distracting focus on the actions we use language to perform. There will be time enough to explain moral statements as something *other than* statements, once the theorist has given reason to think that there is nothing to state.[79] A good moral philosophy will be able to explain moral statements (or pseudo-statements, or non-statements). But it will not focus on moral language as if that were its subject-matter.[80]

Why is the proposed methodological principle sound?

1. Because evaluative and normative language is not distinguished by its usefulness for performing the illocutionary acts of arguing, blaming, praising, insisting, grading, commending, condemning, and so on. All those acts can be performed with descriptive language ('he hasn't had a shot on goal all season' . . .), or with a raised eyebrow. So we cannot understand normative and evaluative language just by pointing out what is done with it.

2. It is true that saying '*this* is good' can be a remarkably effective way of endorsing something. But we can call something *good* without endorsing it. as Bernard Williams has pointed out, there is no logical link between evaluation and endorsement.[81] So pointing out its aptness for performing speech acts does not explain the use of value language.

3. Pointing out that people endorse things is not enough to explain value *or* normativity *or* morality; we need to know whether anything ought to be endorsed. If we had Austin's imaginary complete list of performative uses of value language, we would have an unmanageably impressive catalogue of ways in which people display attitudes, or express preferences, or show emotion, or aim to manipulate other people. But we would still need to make sense of those types of illocutionary act. To understand their significance and their place in people's lives (to do moral philosophy), we would need to ask these questions: can people have reasons for perform-

---

[79] Cf. Bernard Williams's argument against 'the linguistic enterprise' in ethics: *Ethics and the Limits of Philosophy* (1993), ch. 7, 'The Linguistic Turn'.

[80] I do not mean that all the sceptical moral theories I mentioned violate this principle; and since the principle is a matter of focus, it may be unclear whether any particular theory does so. For possible examples see C. L. Stevenson, *Ethics and Language* (London: Oxford University Press, 1944), and R. M. Hare, *The Language of Morals* (Oxford: Oxford University Press, 1952). Hare wrote, 'Ethics, as I conceive it, is the logical study of the language of morals' (p. v).

[81] See his discussion of the merits of hotels in *Ethics and the Limits of Philosophy* (London: Fontana, 1985), 125.

ing them? Or is the sound of those speech acts like the noise of the wind and the waves, as Virginia Woolf described it? '. . . only gigantic chaos streaked with lightning could have been heard tumbling and tossing, as the wind and waves disported themselves like the amorphous bulks of leviathans whose brows are pierced by no light of reason . . .'.[82]

Performatives and Law

Performatives are important in our moral life, but the importance of performatives to moral philosophy is minimal. Ask how Hart put Austin's ideas to work in jurisprudence, and I think we will find corresponding limitations. It is not that performatives are unimportant. It seems to me that their importance in law is very great, and yet their importance for legal theory is minimal. The operative words in conveyances, wills, and other legal documents are all used performatively—that is why such documents are called *instruments*. Judges sentence people by the act of *pronouncing* sentence. The acts of legislatures are typically linguistic acts. And so on. But I do not see any gains to be made from attention to performatives in law, as long as you see that such functions of language exist and that there is nothing bizarre about the notion that, given the right circumstances (including the legal power to change the legal situation by a linguistic act), performative utterances can be effective to do what they purport to do.

Besides pointing it out, what did Hart try to achieve with the insight that people do things with words? He said that 'attention to the various modalities of the performative use of language serves to clarify among other things the idea of legal powers, contracts, and conveyances . . .'.[83] It is not clear what service he has in mind, but it seems to be to refute realists such as Axel Hagerstrom. They thought that only magic words could *really* (e.g.) create a contract. If we don't believe in magic words, we should say that such things cannot happen, so that (e.g.) the contracts we think we enter into don't really exist. The practice of law is clogged with esoteric superstitions.

For clearing up this misconception, Austin's work really is useful—reading his painstaking observations about the conditions in which the utterance of a performative is 'happy' should persuade even a realist that there is no magic in it. Performative uses of language are shown simply to be very sensible, partly rule-governed, ways for people to deal with each other.[84] But this purpose for talking about performatives in legal theory is limited—it is only worthwhile if you need to refute the magic words view. You do not need to talk about performatives if you know that it is possible, and not even mysterious, for example, to commit yourself by saying 'I promise'.

---

[82] Virginia Woolf, *To the Lighthouse* (1927).   [83] *Essays in Jurisprudence and Philosophy*, 4.

[84] Although Austin did not have that effect on Karl Olivecrona. Olivecrona did not think that performative utterances were magic words, but he gave a spurious explanation for their effect (in ordinary life and in law) in terms of 'psychological conditioning'. See his discussion of Austin's work in *Law as Fact*, 2nd edn. (London: Stevens, 1971), 224–6. On the role of performatives in moral and legal theory see also Paul Amselek (ed.), *Théorie des actes de langage, éthique et droit* (Paris: Presses universitaires de France, 1986).

Austin himself hinted at a much more ambitious role for the notion. He made an oblique and offhand suggestion that 'a statement of "the law"' is a performative statement, rather than 'a statement of fact'.[85] Hart seems to have been attracted to the possibility that Austin hints at—in fact it is a view that is almost stated clearly in Hart's early essays, and I propose that it colours the 'practice theory of rules' that is the basis of his later work on the nature of law. The possibility is that the performative functions of language can explain the most basic problem of jurisprudence: the normativity of law.

In his inaugural lecture, Hart rejected Bentham's method of paraphrasis for terms like *right*, and said that a statement like '*A* has a right to be paid £10 by *B*' is not descriptive, but 'may be well called a conclusion of law'.[86] The expression *a right* 'has meaning only as part of a sentence the function of which as a whole is to draw a conclusion of law from a specific kind of legal rule'. It is not quite clear what he means by 'conclusion', but the remark betrays the influence of the charm of performatives: it focuses attention not on what a statement of rights means, but on what people do with it.

Thirty years later Hart retracted the claim.[87] His retraction, in turn, is unclear, but it suggests that he had thought of a 'conclusion of law' as some sort of performative, and that he later came to think that he had confused the (conclusory) force of such a statement with its meaning, and that it was misleading to say that a statement of rights was not descriptive, because saying so obscured the context of such a statement in a system of rules.

It was the notion of a system of rules that he used in his book, *The Concept of Law*, to elucidate statements of legal rights. His 'practice theory of rules' identified a social rule as a regularity of conduct accompanied by a 'distinctive normative attitude' of acceptance, which 'consists in the standing disposition of individuals to take such patterns of conduct both as guides to their own future conduct and as standards of criticism'.[88]

I think the charm of performatives has an influence here too, at the centre of Hart's theory of law—but its influence is oblique. He does not endorse Austin's suggestion that statements of law are performatives; and he holds that statements of law (unlike performatives such as 'I apologise') can be true or false. But note that Hart's interest in statements of law is still focused not on what they mean, but on what people do with them. Occasionally he suggests in *The Concept of Law* that rules are reasons for action[89]—which would imply that statements of law state reasons that people have for acting in one way or another. But taken together, his discussions of acceptance reveal a different view: that people 'treat', 'look upon', 'see', and 'use' rules as reasons.[90] People *take* rules as guides and *use* them to criticize each other and, gener-

---

[85] *How to Do Things with Words*, 4, n. 2.   [86] *Essays in Jurisprudence and Philosophy*, 28.
[87] ibid. 5.
[88] *CL*, 255; this statement of the theory is taken from a résumé in his 'Postscript', written in the 1980s.
[89] *CL*, 84.   [90] *CL*, 90.

ally, to *display an attitude*.[91] Hart actually has nothing to say about the *meaning* of normative statements such as 'A has a right to be paid £10 by B'—except that its meaning is different in law and in morality. He could never explain the difference. It seems that Hart simply thought that there *had* to be a difference in meaning, or it would be impossible for you to state a law you do not approve of. It must be possible for someone to say, as a statement applying English law, 'A has a right to be paid £10 by B', without believing that morality demands the payment. Hart's headache was the thought that, if there was no distinction between the meaning of normative statements in law and in morality, then there was no alternative to a natural law theory of the kind he was trying to avoid.

Raz on Normative Statements

> . . . it is the explanation of the use of normative language which lies
> at the heart of the problem of the normativity of law.[92]

Joseph Raz rejected Hart's claim that normative terms have a distinctive meaning in statements of law. In his view, a normative statement such as 'A has a right to be paid £10 by B' states that B has a certain sort of reason for action. If it is a statement applying the law, it states what B has reason to do from the point of view of the law.[93] Raz's theory of law is part of a theory of practical reasoning in general, and his account of normative statements treats them as having the same meaning (which is to state practical conclusions) in law and in morality. But he dissolves Hart's headache by pointing out that normative statements can be made in a detached way. People can make them without endorsing the point of view from which the reasons they are stating are valid.[94]

Hart's work on the normativity of law betrays the lingering influence of the charm of performatives, and Raz's work shows an alternative that escapes that distracting influence. The good way to use the idea of performatives in legal theory is very restricted; any more ambitious use is disastrous. To understand morality, and to understand law, we need to pay attention to what people state when they make normative statements—it is not enough to point out the attitudes that people display when they utter such statements.

Does the importance of normative statements, which Raz pointed out, belie Raz's own claim that 'there is little that philosophy of language can do to advance one's understanding of law'?[95] Yes, if we view Raz's account of normative statements as

[91] *CL*, 255.
[92] Raz, *Practical Reason and Norms*, 2nd edn. (1990), 169. Cf. 'The problem of the normativity of law is the problem of explaining the use of normative language in describing the law or legal situations', ibid. 170.
[93] ibid. 175. See also 'The Purity of the Pure Theory', in R. Tur and W. Twining (eds.), *Essays on Kelsen* (Oxford: Clarendon Press, 1981).
[94] ibid. 176–7. For Hart's response to Raz's work on the normativity of law, see *Essays on Bentham* (Oxford: Clarendon Press, 1982), 153–61.
[95] See above.

work in the philosophy of language, which it is. But it is a branch of the philosophy of language on which philosophers of language have had little to say. That just means that philosophy of language is so broad that it includes more than the work of professional philosophers of language. Language is not the subject-matter of moral philosophy, but there are areas of the philosophy of language that can only be addressed by moral philosophy.

4 CONCLUSION

Jeremy Bentham foreshadowed much of twentieth-century work on law and language. That is partly because Bentham influenced Hart, and Hart has both expressed valuable insights, and made the most important mistakes in the area. Hart talks as if he had the task of presenting the results of philosophy: he wrote that 'the analytical study of law has been advanced' by the 'insights of modern linguistic philosophy'.[96] But philosophy of language is not a body of results that can be applied to solve jurisprudential problems, in the way that modern biochemistry is (in one aspect) a body of results that can be applied to solve medical problems. Perhaps that is easier to see now, than it was in the 1950s. All the most interesting products of linguistic philosophy, and philosophy of language in general, are extremely controversial. It takes careful argument to distinguish between insights and misconceptions, and it is controversial whether jurisprudence has been advanced by any of Hart's claims about language.

Should we conclude that legal theory needs to say anything about language to accomplish its purposes? The context principle and the diversity principle help to make sense of what judges do in applying the language of the law, and they are crucial reminders of what they need to do in order to apply it truly. An understanding of vagueness points out that the language of the law, and the law itself, cannot always determine the outcome that the law requires, and that the judge must resolve questions left unresolved by the law. Those three principles are crucial to understanding law, and the role of judges. In any conceivable legal system, the main terms of legal doctrine are vague, and have diverse senses that vary with the context. Moreover, these points about language are not *just* points about language: in a system of customary law with no linguistically formulated laws or reports of judicial decisions, courts would still need to see what is relevantly similar among different cases in different contexts, and general legal rights and duties in such a system would typically be vague.

---

[96] *Essays in Jurisprudence and Philosophy*, 4.

The diversity principle and the context principle are also useful—in fact, essential—for the development of useful theoretical terms.

The fourth insight, that language is used to perform other speech acts beside making true or false statements, is of limited use in jurisprudence. Performatives are very important in law, but it is hard to see what problems a theorist can resolve by focusing on them—except to displace misconceptions that you may not have suffered from in the first place.

In summary, a clear understanding of some of the problems of philosophy of language is very useful for legal philosophers. That is not the case because legal philosophy is a branch of philosophy of language. It is because philosophy of language and philosophy of law are cognate parts of political philosophy.

APPENDIX: ON OPEN TEXTURE

Hart borrowed the term *open texture* from Friedrich Waismann, who called it 'the possibility of vagueness.' Several writers have tried to distinguish open texture from 'actual vagueness' in those terms.[97] I think that the distinction lacks any significance for jurisprudence.

The supposed distinction is that a term is vague (and open textured) if there are borderline cases, and open textured (but not vague) if it has no borderline cases, but we could imagine borderline cases. So, for example, it may be that *photon* is not vague, because every object in this world either is clearly a photon, or is clearly not a photon (either by coincidence, or because the laws of physics only allow particles that either clearly have or clearly lack the characteristics of photons). But we could imagine different worlds in which there are particles that have some distinctive features of photons, but are unlike photons in other ways. In such a possible world, the word *photon* would be vague. So *photon* is open-textured but not vague in our world.

This distinction seems to me incoherent, because vagueness is a feature of the meaning of words. If there are possible worlds in which it is unclear whether something counts as a photon, the word *photon* is vague in *this* world. (It is unclear in this world what counts as a photon, even if it is not unclear what in this world counts as a photon.)

For jurisprudence, in any case, the only significance of the distinction is to build into the term *open texture* itself a claim that the language of the law necessarily allows for borderline cases. Even if, Hart seems to say, we used precise language to regulate human behaviour, we could always imagine unclear cases. *That* claim could be made without the incoherent distinction between open texture and vagueness. But there is nothing to be gained in jurisprudence by making the claim in any case. Law is necessarily vague in the more interesting ways that Hart also discusses: that is, law necessarily uses highly vague standards of the sort used by the legal systems we are familiar with to regulate the use of force, the sale of goods, the duty of care in negligence, the duty of one spouse to support the other, and so on and so on. There is

---

[97]   e.g. Andrei Marmor, *Interpretation and Legal Theory* (Oxford: Clarendon Press, 1992), 132; Michael Moore, 'The Semantics of Judging', *Southern California Law Review*, 54 (1981), 151, 201; Frederick Schauer, *Playing by the Rules* (Oxford: Clarendon Press, 1991), 35.

no room for the claim that, even if the laws of a legal system were all precise, we could still imagine borderline cases. The claim is otiose because there is no such thing as a legal system in which all the laws are precise.

FURTHER READING

On philosophy of language and law

Timothy Endicott, *Vagueness in Law* (Oxford: Oxford University Press, 2000).

Thomas Morawetz (ed.), *Law and Language* (Dartmouth: Ashgate, 2000).

Mark D. Greenberg and Harry Litman, 'The Meaning of Original Meaning' *Georgetown Law Journal*, 86 (1998), 569.

Brian Bix, *Law, Language and Legal Determinacy* (Oxford: Clarendon Press, 1996).

Nicos Stavropoulos, *Objectivity in Law* (Oxford: Clarendon Press, 1996).

Stanley Fish, *Doing What Comes Naturally* (Oxford: Clarendon Press, 1989).

Michael Moore, 'A Natural Law Theory of Interpretation', *Southern California Law Review*, 58 (1985), 277.

Glanville Williams, 'Language and the Law', *Law Quarterly Review*, 61 (1945), 71, 179, 293, 384; *Law Quarterly Review*, 62 (1946), 387.

On linguistic analysis of legal language

Peter M. Tiersma, *Legal Language* (Chicago: University of Chicago Press, 1999).

Northwestern University–Washington University Law and Linguistics Conference, *Washington University Law Quarterly*, 73 (1995).

Bernard S. Jackson, *Making Sense in Law: Linguistic, Psychological and Semiotic Perspectives* (Liverpool: Charles Publications, 1995).

John Gibbons (ed.), *Language and the Law* (London: Longman, 1994).

Lawrence M. Solan, *The Language of Judges* (Chicago: University of Chicago Press, 1993).

Judith N. Levi and Anne Graffam Walker, *Language in the Judicial Process* (New York: Plenum, 1990).

Frederick Bowers, *Linguistic Aspects of Legislative Expression* (Vancouver: University of British Columbia Press, 1989).

On the history of English and American legal language

David Mellinkoff, *The Language of the Law* (Boston: Little, Brown, 1963).

CHAPTER 23

LAW AND OBJECTIVITY

BRIAN LEITER

WE can only discuss issues about the objectivity of law if we first have at our disposal some appropriate philosophical tools.

There are two main kinds of philosophical questions about objectivity: metaphysical and epistemological. *Metaphysical* objectivity concerns the extent to which the existence and character of some class of entities depends on the states of mind of persons (i.e. their knowledge, judgment, belief, perception, or response). *Epistemological* objectivity concerns the extent to which we are capable of achieving *knowledge* about those things that are metaphysically objective. Many philosophers working in the Anglo-American traditions also worry about *semantic* objectivity, that is, about whether or not the propositions in some realm of discourse (physics, psychology, ethics, law, etc.) can be evaluated in terms of their truth or falsity. For a discourse to be semantically objective, and for the statements in the discourse to be true, then the things referred to by the terms of that discourse (i.e. quarks, desires, justice, legal facts) must be metaphysically objective.

I am grateful to Professor Yasuji Nosaka for his probing questions and our fruitful discussions of many of these issues during his year as a Visiting Scholar at the University of Texas, 1999–2000. Thanks also to Philip Pettit and Scott Shapiro for comments on earlier versions of portions of this material.

1 METAPHYSICAL OBJECTIVITY

An entity (or a class of entities) is metaphysically objective if its existence and character is *independent* of the human mind. This 'independence requirement' is central to metaphysical objectivity (Brower 1993; Sober 1982), though its proper interpretation raises two important questions: first, *in what way* must a metaphysically objective thing be 'independent' of the human mind; and secondly, *how much* independence of the relevant kind is required?

1.1 What Kind of Independence?

The existence and character of some entity might be *independent* of the human mind in three senses: causally, constitutionally, and cognitively. Only the last two will matter for metaphysical objectivity.

An entity is *causally* independent of the human mind as long as the causal trajectory producing it did not involve the human mind. Shoes, for example, are causally *dependent* on the human mind because the existence and character of any particular pair of shoes depends causally on a cobbler having had certain beliefs and desires (e.g. a desire to make a particular kind of shoe, and true beliefs about what needed to be done to produce such shoes). By contrast, the existence and character of the earth is causally *independent* of the human mind: no human intentions played a causal role in bringing about the existence of the earth or its specific character. Metaphysical objectivity, however, *does not require causal independence.* Even entities that are *causally dependent* on the human mind can be mind-independent in one of the other two senses (below), and thus still be metaphysically objective.

An entity is *constitutionally* independent of the human mind if its existence and character is not constituted by or identical with the mind. Certain historical forms of philosophical 'idealism' (such as those of Bishop Berkeley and Hegel) held that the world was constitutionally *dependent* on the mind (the human mind, or perhaps the mind of God). Conversely, the claim that some entity is metaphysically objective almost always involves denying its constitutional dependence on the mind. The exception is for psychological entities (e.g. beliefs, desires, emotions): such things cannot be constitutionally independent of the mind since they just are facets of the mind. Yet surely psychological facts may also be metaphysically objective. If so, they must be 'independent' of the mind in the final sense.

An entity is *cognitively* independent of the human mind if its existence and character does not depend on any *cognizing* state of persons: for example, belief, sensory perception, judgment, response, and so on. (A 'cognizing' state is one which is receptive to features of the world and thus is a potential source of knowledge of the world.)

A metaphysically objective thing is, accordingly, what it is independent of what anyone *believes* or would be *justified* in believing about it (or what anyone perceives it to be or would perceive it to be under certain conditions, etc.). On this account, psychological facts about a person are metaphysically objective in virtue of not depending on what an observer of that person believes or would be justified in believing about that person's psychological state. (This assumes that mental content is 'narrow', not 'wide', a technical debate in the philosophy of psychology that must be set aside here.)

Any kind of metaphysically objective fact (except for psychological facts) must necessarily be *constitutionally* independent of the mind. All metaphysically objective facts must also be *cognitively* independent. The common-sense picture of the natural world presumes that its contents are metaphysically objective in this sense: ordinary people think that atoms and zebras and sulphur are not simply identical with the mind and that they are what they are independent of what people may believe or be justified in believing about them. Science, then, aspires to epistemological objectivity by trying to accurately depict the way things (objectively) are.

1.2 How Much Independence?

There can be degrees of cognitive *independence*, and thus degrees of objectivity that may be distinguished; not everything that is objective may prove to be objective in the sense in which common sense understands the constituent elements of the natural world to be objective. (This point is important for understanding the objectivity of law, as we will discuss shortly.) The crucial notion for cognitive independence is independence from the *cognizing* states of persons: beliefs, sensory perceptions, judgments, responses, and the like. Thus, this notion of objectivity supposes that there is always a difference between what 'seems right' about some state of affairs and what actually 'is right'. For example, it may seem right to John (based on a sensory perception) that there is a table in front of him, but it may not be right that there is a table there: it could be an optical illusion. The table, then, is objective *in some sense* since its existence is *independent* of what 'seems right' to John.

It is possible, then, to distinguish four kinds of claims about objectivity (Leiter 1993):

- According to *subjectivism*, what seems right to the cognizer determines what is right.
- According to *minimal objectivism*, what seems right to the *community of cognizers* determines what is right.
- According to *modest objectivism*, what seems right to cognizers *under appropriate or ideal conditions* determines what is right.
- According to *strong objectivism*, what seems right to cognizers *never* determines what is right.

Subjectivism and strong objectivism represent the two classical and opposed philosophical positions of antiquity: Protagoras held that 'man is the measure of all things' (subjectivism) (Plato, *Theaetetus*, *152a, *166a–*168b), while Plato embraced a kind of strong objectivism (Plato, *Phaedo*, *741–*75b, *Republic*, *475–*480, *508d–e). The Protagorean position denies the objectivity of the world and everything in it: whatever each individual takes to be the case *is* the case (for that individual), and thus the existence and character of any particular thing depends (epistemically) on the (individual) human mind. By contrast, the Platonist affirms the complete and absolute objectivity of the world: what really is the case about the world is never fixed by what any person or all persons believe, has (or have) reasons to believe, or could have reasons to believe. Mistake, on a global scale, even under ideal epistemic conditions, is a possibility for the Platonist. This latter position is often described as 'realism' (or 'metaphysical realism').

Minimal objectivism and modest objectivism occupy conceptual space between these two familiar, historical positions. Minimal objectivism holds that whatever the community of cognizers takes to be the case is the case. This view, like its pure Protagorean cousin, issues in a kind of relativism (what is the case is relative to a particular community of cognizers), but by abstracting away from the subjectivity of the individual cognizer, it introduces a *minimum* amount of objectivity. It is also a kind of objectivity with some useful domains of application. What is and is not fashionable, for example, is probably minimally objective. What seems right to John about what is fashionable can be objectively wrong: John may be out of sync with the styles of his community, and thus it would be correct to say, 'John is mistaken in thinking that a plaid shirt and striped pants go well together'. But it does not seem that the entire community can be wrong about what is fashionable: in that sense, what seems right to the community determines what really is fashionable.

In most domains, however, minimal objectivity would be viewed as too close to subjectivism for comfort. Modest objectivity thus abstracts even further away from dependence on *actual* cognizers, individual or communal. Something is modestly objective if its existence and character depend only on what cognizers would believe under certain *idealized* conditions for cognition, conditions like full information and evidence, perfect rationality, and the like. (By hypothesis, under *ideal* conditions, all cognizers would come to the same belief about things.) Everyone on the planet can be wrong in his or her beliefs about a modestly objective entity; beliefs formed under ideal epistemic conditions, however, can never be wrong. This latter point is what differentiates modest from strong objectivity.

Some philosophers have defended the idea that truth is at best modestly objective (e.g. the doctrine Hilary Putnam (1981) calls 'Internal Realism'): what is true in any domain is simply whatever inquirers would agree upon under epistemically ideal conditions. Versions of this idea have since been subjected to withering criticisms (Johnston 1993), and it has few adherents. Still, modest objectivity, like the other conceptions, may be particularly apt in certain domains. Consider, for example, facts about colour. It seems natural to say that there are (modestly) objective facts about colour even though the colour of an object is not fully independent of the human mind. For example, we might say that something is red if and only if normal perceivers under normal viewing conditions would be disposed to see it as red. Colour, on this account, depends on the human mind—on human response or perception—but only on human response under *appropriate* conditions. One important recent idea is that evaluative facts might be modestly objective in a similar way (e.g. Pettit 1991): evaluative facts would depend on human responses to morally significant situations under appropriate conditions. In both cases, however, it is important to specify the conditions under which human response fixes the reference of a concept in a non-question-begging way. It obviously will not do, for example, to define 'normalcy' of perceivers and of viewing conditions by reference to their getting the right result (i.e. seeing all and only the red things as red). Some philosophers doubt whether the conditions can be specified in a non-question-begging way (e.g. Wright 1992). We shall consider the prospects for modest objectivity about law below.

2 EPISTEMOLOGICAL OBJECTIVITY

The demand for epistemological objectivity is the demand to be free of *bias* and other factors that *distort* cognition, that prevent the things being cognized from presenting themselves as they really (metaphysically) are. More precisely, epistemological objectivity requires that the cognitive processes and mechanisms by which beliefs about the world are formed be constituted in such a way that they at least *tend* towards the production of accurate representations of how things are. Notice that epistemological objectivity does not require that cognitive processes always yield true representations: that would demand more than is attainable and more than is even expected. Epistemological objectivity obtains when either of the following is true: (1) the cognitive processes at issue *reliably* arrive at accurate representations, or (2) the cognitive processes are free of factors that are known to produce inaccurate representations.

The obstacles to epistemological objectivity will vary with the domain under consideration. In law, bias for or against one party, or ignorance of pertinent rules or facts, will be obvious hindrances to epistemological objectivity. In the sciences, and the social sciences in particular, 'values' are often thought to present a special obstacle to epistemological objectivity in so far as they influence the choice of research topics and, most seriously, the selection and evaluation of evidence. As one contemporary author explains: 'Values are thought to damage inquiry epistemically because they are held to be subjective—they come from us, not the world. Therefore to allow values to influence inquiry into the nature of the world is to allow such inquiry to be subject to a control other than the world itself' (Railton 1985: 818). Epistemic values or norms—for example, norms about when evidence warrants belief—must of course play a role in all scientific inquiry; the worry is about non-epistemic values or norms, like the political ideology of the inquirer or the political climate in which inquiry takes place.

Yet one 'need not require freedom from all value and bias in order to have objective inquiry' since 'there may yet exist mechanisms of belief-formation that incorporate feedback from the object to the inquiring subject' (Railton 1985: 818). The mechanism at issue is *causal*: metaphysically objective things make themselves felt *causally*, whatever our theoretical preconceptions and values. No matter what bias leads me to deny that there is a closed door in front of me, my attempt to walk through it will be thwarted (causally) by reality: the door will stop me.

The causal impact of reality, however, gives us merely an *external* criterion for objectivity, and does not yet show how inquirers could determine whether or not their inquiry is epistemologically objective. Here, however, inquirers might look for certain familiar markers of epistemological objectivity, like the existence of intersubjective agreement in judgment, the publicity of evidence and standards of proof, and the reproducibility of the evidence for a judgment by different inquirers: 'when these conditions are met, subjective contributions and biases will be excluded as far as possible' (Railton 1985: 818). That physics constitutes a cross-cultural, global community of inquirers strongly suggests that it is epistemologically objective: if it were not, then one would expect local differences (in interests, ideology, and the like) to lead to markedly different discourses of physics. Of course, the absence of intersubjective agreement does not *by itself* demonstrate lack of epistemological objectivity; the question is always what the best explanation for lack of such agreement is supposed to be.[1] In the case of the social sciences, where objective truths may conflict with entrenched interests, it should hardly be surprising that there should be no agreement about certain social scientific questions. In other cases, though, the suspicion will be strong that it is entrenched interests and values that distort cognition of the social world and warp scientific inquiry accordingly.

---

[1] Dworkin has often attributed to sceptics about his right-answer thesis a bad verificationist argument to the effect that 'a proposition cannot be true unless there is some agreed test through which its truth might be demonstrated' (1977: 282). But the right way to interpret scepticism about the existence of right answers in hard cases is as a 'best explanation' challenge: where there is deep and intractable disagreement about the right answer, what is the best explanation for that fact? The sceptic says the best explanation in the legal case is that there is no right answer.

3 SEMANTIC OBJECTIVITY

Semantic objectivity is a property of statements, rather than things or cognitive mechanisms. Philosophers in the Anglo-American traditions of the twentieth century, who approach most philosophical problems by framing them first as problems about language and its relationship to the world, have been most concerned with questions of semantic objectivity. Typically, philosophers are concerned with a class of statements characteristic of a particular branch of discourse: say, physics or psychology or ethics or aesthetics. Some branch of discourse enjoys semantic objectivity when its statements are generally apt for evaluation in terms of their truth and falsity. (Not every statement in the discourse need be determinately true or false—the property of 'bivalence'—since few discourses outside pure mathematics are bivalent.) *Cognitivism* is the doctrine that some branch of discourse is semantically objective.[2]

Thus, for example, the discourse of natural science is presumed to be a cognitive discourse: scientific statements about the natural world are generally either true or false. But what of statements in ethics like, 'That distribution of resources is unjust', or 'Harming a defenceless animal is morally wrong'? Many philosophers have thought that there are, *as a metaphysical matter*, no facts in the world corresponding to the 'injustice' of a distribution or the 'moral wrongness' of an action (Gibbard 1990; Mackie 1977; Stevenson 1944). Most philosophers who deny the metaphysical objectivity of morality claim that its semantics is non-cognitive: rather than stating facts (that either obtain or do not obtain), ethical statements, according to *non-cognitivism*, express attitudes or feelings of various kinds (Stevenson 1944 and Gibbard 1990 are the most sophisticated versions of this view). Non-cognitivists bear the burden, then, of explaining away the surface grammar and logical structure of ethical discourse which make it indistinguishable from ordinary empirical discourse (compare: 'This distribution is unjust', with 'That chair is red').

A minority of philosophers, however, agree that morality is *not* metaphysically objective, but none the less maintain that the surface grammar of ethical discourse should be taken at face value: ethical discourse purports to state facts, and is thus a cognitive discourse. It is, unfortunately, a cognitive discourse almost all of whose statements are false (since there are no metaphysically objective moral facts in the world). (The only true ethical statements, on this view, will be *negations* of ethical judgments: 'No, slavery is not really morally wrong'.) This doctrine is known as 'error theory' (Mackie 1977). Error theories about any discourse make it puzzling, however, why the discourse should persist, let alone occupy the central role that ethical

---

[2] Wright (1992) disputes whether truth-aptness is the relevant criterion for demarcating semantically objective discourses; most discourses satisfy the minimum syntactic requirements to make use of the truth-predicate appropriate. The issue about the objectivity of the discourse must be located elsewhere according to Wright.

discourse does in human lives: why would people continue to engage in a putatively fact-stating discourse that never succeeds in stating any facts? Non-cognitivism, as a semantic doctrine, at least identifies an important role for ethical discourse: namely, the expression of feelings and attitudes about matters of real moment to human beings and their social existence.

Most philosophers who accept that ethical discourse is cognitive do so because they also believe that morality is metaphysically objective (in some sense) (Brink 1989; Brower 1993; Pettit 1991; Railton 1986): if there are metaphysically objective moral facts, then moral statements will not be systematically false as error theory has it. How could there be such facts? One important strand of argument (that has also been influential in legal philosophy) presupposes the truth of Kripke–Putnam semantics, according to which there can be necessary truths (e.g. 'water is H_2O') that are discoverable only *a posteriori* (Kripke 1980; Putnam 1975).[3] For those who think moral facts are *strongly* objective (e.g. Brink 1989; Railton 1986), the central idea is that moral facts are simply identical with (or supervenient upon) natural facts: just as there are necessary, *a posteriori* statements of property identity about water, so too there are such statements about moral facts.[4] For example, perhaps the property of being 'morally right' is just identical with the property of 'maximizing human well-being', where the latter may be understood in purely psychological and physiological terms. In that case, whether an action X is morally right is a strongly objective matter, since it is simply a scientific question whether action X will in fact maximize the relevant kinds of psychological and physiological states in the world.[5] The crucial claim, plainly, is that moral facts are to be identified with (or treated as supervenient upon) certain kinds of natural facts. Again, many philosophers are sceptical that this claim can be made out (e.g. Gibbard 1990).

[3] Brink (1988, 2001) provides an accessible introduction to the main themes of the 'new' or 'causal' theory of reference associated with Kripke and Putnam. A more detailed treatment of the issues in philosophical semantics, again with an eye to issues of legal philosophy, may be found in Stavropoulos (1996), 17–34, 53–76.

[4] This allows moral realists to deflect G. E. Moore's famous 'open question' argument. That it was an 'open question' in 1400 whether 'water was H_2O' has no bearing on the necessity of the identity relation, since the necessary identity here was an a posteriori discovery. So too, the fact that it might be an 'open question' whether 'what is pleasurable is good' shows nothing about the real nature of goodness, since what constitutes goodness may also be discoverable only a posteriori.

The Moorean argument can be given a new twist by reframing it in the language of internalism: the doctrine that there is a necessary connection between judging that 'X is good', and feeling some motivational pull to do or have X. Even if there are necessary a posteriori relations between moral facts and natural facts, there does not seem to be any guarantee that discovering a posteriori that 'what is good is pleasure' will necessarily exert any motivational force for the judging agent. 'So pleasure is what is good. So what? Why should I care about pleasure?' seems a completely intelligible question for the judger to ask. Most moral realists (e.g. Railton 1986) respond to this dilemma by simply denying that internalism is true.

[5] Most naturalistic moral realisms are based on versions of utilitarianism, precisely because it is easy to see what the naturalistic base of moral properties would be in a utilitarian schema. One peculiar feature of the moral realism of Moore (1992b) is that it is conjoined with a deontological moral theory, yet within a purportedly naturalistic moral realist framework.

4 LAW AND OBJECTIVITY

In law, issues about objectivity arise along a variety of dimensions.[6] For example: (1) we expect the content of our laws to be objective in the sense of treating people the same unless they are 'relevantly' different. (2) We expect judges to be objective in the sense of not being biased against one party or the other. (3) We expect legal decisions to be objective in the sense of reaching the result that the law *really* requires without letting bias or prejudice intervene. (4) In some areas of law, we expect the law to employ 'objective' standards of conduct (like 'reasonable person' standards) that do not permit actors to excuse their conduct based on their subjective perceptions at the time.

Recently, a substantial literature has emerged on the objectivity of law primarily with respect to the issues posed in (3). Indeed, it is here, in particular, that questions about the objectivity of ethics intersect with those about law. We may think of the central problematic in the following way.

Judges must decide cases. They must consult and interpret the relevant legal sources (statutes, precedent, custom, etc.) in order to determine the governing legal principles and rules, and then decide how these are to apply to the facts of the case. Let us call the 'class of legal reasons' the class of reasons that judges may legitimately consider in deciding a legal question.[7] If the law is 'rationally determinate' on some point that means the class of legal reasons justifies a unique answer on that point: there is, as is commonly said, a single right answer as a matter of law.

We may now speak of the law as *objective* along two possible dimensions:

1. The law is *metaphysically* objective in so far as there exist right answers as a matter of law.
2. The law is *epistemically* objective in so far as the mechanisms for discovering right answers (e.g. adjudication, legal reasoning) are free of distorting factors that would obscure right answers.

Where the law is metaphysically objective, we may say there exists a 'legal fact': if it is rationally determinate, as a matter of law, that 'Leiter is liable for his negligence in these circumstances', then it is a legal fact that Leiter is negligent.

The scope of these claims about the objectivity of law may vary. We may think the law is metaphysically objective only with respect to a narrow range of cases (as the American Legal Realists do), or with respect to nearly all cases (as Dworkin does). We may think the law is epistemically objective some of the time or almost none of the time. The claims to objectivity can diverge as well. The law may be metaphysically objective, but fail to be epistemically objective. On the other hand, the above

[6] See e.g. Greenawalt (1992) for a wide-ranging survey, though one that is a bit thin in its treatment of the philosophical issues.
[7] See Leiter (1995b) for this way of conceptualizing indeterminacy.

characterization of epistemic objectivity presupposes for its intelligibility that the law be metaphysically objective: we can get no purchase on the notion of a 'distorting factor' without reference to the 'things' we are trying to know.[8]

Often, the objectivity of ethics is implicated in the objectivity of law. The metaphysical objectivity of law, as we have seen, is a matter of its rational determinacy, that is, it is a matter of the class of legal reasons justifying a unique outcome. If the class of legal reasons, however, includes *moral* reasons, then the law can be objective only if morality (and moral reasoning) is objective. The class of legal reasons can come to include moral reasons in two ways.

First, and most obviously, the familiar sources of law—like statutes and constitutional provisions—may include moral concepts or considerations. The United States Constitution provides the most familiar examples, since it speaks of 'equal protection', 'liberty', and other inherently moral notions. For courts to apply these provisions is for them necessarily to apply the incorporated moral concepts. For the law to be metaphysically objective in these cases requires that these moral concepts have objective content. Of course, this objective content need not be fixed in virtue of morality being objective: an interpretive principle like 'Interpret each provision as the framers of the provision would have intended' may suffice to make the application of the Equal Protection Clause of the Fourteenth Amendment determinate, without presupposing anything about the 'objective' meaning of 'equality'. Yet in some cases, and under some theories of interpretation, what will be required is precisely to understand what equality *really* requires.[9]

Secondly, moral reasons might be part of the class of legal reasons because they are part of the very criteria of legal validity. Natural lawyers hold that for a norm to be a legal norm it must satisfy moral criteria:[10] thus, a judge wondering whether a particular norm (relevant to a particular case) is a valid legal norm must necessarily engage in moral reasoning. Some Legal Positivists ('Soft' or 'Inclusive' positivists) accept a similar view: they hold that, as a contingent matter, morality can be a criterion of legal validity if it is the practice of legal officials in some society to employ moral considerations as criteria of legal validity. For these positivists—who include the century's leading defender of the doctrine, H. L. A. Hart—legal reasoning in such societies will include moral reasoning.

Of course, even those positivists ('Hard' or 'Exclusive' positivists) who deny that morality is ever a criterion of legality may still hold that it is a judge's duty in exercising discretion in hard cases to reach the morally correct result. Thus, while the objectivity of morality won't, for these positivists, affect the objectivity of law, it will still matter in thinking about what judges ought to do in hard cases.

---

[8] Not all writers accept this link (e.g. Postema 2001). See the further discussion in Section 6.

[9] Examples of this kind of approach include Brink (1988, 2001), Moore (1985), and Stavropoulos (1996).

[10] Satisfying the moral criteria might be *necessary* for a norm to be a legal norm, or it might be both necessary and sufficient. The strongest forms of natural law theory hold the latter.

In all these ways, then, the objectivity of morality may be implicated in how we think about the objectivity of law (or the objectivity of the adjudicative process).

5 HOW OBJECTIVE IS LAW?

Most writers who have considered this question have done so largely within the kind of philosophical framework sketched in the prior sections (e.g. Brink 1988 and 2001; Coleman 1995; Coleman and Leiter 1993; Moore 1985 and 1992*a*; Stavropoulos 1996). Writers like Brink and Moore, for example, have developed an account of law as Strongly Objective, applying the realist semantics (the 'new' or 'causal' theory of reference) of Kripke and Putnam to issues of legal interpretation. As Stavropoulos explains it:

Both Kripke and Putnam attack what they call the traditional theory of reference. That theory holds that an expression refers to whatever fits the description with which speakers associate the expression. The relevant description . . . captures necessary properties of the referent which are knowable *a priori*, as in the case of knowing that a bachelor is an unmarried man. This cannot be true, Kripke and Putnam argue, since expressions refer to the same object in the lips of speakers who can only associate the expression with vague or mistaken descriptions. Indeed, not only individual speakers but the community as a whole can be in error about the true properties of the relevant object. . . . The important suggestion being made by Kripke and Putnam is that reference is *object-dependent*. *Which* object 'Aristotle' or 'water' refers to is not determined by the associated description, but turns instead on a matter of fact, namely which object the name-using or term-using practice is directed at. (1996: 8)

Thus, if on the old view the 'meaning' of an expression (the descriptions speakers associated with it) fixed the reference of the expression, on the new theory, the referent fixes the meaning. 'Water' picks out whatever stuff we happened to baptize with the name 'water' at the beginning of the 'term-using practice'. As it happens, that stuff has a distinctive micro-constitution: it is H_2O. Thus, 'water' refers to stuff that is H_2O, and that is what the term means: the stuff that is H_2O. If we can apply the new theory of reference to the expressions that figure in legal rules, then we can vindicate an account of law as Strongly Objective: the meaning of the rule determines its application, and the meaning is Strongly Objective, that is, the *real* referents of the terms in the legal rule determine the rule's meaning, and the entire community can be mistaken about what that referent is.

Problems arise at several different levels with this account of the law's objectivity, though all are traceable to the reliance on the new theory of reference. To begin, there are reasons to be sceptical about whether the new theory of reference is correct (e.g.

Evans 1973; Blackburn 1988).[11] This debate in philosophical semantics would, however, take us far afield, though the reader should at least be aware that the confidence in the correctness of the theory expressed by Brink, Moore, and others is perhaps not warranted.

Even granting, however, the correctness of the new theory, it is not obvious how it helps in the case of law. After all, the new theory always seemed most plausible for a limited class of expressions: proper names and natural kind terms (i.e. terms that pick out the natural features of the world about which science states lawful generalizations). The reason has to do with the implicit essentialism required for the new theory: unless referents have *essential* characteristics—just as 'water' has a distinctive and essential molecular constitution—they cannot fix meanings. But what is the essence of 'due process' or 'equal protection'? We would first need to accept some version of moral realism before the new theory of reference would help.[12]

Finally, even if the new theory of reference gives the correct account of the meaning of some terms (like natural kind terms), that still does not show that it gives us the right account of meaning for purposes of legal interpretation.[13] Suppose the legislature prohibits the killing of 'fish' within 100 miles of the coast, intending quite clearly (as the legislative history reveals) to protect whales, but not realizing that 'fish' is a natural kind term that does not include whales within its extension. The new theory of reference tells us that the statute protects sea bass but not whales, yet surely a court that interpreted the statute as also protecting whales would not be making a mistake. Indeed, one might think the reverse is true: for a court *not* to protect whales would be to contravene the will of the legislature, and thus, indirectly, the will of the people. What the example suggests is that the correct theory of legal interpretation is *not* a mere matter of philosophical semantics: issues about *political legitimacy*—about the conditions under which the exercise of coercive power by courts can be justified— must inform theories of legal interpretation, and such considerations may even trump considerations of semantics.[14]

---

[11] There are also more general doubts about semantic realism, associated with the work of Michael Dummett, Crispin Wright, and Saul Kripke's reading of Wittgenstein. These problems are reviewed in Coleman and Leiter (1993), 568–72, 605–7.

[12] Both Brink (1989) and Moore (1992b) do accept moral realism. Perhaps for non-moral terms in law, their essential characteristics are *functional* ones, rather than *constitutional*: e.g. since cars can be made out of all kinds of materials, what is essential to 'carhood' is not its molecular constitution but its distinctive *functions*. Cf. Moore (1992b), 207–8.

[13] A version of this point was first made by Munzer (1985), in criticizing Moore (1985).

[14] I take the point in the text to be compatible with Stavropoulos's observation that the real problem is that 'there can be no principled exclusion of whales' from the protection of the statute, and *not* simply a semantic dispute about 'what it is to be a fish' (1996: 192). He continues: 'Mistaken theory of fish-hood prevalent when the statute was drafted *explains* why the word "fish" was mistakenly used to pick out marine life . . . [but] what makes the legislators' view that whales should not be excluded count is the principle justifying the provision' (ibid.). But the justifying principle is, of course, not a deliverance of any philosophical theory of meaning or reference.

Strong Objectivity about legal facts raises another set of problems, apart from the problems in philosophical semantics (cf. Coleman and Leiter 1993: 612–16). If the existence and nature of legal facts are independent of what lawyers and judges (even under ideal conditions) believe about them, then how do judges gain access to such facts? In other words, what reason is there, on the Strong Objectivist view, for thinking that ordinary adjudicative practices are epistemologically objective, that is, involve reliable mechanisms for discovering Strongly Objective legal facts?[15] The 'externalism' about epistemological objectivity discussed earlier (Sect. 2) seems an unhappy answer in the legal context. Recall that on the externalist view, one's beliefs are justified *externally*, that is, independent of one's own experience or awareness of their being justified. *Even if* we had reason to think adjudication was a *reliable* mechanism for generating true beliefs about legal facts—and we have, as yet, no reason for thinking that—it seems bizarre to say that,

1. A legal decision can be justified *even though no lawyers or judges know it to be justified, or may ever know it to be justified*; or
2. A legal decision is not justified *even though all lawyers and judges take it to be justified*.

Yet (1) and (2) follow from the conjunction of Strong Objectivity about legal facts with externalism about justification. Indeed, Strong Objectivity about legal facts alone entails the counter-intuitive claims that,

(A) It is a legal fact that 'Leiter is liable for his negligence' *even though no lawyer or judge believes it, or will ever believe it*; and
(B) It is not a legal fact that 'Leiter is liable for his negligence' *even though all lawyers and judges believe Leiter is liable, indeed even though all lawyers and judges under ideal conditions would believe Leiter is liable.*

If these appeals to intuition are correct, this might suggest that law is only *Modestly* or perhaps *Minimally* objective. Recall that law is Modestly Objective if,

X is a legal fact if *under ideal conditions* lawyers and judges take it to be a legal fact.

Recall that law is Minimally Objective if,

X is a legal fact if the community of lawyers and judges takes it to be a legal fact.

On both accounts, what the law is is *epistemically* constrained. Which view of the objectivity of law—Minimal or Modest—is correct depends, in turn, on whether we think our concept of law is one that allows that all legal practitioners at a given time can be mistaken about what the law 'really' is: if we think that idea is nonsensical, then we are committed to the Minimal Objectivity of law; if we think it makes good sense, then we are committed to the Modest Objectivity of law.[16]

Of course, any account of the law as Modestly Objective must specify the ideal conditions for judgment in a non-question-begging way. What are the conditions such that judgment rendered under them would fix what the legal facts are? Coleman and Leiter describe the ideal judge (i.e. one whose judgments are rendered under ideal epistemic conditions) as:

(1) fully informed both about (*a*) all relevant factual information, and (*b*) all authoritative legal sources (statutes, prior court decisions);
(2) fully rational, for example, observant of the rules of logic;
(3) free of personal bias for or against either party;
(4) maximally empathetic and imaginative, where cases require, for example, the weighing of affected interests; and
(5) conversant with and sensitive to informal cultural and social knowledge of the sort essential to analogical reasoning, in which differences and distinctions must be marked as 'relevant' or 'irrelevant'. (1993: 630)

One might worry though that the notions of 'relevant' facts (in 1), 'maximal' empathy and imagination (in 3), and 'informal' knowledge necessary for judgments of 'relevance' (in 5) cannot themselves be fleshed out in a non-question-begging way, that is, without presupposing what the right answer is as a matter of law.

In addition, we still confront the question of *epistemic* access to legal facts conceived as Modestly Objective. Let us distinguish '*de jure* inaccessibility' from '*de facto* inaccessibility' (Coleman and Leiter 1993: 631). A fact is *de jure* inaccessible if our very concept of the fact means there is no conceptual connection between its existence and our knowledge of it. A fact is *de facto* inaccessible if there is a conceptual connection between the fact and our knowledge of it, but it happens, as a contingent matter in some case, that we do not know what the fact is. According to Strong Objectivity, legal facts are *de jure* inaccessible because what we can epistemically access *never* determines what is the case. (Legal facts may, of course, turn out to be *de facto* accessible.) By contrast, Modestly Objective legal facts will only be *de jure* inaccessible if the ideal conditions specified by the theory are themselves *de jure* (that is, in principle or by the terms of the theory) unattainable by humans. The Modest Objectivist must claim, then, that the ideal epistemic conditions for legal judgment (assuming they can be specified in a non-question-begging way) are realizable by creatures like us. If they are not, of course, then it will follow that legal facts are *de facto* inaccessible as well.

---

[16] Prospects and problems for minimal and modest objectivity are explored in Coleman and Leiter (1993), 616–32 and in Coleman (1995). Dworkin's view might be interpreted as a version of Modest Objectivity, in so far as what Hercules takes the right answer to be seems to fix what the right answer is, and Hercules is just an ideal judge, i.e. one with unlimited time, knowledge, and powers of rational and philosophical reflection (Dworkin 1977: 105). For this kind of reading of Dworkin, see Coleman and Leiter (1993), 633–4. As we will see in the next section, however, Dworkin contests the entire way of conceptualizing objectivity involved in this characterization of his views.

But this suggests a further worry about Strong and Modest Objectivity (cf. Leiter 1993: 207–8). Part of the concept of law is that it is *normative*, or *reason-giving*. Law cannot be normative, however, if *unknown*. This is why we need an answer to the question of epistemic access, for an undetectable legal fact cannot *give* reasons, that is, cannot be normative. Any conception of the law as Strongly or Modestly Objective raises the spectre of the law being unable to fulfil its normative function, in so far as the spectre of *de facto* inaccessibility seems a live one. Only a conception of the law as Minimally Objective is, it seems, guaranteed to be compatible with the normativity of law, precisely because (1) communal consensus is constitutive of legal facts, and (2) such consensus is necessarily accessible to that community.

6 OTHER APPROACHES TO THE OBJECTIVITY OF LAW

Some philosophers recently have disputed whether the traditional ways of conceptualizing objectivity are adequate (Dworkin 1996; McDowell 1997; Nagel 1997; Postema 2001; Putnam 1995b).[17] In particular, these philosophers have raised two kinds of doubts about the earlier characterizations of objectivity. First, these philosophers (especially Dworkin and McDowell) question whether the conception of metaphysical objectivity (especially *strong* metaphysical objectivity) does not presuppose a vantage point on the way things 'really' are to which we can have no access. It is not clear, however, that doubts about, say, the objectivity of morality require such a vantage point: even from 'within' our practices questions can arise about the objectivity of morality because, for example, of the apparent diversity of moral views, or because moral facts do not appear to play a role in causal explanations of experience (Leiter 2001b).[18]

Secondly, some of these philosophers wonder whether the conception of metaphysical objectivity as mind-independence is not a paradigm too closely tied to a picture of the objectivity of the natural world, and thus either does not make sense or should not be applied with respect to the objectivity of domains like ethics or aesthetics. In these evaluative domains, it makes no sense to ask about whether there are evaluative facts 'out there' 'in the world'. The objectivity of evaluative discourse is

---

[17] These revisionary views of objectivity have been extensively criticized (see e.g. Leiter 2001b, Svavarsdóttir 2001; Wright 1992).

[18] Some philosophers who share with Dworkin and McDowell scepticism about the conceptualization of objectivity none the less concede this last point (e.g. Postema 2001).

simply a matter of its susceptibility to reasons, of our ability to subject ethical positions to rational scrutiny and discussion.

According to Dworkin, for example, when we claim that there is an objective fact about whether one interpretation is better than another, or whether one principle is morally better than another, we are not making a claim *external* to the practice of substantive moral or interpretive argument in which these claims arise. 'Slavery is objectively wrong' is simply a *moral* claim internal to the practice of argument in which we offer reasons for the proposition that 'Slavery is wrong'. Two thousand years of metaphysics notwithstanding, there simply are no 'external', *metaphysical* questions about value; there is only ethics, only argument about what is right, what is just, what is good, what is evil, and the like. As Dworkin puts it: 'Any successful—really, any intelligible—argument that evaluative propositions are neither true nor false must be internal to the evaluative domain rather than archimedean about [i.e. external to] it' (1996: 89). Nagel, though not quite agreeing with Dworkin, characterizes the view succinctly: 'the only way to answer skepticism, relativism, and subjectivism about morality is to meet it with first-order moral arguments. [Dworkin] holds that the skeptical positions must themselves be understood as moral claims—that they are unintelligible as anything else' (1997, p. vii).

If we aren't doing metaphysics (or meta-ethics) when we're worrying about 'objectivity', then what are we doing? According to Dworkin, talk about the 'objective' wrongness of abortion, for example, is really just disguised *moral* talk, 'nothing but clarifying or emphatic or metaphorical restatements or elaborations of [the internal moral claim] that abortion is wrong' (1996: 97).

At first sight these remarks seem quite obviously wrong. To claim that abortion is *objectively* wrong is, on a natural reading, not simply to 'repeat' or 'emphasize' that abortion is wrong, but rather to assert a certain metaphysical thesis: to wit, that there exists a property of moral wrongness, which abortion has, and which it has quite independently of what we happen to think about the matter.[19] To talk about 'objective' rightness and wrongness is to talk about metaphysical or ontological issues, about what properties the world contains quite apart from what we happen to know about them. Yet this is precisely what Dworkin seems to deny. Dworkin's arguments have been extensively criticized elsewhere (Leiter 2001*b*); let us focus here on the *crux* of his position.

Dworkin concedes that it *is* a legitimately *external* argument to deny the objectivity of morality on the grounds that it does not meet the constraints imposed by what we might call a 'scientific epistemology' which says—in part, and quite roughly—that: (*a*) only that which makes a causal difference to experience can be known; and

---

[19]   Cf. Brink (1989), 20 ('ethics is objective . . . [in the sense that] it concerns facts that hold independently of anyone's beliefs about what is right or wrong'); Railton (1986), 164 (the issue about objectivity is the issue of 'in what ways, if any, does the existence of moral properties depend upon the actual or possible states of mind of intelligent beings').

(*b*) only that which makes a causal difference to experience is real.[20] Dworkin's response is that such a demand, made about morality, is question-begging. Dworkin objects that the external sceptic's 'hierarchical epistemology . . . tries to establish standards for reliable belief *a priori*, ignoring the differences in content between different domains of belief, and taking no account of the range of beliefs we already hold to be reliable' (1996: 118–19). If a scientific epistemology 'does seem appropriate to beliefs about the physical world' (1996: 119), it makes no sense for moral beliefs '[s]ince morality and the other evaluative domains make no causal claims' (1996: 120). If we accept the demand that moral facts must figure in the 'best explanation' of experience, it will follow that 'no moral (or aesthetic or mathematical or philosophical) belief is reliable. But we can reverse that judgment: if any moral belief is reliable, the "best explanation" test is not universally sound. Either direction of argument . . . begs the question in the same way' (1996: 119).

But the question is begged only if we grant Dworkin's false assumption that the demand for conformity to a scientific epistemology is really an arbitrary, a priori demand.[21] This assumption, however, reveals a complete misunderstanding of what drives the debate between external realist and sceptic about morals. What motivates both 'external' realism and scepticism is precisely the thought that in the post-Enlightenment world, the *only* tenable guide to the real and the unreal is science, and the epistemological standards we have inherited from successful scientific practice. Science (and its associated epistemology) has earned this place of honour by *delivering the goods*: by sending planes into the sky, transplanting hearts, refrigerating food, and so on. A scientific epistemology—predicated on such seemingly simple notions as 'evidence matters' (theories must answer to experience, not simply authority)—is one of the most precious legacies of the Enlightenment, a legacy under attack from those corners of the academy where bad philosophy reigns supreme.

The demand to find a place for moral facts within a scientific epistemology is neither arbitrary nor a priori, but simply the natural question to ask given the a posteriori success of science. It is not that moral claims are simply exempt from a scientific epistemology because they don't involve causal claims; it is, rather, that (crudely speaking) causal power has shown itself over the past few centuries to be the best-going indicia of the knowable and the real, and therefore it is natural to subject any putative fact to this test. Naturalistic moral realists like Brink and Railton aren't 'bad metaphysicians' (Dworkin 1996: 127); rather, they recognize (as Dworkin apparently does not) the epistemological pressure generated by the success of empirical inquiry

[20] A scientific epistemology must, of course, encompass more than a commitment to inference as the best explanation. We need, for example, a basic empiricist doctrine—the senses can be a source of knowledge—as well as certain epistemic norms which satisfy neither the empiricist nor the abductive criteria. These epistemic norms admit of only a *pragmatic* defence, as discussed in the text.

[21] As an aside, let me point out that whether *beliefs* in general and *mathematics* in particular (as distinct from beliefs *about* mathematics) would figure in the best explanation of our experience is an open question—the latter, depending, for example, on whether or not mathematics is indispensable to science.

that honours a scientific epistemology. Given that we have a useful guide to the true and the real already in hand—namely, science and its epistemic norms—why not see, these moral realists essentially ask, whether or not 'moral facts' can meet these demands (rather than suffer the same fate as witches and the ether).

Now no one should be surprised that if we repudiate the demands of a scientific epistemology we get a promiscuous ontology, replete with moral facts, aesthetic facts, theological facts, and the like. But unless we are given a good reason for repudiating this epistemology—other than the patently question-begging reason of making room for our favourite (heretofore) suspect facts—the real question about any putative facts is whether they can answer to our best-going criteria of the knowable and the real.[22] This is what motivates the debate between external realist and external sceptic. Rather than showing their debate to be unintelligible, Dworkin has simply betrayed his misunderstanding of both *what* they are arguing about and *why* they are doing so. What we have yet to find in Dworkin is any *argument* for insulating the domain of morality from the demands of the scientific epistemology which has otherwise served us well.

Recently, Postema (2001) has come to Dworkin's defence on this score.[23] Even if a scientific epistemology has been successful in its domains, this gives us no reason to expect it to apply in all contexts. He writes:

[T]he 'success' of natural science depends at least in part on the fact that it self-consciously brackets, and thus remains silent about, large portions of human experience (notably the normative dimensions of that experience). Moreover, normative discourse does not deal in the base currency of natural science—causal explanations; why, then, should we accept that success in charting the world organized under the category of causation gives license to determine the tools for reasoning our way around the practical world? (2001: 134)

Unfortunately, both claims are, at best, misleading, and at worst, false. What has been distinctive of the growth of science in the twentieth century has *not* been its tendency to 'bracket' domains of human experience, but rather to expand its coverage to subsume them. In the normative domain, one need only think of psychoanalytic accounts of morality and moral motivation at the dawn of the twentieth century or the evolutionary accounts that now dominate scientific study of normative experience at the dawn of the twenty-first. This expansion of science and a scientific epistemology is, indeed, the predictable consequence of its practical success in its original domains of application.

---

[22] Anyone who would repudiate a scientific epistemology must also provide some new, principled account of the distinction between the real and the unreal, demonstrating that while it makes room for e.g. moral facts, it still excludes from our best picture of the world various pseudo-facts.

[23] Postema (2001) defends a conception of objectivity that is *specific* to law—what he calls 'objectivity as publicity'—and which deems legal judgments objective if they issue from a process of public practical reasoning. Cf. the notion of 'procedural objectivity' discussed in Coleman and Leiter (1993: 595–7) and the 'democratic' notion in Putnam (1995a).

Now if in some sense it is true that the 'base currency' of science is 'causal explanations', it is wrong to suggest that 'normative discourse' does not deal in such currency at all. The moral explanations literature (e.g. Sturgeon 1985: 243–5) is replete with examples of the role of causal claims in ordinary normative discourse (e.g. 'Of course he betrayed them, he's an evil person'). It is perfectly reasonable then, even on the terms established by normative discourse itself, to inquire whether these explanations are *good* ones, let alone *best* explanations for the phenomena in question.[24] But whether or not any branch of discourse makes *causal* claims is irrelevant to the applicability of a scientific epistemology: the point is precisely that, so far, *causal power is all we have to go on in ontology.*

This brings us to what Postema calls the 'Pandora's Box argument', which 'puts a challenge to any methodological [i.e. non-metaphysical] account [of objectivity]' to propose an alternative to causal power adequate for distinguishing the objective from the non-objective (2001: 135). Surprisingly, Postema concedes, 'I have no specific test to offer' (2001: 136). Instead, he suggests, a self-referential paradox afflicts a commitment to a scientific epistemology: such an epistemology is not objective by its own criteria (2001: 135).[25] The real argument for embracing a scientific epistemology, however, is not itself epistemic but pragmatic: such an epistemology, as noted earlier, has *delivered the goods.* We have already seen that Postema's attempt to dispute that pragmatic claim failed. Thus, without an alternative criterion of objectivity in hand, Pandora's box is, indeed, opened. In the end, then, Postema is in as vulnerable a position as Dworkin: neither has succeeded in showing how, when thinking about objectivity, we can do *without* metaphysics, nor how we can avoid relying on a scientific epistemology to flesh out this metaphysics.[26]

REFERENCES

Blackburn, Thomas. 1988. 'The Elusiveness of Reference', *Midwest Studies in Philosophy*, 12: 179–94.

Brink, David. 1988. 'Legal Theory, Legal Interpretation, and Judicial Review', *Philosophy & Public Affairs*, 17: 105–48.

——1989. *Moral Realism and the Foundations of Ethics.* New York: Cambridge University Press.

——2001. 'Legal Interpretation, Objectivity, and Morality', in Leiter (2001*a*).

[24] For a negative answer to the question, see Leiter (2001*c*).

[25] Cf. Putnam (1995*b*), 71 for a related objection to the argument in Leiter (1995*a*).

[26] Suppose our metaphysics of legal facts is Modest or Minimal Objectivity: how would that square with a scientific epistemology? Such facts are, of course, mind-independent, *just not to the same degree as Strongly Objective facts.* And they will be causally efficacious to the extent that they (or the psychological facts with which they are identical or on which they supervene) figure in the explanations of e.g. judicial decisions. We have, admittedly, no showing that that will turn out to be the case, but nor has there been any showing of the opposite. The question demands further consideration.

Brower, Bruce. 1993. 'Dispositional Ethical Realism', *Ethics*, 103: 221–49.

Coleman, Jules L. 1995. 'Truth and Objectivity in Law', *Legal Theory*, 1: 33–68.

——and Leiter, Brian. 1993. 'Determinacy, Objectivity and Authority', *University of Pennsylvania Law Review*, 142: 549–637. Also reprinted in A. Marmor (ed.), *Law and Interpretation*. Oxford: Clarendon Press, 1995.

Dworkin, Ronald. 1977. *Taking Rights Seriously*. Cambridge, Mass.: Harvard University Press.

——1996. 'Objectivity and Truth: You'd Better Believe It', *Philosophy & Public Affairs*, 25: 87–139.

Evans, Gareth. 1973. 'The Causal Theory of Names', reprinted in John McDowell (ed.), *The Varieties of Reference*. Oxford: Clarendon Press, 1982.

Gibbard, Allan. 1990. *Wise Choices, Apt Feelings: A Theory of Normative Judgment*. Cambridge, Mass.: Harvard University Press.

Greenawalt, Kent. 1992. *Law and Objectivity*. New York: Oxford University Press.

Johnston, Mark. 1993. 'Objectivity Refigured: Pragmatism without verificationism', in J. Haldane and C. Wright (eds.), *Reality, Representation and Projection*. Oxford: Oxford University Press.

Kripke, Saul. 1980. *Naming and Necessity*. Cambridge, Mass.: Harvard University Press.

Leiter, Brian. 1993. 'Objectivity and the Problems of Jurisprudence', *Texas Law Review*, 72: 187–209.

——1995*a*. 'The Middle Way', *Legal Theory*, 1: 21–31.

——1995*b*. 'Legal Indeterminacy', *Legal Theory*, 1: 481–92.

——(ed.). 2001*a*. *Objectivity in Law and Morals*. New York: Cambridge University Press.

——2001*b*. 'Objectivity, Morality, and Adjudication', in Leiter (2001*a*).

——2001*c*. 'Moral Facts and Best Explanations', *Social Philosophy & Policy*, 18: 79–101.

McDowell, John. 1997. 'Projection and Truth in Ethics', in S. Darwall, A. Gibbard, and P. Railton (eds.), *Moral Discourse and Practice: Some Philosophical Approaches*. New York: Oxford University Press.

Mackie, John. 1977. *Ethics: Inventing Right and Wrong*. London: Penguin.

Moore, Michael S. 1985. 'A Natural Law Theory of Interpretation', *Southern California Law Review*, 58: 277–398.

——1992*a*. 'Law as a Functional Kind', in R. George (ed.), *Natural Law Theory: Contemporary Essays*. Oxford: Clarendon Press.

——1992*b*. 'Moral Reality Revisited', *Michigan Law Review*, 90: 2424–533.

Munzer, Stephen R. 1985. 'Realistic Limits on Realist Interpretation', *Southern California Law Review*, 58: 459–75.

Nagel, Thomas. 1997. *The Last Word*. New York: Oxford University Press.

Pettit, Philip. 1991. 'Realism and Response-Dependence', *Mind*, 100: 587–626.

Postema, Gerald. 2001. 'Objectivity Fit for Law', in Leiter (2001*a*).

Putnam, Hilary. 1975. 'The Meaning of "Meaning",' in *Mind, Language and Reality: Philosophical Papers*, ii. Cambridge: Cambridge University Press.

——1981. *Reason, Truth and History*. Cambridge: Cambridge University Press.

——1995*a*. 'Are Moral and Legal Values Made or Discovered?', *Legal Theory*, 1: 5–19.

——1995*b*. 'Replies to Brian Leiter and Jules Coleman', *Legal Theory*, 1: 69–80.

Railton, Peter. 1985. 'Marx and the Objectivity of Science', in F. Suppe and P. Asquith (eds.), *PSA 1984*, ii. Lansing, Mich.: Philosophy of Science Association. Also reprinted in R. Boyd, P. Gasper, and J. D. Trout (eds.), *The Philosophy of Science*. Cambridge, Mass.: MIT Press, 1991.

—— 1986. 'Moral Realism', *Philosophical Review*, 95: 163–207.

Sayre-McCord, Geoffrey (ed.). 1988. *Essays on Moral Realism*. Ithaca, NY: Cornell University Press.

Sober, Elliott. 1982. 'Realism and Independence', *Noûs*, 16: 369–85.

Stavropoulos, Nicos. 1996. *Objectivity in Law*. Oxford: Clarendon Press.

Stevenson, Charles. 1944. *Ethics and Language*. New Haven: Yale University Press.

Sturgeon, Nicholas. 1985. 'Moral Explanations', reprinted in Sayre-McCord (1988).

Svavarsdóttir, Sigrún. 2001. 'Objective Values: Does Metaethics Rest on a Mistake?' in Leiter (2001*a*).

Wright, Crispin. 1992. *Truth and Objectivity*. Cambridge, Mass.: Harvard University Press.

CHAPTER 24

LAW, SEXUAL ORIENTATION, AND GENDER

EDWARD STEIN

1 INTRODUCTION

In the last half-century, legal, political, and social questions concerning homosexuality have become central questions in various contexts in many parts of the world. In particular, questions relating to the permissibility of sexual activities among people of the same sex, the desire to engage in such activities, the status of lesbian and gay relationships, the recognition of lesbian and gay community institutions, and the appropriateness of discrimination against lesbians, gay men, and other sexual minorities have emerged as among the most challenging questions facing judges, legislators, and executives.

This chapter looks at some theoretical questions about sexual orientations and examines two significant legal and ethical arguments for lesbian and gay rights that relate to these theoretical questions. In Section 2, I consider the following foundational issues: what is a sexual orientation? What is the relationship between sexual orientation and gender? Are sexual orientations socially constructed or are they 'real'? What does scientific research show us about human sexual orientation? My

Thanks to Cheshire Calhoun, Jules Coleman, William Eskridge, Janet Halley, Elizabeth Hillman, Paul Kahn, Andrew Koppelman, Steve Lin, Morris Kaplan, Scott Shapiro, Reva Siegel, and Kenji Yoshino for help at various stages of writing this chapter. Romilda Crocamo and Lisa Tuntigian provided valuable research assistance.

purpose here is not to explore these issues extensively[1] but to use them as a starting-point to consider two legal arguments relating to sexual orientation.

The first legal[2] argument for lesbian and gay rights that I address is the 'born that way' argument. This argument, which has received favourable attention among legal theorists and others interested in lesbian and gay rights, appeals to the claim that sexual orientations are not chosen or are immutable. Intuitively, the argument is that a person should not be punished or in any way discriminated against for a characteristic that he or she did not choose.[3] Advocates of this intuitive argument appeal to scientific research that is supposed to prove sexual orientations are innate or biologically determined.[4] Legal scholars and litigators sympathetic to lesbian and gay rights have tried to fit this intuitive argument into US constitutional jurisprudence and the legal rights framework of other countries.[5]

---

[1] I have done so elsewhere. See Edward Stein, *The Mismeasure of Desire: The Science, Theory and Ethics of Sexual Orientation* (New York: Oxford University Press, 1999).

[2] This chapter does not explicitly focus on general moral and ethical arguments for lesbian and gay rights. I do, however, discuss moral and ethical problems with some legal arguments for lesbian and gay rights and, more generally, moral and ethical arguments that are associated with the specific legal arguments I consider. For many of the moral arguments, see e.g. Edward Batchelor, ed., *Homosexuality and Ethics* (New York: Pilgrim Press, 1980); Jeremy Bentham, 'An Essay on "Paederasty"', in *Philosophy and Sex*, ed. Robert Baker and Frederick Elliston, rev. edn. (Buffalo: Prometheus Books, 1984); John Finnis, 'Law, Morality and "Sexual Orientation"', *Notre Dame Law Review*, 69 (1994), 1049; Andrew Koppelman, 'Homosexual Conduct: A Reply to the New Natural Lawyers', in *Same Sex: Debating the Ethics, Science and Culture of Homosexuality*, ed. John Corvino (Lanham, MD: Rowman and Littlefield, 1997), 44; Richard Mohr, *Gays/Justice: A Study in Society, Ethics and Law* (New York: Columbia University Press, 1990); Gayle Rubin, 'Thinking Sex: Notes for a Radical Theory of the Politics of Sexuality', in *Pleasure and Danger: Exploring Female Sexuality*, ed. Carol Vance (Boston: Routledge & Kegan Paul, 1984), 267; David Richards, *Identity and the Case for Gay Rights* (Chicago: University of Chicago Press, 1999); and Michael Ruse, *Homosexuality: A Philosophical Inquiry* (New York: Blackwell, 1988).

[3] See e.g. Simon LeVay, *Queer Science: The Use and Abuse of Research into Homosexuality* (Cambridge, Mass.: MIT Press, 1996), 231–54; Andrew Sullivan, *Virtually Normal: An Argument about Homosexuality* (New York: Knopf, 1995); and Bruce Bawer, *A Place at the Table: The Gay Individual in American Society* (New York: Poseidon, 1993).

[4] The three most widely cited scientific studies on the origins of sexual orientation are Simon LeVay, 'A Difference in Hypothalamic Structure Between Heterosexual and Homosexual Men', *Science*, 253 (1991), 1034; J. Michael Bailey and Richard Pillard, 'A Genetic Study of Male Sexual Orientation', *Archives of General Psychiatry*, 48 (1991), 1089; Dean Hamer, Stella Hu, Victoria Magnuson, Nan Hu, and Angela Pattatucci, 'A Linkage Between DNA Markers on the X Chromosome and Male Sexual Orientation', *Science*, 261 (1993), 321. For more accessible defences of scientific research on sexual orientation, see LeVay, above n. 3; Dean Hamer and Peter Copeland, *The Science of Desire: The Search for the Gay Gene and the Biology of Behavior* (New York: Simon & Schuster, 1994); and Michael Bailey, 'Biological Perspectives on Sexual Orientation', in *Lesbian, Gay and Bisexual Identities over the Lifespan*, ed. Anthony D'Augeli and Charlotte Patterson (New York: Oxford University Press, 1995).

[5] See e.g. Richard Green, 'The Immutability of (Homo)sexual Orientation: Behavioral Science Implications for a Constitutional (Legal) Analysis', *Journal of Psychiatry & Law*, 16 (1988), 537; and Robert Wintemute, *Sexual Orientation and Human Rights: The United States Constitution, the European Convention, and the Canadian Charter* (Oxford: Oxford University Press, 1995). See also Lisa Keen and Suzanne Goldberg, *Strangers to the Law: Gay People on Trial* (Ann Arbor, MI: University of Michigan Press, 1998) (discussing the decision of litigators to include testimony from scientists at the trial court in *Romer v Evans*, 517 US 620 (1996)).

The second argument I consider, which I call the *sex-discrimination argument*, has also received some favourable attention. According to this argument, any form of discrimination against lesbians, gay men, and bisexuals constitutes sex discrimination.[6] One version of this argument, for example, says that a law prohibiting oral sex between two men or two women, but *not* between one man and one woman, discriminates on the basis of sex because it prohibits a woman from doing something (namely, having oral sex with a woman) that it allows a man to do.[7]

In addition to the foundational questions considered in Section 2, to set up my critical discussion of these two arguments for lesbian and gay rights, in Section 2 I provide some background on the current legal situation of lesbians and gay men in order to illustrate the work that arguments for lesbian and gay rights need to do; the two arguments for lesbian and gay rights on which I focus are usefully evaluated against a specific legal backdrop. I emphasize the context of the United States, but my general analysis is applicable to many democratic countries in the world that have grappled with issues relating to sexual orientation.[8]

I turn next to a critical evaluation of the 'born that way' argument. I show that this argument is legally and ethically flawed and that its scientific premises are unsupported at best. I then turn to a critical evaluation of the sex-discrimination argument. I elaborate the sex-discrimination argument and then I offer three related principled objections to it. I show that, as an argument for lesbian and gay rights, the sex-discrimination argument is sociologically, theoretically, and morally flawed. Having exposed the principled flaws of these two arguments, I show how these flaws lead to pragmatic problems for the two arguments. Because of the practical pitfalls combined with the principled flaws of these arguments, neither offers a strong legal strategy for obtaining lesbian and gay rights.

---

[6] For articulation of various versions of this argument, see e.g. Sylvia Law, 'Homosexuality and the Social Meaning of Gender', *Wisconsin Law Review* (1988), 187; Andrew Koppelman, 'The Miscegenation Analogy: Sodomy Law as Sex Discrimination', *Yale Law Journal*, 98 (1988), 1145; Koppelman, 'Why Sexual Orientation Discrimination is Sex Discrimination', *New York University Law Review*, 69 (1994), 197; Cass Sunstein, 'Homosexuality and the Constitution', *Indiana Law Journal*, 70 (1994), 1; Wintemute, above n. 5; and William Eskridge, Jr., *Gaylaw: Challenging the Apartheid of the Closet* (Boston: Harvard University Press, 1999). For a more detailed critical discussion of this argument, see Edward Stein, 'Evaluating the Sex Discrimination Argument for Lesbian and Gay Rights', *University of California, Los Angeles Law Review*, 49 (forthcoming).

[7] See *State v Walsh*, 713 SW 2d 508, 510 (Mo. 1986) (considering and rejecting the sex-discrimination argument applied to state's sodomy law); *Lawrence v State*, 41 SW 3d 349 (Tex.App. 2001) (same); *Picado v Jegley*, No. CV-99-7048 (Ark. Cir. Ct. 23 Mar. 2001) (finding the state's sodomy law unconstitutional on sex-discrimination grounds as well as on privacy grounds); and Koppelman, *The Miscegenation Analogy*, above n. 6 (applying the sex-discrimination argument to sodomy laws).

[8] See Wintemute, above n. 5 (discussing the sex-discrimination argument and the 'born that way' argument in the context of the Canadian Charter, the US Constitution, and the European Convention).

2 THEORETICAL BACKGROUND

In Plato's *Symposium*, the character Aristophanes offers a myth that many people interpret as being about the origins of human sexual orientations.[9] According to this myth, humans were once anatomically quite different: each human was 'globular in shape, with ... four arms and legs, and two faces ... [on] one head, with one face on one side and one on the other, ... and two lots of privates ...';[10] the globular humans came in three sexes: male, female and 'a third which partook of the nature of both, [called] ... "hermaphrodite", ... a being which was half male and half female'.[11] Because these globular humans threatened the power of the gods, Zeus split them in half down the middle, leaving 'each half with a desperate yearning for the other ...'.[12] Once they had been divided, the three original types of humans gave rise to four different types of people defined by the kind of other half he or she desired. A natural (though contentious)[13] interpretation of this story sees Aristophanes as talking about male and female heterosexuals (humans that result from the splitting of a globular hermaphrodite), lesbians (females that result from the splitting of a globular female), and gay men (males that result from the splitting of a globular male). Further, Aristophanes' story can be interpreted as saying that a person's sexual orientation is an important, defining, and inborn characteristic. Whether this is the correct interpretation of Aristophanes' myth is a question that is beyond the scope of this chapter. What is important about this interpretation of the myth is that it raises several theoretical questions about human sexual desires to which I now turn.

2.1 What is a Sexual Orientation?

Implicit in Aristophanes' myth is the idea that people can be grouped into different types in terms of the sex of the person with whom they want to be intertwined. Implicit in our contemporary concept of a sexual orientation is a similar idea: we think that a person's sexual orientation is in some way related to a person's sex (or gender) and the sex (or gender) of the people to whom that person is sexually

---

[9] See e.g. John Boswell, 'Concepts, Experience and Sexuality', in *Forms of Desire: Sexual Orientation and the Social Constructionist Controversy*, ed. Edward Stein (New York: Routledge, 1992), 163–4; and John Boswell, 'Revolutions, Universals and Sexual Categories', in *Hidden From History: Reclaiming the Gay and Lesbian Past*, M. Duberman, M. Vicinus, and G. Chauncey (New York: New American Library, 1989), 25.

[10] Plato, *Symposium*, at 189e–190, trans. Michael Joyce (1935).   [11] ibid., 189d–e.

[12] ibid. 191.

[13] See e.g. David Halperin, *One Hundred Years of Homosexuality and Other Essays in Greek Love* (New York: Routledge, 1990).

attracted and/or with whom that person engages in sexual activity.[14] Both as a theoretical and practical matter, it can be hard to say what constitutes a person's sex and to determine what sex each person is. This poses a problem for offering a straightforward account of sexual orientation.[15]

Consider the standard distinction between sex and gender. Typically, this distinction is drawn by saying that *sex* (male or female) is biologically determined (i.e. related to one's chromosomes, internal and/or external genitalia, etc.) while *gender* (man or woman) is determined by the characteristics and traits that members of a culture see as associated with a particular sex (hair length, choice of clothing, personality characteristics, etc.).[16] The idea, in a slogan, is that sex is between the legs, under the shirt and in the genes, while gender is in the culture. Legal and non-legal scholars have criticized this distinction on various grounds, most notably by arguing that our views (scientific and non-scientific) about which biological characteristics are necessary and/or sufficient to distinguish males from females (or vice versa) are laden with cultural assumptions about gender and gender roles and, as such, may be mistaken.[17] One common view about what distinguishes males from females focuses on genitalia.[18] Having a particular kind of genitalia (i.e., testes and ovaries (internal genitalia) and/or penises and clitorises (external genitalia)) is, however, neither a necessary nor a sufficient condition for being a male or female, especially in light of the existence of people who have one testis and one ovary[19] and of people who have 'ambiguous' external genitalia.[20] Generally, the existence of *intersexed* people (people

---

[14] This is a bit of a simplification, especially if there are 'true' bisexuals, people who are equally attracted to men and women. The sexual orientation of a true bisexual arguably can be determined without knowing his or her sex. However, it is not clear that all or most bisexuals are true bisexuals. See Martin Weinberg, Colin Williams, and Douglas Pryor, *Dual Attraction: Understanding Bisexuality* (New York: Oxford University Press, 1994). For a legal and theoretical discussion of bisexuality, see Kenji Yoshino, 'The Epistemic Contract of Bisexual Erasure', *Stanford Law Review*, 52 (2000), 353.

[15] See Stein, above n. 1, at 1–38.

[16] See e.g. Roger Brown, *Social Psychology: The Second Edition* (New York: Free Press, 1986); and Stein, above n. 1, at 24–38. Justice Antonin Scalia appealed to this distinction when he said that 'the word "gender" . . . connot[es] . . . cultural or attitudinal characteristics (as opposed to physical characteristics) distinctive to the sexes'. See *J.E.B. v Alabama ex rel* TB, 511 US 127, 157 n.1 (1994) (Scalia, J., dissenting).

[17] See e.g. Anne Fausto-Sterling, *Myths of Gender: Biological Theories about Men and Women*, rev. ed. (New York: Basic Books, 1992); Suzanne Kessler and Wendy McKenna, *Gender: An Ethnomethodological Approach* (New York: Wiley, 1978); Judith Butler, *Gender Trouble: Feminism and the Subversion of Identity* (New York: Routledge, 1990); and Katherine Franke, 'The Central Mistake of Sex Discrimination Law: The Disaggregation of Sex from Gender', *University of Pennsylvania Law Review*, 144 (1995), 1, 9–10.

[18] Among the other criteria, in addition to internal and external genitalia, that are often considered as relevant to distinguishing males and females are the so-called sex chromosomes, gonads, pre-natal hormone levels, pubertal hormonal levels, and H-Y antigen levels. See e.g. John Money, *Gay, Straight and In-Between: The Sexology of Erotic Orientation* (New York: Oxford University Press, 1988), 28–9.

[19] For a discussion, see e.g. Anne Fausto-Sterling, 'The Five Sexes: Why Male and Female Are Not Enough', *The Sciences* (Mar./Apr. 1993), at 20.

[20] See e.g. Suzanne Kessler, *Lessons from the Intersexed* (New Brunswick, NJ: Rutgers University Press, 1998).

who are anatomically or physiologically part male and part female or who have genitalia that are in between male-typical and female-typical genitalia)[21] and *transgendered* people (people who feel that their body sex differs from their feeling of which sex they belong to—known as their *gender identity*—whether or not they have had or may plan to have 'sex-reassignment' surgery—known respectively as *post-operative* and *pre-operative transsexuals*)[22] cause trouble for standard definitions of male and female both inside and outside of the law.

As an example of a legal problem that arises relating to the definition of sex, consider a recent case in Texas. Littleton, a *post-operative male-to-female transsexual* (i.e. Littleton, was classified male at birth, but went through 'sex reassignment' surgery to become female). Thereafter, in Kentucky, Littleton legally changed the sex that was listed on her birth certificate to 'female', married a man, and obtained a valid marriage licence. Littleton's husband subsequently died, allegedly as a result of a doctor's negligence, and Littleton filed a wrongful death action in Texas. The Texas court held that Littleton could not maintain a wrongful death action for the loss of her husband because, for the purposes of Texas marriage law, which explicitly prohibits same-sex marriage, sex at birth is permanent and unalterable.[23] Ironically, perhaps, the *Littleton* decision has led at least two same-sex couples consisting of one female and one male-to-female transsexual to get married in Texas.[24] The problems faced by the standard account of how to distinguish between male and female in turn create problems for a straightforward account of sexual orientation. It seems clear that in some way a person's sexual orientation is related to a person's sex (or gender) and that of the people to whom he or she is attracted, but, especially in light of these conceptual problems with sex, how they are related is unclear.[25]

2.2 How to Identify a Person's Sexual Orientation

Also implicit in the straightforward interpretation of Aristophanes' myth is a view of how to identify a person's sexual orientation. On this view, it is easy to tell what a person's orientation is, because the behaviours, desires, and identities related to a person's sexual orientation point in the same direction. The females who result from the original globular hermaphrodites desire to be intertwined with a male, behave in

[21] ibid.
[22] See e.g. Holly Devor, *FTM: Female-to-Male Transsexuals* (Bloomington, IN: Indiana University Press, 1997); and Bernice Hausman, *Changing Sex: Transsexualism, Technology and the Idea of Gender* (Durham, NC: Duke University Press, 1995).
[23] *Littleton v Prange*, 9 SW 3d 223 (Tex. App-San Antonio 1999), *cert. denied* 121 S.Ct. 17468 (2000). For discussion, see Julie Greenberg, 'When is a Man a Man and When is a Woman a Woman?', *Florida Law Review*, 52 (2000), 745.
[24] See e.g. 'Marriage of Transsexual Draws Protest in Texas', *NY Times*, 18 Sept. 2000.
[25] See e.g. Stein, above n. 1, at 61–4 (critiquing Money, above n. 18).

accordance with this desire by doing things like 'running after men',[26] and would identify themselves as having this desire and engaging in this behaviour. Matters are not so simple because a person's sexual behaviours, sexual desires, and sexual identity can be discordant. Three different accounts of how to identify a person's sexual orientation can be developed, each associated with a different aspect of Aristophanes' implicit account of sexual orientation.

2.2.1 *The Behavioural View*

Consider a simple account of sexual orientation according to which one's sexual orientation is determined by the sex of the people that he or she has sex with: if a person has sex with people of the same sex, then one is a homosexual; if one has sex with people not of the same sex, then one is a heterosexual. On this view, a person's behaviour determines her sexual orientation. I therefore call this the *behavioural view* of sexual orientation.[27] The behavioural view has the advantage of characterizing sexual orientations in an objective and scientifically accessible fashion. On this view, a person's sexual orientation is determined by the sexual acts he has performed. These acts may be unknown to all but the person and his sexual partners, but they are in principle knowable. This account of sexual orientation has connections with behaviourism, a popular psychological and philosophical view of the early twentieth century according to which one can find out everything psychologically interesting about a person by observing her behaviour.[28] Although behaviourism has the advantage of making a person's psychology transparent to an observer, there are legions of problems with it. Most importantly, according to behaviourism, others will typically be in a better position to assess my mental states than I am; it seems, however, that I have special access to at least a substantial part of my mental life. With respect to sexual orientation, the behavioural view is committed to the idea that anyone who can observe my sexual activity knows everything about my sexual orientation. In fact, I know more about my sexual orientation than an observer does because I know something about my sexual desires and unexpressed sexual feelings. This alone is enough to seriously undermine the behavioural view of sexual orientation.[29]

---

[26] See Plato, above n. 10, at 191d.

[27] See Janet Halley, 'Reasoning About Sodomy: Act and Identity in and after *Bowers v. Hardwick*', *Virginia Law Review*, 79 (1993), 1721 (showing that the behavioural view, as well as something like the dispositional view discussed below, is implicit in the Supreme Court's ruling in *Bowers v Hardwick*, 478 US 186 (1986). See also Janet Halley, *Don't: A Reader's Guide to the Military's Anti-Gay Policy* (1999).

[28] For defences of behaviourism, see John B. Watson, 'Psychology as the Behaviorist Views It', *Psychological Review*, 20 (1913), 158; and B. F. Skinner, *Science and Human Behavior* (New York: Free Press, 1965). For a classic critique of behaviourism, see Noam Chomsky, 'A Review of B. F. Skinner's Verbal Behavior', in *Readings in Philosophy of Psychology*, ed. Ned Block (Cambridge, Mass.: Harvard University Press, 1980), 48.

[29] See Stein, above n. 1, at 41–4.

2.2.2 *The Self-Identification View*

One alternative to the behavioural view is the *self-identification view*, according to which one's sexual orientation is based on a person's own assessment of his or her sexual orientation. The self-identification view says that if someone really believes he is a heterosexual, then he is. Unlike the behavioural view, the self-identification view allows that a person can have a sexual orientation that is discordant with his sexual behaviour. This view, however, has the problem of not allowing for self-deception. It is possible for someone to be gay without believing, even in his heart of hearts, that he is a homosexual. It is possible for a young person to be attracted to people of the same sex without realizing it, perhaps because she lives in a society in which homosexuality is invisible and not talked about. Such a person would not have the concept of homosexuality or even the concept of having sex with a person of the same sex, and would not be able to self-identify as homosexual. In fact, however, it seems possible that a person could be a homosexual if he or she has sexual desires and fantasies about people of the same sex even though these desires are deeply repressed in that person's subconscious. This is a possibility, but the self-identification view does not allow for it.

2.2.3 *The Dispositional View*

A view that seems to incorporate the virtues of the behavioural and self-identification views while avoiding their vices is the *dispositional view* of sexual orientation, according to which a person's sexual orientation is based on her sexual desires and fantasies and the sexual behaviours to which she is disposed. If a person has sexual desires and fantasies about having sex primarily with people of the same sex and is inclined, when there is sexual freedom and a variety of appealing sexual partners available, to engage in sexual acts primarily with such people, then that person is a homosexual. In contrast to the behavioural view, the dispositional view allows that people can have sexual orientations before they actually have sex. In contrast to the self-identification view, the dispositional view allows that, although people usually have some special insight into what their sexual orientations are, a person can repress his sexual orientation. The dispositional view shares with the behavioural view the virtue of taking a person's behaviour into consideration, although the dispositional view does so less directly: according to the dispositional view, certain sexual behaviours are relevant because they reflect a person's dispositions. The dispositional view shares with the self-identification view the virtue of giving weight to one's sense of one's sexual orientation, although the dispositional view gives it less weight. For these and other reasons, the dispositional view best fits with the contemporary concept of a sexual orientation.[30]

[30] See Stein, above n. 1, at 45–9. See also the classic studies of Alfred Kinsey, which implicitly adopt the dispositional view: Alfred Kinsey, Wardell Pomeroy, and Clyde Martin, *Sexual Behavior in the Human Male* (1948); and Alfred Kinsey, Wardell Pomeroy, Clyde Martin, and Paul Gebhard, *Sexual Behavior in the Human Female* (Philadelphia: W. B. Saunders, 1953).

2.3   Are Sexual Orientations 'Natural Human Kinds'?

In the last decade or so, a new interdisciplinary academic field dedicated to the study of sexual orientation has developed within the humanities and the social sciences.[31] Within this field, known as *lesbian and gay studies*, the reigning paradigm for thinking about sexual orientation is *constructionism*, a view with roots in the philosophical work of Michel Foucault and in various approaches to sociology and anthropology.[32] Constructionism about sexual orientation emphasizes the historical and cultural contingencies of sexual orientation and sexuality. Constructionism is in conflict with the reigning scientific approach to sexual orientation because such scientific research is connected to *essentialism*, according to which our contemporary categories of sexual orientation can be applied to people in any culture and at any point in history.

Returning to the *Symposium*, some scholars interpret Aristophanes' speech as talking about homosexuals and heterosexuals. Others say that this interpretation unjustifiably and mistakenly projects our categories onto a culture where sexual desire was constructed quite differently. This alternative reading draws support from historical evidence that the Greeks thought about people's sexual desires quite differently than we do. In Attic Greece, a person's social status—that is, whether the person was a citizen or non-citizen, a slave or a free person, an adult or a child, a woman or a man—was important to how the culture viewed his or her sexual desires. In terms of law and social custom, a citizen was allowed to penetrate but not be penetrated by a non-citizen (non-citizens included all slaves, children, women, and foreigners) and was not allowed to penetrate or to be penetrated by another citizen. Thus, the important categories of sexual desire revolved around a person's civic status and whether he wanted to penetrate or be penetrated. This historical evidence is supposed to indicate that Aristophanes and his contemporaries did not have anything like our categories of sexual orientation and that it is anachronistic to interpret Aristophanes as talking about heterosexuals, lesbians, and gay men because this interpretation projects into his mind notions he could not possibly have had.[33]

Underlying the conflict between essentialism and constructionism is a question concerning *natural kinds*. A natural kind is a grouping of entities that plays a central role in the correct scientific laws and explanations. A group is a natural kind in virtue

[31] See e.g. Henry Abelove, Michèle Aina Barale, and David Halperin, *The Lesbian and Gay Studies Reader* (1993).

[32] See e.g. Michel Foucault, *History of Sexuality: An Introduction*, trans. Robert Hurley (New York: Random House, 1978; orig. publ. Paris: Editions Gallimard, 1976); Mary McIntosh, 'The Homosexual Role', *Social Problems*, 16 (1968), 182; and John Gagnon and William Simon, *Sexual Conduct* (Chicago: Aldine, 1973). For opposing views, see e.g. Boswell, above n. 9; and Richard Mohr, 'The Thing of It Is: Some Problems with Models for the Social Construction of Homosexuality', in *Gay Ideas: Outing and Other Controversies* (Boston: Beacon, 1992). See also *Forms of Desire*, above n. 9.

[33] See Halperin, above n. 13; Morris Kaplan, *Sexual Justice* (New York, Routledge, 1997); and Stein, above n. 1, at 94–9.

of the properties its members share or the functions they play independent of how we conceive of them. For example, if current chemical, physical, and physiological theories are correct, then gold, electrons, haemoglobin, and hearts are natural kinds, while chairs, teddy bears, and diet soft drinks are not.[34] Some groups that we think are natural kinds probably will turn out not to be. As a historical example, consider *phlogiston*.[35] Until the late 1700s, scientists thought that phlogiston was an element found in high concentrations in substances that burned while exposed to air. We now know that there is no such substance as phlogiston. Although phlogiston was thought to be a natural kind, the scientific laws in which phlogiston played an explanatory role are false.

Some natural kinds apply to people. I call groupings of people that play a central role in scientific explanations and laws *natural human kinds*.[36] An example of a natural human kind would be the group of people with blood type AB. People with blood type AB constitute a natural human kind because having blood type AB plays a role in laws about what sorts of people a person can donate blood to and receive blood from. Just as there are many groups of things that are *not* natural kinds, there are many groups of people that are not natural human kinds; I call them *social* human kinds. An example would be a registered member of the Democratic Party. Such a grouping does not play an explanatory role in scientific explanations. Similarly, just as there are groups that were mistakenly identified as natural kinds, there are groups of people that were supposed to be natural human kinds, but which are not. As an example, consider the hysteric woman,[37] a woman who allegedly suffers from a disease, called hysteria, the symptoms of which include uncontrollable outbursts, spasms, paralysis, swelling, blindness, and deafness. Originally thought to be caused by a 'wandering' womb, hysteria came to be seen as a specific neurotic illness primarily affecting women. Many people were diagnosed as having hysteria when, in fact, they had some other unidentified illness or were depressed, tired, or nervous. Today, no one believes that hysteria is an actual medical condition.

It is relatively straightforward to use the notion of a natural human kind to precisely define constructionism and essentialism[38] about sexual orientation. Essentialism about sexual orientation is the view that sexual orientations are natural

[34] Ian Hacking, 'A Tradition of Natural Kinds', *Philosophical Studies*, 61 (1991), 109; Richard Boyd, 'Realism, Anti-Foundationalism and the Enthusiasm for Natural Kinds', *Philosophical Studies*, 61 (1991), 127; Frank Kiel, *Concepts, Kinds and Cognitive Development* (Cambridge, Mass.: MIT Press, 1989); and Stein, above n. 1, at 71–92.

[35] James Bryant Conant, *The Overthrow of Phlogiston Theory: The Chemical Revolution of 1775–1789* (Cambridge, Mass.: Harvard University Press, 1950).

[36] See Stein, above n. 1, at 84–92.

[37] Neil Micklem, *The Nature of Hysteria* (New York: Routledge, 1996).

[38] Some philosophers use the term 'essentialism' for the view that a grouping is a natural kind if and only if all and only members of that kind share an intrinsic property (or a set of intrinsic properties). Essentialism in the sense of the term I mean it here does not necessarily entail this sense of the term. Following Boyd, above n. 34, I hold that some natural kinds are defined by a cluster of relevant causal conditions, none of which are necessary or sufficient.

human kinds, while constructionism about sexual orientation is the view that sexual orientations are not natural human kinds.[39] The debate between essentialism and constructionism about sexual orientation is a debate about whether sexual orientations are natural human kinds, in other words, whether sexual orientations will function in scientific laws and scientific explanations. Understanding this debate is a necessary precondition for answering metaphysical, scientific, and ethical questions about sexual orientation.

We live in a culture in which one's sexual orientation is an important fact about a person, a fact that seems deep and open to scientific explanation. Essentialists about sexual orientation try to build on this fact about our culture to argue for the claim that heterosexuals and homosexuals are natural human kinds. In contrast, constructionists deny that our categories of sexual orientation refer to natural human kinds. Properly understood, the debate between essentialism and constructionism about sexual orientation is an empirical debate: if we want to determine whether sexual orientation is best understood using the standard tools of science, we need to determine whether homosexuals and heterosexuals are natural human kinds and whether they can figure in scientific laws and scientific explanations. This is not to say that the essentialism-constructionism debate reduces to the nature-nurture debate, a point I emphasize in the section that follows.

2.4 Are Sexual Orientations Innate?

The debate between constructionism and essentialism is commonly confused with whether sexual orientations are innate (*nativism*) or the result of environmental factors (*environmentalism*). As typically discussed, the issue between nativism and environmentalism is based on a false dichotomy: no human trait is strictly the result of genetics or strictly the result of environmental factors; all human traits are the result of both. There are genetic and neurological factors that affect even the most seemingly environmental traits, like, for example, what a person's major will be in college. On the other hand, environmental factors contribute to the development of even the most seemingly genetic traits, for example, eye colour—if I had not gotten enough of

---

[39] Some philosophers think that there are no natural kinds. See e.g. Nelson Goodman, *Ways of Worldmaking* (Indianapolis: Hackett, 1978). For discussion, see David Armstrong, *Universals: An Opinionated Introduction* (Boulder, CO: Westview, 1989); Hacking, above n. 34; and Boyd, above n. 34. From this view it follows that there are no natural human kinds, and, thus, that sexual orientations are not natural human kinds. While the position that there are no natural *human* kinds is an interesting general philosophical position, it is not an interesting position about sexual orientation. Constructionism about sexual orientation at least implicitly involves the claim that while sexual orientations are not natural human kinds, there are at least some natural kinds. If there are no natural kinds, then there is nothing special about sexual orientation; sexual orientations would not be natural kinds but neither would having a Y chromosome or being a proton. Constructionism is an interesting position *about sexual orientation* only if there are some natural kinds.

certain sorts of vitamins and minerals at crucial times, even though my genes would be the same, my eyes might be a different colour than they are. There is, however, a range of how much genes constrain a trait—one's blood type is more tightly constrained by genetic factors than is one's major in college. I have genes that make it almost certain that my blood type will be B, but I do not have genes that make it almost certain that I will major in philosophy. The nativism-environmentalism debate about sexual orientation, properly understood, concerns where sexual orientation fits on the continuum between blood type and college major.

Many people assume that if essentialism about sexual orientation is true, then nativism about sexual orientation is true, and if constructionism about sexual orientation is true, then environmentalism about sexual orientation is true. This is not the case. Essentialism could still be true even if environmentalism is true. For example, if, as seems unlikely,[40] a person's sexual orientation is connected to his emotional interactions with his parents[41] or with the nature of his first sexual encounter,[42] then sexual orientations could still be natural human kinds. If once the environment has had its effects, a person has a naturalistically determinate sexual orientation and her brain instantiates a particular psychological state in virtue of which she is a heterosexual or homosexual, then certain scientific laws thereby apply to her and sexual orientation would be a natural human kind, even though it is not primarily genetic. The same example will suffice to show that if sexual orientation is shaped primarily by environmental factors, constructionism does not necessarily follow.[43] This makes clear that constructionism and essentialism are *empirical* theses, they are claims that can only be established by observation and/or experimentation.

In the last several years, scientific research on sexual orientation has garnered a great deal of attention in various realms. A series of scientific studies published in leading scientific journals have argued that sexual orientations are innate or fixed at a very early age.[44] While these studies have, for the most part, not been replicated and have been criticized by some researchers and scholars,[45] some scientists and some

[40] Alan Bell, Martin Weinberg, and Susan Hammesmith, *Sexual Preference: Its Development in Men and Women* (Bloomington, IN: Indiana University Press, 1981); and Stein, above n. 1, at 229–57.

[41] See e.g. Sigmund Freud, *Three Essays on the Theory of Sexuality*, trans. James Strachey (New York: Basic Books, 1975; orig. publ. 1905).

[42] See e.g. R. J. McGuire, J. M. Carlisle, and B. G. Young, 'Sexual Deviations as Conditioned Behavior: A Hypothesis', *Behavior Research and Therapy*, 2 (1965), 185.

[43] The commonly held view that there is a connection between essentialism and constructionism, on the one hand, and nativism and environmentalism, on the other, is not, however, completely wrong. If sexual orientations are innate, then constructionism about sexual orientation is false and essentialism is true. Suppose that a person's sexual orientation is primarily determined by genetic factors. In this case, sexual orientations would be innate. In virtue of the genes I am positing as responsible for sexual orientation, there would be natural human kinds associated with sexual orientations; sexual orientations would appear in scientific laws involving these genes. If this were the case, then constructionism would be false.

[44] See above n. 4.

[45] See e.g. Stein, above n. 1, at 164–228; Janet Halley, 'Sexual Orientation and the Politics of Biology: A Critique of the New Argument from Immutability', *Stanford Law Review*, 46 (1994), 503; Fausto-Sterling, above n. 17; and William Byne, 'Biology and Sexual Orientation: Implications of

non-scientist commentators have gone so far as to suggest that a *new scientific paradigm* for the study of human sexuality is emerging.[46] This is not the place to present a detailed discussion of this scientific evidence and its merits. For now, I offer my own assessment of the 'emerging scientific research paradigm' for sexual orientation.

First, the emerging research paradigm rests, in various ways, on an analogy between animal (in particular, rat) and human sexual behaviours and desires.[47] However, as animal sexual behaviour varies wildly among different species,[48] there is no strong reason for thinking that any *particular* animal constitutes an adequate model of human sexual orientation. The strength of an analogy with any particular animal is undermined by the diversity of animal sexual behaviours unless specific evidence is given as to why one animal species is more like humans in terms of sexual behaviours than other species. Further, many attempts to apply research on animal sexual behaviour to human sexual desires are guilty of anthropomorphism.

Secondly, although the main studies that are supposed to support the emerging research paradigm are well placed, widely cited, and widely believed, there are serious methodological and interpretive problems facing each of them. Studies in the emerging scientific paradigm embrace—explicitly or implicitly—a problematic account of what a sexual orientation is, have problems finding an appropriate subject pool to study, accept unjustified assumptions about the base rate of homosexuality, and make a variety of implicit, widely varied, and unjustified assumptions about homosexuality.[49] Space does not permit a discussion of all of these problems but I want to mention just two.

One specific assumption made as part of the emerging research paradigm, which I call the *inversion assumption,* is that sexual orientation is a trait with two forms, a male form that causes sexual attraction to women (shared by heterosexual men and lesbians) and a female form that causes sexual attraction to men (shared by heterosexual women and gay men). This assumption is evident, for example, in the equation of same-sex sexual activity in men with effeminacy. Research premised on the inversion assumption typically proceeds by first trying to identify sex differences and then seeing if any alleged sex difference is inverted in homosexuals. There are alternatives to the inversion assumption. Perhaps, from the physiological point of view, gay men and lesbians should be grouped together and heterosexual men and women

---

Endocronological and Neuroanatomical Research', in *Comprehensive Textbook of Homosexuality,* ed. R. Cabaj and T. Stein (Washington DC: American Psychiatric Press, 1996).

[46] See e.g. LeVay, above n. 3; and Hamer and Copeland, above n. 4.

[47] See e.g. Stein, above n. 1, at 164–79; Anne Fausto-Sterling, 'Animal Models for the Development of Human Sexuality: A Critical Evaluation', *Journal of Homosexuality,* 28 (1995), 217; William Byne, 'Science and Belief: Psychobiological Research on Sexual Orientation', *Journal of Homosexuality,* 28 (1995), 303; and Byne, above n. 45.

[48] See e.g. Bruce Bagemihl, *Biological Exuberance: Animal Homosexuality and Human Diversity* (New York: St Martin's Press, 1999).

[49] See e.g. Stein, above n. 1, at 190–228; and Byne, above n. 45.

should be grouped together. This would be the case if heterosexuals had a brain structure or physiology that disposed them to be sexually attracted to people of the opposite sex while lesbians and gay men had a brain that disposed them to be sexually attracted to people of the same sex. Or, more plausibly, there might be no interesting generalizable differences in brains that correlate with these categories of sexual orientation. This would be the case if sexual orientations come in more than two forms.[50] Further, this would be the case even if there are just two sexual orientations but the conscious and unconscious motivations associated with sexual attraction differ among individuals of the same sex and sexual orientation, that is, if experiences (and subjective interpretations of them) interact to lead different individuals to the same relative degree of sexual attraction to men, women, or both. Because, for example, sexual attraction to women, could be driven by various different psychological factors, there is no reason to expect that all individuals attracted to women should share any particular physiology that distinguishes them from individuals attracted to men.[51]

Another specific assumption made by the emerging research paradigm concerns essentialism about sexual orientation. I showed above that essentialism is an empirical thesis to which scientific research on sexual orientation is relevant. However, in order to *establish* essentialism, a study cannot unquestionably *assume* essentialism. If a study is to have a chance of providing support for an empirical thesis, it has to be possible that the study can produce results that count against the thesis.[52]

I have not made a conclusive argument against the emerging research paradigm. It is possible, as some scientists have suggested, that there is a gene on the X chromosome that codes for a certain pattern of protein synthesis that, in turn, leads to certain patterns of prenatal hormonal secretions and/or to certain kinds of reactions to certain hormones that, in turn, lead to the development of certain psychological mechanisms, based in specific regions of the hypothalamus, that dispose men to desire sexual activity with other men.[53] This theory *may* be true but, for reasons I have

[50] See e.g. Stein, above n. 1, at 49–67.

[51] I am not denying that the inversion assumption is intuitively plausible to many people in our culture, but I am suggesting that the basis for this assumption is not scientific. Rather, this assumption is based on a particular cultural picture according to which gay men are feminine and lesbians are masculine. This cultural view is hardly universal. In some cultures, sexual activity between males was associated with warrior status—see e.g. T. Watanabe and J. Iwata, *The Love of the Samurai: A Thousand Years of Japanese Homosexuality*, trans. D. R. Roberts (London: Gay Men's Press, 1989)—while in others receptive same-sex sexual activity was practised by all males and believed to be essential to their virility— see e.g. Gil Herdt, 'Semen Transaction in Sambia Culture', in *Ritualized Homosexuality in Melanesia* (Berkeley: University of California Press, 1984). That the inversion assumption would not have been plausible in some cultures does not show that it is false. Together, however, the lack of scientific evidence to support the inversion assumption and the fact that it is not culturally universal suggest that it is primarily based on our cultural biases.

[52] See e.g. Stein, above n. 1, at 205–6.

[53] See e.g. Simon LeVay and Dean Hamer, 'Evidence for a Biological Influence in Male Homosexuality', *Scientific American*, 270 (1994), 44.

sketched in the preceding paragraphs and developed elsewhere, I do not think that it or any other specific theory that is part of the emerging scientific research paradigm is particularly *plausible*.[54] In fact, it is at least as plausible that sexual orientations as we conceive of them are *not* natural human kinds.

The emerging scientific research paradigm has the character of a not yet established research paradigm. Thomas Kuhn, in his classic work, *The Structure of Scientific Revolutions*,[55] distinguished between periods of 'normal science' and 'scientific revolutions'. During periods of normal science, the basic theoretical and metaphysical assumptions of a scientific field are accepted and held constant. Practitioners in such a field conduct experiments using a well-established framework. In contrast, during revolutionary periods, significant chunks of a field's paradigm are up for grabs. The scientific study of human sexual desire is, at best, going through a period of revolution. Practitioners in the field have not yet established a paradigm in which 'normal science' can proceed. A decade or so from now, the emerging research paradigm may well turn out to have been a false start in the search for an account of how human sexual desires develop.

2.5 Is a Person's Sexual Orientation a Choice?

Another important fundamental question about sexual orientation is whether a person's sexual orientation is a choice. There is a basic problem with this question: what it is for a characteristic to be a choice is both vague and ambiguous. First, just because a trait is not chosen does not mean that the trait is biologically determined. For example, people do not choose their native language, but this does not entail that one's native language is genetically determined. Secondly, just because a trait is biologically determined does not entail that choice plays no role in the expression and development of that trait. It might be, for example, that I am born with a special musical ability that few people have. I still can choose not to develop or express this ability. Not all biologically based traits are like this—no choice is involved in the development of blood type—but some traits, though biological, require choices in order to be expressed. Thirdly, some characteristics can be determined as the result of choices that, on the surface, seem to have nothing to do with the characteristic that they fix. For example, my childhood decision to regularly watch a particular television show may have unintentionally led to my developing certain personality characteristics. I never *decided* to have these personality traits, but my decision to watch that television show may have led to these traits. Would it be correct to say that I *chose* to have them? Consider the distinction between a *direct* choice and an *indirect* choice. A person

54 See e.g. Stein, above n. 1, at 225–8.
55 Thomas Kuhn, *The Structure of Scientific Revolutions*, rev. edn. (Chicago: University of Chicago Press, 1970).

makes a direct choice to X if she does something with the conscious intention of doing X, while a person makes an *indirect* choice to X if she does something *without* the conscious intention of doing X. I made a direct choice to watch that television show when I was a child, but, in doing so, I made an indirect choice to have certain personality characteristics.

I turn now to three related points about sexual orientation. First, environmentalism about sexual orientation is consistent with sexual orientation not being a choice. Thus, sexual orientation does not need to be biologically determined in order to be immutable. In fact, whatever the merit of scientific research on sexual orientation, the evidence is overwhelming that an adult's sexual orientation is almost impossible to change.[56] This evidence alone should be adequate to establish that sexual orientations are for relevant purposes immutable. Secondly, nativism about sexual orientation is consistent with choices playing a significant role in the development or expression of a sexual orientation. Even if a person is gay in virtue of biology, a person still has to *choose* to be openly gay, to show affection towards people of the same sex, and to have sex with or build families with people of the same sex. Thirdly, sexual orientation might be the result of *indirect* choices. For all we know, one's sexual orientation might be the result of a decision to play basketball more often than chess, to play with soldiers more often than with dolls, to eat spinach more often than Jell-O, or some combination of other choices that one might have made.[57] This is not to say that people develop their underlying sexual desires simply by deciding what their sexual orientation is in much the way one might decide what candidate to vote for in an election.[58] My point here is that questions about sexual orientation and choice are complicated and care needs to be taken when thinking about them. Even a genetic theory of sexual orientation has to allow that, for at least a significant number of

[56] See e.g. D. C. Haldeman, 'Sexual Orientation Conversion Therapy for Gay Men and Lesbians: A Scientific Examination', in *Homosexuality: Research Implications for Public Policy*, ed. J. C. Gonsiorek and James Weinrich (1991); Haldeman, 'The Practice and Ethics of Sexual Orientation Conversion Therapy', *Journal of Consulting and Clinical Psychology*, 62 (1994), 221; Timothy Murphy, 'Redirecting Sexual Orientation: Techniques and Justifications', *Journal of Sex Research*, 29 (1992), 501; and Charles Silverstein, 'Psychological and Medical Treatments of Homosexuality, in *Homosexuality*. Note that this evidence is not necessarily inconsistent with the feelings of many women and some men who feel their sexual orientations are fluid and that some conscious choice is involved in the development of sexual orientation. See e.g. Claudia Card, *Lesbian Choices* (New York: Columbia University Press, 1995), 47–57; Carla Golden, 'Diversity and Variability in Women's Sexual Identities', in *Lesbian Psychologies: Explorations and Challenges*, ed. Boston Women's Psychologies Collective (Urbana, IL: University of Illinois Press, 1987); Vera Whisman, *Queer By Choice: Lesbians, Gay Men and the Politics of Identity* (New York: Routledge, 1996).

[57] See e.g. Stein, above n. 1, at 265–70.

[58] As Joyce Trebilcot, 'Taking Responsibility for Sexuality', in *Philosophy and Sex*, above n. 2; and Sandra Lee Bartky, 'Feminine Masochism and the Politics of Personal Transformation', in *Femininity and Domination* (first published in *Women's Studies International Forum* 7 (1984), 323–4) (New York, Routledge, 1990) have shown, wanting to be a lesbian (or a gay man) for political or philosophical reasons does not necessarily lead to a change in one's sexual attractions—a woman, even if she wants to become a lesbian, might still be sexually attracted to men and not sexually attracted to women.

people, sexual orientation is caused by environmental factors that differ even among identical twins raised together.[59] Choices that individuals make, whether direct or indirect, might explain why at least half of the pairs of identical twins at least one of whom is gay is discordant for sexual orientation.

Various thinkers have tried to connect the question of whether a person's sexual orientation is a choice to the debate between essentialists and constructionists about sexual orientation in the following fashion: constructionists must think that sexual orientations are chosen (*voluntarism*) and essentialists must think that sexual orientations are not chosen (*determinism*).[60] While it may turn out that many constructionists are voluntarists and many essentialists are determinists, constructionism is compatible with determinism.[61] Consider the category of being a peasant or being a member of royalty. These are surely paradigmatic examples of *social* human kinds, but having one of these properties might very well *not* be a choice. Just as one might not be able to choose to be a member of any social or economic class even though membership in such a class constitutes a social human kind, so too it might be that sexual orientation is not chosen even if sexual orientation is a social human kind. Further, essentialism is compatible with voluntarism; it is possible that sexual orientations are natural human kinds and that choice plays a role in the development of sexual orientations. An example of a theory of the origins of sexual orientations that is essentialist and voluntarist is the first encounter theory, one version of which says that one's sexual orientation is fixed by one's first sexual experience.[62] On such a view, being a heterosexual or homosexual is a natural human kind, but one can effectively choose what his sexual orientation is by appropriately choosing the first person with whom he has sex. Given that essentialism and voluntarism are compatible, and that constructionism and determinism are compatible, it is a mistake to collapse the distinction between constructionism and essentialism into the distinction between determinism and voluntarism or vice versa. We cannot determine whether sexual orientation is a choice by turning to the question of whether sexual orientations are natural human kinds.

[59] Bailey and Pillard, above n. 4; J. Michael Bailey, Richard Pillard, and Yvonne Agyei, 'Heritable Factors Influence Sexual Orientation in Woman', *Archives of General Psychiatry*, 50 (1993), 217; Bailey, M. P. Dunne, and M. P. Martin, 'Genetic and Environmental Influences on Sexual Orientation and Its Correlates in an Australian Twin Sample', *Journal of Personality & Social Psychiatry*, 78 (2000), 524; and Bailey, K. M. Kirk, G. Zhu, M. P. Dunne, and M. P. Martin, 'Do Individual Differences in Sociosexuality Represent Genetic or Environmentally Contingent Strategies? Evidence from the Australian Twin Registry', *Journal of Personality & Social Psychiatry*, 78 (2000), 537. For a critical discussion, see Stein, above n. 1, at 140–53, 191–5, 201–16.

[60] See e.g. Steven Epstein, 'Gay Politics, Ethnic Identity: The Limits of Social Constructionism', in *Forms of Desire*, above n. 9, at 239; and Robert Padgug, 'Sexual Matters: On Conceptualizing Sexuality in History', in *Forms of Desire*, at 43.

[61] See e.g. Halperin, above n. 13, at 41–53.   [62] See above n. 42.

3 LESBIAN AND GAY RIGHTS

In this part, I discuss some of the legal issues relating to sexual orientations to provide a context for assessing two arguments for lesbian and gay rights. Claims for lesbian and gay rights fit into three somewhat overlapping categories: claims for the decriminalization of same-sex sexual activity, claims for the protection against discrimination on the basis of sexual orientation, and claims for the recognition of lesbian and gay relationships and institutions.[63] I briefly consider the status of these three types of claims in the United States.

In the United States, fifteen states as well as the military, which is a separate criminal jurisdiction, have laws that criminalize most forms of same-sex sexual activity.[64] Decriminalization involves the repeal of such laws (collectively known as sodomy laws) and other laws that regulate consensual same-sex sexual activity. Claims for decriminalization of same-sex sexual activity argue that such laws violate the right to privacy, are examples of 'victimless crimes' that should not be criminalized, and that such laws, even when not enforced, harm sexual minorities in unjustifiable ways.

The second type of claim for lesbian and gay rights concerns protection against discrimination on the basis of sexual orientation. Currently, thirty-nine states lack protection against such discrimination, that is, it is legal in these states for a non-state entity to discriminate in terms of hiring and housing against a person in virtue of her sexual orientation.[65] Further, Title VII, the federal statute that prohibits discrimination in employment on the basis of race, sex, and some other characteristics, does not prevent employers from discriminating on the basis of sexual orientations.[66] In a nutshell, a lesbian (or a gay man or bisexual)—even if she can prove that sexual orientation was the only reason she was not hired for or fired from a job—has no legal recourse in most states. Advocates of lesbian and gay rights argue that just as the state protects against discrimination on the basis of race and other such inappropriate

[63] See e.g. Kaplan, above n. 33, at 14–17; and Stein, above n. 1, at 204.

[64] Of these states, three have laws that criminalize certain sexual acts only when they are committed by two people of the same sex. Although no state regularly enforces these laws, such laws are selectively enforced in some states, especially against lesbians, gay men, and bisexuals. Even in states where such laws are not generally enforced, the mere existence of laws against sexual activity between people of the same sex is used to support and justify other laws and social practices relating to homosexuality. See e.g. Christopher Leslie, 'Creating Criminals: The Injuries Inflicted by "Unenforced" Sodomy Laws', *Harvard Civil Rights–Civil Liberties Law Review*, 35 (2000), 103.

[65] See Lambda Legal Defense and Education Fund, 'Summary of States which Prohibit Discrimination Based on Sexual Orientation', <www.lambdalegal.org/cgi-bin/pages/documents/record?record=185>.

[66] See e.g. *Smith v Liberty Mutual Insurance Company*, 569 F.2d 325 (5th Cir. 1978); *DeSantis v Pacific Telephone and Telegraph Co.*, 608 F.2d 327 (9th Cir. 1979); and *Dillon v Frank*, 1992 WL 5436 (6th Cir. 1992).

characteristics, so too the state should act as a 'civil shield'[67] against practices that discriminate against lesbians and gay men.[68]

The third category of claims for lesbian and gay rights is less straightforward. Lesbians and gay men argue that their relationships and institutions deserve recognition and that, under the current legal regime, they do not get this recognition. Most notably, no state allows same-sex couples to get married and thereby obtain the wide range of rights, benefits, and privileges that are associated with marriage.[69] Vermont does now allow same-sex couples to enter civil unions, which offer the full range of rights, benefits, and responsibilities that come with marriage in Vermont.[70] However, even if some state were to allow same-sex couples to marry, such couples would not be able to have their marriages recognized in most states or by the federal government.[71] In addition to being unable, for the most part, to have their intimate relationships legally recognized and sanctioned, lesbian and gay employees of state agencies and lesbian and gay students in government-funded schools are often denied funding for their organizations. Such asymmetries also appear with respect to various manifestations of lesbian and gay culture and the speech of lesbian and gay men. For example, artistic expressions that reflect lesbian and gay culture have been banned from receiving government support and representations of and by lesbians, gay men, and bisexuals have played a central role in debates over government funding of the arts and public standards of 'decency'. Further, when the state attempts to regulate speech in cyberspace, the speech of sexual minorities is among the speech typically restricted.

In the United States, legal arguments for lesbian and gay rights can be divided, for the most part, into two types: *equality*-based arguments and *privacy*-based argu-

[67] See Mohr, above n. 2, at 137–87.

[68] Some critics of laws that protect against discrimination on the basis of sexual orientation have argued that such laws give gay men and lesbians 'special rights'. See e.g. *Romer v Evans*, 517 US 620, 626–34 (1996) (discussing whether the amendments at issue merely undercut the claim by homosexuals for 'special rights'); and ibid. at 647–9 (Scalia, J. dissenting) (same). The majority in Romer rejected this criticism of protecting against discrimination on the basis of sexual orientation.

[69] See e.g. William Eskridge, Jr., *The Case for Same-Sex Marriage: From Sexual Liberty to Civilized Commitment* (New York: Free Press, 1996).

[70] An Act Relating to Civil Unions, 2000 Vt. Laws P.A. 91. This law was in response to *Baker v Vermont*, 744 A.2d 864 (Vt. 1999) (holding that same-sex couples must receive the same 'benefits and protections' that the state provides for married male-female couples).

[71] The Defense of Marriage Act of 1996 (DOMA), exempts same-sex marriage from receiving full faith and credit by saying that no State '. . . shall be required to give effect to any public act, record or judicial proceeding of any other State . . . respecting a relationship between persons of the same sex that is treated as a marriage under the laws of such other State . . . or a right or claim arising from such relationship'. 28 USC §1738C. More than thirty States have passed state versions of DOMA. Some people have argued that these laws are unconstitutional because they violate the Full Faith and Credit Clause of the US Constitution, US Constitution art. IV, §1. See e.g. Mark Strasser, 'Ex Post Facto Laws, Bills of Attainder, and the Definition of Punishment: On DOMA, the Hawaii Amendment, and Federal Constitutional Constraints', *Syracuse Law Review*, 48 (1998), 227; and Andrew Koppelman, 'Dumb and DOMA: Why the Defense of Marriage Act Is Unconstitutional', *Iowa Law Review*, 83 (1997), 1.

ments. A line of cases starting in 1965 with *Griswold v Connecticut*[72] and including *Roe v Wade*[73] found a right to privacy in the United States Constitution. By the late 1970s and early 1980s, buttressed by these decisions, many advocates of lesbian and gay rights expected that it was only a matter of time until the privacy line of cases would be extended to encompass the right to engage in sexual activities with people of the same sex and that privacy arguments would take the lead in making the case for lesbian and gay rights generally.[74] In fact, this was the primary argument made before the Supreme Court by lawyers for Michael Hardwick, an openly gay man who was arrested for engaging in consensual sodomy (specifically, oral sex) with another man in his own bedroom.[75] In a five–four decision, the Supreme Court rejected this argument, holding that the privacy right articulated in earlier cases applies only when there is a connection to 'family, marriage or procreation'.[76] According to the *Bowers* majority, the right to privacy, as it appears in the US Constitution, does not require either that 'any kind of private sexual conduct between consenting adults is constitutionally insulated from state proscription'[77] or that there is a 'fundamental right to homosexual sodomy'.[78]

After *Bowers*, litigators and legal theorists advocating lesbian and gay rights mostly abandoned privacy arguments—although they continued to use them in state courts[79]—and began the task of 'arguing around [*Bowers v*] *Hardwick*'.[80] To do so, they turned to equality-based arguments that draw from the Equal Protection Clause of the Fourteenth Amendment and away from privacy-based arguments that draw on the due process clauses of the Fifth and Fourteenth Amendments.[81] This move was coupled with a move away from a focus on repealing laws that criminalize same-sex sexual activities to a focus on repealing laws that discriminate on the basis of sexual orientation.

The Supreme Court has interpreted the Fourteenth Amendment as requiring scepticism towards statutes that make use of various classifications including race,

[72] *Griswold v Connecticut*, 381 US 479 (1965) (overturning law prohibiting birth control devices as violating the right to privacy of married couples).

[73] *Roe v Wade*, 410 US 113 (1973) (overturning anti-abortion statutes on privacy grounds).

[74] See e.g. Note, 'The Constitutionality of Laws Forbidding Private Homosexual Conduct', *Michigan Law Review*, 72 (1974), 1613, 1637; David Richards, 'Sexual Autonomy and the Constitutional Right to Privacy', *Hastings Law Journal*, 30 (1979), 957; and Kenneth Karst, 'The Freedom of Intimate Association', *Yale Law Journal*, 89 (1980), 624.

[75] Brief for Respondent, *Bowers v Hardwick*, 478 US 186 (1986) (Nos. 85–140) (arguing that Supreme Court precedent regarding the right to privacy demands a substantial justification for declaring criminal consensual sexual intimacies between adults engaged in one's bedroom).

[76] *Bowers v Hardwick*, 478 US 186, 191.   [77] ibid.   [78] ibid.

[79] See Melanie Price, 'The Privacy Paradox: The Divergent Paths of the United States Supreme Court and State Courts on Issues of Sexuality', *Indiana Law Review*, 33 (2000), 863.

[80] Patricia Cain, 'Litigating for Lesbian and Gay Rights: A Legal History', *Virginia Law Review*, 79 (1993), 1551, 1640.

[81] Some have argued that, even setting *Bowers* aside, privacy-based arguments are limited in what they can offer lesbians and gay men. See e.g. Kendall Thomas, 'Beyond the Privacy Principle', *Columbia Law Review*, 92 (1992), 1431; Kaplan, above n. 33, at 17–46, 211–27.

ethnicity, national origin, legitimacy, and sex.[82] Litigators and legal scholars attempting to 'argue around *Bowers*' say that statutes that make use of sexual-orientation
classifications, like those that make use of racial and other suspect classifications,
should be subject to heightened scrutiny.[83] The hope is that if courts give heightened
scrutiny to statutes that make use of sexual-orientation classifications, then such
statutes will be found to violate equal protection.

Conceptually, this is where the 'born that way' argument and the sex-discrimination
argument fit. They are attempts to craft equality-based arguments for lesbian and gay
rights. The 'born that way' argument is based on the idea that a person should not be
punished or discriminated against in virtue of a characteristic that she did not choose.
The sex-discrimination argument is based on the idea that sexual-orientation discrimination necessarily involves sex discrimination. In the US context, both arguments try
to fit into existing Supreme Court equal-protection jurisprudence. The Supreme Court
has not directly ruled on the question of whether statutes that make use of sexual-
orientation classifications deserve heightened scrutiny. Most US courts that have considered this question have held that sexual-orientation classifications do *not* deserve
heightened scrutiny.[84] The few courts that have ruled that sexual-orientation classifications warrant heightened scrutiny have had their decisions overruled or vacated.[85] The
sex-discrimination argument attempts to show that sexual-orientation classifications

[82] See e.g *Yick Wo v Hopkins*, 118 US 356 (1886) (interpreting the Fourteenth Amendment as requiring
heightened scrutiny for ethnic classifications); *Hernandez v Texas*, 347 US 475 (1954) (same for national
origin); *Plyler v Doe*, 457 US 202, 218–23 (1982) (alienage); *Levy v Louisiana*, 391 US 68 (1968) (legitimacy);
and *Mississippi University for Women v Hogan*, 458 US 718, 723–4 (1982) (sex). Some scholars have argued
that the enacting Congress intended the Fourteenth Amendment to apply to other classifications besides
race. See e.g. Nina Morais, 'Sex Discrimination and the Fourteenth Amendment: Lost History', *Yale Law
Journal*, 97 (1988), 1153.

[83] The Supreme Court distinguishes between strict scrutiny and intermediate scrutiny. While it has
held that racial classifications warrant strict scrutiny, it has not explicitly held that sex classifications
warrant strict scrutiny. However, in *United States v. Virginia*, 518 US 515 (1996), the Supreme Court
argued forcefully against laws that enforce gender stereotypes and somewhat blurred the boundaries
between strict and intermediate scrutiny. Following Kenji Yoshino, 'Assimilationist Bias in Equal
Protection: The Visibility Presumption and the Case of "Don't Ask, Don't Tell"', *Yale Law Journal*, 108
(1998), 485, 488 n. 6, I use the term 'heightened' scrutiny to encompass both strict scrutiny and intermediate scrutiny. By doing so, I do not deny that these two levels of scrutiny can be differentiated.

[84] See e.g. *Ben-Shalom v Marsh*, 881 F.2d 454, 464 (7th Cir. 1989) (refusing to grant heightened scrutiny
for sexual-orientation classifications in the context of military's policy on homosexuality); *Padula v
Webster*, 822 F.2d 97, 103 (D.C. Cir. 1987) (same in the context of the FBI); and *Thomasson v Perry*, 80 F.3d
915 (4th Cir. 1996) (en banc) (same in the context of military's 'Don't Ask, Don't Tell' policy). The exception is *Tanner v Oregon Health Sciences University*, 91 P.2d 534 (Ore. App. 1998), *review denied* 994 P.2d
129 (Ore. 1999) (holding that lesbians and gay men are 'members of a suspect class to which certain privileges and immunities are not made available').

[85] See e.g. *Watkins v United States Army*, 847 F.2d 1329 (9th Cir. 1988) (holding that sexual-orientation
classifications deserve heightened scrutiny and, under this standard of review, that the US military's pre-
1992 policy of discharging homosexuals was unconstitutional), *vacated and affirmed on other grounds*,
875 F.2d 699 (9th Cir. 1989) (en banc); *High Tech Gays v Defense Industry Security Clearance Office*, 668 F.
Supp. 1361 (N.D. Cal. 1987) (holding that homosexuals or those perceived as homosexuals deserve
heightened scrutiny under equal protection), *reversed* 895 F.2d 563 (9th Cir. 1990); and *Jantz v Muci*, 759
F. Supp. 1543, 1546 (1991) (same), *reversed* 976 F.2d 623 (10th Cir. 1992).

deserve heightened scrutiny by piggybacking arguments for lesbian and gay rights on sex-discrimination jurisprudence. The 'born that way' argument attempts to show that sexual-orientation classifications deserve heightened scrutiny by picking up on the notion, endorsed on some occasions by the Supreme Court, that whether a group is distinguished by an immutable characteristic is relevant to the level of scrutiny it deserves. Given the need for strong arguments for lesbian and gay rights, both the sex-discrimination argument and the 'born that way' argument warrant serious consideration. It is to such consideration that I turn in the sections that follow.

4 THE 'BORN THAT WAY' ARGUMENT FOR LESBIAN AND GAY RIGHTS

4.1 The Argument

In the last couple of decades, scientific research concerning how sexual orientations develop has captured the attention of many Americans. Some researchers, citing evidence from neurology, genetics, and psychology, claim that sexual orientation is either inborn or fixed at an early age.[86] Many lesbians, gay men, and bisexuals have welcomed this claim, finding in it confirmation of their sense that they did not choose to be attracted to people of the same sex. Some parents of lesbians and gay men have also found solace in such research, because it offers assurance that nothing they did made their children homosexual. Advocates for lesbian and gay rights have tried to parlay this research into good news for lesbian and gay rights.[87] Their argument is that if people do not choose to be lesbian, gay, or bisexual, it is wrong to criminalize their sexual behaviour, discriminate against them, and withhold from them benefits that heterosexuals take for granted. This form of the 'born that way' argument has intuitive appeal and is deployed with increasing frequency by people who think that science will secure gay rights.

Although this argument can be made in various jurisdictions,[88] in the context of the United States, the 'born that way' argument attempts to get heightened scrutiny for sexual-orientation classifications by drawing on one of the factors that the Supreme Court has said should be considered in assessing when more than a rational basis is required to evaluate the constitutionality of a statute that invokes a classification. The Court has said that it will consider whether a classification has historically been used to intentionally discriminate against a particular group,[89] whether the use

---

[86] See above n. 4.   [87] See above nn. 3 and 5.   [88] See e.g. Wintemunte, above n. 5.
[89] *Frontiero v Richardson*, 411 US 677 (1973).

of this classification bears any 'relation to ability to perform or contribute to society',[90] whether any groups demarcated by this classification lack the political power to combat the discrimination,[91] and whether groups demarcated by this classification exhibit obvious, immutable, or distinguishing characteristics that define them as a discrete and insular group.[92] That the Supreme Court sometimes considers whether a characteristic is immutable as part of its consideration of whether a classification warrants heightened scrutiny is seen by advocates of the 'born that way' argument as creating an opening for the immutability of sexual orientations to be relevant to lesbian and gay rights.

4.2 Three Problems with the Argument

4.2.1 *Empirical Problems*

Above, I described what amount to several empirical problems for the various forms of the 'born that way' argument. First, it is far from established that sexual orientations are biologically based. Most current scientific research on sexual orientation faces serious methodological objections and is based on a set of unjustified assumptions about sexual orientations generally and homosexuality in particular, for example, such research typically assumes that gay men are in some biological way female-like and that lesbians are male-like. Secondly, it is not even clear that sexual orientations are natural kinds. For all we know, sexual orientations are primarily social categories that do not play any role in scientific explanations. And, thirdly, although it is clear that people do not choose their sexual orientations in the way that they choose how to vote in an election, it is not clear that choices play no role in the development of sexual orientations. Determinism, at least in some senses of the term, about sexual orientation is far from established. For these reasons, the empirical premises of the 'born that way' argument (namely, that lesbians, gay men, and bisexuals are born with their sexual orientations or that choice plays no role in their development) are at best dubious.

4.2.2 *Moral Problems*

More importantly, the 'born that way' argument faces a serious moral objection. Even if one's sexual orientation is primarily biological and not a choice, much of what is legally and ethically relevant about being a lesbian or a gay man is neither biologically based nor determined and, thus, these central aspects of being lesbian or gay would not be reached by the 'born that way' argument. For example, even if sexual

---

[90]   *Frontiero v Richardson*, 411 US 677 (1973) at 686.
[91]   *City of Cleburne v Cleburne Living Center*, 473 US 432, 441 (1985).
[92]   *Bowen v Gilliard*, 483 US 587, 602 (1987).

orientations are genetically based, engaging in sexual acts with a person of the same sex, identifying as a lesbian or a gay man, and deciding to establish a household with a person of the same sex are *choices*, choices that one might not make (in other words, one can decide to be celibate, closeted, and companion-less). Someone who was convinced that lesbians and gay men deserve rights only because sexual orientation is biologically based and not the result of a choice would allow that people can be treated differently on the basis of choices relating to sexual desires. One who thinks that gay men and lesbians are born with their sexual orientations might accept that such people should not be discriminated against on the basis of having sexual desires for people of the same sex. This is perfectly compatible, however, with thinking that people who engage in sexual acts *are* appropriate targets of discrimination, criminal penalties, and the like. Consider, for example, the attitudes of some religious conservatives towards homosexuality. Such people claim that *being homosexual*—namely, having the desire to have sex with people of the same sex—is not a sin, is not immoral, and does not warrant prejudice or discrimination. But expressing this desire by engaging in sex with someone of the same sex, having a romantic relationship with such a person, or advocating homosexuality are, on this view, morally problematic. This view about homosexuality—which is surely not compatible with any robust version of lesbian and gay rights—is compatible with the 'born that way' argument. At best, then, the 'born that way' argument has the potential to protect a person from being discriminated against on the basis of having a desire to have sex with people of the same sex, a quite limited protection.[93]

Even assuming that sexual orientations are immutable, lesbians and gay men deserve protection against discrimination and recognition for their relationships and institutions with respect to their *actions* and *decisions* rather than for their mere orientations. It is when they engage in same-sex sexual acts, identify as gay men and lesbians, and create lesbian and gay families that they especially need lesbian and gay rights. The 'born that way' argument cannot provide support for claims related to rights based on choices even if the choices are related to desires that, for the sake of argument, might be innate.

This problem with the 'born that way' argument can be seen, for example, as part of the contentious issue of whether lesbians and gay men can openly serve in the United States Armed Forces. Under existing law and the Department of Defense

---

[93] Martha Nussbaum, 'Millean Liberty and Sexual Orientation: A Discussion of Edward Stein's *The Mismeasure of Desire*', *Law and Philosophy* (forthcoming 2001), tries to formulate a more sophisticated version of the 'born that way' argument. A crucial premise in this argument, which Nussbaum says most Americans accept, is that society should not put impediments in the way of satisfying a person's sex drive. For my reply to Nussbaum's sophisticated version of the 'born that way' argument, see Edward Stein, 'Reply to Martha Nussbaum and Ian Hacking', *Law and Philosophy* (forthcoming 2001). In a nutshell, I argue that Nussbaum's premise is not accepted by most Americans, and her more sophisticated version of the 'born that way' argument faces the same objections that are fatal to the standard version of this argument.

directives that implement it[94]—together known as the 'Don't Ask, Don't Tell' policy—a service member may be discharged from the Armed Forces if he or she states that 'he or she is homosexual or bisexual',[95] if he or she holds hands or engages in any other bodily contact with a person of the same sex that 'demonstrates a propensity or intent to engage in sexual contact',[96] or 'attempt[s] to marry a person known to be of the same biological sex'.[97] Even though the policy, charitably interpreted, protects lesbians and gay men from being discriminated against in virtue of their sexual desires for people of the same sex, a person can be discharged for any public expression of homosexuality, any evidence of romantic relationships with people of the same sex, and any form of remotely intimate physical contact with people of the same sex. The 'Don't Ask, Don't Tell' policy, as implemented and enforced, fails to protect lesbians and gay men. This exemplifies the sort of laws that are likely to be implemented in the face of the 'born that way' argument. Such laws protect people for the mere having of a sexual orientation but not for any behaviour that might result from such desires.[98]

4.2.3 *Legal Problems*

Some advocates of lesbian and gay rights have articulated a version of the immutability argument in the context of the US Constitution.[99] As explained above, while the Supreme Court has not ruled on whether sexual-orientation classifications are suspect, the Court has articulated some factors that should be considered in assessing when more than a rational basis is required to evaluate the constitutionality of a statute that invokes a classification. One of these factors is whether a group demarcated by a classification exhibits immutable characteristics in virtue of which the group is discrete and insular.[100] The importance of immutability in determining whether a classification is suspect is, however, unclear. The Supreme Court has, on some occasions, discussed heightened scrutiny without mentioning immutability.[101] Further, various legal scholars have argued that immutability is not and should not be important in determining whether a classification is suspect.[102]

---

[94] 10 USC §654 (1994); Separation of Regular Commissioned Officers, Department of Defense Directive 1332.30 (5 Feb. 1994); Qualification Standards for Enlistment, Appointment, and Induction, Department of Defense Directive 1304.26 (5 Feb. 1994); and Enlisted Administrative Separations, Department of Defense Directive 1304.26 (5 Feb. 1994).

[95] Department of Defense Directive 1304.26, H.1.b.(2).

[96] 10 USC §654 (f)(3)(B).   [97] ibid. at §654 (b)(3).

[98] For further discussion of the military's policy towards homosexuality, see Halley, *Don't*, above n. 27.

[99] See e.g. Green, above n. 5. For critical discussion, see Halley, above n. 45; and Yoshino, above n. 83.

[100] See e.g. *Bowen v Gilliard*, 483 US 587, 602 (1987).

[101] *Cleburne*, 473 US at 440–1; *Massachusetts Board of Retirement v Murgia*, 427 US 307, 313 (1976); *Plyler v Doe*, 457 US 202, 218–23 (1982). For discussion, see Yoshino, above n. 83.

[102] See e.g. Halley, above n. 43; Richards, above n. 2; and Yoshino, above n. 83.

In *Romer v Evans*, the Supreme Court overturned an amendment to Colorado's constitution that restricted the rights of lesbians, gay men, and bisexuals.[103] Interestingly, the Court held that the Colorado amendment violated the Equal Protection Clause but it reached its conclusion *without* employing heightened scrutiny, at least not in a technical sense. The Court found that this amendment violated the Equal Protection Clause because it failed to bear any rational relation to a legitimate state interest.[104] In *Romer*, the immutability of sexual orientations had nothing to do with the Court's decision about the rights of lesbians and gay men. This provides just one recent example of a court ruling in favour of lesbian and gay rights without relying on whether lesbians and gay men are 'born that way'.

5 THE SEX-DISCRIMINATION ARGUMENT FOR LESBIAN AND GAY RIGHTS

5.1 The Formal Sex-Discrimination Argument

The basic idea of the sex-discrimination argument is that any law that discriminates on the basis of sexual orientation will also necessarily discriminate on the basis of sex. The argument is simple, formal, and straightforward. If a person's sexual orientation is a dispositional property that concerns the sex of people to whom he or she is attracted, then to determine a person's sexual orientation, one needs to know the person's sex and the sex of the people to whom he or she is primarily sexually attracted. In virtue of what a sexual orientation is, it seems that any law that discriminates on the basis of sexual orientation necessarily discriminates on the basis of sex.

To see the formal version of the sex-discrimination argument in action, consider two laws that affect lesbians and gay men: a law prohibiting same-sex sodomy and a law permitting only opposite-sex marriage. First, consider the Missouri sodomy law that makes it a crime for a person to have 'deviant sexual intercourse with another person of the same sex'.[105] The law defines 'deviant sexual intercourse' as 'any act involving the genitals of one person and the mouth, tongue, or anus of another, or a sexual act involving the penetration, however slight, of the male or female sex organs

---

[103] *Romer v Evans*, 517 US 620 (1996). The amendment at issue precluded state and local legislative, executive, and judicial action protecting homosexual and/or bisexual orientation, conduct, practices, and relationships.

[104] ibid. at 631–6.

[105] *Missouri Annotated Statutes* §566.090 (1998) (enacted 1977). The Missouri sodomy law remains on the books, although a state appellate court, in *State v Cogshell*, 997 S.W.2d 534 (Mo. App. 1999), held that it cannot be used to prosecute consensual sexual activities.

or the anus by a finger, instrument, or object done for the purpose of arousing or gratifying the sexual desire of any person'.[106] Under this law, it is illegal, for example, for a woman to insert her finger into another woman's anus, while it is legal for a man to insert his finger into a woman's anus. As this law prohibits a woman from doing things that it allows men to do, the law thus discriminates on the basis of sex. Secondly, consider the Hawaii marriage law that limits marriages to couples consisting of one man and one woman.[107] According to the sex-discrimination argument, this law discriminates on the basis of sex because it allows a man to marry a woman while prohibiting a woman from marrying a woman. These two examples show how laws that discriminate on the basis of sexual orientation can be seen through the lens of sex discrimination.

Persuading courts that laws which discriminate on the basis of sexual orientation thereby discriminate on the basis of sex may not be enough to convince courts to overturn laws which discriminate on the basis of sexual orientation. Sometimes, courts may find that a law is justified in making use of sex classifications. Although I argue that the sex-discrimination argument is not strong, I admit that if it can persuade judges to apply heightened scrutiny to laws that discriminate on the basis of sexual orientation, this would be a significant accomplishment for lesbian and gay rights. In this section, I raise doubts about whether the sex-discrimination argument will be successful in obtaining heightened scrutiny for such laws.

5.2 Is There *Really* Sex Discrimination?

The sex-discrimination argument as presented thus far faces a straightforward objection. One can deny that statutes which discriminate on the basis of sexual orientation also discriminate on the basis of sex. According to this objection, laws that discriminate on the basis of sexual orientation apply to both sexes equally.

Consider, as an example of this objection, a recent European court decision that directly addressed the sex-discrimination argument.[108] Several years ago, Lisa Grant took a job working for Southwest Trains, Ltd. (SWT), a railway company in England, replacing a man who had held the job for several years and who had received as a benefit a travel pass for his non-marital female partner. Grant applied to SWT for the same travel benefits for her non-marital female partner. SWT refused to provide

---

[106] *Missouri Annotated Statutes* §566.010 (1998) (enacted 1977).

[107] *Hawaii Revised Statutes* §572–1 (1994). This law was found unconstitutional by *Baehr v Miike*, 65 USLW 2399 (Haw. Cir. Ct. 1996) (finding that the state failed to demonstrate a compelling interest in using sex classifications in its marriage laws). However, after a constitutional referendum amended Hawaii's constitution to give the state legislature the power to limit a marriage to a relationship between one man and one women, Hawii Constitution, art. 1, §23 (1998), Hawaii's Supreme Court, in *Baehr v Miike*, No. 20371, 1999 Haw. LEXIS 391 (Haw. 9 Dec. 1999), held that the amendment rendered moot the constitutional challenge to Hawaii's marriage laws.

[108] *Grant v Southwest Trains*, Case C-249/96, ECJ (1998).

Grant's partner with such benefits on the grounds that Grant and her partner were of the same sex. Grant then sued, arguing that SWT violated Article 119 of the treaty establishing the European Community (EC), which says, in part, that 'men and women should receive equal pay for equal work'.[109] In particular, Grant argued that SWT failed to give her equal pay by denying her benefits it gave to a man who occupied the same position. SWT defended itself saying that, first, there is nothing in the EC Treaty that prohibits discrimination on the basis of sexual orientation and, secondly, that it was not guilty of sex discrimination because its policy was sex-neutral: no one, regardless of sex, was eligible for travel benefits for a same-sex partner. The case eventually reached the European Court of Justice (ECJ) to determine whether the EC Treaty's principle of equal pay for men and women prohibits discrimination based on an employee's sexual orientation. The ECJ held that SWT's policy does not constitute sex discrimination because its policy 'applies the same way to female and male workers [and therefore] cannot be regarded as constituting discrimination directly based on sex';[110] both men and women receive the same benefits for their partners under precisely the same circumstances, namely, only if they have an opposite-sex partner.[111] By making this decision, the ECJ denied that discrimination on the basis of sexual orientation constitutes sex discrimination.

This same response to the sex-discrimination argument can be used to defend the Missouri sodomy law. The idea is that Missouri's sodomy law applies equally to men and women: both are prohibited from engaging in 'deviant sexual intercourse' with people of the same sex and both are permitted to engage in 'deviant sexual intercourse' with people of the opposite sex. This is precisely how the Missouri Supreme Court ruled on a sex-discrimination challenge to the state's sodomy law in *State v Walsh*:[112] it held that the sodomy law did not discriminate on the basis of sex because it prohibited both men and women from having sex with people of the same sex and allowed both men and women to have sex with people of the opposite sex.[113]

The problem facing the sex-discrimination argument for lesbian and gay rights is that statutes which use sex classifications to limit lesbian and gay rights can be interpreted in two ways: they can be seen as treating men and women *equally* or they can be seen as treating men and women *differently*.[114] The Missouri sodomy law, for example, can be seen as prohibiting women from engaging in certain sexual acts that men are permitted to engage in or it can be seen as prohibiting both men and women

[109] EC Treaty, art. 119.   [110] *Grant*, at ¶ 5.

[111] The railway company subsequently changed its policy to extend benefits to same-sex partners of employees. See e.g. 'Gay Rail Workers Win Travel Benefits', *Evening Standard* (England), 5 Oct. 1999, at 5.

[112] *State v Walsh*, 713 S.W.2d 508, 510 (Mo. 1986).

[113] An appeals court in the State of Washington adopted this same approach with respect to a sex-discrimination challenge to its marriage law in *Singer v Hara*. It held that the marriage law does not discriminate on the basis of sex because both men and women are prohibited from marrying a person of the same sex and both are permitted to marry a person of the opposite sex. *Singer v Hara*, 55 P.2d 1187, 1191 (Wash. App. 1974); see also *Baehr v Lewin*, 852 P.2d 44, 70–2 (Haw. 1993) (Heen, J. dissenting).

[114] See Stein, above n. 1, at 54–61 (discussing this problem in the context of scientific studies of sexual orientation).

from engaging in certain sexual acts with people of the same sex. When presented with the sex-discrimination argument, many courts—even those sympathetic to lesbian and gay rights—would hold that laws that restrict lesbian and gay rights apply equally to men and women and thus do not constitute sex discrimination. In fact, in *Baker v. Vermont*, the Supreme Court of Vermont, although it held that the failure to provide spousal benefits to same-sex couples violates the Vermont state constitution, rejected the sex-discrimination argument in the same way as did the *Walsh* court.[115] The Court addressed the plaintiff's sex-discrimination argument and held that Vermont's 'marriage laws are facially neutral; they do not single-out men or women as a class for disparate treatment, but rather prohibit men and women equally from marrying a person of the same sex'.[116] All but one of the justices found that sex discrimination is not 'a useful analytic framework'[117] for analysing discrimination on the basis of sexual orientation.[118]

5.3 The *Loving* Analogy

Advocates of the sex-discrimination argument for lesbian and gay rights are aware of this problem facing their argument and they have a strong reply: the mere equal application of a law with respect to two different groups does not entail that the law does not discriminate on the basis of membership in such a group. In the United States, this reply involves the principle that the mere equal application of a law is not enough to show that the law passes muster under the Equal Protection Clause of the US Constitution. Whether laws that discriminate on the basis of sexual orientation really involve sex discrimination is a form of a general problem not unique to laws concerning sexual orientation. The same type of problem arose in the context of racial discrimination. In considering laws against interracial marriage and various forms of interracial 'familial' and sexual activity, courts had to grapple with arguments made on behalf of such laws that claimed these laws applied equally to all races and, thus, did not constitute racial discrimination.[119] In *Loving v Virginia*, the Supreme Court considered a Virginia law prohibiting interracial marriages. Virginia defended its law by claiming that the law applied equally to all individuals regardless

---

[115] *Baker v Vermont*, 744 A.2d 864, 880 n. 13 (citing *Singer* and *Walsh*).

[116] ibid. at 880, n. 13.   [117] ibid.

[118] ibid. at 889 (Dooley, J., concurring) (implicitly accepting the majority's rejection of the sex-discrimination argument); ibid. at 897 (Johnson, J., concurring in part and dissenting in part) (applying the sex-discrimination argument to Vermont's marriage law and finding that law to be unconstitutional because it discriminates on the basis of sex).

[119] See e.g. *Pace v Alabama*, 106 US 583 (1883) (upholding a law prohibiting interracial adultery or fornication on the grounds that such a law applies equally to blacks and whites, and hence is consistent with the Equal Protection Clause). But cf., *Loving v Virginia*, 388 US 1 (1967) (rejecting this argument and overturning laws prohibiting interracial marriage); and *McLaughlin v Florida*, 379 US 184 (1965) (overturning a law against interracial cohabitation).

of their race, namely both whites and non-whites were prohibited from marrying outside of their race.[120] The Supreme Court rejected this reasoning holding that, even if the law prohibiting interracial marriage applied equally to whites and non-whites, it was unconstitutional because it made use of racial classifications that could not be given an exceedingly compelling justification.[121] The Court's holding involved two main parts. First, the Court 'reject[ed] the notion that the mere equal application of a statute containing racial classifications is enough to remove the classifications from the Fourteenth Amendment's proscription of all invidious racial discriminations'.[122] Secondly, the Court held that 'Virginia's miscegenation statutes rest solely upon distinctions drawn according to race. The statutes proscribe generally accepted conduct if engaged in by members of different races . . . '.[123] Even granting that the Virginia marriage law applied equally to all races, because the law makes use of racial classifications, the state must provide an especially strong justification for the law. The Court held that the law violated the Equal Protection Clause because the state failed to provide such a justification for its use of racial classifications.

Loving stands, in part, for the principle that the mere equal application of a statute that makes use of a suspect classification is not enough to show that the statute passes muster under the Equal Protection Clause. Rather, in so far as a statute makes use of a suspect classification, to satisfy the Equal Protection Clause, the state must show that there is a compelling justification for the use of that classification. Advocates of the sex-discrimination argument for lesbian and gay rights make use of this principle from *Loving*. These advocates note that simply showing that a law which makes use of sex classifications applies equally to men and women is not enough to establish that this law is constitutional under the Equal Protection Clause. That mere equal application is not enough provides an answer to the objection to the sex-discrimination argument discussed above, but there remain serious problems facing the sex-discrimination argument.

5.4 The Cultural Claim of the Sex-Discrimination Argument

Comparing the sex-discrimination argument and the central argument of cases like *Loving*,[124] a potential disanalogy appears. In cases like *Loving* involving the equal

---

[120] This is a bit of a simplification because the law only prohibited whites from marrying 'colored' people; a 'colored' man and a 'colored' woman of different races were, under Virginia law, permitted to marry each other (for example, a 'Negro' woman and an 'American Indian' man could marry).

[121] ibid. at 11.   [122] ibid. at 8 (internal quotations omitted).   [123] ibid. at 11.

[124] As, for example, the Hawaii Supreme Court did in *Baehr v Lewin*, 852 P.2d 44 (Haw. 1993), when it said the conclusion that Hawaii's marriage law made use of sex classifications in such a way that requires a compelling state interest followed from a simple adaptation of Loving: '[s]ubstitut[ing] "sex" for "race" and article I, section 5 [of Hawaii's constitution (which explicitly prohibits sex discrimination)] for the Fourteenth Amendment [in *Loving*] yields the precise case before us together with the conclusion that we have reached'. Ibid. at 68.

application of a statute that makes use of racial classifications, there is a fit between the class disadvantaged by the law and the suspect classification the law employs.[125] The Virginia anti-miscegenation law employed racial classifications and disadvantaged blacks and other non-whites. Similarly, the law at issue in *Reed v Reed*[126]—in which men were, all else being equal, chosen over women as executors of estates—employed sex classifications and disadvantaged women. In contrast, laws that discriminate on the basis of sexual orientation, as characterized by the sex-discrimination argument, lack this fit: such laws make use of sex classifications but they seem to disadvantage lesbians, gay men, and bisexuals. Table 24.1 depicts this disanalogy: in the first two rows, there is a fit between the suspect classification used in the law and the class disadvantaged by the law; in the third row, there is no such fit.[127]

Table 24.1 The Analogy at the Heart of the Sex-Discrimination Argument for Lesbian and Gay Rights

Law	Suspect classification used in the law	Class disadvantaged by the law
Virginia's anti-miscegenation law	race	people of colour
The law at issue in *Reed v Reed*	sex	women
Missouri's sodomy law	sex	gay men, lesbians, bisexuals

Advocates of the sex-discrimination argument have addressed this potential disanalogy in great detail, arguing that in order to understand the discrimination involved in laws that limit lesbian and gay rights, we must look to the theoretical underpinnings of discriminatory laws generally and of laws that discriminate on the basis of sexual orientation in particular. The thought is that looking at the underpinnings of these laws will reveal that the underlying justification for discrimination against lesbians, gay men, and bisexuals is sexism and the related idea that men and women should play different roles in our society. This aspect of the sex-discrimination argument supple-

---

[125] This is a somewhat simplified analysis of *Loving*. Arguably, the class disadvantaged by the law at issue in *Loving* is the class of people, regardless of race, who want to marry outside of their race. Such people are called 'miscegenosexuals', following Samuel A. Marcosson, 'Harassment on the Basis of Sexual Orientation: A Claim of Sex Discrimination Under Title VII', *Georgia Law Journal*, 81 (1992), 1, 6. See also Eskridge, above n. 6, at 220.

[126] *Reed v Reed*, 404 US 71 (1971). *Reed* was decided on rational review, not under heightened scrutiny, but I gloss over this fact in my subsequent use of *Reed*.

[127] Table 24.1 is a somewhat modified and abbreviated form of tables used in Eskridge, above n. 6, at 220; and Eskridge, above n. 69 at 167.

ments the formal argument with cultural evidence. The formal claim is that any law that makes use of or involves sexual orientation necessarily involves sex because a person's sexual orientation is indexed to a person's sex and the sex of the people to whom he or she is sexually attracted. The cultural claim is that sexism and homophobia are intimately interconnected.

In a detailed articulation of the sex-discrimination argument, Andrew Koppelman offers evidence from sociology, anthropology, social psychology, and history relating to homophobia and its origins in order to develop the analogy between the role of racial classifications in anti-miscegenation laws, on the one hand, and the role of sex classifications in laws that discriminate on the basis of sexual orientation, on the other.

Much of the connection between sexism and [homophobia] lies in social meanings that are accessible to everyone. It should be clear from ordinary experience that the stigmatization of the homosexual has something to do with the homosexual's supposed deviation from traditional sex roles. . . . Most Americans learn no later than high school that one of the nastier sanctions that one will suffer if one deviates from the behaviour traditionally deemed appropriate for one's sex is the imputation of homosexuality. . . . There is nothing esoteric or sociologically abstract in the claim that the homosexuality taboo enforces traditional sex roles.[128]

He concludes that

[T]he homosexuality taboo . . . is crucially dependent on sexism, without which it might well not exist. . . . [W]hen the state enforces that taboo, it is giving its imprimatur to sexism. . . . [T]he effect that the taboo against homosexuality has in modern American society is, in large part, the maintenance of illegitimate hierarchy; the taboo accomplishes this by reinforcing the identity of the superior caste in the hierarchy, and this effect is at least in large part the reason why the taboo persists. Laws that discriminate against gays are the product of a political decisionmaking process that is biased by sexism. They implicitly stigmatize women, and they reinforce the hierarchy of men over women.[129]

Koppelman's sociological claim that laws restricting lesbian and gay rights are crucially dependent on sexism is central to the sex-discrimination argument. Table 24.2 depicts the structure of the sex-discrimination argument that appeals to sociological evidence about sexism and homophobia.[130]

Table 24.2 depicts three features of a law: the group whose behaviour the law regulates, the class the law disadvantages, and the belief system that justifies the law. Looking at the first row, the claim is that the law at issue in *Loving* regulated miscegenosexuals (more precisely, *heterosexual* miscegenosexuals) by preventing them from marrying the people they want to, it disadvantaged people of colour and miscegenosexuals, and it was justified by racism. The law at issue in *Loving* disadvantaged people of colour even though it applied equally to whites and non-whites

[128] Koppelman, 'Why Sexual Orientation Discrimination is Sex Discrimination', above n. 6, at 234–5.
[129] ibid. at 255–7.
[130] Table 24.2 is an adaptation and modification of tables from Eskridge, above n. 69, at 171; and Eskridge, above n. 6, at 220–1.

Table 24.2 More Sophisticated Way of Understanding the Analogy at the Heart of the Sex-Discrimination Argument for Lesbian and Gay Rights

Law	Group whose behaviour is regulated by the law	Class disadvantaged by the law	Belief system that justifies the law
Virginia's anti-miscegenation law	miscegenosexuals (people who want to marry outside their race)	people of colour, miscegenosexuals	racism
The law at issue in *Reed v Reed*	women who are potential executors of estates	women	sexism
Missouri's sodomy law	people who have (or want to have) sex with people of the same sex	women, gay men, lesbians, bisexuals	sexism

because it enforced the separation of the races and the idea that whites are better than non-whites. Looking at the second row, the law at issue in *Reed* regulated how executors are chosen (men were preferred over women), disadvantaged women, and was justified by sexism. According to the sex-discrimination argument as depicted in the third row of Table 24.2, Missouri's sodomy law regulates lesbians, gay men and bisexuals (i.e. people who have and/or who want to have sex with people of the same sex), disadvantages women, lesbians, gay men, and bisexuals, and is justified by sexism. The Missouri sodomy law disadvantages women because, even though the law applies equally to men and women, it perpetuates the notion that men and women should play different social roles and thereby reinforces gender stereotypes; for this reason, such laws should be subject to heightened scrutiny. Table 24.2 reveals the structure of the strongest form of the sex-discrimination argument: not only do laws that discriminate on the basis of sexual orientation formally involve sex classifications but, more significantly, as a cultural fact, such laws are justified and maintained by sexism.

5.5 Three Objections to the Sex-Discrimination Argument

5.5.1 *A Hypothetical Sex-Discrimination Argument for Racial Equality*

In order to elucidate the problems with the sex-discrimination argument, consider a hypothetical argument that could be made against anti-miscegenation laws. Various scholars have noted that there were sex hierarchies implicit in anti-miscegenation statutes, namely, a significant purpose of such laws was to protect white women from black men.[131] Sex classifications clearly played a role in the development and articulation of anti-miscegenation laws. In light of this fact, one could make a sex-discrimination argument against anti-miscegenation laws.[132] Such an argument would point out that women were disadvantaged by anti-miscegenation laws and that such laws were justified by sexism. Table 24.3 depicts the analogy that is central to the hypothetical sex-discrimination argument against racial discrimination.

Table 24.3 The Analogy at the Heart of the Hypothetical Sex-Discrimination
            Argument Against Anti-Miscegenation Laws

Law	Group whose behaviour is regulated by the law	Class disadvantaged by the law	Belief system that justifies the law
The law at issue in *Reed v Reed*	women who are potential executors of estates	women	sexism
Virginia's anti-miscegenation law	miscegenosexuals	women, people of colour, miscegenosexuals	sexism

Something is, however, seriously wrong with Table 24.3 and the hypothetical argument that is based on it. Overturning anti-miscegenation laws because they discriminate on the basis of sex would mischaracterize the core of the problem with such laws.

   To put a finer point on my claim, there are three related problems with the sex-discrimination argument against anti-miscegenation laws in particular and against racially discriminatory laws in general. First, this argument misidentifies the class disadvantaged by anti-miscegenation laws. Non-whites, more than women, are disadvantaged by such a law. Call this the *sociological* mistake of the sex-discrimination argument against anti-miscegenation laws. The sex-discrimination argument against anti-miscegenation laws overemphasizes the ways these laws disadvantage women as compared to the ways they disadvantage people of colour. Looking at Table 24.3, the sociological mistake with the hypothetical sex-discrimination argument is that anti-miscegenation laws are better depicted if the word 'women' is taken out of

---

[131] See e.g. Eva Saks, 'Representing Miscegenation Law', *Raritan*, 8 (1988), 39, 42 (noting that the first miscegenation statute in the United States, passed in Maryland in 1661, prohibited black men from marrying white women but *not* white men from marrying black women).

[132] I am not suggesting that such an argument could have actually been made in the United States against anti-miscegenation laws. This would have been historically improbable because sex-discrimination doctrine was not as well developed as race-discrimination doctrine when *Loving* and *McLaughlin* were decided.

the third cell of the last row. Anti-miscegenation laws are more accurately character-ized as being disadvantageous primarily to people of colour.

Secondly, the sex-discrimination argument against anti-miscegenation laws misidentifies the belief system that justifies anti-miscegenation laws. Even granting that racism and sexism complement each other in providing the justification of anti-miscegenation laws, racism, not sexism, is the belief system that primarily underlies anti-miscegenation laws. Call this the *theoretical* mistake of the sex-discrimination argument against anti-miscegenation laws. Returning to Table 24.3, the anti-miscegenation laws would be more accurately characterized if 'racism' rather than 'sexism' appeared in the fourth column of the last row.

Thirdly, a court that overturned an anti-miscegenation law on the grounds that the law discriminated on the basis of sex would, in so doing, fail to take a stand on the central moral issue underlying the legal questions about anti-miscegenation laws, namely, that racial discrimination is morally wrong. If the *Loving* Court, in overturning Virginia's anti-miscegenation law, had focused on the sexist rather than the racist assumptions that justified the law, they would have made a moral mistake, not just a theoretical one. Call this the *moral* mistake of the sex-discrimi-nation argument against anti-miscegenation laws. The three mistakes of the sex-discrimination argument against anti-miscegenation laws—the sociological, the theoretical, and the moral—are interconnected. The theoretical mistake builds on the sociological mistake: if women are in fact greatly disadvantaged by anti-misce-genation laws, then it would make sense to say that sexism plays a role in the justifi-cation of such laws. The moral mistake builds on the other two: it is tempting to see the moral issue of anti-miscegenation laws in terms of mistaken and unjust views of women because of the sociological and theoretical claims linking racism and sexism. The three problems with the sex-discrimination argument against anti-miscegenation laws parallel problems with the sex-discrimination argument applied to laws that discriminate against lesbians, gay men, and bisexuals. I turn now to these parallel problems with the sex-discrimination argument for lesbian and gay rights.

5.5.2 *The Sociological and Theoretical Mistakes of the Sex-Discrimination Argument*

The strongest form of the sex-discrimination argument not only makes a formal claim about the connection between sex and sexual orientation, but it also makes a sociological claim and a theoretical claim. The sociological claim is that laws which discriminate on the basis of sexual orientation disadvantage women as well as les-bians, gay men, and bisexuals because these laws perpetuate a social system in which women play different social roles than men. The theoretical claim is that these laws are justified by sexism. In this section, I argue that both the sociological claim and the theoretical claim are mistaken because sex and sexual orientation are culturally and conceptually distinct. In doing so, I build on my earlier theoretical discussion about the relationship between sex and sexual orientation.

Various scholars have argued for the need to analyse sexual orientation and sex separately.[133] For example, Cheshire Calhoun, in her article 'Separating Lesbian Theory from Feminist Theory', says that:

> Patriarchy and heterosexual dominance are two, in principle, separable systems. Even when they work together, it is possible conceptually to pull the patriarchal aspect of male-female relationships apart from their heterosexual dimensions. . . . Even if empirically and histori-cally heterosexual dominance and patriarchy are completely intertwined, it does not follow from this fact that the collapse [or weakening] of patriarchy will bring about the collapse [or weakening] of heterosexual dominance.[134]

While an advocate of the sex-discrimination argument might admit that sexual-ori-entation inequality and homophobia could continue to exist even if there were sex equality and no sexism,[135] I want to make a stronger claim. Building on the work of Calhoun and others,[136] I claim that there are actual and significant differences between sexism and homophobia in contemporary American and other 'Western' societies. Simply put, sexism and homophobia are coming apart. Consider, for example, that it has become unacceptable in most circles to say that women are infe-rior to men, but it is still acceptable to say that lesbians and gay men are defective and immoral in ways that heterosexuals are not. Attitudes like this illustrate how homo-phobia, even as it has gradually become disentangled from sexism, remains entrenched in our society. While many laws that discriminate on the basis of sexual orientation have their origins in sexism, these laws are maintained because of homo-phobia and despite the repeal of many sexist laws. That homophobia and sexism have come apart presents a serious problem for the sex-discrimination argument.

Basically, the existence of these differences calls into question whether sexism—rather than homophobia—is at the core of laws that limit lesbian and gay rights and whether such laws disadvantage women as much as they disadvantage lesbians, gay men, and bisexuals. While sexism plays a role in the justification of laws that dis-criminate against lesbians, gay men, and bisexuals, homophobia plays a more central role. Sexism and homophobia are mutually supporting but distinct belief systems. It mischaracterizes the nature of laws that discriminate against lesbians and gay men to see them as primarily harming women (or even as harming women as much as they harm gay men, lesbians, and bisexuals) and to see them as primarily justified by sex-ism rather than homophobia.

[133] See e.g. Cheshire Calhoun, 'Separating Lesbian Theory from Feminist Theory', *Ethics*, 104 (1994), 558; Rubin, above n. 2; Eve Kosofsky Sedgwick, *Epistemology of the Closet* (Berkeley: University of California Press, 1990), 27–35; Ruthann Robson, *Lesbian (Out)Law* (New York: Ithaca, 1992), 85; and Halley, above n. 27, at 1724.

[134] Calhoun, above n. 133 at 562.

[135] See Koppelman, 'Why Sexual Orientation Discrimination Is Sex Discrimination', above n. 6, at 249.

[136] See above n. 133.

Looking back at Table 24.2 from Section 3, the *sociological* mistake of the sex-discrimination argument is that 'women' should not appear in the third cell of the last row. Laws like Missouri's sodomy law disadvantage lesbians, gay men, and bisexuals. Such laws prohibit them from sexually expressing their intimate relationships and from having sex with the people to whom they are sexually attracted. Relatedly, the *theoretical* mistake of the sex-discrimination argument is that 'homophobia'— not 'sexism'—should appear in the last cell of the last row. Sodomy laws like Missouri's that single out same-sex sexual activity for prohibition are primarily motivated by homophobia. Despite the fact that sexism played a role in their development, such laws are now maintained primarily by animus towards lesbians and gay men, and repulsion towards them and the sexual activities they engage in (as well as sexual activities generally). Therefore, to simply deploy the sex-discrimination argument against sodomy laws would, for example, ignore the central role that conceptions of sexual desire play in such laws. Making the sex-discrimination argument also overlooks the distinctive role that 'the closet'[137] and the associated invisibility of lesbians, gay men, and bisexuals[138] play, for example, in the justification and maintenance of sodomy laws and sexual-orientation discrimination generally.

An advocate of the sex-discrimination argument might respond to the sociological and the theoretical objections raised here by pointing out that just because a law has one problematic feature does not mean that nothing else is wrong with it. Specifically, there might be more than one class disadvantaged by a law and there might be more than one belief system that justifies a law. In particular, in response to the sociological objection, one might say that gay men, lesbians, bisexuals, *and* women are disadvantaged by laws that discriminate on the basis of sexual orientation.[139] Similarly, in response to the theoretical objection, one might say that *both* homophobia and sexism provide the theoretical justification for laws like Missouri's sodomy law.

I agree that some laws that disadvantage one group may also disadvantage another and that more than one belief system may undergird some laws. Sometimes, however, one group may be more disadvantaged than another and one belief system may play a much more central role than another. Granting that women were more disadvantaged than men by anti-miscegenation laws does not entail that *Loving* was decided on the wrong grounds because it failed to discuss the harm to women involved in anti-miscegenation laws. Granting that sexism played a role in justifying anti-miscegenation laws does not entail that the Supreme Court's reasoning in

---

[137] For discussion of the centrality of the closet to the lives of lesbians, gay men and bisexuals, see e.g. Sedgwick, above n. 133; and Janet Halley, 'The Politics of the Closet: Towards Equal Protection for Gay, Lesbian and Bisexual Identity', *UCLA Law Review*, 36 (1989), 915.

[138] See Yoshino, above n. 14; and Yoshino, above n. 83.

[139] Andrew Koppelman, *The Gay Rights Question in Contemporary American Law*, ch. 3, makes precisely this reply, saying 'discrimination can [ ] be based on sex and on sexual orientation at the same time'.

Loving was incomplete because it failed to discuss the sexism implicit in anti-misce-genation laws. Rather, the *Loving* Court rightly focused on the harm to people of colour and the central role of racial hierarchies (specifically, white supremacy) in the justification of the Virginia law. A parallel point can be made concerning the sex-discrimination argument for lesbian and gay rights: women, compared to men, may be more disadvantaged by laws that discriminate on the basis of sexual orienta-tion,[140] but lesbians, gay men, and bisexuals are more significantly disadvantaged than women by such laws. Similarly, while sexism plays a role in maintaining laws relating to sexual orientation, homophobia plays a much more central role.

Both the sociological and the theoretical objections to the sex-discrimination argument relate to the observation that sexism and homophobia have become disen-tangled. The sociological objection is that, as a cultural fact, lesbians and gay men, not women, suffer the greatest harm from laws that discriminate on the basis of sex-ual orientation. The theoretical objection is that laws that discriminate on the basis of sexual orientation are primarily maintained by homophobia, not sexism. Together, the sociological and the theoretical objections create a serious problem for the sex-discrimination argument.

5.5.3 *The Moral Mistake of the Sex-Discrimination Argument*

In an essay written before *Loving* but after *Brown v Board of Education*,[141] Herbert Wechsler argued that the questions posed by state-enforced segregation (in both education and marriage) do not primarily concern discrimination or equal protec-tion but rather primarily concern the right to free association.[142] He argued that the prohibition of miscegenation affected both whites and non-whites; the prohibition, properly understood, did not discriminate against blacks and did not violate the Equal Protection Clause but rather restricted the freedom of association of everyone, regardless of race. Charles Black, in a response, argued that Wechsler ignored the obvious ways in which segregation (in marriage, education, and other contexts) clearly offends equality.[143] Black convincingly—and presciently (in light of the Court's decision in *Loving*)—argued that there was no doubt why segregation laws existed, namely to keep African-Americans 'in their place' and to sustain white

---

[140] As an empirical claim, this is far from obviously true. In fact, it seems that some laws that dis-criminate on the basis of sexual orientation might harm gay men more than lesbians—e.g. sodomy laws; for discussion, see Robson, above n. 133, at 47–59—some might harm lesbians more than gay men—e.g. the military's various policies concerning homosexuality; see Michelle Benecke and Kristin Dodge, 'Military Women in Nontraditional Fields: Casualties of the Armed Forces' War on Homosexuals', *Harvard Women's Law Journal*, 13 (1990), 215—while some might harm gay men and lesbians roughly the same amount.

[141] *Brown v Board of Education*, 347 US 483 (1957) (holding that segregated public schools are uncon-stitutional).

[142] Herbert Wechsler, 'Towards Neutral Principles', in *Principles, Politics and Fundamental Law* (Cambridge, Mass.: Harvard University Press, 1961), 43–7.

[143] Charles Black, 'The Lawfulness of the Segregation Decisions', *Yale Law Journal*, 69 (1960), 421.

supremacy. Further, knowing the Constitution, he had no doubt what is wrong with such laws, namely, segregation violates equal protection and is justified only by racism. It was, said Black, simply 'laughable' to say that such laws are unconstitutional because they restrict the right to free association.

The moral objection to the sex-discrimination argument is similar to Black's objection to Wechsler's argument against segregation: laws that discriminate against lesbians, gay men, and bisexuals should be overturned on the grounds that they make invidious distinctions on the basis of sexual orientation, not on other grounds. Overturning laws that discriminate on the basis of sexual orientation because they discriminate on the basis of sex mischaracterizes the core wrong of these laws.[144] Laws restricting the rights of gay men and lesbians violate principles of equality primarily because such laws discriminate on the basis of sexual orientation, *not* because they discriminate on the basis of sex. By failing to address arguments about the morality of same-sex sexual acts and the moral character of lesbians, gay men, and bisexuals, the sex-discrimination argument 'closets', rather than confronts, homophobia. While the connection between sex discrimination and laws that restrict the rights of lesbians, gay men, and bisexuals is closer than the connection between segregation and the restriction on free association, my objection to the sex-discrimination argument for lesbian and gay rights is a variant of Black's objection to Wechsler: as members of this society, we understand, for example, the goal of Hawaii's constitutional amendment restricting marriage to only opposite sex couples[145] and the goal of sodomy laws that prohibit same-sex—but not opposite-sex—sexual activities. Such laws restrict the rights of lesbians, gay men, and bisexuals and should be overturned for this reason.

In summary, the sex-discrimination argument for lesbian and gay rights, even in its strongest form, faces three serious and related objections. By focusing on the harm to women and the sexist assumptions of laws that discriminate on the basis of sexual orientation, this argument rests on a cultural mischaracterization and theoretical misalignment. These mistakes lead the sex-discrimination argument to provide the wrong analysis of laws that discriminate on the basis of sexual orientation. For these reasons, Table 24.4, rather than Table 24.2, correctly depicts the analogy that should be made concerning laws that discriminate against lesbians, gay men, and bisexuals. As Table 24.4 indicates, lesbians, gay men, and bisexuals constitute the class disadvantaged by laws that discriminate on the basis of sexual orientation and homophobia is the belief system that justifies such laws.[146]

---

[144] For a similar argument, see John Gardner, 'On the Ground of Her Sex(uality)', *Oxford Journal of Legal Studies*, 18 (1998), 167.

[145] Hawaii Constitution, art. 1, §23 (1998).

[146] Drawing on the sex–gender distinction, see above, section 2.1, and building on a trend among some US courts to interpret sex discrimination expansively to include *gender* discrimination—see e.g. *Price Waterhouse v Hopkins*, 490 US 228 (1989) (holding Title VII's prohibition of sex discrimination reaches 'giving credence and effect' to sex stereotypes)—one might try to develop a *gender* discrimination version of the sex-discrimination argument. According to this argument, which I shall call the *gender-discrimination argument for lesbian and gay rights*, a law that discriminates on the basis of sexual

Table 24.4 The More Apt Analogy for Understanding Lesbian and Gay Rights

Law	Suspect classification used in the law	Class disadvantaged by the law	Belief system that justifies the law
Virginia's anti-miscegenation law	race	people of colour, miscegenosexuals	racism
The law at issue in *Reed v. Reed*	sex	women	sexism
Missouri's sodomy law	sex	gay men, lesbians, bisexuals	homophobia

6 A PRAGMATIC EVALUATION OF THE TWO ARGUMENTS

6.1 The Pragmatic Virtues of the Two Arguments

Some advocates of the 'born that way' and the sex-discrimination arguments might grant that there are legal, ethical and empirical problems with these arguments but still insist that there are pragmatic reasons for making them. The thought is that despite their failings, these arguments have pragmatic virtues; people—particularly, voters, legislators, executive, and judges—will be persuaded by these arguments. Various opinion polls have shown that people who think that homosexuality is bio-logically based or that people do not choose their sexual orientations are more likely

orientation discriminates on the basis of gender, in virtue of discriminating in terms of gender-role stereotypes (that is, gay men and lesbians are treated differently in virtue of their gender deviance). For an optimistic and simple statement of this argument, see e.g. Jess Bravin, 'Courts Open Alternate Route to Extend Job-Bias Laws to Homosexuals', *Wall Street Journal*, 22 Sept. 2000 at B1. This argument suffers from the same theoretical and pragmatic problems facing the sex-discrimination argument discussed in this chapter. Further, this argument seems open to the practical objection that far from all gay men and lesbians are, respectively, feminine or masculine, and thus some homosexuals might not be covered by the gender-discrimination argument. Alternatively, an advocate of the gender-discrimination argument might try to argue that, in general, gay men and lesbians are members of a third and/or fourth gender. While this argument may have some theoretical and some sociological support—see e.g. Stein, above n. 1, at 34–5; and Gilbert Herdt, ed., *Third Sex: Third Gender: Beyond Sexual Dimorphism in Culture and History* (New York: Zone Books, 1994)—it is highly unlikely that judges will accept the claim that homosexuals belong to a different gender and, on that basis, count laws that discriminate on the basis of sexual orientation as a type of gender—and hence sex—discrimination.

to favour lesbian and gay rights than those who do not.[147] In light of this evidence and similar anecdotal evidence, some advocates of lesbian and gay rights claim that the 'born that way' argument should be embraced because it persuades people.[148]

Similarly, an advocate of the sex-discrimination argument might agree with my criticisms of this argument while maintaining that it should be a central part of a viable gay rights litigation strategy. In particular, there are three noteworthy pragmatic virtues of the sex-discrimination argument. First, the argument does sometimes persuade judges.[149] Secondly, the sex-discrimination argument, in contrast to some other legal arguments that have been made for lesbian and gay rights, has at least the potential to deliver heightened scrutiny to laws that restrict the rights of lesbians and gay men. Thirdly, given the current legal and social climate facing lesbians, gay men, and bisexuals, it is simply easier for courts and legislatures to frame a decision in terms of protecting women and combating sexism than in terms of protecting lesbians, gay men, and bisexuals and combating homophobia. In the sections that follow, I explore the pragmatic pitfalls of both of these arguments.

6.2 Practical Problems for the 'Born That Way' Argument

6.2.1 *Will it Work?*

To begin, there is historical evidence for doubting the pragmatic value of the 'born that way' argument. In Nazi Germany, for example, the sexologist Magnus Hirschfeld

---

[147] See e.g. Kurt Ernulf, Sune Innala, and Frederick Whitam, 'Biological Explanation, Psychological Explanation and Tolerance of Homosexuals: A Cross-National Analysis of Beliefs and Attitudes', *Psychological Reports*, 65 (1989), 1003; J. Piskur and D. Delegman, 'Effect of Reading a Summary of Research about Biological Bases of Homosexual Orientation on Attitudes Towards Homosexuals', *Psychological Reports*, 71 (1992), 1219; B. E. Whitley, 'The Relationship of Heterosexuals' Attributions for the Causes of Homosexuality to Attitudes Towards Lesbians and Gay Men', *Personality and Social Psychiatry Bulletin*, 16 (1990), 369. Note that these polls provide evidence of correlation but do not settle the causal question. It is possible that the results of these studies are to be explained by the fact that people who are sympathetic to lesbian and gay rights are more likely to embrace nativist theories about sexual orientation.

[148] See e.g. LeVay, above n. 3, at 1–9.

[149] The Hawaii Supreme Court embraced this argument in *Baehr v Lewin*, 852 P.2d 44 (Haw. 1993), even though the argument was, for the most part, not mentioned in the briefs on behalf of the plaintiffs challenging Hawaii's marriage law (see *Baehr v Miike*, No. 20371, 1999 Haw. LEXIS 391 (Haw. 9 Dec., 1999) at *10 n. 3 (Haw., 9 Dec. 1999) (Ramil, J., concurring)) and the Human Rights Committee of the United Nations embraced this argument in *Toonen v Australia*, Case 488/1992, UN GAOR, Hum. Rts. Comm., 49th Sess., Supp. No. 40, Vol. II at 226, UN Doc. A/49/40 (1994), which considered a challenge to Tasmanian's sodomy law, even though the argument was not raised by any of the parties to the case. See also *Brause v Bureau of Vital Statistics*, 1998 WL 88743 (Alaska Super.); and *Lawrence v State*, 2000 WL 729417 (Tex. App.-Hous. (14th Dist.)). Note, however, that when the sex-discrimination argument is embraced by courts, the reasoning is often reject on appeal. The decision in *Brause*—like that in *Baehr v Lewin* (see below, n. 175 and accompanying text)—was mooted by an amendment to the state constitution. See Alaska Constitution, art. I, § 24. Also, the decision in *Lawrence* was overturned by a higher court in *Lawrence v. State*, 41 S.W. 3d 349 (Tex. App. 2001).

argued on behalf of legal protections for homosexuals on the grounds that they constituted a third sex. Hirschfeld's belief in a strong biological basis for sexual orientation led him to lobby for lesbian and gay rights, but it also led him to refer some gay
men for surgery to reduce their 'homosexual inclinations'.[150] Prior to his death,
Hirschfeld conceded that not only had he failed to prove his biological thesis, but that
he had unwittingly contributed to the persecution of homosexuals by stigmatizing
them as biologically defective. He presumably had in mind the fact that, in Germany,
lesbians, gay men, and other sexual minorities were imprisoned, castrated, mutilated
in other ways, and sent to death camps to remove them from the breeding stock.[151]
The example of Germany shows that seeing sexual orientation as biologically based
in no way guarantees a positive result for lesbians and gay men. Even in contemporary times in the United States, it is far from obvious that the appeal to innateness will
persuade. The genetic basis of skin pigmentation, for example, does not seem to have
a mitigating effect on racism.

6.2.2 Risky Strategy

Linking lesbian and gay rights to the ups and downs of scientific research is risky,
especially because, as I have argued above, such research is, at best, still in its early
stages and, further, because biological research into sexual orientation has a poor
track record when it comes to reliability.[152] Making lesbian and gay rights contingent
on a particular scientific finding is simply too risky. That people are persuaded by
biological arguments for lesbian and gay rights may suggest a public relations strategy that will be successful in the short term, but it does not suggest a strategy suited
to grounding rights that are deeply important and that profoundly impact on
people's lives.

As an example of the risks of connecting particular scientific theories to lesbian
and gay politics, consider the relationship of the lesbian and gay movement in
America to psychiatry.[153] In the United States, from World War II to the late 1960s,
many lesbians and gay men embraced psychiatry and its language, partly on political
grounds. The idea was that psychiatry could help legitimate lesbians and gay men
and their organizations.[154] But as the gay movement grew, it began to question

[150] Rainer Herrn, 'On the History of Biological Theories of Homosexuality', *Journal of
Homosexuality*, 28 (1995), 31.

[151] See e.g. Richard Plant, *The Pink Triangle: The Nazi War Against Homosexuals* (New York: Henry
Holt, 1986). The Nazis also espoused social theories of homosexuality. Thus, homosexuals were imprisoned and sent to death camps to prevent 'contamination' of the German youth by exposure to adult
homosexuals. This underscores that, in the presence of animus towards lesbians and gay men, any
theory of the origins of sexual orientation may be used to make the case against lesbian and gay rights.

[152] See e.g. Byne, above n. 47.

[153] Ronald Bayer, *Homosexuality and American Psychiatry*, 2nd edn. (Princeton: Princeton
University Press, 1987).

[154] John D'Emilio, *Sexual Politics, Sexual Communities: The Making of a Homosexual Minority in the
United States, 1940-1970* (Chicago: University of Chicago Press, 1983) at 116–17.

psychiatry, ultimately protesting against the American Psychiatric Association's classification of homosexuality as a psychological disorder.[155] This example shows that science is, at best, a double-edged sword, which is a tricky ethical and political weapon.

6.2.3 *Genetic Engineering*

Finally, even if belief in a biological basis for homosexuality would persuade people to favour lesbian and gay rights in the short run, it might spark calls for genetic engineering to prevent homosexuality and for the development of techniques for the detection of homosexuality so as to enable the abortion of foetuses believed to have the potential to develop into homosexuals.[156] Many biologically based characteristics (including, in some cultures, being a woman)[157] are viewed as undesirable and shameful. Some such characteristics are seen by some to warrant the use of genetic engineering to avoid having children who develop them.

The availability and use of procedures to screen for or select against homosexuality would suggest that screening for homosexuality is a reasonable and sanctioned medical procedure. This could potentially tip the scales of public opinion back towards seeing homosexuality as a physical/mental disorder. Further, the availability and use of such procedures could increase the pressure to hide one's homosexuality and decrease the collective power of lesbians and gay men. Genetic engineering procedures to select against non-heterosexuals could engender and perpetuate attitudes that lesbians and gay men are undesirable and not valuable, policies that discriminate against lesbians and gay men, violence against lesbians and gay men, and the very conditions that give rise to the preference for heterosexuals rather than non-heterosexuals.[158]

To summarize, some people have argued that the 'born that way' argument, even despite its problems, should be embraced. I have argued that even viewed pragmatically, the argument should not be embraced because it may well not work, it is risky, and, in fact, it may actually engender the social conditions it is supposed to combat.[159]

---

[155] Bayer, above n. 153.

[156] See Stein, above n. 1, at 305–27; and Timothy Murphy, *Gay Science: The Ethics of Sexual Orientation Research* (New York: Columbia University Press, 1997), 103–36.

[157] See e.g. Mary Anne Warren, *Gendercide: The Implications of Sex Research* (Totowa, NJ: Rowman and Allenfeld, 1985); Owen Jones, 'Sex Selection: Regulating Technology Enabling the Predetermination of a Child's Gender', *Harvard Journal of Law and Technology*, 6 (1992), 1; and Joni Danis, 'Sexism and "the Superfluous Female": Arguments for Regulating Pre-implantation Sex Selection', *Harvard Women's Law Journal*, 18 (1995), 219.

[158] See above n. 156; and Fredrick Suppe, 'Curing Homosexuality', in *Philosophy and Sex*, above n. 2, at 401–14.

[159] The question remains why lesbians and gay men should have to appeal to the 'born that way' argument to begin with. The issues of choice and immutability seem to be selectively applied to homosexuals and not to other marginalized groups. Members of religious minorities are not asked to demonstrate that either their religious affiliation or their religious practices are innate or immutable. Despite the fact that a person's religious affiliation is not genetic and a person can convert from one religion to another, most modern democracies protect religious liberty.

6.3 Practical Problems for the Sex-Discrimination Argument

I turn now to an assessment of the pragmatic considerations concerning the sex-discrimination argument. Although some people seem to feel that there is something tricky about the sex-discrimination argument, some courts have been persuaded by this argument. I turn to a discussion of some practical problems with making the sex-discrimination argument.

6.3.1 *The Problem of 'Actual Differences' between Men and Women*

Several courts that considered the sex-discrimination argument for lesbian and gay rights responded to the argument by saying there are 'actual differences'[160] between men and women that justify making use of sex classifications, especially in laws related to sexual activity, marriage, procreation, and the like.[161] Although it is not clear how many 'actual differences' really exist between men and women,[162] and how much significance courts are willing to find in the existence of these differences, it is clear that courts will frequently appeal to differences between men and women to justify the use of sex classifications in the face of the sex-discrimination argument. That some courts are willing to allow 'actual differences' between men and women to justify the use of sex classifications creates a substantial practical problem for the sex-discrimination argument.

6.3.2 *Some Anti-gay Laws Do Not Make Use of Sex Classifications*

In virtue of the fact that sex and sexual orientation are conceptually and culturally distinct, not all laws that discriminate on the basis of sexual orientation in fact make use of sex classifications. William Eskridge has usefully distinguished among three different types of laws that discriminate on the basis of sexual orientation: (1) laws that explicitly discriminate on the basis of sexual orientation (*type-1 laws*; an example would be the military's policy concerning homosexuality); (2) laws that discriminate on the basis of sex but which have their primary effect on gay people (*type-2 laws*; an example would be marriage laws that prohibit same-sex couples from marrying); and (3) other laws that do not facially discriminate against either sex or sexual

[160] For cases not related to lesbian and gay rights where the Supreme Court has appealed to 'actual differences', see e.g. *Miller v Albright*, 523 US 420 (1998); *Michael M. v Superior Court*, 450 U.S 464 (1981) (plurality opinion) (upholding use of sex classification in a statutory rape law that made sexual intercourse between a male and a female both under the age of eighteen a crime for the male but not for the female); and *Rostker v Goldberg*, 453 US 57 (1981) (upholding male-only draft registration system).

[161] The 'actual differences' response has been used against versions of the sex-discrimination argument in various cases. See e.g. *Singer v Hara*, 55 P.2d 1187 (Wash. App. 1974) (focusing on the reproductive capacities of male-female couples compared to same-sex couples); *Baker v Nelson*, 191 N.W.2d 185, 186 (Minn. 1977), *appeal dismissed*, 409 U.S. 810 (1977) (upholding Minnesota's marriage law on the grounds that 'the institution of marriage as a union of man and woman uniquely involv[es] the procreation and rearing of children within a family').

[162] See e.g. Fausto-Sterling, above n. 17.

orientation but that have discriminatory effects on lesbians and gay men (*type-3 laws*; an example would be sodomy laws that facially apply to sexual acts between people of both the same sex and the opposite sex but which are enforced only applied to sexual acts between people of the same sex).[163]

The sex-discrimination argument has its greatest potential applied to type-2 laws, that is, laws that discriminate on the basis of sex. The sex-discrimination argument will, however, be much harder for judges to accept when it is applied to type-1 laws or type-3 laws, that is, laws that discriminate on the basis of sexual orientation that do *not* make use of sex classifications. Consider the military's policy concerning homosexuality[164] as an example of a type-1 law because it does not facially discriminate on the basis of sex or even mention sex classifications. Under this policy, one of the several ways that lesbians, gay men, and bisexuals can be discharged is if they engage in sexual activities with people of the same sex. This policy does not, however, discharge heterosexuals who engage in same-sex sexual acts (as some heterosexuals do). Specifically, the law does not provide for the discharge of a member of the armed forces who 'engage[s] in a homosexual act . . . [if] such conduct is a departure from the member's usual and customary behaviour; such conduct . . . is unlikely to recur; . . . and the member does not have a propensity or intent to engage in homosexual acts'.[165] In other words, heterosexuals, even though they might occasionally engage in same-sex sexual acts, will not, as a rule, be discharged for engaging in such acts. Only lesbians, gay men, and bisexuals, will be discharged for engaging in same-sex sexual acts, because, in virtue of their sexual orientations, only they have the propensity to engage in such acts. This part of the military policy is an example of a type-1 law: it does not discriminate on the basis of sex but it discriminates on the basis of sexual orientation—it discharges lesbians, gay men, and bisexuals for engaging in a behaviour for which heterosexuals are not discharged. The sex-discrimination argument will have much less practical force when type-1 laws are involved. This is a serious practical limitation of the sex-discrimination argument.

6.3.3 *Immunizing Anti-gay Laws against the Sex-Discrimination Argument*

Given the difference between type-2 laws and type-1 laws, legislatures that wish to restrict lesbian and gay rights might try to immunize themselves against the sex-discrimination argument by not using sex classifications in laws relating to sexual orientation and by explicitly stating that such laws do not discriminate against sex. In other words, legislatures will recast type-2 laws as type-1 (or type-3) laws. As an illustration, consider the 1993 plurality opinion in *Baehr v Lewin*.[166] In its opinion, widely touted by advocates of lesbian and gay rights, the Court made a distinction between

---

[163] Eskridge, above n. 6, at 205.
[164] See above n. 94.
[165] 10 USC § 654 (b)(1).
[166] *Baehr v Lewin*, 852 P.2d 44 (Haw. 1993).

same-sex marriage (a marriage between two people of the same sex) and *homosexual* marriage (a marriage between homosexuals).

'Homosexual' and 'same-sex' marriages are not synonymous; by the same token, a 'heterosexual' same-sex marriage is, in theory, not oxymoronic. . . . Parties to 'a union between a man and a woman' may or may not be homosexuals. Parties to a same-sex marriage could theoretically be either homosexuals or heterosexuals.[167]

In light of this distinction, *Baehr v Lewin* can be understood as holding that prohibitions on same-sex marriages require a strong justification because they discriminate on the basis of sex, while prohibitions on homosexual marriages do not require such a strong justification.

Consistent with the 1993 decision in *Baehr v Lewin*, a legislature could pass a marriage law that allows same-sex couples to marry but prohibits homosexuals from doing so. The rationale for this hypothetical law would be to allow same-sex marriage in order to avoid the charge of sex discrimination while still prohibiting homosexual marriages. While this may seem an odd law, it is actually similar to the 'Don't Ask, Don't Tell' policy, which permits heterosexuals, but not lesbians, gay men, and bisexuals, to engage in same-sex sexual activities.[168] Among the additional reasons a legislature might offer for this law are that marriage is related to child-rearing (and it believes that lesbians and gay men are bad parents compared to heterosexuals), that lesbians and gay men are less able to sustain the sort of long-term commitments the state wants to encourage in its citizens, and the incidence of sodomy can be reduced by preventing homosexuals from marrying.[169]

Assuming a legislature enacts this hypothetical marriage law, it would be constitutional so far as the sex-discrimination argument for lesbian and gay rights is concerned because it does not discriminate on the basis of sex.[170] That a law which discriminates on the basis of sexual orientation can be immune to the

[167] ibid., at 52 n. 11.

[168] It is also similar to Florida's ban on adoption of children by homosexuals, Florida Statutes Annotated §63.042 (3), as well as to some courts' understanding of same-sex sexual harassment under Title VII—which seems to have been formally overruled by *Oncale v Sundowner Offshore Serv., Inc.*, 523 US 75 (1998)—whereby same-sex harassment would be actionable only when the harasser was a homosexual. See *McWilliams v Fairfax County Bd. of Supervisors*, 72 F.3d 1191 (4th Cir. 1996); *Wrightson v Pizza Hut of Am.*, 99 F.3d 138 (4th Cir. 1996). Although the Supreme Court ruled in *Oncale* that same-sex sexual harassment is covered by Title VII when such harassment is discrimination 'because of sex', the Court seemed to leave open the possibility that a harasser's sexual orientation could be relevant to determining whether the harassment is actionable.

[169] Some of these are among the reasons offered by Hawaii and Vermont in defence of their marriage laws. These reasons were rejected, respectively by the trial court on remand in *Baehr v Miike*, 65 USLW 2399 (Haw. Cir. Ct. 1996) and the Supreme Court of Vermont in *Baker v Vermont*, 744 A.2d 864 (Vt. 1999). For discussion of some of these issues, see e.g. the exchange between Lynn Wardle, 'The Potential Impact of Homosexual Parenting on Children', *University of Illinois Law Review*, (1997), 833, and Carlos Ball and Janice Pea, 'Warring with Wardle: Morality, Social Science and Gay and Lesbian Parents', *University of Illinois Law Review*, (1998), 253.

[170] It is not, however, clear whether the Supreme Court's reasoning in *Romer v Evans*, 517 US 620 (1996), would overturn my hypothetical marriage law.

sex-discrimination argument follows from the fact, discussed above, that sexual orientation and sex are conceptually distinct. This discussion shows that not all laws that adversely effect lesbians, gay men, and bisexuals can be analysed as involving sex discrimination.

The moral of this hypothetical marriage law is that it is possible for a legislature to craft a law (or a court to interpret a law) in such a way that it discriminates on the basis of sexual orientation but not on the basis of sex. The hypothetical shows how a law that discriminates on the basis of sexual orientation through the use of sex classifications can be easily reworked to discriminate on the basis of sexual orientation without making use of sex classifications. (In other words, type-2 laws can be converted into type-1 laws.) This shows that any victories obtained by the sex-discrimination argument might very well be short-lived. If the sex-discrimination argument is deployed, we can expect to see more laws like the 'Don't Ask, Don't Tell' policy, namely, laws that discriminate on the basis of sexual orientation without discriminating on the basis of sex.

The Hawaii Supreme Court's recent decision upholding the constitutionality of the state's marriage law provides an example of a more blunt way of immunizing laws that discriminate on the basis of sexual orientation against the sex-discrimination argument.[171] In 1998, through a state referendum, Hawaii amended its constitution to allow the state legislature to limit marriages to male-female couples.[172] The Hawaii Supreme Court held that this amendment rendered moot the challenge to Hawaii's marriage law. In effect, the court ruled that the constitutional amendment declared that a law that discriminates on the basis of sexual orientation, even in the form of a law that facially makes use of sex classifications, does not violate Hawaii's constitution and is consistent with its sex-discrimination jurisprudence. This failure of the sex-discrimination argument, combined with the existence of laws like the 'Don't Ask, Don't Tell' policy, shows how the sex-discrimination argument, as a practical matter, may well fail.

6.3.4 *The Risk of Backlash*

The fourth practical problem for the sex-discrimination argument is that its practical successes could lead to weakened protections against sex discrimination because a strong backlash typically occurs when lesbians, gay men, and bisexuals make legal and political advances.[173] In fact, some have suggested that the link to lesbian and gay rights, especially to same-sex marriage, had a deleterious effect on the Equal Rights

---

[171]   *Baehr v Miike*, No. 20371, 1999 Haw. LEXIS 391, at *6 (Haw. 9 Dec. 1999).

[172]   Hawii Constitution, art. 1, §23 (1998). A similar scenario was played out in Alaska.

[173]   The mere *possibility* that Hawaii or Vermont might allow same-sex couples to marry so inflamed many people that over half of the state legislatures enacted measures to ensure that same-sex marriages would not be recognized in their jurisdictions and Congress enacted the Defense of Marriage Act. See above n. 71.

Amendment.[174] A backlash to any success of the sex-discrimination argument could undermine both women's rights and lesbian and gay rights. In effect, this is what happened in Hawaii. The 1999 decision of the state's Supreme Court construed the 1998 constitutional amendment as taking Hawaii's marriage law 'out of the ambit of the equal protection clause of Hawaii's constitution',[175] thereby weakening sex-discrimination jurisprudence in Hawaii.

To summarize, the sex-discrimination argument only has the potential to persuade courts with respect to one of the three types of laws that discriminate on the basis of sexual orientation. It is unlikely to persuade judges, even those sympathetic to lesbian and gay rights,[176] particularly because judges may appeal to actual differences between men and women. Further, any victories obtained by the sex-discrimination argument may be short-lived and may have deleterious effects on sex-discrimination jurisprudence. In light of these practical problems and the sociological, theoretical, and moral problems discussed above, advocates of lesbian and gay rights should avoid relying on the sex-discrimination argument.

6.3.5 *Sex Discrimination as an Argument in the Alternative*

Some advocates of lesbian and gay rights have suggested making the sex-discrimination argument in the alternative coupled with other arguments for lesbian and gay rights.[177] Given that the sex-discrimination argument sometimes does persuade judges, why not offer this argument in the alternative, especially when this 'double-barrelled' approach has proved effective?[178] I have argued that the sex-discrimination argument faces both practical pitfalls and principled objections. I have *not*, however, argued that the sex-discrimination argument for lesbian and gay rights should *never* be made. Weak arguments do sometimes persuade judges. Especially when a law that discriminates on the basis of sexual orientation makes explicit use of sex classifications (a type-2 law) and when the sexual-orientation discrimination involved in such a law is closely related to sex-role stereotypes, some judges may be persuaded to overturn laws that restrict lesbian and gay rights. Similarly, the sex-discrimination argument might provide a welcome alternative to judges who are sym-

[174] See e.g. Jane Mansbridge, *Why We Lost the ERA* (Chicago: University of Chicago Press, 1986), 128–9 and 144–5.

[175] *Baehr v Miike*, No. 20371, at *6.

[176] See above text accompanying nn. 115–18 (discussing *Baker v Vermont*, 744 A.2d 864 (Vt. 1999)).

[177] See e.g. Eskridge, above n. 69, at 182 (advocating a 'double-barrelled' approach to making the case for same-sex marriage); and Koppelman, above n. 139 ('sex discrimination argument is . . . only . . . one arrow in the quiver').

[178] See,e.g. *Nabozny v Podlesny*, 92 F.3d 446 (7th Cir. 1996) (holding that school administrators violated the Equal Protection Clause when they discriminated on the basis of *both* sex and sexual orientation when they did nothing to prevent the repeated abuse of an openly gay student); and *Baker*, 744 A.2d 864, in which the sex-discrimination argument was made as an argument in the alternative both in the briefs and in the oral arguments with the result that one of the five judges was persuaded by the sex-discrimination argument and the remaining four judges were persuaded by other arguments for lesbian and gay rights, see above text accompanying nn. 115–18.

pathetic to lesbian and gay rights but who are hesitant to break new doctrinal ground. Despite these points, my view is that the sex-discrimination argument, given its practical and theoretical pitfalls, if presented at all, should be used with great caution. Making this argument in the alternative in conjunction with other sorts of arguments for lesbian and gay rights might mitigate some of the practical problems with the sex-discrimination argument, but some serious worries would remain. A law that discriminates on the basis of sexual orientation that is overturned in the face of the sex-discrimination argument could reappear in a slightly different form, recast so that it does not make use of sex classifications. Further, when a law that discriminates on the basis of sexual orientation is overturned in the face of the sex-discrimination argument, the central moral debates about homosexuality are bracketed. Perhaps Herbert Wechsler's argument that appealed to the right to free association[179] would have worked to persuade judges who otherwise upheld racial segregation, but such an argument would have lacked the moral force of the Supreme Court's opinion in *Loving*. When the basic human rights of a despised minority are at issue, the judiciary needs to speak in a strong moral voice. Both the sex-discrimination argument and the 'born that way' argument fail to do so.

7 CONCLUSION

More than a decade ago, political theorist Michael Sandel showed how arguments for lesbian and gay rights that appeal to the 'liberal toleration' of homosexuality avoid the difficult moral issues relating to homosexuality[180] and will, at best, produce weak, short-term gains for lesbian and gay rights.[181] Both of the arguments for lesbian and gay rights I focus on in this essay—the sex-discrimination argument and the 'born that way' argument—fail to address the actual wrongs with discrimination on the basis of sexual orientation and with the failure to recognize claims of lesbians and gay men more generally. In doing so, they fail to argue that same-sex sexual desire should be of the same legal and ethical status as opposite-sex sexual desire, that same-sex sexual acts should be of the same legal and ethical status as opposite-sex sexual acts, and that relationships between people of the same sex should have the same legal and ethical status as relationships between people of the opposite sex. These issues need to be faced to obtain and maintain robust rights for bisexuals, lesbians, and gay

[179] See Wechsler, above n. 142.
[180] Michael Sandel, 'Moral Argument and Liberal Toleration: Abortion and Homosexuality', *California Law Review*, 77 (1989), 521.
[181] ibid. at 537.

men.[182] By failing to make the necessary legal and ethical arguments, both arguments avoid rather than address the issues at the core of claims for lesbian and gay rights.

I have argued that these two arguments have other failings. The sex-discrimination argument makes the sociological mistake of failing to acknowledge the cultural distinctness of sexism and homophobia and of sex discrimination and sexual-orientation discrimination. The 'born that way' argument crucially rests on dubious empirical premises about how human sexual orientations develop and, when made in the context of the US Constitution, it rests on dubious equal protection jurisprudence. These principled problems with both arguments are related to the theoretical issues discussed in Section 2 of this chapter and lead to practical problems with basing a litigation strategy on either of these two arguments.

The legal situation for lesbians and gay men, while better than it has been in the past, is hardly rosy. Given this situation, advocates of lesbian and gay rights may be tempted by any argument that might prove successful in obtaining lesbian and gay rights. The 'born that way' argument and the sex-discrimination argument are each, in various ways, tempting arguments. But I have shown that both face serious problems. There exist, however, other strong legal and ethical arguments to be made for lesbian and gay rights and, although there are difficulties facing attempts to formulate practical arguments for lesbian and gay rights, I think there are some promising practical strategies. I do not, however, think that there is a single argument for lesbian and gay rights that will work in all contexts. Fifteen years after *Bowers v Hardwick*, privacy arguments have some continued viability, especially when made in conjunction with some equality-based arguments.[183] Further, I think that equality-based arguments, especially those that draw on analogies[184] to race, sex (note that this is different from the sex-discrimination argument, which argues the sexual-orientation discrimination is an instance of sex discrimination not that it is like sex discrimination) and perhaps religious liberty.[185] The Supreme Court's reasoning in *Romer v Evans*, although limited in various ways, may be a first step towards this approach.[186]

---

[182] See Richards, above n. 2.   [183] See, e.g., Kaplan, above n. 33.

[184] See e.g. Richards, above n. 2.

[185] The basic principles that underlie the United States Constitution's protection of religious liberty (namely, freedom of conscience, freedom of association, and the rights to free speech and free assembly) also provide a robust defence of lesbian and gay rights. See e.g. David Richards, 'Sexual Preference as a Suspect (Religious) Classification: An Alternative Perspective on the Unconstitutionality of Anti Lesbian/Gay Initiatives', *Ohio State Law Journal*, 55 (1994), 491; and William Eskridge, 'A Jurisprudence of "Coming Out": Religion, Homosexuality, and Collisions of Liberty and Equality in American Public Law', *Yale Law Journal*, 106 (1997), 2411.

[186] See e.g. Cass Sunstein, 'The Supreme Court 1995 Term: Foreword: Leaving Things Undecided', *Harvard Law Review*, 110 (1996), 6; Matt Coles, 'The Meaning of Romer v. Evans', *Hastings Law Journal*, 48 (1997), 1343; and Lynn Baker, 'The Missing Pages in the Majority Opinion in *Romer v Evans*', *University of Colorado Law Review*, 68, 387.

INDEX